UNDERSTANDING IMMIGRATION LAW
Second Edition

UNDERSTANDING IMMIGRATION LAW

Second Edition

Kevin R. Johnson
*Dean and Mabie-Apallas Professor of Public Interest
Law and Chicana/o Studies
University of California, Davis*

Raquel Aldana
*Associate Dean for Faculty Scholarship, Professor of Law,
and Director of the Inter-American Program University of
the Pacific McGeorge School of Law*

Bill Ong Hing
*Professor of Law
University of San Francisco
Professor of Law Emeritus
University of California, Davis*

Leticia M. Saucedo
*Professor of Law
University of California, Davis*

Enid Trucios-Haynes
*Professor of Law
Brandeis School of Law, Louisville*

ISBN: 978-0-7698-8196-6
eBook ISBN: 978-0-7698-8197-3

Library of Congress Cataloging-in-Publication Data
Understanding immigration law / Kevin R. Johnson, Dean and Mabie-Apallas Professor of Public Interest Law and Chicana/o Studies University of California, Davis [and four others]. — Second edition.
    pages cm
    Includes index.
    ISBN 978-0-7698-8196-6 (softbound)
    1. Emigration and immigration law—United States. 2. United States—Emigration and immigration—Government policy. 3. Immigration enforcement—United States. I. Johnson, Kevin R., author.
    KF4819.U53 2015
    342.7308'2—dc23
                                                                                    2015012321

This publication is designed to provide authoritative information in regard to the subject matter covered. It is sold with the understanding that the publisher is not engaged in rendering legal, accounting, or other professional services. If legal advice or other expert assistance is required, the services of a competent professional should be sought.

NOTE TO USERS

To ensure that you are using the latest materials available in this area, please be sure to periodically check the LexisNexis Law School web site for downloadable updates and supplements at www.lexisnexis.com/lawschool.

Editorial Offices
630 Central Ave., New Providence, NJ 07974 (908) 464-6800
201 Mission St., San Francisco, CA 94105-1831 (415) 908-3200
www.lexisnexis.com

MATTHEW●BENDER

Preface

In preparing the first edition of *Understanding Immigration Law*, we faced a formidable set of challenges. Commencing work on the second edition, we, to our surprise, found that the challenges may have become even more formidable.

First, this book analyzes one of the most disputed public policy issues facing the United States. A heated national debate over immigration reform has spanned the 15 years of the new millennium, with no end in sight. Its contentiousness is a function of the complex, important, and, in certain respects, personal issues implicated by the policy choices that the nation must make. Immigration law and policy responds to a number of competing demands and interests that touch on contested conceptions of national identity, class and socioeconomic status, and related issues. Simply finding the proper tone to encourage rational discussion of the legitimate differences of opinion can at times prove to be challenging.

Second, U.S. immigration law is incredibly complex. Part of the law's complexity arises from the fact that it deviates in important respects from mainstream public law, a characteristic known as "immigration exceptionalism." As the Supreme Court has emphasized, "[i]n the exercise of its broad power over naturalization and immigration, Congress regularly makes rules that would be unacceptable if applied to citizens." *Mathews v. Diaz*, 426 U.S. 67, 79–80 (1976). The fundamental question of the role of the judiciary in reviewing the constitutionality of immigration laws remains in dispute. The Supreme Court has never overruled its foundational decisions upholding immigration laws that were racially discriminatory. *See, e.g., Chae Chan Ping v. United States* (The Chinese Exclusion Case), 130 U.S. 581 (1889). It has not disturbed the ruling that the courts lack the power to review the constitutionality of the substantive immigration admissions criteria passed by Congress. *See* Gabriel J. Chin, *Segregation's Last Stronghold: Race Discrimination and the Constitutional Law of Immigration*, 46 UCLA L. REV. 1 (1998). Indeed, it remains contested whether the U.S. Constitution applies to the review of the immigration laws and what precise protections it extends to noncitizens. Put simply, immigration exceptionalism requires a fair amount of explanation.

Nor is the Immigration & Nationality Act of 1952 (INA), which is the centerpiece of American immigration law, known for its accessibility to students and lawyers. To the contrary, only the much-maligned Internal Revenue Code rivals the intricate, lengthy, and all too often obtuse INA. *See Castro-O'Ryan v. INS*, 847 F.2d 1307, 1312 (9th Cir. 1988) ("With only a small degree of hyperbole, the immigration laws have been termed 'second only to the Internal Revenue Code in complexity.' ") (citation omitted); *Lok v. INS*, 548 F.2d 37, 38 (2d Cir. 1977) (stating that U.S. immigration laws resemble "King Minos's labyrinth in ancient Crete"). Consequently, explaining concisely and clearly the statute's complexities and nuances requires great care and attention. In addition, striking a balance in one volume between simplifying while not dumbing down the fundamentals of U.S. immigration law proves to be difficult. Seeing the forest through the trees often proves most difficult for both the expert in, as well as the newcomer to, immigration law. We strive throughout *Understanding Immigration Law* to provide the reader with the basics of immigration law without getting lost in the minutiae.

To exacerbate the complexities of immigration law, Congress amends the Immigration & Nationality Act (INA) just about every year, with the changes slowly making the law

Preface

lengthier and more complex, if not clearer and easier to understand. Moreover, the immigration bureaucracy (*see* Chapter 5) regularly promulgates new regulations and amends existing ones. The courts and the Board of Immigration Appeals issue many opinions in immigration cases. Changes in the law, including the Supreme Court's decision in *Arizona v. United States*, 132 S. Ct. 2492 (2012) and the Obama administration's announcement in 2012 of the Deferred Action for Childhood Arrivals program (and its controversial expansion in 2014), which provides relief to certain undocumented immigrants, *see* Chapter 12, required extensive changes from the first edition of *Understanding Immigration Law*. Scholars must work diligently to just keep up with the frequent changes in this highly technical body of law.

Change in the law — perhaps even wholesale "comprehensive immigration reform" — in the near future is a distinct possibility. Discussion of immigration reform has been in the air for well over a decade. Massive changes in the law can come with little notice. In 1990, to the surprise of many informed observers, Congress overhauled the immigration laws and expanded lawful immigration. In 1996, Congress passed far-reaching, reforms that one informed observer characterized as "the most radical reform of immigration law in decades — or perhaps ever." PETER H. SCHUCK, CITIZENS, STRANGERS, AND IN-BETWEENS 143 (1998). Within months of September 11, 2001, Congress passed the USA PATRIOT Act, which added tough new immigration provisions ostensibly designed to combat terrorism.

Since publication of the first edition in 2009, rumblings in Congress of comprehensive immigration reform repeatedly have come and gone. Although much-debated, Congress has failed to pass a major immigration reform package. It also has been unable to pass any of the versions of the DREAM Act introduced in Congress that would have benefited undocumented college students. *See* Chapter 18.

The inability of Congress to enact immigration reform legislation has contributed to the long-running, and often over-heated, national debate over immigration. President Obama's 2014 executive action, including expansion of the deferred action program, provoked great controversy and is tangled in legal challenges. A growing number of state and local governments have passed laws designed to facilitate enforcement of the immigration laws. Chapter 4, which has been substantially revised since the first edition, critically reviews the constitutionality of such efforts, and whether they intrude on the federal power to regulate immigration.

Current events also regularly transform the immigration landscape. In 2014, for example, public attention and the Obama Administration focused on the much-publicized increase in unaccompanied minors from Central America. *See* Frances Robles, *Fleeing Gangs, Children Head to U.S. Border*, N.Y. TIMES, July 9, 2014. We attempt to integrate such developments into *Understanding Immigration Law* but cannot always predict how significant and lasting they will be.

Despite the many challenges, the second edition of *Understanding Immigration Law* strives to lay out the basics of U.S. immigration law in a way accessible to newcomers to the field. Readers can judge whether we met our goal.

The early chapters of this volume offer background about the intellectual, historical, and constitutional foundations of U.S. immigration law. They also identify factors that have historically fueled migration to the United States, including the economic "pull" of jobs and family in the United States and the "push" of economic hardship, political

Preface

instability, and other aspects of life in the sending country. The middle chapters provide a capsule summary of the law concerning admissions and removals under the Immigration and Nationality Act, as amended, and implementing regulations. We end with a chapter making some tentative speculations about the future of U.S. immigration law.

Understanding Immigration Law has been designed to be used by students as a supplement to the most-widely adopted immigration law casebooks, including STEPHEN H. LEGOMSKY & CRISTINA M. RODRÍGUEZ, IMMIGRATION AND REFUGEE LAW AND POLICY (5th ed. 2009), THOMAS ALEXANDER ALEINIKOFF, DAVID A. MARTIN, HIROSHI MOTOMURA & MARYELLEN FULLERTON, IMMIGRATION AND CITIZENSHIP: PROCESS AND POLICY (7th ed. 2012), and other leading immigration law casebooks. The background to leading Supreme Court immigration decisions can be found in IMMIGRATION STORIES (David A. Martin & Peter H. Schuck eds., 2005).

Immigration is the topic of many websites and blogs. For up-to-date immigration law news and analysis, visit the Immigration Prof blog, http://lawprofessors.typepad.com/immigration/, which is managed by two co-authors (Kevin R. Johnson and Bill Hing) of *Understanding Immigration Law*. LexisNexis Immigration Law Newsroom (http://www.lexisnexis.com/legalnewsroom/immigration/default.aspx) also provides comprehensive immigration news, court decisions, and other immigration materials.

A Note on Terminology

Although not defined in the Immigration & Nationality Act, the emotion-laden phrase "illegal aliens" often is employed in the public debate over immigration. *See generally* MAE M. NGAL, IMPOSSIBLE SUBJECTS: ILLEGAL ALIENS AND THE MAKING OF MODERN AMERICA (2004). Because the lawfulness of the status of some undocumented immigrants is not always clear, characterizing them as "illegal" is not entirely accurate. Restrictionists frequently decry "illegal aliens" and advocate their mass deportation from the United States. The use of the very term "illegal aliens" ordinarily betrays a restrictionist bias in the speaker. We avoid use of the term in this book. Similarly, the term "alien," although literally the DNA of the INA, which addresses in general terms the treatment of "aliens," as opposed to citizens, has negative connotations. *See* Kevin R. Johnson, *"Aliens" and the U.S. Immigration Laws: The Social and Legal Construction of Nonpersons*, 28 U. MIAMI INTER-AM. L. REV. 263 (1996–97); D. Carolina Nuñez, *War of the Words: Aliens, Immigrants, Citizens, and the Language of Exclusion*, 2013 BYU L. REV. 1517. Because the term "aliens" is effectively the organizing term of the entire immigration statute, we must employ it, although we strive to do so carefully and sensitively throughout.

Kevin R. Johnson
Raquel Aldana
Bill Ong Hing
Leticia M. Saucedo
Enid Trucios-Haynes

Table of Contents

Table of Contents

Table of Contents

Table of Contents

Table of Contents

Table of Contents

Table of Contents

Table of Contents

Table of Contents

Table of Contents

Table of Contents

Table of Contents

Table of Contents

Table of Contents

Chapter 1

UNDERSTANDING AND EVALUATING U.S. IMMIGRATION LAW AND POLICY

Migration is the result of the complex interaction of individual and societal processes influenced by innumerable variables. This chapter outlines the various factors affecting these processes as well as public concerns frequently voiced with immigration and immigrants. The intention is to help students better appreciate the overall backdrop against which the U.S. immigration laws and their enforcement operate.

Immigrants are influenced by the myriad of factors that make people want to leave all that they call home to uproot themselves and, at times, family.[1] Some of the reasons for migrating are rather ordinary, namely migration for economic opportunity or to rejoin family members. Other decisions are motivated by dramatic events, such as the migration of persons who flee civil war or persecution on account of their political views, religion, or race, or who leave their homeland because of war and natural disaster, such as hurricane, earthquake, or famine.

Importantly, most people, if for no reason other than inertia, live and die in their nation of birth:

> Most people have no inclination to leave their native soil, no matter how onerous conditions become. Would-be emigrants must fight off the ties of family, the comfort of familiar surroundings, the rootedness in one's culture, the security of being among "one's own," and the power of plain inertia. Conversely, being uprooted carries daunting prospects: adjusting to alien ways, learning a new language, the absence of kith and kin, the sheer uncertainty of it all.[2]

Despite the human pressures against movement, fears run rampant in many Western nations that the reduction of border controls — or, alternatively, the failure to bolster them — will open the "floodgates"[3] and that millions of immigrants from around the world will overwhelm their homeland. This deep-seated fear indelibly influences the formulation and enforcement of the U.S. immigration laws.

Contrary to popular intuition, free movement need not necessarily result in mass migration. Unrestrained movement *within* the United States, for example, ordinarily has not led to mass migration among the states. This is the case despite the

---

[1] For the classic study of the immigrant experience, see OSCAR HANDLIN, THE UPROOTED (2d ed. 1973).

[2] ALAN DOWTY, CLOSED BORDERS: THE CONTEMPORARY ASSAULT ON FREEDOM OF MOVEMENT 223 (1987).

[3] This fear inspired the title of KEVIN R. JOHNSON, OPENING THE FLOODGATES: WHY AMERICA NEEDS TO RETHINK ITS BORDERS AND IMMIGRATION LAWS (2007), from which certain parts of this chapter have been adapted. For analysis of the fear that relaxing immigration restrictions will open the proverbial floodgates, see *Id.* at 26–31; *see also* Ediberto Román, *The Alien Invasion?*, 45 HOUS. L. REV. 841 (2008) (questioning the characterization of flow of immigrants to the United States on an "invasion").

fact that significant economic, social, and other disparities exist among the states, such as between Mississippi and California, or New York and South Dakota.[4] Most Mississippians remain in Mississippi even though superior economic opportunities exist in California, New York, and Texas. Similarly, migration from Puerto Rico, a U.S. territory, is relatively stable despite the existence of economic disparities between the island and the mainland and that all Puerto Ricans as American citizens can legally migrate to the U.S. mainland.[5]

The truth of the matter is that most people the world over would prefer to stay put in their native lands. Most Mexicans, for example, prefer to — and in fact do — stay in Mexico. The feared mass migration in the expanding European Union, which generally permits labor migration between member nations, has not come to pass. *See* Ch. 18.

Despite the reality of human inertia as well as the general affinity for family and homeland, debate about immigration — from relatively minor reform efforts to broader ones — almost invariably confronts the concern that the United States risks being overrun by immigrants of different races, cultures, and creeds.

Modern times have witnessed the globalization of the international economy and greatly improved transportation, with increased migration a result. In light of the existing economic disparities between nations, migration to the United States from Latin America today arguably is a fact of modern life. Chapter 18 discusses future possibilities for changes in the U.S. immigration laws that might bring them more into line with the realities of global integration and the increased movement of people the world over.

This chapter outlines the arguments concerning the morality of immigration restrictions and the devotion of the nation-state to the exercise of sovereign power over its borders. It proceeds to outline some of the public concerns with immigration, including its real and perceived economic impacts, which influence the public debate about immigration and reform of the current U.S. immigration laws.

A.   THE MORALITY OF IMMIGRATION RESTRICTIONS

Liberal theory, with its devotion to the protection of individual rights from intrusion by the state, serves as the bedrock of the U.S. legal structure. The U.S. Constitution, especially the Bill of Rights, powerfully symbolizes the nation's commitment to individual rights.

One could reasonably argue that liberal theory with its emphasis on individual rights militates in favor of an immigration system with freedom to migrate. Contending that border controls infringe on individual rights to free movement, political theorist Joseph Carens in a famous article advocates for free migration

---

[4] *See* Raven Molloy, Christopher L. Smith, & Abigail Wozniak, *Internal Migration in the United States*, 25 J. ECON. PERS. 173 (2011) (analyzing the declining internal migration between the various states of the United States).

[5] *See* JOHNSON, *supra* note 3, at 26–31.

across national boundaries.[6]

Carens' open border regime would only allow for narrow restrictions on migration of persons outside the country. Recognizing the need to take steps against a clear "threat to the public order," Carens would allow measures in his more open system so as to bar mass migration that would threaten chaos and the potential collapse of liberal society.[7]

Michael Walzer's influential book *Spheres of Justice* (1983)[8] offers a communitarian defense of restrictive immigration policies. He contends that the community should be able to limit the admission of outsiders in order (1) to preserve community self-definition; and (2) to allow the community to make decisions that reflect shared community values. "The heart of Walzer's argument is that admissions decisions are the legitimate and essential prerogative of the current members of any particular national community."[9] At the same time, Walzer would recognize that moral limits exist on the admissions criteria adopted by any community; racial restrictions, for example, must be classified as invidious and impermissible.[10]

Ultimately, liberal theory is difficult to reconcile with a system of closed borders. However, the American legal system has long been deeply committed both to individual rights for people in the country and greatly limited admissions of people outside the country. A tension between these two conflicting strands of thought plays out throughout U.S. immigration law, with great ambivalence about the full extension of rights to noncitizens.[11]

Contemporary immigrant rights advocates put forth strong moral claims for more liberal admissions.[12] Religious-based arguments for more open admissions and more generous treatment of immigrants have been made with increasing frequency.[13] Indeed, one law professor relies on Catholic social thought to advocate

---

[6] *See* Joseph H. Carens, *Aliens and Citizens: The Case for Open Borders*, 49 REV. POL. 251, 251 (1987). JOSEPH H. CARENS, THE ETHICS OF IMMIGRATION LAW 225–54 (2013) argues for open borders to promote human freedom and equality. Analysis of ethical and moral issues implicated by the regulation of migration can be found in BRUCE ACKERMAN, SOCIAL JUSTICE IN THE LIBERAL STATE 93–95 (1980); and Timothy King, *Immigration from Developing Countries: Some Philosophical Issues*, ETHICS, Apr. 1983, at 525–31.

[7] Carens, *supra* note 6, at 259. In a similar vein, JOSEPH H. CARENS, IMMIGRANTS AND THE RIGHT TO STAY 3–51 (2010) argues that the longer a migrant remains within a state's borders, the stronger the moral claim to remain within the state.

[8] MICHAEL WALZER, SPHERES OF JUSTICE (1983).

[9] Linda S. Bosniak, *Membership, Equality, and the Difference That Alienage Makes*, 69 N.Y.U. L. REV. 1047, 1072 (1994).

[10] *See* WALZER, *supra* note 8, at 40.

[11] *See generally* LINDA BOSNIAK, THE CITIZEN AND THE ALIEN: DISCUSSIONS OF CONTEMPORARY MEMBERSHIP (2006) (analyzing the ambiguous status of immigrants in American law and society); JUDITH GANS, ELAINE M. REPLOGLE, & DANIEL J. TICHENOR, DEBATES OF U.S. IMMIGRATION 11–120 (2012) (studying admission of immigrants into the United States and membership in U.S. society); DANIEL J. TICHENOR, DIVIDING LINES: THE POLITICS OF IMMIGRATION CONTROL IN AMERICA (2009) (analyzing the historical allocation of rights between citizens and noncitizens in the United States).

[12] *See, e.g.*, Saby Ghosray, *Is There a Human-Rights Dimension to Immigration? Seeking Clarity Through the Prism of Morality and Human Survival*, 84 DEN. U.L. REV. 1151 (2007).

[13] *See, e.g.*, Michael Churgin, *Lobbying by Jewish Organizations Concerning Immigration: A*

for comprehensive immigration reform.[14]

B.   NATIONAL SOVEREIGNTY AND BORDERS

Among much of the world, there is an almost natural assumption that nations have unfettered sovereign power to maintain closed borders. The U.S. Supreme Court's approach to American immigration law is consistent with this premise. *See* Ch. 3. Despite the assumed dominance of national sovereign power over borders, international law increasingly limits the sovereign powers of nation-states to restrict migration into their territories.

1.   Expansive Notions of National Sovereignty

In *Chae Chan Ping v. United States* (The Chinese Exclusion Case),[15] the Supreme Court upheld an infamous late nineteenth century law — one in a series of laws known as the "Chinese exclusion laws" — prohibiting virtually all immigration from China. In so doing, the Court emphasized that "[t]he power of exclusion of foreigners [is] an *incident of sovereignty* belonging to the government of the United States, as part of [its] *sovereign powers delegated by the Constitution*."[16] The Court elaborated:

> the United States, in [its] relation to foreign countries and [its] subjects or citizens are one nation, invested with powers which belong to independent nations, the exercise of which can be invoked for the absolute independence and security throughout its entire territory. . . . *To preserve its independence, and give security against foreign aggression and encroachment, is the highest duty of every nation, and to attain these ends nearly all other considerations are to be subordinated. It matters not in what form such*

Historical Study, 83 U. Det. Mercy L. Rev. 947 (2006); James Parry Eyster, *Pope John Paul II and Immigration Law and Policy,* 6 Ave Maria L. Rev. 85 (2007); Stephen H. Legomsky, *Emigration, Obligation, and Evil: A Response to Michael Scaperlanda's Keynote Address at Fordham University School of Law Delivered Feb. 25, 2005,* 83 U. Det. Mercy L. Rev. 849 (2006); Michael Scaperlanda, *Immigration and Evil: The Religious Challenge,* 83 U. Det. Mercy L. Rev. 835 (2006); *see also* Michele R. Pistone & John J. Hoeffner, Stepping Out of The Brain Drain: Catholic Social Teaching in a New Era of Migration (2007) (analyzing through the lens of Catholicism the impacts of migration of skilled workers on sending and receiving countries); Victor C. Romero, *Christian Realism and Immigration Reform,* 7 U. St. Thomas L.J. 310, 312 (2010) ("[I]f our ultimate goal is to mirror God's kingdom here on earth, then Christian leaders should take seriously the notion that a more open border policy best approximates the ideal City of God than settling for compromises based on man-made values, fears and concerns."). *See generally* Religious and Ethical Perspectives on Global Migration (Elizabeth M. Collier & Charles R. Strain eds., 2014) (examining the ethics of migration and migration controls in an era of global migration); Ched Myers & Matthew Colwell, Our God is Undocumented: Biblical Faith and Immigrant Justice (2012) (offering arguments for open borders based on the biblical tradition).

[14] *See* Michael A. Scaperlanda, *Reflections on Immigration Reform, the Workplace and the Family,* 4 U. St. Thomas L.J. 508, 518–28 (2007).

[15] 130 U.S. 581 (1889).

[16] *Id.* at 609 (emphasis added); *see* Fong Yue Ting v. United States, 149 U.S. 698, 707 (1893) ("The right of a nation to expel or deport foreigners . . . is as absolute and unqualified as the right to prohibit and prevent their entrance into the country.").

*aggression and encroachment come, whether from the foreign nation
acting in its national character or from vast hordes of its people crowding
in upon us.*[17]

Courts, political leaders, and commentators continue to invoke robust conceptions of national sovereignty to justify the many restrictive elements of the U.S.
immigration laws. *See* Ch. 9. However, commentators have acknowledged that
international law has increasingly imposed limits on the sovereign power of nations
to exclude outsiders.[18] For example, the United Nations Protocol Relating to the
Status of Refugees[19] restricts the powers of nation-states to return to their
homelands certain noncitizens who have fled actual or feared persecution. The
Convention against Torture and Other Cruel, Inhuman or Degrading Treatment or
Punishment,[20] also prohibits a nation from returning a noncitizen to likely torture
in his or her native country.

Despite the expansion of rights of migrants in international law, American
political leaders often invoke the nation's unfettered sovereign power over border
security. The U.S. government greatly fortified its borders in the name of national
security after the loss of life on September 11, 2001. *See* Ch. 14. Echoes of
sovereignty discourse can be seen in the arguments of critics who contend that
global trade agreements and the creation of international institutions effectively
surrender national sovereignty. *See* Ch. 18. Nations often prefer to view immigration as a wholly domestic matter, although it unquestionably implicates foreign
nations, their citizens, relations between nations, and international law.

2.   Borders and Border Controls

Generally speaking, nation-states are organized with borders between nations.
Those borders often, although not always, are accompanied by border controls.
Strict border enforcement is especially popular in the developed nations of the
West, which often fear mass migration of foreign citizens because of the high
demand for immigration to their countries.

Border controls often are thought of as an important symbol of national
sovereignty. Beginning in the 1990s, the United States has unquestionably fortified
its borders. *See* Ch. 2. The European Union, while allowing for labor migration
among the member nations, has fortified its border controls at the outer perimeter
of the common market to such an extent that it is frequently referred to as the
"Fortress Europe." *See* Ch. 18.

Even assuming that nation-states possess sovereign power to establish border
controls, this does not mean that nation-states *must* have border controls that
strictly limit entry. Nations can exercise their sovereign power to decide that less
restrictive immigration laws and policies are the most sensible for the country and

---

[17] *Chinese Exclusion Case*, 130 U.S. at 604, 606 (emphasis added).

[18] *See* James A.R. Nafziger, *The General Admission of Aliens Under International Law*, 77 Am. J.
Int'l L. 804 (1983).

[19] 19 U.S.T. 6223, 606 U.N.T.S. 267 (1967).

[20] 1465 U.N.T.S. 85 (1984).

its residents. For discussion of more liberal admissions schemes than that which is currently in place in the United States, see Ch. 18.

3. The Social Contract and Community Membership

The nation-state unquestionably has sovereign power over all residents — immigrants and citizens — within its jurisdiction. A "social contract" binds the residents of a nation-state and its government. Professor Juliet Stumpf cogently explains the notion of the social contract with residents of the United States:

> Social contract principles focus on "the consent of a particular population to be governed" and seek to identify who is entitled by that consent to the protections of the Constitution.
>
> Who is entitled to constitutional guarantees is not obvious from the text of the Constitution. Although the Constitution begins with the phrase "We the People," it does not define who those "People" are. Few provisions of the Constitution specify that they apply exclusively to citizens. Most provisions, particularly the Bill of Rights, either address "the people" or "persons" or couch their application in more general terms. The acquisition of citizenship appears once in the body of the Constitution, empowering Congress to enact "an uniform Rule of Naturalization."
>
> Social contract theory has attempted to identify who "the People" are. The social contract approach begins with the premise that "members of the citizenry have agreed to be governed in a particular manner." [The Supreme Court in] *McCulloch v. Maryland* [17 U.S. (4 Wheat.) 316, 404–05 (1819)] took this approach in its description of the constitutional bargain struck between the people and their government. It asserted that "[t]he government proceeds directly from the people" and that "[i]ts powers are granted by them, and are to be exercised directly on them, and for their benefit." From that contractual premise, "[o]nly members and beneficiaries of the social contract are able to make claims against the government." Conversely, "the government may act outside of the contract's constraints against" non-members.[21]

The terms and conditions of a social contract with noncitizens — including those that fall into different immigration categories (lawful permanent residents, temporary visitors, undocumented immigrants, etc.) — has never been clear in American law.[22] The United States historically has been deeply ambivalent about the rights

---

[21] Juliet Stumpf, *Citizens of an Enemy Land: Enemy Combatants, Aliens, and the Constitutional Rights of the Pseudo-Citizen*, 38 U.C. Davis L. Rev. 79, 87–89 (2004) (footnotes omitted).

[22] *See* Dowell Myers, Immigrants and Boomers: Forging a New Social Contract for the Future of America (2007) (calling for a new social contract between an aging native-born American population and younger immigrants); Robert S. Chang, *Centering the Immigrant in the Inter/national Imagination (Part III): Aoki, Rawls, and Immigration*, 90 Or. L. Rev. 1319 (2012) (analyzing the application of social contract theory to immigrants); Berta Hernández-Truyol & Justin Luna, *Children and Immigration: International, Local, and Social Responsibilities*, 15 B.U. Pub. Int. L.J. 297 (2006) (proposing a reformed social contract grounded in human rights principles that promote health, education, and welfare protections for children regardless of immigration status).

held by noncitizens with the courts vacillating in its extension of rights to noncitizens.[23] Generally speaking, potential entrants hold the fewest rights of all noncitizens. Legal immigrants unquestionably have more rights than undocumented immigrants and, in some ways, hold similar bundles of rights as citizens. However, in important instances, legal immigrants do not and, for example, generally cannot vote in elections or serve on juries.

Undocumented immigrants possess the smallest bundle of legal rights of all residents of the United States. However, in a few instances, they hold rights similar to U.S. citizens and legal immigrants. For example, the Supreme Court has held that undocumented immigrants have a right to a public elementary and secondary education under the Constitution.[24] Chapter 3 outlines the law concerning the constitutional rights possessed by noncitizens.

C. INTERNATIONAL HUMAN RIGHTS LIMITATIONS ON SOVEREIGN POWER OVER BORDERS

1. The Rights of Immigrants

a. A Right to Migrate?

A rich body of international law deals with the former Soviet Union and a small number of nations that barred emigration out of the country.[25] This was a significant problem in the days of the Cold War, with communist nations often stringently restricting the ability of its citizens to leave their respective countries.[26]

---

[23] *See generally* BOSNIAK, *supra* note 11 (analyzing the ambiguous legal status of immigrants in U.S. society).

[24] *See* Plyler v. Doe, 457 U.S. 202 (1982) (invalidating Texas law effectively barring undocumented children from public elementary and secondary schools). For analysis of the circumstances surrounding *Plyler v. Doe*, see Michael A. Olivas, Plyler v. Doe, *The Education of Undocumented Children, and the Polity, in* IMMIGRATION STORIES 197 (David A. Martin & Peter H. Schuck eds., 2005).

[25] *See* Thomas Kleven, *Why International Law Favors Emigration over Immigration*, 33 U. MIAMI INTER-AM. L. REV. 70 (2002); *see also* Joy M. Purcell, Note, *A Right to Leave, But Nowhere to Go: Reconciling an Emigrant's Right to Leave with the Sovereign's Right to Exclude*, 39 U. MIAMI INTER-AM. L. REV. 177, 178 (2007) ("[W]hile most nations are quick to criticize other nations for restrictive emigration policies, there has never been widespread international recognition of a corresponding right to immigrate."). Increasing scholarly attention has been paid to emigration, specifically emigrants' continuing ties with their native countries. *See, e.g.*, Kim Barry, *Home and Away: The Construction of Citizenship in an Emigration Context*, 81 NYU L. REV. 11 (2006); Anupam Chander, *Diaspora Bonds*, 76 NYU L. REV. 1005 (2001); Michael J. Trebilcock & Matthew Sudak, *The Political Economy of Emigration and Immigration*, 81 NYU L. REV. 234 (2006); *see also* Anu Bradford, *Sharing the Risks and Rewards of Economic Migration*, 80 U. CHI. L. REV. 29 (2013) (analyzing the competing national interests of emigration and immigration concerning who should migrate and arguing that existing restrictions on migration are economically inefficient).

[26] *See, e.g.*, Rodriguez-Roman v. INS, 98 F.3d 416 (9th Cir. 1996) (deciding the claim of an asylum-seeker who had fled Cuba); Dimitry Kochenov, *The Right to Leave Any Country Including Your Own in International Law*, 28 CONN. J. INT'L. L. 43 (2012) (analyzing the evolution of the right to leave a country under international law); Matthew A. Light, *What Does It Mean to Control Migration? Society Mobility Policies in Comparative Perspective*, 37 LAW & SOC. INQ. 395 (2012) (analyzing restrictive migration policies of the former Soviet Union); Eric Retter, Comment, *You Can Check Out Any Time You*

A much more limited body of international law deals with immigration and the ability of states to close the borders to outsiders. An expanding body of international human rights law, such as the United Nations Protocol Relating to the Status of Refugees[27] and Convention against Torture,[28] restricts the sovereign power of nations to limit migration of certain categories of noncitizens into their territory. Scholars have emphasized the increasing importance of human rights principles in immigration law.[29]

James A.R. Nafziger has forcefully argued that

> [t]he international significance of migration and the interdependence of states lend support to the argument that the general admission of aliens should not be regarded as an untrammeled discretionary power within the exclusive domestic jurisdiction of states. Therefore, although a state has no duty to admit all aliens who might seek to enter its territory, [states have] a qualified duty to admit aliens when they pose no danger to the public safety, security, general welfare, or essential institutions of a recipient state.[30]

International law provides limited rights to migrate into, and remain in, a nation. However, the 2012 International Law Commission's Draft Articles on the Expulsion of Aliens, provisionally adopted by the United Nation's General Assembly, generally "recognize a general right of a state to expel aliens from its territory but only in accordance with the present draft articles and other applicable rules of international law, in particular those relating to human rights."[31]

Like, But We Might Not Let You Leave: Cuba's Travel Policy in the Wake of Signing the International Covenant on Civil and Political Rights, 23 EMORY INT'L L. REV. 651 (2009) (analyzing Cuba's historical travel restrictions under international law). In 2012, the Cuban government eased travel restrictions on its citizens. *See* Victoria Burnett, *After Decades, Cuba Eases Travel Rules to Maintain Ties*, N.Y. TIMES, Oct. 16, 2012.

[27] 19 U.S.T. 6223, 606 U.N.T.S. 267 (1967).

[28] 1465 U.N.T.S. 85 (1984).

[29] *See, e.g.*, Elizabeth M. Bruch, *Open or Closed: Balancing Border Policy with Human Rights*, 96 KY L.J. 197 (2007/08); Vincent Chetail, *The Human Rights of Migrants in International Law: From Minimum Standards to Fundamental Rights*, 28 GEO. IMMIGR. L.J. 225 (2013); Jaya Ramji-Nogales, *A Global Approach to Secret Evidence: How Human Rights Law Can Reform Our Immigration System*, 39 COLUM. HUM. RTS. L. REV. 287 (2008); Lesley Wexler, *Human Rights Impact Statements: An Immigration Case Study*, 22 GEO. IMMIGR. L.J. 285 (2008); Lesley Wexler, *The Non-Legal Role of International Human Rights Law in Addressing Immigration*, 2007 U. CHI. LEG. F. 359 (2007); *see also* Sonja Starr & Lea Brilmayer, *Family Separation as a Violation of International Law*, 21 BERKELEY J. INT'L L. 213 (2003) (analyzing involuntary family separation as violation of international law); Chantal Thomas, *What Does the Emerging International Law of Migration Mean for Sovereignty?*, 14 MELBOURNE J. INT'L L. 1 (2013) (considering the impacts of emerging international law of migration on the meaning of sovereignty); J. Brian Johns, Note, *Filling the Void: Incorporating International Human Rights Protections into United States Immigration Policy*, 43 RUTGERS L.J. 541 (2013) (proposing changes to U.S. immigration law that would bring it into conformity with international human rights norms). *See generally* RUTH RUBIO MARIN, HUMAN RIGHTS AND IMMIGRATION (2012) (advocating the protections of the human rights of migrants).

[30] Nafziger, *supra* note 18, at 805.

[31] U.N. Int'l Law Comm'n 64th Sess., May 7–June 1, July 3–August 3, 2012, U.N. Doc. A/CN.4/L.797. For analysis of the draft articles, see Sean D. Murphy, *The Expulsion of Aliens and Other Topics: The Sixty-Fourth Session of the International Law Commission*, 107 AM. J. INT'L L. 164 (2013); *see also*

b. The "Stake" Theory — A Sliding Scale of Rights for Noncitizens

"Some scholars have argued that the interests of immigrants, including undocumented immigrants, should increase as the immigrants' "stake" in the [United States] increases. By "stake" they mean particular attachments and commitments and expectations that develop over time through relationship."[32] Joseph Carens has offered a philosophical justification for the stake theory, with rights of an undocumented immigrant growing the longer that he or she resides in a country.[33]

The U.S. courts have not expressly embraced the stake theory to justify its reasoning in decisions involving the rights of immigrants. *See* Ch. 3. However, the theory provides a helpful way to rationalize in a rough fashion the results of many judicial decisions addressing the rights of immigrants. As you read through this volume, consider how the stake theory helps explain a court decision implicating the rights of immigrants.

Under American law, there is a sort of hierarchy of noncitizens in terms of the recognition of legal rights, all loosely correlated with their legal and other roots — their "stake" — in the United States. The stake theory is implicitly recognized in forms of relief from removal that include a period of residency in the United States as a requirement for eligibility. *See* Ch. 12. Undocumented immigrants have relatively few rights. Temporary visitors have more. And lawful permanent residents possess the most rights, but not quite as many as U.S. citizens. These differential rights are all more or less tied to the respective noncitizens' "stake" in the community. *See* Ch. 3.

International law has focused increasingly on protecting the rights of undocumented immigrants.[34] In 2003, the International Convention on the Protection of

---

Chantal Thomas, *Convergences and Divergences in International Legal Norms on Migrant Labor*, 32 COMP. LAB L. & POL'Y J. 405 (2011) (analyzing labor and other rights of migrants in international instruments). The European Union proposed amendments to the draft articles. *See* EU Statement — United Nations 6th Comm.: Report of International Law Commission Expulsion of Aliens (2012), *available at* http://www.eu-un.europa.eu/articles/en/article_12789_en.htm (last visited July 7, 2014).

[32] Linda S. Bosniak, *Opposing Prop. 187: Undocumented Immigrants and the National Imagination*, 28 CONN. L. REV. 555, 619 n.99 (1996) (citing David A. Martin, *Due Process and Membership in the National Community: Political Asylum and Beyond*, 44 U. PITT. L. REV. 165 (1983)); *Developments in the Law: Policy and the Rights of Aliens*, 96 HARV. L. REV. 1286, 1289–90 (1983).

[33] *See* CARENS, *supra* note 7, at 18 (arguing that "[p]eople who live and work and raise their families in a society become members, whatever their legal status"); GORDON H. HANSON, REGULATING LOW-SKILLED IMMIGRATION IN THE UNITED STATES 3–23 (2010) (contending that undocumented immigrants acquire a de facto right to remain in the United States by finding work and staying out of trouble). Some commentators have contended that undocumented immigrants' long-term presence in the United States affords them a right to remain akin to the doctrine of adverse possession in property law. *See* Timothy J. Lukes & Minh T. Hoang, *Open and Notorious: Adverse Possession and Immigration Reform*, 27 WASH. U. J. L. & POL'Y 123 (2008); Monica Gomez, Note, *Immigration by Adverse Possession: Common Law Amnesty for the Long-Residing Illegal Immigrants in the United States*, 22 GEO. IMMIGR. L.J. 105 (2007).

[34] *See* Linda S. Bosniak, *Human Rights, State Sovereignty and the Protection of Undocumented Migrants Under the International Migrant Workers Convention*, 25 INT'L MIGRATION REV. 737 (1991); Beth Lyon, *Tipping the Balance: Why Courts Should Look to International and Foreign Law on Unauthorized Immigrant Worker Rights*, 29 U. PA. J. INTL'L L. 169 (2007); Sandesh Sivakumaran, *The*

the Rights of All Migrant Workers and Members of Their Families[35] entered into force. To date, the United States has not ratified the convention.

2. Refugees

The protection of refugees and displaced peoples is at the core of international human rights law. The U.S. government as well as the international community often speaks about the obligations of nations to not return a person to his or her homeland if he or she has fled, or fears political, racial, religious, and related forms of persecution.

The United Nations Protocol Relating to the Status of Refugees,[36] as implemented in the United States by the Refugee Act of 1980,[37] demonstrates a commitment to humanitarian treatment of refugees. The Convention against Torture reflects a similar commitment.[38] Chapter 10 discusses the law's treatment of persons who suffered, or fear, persecution or torture.

D. DETERMINANTS OF MIGRATION: THE TRADITIONAL PUSH AND PULL FACTOR ANALYSIS

The causes of immigration to the United States have traditionally been explained by "push factors" and "pull factors."[39] These factors show that migration is a dynamic process based on relative economic, social, and political conditions between different countries.

Many migrants leave home for greater economic opportunity and to rejoin family.[40] Political and other freedoms in America also attract some immigrants.

Rights of Migrant Workers One Year on: Transformation or Consolidation?, 36 Geo J. Int'l L. 113 (2004); *see also* Eleanor Acer & Jake Goodman, *Reaffirming Rights: Human Rights Protections of Migrants, Asylum Seekers, and Refugees in Immigration Detention*, 24 Geo. Immigr. L.J. 507 (2010) (analyzing the protections available to immigrants under human rights treaties and the failure of nations, including the United States, to comply with international law). *But see* Kevin R. Johnson, *The Moral High Ground? The Relevance of International Law to Remedying Race Discrimination in U.S. Immigrations Laws*, in Moral Imperialism: A Critical Anthology 285 (Berta Esperanza Hernández-Truyol eds., 2002) (questioning the U.S. government's true commitment to compliance with international law in American immigration law).

[35] International Convention on the Protection of the Rights of All Migrant Workers and their Families (Dec. 1990), *available at* http://www2.ohchr.org/english/bodies/cmw/cmw.htm (last visited July 17, 2014); *see* Ryszard Cholewinski, *Human Rights of Migrants: The Dawn of A New Era?*, 24 Geo. Immigr. L.J. 585 (2010).

[36] 19 U.S.T. 6223, 606 U.N.T.S. 267 (1967).

[37] Refugee Act of 1980, Pub. L. No. 96-212, 94 Stat. 102 (1980). *See generally* Deborah E. Anker & Michael H. Posner, *The Forty Year Crisis: A Legislative History of the Refugee Act of 1980*, 19 San Diego L. Rev. 9 (1981) (summarizing the legislative history of the Refugee Act of 1980).

[38] 1465 U.N.T.S. 85 (1984).

[39] *See* Örn B. Bodvarsson & Hendrik Van den Berg, The Economics of Immigration: Theory and Policy 6 (2d ed. 2013).

[40] *See generally* Wayne A. Cornelius, Mexican Migration to the United States: The Limits of Governmental Intervention, Working Papers in U.S.-Mexican Studies (1981) (analyzing the determinants of migration from Mexico to the United States).

These factors constitute "pull factors."

Conversely, the lack of economic opportunity or the lack of political freedoms in one's native country may constitute "push" factors, which serve as incentives for people to leave their native countries.

Importantly, traditional push/pull analysis has limits in explaining national and individual migration decisions.[41] Family and social networks developed over generations of migration, for example, contribute significantly to migration patterns.[42]

Although war and violence as well as netural disasters contribute to migration pressures, modern immigration to the United States largely represents labor migration — the movement of workers across national boundaries for jobs and economic opportunity.[43] Due largely to transportation improvements, such migration is far easier today than it was in the past.

The information age also has meant that information can move quickly around the world. Workers in India, for example, can easily learn of job opportunities in California's Silicon Valley. Today's immigrants thus have easier access to knowledge about jobs, and U.S. society generally, than those of the 1800s.

Recent years have seen repeated attempts at major immigration reform in the United States. *See* Ch. 18. For reform efforts to be successful, the law must address both the traditional push and pull factors, as well as the influence of family and social networks, war and related events, and natural disasters, which fuel migration to the United States.

1. Economics

a. Push: Poverty and Limited Economic Opportunity

Poverty in the developing world has contributed to migration pressures. As mentioned above, the lack of economic opportunity tends to "push" people from a country to places where they will have greater economic opportunities:

> As early as 1885, E.G. Ravenstein, described as "the founding father of modern migration research," suggested that the primary causes of migration are economic . . . . The decision to emigrate is a very personal one, influenced by a myriad of factors that are often difficult to identify and quantify. *However, while no single cause can explain migration, most*

---

[41] *See* Alejandro Portes & József Böröcz, *Contemporary Immigration: Theoretical Perspectives on its Determinants and Modes of Incorporation*, 23 Int'l Migration Rev. 606, 607–14 (1989).

[42] *See* Douglas S. Massey, *The Social and Economic Origins of Immigration*, 510 Annals 60, 68–70 (1990).

[43] *See* Johnson, *supra* note 3, at 131–37; *see also* Jagdeep S. Bhandari, *World Migration and Trading Regimes*, 3 Alb. Gov't L. Rev. 169 (2010) (examining the relationship between international trade and international migration and the effect of trade on incentives to migrate); Jagdeep S. Bhandari, *International Migration and Trade: A Multi-Disciplinary Synthesis*, 6 Rich. J. Global L. & Bus. 113 (2006) (same); Trebilcock & Sudak, *supra* note 25 (studying economic impacts of immigration and emigration of labor). *See generally* Giovanni Peri, Immigration, Labor Markets, and Productivity (2012) (studying immigrant workers and their effect on the U.S. labor market).

indications are that economic considerations are among the more impor-tant factors. The use of skills-based programs in Canada, Australia, . . . New Zealand, and the U.S. . . . all suggest that immigration countries realize that a significant portion of emigrants are motivated by economic concerns.[44]

b. Pull: The Demand for Labor

The availability of jobs and economic opportunity in the United States has served for generations as a powerful magnet pulling immigrants, including undocumented workers, to this country. Many undocumented immigrants come for employment — including in skilled as well as unskilled jobs — available in the United States. Lawful avenues of immigration often are unavailable to low-and medium-skilled workers.

Calls often have been to make U.S. immigration law more consistent with the nation's labor needs.[45] Billionaire Bill Gates, founder of Microsoft, regularly testifies before Congress about the need for more liberal admissions of skilled labor into the United States.[46]

2. Pull: Family Reunification

Many immigrants come to the United States to rejoin family. One of the principal goals of the U.S. immigration laws is to promote family reunification.[47] As you read through this book, consider how successfully the law achieves this goal.

---

[44] Trebilcock & Sudak, *supra* note 25, at 241, 246–47 (emphasis added) (footnotes omitted).

[45] *See, e.g.*, Susan Martin & B. Lindsay Lowell, *Competing for Skills: U.S. Immigration Policy Since 1990*, 11 L. & Bus. Rev. Am. 387 (2005); Anton F. Mertens, *Build A Better Mousetrap and the World Will Beat A Path to Your Door: Can the Employment-Based Immigration Process Be Improved?*, 5 J. Marshall L.J. 513 (2012); Devon M. Collins, Note, *Toward a More Federalist Employment-Based Immigration System*, 25 Yale L. & Pol'y Rev. 349 (2007); Jonathan G. Goodrich, Comment, *Help Wanted: Looking for a Visa System that Promotes the U.S. Economy and National Security*, 42 U. Rich. L. Rev. 975 (2008).

[46] *See, e.g.*, Bill Gates, Transcript of Remarks by Microsoft Chairman Bill Gates Before the Committee on Science and Technology, U.S. House of Representatives (Mar. 12, 2008), *available at* http://www.microsoft.com/en-us/news/exec/billg/speeches/2008/congress.aspx (last visited July 14, 2014); Kim Hart, *Gates Calls on Congress for Science Education, Visas*, Wash. Post, Mar. 13, 2008 at D3; Robert Pear, *High-Tech Titans Strike Out on Immigration Bill*, N.Y. Times, June 25, 2007. Business leaders have advocated for an immigration policy that expands opportunities for immigrants to lawfully enter the American labor force. *See* Nathanial Parish Flannery, *Can Business Leaders Push Congress to Act On Immigration Reform?*, Forbes, Nov. 8, 2013. *See generally* Ayelet Shachar, *The Race for Talent: Highly Skilled Migrants and Competitive Immigrant Regimes*, 81 NYU L. Rev. 148 (2006) (analyzing the competition between nations for highly skilled labor).

[47] *See* Stephen H. Legomsky & Cristina M. Rodríguez, Immigration and Refugee Law and Policy 262 (5th ed. 2009) (stating that the Immigration and Nationality Act of 1952 "established the first comprehensive set of family-based preferences. Since then, one central value that United States immigration laws have long promoted, albeit to varying degrees, is family unity.") (footnote omitted).

3. Push: Migration Pressures Generated by U.S. Foreign Policy

With the globalization of the economy, increasing attention has been paid to the relationship between migration and international trade.[48] The North American Free Trade Agreement (NAFTA), European Union, World Trade Organization, and other free trade arrangements unquestionably have significant impacts on immigration. *See* Ch. 18.

Some critics contend that trade agreements exacerbate economic inequality between nations and adversely affect workers. U.S. international economic policies have been accused of increasing poverty and wealth inequality between the United States and other nations, which in turn has contributed to pressures for migration. Some observers claim that NAFTA, which did not squarely address migration,[49] *see* Ch. 18, caused economic dislocation in Mexico that contributed to pressures for its nationals to migrate to the United States.[50]

Similarly, U.S. foreign policy arguably has at times contributed to civil war and violence. Civil wars in El Salvador and Guatemala in the 1980s, for example, resulted in the migration of hundreds of thousands of people from those countries, with many migrants making their way to the United States.[51] Some commentators contend that political and economic support for authoritarian regimes by the U.S. government contributed to the civil strife and political turmoil in Central America and that the nation should have more generously treated asylum seekers from there.[52] Similar arguments have been made with respect to Haiti in the 1980s and 1990s[53] and Central America in 2014.[54]

---

[48] *See* Patricia Fernandez-Kelly, *Introduction: NAFTA and Beyond: Alternative Perspectives in the Study of Global Trade and Development*, 610 Annals 6 (2007).

[49] *See* Kevin R. Johnson, *Free Trade and Closed Borders: NAFTA and Mexican Immigration to the United States*, 27 UC Davis L. Rev. 937, 954–59 (1994).

[50] *See* Teresa A. Miller, *A New Neo-Liberal Economic Policies and the Criminalization of Undocumented Migration*, 61 SMU L. Rev. 171, 178–80 (2008); Ranko Shiraki Olivier, *In the Twelve Years of NAFTA, the Treaty Gave to Me . . . What Exactly?: An Assessment of Economic, Social, and Political Developments in Mexico Since 1994 and Their Impact on Mexican Immigration into the United States*, 10 Harv. Latino L. Rev. 53 (2007); Cody Jacobs, Note, *Trade We Can Believe in: Renegotiating NAFTA's Labor Provisions to Create More Equitable Growth in North America*, 17 Geo. J. Poverty L. & Pol'y 127, 135 (2010). *See generally* Bill Ong Hing, Ethical Borders, NAFTA, Globalization, and Mexican Migration (2010) (analyzing the relationship between the North American Free Trade Agreement and immigration to the United States from Mexico).

[51] *See* Orantes-Hernandez v. Thornburgh, 919 F.2d 549 (9th Cir. 1990) (holding that the U.S. government engaged in the pattern and practice of violating the rights of Salvadoran and Guatemalan asylum-seekers).

[52] *See* Susan Bibler Coutin, *Failing Outside: Excavating the History of Central American Asylum Seekers*, 36 Law & Soc. Inq. 569 (2011) (evaluating U.S. government's treatment of asylum seekers from Central America); Ann Aita, Note, *What About Us? NACARA'S Legacy and the Need to Provide Equal Protection to Guatemalan, Nicaraguan, Salvadoran, and Honduran Residency-Seekers in the United States*, 32 Rutgers L.J. 341 (2000) (analyzing treatment of Central American asylum seekers under American law); Eli Coffino, Note, *A Long Road to Residency: The Legal History of Salvadoran & Guatemalan Immigration to the United States with a Focus on NACARA*, 14 Cardozo J. Int'l & Comp. L. 177, 178 (2006) (same).

[53] *See, e.g.*, Sale v. Haitian Centers Council, Inc., 509 U.S. 155 (1993) (upholding U.S. government's

Military conflicts has unquestionably resulted in migration flows. The U.S. government's waging of war in Iraq after September 11, 2001 led to flows of refugees out of that country.[55] A similar flow of refugees took place in the aftermath of the Vietnam conflict.[56] Widespread violence in Sudan, Kenya, and other African nations likewise has resulted in population displacements in recent years.[57] Political violence in Syria in 2013–14 made it a refugee-sending country.[58]

Environmental disasters also can result in migration.[59] Severe economic circumstances can as well.[60] The Irish potato famine of the 1800s is a memorable historical example of an environmental catastrophe leading to severe economic dislocation.[61] A combination of economic crisis, political violence, and natural disaster has contributed to flows of migrants from Haiti for decades.

E.   THE IMPACTS OF IMMIGRATION ON THE UNITED STATES

The impacts of immigration on the United States are often hotly contested, with the perceived impacts greatly influencing the public dialogue over immigration.

---

interdiction and repatriation program in which persons fleeing Haiti were returned there). For criticism of the Haitian interdiction program, see Harold H. Koh, *The "Haiti Paradigm" in United States Human Rights Policy*, 103 YALE L.J. 2391 (1994); Harold H. Koh, *Reflections on Refoulment and Haitian Centers Council*, 35 HARV. INT'L L.J. 1 (1994).

[54] *See* Frances Robles, *Fleeing Gangs, Children Head to U.S. Border*, N.Y. TIMES, July 9, 2014.

[55] *See generally* UNITED NATIONS REFUGEE AGENCY, 2013 MID-YEAR TRENDS (June 2013) [hereinafter UN 2013 MID-YEAR TRENDS], *available at* http://www.unhcr.org/52af08d26.html (last visited July 14, 2014) (offering a statistical picture of refugees, asylum seekers, internally displaced persons, and stateless persons).

[56] *See* Harvey Gee, *Some Thoughts and Truths About Immigration Myths: The "Huddled Masses" Myth: Immigration and Civil Rights*, 39 VAL. U. L. REV. 939, 946–51 (2005) (book review) (discussing nativist reaction in the United States to Vietnamese refugees that contributed to passage of the Refugee Act of 1980); Harvey Gee, *The Refugee Burden: A Closer Look at the Refugee Act of 1980*, 26 N.C.J. INT'L L. & COM. Reg. 559 (2001) (same).

[57] *See* UN 2013 MID-YEAR TRENDS, *supra* note 55; M. Rafiqul Islam, *The Sudanese Darfur Crisis and Internally Displaced Persons in International Law: The Least Protection for the Most Vulnerable*, 18 INT'L J. REFUGEE L. 354 (2006); Zachary A. Lomo, *The Struggle for Protection of the Rights of Refugees and IDPS in Africa: Making the Existing International Legal Regime Work*, 18 BERKELEY J. INT'L L. 268 (2000); Charles Mwalimu, *The Legal Framework on Admission and Resettlement of African Refugees with an Emphasis on Kenya, Tanzania, and Uganda*, 18 EMORY INT'L L. REV. 455 (2004).

[58] *See* Patricia Zengerle, *U.S. Eases Rules to Admit More Syrian Refugees, After 31 Last Year*, REUTERS, Feb. 5, 2014, *available at* http://www.reuters.com/article/2014/02/05/us-syria-crisis-usa-refugees-idUSBREA141ZQ20140205 (last visited July 14, 2014).

[59] *See* Brooke Havard, Comment, *Seeking Protection: Recognition of Environmentally Displaced Persons Under International Human Rights Law*, 18 VILL. ENVIRON'L L. REV. 65 (2007).

[60] *See* Francis Gabor & John B. Rosenquest IV, *The Unsettled Status of Economic Refugees from the American and International Legal Perspectives — A Proposal for Recognition Under Existing International Law*, 41 TEX. INT'L L.J. 275 (2006).

[61] *See* BODVARSSON & VAN DEN BERG, *supra note 39*, at 437–40; OSCAR HANDLIN, BOSTON'S IMMIGRANTS: A STUDY IN ACCULTURATION 50–51 (1959); STEPHEN THERNSTROM, POVERTY AND PROGRESS: SOCIAL MOBILITY IN A NINETEENTH CENTURY CITY 17–21, 25–26 (1977); Lolita Buckner Innis, *Dutch Uncle Sam: Immigration Reform and Notions of Family*, 36 BRANDEIS J. FAM. L. 177, 185–86 (1997/98).

1.   Economic Impacts — The Labor Market

From an economic perspective, labor and capital are factors of production in a market economy. Migration to the United States directly affects the nation's supply of labor and thus directly impacts the domestic economy.[62] An increase to a factor of production ordinarily would be viewed as a net positive to the economy. However, matters are complicated when it comes to immigration — and the movement of people. Indeed, restrictionists and immigrant rights advocates often debate whether immigrants help or hurt the U.S. economy.[63]

Immigrants tend to be over-represented in the highest and lowest skilled jobs in the United States.[64] As two influential commentators have observed,

> high demand exists, at the low end, for unskilled and menial service workers and, at the high end, for professionals and technicians — with diminishing opportunities for well-paid employment in between. . . . Contemporary immigration has responded to this new "hourglass" economy by bifurcating, in turn, into major occupational categories. . . . The increasing heterogeneity of the contemporary foreign-born population in the wake of these legal and labor-market changes requires additional emphasis as a counterpart of the common popular description of immigration as a homogenous phenomenon.[65]

Thousands of skilled workers migrate to this country annually. However, there are many obstacles to lawful migration of skilled workers to the United States. The employment visa process "has been widely criticized as a broken system that is, at best grossly inefficient and, at worst, irrational."[66] Skilled workers must navigate a complex set of time-consuming and costly requirements that necessitate the assistance of skilled attorneys. Employers frequently complain about the time and expense of the labor certification process for the legal immigration of skilled workers to the United States. *See* Chs. 7, 8. The law, as it was designed, significantly inhibits the migration of skilled workers.

Economists often marshal arguments favoring liberal migration between nations and the ready mobility of labor. The benefits to the labor market derived from immigrant workers in the United States are undeniable. Nonetheless, as one policy analyst put it,

---

[62] For analysis of immigrants in the U.S. labor market, see CONGRESSIONAL BUDGET OFFICE, THE ROLE OF IMMIGRANTS IN THE U.S. LABOR MARKET (2005).

[63] *See* JOHNSON, *supra* note 3, at 131–67; BILL ONG HING, TO BE AN AMERICAN: CULTURAL PLURALISM AND THE RHETORIC OF ASSIMILATION 76–145 (2000).

[64] *See* JEFFREY S. PASSEL, BACKGROUND BRIEFING PREPARED FOR TASK FORCE ON IMMIGRATION AND AMERICA'S FUTURE 24 (Pew Hispanic Center 2005) ("Some have characterized the educational distribution of immigrants as an 'hourglass' because immigrants tend to be over-represented at both extremes [of education] relative to natives . . . ."), *available at* http://pewhispanic.org/files/reports/46.pdf (last visited July 17, 2014).

[65] ALEJANDRO PORTES & RUBÉN G. RUMBAUT, IMMIGRANT AMERICA: A PORTRAIT 27, 29 (4th ed. 2014).

[66] Enid Trucios-Haynes, *Temporary Workers and Future Immigration Policy Conflicts: Protecting U.S. Workers and Satisfying the Demand for Global Human Capital*, 40 BRANDEIS L.J. 967, 986 (2002) (footnote omitted).

U.S. immigration policy is based on denial. Most lawmakers in the United States have largely embraced the process of economic "globalization," yet stubbornly refuse to acknowledge that increased migration, especially from developing nations, is an integral and inevitable part of this process. Instead, they continue in an impossible quest that began shortly after World War II: the creation of a transnational market in goods and services without a corresponding transnational market for the workers who make those goods and provide those services. *In defiance of economic logic, U.S. lawmakers formulate immigration policies to regulate the entry of foreign workers into the country that are largely unrelated to the economic policies they formulate to regulate international commerce.* Even in the case of Mexico . . . , the U.S. government tries to impose the same arbitrary limits on immigration as it does on a country as remote as Mongolia. Moreover, while the global trade of goods, services, and capital is regulated through multilateral institutions and agreements, U.S. policymakers persist in viewing immigration as primarily a matter of domestic law enforcement. . . . Lawmakers must devise a realistic solution to this dilemma. *Perpetuating the status quo by pouring ever larger amounts of money into the enforcement of immigration policies that are in conflict with economic reality will do nothing to address the underlying problem.*[67]

In a similar vein, the Immigration Policy Center contends that "current U.S. immigration policies remain largely unresponsive to the labor needs of the U.S. economy by imposing arbitrary and static limits on employment-based immigration that have merely diverted labor migration to the undocumented channels or further clogged the family-based immigration system."[68]

Because the global economy has become increasingly competitive, focusing immigration law on labor migration is imperative. Some U.S. employers rely on undocumented labor in order to compete in the global marketplace. Low-cost immigrant labor increases a business's capacity to compete and benefits employers and the U.S. economy as a whole. Employers in agriculture, meat and poultry processing, and the hotel and restaurant industries, for example, often employ undocumented labor. Consumers benefit through lower prices for many commodities, including fruits, vegetables, meat, and poultry, and for services, such as domestic service work, hotels and restaurants, and construction.

Dependence on undocumented labor has led to employer resistance to various federal immigration enforcement efforts, especially workplace enforcement. For example, when the federal government began an operation to enforce the laws barring the employment of undocumented immigrants in the meat packing industry

---

[67] Walter A. Ewing, *From Denial to Acceptance: Effectively Regulating Immigration to the United States*, 16 STAN. L. & POL'Y REV. 445, 445–46 (2005) (emphasis added).

[68] IMMIGRATION POLICY CENTER, ECONOMIC GROWTH & IMMIGRATION: BRIDGING THE DEMOGRAPHIC DIVIDE (Nov. 2005). Some commentators have claimed that restrictive U.S. immigration laws have driven employers to outsource jobs to countries, including China and India, which would otherwise be performed by workers in the United States. *See, e.g.,* Mary Therese O'Sullivan, *A Paradox in Employment: The Contradiction that Exists Between Immigration Laws and Outsourcing Practices, and Its Impact on the Legal and Illegal Minority Working Classes*, 6 DEPAUL J. SOC. JUST. 111 (2012).

in Nebraska in 1999, state and local political leaders protested because of the impacts on the state economy.[69] For similar reasons, agricultural employers often support measures that would ease restrictions on access to immigrant workers. An American Farm Bureau Federation study concluded that, "*if agriculture's access to migrant labor were cut off, as much as $5–9 billion in annual production of . . . commodities . . . would be lost in the short term. Over the longer term, this annual loss would increase to $6.5–12 billion . . . .*"[70]

Many economists have observed that the domestic economy benefits from an expanding labor force that allows steady economic growth with a minimum of inflation. In fact, economists have credited the influx of immigrant labor with helping to spark the American economic boom of the 1990s, one of the more sustained periods of economic growth in U.S. history.[71] Respected former chair of the Federal Reserve Board Alan Greenspan opined that immigrants contributed more than their fair share to the economy.[72] Many immigrants take low-wage jobs that are not particularly easy for employers to fill at the wage rate that they want to pay.[73]

In addition, the money spent by immigrants have ripple effects, referred to by economists as "multiplier effects," with positive reverberations throughout the entire U.S. economy.[74] As the undocumented immigrant population has grown in this country, so has its purchasing power, and thus its importance to the nation's overall economic activity. Not surprisingly, many businesses now compete for business in the growing immigrant market. Increasing numbers of banks, health insurers, savings and loans, and home mortgage companies today accept foreign identification cards, rather than requiring official U.S. identification. For obvious reasons, businesses are eager to access new market opportunities with little concern about the immigration status of paying customers.[75]

There is one critically important — and rather obvious — difference between free trade in goods and services and free movement of labor. As Max Frisch observed about guest workers in Germany, "[w]e wanted workers, but humans

---

[69] *See* David Bacon, *And the Winner Is . . .* , AM. PROSPECT, Nov. 2005, at A12.

[70] AMERICAN FARM BUREAU FEDERATION, IMPACT OF MIGRANT LABOR RESTRICTIONS ON THE AGRICULTURAL SECTOR 1 (2006) (emphasis added).

[71] *See* AMERICAN IMMIGRATION LAW FOUNDATION, MEXICAN IMMIGRANT WORKERS AND THE U.S. ECONOMY: AN INCREASINGLY VITAL ROLE (2002); ANDREW SUM ET AL., IMMIGRANT WORKERS AND THE GREAT AMERICAN JOB MACHINE: THE CONTRIBUTIONS OF NEW FOREIGN IMMIGRATION TO NATIONAL AND REGIONAL LABOR FORCE GROWTH IN THE 1990s (National Business Roundtable, 2002).

[72] *See* Richard W. Stevenson, *Greenspan Holds Forth Before a Friendly Panel*, N.Y. TIMES, Jan. 27, 2000, at C1; *Alan Greenspan Is Embraced as a Champion of the Huddled Masses*, WALL ST. J., Mar. 14, 2000.

[73] *See* RAKESH KOCHHAR, LATINO LABOR REPORT, 2004: MORE JOBS BUT AT LOWER WAGES 1–2 (Pew Hispanic Center, May 2005), at http://pewhispanic.org/files/reports/45.pdf (last visited July 7, 2014).

[74] *See* JOHNSON, *supra* note 3, at 139–41.

[75] For a discussion of competition for the business of immigrants, see Laura Sonderup, *The Business of Immigrant Markets: Providing Access to Financial Services*, 60 CONSUMER FIN. L.Q. REP. 503 (2006); Tisha R. Tallman, *Liberty, Justice, and Equality: An Examination of Past, Present, and Proposed Immigration Policy Reform Legislation*, 30 N.C. J. INT'L L. & COM. REG. 869, 881–82 (2005).

came."[76] New people from foreign countries bring new families, cultures, languages, and change to the nation. What they bring therefore is qualitatively different than that brought by an influx of foreign capital or goods. Many Americans fear the cultural and other changes brought by immigrants.[77]

2. Economic Benefits for Employers and Business

At various times in U.S. history, business interests have vigorously supported less restrictive immigration laws.[78] Driven by the profit motive, employers may be expected to support policies, including guest worker programs and lax enforcement of the laws barring businesses from employing undocumented immigrants, which allow ready access to relatively inexpensive immigrant labor. For similar reasons, employers resist efforts at enforcement of the immigration laws. Even with congressional passage of the Immigration Reform and Control Act of 1986,[79] which made employers subject to sanctions for the employment of undocumented immigrants, *see* Ch. 14, many employers continue to employ them.

Businesses have strong economic incentives to advocate law and policies that ensure access to immigrant labor. Business interests often favor fewer immigration restrictions. One wing of the Republican Party supports more liberal immigration admissions. Another wing of the Party opposes the change brought by immigrants and calls for more restrictive laws and greater enforcement. The complex politics surrounding immigration greatly complicate efforts at reforming the U.S. immigration laws. *See* Ch. 18.

3. Benefits to Immigrant Workers

Of course, employers are not the only economic actors to benefit from immigration. Many immigrants come to this country for jobs that pay more than those in their homeland. Earnings that are low by American standards represent real improvements over what many migrants would earn at home. Employment, even if substandard by American standards, may well represent wage gains to the migrant worker from the developing world.

Upon migrating to the United States, immigrants often see tangible economic gains through higher wages. Indeed, economic opportunity is unquestionably one of the primary motivators behind many migrants' decisions to leave their homeland and come to this country. Not surprisingly, the immigrants most likely to migrate

---

[76] Max Frisch, *Uberfremdung I, in* SCHWEIZ ALS HEIMAT? 219 (1990).

[77] *See, e.g.*, PETER BRIMELOW, ALIEN NATION: COMMON SENSE ABOUT AMERICA'S IMMIGRATION DISASTER (1995); VICTOR DAVIS HANSON, MEXIFORNIA: A STATE OF BECOMING (2003); SAMUEL P. HUNTINGTON, WHO ARE WE?: THE CHALLENGES TO AMERICA'S NATIONAL IDENTITY (2004).

[78] *See* KITTY CALAVITA, U.S. IMMIGRATION LAW AND THE CONTROL OF LABOR, 1820–1924, at 151–57 (1984) (analyzing efforts of business to loosen immigration restrictions in the 1920s); JULIAN SAMORA, LOS MOJADOS: THE WETBACK STORY 33–57 (1971) (contending that the Border Patrol's enforcement efforts were closely aligned to the labor needs of growers); John A. Scanlan, *Immigration Law and the Illusion of Numerical Control*, 36 U. MIAMI L. REV. 819, 836 (1982) (recognizing efforts of business to ease restrictive U.S. immigration policies).

[79] Pub. L. No. 99-603, 100 Stat. 3359 (1986).

to the United States come from the developing world, where wages and economic opportunities are less than those in this country.

4. Aggregate Benefits to the National Economy

The 2005 Economic Report of the President, then George W. Bush, unequivocally concluded that *"[a] comprehensive accounting of the benefits and costs of immigration shows that the benefits of immigration exceed the costs."*[80] The 2013 Economic Report of the President, with Barack Obama at the helm, continued to emphasize the economic benefits of immigration, as well as the possible economic gains from of immigration reform:

> Immigrants add to the labor force and increase the economy's total output. The gains accrue to natives whose productivity is enhanced by immigrant workers — often referred to as complementary factors — as well as to capital owners. . . . A recent Congressional Budget Office study . . . found that allowing undocumented immigrants a pathway to citizenship is likely to help the Federal budget. The study estimates, that had a pathway had been established, Federal revenues would have increased by $48.3 billion while Federal outlays would have increased by $22.7 billion over the 2008–12 period, leading to a surplus of $25.6 billion.[81]

The federal government is not alone in the conclusion that immigration benefits the national economy. Long an unabashed supporter of free labor migration, the *Wall Street Journal* proclaimed in 1984 that "[i]f Washington still wants to 'do something' about immigration, we propose a five-word [constitutional] amendment: *There shall be open borders."*[82] As discussed above, employers and businesses gain economically from the ready availability of relatively inexpensive labor, which is especially advantageous in highly competitive industries.

Immigrants have helped to economically revitalize rundown urban centers. New York and Los Angeles are two well-known examples of metropolises that have seen urban decay transformed into economic renewal through immigration.[83] Immigrants come to these urban areas in search of economic opportunity. These areas often tend to be areas of high economic growth and great economic activity, which makes economic sense because migrants have no incentive to migrate to places where jobs and opportunities are not available.

In a regime of limited immigration opportunities, like that which exists under current U.S. immigration law, undocumented immigration provides concrete economic benefits to the national economy. As one economist aptly put it:

> It is not easy to fashion a convincing economic argument against an open door toward temporary workers with employer sponsorship, and thus illegal immigration may be in large part the result of economically unsound

---

[80] Economic Report of the President 93 (2005) (emphasis added).

[81] Economic Report of the President 154, 156 (2013).

[82] *In Praise of Huddled Masses*, Wall St. J., July 3, 1984, at 24 (emphasis added); *see The Simpson Curtain*, Wall St. J., Feb. 1, 1990, at A8 ("Our view is, borders should be open.").

[83] *See* Hing, *supra* note 63, at 54–56.

U.S. policies. Furthermore, because illegal aliens participate only minimally in entitlement programs, do not vote, and usually pay taxes like other workers, it is by no means clear that their presence should be viewed as a "problem." Without an appropriate policy regarding the admission of temporary workers, illegal immigration may be a "second-best" response to the resulting economic inefficiencies.[84]

The economic arguments in favor of more open immigration policies resemble those employed by international trade advocates for the free trade of goods and services across national boundaries. "Economists . . . recommend liberalized trade as a policy that is likely to produce gains for each national economy. Economists recognize that the same theory that applies to goods also applies to international trade in other markets. Nations can gain from not only the free movement of goods across national boundaries but also free movement of labor across national boundaries."[85]

Relying on international trade economics, Howard Chang has argued that liberalizing immigration policies would likely increase national and global economic welfare. In his estimation and that of others economists, freer migration policies would permit a more efficient use of the untapped source of relatively low-wage labor in countries across the world.[86] One influential econometric study found that "[a]lthough highly speculative, the calculations . . . clearly suggest large potential worldwide efficiency gains from moving toward a worldwide labor market free of immigration controls."[87]

The proliferation of trade agreements, including regional arrangements such as the European Union and the North American Free Trade Agreement, and global institutions, like the World Trade Organization, show the current popularity of free trade. *See* Ch. 18. Recognizing the economic benefits, leaders of many nations have promoted eliminating the barriers to the exchange of capital, goods, and services.

Immigration arguably contributes to the greater global good. Celebrated economist John Kenneth Galbraith observed that "[m]igration . . . is the oldest action against poverty. It selects those who most want help. *It is good for the*

---

[84] Alan O. Sykes, *The Welfare Economics of Immigration Law: A Theoretical Survey with an Analysis of U.S. Policy, in* Justice In Immigration 158, 159 (Warren A. Schwartz, ed., 1995).

[85] Howard F. Chang, *The Economics of International Labor Migration and the Case for Global Distributive Justice in Liberal Political Theory*, 41 Cornell Int'l L.J. 1, 1 (2008) (footnote omitted).

[86] *See* Donald J. Boudreaux, *Some Basic Economics of Immigration*, 5 J.L. Econ. & Pol'y 199 (2009); Howard F. Chang, *Liberalized Immigration as Free Trade: Economic Welfare and the Optimal Immigration Policy*, 145 U. Pa. L. Rev. 1147 (1997); Howard F. Chang, *Migration as International Trade: The Economic Gains from the Liberalized Movement of Labor*, 3 UCLA J. Int'l L. & Foreign Aff. 371 (1999) [hereinafter Chang, *Migration as International Trade*]; *see also* Jake Lichter, Note, *Mode IV and the Future of a Liberalized Global Immigration Policy*, 27 Geo. Immigr. L.J. 187 (2012) (analyzing the pros and cons of liberalized immigration policy and examining the World Trade Organization's restrictions on the movement of peoples). *But see* Julian L. Simon, The Economic Consequences of Immigration 365–66 (2d ed. 1999) (disputing that international trade and immigration are economically equivalent); Jennifer Gordon, *People Are Not Bananas: How Immigration Differs from Trade*, 104 Nw. U.L. Rev. 1109 (2010) (to the same effect).

[87] Bob Hamilton & John Whalley, *Efficiency and Distributional Implications of Global Restrictions on Labor Mobility*, 14 J. Dev. Econ. 61, 74 (1984).

country to which they go; it helps to break the equilibrium of poverty in the country from which they come."[88]

The economic benefits of immigration, however, are not all easy to quantify, or to identify concretely. It is difficult, for example, to estimate the precise impact of the ready availability of immigrant labor on consumer prices. The costs of immigration to a nation — such as the costs of providing a public education and emergency services by state and local governments — are easier to quantify. For this and other reasons, the costs of immigration tend to dominate the discussion of the economics of immigration. The advocates of immigration restrictions frequently present the economic impacts of immigration in a one-sided fashion by employing a cost/benefit analysis without a good estimate of the aggregate economic benefits.

5. Does Increased Immigration Enforcement Make Economic Sense?

Despite the tangible economic benefits of immigration, U.S. immigration law has been deeply ambivalent about immigration and immigrant workers.

The U.S. government often fails to consider basic labor economics in formulating immigration law and policy. As a result, the nation has created a system in which undocumented workers are integral to the national economy but, at the very same time, find themselves exploited and marginalized in American social life. To make matters worse, because the labor pool depends on the vagaries of immigration enforcement, employers may face fluctuating supplies of labor, which adversely affects productivity and economic efficiency.

Do aggressive immigration enforcement measures make economic sense? The answer to this question is far from clear. Economist John Kenneth Galbraith has emphasized that

> [w]ere all the illegals in the United States suddenly to return home, the effect on the United States economy would . . . be little less than disastrous . . . . A large amount of useful, if often tedious, work . . . would go unperformed. Fruits and vegetables in Florida, Texas, and California would go unharvested. Food prices would rise spectacularly. Mexicans wish to come to the United States; they are wanted; they add visibly to our well-being. . . . Without them, the American economy would suffer . . . .[89]

The administration of George W. Bush increased the use of workplace raids as a tool of immigration enforcement.[90] In May 2008, in Postville, Iowa, the U.S. government engaged in the largest raid on undocumented workers at a single site

---

[88] JOHN KENNETH GALBRAITH, THE NATURE OF MASS POVERTY 136 (1979) (emphasis added).

[89] *Id.* at 134.

[90] *See* Raquel Aldana, *Of Katz and "Aliens": Privacy Expectations and the Immigration Raids*, 41 UC DAVIS L. REV. 1081, 1092–96 (2008); Anil Kalhan, *The Fourth Amendment and Privacy Implications of Interior Immigration Enforcement*, 41 UC DAVIS L. REV. 1137 (2008); David B. Thronson, *Immigration Raids and the Destabilization of Immigrant Families*, 43 WAKE FOREST L. REV. 391 (2008); *see also* Shoba Sivaprasad Wadhia, *Under Arrest: Immigrants' Rights and the Rule of Law*, 38 U. MEMP. L. REV.

in U.S. history; nearly 900 agents surrounded the Agriprocessors plant, the nation's largest kosher slaughterhouse and meat processing plant.[91] Following the raids, many of the workers pled guilty to criminal immigration charges in mass proceedings.[92]

The Obama administration has generally opted for measures other than workplace raids to enforce the immigration laws in the interior of the United States. United ended in 2014, Secure Communities, which required state and local law enforcement authorities to cooperate with U.S. immigration enforcement agencies in sharing information on noncitizens who are arrested, WCS the administration's signature immigration enforcement program. *See* Ch. 4. Through Secure Communities and other enforcement measures, the Obama administration has removed record numbers of immigrants from the United States, in the neighborhood of 400,000 annually. *See* Ch. 12.

While the clamor for immigration enforcement continues, attention to the aggregate economic consequences of immigration has been minimal. Globalization of the world economy has been steadily proceeding over the post-World War II period. By the end of the twentieth century, integration of national economies had been achieved to a level never previously attained. Despite that economic integration, border enforcement continues to be aggressively employed to limit the movement of people into the United States. The U.S. government thus embraces comprehensive immigration restrictions as it simultaneously opens its borders to trade and flows of capital, goods, and services. "[T]he irony is that in this period of globalization marked by its free movement of capital and goods, the movement of labor is subject to greater restrictions than at the dawn of the Industrial Revolution."[93]

853, 862–88 (2008) (analyzing the rights of immigrants in workplace enforcement of the U.S. immigration laws).

[91] *See* Kevin R. Johnson, *The Intersection of Race and Class in U.S. Immigration Law and Enforcement*, 72 LAW & CONTEMP. PROBS. 1, 30–34 (2009); Allison L. McCarthy, *The May 12, 2008 Postville, Iowa Immigration Raid: A Human Rights Perspective*, 19 TRANSNAT'L & CONTEMP. PROBS. 293 (2010); Karla Mari McKanders, *The Unspoken Voices of Indigenous Women in Immigration Raids*, 14 J. GENDER RACE & JUST. 1 (2010); Marcela Mendoza & Edward M. Olivos, *Advocating for Control with Compassion: The Impacts of Raids and Deportations on Children and Families*, 11 OR. REV. INT'L L. 111 (2009).

[92] *See* ERIK CAMAYD-FREIXAS, U.S. IMMIGRATION REFORM AND ITS GLOBAL IMPACT: LESSONS FROM THE POSTVILLE RAID (2013); *see also* Evelyn H. Cruz, *Component Voices: Noncitizen Defendants and the Right to Know the Immigration Consequences of Plea Agreement*, 13 HARV. LATINO L. REV. 47 (2010) (reviewing the due process protections afforded to noncitizens in criminal proceedings with a focus on the Postville raid); Donna Ackermann, Note, *A Matter of Interpretation: How the Language Barrier and the Trend of Criminalizing Illegal Immigration Caused a Deprivation of Due Process Following the Agriprocessors, Inc. Raids*, 43 COLUM. J.L. SOC. PROBS. 363 (2010) (arguing that the due process rights of Agriprocessor workers were violated in the legal proceedings).

[93] CALAVITA, *supra* note 78, at 152.

6. The Economic Costs of Immigration

Studies attempting to measure the overall economic impacts of immigration have not been entirely consistent. Some studies conclude that the costs of immigration outweigh any benefits.[94] Others, including studies by the U.S. government,[95] contend that the alleged economic costs of immigration are overstated and are greatly outweighed by the benefits.[96] The most comprehensive empirical studies conclude that, in the larger scheme of things, any negative economic impacts of immigration on some segments of the U.S. labor face are relatively small and outweighed by the overall aggregate benefits to the national economy.[97]

Even assuming that the costs of immigration on some discrete segments of the U.S. economy do somewhat outweigh its benefits, more liberal admission policies might still offer net welfare gains to the entire nation. Enhanced labor mobility might benefit the national economy. Many economists, including some who criticize contemporary U.S. immigration policy, advocate this strategy.[98]

a. Downward Wage Pressures

Workers in the United States historically have feared labor competition from immigrant labor and the accompanying downward pressure on wages. Labor unions at various times have supported restrictionist immigration laws and policies, such as the employer sanctions of the 1986 immigration reform. See Ch. 14. Union support for the Chinese exclusion laws in the nineteenth century, discussed in Chs. 2, 3, and 6, is another well-known example. As discussed later in this Chapter, organized labor's position on immigration has changed significantly in recent years.

Immigrants often are blamed in contemporary public discussions of immigration for placing downward pressure on wages. The fear stems from the idea that immigrants will work for lower wages than U.S. citizens are willing to accept and that employers will consequently become unwilling to pay more than immigrants are willing to take. Employers and immigrant advocates counter with the claim that

---

[94] See, e.g., ROY BECK, THE CASE AGAINST IMMIGRATION: THE MORAL, ECONOMIC, SOCIAL, AND ENVIRONMENTAL REASONSFOR REDUCING U.S. IMMIGRATION BACK TO TRADITIONAL LEVELS (1996); GEORGE J. BORJAS, HEAVEN'S DOOR: IMMIGRATION POLICY AND THE AMERICAN ECONOMY (1999); BRIMELOW, supra note 77, at 137–77.

[95] See supra text accompany notes & notes 80–81.

[96] See, e.g., SIMON, supra note 86; see also Michael A. Olivas, Immigration Law Teaching and Scholarship in the Ivory Tower: A Response to Race Matters, 2000 U. ILL. L. REV. 613, 632–35 (reviewing studies on the economic costs and benefits of immigration to the United States).

[97] See NATIONAL RESEARCH COUNCIL, THE IMMIGRATION DEBATE: STUDIES ON THE ECONOMIC, DEMOGRAPHIC, AND FISCAL EFFECTS OF IMMIGRATION (1998); see also HING, supra note 63, at 76–106 (summarizing various studies on the economic consequences of immigration); LEGOMSKY & RODRÍGUEZ, supra note 47, at 71–85 (same); Bradford, supra note 25, at 31 (discussing the distribution of the economic costs and benefits of migration); Peter H. Schuck, Alien Rumination, 105 YALE L.J. 1963, 1981–87 (1996) (book review) (analyzing various economic studies on immigration and concluding that any adverse economic impacts were small compared to the overall size of the U.S. economy).

[98] See, e.g., BORJAS, supra note 94; SIMON, supra note 86; Gary S. Becker, Give Us Your Skilled Masses, WALL STREET J., Nov. 30, 2005, at A18.

immigrants are willing to do work that Americans simply will not do.[99]

There is evidence that low wage immigrant workers have negative effects on the wage scale of the lowest paid workers in the United States.[100] Unskilled U.S. citizens in urban, high immigration areas are the most directly affected. One much-cited 2005 study by Harvard economists George Borjas and Lawrence Katz attributed wage reductions for low skilled workers in the United States to undocumented immigration from Mexico.[101] Other empirical studies, however, reach contrary conclusions.[102] One study shows that immigration generally increases the wage level and accounts for only a small fraction of the increase in the wage gap between college educated students and high school dropouts from 1990 to 2004.[103] Any growth in wage disparities may be attributable to factors other than immigration, such as increasing worldwide competition and declining unionization in the United States.[104]

Even if the overall effects of immigration on unskilled citizens are relatively small, the impacts on discrete parts of the labor force are tangible and help generate tension between citizens and immigrants.[105] Immigration unquestionably has transformed — and continues to transform — certain labor markets. Over the last few decades, for example, jobs in the poultry and beef industries in the Midwest and Southeast and the janitorial industry in Los Angeles, have shifted from citizens to immigrant workers. In some circumstances, jobs have moved from being held predominantly by African American citizens to mostly Latina/o immigrants.[106]

---

[99] Others argue that Americans would in fact take these jobs if they paid a higher wage. Based on this argument, some commentators have embraced immigration restrictions as a way of improving the wages and working conditions of unskilled workers in certain industries, such as agriculture. *See, e.g.*, PHILIP L. MARTIN & DAVID A. MARTIN, THE ENDLESS QUEST: HELPING AMERICA'S FARM WORKERS (1994).

[100] *See, e.g.*, BORJAS, *supra* note 94.

[101] *See* GEORGE J. BORJAS & LAWRENCE F. KATZ, THE EVOLUTION OF THE MEXICAN BORN WORKFORCE IN THE UNITED STATES (2005).

[102] *See* Chang, *Migration as International Trade, supra* note 86, at 408–09 (citing and summarizing studies).

[103] *See* GIANMARCO I.P. OTTAVIANO & GIOVANNI PERI, RETHINKING THE EFFECTS OF IMMIGRATION ON WAGES (July 2006); *see also* GIANMARCO I.P. OTTAVIANO & GIOVANNI PERI, RETHINKING THE EFFECTS OF IMMIGRATION ON WAGES (2012) (reaching similar conclusions); GIOVANNI PERI & CHAD SPARBER, TASK SPECIALIZATION, IMMIGRATION, AND WAGES (July 2009) (same).

[104] *See* Eduardo Porter, *Cost of Illegal Immigration May Be Less Than Meets the Eye*, N.Y. TIMES, Apr. 16, 2006, at § 3, p. 3.

[105] *See* ROGER WALDINGER & MICHAEL I. LICHTER, HOW THE OTHER HALF WORKS: IMMIGRATION AND THE SOCIAL ORGANIZATION OF LABOR (2003); ETHNIC LOS ANGELES (Roger Waldinger & Mehdi Bozorgmehr eds., 1996); ROGER WALDINGER, STILL THE PROMISED CITY? AFRICAN-AMERICANS AND NEW IMMIGRANTS IN POSTINDUSTRIAL NEW YORK (1996).

[106] For analysis of the emergence of the "brown collar" workplace, see Leticia M. Saucedo, *Immigrants, Cultural Narratives, and National Origin*, 44 ARIZ. ST. L.J. 305 (2013); Leticia M. Saucedo, *The Browning of the American Workplace: Protecting Workers in Increasingly Latino-ized Occupations*, 80 NOTRE DAME L. REV. 303 (2004); Leticia M. Saucedo, *The Employer Preference for the Subservient Worker and the Making of the Brown Collar Workplace*, 67 OHIO ST. L.J. 961 (2006); Leticia M. Saucedo, *Addressing Segregation in the Brown Collar Workplace: Toward a Solution for the Inexorable 100%*, 41 U. MICH. J.L. REFORM 447 (2008).

Despite these costs, economists have identified many oft-ignored economic benefits from the migration of unskilled labor. Unskilled labor tends to increase demand for middle and higher skilled immigrants who are needed in order to efficiently utilize that unskilled labor. Complementarity of skills must be considered in evaluating the net benefit of immigrants on the labor market.[107] As one economist has noted,

> [f]oreign-born workers do not substitute perfectly for, and therefore do not compete with, most native-born workers. Rather the complementary nature of the skills, occupations, and abilities of foreign-born increases the productivity of natives, stimulates investment, and enhances the choices available to consumers. *As a result, immigration increases the average wages of all native-born workers, except those who do not have a high-school diploma. Even for the small and shrinking number of native-born workers without a high school diploma, the decline in wages from immigration is much smaller than some have estimated.*[108]

Moreover, as discussed previously, immigrants may contribute to overall gains to the national economy, which ultimately translates into an overall increase in average wages for *all* workers.[109] Put simply, the labor added by migrants adds to the overall economic growth of the United States.

Despite the overall benefits of immigrants to the economy, organized labor has often taken restrictionist positions in national debates on immigration. Unions historically have greatly feared downward pressures on the wage scale resulting from an influx of immigrant workers. The impact of immigrants on the job market is a bread-and-butter concern that has contributed greatly to periodic xenophobic outbursts that culminated in restrictionist immigration laws. *See* Ch. 2. Historically, labor unions have supported restrictionist measures, including the Chinese exclusion laws of the late nineteenth century.[110]

In recent years, major labor unions in the United States have shifted their position on immigration and are now exploring ways of organizing immigrant labor[111] and unionizing across national boundaries.[112] The AFL-CIO currently

---

[107] *See* Lawrence F. Katz & Kevin M. Murphy, *Changes in Relative Wages, 1963–1987: Supply and Demand Factors*, 107 Q. J. ECON. 35 (1992).

[108] GIOVANNI PERI, IMMIGRANTS, SKILLS, AND WAGES: REASSESSING THE ECONOMIC GAINS FROM IMMIGRATION (Immigration Policy Center, 2006) (emphasis added); *see* DAVID CARD, IS THE NEW IMMIGRATION REALLY SO BAD? (Nat'l Bureau of Economic Research Working Paper, 2005); GIOVANNI PERI, RETHINKING THE AREA APPROACH: IMMIGRANTS AND THE LABOR MARKET IN CALIFORNIA, 1960–2005 (Nat'l Bureau of Economic Research Working Paper, 2010).

[109] *See* GIANMARCO I.P. OTTAVIANO, RETHINKING GAINS FROM IMMIGRATION: THEORY AND EVIDENCE FROM THE U.S. (Nat'l Bureau of Economic Research Working Paper, 2005).

[110] *See* 3 PHILIP S. FONER, HISTORY OF THE LABOR MOVEMENT IN THE UNITED STATES 256–81 (1964) (describing the traditionally restrictionist positions of the American Federation of Labor).

[111] *See* Marion Crain & Ken Matheny, *Labor's Identity Crisis*, 89 CAL. L. REV. 1767, 1828–30 (2001).

[112] *See* Frederick M. Abbott, *Foundation-Building for Western Hemispheric Integration*, 17 Nw. J. INT'L L. & BUS. 900, 922 (1996–97). *See generally* DALE HATHAWAY, ALLIES ACROSS THE BORDER: MEXICO'S "AUTHENTIC LABOR FRONT" AND GLOBAL SOLIDARITY (2000) (analyzing efforts by labor unions to organize workers across borders).

supports immigration reform, including a path to legalization for undocumented workers.[113] It evidently came to the realization that border controls and aggressive border enforcement have not prevented immigrant labor from entering the country and are unlikely to do so in the foreseeable future.[114]

b. Wage Costs to Minorities

The claim that immigrant labor adversely affects *minority* citizens in low-wage jobs often finds its way into the immigration debate in the United States.[115] Some observers forcefully contend that immigration has adversely affected the economic fortunes of African Americans.[116]

Especially in major urban areas, immigrants — many of them Latina/o — may find themselves in competition with African American workers for low wage jobs.[117] In addition, migration may not only affect the labor markets in high immigration areas, where wages may be depressed, but may also lead to migration of citizens outside of those areas.[118] As for workers generally, immigrant labor appears to have a small overall impact on the wages of workers without high school diplomas. Such impacts, although small, affect the most vulnerable in the job market and can lead to strong resistance to more liberal immigrant admissions policies.

c. Increased Economic Inequality

A fear related to the concern that immigrant labor undercuts the domestic wage scale is that easy migration increases wealth inequality. This line of reasoning, which finds some support empirically, sees inexpensive labor as allowing businesses to reap greater profits, accumulate more wealth, and gain at the expense of workers. This phenomenon, however, may well be an enduring characteristic of a

---

[113] *See* AFL-CIO and Change to Win, The Labor Movement's Principles for Comprehensive Immigration Reform (2009), *available at* http://www.aflcio.org/content/download/60511/854621/ UnityFrameworkAug2009.pdf (last visited July 7, 2014).

[114] *See* Linda Bosniak, *Citizenship and Work*, 27 N.C. J. INT'L L. & COM. REG. 497, 503–05 (2002).

[115] *See, e.g.*, VERNON M. BRIGGS, JR., MASS IMMIGRATION AND THE NATIONAL INTEREST 211–15 (1992); MICHAEL LIND, THE NEXT AMERICAN NATION: THE NEW NATIONALISM AND THE FOURTH AMERICAN REVOLUTION 181–216 (1996).

[116] *See, e.g.*, BRIGGS, *supra* note 115, at 213–15; MICHAEL LIND, NEXT AMERICAN NATION: THE NEW NATIONALISM AND THE FOURTH AMERICAN REVOLUTION 139–216 (1996); HELP OR HINDRANCE? THE ECONOMIC IMPLICATIONS OF IMMIGRATION FOR AFRICAN AMERICANS (Daniel S. Hamermesh & Frank D. Bean, eds., 1998); STRANGERS AT THE GATES: NEW IMMIGRANTS IN URBAN AMERICA (Roger Waldinger ed., 2001); ROGER WALDINGER, STILL THE PROMISED CITY? AFRICAN-AMERICANS AND NEW IMMIGRANTS IN POST INDUSTRIAL NEW YORK (1996); Steven Schulman & Robert C. Smith, *Immigration and African Americans, in* AFRICAN AMERICANS IN THE U.S. ECONOMY 199 (Cecilia A. Conrad, John Whitehead, Patrick Mason, & James Stewart eds., 2005); *see also* Jennifer Gordon & R.A. Lenhardt, *Rethinking Work and Citizenship*, 55 UCLA L. REV. 1161 (2008) (evaluating the status of Latina/o and African American workers through different labor market and citizenship experiences). For analysis of the complex politics of immigration among the African American and Latina/o communities, see Maritza I. Reyes, *Opening Borders: African Americans and Latinos Through the Lens of Immigration*, 17 HARV. LATINO L. REV. 1 (2014).

[117] *See* Roger Waldinger, *Black/Immigrant Competition Re-Assessed: New Evidence from Los Angeles*, 40 SOC. PERSPECTIVES 365 (1997).

[118] *See* RONALD G. EHRENBERG & ROBERT S. SMITH, MODERN LABOR ECONOMICS: THEORY AND PUBLIC POLICY 356 (11th ed. 2011).

market economy rather than unique to immigration and liberal admissions policies. Even if such fears were real ones, it may not be possible through border enforcement measures to halt highly motivated immigrants pursuing economic opportunity from entering the United States. Other policies, such as the use of the tax system, might better address the wealth distribution impacts of immigration.[119]

According to some observers, globalization has led to increased economic inequality, with capital gaining at the expense of labor.[120] Such concerns have generated controversy and, at times, protests. Opposition to free trade, as exemplified by the, at times, violent protests in the 1990s against the World Trade Organization,[121] has been voiced at various times in the modern era.

Restrictionists often make forceful economic arguments for the maintenance of a limited entry immigration system.[122] One major argument is that, although employers stand to benefit from a more liberal admissions system, the concomitant costs are imposed on poor and working people. Fears of greater economic inequality in the United States due to liberal immigration policies — with businesses getting wealthier while real workers' wages decline with the influx of low wage immigrant workers — often contribute to the populist nature of anti-immigrant movements.

7. Public Benefits

Congress historically has limited the immigration of poor and working noncitizens to the United States.[123] Fears that the poor would empty the public coffers and fill the poor houses animate various provisions of the U.S. immigration laws, such as the exclusion of immigrants likely to become "public charges." *See* Ch. 9. The underlying concern is that poor and working noncitizens who come to this country will consume public benefits, exhaust scarce resources, and thus constitute a net drag on the national economy.[124]

---

[119] *See* Chang, *Migration as International Trade, supra* note 86, at 409–10.

[120] *See, e.g.*, Fran Ansley, *Inclusive Boundaries and Other (Im)possible Paths Toward Community Development in a Global World*, 150 U. PA. L. REV. 353 (2001); Gil Gott, *Critical Race Globalism? Global Political Economy, and the Intersections of Race, Nation, and Class*, 33 UC DAVIS L. REV. 1503 (2000); Sylvia R. Lazos Vargas, *Globalization or Global Subordination? How LatCrit Links the Local to Global and the Global to the Local*, 33 UC DAVIS L. REV. 1429, 1436–50 (2000); Chantal Thomas, *Globalization and the Reproduction of Hierarchy*, 33 UC DAVIS L. REV. 1451 (2000).

[121] *See* Ibrahim J. Gassama, *Confronting Globalization: Lessons from the Banana Wars and the Seattle Protests*, 81 OR. L. REV. 707, 730 (2002); Clyde Summers, *The Battle in Seattle: Free Trade, Labor Rights, and Societal Values*, 22 U. PA. J. INT'L ECON. L. 61 (2001); Susan Tiefenbrun, *Free Trade and Protectionism: The Semiotics of Seattle*, 17 ARIZ. J. INT'L & COMP. L. 257 (2000); *see also* Adam Warden, *A Brief History of the Anti-Globalization Movement*, 12 U. MIAMI INT'L & COMP. L. REV. 237 (2004) (summarizing the contemporary political movement against globalization).

[122] *See* Chandran Kukathas, *The Case for Open Migration, in* CONTEMPORARY DEBATES IN APPLIED ETHICS 207, 211–14 (Andrew I. Cohen & Christopher Heath Wellman eds., 2005).

[123] *See generally* Kevin R. Johnson, *Public Benefits and Immigration: The Intersection of Immigration Status, Ethnicity, Gender, and Class*, 42 UCLA L. REV. 1509 (1995).

[124] *See* Howard F. Chang, *The Immigration Paradox: Poverty, Distributive Justice, and Liberal Egalitarianism*, 52 DEPAUL L. REV. 759 (2003).

California's Proposition 187, which voters passed by a 2-1 margin in 1994, exemplifies the heated public reaction to the belief that undocumented immigrants are excessively using public benefits.[125] If it had been implemented, this measure would have denied undocumented students access to the public schools (contrary to Supreme Court precedent)[126] and would have rendered them ineligible for virtually almost all public benefits. The campaign that culminated in the passage of Proposition 187 was marred by anti-immigrant, and often anti-Mexican, rhetoric. A federal court barred most of Proposition 187 from going into effect because the state law intruded on the federal power to regulate immigration.[127] Its passage nonetheless demonstrates how fears of public benefits receipt by immigrants may translate into anti-immigrant laws. The political pressures behind Proposition 187 contributed to congressional passage of federal welfare reform in 1996 that eliminated eligibility of many legal immigrants for major federal benefit programs.[128]

States also have passed laws designed to restrict immigration and, in some instances, limited immigrant public benefit eligibility. In 2010, the Arizona legislature passed SB 1070, an immigration enforcement law designed to encourage the removal of undocumented immigrants in the state. A number of states, including Alabama, Georgia, Indiana, South Carolina, and Utah passed similar legislation. In 2012, the Supreme Court struck down several core provisions of the Arizona law.[129] *See* Ch. 4.

As discussed previously, the available data suggests that immigrants benefit the U.S. economy more than they cost it. Nevertheless, the fear of immigrant welfare abusers deeply influences the public discussion of immigration. Stereotypes of fertile Mexican women sneaking into the United States to give birth to U.S. citizen children[130] adds fuel to the fire, just as images of the Black welfare "queen" influence the public policy debates over welfare.[131]

---

[125] *See generally* Bosniak, *supra* note 32 (analyzing nature of opposition to Proposition 187); Johnson, *supra* note 123 (analyzing the impacts of Proposition 187 in light of the history of concern with immigrant public benefit receipt); Kevin R. Johnson, *An Essay on Immigration Politics, Popular Democracy, and California's Proposition 187: The Political Relevance and Legal Irrelevance of Race*, 70 Wash. L. Rev. 629 (1995) (analyzing the anti-Mexican sentiment at the core of the initiative campaign); Ruben J. Garcia, Comment, *Critical Race Theory and Proposition 187: The Racial Politics of Immigration Law*, 17 Chicano-Latino L. Rev. 118 (1995) (same).

[126] *See supra* text accompanying note & note 24 (citing Plyler v. Doe, 457 U.S. 202 (1982)).

[127] *See* League of United Latin Am. Citizens v. Wilson, 908 F. Supp. 755 (C.D. Cal. 1995).

[128] *See* Personal Responsibility and Work Opportunity Reconciliation Act of 1996, Pub. L. No. 104-193, 110 Stat. 2105.

[129] *See* Arizona v. United States, 132 S. Ct. 2492 (2012). For further analysis of the Supreme Court's decision in *Arizona v. United States*, see Ch. 4.

[130] *See* Catherine R. Albiston & Laura B. Nielsen, *Welfare Queens and Other Fairy Tales: Welfare Reform and Unconstitutional Reproductive Controls*, 38 How. L.J. 473, 476–88 (1995); Angela Onwuachi-Willig, *The Return of the Ring: Welfare Reform's Marriage Cure as the Revival of Post-Bellum Control*, 93 Cal. L. Rev. 1647, 1665–73 (2005).

[131] *See generally* Steven W. Bender, Greasers and Gringos: Latinos, Law, and the American Imagination (2003) (analyzing critically various stereotypes about Latina/os in American popular culture); Leo R. Chavez, The Latino Threat: Constructing Immigrants, Citizens, and the Nation (2008) (studying negative stereotypes of Latina/o immigrants).

The concern with public benefit receipt often influences controversies involving the rights of immigrants. For example, undocumented immigrant eligibility for a driver's license — an important public safety concern — has been challenged by opponents contending that undocumented immigrants should not be entitled to the "public benefit" of a license to drive.[132]

Immigrants are not eligible for the most costly federal public benefits programs. In 1996, Congress enacted welfare reform that made both lawful and undocumented immigrants ineligible for Temporary Assistance to Needy Families (TANF) and Food Stamps, two major federal public welfare programs.[133] Previously, lawful immigrants had been eligible for these benefits. Since 2009, states have had the option of covering lawful immigrants in TANF and some other programs.[134] Importantly, *undocumented* immigrants have *never* been eligible for the major — and most costly — federal public benefits programs.

Many immigrants pay taxes, a fact often ignored in the debate over immigrant public benefit receipt. Indeed, "each year undocumented immigrants add billions of dollars in sales, excise, property, income and payroll taxes, including Social Security, Medicare and unemployment taxes, to federal, state and local coffers. Hundreds of thousands of undocumented immigrants annually file federal and state income tax returns."[135]

Despite not having a Social Security number, many undocumented immigrants pay federal taxes by securing a Taxpayer Identification Number. Undocumented immigrants are often counseled to do so in order to improve their chances of later regularizing their immigration status. Nonetheless, ineligible for major public benefit programs, undocumented immigrants see limited direct benefits from their tax payments in terms of public benefit programs. Moreover, hundreds of thousands of undocumented immigrants work under assumed names and false Social Security numbers. Undocumented immigrants thus contribute billions of

---

[132] *See* Kevin R. Johnson, *Driver's Licenses and Undocumented Immigrants: The Future of Civil Rights Law?*, 5 NEV. L.J. 213 (2004); María Pabón Lopez, *More than a License to Drive: State Restrictions on the Use of Driver's Licenses by Noncitizens*, 29 S. ILL. U. L.J. 91 (2004/05); Sylvia R. Lazos Vargas, *Missouri, the "War on Terrorism," and Immigrants: Legal Challenges Post 9/11*, 67 Mo. L. REV. 775, 798–807 (2002).

[133] *See* Responsibility and Work Opportunity Reconciliation Act of 1996, Pub. L. No. 104-193, § 402, 110 Stat. 2105, 2260. Congress later restored certain benefits to certain categories of legal immigrants. *See* Noncitizen Benefit Clarification and Other Technical Amendments of 1998, Pub. L. No. 105-306, 112 Stat. 2926 (1998).

[134] For current eligibility of federal welfare and other public benefit programs, see U.S. Dep't of Heath & Human Services, Overview of Immigrants' Eligibility for SNAP, TANF, Medicaid, and CHIP (2012), *available at* http://aspe.hhs.gov/hsp/11/ImmigrantAccess/Eligibility/ib.shtml (last visited July 7, 2014); Nat'l Immigration Law Center, Overview of Immigrant Eligibility for Federal Programs (2011), *available at* http://www.nilc.org/overview-immeligfedprograms.html (last visited July 7, 2014).

[135] Francine J. Lipman, *The Taxation of Undocumented Immigrants: Separate, Unequal and Without Representation*, 9 HARV. LATINO L. REV. 1, 5 (2006) (footnotes omitted); *see* Francine J. Lipman, *The "Illegal" Tax*, 11 CONN. PUB. INT. L.J. 93 (2011) (dispelling the myth that immigrants do not pay taxes); Erin E. Stefonick, *The Alienability of Alien Sufferance: Taxation Without Representation in 2009*, 10 FLA. COASTAL L. REV. 691 (2009) (analyzing the disparity of access to public benefits between noncitizens and citizens despite the fact that both pay taxes).

dollars to help keep afloat the financially-strapped Social Security system and will never collect benefits.[136]

One of the major sources of state/federal tension results from the current allocation of costs and benefits of immigration between the state and federal governments. Many of the economic benefits stemming from immigration accrue to the federal government through the collection of tax revenues from employers who are increasingly profitable due to the access to immigrant labor. State and local governments, on the other hand, do not receive the bulk of the tax benefits, but are obliged to pay for public services, such as a public education and emergency health care, provided to immigrants. This fiscal disconnect is often at the crux of the dispute over the costs of immigration and proliferation of state and local laws seeking to regulate immigration and immigrants. *See* Ch. 4.

A few high-immigration states have aggressively pursued federal funds to help pay for the costs of immigration incurred at the state and local levels. Arizona, California, Florida, New Jersey, New York, and Texas have sued the U.S. government for compensation for the costs of immigration.[137] In 2005, Arizona and New Mexico sought to offset the costs of immigration by declaring immigration states of emergency, thus becoming eligible for federal emergency funding.[138] The federal government at various times has provided funds to states experiencing high rates of immigration in order to help offset the associated costs.[139]

8. Social and Cultural Impacts

The effects of immigration on the fabric of U.S. society have arisen time and again in American history. The United States has a checkered history of responding to immigrants. U.S. immigration law is famous for its cyclical nature. *See* Ch. 2.

At times, the nation has embraced some of the most liberal immigration admissions laws and policies in the world. The nation's immigration laws, during these times, have been truer to the ideal of offering open arms to the "huddled masses," as inscribed on the Statue of Liberty, than they are today. Despite the law's current restrictions on immigration, U.S. law remains more open in terms of admissions and access to citizenship than the laws of many developed nations.

At other times in U.S. history, the nation has embraced immigration laws and policies that, in retrospect, make us cringe with regret.[140] Time and time again,

---

[136] *See* Eduardo Porter, *Illegal Immigrants Are Bolstering Social Security with Billions*, N.Y. TIMES, Apr. 5, 2005, at 1.

[137] *See* Arizona v. United States, 104 F.3d 1095 (9th Cir.), *cert. denied*, 522 U.S. 806 (1997); Texas v. United States, 106 F.3d 661 (5th Cir. 1997); California v. United States, 104 F.3d 1086 (9th Cir. 1997); New Jersey v. United States, 91 F.3d 463 (3d Cir. 1996); Padavan v. United States, 82 F.3d 23 (2d Cir. 1996); Chiles v. United States, 69 F.3d 1094 (11th Cir. 1995), *cert. denied*, 517 U.S. 1188 (1996).

[138] *See* JOHNSON, *supra* note 3, at 153–54.

[139] *See* Hiroshi Motomura, *Federalism, International Human Rights, and Immigration Exceptionalism*, 70 U. COLO. L. REV. 1361, 1366–68 (1999); Jay T. Jorgensen, Comment, *The Practical Power of State and Local Governments to Enforce Federal Immigration Laws*, 1997 BYU L. REV. 899, 937–39.

[140] *See generally* JOHN HIGHAM, STRANGERS TO THE LAND: PATTERNS OF AMERICAN NATIVISM 1860–1925 (8th

fear and social stress have sparked fiery attacks on the nation's most vulnerable outsiders. *See* Ch. 2. Punitive immigration laws and tough enforcement, as well as harsh treatment of immigrants and minorities who shared similar characteristics, can be found repeatedly in the annals of American history.

The cyclical nature of immigration politics — and thus U.S. immigration law and policy — often has been directly linked to the overall state of the domestic economy and the perceived social evils of the day. War, political and economic turmoil, and other tensions also have influenced the nation's collective attitude toward immigration. Social stresses, like fears of terrorism after September 11, 2001, find a ready outlet in immigration law and its enforcement, with much more limited constitutional constraints than in other areas of law.

a. "Illegal Aliens" and the Influence of Racism, Nativism, Etc.

Immigrants often have a distinctively negative image in popular culture. Although not officially defined by the Immigration & Nationality Act of 1952, the emotion-laden phrase "illegal aliens" figures prominently in popular debate over immigration.[141] "Illegal aliens," as their moniker strongly implies, are characterized as law-breakers, abusers, and intruders, undesirables we want excluded from U.S. society. The very use of the term "illegal aliens" frequently betrays a restrictionist bias in the speaker. By stripping people of their humanity, the terminology helps rationalize the harsh treatment of undocumented immigrants under the immigration laws.

Although its precise impacts are difficult to measure, intolerance, particularly in the form of racism and nativism, unquestionably at various times, has influenced U.S. immigration law and policy. *See* Chs. 2, 3, 6. To make matters worse, the courts have often refused to intervene to halt the excesses of the political process. *See* Ch. 6. Consequently, periodic waves of harsh exclusions and deportation campaigns dominate the history of U.S. immigration law and its enforcement. Restrictionist measures, such as the Chinese exclusion laws, the discriminatory national origins quotas system, and sporadic deportation campaigns that target Mexican nationals, are monuments to times when anti-immigrant sentiment carried the day in the political process. *See* Ch. 2.

As summarized in Chapter 2, the United States has historically excluded disfavored groups from the nation's shores. In the early days of the Republic, political dissidents were punished through deputation under the Alien and Sedition Acts. During the Red Scare after World War I and the McCarthy era of the 1950s,

---

ed. 2008); BILL ONG HING, DEFINING AMERICA THROUGH IMMIGRATION POLICY (2004); KEVIN R. JOHNSON, THE "HUDDLED MASSES" MYTH: IMMIGRATION AND CIVIL RIGHTS (2004); LUCY E. SALYER, LAWS HARSH AS TIGERS: CHINESE IMMIGRANTS AND THE SHAPING OF MODERN IMMIGRATION LAW (1995).

[141] *See* MAE M. NGAI, IMPOSSIBLE SUBJECTS: ILLEGAL ALIENS AND THE MAKING OF MODERN AMERICA (2004). For analysis of the negative connotations of the term "alien," which is the centerpiece of the comprehensive Immigration and Nationality Act, see Kevin R. Johnson, *"Aliens" and the U.S. Immigration Laws: The Social and Legal Construction of Nonpersons,* 28 U. MIAMI INTER-AM. L. REV. 263 (1996–97); D. Carolina Nuñez, *War of the Word: Aliens, Immigrants, Citizens, and the Language of Exclusion,* 2013 BYU L. REV. 1517.

communist sympathies of the loosest variety could result in the deportation of a noncitizen. In one such case, a long-term lawful permanent resident faced the prospect of indefinite detention on Ellis Island for alleged communist ties based on secret evidence after his native land refused to accept his return.[142]

There is nothing more inconsistent with the nation's oft-repeated commitment to the "huddled masses" of the world than to bar poor and working immigrants from coming to the United States. But poor and working class immigrants have legally been excluded in large numbers from this country for much of U.S. history. *See* Ch. 2. The driving force behind their exclusion has been the idea that the nation cannot admit immigrants who would contribute little to the U.S. economy and might exhaust precious public benefits.

The immigration laws have also sought to keep out immigrants who shared characteristics with unpopular groups in the United States. The historical exclusion of gay men and lesbians, the disabled, and many other groups have reflected biases in U.S. society generally.[143] Indeed, until 1990, the immigration laws classified homosexuals as "psychopathic personalities" who could be lawfully barred from the United States.[144]

In restricting the admission of undesirable noncitizens, immigration law has been used to systematically maintain the racial demographics of the United States. For much of U.S. history, race has been expressly incorporated into the immigration laws and their enforcement. Laws like the Chinese exclusion laws, the national origins quota system, which preferred immigration from northern Europe,[145] and the requirement that an immigrant be "white" to naturalize, which was the law of the land from 1790 until 1952,[146] exemplify this racial bias.

The triumph of the civil rights movement and its embrace of the antidiscrimination principle, led Congress to remove race-based exclusions from the immigration laws. The Immigration Act of 1965[147] eliminated the discriminatory national

---

[142] *See* Shaughnessy v. United States *ex rel.* Mezei, 345 U.S. 206 (1953); *see also* United States *ex rel.* Knauff v. Shaughnessy, 338 U.S. 537 (1950) (declining to disturb the U.S. government's refusal to allow a noncitizen to come to the United States to be with her U.S. citizen spouse based on secret evidence that she was a danger to national security). *See generally* Charles D. Weisselberg, *The Exclusion and Detention of Aliens: Lessons from the Lives of Ellen Knauff and Ignatz Mezei*, 143 U. Pa. L. Rev. 933 (1995) (discussing the facts surrounding the circumstances surrounding the cases of Mezei and Knauff).

[143] *See generally* Johnson, *supra* note 140.

[144] *See id.* at 140–51; *see, e.g.*, Boutilier v. INS, 387 U.S. 118 (1967) (holding that Congress intended to include homosexuals as "psychopathic personalities" subject to exclusion from the United States). Changes in the immigration laws have come as domestic sensibilities have changed. For example, after the U.S. Supreme Court in *United States v. Windsor*, 133 S. Ct. 2675 (2013) invalidated the core of the Defense of Marriage Act, U.S. immigration authorities began to process immigration visa petitions filed on behalf of same-sex spouses. *See* Statement by Former Secretary of Homeland Security Janet Napolitano, Implementation of the Supreme Court Ruling on the Defense of Marriage Act (July 1, 2013), *available at* https://www.hsdl.org/?view&did=739720.

[145] *See supra* note 140 (citing authorities).

[146] *See generally* Ian Haney Lopez, White by Law: The Legal Construction of Race (10th commemorative ed. 2006) (analyzing the requirement that an immigrant be white to naturalize).

[147] Pub. L. No. 89-236, 79 Stat. 911 (1965). For analysis of the 1965 Act's restrictions on Latina/o immigration as a compromise necessary to secure the elimination of the national origins quotas system,

origins quotas system and embraced color-blindness in immigrant admissions. Since 1965, immigration from Asia to the United States has increased.[148] This change in migration patterns has worried some Americans concerned about maintaining the American national identity as well as those concerned about immigration's impact on labor markets and wages.

Even though color blind on their face, the modern U.S. immigration laws continue to have disproportionate impacts on noncitizens of color.[149] People of color from the developing world, particularly those from nations that send relatively large numbers of immigrants to the United States, are the most disadvantaged of all groups — especially those of a select few high immigration nations. They suffer disproportionately from tighter entry requirements and heightened immigration enforcement. For example, under certain visa categories, noncitizens from India, the Philippines, and Mexico experience much longer waits for entry into the United States than similarly situated noncitizens from other nations.[150]

b. National Identity

Throughout U.S. history, restrictionists have regularly called for drastic reductions of immigration to the United States. Today, anti-immigrant positions grab the headlines, add sensational flare to Fox News, and sell well in bookstores.

Alarmist books about the evils of immigration have a long, if not illustrious, history. Early in the twentieth century, many books appealed to claims of white racial superiority, antipathy for immigration and immigrants, and looming "crisis."[151] This fervently anti-immigrant literature offered intellectual justification for the discriminatory national origins quotas system enacted by Congress in 1924. *See* Ch. 2. That system, which favored immigrants from northern Europe over all others, were unquestionably based on racially discriminatory views and the belief

---

see Kevin R. Johnson, *The Beginning of the End: The Immigration Act of 1965 and the Emergence of the Modern U.S./Mexico Border State*, IMMIGRATION & NATIONALITY L. REV. (forthcoming 2015), *available at* http://papers.ssrn.com/sol3/papers.cfm?abstract_id=2362478.

[148] *See* Gabriel J. Chin, *The Civil Rights Revolution Comes to Immigration Law: A New Look at the Immigration and Nationality Act of 1965*, 75 N.C. L. REV. 273 (1996).

[149] *See* Kevin R. Johnson, *The Immigration Laws, and Domestic Race Relations: A "Magic Mirror" into the Heart of Darkness*, 73 IND. L.J. 1111 (1998).

[150] *See* Bernard Trujillo, *Immigrant Visa Distribution: The Case of Mexico*, 2000 WIS. L. REV. 713 (showing how annual ceilings on certain immigrant admissions from a single country apply to all nations but have a disproportionate impact on prospective immigrants from Mexico, and noncitizens from several other developing nations, because demand for immigration from those nations greatly exceeds the ceiling); Jennifer M. Chacón, *Loving Across Borders: Immigration Law and the Limits of Loving*, 2007 WIS. L. REV. 345, 359–60 (same); Stephen H. Legomsky, *Immigration Equality and Diversity*, 31 COLUM. J. TRANSNAT'L L. 319, 321 (1993) (commenting on disparate racial impacts of per country ceilings); Jan C. Ting, *"Other than a Chinaman": How U.S. Immigration Law Resulted From and Still Reflects a Policy of Excluding and Restricting Asian Immigration*, 4 TEMPLE POL. & CIV. RTS. L. REV. 301, 309 (1995) (same). The U.S. DEP'T OF STATE, BUREAU OF CONSULAR AFFAIRS, VISA BULLETIN for July 2014, *available at* http://travel.state.gov/content/visas/english/law-and-policy/bulletin/2014/visa-bulletin-for-july-2014.html (last visited July 7, 2014) (shows year long waits, some as long as 20 years, for certain categories of visas for noncitizens from Mexico, India, and the Philippines).

[151] *See* MADISON GRANT, THE PASSING OF THE GREAT RACE, OR THE RACIAL BASIS OF EUROPEAN HISTORY (1916); LOTHROP STODDARD, THE RISING TIDE OF COLOR AGAINST WHITE WORLD SUPREMACY (1920).

that it was necessary and proper to curtail immigration to ensure white supremacy in the United States.

Concerns with the racial composition of the United States constitute a link between the restrictionists of yesterday and today. Many of best-selling books advocates the need to drastically reduce the current levels of immigration to the United States.[152] Importantly, commentators of many different political persuasions advocate restrictionist positions. Some progressives embrace reducing immigration to protect poor, minority, and working U.S. citizens.[153]

In *Who Are We?: The Challenges to America's National Identity*,[154] Samuel Huntington expressed the fear that the increasingly multicultural United States could disintegrate into the type of ethnic strife that destroyed the former Yugoslavia in the 1990s, or, in less dramatic fashion, divided Quebec for much of the twentieth century. A most controversial part of the book is Huntington's claim that immigration from Mexico is a threat to American national identity and national unity. He asserts that Mexican immigrants differ from other immigrant groups because of the proximity of Mexico to the United States and the number of immigrants — legal and undocumented — from Mexico in this country.[155]

In modern times, the United States continues to use its immigration law and policy to respond to the perceived social problems of the day. Today, commentators, such as Samuel Huntington, in the United States view Mexican migration as a serious social problem. Some Americans believe that the United States has "lost control" of its borders[156] and that excessive numbers of immigrants are coming to this country.

At various times in American history, the U.S. government has attempted to coerce immigrants and people of color to assimilate into the mainstream and adopt "American" ways. Coerced assimilation of noncitizens was popular early in the twentieth century. The emergence of the public commitment to the tolerance of different cultures in the form of multiculturalism has made it more difficult to adopt

---

[152] Bestsellers in the restrictionist genre include BRIMELOW, *supra* note 77; PATRICK J. BUCHANAN, DEATH OF THE WEST: HOW DYING POPULATIONS AND IMMIGRANT INVASIONS IMPERIL OUR COUNTRY AND CIVILIZATION (2002); HANSON, *supra* note 77; MICHELLE MALKIN, INVASION: HOW AMERICA STILL WELCOMES TERRORISTS, CRIMINALS, AND OTHER FOREIGN MENACES TO OUR SHORES (2002).

[153] *See e.g.*, ROY BECK, THE CASE AGAINST IMMIGRATION: THE MORAL, ECONOMIC, SOCIAL, AND ENVIRONMENTAL REASONS FOR REDUCING U.S. IMMIGRATION BACK TO TRADITIONAL LEVELS (1996); TODD GITLIN, THE TWILIGHT OF COMMON DREAMS: WHY AMERICA IS WRACKED BY CULTURE WARS (1995), MICHAEL LIND, NEXT AMERICAN NATION: THE NEW NATIONALISM AND THE FOURTH AMERICAN REVOLUTION (1996).

[154] *See* HUNTINGTON, *supra* note 77.

[155] For a response to Huntington's claims, see Kevin R. Johnson & Bill Ong Hing, *National Identity in a Multicultural Nation: The Challenge of Immigration Law and Immigrants*, 103 MICH. L. REV. 1347, 1364–68 (2005); *see also* George A. Martínez, *Immigration: Deportation and the Psuedo-Science of Unassimilable Peoples*, 61 SMU L. REV. 7, 10–11 (2008) (questioning claims by Huntington and others that immigrants today fail to assimilate).

[156] *See* Immigration Reform and Control Act of 1983: Hearings on H.R. 1510 Before the Subcomm. On Immigration, Refugees, and International Law of the House Comm. of the Judiciary, 98th Cong., 1st Sess. 6 (1983) (testimony of Attorney General William French Smith) ("We have lost control of our borders. We have pursued unrealistic policies. We have failed to enforce our laws effectively.").

coercive measures that mandate assimilation or to criticize the culture of people of Mexican ancestry as inferior.[157]

Nonetheless, demands for immigrant assimilation, and complaints about the failure of today's immigrants to assimilate, reappear in the public debate with remarkable consistency. Such demands persist even though English language programs that would promote assimilation go underfunded by government and access to such programs is limited for most immigrants.[158] Assimilation demands tend to be more refined than in the past. Relatively few claims are made — at least in polite company — that the racial inferiority of today's immigrants makes their assimilation next to impossible.

c. National Security Anxieties

The anti-terrorism policies adopted after September 11, 2001 negatively affected the civil rights of immigrants, and certain groups of U.S. citizens, in the United States. Muslims and Arab communities initially were targeted for arrest, detention, and interrogation and an entire array of special immigration requirements and program.[159] Immigration law, known for delegating vast powers to the Executive Branch and Congress, see Ch. 6, became the focal point of the nation's domestic war on terror. In the USA PATRIOT (Uniting and Strengthening America by Providing Appropriate Tools Required to Intercept and Obstruct Terrorism) Act,[160] Congress expanded the definition of "terrorist activity" and also afforded the Executive Branch greater authority to act in the name of national security.

Other immigrant groups have also suffered the ripple effects of the "war on terror." For example, the deportation of Mexican and Central American immigrants escalated dramatically in the years after September 11, 2001.[161] Enforcement of the

---

[157] See George A. Martínez, *Latinos, Assimilation and the Law: A Philosophical Perspective*, 20 CHICANO-LATINO L. REV. 1, 13–18 (1999) (analyzing the relationship between multiculturalism and assimilation); George A. Martínez, *Immigration and the Meaning of United States Citizenship: Whiteness and Assimilation*, 46 WASHBURN L.J. 335 (2007) (analyzing the requirement of assimilation as a prerequisite for full U.S. citizenship); *see also* George A. Martínez, *Race, American Law, and the State of Nature*, 112 W. VA. L. REV. 799 (2010) (articulating the philosophical explanation for harsh treatment of racial minorities under U.S. immigration laws).

[158] See James Thomas Tucker, *The ESL Logjam: Waiting Times for ESL Classes and the Impact on English Learners; English as a Second Language*, NAT'L CIVIC REV., Mar. 22, 2007, vol. 96, No. 1. Increasingly, the private sector has promoted immigrant assimilation with employers, among other policies, promoting English language acquisition. *See* Pamela Constable & N.C. Aizenman, *Companies Take Lead in Assimilation Efforts*, WASH. POST, Aug. 9, 2008, at B1.

[159] See Susan M. Akram & Kevin R. Johnson, *Race, Civil Rights, and Immigration Law After September 11, 2001: The Targeting of Arabs and Muslims*, 58 NYU ANN. SURV. AM. L. 295 (2002); Muneer I. Ahmad, *A Rage Shared by Law: Post-September 11 Racial Violence as Crimes of Passion*, 92 CAL. L. REV. 1259 (2004); Bill Ong Hing, *Vigilante Racism: The De-Americanization of Immigrant America*, 7 MICH. J. RACE & L. 1441 (2002); Leti Volpp, *The Citizen and the Terrorist*, 49 UCLA L. REV. 1575 (2002).

[160] Pub. L. No. 107-56, 115 Stat. 272 (2001). In 2006, Congress extended, as modified, the Act but narrowed it in response to certain criticisms. *See* Pub. L. No. 109-177, 120 Stat. 192 (2006).

[161] See Kevin R. Johnson & Bernard Trujillo, *Immigration Reform, National Security After September 11, and the Future of North American Integration*, 91 MINN. L. REV. 1369 (2007); Kevin R. Johnson, *September 11 and Mexican Immigrants: Collateral Damage Comes Home*, 52 DEPAUL L. REV. 849 (2003).

U.S./Mexico border has emerged as national security concern.

9. Crime

The 1990s saw nothing less than a monumental shift toward aggressive immigration enforcement in the United States. Border enforcement became one of the nation's highest priorities. *See* Ch. 2. In 1996, Congress enthusiastically joined the fray. Bent on curbing undocumented immigration, deporting criminal aliens, protecting the nation from terrorists, and guarding the public fisc, Congress passed a series of tough immigration laws.[162] Detention of many aliens became mandatory, with the number of immigrants detained increasing dramatically in local jails, federal penitentiaries, and privately run detention facilities. "Criminal aliens" — with the vast majority from Mexico and Central America — have been detained and deported in record numbers since 1996.[163]

In recent years, the U.S. government has focused enforcement efforts on the deportation of criminal aliens,[164] including but not limited to so-called gang members.[165] The U.S. government has prosecuted immigration crimes, such as illegal re-entry into the country, at record rates and the cases often clog the federal courts of the U.S./Mexico border region.[166]

Despite popular stereotypes about the criminal alien, there is little evidence that the crime rate among immigrants in the United States is any higher than that among the general population. As Peter Schuck stated in a comprehensive review of the data,

> [a]lthough the systematic data on point are somewhat dated, legal immigrants do not appear to commit any more crime than demographically similar Americans; they may even commit less, and that crime may be less serious. Nor does today's immigrant crime appear to be worse than in earlier eras. The immigrants who flooded American cities around the

---

[162] *See* Illegal Immigration Reform and Immigrant Responsibility Act, Pub. L. No. 104-208, 110 Stat. 3009 (1996); Antiterrorism and Effective Death Penalty Act, Pub. L. No. 104-132, 110 Stat. 1214 (1996); Personal Responsibility and Work Opportunity Act, Pub. L. No. 104-193, 110 Stat. 2105 (1996); see also Deborah Weissman, *The Politics of Narrative: Law and the Representation of Mexican Criminality*, 38 Fordham Int'l L.J. 141 (2015) (analyzing impacts of Mexican-as-criminal narrative).

[163] Detention of immigrants is costly. *See* National Immigration Forum, The Math of Immigration Detention: Runaway Costs for Immigration Detention Do Not Add Up to Sensible Policies (2013), *available at* http://www.immigrationforum.org/images/uploads/mathofimmigrationdetention.pdf (last visited July 7, 2014).

[164] *See generally* Allegra M. McLeod, *The U.S. Criminal-Immigration Convergence and Its Possible Undoing*, 49 Am. Crim. L. Rev. 105 (2012); Jennifer M. Chacón, *Unsecured Borders: Immigration Restrictions, Crime Control and National Security*, 39 Conn. L. Rev. 1827 (2007); Stephen H. Legomsky, *The New Path of Immigration law: Asymmetric Incorporation of Criminal Justice Norms*, 64 Wash. & Lee L. Rev. 469 (2007); Teresa Miller, *Blurring the Boundaries Between Immigration and Crime Control After September 11*, 25 B.C. Third World L.J. 81 (2005); Juliet Stumpf, *The Crimmigration Crisis: Immigrants, Crime, and Sovereign Power*, 56 Am. U. L. Rev. 367 (2006). *See generally* Ch. 15 (discussing the criminalization of U.S. immigration law).

[165] *See* Jennifer M. Chacón, *Whose Community Shield?: Examining the Removal of the "Criminal Street Gang Member"*, 2007 U. Chi. Leg. F. 317.

[166] *See* Chacón, *supra* note 164, at 1846–48.

turn of the century (the ancestors of many of today's Americans) were also excoriated as congenitally vicious and usually crime-prone . . . . The evidence suggests that those claims were false then, and similar claims appear to be false now.[167]

A number of recent studies suggest that immigrants are less, not more, prone to crime than the native born.[168] A 2005 study found that "[o]ver the 1990s,. . . . immigrants who chose to come to the United States *were less likely to be involved in criminal activity than earlier immigrants and the native born.*"[169] One 2006 commentary published in the *Wall Street Journal* speculated that the drop in national crime rates may be attributable to increased immigration.[170]

Nonetheless, concerns with criminal aliens remain politically popular and the U.S. government has focused much time and effort deporting them. Increasingly, the federal government has coordinated with state and local governments to facilitate noncitizens convicted of crimes.[171] *See* Ch. 4.

Like some U.S. citizens, some noncitizens in the United States commit crimes and are incarcerated. State and local governments prosecute many of these crimes, and pay for the incarceration of many convicted criminals. Such costs may be substantial in high immigration states. As a result of the "war on drugs," and the ever-increasing rates of incarceration of young men, such costs have swelled over the last few decades.

Like the immigrant benefit recipient, the "criminal alien" generates great fear among the general public. Criminals have few defenders in the political process. "Criminal aliens" have even fewer political allies. Consequently, fears of criminal

---

[167] Schuck, *supra* note 97, at 1988–89 (emphasis added); *see* Chacón, *supra* note 164, at 1879 ("In spite of the persistent belief that immigrant groups are more likely to commit crime than the native born, the available evidence suggests that the belief is unfounded.").

[168] *See* KRISTIN E. BUTCHER & ANNE MORRISON PIEHL, CRIME, CORRECTIONS, AND CALIFORNIA (Public Policy Institute of California 2008); RUBÉN G. RUMBAUT & WALTER EWING, THE MYTH OF IMMIGRANT CRIMINALITY AND THE PARADOX OF ASSIMILATION: INCARCERATION RATES AMONG NATIVE AND FOREIGN-BORN MEN (2007). One analysis found that "data from New Jersey and California once again confirms what researchers have found repeatedly over the past 100 years; immigrants are *less* likely than the native-born to be in prison, and high rates of immigration are *not* associated with higher rates of crime." IMMIGRATION POLICY CENTER, NEW STATE-LEVEL RESEARCH DEBUNKS THE MYTH OF IMMIGRANT CRIMINALITY (July 17, 2008) (emphasis in original).

[169] KRISTIN F. BUTCHER & A.M. PIEHL, WHY ARE IMMIGRANTS' INCARCERATION RATES SO LOW? EVIDENCE OF SELECTIVE IMMIGRATION, DETERRENCE, AND PUNISHMENT 2 (Federal Reserve Bank of Chicago, Nov. 2005) (emphasis added).

[170] *See* Robert J. Sampson, *Open Doors Don't Invite Criminals*, WALL STREET J., Mar. 11, 2006, at A27.

[171] *See* Peter H. Schuck & John Williams, *Removing Criminal Aliens: The Pitfalls and Promises of Federalism*, 22 HARV. J.L. & PUB. POL'Y 367 (1999); U.S. Senator Jeff Sessions & Cynthia Hayden, *Immigration in the Twenty-First Century: The Growing Role for State & Local Law Enforcement in the Realm of Immigration Law*, 16 STAN. L. & POL'Y REV. 323 (2005). For criticism, see Huyen Pham, *The Inherent Flaws in the Inherent Authority Position: Why Inviting Local Enforcement of Immigration Laws Violates the Constitution*, 31 FLA. ST. U. L. REV. 965 (2004); Michael J. Wishnie, *Civil Liberties in a New America: State and Local Police Enforcement of Immigration Laws*, 6 U. PA. J. CONST. L. 1084 (2004).

aliens have resulted in stringent provisions in the immigration laws directed at noncitizens convicted of crimes.[172]

Immigration reforms in 1996 made deportation of criminal noncitizens a top priority and dramatically expanded the criminal removal grounds. Increasingly greater numbers of crimes subjected noncitizens to removals. A crime classified as an "aggravated felony" under the immigration laws was transformed to include crimes that are not always particularly "aggravated" or a "felony" under current law. See Chs. 12, 15. The 1996 reforms also made detention of criminals awaiting deportation much more common, even mandatory in certain cases. See Ch. 6. Following the passage of the reforms, the federal government aggressively pursued criminal deportations. Consequently, removals of criminal aliens have occurred at record levels over the last decade.[173] At the same time, the Supreme Court has regularly rejected arguments of the U.S. government for mandatory removal of lawful permanent residents who have been convicted of relatively minor crimes.[174]

10. Environmental Costs

Concerns frequently have been raised about the environmental consequences of immigration. Restrictionists argue that hundreds of thousands of immigrants coming to the United States have resulted in overpopulation. The argument effectively amounts to an economic concern with the allocation of a perceived scarce resource, in this case access to this country. Limits on immigration promise to keep a lid on population growth. Concerns with the world population, as well as the global environment, are secondary to those who adopt this type of "America-first" attitude. Environmental concerns periodically have been raised in the debate over immigration and likely will reappear in the future.[175]

The Sierra Club, an influential American environmental group, has experienced internal division over immigration. For years, the organization did not formally take a position on immigration,[176] as it vigorously debated the issue.[177] Members in

---

[172] See, e.g., Daniel Kanstroom, *Deportation, Social Control, and Punishment: Some Thoughts About Why Hard Laws Make Bad Cases*, 113 HARV. L. REV. 1890 (2000); Teresa A. Miller, *Citizenship & Severity: Recent Immigration Reforms and the New Penology*, 17 GEO. IMMIGR. L.J. 611, 616–620 (2003); Nancy Morawetz, *Understanding the Impact of the 1996 Deportation Laws and the Limited Scope of Proposed Reforms*, 113 HARV. L. REV. 1936 (2000). In 2010, the Supreme Court expanded the protections for noncitizens in criminal prosecutions in a landmark case involving a lawful permanent resident facing removal. See Padilla v. Kentucky, 559 U.S. 356 (2010) (holding that the Sixth Amendment requires attorneys in criminal cases to advise noncitizen defendant of the possible immigration consequences of a plea bargain); Ch. 15 (discussing *Padilla v. Kentucky*).

[173] See Johnson, *supra* note 161, at 853–55.

[174] See, e.g., Moncrieffe v. Holder, 133 S. Ct. 1678 (2013) (marijuana possession); Carachuri-Rosendo v. Holder, 560 U.S. 563 (2010) (prescription drug possession)

[175] See Dan Blankenau, *Ecosystem Protection Versus Immigration: The Coming Conflict*, 12 GREAT PLAINS NAT. RESOURCES J. 1 (2007); Richard D. Lamm, *Immigration: The Ultimate Environmental Issue*, 84 DEN. U.L. REV. 1003 (2007).

[176] The Sierra Club, *Immigration* (adopted Nov. 17, 2007), *available at* https://www.sierraclub.org/sites/www.sierraclub.org/files/immigration.pdf (last visited July 14, 2014).

[177] See Eric K. Yamamoto & Jen-L W. Lyman, *Racializing Environmental Justice*, 72 U. COLO. L. REV. 311, 349–51 (2001).

favor of stricter immigration policies contended that limiting immigration in this country is crucial to decreasing sprawl and pollution.[178] Other members opposed restrictionist measures. The executive director of the Sierra Club once stated that supporters of stricter immigration policies were "in bed with racists."[179] In 2013, the Sierra Club announced that it would support a proposal for comprehensive immigration reform that included a path to citizenship for undocumented immigrants.[180]

---

[178] *See* Traci Watson, *Sierra Club Could Add Immigration to Green Agenda*, USA TODAY, Mar. 8, 2004, at 3A.

[179] *See* Felicity Barringer, *Bitter Division of Sierra Club on Immigration*, N.Y. TIMES, Mar. 16, 2004, at A1.

[180] *See* Press Release, The Sierra Club (Apr. 25, 2013), *available at* http://content.sierraclub.org/press-releases/2013/04/sierra-club-supports-path-citizenship-undocumented-immigrants (last visited July 14, 2014); Anna Palmer & Darren Samuelsohn, *Sierra Club Backs Immigration Reform*, POLITICO PRO, Mar. 24, 2013, *available at* http://www.politico.com/story/2013/04/sierra-club-immigration-reform-90615.html (last visited July 14, 2014); Jorge Rivas, *Sierra Club Official Endorses Immigration Reform*, COLORLINES NEWS, Apr. 25, 2013, *available at* http://colorlines.com/archives/2013/04/sierra_club_officially_endorses_immigration_reform.html (last visited July 14, 2014).

Chapter 2

THE EVOLUTION OF U.S. IMMIGRATION LAW AND POLICY

A. COLONIAL IMMIGRATION

Prior to Columbus's arrival to the islands off our southeastern shores, perhaps 18 million Native Americans resided in what is now the United States and Canada. Although the first people to colonize the New World were the Spanish and French, the European explorers who followed Christopher Columbus to North America in the sixteenth century had no notion of founding a new nation. Neither did the first European settlers who populated the 13 colonies on the eastern shores of the continent in the seventeenth and eighteenth centuries. They regarded America as but the western rim of a transatlantic European world.

Life in the New World made the colonists different from their European cousins, and eventually, during the American Revolution, these new Americans came to embrace a vision of their country as an independent nation. They had much in common to begin with. The colonies had been *British* colonies. Most came determined to create an agricultural society modeled on English customs. Conditions in the New World deepened their common bonds. Most learned to live lives unfettered by the tyrannies of royal authority, official religion, and social hierarchies that they had left behind. They grew to cherish ideals that became synonymous with American life — reverence for individual liberty, self-government, religious tolerance, and economic opportunity. The original colonists and their progeny became the "founders" of a new nation, and as such they have come to be regarded as the original Americans. By accepting this notion, we have come to accept the idea that an "American" is someone attached to the United States of America; thus the founders of the United States were the original, new Americans. Almost immediately, the original Americans displayed a willingness to exclude certain others from the concept of a true American. They displayed a willingness to subjugate outsiders — first Indians, who were nearly annihilated through war and disease, and then Africans, who were brought in chains to serve as slave labor, especially on the tobacco, rice, and indigo plantations of the southern colonies.

But if the settlement experience gave people a common stock of values, both good and bad, it also divided them. The 13 colonies were quite different from one another. Puritans carved right, pious, and relatively democratic communities of small family farms out of rocky-soiled New England. Theirs was a homogeneous world in comparison to most of the southern colonies, where large landholders, mostly Anglicans, built plantations along the coast from which they lorded over a labor force of black slaves and looked down upon the poor white farmers who settled the backcountry. Different still were the middle colonies stretching from New York to Delaware. There, diversity reigned. Well-to-do merchants put their stamp on New York City, as Quakers did on Pennsylvania, while out in the countryside sprawling estates were interspersed with modest homesteads. Within individual colonies, conflicts festered over economic interests, ethnic rivalries, and religious practices. All those clashes made it difficult for colonists to imagine that they were a single people with a common identity much less that they ought to break free from Britain. British tyranny unified the colonies, and a new nation was born, peopled by those who were openly welcomed, those who withstood discouraging sentiment, and slaves.

During the early Colonial Period, some individual colonies attempted to regulate immigration, but essentially there was no integrated immigration policy. The first settlers were French and Spanish. Prior to 1680, most newcomers were English Protestants. A combination of religious, political, and economic motives brought these settlers to the New World. However, when English emigration began to decline in the 1680s, colonies — particularly Pennsylvania and North Carolina — began to promote the immigration of certain other nationalities and ethnic groups while attempting to exclude undesirables. This produced an influx of French Huguenots, Irish Quakers, and German Pietists. Newcomers from Scotland, Portugal, Spain, Switzerland, the Netherlands, and the Rhineland followed. About 450,000 immigrants — representing a dozen nationalities — arrived during the eighteenth century.

These new immigrants came for a myriad of reasons. German Pietist sects, including the Mennonites and Moravians, also fled persecution in search of religious freedom, many in response to the sympathetic Quaker teachings of William Penn. A later German group, the Hessians, came to fight as mercenaries with the British in the American Revolution, and 5,000 stayed to become immigrants. Dutch and Swedes came for political freedom and economic opportunity, and the Scotch-Irish came throughout the eighteenth century for economic, religious, and political motives. European migration was not limited to the original 13 colonies. Spain wanted to expand the Spanish Empire and sent immigrants to California, Florida, and Mexico to search for gold, to trade with Native Americans, and to convert them to Christianity. French settlers came to Louisiana and Canada to seek land and business opportunities, convert the Native Americans, and to protect French trading interests. The French Huguenots immigrated to flee religious persecution after the revocation of the Edict of Nantes in 1685.

Even during this "open" era of immigration, the original colonies attempted to define their new America by promoting immigration only to select groups. When the first census was taken in 1790, the total population was recorded at 3,227,000. English, Scots, and Scotch-Irish accounted for 75 percent; Germans made up 8 percent; and other nationalities with substantial numbers included the Dutch, French, Swedes, and Spanish. In addition, the 1790 census recorded a population of 750,000 blacks, a result of the involuntary migration of the 350,000 African slaves into the colonies. By the census of 1810, the white population had increased to approximately six million, and the black population to approximately 1,378,000.

B. EARLY STATE AND FEDERAL IMMIGRATION LAW AND POLICY

As the new nation emerged, "immigration policies" continued to be handled by individual states with little federal intervention. As in the Colonial Period, these policies were aimed at the exclusion of certain undesirables, as individual states begin to delineate who should become part of their community. Yet beyond those who were not wanted, the doors were open in unlimited numbers to able-bodied souls who made the trek to the new nation. In fact, one of the complaints the authors of the Declaration of Independence made against King George III was that his policies sharply restricted immigration. King George saw burgeoning population as a threat to his hold on the colonies and tried to strangle further influx. Thus, in the Declaration of Independence, King George was castigated as having " . . . endeavored to prevent the population of these States; for that purpose obstructing the laws for naturalization of foreigners, refusing to pass others to encourage their migrations hither, and raising the conditions of new appropriations of lands."

Prior to 1875, state immigration provisions that often applied to interstate as well as to foreign migrants, regulated at least four groups: criminals, paupers, slaves or free blacks, and certain religions. A fifth category involved those espousing unorthodox or unpopular views, although state colonial screening on the basis of political belief was implemented on a limited basis. This early sentiment — seeking only those who would become patriotic loyalists — represents an early version of a viewpoint (manifested in anti-communist, anti-anarchist, and anti-terrorist screening) that has remained an important part of the immigration policy debate throughout the nation's history. While the migration of a sixth group of individuals — those suspected of carrying contagious diseases — raised concerns among the colonists, regulation through quarantine was not immigrant-specific.

1. Criminals

The early colonies opposed the immigration of persons convicted of crimes. Under modern immigration laws, individuals with certain criminal backgrounds are barred from entering the country. Thus for example, an individual who might fall into an immigration category reserved for relatives of U.S. citizens or for those with special job skills, can still be excluded if immigration officials discover that the applicant has been convicted of a narcotics offense or a crime involving moral turpitude. In the seventeenth and eighteenth centuries, however, British attempts to transport criminals to the U.S. concerned the colonists. English judges could sentence felons to the colonies as punishment, and felons could also be shipped to the colonies as indentured servants. Several colonies enacted restrictions on the entry of such individuals, only to be overruled by the British government. The British lost this veto authority after the war of independence, but even after 1783, the British continued to send convicts as indentured servants. In 1788, the Congress of the Confederation adopted a resolution recommending that states "pass proper laws for preventing the transportation of convicted malefactors from foreign countries into the U.S." Within a year, several states responded. Massachusetts, Pennsylvania, South Carolina, and Virginia prohibited the importation of person who had ever been convicted of a crime. In later years, after the federal Constitution had taken effect, further states enacted similar legislation: Maine, Maryland, New Jersey, New York, and Rhode Island.

2.   Paupers

The Statue of Liberty's "give us your tired, your poor" refrain [written by political dissenter Emma Lazarus in 1883] was definitely not the philosophy of the colonies, nor is it today's philosophy as modern laws exclude those immigrants who are "likely to become a public charge." The colonists were comfortable with the notion of members of the lower class fleeing the overcrowded, rigid social structure of Europe, as long as they were hard-working and honest. But the colonists feared that Europe was using the new world as a dumping ground for the lazy and disabled. After all, English judges could also banish vagrants along with felons to the colonies. Thus, after independence, a number of states instituted legislation aimed at the poor from abroad as well as those from other states. In Massachusetts, the 1794 poor laws imposed a penalty on any person who knowingly brought a pauper or indigent person into any town in the Commonwealth and left him there. This applied to intrastate, interstate, and international transporting of the poor. Beginning in 1820, Massachusetts returned to the colonial system of demanding security from masters of vessels when their passengers seemed likely to become paupers. In New York, a 1788 statute authorized the justice of the peace to order a newcomer removed if it was determined that the person would likely become a public charge within the first year of residence. Until 1813, paupers who returned after removal were subject to severe corporal punishment as well as retransportation. The 1788 poor law required masters of vessels arriving in the New York City harbor to report within 24 hours the names and occupations of all passengers; if any passenger appeared likely to become a charge, the vessel was required to either return the passenger or post a bond.

3.   Blacks

Prior to the Civil War, Southern slave states adopted legislation prohibiting the migration of free blacks and urged free Northern states to do the same. Since many white inhabitants of the North were prejudiced against blacks, several free states obliged. They did so by either blocking the movement of blacks into the state, or requiring good behavior and assurances that blacks would not become public charges. Slave states also subjected their free black residents to more stringent regulations and criminal laws than whites. The sentiment behind some of these laws was related to immigration from abroad. Many states did not welcome fleeing French slaveowners who brought slaves that may have been influenced by the ideals of freedom. These fears were not entirely unfounded. A successful slave revolt in Saint Dominique ultimately produced the nation of Haiti. In 1803, Southern states succeeded in pushing for federal legislation prohibiting the importation of foreign blacks into states whose laws prohibited their entry. Relatedly, in the early 1800s, Southern states regulated free black sailors aboard vessels arriving in Southern ports. States such as South Carolina did not want black sailors wandering its streets, even temporarily. As such, South Carolina and other states required black seamen to be held in jail or quarantined on the ship, barring communication with local blacks.

In addition to legislation adopted by the states, blacks were also attacked through early federal immigration policy. In the First Congress, on March 26, 1790 a provision was made, pursuant to constitutional power (Art. 1, § 8, clause 4), to establish a uniform rule of naturalization, for aliens who were "free white males" who had two years residence. This provision excluded indentured servants, slaves, and most women, all of whom were considered dependents and thus incapable of casting an independent vote. The person had to be of good moral character, a requirement that remains today.

4. Religious Views

Religious belief often limited one's choice of domicile in the New World. In the spirit of the time, colonial charters frequently denied admission to Catholics. Virginia is an example of one such state that denied admission on the basis of religious belief. The first settlers to Virginia were emigrants from England who were of the English church, at a point in time when the church was flushed with complete victory over the religions of all other persuasions. Yet the settlers showed intolerance with their Presbyterian brethren, who had emigrated to the northern colonies. Furthermore, Virginia passed several laws aimed at Quakers, who had fled from persecution in England and cast their eyes on the New World as an asylum of civil and religious freedom. Sadly, the Quakers found the New World free only from the reigning sect. Several acts of the Virginia assembly of 1659, 1662, and 1693 aimed at Quakers espoused Virginia's strong religious beliefs. These laws made it a crime for parents to refuse to have their children baptized, prohibited the unlawful assembling of Quakers, and penalized any master of a vessel bringing a Quaker into the state. The laws further ordered Quakers already present in Virginia and Quakers that attempted to enter the state to be imprisoned until they left the country, providing a mild punishment for their first and second return, and death for the third. In addition, the laws inhibited all persons from holding Quaker meetings in or near their homes, entertaining Quakers individually, or disposing of books that supported Quaker tenets. Statutory oppressions of religion were wiped away in 1776.

In contrast to Virginia's stringent anti-Quaker laws, Pennsylvania espoused a broader religious philosophy. King Charles II granted the charter for Pennsylvania to William Penn in 1681. Penn, a Quaker, was driven by two principal motives in founding the colony, "the desire to found a free commonwealth on liberal and humane principles, and the desire to provide a safe home for persecuted Friends." English Quakers were the dominant element, although many English settlers were Anglican.

Penn was far in advance of his time in his views of mankind's capacity for democratic government, and equally so in his broad-minded tolerance of different religious beliefs. The 1701 declaration of his final charter of privileges was not:

> Intended as the fundamental law of the Province and declaration of religious liberty on the broadest character and about which there could be no doubt of uncertainty. It [was] a declaration not of toleration but of religious equality and brought within its protection all who professed one Almighty God, — Roman Catholics, and Protestants, Unitarians, Trinitarians, Christians, Jews, and Mohammedans, and excluded only Atheists and Polytheists.

His toleration of other forms of religious belief was in no way half-hearted and imbued the Society of Friends with feelings of kindness toward Catholics, or at least accentuated those feelings in them. In the 1720s, a Catholic chapel was erected in Pennsylvania, which was thought to be contrary to the laws of Parliament. The chapel was not suppressed pending a decision of the British Government upon the question of whether immunity granted by the Pennsylvania law did not protect Catholics. When, after Braddock's defeat during the French War, hostility to France led to an attack upon the Pennsylvania Catholics by a mob, the Quakers protected them. It has been said of Pennsylvania that no other American colony had "such a mixture of languages, nationalities and religions. Dutch, Swedes, English, Germans, Scotch-Irish and Welsh; Quakers, Presbyterians, Episcopalians, Lutherans, Reformed, Mennonites, Tunkers, and Moravians all had a share in creating it." Although the Constitution of Pennsylvania protected religious freedom, it was held that Christianity is part of the common law of Pennsylvania; not Christianity founded on any particular tenets, but Christianity with liberty of conscience to all men.

Another example of religious tolerance was New York, a colony that accommodated Quakers in its constitutional convention. In its provision related to requirements of voters, the convention provided, "[t]hat every elector, before he is admitted to vote, shall, if required by the returning-officer or either of the inspectors, take an oath, or, if of the people called Quakers, an affirmation, of allegiance to the State." In fact, although the convention affirmed that the "common law of England" would continue to be the law of the state, any "such parts of the said common law . . . as may be construed to establish or maintain any particular denomination of Christians or their ministers . . . are abrogated and rejected."

Anti-Catholicism in some quarters persisted after the American Revolution. Several states enacted legislation against the Catholic religion. The Carolinas had a law preventing a Catholic from holding office, and New Hampshire had a similar provision in its constitution. Anti-Catholic violence occurred in 1834, when the Ursuline Convent in Charleston was burned. In Philadelphia in 1844, anti-Catholicism led to riots that lasted three days.

5. Unorthodox Views

Some colonies attempted to exclude or screen would-be immigrants on the basis of political belief or affiliation. For example, a 1727 Pennsylvania act required immigrants "to take an oath of allegiance to the king and fidelity to the proprietors and the provincial constitution." Banishment — the probable antecedent of deportation as an instrument of immigration policy — was sometimes used during the colonial era to punish persons espousing unorthodox or unpopular views.

Several of the nation's most prominent people spoke out about foreign influence during this time period. Benjamin Franklin's 1755 expression against further German migration to Pennsylvania was not simply about language:

> [W]hy should the Palatine [German] boors be suffered to swarm in our settlements and, by herding together, establish their language and *manners* to the exclusion of ours? Why should Pennsylvania, founded by the English, become a colony of *aliens*, who will shortly be so numerous as to *germanize* us instead of our anglifying them? [emphasis added]

Franklin continued these expressions during the Continental Congress, warning of the increasing German influence in American society. Similarly, in 1788 John Jay (a year later appointed to be the first chief justice of the Supreme Court by George Washington) noted in The Federalist Number 2:

> Providence has been pleased to give this one connected country to one united people-a people descended from the same ancestors, speaking the same language, professing the same religion, *attached to the same principles of government, very similar in their manners and customs*, and who, by their joint counsels, arms, and efforts, fighting side by side throughout a long and bloody war, have nobly established general liberty and independence. [emphasis added]

And in the same vein, Thomas Jefferson stated:

> [I]t is impossible not to look forward to distant times, when our rapid multiplication will expand itself . . . [and] cover the whole northern, if not the southern continent, with a people speaking the same language, governed in similar forms, [and] by similar laws; nor can we contemplate with satisfaction either *blot or mixture on that surface*. [emphasis added]

In addition to Franklin and Jefferson, John Adams, a Federalist and the nation's second president, was also wary of foreign influence. In his inaugural address, March 4, 1797, he warned that the nation should never "lose sight of the danger to our liberties if anything partial or extraneous should infect the purity of our free, fair, virtuous, and independent elections. . . . If that solitary suffrage can be obtained by foreign nations by flattery or menaces, by fraud or violence, by terror, intrigue, or venality, the Government may not be the choice of the American people, but of foreign nations. . . . [It is] the pestilence of foreign influence, which is the angel of destruction to elective governments . . . ."

Fears of foreign influence led to an early attempt at federal immigration control. The 1798 Alien and Sedition Laws, a series of four laws passed by the Federalist-controlled U.S. Congress and signed by President Adams, purportedly was enacted not only in response to hostile actions of the French Revolutionary government on the seas, but also designed to quell political opposition from the Democratic-Republican Party, led by Thomas Jefferson and James Madison. The first of the laws was the Naturalization Act, passed by Congress on June 18. This act required that aliens be residents for 14 years instead of five before they became eligible for U.S. citizenship. This adversely affected Jefferson's party that depended on recent arrivals from Europe for much of its voting strength. Congress then passed the Alien Friends Act on June 25, authorizing the President to deport aliens "dangerous to the peace and safety of the United States" during peacetime. The naturalization and alien acts were aimed largely at Irish immigrants and French refugees who had participated in political activities critical of the Adams administration. The third law, the Alien Enemies Act, was enacted by Congress on July 6. This act allowed the wartime arrest, imprisonment, and deportation of any alien subject to an enemy power. President Adams made no use of the alien acts. The last of the laws, the Sedition Act, passed on July 14, declared that any treasonable activity, including the publication of "any false, scandalous and malicious writing," was a high misdemeanor, punishable by fine and imprisonment. Under this legislation, 25 men, most of them editors of Democratic-Republican newspapers, were arrested and the newspapers were forced to shut down. One of the men arrested was Benjamin Franklin's grandson, Benjamin Franklin Bache, editor of the Philadelphia Democrat-Republican Aurora. Charged with libeling President Adams, Bache's arrest erupted in a public outcry against all of the Alien and Sedition Acts. Resolutions against the acts became part of the Democratic-Republican platform in the 1800 presidential election, and were partly responsible for the election of Jefferson to the presidency. Once in office, Jefferson pardoned all those convicted under the Sedition Act, and Congress restored all fines paid with interest. The Alien Friends Act and the Sedition Act expired by 1801; Congress repealed the Naturalization Act in 1802 (restoring the residency requirement to five years), and the Alien Enemies Act was amended.

The impetus behind the Alien and Sedition Acts was fear of foreign influence. For example, in the Sedition Act, the United States government was in effect declaring war upon the ideas of the French Revolution. To protect the American way — as interpreted by the Federalists — the people were to be safeguarded against the dangerous opinions spreading over the world. According to this theory, the only way to preserve the health of the body politic was to impose a "quarantine upon ideas." Federalists believed that many Republicans, being more French than American at heart, would join a French army of invasion should it land on American shores. The Federalists craved security from the threat of Bonaparte's army, revolutions, and subversive ideas. As upholders of the implied and inherent powers of the national government, the Federalists found support for the Alien Act in the right of Congress to defend the country against foreign aggression. To them, self-preservation was the higher law — a power with which every government was endowed. Every morning Secretary of State Timothy Pickering methodically pored over the Republican newspapers in search of seditious material. He demanded all U.S. District Attorneys to closely scrutinize Republican newspapers published in their districts, insisting on prosecution of both author and publisher.

In spite of these early colonial, state, and federal expressions of exclusion, until Chinese were excluded in 1882, no limits on the numbers of immigrants or refugees to what has become the United States existed. Immigration was limited or discouraged principally by the cost of travel, diseases, conflict with indigenous inhabitants, or racial, religious, or political discrimination by prior immigrant groups.

As long as they were the *right kind* of immigrants, the new nation wanted them. In 1791, Alexander Hamilton warned Congress that if the United States were to develop into an industrial power, immigration would have to be encouraged so as to offset the "scarcity of hands" and the "dearness of labor." The nineteenth century witnessed recruitment efforts by the U.S. government and the states, as well as private employers, who saturated Europe with promotional campaigns to stir up emigration to the United States. Substantial European immigration, especially from Germany, occurred in the two decades prior to the Civil War. As Andrew Carnegie explained it, "The value to the country of the annual foreign influx is very great indeed. . . . These adults are surely worth $1,500 each — for in former days an efficient slave sold for that sum." To Carnegie, immigration was a "golden steam which flows into the country each year." Policy makers throughout the nineteenth century extolled the economic benefits of abundant immigration and fashioned U.S. immigration policies to maximize the flow.

The Republican Party platform of 1864, that Abraham Lincoln helped to draft, fostered the same philosophy:

> Foreign immigration which in the past has added so much to the wealth, resources, and increase of power to this nation — the asylum of the oppressed of all nations — should be fostered and encouraged by a liberal and just policy.

Months earlier, on December 8, 1863, President Lincoln strongly recommended legislation to the 37th Congress that would encourage immigration:

> I again submit to your consideration the expediency of establishing a system for the encouragement of immigration. Although this source of national wealth and strength is again flowing with greater freedom than for several years before the insurrection occurred, there is still a great deficiency of laborers in every field of industry, especially in agriculture and in our mines, as well of iron and coal as of the precious metals. While the demand for labor is thus increased here, tens of thousands of persons destitute of remunerative occupation are thronging our foreign consulates and offering to emigrate to the United States if essential but very cheap assistance can be afforded them. It is very easy to see that under the sharp discipline of civil war the Nation is beginning a new life. This noble effort demands the aid and ought to receive the attention and support of the Government.

Not surprisingly, the first comprehensive federal immigration law, passed in 1864, was an Act to Encourage Immigration. This law established the first U.S. Immigration Bureau, whose primary function was to increase immigration so that American industries would have an adequate supply of workers to meet production needs during the Civil War. In addition, in an effort to reduce the number of immigrants who left industry for homesteading or army enlistment, the law made pre-emigration contracts binding. Although the law was repealed in 1868, it spawned the host of private labor recruitment agencies that for many years continued to be a significant force behind European emigration.

Of course immigration was not without its critics. During the decades preceding the Civil War, when the massive wave of immigrants, mostly from Ireland and Germany, came to America, prejudice or nativism reached new heights. The Irish were Catholic, a fact that fed Protestant fears that the papacy intended to take over the U.S. government. Even though the immigrants were vital to the industrial and economic expansion of the nation, many natives attacked them as foes of the Republic. Some joined nativist groups to combat the "alien menace." Others pressured the Whigs and Democrats to pass anti-immigrant legislation, such as laws lengthening the time it took to become a citizen. Several such groups combined to form the Order of the Star-Spangled Banner that adopted a pledge of secrecy; if people asked them about their program, they responded "I know nothing." The organization became the most powerful nativist organization of the era. The basic tenets that defined the order's ideology included a belief that Protestantism sustained and preserved the Republic because it emphasized individualism, democracy, and equality, while Roman Catholicism threatened the Republic because it emphasized authoritarianism, opposed freedom of thought, dictated how Catholics should vote, and insisted that priests act as intercessors between God and the faithful. This culminated with the birth of the American or Know-Nothing Party in the 1850s. In 1856, the American Party nominated ex-President Millard Fillmore as their presidential candidate, who attracted almost 900,000 votes. The American Party platform included the following planks:

> III. *Americans must rule America*; and to this end, *native*-born citizens should be selected for all state, federal, or municipal offices of government employment, in preference to naturalized citizens. . . .

> IX. A change in the laws of naturalization, making continued residence of twenty-one years, of all not heretofore provided for, an indispensable requisite for citizenship hereafter. . . .

Yet, mostly pro-immigration sentiment prevailed through the 1800s.

The mass migration of the nineteenth century was the result of a near perfect match between the needs of a new country and overcrowded Europe. Europe at this time was undergoing drastic social change and economic reorganization, severely compounded by overpopulation. An extraordinary increase in population coincided with the breakup of the old agricultural order which had been in place since medieval times throughout much of Europe. Commonly held lands were broken up into individual owned farms, resulting in landless status for peasants from Ireland to Russia. At approximately the same time, the industrial revolution was underway, moving from Great Britain to Western Europe, and then to Southern and Eastern Europe. For Germany, Sweden, Russia, and Japan, the highest points of emigrants coincided with the beginnings of industrialization and the ensuing general disruption of employment patterns. The artisans joined the peasants evicted from their land as immigrants to the United States. Population pressure and related economic problems, sometimes in the extreme form of famine, were the major causes of the mass migration of this long period, followed by religious persecution and the desire for political freedom.

America, on the other hand, had a boundless need for people to push back the frontier, to build the railways, to defend unstable boundaries, and to populate new States. The belief in America as a land of asylum for the oppressed was reinforced by the commitment to the philosophy of manifest destiny. Immigration was required for settlement, defense, and economic well-being.

C. ENSLAVEMENT OF AFRICAN WORKERS AS FORCED IMMIGRATION POLICY

The forces of racism have become embodied in U.S. immigration laws. As these laws are enforced, they are accepted as common practice, in spite of their racial effects. We may not like particular laws or enforcement policies because of their harshness or their violations of human dignity or civil rights, but many of us do not sense the inherent racism because we are not cognizant of the dominant racial framework. Understanding the evolution of U.S. immigration laws and enforcement provides us with a better awareness of the institutional racism that controls those policies. As we look closely at the evolution of immigration laws and enforcement policies, we come to realize that the history begins with slavery. Forced African labor migration set the stage for the Mexicans and the Chinese.

Professor Rhonda Magee has made the case that the notion of immigrant must include the forced immigration system of chattel slavery and that the law and policy of chattel slavery is a relevant historical antecedent to today's immigration law. She notes:

> [S]lavery was, in significant part (though hardly exclusively), an immigra-tion system of a particularly reprehensible sort: a system of state-sponsored forced migration human trafficking, endorsed by Congress, important to the public fisc as a source of tax revenue, and aimed at fulfilling the need for a controllable labor population in the colonies, and then in the states, at an artificially low economic cost.
>
> . . . Viewing immigration as a function of slavery helps us articulate an important irony: that with respect to immigration, slavery — our racially based forced migration system — laid a foundation for both a racially segmented labor-based immigration system, and a racially diverse (even if racially hierarchical) "nation of immigrants." These legacies which the founders may not have set out to leave, but which are among the United States' most pernicious and most precious gifts to civilization.[1]

Scholars generally trace the beginning of racially restrictive U.S. immigration policies to laws directed at various immigrant groups. Prior to 1870, the subordi-nation of people of African descent was further underscored by the fact that people from Africa could not become U.S. citizens through naturalization. The Nationality

---

[1] RHONDA V. MAGEE, *Slavery as Immigration?*, 44 U.S.F. L. REV. 273, 277, 289–99 (2009).

Act of 1790 limited naturalization to "free white persons" and specifically excluded African Americans and Native Americans.[2] However, in 1870, Congress extended naturalization rights to anyone of African descent.[3]

Throughout the immigration history of the United States, Africans have been underrepresented as a voluntary immigrant group. Before 1965, Africans represented less than 1 percent of the total immigrant population.[4] In 1990, Africans still constituted only 2.3 percent of all immigrants.[5]

Newcomers of African descent can be found in the United States of course. In the first two decades of the nineteenth century, Africans from the small island of Cape Verde began to settle in the northeast in places like New Bedford, Massachusetts. They worked in seafaring occupations and as agricultural laborers in the cranberry industry. Members of the immigrant community dissociated themselves from African-Americans and maintained an ethnicity as Portuguese colonists.[6] By 1850, there were 551 African immigrants in the United States and 2,539 in 1900. Between 1900 and1950, 31,000 Africans entered the country. Many came as students sponsored by missionaries, and returned to Africa to spread their faith to their former townspeople and tribesmen.[7] Significant increases did not occur until the 1960s. In 1960 there were 35,355 African migrants, but by 1990, the number was 363,819. By 2000, the figure reached 881,300, but the number represented only 3 percent of the total immigrant population in the United States.[8] However, the African migrant population almost doubled within 10 years, and the 2010 census counted a total of almost 1.7 million.[9] The largest subgroups of African descent are illustrated in Table 1.

---

[2] Act of Mar. 26, 1790, Ch. 3, 1 Stat. 103–04 (1790). Years later, when Japanese immigrants unsuccessfully sought naturalization as "free white persons," the Supreme Court reaffirmed that the 1790 naturalization statute intended that "Negroes and Indians" were to be denied naturalization. Ozawa v. United States, 260 U.S. 178, 196 (1922).

[3] Act of July 14, 1870, Ch. 254, 16 Stat. 254 (1870).

[4] U.S. Immigr. And Naturalization Service Stat. Y.B. of the Immigr. And Naturalization Serv., 1989, at xvii (1990).

[5] U.S. Immigr. And Naturalization Service Stat. Y.B. of the Immigr. And Naturalization Serv., 1990, at 53 tbl.3 (1991).

[6] John W. Frazier, Joe T. Darden, & Norah F. Henry, The African Diaspora in the U.S. and Canada at the Dawn of the 21st Century 97 (2010).

[7] Id.

[8] Olanipekun Laosebikan, From Student to Immigrant: Diasporization of the African Student in the United States 6 (2012) (Ph.D. dissertation, University of Illinois at Urbana-Champaign) (on file with author); Shimantini Shome, Assimilation of Somali Refugees and Immigrants in the Kansas City Area 12 (2011) (Ph.D. dissertation, University of Kansas) (on file with author).

[9] Immigration Policy Center, African Immigrants in America: A Demographic Overview (June 2012), available at http://www.immigrationpolicy.org/just-facts/african-immigrants-america-demographic-overview.

Table 1 Largest African Migrant Communities in U.S., 2012[10]

Nigerians	228,166
Ethiopians	177,909
Egyptians	153,735
Ghanaians	127,802
Kenyans	99,115
Somalis	85,700

This boom is surprising on many levels; given the segregation and open racial antipathy that existed in the United States up until the Civil Rights movement, many Africans who emigrated in the last century chose to migrate to European countries.[11] The 1994 implementation of the 1990 Immigration Act, which established the Diversity Visa Program,[12] was arguably meant to allow skilled Africans, among other immigrants, a means to enter the country. This program, pushed for by business leaders looking to employ skilled laborers, established a lottery for prospective immigrants to the United States. Under the law, individuals who have a high school diploma (or its equivalent), as well as two years of work experience in an occupation which requires a minimum of two years of training or experience, may enter a visa lottery for one of 50,000 immigrant visas to enter the United States.[13] This requirement threatened to shut out African immigrants who could otherwise benefit from the program; according to 2013 statistics from the UNESCO organization, 38 percent of African adults are illiterate.[14] Two-thirds of these adults are women. Applicants are also required to apply electronically, and data reveals that an average of 15 percent of Africans have internet access.[15]

A close look at African migrants to the United States reveals that the vast majority entered as refugees or under diversity visa lottery program. Thus, the 1965 Act played little role in facilitating their entry. However, the framework of the Act has provided the basis for some African migration and, if continued, will serve as the foundation for future African immigrants to the United States much as it did for the remaking of Asian America.[16]

---

[10] 2012 American Community Survey, Table B05006: "Place of Birth for the Foreign-Born Population in the United States." The Somali figure is a 2010 estimate.

[11] Bill Ong Hing, *Immigration Policies: Messages of Exclusion to African Americans*, 37 Howard L.J. 237 (1994).

[12] Immigration Act of 1990, PL 101–649, Nov. 29, 1990, 104 Stat. 4978.

[13] 8 U.S.C. § 1153(c).

[14] United Nations Educational, Scientific and Cultural Organization, Literacy and non-formal education, *available at* http://www.unesco.org/new/en/dakar/education/literacy/.

[15] The World Bank: Internet Users per 100 people, *available at* http://data.worldbank.org/indicator/IT.NET.USER.P2/countries?display=map.

[16] Bill Ong Hing, Making and Remaking Asian American Through Immigration Policy, 1850–1990 (1993).

D.   THE RISE OF COMPREHENSIVE FEDERAL REGULATION: THE CHINESE EXCLUSION ERA AND BEYOND

1.   The Evolution of Chinese Exclusion

The discovery of gold, a rice shortage, and the recruitment of Asian labor led to the initiation of noticeable Asian migration in the nineteenth century, in turn triggering a backlash against that migration. Examining the impetus and development of exclusion laws directed first at Chinese and eventually at all Asian immigrants reveal a sordid tale of racism and xenophobia. The antipathy demonstrated toward Asians paralleled the repugnance that America showed to African slaves. The attack on Asian immigrants represented the first comprehensive federal regulation of immigration that would later serve as the model for exclusion of eastern and southern Europeans.

Early on, the Chinese were officially welcomed in the United States. The simultaneous opening of both China and the American West, along with the discovery of gold in 1848, led to a growing demand for and a ready supply of Chinese labor. Chinese were actively recruited to fill needs in railroad construction, laundries, and domestic service. In 1852, the governor of California even recommended a system of land grants to induce the immigration and settlement of Chinese. A decade later, a select committee of the California legislature advocated continued support of Chinese immigration. It reported that the 50,000 Chinese in the state paid almost $14 million annually in taxes, licenses, duties, freights, and other charges, that their cheap labor would be of great value in developing the new industries of the state, and that trade with China should be fostered. After the Civil War, some Southern plantation owners seriously considered replacing their former slaves with Chinese laborers. By 1882, about 300,000 Chinese had entered and worked on the West Coast.

Favorable sentiment was certainly not universal. In 1857 at the Oregon constitutional convention, a nativist amendment was introduced to exclude Chinese. It failed principally because most in attendance felt that Chinese made "good washers, good cooks, and good servants."[17] Despite official encouragement of importing Chinese labor by some, the Chinese who arrived encountered fierce racial animosity by the 1840s, as did miners from Mexico, South America, Hawaii, and even France. Irish Roman Catholics in California, replicating the prejudice they had suffered on the East Coast, rallied against the brown, black, and yellow foreigners in the mines. This racial prejudice, exacerbated by fear of competition from aliens, prompted calls for restrictive federal immigration laws.

For a time this sentiment gained powerful political backing from the newly formed Know-Nothing party. Organized in the 1850s, this secretive political organization was formed to push for the exclusion of all foreign-born citizens from office, to discourage immigration, and to "keep America pure." The organization also demanded a 21-year naturalization period. On the East Coast it fought against

---

[17] MARY R. COOLIDGE, CHINESE IMMIGRATION 21 (1909).

Irish Catholic immigration, while on the West Coast the target was usually the Chinese. Members fostered the attitude that these immigrants were subversive influences, and induced the federal government to pass restrictive regulations governing the entry of foreign workers. If asked about the members or program of the party, which eventually adopted the name American Party, its members were instructed to answer, "I know nothing about it." A division within the party over the question of slavery, and the voluntary enlistment of thousands of immigrants (principally on the East Coast) into the Union armies during the Civil War, led to the demise of the Know-Nothings in the 1860s.

The demise of the Know-Nothing party notwithstanding, by the late 1860s, the Chinese question became a major issue in California and Oregon politics. Many white workers felt threatened by the competition they perceived from the Chinese, while many employers continued to seek them as inexpensive laborers and subservient domestics. Employment of Chinese by the Central Pacific Railroad was by this time at its peak. Anti-coolie clubs increased in number, and mob attacks against Chinese became frequent. Seldom outdone in such matters, many newly organized labor unions were by then demanding legislation against Chinese immigration. Chinese were at once admired and resented for their resourcefulness in turning a profit on abandoned mines and for their reputed frugality. Much of this resentment was transformed into or sustained by a need to preserve "racial purity" and "Western civilization."[18]

Eventually, Sinophobic sentiment prevailed. First, Chinese immigrants were judged unworthy of citizenship. In amending the Nationality Act of 1790, that had limited citizenship through naturalization to "free white persons" (specifically excluding African Americans and Native Americans), Congress in 1870 extended the right to naturalize to aliens of African descent. But it deliberately denied Chinese that right because of their "undesirable qualities."[19] Then, responding to law-enforcement claims that Chinese women were being imported for prostitution, Congress in 1875 passed legislation prohibiting their importation for immoral purposes. The overzealous enforcement of the statute, commonly referred to as the Page Law, effectively barred Chinese women and further worsened an already imbalanced sex ratio among Chinese.

The exclusion of prostitutes marked the beginning of direct federal regulation of immigration, though it did little to stem nationwide pressure for further significant curbs on Chinese immigration. During the 1881 session of Congress, 25 anti-Chinese petitions were presented by a number of civic groups, like the Methodist Church and the New York Union League Corps, and from many states, including Alabama, Ohio, West Virginia, and Wisconsin. The California legislature declared a legal holiday to facilitate anti-Chinese public rallies that attracted thousands of demonstrators.

Responding to this national clamor, the 47th Congress enacted the Chinese Exclusion Act of May 6, 1882. The law excluded laborers for 10 years, and

---

[18] ROGER DANIELS, THE POLITICS OF PREJUDICE: THE ANTI-JAPANESE MOVEMENT IN CALIFORNIA AND THE STRUGGLE FOR JAPANESE EXCLUSION 19 (1962).

[19] EDWARD HUTCHINSON, LEGISLATIVE HISTORY OF AMERICAN IMMIGRATION POLICY 5–6 (1981).

effectively slammed the door on all Chinese immigration. It did permit the entry of teachers, students, and merchants, but their quota was quite small.

The act crippled the development of the Chinese American community because Chinese women were defined as laborers. Chinese laborers who had already immigrated therefore had no way to bring wives and families left behind. Chinese pleas for a different statutory interpretation were to no avail. Initially men could leave and return, but they could not bring their spouses with them. As a result, the only women permitted to enter were the wives of American-born Chinese and of a few merchants. The ban on laborers' spouses effectively halted the immigration of Chinese women, thereby exacerbating the restraints imposed by the exclusion of women through expanded enforcement of the Page Law and preventing family formation for Chinese immigrants.

Leaders of the anti-Chinese movement, however, were not satisfied. They pressed for something beyond the 10-year exclusion period. They succeeded, over the next dozen years, through a series of treaties and new laws that led to an indefinite ban on Chinese immigration in 1904. The 1904 legislation extending Chinese exclusion indefinitely marked the culmination of a 35-year series of laws that, beginning with the 1870 naturalization act specifically barring Chinese, limited and then excluded Chinese immigrants. Not until the alliance with China during World War II would Congress reconsider any aspect of those barriers to membership; Chinese simply were not viewed as worthy of being American. And not until 1965 would Congress substantially alter nearly a century of laws aimed at keeping the Chinese marginalized.

2. The Gentlemen's Agreement with Japan

Not coincidentally, the first appreciable number of Japanese immigrants entered at the height of the Chinese exclusion movement. Agricultural labor demands, particularly in Hawaii and California, led to increased efforts to attract Japanese workers after the exclusion of the Chinese. In 1884, two years after the Chinese Exclusion Act, the Japanese government yielded to internal pressures to permit laborers to emigrate to work on Hawaiian sugar plantations. The next year, in the midst of Meiji Japan's new-found interest in foreign lands, the Japanese Diet passed the country's first modern emigration law, allowing government-sponsored contract laborers to travel to Hawaii.

Like the initial wave of Chinese immigrants, Japanese laborers were at first warmly received by employers. These young and healthy men were needed to perform the strenuous work on Hawaiian sugar plantations. So many of them came that the Japanese became the largest group of foreigners on the islands. Few came to the mainland, so little effective political pressure was incited to exclude them. In San Francisco in 1869, the new immigrants were described as "gentlemen of refinement and culture . . . [who] have brought their wives, children, and . . . new industries among us."[20] By 1894, as Chinese exclusion was being extended, Japan and the United States reaffirmed their commitment to open travel, each promising the other's citizens liberty to enter, travel, and reside in the receiving country.

---

[20] PETER IRONS, JUSTICE AT WAR 9 (1983).

By the turn of the century, unfavorable sentiment toward the Japanese laborers grew as they began to migrate to the western United States. After Hawaii was annexed in 1898, the Japanese were able to use it as a stepping stone to the mainland, where the majority engaged in agricultural work. Economic competition with white farm workers soon erupted.

By the 1890s, when economic xenophobia was gaining greater acceptance on the East Coast, nativists — many motivated by racial dislike for Asians — with the backing of organized labor in California formed the Japanese and Korean Exclusion League (later renamed the Asiatic Exclusion League). The league joined forces (and membership often overlapped) with smaller organizations such as the Anti-Jap Laundry League and the Anti-Japanese League of Alameda County. Exclusion once again became a major political issue, only this time the Japanese were the target.

After Japan's crushing victories over China in 1895 and Russia in 1905, policymakers viewed exclusion as a means of controlling a potential enemy. Many Americans had regarded Japan as an eager student at the knee of the United States. But the Japanese Navy defeated its Russian counterpart, signaling a turning point in relations between the United States and Japan.

In the wake of the 1906 San Francisco earthquake, fierce anti-Japanese rioting resulted in countless incidents of physical violence. Japanese students in San Francisco were ordered to segregated schools — an act that incensed Japan and later proved a major stumbling block in negotiations over restrictions on Japanese laborers. Demands for limits on Japanese immigration resonated.

Japanese laborers were eventually restricted but not in conventional legislative fashion. Japan's emergence as a major world power meant that the United States could not restrict Japanese immigration in the heavy-handed, self-serving fashion with which it had curtailed Chinese immigration. To do so would have offended an increasingly assertive Japan when the United States was concerned about keeping an open door to Japanese markets. To minimize potential disharmony between the two nations while retaining the initiative to control immigration, President Roosevelt negotiated an informal agreement with Japan. Under the terms of the so-called Gentlemen's Agreement reached in 1907 and 1908, the Japanese government refrained from issuing travel documents to laborers destined for the United States. In exchange for this severe but voluntary limitation, Japanese wives and children could be reunited with their husbands and fathers in the United States, and the San Francisco school board would be pressured into rescinding its segregation order. The ability for Japanese immigrants to have and form families ensured the community of natural growth, distinguishing it from the more bachelor-oriented Chinese immigrant community whose population began to decline after the Chinese exclusion laws.

Japanese immigrants attempted to attack their preclusion from citizenship through naturalization without success. In *Takao Ozawa v. United States* (1922), one Japanese immigrant took his claim to the Supreme Court, arguing that he should be regarded a "free white person" under the naturalization laws. The Court disagreed, simply concluding:

[T]o adopt the color test alone would result in a confused overlapping of races and a gradual merging of one into the other, without any practical line of separation. . . . [T]he federal and state courts, in an almost unbroken line, have held that the words "white person" were meant to indicate only a person of what is *popularly known* as the Caucasian race. . . . With the conclusion reached in these several decisions we see no reason to differ. [emphasis added]

3. Filipinos and Asian Indians

At the turn of the century, the United States was beginning its relationship with the Philippines as it was changing its view toward Japan. After the U.S. victory over Spain in the 1898 Spanish-American War, President McKinley concluded that the people of the Philippines, then a Spanish colony, were "unfit for self-government" and that "there was nothing left for [the United States] to do but to take them all, and to educate the Filipinos, and uplift and civilize and Christianize them.[21] The sentiment was a clear expression that the President did not view The U.S. takeover met with violent resistance from many Filipinos who had struggled for independence from colonial domination.

Ironically, the fact that the Philippines became U.S. colony meant that Filipinos automatically became noncitizen nationals of the United States. They could travel in and out of the United States without regard to immigration laws, they were not subject to exclusion or deportation, and requirements for obtaining full citizenship were relaxed. When appreciable numbers of Filipinos came in after World War I (when Chinese and Japanese workers could no longer be recruited) exclusionary efforts against them began.

The advent of the twentieth century witnessed the entry of other Asians, such as Asian Indians, but in small numbers. Even though those seeking trade were among some of the earliest migrants to the United States, Indians had insignificant contacts with this country during the nineteenth century. The poorer workers among them found labor opportunities in British colonies. The few thousand who did come, most of them men, settled primarily in California, and most of them found agricultural jobs.[22] Their families remained in India while husbands and fathers worked to earn money to send for them or to return. A small number of more educated Indians also entered.

Even small numbers of Asian Indians managed to agitate the Asiatic Exclusion League, which had sprung up in response to Japanese and Korean immigration. Racial and economic nativism was again at the core of the agitation. Asian Indians competed for agricultural jobs and were willing to work for lower wages in other jobs, so nativists used violence to force them out of local jobs. Not satisfied with making life in the United States miserable and even dangerous, exclusionists also persuaded federal immigration authorities to block their entry. The California commissioner of state labor statistics concluded that the "Hindu is the most

---

[21] JAMES PATTERSON, AMERICA IN THE TWENTIETH CENTURY 94 (1983).

[22] Many Asian Indians who migrated to the Western Hemisphere settled in Canada first, because of the British Commonwealth connection.

undesirable immigrant in the state. His lack of personal cleanliness, his low morals and his blind adherence to theories and teachings, so entirely repugnant to American principles, make him unfit for association with American people."[23] Although about 2,000 Asian Indians immigrated from 1911 to 1917, more than 1,700 were denied entry during the same period, mostly on the grounds that they would need public assistance.

Like the Chinese and Japanese before them, many Asian Indians fought for acceptance. Some sought to have laws discriminating against them overturned by the courts. Lower federal courts had granted them the right to naturalize on the grounds that they were Caucasians and thus eligible "white persons" under the citizenship laws of 1790 and 1870. But in *United States v. Bhagat Singh Thind* (1923), the Supreme Court reversed this racial stance, deciding that Indians, like Japanese, would no longer be considered white persons, and were therefore ineligible to become naturalized citizens.

But barring Asian Indian and other Asian immigrants from naturalization was not enough to keep them from exclusion from the definition of American if immigration bars were not erected. Strict control of Chinese and Japanese immigration had done little to satisfy the demands of American nativists who maintained a closed view of the American society. They insisted that all Asians were racially inferior to whites and should be completely barred.

Congress responded to this anti-Asian clamor and a renewed xenophobia aroused by the influx of southern and eastern Europeans by passing the Act of February 5, 1917. The constant flow of Italians, Russians, and Hungarians that peaked in the first decade of the century, fueled racial nativism and anti-Catholicism, culminating in a controversial requirement that excluded aliens "who cannot read and understand some language or dialect. But the act also created the "Asiatic barred zone" by extending the Chinese exclusion laws to all other Asians. The zone covered South Asia from Arabia to Indochina, as well as the adjacent islands. It included India, Burma, Thailand, the Malay States, the East Indian Islands, Asiatic Russia, the Polynesian Islands, and parts of Arabia and Afghanistan. China and Japan did not have to be included because of the Chinese exclusion laws and the Gentlemen's Agreement. But together these provisions declared inadmissible all Asians except teachers, merchants, and students. Only Filipinos and Guamanians, under U.S. jurisdiction at the time, were not included.

The reactionary, isolationist political climate that followed World War I, manifested in the Red Scare of 1919–20, led to even greater exclusionist demands. The landmark Immigration Act of 1924, opposed by only six senators, once again took direct aim at southern and eastern Europeans, whom the Protestant majority in the United States viewed with dogmatic disapproval. The arguments advanced in support of the bill stressed recurring themes: the racial superiority of Anglo-Saxons, the fact that immigrants would cause the lowering of wages, and the unassimilability of foreigners, while citing the usual threats to the nation's social unity and order posed by immigration.

---

[23] California Board of Control, *California and the Oriental: Japanese, Chinese, and Hindus* 101–2 (Sacramento: State Printing Office 1920).

The act restructured criteria for admission to respond to nativist demands and represented a general selection policy that remained in place until 1952. The scheme provided that immigrants of any particular country be limited to 2 percent of their nationality in 1890. The law struck most deeply at Jews, Italians, Slavs, and Greeks who had immigrated in great numbers after 1890, and who would be most disfavored by such a quota system.

Though sponsors of the act were primarily concerned with limiting immigration from southern and eastern Europe, they simultaneously eliminated the few remaining categories for Asians. The act provided for the permanent exclusion of any "alien ineligible to citizenship." Since Asians were barred from naturalization under the 1790 and 1870 laws, the possibility of their entry was cut off indefinitely. Asians were not allowed even under the 2 percent quota rule. The primary target were the Japanese, who, while subject to the Gentlemen's Agreement, had never been totally barred by federal immigration law until then.

The only Asians not affected by the 1924 Act were Filipinos, who remained exempt as nationals and who by then had settled into a familiar pattern of immigration. Before 1920, a few resided mostly in Hawaii; their presence on the islands helped establish conditions later conducive to a more substantial labor migration. They became a convenient source of cheap labor after Japanese immigration was restricted in 1908. Just as the Chinese exclusion law had encouraged employers to look to Japan, so the limitations on Japanese immigrants led to an intense recruitment, especially by the Hawaiian Sugar Planters' Association, of Filipino laborers because of their open travel status as noncitizen nationals.

By the late 1920s, Filipino laborers began to look beyond Hawaii, where the demand for their labor was shrinking, to the mainland where the need for cheap labor, especially in agriculture, was growing. Many left Hawaii partly in response to employers' recruitment efforts. Most Filipinos who had come to the mainland previously had been students. But in the late 1920s, laborers came to California predominantly to work on citrus and vegetable farms.

Because of their special immigration status, Filipinos considered themselves American in important respects. Still, on their arrival familiar cycles of rejection quickly surfaced, much to their consternation. They were met with acceptance by eager employers and then, almost immediately, resentment from white workers, particularly as their numbers increased on the mainland in the late 1920s.

To white workers in California, the privileged immigration status of Filipinos did not change the fact that they were an economic threat who had the physical characteristics of Asiatics. They were just another undesirable Asian race who had a disturbing attitude, because they knew something of American culture, could speak English, and in some cases lived with white women. They also seemed to be taking over white jobs and lowering standards for white wages and working conditions. As it had toward Chinese and Japanese, white resentment of Filipinos soon boiled over into violence, and numerous anti-Filipino outbursts erupted in California between 1929 and 1934. Their strong concentration in agriculture made them visible and competitive (of the 45,000 reported on the mainland in 1930, about 82 percent were farm laborers) especially during the severe unemployment of the

Great Depression. Since Filipinos were often on the bottom of the economic ladder, the depression struck them particularly hard. Exclusionists suggested that the United States ought to repatriate unemployed Filipino workers, for their own benefit as well as for that of the United States.

Calls for the exclusion of Filipino workers were warmly received in Congress, which welcomed any seemingly uncomplicated proposal that promised relief for the depression's high unemployment. For policymakers, however, dealing with anti-Filipino agitation was not as simple as responding to earlier anti-Chinese, anti-Asian Indian, and even anti-Japanese campaigns. They could travel in and out of the country without constraint, so until the Philippines was granted independence, Congress could not exclude Filipinos.

An unlikely coalition of exclusionists, anti-colonialists, and Filipino nationalists managed to band together to promote the passage of the Tydings-McDuffie Act in 1934. Many of the exclusionists had initially wished to keep the Philippines, but they soon realized that to exclude Filipino laborers they had to support Filipino nationalists and anti-colonialists and grant the nation its freedom. Independence and exclusion became so intertwined that the former was often used as a motive for the latter.

Tydings-McDuffie was everything exclusionists could hope for. When their nation would become independent on July 4, 1946, Filipinos would lose their status as nationals of the United States, regardless of where they lived. Those in the United States would be deported unless they became immigrants. Between 1934 and 1946, however, any Filipino who desired to immigrate became subject to the immigration acts of 1917 and 1924, and the Philippines was considered a separate country with an annual quota of only 50 visas!

The passage of Tydings-McDuffie, the last congressional act excluding immigration from Asia, signaled the formal end of an era. The refusal to extend Asians the right to naturalize, the laws against the Chinese, the Gentlemen's Agreement with Japan, the 1917 and 1924 immigration acts, and Tydings-McDuffie were the legacy of the schizophrenic attempt by Congress to satisfy economic ambitions, some egalitarian views of the world, and nativist prejudice. These exclusion laws remained in full force throughout the 1930s and much of the 1940s, symbolizing a peak in anti-immigrant power.

E. THE NATIONAL ORIGINS QUOTA SYSTEM

Manifested in the Red Scare of 1919–20, the reactionary, isolationist political climate that followed World War I led to even greater exclusionist demands. To many Americans, the ghost of Bolshevism seemed to haunt the land in the specter of immigrant radicals, especially after the 1919 wave of industrial unrest in immigrant-dominated workforces of the coal, steel, meatpacking, and transportation industries. In reaction to the isolationist political climate, Congress passed a variety of laws placing numerical restrictions on immigration.

The reactionary exclusionist sentiment of the time was combined with the ethnic. The 1917 literacy law was inadequate for restrictionists who remained concerned about the continuing entry of southern and eastern Europeans. Southern and eastern European immigrants numbered 4.5 million in 1910, and by 1920 the figure surged again to 5.67 million. The 100 percent American campaign was alarmed that one-fifth of the California population was Italian American by then.

In addition to the menace of leftist political influence emanating from parts of Europe, public and congressional arguments in support of more restrictive legislation stressed recurring themes: the racial superiority of Anglo-Saxons, the fact that immigrants would cause the lowering of wages, the unassimilability of foreigners, and the usual threats to the nation's social unity and order posed by immigration. Popular biological theories of the period alleging the superiority of certain races also were influential.

The result of the continued assault on southern and eastern European immigrants was the Quota Law of 1921, enacted as a temporary measure. This legislation introduced for the first time numerical limitations on immigration. With certain exceptions, the law allocated quotas to each nationality totaling 3 percent of the foreign-born persons of that nationality residing in the United States in 1910, for an annual total of approximately 350,000. Since most of those living in the United States in 1910 were northern or western European, the quota for southern and eastern Europeans was smaller (about 45,000 less). The latter groups filled their quotas easily, but northern and western European countries did not fill their quotas under this law.[24] This law was scheduled to expire in 1922, but was extended to June 30, 1924.

A permanent policy of numerical restrictions was enacted in 1924. One problem with the 1910 model for the 1921 law was that the period between 1900 to 1910 witnessed a large influx of southern and eastern Europeans. So a 1910 population model would include a higher proportion of southern and eastern Europeans than earlier years. So the landmark Immigration Act of 1924, opposed by only six senators, took an even greater malicious aim at southern and eastern Europeans, whom the Protestant majority in the U.S. viewed with dogmatic disapproval.

The 1924 legislation adopted a national origins formula that eventually based the quota for each nationality on the number of foreign-born persons of their national origin in the United States in 1890 — prior to the major wave of southern and eastern Europeans. The law provided that immigrants of any particular country be reduced from 3 percent under the 1921 law to 2 percent of the group's population under the new law. And instead of 1910 as the population model year for determining how many could enter, the 2 percent was based on a particular nationality's population in 1890, when even fewer immigrants from southern and eastern Europe lived in the United States. The quota formula was hailed as the "most far reaching change that occurred in America during the course of this quarter century," enabling a halt to "the tendency toward a change in the fundamental composition of the American stock."

---

[24] There was a non-quota exception of which some southern and eastern Europeans took advantage. The law permitted a person to be admitted to the United States as an immigrant if the individual had resided in the Western Hemisphere for one year (later changed to five years). So by temporarily living in a Western Hemisphere country, the quota could be avoided.

This formula resulted in a sharp curtailment of immigrants from southern and eastern Europe, and struck most deeply at Jews, Italians, Slavs, and Greeks. Quota immigrants were limited to approximately 165,000 per year, with the proportion and number even smaller for southern and eastern Europeans than before. However, natives of the Western Hemisphere countries could enter without numerical restriction. Other nonquota groups included wives and children of U.S. citizens and return lawful residents. Those who entered in violation of visa and quota requirements were deportable without time limitation. Another provision, aimed at Asians, barred all aliens ineligible to citizenship, thus completely barring Japanese (as well as all other Asians), some of whom had continued to enter under the 1907 Gentlemen's Agreement.

The impact of the national origins quota system on the southern and eastern European population in the United States is evident from census information on the foreign-born population of the country. They numbered about 1.67 million in 1900. After the big immigrant wave of the first decade of the twentieth century, the figure almost tripled to 4.5 million in 1910. The population surged again in the next decade to 5.67 million in 1920. However, after the quota systems of 1921 and 1924 took effect, the number of immigrants from those regions of Europe declined. The population increased to only 5.92 million by 1930. The figures for immigrants from specific countries are also telling. The population of Italian immigrants increased only 11.18 percent between 1920 and 1930, after experiencing a 176 percent jump in the first decade of the century. The number of Polish immigrants in the United States increased only 11.4 percent during the 1920s, and the number of Hungarians in the country actually declined from 397,283 to 274,450.

F.   THE IMMIGRATION AND NATIONALITY ACT OF 1952

Influenced by the cold war atmosphere and anti-communist fervor of the post-World War II era and the onset of the Korean War, the McCarran-Walter Act of 1952 was enacted, overhauling the country's immigration laws in major ways. While the quota system of the 1920s was influenced by the Red Scare of 1919–1920, the limitation on southern and eastern Europeans was not an explicit limitation on the entry of communists and subversives. The 1952 law was more direct and reminiscent of the alien and sedition laws of early America: individuals who held certain political viewpoints were not welcome; certain viewpoints were un-American. Moreover, the 1952 law lays the groundwork to exclude another social group that was un-American: homosexuals.

The fear of communism and other "non-democratic" ideas played an important part of the national psyche leading up to the law. The Smith Act of 1940, that made it illegal to advocate the overthrow of the government by force or to belong to an organization advocating such a position, was used by the Truman administration to jail leaders of the American Communist Party. In response to criticism, particularly from the House Committee on Un-American Activities, that his administration was "soft on communism," Truman established the Loyalty Review Board in 1947 to review government employees. In 1950, Senator Pat McCarran of Nevada (the co-author of the 1952 legislation) sponsored the Internal Security Act that required communist-front organizations to register with the attorney general and barred their members from defense work and travel abroad. The same year, Alger Hiss, a former State Department official who had become president of the Carnegie Endowment for International Peace, was convicted of perjury, following allegations that he was a communist who had supplied classified documents to the Soviet Union. Also in 1950, Julius and Ethel Rosenberg, as well as Harry Gold, were charged with and convicted of giving atomic secrets to the Soviet Union, and eventually the Rosenbergs were executed. Earlier in 1950, Senator Joseph R. McCarthy embarked on his infamous hunt for subversives, stating that he had a list of known communists who were working in the State Department; later his attacks expanded to include diplomats, scholars, and filmmakers.

With this backdrop, little wonder that the 1952 Act contained several provisions relating to the exclusion and deportation of subversives and communists. For example, the law provided these exclusion provisions that, in large part, have endured:

Aliens who are, or at any time have been, members of any of the following classes:

(A) Aliens who are anarchists;

(B) Aliens who advocate or teach, or who are members of or affiliated with any organization that advocates or teaches, opposition to all organized government;

(C) Aliens who are members or affiliated with (i) the Communist Party of the United States, (ii) any other totalitarian party of the United States, (iii) the Communist Political Association, (iv) the Communist or any other totalitarian party of any State of the United States, of any foreign state, or of any political or geographical subdivision of any foreign state . . . *Provided*, that nothing in this paragraph, or in any other provision of this Act, shall be construed as declaring that the Communist Party does not advocate the overthrow of the Government of the United States by force, violence, or other unconstitutional means;

(D) Aliens . . . who advocate the economic, international, and governmental doctrines of world communism or the establishment in the United States of a totalitarian dictatorship, or who are members of or affiliated with any organization that advocates the economic, or international, and governmental doctrines of world communism . . . ;

(G) Aliens who write or publish, or cause to be written or published, or who knowingly circulate, distribute, print, or display . . . any written or printed matter, advocating or teaching opposition to all organized government, or advocating or teaching . . . the overthrow by force, violence, or other unconstitutional means of the Government of the United States or of all forms of law . . . .[25]

---

[25] 8 U.S.C. § 1182(a)(28) (1952).

The act also called for grounds for exclusion, that contained detailed provisions relating to health, criminal, moral, economic, and subversive criteria. Expulsion was authorized without time limitation of aliens who enter unlawfully, nonimmigrants who overstay their allotted time, and those who are guilty of certain misconduct such as criminals, narcotics violators, prostitutes, and of course subversives.

In spite of his sensitivity to being called "soft on communism," President Truman opposed the enactment of the 1952 Act. His veto, which was easily overridden by Congress, was not based on opposition to the subversion and anti-communism provisions nor the new entry or deportation sections. In fact, he was certainly not averse to jailing or throwing communists out of the country. The act continued the national origins quota selection system of the 1920s, perpetuating the policy that immigrants from one part of the world were better than others. This continuation of the racialized quota system triggered Truman's adamant opposition to the legislation. But on June 27, 1952, Congress passed the bill over Truman's veto.[26]

In addition to continuing the national origins quota system for the Eastern Hemisphere, the 1952 Act also established a four-category selection system. Fifty percent of each national quota was allocated for first preference distribution to aliens with high education or exceptional abilities, and the remaining three preferences were divided among specified relatives of U.S. citizens and lawful permanent resident aliens. This four-point selection system was the antecedent of the current preference system that places higher priority on family reunification than on needed skills. However, under the 1952 law national origins remained the determining factor in immigrant admissions, and Northern and Western Europe were heavily favored. As in the past, the Western Hemisphere was not subject to numerical limitations. Although the Asian exclusion laws were finally deleted, in its place a new "Asia-Pacific Triangle" was established with a trivial 2,000 annual quota, continuing the blatant form of racial and ethnic discrimination that epitomized the retained quota laws.

The ostracism that gays and lesbians endure in American life also has immigration-related underpinnings partially rooted in the 1952 law. The immigration laws of the nation, especially provisions related to who can enter, who cannot enter, and who can be removed, represent the judgment of our elected leaders as to whom we would allow or not allow to enter and become an American. For decades, the immigration laws contained provisions that were intended to keep immigrant homosexuals out of the country, thereby institutionalizing the sentiment that homosexuals should not be Americans. Homosexuals were first statutorily excluded from entry by the Immigration Act of 1917, which prohibited the admission of "persons of constitutional psychopathic inferiority" certified by a physician to be "mentally. . . . defective."[27] In 1950, the Senate subcommittee that eventually recommended the overhaul to the Immigration and Nationality Act reported that the "purpose of [an existing] provision against 'persons with constitutional psychopathic inferiority' will be more adequately served by changing that term to 'persons afflicted with psychopathic personality,' and that the classes of mentally defectives

---

[26] Pub. L. No. 414, 82d Congress (66 Stat. 163).

[27] Ch. 29, § 3, 39 Stat. 874 (1917) (repealed 1952).

should be enlarged to include homosexuals and other sex perverts."[28] Thus, among the major changes to the immigration laws that resulted in 1952, Congress included in the list of individuals to be excluded those "afflicted with psychopathic personality."[29]

In 1962, the federal Ninth Circuit Court of Appeals, in *Fleuti v. Rosenberg*,[30] allowed a homosexual man to reenter the country, ruling that the term "psychopathic personality" was too vague to encompass homosexuals under certain circumstances. In response, in 1965 Congress amended the law to include the words "sexual deviation" in order to "serve the purpose of resolving any doubt on this point."[31] Now the law excluded "aliens afflicted with psychopathic personality, sexual deviation, or a mental defect."[32]

The constitutionality of the exclusion of homosexuals was resolved by the Supreme Court a few years later in *Boutlier v. INS* (1967),[33] a deportation case. The Supreme Court held that the legislative history of the provision indicated "beyond a shadow of a doubt" that Congress intended to exclude immigrants who were homosexuals via the "psychopathic personality" provision. As a result, the Court upheld Boutilier's deportation, because prior to his entry in the United States when he was 21 years old, he had engaged in homosexual activity on a regular basis. Since he was excludable at the time of his immigration, he could now be deported.

In spite of Congress' clear intent to exclude homosexuals and the Supreme Court's finding of constitutionality to do so, the ability of INS to enforce the homosexual exclusion provision continued to be tested. After years of intense debate over the exclusion of homosexuals, the Immigration Act of 1990 removed the psychopathic personality and sexual deviation language from the exclusion provisions along with all language referring to mental retardation, insanity, and mental defects.

G.   THE IMMIGRATION REFORM AND CONTROL ACT OF 1986 (IRCA)

Concerns over the number of undocumented workers (predominantly Mexican) in the United States deepened in the 1970s and early 1980s. While no one knew the exact number, some of the more hysterical estimates ranged from eight to 12 million. In spite of increased authority and resources for Border Patrol efforts, INS efforts were perceived as ineffectual. Proposals were made to address the situation from a different perspective — by penalizing employers who were hiring undocumented workers, through what was called "employer sanctions." By 1986, employer sanctions became part of the nation's immigration laws. The passage of the

---

[28] S. Rep. No. 1515, 81st Cong, 2d Sess., p. 345.

[29] 8 U.S.C. § 1182(a)(4) (1952).

[30] 302 F.2d 652 (9th Cir. 1962), *vacated on other grounds*, 374 U.S. 449 (1963).

[31] S. Rep. No. 748, 89th Cong., 1st Sess. 19, reprinted in 1965 U.S. Code Cong. & Ad. News 3328, 3337; H.R. Rep. No. 745, 89th Cong., 1st Sess. 16 (1965).

[32] 8 U.S.C. § 1182(a)(4) (1976).

[33] 387 U.S. 118 (1967).

Immigration Reform and Control Act (IRCA) represented the culmination of years of social, political and congressional debate about the perceived lack of control over our southern border. The belief that something had to be done about the large numbers of undocumented workers who had entered the U.S. from Mexico in the 1970s was reinforced by the flood of Central Americans that began arriving in the early 1980s. While the political turmoil of civil war in El Salvador, Guatemala, and Nicaragua drove many Central Americans from their homeland, they, along with the Mexicans who continued to arrive, were generally labeled economic migrants by the Reagan Administration, the INS, and the courts.

Employer sanctions had earlier iterations. In 1952 — when the immigration laws were overhauled to clamp down on subversives and communists, the notion of punishing employers got nowhere. As a provision outlawing willful importation, transportation, or harboring of undocumented aliens was debated, an amendment was proposed imposing criminal penalties for the employment of undocumented aliens if the employer had "reasonable grounds to believe a worker was not legally in the United States." The amendment was soundly defeated, but beginning in 1971, legislative proposals featuring employer sanctions as a centerpiece reappeared and were touted as the tool needed to resolve the undocumented alien problem. By the end of the Carter Administration in 1980, the Select Commission on Immigration and Refugee Policy portrayed legalization as a necessary balance to sanctions. However, the story of congressional support for IRCA is complicated. Although some broader-mined members of Congress may have wanted legalization to be implemented generously once enacted, Congress' support for legalization itself was decidedly underwhelming.

So within 30 years of the 1952 rejection of employer sanctions, things had changed. Most Americans were convinced that a crisis over undocumented immigration — especially undocumented *Mexican* migration — existed and that something had to be done. The desire to rid the country of the unwanted was too strong. The power of employers to resist sanctions collapsed, and by 1986 federal employer sanctions were enacted as the major feature of reform. By a bare swing vote of only four members of the House of Representatives, legalization (amnesty) provisions (one part for those who entered prior to 1982, and another for certain agricultural workers) were also made part of the package to address the undocumented immigrant issue. Although on paper the appearance of a deal of employer sanctions for amnesty was struck, there was no political tradeoff; IRCA would have gone forward if legalization were dropped by the House, and its effective implementation in the hands of an inept Immigration and Naturalization Service was seriously in doubt.

1. Reasons Given for Legalization

The major justifications advanced by legislative supporters of a legalization program were varied.

a. No Alternative to Legalization

How could Congress deal with the huge number of undocumented aliens living in the United States? Members of Congress only had a handful of alternatives: first, legalize some or all of the aliens; second, find and deport some or all of them; or third, do nothing. The second alternative would have required a huge effort to "round up" aliens, would probably have violated many civil rights and therefore engendered a horde of lawsuits, would have cost a fortune, and simply would never have worked. The third alternative was not possible since Congress was under pressure to do something about the perceived undocumented problem. Legalization was the only alternative.

Thus, in a real sense, this argument boiled down to a logistically realistic response to the "problem of undocumented aliens." Existing enforcement was failing and massive deportations would certainly never have worked. Thus, one could argue that the program had to be generous if the goal was to rid the country of undocumented aliens. Yet the cutoff date adopted for legalization was not generous, and the "no alternatives" argument was not the only reasoning offered to support legalization.

b. Spread INS Resources

A different justification for legalizing undocumented residents was that this would allow the INS to stop concentrating its enforcement resources on locating and apprehending longtime residents and concentrate instead on enforcement of the border against newly arriving, undocumented aliens.

c. Elimination of the Underclass

For some, legalization was the mechanism to address the fact that many undocumented aliens lived in what some described as an "underclass" in poverty without the protection of labor or health laws. The Select Commission had complained of the existence of a "second class" society. And many members of Congress hoped that legalization would eliminate the underclass.[34] A spokesman for the Mexican American Legal Defense and Education Fund (MALDEF) was typical of supporters who contended that "[l]egalization is the only realistic and meaningful way to bring the undocumented population 'out of the shadows' and into the mainstream of American life with the minimum of disruption and expense."[35] And on signing the legislation, even President Reagan, who was more interested in the employer sanctions provisions of the law, expressed hope that the legalization program would remove people from "the shadows."[36]

---

[34] *See, e.g.*, 132 Cong. Rec. 30,064 (1986) (statement of Rep. Bill Richardson).

[35] Housing Hearing 28 at 128 (statement of Richard Fajardo, MALDEF).

[36] Statement on Signing the Immigration Reform and Control Act of 1986, 1986 Pub. Papers 1522.

d. Equity, Fairness, Dignity, Compassion, and Reality

Many lawmakers supported the legalization program because of the contributions that undocumented workers had already made to the country, and charged the nation with a responsibility to account for those contributions. This view was used to respond to complaints that legalization was not fair to prospective immigrants waiting in line abroad or that it might be a "magnet" for further unlawful entrants thinking they could cheat their way into the program. Indeed, the House Report argued that legalization was "equitable" to the undocumented aliens working in the United States, and in President Reagan's words, "fair to the countless thousands of people throughout the world who seek legally to come to America."[37]

For others, it demonstrated "compassion" for those now part of American society, giving "dignity" and "honor" to those working without permission in America; in short, it was "necessary," "humanitarian," and the "American way."[38] Even the INS Commissioner touted legalization as a compromise between a "humanitarian recognition of illegals who have significant equities in the U.S." and "fair and reasonable screening requirements that do not reward proven criminals."[39]

2. Intent of the Special Agricultural Worker Program

Evidence of the scope and intent behind the Special Agricultural Worker (SAW) legalization program is sketchy. The program made its way to inclusion in IRCA virtually without congressional debate and without any attempts to change it. Naturally, the program had its supporters and detractors. But few made statements revealing the intended scope of the program or the reasoning behind its structure. Several legislators viewed the SAW program as a compromise between growers and workers. No one seemed to think the SAW program was primarily for the benefit of laborers, although the legislative history makes it apparent that Congress was mindful not to reenact elements of the Bracero guestworker program from the 1950s.

3. What Legalization Entailed

IRCA contained two major amnesty or legalization provisions that had the potential of benefiting millions of undocumented aliens. The first provided permanent residence status to aliens who had resided in the United States since before January 1, 1982. The other afforded permanent residence status to farm workers or Special Agriculture Workers (SAWS) who had performed agricultural work for at least 90 days between May 1, 1985 and May 1, 1986."

Those who commonly fell under the first program either entered by crossing the border without inspection prior to January 1, 1982, or entered on a visitor or student visa and worked without permission or overstayed the permitted length of stay prior to that date. About 70 percent who ultimately applied under the pre 1982

---

[37] H.R. Rep. No. 682-1, at 71; Statement on Signing of IRCA, at 1522.

[38] Statements of Representative H. Fish and Senator D. Moynihan.

[39] House Hearing 28, at 203 (statement of Alan Nelson, Commissioner, INS).

program were Mexican; the next largest groups were Salvadoran (8.1 percent) and Guatemalan (3 percent). However, the percentages may simply reflect the results of publicity priorities of the INS and community based organizations (CBOs). Demographers who scrutinized the 1980 census data prior to IRCA concluded that only 55 percent of the undocumented population was Mexican in origin.

Those qualifying under the farm worker program were also mostly Mexican. They predominated with 81.6 percent of the SAW applications. Haitians received 3.4 percent, El Salvadorans 2 percent, and Guatemalans and Asian Indians 1.4 percent each.

Ultimately, 1.7 million applicants filed under the pre-1982 program and 1.2 million applied as SAWs. The number for the pre-1982 program was far below most estimates, while the figure for agricultural workers was higher than expected.

4. Employer Sanctions

Under IRCA, for the first time Congress prohibited employers from hiring workers who are not authorized to work in the United States, imposing civil and criminal penalties on violators. IRCA was the product of years of debate regarding the impact of undocumented immigrant workers on the United States. Employer sanctions were the centerpiece of the legislation, but employers also became subject to penalties for new employment discrimination laws.

In response to intense lobbying by civil rights advocates and concerned members of Congress who feared that employer sanctions would cause employment discrimination, protections were included in the law intended to safeguard against discrimination. IRCA contained provisions that attempted to insure that employers would not use the new employer sanctions law as a pretext for discriminating against immigrant workers. Prior to IRCA, private employers could require employees to be U.S. citizens, but after IRCA, employers had to hire a qualified immigrant job applicant, unless a citizen was equally qualified applied for the job. Employers could be fined for such discriminatory hiring practices, as well as for requiring new immigrant employees to come up with more proof than necessary to establish eligibility to work.

IRCA mandated the General Accounting Office (GAO), the investigative arm of Congress, to conduct three annual studies from 1987 to 1989 to determine whether employer sanctions had resulted in "widespread discrimination." A "sunset" provision further stipulated that employer sanctions could be repealed if the GAO concluded that compliance caused employers to discriminate.

The first two status reports on employer sanctions by the GAO found that "one in every six employers in GAO's survey who were aware of the law may have begun or increased the practice of (1) asking only foreign-looking persons for work authorization documents or (2) hiring only U.S. citizens." In spite of the fact that almost 17 percent of employers admitted to practices that violated the discrimination provisions of IRCA, GAO concluded that the findings did not establish a pattern of "widespread discrimination," citing lack of conclusive evidence that the employer sanctions requirements were the cause of discrimination.

In 1989, a number of groups across the country began to compile information that they had received from individuals of mostly Asian, Latino, and Middle Eastern descent regarding discriminatory treatment they had experienced while seeking new employment or working in the current positions. Several civil rights organizations issued reports of the anecdotal evidence collected. While the reports documented disturbing accounts of discrimination, proponents of employer sanctions dismissed the data collected by advocacy groups as unreliable.

Eventually, some of the independent research could not be ignored by the GAO. A methodological survey of 416 San Francisco employers was conducted in San Francisco, revealing that an overwhelming 97 percent of the firms regularly engaged in at least one employment practice that could be discriminatory under IRCA or other anti-discrimination laws. Another 53 percent reported that they engaged in three or more such practices. The research was submitted to the GAO in September 1989, and influenced the GAO's third report.[40]

Despite the GAO's findings of "widespread" IRCA-related employment discrimination and similar evidence by independent researchers in its final two reports, Congress did not repeal employer sanctions. The findings were routinely dismissed by anti-immigrant groups, Senator Alan Simpson (a co-sponsor of IRCA), and the AFL-CIO as insignificant or unreliable. Several bills to repeal employer sanctions were introduced in Congress in 1990 and 1991, but none reached the floor of Congress (in spite of bi-partisan support from Senators Kennedy and Hatch).

Although employer sanctions were not repealed, the Immigration Act of 1990 did strengthen IRCA's anti-discrimination provisions. The law increased employer and employee education, added Special Agricultural Workers to the category of protected workers, changed the penalties for discrimination to conform with those for employer sanctions penalties, made document abuse an unfair immigration-related employment practice, prohibited retaliation against those who file charges, made it easier to prosecute for document abuse by adding civil, as well as criminal penalties, and eliminated the requirement that a noncitizen who makes a discrimination charge must have filed an official "declaration of intent" to become a citizen.

By the early 1990s, many members of Congress, most notably Senator Simpson, contended that no further employer education was necessary to decrease employment discrimination. In fact, Simpson argued at a 1992 Senate Judiciary Committee hearing that the employer sanctions provisions, both the documentation requirements and the anti-discrimination protections, were as familiar to employers as were the requirements to pay taxes.

Only a fraction of U.S. employers and workers have received education from the Office of Special Counsel, which spent approximately $14 million on educational outreach between 1990 and 1996. OSC's education program did not begin in earnest until 1990, when it initiated a grants program, contracting with local groups to

---

[40] Lina M. Avidan, *Employment and Hiring Practices Under the Immigration Reform and Control Act of 1986; A Survey of San Francisco Businesses*, Coalition for Immigrant and Refugee Rights and Services, 1989.

conduct educational campaigns. The OSC is located in Washington, D.C., with no branch offices. Between 1987 and 1996, the OSC received 4,868 charges of discrimination from workers, but only 145 formal complaints were filed by the OSC against employers, 83 of whom were fined for IRCA-related unfair employment practices. Distribution of INS' *Handbook for Employers* that explains the regulations and has pictures of acceptable documents has also been inadequate. Only two nationwide distributions of the handbook took place by 1996: one in 1987 and again in 1991.

Although employer sanctions remain part of the immigration laws, by 2001, the concept had lost one of its ardent supporters. As organized labor, including the AFL-CIO, realized that its future viability rested solidly on the shoulders of immigrant workers, unions called for the repeal of employer sanctions and for the legalization of undocumented workers.

H.   THE 1965 AMENDMENTS AND THE IMMIGRATION ACT OF 1990

1.   The 1965 Framework for Selection

Since the 1952 Act changed little in the immigration selection system, the question over which immigrants to admit to the United States remained a battlefront. The survival of the national origins quota system of the 1920s through the 1952 Act continued the Western European dominance over immigration to the United States. The law continued to exasperate many observers, including President Truman, who vetoed the 1952 legislation largely due to its failure to repudiate the quota system. Congress, however, overrode Truman's veto, and critics were resigned to cite the law as an embarrassment that was inconsistent with our stature as leader of the free world.

Truman and others did not relent. Soon after the enactment of the 1952 law, he appointed a special Commission on Immigration and Naturalization to study the system. A 319-page report issued in 1953 strongly urged the abolition of the national origins system and recommended quotas without regard to national origin, race, creed, or color. President Eisenhower embraced the findings, but his push for corrective legislation failed. Despite repeated attempts at new legislation, no major action was taken on any of the commission's recommendations until more than 10 years later.

Entering office in January 1961, President Kennedy submitted a comprehensive program that provided the impetus for ultimate reform. His proposals reflected his long-standing interest in immigration reform. Kennedy called for the repeal of the discriminatory national origins quota system and the racial exclusion from the Asia-Pacific triangle, while assailing the nativism that led to the infamous Chinese exclusion laws. He envisioned a system governed by the skills of the immigrant and family reunification. For him, his proposed changes meant both an increase in fairness to applicants and in benefits to the United States.

President Kennedy's hopes for abolishing the quota system were realized when the 1965 amendments were enacted. The Asia-Pacific Triangle geographic restrictions were also eliminated (although the ceiling of 2,000 visas for that area had already been deleted in 1961). But his egalitarian vision of visas on a first-come, first-served basis gave way to a narrower and more historically parochial framework that provided few, if any, obvious advantages for prospective Asian immigrants. The new law allowed 20,000 immigrant visas annually for every country not in the Western Hemisphere. The allotment was made regardless of size of a country, so that mainland China had the same quota as Tunisia. Of the 170,000 visas set aside for the Eastern Hemisphere, 75 percent were for specified "preference" relatives of citizens and lawful permanent residents, and an unlimited number was available to immediate relatives (parents of adults, minor unmarried children, and spouses) of U.S. citizens. First preference was for the adult, unmarried sons and daughters of U.S. citizens, second preference for the spouses and unmarried children of lawful permanent resident aliens, fourth preference for married sons and daughters of U.S. citizens, and fifth preference for the siblings of U.S. citizens. Two occupational categories and a nonpreference category were also established. The occupational categories helped professionals and other aliens who filled jobs for which qualified U.S. workers were not available; although, for the first time, aliens seeking entry as skilled and unskilled labor were required to have approval of the Secretary of Labor. Under the nonpreference category, an alien who invested $40,000 in a business could qualify for immigration to the United States. A seventh preference was a refugee-like category for conditional entrants who were fleeing communist-dominated countries or the Middle East.

2.   Restraints on Mexican Immigration in the 1970s

Although the 1952 Act did not place a numerical limit on immigration from these areas, Congress included the Western Hemisphere quota of 120,000 in the 1965 amendments as a compromise for abolishing the national origins system. Concern was raised over the fact that immigration was on the increase from countries of the Western Hemisphere, particularly from Mexico.

Thus, while the rest of the world enjoyed an expansion of numerical limitations and a definite preference system after 1965, Mexico and the Western Hemisphere were suddenly faced with numerical restrictions for the first time. The Western Hemisphere was allotted a total of 120,000 immigrant visas each year, and while the first-come, first-served basis for immigration sounded fair, applicants had to meet strict labor certification requirements and demonstrate that they would not be displacing U.S. workers. Waivers of the labor certification requirement were available, however, for certain applicants, e.g., parents of U.S. citizen children. As one might expect given the new numerical limitations, by 1976 the procedure resulted in a severe backlog of approximately three years and a waiting list with nearly 300,000 names.[41]

As the immigration of Mexicans became the focus of more debate, Congress enacted legislation in 1976, curtailing Mexican migration even more. The law imposed the preference system on Mexico and the Western Hemisphere along with

---

[41] *See* CHARLES GORDON & STANLEY MAILMAN, IMMIGRATION LAW AND PROCEDURE § 1.4c (1993); Memorandum for the Associate Attorney General, Re: Allocation of Visas under *Silva v. Levi*, Deputy Assistant Attorney General, Office of Legal Counsel, Department of Justice, 3 (May 15, 1978).

a 20,000 visa per country numerical limitation. Thus Mexico's annual visa usage rate (which had been about 40,000) was virtually cut in half overnight, and thousands were left stranded on the old system's waiting list.[42] In 1978, the 120,000 Western Hemisphere and 170,000 Eastern Hemisphere quotas were merged into a single 290,000 worldwide numerical limit on immigration.

An 11-year misallocation of visas to Cuba eventually led to the permanent injunction and a "recapturing" of the wrongfully issued visas in lawsuit *Silva v. Bell*.[43] Finally, people who would have been able to immigrate years earlier, but for the mistake in taking away visas from the Western Hemisphere allocation, were able to now lawfully immigrate. However, Mexicans again received the short end of the stick when the State Department's formula for reallocation, which failed to provide sufficient visas for thousands of Mexicans on the *Silva* waiting list, was upheld. As a result, in February 1982, INS authorities began to round up those *Silva* class members who had not been accorded immigrant visa, advising them that they were now deportable and that work permission was terminated. The recipients were further informed that unless provisions of the existing immigration law qualified them to remain in the United States, they would have 30 days for voluntary departure. Although INS delayed enforcement for awhile, by February 1, 1983, the Enforcement Branch of the INS resumed the roundup of *Silva* class members.[44]

To make matters worse, in the first year of the new Western Hemisphere preference system and 20,000 limit on countries in the region, Mexico lost 14,000 visas due to a congressional mistake. The enactment date of the new law was January 1, 1977. However since the government's fiscal year runs from October 1 to September 30, the amendments did not become effective until after one full quarter of fiscal year 1977 had expired. During that first quarter, 14,203 visas were issued to Mexicans pursuant to the immigration system that prevailed in the Western Hemisphere before the new law became effective. The State Department nevertheless charged those visas against the newly-imposed national quota of 20,000, leaving only 5,797 visas available for Mexican immigrants between January 1 and September 30, 1977. In *De Avila v. Civiletti*,[45] the Seventh Circuit Court of Appeals sustained the State Department's approach even though it was "obvious that Congress . . . through inadvertence failed to inform the State Department how to administer during a fraction of the fiscal year a statute designed to apply on a full fiscal year basis."

---

[42] Act of Oct. 20, 1976, Pub. L. No. 94-571, 90 Stat. 2703 (1976); Silva v. Bell, 605 F.2d 978 (7th Cir. 1979) at 980–982.

[43] Silva v. Bell, 1978 U.S. Dist. LEXIS 15038 (N.D. Ill. Oct. 10, 1978) (order granting permanent injunction); *See also* No. 76C 1456 (N.D. Ill. June 21, 1977) (final judgment order-visas recaptured).

[44] Telegraphic Message of Hugh J. Brian, Asst. Commr. Detention and Deportation, Central Office Immigration and Naturalization Service, CO 242.4-P (Aug. 20, 1982); Memorandum from E. B. Duarte, Jr, Director, Outreach Program, Central Office Immigration and Naturalization Service, To Outreach Centers, Subject: Silva Update (February 3, 1983).

[45] 643 F.2d 471, 476 (7th Cir. 1981).

3. Affirmative Action for Western Europeans: "Diversity" in the 1980s and 1990s

By the end of the 1970s and through the 1980s, immigrant visa demands from Mexico remained high, and demand from certain Asian countries surged. By 1990, immigrants from Mexico, the Philippines, India, Korea, and Chinese from China, Taiwan, and Hong Kong dominated legal immigration categories. Given the per-country numerical limitations, Mexico and Asian countries shared (and continue to share) the largest backlogs in family reunification categories. This was especially true for preference categories reserved for siblings of U.S. citizens and relatives of lawful permanent resident aliens. Yet, in 1982, as part of a major legislative package, Republican Senator Alan Simpson of Wyoming initiated a crusade to eliminate the immigration category allowing U.S. citizens to be reunited with siblings and persisted in his efforts to abolish the category until his retirement in 1996.

In 1986, Congress responded to the rising domination of Asian and Latinos in immigration totals in a different manner. Although the country's population was still overwhelmingly white and of European descent, Congress added a little publicized provision in the Immigration Reform and Control Act to help 36 countries that had been "adversely affected" by the 1965 changes. To be considered "adversely affected," a country must have been issued fewer visas after 1965 than before. Thus, the list included such countries as Great Britain, Germany, and France, but no countries from Africa who sent few immigrants prior to 1965. So the so-called "diversity" program was not about diversifying the country, which of course remained overwhelmingly white. It also was not about helping immigrants from countries that had little ability to voluntarily immigrate to the United States historically, e.g., African nations. The "diversity" program was actually an affirmative action program for natives of countries who already made up the vast ethnic background of the country, such as Western European countries.

The new allocations were significant. The 1986 law provided an extra 5,000 such visas a year for 1987 and 1988, but the number increased to 15,000 per year for 1989 and 1990 through additional legislation. These visas were above and beyond the 20,000 visas that were already available for immigrants from each of the "diversity" countries under the preference system. But in order to qualify for the diversity visas, applicants did not have to have close relatives already in the United States or special job skills that would benefit the country. The program was a "first-come-first-served" worldwide mail registration program, benefiting the earliest-registered applicants and their immediate families, requiring them only to meet the nationality, health, and morals qualifications of immigration laws.

Part of the impetus for the "diversity" program was the fact that many Irish nationals who came to the United States were unable to fit into the regular immigration categories. They did not have close relatives who could petition for them, and many did not have special job skills. In the 1980s, a severe economic downturn in Ireland motivated many of its young professionals to look for work abroad. Ireland's gross domestic product (GDP) grew an average of only 1.8 percent each year from 1980 to 1985. Its national debt rivaled that of many Third

World countries; in 1986, the debt stood at 134 percent of the GNP.[46] Ireland's foreign debt, in per capita terms, was one of the highest in the world — three times as high as Mexico's. One out of every five Irish workers was out of a job by 1987, and the unemployment rate was worse in major cities such as Dublin.[47]

Discouraged by the economy in Ireland, many of its young residents traveled to the United States, usually on temporary visas such as for tourism. Eventually they overstayed their visas. By 1989, the Irish government estimated that perhaps 50,000 Irish nationals resided in the United States in undocumented status.

So in 1988, Congress set aside an extra 20,000 visas to increase immigration diversity over a period of another two years. This time, the "OP-1" lottery for the visas was available to nationals of countries that were "underrepresented," namely a foreign state that used less than 25 percent of its 20,000 preference visas in 1988. As a result, all but 13 countries in the world were eligible. Mexico, the Philippines, China, Korea, and India were among the countries that were not eligible. Over 3.2 million applicants were received for the 20,000 visas.

Legislation in 1990 extended the diversity visa concept even more. Until October 1, 1994, a transition diversity program would provide 40,000 visas per year for countries "adversely affected" by the 1965 amendments, except that 40 percent of the visas were effectively designated for Irish nationals. True, displaced Tibetans residing in India or Nepal were also given extra numbers, but the overwhelming diversity beneficiaries would be white. After October 1, 1994, 55,000 diversity visas would be available annually in a lottery-type program to natives of countries from which immigration was lower than 50,000 over the preceding five years — certainly not Mexico, China, South Korea, the Philippines, or India. Under a complicated formula that weighs countries and regions of the world and uses relative populations, the State Department determines the distribution of lottery visas. A single state can never get more than 7 percent (3,850) of the total diversity visas available each year. In one early projection of the formula, the first year's regional distribution looked like this: Africa 20,900, Asia 6,380, North America 0, Europe 24,310, Latin America 2,530, and Oceania 880.

In order to take part in the lottery program in 1988, an applicant needed only to submit a letter with family and other biographical data. Under the 1990 diversity program, however, the applicant must have a high school education, or within five years of application, the applicant must have at least two years of work experience in an occupation that requires at least two years of training or experience. That left out most Africans who wanted to immigrate.

The justification for special treatment for Irish nationals at various junctures of the diversity program was the recognition that under the primarily family-based immigration system, a special seed or pipeline category needed to be established. Only then could a significant number of people immigrate who could then take advantage of the family reunification categories by becoming U.S. citizens or filing

---

[46] Karen DeYoung, *Irish Again Look Abroad for Economic Opportunities; Emigraion Rates Have Risen Sharply*, THE WASHINGTON POST, Dec. 6, 1986, at A1.

[47] Ray Moseley, *In Ireland, an Election, a Dilemma*, CHICAGO TRIB., Feb. 8, 1987, at C12; *Poorest of the Rich*, THE ECONOMIST, Jan. 16, 1988, at 10.

under the category reserved for relatives of lawful permanent resident aliens.

4. Debating Foreign Professional Workers

The historical tensions between employers and the native work force over strategies of filling jobs with foreign workers (seen vividly in the agricultural industry) was highlighted in the battle over visas for skilled and professional workers in the 1980s and 1990s.

The battle also coincided with parallel attacks on the family immigration system — which had been the foundation of the immigration laws since the 1965 amendments. Prior to 1990, 80 percent of the worldwide preference system quota of 270,000 was reserved for kinship provisions, and the category of immediate relatives of the United States citizens was numerically unlimited. The effect of this priority was demonstrated vividly in the subsequent flow of Asian immigration, even though nations such as those in Africa and Asia, with low rates of immigration prior to 1965, were handicapped. In other words, the nations with large numbers of descendants in the United States were expected to benefit from a kinship-based system, and in 1965, less than a million Asian Americans resided in the country. Although the kinship priority meant that Asians were beginning on an unequal footing, at least Asians were on par numerically, in terms of the per country quotas. Gradually, by using the family categories to the extent they could be used and the labor employment route, Asians built a family base from which to use the kinship categories more and more. By the late 1980s, well over 90 percent of all Asian immigration to the United States was through the kinship categories, as with virtually all immigration to the United States.

The genesis for the legislation that ultimately became the Immigration Act of 1990 came in the form of Senate bill S. 358, whose primary sponsor was Republican Senator Alan Simpson, and House bill H.R. 4300, led by Democratic Congressman Bruce Morrison. Simpson had been a member of the Select Commission on Immigration and Refugee Policy that issued a report in 1981 calling for major changes in the immigration laws. After IRCA was enacted in 1986 to address issue of undocumented migration through employer sanctions and legalization, Simpson turned his attention to legal immigration categories. At the time, although 20 percent of preference categories were available to labor employment immigrants (54,000), when the unrestricted immediate relative immigration categories were added to the total number of immigrants each year, less than 10 percent of immigrants who were entering each year were doing so on the basis of job skills.

At a time when legal immigration continued to be dominated by Asians and Latinos even after "diversity programs" were being implemented to aid non-Asian and non-Mexican immigrants, Simpson wanted the family immigration numbers reduced or at least managed. S. 358 was approved by the Senate in July 1989, which would establish a ceiling of 630,000 legal immigrants for three years. Of the total, 480,000 would be reserved for all types of family immigration and 150,000 would be set aside for immigrants without family connections but with skills or job related assets. Yet after numerous markups and hearings, the House of Representative passed Morrison's H.R. 4300, a rather different bill, on Oct. 3, 1990. The bill actually would reduce family immigration more dramatically — thereby reducing the number of Asian and Latino family immigrants, providing 185,000 family-based visas and 95,000 employment-based visas annually.

As originally introduced, H.R. 4300 revamped most immigrant and nonimmigrant work visa categories. It created four categories, which would have priority within the 95,000 total visas for employer sponsored immigrants. These aliens would also be exempt from the labor certification requirement which had demanded that employers demonstrate the unavailability of U.S. workers. The bill would also allow up to 1,000 foreign investors to obtain a two-year conditional resident status by investing at least $1 million and creating 10 new jobs for unrelated U.S. citizens or other workers. Critics noted that this would essentially allow foreign investors to buy citizenship. Employers could also sponsor other aliens provided they prove a shortage of U.S. workers.

As passed, H.R. 4300 would increase the number of legal immigrants to 775,000 a year from the prior 540,000. It would also speed the process of uniting families, attract more skilled workers, and create a new diversity category for immigrants from countries whose nationals have largely been excluded in the past. After passing the bill, the House changed the bill number to S. 358 to enable it to go to a joint House-Senate conference. However, many were opposed to the more liberal House bill and negotiated to cap legal immigration and place new measures to control illegal immigration, including tougher provisions against criminal aliens.

Enacted on Oct. 26, 1990, the compromise bill would allow 700,000 immigrants from 1992–94 and 675,000 annually in subsequent years.[48] For the time being, proposals to cut back on family immigration were defeated, and the Immigration Act of 1990 had responded to lobbying efforts by American businesses. The Act was a significant, and to some a revolutionary, revision of the focus of U.S. immigration law. After passage of the Act, although the main thrust of immigration law continued to be family immigration, highly-skilled immigrations would be deliberately encouraged to resettle in the United States more than ever before. In the long run, the number of employment based visas would nearly triple from 54,000 to 140,000 per year. Predictably, the bill met with a great deal of resistance from labor organizations. They were mollified, however, by the fact that the labor certification requirements remained essentially the same as they were prior to passage of the Act, and were not streamlined even though an earlier House version of the bill had called for that.

Under the new law, that remains part of today's system, occupational visas were divided into five categories: (1) 40,000 visas for priority workers who possess extraordinary ability in the arts, sciences, education, business, or athletics, or outstanding professors and researchers, and certain multinational executives; (2) 40,000 visas for professionals holding advanced degrees or aliens of exceptional ability; (3) 40,000 visas for skilled workers, professionals with baccalaureate

---

[48] The compromise included portions of S. 3055 sponsored by Simpson, which would speed deportations of criminal aliens. Section 501 expanded the definition of "aggravated felony" to include illicit trafficking in any controlled substance, money laundering, and any crime of violence with a 5-year imprisonment imposed. The bill also included both federal and state crimes. Aliens convicted of aggravated felonies would have expedited deportation hearings and would not be released from custody while in deportation proceedings. 67 IR 1229–31.

degrees, and unskilled workers for jobs for which qualified American workers are not available (only 10,000 visas can be issued for unskilled workers); (4) 10,000 visas for special immigrants; and (5) 10,000 visas for employment creation immigrants, specifically investors of $500,000 to $3 million whose investments create at least 10 new jobs.

Most of the available immigrant visas are still reserved for relatives of U.S. citizens and lawful permanent resident aliens. However, the near tripling of occupational visas from 54,000 to 140,000 in the 1990 legislation signaled the beginning of a shift in the focus of U.S. immigration law from concern with family reunification toward a policy of importing skilled workers. In fact, before 1990, up to one-half of the 54,000 occupational visas could be used for unskilled workers who were not displacing American workers; but the figure for unskilled workers was reduced to 10,000 by the 1990 law.

The creation of the investor or employment-creation visa was also noteworthy. This new category was designed for immigrants seeking to engage in a new commercial enterprise. The law requires that the investment be at least $1 million, but the amount is reduced to $500,000 if the enterprise is located in a targeted employment area, such as a rural area or any area that has experienced high unemployment of at least 150 percent of the national average rate. No fewer than 3,000 of the 10,000 visas are reserved for applicants whose enterprises will be located in targeted employment areas.

5.   More Visas for Temporary Workers: the H-1B Category

The Immigration Act of 1990 also implemented at new H-1B program that has proven to be quite popular with U.S. businesses, but also opposed by some who think businesses should hire available U.S. workers and groups that have seen the program used mostly by professionals from India and China.

Prior to 1990, an unlimited number of nonimmigrant H-1 work visas were available to individuals of "distinguished merit and ability."[49] This requirement was easily satisfied by professional-level employees. The law did not require the person to have an advanced degree or to be renowned in the field. In essence, all that was required was that the alien have at least a baccalaureate degree or its equivalent in a given field, and that the knowledge required for a particular job be a realistic prerequisite to entry into a particular field of endeavor.[50] As a result, tens of thousands of nonimmigrants entered annually in this H-1 professional category.

In 1990, the old H-1 program was replaced with the H-1B program for nonimmigrants entering "in a specialty occupation."[51] Like its predecessor, this provision provides a convenient way for professional workers to enter for temporary employment purposes. Again, the main requirement is that the occupation requires at least a bachelor's degree in the particular specialty. But an important new requirement was added; the employer must submit a Labor

---

[49] 8 C.F.R. § 214.2(h) (1989).

[50] Matter of Shin, 11 I.&N. Dec. 686 (Dist. Dir. 1966).

[51] 8 U.S.C. § 1101(a)(15)(H)(i)(b).

Condition Application (LCA) to the Department of Labor, attesting that the foreign worker's employment does not adversely impact similarly-employed U.S. workers. In other words, H-1B workers cannot be exploited and must be paid at least the prevailing wage in the industry, and working conditions must be the same as similarly-employed workers in the same area of employment.

A critical difference, however, between the former H-1 program and the newer H-1B program has to do with numbers. The 1990 law imposed a 65,000 limit on the number of aliens who could be given H-1B status each year. This number proved highly controversial and subject to much political struggle, as the quotas were easily reached in the late 1990s at the height of the high-tech boom. More than half of the visas were issued to nonimmigrants (mostly engineers) from India, and another 10 percent were issued to nationals of the Republic of China. Also, some 60 percent of the visas were issued for computer and systems analyst positions.

Led by the high technology industry in the late 1990s, businesses lobbied Congress to increase the H-1B visa numbers. In spite of critics who argued unconvincingly that U.S. workers were available to fill these positions, in October 2000 Congress cleared the backlog of pending H-1B cases and increased the annual allotment to 195,000 for 2001, 2002, and 2003. Much of these efforts proved unnecessary as hundreds of high-tech industries went belly-up in 2001 and 2002, and the need for H-1B workers went dry. With the recession over, the demand for H-1B visas is greater than ever. Today, the 65,000 visas available are quickly used up each year.

I. IMMIGRATION REFORM IN 1996

1. Antiterrorism and Effective Death Penalty Act of 1996

Although the primary focus of the Immigration Act of 1990 was on the debate over the number of visas for kinship categories versus employment categories, Senator Alan Simpson insisted on stronger provisions to deal with aliens convicted of crimes as well. The compromise included portions of S. 3055 sponsored by Simpson, which would speed deportations of criminal aliens. Section 501 expanded the definition of "aggravated felony" to include illicit trafficking in any controlled substance, money laundering, and any crime of violence with a five-year imprisonment imposed. Aliens convicted of aggravated felonies would have expedited deportation hearings and would not be released from custody while in deportation proceedings.[52]

The 1990 enforcement provisions stemmed from Congress' belief that aliens in deportation proceedings and those convicted of crimes had too many rights.[53] Congress also presumed that aliens and their attorneys unnecessarily delayed deportation proceedings through frivolous motions and appeals. After the passage of the Immigration Act of 1990, other acts of Congress further limited the rights of aliens convicted of aggravated felonies through the Immigration and Technical

---

[52] 67 IR 1229–31.

[53] 68 IR 197.

Corrections Act of 1994, the Illegal Immigration Reform and Immigration Responsibility Act of 1996, and the Antiterrorism and Effective Death Penalty Act of 1996 (AEDPA).

On April 24, 1996, President Clinton signed AEDPA into law. The act was passed with broad bipartisan support by Congress (91-8-1 in the United States Senate, 293-133-7 in the House of Representatives) the Antiterrorism and Effective Death Penalty Act of 1996 (AEDPA). The law expanded the government's ability to take antiterrorism measures, increased circumstances under which victims of crime can receive restitution from defendants, and narrowed habeas jurisdiction, and eased standards required to deport immigrants.

AEDA included very significant changes to the immigration laws relating to exclusion, criminal aliens, and special removal proceedings for alien terrorists. Special removal procedures for alien terrorists set forth the establishment of a new removal court composed of five federal district court judges appointed by the chief justice of the U.S. Supreme Court. The court could hear a case whenever the attorney general certified that an alien terrorist physically present in the United States would pose a risk to national security if removed by normal deportation procedures. A judge could then grant the application for removal, ordering the alien detained pending removal. If an alien removed attempted to reenter without authorization, he or she would be subject to imprisonment for 10 years. The bill denied other forms of relief for terrorists, including asylum and voluntary departure. Habeas corpus was also foreclosed.

AEDPA's provisions affecting the treatment of criminal aliens included several immigration offenses to be predicate offenses for Racketeer Influenced and Corrupt Organization (RICO) convictions. The new RICO-predicate offenses included document fraud and trafficking in aliens. Other criminal alien provisions included long-distance relocation plans for any criminal alien who had attempted illegal entry into the United States at least three times. AEDPA also provided for deportation of criminals before their entire prison sentence is served. If such an alien were to later illegally enter the United States, that alien would have to serve the remainder of the prison sentence at that time.

AEDPA added crimes to the list of aggravated felonies for which a criminal alien would be subject to expedited removal. These offenses include: forgery of a passport or other document for entry into the United States and running a gambling business. It also modified the expedited procedures, including extreme limits on any challenge to the removal order and limitations on discretionary review of a removal order.

2.   Welfare Reform

On the eve of the 1996 Democratic National Convention, President Clinton signed into law a sweeping reform bill, the Personal Responsibility and Work Opportunity Reconciliation Act of 1996 (the "Act").[54] By eliminating a federal commitment to provide even a minimal level of assistance to America's poorest, the

---

[54] Pub. L. No. 104-193, 110 Stat. 2105 (1996).

legislation carried harsh consequences for a range of economically vulnerable individuals and families. Since the Act specifically targeted immigrants for major cuts, its effects were felt quickly and severely by noncitizen immigrants in economic need.

The Act made legal immigrants ineligible to receive a number of federally-funded public benefits. It similarly authorized state and local governments to deny locally-funded benefits to legal immigrants, transgressing the long-held constitutional requirement that states treat citizens and legal immigrants alike in terms of public benefits eligibility. The legislation also tightened restrictions affecting undocumented immigrants, further marginalizing a group that was already ineligible for most benefits and services.

Social welfare laws commonly distinguish between the eligibility of *undocumented* immigrants and *documented* immigrants (which includes refugees). The 1996 Act originally barred both groups of immigrants from participating in two federal benefits programs: Supplemental Security Income (SSI) and food stamps. Until the 1997 budget compromise reached by Congress and President Clinton restored benefits to documented immigrants who were in the country as of August 26, 1996, data from the Social Security Administration indicated that approximately half a million immigrants would lose SSI as a result of the new law; a million were likely to lose food stamps.

Certain classes of legal immigrants were exempt from these restrictions: (1) refugees, asylees, and individuals granted withholding of deportation, but only for the first five years after being granted that status; (2) active duty service members, veterans, and their direct family members; and (3) permanent residents who can prove that they have worked at least 40 qualifying quarters, or 10 years, for social security purposes. All *future* immigrants would be barred for a period of five years after "entry" from any federal means-tested program, again certain classes of legal immigrants were exempt. In addition to barring future immigrants from receiving SSI and Food stamps, the Act authorized states to pass legislation denying legal immigrants access to a range of state-administered federal programs. As the costs of social welfare programs shifted to the states, they were increasingly tempted to deny legal immigrants assistance under these programs.

While the Act directly excluded legal immigrants from receiving some benefits and enables states to restrict eligibility for others, the Act also made changes that affect immigrant eligibility indirectly. In particular, the legislation toughened standards for immigrants whose eligibility depended on a sponsor. Applicants for family-based immigrant visas had to demonstrate that they were not likely to become a public charge. In making this demonstration, petitioning relatives of visa applicants were now required to submit a legally binding affidavit, agreeing to provide financial support to the applicant. Some programs included the sponsor's income in calculating eligibility, a practice called "sponsor-deeming."

The Act was also harsh to immigrants in unprecedented semantic ways. Immigrants who did not meet the Act's definition of "qualified" immigrants were considered "unqualified," including immigrants who were residing in the United States legally or with the permission of immigration authorities. The legislation barred unqualified immigrants from receiving any "federal public benefit," including any of the major federal public benefit programs: Temporary Assistance for Needy Families (TANF, which replaced Aid To Families with Dependent Children), Food stamps, Medicaid, SSI, unemployment compensation, school loans and grants, and subsidized housing. Many of these programs historically were closed to undocumented immigrants. Under prior law, however, immigrants were eligible to receive Medicaid, SSI, and AFDC if they were "permanently residing in the United States under color of law" (PRUCOL), a category eliminated by the Act's blanket exclusion of unqualified immigrants. All immigrants could qualify for social security benefits and unemployment insurance compensation if they had employment authorization and a valid social security number. These programs were now completely closed to those considered "unqualified."

In the wake of the 1996 Act, many legal immigrants began the process of naturalization, since citizens would still be eligible for benefits, albeit subject to many new restrictions. Welfare reform thus contributed to record-setting naturalization applications during much of 1997. Some who failed or who were not eligible for naturalization may have had access to local cash assistance programs such as General Assistance. Others who were frightened by the prospect of losing benefits committed or contemplated committing suicide. The financial outlook for these groups was very grim.

By August 5, 1997, a year after the passage of the welfare reform legislation, the Clinton administration and congressional leaders compromised and restored most disability and health benefits to immigrants who were in the country and covered before the initial legislation. Reached as part of a budget agreement, this re-reform allowed legal immigrants to remain eligible for SSI and Medicaid if they were receiving such benefits on August 22, 1996, when the 1996 welfare reform law was enacted. Lawful immigrants who were not yet receiving benefits, but were residing in the United States as of the enactment date, were eligible for SSI and Medicaid if they became disabled. The exemption from SSI and Medicaid restrictions for refugees was extended from five to seven years. However, restrictions on most programs other than SSI including the bar on food stamps, deeming provisions, and binding affidavits of support were retained.

3.   Illegal Immigration Reform and Immigrant Responsibility Act

The Illegal Immigration Reform and Immigrant Responsibility Act of 1996 (IIRIRA)[55] made vast changed the immigration laws. One major change eliminated basic relief from deportation for long term lawful permanent residents who have been convicted of an aggravated felony. Prior to IIRIRA, such individuals could seek a discretionary waiver of deportation if they could demonstrate rehabilitation, remorse, and important family and community ties. However, the 1996 law renders aggravated felons ineligible for such discretionary relief.[56] An aggravated felony is defined in 8 U.S.C. 1227(a)(2)(A) as murder, rape, sexual abuse of a minor, any illicit trafficking in any controlled substance (including drugs, firearms, or

---

[55]   Pub. L. 104-208, 110 Stat. 3009.

[56]   8 U.S.C. 1229(a).

destructive materials), money laundering, or any crime of violence (except for purely political offenses) for which the term of imprisonment imposed is at least one year. The definition also includes offenses of theft, if the term of imprisonment imposed is at least one year.

IIRIRA also affected asylum seekers. The law created procedures to remove aliens appearing at the border without documentation and required that anyone desiring asylum must file within one year of entering the country. The expedited procedures were designed to remove aliens who arrived in the United States without proper travel documents or who were suspected of carrying documents procured by fraud. A single immigration officer at an airport or other port of entry screens individuals to determine whether they intend to apply for asylum or fear persecution. If the officer thinks that the person does not fear persecution, the officer can order the person summarily removed from the country and bar the person from reentering the country for five years, without any further hearing or judicial review.

Those persons arriving who do express fear or want to apply for asylum immediately are transferred to a detention center. They may be placed in handcuffs, even shackles, at the airport, then transported to detention centers or jails. Although they are not charged with any crimes, they remain locked up at least until asylum officers can conduct extensive interviews to determine whether the applicants have a "credible fear" of persecution. If the asylum officer determines that the person does not have a credible fear of persecution, then the person must affirmatively request a review by an immigration judge. There is no right to judicial review. The review before an immigration judge is expedited and limited. The review must be concluded no later than seven days after the credible fear determination and need not even be conducted in person; it can be conducted by telephone or video connection. Counsel cannot be present, no evidence can be submitted, and no witness can be called.

J.   NATIONAL SECURITY AND POST-9/11 MEASURES

Since 9/11 Congress and the President have screened immigration policy proposals and enforcement procedures through the lens of national security. For anti-immigrant forces in the United States, 9/11 provided a once-in-a-lifetime opportunity to use the tragic events to draw linkages with virtually every aspect of their nativist agenda. But this is a neo-nativist agenda born of old hate cloaked in suggestions of international intrigue.

The Bush White House helped fuel the neo-nativist agenda in its legislative proposals that led to the USA PATRIOT Act, authorizing broad sweeps and scare tactics. The Bush White House epitomized its philosophy by words such as these in its July 2002 National Strategy for Homeland Security:

> Our great power leaves these enemies with few conventional options for doing us harm. One such option is to take advantage of our freedom and openness by *secretly inserting terrorists into our country* to attack our homeland. Homeland security seeks to deny this avenue of attack to our

enemies and thus to provide a secure foundation for America's ongoing global engagement.[57]

A restrictionist organization like the Center for Immigration Studies (CIS) takes these words and argues that in the Department of Homeland Security's

> expansive portfolio, immigration is central. The reason is elementary: no matter the weapon or delivery system — hijacked airliners, shipping containers, suitcase nukes, anthrax spores — operatives are required to carry out the attacks. Those operatives have to enter and work in the United States. . . . Thus keeping the terrorists out or apprehending them after they get in is indispensable to victory.[58]

Thus, CIS used the opportunity presented by 9/11 to argue against issuing driver's licenses to undocumented people and to advocate for sweeps and apprehensions. Apparently, the idea is to make it hard for potential terrorists (i.e., foreigners) to move around or make a living, so they will become discouraged and leave. And who can argue against keeping terrorists out or apprehending them after they arrive?

Congress and the Bush administration heeded the appeals to implement harsh immigration policies. The events of 9/11 and the ensuing call to action from many quarters — including the anti-immigrant lobby — resulted in far-reaching legislative and enforcement actions. These enforcement actions had implications not only for suspected terrorists but also for immigrants already in the United States and noncitizens trying to enter as immigrants or with nonimmigrant visas.

The USA PATRIOT Act is the most notable enactment.[59] The Act passed Congress with near unanimous support, and the President signed it into law a mere six weeks after 9/11. The vast powers embodied in the law provide expanded authority to search, monitor, and detain citizens and noncitizens alike, but its implementation since passage has preyed most heavily on noncitizen Arabs, Muslims, and Sikhs. Authority to detain, deport, or file criminal charges against noncitizens is specifically broadened. Consider the following noncitizen-related provisions in the law:

- Noncitizens are denied admission if they "endorse or espouse terrorist activity," or "persuade others to support terrorist activity or a terrorist organization," in ways that the State Department determines impede U.S. efforts to combat terrorism.

- The Act defines "terrorist activity" expansively to include support of otherwise lawful and nonviolent activities of almost any group that used violence.

---

[57] President Releases National Strategy for Homeland Security, July 16, 2002, *available at* http://georgewbush-whitehouse.archives.gov/news/releases/2002/07/20020716-2.html (emphasis added).

[58] Mark Krikorian, *Keeping Terror Out — Immigration Policy and Asymmetric Warfare*, THE NATIONAL INTEREST (Spring 2004).

[59] The clumsy, complete title is the Uniting and Strengthening America by Providing Appropriate Tools Required to Intercept and Obstruct Terrorism Act, *voila* the USA PATRIOT Act (Pub. L. No. 107-56).

- Noncitizens are deportable for wholly innocent associational activity, excludable for pure speech, and subject to incarceration without a finding that they pose a danger or flight risk.

- Foreign nationals can be detained for up to seven days while the government decides whether or not to file criminal or immigration charges.

- The Attorney General has broad preventive detention authority to incarcerate noncitizens by certifying there are "reasonable grounds to believe" that a person is "described in" the antiterrorism provisions of the immigration law, and the individual is then subject to potentially indefinite detention.

- The Attorney General can detain noncitizens indefinitely even after prevailing in a removal proceeding "until the Attorney General determines that the noncitizen is no longer a noncitizen who may be certified [as a suspected terrorist.]"

- Wiretaps and searches are authorized without a showing of probable criminal conduct if the target is an "agent of a foreign power," including any officer or employee of a foreign-based political organization.

To further emphasize how future visa issuance and immigration enforcement must be screened through the lens of national security, the Immigration and Naturalization Service (INS) was subsumed into the Department of Homeland Security (DHS) on November 25, 2002. Previously, the INS was under the control of the Attorney General's Justice Department — an enforcement-minded institution, but now the Administration has institutionalized the clamping down on noncitizens in the name of national security. The new Cabinet-level department merged all or parts of 22 federal agencies, with a combined budget of $40 billion and 170,000 workers, representing the biggest government reorganization in 50 years. DHS placed INS functions into two divisions: US Citizenship and Immigration Services (USCIS) which handles immigrant visa petitions, naturalization, and asylum and refugee applications and the Under Secretary for Border and Transportation Security, which includes the Bureau of Customs and Border Protection along with Immigration and Customs Enforcement units, for handling enforcement matters.

Before and after DHS' creation, and presumably using pre-existing authority and new-found power under the PATRIOT Act, the administration implemented a number of policies and actions aimed at noncitizens in the name of national security:

- Amending its own regulations on September 17, 2001, INS authorizes the detention of any alien for 48 hours without charge with the possibility of extending the detention for an additional "reasonable period of time" in the event of an "emergency or other extraordinary circumstance."

- On September 21, 2001, the chief immigration judge orders new procedures requiring all immigration judges to hold "secure" hearings separately from all other cases, to close the hearings to the public, and to avoid discussing the case or disclosing any information about the case to anyone outside the immigration court.[60]

- On October 31, 2001, Attorney General John Ashcroft asks the Secretary of State to designate 46 new groups as terrorist organizations pursuant to the PATRIOT Act.

- On November 9, 2001, Attorney General Ashcroft calls for the "voluntary" interviews of up to 5,000 aliens from countries suspected of harboring relatively large numbers of terrorists; interviewees may be jailed without bond the Attorney General finds they are violating immigration laws.

- On November 9, 2001, the State Department slows the process for granting visas for men, ages 16 to 45, from certain Arab and Muslim countries by about 20 days.

- On November 13, President Bush issues an executive order authorizing the creation of military tribunals to try noncitizens on charges of terrorism.

- On December 4, 2001, U.S. Senator Russ Feingold holds hearings on the status of detainees. Attorney General Ashcroft suggests that those who question his policies are "aiding and abetting terrorism."

- On December 6, 2001, INS Commissioner James Ziglar announces that the INS will send the names of more than 300,000 aliens who remain in the United States, despite prior deportation or removal orders, to the FBI for inclusion in the National Crime Information Center database. This becomes known as the Alien Absconder Initiative.

- On January 8, 2002, the Department of Justice adds to the FBI's National Crime Information Center database the names of about 6,000 men from countries believed to be harboring al-Qaeda members who have ignored deportation or removal orders.

- On January 25, 2002, the Deputy Attorney General issues instructions for the Alien Absconder Initiative to locate 314,000 people who have a final deportation order, but who have failed to surrender for removal. The Deputy Attorney General designates several thousand men from "countries in which there has been al-Qaeda terrorist presence or activity" as "priority absconders" and enters them first into the National Crime Information Center database.

- On March 19, 2002, the Department of Justice announces interviews with 3,000 more Arabs and Muslims present in the United States as visitors or students.

- In June 2002, the INS proposes broadening special registration requirements for nonimmigrants from certain designated countries.

- On July 15, 2002, the Department of Justice announces a surveillance pilot program whereby U.S. citizens, including truckers, bus drivers, and others,

---

[60] A subsequent proposal by the National Association of Immigration Judges (NAIJ) is noteworthy. On January 2002, NAIJ proposed the creation of a separate executive branch agency to house the trial-level immigration courts and Board of Immigration Appeals, citing "disturbing encroachments on judicial independence" taken by the Present, the Attorney General and the Department of Justice in the aftermath of 9/11.

can act as informants to report "suspicious activity." The program is to be called Operation TIPS (Terrorism Information and Prevention System).

- On July 24, 2002, the Department of Justice authorizes any state or local law enforcement officer — with the consent of those who cover the jurisdiction where the law enforcement officer is serving — to perform certain functions of INS officers during the period of a declared "mass influx of aliens."

- On August 21, 2002, the INS deports approximately 100 Pakistanis arrested on immigration violations.

- On September 16, 2002, Attorney General Ashcroft orders the INS to launch a "prompt review" of political asylum cases to identify any immigrants who have admitted to accusations of terrorist activity or being members of any terrorist organizations.

- On November 6, 2002, INS expands the special registration or National Security Entry-Exit Registration System (NSEERS) by requiring certain male nationals and citizens of Iran, Iraq, Libya, Sudan, and Syria admitted to the United States prior to September 10, 2002 to register with INS. Failure to report to an INS office for fingerprinting, a photo, and an interview will result in deportation. On December 16, 2002, nonimmigrant males 16 years or older from Saudi Arabia and Pakistan are added to this list. On January 16, 2003, five more countries — Bangladesh, Egypt, Indonesia, Jordan, and Kuwait — are added to the list of 20 whose male citizens must register with INS.

- On November 18, 2002, the Foreign Intelligence Surveillance Act (FISA) Court of Review rules that the USA PATRIOT Act gives the Department of Justice broad authority to conduct wiretaps and other surveillance on terrorism suspects in the United States.

- On March 17, 2003, the Bush administration launches Operation Liberty Shield to "increase security and readiness in the United States." As part of this effort, DHS implements a temporary policy of detaining asylum seekers from three countries where al-Qaeda is known to have operated.

- On March 20, 2003, the Attorney General reveals that since December 18, 2002, FBI agents and U.S. marshals have detained foreign nationals for alleged immigration violations in cases where there is not enough evidence to hold them on criminal charges.

- In late 2005, President Bush confirmed that the U.S. had engaged in secret wiretapping of telephone calls of U.S. citizens with others from abroad without going to the FISA court for authorization.

In 2002, Congress created the National Commission on Terrorist Attacks Upon the United States (better known as the 9/11 Commission) that Congress charged with investigating the circumstances surrounding the 9/11 terrorist attacks and recommending responses. It released its final report and recommendations in July 2004. Soon after the Commission's report, Congress drafted legislation to implement its recommendations. During debates on the legislation, several members of Congress, most notably Representative James Sensenbrenner (R-Wis), the Chair of the House Judiciary Committee, argued for the inclusion of a number of contentious immigration measures. These measures went beyond the Commission's specific recommendations, nearly preventing the legislation's passage. The immigration-related proposals would have expanded the government's authority to arrest, detain, and deport immigrants, restricted judicial review and oversight, and reduced the number of documents immigrants may use to establish their identity. Sensenbrenner wanted to include a provision barring states issuing driver's licenses to undocumented aliens. But Commission members and 9/11 victims' relatives spoke out against these provisions, arguing that the debate was delaying legislation and would not make any significant contribution to public safety and security. Congress removed Sensenbrenner's proposal and the other anti-immigrant measures from the final version of the legislation, and Congress passed the Intelligence Reform and Terrorism Prevention Act of 2004.

In early 2005, Representative Sensenbrenner quickly reintroduced the contro-versial provisions (dubbed the REAL ID Act) he had removed, and on February 10, the House of Representatives passed Sensenbrenner's full package. One month later, the same legislation was attached to a huge emergency appropriations bill — a must-sign piece of legislation — to fund U.S. military efforts in Iraq and Afghanistan. The House passed this massive funding bill without any public debate or hearings. When the debate shifted to the Senate, the legislation did not include the REAL ID Act. But when the bill went to the Conference Committee, House supporters pushed strongly for the provisions to be included. During debates legislators removed a few of the most unsavory proposals, including one that would have created private bounty hunters to enforce immigration law. But the REAL ID Act provisions remained, and the Act was part of the package signed into law.[61]

K. THE JEKYLL AND HYDE OBAMA ERA

The history of the Obama Administration related to immigration law and policy features President Obama as the "deporter-in-chief" versus the president who exercised executive discretion granting deferred action and employment permission to undocumented students. This split personality image is a reflection of a president who is at once deporting individuals at a record-setting pace, yet touting the need for legalization with a path to citizenship for hard working immigrants who contribute mightily to our economy. The Obama administration also played an important role in successfully challenging anti-immigrant state laws such as Arizona's SB 1070.[62] Yet, the administration opposed the granting of law licenses to undocumented law graduates who have passed the state bar examination.[63] In the

---

[61] The REAL ID Act affects everyone in the United States. Beginning in 2008, anyone living or working in the United States must have a federally approved ID card to travel on an airplane, open a bank account, collect Social Security payments, or take advantage of nearly any government service. Practically speaking, every driver's license likely will have to be reissued to meet federal standards. The REAL ID Act hands the Department of Homeland Security the power to set these standards and determine whether state drivers' licenses and other ID cards pass muster.

[62] Arizona v. United States, 567 U.S. ___ (2012).

[63] *See* Maura Dolan, *Justice Department opposes illegal immigrant's bid to practice law*, L.A. TIMES, Aug. 12, 2012.

process, President Obama has attracted strong criticism from both the right and the left on immigration issues.

1. Secure Communities

The Obama Administration has engaged in a record-breaking pace of removals, reaching the two million mark in the middle of its sixth year. In achieving this number, the strategies included an expansion of the Secure Communities Program, ICE detainers, and increased detentions. Secure Communities relies on partnerships and biometric technology to build deportation capacity. ICE and the FBI work together to take advantage of the strong relationships already forged between the FBI and state and local law enforcement agencies. For every person booked into jail, local authorities run fingerprints against federal immigration and criminal databases. Ordinarily, the fingerprints of county and state arrestees are submitted to the FBI only. Under Secure Communities, the prints go to ICE too. If an individual's fingerprints match those of a non U.S. citizen (including legal resident), an automated process notifies the Law Enforcement Support Center (LESC) of ICE. Officials then evaluate the case, based on immigration status and criminal history.

Although the Bush Administration piloted the Secure Communities Program in 2008, the Obama Administration expanded it exponentially into a program where all local enforcement authorities must share fingerprints of anyone arrested with ICE. According to ICE, the mission of Secure Communities is "to improve public safety by implementing a comprehensive, integrated approach to identify and remove criminal aliens from the United States."[64] By 2013, Secure Communities was operating in all 3,141 jurisdictions (state, county, and local jails and prisons) in the country. The net effect is to "create a virtual ICE presence at every local jail."[65]

As of September 30, 2011, there were 692,788 matches in the database that resulted in the removal of more than 142,000 persons.[66] However, the program resulted in the wrongly arrest of approximately 3,600 U.S. citizens by April 2011.[67] Since the implementation of the program, there has been disproportionate effect on Latinos as 93 percent of the people identified for deportation proceedings are from Latin America in comparison to 2 percent from Asia and 1 percent from Canada and Europe.[68] Since deportation is not considered to be a criminal proceeding, no appointed counsel is provided during appearances before an immigration judge.[69]

---

[64] http://www.ice.gov/doclib/foia/secure_communities/securecommunitiespresentations.pdf.

[65] ICE News Release, Harris County Sheriff's Office first of several sites in the nation to receive full interoperability technology to help identify criminal aliens, Oct. 29, 2008, http://www.ice.gov/news/releases/0810/081029houston.htm.

[66] http://www.immigrationpolicy.org/just-facts/secure-communities-fact-sheet.

[67] http://www.law.berkeley.edu/files/Secure_Communities_by_the_Numbers.pdf.

[68] http://www.law.berkeley.edu/files/Secure_Communitimilarly, a federal court in Rhode Island held that both state and federal officials bore responsibility fores_by_the_Numbers.pdf.

[69] http://www.law.berkeley.edu/files/Secure_Communities_by_the_Numbers.pdf.

In spite of ICE's assertion that it "prioritizes the removal of criminal aliens, those who pose a threat to public safety, repeat immigration violators . . . [and] the most dangerous and violent offenders [,]" ICE has inconsistently deported only 19 percent level 2 and 26 percent level 1 illegal immigrations from all the deportations. Thus, well over half of the deportees are those with minor or no offenses. In addition to these problematic results, there are additional concerns such as: obstacles to community policing as community members may view local police officers as immigration agents, issue of profiling and pretextual arrests, lack of clear complaint mechanisms for those who believe they have been erroneously been identified as deportable aliens, and strong concern about the lack of oversight and transparency, especially when it comes to supervising local partnerships.[70]

On November 20, 2014, as part of his Executive Action to defer the deportation of more DREAMers and parents of U.S. citizens and lawful permanent residents, President Obama announced the end of the Secure Communities Program. To immigrant advocates, the Secure Communities program symbolized what was wrong with the nation's immigration enforcement strategy. Saying federal agents should focus on deporting "felons, not families," President Obama announced a new initiative, the Priority Enforcement Program, which officials said would target only those who have been convicted of certain serious crimes or who pose a danger to national security. However, skeptics have voiced concern that the PEP program will continue the federal entanglement with local law enforcement that threatens public safety because it invites police to select people for deportation instead of protecting their welfare.[71]

2. ICE Detainers

When there is a match, ICE may choose to place a "detainer" on the individual. This is a request for the jail to hold that person for up to 48 hours beyond the scheduled release date, so that ICE can take custody and initiate deportation proceedings. The local jail bed becomes an immigration bed, and the additional time in custody is usually 48 hours plus weekends/holidays. In the meantime, the person is denied bail and pretrial diversion programs. The process actually may end up being two to three weeks or longer.

Over time, momentum grew among states and localities that rejected the federal government's requests these detainer requests to imprison people in state and local jails while their immigration status is investigated. Places like Santa Clara County (San Jose), California, San Francisco, Chicago, Philadelphia, Massachusetts, the District of Columbia, and several Oregon counties announced that they would no longer comply with ICE detainer requests after criminal custody had ended.

Most policies rejecting ICE holds were based on an understanding by local law enforcement officials that getting involved in immigration enforcement undermined community trust in the police making everyone less safe. Instead, the detainers resulted in the detention and deportation of people with minor infractions or no

---

[70] http://www.immigrationpolicy.org/just-facts/secure-communities-fact-sheet.

[71] Aura Bogado, *Goodbye, Secure Communities. Hello, Priority Enforcement Program*, COLORLI-NES.COM, Nov. 21, 2014.

criminal history at all. Nearly 48 percent of the immigrants who triggered an ICE detainer had no criminal convictions, not even traffic violations. In some instances, undocumented victims of spousal abuse were deported following an ICE detainer triggered by a Secure Communities finger print check.

Rejecting ICE holds were more than about protecting public safety; they also recognized that ICE holds are, at their core, unconstitutional violations of the rights of individuals detained. The Obama administration deportation records were achieved in no small part by leaning on state and local law enforcement agencies. ICE funneled hundreds of thousands of people into the deportation pipeline by issuing immigration "detainers."

A major example of resistance to ICE detainers was California's enactment of the TRUST Act that went into effect in January 2014. The law required all California sheriffs to disregard an ICE detainer request, unless the immigrant is charged with or convicted of a serious offense. By April, law enforcement agencies showed a 44 percent drop in people held for possible deportation.

By summer of 2014, sheriffs around the nation were openly rejecting ICE detainer requests. The numbers grew after a federal judge in Oregon ruled that a sheriff there had violated one immigrant woman's civil rights by holding her in the county jail solely at the request of federal agents, subjecting the sheriff to civil damages.[72] Philadelphia's policy came on the heels of the Third Circuit Federal Appeals Court's decision that recognized that ICE detainers are merely requests, not orders — and that if states and localities choose to detain people on that basis, they can be liable in court for violating the Constitution.[73] Similarly, a federal court in Rhode Island held that both state and federal officials bore responsibility for detaining a U.S. citizen on an ICE detainer without an adequate legal basis.[74] The local decisions began to limit the Obama administration's deportation enforcement strategies.

3. Detention

Over the course of the Obama Administration, DHS officials detained record numbers of immigrants, driven by a little-known congressional directive known on Capitol Hill as the "bed mandate." Congressional appropriations language covering ICE's detention budget, for example in the Continuing Appropriations Act of 2014, states "[t]hat funding made available under this heading shall maintain a level of not less than 34,000 detention beds." The policy has been interpreted as requiring ICE to keep an average of 34,000 detainees per day in its custody, a quota that has steadily risen since it was established in 2006 by conservative lawmakers who insisted that the agency was not doing enough to deport unlawful immigrants.

But before the unaccompanied immigrant children crisis occurred in 2014, illicit crossings from Mexico had fallen to near their lowest levels since the early 1970s,

---

[72] Maria Miranda-Olivares v. Clackamas County, 2014 U.S. Dist. LEXIS 50340 (D. Ct. Or. Apr. 11, 2014),

[73] Galarza v. Szalczyk, 745 F.3d 634 (3d Cir. 2014).

[74] Morales v. Chadbourne, 996 F. Supp. 2d 19 (D.R.I. 2014).

and ICE began meeting Congress's immigration detention goals by reaching deeper into the criminal justice system to arrest foreign-born, legal U.S. residents convicted of any crimes that could render them eligible for deportation. The agency also greatly expanded the number of undocumented immigrants taken into custody after traffic stops by local police, often via the Secure Communities Program. Four countries — Mexico, Guatemala, Honduras, and El Salvador — accounted for 88 percent of all immigration detainees in 2011.

The majority of ICE detainees are not violent offenders. A 2009 internal ICE review found that only 11 percent of detainees had been convicted of violent crimes. Almost half of all potential deportees who appear in immigration court are allowed to remain in the United States. But many end up spending months, even years, in costly federal custody while they await a ruling, even when far cheaper alternatives are available, such as ankle bracelets and other forms of electronic monitoring. Those alternatives can cost less than $10 a day, while the cost of keeping someone in ICE custody exceeds $150.

With federal spending on immigration detention and deportation reaching $2.8 billion a year, more than doubling since 2006, the mandate has met growing skepticism from budget hawks in both parties, particularly after DHS officials told Congress during the "sequestration" debate in April 2014 that the agency could save money by lowering the bed mandate to 31,800 and relying on cheaper alternatives to jails. But House Republicans successfully pushed back, set the mandate at 34,000 detainees and ordered ICE officials to spend nearly $400 million more than they requested. Congress's expanding detention goals have been a boon to private prison contractors, especially Florida-based GEO Group and Tennessee-based Corrections Corp. of America. The two companies have won hundreds of millions of dollars' worth of ICE contracts in recent years while lobbying Congress on immigration enforcement issues.

Since the explicit purpose of ICE detaining people is to make sure they show up for their immigration hearings, it would make sense to consider less costly, more humane alternatives that meet that same goal. ICE officials have testified to Congress that Alternatives to Detention programs — geared toward legal residents with family and community ties — have had compliance rates of 96 percent with court-ordered appearances. Yet the agency's budget for alternatives is less than $100 million, dwarfed by its detention budget.

ICE officials argue that they have limited discretion over which detainees are eligible for alternative forms of supervision. The Illegal Immigration Reform and Immigrant Responsibility Act of 1996 greatly expanded the scope of crimes that could trigger deportation. According to ICE, more than two-thirds of the immigrants in custody are "mandatory detention" cases, including drug offenders, violent offenders, and anyone involved in prostitution-related crimes, among other violations that trigger automatic detention. INA. § 236(c) requires that noncitizens be detained after they are released from criminal custody, and that they remain detained while removal proceedings are pending against them.

The mandatory detention grounds include various grounds of inadmissibility from INA § 212(a), including the commission of a crime involving moral turpitude, multiple convictions where the aggregate sentence is five years or more of imprisonment, a controlled substance offense, a prostitution-related offense, terrorist activity, significant human trafficking, or money laundering. Detention is also mandatory for those who are deportable based on criminal convictions (found in INA § 237) including for a crime involving moral turpitude, two or more crimes involving moral turpitude, an aggravated felony, a firearms offense, a controlled substance conviction other than a single offense for possession for your own use of 30 grams or less of marijuana, drug abuse or addiction, or espionage, sabotage, or treason.

The Supreme Court has held, however, that indefinite detention is not permitted when removal is unlikely.[75] The Ninth Circuit Court of Appeals has ruled that immigrants who have experienced prolonged detention — even pending deportation proceedings — have a right to a bond hearing to determine whether or not they should continue to be detained. The court upheld the District Court order requiring bond hearings for detainees who have been locked up for six months or longer.[76]

4. Prosecutorial Discretion

In contrast to the Obama Administration's deportation and detention face, the president did have DHS implement key administrative discretion programs intended to avert removal for many deportable aliens in the absence of Congressional passage of comprehensive immigration reform on behalf of undocumented immigrants. One action was embodied in a June 17, 2011, memorandum by ICE Director John Morton on the use of prosecutorial discretion in immigration matters.[77] Prosecutorial discretion refers to the agency's authority to not enforce immigration laws against certain individuals and groups. The "Morton memo" called on ICE attorneys and employees to refrain from pursuing noncitizens with close family, educational, military, or other ties in the United States and instead spend the agency's limited resources on persons who pose a serious threat to public safety or national security.

The Morton memo was greeted with fanfare by immigrant rights advocates. Some 400,000 pending deportation cases would be reviewed to cull out the low priority immigrants for cancellation of proceedings.[78] Others with strong equities

---

[75] Zadvydas v. Davis and Ashcroft v. Kim Ho Ma, 533 U.S. 678 (2001); *cf.*, Demore v. Hyung Joon Kim, 538 U.S. 510 (2003).

[76] Rodriguez v. Robbins, 715 F. 3d 1127 (9th Cir. 2013).

[77] *See* John Morton, Exercising Prosecutorial Discretion Consistent with the Civil Immigration Enforcement Priorities of the Agency for the Apprehension, Detention, and Removal of Aliens, US Immigration and Customs Enforcement, June 11, 2011, http://www.ice.gov/doclib/secure-communities/pdf/prosecutorial-discretion-memo.pdf ("Morton memo"). Director Morton actually issued two memoranda on prosecutorial discretion that day. Morton's second memo focuses on exercising discretion in cases involving victims, witnesses to crimes, and plaintiffs in good faith civil rights lawsuits. That memo instructs "[a]bsent special circumstances or aggravating factors, it is against ICE policy to initiate removal proceedings against an individual known to be the immediate victim or witness to a crime." John Morton, Prosecutorial Discretion: Certain Victims, Witnesses and Plaintiffs, US Immigration and Customs Enforcement, June 11, 2011, http://www.aila.org/content/default.aspx?docid=35939.

[78] *See* Esther J. Cepeda, *Immigration Reform Chump-Change*, NBC Latino.Com, June 20, 2012, http://nbclatino.tumblr.com/post/25538630476/opinion-immigration-reform-chump-change

without serious criminal problems honestly believed that their removal would be averted. They found hope in what President Obama said on the 2012 campaign trail:

> What I've also said is if we're going to go after folks who are here illegally, we should do it smartly and go after folks who are criminals, gang bangers, people who are hurting the community, not after students, not after folks who are here just because they're trying to figure out how to feed their families. *And that's what we've done.*[79]

Unfortunately, what may have been intended by the president and ICE Director Morton was not uniformly implemented in the field. Many individuals, including DREAMers, were forced to leave the country after living in the United States in undocumented status for years without criminal problems and with solid equities.[80]

---

[79] *Second Presidential Debate Full Transcript*, ABC NEWS, Oct. 17, 2012, (emphasis added), http://abcnews.go.com/Politics/OTUS/2012-presidential-debate-full-transcript-oct-16/story?id=17493848#.UILgCcXoQmo

[80] Bill Ong Hing, *The Failure of Prosecutorial Discretion and the Deportation of Oscar Martinez*, 15 SCHOLAR 437 (2013). Consider these cases:

> Enrique Candia lives a quiet life in Oakland. When he's not working, he takes care of his ailing wife and his three grandchildren and makes sure his son is on track to finish college. Now, although he has no criminal record, the 56-year-old is facing a court battle that could take him away from his family for years. In June 2010, federal agents arrested Candia for working in the United States without proper authorization. A Mexican national who has lived in this country for almost 20 years, Candia was sent to an Immigrations and Customs Enforcement detention center.

Shoshana Walter, *After Almost 20 Years in U.S., Immigrant Faces Major Court Battle over Deportation*, SAN FRANCISCO CHRONICLE, Aug. 13, 2012. On July 27, 2012, Antonio Martinez Lara was arrested in Georgia for driving without a license and transferred to ICE because of he was undocumented. He was a 50-years-old, Mexican national who lived in the United States for 24, with three U.S. citizen grandchildren. *See Dreamer's Father Detained with an ICE Hold*, http://latino.foxnews.com/latino/politics/2011/09/08/dreamers-released-after-arrest-at-immigration-protest-officials-say-wont-face/. Agapito Hernandez entered with his family when he was fourteen. Eventually, he got married and was known as a "sweet" family man. However, the 38-year-old Agapito, who has no other criminal record, was arrested after he accidentally drove his sport utility vehicle into the bay when his brakes malfunction. Although he was found not guilty of reckless driving, he was taken into ICE custody to face deportation. Mike Aldax, *High and dry after plunge*, SAN FRANCISCO EXAMINER, Apr. 19, 2012. Forty-five members of Buen Pastor Church of Raleigh, North Carolina, were arrested by immigration agents when their church vans were pulled over in Louisiana after attending a religious retreat. Twenty-two faced deportation; eventually 18 were granted prosecutorial discretion, on member was denied, and three sought relief in deportation hearings. *See* National Network for Immigrant and Refugee Rights, *Buen Pastor Church Case*, Apr. 14, 2012 (on file with author). After dropping off his wife and son at a Wal-Mart, Claudio Molina stayed in the parking lot but went into a diabetic shock in reaction to medication he was taking for his diabetes. Police responded to a call from a concerned bystander, but the police arrested Molina on suspicion of driving while intoxicated. But even after things were cleared up, Molina, a native of Argentina, was turned over to ICE for deportation. Julianne Hing, *As SB 1070 Heads to Court, a Father's Case Reveals the Larger Problem*, COLORLINES, Apr. 24, 2012, http://colorlines.com/archives/2012/04/new_york_fathers_case_tests_obamas_deportation_policies.html. In February 2012, the United States Ninth Circuit Court of Appeals place five deportation cases on hold and asked federal attorneys how the immigrants, mostly longtime residents with U.S. citizen children, fit into the Morton memo plan to focus on removing the most dangerous deportable aliens. Bob Egelko, *Appeals court puts 5 deportation cases on hold*, SAN FRANCISCO CHRONICLE, Feb. 7, 2012. But after it became clear that the implementation of the Morton memo was not producing consistent results, the court proceeded with the cases.

The hard lesson learned in these cases is that what seems clear on paper from ICE headquarters does not necessarily get translated to what gets implemented on the ground. Disappointed officials in Washington, D.C., can do little about an isolated case.

A few days after the Morton memo was issued, the ICE union issued its own press release warning: "Any American concerned about immigration needs to brace themselves for what's coming. . . . The desires of foreign nationals illegally in the United States were the framework from which these policies were developed. . . . [T]he result is a means for every person here illegally to avoid arrest or detention; as officers we will never know who we can or cannot arrest."[81] Then a year later, in August 2012, 10 ICE agents filed a lawsuit against DHS Secretary Napolitano alleging that the prosecutorial discretion policies announced in the Morton memo prevented them from doing their job and "defending the Constitution."[82] The lawsuit was funded by the anti-immigrant organization Numbers USA, and the lead counsel was Kris Kobach, the architect of several anti-immigrant state laws, such as Arizona's SB 1070.[83]

Although the ICE union lawsuits have been dismissed, immigrants and their advocates continued to learn the lesson that relying on administrative good faith is a mistake. Inconsistent implementation of administrative policy statements is difficult to control against. Given the range of factors that can affect the exercise of discretion, such as the enforcement backgrounds of local decision makers, harsh decisions are not surprising.

5. DACA

Although the Morton memo of June 17, 2011, did result in the termination of some deportation proceedings involving DREAMers, the removal of many DREAMers with no criminal backgrounds continued.[84] For example, Ramon Aguirre, who had entered the United States at the age of seven and became a talented artist in high school, was deported even though he had a four-year old son.[85] Cesar Montoya faced deportation after being stopped for driving without a license.[86] In Denver, a recent high school graduate who was brought to the United States as an undocumented minor by his mother when he was seven years old was

---

[81] *ICE Agent's Union Speaks Out on Director's "Discretionary Memo" Calls on the public to take action*, June 23, 2011, http://iceunion.org/news/ice-agent%E2%80%99s-union-speaks-out-director%E2%80%99s-%E2%80%9Cdiscretionary-memo%E2%80%9D-calls-public-take-action-click-her

[82] Elise Foley, *Kris Kobach Represents Immigration Agents in Lawsuit Against Obama Administration*, Huffington Post, Aug. 23, 2012, *available at* http://www.huffingtonpost.com/2012/08/23/kris-kobach-immigration-lawsuit-obama_n_1825272.html. In addition to the Morton memo, the lawsuit challenged the deferred action program specifically for DREAMers that was announced on June 15, 2012 by the Obama administration.

[83] Elise Foley, *Kris Kobach Represents . . . .*

[84] *See, e.g.,* AILA report cases (11/10/11) for places like Atlanta.

[85] Ani Palacios McBride, *Dream Activist Blames Senators Reid and Durbin for Deportations*, La Columna, Oct. 12, 2011, *available at* http://contacto-latino.com/ideas-latinas/la-columna/2003/dream-activist-blames-senators-reid-and-durbin-for-deportations/.

[86] *Id.*

first told that he would be granted prosecutorial discretion, but later on the local ICE Chief Counsel said there was a "mix-up" and that the young man would not be receiving prosecutorial discretion.[87] Also, DREAMers who had minor criminal records were removed. For example, 22-year-old Yanelli Hernandez was removed to Mexico in January 2012, because she was undocumented and had convictions for driving under the influence and forgery.[88] Hernandez, a factory worker with mental problems, had attempted suicide twice.[89]

DREAMers and their supporters were disappointed in the Morton memo results and called on the president to do more.[90] So on June 15, 2012, to make his intent very clear to ICE officials in the field, President Obama specifically announced that DREAMers would be granted deferred action and employment authorization for at least two years.[91] Not coincidentally, his decision came after DREAM activist Gaby Pacheco met with Republican Senator Marco Rubio and a weeklong protest and sit-in at the Obama campaign office in Denver, Colorado.[92]

Under the directive, deferred action could be granted on a case-by-case basis to individuals who meet the following criteria: they came to the United States when they were younger than 16, they have continuously resided in the United States for at least five years, and they are in school, have graduated from high school, have obtained a GED or are honorably discharged veterans of the armed forces. The individuals could qualify if they had not been convicted of a felony, significant misdemeanor offense or multiple misdemeanor offenses, or otherwise posed a threat to national security or public safety.[93] And they had to be under age 31.

Deferred Action for Childhood Arrivals (DACA) status was granted to 553,197 applicants by March 2014. Only 20,311 applicants were denied. After the initial two-

---

[87] Email from Violeta Raquel Chapin to immprof@listserv.unc.edu, Apr. 9, 2012 (on file with author).

[88] *ICE Deports Former Reading Woman*, CINCINNATI INQUIRER, Jan. 31, 2012.

[89] *Id.*

[90] *President Obama to Halt Deportation of DREAMers*, June 15, 2012, *available at*, http://immigrationimpact.com/2012/06/15/president-obama-to-halt-removal-of-dreamers/

[91] *Id.* When the Morton memo was issued, supporters of same-sex couples sought explicit assurances from DHS and the White House that the foreign-born partner of a U.S. citizen would be granted prosecutorial discretion. Administration officials had stated that being in a same-sex relationship would be considered in the context of the "community contributions" and "family relationships" factors in the Morton memo. But activists and Democratic lawmakers sought additional assurances that bi-national same-sex couples would not be left out. Chris Johnson, *Lawmakers seek added protections for bi-national gay couple*, WASHINGTONBLADE.COM, Sept. 27, 2011, http://www.washingtonblade.com/2011/09/27/lawmakers-seek-added-protections-for-bi-national-gay-couples/. Finally, more than a year later, DHS Secretary Napolitano announced: "In an effort to make clear the definition of the phrase 'family relationships,' I have directed ICE to disseminate written guidance to the field that the interpretation of the phrase 'family relationships' includes long-term, same-sex partners." Miranda Leitsinger, *US Immigration Chief: Same-sex ties are family ties*, NBC NEWS.COM, Sept. 28, 2012, http://usnews.nbcnews.com/_news/2012/09/28/14140024-us-immigration-chief-same-sex-ties-are-family-ties?lite.

[92] Julia Preston, *Young Immigrants Say It's Obama's Time to Act*, NY TIMES, Nov. 30, 2012; Julianne Hing, *DREAMers Stage Sit-Ins at Obama Office to Force Deportation Standoff*, COLORLINES, June 13, 2012, http://colorlines.com/archives/2012/06/dreamers_planned_obama_campaign_office_sit-ins_force_deportation_standoff.html

[93] *A Breakdown of DHS's Deferred Action for DREAMers*, June 18, 2012, *available at* http://immigrationimpact.com/2012/06/18/a-breakdown-of-dhss-deferred-action-for-dreamers/

year period, individuals could request DACA renewal if they continued to meet the initial criteria and these additional guidelines: (a) did not depart the United States on or after Aug. 15, 2012, without advance parole; (b) continuously resided in the United States since they submitted their most recent DACA request that was approved; and (c) had not been convicted of a felony, a significant misdemeanor or three or more misdemeanors, and do not otherwise pose a threat to national security or public safety.

On November 20, 2014, the President took further executive action on behalf of DACA recipients and to block the deportation of four to five million more undocumented immigrants, primarily the parents of U.S. citizen children or lawful permanent resident children.[94] The program for parents is referred to as the Deferred Action for Parents of Americans and Lawful Permanent Residents (DAPA) program. The President's announcement even included the intent to end the Secure Communities program.[95] Republicans claimed that the President acted unconstitutionally,[96] and legal challenges were filed.[97] In the meantime, the White House and community based organizations prepared for the implementation of the new program.[98]

6.   Same-Sex, Binational Couples

Under the Immigration and Nationality Act, U.S. citizens and legal permanent residents may sponsor their spouses (and other immediate family members) for immigration purposes. But until the Supreme Court ruled the Defense of Marriage Act (DOMA) unconstitutional in *United States v. Windsor*,[99] same-sex partners of U.S. citizens and permanent residents were not considered "spouses" and their partners could not sponsor them for family-based immigration.[100] Before the *Windsor* case reached the Supreme Court, the Obama administration refused to defend DOMA. On February 23, 2011, U.S. Attorney General Eric Holder issued a

---

[94] Elise Foley, *Obama Moves to Protect Millions from Deportation*, HUFFINGTON POST, Nov. 20, 2014, *available at* http://www.huffingtonpost.com/2014/11/20/obama-immigration-plan_n_6178774.html.

[95] *Obama was wise to end Secure Communities program*, *SFGATE* (Nov. 28, 2014), *available at* http://www.sfgate.com/opinion/editorials/article/Obama-was-wise-to-end-Secure-Communities-program-5923254.php.

[96] Julia Preston, *House Republicans and White House Clash on Obama Immigration Plan*, N.Y. TIMES, Dec. 2, 2014, *available at* http://www.nytimes.com/2014/12/03/us/politics/jeh-johnson-testifies-before-house-homeland-security-committee.html?_r=0.

[97] David Montgomery & Julia Preston, *17 States Suing on Immigration*, N.Y. TIMES, Dec. 3, 2014, *available at* http://www.nytimes.com/2014/12/04/us/executive-action-on-immigration-prompts-texas-to-sue.html.

[98] Winnie Hu, *New York Immigration Groups Prepare to Meet Demands of New Policy*, N.Y. TIMES, Nov. 28, 2014, *available at* http://www.nytimes.com/2014/11/29/nyregion/new-york-agencies-gear-up-to-meet-demands-of-new-immigration-policy.html.

[99] 570 U.S. 12 (2013).

[100] In *Adams v. Howerton*, 673 F.2d 1036 (9th Cir. 1982), *cert. denied*, 458 U.S. 1111 (1982) the United States Court of Appeals for the Ninth Circuit held that the term "spouse" refers to an opposite-sex partner for the purposes of immigration law. The court held that "Congress's decision to confer spouse status under [the law] only upon the parties to heterosexual marriages has a rational basis. . . . Congress rationally intended to deny preferential status to the spouses of [same-sex] marriages."

statement from the Obama administration that agreed with the plaintiff's position that DOMA violated the U.S. Constitution and said he would no longer defend the law in court. Significantly, the Obama administration also had announced prior to *Windsor* that in considering whether prosecutorial discretion should be exercised favorably, "family relationships" should include same-sex partners — including domestic partners.[101]

The demise of DOMA opened the door to immigration possibilities for same-sex, bi-national couples for the Obama administration. After the decision, President Obama directed federal departments to ensure the decision and its implication for federal benefits for same-sex legally married couples be implemented swiftly and smoothly. To that end, DHS Secretary Janet Napolitano directed U.S. Citizenship and Immigration Services (USCIS) to review immigration visa petitions filed on behalf of a same-sex spouse in the same manner as those filed on behalf of an opposite-sex spouse. As long as the same-sex marriage in valid in the jurisdiction where the marriage to place, the marriage would be recognized for U.S. immigration purposes.[102]

Today, an estimated 40,000 bi-national same-sex couples reside in the United States. Too many are kept apart from overseas partners, or forced to live in the precarious state in which one partner in constant fear of deportation. Although the end of DOMO is helpful, that does not completely resolve the problem under the federal immigration system because so many immigrants live in jurisdictions where there is no legally-recognized same sex marriage.

L.   THE PUSH FOR IMMIGRATION REFORM

The furor over illegal immigration is palpable. Rightly or wrongly, segments of the United States media, policy leaders, and populace continue to be obsessed with the issue of undocumented immigration to the United States. With an estimated 11 million undocumented aliens in the United States, advocates for immigration reform have become louder and more visible. Over the past few years, immigrant rights advocates have called for a broad legalization program, while restrictionists unrealistically demand that the entire undocumented population be rounded up and deported and that the border somehow be secured.

President Bush re-ignited a discussion beyond a let's-round-up-and-deport-them approach with a proposal for a large-scale guestworker plan. In many respects, his plan reflected smart politics as well as a method to address the undocumented challenge. Under Bush's plan, first presented on January 7, 2004, and reiterated shortly after his re-election, each year 300,000 undocumented immigrants and workers from abroad would be able to apply for a three-year work permit; the permit could be extended once for a total of six years. Workers would be allowed to switch jobs and to move from one type of work to another. Those coming from

---

[101] *See* Victoria Neilson, *Prosecutorial Discretion Memo Extends "Family Relationships" to Include LGBT Partners*, Oct. 9, 2012, at http://www.immigrationequality.org/wp-content/uploads/2012/01/LGBT-PD-advisory.pdf.

[102] *See* Janet Napolitano, *Same-Sex Marriages*, July 1, 2013, at http://www.uscis.gov/family/same-sex-marriages.

abroad would be able to bring family members.[103] The shrewdness of the proposal began with the fact that no automatic path toward citizenship was provided to the workers, addressing concerns of some anti-immigrant groups. But by providing an opportunity to work for up to six years, many undocumented workers would step forward and reveal themselves, while a large pool of low-wage workers would make the business community extremely happy. In fact, providing a perpetual pool of low-wage workers would revolutionize the labor market.

The debate over the guestworker solution does not divide along neat partisan lines. Democratic U.S. Senator Dianne Feinstein, the AFL-CIO, and immigrant rights organizations who recall the abuses of the Bracero program have opposed guestworker programs. Republican Senator Marco Rubio as well as the restriction-ist Federation for American Immigration Reform are also quite vocal in their opposition. Yet in 2005 and 2006, a bipartisan group of legislators, businesses, and even some farmworker organizations came to embrace guestworker proposals.

By the time 2007 rolled around, the presidential race began in earnest and all bets were off. In order to appease the far right of the Republican Party, John McCain withdrew his support from his 2006 McCain-Kennedy legislation, and comprehensive legislation took a far turn to the right. The theme was that the border had to be secured before any steps toward legalization could be taken, and from left field a provision eliminating family immigration categories became part of a compromise package that would install an elitist point system for immigration categories instead.

By the end of 2007, any possibility of comprehensive immigration reform was derailed by those who viewed guestworkers and even a burdensome legalization plan as amnesty. Even the immigrant rights community was splintered by then — some arguing that getting something would be better than nothing, while others maintaining that eliminating family categories and accepting a burdensome legal-ization plan was not worth the price. Congress dropped any serious work on comprehensive reform during the 2008 presidential campaign, as both parties appeared hesitant to take on the political hot potato of immigration reform.

Coming into office, President Obama pledged to make efforts to pass compre-hensive immigration reform one of his top priorities. However, the challenges of the economic downturn, a focus on health care reform, and anti-immigrant forces derailed those efforts in his first term. Although the DREAM Act passed the then-Democratically controlled House of Representatives in late 2010, the legisla-tion fell five votes short of breaking a Republican filibuster in the Senate. The proposal would grant legalization to those who came to the United States at age 15 or younger, have been in the country at least five years before the bill's enactment date, and are currently age 29 or younger. Perhaps 700,000 individuals would benefit from its enactment.

In President Obama's second term, a bipartisan group of Senators forged a broad agreement on immigration, and the Senate passed the Border Security, Economic Opportunity and Immigration Modernization Act of 2013 (S.744), which, if enacted, would comprise the largest-scale overhaul of our immigration system in more than

---

[103] Ricardo Alonso-Zaldivar, *Bush Would Open U.S. to Guest Workers*, L.A. Times, Jan. 8, 2004, at A1.

25 years. Significantly, the bill would provide a road to U.S. citizenship for perhaps as many as 11 million unauthorized immigrants, allocate billions for militarization of the southern border, and restructure the family immigration system. The bill also would create stringent enforcement and deportation measures, and ramp up workplace enforcement by mandating that employers use an electronic employment eligibility verification system (E-Verify). The main portions of S. 744 were as follows:

TITLE I: BORDER SECURITY

Initial implementation. Within 6 months of the bill's passage, the secretary of the U.S. Department of Homeland Security (DHS) would be required to craft a strategy to increase surveillance at all southern border sectors and to extend the existing barriers along the U.S.-Mexico border so that they total 700 miles of barriers/fencing. The goal of the strategy would be to apprehend 9 out of every 10 immigrants who attempt to enter the country at these border sectors without permission (also known as a 90 percent effectiveness rate).

Funding. The bill allocates an astronomical $46.3 billion for border enforcement.

Commission. An advisory Southern Border Security Commission would be established no later than one year after the bill's enactment. The DHS secretary may use $2 billion in funding to carry out the activities recommended by the commission.

Use of force. Use-of-force policies and trainings would be implemented, along with a complaint procedure. U.S. Customs and Border Patrol officers, along with other federal law enforcement officials, would be subject to a prohibition on racial or ethnic profiling.

Trigger to begin legalization. Before registered provisional immigrant (RPI) status is granted to unauthorized immigrants, the DHS secretary must certify that implementation of the U.S.-Mexico border strategy has begun.

LPR trigger. Before RPIs can adjust to lawful permanent resident (LPR) status (i.e., obtain a "green card"), the DHS secretary must:

- Certify that the U.S.-Mexico border surveillance and fencing strategy has been "substantially deployed" and is "substantially operational";
- Deploy 38,405 full-time active-duty Border Patrol agents along the southern border;
- Implement a mandatory electronic employment eligibility verification system (E 'Verify), to be used by all employers in the U.S.; and
- State that DHS is using an electronic system to identify those who are exiting the country at air and sea ports of entry.

TITLE II: IMMIGRANT VISAS

Registered Provisional Immigrant (RPI) Status

In order to be eligible for RPI status, a person must:

- Have been physically present in the U.S. on or before Dec. 31, 2011,

- Have maintained continuous presence up until the date of application,

- Have settled any assessed federal tax liability,

- Not have been convicted of certain criminal offenses, and

- Not have been a lawful permanent resident, asylee, refugee, or present in the U.S. in a lawful nonimmigrant status.

- After 6 years of having RPI status, the person to whom it was granted must apply to renew it. After 10 years in RPI status, the person would be eligible to apply for LPR (or "green card") status. An additional 3 years in LPR status is required before individuals may apply for U.S. citizenship.

Fees and fines. Fees paid by the applicant must cover the cost of the application process, and fines would be assessed as follows: $1000 at RPI application ($500 may be paid when filing the initial application and $500 at renewal), and $1000 at adjustment to a green card.

Back taxes. A person with RPI status must also pay any back taxes owed since he or she was granted the status.

Time limit to file. Immigrants may file for RPI status up to one year after the time that the final regulations are published by DHS. The DHS secretary may extend this limit for an additional 18 months.

Ability to apply for family members. A person with RPI status would also be able to apply for RPI status for dependent children or his/her spouse, provided they were in the U.S. on the date the RPI status was granted to the principal applicant and also that they were present in the U.S. on or before Dec. 30, 2012.

Individuals in custody or removal proceedings. Individuals who are apprehended by immigration authorities before the application period, are in removal proceedings, or have been ordered removed would be able to apply after establishing eligibility for RPI status.

Individuals outside the U.S. Individuals who departed from the U.S. subject to an order of exclusion, deportation, removal, or voluntary departure, and who are outside the U.S. or who reentered unlawfully after Dec. 31, 2011, without receiving DHS consent to reapply for admission would not be eligible to apply for RPI status. However the DHS secretary may waive this bar for spouses or children of a U.S. citizen or LPR, parents of a child who is a U.S. citizen or LPR, or individuals who meet certain requirements under the DREAM-related provisions that are included in the bill. In addition, prior to granting this waiver, DHS must determine whether the person has a criminal conviction, notify and consult with any victim to determine whether to grant the waiver, and notify the victim that the waiver was granted.

Who is not eligible. Those who have been convicted of the following are not eligible for RPI status: a felony, an aggravated felony, 3 or more misdemeanors (other than immigration status-related convictions), certain foreign offenses, and unlawful voting. Aggravated felonies can include minor offenses such as shoplifting.

Nationality-based additional security screening. DHS is required to conduct an additional security screening of RPI applicants, spouses, and children who resided in a country or region "known to pose a threat, or that contains groups or organizations that pose a threat to the U.S."

Requirements for renewal. At renewal, RPIs must demonstrate that they have been employed regularly and are not likely to fall below the federal poverty level.

Requirements for lawful permanent residence (LPR status or "green card"). At the stage of applying for adjustment to LPR status, RPIs must demonstrate that they are employed regularly and show that they are likely to have income or resources at 125 percent of federal poverty level wages or satisfy certain education requirements. They must also demonstrate that they are pursuing a course of study in English and U.S. history/civics.

Waiver. The DHS secretary would have the authority to waive certain restrictions for humanitarian purposes, to ensure family unity, or if it is in the national interest.

DREAM

An expedited road to citizenship would be available to those who entered the U.S. before the age of 16, graduated from high school (or received a GED) in the United States, and attended at least 2 years of college or served 4 years in the uniformed services. DREAMers would apply for RPI status, and, after 5 years, would be eligible to apply for adjustment to LPR status. They then would be able to apply immediately for U.S. citizenship.

No age cap. There would be no upper-age limit for those who apply under this provision. This makes sense, since the relevant issue is the person's age at the time of entry into the U.S., not his or her current age.

DACA streamlining. The DHS secretary would have the discretion to establish streamlined procedures for people already granted Deferred Action for Childhood Arrivals (DACA).

No penalty for offering in-state tuition. The bill would repeal a provision of the Illegal Immigration Reform and Immigrant Responsibility Act of 1996 that prohibited public universities from offering in-state tuition rates to undocumented students on the basis of residence in the state, unless they offered the same rates to nonresidents of the state.

Educational loans. RPIs who entered the U.S. prior to age 16 (and agricultural workers with blue card status) may qualify for federal work-study and federal student loans. They remain ineligible for federal Pell grants until they adjust to LPR status.

Family-and Employment-based Immigration

The bill provides for significant changes to the family-and employment-based immigration system, including the elimination of certain immigration/visa categories altogether and the lifting of visa caps for others. A new "merit-based" system would be created, and the substantial backlog in the current preference system would be eliminated.

Eliminated categories. The bill would eliminate family-based visas for siblings of U.S. citizens and set a cap at age 31 for married sons and daughters of U.S. citizens seeking immigrant visas. These changes would take effect prospectively, 18 months after the date of enactment of the bill, and people could file visa petitions to immigrate these relatives up until this effective date.

Uncapped categories. Importantly, spouses and children of LPRs would be considered immediate family members and therefore would no longer be subject to arbitrary visa caps. Spouses and children of those receiving Science Technology Engineering and Math (STEM) visas, other professionals, and foreign doctors would also be able to have their spouses and children join them.

Merit-based "Track One" immigrant visas. The bill initially would allocate 120,000 immigrant visas per year for Track One visas, a number that could increase by as much as 5 percent each subsequent year as long as unemployment remains under 8.5 percent, up to a cap of 250,000 visas. The visas would be allocated based on a point system that takes into account various factors, including educational degrees, employment experience, the needs of U.S. employers, U.S. citizen relatives, and age.

Merit-based "Track Two" visas. Track Two visas would be available for people who are currently beneficiaries of backlogged employment- and family-based visa petitions, for immigrants who have been waiting for a visa for at least 5 years, and also for individuals who have been lawfully present in the U.S. for at least 10 years. Family members with pending petitions would be allocated transitional merit-based visas such that they should all be allocated over the 7-year period from 2015 to 2021.

Repeal of the Diversity Visa Program. The Diversity Visa Program would be repealed as of Oct. 1, 2014, although noncitizens who were selected in the diversity visa lottery in fiscal year 2013 or 2014 would remain eligible to receive a visa under the program.

V nonimmigrant visas. The bill would create a new nonimmigrant V visa for the beneficiaries of family visa petitions to live and work in the U.S. while waiting for their immigrant visas to be approved.

No provision for same-sex couples. The Uniting American Families Act is not included in the bill.

W nonimmigrant visas. The bill would create a new worker program for low-skilled workers who will work for 3 years for registered employers in an occupation with labor shortages, with the ability to renew the visa for an additional 3 years. W visa holders would have the ability to eventually apply for merit-based green cards and to switch to another registered employer and job at will. Dependents would be able to join the W visa-holder and would receive work authorization.

Access to Public Benefits and the Affordable Care Act (ACA)

Federal public benefit programs. Individuals granted RPI status, "blue card" status (agricultural workers), and V nonimmigrant visas will not be eligible for the following "federal means-tested public benefits" programs: nonemergency Medicaid, Children's Health Insurance Program (CHIP), Supplemental Nutrition Assistance Program (SNAP or food stamps), Temporary Assistance for Needy Families (TANF), and Supplemental Security Income (SSI) for the duration of their provisional status. When most of these individuals adjust to LPR status, they will be forced to wait at least five additional years before becoming eligible for these programs. As a result, an individual with RPI status who is otherwise eligible for public benefits would not be able to enroll in programs such as Medicaid and SNAP for 15 years.

Social Security credit. Individuals with RPI status and visa over-stayers may not claim credit for any quarter of coverage earned between 2004 and 2014 in which they were not authorized to work. This provision applies to quarters used in determining eligibility for Title II Social Security retirement benefits as well as Social Security Disability Insurance (SSDI).

Affordable Care Act. Individuals granted RPI, blue-card, or V nonimmigrant visa status will be able to buy private health insurance at full cost through the insurance marketplaces created under the Affordable Care Act (ACA). However, during the duration of their provisional status, these individuals will not be eligible for the ACA's premium tax credits and cost-sharing reductions that will help make health insurance affordable for low- and middle-income, working families. Also, those with RPI, blue-card or V nonimmigrant visa status will not be subject to the ACA's requirement to have health insurance or pay a tax penalty.

Currently eligible individuals with a B visa (temporary visitors for business or pleasure) or F visa (students, as well as their spouses and children) will also be excluded from the ACA's premium tax credits and cost-sharing reductions and also are not subject to the ACA's health insurance requirement or tax penalty. However, unlike individuals granted RPI, blue-card, or V nonimmigrant status, B and F visa holders won't be able to purchase private health insurance full cost through the ACA-created insurance marketplaces.

Other categories of immigration status that are included in the bill, including workers in expanded H-category visas, low-skilled workers who obtain W visas, and individuals who adjust to LPR status from RPI or blue-card status or through the clearing of the visa backlogs, will be eligible for the ACA and related subsidies under existing law while in that status. They will not be eligible for federal means-tested public benefits until they adjust to LPR status and then meet the five-year waiting period.

TITLE III: INTERIOR ENFORCEMENT

This title contains many subparts, including: a section that requires employers to use an electronic employment eligibility verification system; worker protections, including the POWER Act; asylum and refugee provisions; immigration court reform; and new provisions related to violations of immigration law that constitute crimes.

Electronic Employment Eligibility Verification System (EEVS)

The bill would require all employers to use the federal government's EEVS to verify the employment eligibility of newly hired employees; the requirement would be phased in by employer size. The EEVS provision contains significant due process and worker protections for U.S. citizens and employment-authorized individuals who are affected by a system error. An example of an electronic employment eligibility verification system is E-Verify.

Implementation. Employers with more than 5,000 employees must begin using the EEVS, for newly hired employees and employees with expiring work-authorization documents, within 2 years after the regulations are published. Similarly, employers with more than 500 employees must begin using the EEVS within 3 years, and agricultural employers and all other employers must begin using the EEVS within 4 years.

Increased Worker Protections

Hoffman Plastic fix. The bill would create an important legislative fix of the Supreme Court's decision in *Hoffman Plastic Compound, Inc. v. NLRB*,[104] by specifying that neither back pay nor any other damages (except any reinstatement remedy prohibited under federal law) shall be denied to an individual based on his or her immigration status.

POWER Act. The bill increases legal protections for immigrant workers who are wrongfully terminated or who experience significant workplace abuse. The bill would bolster legal remedies to immigrant workers who are fired in violation of labor laws, while providing for U-visa relief for whistleblowers who experience serious workplace abuse, exploitation, or retaliation.

S. 744 was attacked from the right and from the left. The Tea Party, the Center for Immigration Studies, and the Federation for American Immigration Reform (FAIR) remain staunchly opposed to any legislation that provides legalization —

---

[104] 535 U.S. 137 (2002).

especially one that provides a path to citizenship — to undocumented immigrants. Many immigrant rights organizations opposed S.744 because of billions in increased funding for border militarization as well as a nebulous path to citizenship that could take up to 15 years for undocumented immigrants.

In contrast to the Senate's successful bipartisan efforts on a broad immigration bill, efforts in the House of Representatives languished. More than a year after S.744 passed the Senate, the prospects for immigration reform legislation in the House were declared dead. In response, immigrant rights advocates focused on pressuring President Obama to expand his executive actions to benefit more undocumented immigrants. These efforts continued in the midst of the unaccompanied immigrant children challenge at the border that provided another basis for anti-immigrant politicians and organizations to oppose legislation, blaming the president for the crisis.

Chapter 3

THE FEDERAL IMMIGRATION POWER

This chapter considers the power of the federal government under the U.S. Constitution to regulate immigration.

As the Supreme Court has interpreted the Constitution, the federal government possesses primary responsibility for regulating immigration to the United States.[1]

---

[1] The Supreme Court's most recent pronouncement on the federal government's power over

Congress passes the immigration laws; courts ordinarily defer to the substantive immigration judgments of Congress, such as to which categories of immigrants to admit to, and deport from, the country. Administration of the immigration laws is in the hands of the Executive Branch of the national government. Chapter 5 lays out the functions of the various federal agencies that regulate immigration.

To the extent that it intervenes in immigration matters, the Supreme Court generally focuses on ensuring adherence to proper procedures for noncitizens — specifically compliance with Due Process norms — facing removal from the United States as well as the proper interpretation of the comprehensive federal immigration statute, the Immigration and Nationality Act.[2] One question addressed by the Court in recent years is whether any — and, if so, how much — residual authority on immigration matters resides with the state and local governments.

State and local governments in the modern era have attempted to facilitate enforcement of the U.S. immigration laws. Chapter 4 analyzes the constitutionally appropriate role of state and local government in immigration regulation. In deciding challenges to two Arizona immigration enforcement laws in the last few years,[3] the Supreme Court significantly reined in the state's more aggressive attempts at immigration regulation, making it clear that the federal government has primary authority over immigration.

In 2014, a national controversy commenced over the distribution of immigration authority between the Executive Branch and Congress. After repeated failures by Congress to pass immigration reform legislation, *see* Chapter 18, President Obama decided to act in an interim fashion and the administration took a number of immigration measures that critics challenged as usurping congressional authority. After initiating in 2012 a "deferred action" program for undocumented immigrants who arrived as children, President Obama expanded the program in 2014. That executive action sparked nothing less than a firestorm of controversy. As will be discussed later in this chapter, 26 states challenged the lawfulness of the expanded deferred action program and, in February 2015, a district court entered a preliminary injunction barring the new program form going into effect.

A. THE CONSTITUTIONAL POWER TO REGULATE IMMIGRATION

No provision of the U.S. Constitution unequivocally authorizes the federal government to regulate immigration and immigrants in the comprehensive way that we see in the modern United States. Indeed, not much in the Constitution specifically pertains to immigration.

---

immigration law and its enforcement vis-à-vis the states can be found in Arizona v. United States, 132 S. Ct. 2492 (2012). *See* Ch. 4.

[2] Pub. L. No. 82-414, 66 Stat. 163 (1952) (codified as amended in scattered sections of 8, 18, & 22 U.S.C.).

[3] *See* Arizona v. United States, 132 S. Ct. 2492 (2012); Chamber of Commerce v. Whiting, 131 S. Ct. 1968 (2011).

Immigration evidently was not a pressing concern to framers of the Constitution. The framers focused more on establishing a national government that would attract persons to settle the new nation than on restricting immigration.

One commentator has observed that

> [t]here is also little reason to believe that the Framers contemplated creating a federal immigration power. *One of the grievances directed against the Crown in the Declaration of Independence was that the King had obstructed free immigration to the colonies. And at the time of the framing, the United States generally encouraged free immigration, while various states maintained laws authorizing the expulsion of aliens deemed undesirable.* In 1788, after the Constitutional Convention, the Congress of the Confederation recommended that the several states "pass proper laws for preventing the transportation of convicted malefactors from foreign counties into the United States." The action was later viewed by some as confirming the states' primacy in regulating the entry and exit of aliens.[4]

Scholars have struggled in search of a constitutional justification for the general exercise of federal power over immigration regulation.[5] Despite the lack of clear constitutional authority, comprehensive federal regulation of immigration has been the rule since the late nineteenth century.[6]

1. Enumerated Powers

A fundamental principle of American constitutional law is that the federal government is one of "enumerated powers."[7] That means that the federal government can exercise power only insofar as the Constitution, which specifically reserves most powers to the states, expressly authorizes it. *See* U.S. Const. X Amendment ("The powers not delegated to the United States by the Constitution, nor prohibited by it to the states, are reserved to the states respectively, or to the people.").

Given that the Constitution says little about the national government's power to regulate immigration, the enumerated powers principle poses difficulties for its exercise of constitutional authority to regulate immigration. Because immigration implicated the movement of slaves, and thus the institution of slavery — an issue of

---

[4] Sarah H. Cleveland, *Powers Inherent in Sovereignty: Indians, Aliens, Territories, and the Nineteenth Century Origins of Plenary Power over Foreign Affairs*, 81 Tex. L. Rev. 1, 98 (2002) (emphasis added) (footnotes omitted).

[5] *See* Clare Huntington, *The Constitutional Dimension of Immigration Federalism*, 61 Vand. L. Rev. 787, 812–13 (2008) (questioning whether the U.S. Constitution grants exclusive authority to the national government to regulate immigration).

[6] For analysis of the development of the federal immigration power, see Cleveland, *supra* note 4, at 81–163.

[7] *See, e.g.*, The Federalist No. 45, at 292 (James Madison) (Clinton Rossiter ed., 1961) ("The powers delegated by the proposed Constitution to the federal government are few and defined. Those which are to remain in the State governments are numerous and indefinite.").

considerable contention in the framing of the Constitution — the framers were reluctant to directly address the topic.[8]

a. The Naturalization Power

Before ratification of the Constitution, states had widely differing rules for the granting of citizenship.[9] Some states granted citizenship immediately to all who landed on their shores; other states established a waiting period.[10] To prevent the confusion that might arise from varying state citizenship laws,[11] the Constitution expressly delegated the power to Congress "[t]o establish a *uniform* Rule of Naturalization."[12]

Since early in this nation's history, Congress has exercised the naturalization power. The result has been a single uniform set of naturalization rules for the entire nation. The Executive Branch for the most part has administered the naturalization rules established by Congress and does so today.

Chapter 17 reviews the modern process and requirements for naturalization. Importantly, the U.S. naturalization laws, although generous in many respects, such as requiring a relatively short five years of residency to be eligible for naturalization, have not always been laudable. From 1790–1952, for example, the law required that a noncitizen be "white" to naturalize, a requirement that the Supreme Court interpreted on several occasions.[13]

The constitutional power to establish a process and requirements for immigrants to naturalize and become citizens does not inexorably lead to the conclusion that the national government possesses the power to establish immigrant admissions criteria and deportation grounds. As as a practical matter, however, it is difficult to see, as would be the case with varying state naturalization rules and procedures, how the nation could cope with a hodge-podge of different state immigration laws regulating the admission and removal of immigrants.[14]

---

[8] *See* ARISTIDE R. ZOLBERG, A NATION OF DESIGN: IMMIGRATION POLICY IN THE FASHIONING OF AMERICA 78 (2006); Cleveland, *supra* note 4, at 788; Gerald L. Neuman, A *Lost Century of American Immigration Law (1776–1875)*, 93 COLUM. L. REV 1833, 1866–67 (1993).

[9] *See* James E. Pfander & Theresa R. Wardon, *Reclaiming the Immigration Constitution of the Early Republic: Prospectivity, Uniformity, and Transparency*, 96 VA. L. REV. 359, 383–85 (2010) (reviewing early state citizenship rules).

[10] *See* Ricardo Gonzalez Cedillo, *A Constitutional Analysis of the English Literacy Requirement of the Naturalization Act*, 14 ST. MARY'S L.J. 899, 912–14 (1983).

[11] *See* JAMES H. KETTNER, THE DEVELOPMENT OF AMERICAN CITIZENSHIP, 1608–1870, at 224–25 (1978).

[12] U.S. CONST. ART. I, § 8, cl. 4 (emphasis added).

[13] *See* An Act to Establish an Uniform Rule of Naturalization, Ch. 3, 1 Stat. 103 (1790) (limiting naturalized citizenship to "free white person[s]"); *see, e.g.*, Ozawa v. United States, 260 U.S. 178 (1922) (holding that an immigrant from Japan was not "white" and thus ineligible for naturalization); United States v. Thind, 261 U.S. 204 (1923) (ruling to the same effect with respect to an immigrant from India). *See generally* IAN HANEY-LÓPEZ, WHITE BY LAW (10th anniversary ed. 2006) (analyzing caselaw, interpreting the requirement in place from 1790 to 1952 that immigrants be "white" to naturalize).

[14] *See* Arizona v. United States, 132 S. Ct. 2492, 2498 (2012) ("It is fundamental that foreign countries concerned about the status, safety, and security of their nationals in the United States must be able to

At the time of the framing of the Constitution, the magnitude and ease of migration differed substantially from that which exists in modern times. The federalization of the immigration laws occurred at a time when immigration to the United States had increased, generated national concern, and provoked a congressional — and national — response. The impracticality of state regulation of admissions and removals of immigrants arguably are greater today than in the past.

b. The Commerce Power

Article I, § 8, clause 3, of the Constitution provides Congress with the power "[t]o regulate Commerce with foreign Nations, and among the several States, and with the Indian Tribes . . . ." In the earliest immigration cases, the Supreme Court viewed the federal government's power to regulate immigration as based on its power to regulate commerce. It relied on the Commerce Clause to invalidate a number of state laws that sought to regulate immigration through the imposition of taxes or other regulations on carriers.[15]

In *Smith v. Turner (The Passenger Cases)*,[16] the Supreme Court in 1849 relied upon the Commerce Clause to bar the imposition of fees by states on immigrants disembarking at ports. Similarly, in *People v. Compagnie Generale Transalantique*,[17] the Court in 1883 struck down New York's one-dollar tax on each foreign passenger arriving at the Port of New York, emphasizing that "[i]t has been so repeatedly decided by this court that such a tax as this is a regulation of commerce with foreign nations, confided by the Constitution to the exclusive control of congress . . . ."

The next year, in the *Head Money Cases*,[18] the Court relied on the commerce power to uphold a federal fee on immigrants and emphasized that "Congress [has] the power to pass a law regulating immigration as *a part of commerce of this country with foreign nations.*" Less than a decade later, in *Nishimura Ekiu v. United States*,[19] the Court listed the Commerce Clause as one of many constitutional provisions that afforded the national government the power to regulate immigration.

In 1941, the Supreme Court in *Edwards v. California*[20] struck down a California law that made it a crime to bring an indigent person into the state on the ground that it interfered with the power of Congress to regulate interstate commerce. The Court stated emphatically that "it is settled beyond question that the transportation

---

confer and communicate on this subject *with one national sovereign, not the 50 separate States.*") (emphasis added).

[15] *See, e.g.*, Chy Lung v. Freeman, 92 U.S. 275 (1876) (invalidating a state law requiring noncitizens to secure a bond or face exclusion from the state); Henderson v. New York, 92 U.S. 259 (1876) (striking down a New York law requiring that ship masters pay $1.50 tax per passenger brought to the state or provide $300 bond to indemnify the city for relief expenses).

[16] 48 U.S. (7 How.) 283, 306–07 (1849).

[17] 107 U.S. 59, 60 (1883).

[18] 112 U.S. 580, 600 (1884) (emphasis added).

[19] 142 U.S. 651, 658 (1892).

[20] 314 U.S. 160 (1941).

of persons is 'commerce.' "[21] In a concurring opinion, Justice Jackson asserted that, although the California law violated the Privileges or Immunities Clause of the Fourteenth Amendment, human beings "do not fit easily into my notions of what is commerce. To hold that the measure of his rights is the commerce clause is likely to result eventually either in distorting the commercial law or in denaturing human rights."[22]

Professor Mary Sarah Bilder has cogently summarized the Supreme Court's reliance on the Commerce Clause as a constitutional rationale for federal immigration regulation as follows:

> People are articles of commerce, or so the United States Supreme Court held in 1941, emphasizing that the issue was "settled beyond question." [citing *Edwards v. California*, 314 U.S. 160, 172 (1941)]. . . . For the first hundred years, the Court debated the question of immigration power under the Commerce Clause. The consequences of the unsettled jurisprudence reappear in every constitutional law casebook; the classic line of commerce cases stretching from *Gibbons* [*v. Ogden*, 22 U.S. (9 Wheat) 1 (1824),] through [*Mayor of New York v. Miln*, 36 U.S. (11 Pet.) 102 (1837),] to *The Passenger Cases* [Smith v. Turner, Norris v. Boston, 36 US. (11 Pet. 102 (1837)]. In 1876, the Court finally unanimously decided to link immigration to the exclusive federal commerce power based on the perception that immigrants were "articles of commerce." [*Henderson v. Mayor of New York*, 92 U.S. 259 (1876)].[23]

The Commerce Clause is a convenient constitutional justification for the federal power to regulate immigration. Migration and commerce, international and domestic, are obviously linked. Immigration often is attributable to the movement of labor, which has economic (i.e., commercial) impacts. Perceived economic benefits (or costs) of immigration often are employed to justify tighter or looser immigration laws.[24] *See* Ch. 1.

At the same time, as Justice Jackson stated in *Edwards v. California*, it may seem insensitive to commodify immigrants as "articles" of commerce. Given the problematic history of slavery in the United States, we understandably are skittish over classifying people as anything less than human.[25] Nonetheless, immigration unquestionably has an impact on both interstate and international commerce, thus making the Commerce Clause one possible justification for the national regulation of immigration.

---

[21] *Id.* at 172.

[22] *Edwards v. California*, 314 U.S. at 182 (Jackson, J., concurring).

[23] Mary Sarah Bilder, *The Struggle over Immigration: Indentured Servants, Slaves, and Articles of Commerce*, 61 Mo. L. Rev. 743, 745–46 (1996).

[24] *See* Kevin R. Johnson, Opening the Floodgates: Why America Needs to Rethink Its Borders and Immigration Laws 131–67 (2009) (summarizing literature on economic impacts on immigration).

[25] *See generally* Rethinking Commodification: Cases and Readings in Law and Culture (Martha M. Ertman & Joan C. Williams eds., 2005).

c.   Migration and Importation Clause

Article I, § 9, clause 1, of the Constitution provides that "[t]he Migration or Importation of such Persons as any of the States now existing shall think proper to admit, shall not be prohibited by the Congress prior to the year one thousand eight hundred and eight but a Tax or duty on such importation, not exceeding ten dollars for each Person."[26] That clause has generally been understood as prohibiting congressional attempts to end the slave trade before 1808. It represented a political compromise central to the ratification of the entire Constitution. Congress subsequently banned the importation of slaves effective January 1, 1808.[27]

During the framing of the Constitution, considerable debate about the meaning of the Migration and Importation Clause ensued.[28] It was widely agreed that slaves as articles of commerce were "imports" and thus subject to taxation.[29] The primary disagreement concerned whether this clause allowed for the taxation of free immigrants admitted to the United States.[30]

One might argue that constitutional limits on Congress regulating the "Migration or Importation" of persons by implication authorizes the power to regulate the migration or importation of persons after 1808. The framers, however, seem to have intended the Migration and Importation Clause to limit as a primary matter congressional power to end the importation of slaves, not to afford the national government the general power to regulate migration.

d.   War Power and the National Government's Obligation to Protect the States Against Invasion

Under Article I, § 8, clause 11, Congress possesses the authority "[t]o declare War." The Supreme Court has held that the so-called War Power authorizes federal laws providing for the exclusion and expulsion of "enemy aliens," such as through the Alien and Sedition Acts of the 1790s.[31] The Court has upheld the constitution-

---

[26] *See* Rhonda v. Magee, *Slavery as Immigration?*, 44 U.S.F. L. Rev. 273 (2009) (analyzing Article I, § 9, cl. 1 of the U.S. Constitution from an immigration perspective). For analysis of the clause, see David B. Davis, The Problem of Slavery in the Age of Revolution, 1770–1823, at 119–31 (1975); Walter Berns, *The Constitution and the Migration of Slaves*, 78 Yale L.J. 198 (1968).

[27] *See* Act of March 2, 1807, Ch. 22, 2 Stat. 425.

[28] Bilder, *supra* note 23, at 787 (reviewing different views at the time of the framing of the Constitution of the meaning of the Migration and Importation Clause).

[29] *See id.* at 784.

[30] Some delegates to the constitutional convention, including James Madison, believed that this clause only governed the importation of slaves. *See id.* at 785. In contrast, Luther Martin and Gouverneur Morris stated that, even if the framers intended it only to apply to slaves, the text of the Migration and Importation Clause would allow for the taxation of all immigrants. *See id.* at 787.

[31] *See* Kevin R. Johnson, *The Antiterrorism Act, the Immigration Reform Act, and Ideological Regulation in the Immigration Laws: Important Lessons for Citizens and Noncitizens*, 28 St. Mary's L.J. 833, 865–69 (1997); *see also* Gregory Fehlings, *Storm on the Constitution: The First Deportation Law*, 10 Tulsa J. Comp. & Int'l L. 63, 63–70 (2002) (analyzing congressional passage of the Alien and Sedition Acts); Jules Lobel, *The War on Terrorism and Civil Liberties*, 63 U. Pitt. L. Rev. 767, 767–70 (2002) (observing that the Alien and Sedition Acts were the first laws that allowed Presidents to exercise the deportation power); Robert R. Reinstein, *Foreword: Balancing Security and Liberty in the New*

ality of such laws.[32]

Dissenting in *The Passenger Cases*,[33] Justice Daniel conceded that the War Power Clause authorizes Congress to regulate "alien enemies" — i.e., nationals of countries with which the United States is at war, but doubted whether it could justify the general regulation of immigration. As Justice Daniel observed, there are limits on the War Power as a justification for immigration regulation by the federal government. Namely, only a small number of a nation's admissions and deportations truly implicate the specter of war.

Related to the War Power, the federal government owes a duty to the states under Article IV § 4 of the Constitution: "The United States shall . . . protect each [State] against Invasion . . . ." Some observers have claimed that this effectively requires the national government to regulate immigration.[34] In response to, among other things, concerns over the costs of immigration, several states in recent years have unsuccessfully sought to invoke the Invasion Clause in actions against the federal government for allegedly failing to effectively enforce the immigration laws. California, for example, sued the federal government for alleged violation of Article IV to recover monies paid in emergency medical care, criminal incarceration, parole supervision, and education as the result of an "invasion" of immigrants into the state.[35] Other states have brought similar unsuccessful claims against the federal government.[36]

One might argue that the federal government must be permitted to regulate immigration in order to fulfill its obligations to the states under the Invasion Clause. This, of course, implicitly treats all migrants as unwanted "invaders" and plays into the popular conception of immigrants as a social problem. *See* Chs. 1 and 2.

Century, 14 TEMP. POL. & CIV. RTS. L. 329, 33 (2005) (asserting that Congress passed the Alien and Sedition Acts because the Federalists feared that immigrants were disloyal to the United States). *See generally* JOHN C. MILLER, CRISIS IN FREEDOM: THE ALIEN AND SEDITION LAWS (1951) (analyzing history surrounding the enactment of the Alien and Sedition laws); JAMES MORTON SMITH, FREEDOM'S FETTERS: THE ALIEN AND SEDITION LAWS AND AMERICAN CIVIL LIBERTIES (1956) (to the same effect).

[32] *See, e.g.*, Ludecke v. Watkins, 335 U.S. 160 (1948). For analysis of the national security rationale for the plenary power doctrine immunizing the immigration laws from judicial review, see Matthew J. Lindsay, *Immigration, Sovereignty, and the Constitution of Foreignness*, 45 CONN. L. REV. 743 (2013); Matthew J. Lindsay, *Immigration as Invasion: Sovereignty, Security, and the Origins of the Federal Immigration Power*, 45 HARV. C.R.-C.L. L. REV. 1, 3 (2010).

[33] 48 U.S. (7 How.) 283, 509–10 (1849) (Daniel, J., dissenting).

[34] *See* Melissa Blair, Comment, *Terrorism, America's Porous Borders, and the Role of the Invasion Clause Post-9/11/2011*, 87 MARQ. L. REV. 167 (2003); Heather Dwyer, Note & Comment, *The State War Power: A Forgotten Constitutional Clause*, 33 U. LA VERNE L. REV. 319, 337–39 (2012); Justin C. Glon, Note, *"Good Fences Make Good Neighbors": National Security and Terrorism — Time to Fence in Our Southern Border*, 15 IND. INT'L & COMP. L. REV. 349, 386–87 (2005).

[35] *See* California v. United States, 104 F.3d 1086, 1089–90 & n.3 (9th Cir. 1997) (holding that the claim against the U.S. government under the Invasion Clause was a nonjusticiable political question).

[36] *See* Arizona v. United States, 104 F.3d 1095, 1096 (9th Cir. 1997), *cert. denied*, 522 U.S. 806 (1997); New Jersey v. United States, 91 F.3d 463, 468–69 (3d Cir. 1996); Padavan v. United States, 82 F.3d 23, 28 (2d Cir. 1996); Chiles v. United States, 69 F.3d 1094 (11th Cir. 1995), *cert. denied*, 517 U.S. 1188 (1996); People of Colo. *ex rel.* Suthers v. Gonzales, 558 F. Supp. 2d 1158 (D. Colo. 2007); *see also* Texas v. United States, 106 F.3d 661 (5th Cir. 1997) (seeking federal monies based on alleged constitutional and statutory violations resulting from the failure of the U.S. government to adequately enforce the immigration laws).

Ultimately, it seems a stretch to claim that the War and Invasion Clauses of the U.S. Constitution provide the general constitutional authorization to Congress to regulate immigration. Some immigration decisions may impact U.S. relations with nations with which it is at war and may combat unwanted "invasions." Most such decisions do not implicate war and invasion, however.

e. Immigration-Related Provisions in the Contemporary Public Debate

Two provisions of the Constitution that touch on immigration and nationality have been in the news in recent years. Neither provide much of an argument that the national government has the broad power to regulate immigration.

Article II, § I, clause 5 provides that "[n]o Person except a natural born Citizen . . . shall be eligible to the Office of the President."[37] This is the only constitutionally compelled "natural born" citizenship requirement for a U.S. government office, which Robert Post has identified as the "worst" provision of the Constitution.[38] *See* Ch. 17.

The "natural born Citizen" requirement for President emerged as a bone of contention in the 2008 presidential election. Republican nominee Senator John McCain's eligibility to be President was questioned because he was born in the Panama Canal Zone, not the territorial United States.[39] The provision subsequently became a much more contentious issue as some vocal opponents of the candidacy of Senator Barack Obama, whose father was Kenyan, claimed that he was not in fact

---

[37] Charles Gordon, *Who Can Be President of the United States: The Unresolved Enigma*, 28 Md. L. Rev. 1 (1968) is the classic analyses of this constitutional provision. Much of the contemporary attention to the issue comes from public discussion of the ineligibility for the Presidency of former California Governor Arnold Schwarzenegger, an immigrant from Austria. *See, e.g.*, Sarah Helene Duggin & Mary Beth Collins, *"Natural Born" in the USA: The Striking Unfairness and Dangerous Ambiguity of the Constitution's Presidential Qualifications Clause and Why We Need to Fix It*, 85 B.U. L. Rev. 53 (2005); Lawrence Friedman, *An Idea Whose Time Has Come — The Curious History, Uncertain Effect, and the Need for Amendment of the "Natural Born Citizen" Requirement for the Presidency*, 52 St. Louis L.J. 137 (2007); William T. Han, *Beyond Presidential Eligibility: The Natural Born Citizen Clause as a Source of Birthright Citizenship*, 58 Drake L. Rev. 457 (2010); Christina S. Lohman, *Presidential Eligibility: The Meaning of the Natural-Born Citizen Requirement: Globalization as the Impetus and the Obstacle*, 81 Chi.-Kent L. Rev. 275 (2006); Claudine Pease-Wingenter, *Empowering Our Children to Dream Without Limitations: A Call to Revisit the "Natural Born Citizen" Requirement in the Obama Era*, 29 Chicana/o-Latina/o L. Rev. 43 (2010); John R. Hein, Comment, *Born in the U.S.A., but Not Natural Born: How Congressional Territorial Policy Bars Native-Born Puerto Ricans from the Presidency*, 11 U. Pa. J. Const. L. 423 (2009); Andrew D. Miller, Note, *Terminating the "Just Not American Enough" Idea: Saying "Hasta La Vista" to the Natural-Born-Citizen Requirement of Presidential Eligibility*, 57 Syr. L. Rev. 97 (2006).

[38] *See* Robert Post, *What Is the Constitution's Worst Provision?*, 12 Const. Commentary 191 (1995).

[39] *See* Gabriel J. Chin, *Why Senator John McCain Cannot Be President: Eleven Months and a Hundred Yards Short of Citizenship*, 107 Mich. L. Rev. First Impressions 1 (2008), *available at* http://www.michiganlawreview.org/articles/why-senator-john-mccain-cannot-be-president-eleven-months-and-a-hundred-yards-short-of-citizenship. At least two lawsuits unsuccessfully challenged Senator McCain's eligibility for the Presidency. *See* Inland Empire Voters v. United States, 1st Amended Complaint for Declaratory Relief, Civil Action ED CV 08-00304 SGL (Opx) (C.D. Cal. filed Mar. 31, 2008); Hollander v. McCain, First Amended Complaint, Civil Action No. 1:08-cv-99-JL (D. N.H. filed Apr. 3, 2008).

born in Hawaii, is not a U.S. citizen by birth, and thus was ineligible for the Presidency.[40] Indeed, the election of President Barack Obama saw the emergence of the full blown "birther" movement.[41] The birthers' accusations spurred President Obama to provide proof of his birth in Hawaii.[42]

Another provision of the Constitution dealing with citizenship grew out of one of the constitutional amendments that ended slavery in the United States. Section 1 of the Fourteenth Amendment provides that "[a]ll persons born or naturalized in the United States, and subject to the jurisdiction thereof, are citizens of the United States and of the state wherein they reside." *See* Ch. 17. This provision ensures full national citizenship of the United States to *all* persons born in the United States as well as those who have naturalized. It was a response to the denial of citizenship to freed slaves under *Dred Scott v. Sandford*,[43] a Supreme Court decision that figured prominently in the outbreak of the American Civil War.

The traditional rule under the Fourteenth Amendment has been that any person born in the United States — whatever the immigration status of the parents — is a U.S. citizen.[44] The rule, which has come under attack, *see* Chapter 17, means that children of undocumented immigrants born in the United States are citizens.

---

[40] *See* Stephen Parks, *The Birthers' Attacks and the Judiciary's Article III "Defense" of the Obama Presidency*, 38 S.U. L. Rev. 179 (2011); *see, e.g.*, Barnett v. Obama, 2009 U.S. Dist. LEXIS 101206 (C.D. Cal. 2009) (dismissing suit alleging that President Obama did not meet the constitutional natural born citizen qualification required to be President).

[41] *See, e.g.*, *The Birthers*, *available at* www.birthers.org, (last visited July 14, 2014); Frank Rich, *The Obama Haters' Silent Enablers*, N.Y. Times, June 14, 2009, at WK8; Samuel Freedman, *In Untruths About Obama, Echoes of a Distant Time*, N.Y. Times, Nov. 1, 2008, at A21. For analysis of the social and political significance of the birther movement, see Kevin R. Johnson, *Immigration and Civil Rights: Is the "New" Birmingham the Same as the "Old" Birmingham?*, 21 Wm. & Mary Bill Rts. J. 367, 382–83 (2012).

[42] *See Birthers Unconvinced by Obama's Certificate*, National Pub. Radio, Apr. 28, 2011, *available at* http://www.npr.org/2011/04/28/135808711/birthers-unconvinced-by-obamas-certificate (last visited July 14, 2014).

[43] *See* Dred Scott v. Sandford, 60 U.S. (19 How.) 393 (1857).

[44] *See* United States v. Wong Kim Ark, 169 U.S. 649 (1898); Garrett Epps, *The Citizenship Clause, A "Legislative History"*, 60 Am. U. L. Rev. 331 (2011). For a summary of the ongoing contemporary dispute over birthright citizenship, see Ch. 17. *Compare* John C. Eastman, *Born in the U.S.A.? Rethinking Birthright Citizenship in the Wake of 9/11*, 42 U. Rich. L. Rev. 955 (2008) (calling for rethinking of interpretation of 14th Amendment's birthright citizenship clause), with James C. Ho, *Birthright Citizenship, The Fourteenth Amendment, and State Authority*, 42 U. Rich. L. Rev. 969 (2008) (defending birthright citizenship). *See* James C. Ho, *"American": Birthright Citizenship and the Original Understanding of the 14th Amendment*, 9 Green Bag 2d 367 (2006); Angela Kim, *The Growing Movement to Redefine Birthright Citizenship and the Fourteenth Amendment*, 25 Geo. Immigr. L.J. 757 (2011); Rachel E. Rosenbloom, *Policing the Borders of Birthright Citizenship: Some Thoughts on the New (and Old) Restrictionism*, 51 Washburn. L.J. 311 (2012); *see also* Matthew Ing, *Birthright Citizenship, Illegal Aliens, and the Original Meaning of the Citizenship Clause*, 45 Akron L. Rev. 719, 768 (2012) (arguing that U.S.-born children of undocumented immigrants are constitutionally entitled to birthright citizenship); Gerald L. Neuman, *Back to Dred Scott?*, 24 San Diego L. Rev. 485 (1987) (book review) (reviewing critically Peter H. Schuck & Rogers M. Smith, Citizenship Without Consent: Illegal Aliens in the American Polity (1985)), which re-evaluates birthright citizenship); Mark Shawhan, *"By Virtue of Being Born Here": Birthright Citizenship and the Civil Right Act of 1866*, 15 Harv. Latino L. Rev. 1 (2012) (analyzing the debates over the Citizenship Clause and defending birthright citizenship).

f. Summary

Nothing in the U.S. Constitution clearly enumerates the federal power to regulate immigration. Nonetheless, federal regulation of immigration continues. Contemporary state and local immigration enforcement efforts have provoked great controversy. The Supreme Court has placed limits on the states, most recently in *Arizona v. United States*,[45] to prevent intrusion on the federal power to regulate immigration. *See* Ch. 4.

However, the naturalization, commerce, and war and related powers afforded to Congress under Article I, in combination offer generalized support for congressional regulation of immigration. These powers, together with the foreign affairs and sovereign powers inherent in the U.S. Constitution (discussed below), offer sensible practical arguments supporting the congressional power to regulate immigration.

2. Implied Powers

a. Foreign Affairs Power

Commentators often refer to the Executive Branch's implied power over foreign affairs to authorize federal regulation of immigration.[46] The Supreme Court has at times as well. In *Chae Chan Ping v. United States* (The Chinese Exclusion Case),[47] the Court in 1889 invoked the national government's power over foreign affairs as the constitutional basis of its power to regulate immigration and upheld a federal immigration law that, among other things, excluded most immigrants from China from American shores. *See* Chs. 2, 6. In the words of Justice Field, "the United States, in their *relation to foreign countries* and their subjects or citizens, are one nation, invested with powers which belong to independent nations. . . . [F]or national purposes, embracing our *relations with foreign nations*, we are but one

---

[45] 132 S. Ct. 2492 (2012).

[46] *See, e.g.,* Raquel Aldana, *The September 11 Immigration Detentions and Unconstitutional Executive Legislation*, 29 S. Ill. U. L.J. 5, 14–21 (2005); Erin J. Delaney, *Justifying Power: Federalism, Immigration, and "Foreign Affairs"*, 8 Duke J. Const. Law & Pub. Pol'y 153 (2013); Anne Y. Lee, *The Unfettered Executive: Is There an Inherent Presidential Power to Exclude Aliens?*, 39 Colum. J.L. & Soc. Probs. 223, 245–48 (2005); Nancy E. Powell, *The Supreme Court as Interpreter of Executive Foreign Affairs Power*, 3 Conn. J. Int'l L. 161, 184–87 (1987). *See generally* Adam B. Cox & Cristina M. Rodríguez, *The President and Immigration Law*, 119 Yale L.J. 458 (2009) (analyzing the inherent executive authority over immigration and the critical immigration policy-making role of the President). For analysis of Presidential power over immigration in connection with the Deferred Action for Childhood Arrivals (DACA) program, which is discussed in Chapter 12, see Lauren Gilbert, *Obama's Ruby Slippers: Enforcement Discretion in the Absence of Immigration Reform*, 116 W. Va. L. Rev. 355 (2013); Peter Margulies, *Taking Care of Immigration Law: Presidential Stewardship, Prosecutorial Discretion, and Separation of Powers*, 94 B.U.L. Rev. 105 (2013). *Compare* Robert J. Delahunty & John C. Yoo, *Dream On: The Obama Administration's Nonenforcement of Immigration Laws, the DREAM Act, and the Take Care Clause*, 91 Tex. L. Rev. 781, 784–85, 856 (2013) (arguing that by authorizing the DACA program, President Obama breached his responsibility to faithfully enforce the immigration laws), *with* Shoba Sivaprasad Wadhia, *In Defense of DACA, Deferred Action, and the DREAM Act*, 91 Tex. L. Rev. See Also 59, 62–68 (2013) (defending the program as consistent with the exercise of prosecutorial discretion by the Executive Branch in the immigration matters), *available at* http://www.texaslrev.com/wp-content/uploads/Wadhia.pdf (last visited July 7, 2014).

[47] 130 U.S. 581, 609 (1889).

people, one nation, one power."[48] The Court further explained that "[t]he power of exclusion of foreigners [is] *an incident of sovereignty belonging to the government of the United States, as a part of those sovereign powers delegated by the Constitution . . . ."*[49] and emphasized

> [t]hat the government of the United States . . . can exclude aliens from its territory is a proposition which we do not think open to controversy. *Jurisdiction over its own territory to that extent is an incident of every independent nation. It is a part of its independence. If it could not exclude aliens, it would be to that extent subject to the control of another power.*[50]

The Constitution fails to expressly enumerate the foreign affairs power of the national government.[51] However, in *United States v. Curtiss-Wright Export Corp.*,[52] the Supreme Court recognized the national government's *inherent* sovereign power over foreign affairs. Although commentators have questioned *Curtiss-Wright*,[53] almost all agree that the national government possesses some foreign affairs power.

The federal government's exclusive power to conduct foreign affairs has led courts to invalidate *state* statutes that attempt to regulate immigration. The classic statement of that position is found in the 1875 decision of *Chy Lung v. Freeman*:

> The passage of laws which concern the admission of citizens and subjects of foreign nations to our shores belongs to Congress, and not to the States. It has the power to regulate commerce with foreign nations; the responsibility for the character of those regulations, and for the manner of their execution, belongs solely to the national government. *If it be otherwise, a single State can, at her pleasure, embroil us in disastrous quarrels with other nations.*[54]

---

[48] *Id.* at 604, 606 (emphasis added).

[49] *Id.* at 609 (emphasis added).

[50] *Id.* at 603–04 (emphasis added).

[51] *See* LOUIS HENKIN, FOREIGN AFFAIRS AND THE CONSTITUTION 16–18 (1972); Curtis A. Bradley, *Executive Power Essentialism and Foreign Affairs*, 102 MICH. L. REV. 545, 660–64 (2004); David Gartner, *Foreign Relations, Strategic Doctrine, and Presidential Power*, 63 ALA. L. REV. 499 (2012); Saikrishna B. Prakash & Michael D. Ramsey, *The Executive Power over Foreign Affairs*, 111 YALE L.J. 231 (2001); Michael D. Ramsey, *The Power of the State in Foreign Affairs: The Original Understanding of Foreign Policy Federalism*, 75 NOTRE DAME L. REV. 341, 396–99 (1999); Michael D. Ramsey, *The Myth of Extraconstitutional Foreign Affairs Power*, 42 WM. & MARY L. REV. 379, 403–06 (2000); Michael P. Van Alstine, *Executive Aggrandizement in Foreign Affairs Lawmaking*, 54 UCLA L. REV. 309, 316–20 (2006).

[52] 299 U.S. 304, 315–18 (1936).

[53] *See* HENKIN, *supra* note 51, at 23–26; Cleveland, *supra* note 4; Malvinia Halberstam, *The Powers of Congress and the President on Matters that Affect U.S. Foreign Affairs*, 19 ILSA J. INT'L & COMP. L. 335 (2013); Charles A. Lofgren, United States v. Curtiss-Wright Export Corporation: *An Historical Reassessment*, 83 YALE L.J. 1 (1973); Richard F. Hahn, Note, *Constitutional Limits on the Power to Exclude Aliens*, 82 COLUM. L. REV. 995 (1982); *see also* Kimberly L. Fletcher, *The Court's Decisive Hand Shapes the Executive's Foreign Affairs Policymaking Power*, 73 MD. L. REV. 247 (2013) (analyzing the Supreme Court's role in defining executive power over foreign policy).

[54] 92 U.S. 275, 280 (1876) (emphasis added); *see* Hines v. Davidowitz, 312 U.S. 52, 62 (1941) (invalidating Pennsylvania's Alien Registration Act and emphasizing "[t]hat the supremacy of the national power in the general field of foreign affairs, including power over immigration, naturalization

Similarly, in *Nishimura Ekiu v. United States*,[55] the Supreme Court upheld the federal Immigration Act of 1891 and stated that

> [i]t is an accepted maxim of international law, that every sovereign nation has the power, as inherent in sovereignty, and essential to preservation, to forbid the entrance of foreigners within its dominions, or to admit them only in such cases and upon such conditions as it may see fit to prescribe. *In the United States, this power is vested in the national government, to which the Constitution has committed the entire control of international relations, in peace as well as in war.*

Most recently, in *Arizona v. United States*,[56] the Supreme Court in 2012 invalidated core provisions of a controversial state immigration enforcement law known as SB 1070 and emphasized that "the Government of the United States has *broad, undoubted power* over the subject of immigration and the status of aliens. *This authority rests, in part, on the National Government's . . . inherent power as sovereign to control and conduct relations with foreign nations.*" The Court elaborated:

> [t]he federal power to determine immigration policy is well settled. Immigration policy can affect trade, investment, tourism, and diplomatic relations for the entire Nation, as well as the perceptions and expectations of aliens in this country who seek the full protection of its laws. . . . Perceived mistreatment of aliens in the United States may lead to harmful reciprocal treatment of American citizens abroad. . . .
>
>   It is fundamental that foreign countries concerned about the status, safety, and security of their nationals in the United States must be able to confer and communicate on this subject with one national sovereign, not the 50 separate States. This Court has reaffirmed that "[o]ne of the most important and delicate of all international relationships . . . has to do with the protection of the just rights of a country's own nationals when those nationals are in another country." . . .
>
> Federal governance of immigration and alien status is extensive and complex. . . . [57]

As *Arizona v. United States* demonstrates, the Supreme Court continues to rely on the foreign relations power as a justification for the federal exercise of authority over immigration.[58] In another important decision, *Sale v. Haitian Centers Council,*

---

and deportation, is made clear by the Constitution, was pointed out by the authors of the Federalist in 1787, and has since been given continuous recognition by this Court") (footnotes omitted).

[55]   142 U.S. 651, 658 (1892) (emphasis added).

[56]   Arizona v. United States, 132 S. Ct. 2492, 2498 (2012) (emphasis added) (citations omitted).

[57]   *Id.* at 2498–99 (citations omitted).

[58]   *See, e.g.,* INS v. Aguirre-Aguirre, 526 U.S. 415, 425 (1999) ("We have recognized that judicial deference to the Executive Branch is *especially appropriate in the context where officials 'exercise especially sensitive political functions that implicate questions of foreign relations.'*") (citation omitted) (emphasis added); Mathews v. Diaz, 426 U.S. 67, 81 (1976) (to the same effect); *see also* Harisiades v. Shaughnessy, 342 U.S. 580, 588–89 (1952) (noting that immigration policy is "virtually and intricately interwoven" with foreign relations, war power, and maintenance of a republican form of government).

Inc.,[59] the Court cited *United States v. Curtiss-Wright Export Corp.* and upheld the U.S. government's interdiction of Haitians on the high seas, rejecting arguments that the interdiction program violated international and domestic law; in so doing, the Court emphasized that "we are construing treaty and statutory provisions that may involve *foreign and military affairs* for which the President has unique responsibility."

b. Necessity and Structural Justifications

One leading immigration law casebook suggests that the federal power over immigration is necessary to the successful operation of the constitutional framework and thus must be implied into the Constitution:

> The primary purpose of the Constitution is to establish a system of government for a nation, a nation encompassing territory and members ("citizens"). A system of government is the process by which citizens establish rules of conduct for persons within the territory. From these premises, two sorts of structural arguments may follow.
>
> *First, to be a sovereign nation, a people must have control over their territory.* A nation of open borders runs the risk of not being able to govern itself because its sovereignty, to some extent, is in the hands of the other nations of the world. It seems reasonable to believe that the persons who wrote and ratified the Constitution thought (or hoped) they were creating a nation that would be able to take its place among other nations as an equal; one that would possess the powers of sovereignty generally possessed by all other nations. *Second, the relationship of the citizen to the nation is crucial.* Citizens, through the process of government, argue about, protect and further values. Immigration decisions give citizens the ability to regulate who the participants in the discussion will be. By deciding whom we permit to enter the country, we say much about who we are as a nation.
>
> Thus, we have identified two kinds of structural arguments to justify the immigration power, one based on *self-preservation*, the other on *self-definition.*[60]

There arguably is no real alternative but for the federal government to regulate immigration — especially in the modern world with relatively easy travel and heavy demand for migration to the United States. Although it is true that federal immigration regulation did not exist in its current form for the first century of the nation's existence,[61] times, as they say, have changed. We today have a nation that no longer focuses primarily on promoting settlement of the great frontier in its

---

[59] 509 U.S. 155, 188 (1993) (emphasis added); *see* Harold Hongju Koh, *The Human Face of the Haitian Interdiction Program,* 33 VA. J. INT'L L. 483, 487 (1993) (characterizing the policy of the U.S. government as "not only lawless, but also heartless and mindless"); Harold Hongju Koh, *Reflections on Refoulment and Haitian Centers Council,* 35 HARV. INT'L L.J. 1 (1994) (to the same effect).

[60] T. ALEXANDER ALEINIKOFF, DAVID A. MARTIN, HIROSHI MOTOMURA & MARYELLEN FULLERTON, IMMIGRATION AND CITIZENSHIP: PROCESS AND POLICY 193–94 (7th ed. 2012) (emphasis added).

[61] *See* Neuman, *supra* note 8, at 1833–34.

migration laws and policies. Nor is the movement of people, generally speaking, nearly as difficult and rare as it was in the past. One might reasonably pose the question what choice is there today but for the national government to regulate immigration?

It is difficult to dispute that the need for sovereign control over borders to ensure the existence of the nation as well as the power to define a national identity, are legitimate goals for the national government. Whatever their common-sense appeal, however, the powers to pursue these goals are not expressly enumerated in the U.S. Constitution.

B.   THE SCOPE OF THE FEDERAL POWER TO REGULATE IMMIGRATION

In the last decades of the nineteenth century, Congress passed laws that comprehensively regulated immigration. By the end of the century, the federal government firmly was in charge of immigration regulation and states had been effectively removed from much of a role in that arena.

Despite the lack of clear constitutional authority to regulate immigration, the Supreme Court has declared the scope of the federal power to regulate immigration to be broad and expansive, with a limited role of the Judiciary in reviewing the immigration laws passed by Congress and the implementation by the Executive Branch.

1.   The Plenary Power Doctrine

The judicially created "plenary power" doctrine emerged originally to shield from judicial review the laws greatly limiting Chinese immigration in the late nineteenth century. It continues to protect from judicial scrutiny the substantive decisions of Congress on immigration admissions and removal criteria.

In *The Chinese Exclusion Case*,[62] the Supreme Court rejected a constitutional challenge to the Chinese Exclusion Act and emphasized that courts lack power to review congressional exercise of its "plenary power" over immigration. Note that, although it is difficult to identify the specific authority in the text of the Constitution for Congress to regulate immigration, the Court nevertheless recognizes that power and, at the same time, concludes that the immigration laws are not subject to ordinary judicial review.

---

[62] Chae Chin Ping v. United States (*The Chinese Exclusion Case*), 130 U.S. 581, 609 (1889). *See generally* Gabriel J. Chin, Chae Chan Ping *and* Fong Yue Tin: *The Origins of Plenary Power in* IMMIGRATION STORIES 7 (David A. Martin & Peter H. Schuck ed., 2005). Although the conventional wisdom is that the Chinese exclusion laws culminated the federalization of the immigration laws, one commentator argues that "[t]he regulation of marriage and morality played a pivotal role in the federalization of immigration law." Kerry Abrams, *Polygamy, Prostitution, and the Federalization of Immigration Law,* 105 COLUM. L. REV. 641, 642 (2005); *see also* Matthew Lindsay, *Preserving the Exceptional Republic: Political Economy, Race, and the Federalization of American Immigration Law,* 17 YALE J.L. & HUMANITIES 181 (2005) (analyzing the factors contributing to federalization of immigration law).

Scholars have consistently criticized the plenary power doctrine, which allows noncitizens to be treated in ways that would be unconstitutional if they were citizens.[63] *See* Ch. 6. To date, there have been no successful challenges to laws passed by Congress that refuse admission to certain classes of noncitizens or authorize the removal of specific categories of noncitizens from the country.

Under the plenary power doctrine, *see* Chapter 6, the courts generally defer to the political branches of government on immigration matters. In 1977, the Supreme Court stated unequivocally that: "[t]his Court has repeatedly emphasized that 'over no conceivable subject is the legislative power of Congress more complete than it is over' the admission of aliens."[64] The Court, for example, has upheld exclusions and deportations of noncitizens of certain races and nationalities, as well as those with particular political views (including views protected by the First Amendment if held by U.S. citizens in the United States), and has permitted indefinite detention of immigrants.[65] The Supreme Court aggressively invoked the plenary power doctrine during the Cold War to shield from judicial review some particularly harsh immigration admissions decisions.[66]

Three immigration cases decided by the Supreme Court in 2001 suggested the decline of the plenary power doctrine. In *Zadvydas v. Davis*,[67] the Court refused to invoke the doctrine to shield from review the Executive Branch's indefinite detention of noncitizens awaiting deportation from the United States. Stating that the power of Congress over immigration is "subject to important constitutional limitations,"[68] the Court decided the case on statutory grounds and held that a reasonable time limitation on post-removal detention must be inferred into the statute because "a statute permitting indefinite detention would raise a serious constitutional problem."[69] In the same Term, the Court emphasized that Congress must clearly state the elimination of judicial review of removal orders and, because it had not (and because to do so would raise "serious constitutional questions"), refused to read 1996 reform legislation as eliminating habeas corpus review of a

---

[63] For criticism of the plenary power doctrine, see T. ALEXANDER ALEINIKOFF, SEMBLANCES OF SOVEREIGNTY: THE CONSTITUTION, THE STATE, & AMERICAN CITIZENSHIP (2002); GERALD L. NEUMAN, STRANGERS TO THE CONSTITUTION: IMMIGRANTS, BORDERS, & FUNDAMENTAL LAW (1996); Kif Augustine-Adams, *Plenary Power Doctrine After September 11*, 38 UC DAVIS L. REV. 701 (2005); Gabriel J. Chin, *Segregation's Last Stronghold: Race, Discrimination and the Constitutional Law of Immigration*, 46 UCLA L. REV. 1 (1998); Stephen H. Legomsky, *Immigration Law and the Principal of Plenary Congressional Power,* 1984 S. CT. REV. 255.

[64] Fiallo v. Bell, 430 U.S. 787, 792 (1977) (quoting Oceanic Navigation Co. v. Stranahan, 214 U.S. 320, 339 (1909)).

[65] *See, e.g.*, Chae Chin Ping v. United States (*The Chinese Exclusion Case*), 130 U.S. 581, 609 (1889) (refusing to disturb Chinese exclusion law); Harisiades v. Shaughnessy, 342 U.S. 580 (1952) (upholding deportation of former Communist party members).

[66] *See, e.g.*, United States *ex rel.* Knauff v. Shaughnessy, 338 U.S. 537, 546–47 (1950) (refusing to admit the wife of a U.S. citizen based on secret evidence); Shaughnessy v. United States *ex rel.* Mezei, 345 U.S. 206, 215–16 (1953) (allowing long term lawful permanent resident to be subject to indefinite detention based on secret evidence upon seeking reentry into the United States).

[67] 533 U.S. 678, 695–96 (2001).

[68] *Id.* at 695.

[69] *Id.* at 690.

removal order.[70] Finally, in *Nguyen v. INS*,[71] the Court upheld a distinction in the award of citizenship in the Immigration and Nationality Act between illegitimate children of U.S. citizen fathers and mothers but applied the same constitutional scrutiny that it applies to other gender classifications. The Court declined to address the "wide deference accorded to Congress in the exercise of its immigration and naturalization power."[72]

Outside the immigration laws, the Court has not hesitated to invalidate distinctions based on gender stereotypes.[73] However, an equally divided 4-4 Court[74] in 2011 in *Flores-Villar v. United States* affirmed a court of appeals ruling that upheld different standards for children born out of wedlock outside of the United States to obtain U.S. citizenship, resting on whether the child's mother or father was a U.S. citizen.[75] It is one of several occasions in which the Court in recent years has grappled with the constitutionality of gender-based distinctions in the immigration and nationality laws.[76] At least four Justices apparently rejected application of the plenary power doctrine to shield the law in question from judicial review and would have struck down the gender-based distinction. The fact that the Supreme Court was equally divided in *Flores-Villar v. United States* places in doubt the future of the plenary power doctrine.

At various times, some immigration scholars declared that the plenary power doctrine was in decline.[77] However, after the events of September 11, 2001, the Bush administration relied on the doctrine to justify the "special registration" program directed at Arab and Muslim noncitizens.[78] The Attorney General

---

[70] *See* INS v. St. Cyr, 533 U.S. 289, 310–14 (2001).

[71] 533 U.S. 53 (2001).

[72] *Id.* at 72–73.

[73] *See, e.g.*, United States v. Virginia, 518 U.S. 515 (1996) (striking down Virginia Military Institute's male-only admission policy); Mississippi Univ. for Women v. Hogan, 458 U.S. 718 (1982) (invalidating the university's single sex admission policy).

[74] Flores-Villar v. United States, 131 S. Ct. 2312 (2011).

[75] *See* United States v. Flores-Villar, 536 F.3d 990, 994–98 (9th Cir. 2008).

[76] *See* Nguyen v. INS, 533 U.S. 53 (2001) (upholding a U.S. citizenship provision favoring illegitimate children of naturalized mothers over fathers); Miller v. Albright, 523 U.S. 420 (1998) (to the same effect); *see also* Pierre v. Holder, 588 F.3d 767 (2d Cir. 2009) (rejecting the claim that gender discrimination in U.S. nationality law violated the Equal Protection Clause). For analysis of the Supreme Court decisions in this area, see Albertina Antognini, *From Citizenship to Custody: Unwed Fathers Abroad and at Home*, 36 HARV. J. L. & GENDER 405 (2013); Nina Pillard, *Plenary Power Underground in* Nguyen v. INS: *A Response to Professor Spiro*, 16 GEO. IMMIGR. L.J. 835 (2002); Jessica Portmess, Comment, *Until the Plenary Power Do Us Part: Judicial Scrutiny of the Defense of Marriage Act in Immigration After* Flores-Villar, 61 AM. U.L. REV. 1825 (2012). The genesis of the gender-based nationality distinctions as part of an effort to enforce racial exclusions in the immigration laws is discussed in Kristin A. Collins, *Illegitimate Borders: Jus Sanguinis Citizenship and the Legal Construction of Family, Race, and Nation*, 123 YALE L.J. 2134 (2014).

[77] *See, e.g.*, Gabriel J. Chin, *Is There a Plenary Power Doctrine? A Tentative Apology and Prediction for Our Strange but Unexceptional Constitutional Immigration Law*, 14 GEO. IMMIGR. L.J. 257 (2000); Cornelia T.L. Pillard & T. Alexander Aleinikoff, *Skeptical Scrutiny of Plenary Power: Judicial and Executive Branch Decision Making in* Miller v. Albright, 1998 SUP. CT. REV. 1 (1998); Peter J. Spiro, *Explaining the End of Plenary Power*, 16 GEO. IMMIGR. L.J. 339 (2002).

[78] *See, e.g.*, Registration and Monitoring of Certain Nonimmigrants, 67 Fed. Reg. 52,584 (Aug. 12,

explained that "[t]he political branches of the government have plenary authority in the immigration area."[79] In addition, the Supreme Court subtly moved in a similar direction after September 11. In *Demore v. Kim*,[80] the Court backed away from a 2001 decision and upheld the mandatory detention of certain noncitizens pending their deportation and emphasized that the "this Court has firmly and repeatedly endorsed the proposition that Congress may make rules as to aliens that would be unacceptable if applied to citizens."

Besides applying the plenary power doctrine to the review of admission and removal criteria in the immigration laws, the Supreme Court has invoked the doctrine to immunize from judicial review federal laws that discriminate against immigrants residing in the United States. For example, in finding that Congress could limit the eligibility of lawful immigrants for a federal medical benefits program, the Court emphasized that

> [i]n the exercise of its broad power over naturalization and immigration, Congress regularly makes rules that would be unacceptable if applied to citizens. The exclusion of aliens and the reservation of the power to deport have no permissible counterpart in the Federal Government's power to regulate the conduct of its own citizenry. The fact that an Act of Congress treats aliens differently from citizens does not itself imply that such disparate treatment is "invidious."[81]

In short, there is a long history of judicial deference to decisions by Congress and the Executive Branch on issues of immigrant admission and removal and allowing for differential treatment of immigrants and citizens. The courts ordinarily decline

---

2002) (requiring "special registration" of certain noncitizens from nations populated predominantly by Arabs and Muslims). The courts rejected legal challenges to the "special registration" program. *See* Kandamar v. Gonzales, 464 F.3d 65, 73–74 (1st Cir. 2006); Ahmed v. Gonzales, 447 F.3d 433, 439–40 (5th Cir. 2006); Ali v. Gonzales, 440 F.3d 678, 681–82 (5th Cir. 2006); Roudnahal v. Ridge, 310 F. Supp. 2d 884, 892 (N.D. Ohio 2003).

For general discussion of how contemporary U.S. immigration enforcement responds to national security concerns, see Ch. 14. For an overview of governmental actions after September 11, 2001 targeting Arab and Muslim citizens and noncitizens, see Susan M. Akram & Kevin R. Johnson, *Race, Civil Rights, and Immigration Law After September 11, 2001: The Targeting of Arabs and Muslims*, 58 NYU ANN. SURV. AM. L. 295 (2002); Susan M. Akram & Maritza Karmely, *Immigration and Constitutional Consequences of Post-9/11 Policies Involving Arabs and Muslims in the United States: Is Alienage a Distinction Without a Difference?*, 38 UC DAVIS L. REV. 609 (2005); Karen. C. Tumlin, Comment, *Suspect First: How Terrorism Policy Is Reshaping Immigration Policy*, 92 CAL. L. REV. 1173 (2004).

[79] 67 Fed. Reg. at 52, 585 (citing Fiallo v. Bell, 430 U.S. 787, 792 (1977); Mathews v. Diaz, 426 U.S. 67, 80–82 (1976)).

[80] 538 U.S. 510, 522 (2003) (citations omitted); *see* M. Isabel Medina, Demore v. Kim — *A Dance of Power and Human Rights*, 18 GEO. IMMIGR. L.J. 697 (2004) (criticizing the Court's decision in *Demore v. Kim*); Margaret H. Taylor, Demore v. Kim: *Judicial Deference to Congressional Folly, in* IMMIGRATION STORIES, *supra* note 123, at 343 (contending that the Supreme Court's decision in *Demore v. Kim* was a response to the "war on terror" after September 11, 2001 and that the Court was reluctant to interfere with the U.S. government's detention of noncitizens that it viewed to be a threat to public safety).

[81] Mathews v. Diaz, 426 U.S. 67, 79–80 (1976) (emphasis added) (footnotes omitted); *see, e.g.*, Demore v. Kim, 538 U.S. 510, 521–22 (2003) (quoting *Mathews v. Diaz*); Reno v. Flores, 507 U.S. 292, 305–06 (1993) (invoking the plenary power doctrine and upholding regulation limiting release from detention of juvenile noncitizens); Fiallo v. Bell, 430 U.S. 787, 792 (1977) (quoting *Mathews v. Diaz*).

to interfere with the substantive decisions of the political branches of government on immigration matters. As we shall see later in this Chapter, judicial intervention in the U.S. immigration laws has ordinarily been limited to ensuring that proper procedural protections, such as judicial review, are in place and that the Executive Branch properly interpreted the immigration laws.

At the same time, there is room for judicial review of the implementation of the immigration statute. In *McNary v. Haitian Refugee Center*,[82] for example, the Supreme Court held that challenges to the constitutionality of the practices of the Immigration and Naturalization Service were proper subjects for judicial review. Courts continue to review the practices of immigration authorities even though Congress has attempted to restrict judicial review. *See* Ch. 6. In 2001, the Court reiterated the "strong presumption in favor of judicial review of administrative action" and that, in arguing against judicial review of removal orders, the U.S. government must overcome "the longstanding rule requiring a clear statement of congressional intent to repeal habeas jurisdiction."[83]

2.   Federal Preemption of State and Local Immigration Enforcement Laws

Since the late nineteenth century, the federal government has comprehensively regulated immigration. The states previously had regulated migration into their jurisdictions in certain respects, with a particular emphasis on discouraging the poor and criminals from entering their respective jurisdictions.[84]

In recent years, the place of the states in immigration enforcement has emerged as an issue of contention. In *DeCanas v. Bica*,[85] the Supreme Court in 1976 held that federal law did not preempt a California law barring the employment of undocumented immigrants.[86] The Court nonetheless acknowledged that "[p]ower to regulate immigration is *unquestionably exlusively a federal power.*"[87] The Court reiterated federal primacy over immigration in 2011 but again, based on 1986 legislation, upheld a state law imposing sanctions on employers of undocumented immigrants.[88]

Increasingly, state and local governments have challenged federal primacy over immigration regulation. This trend began in a preliminary way in 1994, when

---

[82]   498 U.S. 479, 498–99 (1991).

[83]   INS v. St. Cyr, 533 U.S. 289, 298 (2001) (citations omitted).

[84]   *See* Neuman, *supra* note 8, at 1841–59.

[85]   424 U.S. 351, 364–65 (1976).

[86]   In 1986, Congress enacted the Immigration Reform and Control Act, Pub. L. No. 99-603, 100 Stat. 3359 (1986), which provides for the imposition of sanctions on employers of undocumented immigrants and expressly preempts most state laws in this area of immigration regulation. *See* Chs. 2, 14.

[87]   *DeCanas v. Bica*, 424 U.S. at 354 (citing *Passenger Cases*, 48 U.S. (7 How.) 283 (1849); Henderson v. Mayor of New York, 92 U.S. 259 (1876); Chy Lung v. Freeman, 92 U.S. 275 (1876); Fong Yue Ting v. United States, 149 U.S. 698 (1893)) (emphasis added).

[88]   *See* Chamber of Commerce v. Whiting, 131 S. Ct. 1968, 1970 (2011) (" '[P]ower to regulate immigration is unquestionably . . . a federal power.' ") (quoting DeCanas v. Bica, 424 U.S. 351, 354 (1976)).

California voters passed Proposition 187, a measure that effectively was found to regulate immigration by, among other steps, denying public benefits to undocumented immigrants.[89] A federal court struck down most of the measure as preempted by federal law.[90]

With the repeated failure of Congress to pass comprehensive immigration reform in the new millennium, state and local governments have increased their immigration enforcement efforts.[91] See Ch. 4. The weight of authority is on the side of federal preemption of state immigration enforcement laws.[92] In 2012, the

---

[89] See, e.g., Linda S. Bosniak, *Opposing Proposition 187: Undocumented Immigrants and the National Imagination,* 28 Conn. L. Rev. 555 (1996); Kevin R. Johnson, *An Essay on Immigration Politics, Popular Democracy, and California's Proposition 187: The Political Relevance and Legal Irrelevance of Race,* 70 Wash. L. Rev. 629, 646 (1995); Kevin R. Johnson, *Public Benefits and Immigration: The Intersection of Immigration Status, Ethnicity, Gender, and Class,* 42 UCLA L. Rev. 1509 (1995); Ruben J. Garcia, Comment, *Critical Race Theory and Proposition 187: The Racial Politics of Immigration Law,* 17 Chicano-Latino L. Rev. 138 (1995).

[90] See League of United Latin American Citizens v. Wilson, 997 F. Supp. 1244 (C.D. Cal. 1997).

[91] See Sosa Thomas, Comment, *"Mi Casa No Es Su Casa": How Far is Too Far When States and Localities Take Immigration Matters into Their Own Hands,* 29 Chicana/o-Latina/o L. Rev. 103, 109 (2010). For discussion of congressional efforts to pass comprehensive immigration reform, see Ch. 18.

[92] *Compare* City of Hazelton v. Lozano, 724 F.3d 297 (3d Cir. 2013), *cert. denied,* 134 S. Ct. 1491 (2014) (invalidating city immigration ordinance on federal preemption grounds), *with* Keller v. City of Fremont, 719 F.3d 931 (8th Cir. 2013), *cert. denied,* 134 S. Ct. 2140 (2014) (finding that local immigration enforcement ordinance was not preempted by federal law). For critical analysis of state and local attempts to regulate immigration, see Kevin R. Johnson, *Immigration and Civil Rights: State and Local Efforts to Regulate Immigration,* 46 Ga. L. Rev. 609 (2012); Michael A. Olivas, *Immigration-Related State and Local Ordinances: Preemption, Prejudice, and the Proper Role for Enforcement,* 2007 U. Chi. Legal F. 27; Huyen Pham, *The Inherent Flaws in the Inherent Authority Position: Why Inviting Local Enforcement of Immigration Laws Violates the Constitution,* 31 Fla. St. U.L. Rev. 965 (2004); Michael J. Wishnie, *Laboratories of Bigotry? Devolution of the Immigration Power, Equal Protection, and Federalism,* 76 NYU L. Rev 49 (2001); *see also* Jennifer M. Chacón, *The Transformation of Immigration Federalism,* 21 Wm. & Mary Bill Rts. J. 577 (2012) (outlining the Supreme Court's immigration federalism jurisprudence and discussing the Supreme Court's somewhat conflicting views about the role of states in immigration enforcement); Orde F. Kittrie, *Federalism, Deportation, and Crime Victims Afraid to Call the Police,* 91 Iowa L. Rev. 1449 (2006) (analyzing federalism issues raised in immigration enforcement); Michael A. Olivas, *Preempting Preemption: Foreign Affairs, State Rights, and Alienage Classifications,* 35 Va. J. Int'l L. 217 (1994) (arguing for adherence to the general rule that state regulation of immigration is preempted by federal law); *cf.* Rose Cuison Villazor, *What Is a "Sanctuary"?,* 61 SMU L. Rev. 133 (2008) (analyzing the "sanctuary" cities, which do not assist in federal immigration enforcement efforts, in the United States).

Some scholars have called for greater state and local involvement in immigration regulation. *See, e.g.,* Huntington, *supra* note 5; Kris W. Kobach, *The Quintessential Force Multiplier: The Inherent Authority of Local Police to Make Immigration Arrests,* 69 Alb. L. Rev. 179 (2005); Peter H. Schuck, *Taking Immigration Federalism Seriously,* 2007 U. Chi. Legal F. 57; Peter J. Spiro, *The States and Immigration in an Era of Demi-Sovereignties,* 35 Va. J. Int'l L. 121 (1994); *see also* Matthew Parlow, *A Localist's Case for Decentralizing Immigration Policy,* 84 Den. U. L. Rev. 1061 (2007) (contending that local governments should be permitted to regulate immigration in a manner consistent with federal immigration law and policy); David P. Weber, *State and Local Regulation of Immigration: The Need for a Bilateral (Reciprocal) Ratchet,* 18 ILSA J. Int'l & Comp. L. 707, 732–38 (2012) (proposing that states be given a role in shaping current immigration legislation); Brett Merritt, Note, *Collaborative Regulation: Cooperation Between State and Federal Governments Is Key to Successful Immigration Reform,* 66 Okla. L. Rev. 401, 423–29 (2014) (to similar effect). Analysis of the authority of states to adopt immigration enforcement measures after *Arizona v. United States* can be found in Lucas Guttentag,

Supreme Court in *Arizona v. United States*[93] struck down core provisions of a controversial Arizona immigration enforcement statute on federal preemption grounds.

One way of rationalizing the role of the two coordinate bodies of government with respect to immigration is to allow the federal government to regulate admission and removal of noncitizens and enforce the immigration laws with state and local assistance as authorized by the U.S. government. State and local governments also can play an important role in facilitating the integration of immigrants into American society.[94]

3.   Constitutional Protections for Immigrants

Noncitizens seeking entry into the United States at the border possess limited rights. Indeed, the Supreme Court in 1982 restated the essence of the plenary power doctrine that "an alien seeking initial admission has *no* constitutional rights regarding his application, for the power to admit or exclude aliens is a sovereign prerogative."[95] Generally speaking, noncitizens within the territory of the United States have more rights but not as many as U.S. citizens. Commentators have called for greater protection of the rights of immigrants residing in the United States.[96]

Immigration Preemption and the Limits of State Power: Reflections on Arizona v. United States, 9 STAN. J. CIV. RTS. & CIV. LIB. 1 (2013); Ch. 4.

[93] 132 S. Ct. 2492 (2012). For the contention that the plenary power doctrine, by reserving near-complete power to regulate immigration the federal government, serves to protect the rights of noncitizens by, and avoid negative foreign policy consequences resulting from, state immigration enforcement laws, see Mary Fan, *Rebellious State Crimmigration Enforcement and the Foreign Affairs Power*, 89 WASH. U.L. REV. 1269 (2012).

[94] *See* Cristina Rodríguez, *The Significance of the Local in Immigration Regulation*, 106 MICH. L. REV. 567 (2008).

[95] Landon v. Plasencia, 459 U.S. 21, 32 (1982) (citing, *inter alia*, United States *ex rel* Knauff v. Shaughnessy, 338 U.S. 537, 542 (1950); Fiallo v. Bell, 430 U.S. 787, 799 (1977); Kleindienst v. Mandel, 408 U.S. 753 (1972)) (emphasis added).

[96] *See, e.g.*, Aldana, *supra* note 46, at 13–39; Victor C. Romero, *The Congruence Principle Applied: Rethinking Equal Protection Review of Federal Alienage Classifications After* Adarand Constructors, Inc. v. Peña, 76 OR. L. REV. 425, 439–54 (1997); *Developments in the Law–Immigration Policy and the Rights of Aliens*, 96 HARV. L. REV. 1286, 1408 nn.57–58 (1983); *see also* Akiesha R. Gilcrist, *Undocumented Immigrants: Lack of Equal Protection and Its Impact on Public Heath*, 34 J. LEGAL MED. 403 (2013) (advocating for equal protection rights for undocumented immigrants and equal access to welfare benefits); Lori A. Nessel, *Undocumented Immigrants in the Workplace: The Fallacy of Labor Protection and the Need for Reform*, 36 HAR. C.R.-C.L. L. REV. 345 (2001) (arguing for equal enforcement of the labor laws without regard to immigration status); Elizabeth R. Chesler, Note, *Denying Undocumented Immigrants Access to Medicaid: A Denial of Their Equal Protection Rights?*, 17 B.U. PUB. INT. L.J. 255 (2008) (advocating the provision of health benefits to undocumented immigrants).

a. Individual Rights

i.   Procedural Due Process

Noncitizens in removal, also referred to as deportation, proceedings have long been entitled to the protections of the Due Process Clause.[97] The Court initially defined the due process rights of noncitizens narrowly — for example, finding that the lack of knowledge of English in a deportation hearing conducted in English did not violate due process.[98] However, the due process rights of noncitizens in removal and other immigration proceedings have expanded consistent with the general expansion of due process rights over the twentieth century. This expansion demonstrated the sensitivity to the weighty life and liberty interests at stake in removal proceedings.[99]

In 1982, the Supreme Court in *Landon v. Plasencia*[100] held that a lawful permanent resident who had briefly left the country could be denied entry and have her right to return decided in a hearing so long as that hearing comported with due process. The Court adhered to its previous holding[101] that an "innocent, casual and brief excursion" outside the United States by a lawful permanent resident would not, upon her return, mean that she was engaged in a new "entry" into the country. The question of the nature and meaning of the "excursion," however, need not be resolved in a full-blown deportation hearing, which at the time generally afforded the noncitizen a full array of procedural protections; the immigration statute in place at the time "clearly reflect[ed] a congressional intent that, whether or not the alien is a permanent resident, admissibility shall be determined in an exclusion hearing," with such hearings at the time offering fewer procedural protections than afforded noncitizens in deportation hearings.[102] The Court thus permitted the issue of Plasencia's alleged "entry" to be resolved in an exclusion hearing but only so long as that hearing comported with Due Process.

The Court in *Landon v. Plasencia* restated the essence of the plenary power doctrine that "an alien seeking initial admission has *no* constitutional rights regarding his application, for the power to admit or exclude aliens is a sovereign prerogative."[103] However, the Court went on to observe that "once an alien gains admission to our country and begins to develop the ties that go with permanent

---

[97] *See* Yamatcya v. Fisher (The Japanese Immigrant Case), 189 U.S. 86, 100–01 (1903).

[98] *See id.* at 101–02.

[99] *See* Fong Haw Tan v. Phelan, 333 U.S. 6, 10 (1948) ("Deportation is a drastic measure and at times the equivalent of banishment or exile."); Bridges v. Wixon, 326 U.S. 135, 147 (1945) (emphasizing that "deportation may result in the loss 'of all that makes life worth living' ") (citation omitted).

[100] 459 U.S. 21 (1982).

[101] Rosenberg v. Fleuti, 374 U.S. 449, 462 (1963).

[102] *Landon v. Plasencia*, 459 U.S. at 28; *see* All Star Bail Bonds, Inc. v. Eighth Jud. Dist. Court, 326 P.3d 1107, 1109 (Nev. 2014) (citing *Landon v. Plasencia* and recognizing the distinction between "exclusion" and "deportation" proceedings). For fuller analysis of the decision, see Kevin R. Johnson, *Maria and Joseph Plasencia's Lost Weekend: The Case of* Landon v. Plasencia, *in* IMMIGRATION STORIES, *infra* note 33, at 221; Ch. 6. In 1996, Congress combined the exclusion and deportation proceedings into a single "removal proceeding." *See* Vartelas v. Holder, 132 S. Ct. 1479, 1485 n.3 (2012); Ch. 13.

[103] *Landon v. Plasencia*, 459 U.S. at 32 (citing, *inter alia*, United States *ex rel.* Knauff v.

residence, his constitutional status changes accordingly. Our cases have frequently suggested that a continuously present resident alien is entitled to a fair hearing when threatened with deportation . . . ."[104] The Court further emphasized that "[w]e need not now decide the scope of [the plenary power doctrine]; it does not govern this case, for Plasencia was absent from the country only a few days, and *the United States has conceded that she has a right to due process*."[105]

The Court stated that the flexible *Mathews v. Eldridge* balancing test — the general test previously articulated by the Court for evaluating whether governmental procedures comply with Due Process — applied to determining the specific procedures that Due Process required in Plasencia's case:

> the courts must consider the interest at stake for the individual, the risk of an erroneous deprivation of the interest through the procedures used as well as the probable value of additional or different procedural safeguards, and the interest of the government in using the current procedures rather than additional or different procedures.[106]

Although declining to itself strike the balance in Plasencia's case, the Court acknowledged that she had a "weighty" interest at stake because she "stands to lose the right 'to stay and live and work in this land of freedom' " and "may lose the right to rejoin her immediate family, a right that ranks high among the interests of the individual."[107] It further observed that "[t]he government's interest in efficient administration of the immigration laws at the border also is weighty."[108] The Court reminded the lower court that, on remand, it could only decide "whether the procedures meet the essential standard of fairness under the Due Process Clause and [could not impose] procedures that merely displace congressional choices of policy."[109]

The courts have followed the Supreme Court's holding in *Landon v. Plasencia* that, when seeking re-entry into the country, a lawful permanent resident's claim of admissibility must be determined in proceedings that comply with Due Process.[110]

Shaughnessy, 338 U.S. 537, 542 (1950); Fiallo v. Bell, 430 U.S. 787, 799 (1977); Kleindienst v. Mandel, 408 U.S. 753 (1972)) (emphasis added).

[104]   Landon v. Plasencia, 459 U.S. at 32 (citations omitted). One of the authorities relied on by the Court for this proposition was *Johnson v. Eisentrager*, 339 U.S. 763, 770 (1950), which was much-debated in connection with the indefinite detention after September 11, 2001 of two U.S. citizens, Jose Padilla and Yaser Hamdi, who the Executive Branch classified as "enemy combatants." *See* Hamdi v. Rumsfeld, 542 U.S. 507 (2004) (ruling that a U.S. citizen held as "enemy combatant" had the right to a hearing to challenge that classification); Rumsfeld v. Padilla, 542 U.S. 426 (2004) (finding that the court in which action was filed lacked jurisdiction over Padilla and could not entertain a challenge to his detention as an "enemy combatant"). In *Eisentrager*, 339 U.S. at 770, the Court observed that the rights of a noncitizen who had resided in the United States ordinarily increased with the length of residence, which stood in stark contrast to the lack of rights of "enemy aliens" in times of war.

[105]   *Landon v. Plasencia*, 459 U.S. at 34 (citation omitted) (emphasis added).

[106]   *Id.* (citing Mathews v. Eldridge, 424 U.S. 319, 334–35 (1976)).

[107]   *Landon v. Plasencia*, 459 U.S. at 34 (citations omitted).

[108]   *Id.*

[109]   *Id.* at 34–35.

[110]   *See, e.g.*, INS v. Phinpathya, 464 U.S. 183, 193 (1984); Ali v. Reno, 22 F.3d 442, 448 (2d Cir. 1994).

Some courts also expressed the view that *Landon v. Plasencia* as standing for the proposition that the rights of lawful permanent residents increase as the length of their time in the country grows and thus are greater than those of first-time entrants.[111] In contrast, some courts have highlighted language from the decision to support Congress's plenary power with respect to the procedures afforded to certain noncitizens seeking initial entry into the country.[112]

Importantly, courts have understood *Landon v. Plasencia* to require that the *Mathews v. Eldridge* balancing test applies to evaluating whether hearing procedures are consistent with the Due Process Clause.[113] In 1988, the Board of Immigration Appeals ruled that a returning lawful permanent resident like Plasencia must be given reasonable notice of the charges, as well as a procedurally fair hearing with the government bearing the burden of proof; the lawful permanent resident could be excluded from the United States only upon a showing of clear, unequivocal, and convincing evidence.[114]

Some immigration law scholars read *Landon v. Plasencia* as opening the door for expanded constitutional protections for noncitizens seeking entry into the United States.[115] Other commentators, however, are more circumspect, emphasizing that the decision includes language endorsing the plenary power doctrine and failed to define with specificity the constitutional rights of lawful permanent residents.[116]

Responding to *Landon v. Plasencia*, Congress in 1996 amended the immigration laws to provide that returning lawful permanent residents seeking to enter the country are generally not subject to the same procedures and inadmissibility grounds as first-time entrants. *See* Chs. 9, 11–12. The new law provides that a lawful permanent resident at the border generally is *not* treated as seeking initial

---

[111] *See, e.g.*, Galluzzo v. Holder, 633 F.3d 111, 114 (2d Cir. 2011); Rhoden v. United States, 55 F.3d 428, 432 (9th Cir. 1995); Campos v. INS, 961 F.2d 309, 316 (1st Cir. 1992); Chen v. Aitken, 917 F. Supp. 2d 1013, 1016–17 (N.D. Cal. 2013).

[112] *See, e.g.*, Angov v. Holder, 736 F.3d 1263, 1272–73 (9th Cir. 2013); Cuban Am. Bar Ass'n v. Christopher, 43 F.3d 1412, 1428 (11th Cir. 1995), *cert. denied*, 516 U.S. 913 (1995); Haitian Ctrs. Council v. McNary, 969 F.2d 1326, 1340 (2d Cir. 1992), *vacated sub nom. as moot*, 509 U.S. 918 (1993).

[113] *See, e.g.*, Zadvydas v. Davis, 533 U.S. 678, 694 (2001); Oshodi v. Holder, 729 F.3d 883, 894–96 (9th Cir. 2013) (en banc); Ching v. Mayorkas, 725 F.3d 1149, 1157–59 (9th Cir. 2013); Flores v. Meese, 934 F.2d 991, 1013 (9th Cir. 1990), *rev'd on other grounds*, 507 U.S. 291 (1993).

[114] *See* Matter of Huang, 19 I.&N. Dec. 749, 753–54 (BIA 1988); *see, e.g.*, Khodagholian v. Ashcroft, 335 F.3d 1003, 1006 (9th Cir. 2003); Rosendo-Ramirez v. INS, 32 F.3d 1085, 1090 (7th Cir. 1994).

[115] *See, e.g.*, David A. Martin, *Due Process and Membership in the National Community: Political Asylum and Beyond*, 44 U. PITT. L. REV. 165, 214–15 (1983); Hiroshi Motomura, *The Curious Evolution of Immigration Law: Procedural Surrogates for Substantive Constitutional Rights*, 92 COLUM. L. REV. 1625, 1652–56 (1992) [hereinafter, Motomura, *The Curious Evolution of Immigration Law*]; Hiroshi Motomura, *Immigration Law After a Century of Plenary Power: Phantom Constitutional Norms and Statutory Interpretation*, 100 YALE L.J. 545, 578–780 (1990); Michael Scaperlanda, *Partial Membership: Aliens and the Constitutional Community*, 81 IOWA L. REV. 707, 744–45 (1996).

[116] *See* T. Alexander Aleinikoff, *Immigrants in American Law: Aliens, Due Process and "Community Ties": A Response to Martin*, 44 U. PITT. L. REV. 237, 260 n.65 (1983); Legomsky, *supra* note 63, at 260 nn.25–26; Peter H. Schuck, *The Transformation of Immigration Law*, 84 COLUM. L. REV. 1, 62–63 & n.342 (1984).

admission into the country.[117] Most lawful permanent residents at the border now are entitled to a removal proceeding with broader procedural protections than they would have enjoyed before the Supreme Court decided *Landon v. Plasencia.*

ii.   Substantive Due Process

Noncitizens in the United States have limited substantive due process rights.[118] In *Flores v. Reno*,[119] the Supreme Court rejected the substantive due process claim of unaccompanied minors to be released to persons not their parents, close relatives, or legal guardians. The Court found no substantive due process violation, emphasizing that only the rights of *aliens* were at stake.[120]

In subsequent cases, the Court has vacillated in extending substantive due process rights to noncitizens in detention. In *Zadvydas v. Davis*,[121] the Court refused to invoke the plenary power doctrine to shield from review the indefinite detention of noncitizens awaiting deportation and held that regular review for possible release was required. However, in *Demore v. Kim*,[122] the Court restated the doctrine and upheld mandatory detention of certain noncitizens pending their removal from the United States. One explanation for the different results in the two cases is that the events of September 11, 2001 raised national security concerns that influenced the Court's approach to the constitutionality of detention of noncitizens convicted of crimes.[123]

iii.   Equal Protection

The Equal Protection rights under the Fifth and Fourteenth Amendments are diluted when it comes to noncitizens living in the United States. The Supreme Court has invoked the plenary power doctrine to immunize from meaningful judicial review *federal* laws that discriminate against lawful immigrants who live in the United States.[124] In so doing, the Court has generally applied lenient rational basis review to the federal alienage classification,[125] demonstrating that noncitizens in the United States possess *some* Equal Protection rights.

---

[117] Immigration and Nationality Act § 101(a)(13)(C), 8 U.S.C. § 1101(a)(13)(C) (amended by Illegal Immigration Reform and Immigrant Responsibility Act of 1996 by § 301(a), Pub. L. No. 104-208, 110 Stat. 3009-546, 3009-575 (1996)), provides that a lawful permanent resident ordinarily "shall not be regarded as seeking admission into the United States for purposes of the immigration laws . . . ."

[118] For analysis of the state of substantive due process doctrine, see Daniel O. Conkle, *Three Theories of Substantive Due Process*, 85 N.C. L. Rev. 63 (2006); Michael A. Scaperlanda, *Illusions of Liberty and Equality: An "Alien's" View of Tiered Scrutiny, Ad Hoc Balancing, Governmental Power, and Judicial Imperialism*, 55 Cath. U.L. Rev. 5 (2005).

[119] 507 U.S. 292 (1993).

[120] *See id.* at 301–06 (citing, *inter alia*, Mathews v. Diaz, 426 U.S. 67, 81 (1976) and other plenary power doctrine cases).

[121] 533 U.S. 678, 695–96 (2001).

[122] 538 U.S. 510, 522 (2003).

[123] *See* Taylor, *supra* note 80.

[124] *See, e.g.*, Mathews v. Diaz, 426 U.S. 67, 79–80 (1976).

[125] *See id.* at 81–82.

The Supreme Court at times has struck down limitations on the rights of lawful immigrants on Equal Protection grounds.[126] The Court occasionally has employed strict scrutiny to review *state* laws that discriminate against lawful permanent residents.[127] However, the Court has permitted state governments to impose citizenship requirements on state jobs that perform a "political function."[128]

Discrimination based on alienage can have disparate impacts on particular national origin groups. In *Cabell v. Chavez-Salido*,[129] the Supreme Court rejected an Equal Protection challenge to a California law requiring probation officers to be U.S. citizens. Based on that law, Los Angeles County declined to hire for a probation officer position a lawful permanent resident, who was born in Mexico and had lived in the United States for more than twenty-five years.[130] Mexicans constitute the largest group of lawful permanent residents and are thus affected by laws like the one at issue in *Cabell v. Chavez-Salido* in larger numbers than other national origin groups.

The highwater mark of noncitizen rights under the Equal Protection Clause is *Plyler v. Doe*,[131] which held that the state of Texas could not constitutionally bar undocumented immigrant children from the elementary and secondary public schools. A 5-4 Court emphasized that "[a]liens, even aliens whose presence in the country is unlawful, have long been recognized as 'persons' guaranteed due process

---

[126] *See, e.g.*, Takahashi v. Fish & Game Comm'n, 334 U.S. 410, 420 (1948) (striking down a state law restricting fishing by noncitizens); Truax v. Raich, 239 U.S. 33 (1915) (invalidating Arizona law requiring a certain number of employees in the workplace to be citizens); Yick Wo v. Hopkins, 118 U.S. 356 (1886) (holding that discriminatory enforcement of local ordinances against persons of Chinese ancestry violated Equal Protection Clause). For a rare but much-cited case invalidating an immigration relief provision as limited by the Executive Branch as a violation of the Equal Protection Clause, see Francis v. INS, 532 F.2d 268 (2d Cir. 1976).

[127] *See, e.g.*, Bernal v. Fainter, 467 U.S. 216, 220 (1984) (applying strict scrutiny in holding that a state citizenship requirement for notary publics was unconstitutional); Sugarman v. Dougall, 413 U.S. 634, 641–46 (1973) (finding aliens to be a discrete and insular minority, applying strict scrutiny, and invalidating a citizenship requirement for a state civil service position); Graham v. Richardson, 403 U.S. 365, 370–76 (1971) (applying strict scrutiny to an alienage classification and striking down a bar of state welfare benefits to lawful residents).

[128] *See, e.g.*, Cabell v. Chavez-Salido, 454 U.S. 432 (1982) (upholding a state law requiring "peace officers" to be U.S. citizens); Ambach v. Norwick, 441 U.S. 68 (1979) (public school teacher); Foley v. Connelie, 435 U.S. 291 (1978) (police officers).

[129] 454 U.S. 432 (1982).

[130] In dissent, Justice Blackmun lamented: "I can only conclude that California's exclusion of these appellees from the position of deputy probation officer stems solely from state parochialism and hostility toward foreigners who have come to this country lawfully." *Id.* at 463 (Blackmun, J., dissenting).

[131] 457 U.S. 202 (1982); *see* Michael A. Olivas, Plyler v. Doe, *The Education of Undocumented Children, and the Polity, in* IMMIGRATION STORIES, *supra* note 24, at 197; Ch. 1 (analyzing the background of the case). For further analysis of the decision, see Nancy B. Anderson, *The Promise of* Plyler: *Public Institutional In-State Tuition Policies for Undocumented Students and Compliance with Federal Law*, 70 WASH. & LEE L. REV. 2339 (2013); Udi Ofer, *Protecting* Plyler: *New Challenges to the Right of Immigrant Children to Access a Public School Education*, 1 COLUM. J. RACE & L. 187 (2012); Michael A. Olivas, *From a "Legal Organization of Militants" into a "Law Firm for the Latino Community": MALDEF and the Purposive Cases of* Keyes, Rodriguez, *and* Plyler, 90 DEN. U.L. REV. 1151, 1163–1207 (2013); Michael A. Olivas, *The Political Efficacy of* Plyler v. Doe: *The Danger and the Discourse*, 45 UC DAVIS L. REV. 1, 8 (2011); Michael A. Olivas & Kristi L. Bowman, Plyler's *Legacy: Immigration and Higher Education in the 21st Century*, 2011 MICH. ST. L. REV. 261, 262 (2011).

of law by the Fifth and Fourteenth Amendments. . . . Indeed, we have clearly held that the Fifth Amendment protects aliens whose presence in this country is unlawful from invidious discrimination by the Federal Government."[132] The Court further stated that "[i]t would be incongruous to hold that the United States . . . is barred from invidious discrimination with respect to unlawful aliens, while exempting the States from a similar limitation."[133] Although not finding undocumented immigrants to be a suspect class, or that education is a fundamental right,[134] the Court found that the Texas law that would have effectively barred undocumented children from the public schools violated the Equal Protection Clause.

The dangers of discrimination against unpopular groups of noncitizens can be seen in the various measures implemented by the federal government after September 11, 2001. There was legal precedent for the measures. In *Narenji v. Civiletti*,[135] while a group of Americans were held hostage in Iran, a court of appeals in 1979 upheld special procedures requiring nonimmigrant Iranians attending post-secondary school to report to the local Immigration and Naturalization Service office. The court emphasized that "classifications among aliens based upon nationality are consistent with due process and equal protection if supported by a rational basis."[136] The court found that the regulation satisfied that test and stated that "it is not the business of courts to pass judgment on the decisions of the President in the field of foreign policy."[137]

After September 11, 2001, the President instituted a "special registration" program known as the National Security Entry-Exit Registration System that applied to certain noncitizens from nations populated predominantly by Arabs and Muslims. *See* Ch. 14. In creating the program, the Attorney General emphasized that "[t]he political branches of the government have plenary authority in the immigration area."[138] The courts refused to disturb the program.[139] In *Kandamar*

---

[132] *Plyler v. Doe*, 457 U.S. at 210 (citing, *inter alia*, Yick Wo v. Hopkins, 118 U.S. 356, 369 (1886) and Mathews v. Diaz, 426 U.S. 67, 77 (1976)).

[133] *Plyler v. Doe*, 457 U.S. at 210 (citation omitted).

[134] *See id.* at 219, 221.

[135] 617 F.2d 745, 746–47 (D.C. Cir. 1979).

[136] *Id.* at 748; *see* Ghaelian v. INS, 717 F.2d 950, 953 (6th Cir. 1983); Nademi v. INS, 679 F.2d 811 (10th Cir. 1982); Dastmalchi v. INS, 660 F.2d 880, 892 (3d Cir. 1981); Malek-Marzban v. INS, 653 F.2d 113 (4th Cir. 1981).

[137] Narenji v. Civiletti, 617 F.2d at 748. Later, President George Bush responded to the Iraqi invasion of Kuwait by requiring fingerprinting and photographing of nonimmigrants with Iraqi and Kuwaiti travel documents. *See* 56 Fed. Reg. 1566 (1991) (codified at 8 C.F.R. pt. 264).

[138] Registration and Monitoring of Certain Nonimmigrants, 67 Fed. Reg. 52,584, 52,585 (Aug. 12, 2002) (citing Fiallo v. Bell, 430 U.S. 787, 792 (1977); Mathews v. Diaz, 426 U.S. 67, 80–82 (1976)).

[139] *See, e.g.*, Kandamar v. Gonzales, 464 F.3d 65, 73–74 (1st Cir. 2006); Ahmed v. Gonzales, 447 F.3d 433, 439–40 (5th Cir. 2006); Ali v. Gonzales, 440 F.3d 678, 681–82 (5th Cir. 2006); Roudnahal v. Ridge, 310 F. Supp. 2d 884, 892 (N.D. Ohio 2003). For criticism of the special registration program, see Sahar F. Aziz, *Policing Terrorists in the Community*, 5 HARV. NAT'L SEC. J. 147, 219–20 (2014); Anya Bernstein, *The Hidden Costs of Terrorist Watch Lists*, 61 BUFFALO L. REV. 461, 524–25 (2013); Ty S. Wahab Twibell, *The Road to Internment: Special Registration and Other Human Rights Violations of Arabs and Muslims in the United States*, 29 VT. L. REV. 407, 527–35 (2005); Kathryn Lohmeyer, Note and Comment, *The*

v. Gonzales,[140] the court of appeals rejected a constitutional challenge to the special registration program and emphasized that

> we . . . give deference to the Attorney General's requirement that young males from certain countries be subject to special registration. We hold that a special registration system serves legitimate government objectives of monitoring nationals from certain countries to prevent terrorism and is rationally related to achieving these monitoring objectives. [citing *Narenji v. Civiletti*].

b. Separation of Powers

A heated controversy arose during the Obama presidency concerning the power of the President on immigration.

In 2012, the U.S. Department of Homeland Security announced the Deferred Action for Childhood Arrivals (DACA) program, which provides temporary relief known as deferred action from removal given on a case-by-case basis to noncitizens who entered the United States as children and satisfied certain eligibility requirements.[141] See Chs. 12, 18. With their potential removal designated as "low priority cases," eligible noncitizens may apply for deferred action from removal,[142] which is temporary in duration. DACA relief allows a noncitizen to obtain employment authorization and a Social Security number.[143] Importantly, DACA "is not a permanent solution and does not grant [recipients] any long-term immigration status stability."[144]

The Obama administration characterized DACA as an exercise of prosecutorial discretion in selecting which removal cases to which the Executive Branch devotes its limited immigration enforcement resources.[145] As this volume goes to press, a

---

Pitfalls of Plenary Power: A Call for Meaningful Review of NSEERS "Special Registration," 25 WHITTIER L. REV. 139 (2003); Heidee Stoller et al., Developments in Law and Policy, *The Costs of Post-9/11 National Security Strategy*, 22 YALE L. & POL. REV. 197, 220–22 (2004); *see also* Hiroshi Motomura, *Immigration and We the People After September 11*, 66 ALB. L. REV. 413, 420–21 (2003) (calling for the need for a deeper understanding of immigration decisions with the hopes of preventing the anti-terrorism measures from dividing the nation).

In 2011, the Department of Homeland Security announced the end of the special registration program. *See* Department of Homeland Security Office of the Secretary, Notice Removing Designated Countries from the National Security Entry-Exit Registration system (NSEERS) (2011), *available at* www://gpo. gov/fdsys/pkg/FR-2011-04-28/pdf/2011-10305.pdf (last visited July 7, 2014).

[140] 464 F.2d 65, 73–74 (1st Cir. 2006) (citation omitted).

[141] U.S. Dep't of Homeland Security Memorandum, *Exercising Prosecutorial Discretion With Respect to Individuals Who Came to the United States as Children* (June 15, 2012), *available at* http://www.dhs.gov/xlibrary/assets/s1-exercising-prosecutorial-discretion-individuals-who-came-to-us-as-children.pdf [hereinafter DHS Memorandum], last checked Apr. 22, 2015; *see* Ch. 12.

[142] *See id.*

[143] *See* National Immigration Law Center, Frequently Asked Questions: The Obama Administration's Deferred Action for Childhood Arrivals (DACA), *available at* http://www.nilc.org/FAQdeferredactionyouth.html (last visited Apr. 22, 2015).

[144] Mariela Olivares, *Renewing the Dream: DREAM Act Redux and Immigration Reform*, 16 HARV. LATINO L. REV. 79, 91 (2013).

[145] See DHS Memorandum, *supra* note 141; *see also* Shoba Sivaprasad Wadhia, *The Role of*

lawsuit, which challenges the program as violating the constitutional requirement that the President "take care that the laws be faithfully executed," has not been finally decided.[146]

In response to Congress's repeated failure to pass immigration reform, *see* Chapter 18, the Obama administration took a number of steps to refine and reform its immigration enforcement efforts. The President expanded the existing DACA program and created a new deferred action program for undocumented parents of U.S. citizens and lawful permanent residents.[147] Notably, the new initiatives did not, as some had hoped, provide deferred action status to the undocumented parents of DACA recipients.[148]

The President's actions sparked a contentious national debate. Although previous Presidents had engaged in similar (although not identical) immigration measures,[149] critics complained that the new deferred action program was unprecedented in scope.[150] Texas and 25 states filed a lawsuit challenging the new program.[151] A federal district court in February 2015 entered a preliminary injunction barring the expanded deferred action program from going into effect, which is on appeal as this book goes to press.[152]

Prosecutorial Discretion in Immigration Law, 9 Conn. Pub Int. L.J. 1 (2009/10) (explaining concept of prosecutorial discretion in immigration removal matters). *See generally* Shoba Sivaprasad Wadia, Beyond Deportation: The Role of Prosecutorial Discretion in Immigration Cases (2010).

[146] *See* Crane v. Napolitano, 2013 U.S. Dist. Lexis 57788 (N.D. Tex. Apr. 23, 2013), *aff'd sub nom.*, Crane v. Johnson, 2015 U.S. App. LEXIS, 5573 (5th Cir. Apr. 7, 2015). For the claim that the DACA program violates the "Take Care" Clause of Article II, §3 (providing that the President "shall take care that the laws be faithfully executed"), see Robert J. Delahunty & John C. Yoo, *Dream On: the Obama Administration's Nonenforcement of Immigration Laws, the DREAM Act, and the Take Care Clause*, 91 Tex. L. Rev 781, 784-85, 856 (2013). *But see* Shoba Sivaprasad Wadhia, *In Defense of DACA, Deferred Action, and the DREAM Act*, 91 Tex. L. Rev. *See also* 59, 62-68 (2013) (defending DACA program as consistent with the executive exercise of prosecutorial discretion in the immigration matters), *available at* http://www.texaslrev.com/wp-content/uploads/Wadhia.pdf (last visited Apr. 22, 2015).

[147] *See* U.S. Dep't of Homeland Security, *Fixing Our Broken Immigration System Through Executive Action — Key Facts* (last published Dec. 5, 2014), *available at* http://www.dhs.gov/immigration-action (last visted Apr. 22, 2015).

[148] The Justice Department's Office of Legal Counsel had concluded that such relief might violate the law. *See* Memorandum on the Department of Homeland Security's Authority to Prioritize Removal of Certain Aliens Unlawfully Present in the United States and to Defer Removal of Others, Karl R. Thompson, Principal Deputy Assistant Attorney General, Office of Legal Counsel dated Nov. 19, 2014, *available at* http://www.justice.gov/sites/default/files/olc/opinions/attachments/2014/11/20/2014-11-19-auth-prioritize-removal.pdf (last visited Apr. 22, 2015).

[149] *See* American Immigration Council, *Immigration Policy Center, Executive Action on Immigration: A Resource Page*, *available at* http://www.immigrationpolicy.org/executive-action-immigration-resource-page (last visited Apr. 22, 2015).

[150] *See* Editorial, *President Obama's Unilateral Action on Immigration Has No Precedent*, Wash. Post, Dec. 3, 2014.

[151] *See* Texas v. United States, Case No. Civil No. B-14-254 (S.D. Tex., filed Dec. 3, 2014), https://www.texasattorneygeneral.gov/files/epress/files/20141203ImmigrationExecutiveOrderLawsuit.pdf.

[152] *See* Texas v. United States, 2015 U.S. Dist. LEXIS 18551 (S.D. Tex. Feb. 16, 2015).

i.   Congressional Limits on Judicial Review

The courts have seen a variety of limits on judicial review imposed over the years. Both the plenary power doctrine and general deference afforded to administrative agencies, discussed in Chapter 6, limit the scope of judicial review of the immigration laws and their administration. In addition, Congress has limited judicial review of immigration decisions by the Executive Branch. Chapter 6 discusses these provisions and the courts' treatment of them.

ii.   *INS v. Chadha*

In *INS v. Chadha*,[153] the Supreme Court found that a provision of the Immigration and Nationality Act authorizing Congress to reverse a decision of the agency in a deportation case violated separation of powers principles. The U.S. government initiated deportation proceedings against Chadha after expiration of his student visa. The immigration court suspended Chadha's deportation due to extreme hardship, a decision vetoed by Congress. The Supreme Court found that the congressional veto violated fundamental separation of powers principles:

> Disagreement with the Attorney General's decision on Chadha's deportation — that is, Congress' decision to deport Chadha — no less than Congress' original choice to delegate to the Attorney General the authority to make that decision, involves determinations of policy that Congress can implement in only one way; bicameral passage followed by presentment to the President. Congress must abide by its delegation of authority until that delegation is legislatively altered or revoked.[154]

Since *INS v. Chadha* was decided, Congress has avoided direct intervention in the decisions of the immigration bureaucracy in individual cases.

---

[153] 462 U.S. 919 (1983).

[154] *Id.* at 954–55 (footnote omitted).

Chapter 4

IMMIGRATION FEDERALISM

Until 1875[1], with the exception of the short-lived Alien and Sedition Acts of 1798,[2] Congress left the U.S. international borders open. States, not the federal government, attempted to restrict immigration flows. States imposed restrictions on transborder movement on the basis of crime, health, public morals, poverty,

---

[1] In 1875, Congress restricted immigration for the first time by including a convict and prostitution immigration restriction in a federal statute. Act of Mar. 3, 1875, Ch. 141, 18 Stat. 477 (repealed 1974).

[2] This package of legislation included three statutes directed specifically towards aliens: the Naturalization Act of 1798, Act of June 18, 1798, Ch. 54, 1 Stat. 566; the Alien Enemies Act, Act of July 6, 1798, Ch. 66, 1 Stat. 577; and the Alien (or Alien Friends) Act, Act of June 25, 1798, Ch. 58, 1 Stat. 570.

disability, and ideology or race.³ Then, with a series of nineteenth century decisions, the Court invalidated certain state immigration restrictions.⁴ Ultimately the Court declared in 1889 that immigration control is an exclusive federal power with the *Chinese Exclusion Case*.⁵

The *Chinese Exclusion Case* originated the doctrine of federal plenary immigration power, but the doctrine did not end state regulation of immigrants. Unable to directly control transborder movement, states turned to restricting the living conditions of immigrants who were perceived as a threat to the well-being of white native residents. In the late nineteenth and early twentieth centuries, these state efforts included employment and property ownership restrictions against mostly Japanese and Chinese immigrants.⁶ In addition, it included language restrictions that targeted German and other Eastern and Southern European immigrants.⁷ These and other state alienage restrictions have continued throughout much of the twentieth century until today, usually heightening in times of economic depression or war.

More recently, especially since the September 11th attacks, several states and local governments have adopted hundreds of laws, local ordinances or resolutions regulating immigrants or immigration. The National Congress of State Legislatures has been tracking the number, content and scope of these laws since at least 2005.⁸ In general, all 50 states, as well as the District of Columbia and Puerto Rico, are engaging in the regulation of immigrants or immigration locally.⁹ Moreover, over the years the number state legislation has increased to more than 400 enacted laws, regulations or resolutions. Several hundreds more have been introduced but have not been adopted.¹⁰ Thematically, these laws touch on various

---

³ *See* Kerry Abrams, *Polygamy, Prostitution, and the Federalization of Immigration Law*, 105 COLUM. L. REV. 641 (2005); Marvin H. Morse and Lucy M. Moran, *Troubling the Waters: Human Cargos*, 33 J. MAR. L. & COM. 1 (2002); and Gerald L. Neuman, *The Lost Century of American Immigration Law (1776–1875)*, 93 COLUM. L. REV. 1833 (1993).

⁴ *See, e.g.*, The Passenger Cases, 48 U.S. 283 (1849) and Henderson v. Mayor of New York, 92 U.S. 259 (1876) (striking down state taxes on certain categories of arriving immigrants).

⁵ Chae Chan Ping v. U.S., 130 U.S. 581 (1889).

⁶ Keith Aoki, *No Right to Own?: The Early Twentieth-Century "Alien Land Laws" as a Prelude to Internment*, 40 B.C. L. REV. 37 (1998); SU CHENG CHAN, THIS BITTER-SWEET SOIL: THE CHINESE IN CALIFORNIA AGRICULTURE, 1860–1910 (1986); ROGER DANIELS, THE POLITICS OF PREJUDICE: THE ANTI-JAPANESE MOVEMENT IN CALIFORNIA AND THE STRUGGLE FOR JAPANESE EXCLUSION (2d. ed. 1977).

⁷ Lupe S. Salinas, *Immigration and Language Rights: The Evolution of Private Racists Attitudes into American Public Law and Policy*, 7 NEV. L.J. 895, 917 (2007).

⁸ NATIONAL CONFERENCE OF STATE LEGISLATURE, http://www.ncsl.org/research/immigration.aspx (last visited Oct. 2014).

⁹ The number of states regulating immigrants per year is as follows: 25 in 2005; 32 in 2006; all 50 in 2007; 41 in 2008; 48 in 2009; 44 in 2010; 46 in 2011; 44 plus Puerto Rico in 2012; and 45 plus the District of Columbia in 2013. *See generally* yearly reports on State Immigration Legislation, *available at* NATIONAL CONFERENCE OF STATE LEGISLATURE, http://www.ncsl.org/research/immigration/state-laws-related-to-immigration-and-immigrants.aspx (last visited Oct. 2014).

¹⁰ The number of enacted local immigrations laws, ordinances or resolutions are as follows: 45 in 2005; 90 in 2006; 240 in 2007; 353 in 2008; 353 in 2009; 346 in 2010; 306 in 2011; 156 in 2012; and 437 in 2013. *See generally* yearly reports on State Immigration Legislation, *available at* NATIONAL CONFERENCE OF STATE LEGISLATURE, http://www.ncsl.org/research/immigration/state-laws-related-to-immigration-and-

subjects that include public benefits, education, employment, human trafficking, identification, driver's licenses, voting, law enforcement, language, legal services, land, and health.[11] Several states have also adopted omnibus immigration legislation, which are laws that combine a range of types of regulation of immigrants into a single law.[12]

From the beginning, constitutional challenges to state anti-immigrant and some pro-immigrant measures have raised individual rights concerns as well as questions of preemption. Initially, the preemption arguments focused on state infringement upon the federal government's commerce — or treaty-making powers. With few exceptions, courts upheld these early local ordinances, holding that they did not conflict with treaty obligations[13] or interfered with commerce.[14] Furthermore, courts held that states could legitimately discriminate and reserve for their citizens the distribution of public moneys and wealth, among which was the access to natural resources and public service jobs.[15]

As federal immigration power solidified and expanded, preemption challenges focused instead on state infringement upon the federal immigration power. As extensively documented in this chapter, generally, the success of federal immigration power preemption claims has been greater when Congress has legislated specifically in the area and when state regulations conflict with federal law or policies. Preemption successes also occur when states deny rights or benefits to documented immigrants in the absence of authorizing federal legislation, especially if these laws target lawful permanent residents. In contrast, state laws are more likely to be upheld when they target the undocumented, are consistent with federal immigration laws or policies, and/or are considered to involve an overriding state interest. At times, however, the federal immigration power preemption doctrine has yielded contradictory judicial results. Such results have prompted scholars to critique the preemption doctrine as unworkable because the line between noncitizen regulation affecting domestic affairs and foreign affairs is impossible to draw.[16]

---

immigrants.aspx (last visited Oct. 2014). The NCSL explains the significant drop in 2012 to the uncertainly in the way the U.S. Supreme Court would rule on *Arizona v. United States*, 132 S. Ct. 2492 (2012), a case in involving a challenge to Arizona's SB1070 law, which is discussed in this chapter in subsection O.

[11] *See generally* yearly reports on State Immigration Legislation, *available at* NATIONAL CONFERENCE OF STATE LEGISLATURE, http://www.ncsl.org/research/immigration/state-laws-related-to-immigration-and-immigrants.aspx (last visited Oct. 2014).

[12] NCSL, Omnibus Immigration Legislation, Aug. 27, 2012, *available at* NATIONAL CONFERENCE OF STATE LEGISLATURE, http://www.ncsl.org/research/immigration/omnibus-immigration-legislation.aspx (last visited Oct. 2014).

[13] *See, e.g.*, Hauenstein v. Lynham, 100 U.S. 483 (1880); Blythe v. Hinckley, 180 U.S. 333 (1901); Patsone v. Pennsylvania, 232 U.S. 138 (1914); Crane v. New York, 239 U.S. 195 (1915); Heim v. McCall, 239 U.S. 175 (1915) and Terrace v. Thompson, 263 U.S. 197 (1923).

[14] McCready v. Virginia, 94 U.S. 391 (1877).

[15] *See, e.g.*, *Lynham*, 100 U.S. at 485–86; *Patsone*, 232 U.S. at 143–44; *McCall*, 239 U.S. at 188–193; *Thompson*, 263 U.S. at 214–224.

[16] *See, e.g.*, Christina M. Rodríguez, *The Significance of the Local in Immigration Regulations*, 106 MICH. L. REV. 567, 616–640 (2008); Pratheepan Gulasekaram, *Aliens with Guns: Equal Protection, Federal Power, and the Second Amendment*, 92 IOWA L. REV. 891, 929–40 (2007).

As the equal rights doctrine also evolved, equality challenges to state alienage restrictions have enjoyed greater success with courts recognizing that alienage-based distinctions are suspect and deserving of strict scrutiny protection.[17] Protection, however, has generally extended only to lawful permanent residents and has excluded the undocumented, with the exception of undocumented children for purposes of K-12 education.[18] Thus, states still have had a wide margin to discriminate against the undocumented, at least when the distinction denies what courts deem a privilege or benefit. Further, Congress has, to a certain extent, devolved to states its authority to discriminate even against lawful residents, at least with regard to public benefits.[19] As a result, some states have seized on this statutory authority to discriminate against lawful residents in the area of public benefits.[20] Finally, states are able to discriminate freely against all noncitizens as to voting and in certain public jobs based on principles of federalism because these areas are viewed as exclusive local political functions.[21] However, other successful rights-based challenges have included those rooted in the First Amendment.[22]

A. THE ALIEN LAND LAWS

Since the U.S. post-colonial period, land ownership became a significant area of local alienage regulation. At this time, alien land laws were largely restrictive and revealed their origins in racism, xenophobia, and anti-communism.[23] During the nineteenth century, however, some states did create property rights for noncitizens; in doing so, these states succeeded in untethering notions of citizenship from notions of ownership and created a more expansive vision of membership in the U.S. polity.[24] Many restrictive alien lands laws, however, still persist today. Many of them remain unchanged from their original form or, if changed, only partially so.[25]

The early U.S. colonies adopted alien land laws from the English common law, which excluded noncitizens from land ownership.[26] Then, from U.S. independence until the late nineteenth century, a tendency to abolish alien land restrictions

---

[17] Graham v. Richardson, 403 U.S. 365, 371–72 (1971).

[18] Plyler v. Doe, 457 U.S. 202, 221–26 (1982).

[19] *See generally* I. Public Benefits.

[20] *Id.*

[21] *See generally* C. Alienage Suffrage and F. The Political-Function Exception.

[22] *See generally* K. 2. Day Laborers and N. Official English/English-Only Laws.

[23] Allison Brownell Tirres, *Property Outliers: Non-Citizens, Property Rights and State Power*, 27 GEO. IMMIGR. L.J. 77, 109 (2012). *See also* Jean Stefansic, *Terrace v. Thompson and the Legacy of Manifest Destiny*, 12 NEV. L.J. 532 (2012).

[24] Allison Brownell Tirres, *Ownership Without Citizenship: The Creation of Noncitizen Property Rights*, 19 MICH. J. RACE & L. 1 (2013).

[25] *Id.*

[26] Polly J. Price, *Alien Land Restrictions in the American Common Law: Exploring the Relative Autonomy Paradigm*, 43 AM. J. LEGAL HIST. 152, 155–66 (1999). *See also* Mark Shapiro, Note, *The Dormant Commerce Clause: A Limit on Alien Land Laws*, 20 BROOK. J. INT'L L. 217, 220 (1993).

emerged.[27] This trend was followed by the enactment of several waves of anti-alien land laws both at the federal and state levels. This was in response to perceived threats of foreign land ownership to national and local interests. Based on fears that large foreign-owned ranches would jeopardize statehood for the territories, Congress passed the Territorial Land Act of 1787.[28] This act forbade extensive alien landholding in the organized territories, except by immigrant farmers who had applied for citizenship. Eleven states passed similar laws as a necessary response to a depressed agricultural condition, as well as to guard against absentee ownership of land.[29]

At the turn of the twentieth century, the Japanese represented an economic threat to native whites in Western states, particularly in agriculture.[30] As a result, in 1913, California adopted the California Alien Land Law.[31] California extended the law in 1920, and several states followed suit, from Washington and Oregon to Kansas, and eventually further east.[32] These laws, *inter alia*, barred "aliens ineligible for citizenship," which in turn affected almost exclusively the Japanese, not only from owning, but also from leasing and transferring in trust, agricultural land.[33] In a series of four cases decided in 1923, the Court upheld the constitutionality of these laws, finding that they neither violated U.S. treaty obligations with Japan nor equal protection.[34] In its reasoning, the Court completely ignored the *Yick Wo v. Hopkins*[35] precedent, which had struck down California's ordinance barring the Chinese from operating laundry mats. The Court also distinguished *Truax v. Raich*,[36] which struck down an Arizona ordinance restricting the employment of noncitizens.[37] The Court distinguished *Truax* by contrasting the Fourteenth Amendment right to earn a living from the privilege of owning or controlling agricultural land within the state.[38] Moreover, the Court held that controlling the quality and allegiance of those who own and occupy farmlands were matters of the highest importance to states.[39] Then, not surprisingly, anti-Japanese sentiment intensified during World War II, prompting some states to enact restrictive alien law statutes aimed specifically at preventing Japanese from moving into states

---

[27] Shapiro, *supra* note 26 at 220. *See also* Tirres, *Ownership Without Citizenship*, *supra* note 24, at 27–31.

[28] 48 U.S.C. §1501–08 (1988).

[29] Shapiro, *supra* note 26, at 221.

[30] Aoki, *No Right to Own?*, *supra* note 6, at 38–55. *See also* Shapiro *supra* note 26, at 222.

[31] The Webb-Haney Alien Land Law of 1913, *available at* http://www.intimeandplace.org/Japanese%20Internment/reading/constitution/alienlandlaw.html.

[32] Aoki, *No Right to Own?*, *supra* note 6, at 53.

[33] *Id.* at 38–9.

[34] *See* Terrace v. Thompson, 263 U.S. 197 (1923); Porterfield v. Webb, 263 U.S. 225 (1923); Webb v. O'Brien, 263 U.S. 313 (1923); Frick v. Webb, 263 U.S. 326 (1923).

[35] Yick Wo v. Hopkins, 118 U.S. 356 (1886).

[36] Truax v. Raich, 239 U.S. 33 (1915).

[37] *See infra* notes 144–62 and accompanying text (discussing the *Yick Wo* and *Truax v. Raich* cases).

[38] *Thompson*, 263 U.S. at 222.

[39] *Id.*

following their release from interment.[40]

After World War II, the Court took initial steps to repeal alien land laws based on equal protection grounds. In *Oyama v. California*, the Court indicated in *dicta* that equal protection did not allow California to prohibit land ownership by foreign nationals who were ineligible for citizenship.[41] Several state supreme courts followed suit and declared their alien land laws unconstitutional in violation of the Fourteenth Amendment,[42] while other state legislatures repealed their laws. More importantly, by 1952, no foreign national was ineligible for citizenship on the basis of race or national origin.[43] As a result, most laws restricting land ownership based on citizenship ineligibility would no longer facially discriminate based on national origin.

Another wave of alien land laws was enacted during the Cold War to limit the rights of foreigners to receive land by inheritance. The purpose of such laws was to prevent the diversion of U.S. wealth to communist governments.[44] In 1968, however, the Supreme Court severely limited this practice when it struck down an Oregon statue that conditioned a foreign national's rights of inheritance on a showing of reciprocal rights granted to U.S. citizens in that national's country of origin.[45] This time, the basis for the challenge was the law's unconstitutional intrusion into the field of foreign affairs;[46] thus, the Court failed once again to declare such laws unconstitutional on equal protection grounds.[47]

A more recent wave of alien land laws occurred in the 1970s, when a number of states reacted to a surge in farmland foreign investment by restricting the *situs* and the amount of land that could be purchased.[48] To date, no court has struck down the validity of these statutes. Moreover, state cases during this era distinguished *Oyama* based on the absence of facial national origin discrimination in the alien land law restrictions.[49]

Many states, even today, continue to have laws that restrict (or affirm) to some degree the rights of noncitizens to own property.[50] Modern alien land laws are quite

---

[40] *See, e.g.*, Gabriel J. Chin, *Citizenship and Exclusion: Wyoming's Anti-Japanese Alien Land Law in Context*, 1 Wyo. L. Rev. 497, 498–503 (2001).

[41] Oyama v. California, 332 U.S. 633 (1948). *See* Rose Cuison Villazor, *Rediscovering Oyama v. California: At the Intersection of Property, Race, and Citizenship*, 87 Wash. U. L. Rev. 979 (2010) for a discussion of the significance of *Oyama* of creating a paradigm shift in the treatment of property rights for Japanese Americans.

[42] *See, e.g.*, Sei Fujii v. State, 242 P.2d. 617, 625 (Cal. 1952); State v. Oakland, 287 P.2d 39, 42 (Mont. 1955); Kenji Namba v. McCourt, 204 P.2d 569, 614 (Or. 1949).

[43] McCarran-Walter Act of 1952, Pub. L. No. 82-414, 66 Stat. 163.

[44] Shapiro, *supra* note 26, at 222.

[45] Zschernig v. Miller, 389 U.S. 429 (1968).

[46] *Id.* at 432.

[47] *Tirres, Property Outliers, supra* note 23, at 107.

[48] *Shapiro, supra* note 26, at 222 (citing to laws enacted in Iowa and Nebraska).

[49] *See, e.g.*, Lehndorff Geneva, Inc. v. Warren, 246 N.W. 2d 815, 824 (Wis. 1976).

[50] *See, e.g., Tirres, Property Outliers, supra* note 23, at 80 (documenting that alien land laws continue to exist in the majority of states and that only 14 states have no alien land restriction of any kind).

different from one another and defy easy categorization. Moreover, these laws change frequently over time.[51] One problem with these laws is that they fail to conform to federal categories on immigration status or impose requirements that are no longer valid under federal immigration law, such as requiring declarations of intent to naturalize.[52] One type of restriction pertains to the acquisition of agricultural land by nonresident foreign nationals or foreign corporations. Other states limit the number of acres that can be owned or simply impose reporting requirements.[53] Non-agricultural restrictions on real property similarly impose limits on the number of acres that can be owned, limit the number of years the property may be held, or impose reporting requirements.[54] A few states still have laws restricting the right of foreign nationals to receive inheritances.[55] Finally, some states do not limit ownership at all but merely require the reporting of certain transaction undertaken by noncitizens.[56]

Despite the number of constitutional challenges available,[57] none are likely to strike down most remaining alien land laws for several reasons.[58] First, the vast majority of current alien land laws restrict only nonresident foreign nationals or foreign corporations from owning land. And whether these laws are equally susceptible to constitutional challenges based on equal protection grounds remains unclear.[59] Moreover, very few statutes impose reciprocity provisions on other nations or any other provision that would trample on the federal government's foreign affairs powers. This includes statutes that would deny foreign nationals specific rights granted to them by treaty.[60] Another potential challenge could be on preemption grounds based on the powers of the federal government to regulate commerce and foreign affairs, and perhaps also in its taxing powers.[61] To date, however, no federal statute that could pertain to alien property restrictions[62] has

---

[51] *Id.* at 97.

[52] *Id.* at 99.

[53] Price, *supra* note 26, at 223. *See also* Tirres, *Property Outliers, supra* note 23, at 99–100 (documenting that nine states have provisions limiting ownership based on either the amount of acreage or the proposed use of the property).

[54] Price, *supra* note 26, at 223.

[55] *Id.*

[56] Tirres, *Property Outliers, supra* note 23, at 100–101.

[57] Professor Allison Brownell Tirres argues, on the other hand, that alienage law remains a property outlier precisely because it has not adopted the core principles of property of alienability, equality, and non-discrimination, such that rights-based challenges in this area remain weak and explain the persistence of discrimination in these laws. Tirres, *Property Outliers, supra* note 23, at 77–78.

[58] *See, e.g.,* Shames v. Nebraska, 323 F. Supp. 1321 (D. Neb. 1971) (upholding a Nebraska statute that prohibited nonresident aliens from inheriting property in the state against preemption and equal protections challenges).

[59] Shapiro, *supra* note 26, at 226.

[60] *Id.* at 228–229.

[61] *Id.* at 230–31.

[62] The statutes include the Alien Property Custodian Regulations, 26 C.F.R. § 303.1 (2014); 28 C.F.R. § 167 (2014); 31 C.F.R. §§ 520.101, 520.102 (1992); the Foreign Asset Control Regulation, 50 U.S.C. §§ 1–44 (1988); the AFIDA, 7 U.S.C. §§ 3501–08 (1988); the International Investment and Trade in Services Survey Act of 1976, 22 U.S.C. §§ 3101–08 (amended 1990); the Foreign Investment in Real

been employed to challenge state alien land laws. This is perhaps because the rights of foreign nationals with respect to real property have been primarily a matter of state regulation.[63] Moreover, Congress has not expressly manifested its intent to preempt state alien land regulation, even when it has legislated to regulate foreign ownership of U.S. real property.[64]

B. FIREARM ALIENAGE RESTRICTIONS

Laws that restrict noncitizens' possession, use, and/or transport of firearms occupy another important area of alienage state regulation. As Professor Pratheepan Gulasekaram has stated, "[a]ccess to, and use of, firearms has helped define ideas o membership in America"; "[c]oncomitanly, however, the gun has also demarcated the borders of exclusion as well.[65]

Historically, state legislatures enacted these gun laws within the first decades of the twentieth century based on fear and prejudices against immigrants. Newly arrived Italian immigrants and so-called foreign anarchists during the red-scare era were objects of such fear.[66] Although many of these laws have been amended or repealed, today over 20 states still impose some form of restriction on noncitizens' possession, use, and/or transport of firearms.[67] In addition, the federal Gun Control Act (GCA), adopted originally in 1968 and amended in 1993,[68] currently forbids ownership, possession, or transport of firearms by nonimmigrants (temporary legal migrants), undocumented immigrants, and former citizens who have renounced their citizenship.[69] Congress enacted the GCA in order to prevent firearms from getting into the hands of perceived dangerous individuals, and noncitizens were included along with persons with prior felony convictions.[70]

Constitutional challenges to firearm alienage restriction laws in a handful of states have focused mostly on equal protection or preemption grounds, with few others raising a right to bear arms under state constitutions. The results have been varied. Courts invalidating state firearm alienage restrictions have relied mostly on

---

Property Tax Act of 1980, 22 U.S.C. § 3104 (c); the Agricultural Foreign Investment Disclosure Act, 7 U.S.C.A. § 3501 (1978).

[63] AMERICAN JURISPRUDENCE, SECOND EDITION, Aliens and Citizens, § 2075, Real Property Rights.

[64] Shapiro, *supra* note 26, at 231–36.

[65] Pratheepan Gulasekaram, *Guns and Membership in the American Polity*, 21 WM. & MARY BILL RTS. J. 619, 620 (2012).

[66] Gulasekaram, *Aliens with Guns*, *supra* note 16, at 908–09.

[67] *Id.* at 895. The first gun control act that mentions noncitizens is the Omnibus Crime Control and Safe Streets Act of 1968, Pub. L. No. 90-351, tit. IV, 82 Stat. 197, 234 (1968) (codified at 18 U.S.C. §§ 921–30 (2000)). Karen A. Michalson, *Constitutional Law — Is 18 U.S.C. § 922 (0)(1) Constitutional? Mere Possession of Self-Created Objects and the Reach of the Commerce Clause*, 28 W. NEW ENG. L. REV. 133, 144 (2005).

[68] Brady Handgun Violence Prevention Act, Pub. L. No. 103-159, 107 Stat. 1536 (1993).

[69] 18 U.S.C. § 922 (g)(5)(A) (2000).

[70] *See* William J. Vizzard, *The Gun Control Act of 1968*, 18 ST. LOUIS U. PUB. L. REV. 79, 87–90 (1999); Franklin E. Zimring, *Firearms and Federal Law: The Gun Control Act of 1968*, 4 J. LEGAL STUD. 133, 140–43 (1975).

equal protection grounds[71] or on the fundamental right to bear arms.[72] Cases upholding state firearm alienage restrictions have either viewed the state police power as creating an exemption to equal protection restrictions,[73] or have rejected preemption challenges based on the interplay between state and federal firearm alienage restrictions.[74] Congress specifically contemplated concurrent state firearm regulation when it enacted the Gun Control Act.[75] In effect, Section 927 of the Act declares that viable preemption challenges are limited to conflict preemption; that is, state laws that are in direct conflict with federal legislation; and not field preemption; that is, state laws that are otherwise consistent with or expand on federal alienage gun restrictions.[76] Thus, a preemption problem would likely arise only if states decreased federal alienage gun restrictions, which currently apply to the undocumented, nonimmigrants, and persons who have denounced their citizenship. In contrast, preemption would not apply if states sought to expand the restriction also to certain lawful permanent residents.[77]

Challenges to federal alienage gun restrictions based on the right to bear arms or on equal protection had also been rejected, namely because a right to bear arms had not been considered an individual right.[78] However, in 2008, the Supreme Court in *District of Columbia v. Heller*[79] recognized the right of an individual to bear arms in the Second Amendment. Additionally, in 2010, in *McDonald v. City of Chicago*,[80] the Court held that the Second Amendment was incorporated against states and localities. Some were convinced these holdings could revive equal protection and right to bear arms challenges to laws restricting alienage use of guns. Not surprisingly, a number of challenges to gun restriction laws based on alienage ensued, with mixed success.

---

[71] *See* Chan v. Troy, 559 N.W.2d 374, 376 (Mich. Ct. App. 1996); State v. Chumphol, 634 P.2d 451 (Nev. 1981); Sandiford v. Com., 217 Va. 117 (Va. 1976); and People v. Rappard, 28 Cal. App. 3d 302 (1972).

[72] *See* People v. Zerillo, 189 N.W. 927 (Mich. 1922).

[73] *See* Ex Parte Rameriz, 226 P. 914 (Cal. 1994); *People v. Cannizaro*, 138 Cal. App. 28 (1934); Utah v. Vlacil, 645 P.2d 677 (Utah 1982); Utah v. Beorchia, 530 P.2d 813 (Utah 1974) and State v. Rheaume, 116 A. 758 (N.H. 1922).

[74] *See* State v. Hernandez-Mercado, 879 P.2d 283 (Wash. 1994).

[75] 18 U.S.C. § 927 (2000).

[76] Gulasekaram, *Aliens with Guns, supra* note 16, at 927.

[77] *Id.*

[78] *See* Lewis v. U.S., 445 U.S. 55, 65 (1980) (reviewing firearm restrictions under rational basis and noting that legislative restrictions on the use of firearms do not trench upon any constitutionally protected liberty); U.S. v. Toner, 728 F.2d 115, 128 (2d Cir. 1984) (holding that the right to possess a gun is a not a fundamental right and that the statute making it a felony for an "illegal alien" to possess or transport "in commerce or affecting commerce . . . any firearm" did not violate the Fifth Amendment right to equal protection).

[79] District of Columbia v. Heller, 554 U.S. 570, 581 (2008).

[80] McDonald v. City of Chicago, 561 U.S. 742 (2010).

The Fourth, Fifth, and Tenth Circuits,[81] as well as at least one district court,[82] have all declined to extend Second Amendment protection to undocumented immigrants charged with crimes for the unlawful possession of guns. For the Fourth and Fifth Circuits, the refusal to extend protection was based on a categorical assertion that "illegal aliens" simply fell outside the scope of the Second Amendment.[83] In contrast, the Tenth Circuit declined to hold that the Second Amendment is inapplicable to noncitizens. Rather, the Tenth Circuit engaged in constitutional avoidance by assuming that the right of the people could include the right of lawful noncitizens to carry guns but, could exclude those rights of "illegal aliens," without violating the Second Amendment or equal protection under rational scrutiny.[84] At least three federal district courts, moreover, have also extended Second Amendment protection to lawful permanent residents challenging state law gun restrictions requiring citizenship.[85]

Part of the explanation for these varied outcomes in the lower courts rests in *Heller* itself, which did not expressly address the issue but hinted that the Second Amendment's use of the word "people" could exclude noncitizens from its protection. The *Heller* Court cited to *U.S. v. Verdugo-Urquidez*,[86] a case involving the meaning of the word "people" in the Fourth Amendment.[87] There, in *dicta*, the Court defined the term as referring to "a class of persons who are part of a national community or who have otherwise developed sufficient connection with this country to be considered part of that community."[88] Lower courts applying this *dictum* have been willing to recognize that "people" includes lawful permanent residents but not undocumented immigrants.[89] It is important to note one significant problematic aspect of cases that exclude undocumented immigrants from the protection of the Second Amendment based on a narrow interpretation of "people." These cases create a contradiction with the extension of Fourth Amendment protections, which also uses the word "people," to criminal defendants who are undocumented.[90] Professor Gulasekaram has also questioned the constitutional validity of an interpretation of "people" to equate it with citizenship, noting as well the historical

---

[81] U.S. v. Izaguirre, 2013 U.S. App. LEXIS 3325 (4th Cir. 2013); U.S. v. Huitron-Guizar, 678 F.3d 1164 (10th Cir. 2012); U.S. v. Carpio-Leon, 701 F.3d 974 (2012); and U.S. v. Portillo-Munoz, 643 F.3d 437 (5th Cir. 2011).

[82] U.S. v. Yanez-Vasquez, 2010 U.S. Dist. LEXIS 8166 (D. Kan. Jan. 28, 2010).

[83] *Izaguirre*, 2013 U.S. App. LEXIS 3325 at 2; *Carpio-Leon*, 701 F.3d at 975 and *Portillo-Munoz*, 643 F.3d at 442.

[84] *Huitron-Guizar*, 678 F.3d at 1167–70.

[85] Fletcher v. Haas, 851 F. Supp. 2d 287 (D. Mass. 2012); Smith v. South Dakota, 781 F. Supp. 2d 879 (D.S.D. 2011); and State v. Ibrahim, 269 P.3d 292 (Wash. Ct. App. 2011).

[86] 494 U.S. 259 (1990).

[87] Heller, 554 U.S. 570, 581.

[88] *Id.* at 265.

[89] *Izaguirre*, 2013 U.S. App. LEXIS 3325 at 2; *Carpio-Leon*, 701 F.3d at 975 and *Portillo-Munoz*, 643 F.3d at 442.

[90] Gulasekaram, *Guns and Membership*, *supra* note 65, at 623 ("[The Fifth Circuit] surprisingly opined that 'the people' of the Second Amendment might be a narrower class of persons than 'the people' of the Fourth Amendment.").

context of gun regulation as motivated by racial animus and xenophobia.[91] Further, Professor Gulasekaram argues that a citizenship-based reading of the right to bear arms is inconsistent with the important role that noncitizens today have in arms-bearing public functions. This includes their substantial military service and the requirement that they must register for selective service.[92]

C. ALIENAGE SUFFRAGE AND OTHER TYPES OF ALIENAGE POLITICAL PARTICIPATION

Historically, states determined who was eligible to vote in both state and federal elections[93] with few exceptions, such as when Congress promoted alien suffrage to encourage immigration in certain U.S. territories.[94] From the founding throughout much of the nineteenth century,[95]states did not restrict voting to citizens. Early support for alienage suffrage was motivated by both democratic and instrumental principles. Not only did states send the message that newcomers would not be excluded from political participation, as it was a natural right (instead exclusion rested on race, gender, property, and wealth), but states also hoped that enfranchising noncitizens would encourage their rapid state settlement.[96]

Wars and the changing faces and needs of immigration into the United States, however, led to a rise in nativism, as well as more restrictive views about who should participate in the community's process of political self-definition.[97] By 1928, no state afforded noncitizen suffrage in statewide or federal elections,[98] a situation that persists until today. Noncitizens are, however, allowed to vote in a few U.S. municipalities, towns, or in school district elections.[99] Even here, however, the

---

[91] Pratheepan Gulasekaram, *"The People" of the Second Amendment: Citizenship and the Right to Bear Arms*, 85 N.Y.U. L. Rev. 1521 (2010).

[92] Gulasekaram, *Aliens with Guns, supra* note 16, at 907.

[93] Gerald L. Neuman, *"We Are the People": Alien Suffrage in German and American Perspective*, 13 Mich. J. Int'l L. 259, 294 (1992).

[94] Jasmin B. Raskin, *Legal Aliens, Local Citizens: The Historical, Constitutional and Theoretical Meanings of Alien Suffrage*, 141 U. Pa. L. Rev. 1391, 1402, 1407 (1993) (discussing the Northwest Ordinance of 1787 and the Organic Acts for the Oregon and Minnesota territories which granted noncitizens the rights to vote in order to produce immigration in those respective territories). Similarly, though Congress did not extend voting rights to noncitizens in lands taken from Mexico during the Mexican war, it did include provisions for alienage suffrage for persons willing to declare their intent to naturalize. *Id.* at 1407–08.

[95] Leon E. Aylsworth, *The Passing of Alien Suffrage*, 25 Am. Pol. Sci. Rev. 114, 114–16 (1931) (documenting that during the nineteenth century the constitutions of at 22 states and territories granted noncitizens the right to vote).

[96] Raskin, *supra* note 94, at 1395.

[97] *See* Neuman, *"We Are the People," supra* note 93, at 296–99; Raskin, *supra* note 94, at 1403–15; Virginia Harper-Ho, *Noncitizen Voting Rights: The History, the Law and Current Prospects for Change*, 18 Law & Ineq. 271, 276 (2000) (discussing the effect of the War of 1812, the Civil War and WWI on alienage suffrage in the United States).

[98] Aylsworth, *supra* note 95, at 114.

[99] Elise Brozovich, *Prospects for Democratic Change: Non-citizen Suffrage in America*, 23 Hamline J. Pub. L. & Pol'y 403 Wm. & Mary Bill Rts. J., 440–44 (2002). *See also* Peter J. Spiro, *The (Dwindling) Rights and Obligations of Citizenship*, 21 899, 908–911.

decision to allow noncitizen vote participation meets resistance. This includes questions over whether localities should be able to make voting eligibility decisions.[100]

Throughout the history of alienage suffrage, the battle to enfranchise noncitizens has been political rather than legal, and the preference has been for state discretion over judicial intervention. Historically, neither the Supreme Court nor lower courts have declared the practice of inclusion unconstitutional.[101] Rather, numerous state courts endorsed alienage suffrage,[102] and even the U.S. Supreme Court indirectly signaled acceptance of the practice based on federalism principles.[103] This treatment of alienage suffrage as a political question appears consistent with constitutional text. Under the U.S. Constitution, alien suffrage is neither constitutionally compelled nor constitutionally forbidden.[104] One oblique reference appears in Article I, which reads that members of the House of Representatives shall be "chosen every second Year by the People of several states,"[105] with "People" possibly being read as narrower than person and imposing a citizenship restriction.[106] The various suffrage amendments (the Fifteenth, Nineteenth, Twenty-fourth, and Twenty-sixth) make explicit reference to citizens.[107] Their language, however, proscribes the exclusion of citizens from voting without prohibiting the inclusion of others. Indeed, just four years after the adoption of the Fifteenth Amendment, the Court in *Minor v. Happersett* did not interpret the word "citizen" to invalidate the common and visible practice of alienage suffrage in several states.[108]

The contemporary practice of alienage suffrage exclusion is likely to be upheld as courts continue to view voting laws as involving political decisions rather than legal mandates.[109] Some scholars have even projected that if Congress were to prohibit

---

[100] *See, e.g.*, Lauren Gilbert, *Reconceiving Citizenship: Noncitizen Voting in New York Municipal Elections as a Case Study in Immigrant Integration and Local Governance*, 2 J. ON MIGRATION & HUMAN SECURITY 223 (2014) (documenting that New York City's attempt to grant voting rights to noncitizens in municipal elections turned on whether City Councils have the authority to decide who "the People" are without approval from the state government in Albany or without a referendum).

[101] Raskin, *supra* note 94, at 1417.

[102] *Id.*

[103] *Id.* at 1717–20 (discussing Dred Scott v. Sanford, 60 U.S. (19 How.) 393, 405 (1856); Minor v. Happersett, 88 U.S. (21 Wall.) 162 (1874); Pope v. Williams, 193 U.S. 621 (1904)).

[104] Neuman, *"We Are the People"*, *supra* note 93, at 292.

[105] U.S. CONST. art.I, § 2, cl. 1.

[106] Neuman, *"We Are the People"*, *supra* note 93, at 292. *See also* notes 86–90 and accompanying text (discussing the U.S. Supreme Court holding in *Verdugo-Urquidez*).

[107] Other constitutional provisions cited in the alienage suffrage debate includes Article IV, § 4, the Republican Guaranty Clause ["The United States shall guarantee to every State in this Union a Republican Form of Government . . . "] and the Fourteenth Amendment, cl. 1, the Privileges and Immunities Clause ["Not state shall make or enforce any law which shall abridge the privileges and immunities of citizens of the United States."]. Alienage suffrage, however, does not contravene the text of either provision. Harper-Ho, *supra* note 97, at 289–290.

[108] 88 U.S. at 177. *See also* Raskin, *supra* note 94, at 1424–30 (arguing that the suffrage amendments to not require states to confine voting to U.S. citizens).

[109] Indeed, subsequent equal protection challenges to laws prohibiting alien suffrage in local elections

alienage suffrage, such law would be upheld under modern constitutional law and federal immigration power.[110] Moreover, despite early arguments to the contrary,[111] equal protection challenges to state alienage suffrage restrictions would likely fall under the political-function exception doctrine.[112] Under this doctrine, alienage discrimination has been upheld in areas of government and politics.[113]

More recently, states have adopted at least four types of alienage voting restrictions laws;[114] those that criminalize voting in an election without proper authorization;[115] those that target public officials who allow noncitizens to vote;[116] those that mandate voters prove their citizenship status for voter registration or at the voting poll;[117] and those that limit the ability of noncitizens to donate to public campaigns.[118] At least with regard to laws that require voters to prove their citizenship to either register to vote or to carry out their vote, the Ninth Circuit struck down Arizona's proposition 200 based on preemption grounds based on the National Voter Registration Act, which the court held superseded the state's voter registration procedures.[119] The Ninth Circuit, however, declined to hold that the law also violated equal protection or the Voting Rights Act. It concluded respectively, that requiring voters to show identification is not invidious discrimination unrelated to voter qualification nor results in the denial or abridgement of the right of any citizen to vote on account of race or color under section (2)(a) of the VRA.[120] Then, on October 18, 2014, the Supreme Court without providing a reasoning,

---

have been unsuccessful. *See, e.g.*, Park v. State, 528 P.2d 785 (Alaska 1974) (upholding law that restricted voting in state elections to citizens); Padilla v. Allison, 38 Cal. App. 3d 784 (1974) (upholding California's Constitutional provision making citizenship a prerequisite to voting).

[110] Neuman, *"We Are the People"*, *supra* note 93, at 324. *But cf.* Harper-Ho, *supra* note 97, at 288–89 and Raskin, *supra* note 94, at 1430–31.

[111] Gerald Rosberg, *Aliens and Equal Protection: Why Not the Right to Vote?*, 75 Mich. L. Rev. 1092, (1977) (arguing that equal protection should be read to guarantee the right of resident noncitizens to vote at all levels of government).

[112] Brozovich, *supra* note 99, at 421–26.

[113] *See generally infra* subsection F. The Political-Function Exception.

[114] At the federal level, some have proposed laws to exclude undocumented citizens from counting for purposes of federal apportionment. *See* Patrick J. Charles, *Representation Without Documentation? Unlawfully Present Aliens, Apportionment, the Doctrine of Allegiance, and the Law*, 25 BYU J. Pub. L. 35, 38 (2011).

[115] *See, e.g.*, S.B. 007, 65th Gen. Assem., 1st Extr. Sess. (Colo. 2006) (making the act of deliberately voting in an election without proper authorization a Class 5 felony)

[116] *See. e.g.*, S.B. 162, 143rd Gen. Assem. Reg. Sess. (Del. 2006) (requiring appointed elected officials to swear they will not knowingly or willfully receive a vote from a noncitizen at a polling place of election).

[117] *See, e.g.*, Arizona Taxpayer and Citizen's Protection Act, Proposition 200 (Ariz. 2004); S.B. 403, 2006 Reg. Sess. (N.H. 2006), S.B. 118, 81st Leg. Assem., Reg. Sess. (S.D 2006); Georgia (2008), New Hampshire (2008), and Washington (2008); H.B. 2067, 2011 Reg. Sess. (2011); S.B. 165, 2011 Gen. Sess., Leg. Gen. Counsel (Utah 2011); Colorado (2012); California (2012); Virginia (2013) (requiring proof of citizenship or clarification documents that may be used for voter registration purposes that are only available to citizens).

[118] *See, e.g.*, National Conference of State Legislature, 2010 Immigration-Related Laws and Resolution in the States, *available at* http://www.ncsl.org/research/immigration/2010-immigration-related-laws-and-resolutions-936.aspx (describing generally laws passed in Alaska, California, and Utah).

[119] Gonzalez et al., v. Arizona, 624 F.3d 1162 (9th Cir. 2010).

[120] *Id.* at 1192–98.

issued an order to permit the state of Texas to use its strict voting identification law in the upcoming elections. The three female Justices joined in a strong dissent saying the order would risks denying the right to vote to hundreds of thousands of eligible voters.[121]

As to alienage proscriptions on campaign contributions, temporary immigrants and undocumented immigrants (but not lawful permanent residents) are, in fact, already prohibited under federal law from making campaign donations under the Bipartisan Campaign Reform Act (BCRA).[122] At least one federal district court has rejected a First Amendment challenge to the BCRA brought by temporary work visa holders.[123] Thus, it is possible that similar state laws would be upheld as long as they do not target lawful permanent residents or unless the state laws are preempted by the BCRA.

Contemporary arguments over alienage suffrage or other types of political participation continue to emphasize the State's discretion to define the political community. This continues even as restrictive voting qualifications as applied to citizens (e.g., literacy or residency requirements) face strict scrutiny equal protection challenges.[124] Local arguments for inclusion have generally focused on the legitimate interest of resident noncitizens in having a say in the rules that govern their conduct and affect their interests in light of their status as subjects of U.S. laws. In addition, it focuses on their degree of contributions and stakes in the community.[125] Others espouse on even stricter commitment to the First Amendment, at least as to political contributions, and argue that the only legitimate restriction to political speech should be based on proven instances of corruption.[126] In contrast, those who oppose alienage suffrage insist on citizenship as an essential precondition for voting. They also question the fairness of including nonmembers and cast doubt on the loyalty of those who decline to declare their allegiance and full commitment to the United States.[127]

D. ALIENS AND JURY SERVICE

Between the twelfth and nineteenth centuries, England experienced the rise and fall of the mixed jury, a special jury comprised of both citizens and aliens to resolve disputes between community members and outsiders.[128] In the United States, the courts in the late eighteenth and early nineteenth centuries followed England in

---

[121] Veasy v. Perry, 135 S. Ct. 9 (2014).

[122] *See* James Ianellli, *Noncitizens and Citizens United*, 56 Loy. L. Rev. 869 (2010) (discussing the BCRA's ban on independent expenditures from foreign sources).

[123] Bluman v. Federal Elections Commission, 800 F. Supp. 2d 281 (D.D.C. 2011).

[124] Neuman, *"We Are the People," supra* note 93, at 313–22.

[125] Raskin, *supra* note 94, at 1441–45.*See also* Harper-Ho, *supra* note 97, at 294–98.

[126] Ianelli, *supra* note 122, at 873.

[127] Neuman, *"We Are the People", supra* note 93, at 325–30. *See also* Charles, *supra* note 114 and Adam B. Cox and Eric A. Posner, *The Rights of Migrants: An Optimal Contract Framework*, 84 N.Y.U. L. Rev. 1403, 1442–44 (2009).

[128] *See generally* Marianne Constable, The Law of the Other: The Mixed Jury and Changing Conceptions of Citizenship, Law, and Knowledge (1994).

providing non-citizens on trial a mixed jury.[129] The disappearance of the practice in England, however, led to its demise in the United States. By 1936, the U.S. Supreme Court declared that the mixed jury practice no longer existed.[130] Today, all states make citizenship a requirement for jury service by law or practice.[131] Challenges under equal protection or Sixth Amendment to these requirements by either the accused or the excluded noncitizen grounds have been unsuccessful.[132]

California would have become in 2013 the first state to allow lawful permanent residents (about 3.5 million living in the state) to serve on juries.[133] However, the law was vetoed by Governor Jerry Brown who likened jury service to voting and said that the responsibility should come only with citizenship.[134] Some constitutional scholars agree with Governor Brown. Professor Vikram David Amar has argued, for example, that jury service, like voting and office holding, was conceived as a political right, as distinguished from a civil right; moreover political rights were excluded from the coverage of the Fourteenth Amendment and were instead included most directly through the voting amendments, beginning with the Fifteenth and running through the Twenty-Sixth.[135] The Sixth Amendment, which guaranties the accused the right to a jury trial, does not explicitly require citizenship,[136] but the U.S. Supreme Court, at least in dicta, has suggested that states may require jurors to be citizens.[137]

The result of the exclusion of all noncitizens from jury service, however, is both numerically significant as well as skewed by race and ethnicity.[138] As a result, some argue that it is possible to challenge noncitizen jury exclusion both on equal protection grounds, from the perspective of those excluded, as well as on Sixth Amendment grounds, from the perspective of the accused who can claim that his peers are not judging him or her.[139] Proponents of noncitizens serving in juries also note that the exclusion of noncitizens from jury service raises concerns related to the quality of the jury's deliberation and decision-making. The concern is that

---

[129] See Lewis H. LaRue, A Jury of One's Peers, 33 Wash. & Lee L. Rev. 841, 850 (1976).

[130] U.S. v. Wood, 299 U.S. 123 (1936).

[131] See, e.g., Mary Lombardi, Reassessing Jury Service Citizenship Requirements, 59 Case W. Res. L. Rev. 725, 728–29 (2009).

[132] Id. at 729–34.

[133] Occasionally, some noncitizens have served on juries in error. This error will not necessarily be remedied with a new trial since the Sixth Amendment guarantees a jury but not an all citizen jury. See, e.g., Owens v. State, 924 A.2d 1072 (Md. 2007), cert. denied, 552 U.S. 1144 (2008).

[134] Jennifer Medina, Veto Halts Bills for Jury Duty by Noncitizens in California, N.Y. Times, Oct. 3, 2013.

[135] Vikram David Amar, Jury Service as Political Participation Akin to Voting, 80 Cornell L. Rev. 203, 204 (1995).

[136] The Sixth Amendment states that "[i]n criminal prosecutions, the accused shall enjoy the right to a speedy and public trial, by an impartial jury of the State and district wherein the crime shall have been committed." U.S. Const. amend. VI.

[137] Amy R. Motomura, Note, The American Jury: Can Noncitizens Still be Excluded? 64 Stan. L. Rev. 1503, 1504–05 (2012) (referencing Thompson v. Utah, 170 U.S. 343 (1898) and Williams v. Florida, 399 U.S. 78 (1970)).

[138] Id. at 1506–1510.

[139] Id. at 1516–1545.

alienage exclusion reduces the diversity of juries, questions the legitimacy of representation by excluding noncitizen parties when many who face crime are themselves noncitizens, and denies many the ability to serve in an important civil institution when they are otherwise well integrated into the fabric of U.S. society.[140]

E.   THE SPECIAL PUBLIC INTEREST DOCTRINE

For most of U.S. history, states have been free to reserve resources for their own citizens or to share them with noncitizens. Throughout the seventeenth century, for example, some states restricted access to natural resources and commercial licenses solely to citizens.[141] What would become known as the special public interest doctrine was subsequently extended into areas of private and public employment, as well as in the area of public benefits.[142] While the original special public interest doctrine did not survive equal protection and preemption scrutiny,[143] even today some states continue to bar all noncitizens (including lawful permanent residents) or only some (i.e., temporary or undocumented) from private and public jobs, professional licenses, from state institutions of higher learning, and from public benefits.[144]

The first time the Court struck down a special public interest ordinance was in 1886 in *Yick Wo v. Hopkins.*[145] A San Francisco local ordinance, while neutral on its face, was used to deny commercial licenses almost exclusively to Chinese laundry mat owners, some of whom had operated their businesses for more than 20 years.[146] The Court acknowledged the racial animus behind the ordinance and applied the Fourteenth Amendment to strike it down.[147] *Yick Wo*, however, did not rid states of the special public interest exception. Many statutes barring noncitizens from jobs or natural resources continued to be upheld by the courts.[148] In addition, courts justified certain types of alienage commercial restrictions based on the states' police powers, which they could employ to protect the health, safety, welfare, and morals of the community.[149]

---

[140] *Id.* at 1511–16. *See also* Lombardi, *supra* note 131, at 737–61.

[141] *See, e.g.*, McCready v. Virginia, 94 U.S. 391 (1876) (local ordinance barring noncitizens from catching and planning oysters in local river).

[142] *See generally infra* subsections F. The Political-Function Exception, G. Private Employment, and I. Public Benefits.

[143] *See infra* subsections F. The Political-Function Exception, G. Private Employment, I. Public Benefits, and J.2. Higher Education.

[144] *See infra* subsections E–J.

[145] Yick Wo v. Hopkins, 118 U.S. 356 (1886).

[146] *Id.* at 358.

[147] *Id.* at 368.

[148] *See, e.g.*, Crane v. New York, 239 U.S. 195 (1915) (government contracts); Heim v. McCall, 239 U.S. 175 (1915) (subway contracts); McCready v. Virginia, 94 U.S. 391 (1876) (oysters at a local river); Patsone v. Commw. of Pennsylvania, 232 U.S. 138 (1914) (hunting wild game).

[149] *See, e.g.*, Trageser v. Gray, 20 A. 905 (Md. 1890) (upholding restriction on selling liquor given the inherent danger of the business). *But see* Templer v. Michigan State Bd. of Examiners of Barbers, 90 N.W. 1058 (Mich. 1902) (striking down restriction on noncitizens from becoming barbers as unnecessary to protect health).

In 1915, the Court limited somewhat the public interest doctrine in *Truax v. Raich*. The Court struck down an Arizona statute forbidding private businesses of more than five persons from filling their work force with more than 20 percent noncitizens.[150] The Court held that states could not bar noncitizens from the "common occupations of the community,"[151] though it left open the permissibility of alienage restrictions in areas outside employment.[152] States thus continued to carve out exceptions to *Truax*, excluding noncitizens from operating certain businesses or engaging in certain occupations. States argued that such alienage restrictions constituted reasonable police regulation to protect the public interest. These exceptions elicited mixed holdings from the courts. In 1927, for example, the Court upheld an Ohio law that barred noncitizens from operating pool halls, considering such places to be potential locations of depravity.[153] Meanwhile, state courts upheld certain alienage restrictions in areas of public employment,[154] transportation services,[155] fishing,[156] and labor union positions.[157] In other states, similar restrictions on commercial licenses or occupations, however, did not survive courts' skepticism that the nature of the business threatened the public welfare. These laws were struck down as violating equal protection or treaty obligations.[158]

Not until 30 years after *Truax* did the Court again reject a public interest rationale for discriminating against noncitizens. In 1948, in *Takahashi v. Fish & Game Commission*, the Court struck down a California law that denied fishing licenses to foreign nationals ineligible for citizenship.[159] The Court required California to establish a rational relation test to the restriction and articulate the state special public interest of regulating the supply of fish.[160] In striking down the law, however, the Court refused to consider the racist legislative purpose of the statute, which targeted the Japanese.[161] The Court did, however, hold that the fishing restriction was preempted by the federal government's plenary power to regulate noncitizens. It stressed that "the power of the state to apply its laws

---

[150] Truax v. Raich, 239 U.S. 33 (1915).

[151] *Id.* at 41.

[152] *Id.* at 41–43.

[153] State of Ohio ex rel. Clarke v. Deckeback, 274 U.S. 392, 396 (1927). Prior state cases have also upheld similar restrictions. *See* Anton v. Winkle, 297 F. 340 (D. Or. 1924); State ex rel. Balli v. Carrel, 124 N.E. 129 (Ohio 1919).

[154] People v. Crane, 108 N.E. 427 (N.Y. 1915); Lee v. City of Lynn, 111 N.E. 700 (Mass. 1916); Cornelius v. City of Seattle, 213 P. 17 (Wash. 1923), overruled by Herriott v. City of Seattle, 500 P.2d 101 (Wash. 1972).

[155] Morin v. Nunan, 103 A. 378 (N.J. 1918) (denying licenses to transport passengers for hire).

[156] Alsos v. Kendall et.al., 227 P. 286 (Or. 1924).

[157] American Fed'n. of Labor v. Mann, 188 S.W. 2d 276 (Tex. Civ. App. 1945).

[158] Abe v. Fish and Game Comm'n of Cal., 9 Cal. App. 2d 300 (1935) (commercial fishing license); Magnani v. Harnett, 257 A.D. 487 (N.Y. App. Div. 1939) (chauffeur licenses); Wormsen v. Moss, 29 N.Y.S.2d 798 (1941) massage parlor operators; State ex rel. Quisor v. Ellis, 184 P.2d 860 (Or. 1947) (barber shop).

[159] 334 U.S. 410 (1948).

[160] *Id.* at 418–20.

[161] *Id.* at 418 (it is "unnecessary to resolve this controversy concerning the [racial] motives that prompted enactment of the legislation").

exclusively to its alien inhabitants as a class is confined within narrow limits."[162] In the meantime, some states continued to rely on the public interest doctrine, at times unsuccessfully, to discriminate against noncitizens, including by barring them from certain jobs.[163]

Takahashi cast doubt on the special public interest doctrine. However, more than two decades passed before the Court rejected the doctrine and granted noncitizens, at least lawful permanent residents, a suspect class status. In 1971, in *Graham v. Richardson*, the Court struck down two state welfare statutes that denied benefits to noncitizens, including legal permanent residents. It did so by applying a strict scrutiny analysis and declaring that "classifications based on alienage . . . are inherently suspect and subject to close judicial scrutiny."[164] The Court also relied on preemption as another reason for invalidating the statutes, stating that laws that restrict welfare eligibility of noncitizens "conflict with . . . overriding national policies in an area constitutionally entrusted to the Federal Government."[165]

Some scholars have dated the death of the special public interest doctrine as early as 1948 or at least 1971, with the Court's holdings in *Takahashi* and *Graham*, respectively.[166] Different doctrines, however, have emerged, such as the political-function exception or the expansion of the federal plenary power doctrine over immigration. Moreover, Congress' legislature devolution of its immigration power to states has permitted localities to restrict their resources for citizens, at least as to certain public jobs or certain public benefits in nearly the same scope as was permitted under the special public interest doctrine.[167] Moreover, since *Graham*, recent constitutional holdings have more clearly narrowed the application of equal protection to a narrower group of noncitizens, primarily lawful permanent residents. These holding have allowed states wide discretion, with the exception of K-12 public education, to exclude undocumented immigrants from the enjoyment of state resources.[168] Further, limitations on the preemption doctrine have expanded the ability of states to discriminate against undocumented or temporary foreign residents, particularly in the area of private employment.[169]

---

[162] *Id.* at 420.

[163] *See, e.g.*, Perotta v. Gregory, 158 N.Y.S.2d 221 (1957) (upholding alienage restriction for garbage collector job); Purdy and Fitzpatrick v. State, 456 P.2d 645 (Cal. 1969) (striking down statute that prohibited noncitizen employment on public works based on preemption); Dep't of Labor and Industry v. Cruz, 212 A.2d 545 (N.J. 1965) (striking down based on equal protection a statute banning noncitizen employment in public works employment); Hsieh v. Civil Serv. Comm'n of City of Seattle, 488 P.2d 515 (Wash. 1971) (striking down citizenship requirement to be a civil engineer); Herriott v. City of Seattle, 500 P.2d 101 (Wash. 1972) (striking down citizenship requirement to become city transit operator).

[164] 403 U.S. 365, 371–72 (1971).

[165] *Id.* at 378.

[166] *See* Michael Scaperlanda, *Partial Membership: Aliens and the Constitutional Community*, 81 IOWA L. REV. 707, 735 (1996).

[167] *See generally infra* subsections F. The Political-Function Exception, H. Private Employment, and I. Public Benefits.

[168] *See generally infra* subsections I. Public Benefits, J.2. Higher Education, K. Worker Rights, L. Driver's Licenses, and M. Landlord/Tenant Immigration Ordinances.

[169] *See generally infra* subsection H. Private Employment.

F.   THE POLITICAL-FUNCTION EXCEPTION

For public service jobs, the U.S. Supreme Court carved out early in its jurisprudence a political-function exception, which has permitted states to restrict certain public jobs for their citizens. In 1915, the same year that the Court decided *Truax* and struck down a citizenship requirement as a condition of private employment, the Court also upheld in *Crane v. New York* a New York statute prohibiting the employment of noncitizens on public works projects.[170] As described above, successful challenges to the special public interest exception put into question the remaining validity of *Crane*; however, it would not be the end of noncitizen public employment restrictions, which would ultimately be upheld under a new doctrine that would become known as the political-function exception.

The first Supreme Court case to allude to the political-function doctrine was *Sugarman v. Dougall*, which struck down a New York State law that limited state competitive civil service positions to U.S. citizens.[171] The Court rejected the broad application of the special public interest doctrine that had earlier restricted noncitizen access to certain public rights and resources.[172] It required instead a substantial state interest and a narrowly tailored law to achieve that interest.[173] *Sugarman*, however, left open the possibility that a citizenship requirement for some public jobs in which the state had a legitimate interest — i.e., "where citizenship bears some rational relationship to the special demands of a particular position" — could pass constitutional muster.[174] This prerogative, the Court explained, resides in a State's power and responsibility "to preserve the basic conception of a political community."[175] This pertains "not only to the qualification of voter, but also to persons holding state elective or important non-elective executive, legislative, and judicial positions."[176] Such public officers, the Court considered, "perform functions that go to the heart of representative government[s]."[177]

After *Sugarman*, the Court began to carve out areas in which states could require citizenship in public employment. In essence, the political-function exception permitted states to show only a rational relationship between the alienage restriction and the interest that were sought to be protected.[178] In *Foley v. Connelie*, decided just a year after *Sugarman*, police officers became the first

---

[170]   Crane v. New York, 239 U.S. 195 (1915).

[171]   413 U.S. 634 (1973).

[172]   John E. Richards, *Public Employment Rights of Aliens*, 31 Baylor L. Rev. 371, 372–74 (1982).

[173]   *Sugarman*, 413 U.S. at 641–46. Interestingly, in 1975, the Supreme Court in Hampton v. Mow Sun Wong, 426 U.S. 88 (1976), struck down a federal regulation barring noncitizens, including lawfully admitted permanent residents, from employment in the federal competitive civil service. In doing so, it rejected the argument that the federal government's plenary power over immigration did not extend to its ability to arbitrarily subject all resident aliens to different substantive rules from those that applied to citizens. *Id.*

[174]   *Id.* at 647 (quoting from Judge Lumbaards' lower court's separate concurrence opinion).

[175]   *Id.* (quoting from Dunn v. Blumstein, 405 U.S. 330, 344 (1972)).

[176]   *Id.*

[177]   *Id.*

[178]   Foley v. Connelie, 435 U.S. 291, 297 (1978).

exception. Here, the Court justified its holding on the basis that police, while they do not formulate policy, use a high degree of judgment and discretion that affect the lives of citizens, and that, moreover, citizens are presumed to be more familiar and sympathetic to U.S. traditions.[179] Both Justice Blackmun's concurrence and Justice Marshall's dissent in *Foley* expressed concern over the watering down of the requirement that important positions must involve policymaking, not merely policy execution.[180]

A year after *Foley*, in *Ambach v. Norwick*, the Court extended the political-function exception to teachers employed in public schools. The Court reasoned that teaching fulfills "a most fundamental obligation of government to its constituency" and is "so bound up with the operation of the state."[181] The Court came to this conclusion because teachers as role models have a unique opportunity "to influence the attitudes of students toward government, the political process and citizens' social responsibility."[182] *Ambach* provoked a strong four-member dissent returning again to the requirement that important public employees must participate directly in policy setting, a role that teachers did not fulfill.[183]

In 1982, in *Cabell v. Chavez-Salido*, the Court not only extended the political-function exception to probation officers,[184] but created an even more flexible rule permitting states to apply it to a broadly worded statute.[185] The statute actually precluded noncitizens from jobs as peace officers. In addition to probation officers, this included 70 different types of jobs such as toll takers, cemetery sextons, fish and game wardens, furniture and bedding inspectors, and Board of Dental Examiners.[186] The Court announced a two-pronged test to decide the issue: first, to examine whether the classification was inclusive (i.e., narrowly tailored); and second, whether the classification involved a non-elective government position of someone who participated directly in the formulation, operation or review of broad public policy.[187] As to the first prong, the Court rejected a standard based solely on the general reach of the statute, inquiring instead into "whether the restriction reaches so far and is so broad and haphazard as to belie the state's claim that it is only attempting to ensure that an important function of the government be in the hands of [citizens]."[188] In essence, as the dissent pointed out, this approach changed the standard of review of alienage classifications challenge as overbroad from one of strict scrutiny to only a requirement of "substantial fit."[189] Thus, while the Court acknowledged that some of the categories had, at best, a "tenuous" connection to

---

[179] *Id.* at 297–300.

[180] *Id.* at 301 (Blackmun, J. concurring); *Id.* at 303–13 (Marshall, J., dissenting).

[181] Ambach v. Norwick, 441 U.S. 68, 69–72 (1979).

[182] *Id.* at 79.

[183] *Id.* at 83.

[184] 454 U.S. 432, (1982).

[185] *Id.*

[186] *Id.* at 450.

[187] *Id.* at 441.

[188] *Id.* at 442.

[189] *Id.* at 453.

usual police activities, it emphasized that the general arrest authority theoretically accorded all peace officers to find the statute "sufficiently tailored" to the aims sought.[190] As to the second prong, the Court reasoned that probation officers' tremendous discretionary and coercive authority over those who have been found to violate the norms of social order met the requirement of the job's political function.[191] Here too, the four-member dissent reiterated similar concerns to the ones expressed in *Ambach* because probation officers also do not directly engage in policy making, nor were their coercive powers over law-breaking citizens unique.[192] With *Cabell*, the dissenting Justices feared, almost every judicial and bureaucratic position would qualify for the political-function exception.[193] As discussed in the section below, however, the Supreme Court has rejected the political function exception in a number of cases, primarily involving noncitizen access to professional licenses that are insufficiently related to a public function.

The political-function exception has been justified as a means to preserve the significance of citizenship within a community, which requires drawing lines between community and outsiders.[194] Disagreement arises still as to where exactly that line should be drawn, as every public employee could suddenly be transformed into a policymaker to exclude noncitizens.[195] Many caution, moreover, that courts have employed the rhetoric of preserving the political community to discriminate against noncitizens who are stereotyped as disloyal and unwilling to adopt U.S. values.[196]

G. PROFESSIONAL OR OCCUPATIONAL LICENSES AND NONCITIZENS

States have traditionally regulated a wide variety of occupations or professions by requiring licensing in order to protect the public health, safety, and welfare.[197] One of the contested issues is whether states have the power to condition license eligibility on immigration status. At least with regard to lawful permanent residents, the latest answer has been no, so long as these professions do not legitimately serve a political-function. In 1975, in *In re Griffiths*, decided the same

---

[190] *Id.* at 444.

[191] *Id.* at 446.

[192] *Id.* at 453.

[193] *Id.* at 461–62. Some lower courts, however, will still strike down broadly worded statutes that ban noncitizens from all public employment, even if as applied they pertain to professions that the Court has found to have a "political function." *See, e.g.*, Chang v. Glynn County School Dist., 457 F. Supp. 2d 1378 (S.D. Ga. 2006) (striking down Georgia's statute that barred noncitizens from all public employment when applied to fire noncitizen public school teacher plaintiffs).

[194] *See* Kiyoko Kamio Knapp, *The Rhetoric of Exclusion: The Art of Drawing a Line Between Aliens and Citizens*, 10 Geo. Immigr. L.J. 401, 412 (1996); Scaperlanda, *supra* note 166, at 736–37.

[195] Knapp, *The Rhetoric of Exclusion, supra* note 194, at 412.

[196] *Id.* at 418–23. *See also* Kenneth L. Karst, Belonging to America: Equal Citizenship and the Constitution 87 (1989).

[197] Jennessa Calvo-Friedman, Note, *The Uncertain Terrain of State Occupational Licensing Laws for Noncitizens: A Preemption Analysis*, 102 Geo. L.J. 1597, 1598 (2014) ("Eight hundred occupations required a license by at least one state during 2003").

day as *Sugarman,* the Court struck down a citizenship requirement of admission to the Connecticut bar and rejected the argument that lawyers, as officers of the court, were formulators of governmental policy.[198] Until then, an overwhelming majority of states prevented even lawful permanent residents from gaining admission to the bar.[199] In striking down the restriction, the Court found that lawyers are not officials of government by virtue of being lawyers as they were not so close to the core of the political process as to make them formulators of government policy.[200] In 1976, the Court also rejected a similar restriction with regard to civil engineers.[201] Then, in 1984, the Court rejected the political-function exception as applied to public notaries.[202] In doing so, the Court reiterated that the political-function exception is supposed to be narrow and should apply only to positions intimately related to the process of democratic self-government.[203]

On the other hand, the exclusion of undocumented noncitizens or even temporary immigrants (or nonimmigrants) from professional jobs has yielded mixed results in the lower courts. In 2005, for example, the Fifth Circuit in *LeClerc v. Webb* upheld Louisiana's exclusion of nonimmigrants from admission to the State Bar.[204] Meanwhile, a federal district court upheld Louisiana's bar of nonimmigrants from obtaining a nursing license in the state.[205] In contrast, the Second Circuit in *Adusumelli v. Steiner* and other lower federal district courts in New York have invalidated New York licensing statutes that precluded nonimmigrants from the pharmacy profession.[206] The circuit split reveals court's disagreement over whether nonimmigrants who are lawfully admitted to the United States, even if temporarily, constitute a suspect class or are subject only to rational review protection.[207] Further, it reveals division on whether federal law preempts such laws insofar as employment restrictions on individuals granted work authorization under the immigration laws are precluded under state law to pursue the very purpose of the visa.[208]

More recently, the contested issue has become whether undocumented law graduates could or should be permitted to seek admission into state bars to become

---

[198] *In re Griffiths,* 413 U.S. 717, 729 (1973).

[199] Kiyoko Kamio Knapp, *Disdain of Alien Lawyers: History of Exclusion,* 7 Seton Hall Const. L.J. 103, 121–40 (1996). *See also* Kevin R. Johnson, *Bias in the Legal System? An Essay on the Eligibility of Undocumented Immigrants to Practice Law,* 46 U.C. Davis L. Rev. 1655, 1658 (2013).

[200] In re Griffiths, 413 U.S. at 729.

[201] Examining Board of Engineers, Architects, and Surveyors v. Flores de Otero, 426 U.S. 572 (1976).

[202] Bernal v. Fainter, 467 U.S. 216 (1984). For a critique of *In re Griffith, see* Sanford Levinson, *National Loyalty, Communalism, and the Professional Identity of Lawyers,* 7 Yale J.L. & Human 49 (1995).

[203] *Id.* at 221.

[204] 419 F.3d 405 (5th Cir. 2005).

[205] Van Staden v. St. Martin, 664 F.3d 56 (2011).

[206] Dandamudi v. Tisch, 686 F. 3d 66 (2012) and Adusumelli v. Steiner, 740 F. Supp. 2d 582 (S.D.N.Y. 2010).

[207] *See, e.g.,* Justin Storch, *Legal Impediments Facing Nonimmigrants Entering Licensed Professions,* 7 Mod. Am. 12 (2011).

[208] Calvo-Friedman, *supra* note 197, at 1609.

licensed to practice law. The issue has arisen in the context of a few states, such as Florida, California, and New York, exploring the legality of granting rather than denying admission to recent law graduates to the profession of law. Because of this, the issue has not turned on equal protection challenges but solely on federal preemption grounds. The basis for the preemption challenge has turned on the language of 8 U.S.C. Section 1621. Interestingly this provision was never mentioned by the Fifth or Second Circuits when deciding *LeClerc and Adusumelli*, implying through omissions, perhaps, that they did not view the provision as relevant.[209] In contrast, however, the Ninth Circuit and the Supreme Court of Florida, as discussed below, view 8 U.S.C. Section 1621 as determinative of whether California and Florida respectively may allow undocumented law students admission into the state bar.

Subsection (d) of Section 1621, which was passed as part of major welfare reform legislation — 1996 Personal Responsibility and Work Opportunity Act, authorized a state, if it so chooses, to affirmatively confer a state or local public benefit to which unqualified noncitizens would otherwise be ineligible. Under the law, undocumented immigrants, but not nonimmigrant, were deemed to be unqualified noncitizens under subsection (a). Subsection (c)(2)(C) of Section 1621 further defined state or local public benefit as including "the issuance of a professional license to, or the renewal of a professional license by, a foreign national not physically present in the United States."[210] Both the Ninth Circuit and the Florida Supreme Court understood this provision to bar undocumented noncitizens from being granted a license to practice law, unless the state affirmatively passed legislation as authorized under Subsection (d).[211] Moreover, while in California the state legislature had passed a law to grant such authorization,[212] the same was not true in Florida when the Florida's Supreme Court ruling was issued. Thus, these two cases, relying on a preemption analysis, yielded different results with California but not Florida authorizing the admission of undocumented law students into the state bar.[213] Subsequently, however, in May 2014, Florida enacted HB 755 into law, which allows undocumented noncitizens to be admitted to the state bar upon fulfilling all the requirements for admission.[214] As of the date of publication, New York's decision

---

[209] *Id.* at 1624.

[210] 8 U.S.C. § 1621(c)(2)(C).

[211] *In re* Garcia, 315 P.3d 117, 128 (Cal. 2014) and Florida Board of Bar Examines re Question as to Whether Undocumented Immigrants are Eligible for Admission to the Florida Bar, 134 So. 3d 432 (Fla. 2014).

[212] California passed AB 1024 into law in response to the Supreme Court arguments in the *In Re Garcia* case in September 2013. AB 1024 added the following language to the California Business and professions Code:

> Upon certification by the examining committee that an applicant who is not lawfully present in the United States has fulfilled the requirements of admission to practice law, the Supreme court may admit that applicant as an attorney of law in all the courts of this state and may direct an order to be entered upon its records to that effect.

Text of AB 1024 *available at* http://leginfo.legislature.ca.gov/faces/billNavClient.xhtml?bill_id= 201320140AB1024.

[213] *Id.*

[214] Fla. Stat. § 454.021(3) reads:

whether to follow California and Florida's lead is still pending.

Finally, it is important to note that both the Florida and California laws condition the admission of undocumented law students as lawyers in the state upon satisfying all of the requirements for admission, including character and fitness and passage of the bar exam. The laws imply, however, that undocumented status alone is not a bar to moral character and fitness, or at least that Board Examiners of those states have not deemed it to be.[215] In fact, the California Supreme Court concluded in its judgment that Sergio Garcia, the undocumented graduate from UCLA, had met his burden of establishing good moral character.[216] Further, the decision to admit undocumented law students into the profession, as the California Supreme Court clarified, does not amount to an authorization to work under the immigration laws. Neither does it alter in any way the ongoing unauthorized stay of the applicant who remains subject to removal.[217]

H. PRIVATE EMPLOYMENT

In 1971, California was in the spotlight for enacting the first law in the nation imposing employer sanctions for knowingly hiring employees who were not at minimum, lawful permanent residents.[218] In a series of lower court battles, however, at least for jobs falling outside the scope of the political-function exception, *Graham v. Richardson* immediately led to the defeat of many similar state laws imposing alienage employment restrictions based on equal protection and/or preemption grounds.[219] That same year, however, the Court decided *De Canas v. Bica*, which upheld the California law.[220] *De Canas* became a landmark victory for states which led to the adoption by other states of laws prohibiting employers from hiring undocumented workers.[221]

Upon certification by the Florida Board of Bar Examiners that an applicant who is not lawfully present in the United States has fulfilled all requirements for admission to practice law in this state, the Supreme Court of Florida may admit that applicant as an attorney at law authorized to practice in this state and may direct an order be entered upon the court's records to that effect.

[215] For a detailed analysis of what may be some issues unique to undocumented law students that could bear on decisions related to character and fitness to practice law, see Raquel Aldana, Beth Lyon, Karla Mari McKanders, *Raising the Bar: Law Schools and Legal Institutions Leading to Educate Undocumented Students*, 44 ARIZ. ST. L.J. 5, 15–37 (2012).

[216] *In re Garcia*, 315 P.3d 117, 128 at 134 (Cal. 2014). The court noted that Garcia was brought to the U.S. undocumented as a child by his parents and had since led an exemplary life with the exception of two problematical incidents that the bar committee did not consider relevant to their finding that Garcia possessed the good moral character for a law license. *Id.* at 134

[217] *Id.* at 132.

[218] Rick Su, *The States of Immigration*, 54 WM. & MARY L. REV. 1339, 1364 (2013).

[219] *See Herriott v. City of Seattle*, 500 P.2d 101 (Wash. 1972) (on transit operators); Sundram v. City of Niagara Falls, 357 N.Y.S.2d 943 (1973) (taxi cab drivers); Mohamed v. Parks, 352 F. Supp. 518 (D. Mass. 1973) (counselors); Wong v. Hohnstrom, 405 F. Supp. 727 (D. Minn. 1975) (pharmacists); C.D.R. Enterprises, LTD., et al., v. Bd. of Educ. of the City of New York, 412 F. Supp. 1164 (E.D.N.Y. 1976) (painting contractors).

[220] 424 U.S. 351 (1976).

[221] Su, *The States of Immigration*, *supra* note 218, at 1367.

The *De Canas* challenge focused on preemption because the California statute was said to encroach upon and interfere with Congress' exercise of its exclusive power over immigration.[222] At this time, however, no federal law existed that proscribed private employers from hiring immigrants, including those without authorization to work in the United States. Indeed, although Congress had considered adopting employer sanctions since as early as 1952 and tried again in 1971 (after California adopted its own law) Congress was unsuccessful until 1986 to federalize employer sanctions for the hiring of undocumented workers.[223]

De Canas established a three-prong test to assess preemption. First, courts must determine whether the state regulation is invalid as a "regulation of immigration."[224] Second, even if the legislation does not regulate immigration, it is still preempted if Congress has shown a "clear and manifest purpose" to completely enact an "ouster of state power — including state power to promulgate laws not in conflict with federal laws."[225] Third, the state law is preempted if it "stands as an obstacle to the accomplishment and execution of the full purposes and objectives of Congress."[226]

In applying the test, the *De Canas* Court generously interpreted the preemption test in favor of the states. On the first prong, the *De Canas* Court reasoned that the "[p]ower to regulate immigration is unquestionably exclusively a federal power."[227] However, it cautioned that "[not] every state enactment which in any way deals with aliens is a regulation of immigration" and is *per se* preempted by federal law.[228] The Court further narrowed the regulation of immigration to include "essentially a determination of who should or should not be admitted into the country, and the conditions under which a legal entrant would remain."[229] The Court, moreover, characterized the California statute as implicating the state's broad policing powers to regulate the employment relationship and to protect workers within the state.[230] Given this rationale, the Court held that it could not conclude that preemption is required because "the nature of the . . . subject matter (regulation of employment of illegal aliens) permits no other conclusion . . . ."[231] While *De Canas* did not extend to bar Congress from regulating the employment of noncitizens, another decade would pass before Congress would make it illegal to hire undocumented workers.[232] Thus, as to the second prong, the Court also could not find preemption

---

[222] 424 U.S. at 353–54.

[223] Su, *The States of Immigration, supra* note 218, at 1364–65.

[224] 424 U.S.at 354.

[225] *Id.* at 357.

[226] *Id.* at 363.

[227] *Id.* at 354.

[228] *Id.* at 355.

[229] *Id.*

[230] *Id.* at 356.

[231] *Id.*

[232] *See infra* notes 237–252 and accompanying text (discussing the Immigration Reform and Control Act of 1986).

given that "Congress ha[d] [not] unmistakably so ordained that result."[233] Finally, as to the third prong, *De Canas* chose to remand the case due to the lack of a complete record on the issue.[234]

Post-*De Canas*, and in the absence of federal legislation regulating the employment of noncitizens, state laws imposing sanctions on private employers for hiring noncitizens survived preemption or equal protection challenges. However, they survived only when these laws pertained to undocumented workers, not to permanent or temporary residents authorized to work in the United States.[235] Interestingly, however, states appeared to be acting more symbolically than out of an actual concern about job displacement of U.S. citizens by immigrants. In fact, little evidence exists that states were actually enforcing their laws.[236]

Then, in 1986, when only about 11 states proscribed the employment of undocumented workers,[237] Congress passed the Immigration Reform and Control Act of 1986 (IRCA). IRCA imposed for the first time federal civil and criminal sanctions on employers for "knowingly" hiring undocumented workers.[238] The rationale for the law was that jobs in the United States attracted undocumented immigrants, which in turn depressed wages and worsened working conditions for eligible U.S workers.[239] Intended to control unauthorized immigration by deterring unauthorized workers, IRCA expressly preempted state or local laws "imposing civil or criminal sanctions (other than through licensing and similar law) upon those who employ, or recruit or refer for a fee for employment, unauthorized aliens."[240] Also in 1996, Congress adopted E-verify as a Basic Pilot Program as part of the Illegal Immigration Reform and Immigrant Responsibility Act (IIRIRA).[241] E-verify was designed to supplement without replacing the I-9 employment verification system created under IRCA under which employees had to present documentation proving their authorization to work in the United States. E-verify would permit an employer to authenticate employment documents by submitting information provided on the I-9 forms over the Internet to the Social Security Administration and/or Department of Homeland Security.[242]

---

[233] *De Canas*, 424 U.S. at 356.

[234] *Id.* at 363.

[235] *See, e.g.*, C.D.R. Enterprises, LTD. v. Bd. of Educ. of City of New York, 412 F. Supp. 1164 (E.D.N.Y. 1976) (striking down as in violation of equal protection a New York labor law providing that employment in the construction of public works must be given to citizens); Rogers v. Larson, 563 F.2d 617 (V.I. Ct. App. 1977) (striking down as preempted a Virgin Islands statute requiring the termination of nonimmigrant workers authorized to work with resident workers).

[236] Su, *The States of Immigration*, *supra* note 218, at 1367.

[237] *Id.* at 1368.

[238] Pub. L. No. 99-603, 100 Stat. 339 (1986).

[239] Michael J. Wishnie, *Prohibiting the Employment of Unauthorized Immigrants: The Experiment Fails*, 2007 U. CHI. LEGAL F. 193, 195–6 (2007).

[240] 8 U.S.C. § 1324 (a)(h)(2) (2000).

[241] Illegal Immigration Reform and Immigrant Responsibility Act of 1996 ("IIRIRA"), Pub. L. No. 104-208, Div. C. 110 Stat. 3009-546, at § 403.

[242] Lauren Gilbert, *Immigrant Laws, Obstacle Preemption and the Lost Legacy of McCulloch*, 33 BERKELEY J. EMP. & LAB. L. 153, 171–72 (2012).

Despite IRCA's express preemption clause, particularly post-9/11, when hostility against immigrants increased, a few states, frustrated over federal under enforcement of IRCA, enacted their own laws imposing sanctions (e.g., denying licensing or government contracts) on employers for hiring unauthorized workers. For example, in 2006, the City of Hazleton, Pennsylvania enacted Ordinance 2006–10, which sought to deny or suspend business licenses to employers who employed unauthorized workers.[243] Similarly, in 2007, Arizona enacted the Legal Arizona Workers Act, which similarly sought to suspend or revoke an employer's business license for knowingly or intentionally hiring the undocumented.[244] Other states followed suit and passed similar laws alone or as part of broader anti-immigrant measures, including Arkansas,[245] Iowa,[246] South Carolina,[247] Oklahoma,[248] Missouri,[249] Texas,[250] Tennessee,[251] and West Virginia.[252]

In addition to employer sanctions for the hiring of undocumented workers, some states required employers to use the federal E-verify database to check the immigration status of their employees and/or new hires or otherwise sanctioned the failure to do so.[253] The Hazleton Ordinance, for example, created a private right of action allowing workers to sue employers for not participating in E-verify as mandated by federal law.[254] The Legal Arizona Workers Act went further than federal law by requiring that all Arizona employers use the E-verity system to confirm the immigration status of its workers.[255] In contrast, under IRRIRA,

---

[243] Marisa S. Cianciarulo, *The "Arizonification" of Immigration Law: Implications of Chamber of Commerce v. Whiting for State and Local Immigration Legislation*, 15 Harv. Latino L. Rev. 85, 102–03 (2012).

[244] A.R.S § 23–211 to 23–214 (Supp. 2007).

[245] H.B. 1699 — Act 545 (2007).

[246] S.B. 562 (2007).

[247] South Carolina Illegal Immigration Reform Act, S. 392, 117th Sess. (2007–2008), *available at* http://www.scstatehouse.gov/sess117_2007-2008/bills/392.htm.

[248] The Oklahoma Taxpayer and Citizen Protection Act of 2007, H.B. 1804, 51st Leg., 1st Sess. (2007).

[249] Missouri Omnibus Immigration Act, S.B. 348 (Aug. 28, 2007), *available at* http://www.senate.mo.gov/07info/BTS_Web/Bill.aspx?SessionType=r&BillID=6818.

[250] HB 1196 (2007).

[251] Tennessee House Bill 729 (Jan. 1, 2008), *available at* http://www.capitol.tn.gov/Bills/108/Bill/HB0729.pdf.

[252] S.B. 70-Chapter 144 (2007).

[253] These other states include Georgia, Colorado, Missouri, Mississippi, Rhode Island, Utah, and Minnesota. *See* Paul Hastings, *Immigration News: Recent E-Verify Developments*, May 20, 2008, *available at* http://www.paulhastings.com/publications-items/details/?id=0078de69-2334-6428-811c-ff00004cbded. *See also* Gilbert, *supra* note 242, at 171 (adding South Carolina, Alabama, and Mississippi to the list of states that like Arizona required all employees to use E-verify and another 11 states that only required government employees to do so).

[254] Cianciarulo, *supra* note 243, at 103.

[255] *Id.* at 117–18. In contrast, at least one state, Illinois, passed legislation to restrict the use of E-verify subject to database improvements. Illinois Public Act 095-0138, H.B. 1744, 820 Ill. Comp. Stat. 55/1, et at seq., § 12(a) (an act amending the Right to Privacy in the Workplace Act), *available at* www.ilga.gov/legislation/publicacts/fulltext.asp?Name=095-0138 ("Employers are prohibited from enrolling in any Employment Eligibility Verification System . . . until the Social Security Administration (SSA) and Department of Homeland Security (DHS) databases are able to make determination of 99%

E-verify, is a voluntary system of employment verification.[256] Only in 2012, and solely through Executive Order, did President Obama require federal contractors to verify employment authorization by using E-verify.[257]

Preemption challenges to state laws imposing employer sanctions for the hiring of the undocumented workers or those that mandated e-verify initially yielded mixed results. For example, the Third Circuit found that the City of Hazleton's licensing provisions conflicted with IRCA in increasing employers' burdens by creating a separate and independent adjudicative system for determining when an employer is guilty of employing unauthorized workers.[258] In contrast, the Ninth Circuit upheld the Legal Arizona Workers Act finding that IRCA did not expressly preempt the law because the licensing provisions did not fall squarely within IRCA's "saving clause."[259] In so holding, the Ninth Circuit reaffirmed the *De Canas*-based principle that "the power to regulate the employment of unauthorized aliens remains within the state's historic police power."[260] Then, in 2010, the U.S. Supreme Court, in a 5-3 vote, resolved the conflict in favor of the Ninth Circuit when it decided *Chamber of Commerce of the United States v. Whiting* and upheld the Legal Arizona Workers Act against IRCA's preemption challenges.[261]

The challengers or the Legal Arizona Workers Act, which included the business community and immigrant advocacy groups, argued that IRCA expressly pre-empted any law "imposing civil or criminal sanctions (other than through licensing and similar laws) upon those who employ, or recruit or refer for a fee for employment, unauthorized aliens.[262] They further argued that the provisions "saving clause" — i.e., the parenthetical — did not apply to the Arizona law because Arizona was not a licensing law at all since it did not provide for the licensing of anyone.[263] As some scholars have noted, the emphasis on express preemption mistakenly deemphasized a stronger claim for implied preemption on which the Third Circuit had replied to strike down the Hazleton Ordinance.[264] In the end, the Court rejected that IRCA expressly preempted the Legal Arizona Workers Act by finding that it constituted a licensing scheme as contemplated in IRCA's savings clause.[265] It also found that in light of this, the law's licensing provisions also could not be conflict preempted, especially when the regulation of businesses through

---

of the tentative non-confirmation notices issued to employers within 3 days, unless otherwise required by law.").

[256] Gilbert, *Immigration Laws*, *supra* note 242, at 171–72.

[257] *See* U.S. CITIZENSHIP AND IMMIGRATION SERVICES, E-VERIFY FOR FEDERAL CONTRACTORS, http://www.uscis.gov/e-verify/federal-contractors/ (last revised Jan. 17, 2014).

[258] Lozano v. City of Hazleton, 620 F.3d 170, 196 (3d. Cir. 2010), *cert. granted, judgment vacated by* 131 S. Ct. 2958 (2011).

[259] *Chicanos Por la Causa, Inc. v. Napolitano*, 558 F.3d 856, 864 (9th Cir. 2009).

[260] *Id.* at 865 (citing De Canas v. Bica, 424 U.S. 351, 360 (1976)).

[261] Chamber of Commerce of the United States v. Whiting, 131 S.Ct. 1968, 1980 (2011).

[262] 8 U.S.C. § 1324a(h)(2).

[263] Brief for the Petitioners at 2-3, 34-26, *Chamber of Commerce v. Whiting*, 131 S. Ct. 1968 (2011).

[264] Gilbert, *Immigration Laws*, *supra* note 242, at 177–79.

[265] *Whiting*, 131 S. Ct. at 1978.

licensing laws has never been considered an area of dominant federal concern.[266] Moreover, despite concerns expressed by some of the Justices that Arizona's mandatory E-verify laws contradicted Congressional intent, the Court also found that the law's imposition of a mandatory use of E-verify on employers was not conflict preempted under the 1996 law that established E-verify, the Illegal Immigration Reform Act. It reasoned that nothing in this law prevented states from making E-verify mandatory; it prevented only the federal government from doing so.[267]

Scholars examining *Whiting* suggest that its holding exposes some of the tensions and contradictions of the Court's modern preemption doctrine. These include, for example, the increasing reluctance of the more conservative Justices of the Court to find implied obstacle preemption either because it must rely on the object and purpose of the law, rather than plain meaning, or because it tramples on state rights without express congressional intent.[268] *Whiting*, and subsequently, *U.S. v. Arizona*,[269] are therefore viewed as cases that significantly expand the territory over which states will be able to continue to regulate immigrants.[270] At least with regard to the City of Hazleton, however, this may not be the case.

Subsequent to the *Whiting* case, the U.S. Supreme Court ordered the Third Circuit to vacate its judgment and revisit anew the preemption challenges to the Hazleton Ordinance, including its employer licensing restrictions and E-verify.[271] Interestingly, on remand, the Third Circuit still found that the Ordinance was preempted.[272] The Third Circuit acknowledged, *inter alia*, that *Whiting* contradicted its earlier conclusion that Hazleton's employment provisions were conflict preempted because they established distinct sanctions as those contemplated under IRCA.[273] The Third Circuit further acknowledged that *Whiting* overruled it with regard to its findings on E-verify because it considered that Congress intended to encourage the expansion of E-verify by states.[274] However, the Third Circuit agreed with plaintiffs that the Hazleton Ordinance was conflict preempted because it applied to a much broader range of actors and activities than Congress intended under IRCA. Namely it included not only employers but also those who are self-employed or are partnerships, corporations, contractors, and subcontractors and not solely employers but also any activity conducted by a business entity.[275] The Third Circuit also relied on the fact that the Hazleton Ordinance created a separate scheme of enforcement that failed to comply with federal procedural protections in

---

[266] *Id.* at 1983.

[267] Gilbert, *Immigration Laws, supra* note 242, at 180–81.

[268] *See id.* at 161–62.

[269] 567 U.S. ___, 132 S. Ct. 2492 (2012). For a fuller discussion of *U.S. v. Arizona*, see *infra* Part O Local Immigration Enforcement.

[270] *See, e.g.*, Gilbert, *Immigration Laws, supra* note 242, at 205–06 and Margaret Hu, *Reverse Commandeering*, 46 U.C. Davis L. Rev. 535 (2012).

[271] City of Hazleton v. Lozano, 131 S. Ct. 2958 (2011).

[272] Lozano v. City of Hazleton, 724 F.3d 297 (3d Cir. 2013).

[273] *Id.* at 305.

[274] *Id.* at 306.

[275] *Id.*

order to distinguish Hazleton's Ordinance from the Arizona case.[276] Furthermore, other attempts by some states, including Arizona, to go even further in sanctioning employers have not been successful. This includes actions such as imposing tax penalties,[277] increasing civil remedies and causes of actions by U.S. workers challenging employers for hiring undocumented workers,[278] or by criminalizing them for failure to comply with the laws.

I. PUBLIC BENEFITS

Congress, and before that states, regulated immigrants' consumption of public benefits not by denying them access to public benefits, but principally by barring the migration of "paupers" or persons likely to become a public charge.[279] In fact, most states conferred public benefits to most of indigent residents irrespective of their immigration status. This was often based on policy considerations[280] and state constitutional or statutory provisions recognizing a duty to aid indigents or the needy who reside in their territory.[281] Similarly, prior to 1996,[282] legal noncitizens were automatically eligible for almost all federally funded public benefits,[283] although fewer programs remained accessible to the undocumented.[284]

Some states, as well as the federal government, however, have restricted public benefits eligibility even for lawful permanent residents. In *Graham*, for example, equal protection and preemption challenges were brought to Arizona and Pennsylvania statutes that restricted public benefits to lawful permanent residents.[285] The Arizona statute imposed a 15-year residency requirement on lawful permanent

---

[276] *Id.* at 309.

[277] In *U.S. v. Alabama*, the Tenth Circuit struck down a provision of the Alabama Taxpayer and Citizen Protection Act based on express preemption that prohibited employers from deducting as a business expense on their state tax filings any compensation paid to undocumented workers. 691 F.3d 1269 (2012).

[278] *Id.*

[279] Neuman, *The Lost Century of American Immigration Law*, *supra* note 3, at 1848 (discussing state pauper immigration restrictions); Richard A. Boswell, *Restrictions on Non-citizens' Access to Public Benefits: Flawed Premise, Unnecessary Response*, 42 U.C.L.A. L. Rev. 1475, 1481–87 (1995) (discussing federal economic based immigration restrictions).

[280] *See* Peter L. Reich, *Public Benefits for Undocumented Aliens: State Law into the Breach Once More*, 21 N.M. L. Rev. 219, 242–48 (1991) (discussing policy reasons for granting public benefits to all immigrants, including health risks to the public when vulnerable groups lack access to basic medical services; the greater contributions as compared to costs of immigrants to U.S. society; and humanitarian values).

[281] *See id.* at 228–41.

[282] In 1996, Congress revamped the entire welfare system and also restricted federal welfare program eligibility for lawful permanent residents. *See infra* notes 310–22 and accompanying text.

[283] Reich, *supra* note 280, at 221, 232–34 (discussing pre-1996 access restrictions to immigrants except permanent residents or persons "permanently residing in the United States color of law"). *See also* Evangeline G. Abriel, *Rethinking Preemption for Purposes of Aliens and Public Benefits*, 42 U.C.L.A. L. Rev. 1597, 1660–62 (1995); Boswell, *supra* note 279, at 1487–92.

[284] Reich, *supra* note 280, at 237; Boswell, *supra* note 279, at 1498–1500.

[285] Graham v. Richardson, 403 U.S. 365, 366–380 (1971).

residents for the receipt of federal assistance programs.[286] The Pennsylvania statute restricted to citizens the receipt of a general assistance program funded solely with state funds.[287] Congress began to enact alienage restrictions on access to public benefits principally in the 1970s.[288] Unlike states, however, the federal government has enjoyed broader discretion to impose alienage restrictions on access to federal public benefits.

In 1976, five years after *Graham*, the Court upheld, as a legitimate exercise of federal immigration power, Congress' imposition of a five-year residency federal requirement on lawful permanent residents seeking Medicare Supplemental Medical Insurance in *Matthews v. Diaz*.[289] *Graham*, in fact, foreshadowed the result in *Diaz*. *Graham*, which also considered a preemption challenge, had held that states may not "add to nor take from the conditions lawfully imposed by Congress upon admission, naturalization and residence of aliens in the United States . . . "[290] Similarly, the *Diaz* Court affirmed that the "relationship between the United States and our alien visitors has been committed to the political branches of the Federal Government."[291] Thus, the Court applied the same lenient rational basis test to federal alienage public benefits restriction that had traditionally applied in the immigration context.[292]

The *Diaz* Court's rationale falls within a broader conception of immigration control. Measures that exclude immigrants from access to rights and benefits of U.S. citizens are viewed as both indirect means of controlling immigration and as a proper preservation of the benefits of membership for those deemed to belong within the moral boundaries of the national community.[293] Critics of *Diaz* question, however, the deterrence immigration control claims, specifically that immigrants do not ordinarily come to the United States to obtain benefits but rather, to work.[294] Moreover, at least when the sovereign consented to their admission in the first place, when immigrants live and work in the political community, they should be treated as members of the community.[295] The mirror image critique is directed at *Graham*, in that states should be allowed to discriminate in favor of citizens who are

---

[286] *Id.*

[287] *Id.* Before *Graham*, citizenship was a classification for old age assistance in Texas. Vernon's Ann. Texas Const. Art. 3, § 51-a. After *Graham*, the legislature amended its statute. *Id.* However, even after *Graham*, Mississippi has not overturned its law requiring one year state residency in order to receive old age assistance. Miss. Code Ann. § 43-9-7.

[288] Boswell, *supra* note 279, at 1492–97.

[289] Matthews v. Diaz, 426 U.S. 67 (1976).

[290] *Graham*, 403 U.S. at 378.

[291] *Diaz*, 426 U.S. at 81.

[292] *Id.* at 79–80.

[293] Linda Bosniak, *Membership, Equality, and the Difference that Alienage Makes*, 69 N.Y.U. L. Rev. 1047, 1053 (1994).

[294] Kevin R. Johnson, *Public Benefits and Immigration: The Intersection of Immigration Status, Ethnicity, Gender and Class*, 42 U.C.L.A. L. Rev. 1509, 1513, n.18 (1995) (citing to several social science studies linking migration patterns to jobs and family unification, not public benefits). *See also* Reich, *supra* note 280, at 226 (same).

[295] Michael Walzer, *The Distribution of Membership*, in Boundaries: National Autonomy and Its Limits 1, 23–32 (Peter J. Brown & Henery Sur, eds., 1981).

the sole full members of the community.[296] Those who defend *Graham* do so for the same reasons that *Diaz* is criticized and emphasize, at least with respect to lawful residents, that noncitizens too have strong claims to membership.[297]

Post *Diaz*, Congress continued to impose further public benefits restrictions on noncitizens. For example, the 1986 IRCA reforms granted lawful status to undocumented persons residing in the United States since before 1982. However, it disqualified them from any federal or joint federal-state assistance program for five years from the date of legalization.[298] Similarly, the Immigration Act of 1990 created a new "temporary protected status" for persons fleeing armed conflict or natural disasters in their home. However, it also prohibited the beneficiaries from participating in most federal benefit programs.[299]

Some states also attempted to duplicate and impose even greater restrictions on noncitizen public benefit eligibility than under federal law, but limited to undocumented immigrants in light of *Graham*. Proposition 187, which California voters overwhelmingly approved in 1994,[300] *inter alia*, barred the undocumented from a host of social services and health care provisions.[301] It also imposed mandatory reporting provisions to immigration and other state agencies when ineligible persons sought these benefits.[302] Proposition 187 took on highly inflated rhetoric, blaming "illegal aliens for the ills of the state." Proponents of the measure in the official Ballot pamphlet warned of an "illegal alien invasion" that would reduce California to "economic bankruptcy."[303] Ironically, the projected enforcement costs of Proposition 187 would have dwarfed any projected savings.[304]

The first challenge to Proposition 187 (*Lulac I*) sought to declare the proposition unconstitutional, mostly based on preemption as applied to the undocumented and on equal protection grounds as applied to undocumented children.[305] *Lulac I, inter alia*, struck down as preempted, Proposition 187's public benefits verification and reporting requirements since these created "an entirely independent set of criteria by which to classify individuals based on immigration status."[306] Further, criteria

---

[296] Gerald L. Neuman, *Aliens as Outlaws: Government Services, Proposition 187, and the Structure of Equal Protection Doctrine*, 42 U.C.L.A. L. Rev. 1425, 1427 (1995).

[297] *Id.*

[298] 8 U.S.C.A. § 1255(h)(1)(A) (Supp. 1991).

[299] Pub. L. No. 101-649, 104 Stat. 4978 (1990).

[300] Proposition 187 was approved by a 59-41 percent margin. California Secretary of State, Statement of Vote, Nov. 8, 1994, at 115.

[301] These services included child welfare and foster care benefits, county general assistance, battered women's counseling, and publicly-funded health services. Johnson, *Public Benefits and Immigration*, *supra* note 294, at 1562–63.

[302] *Id.*, at 1562–63.

[303] Arguments in Favor of Proposition 187, in Proposition 187: Illegal Aliens — Ineligibility for Public Services — Verification and Reporting, § 10, 1994 Cal. Adv. Leg. Serv. B-43 (Deering). *See also* Johnson, *Public Benefits and Immigration*, *supra* note 294, at 1558–61 (discussing the anti-immigrant animus of Proposition 187).

[304] Johnson, *Public Benefits and Immigration*, *supra* note 294, at 1568–71.

[305] League of United Latin Am. Citizens v. Wilson (Lulac I), 908 F. Supp. 755, 764 (C.D. Cal. 1995).

[306] *Id.* at 770 (striking down as preempted Sections 4 through 9 in the preamble).

was aimed solely at reporting violations to effectuate removal.[307] In addition, *Lulac I* held that federal legislation preempted the provision in Proposition 187 that denied state administration of federally funded public social services to the undocumented.[308] In contrast, *Lulac I* upheld Proposition 187's denial of public benefits when based on federal determinations of immigration status.[309]

Shortly after, however, Congress adopted the Personal Responsibility and Work Opportunity Reconciliation Act of 1996 (PRWORA), making the defeat of Proposition 187 short-lived.[310] In fact, some consider Proposition 187 as the impetus for the 1996 anti-immigrant reform.[311] In general, the PRWORA did four things. First, it restricted the eligibility of "qualified aliens,"[312] including certain lawful permanent residents, to receive several federally funded public benefits.[313] Second, it authorized, but did not require states to deny locally funded benefits to "qualified aliens,"[314] despite *Graham's* precedent.[315] Third, the legislation tightened restrictions on the few public benefits once available to certain persons now considered "not qualified," including undocumented persons.[316] In fact, the PRWORA proscribed states from conferring benefits to the undocumented persons except

---

[307] *Id.* at 771.

[308] *Id.* at 786.

[309] *Id.* at 776.

[310] Pub. L. No. 104-193, 110 Stat. 2105 (1996).

[311] Peter J. Spiro, *Learning to Live with Immigration Federalism*, 29 Conn. L. Rev. 1627, 1641–46 (1997) (discussing the "steam-valve" effect of preemption, under which state preferences, frustrated at the local level, are revisited by Congress).

[312] PRWORA classified all foreign nationals into two categories of eligibility for federal, state, or local public benefits: "qualified aliens" and "not-qualified aliens." "Qualified aliens" included, among others, lawful permanent residents, those granted refugee or asylum status, and certain battered spouses or children. "Not-qualified aliens" include the undocumented, as well as persons with temporary visas or nonimmigrant status, those granted temporary protected status, and other persons who have applied for but not yet received legal immigration status. PRWORA § 431[b].

[313] For example, the PRWORA barred "qualified aliens" from receiving supplemental security income (SSI) and food stamps, at least until those eligible attain citizenship or meet additional requirements. PRWORA §§ 401 and 402[a][1]). Certain classes of "qualified aliens" were exempted from SSI and food stamps restrictions: (1) refugees, asylees, and individuals granted withholding of deportation, but only for the first five years after being granted that status; (2) active duty service members, veterans, and their direct family members; and (3) lawful permanent residents who could prove they had worked at least 40 qualifying quarters, or 10 years, for social security purposes. PRWORA § 402[a][2]. PRWORA also restricted lawful permanent residents access to other federal means-tested programs, such as Medicaid and Temporary Assistance for Needy Families (TANF) for the first five years after entry or admission PRWORA § 401[a].

[314] 8 U.S.C. § 1612(b)(1) (2000) (authorizing states to "determine the eligibility" of qualified aliens for Medicaid, TANF, and Title XX block grants); and *id.* § 1622 (a) (authorizing states to "determine the eligibility for any State Public Benefits" or certain qualified and certain nonqualified aliens).

[315] Legislative history, in fact, suggests that *Graham* was an explicit target of several provisions of the PRWORA. Michael J. Wishnie, *Laboratories of Bigotry? Devolution of the Immigration Power, Equal Protection, and Federalism*, 76 N.Y.U. L. Rev. 493, 512–14 (2001).

[316] Under law prior to PRWORA, foreign nationals were eligible to receive Medicaid, SSI, and Aid to Families with Dependent Children (now TANF) if they were "permanently residing in the United States under color of law." PRWORA disallowed such aid. "Not-qualified aliens" are still eligible for some public benefits, however. These include: emergency Medicaid; immunizations; diagnosis and treatment of communicable diseases; short-term, in-kind, noncash emergency or disaster relief services; school lunch,

through affirmative legislative enactment.[317] Finally, the PRWORA delegated to states the administration of public benefits programs. This included the requirement to verify applicant's immigration status and mandatory reporting requirements to immigration authorities for three federal programs (social security income, public housing, and Temporary Assistance for Needy Families) when the agency knows that the applicant is not lawfully present in the United States.[318] In light of the PRWORA, then California Governor Pete Wilson appealed *Lulac I* and moved for reconsideration.[319] However, *Lulac II* found that the PROWA itself preempted most provisions of the state law. The foundation that had supported the initiative also appealed, but the Ninth Circuit affirmed.[320] Two years later in 1999, the Seventh Circuit in City of *Chicago v. Shalala*[321] became one of the first courts to uphold the PWORA under rational basis review.[322]

Recently, the promise of universal healthcare as part of health care reform did not prove true for immigrants. The 2010 Patient Protection Affordable Care Act (ACA) and the Health Care and Education Reconciliation Act, passed a few weeks later to amend the ACA, left out millions of noncitizens from protection.[323] For example, the ACA did not change immigrant eligibility requirements for the Medicaid program under PRWORA. As a result, most LPRs must wait five years after becoming legal residents to be eligible to receive Medicaid benefits, while refuges and asylees must generally wait seven years to become eligible.[324] What this means is that even with the ACA, low-income, recently arrived lawful residents must search for health insurance on the private market or through health exchanges, regardless of whether their states expand Medicaid coverage under the ACA.[325]

Undocumented immigrants, even those granted deferred action, were expressly excluded from virtually all of the ACA's protections. They are also unable to access any of the benefits of the ACA, except for what the PRWORA already permitted: emergency medical services.[326] Moreover, the ACA reduced federal funding for immigration status-blind emergency medical treatment. This will further burden emergency rooms who are supposed to treat all patients regardless of immigration status and ability to pay.[327]

---

breakfast, and other child nutrition programs. STEVEN W. BENDER, ET AL., EVERYDAY LAW FOR LATINOS/AS, 205–206 (2008).

[317] PRWORA § 1621[c] and [d]).

[318] *Id.*, at § 404, amended by Balanced Budget Act of 1997, §§ 564, 5581(a).

[319] United Latin Am. Citizens v. Wilson, 997 F. Supp. 1244, 1252 (C.D. Cal. 1997).

[320] League of United Latin Am. Citizens v. Wilson, 131 F.3d 1297, 1309 (9th Cir. 1997).

[321] 189 F.3d 598 (1999).

[322] Also in 2013, the 9th Circuit upheld the denial of federal student loans to noncitizens ineligible under the PRWORA. Mashiri v. Department of Education, 724 F.3d 1028 (2013).

[323] Vinita Andrapalliyal, *"Healthcare for All?" The Gap Between Rhetoric and Reality in the Affordable Care Act*, 61 UCLA L. REV. Discourse 58, 60 (2013).

[324] *Id.* at 63.

[325] *Id.* at 64.

[326] *Id.* at 66.

[327] *Id.* In fact, some of the ERs are engaging in illegal "self-help" practices of deporting

The eligibility of health benefits under the ACA is murkiest for nonimmigrants, including the approximate two million who have overstayed. For example, the ACA is unclear on whether nonimmigrants are subject to the insurance mandate. At a minimum, nonimmigrants that have overstayed appear to be required to participate since they are considered "lawfully present"; however, nonimmigrants are also ineligible for Medicaid benefits and thus must access health insurance on the private market or through health exchanges.[328]

Several scholars have lamented that the exclusion of noncitizens from the ACA solidified bounded notions of who belongs as a member of U.S. society.[329] Other question the policy choice and argue that extending universal coverage to all noncitizens is a more efficient and better alternative even for U.S. citizens.[330]

With some exceptions, initial state responses to PRWORA were to restore certain benefits to legal immigrants. According to a 2002 study, over half of the states were spending their own money to cover at least some of the immigrants who are ineligible for federally funded programs, although these programs offer fewer benefits.[331] In addition, some states also passed legislation to provide a few public benefits even to the undocumented, such as prenatal care and medical insurance for the elderly, for the disabled, and for children.[332] In contrast, some states heeded the federal government's invitation to strip lawful permanent residents of even greater public benefits than under the PRWORA.[333] Others are imposing stricter verification and mandatory reporting requirements. For example, on November 2, 2004, Arizona voters approved Proposition 200, also known as the Arizona Taxpayer and Citizen Protection Act.[334] Proposition 200 included provisions to deny undocumented individuals benefits for which they were already ineligible under the PRWORA.[335] It also required all Arizona agencies that were responsible for administering public benefits, subject to civil and criminal sanctions, to verify the immigration status of any applicant and report to the immigration authorities any

---

undocumented immigrants to their country of origin in order to avoid ongoing and unreimbursed costs. *See, e.g.*, Lori A. Nessel, *The Practice of Medical Repatriation: The Privatization of Immigration Enforcement and Denial of Human Rights*, 55 Wayne L. Rev. 1725 (2009).

[328] Andrapalliyal, *supra* note 323, at 65.

[329] *See* Nan D. Hunder, *Health Insurance Reform and Intimations of Citizenship*, 159 U. Pa. L. Rev. 1955 (2011) and Janet L. Dolgin and Katherine R. Dieterich, *When Others Get Too Close: Immigrants, Class, and the Health Care Debate*, 19 Cornell J. L. & Pub. Pol'y 283 (2010).

[330] Patrick Glen, *Health Care and the Illegal Immigrant*, 23 Health Matrix 197 (2013).

[331] The National Immigration Law Center (NILC), Guide to Immigrant Eligibility for Federal Programs 3, 102–103, 108, 122–27, 134–35 (4th ed. 2002).

[332] *Id.* at 124–27.

[333] California barred unqualified immigrants from 200 programs. Wendy Zimmerman & Karen C. Tumlin, *Patchwork Policies: State Assistance for Immigrants Under Welfare Reform*, 1999 Urb. Inst. 39–41 (1999), *available at* http://www.urban.org/UploadedPDF/occ24.pdf. Maine cut off immigrant access to health insurance. *Id.* at 41. Minnesota and Maine barred undocumented immigrants from general assistance. *Id.*

[334] Proposition 200, *available at* https://www.azsos.gov/election/2004/Info/PubPamphlet/english/prop200.htm (last visited Jan. 25, 2007) (current version at Ariz. Rev. Stat. Ann. § 46-140.01).

[335] *Id.* at § 6.A

applicant unable to provide it.[336] Proposition 200 proponents claimed that undocumented immigrants cost the state tens of millions of dollars based on unsubstantiated allegations of pernicious fraud for seeking benefits, for which they did not qualify.[337] Here, too many questionable savings would have been dwarfed by the millions of tax dollars necessary to implement the verification requirements.[338] After Arizona's initiative, more than 20 states considered or introduced similar measures to the ones of Proposition 200, responding in great part to budget restrictions resulting from the economic crisis.[339]

The *Diaz* precedent has foreclosed challenges to Congress' authority to enact the PRWORA and deny public benefits to noncitizens.[340] Some scholars argue, nevertheless, that Congress could not legislate to undermine *Graham* simply by devolving its powers to discriminate against noncitizens to states through the PRWORA.[341] However, after PRWORA, courts have resisted preemption and equal protection challenges to restrictive state public benefits measures, so long as the states have followed PRWORA guidelines. A federal district court, for example, lifted its restraining order against Proposition 200's public benefit provisions. It did so after Arizona's Attorney General clarified that the public benefits restrictions applied only to those public benefits programs already governed by federal law and did not include the state's medical insurance or many other state programs.[342] Subsequently, the Ninth Circuit vacated the district court's order and held that the Arizona employee plaintiffs lacked standing to enjoin enforcement of Arizona Proposition 200 for failing to show a "genuine threat of imminent prosecution."[343] Then in 2012 and 2014, the Ninth Circuit also upheld the state of Washington's and Hawaii's termination of state-funded food assistance program for certain legal residents and state-funded health care benefits plans to nonimmigrants respectively because these followed PRWORA guidelines.[344] Similarly, two federal district courts have upheld the state of New Jersey's restoration of the five-year bar for the state-funded Medicaid program to new LPRs since these are also consistent with PRWORA guidelines.[345]

A few challenges to post-PRWORA restrictions on state public benefits have been successful, although based on state constitutional challenges. The state of New York, for example, has interpreted its State Constitution as creating a right to welfare. This trumps federal legislation mandating or permitting state discrimina-

---

[336] *Id.* at § 6.A.

[337] Raquel Aldana, *Federal Citizenship and the "Alien,"* 46 WASHBURN L.J. 263, 276–277 (2007).

[338] *Id.* at 275.

[339] *See* Protect America Now website to promote initiatives in other states, *available at* http://www.protectamerica.com/.

[340] *See* Michael J. Wishnie, *Laboratories of Bigotry?*, *supra* note 315, at 518.

[341] *Id.* at 528–58.

[342] Friendly House v. Napolitano, 419 F.3d 930 (9th Cir. 2005) (order).

[343] Friendly House v. Napolitano, 419 F.3d 930, 932 (9th Cir. 2005).

[344] Pimentel v. Dreyfus, 670 F.3d 1096 (9th Cir. 2012) and Korab v. Fink, 748 F.3d 875 (9th Cir. 2014).

[345] A.B. v. Division of Medical Assistance & Health Services, 971 A.2d 403 (N.J. Super. Ct. 2009) and Guaman v. Velez, 74 A.3d 931 (N.J. Super. Ct. 2013).

tion against noncitizens.[346] Massachusetts as well has applied strict scrutiny to attempts to restrict health insurance benefits only to lawful permanent residents with a five-year residency based on state constitutional law.[347]

Finally, pro-immigrant public benefits state measures seeking to restore PRWORA-stripped benefits to immigrants through state funds have received mixed results based on preemption challenges. A few have struck down such laws based on preemption, viewing the PRWORA as a comprehensive regulatory scheme in the area of public benefits.[348] Others, however, have upheld such laws given that the PRWORA authorized such extensions so long as states adopted affirmative legislation to do so.[349]

The debate of whether states should be able to freely deny public benefits to undocumented immigrants is made more difficult by undocumented immigrants' unauthorized entry. As well as the inability or unwillingness of the federal government to control the border. To some, these factors justify state discrimination when states disproportionately bear the "costs" of the presence of unauthorized migrants who have no right to claim membership in the community.[350] Those who favor equal protection for the undocumented highlight the disparate impact of public benefits restrictions on the most vulnerable subgroup of immigrants, namely poor people of color and women, few of who are eligible to immigrate legally to the United States despite strong pull factors from U.S. employers for these workers.[351] Moreover, their unrepresented, unlawful status and foreignness makes the undocumented the most vulnerable to nativist outbursts of anti-immigrant sentiments and hostile discrimination that requires judicial protection.[352]

J. PUBLIC EDUCATION

1. K-12 Education

Another area that some states have attempted to restrict is access to public education from kindergarten through twelfth grade (K-12). In 1975, for example, Texas passed legislation to bar undocumented children from K-12 public schools or charge them tuition.[353] A group of undocumented children challenged the law on

---

[346] *Id.* at 301–302.

[347] Finch v. Commonwealth Health Insurance Connector Authority & Others, 946 N.E.2d 1262 (Mass. 2011) and Finch v. Commonwealth Health Insurance Connector Authority & Others, 959 N.E.2d 970 (Mass. 2012).

[348] Aldana, *Federal Citizenship, supra* note 337, at 286–87.

[349] *See, e.g.,* Kaider v. Hamos, 975 N.E.2d 667 (Ill. App. Ct. 2012) (upholding program in Illinois granting state funds to pregnant women and undocumented children).

[350] *See* Johnson, *Public Benefits and Immigration, supra* note 294, at 1538–40.

[351] *Id.* at 1542–58.

[352] Neuman, *Aliens as Outlaws, supra* note 296, at 1440–50.

[353] Tex. Educ. Code Ann. Tit. 2, § 21.031 (Vernon 1976). For a more detailed explanation of Texas' law, see Michael A. Olivas, *Plyler v. Doe, the Education of Undocumented Children, and the Policy, in* Immigration Stories 198–199 (David A. Martin and Peter H. Schuck, eds. 2005).

preemption and equal protection grounds[354] in *Plyler v. Doe,* a case the U.S. Supreme Court would ultimately decided in their favor in 1982 in a 5-4 margin.[355] The Court declared that unlike public benefits, access to K-12 education is a quasi-fundamental right, and that the Texas law violated equal protection under the Fourteenth Amendment of the U.S. Constitution.[356] The *Plyler* Court recognized that undocumented immigrants are "persons" under the Fourteenth Amendment; however, it explicitly denied that they constitute a "suspect" class.[357] Nevertheless, the Court accorded undocumented children special status (quasi-suspect) in that children should not be punished for their parents' choice to break the immigration laws.[358] Then, applying intermediate scrutiny,[359] the Court dismissed the State's argument that the law was necessary to preserve the State's "limited resources for the education of its lawful residents,"[360] particularly when the State failed to show significant savings for the state during trial.[361] The Court also rejected the state's justification of the law as a deterrent against unlawful immigration, finding it a "ludicrously ineffectual attempt to stem the tide of illegal immigration."[362] Further, it found it was also an infringement into Congress' exclusive power over immigration.[363] Finally, while the *Plyler* Court was divided on the constitutional question, it was unanimous about the inadvisability to the Texas law. Namely it recognized the law's potential of creating a permanent cast of undocumented residents with no hope of advancement in U.S. society.[364] For many scholars, *Plyler* was a significant civil rights milestone for undocumented children specifically and for immigrants more generally.[365]

At a minimum, *Plyler* requires K-12 schools not to adopt policies or take actions that would deny access to or dissuade the enrollment of undocumented children in public schools. *Plyler* also entitles undocumented students to varied benefits provided by a number of special programs.[366] The rights of undocumented students' access to K-12 public education and programs are settled in the legal

---

[354] For an explanation of the *Plyler* litigation and principal players, see Olivas, *supra* note 353, at 199–208.

[355] 457 U.S. 202 (1982).

[356] *Id.* at 221–28.

[357] *Id.* at 218–219.

[358] *Id.* at 220.

[359] The Court employs a rational basis argument but actually applies a test that is best characterized as intermediate scrutiny in that the State had to meet a "substantial goal." *Id.* at 223–24.

[360] *Id.* at 227.

[361] *Id.* at 229.

[362] *Id.* at 228.

[363] *Id.* at 225–36.

[364] *Id.* at 218–19.

[365] *See, e.g.,* MICHAEL OLIVAS, NO UNDOCUMENTED CHILD LEFT BEHIND: PLYER V. DOE AND THE EDUCATION OF UNDOCUMENTED CHILDREN (NYU Press 2012) and Gabriel J. Chin, *Sweatt v. Painter and Undocumented College Students in Texas,* 36 T. MARSHALL L. REV. 39 (2010).

[366] These programs include: (1) the Emergency Immigrant Education Program (No Child Left Behind Act of 2001, 115 Stat. 1425 at §§ 3241–3248); (2) programs that receive funds under Section 204 of the Immigrant Reform and Control Act (SILG Funds); (3) bilingual or English-language learning programs; (4) Chapter 1 funds, which are used to supplement the educational services provided to

domain, despite post-*Plyler* attempts by some states to sidestep the decision. For example, in clear violation of *Plyler*, California's Proposition 187 included provisions barring undocumented children from public schools.[367] However, this was struck down as unconstitutional early in the litigation.[368] Moreover, in 1996, Congress considered federal legislation to reverse *Plyler*, known as the Gallegly Amendment.[369] Ultimately, however, the PRWORA preserved *Plyler* by prohibiting states from denying children access to elementary public schools.[370] Still, some states have chosen to deny access to K-12 schools to nonimmigrant children given that *Plyler* did not directly address the issue.[371] Others have focused on calculating the cost of educating undocumented children in the hope of overturning *Plyler* on the facts — i.e., showing a substantial financial interest to educate lawful residents.[372]

2. Higher Education

States' involvement in noncitizen access to higher education has implicated issues of admission, in-state tuition, and other financial benefits eligibility, such as financial aid and scholarships. It is well-settled law that states that deny any of these benefits to lawful permanent residents run afoul of equal protection. In 1977, in *Nyquist v. Mauclet*, the Court applied strict scrutiny equal protection analysis to strike down a New York state financial assistance program. This program was limited solely to citizens or certain noncitizens who were either refugees or had applied or intended to apply for citizenship.[373]

Challenges to denial of these same benefits to nonimmigrants and the undocumented, however, have been tested solely for preemption validity, not for equality or substantive due process principles. In 1982, in *Toll v. Moreno*, the Court struck down on preemption grounds a 1973 Maryland statute that granted in-state tuition benefits solely to U.S. citizens and lawful permanent residents.[374] The plaintiffs in that case, who held "G-4" nonimmigrant visa status, challenged the legislation on the basis that it conflicted with federal immigration policy. Under this policy, in contrast to other nonimmigrant holders, they were permitted to establish

---

low-achieving students in low-income neighborhoods; (5) Head Start programs; (6) special education; and (7) free and reduced meal programs.

[367] Section 7 of Proposition 187, California ballot Pamphlet: General Election Nov. 8, 1994, at 92 (1994) (adding Cal. Educ. Code § 48125).

[368] League of United Latin American Citizens v. Wilson, 908 F. Supp. 755 (C.D. Cal. 1995).

[369] H.R. 4134, 104th Cong. § 1 (1996).

[370] 8 U.S.C. §§ 1643(a)(2) (2000).

[371] BENDER, ET AL., *supra* note 316, at 89. *See also* Udi Ofer, *Protecting Plyler: New Challenges to the Right of Immigrant Children to Access a Public School Education*, 1 COLUM. J. RACE & L. 187 (2012).

[372] BENDER, ET AL., *supra* note 316, at 89. *See also* Maria Pabón López et al., *The Prospects and Challenges of Educational Reform for Latino Undocumented Children: An Essay Examining Alabama's H.B. 56 and Other State Immigration Measures*, 6 FIU L. REV. 231 (2011).

[373] 432 U.S. 1 (1977). *See also* Jagnandan v. Giles, 379 F. Supp. 1178 (N.D. Miss. 1974) (declaring a Mississippi statute classifying all noncitizens, including permanent resident plaintiffs, as nonresidents for purposes of charging them higher tuition and fees, unconstitutional under equal protection and due process).

[374] 458 U.S. 1, 3–4 (1982).

domicile in the U.S.[375] The Court agreed that barring domiciled nonimmigrants from acquiring in-state status for purposes of college tuition violated the Supremacy Clause.[376] The case, however, did not address the law's legality as applied to non-domiciled nonimmigrants under federal immigration law or undocumented students.

Subsequent state cases addressing states' ability to employ federal immigration criteria to postsecondary in-state tuition determinations, moreover, yielded mixed results.[377] This area of the law, which has become increasingly pertinent as states legislate to either grant or deny these benefits to undocumented students, remains unsettled. Since 2001, at least 14 states have legislated to grant undocumented students in-state tuition,[378] while three — Arizona, Georgia, and Indiana — have legislated against it.[379] In addition, states' Attorney Generals, Board of Regents, or Departments of Education have weighed in on the issue with mixed results.[380] In addition, at least five states — California, Minnesota, New Mexico, Texas, and Washington, allow undocumented students to receive state financial aid.[381] In general, those states that grant in-state tuition benefits and/or state funded-student aid, delineate requirements of eligibility that include that the student must live in state and have attended high school in the state for a specified number of

---

[375] *Id.* at 7–8.

[376] *Id.* at 17.

[377] Challenges based on preemption to California's decision in the 1980s to allow undocumented students establish residency for tuition purposes, for example, produced inconsistent rulings in California courts. For a thorough examination of this litigation, see Michael A. Olivas, *Storytelling Out of School: Undocumented College Residency, Race, and Reaction*, 22 HASTINGS CONST. L.Q. 1019, 1051–1060 (1995).

[378] *See* NATIONAL CONFERENCE OF STATE LEGISLATURES, UNDOCUMENTED STUDENT TUITION: STATE ACTION, June 12, 2014, *available at* http://www.ncsl.org/research/education/undocumented-student-tuition-state-action.aspx (last visited Oct. 15, 2014). These states are Colorado, Connecticut, Florida, Illinois, Kansas, Maryland, Minnesota, Nebraska, New Mexico, New Jersey, New York, Oregon, Texas, Utah, and Washington. For an analysis of Utah's law granting in-state tuition to undocumented students, see Juliet Stewart and Thomas Christian Quinn, *To Include or Exclude: A Comparative Study of State Laws on In-State Tuition for Undocumented Students in the United States*, 18 TEX. HISP. J. L. & POL'Y 1, 32-36 (2012).

[379] These states are Arizona, Georgia, and Mississippi. *Id.* For an analysis of Georgia's law, see Azadeh Shahshahani and Chaka Washington, *Shattered Dreams: An Analysis of the Georgia Board of Regent's Admissions Ban From a Constitutional and International Human Rights Perspective*, 10 HASTINGS RACE & POVERTY L.J. 1 (2013).

[380] *Compare* Ark. Op. Atty. Gen. No. 2008-109, 2008 WL 4198411 (Ark. A.G.) (concluding that colleges and university may enroll undocumented students and are not obliged to verify citizenship in the absence of a rule or regulation to the contrary) with Co. Atty. Gen., Formal Opinion No. 06-01, 2006 WL 1370998 (Colo. A.G.) (concluding that community colleges lack statutory authority to establish a policy or regulating granting in-state tuition status to undocumented students).

[381] *See* NCSL, *Undocumented Student Tuition, supra* note 378. In contrast, in New Jersey, the Higher Education Student Assistance Authority, and in Florida, the Florida State Board of Education and the Florida Board of Governors, attempted to deny tuition grant aid to U.S. citizen students on the basis of her parents' status as undocumented immigrants. In 2012, a New Jersey district court and a Florida federal district court respectively voided the decision as unconstitutional. A.Z., v. Higher Education Student Assistance Authority, 48 A.3d 1151 (N.J. Super. Ct. 2012) and Ruiz v. Robinson, 892 F. Supp. 2d 1321 (S.D. Fla. 2012).

years.[382] Also, while the decision to either deny or grant admission and/or in-state tuition to undocumented students is framed generally in terms of colleges and universities, the question bears also on graduate schools.[383]

To date, the debate over the legality of in-state tuition for undocumented students has centered on whether states that charge in-state tuition to undocumented students are preempted by the Illegal Immigration Reform and Immigrant Responsibility Act of 1996 (IIRIRA).[384] Chapter 14 of IIRIRA, which deals with restricting welfare and public benefits, contains two provisions relevant to noncitizens in postsecondary education. Section 1621 included in the definition of restricted "[s]tate or local public benefit[s]" "any . . . postsecondary education . . . benefit for which payments or assistance are provided to an individual, household, or family eligibility unit by an agency of a State or local government or by appropriated funds of a State or local government."[385] Section 1621 further prescribes that only states which have specifically enacted legislation after August 22, 1996 to affirmative grant eligibility could make such state or local public benefits available to noncitizens excluded from benefits under the legislation.[386] More on point, Section 1623 of IIRIRA provides that "an alien who is not lawfully present in the United States shall not be eligible on the basis of residency within a State (or a political subdivision) for any postsecondary education benefit unless a citizen or national of the Unites States is eligible for such a benefit (in no less an amount, duration, and scope) without regard to whether the citizen or national is such a resident."[387]

Professor Kris W. Kobach has relied on IIRIRA § 1623 to publish articles and to participate in litigation to challenge state laws that offer in-state college tuition to undocumented students.[388] Kobach argues, *inter alia*, that the plain text of § 1623 displaces state laws that offer in-state tuition to undocumented students without offering the same to out-of-state residents through express preemption.[389] Most states offering in-state tuition to undocumented students, however, do so not on the

---

[382] *Id.* Some scholars have documented, however, that despite the existence of favorable laws and/or policies toward undocumented students, undocumented students multiple barriers. Marina Alexio, et al., *An Analysis of Policies Toward Applications from Undocumented Immigrant Students at Big Ten Schools*, 30 Law & Ineq. 1 (2012).

[383] *See, e.g.*, Aldana et al., *Raising the Bar, supra* note 215.

[384] Illegal Immigration Reform and Immigrant Responsibility Act (IIRIRA) of 1996, Pub. L. No. 104-208, div. C, 110 Stat. 3009-546-3009-724.

[385] *Id.* at § 1621.

[386] *Id.* ("A State may provide that an alien who is not lawfully present in the United States is eligible for any State or local public benefit which such alien would otherwise be ineligible under subsection (a) of this section only through the enactment of State law after August 22, 1996, which affirmatively provides for such eligibility.").

[387] *Id.* at § 1623.

[388] Kris W. Kobach, *Immigration Nullification: In-State Tuition and Lawmakers who Disregard the Law*, 10 N.Y.U. J. Legis. & Pub. Pol'y 473, 503–17 (2006–2007).Kobach represents the U.S. citizens' plaintiffs challenging the laws granting in-state tuition to undocumented students in Kansan and California. *Id.* at FN a1.

[389] *Id.* at 507–08. Kobach also makes an argument for implied preemption through other provisions of the INA in that such laws conflict with the objectives of Congress to curtail undocumented migration,

basis of residency but rather contingent upon attending high school in the state for three years.[390] Kobach views this approach as states' attempt to evade § 1623.[391] He argues that Congress intended the phrase "eligible on the basis of residence within the State . . . for any postsecondary education benefit" to expressly bar undocumented students from resident tuition rates, discounts, and scholarships available to state residents.[392] Any other reading of the statute, Kobach characterizes as implausible because it allows states to create a semantic loophole to obliterate the proscription so long as the word "residence" is avoided. This would, in turn, violate the "whole act" rule of statutory construction by ignoring the rest of the IIRIRA and the manifest intent of Congress.[393] As a matter of public policy, Kobach espouses the view that persons who have violated federal immigration laws should not be rewarded with taxpayer-subsidized tuition. This is in light of limited resources and the increasing financial burden born by U.S. taxpayers and U.S. citizen parents to educate their children.[394]

Professor Michael A. Olivas adopts different constitutional, statutory, and policy approaches to the issue of in-state resident tuition policies for noncitizens. Olivas views states' apportionment of tuition benefits and state residency determinations as appropriately a state role when such laws incorporate but do not determine immigrant status.[395] Indeed, for more than a century, states have exercised sole authority to set admission and resident tuition policies at public universities.[396] Moreover, in-state residency is solely a state-determined benefit or status as no federal funds attach to the classification.[397] Thus, Olivas rejects the argument that in-state tuition laws for undocumented students are impinging on federal immigration powers.[398]

Olivas also does not read IIRIRA as precluding states from granting in-state tuition to undocumented students. Olivas reads Sections1621 and 1623 of IIRIRA together (the latter which Kobach mostly ignores) to conclude that IIRIRA allows states to confer (or not to confer) residency status upon the undocumented in their public postsecondary institutions.[399] Section 1623 merely modifies the authority of states to confer state postsecondary benefits such that undocumented students are

---

represent a general obstacle to enforcement, and require state officers to make independent judgments about students' immigration status. *Id.* at 513–17.

[390] *Id.* at 506.

[391] *Id.*

[392] *Id.* at 510.

[393] *Id.* at 511.

[394] *Id.* at 498–503.

[395] Michael A. Olivas, *Lawmakers Gone Wild? College Residency and the Response to Professor Kobach*, 61 S.M.U. L. Rev. 99, 106 (2008).

[396] *See* Michael A. Olivas, *Storytelling Out of School: Undocumented College Residency, Race, and Reaction*, supra note 377, at 1027 (tracing court cases dating back to 1882 that held that only states can set residency and tuition policies for institutions of higher learning).

[397] Olivas, *Lawmakers Gone Wild?*, *supra* note 395, at 122.

[398] *Id.*

[399] *Id.*

not favored over out-of-state residents.[400] All 10 state statutes currently conferring in-state tuition to undocumented students require of them state high school attendance and three years residency, which are not required of citizen non-residents.[401] As such, undocumented students are not favored over other nonresident applicants. Further, Olivas reads the term "benefit" as used in both provisions as proscribing monetary postsecondary benefits, not status-based residency classifications.[402] As a matter of public policy, Olivas challenges the overstated claims of U.S. citizen student displacement by undocumented students. He also critiques the short-sightedness of opposing the integration of long-term undocumented students as productive contributors of society.[403]

Plaintiffs on either side of the debate are relying on the Supremacy Clause to challenge the validity of laws that grant or deny in-state tuition or other postsecondary benefits to undocumented students. For example, students and unincorporated organizations challenged Virginia's post-secondary institutions' policy of denying admissions to undocumented students based, *inter alia*, on preemption.[404] Nonresident citizen students asserted preemption to challenge a Kansas statute allowing undocumented students to attend Kansas universities and pay in-state tuition.[405] The Kansas litigation never reached the merits because the Tenth Circuit affirmed the district court's case dismissal for lack of standing.[406]

The Virginia federal district court holding applied the *De Canas* three-prong preemption test[407] to uphold the validity of admission denials to postsecondary schools to undocumented students. Like Olivas, the court affirmed that federal

---

[400] *Id.* at 123.

[401] *Id.*

[402] To make this argument, Olivas examines the textual modifications of "benefit" employed in the provisions — such as "for which payments or assistance are provided to an individual, household, or family eligibility . . . under 1621(c) (1)(B) and "amount, duration, and scope" in section 1623. *Id.* at 124. See also Laura A. Hernández, *Dreams Deferred — Why In-State College Tuition Rates Are Not a Benefit Under the IIRIRA And How this Interpretation Violates the Spirit of Plyer*, 21 Cornell J. L. & Pub. Pol'y 525 (2012).

[403] Olivas, *Storytelling Out of School, supra* note 377, at 1085–86.

[404] Equal Access Education v. Merten, 305 F. Supp. 2d 585 (E.D. Va. 2004).

[405] Day v. Bond, 511 F.3d 1030 (10th Cir. 2007).

[406] *Id.* at 1139. Another case in Oklahoma against a statute that included 14 distinct anti-immigration sections, including Section 11 denying resident tuition, financial aid, and scholarship to undocumented students was also dismissed for lack of standing. That case, however, did not include student plaintiffs challenging that specific provision of the law. Nevertheless, it is worth noting that while certain other undocumented persons denied driver's licenses or who faced eviction from their homes based on their status could prove injury, they were denied standing nonetheless on a theory of "unclean hands." The decision reads in relevant part:

> An Illegal alien, in willful violation of federal immigration law, is without standing to challenge the constitutionality of a state law, when compliance with federal law would absolve the illegal alien's constitutional dilemma . . . "

National Coalition of Latino Clergy, Inc., et al. v. Henry, 2007 U.S. Dist. LEXIS 94871 (N.D. Okla. 2007). This same logic could apply to deny standing to undocumented students challenging laws that deny them in-state tuition.

[407] 424 U.S. 351 (1976). *See supra* notes 220–34 and accompanying text for a description of the *De Canas* test.

immigration laws and those more specifically pertaining to noncitizen postsecondary benefits do not preclude state regulation of noncitizen access to higher education benefits.[408] In dicta, however, on the specific interpretation of IIRIRA Section 1623, the court inferred that "aliens cannot receive in-state tuition unless out-of-state United States citizens receive this benefit."[409] This reading is more consistent with Kobach's interpretation of the same section.

Interestingly, a 2008 ICE letter to North Carolina's Attorney General's office on the issue of federal laws' regulation of higher education benefits to the undocumented concluded that "*admissions* to public post-secondary educational institutions is not one of the benefits regulated by the [IIRIRA]. Further it concluded that it is not a public benefit under the [PWORA]."[410] The letter did not address the issue of in-state tuition benefits. In 2010, the Supreme Court of California considered whether a state statute granting in-state tuition to undocumented students violates Section 505 of IIRIRA.[411] The court held that IRRIRA did not preempt the California statute since its exemption from paying nonresident tuition to undocumented students is not based on residence. Instead it was based on other criteria, including possessing a California high school degree or equivalent.[412] The California highest court also rejected a challenge to California's in-state tuition law based on the Privileges and Immunities Clause of the U.S. constitution. It concluded that the clause does not prohibit states from granting certain benefits to noncitizens that it does not confer on citizens.[413] Also in 2010, a federal Texas district court refused standing to plaintiffs who attempted to challenge Texas decision to grant in-state tuition to undocumented students.[414] In 2012, an Alabama federal district court enjoined provisions of the Alabama law denying undocumented students admission to state colleges and universities. It did so on the basis that the statute's classification of those permitted enrollment — those possessing lawful permanent residence or an appropriate nonimmigrant visa under federal law — constituted an unconstitutional classification of aliens.[415] Ultimately, the Alabama legislature amended the law to strike out the unconstitutional classification and subsequently the Eleventh Circuit vacated the

---

[408] For example, the court rejects the argument that state determinations of students' immigration status is preempted by federal immigration law because Virginia adopts federal immigration classifications. *Equal Access Education v. Merten*, 305 F. Supp. 2d at 603 (E.D. Va. 2004). As well, the court rejects that Virginia is attempting to regulate in a field that is completely occupied by the federal government. *Id* at 605.

[409] *Id.* at 606–07.

[410] Letter from Sheriff (Ret.) Jim Pendergraph, Executive Director, Office of State and Local Coordination, U.S. Dept. of Homeland Security to Thomas J. Ziko, Special Deputy Attorney General, N.C. Department of Justice (July 9, 2008) (cited in Ark. Op. Atty. Gen. No. 2008-109, 2008 WL 4198411, at *3 (Ark. A.G.))

[411] Martinez v. Regents of the University of Cal., 241 P.3d 855 (Cal. 2010).

[412] *Id.* at 863. The California highest court also considered but rejected arguments that the PRWORA preempted the California in-state tuition statute, namely because the California law did not mention the PRWORA and because it did not use the words "illegal alien." *Id.* at 868.

[413] *Id.* at 869.

[414] Immigration Reform Coal. of Texas v. Texas, 706 F. Supp. 2d 760, 765 (S.D. Tex. 2010).

[415] Hispanic Interest Coal. of Ala. v. Governor of Ala., 691 F.3d 1236 (11th Cir. 2012).

district court's injunction.[416] Then in 2013, a Texas court of appeals recognized standing for a group of taxpayers to challenge on preemption grounds Texas' decision to grant in-state tuition to undocumented students.[417] This was in sharp contrast to a very similar lawsuit filed by taxpayers in 2010 which was dismissed for lack of standing by a Texas federal district court.[418]

None of the above decisions and/or opinions definitively resolves the issue of whether federal law or state law governs issues of admission and/or in-state tuition benefits for undocumented students. The issue of in-state tuition is certainly permitting localities to define membership[419] in ways that some scholars view as positive and constitutional.[420] Some scholars, however, have expressed concern over the lack of uniformity that has resulted from the piecemeal approach and have argued in favor of national policy in this area.[421] Others also note, for example, that racial composition of state legislatures and their political affiliation, as well as racial bias, appear to be determining the outcome of whether to grant or deny in-state tuition in the localities.[422]

Congress could ultimately legislate to definitively "occupy" the field of postsecondary education benefits for noncitizens. Since 2001, Congress has attempted, but failed to pass the legislation most commonly known as the Development Relief and Education for Alien Minors (DREAM) Act. The DREAM Act would permit states to offer in-state tuition rates to undocumented students and would offer legalization to noncitizens who possess good moral character, can establish five-year residency in the U.S., are under 21 years of age, earn a high school degree, and complete at least two years of college or military service.[423] Were this law to pass, it would preempt inconsistent state legislation, although states might still be able to regulate to grant or deny benefits to undocumented students ineligible for benefits under the DREAM Act.

In the meantime, the Obama administration's decision to implement that Deferred Action for Childhood Arrivals (DACA) program, which has allowed more than half a million undocumented youths to avoid deportation and be granted work

---

[416] *Id.* at 1243.

[417] Lone Star College System v. Immigration Reform Coal., 418 S.W. 3d 263 (Tex. App. 2013).

[418] Immigration Reform Coalition of Texas v. Texas, 706 F. Supp. 2d 760 (S.D. Tex. 2010).

[419] *See, e.g.,* Angela M. Banks, *Members Only: Undocumented Students & In-State Tuition,* 2013 B.Y.U. L. Rev. 1425 (2013).

[420] *See, e.g.,* Sallie Dietrich, *Redefining "American": The Constitutionality of State Dream Acts,* 31 Law & Ineq. 165 (2012) and Victor C. Romero, *Immigrant Education and the Promise of Integrative Egalitarianism,* 2001 Mich. St. L. Rev. 275 (2011).

[421] Stephen L. Nelson, Kara Hetrick Glaubitz, and Jennifer L. Robinson, *Reduced Tuition Benefits for Undocumented Immigrant Students: The Implications of a Piecemeal Approach to Policymaking,* 53 Santa Clara L. Rev. 897 (2013).

[422] *See, e.g.,* Stephen L. Nelson, et al., *States Taking Charge: Examining of the Role of Race, Party Affiliation, and Preemption in the Development of In-State Tuition Laws for Undocumented Immigrant Students,* 19 Mich. J. Race & L. 247 (2014) and Marcia A. Yablon-Zug and Danielle R. Holley-Walker, *Not Very Collegial: Exploring Bans on Undocumented Immigrant Admissions to State Colleges and Universities,* 3 Charleston L. Rev. 421 (2009).

[423] *See* Regini Shah, *Sharing the Dream: Toward Formalizing the Status of Long-Term Undocumented Children in the United States,* 39 Colum. Hm. Rts. L. Rev. 637 (2008).

authorization and a Social Security Number, has sparked new litigation in states that still refuse to admit or grant them in-state tuition.[424] DACA strengthens the undocumented students' position that they are now in "lawful presence" in the United States and that denial of in-state tuition to them would violate federal immigration guidelines on the establishment of residency status.[425] Indeed, post-DACA, Virginia's Attorney General agreed that undocumented students would not be eligible for in-state tuition since they now can establish lawful presence, so long as they also satisfy the domicile requirements under state law.[426]

K. WORKER RIGHTS

1. State Employment and Labor Laws

Undocumented workers struggle for workplace protections, but their immigration status functions as a liability. Ample research has documented the challenges with low-wage work and the particular vulnerability of unauthorized immigrant workers.[427] Despite this, in the last four decades especially, the law has shifted to make it even more difficult for undocumented workers to find protection under U.S. labor and worker protection laws.[428] Some scholars lament this shift in law for its failure to recognize indicators of membership in favor of status-based considerations that in the end undermine the goals of labor and employment law.[429]

The passage of IRCA in 1986 with its establishment of employer sanctions for the hiring of undocumented workers muddled the waters for the protection of undocumented workers under U.S. labor and worker laws. Prior to IRCA's passage, worker rights and benefits, with the exception of unemployment benefits,[430] had generally been available to all workers, regardless of immigration

---

[424] *See, e.g.*, April 29, 2014 letter to the Hon. John J. Goger by Immigration Professors of amicus Curiae Brief in DACA Beneficiary Georgia College Students v. University Systems of Georgia's Board of Regents case (on file with author) and Justin Jouvenal, *Immigrant Students in Va. Seeking In-State college Tuition*, THE WASHINGTON POST, Dec. 17, 2013.

[425] Letter to the Hon. John J. Goger by Immigration Professors, *supra* note 424.

[426] Media communication from the Office of the Commonwealth of Virginia, Office of the Attorney General, Mark Herring, Herring Advises that Virginia "Dreamers" can Qualify for In-State Tuition, *available at* http://www.oag.state.va.us/index.php/media-center/news-releases/122-herring-advises-that-virginia-dreamers-can-qualify-for-in-state-tuition-april-29-2014.

[427] *See, e.g.*, Kati L. Griffith, *Undocumented Workers: Crossing the Borders of Immigration and Workplace Law*, 22 CORNELL J.L. & PUB. POL'Y 611 (2012); Shannon Gleeson, *Labor Rights for All? The Role of Undocumented Immigrants Status for Worker Claims Making*, 35 LAW & SOC. INQUIRY 561 (2010) and Justin McDevitt, *Compromise Is Complicity: Why There Is No Middle Road in the Struggle to Protect Daylaborers in the United States*, 26 ABA J. LAB. & EMP. L. 101 (2010).

[428] *See, e.g.*, Kati L. Griffith, *U.S. Migrant Worker Law: The Interstices of Immigration Law and Labor Law and Employment Law*, 31 COMP. LAB. L. & POL'Y 125 (2009).

[429] *See e.g.*, D. Carolina Núñez, *Fractured Membership: Deconstructing Territoriality to Secure Rights and Remedies for the Undocumented Worker*, 2010 WIS. L. REV. 817 (2010).

[430] *See, e.g.*, Alonso v. State of California, 50 Cal. App. 3d 242 (1975); Pinilla v. Bd. of Review in Dep't of Labor, 382 A.2d 921 (N.J. Super. Ct. 1978); Flores v. Dep't of Jobs and Training, 411 N.W. 2d 499 (Minn. 1987); and Ruiz v. Unemployment Compensation Bd. of Review, 911 A.2d 600 (Pa. Cmmw. Ct. 2006) (barring unauthorized workers from unemployment benefits).

status.[431] Since IRCA's passage, however, a number of employers challenged workers' compensation claims by unauthorized workers, although generally state courts found no conflict between IRCA's employer sanctions for the hiring of undocumented persons and state laws protecting workers.[432] In passing IRCA, in fact, legislative history leaves clear that the law's intention was not to limit workplace protections afforded to undocumented workers.[433]

Despite IRCA's legislative history, in 2002 the U.S. Supreme Court decided *Hoffman Plastic Compounds, Inc. v. National Labor Relations Board*.[434] The Court held that an undocumented worker fired in retaliation for his support of union organizing was ineligible for backpay (i.e., lost wages resulting from unlawful termination) because such an award would conflict with IRCA's bar on the hiring of undocumented workers. *Hoffman Plastic* was a departure from the Court's decision nearly two decades earlier in 1984 in *Sure-Tan, Inc. v. NLRB*.[435] There, the Court found no difficulty harmonizing NLRA coverage with a worker's violation of the immigration laws.[436] *Sure-Tan* held that undocumented workers are "employees" under the NLRA, and thus, found that NLRA statutory remedies applied equally to undocumented workers.[437] But even in *Sure-Tan*, decided pre-IRCA, the issue of backpay was more controversial. It ultimately lead to a 5-4 majority disapproving an award of six months backpay for workers who had accepted voluntary departure in lieu of deportation. This was based on concerns over undermining the deterrence of unauthorized migration embodied in the immigration laws.[438] *Hoffman Plastic*, however, did not rely on *Sure-Tan* to deny backpay remedies. It choose instead to conclude that IRCA has significantly altered the "legal landscape,"[439] for it has " 'forcefully' made combating the employment of illegal aliens central to '[t]he policy of immigration law.' "[440] More recently, the Second Circuit and several other federal district courts have affirmed the denial of backpay awards for employer violations of the National Labor Relations Act. They have also required employees to disclose their immigration status as part of discovery when back pay remedies are at issue.[441]

---

[431] *See* Keith Cunningham-Parmeter, *Redefining the Rights of Undocumented Workers*, 58 Am. U. L. Rev. 1361 (2009) and Anne Marie O'Donovon, *Immigrant Workers and Workers' Compensation After Hoffman Plastics Compounds, Ind. v. N.L.R.B.*, 30 N.Y.U. Rev. L. & Soc. Change 299, 303–04 (2006).

[432] *Id.*

[433] H.R. Rep. No. 99-682, pt. 1, at 49; H.R. Rep. No. 99-682, pt. 2, at 8–9.

[434] 535 U.S. 137 (2002).

[435] 467 U.S. 883 (1984).

[436] *Id.* at 893–94.

[437] *Id.*

[438] *Id.* at 903.

[439] *Hoffman Plastic*, 535 U.S. at 147 (quoting INS v. Nat'l Ctr. For Immigrants' Rights, Inc., 502 U.S. 183, 194 & n.8 (1991)).

[440] *Id.* at 148.

[441] See Palma v. National Labor Relations Board, 723 F.3d 176 (2d Cir. 2013) and National Labor Relations Board v. Domsey Trading Corporation, 636 F.3d 33 (2d Cir. 2011). *See also* Bermudez v. Karoline's International Restaurant Bakery Corp., 2013 U.S. Dist. LEXIS 169066 (E.D.N.Y. Nov. 21, 2013), Hernandez v. Alexander, 2009 U.S. Dist. LEXIS 61017 (N.D. Miss. 2009). But see Sandoval v. Rizzuti Farms, LTD, 656 F. Supp. 2d 1265 (E.D. Wash. 2009) (barring early discovery of immigration

Post-*Hoffman Plastics*, some states have relied on the opinion's IRCA interpretation to deny state worker rights to undocumented workers. Other states have rejected the expansion of *Hoffman Plastics* to state workplace laws.[442] For example, while almost all state workers' compensation statutes cover undocumented workers,[443] some courts have relied on *Hoffman Plastics* to deny some or all workers' compensation remedies to undocumented workers. They focused on the worker's wrongdoing of working without authorization and IRCA's goal of deterring unauthorized migration.[444] In addition, a few state legislatures have contemplated proposals to exclude the undocumented from worker compensation benefits based on alleged worker misconduct.[445] Similarly, tort actions filed by undocumented workers against employers for work injuries have yielded mixed results, at least as to lost wages resulting from the injury.[446] Those courts denying lost wages view this remedy as similar to back pay, given that it awards damages for "would have" rather than already earned wages in contravention of IRCA.[447] In addition, some state courts have denied worker remedies for wrongful termination under state anti-discrimination statutes based

---

status to prevent manifest injustice even in cases involving back pay claims).

[442] *See generally* María Pabón López, *The Place of the Undocumented Workers in the United States Legal System After Hoffman Plastics Compounds: An Assessment and Comparison with Argentina's Legal System*, 15 IND. INT'L & COMP. L. REV. 301 (2005).

[443] Jeffrey Klamut, *The Invisible Fence: De Facto Exclusion of Undocumented Workers from State Workers' Compensation Systems*, 16 KANS. J. L. & PUB. POL'Y 174, 182 (2006–7) (explaining that many statutes include undocumented workers explicitly in their statutory definition of employee, while others do so only implicitly through broad language that includes all workers employed under a contract of hire). Still, most undocumented workers are de facto excluded from coverage because most work in industries where statutory exemptions and employer evasion schemes limit access to worker compensation benefits. *Id.* at 188–204.

[444] *See, e.g.*, Torres v. Precision Industries, P.I. Inc., 2014 Tenn. App. LEXIS 470 (Tenn. Ct. App. 2014) (denying retaliatory discharge claim after undocumented workers injured his back); Gonzalez v. Performance Painting, Inc., 303 P.3d 802 (N.M. 2013) (denying modifier benefits after injury); Sanchez v. Eagle Alloy, Inc. 658 N.W. 2d 510, 515 (Mich. Ct. App. 2003) (limiting undocumented worker's compensation benefits to the date when his undocumented status was discovered because of the worker's criminal act of obtaining employment fraudulently); Reinforced Earth Co. v. Workers' Com. Appeal Bd. (Astudillo), 810 A.2d 99, 108–09 & n.12 (Pa. 2002) (holding that while *Hoffman Plastics* did not bar medical benefits for injuries sustained by undocumented workers, it did suspend their eligibility for wage replacement benefits); Tarango v. State Indus. Ins. Sys., 25 P.3d 175 (Nev. 2001) (holding while undocumented workers are eligible for medical compensation for injuries, not so for vocational rehabilitation because of their unauthorized entry).*See also* Roxana Mondragón, Injured *Undocumented Workers and Their Workplace Rights: Advocating for a Retaliation Per se Rule*, 44 COLUM. J. L. & SOC. PROBLS. 447 (2011).

[445] Klamut, *supra* note 443, at 204–207 (discussing proposals in South Carolina and Maryland).

[446] *Compare* Veliz v. Rental Serv. Corp. USA, 313 F. Supp. 2d 1317, 1337 (M.D. Fla. 2003) *and* Hernandez-Cortez v. Hernandez, 2003 U.S. Dist. LEXIS 19780 (D. Kan. Nov. 4, 2003) (relying on *Hoffman Plastics* to deny lost wages as a remedy for the work-related death of a worker) with Grocers Supply, Inc. v. Cabello, 390 S.W. 3d 707 (Tex. App. 2012), Wielgus v. Ryobi Technologies, Inc., 875 F. Supp. 2d 854 (N.D. Ill. 2012), Kalyta v. Versa Products, Inc., 2011 U.S. Dist. LEXIS 27719 (D.N.J. Mar. 17, 2011), Silva v. Wilcox, 223 P.3d 127 (Colo. Ct. App. 2009), Majlinger v. Casino Contracting Corp., 25 A.D.3d 14 (N.Y. App. Div. 2005) and Tyson Foods, Inc. v. Guzman, 116 S.W.3d 233 (Tex. App. 2003) (awarding lost wages to undocumented worker).

[447] *Veliz*, 313 F. Supp. 2d at 1337.

also on IRCA's deterrence rationale.[448] Some scholars question the legitimacy of using the concept of fault to deny undocumented workers compensation that they are otherwise owed under workplace or tort laws.[449]

Several states, however, have refused to extend *Hoffman Plastics* to state worker compensation statutes. They have reasoned that it is the role of states to regulate workplace safety and finding strong policy grounds to protect workers within the state.[450] Courts that have granted lost wages emphasize instead the prevalence of the states' interest in protecting workers, absent an explicit mandate from Congress.[451] In the same way that the undocumented worker in *Hoffman Plastics* was eligible for compensation for work already performed, less affected have been worker protections for work already performed, such as state prevailing wage requirements or laws imposing penalties for unpaid wages.[452] Finally, it is

---

[448] Crespo v. Evergo Corp., 841 A.2d 471 (N.J. Super. Ct. 2004) (denying remedies to undocumented worker fired for being pregnant); Morejon v. Hinge, 2003 Cal. App. Unpub. LEXIS 10394 (Nov. 4, 2003) (unpublished) (denying remedies to undocumented worker who was fired after requesting leave to undergo surgery to treat ovarian cancer).

[449] Christine M. Cimini, *Undocumented Workers and Concepts of Fault: Are Courts Engaged in Legitimate Decision making?*, 65 Vand. L. Rev. 389 (2012).

[450] *See, e.g.*, Bollinger Shipyards, Inc. v. Director, Office of Worker's Compensation Programs, 604 F.3d 864 (5th Cir. 2010) (holding that undocumented workers are eligible to recover worker's compensation benefits under the LHWCA); Madeira v. Affordable Hous. Found, Inc., 469 F.3d 219, 228 (2d Cir. 2006) (concluding that states enjoy broad authority under their police powers to enact laws affecting occupational health and safety and holding that undocumented worker was eligible for lost earnings damages). *See also* New York Medical Center of Queens, v. Microtech Contracting Corp., 22 N.Y.3d 501 (N.Y. 2014) (allowing recovery for injuries under state law); Fernandez v. McDonald's, 292 P.3d 311 (Kan. 2013) (upholding permanent disability claim); Delaware Valley Field Services v. Ramirez, 2012 Del. Super. LEXIS 622 (Del. Super. Ct. Sept. 13, 2012) (awarding total disability benefits even after worker's deportation); HDV Construction Systems, Inc. v. Aragon, 66 So. 3d 331 (Fla. Dist. Ct. App. 2011) (allowing permanent disability claim); Abel Verdon Construction v. Rivera, 348 S.W.3d 749 (Ky. 2011) (allowing partial disability recovery); Staff Management v. Jimenez, 839 N.W.3d 640 (Iowa 2013) (allowing healing period benefits); Asylum Co. v. DC Department of Employment Services, 10 A.3d 619 (DC Ct. App. 2010) (allowing total disability claim); Salas v. Sierra Chemical Co., 327 P.3d 797 (2014) (permitting disability discrimination claim following work injury); Balbuena v. IDR Realty LLC, 845 N.E.2d 1246 (N.Y. 2006) (awarding lost earnings); Design Kitchen & Baths v. Lagos, 882 A.2d 817 (Md. 2005) (awarding medical benefits); Correa v. Waymouth Farms, Inc., 664 N.W. 2d 324 (Minn. 2003) (awarding temporary total disability benefits to undocumented worker); Cherokee Indus., Inc. v. Alvarez, 84 P.3d 798 (Okla. Civ. App. 2003) (awarding total disability benefits).

[451] *Majlinger*, 25 A.D. 3d at 14.

[452] *See, e.g.*, Lamonica v. Safe Hurricane, 711 F.3d 1299 (11th Cir. 2013) (upholding undocumented worker action against employer for overtime wages); Lucas v. Jerusalem Cafe, LLC, 721 F.3d 927 (8th Cir. 2013) (upholding undocumented workers claims for overtime wages and minimum wage); Rodriguez v. The Pie of Port Jefferson Corp., 2014 U.S. Dist. LEXIS 138738 (E.D.N.Y. Sept. 24, 2014) (upholding unpaid overtime wages claim); Bautista Hernandez v. Tadala's Nursery, Inc., 2014 U.S. Dist. LEXIS 106791 (S.D. Fla. July 3, 2014) (allowing overtime violations); Grocers Supply, Inc. v. Cabello, 390 S.W. 3d 707 (Tex. App. 2012) (award of lost wages); Jin-Ming Lin et al., v. Chinatown Restaurant Corp., 771 F. Supp. 2d 185 (D. Mass. 2011) (allowing unpaid minimum and overtime wages); Villareal v. El Chile, Inc., 266 F.R.D. 207 (N.D. Ill. 2010) (immigration status not relevant to unpaid wages claim); Serrano v. Underground Utilities Corp., 970 A.2d 1054 (N.J. Super. Ct. 2009) (employers precluded from asking about immigration status in prevailing wage suit); Coma Corp. v. Kansas Dept. of Labor, 154 P.3d 1080 (Kan. 2007) (holding that IRCA did not preempt Kansas Wage Payment Act on the issue of earned but unpaid wages and that employer was subject to statutory penalty for willfully failing to pay undocumented worker his earned wages); Reyes v. Van Elk, Ltd., 148 Cal. App. 4th 604 (2007) (holding

important to note that some local governments have responded to deficiencies in federal labor and employment law protections with their own innovations to improve the rights of low wage and immigrant workers, including undocumented domestic workers.[453]

2. Day Laborers

Local governments have also acted to regulate the growing presence of day laborers in their communities. Day laborers who generally congregate at informal hiring places such as a street corner, parking lot, sidewalks, or park to wait for temporary or permanent employment, are overwhelmingly Latino and undocumented.[454] Their visibility has created tensions in communities, especially with some anti-immigrant groups who portray them as violent criminals and sexual harassers[455] or simply as public nuisances or traffic safety hazards.[456] As well, localities have been concerned over day laborer's all too common experiences of labor exploitation and other types of victimization, including hate crimes.[457] Scholars, however, contest that the strategy of exclusion ignores economic theory. This justifies the presence of day labor markets in public space, and is at odds with economic and demographic changes that have increased demand for day laborers — whether undocumented or not.[458]

Localities have either moved to harass or displace day laborers or they have attempted to improve their lot. They have done so by imposing license restrictions on those who hire them or by promoting and regulating work centers that provide improved facilities, education, and legal representation to exploited workers.[459] Either response has faced court challenges with largely positive results for day laborers. Despite the litigation successes documented below, some scholars are still seeing a wide gap between the legal successes and actual victory of increased worker protections for day laborers.[460]

---

that IRCA did not preempt the states wage and hour legislation in undocumented workers' claim for unpaid prevailing wages). *But see* Zavala v. Wal-Mart Stores Inc., 691 F.3d 527 (3d Cir. 2013) (denying class action certification to undocumented workers seeking to recover lost wages).

[453] *See, e.g.*, Donna E. Young, *The Constitutional Parameters of New York State's Domestic Workers Bill of Rights: Balancing the Rights of Workers and Employers*, 74 ALB. L. REV. 1769 (2010–2011) and Scott L. Cummings and Steven A. Boutcher, *Mobilizing Local Government Law for Low-Wage Workers*, 1 U. CHI. LEGAL F. 187 (2009).

[454] Abel Valenzuela Jr., et al., *On the Corner: Day Labor in the United States* (2006), *available at* http://www.sscnet.ucla.edu/issr/csup/uploaded_files/Natl_DayLabor-On_the_Corner1.pdf.

[455] *See, e.g.*, DAY LABORERS, http://www.daylaborers.org/index.htm (website portraying daylaborers as violent criminals and sexual deviants) (last visited October 2014).

[456] Mauricio A. España, *Day Laborers, Friend or Foe: A Survey of Community Responses*, 30 FORDHAM URB. L.J. 1979, 1993–2000 (2003).

[457] *Id.* at 1991–1993, 2001–2002.

[458] *See, e.g.*, Gregg W. Kettles, *Day Labor Markets and Public Space*, 78 UMKC L. REV. 139 (2009).

[459] *See, e.g.*, Victor Narro, *Impacting Next Wave Organizing: Creative Campaign Strategies of the Los Angeles Worker Center*, 50 N.Y.L. SCH. L. REV. 465, 486–95 (2005–2006) (describing the work of worker centers with day laborers). *See also* Rodriguez, *The Significance of the Local*, *supra* note 16, at 597–99 (same).

[460] See Kristina M. Campbell, *The High Cost of Free Speech: Anti-Solicitation Ordinances, Day*

One common type of regulation, for example, has been laws or ordinances that impose a traffic violation on day laborers or persons who hire them for congregating at informal hiring places to seek jobs or for picking up the workers at these places.[461] Such laws have been successfully struck down under First Amendment challenges[462] as impermissible content-based regulation (of protected commercial speech).[463] Even if deemed content-neutral, it has also been struck down for lacking a substantial state interest,[464] or for not being narrowly tailored to meet that interest.[465] In contrast, First Amendment challenges to registration requirements based on a theory of impermissible prior restraints on the commercial speech of those who employ day laborers have not been successful. This is true as long as the law establishes clear guidelines and accords sufficient due process to registrants, including judicial review.[466]

Equal protection challenges have also been raised against selective law enforcement practices by local police or against ordinances designed to curb day labor practices. For example, a successful equal protection challenge was brought against the mayor and police of the Village of Mamaroneck in New York. This was done after they waged an intense law enforcement campaign to reduce the number of workers that included increasing police presence in the area, intimidating workers, and aggressively issuing traffic tickets to contractors who entered the area to pick up day laborers.[467] In contrast, another court upheld a housing overcrowding ordinance adopted by the Town of Jupiter, Florida. This was then enforced against properties primarily occupied by Hispanic residents in an effort to drive out day laborers congregating in the neighborhood.[468] The different outcomes in the cases turned on whether plaintiffs factually proved to the court that selective enforcement was intentionally racist against Latinos as opposed to discriminatory based on non-suspect characteristics.[469]

The public sponsorship of work centers for day laborers has also been challenged. In the town of Herndon, for example, taxpayers sponsored by Judicial

---

Laborers, and the Impact of "Backdoor" Local Immigration Regulations, 25 GEO. IMMIGR. L.J. 1 (2010).

[461] *See, e.g.*, § 72.17(C) of the Town of Cave Creek, Arizona Code (Oct. 24, 2007) (making it unlawful for "[any] person to stand on or adjacent to a street or highway and solicit, or attempt to solicit, employment, business or contributions from the occupant of any vehicle").

[462] For a thoughtful discussion of day laborers social movements and litigation strategies, see Scott L. Cummings, *Litigation at Work: Defending Day Labor in Los Angeles*, 58 UCLA L. REV. 1617 (2011).

[463] Valle Del Sol Inc. v. Whiting, 709 F.3d 808 (9th Cir. 2013) (affirming preliminary injunction against day laborer provision) and Lopez v. Town of Cave Creek, 559 F. Supp. 2d 1030 (D. Ariz. 2008).

[464] Coal. for Humane Immigrant Rights of Los Angeles v. Burke, 2000 U.S. Dist. LEXIS 16520 (C.D. Cal. Sept. 12, 2000) (unpublished opinion).

[465] Comite Jornaleros de Redondo Beach v. City of Redondo Beach, 657 F.3d 936 (9th Cir. 2011) and Jornaleros de la Palmas v. City of League City, 945 F. Supp. 2d 779 (S.D. Texas 2013).

[466] *See, e.g.*, Calderon v. City of Vista, 2006 U.S. Dist. LEXIS 54736 (S.D. Cal. Aug. 1, 2006) (unpublished opinion).

[467] *See, e.g.*, Doe v. Vill. of Mamaroneck, 462 F. Supp. 2d 520, 527 (S.D.N.Y. 2006).

[468] Young Apartments, Inc. v. Town of Jupiter, Florida, 2007 U.S. Dist. LEXIS 36814 (S.D. Fla. May 21, 2007).

[469] *Compare* Vill. of Mamanoreck, 462 F. Supp. 2d at 547–553 *with* Young Apartments, Inc., 2007 U.S. Dist. LEXIS 36814, at *5.

Watch, a conservative political group, raised a preemption challenge. They argued that the work centers facilitate the hiring of undocumented workers in violation of IRCA.[470] This litigation ultimately became moot when the town of Herndon closed the center's doors in 2007 after facing significant public pressure against it.[471]

L. DRIVER'S LICENSES

Post 9/11, the issue of driver's license restrictions for noncitizens took center stage.[472] With few exceptions, prior to that time, most noncitizens could obtain driver's licenses notwithstanding their immigration status.[473] Suddenly, however, driver's licenses became an issue of national security, rather than a local road safety regulation.[474] In fact, in 2004, Congress signed into law the Intelligence Reform and Terrorism Prevention Act (IRTPA)[475] and the REAL ID Act in 2005.[476] These Acts "federalized" driver's licenses by imposing national standards for their issuance.[477] The REAL ID Act specifically affected noncitizens by imposing Social Security Numbers (SSN) and legal residency requirements on state-issued driver's licenses for these to be used as a form of identification before federal agencies for official purposes.[478] As well, the REAL ID act contemplated only temporary driver's licenses and identification cards for noncitizens with temporary visas or those whose petitions were pending with an expiration date matching that of the visa or after one year if there was no definite end period.[479]

By the time Congress acted, at least 24 states had already legislated to require lawful presence for the issuance of driver's licenses, with only 11 states that expressly did not.[480] The federalization of driver's licenses, however, also prompted

---

[470] *See, e.g.,* Karunakarum v. Town of Herndon, 2006 Va. Cir. LEXIS 33 (Va. Cir. Ct. 2006) (unpublished opinion) (granting standing to taxpayers). For the background to the litigation see Margaret Hobbins, Note, *The Day Laborer Debate: Small Towns, U.S.A. Takes on Federal Immigration Law Regarding Undocumented Workers,* 6 CONN. PUB. INT. L.J. 111, 113–117 (2006).

[471] Rodríguez, *The Significance of the Local, supra* note 16, at 599.

[472] Aldana, *Federal Citizenship, supra* note 337, at 281–82. *See also* María Pabón López, *More than a License to Drive: State Restrictions on the Use of Driver's Licenses by Noncitizens,* 29 S. ILL. U. L.J. 9, 95–109 (2005).

[473] Some exceptions included Illinois and California, which, since the 1970s and 1990s respectively, required applicants for driver's licenses to have social security numbers. See Doe v. Edgar, 1989 U.S. Dist. LEXIS 9498 (N.D. Ill. Aug. 2, 1989) (unpublished) (discussing Ill. Rev. Stat. Ch. 95 1/2, para 6_1.06); Lauderbach v. Zolin, 36 Cal. App. 4th 454G (1995) (discussing California's 1992 Trial Court Realignment and Efficiency Act). *See also* Kevin R. Johnson, *Driver's Licenses and Undocumented Immigrants: The Future of Civil rights Law?,* 5 NEV. L.J. 213, 232 (2004) (discussing the anti-immigrant animus behind California's law).

[474] Aldana, *Federal Citizenship, supra* note 337, at 282.

[475] Pub. L. No. 108-458, § 7212(b)(2)(A)–(F), 118 Stat. 3638 (Dec. 17, 2004).

[476] Pub. L. No. 109-13, 119 Stat. 231 (May 10, 2005).

[477] Aldana, *Federal Citizenship, supra* note 337, at 282.

[478] Real ID Act, supra note 476, at § 202(c).

[479] *Id.*

[480] Aldana, *Federal Citizenship, supra* note 337, at 282.

many more states to legislate in the area,[481] despite significant concerns over costs and other burdens on states.[482] As of September 2014, most states continue to restrict noncitizen access to driver's licenses either by requiring an SSN, with or without exceptions for the issuance of a license, or by imposing a lawful presence requirement through legislation and/or agency practice. Persons with immigration status, even if temporary, can usually satisfy the lawful presence requirement, although sometimes the license will expire on the same date that their immigration status expires. For this reason, youths granted deferred action became eligible for driver's licenses in every state, except in Arizona and Nebraska. These two states attempted to deny driver's licenses even to youths who have been granted DACA.[483] In contrast, 13 states or localities have now passed laws that either grant access to permanent or temporary driver's licenses or driver authorization cards to applicants who reside in their state regardless of immigration status.[484] A controversial aspect of driver authorization cards is that attempts to distinguish these from driver's licenses has meant the inclusion of labels like "No Lawful Status" or "For Driving Purposes Only." Many feel this stigmatizes or worse, increases the person's risk of removal by signaling their immigration status to law enforcement such as local police their immigration status as part of a routine traffic stop.[485]

Proponents of granting driver's licenses to all noncitizens challenge the claim that their exclusion would improve national security; as well they raise civil liberties and state rights concerns.[486] The conferral of driver's license to noncitizens would create a fuller record of the identity of undocumented persons in the U.S., furthering the government's law enforcement goals.[487] In contrast, the denial of identification to undocumented persons affects their ability to conduct the most "ordinary living" tasks, such as driving, opening up a bank account, or renting an apartment.[488] Moreover, racial and anti-immigrant animus has motivated many of the local driver's license restriction legislation, which is viewed as a type of immigration control.[489] Undocumented persons, however, do not go away and find

---

[481] Within four months of the REAL ID Act's passage, 24 states introduced legislation to conform state law to the federal requirements *Id.* at 283.

[482] *See* National Governors Association, National Conference of State Legislatures, American Association of Motor Vehicle Administration, The Real ID Act: National Impact Analysis 2 (Sept. 2006), *available at* http://www.ncsl.org/print/statefed/Real_ID_Impact_Report_FINAL_Sept19.pdf (concluding that Real ID would cost more than $11 billion over five years and have a major impact on services to the public and impose unrealistic burden on state compliance).

[483] National Immigration Law Center, Access to Driver's Licenses for Immigrant Youth Granted DACA, http://www.nilc.org/dacadriverslicenses2.html (last visited Oct. 21, 2014).

[484] These states are: California, Colorado, Connecticut, Washington D.C., Illinois, Maryland, New Mexico, Nevada, Oregon, Puerto Rico, Utah, Vermont, and Washington. *See* http://www.nilc.org/driverlicensemap.html (last visited Oct. 21, 2014).

[485] *See, e.g.*, Tung Sing Wong, *Branded to Drive: Obstacles Preemption of North Carolina's Licenses to DACA Recipients*, 37 Hamline L. Rev. 81 (2014).

[486] *See, e.g.*, Raquel Aldana & Sylvia R. Lazos Vargas, *"Aliens" in Our Midst Post 9-11: Legislating Outsiderness Within the Border*, 38 U.S.C. Davis L. Rev. 1683, 1711–19 (2005).

[487] Donald Kervin & Margaret D. Stock, *The Role of Immigration in a Coordinated National Security Policy*, 21 Geo. Immigr. L.J. 383, 411–13 (2007).

[488] Johnson, *Driver's Licenses and Undocumented Immigrants, supra* note 473, at 223–232.

[489] *Id.* at 223–24.

alternatives to live and drive without U.S. driving authorization and identification. The consequences of this fact not only deteriorate road safety but expose immigrants to harm, such as increased exploitation, profiling, and criminalization.[490] Proponents of denying driver's licenses to undocumented immigrants focus on concerns over legitimizing the illegal conduct of persons who entered the U.S. illegally and continue to reside within the U.S. without authorization.[491]

A number of states have also openly opposed the federalization of driver's licenses, citing in addition to cost, state sovereignty, road safety, and privacy concerns.[492] In January of 2008, Maine became the first state to pass a resolution in opposition of REAL ID compliance, joined subsequently by Arkansas, Idaho, Montana, and Washington.[493] In addition, at least 24 other states have considered opting out of REAL ID or placing conditions on their participation.[494]

Court challenges to driver's license restrictions for noncitizens have generally been unsuccessful because those affected — namely undocumented immigrants — are not treated as a protected group and the restriction is not considered a fundamental right. The Sixth Circuit, for example, upheld Tennessee's driver certificate program against an equal protection challenge filed by temporary residents.[495] To do so, the court declined to extend suspect class status to nonimmigrants or to recognize driver's license denials as violating the fundamental right to travel.[496] Similar results have occurred in Iowa, Georgia, and North Dakota where bars to driver's licenses to undocumented persons have been upheld against equal protection challenges, despite the absence of a driving certificate.[497]

Substantive due process challenges also have not succeeded, because the denial of driver's license is viewed as a privilege to drive, not as a fundamental liberty interest.[498] Separate right to travel challenges have also been dismissed, at least for

---

[490] *Id.* (documenting, *inter alia*, the imposition of criminal sanctions for driving without a license).

[491] *See, e.g.*, Gregory A. Odegaard, *A Yes or No Answer: Plea to End the Oversimplification of the Debate on Licensing Aliens*, 24 J. L. & Pol. 435, 436 (2008).

[492] *See* Manoj Govindaich, *Driver Licensing Under the Real ID Act: Can Current Technology Balance Security and Policy*, 2006 U. Ill. L.J. L. Tech. & Pol'y 201 (2006) (discussing Real ID's privacy concerns).

[493] State objection to the Real ID Act has grown to twenty seven states which have either passed statutory objections or resolutions in the House or Senator or both in opposition. See National Conference on State Legislatures, State Legislative Activity in Opposition to the Real ID (Jan. 2014), *available at* http://www.ncsl.org/documents/standcomm/sctran/REALIDComplianceReport.pdf.

[494] Nat'l Immig. L. Ctr., 2007 State REAL ID Legislation (April 2007), *available at* http://www.nilc.org/immspbs/DLs/state_real_id_proposals_2007-04-23.pdf.

[495] LULAC v. Bredesen, 500 F.3d 523 (6th Cir. 2007).

[496] *Id.* The right to travel challenge in this case was made more difficult by Tennessee's issuance of driving certificates, which the court viewed as hardly an attempt of the state to deter or penalize travel. *Id.*

[497] Sanchez v. Iowa, 692 N.W.2d 812 (Iowa 2005); John Doe 1 v. Georgia Dep't of Pub. Safety, 147 F. Supp. 2d 1369 (N.D. Ga. 2001); Doe v. Edgar, 1989 U.S. Dist. LEXIS 9498 (N.D. Ill. Aug. 2, 1989) (unpublished opinion). *But see* People v. Quiroga-Puma, 848 N.Y.S.2d 853 (N.Y. Just. Ct. 2007) (applying equal protection strict scrutiny to a New York statute that resulted in the denial of driver's licenses to undocumented persons).

[498] *Sanchez*, 692 N.W.2d at 819–20.

undocumented persons, whose presence in the U.S. in violation of federal law makes their "right to travel" claims untenable to some courts.[499] Several challenges have been addressed to motor vehicle departments alleging misapplication of statutes or administrative overreach. This occurs when their practices have imposed requirements that immigrant applicants have been unable to meet to obtain driver's licenses.[500] More recently, DACA recipients have experienced mixed early success when challenging Arizona and Nebraska's attempt to deny them driver's licenses. In July 2014, the Ninth Circuit granted injunctive relief to DACA recipients denied driver's licenses in Arizona based on a pending equal protection challenge;[501] in contrast, a federal district court denied injunctive relief on a preemption and equal protection claim raised in a similar lawsuit.[502]

M.   LANDLORD/TENANT IMMIGRATION ORDINANCES

Immigrant communities have already been disproportionately affected by facially neutral housing code ordinances, such as those that purport to limit nontraditional family units or occupancy rates.[503] Beginning in 2006, however, localities began to adopt ordinances that explicitly sought to bar undocumented immigrants from rental properties based on their immigration status.[504] Hazleton, Pennsylvania became the first municipality to adopt an anti-immigrant tenancy ordinance, and it became the model to hundreds of other localities in about 29 states considering similar provisions.[505] By mid-2008, localities had passed at least 42 ordinances containing immigrant tenancy restrictions,[506] relying on states' police power to protect the health, safety, and welfare of their citizens.[507]

---

[499] *Doe v. Georgia Dep't of Pub. Safety*, 147 F. Supp. 2d at 1373–75. *See also* LULAC v. Bredesen, 500 F.3d 523 (6th Cir. 2007) (dismissing right to travel claim when driving certificates had been issued).

[500] Cubas v. Martinez, 870 N.E.2d 133 (N.Y. 2007) (upholding New York's DMV's statutory authority for proof-of identity requirements); Fahy v. Comm'n, New Hampshire Department of Safety, 2006 U.S. Dist. LEXIS 78342 (D.N.H. Oct. 26, 2006) (unpublished opinion) (striking down practice of imposing a shorter expiration date on driver's licenses for, *inter alia*, lawful permanent residents when practice not statutorily mandated nor authorized); Villegas v. Silverman, 832 N.E.2d 598 (Ind. 2005) (enjoining Indiana's Bureau of Motor Vehicles identification requirements based on overreach of statutory authority and violation of administrative rule-making procedures); Lauderbach v. Zolin, 35 Cal. App. 4th 578 (1995) (upholding San Francisco's DMV's statutory authority to require social security numbers for the issuance of driver's licenses).

[501] Arizona Dream Act Coalition v. Brewer, 757 F.3d 1053 (9th Cir. 2014).

[502] Saldana v. Lahm, 2013 U.S. Dist. LEXIS 148209 (D. Neb. Oct. 11, 2013).

[503] Guadalupe T. Luna, *Immigrants, Cops and Slumlords in the Midwest*, 29 S. ILL. U. L.J. 61, 73–77 (2005).

[504] Rigel C. Oliveri, *Between a Rock and a Hard Place: Landlords, Latinos, Anti-Illegal Immigrant Ordinances, and Housing Discrimination*, 62 VAND. L. REV. 55, 59–72 (2009).

[505] *Id.* at 60.

[506] *Id.*

[507] *See, e.g.*, Villas at Parkside Partners v. The City of Farmers Branch, 577 F. Supp. 2d 858 (N.D. Tex. 2008) (citing to the preamble of Ordinance 2892, which read in part that "the city of Farmers has determined that it is a necessity to adopt . . . immigration certification . . . for apartment complexes to safeguard the public . . . ").

Generally, these tenancy ordinances include renting to certain noncitizens as part of the definition of "harboring"[508] and impose on tenants the need to provide proof of legal citizenship and/or residency requirements.[509] Under some ordinances, such as the City of Farmers Branch, landlords directly would be responsible for immigration verification and recordkeeping.[510] Other ordinances, such as Hazleton's, require that all tenants obtain an occupancy permit from the City, which they could obtain only after providing proof of immigration eligibility.[511] Or, as in the case of the City of Escondido, some ordinances sought to rely on federal cooperation or resources for immigration verification.[512] Generally, enforcement relies on any individual filing a complaint with the municipality that a resident of a dwelling unit is an unauthorized immigrant.[513] In addition, in some cases, landlords may exercise a "safe harbor" provision and seek to verify a tenant's immigration eligibility even without a complaint.[514] In all cases, tenants unable to comply with immigration eligibility to rent are subject to eviction within days.[515] Landlords who fail to evict must face suspension of their licenses to rent,[516] civil penalties,[517] or, in some cases, criminal sanctions.[518]

---

[508] *See, e.g.*, City of Hazleton Ordinance 2006–18, The Illegal Immigration Relief Act Ordinance (IIRA), Sept. 21, 2006, at § 5 and 7.B, *available at* https://www.aclu.org/files/pdfs/immigrants/escondido_ordinance.pdf; Okla. Stat. tit. 21, § 446 (2007) and City of Escondido Ordinance No. 2006-38R, "Establishing Penalties for Harboring of Illegal Aliens in the City of Escondido," § 3, 16E-1, *available at* https://www.aclu.org/files/pdfs/immigrants/escondido_ordinance.pdf.

[509] *See, e.g.*, City of Farmers Branch, Ordinance No. 2892, "An Ordinance Amending Chapter 26, Businesses, Article IV Apartment Complex Rental, Mandating a Citizenship Certification Pursuant to 24 CFR 5 et seq;" § 2, *available at* http://www.americanbar.org/content/dam/aba/publishing/insights_law_society/news3.authcheckdam.pdf; City of Hazleton Ordinance 2006–13, Establishing a Registration Program for Residential Rental Properties . . . " "Tenant Registration Ordinance," Aug. 15, 2006, at 7.b.1.g.

[510] City of Farmer's Branch Ordinance No. 2892, *supra* note 509, at § 2, (2)–(4).

[511] Hazleton Ordinance 2006–13, *supra* note 509, at 7.b.1.g. Another example is Valley Park. *See* Oliveri, *supra* note 504, at 63–64.

[512] City of Escondido Ordinance No. 2006-38R, *supra* note 508, at § 3, 16E-2(c).

[513] Oliveri, *supra* note 505, at 62–63 (describing complaint procedures under ordinances enacted by Hazleton, Cherokee County, Escondido, Riverside, and Valley Park).

[514] *Id.* at 62 (discussing Hazleton's "safe harbor" provision).

[515] *Id.* at 62–63 (describing procedures leading up to eviction in Hazleton, Cherokee County, Riverside, and Valley Park).

[516] *See, e.g.*, Escondido Ordinance No. 2006-38R, *supra* note 508, at § 3, 16E-2(d); Hazleton Ordinance, 2006–18, *supra* note 508, at § 5.B(4).

[517] *See, e.g.*, Hazleton Ordinance, 2006–13, *supra* note 509, at § 10.b ($1,000.00 fine for each occupant without a permit and $100 per day per occupant not evicted). *See also* Oliveri, *supra* note 505, at 63 n.22 (discussing fines imposed by Valley Park, Farmer's Branch, Escondido, and Riverside).

[518] *See, e.g.*, Farmers Branch Ordinance No. 2892, *supra* note 510 at § 4 (misdemeanor punishable with a $500 per day per violation).

Several of the ordinances have been challenged in court,[519] with some being dismissed after localities voluntarily amended or withdrew the ordinances.[520] Legal challenges have raised constitutional claims of preemption, due process and equal protection violations, as well claims based on federal civil rights statutes and state laws. As of the date of this writing, the Third and Fifth Circuits have struck down the city ordinances on preemption grounds.[521] In May 2014 the Supreme Court rejected attempts by the towns of in Texas and Pennsylvania to revive the local laws by denying certiorari.[522] The Third Circuit considered that the City of Hazleton's housing and rental registration ordinances were both field and conflict preempted respectively. It did so because these laws attempted to regulate residence based solely on immigration status or intruded in the field of alien registration. In addition it found they interfered with the federal government's discretion to control the removal process.[523]

The Fifth Circuit found that the imposition of criminal sanctions and licensing penalties imposed by the City of Farmer's Branch conflicted with federal immigration law. It found that these sanctions constituted concurrent enforcement of the immigration laws but either created new criminal offenses that did not exist under federal immigration law or provided a different mechanism to criminalize conduct already criminalized by the federal anti-harboring laws.[524] In contrast, the Eighth Circuit reversed an earlier holding of the district court. It held instead that Freemont, Nebraska's law proscribing the renting of housing to unauthorized aliens was neither field nor conflict preempted by federal law. Moreover plaintiffs failed to satisfy a disparate impact claim.[525] The Eighth Circuit reasoned that laws

---

[519] Oliveri, *supra* note 504, at 65–72 (discussing litigation in Hazleton, Pennsylvania, Valley Park, Missouri, Farmers Branch, Texas, Cherokee County, Georgia, Escondido, Texas, Riverside, New Jersey). In addition, tenant plaintiffs filed a complaint in Oklahoma Nat'l Coal. of Latino Clergy, Inc., et al., v. Henry, 2007 U.S. Dist. LEXIS 94871 (N.D. Okla. Dec. 28, 2007).

[520] *Id.* at 65, note 38 (discussing the results in Valley Parks, Cherokee Country, Escondido, Riverside, and Farmer's Branch).

[521] Lozano v. City of Hazelton, 724 F.3d 297 (3d Cir. 2013) and Villas at Parkside Partners v. The City of Farmers Branch, Texas, 726 F.3d 524 (5th Cir. 2013).

[522] Lawrence Hurley, *U.S. Supreme Court Declines Immigration Cases*, http://www.reuters.com/article/2014/03/03/us-usa-court-immigration-idUSBREA221C220140303 (last visited Oct. 21, 2014).

[523] *City of Hazelton*, 724 F.3d at 316–23.

[524] *City of Farmer's Branch*, 726 F.3d at 528–31.

[525] Keller v. City of Freemont, 719 F.3d 931 (8th Cir. 2013). Interestingly, the City of Alabama, which resides within the 8th Circuit, amended its tenancy law when a district court declared it to be preempted in 2011, before the Eighth Circuit would rule against preemption. Specifically, Section 30 of the Beason-Hammon Alabama Taxpayer and Citizenship Protection Act (HB 56) prohibited individuals who could not prove their citizenship status form staying in their manufactured homes. Central Alabama Fair Housing Center v. Magee, 835 F. Supp. 2d 1165 (M.D. Ala. 2011), *opinion vacated by* Central Alabama Fair Housing Center v. Commissioner, Alabama Dept. of Revenue, 2013 U.S. App. LEXIS 11316 (11th Cir. May 17, 2013). By the time the case reached the Eighth Circuit in 2013, the court declared the case moot since the amendments to the Alabama code would not make the case applicable to future mobile home transactions. Central Alabama Fair Housing Center v. Commissioner, Alabama Dept. of Revenue, 2013 U.S. App. LEXIS 11316 (11th Cir. May 17, 2013). For a discussion of the Freemont Ordinance, see Ashleigh Bausch Varly and Mary C. Snow, *Don't You Dare Live Here: The Constitutionality of the Anti-Immigrant Employment and Housing Ordinances at Issue in Keller v. City of Freemont*, 45 CREIGHTON L. REV. 503 (2012).

designated to deter or prohibit unlawfully present aliens from residing within a particular locality are not tantamount of immigration laws.[526] The Eighth Circuit further found that the law's licensing scheme were not field preempted by federal alien registration laws. It found that they did not apply to all aliens since not all are renters. They were also not preempted by the federal anti-harboring provisions when these did not expressly preclude states from imposing different penalties for violating state laws.[527] As well, the Eight Circuit rejected the argument that simply alleging that the law would have a disparate impact on Latinos without actual evidence failed to establish a prima facie case based on equal protection grounds.[528] Some scholars predict that this Circuit split may prompt the Supreme Court to once again take up the issue of when immigration-related laws are preempted under federal immigration law.[529]

Property scholars have begun to weigh in on localities' attempts to regulate immigration through property law. Some suggest that courts are getting it wrong by excluding traditional core principles of property law into the analysis of these cases.[530] Others emphasize the need for courts to adopt a more robust equality principle for scrutinizing these laws.[531]

N. THE OFFICIAL ENGLISH/ENGLISH-ONLY LAWS

The large presence of foreign nationals in the United States has also raised questions and tensions around language rights, especially when localities have moved to enact laws or policies. Such policies includes constitutional amendments, that either declare English to be the official language or that mandate the use of either English-only and that even require bilingualism.

State Official English/English-only laws date back to 1811, when Louisiana became the first state to adopt English as the state's official language.[532] During the early 1900s a few states followed suit, motivated by a growing hostility toward immigrants from Southern and Eastern Europe.[533] A new wave of similar laws surfaced in the 1980s, spearheaded by organizations such as U.S. English.[534] This

---

[526] *Keller*, 719 F.3d at 941.

[527] *Id.* at 942–43.

[528] *Id.* at 948–49.

[529] *See* Jennifer Coleman, *A Divisive Split in the Eighth, Fifth, and Third Circuits: What the Courts Have to Say About States and Communities Taking Immigration into Their Own Hands*, 27 GEO. IMMIGR. L.J. 871 (2013).

[530] *See, e.g.*, David A. Super, *A New Property*, 113 COLUM. L. REV. 1773 (2013) and Tirres, *Property Outliers, supra* note 23, at 77.

[531] *See, e.g.*, Laura A. Hernández, *Anchor Babies: Something Less than Equal Under the Equal Protection Clause*, 19 S. CAL. REV. L & SOC. JUST. 331 (2010) and Rigel C. Oliveri, *Between a Rock and A Hard Place, supra* note 504, at 55.

[532] LOUISIANA ENABLING ACT, 2 U.S. Stat. 641 § 3 (1811).

[533] Steven W. Bender, *Consumer Protection for Latinos: Overcoming Language Fraud and English-Only in the Marketplace*, 45 AM. U. L. REV. 1027, 1046–47 (1996).

[534] Kenya Hart, *Defending Against a "Death by English": English-Only, Spanish-Only, and a*

time directed toward Latino/a and Asian immigrants.[535] Those efforts lost momentum by the end of the decade, when, in fact, some legislatures even adopted multilingual resolutions.[536] The success of the California's Proposition 187 campaign, however, led many other states to adopt Official English or English-Only laws.[537] More recently, the post-9/11 anti-immigrant climate has also resulted in greater language restrictions targeting immigrants. As of the time of this writing, a total of 31 states, have adopted such laws with Oklahoma being the most recent to do so in 2010.[538]

Official English/English-only laws have been adopted by states as constitutional amendments, as statutes, or through referenda. A more recent trend has only involved the enactment of English-only laws through ordinances by cities and other localities.[539] The content of these laws differs substantially from state to state, which may determine the reach of its implementation as well as their legality, neither of which is settled.[540] There are, for example, several states whose laws simply declare English the "official" state language,[541] with others adding enforcement provisions,[542] while the majority of states specifically bar or limit the use of any language other than English to conduct state business.[543] Certainly, the latter tend to be the most restrictive, but even those laws solely declaring English the official language are not always purely symbolic. They have also prompted some legislatures or agencies to adopt English-only policies as a direct result of the law's adoption.[544] As well, some state agencies have adopted English-only policies, even in the absence of Official English/English only laws in the state, such as, for

---

Gringa's Suggestions for Community Support of Language Rights, 14 BERKELEY LA RAZA L.J. 177, 178–79 (2003).

[535] Bender, *supra* note 533, at 1047.

[536] *Id.* at 1047–48 (discussing multilingual measures in New Mexico, Oregon, and Washington).

[537] Bender, *supra* note 533, at 1048–49.

[538] The 30 states and date of adoption of the latest law in that state are as follows: Louisiana (1811); Nebraska (1920); Illinois (1969); Massachusetts (1975); Hawaii (1978, note with native Hawaiian); Virgina (1981 & 1996); Kentucky (1984); Indiana (1984); Tennessee (1984); California (1986); Georgia (1986 & 1996); Arkansas (1987); Mississippi (1987); North Carolina (1987); North Dakota (1987); South Carolina (1987); Colorado (1988); Florida (1988); Alabama (1990); Montana (1995); New Hampshire (1995); South Dakota (1995); Wyoming (1996); Alaska (1998); Missouri (1998); Utah (2000); Iowa (2002); Arizona (2006); Idaho (2007); Kansas (2007); and Oklahoma (2010). States with Official English Laws, U.S. English, *available at* http://www.us-english.org/view/13 (last visited Oct. 23, 2014). *See also* Josh Hill et al., *Watch Your Language: The Kansas Law Review Survey of Official English and English-Only Laws and Policies*, 57 U. KAN. L. REV. 669 (2009).

[539] *See* Lupe S. Salinas, *Immigration and Language Rights, supra* note 7, at 927 (stating that at least 50 local governments have adopted or are planning to adopt similar Official English/English-Only ordinances).

[540] Bender, *supra* note 533, at 1049.

[541] These include: Hawaii, Illinois, Indiana, Kentucky, Massachusetts, North Dakota, and Mississippi.

[542] These include: Alabama, Arkansas, California, Colorado, Florida, Missouri, and North Carolina.

[543] These include: Alaska, Kansas, Louisiana, Georgia, Idaho, Iowa, Montana, Nebraska, New Hampshire, Tennessee, South Carolina, South Dakota, Utah, Virginia, and Wyoming.

[544] Such was the case, for example, where the Alabama Department of Public Safety decided to administer the driver's license examination only in English after the state adopted a constitutional amendment declaring English the official language of the state. Alexander v. Sandoval, 532 U.S. 275, 278–79 (2001). *See also* Bender, *supra* note 533, at 1054 ("Once enacted, a 'symbolic' Official English law

example, no Spanish rules in schools.[545] In addition, some states, have adopted special laws barring bilingualism or multilingualism in specific government functions, such as, for example, a prohibition against bilingual instruction in schools.[546]

These Official English/English-Only laws have either promoted or been adopted in the context of English-Only practices in the provision of public services or in English-Only policies in the workplace. In addition, language discrimination issues have arisen in the context of jury composition and prisoners' rights. Challenges to English-Only laws, policies, or practices have been brought under free speech and equal protection, the latter generally under federal civil rights statutes. The nature of the challenge and outcomes has varied according to whether the challenge involves a public function or the private sphere. There are also distinctions based on the type of public function involved.

In the public sphere, in 1923, the U.S. Supreme Court struck down a Nebraska statute that forbade any teacher "to teach any subject to any person in any language other than the English language." It struck it down for infringing on the free speech right of the teacher to teach and the equivalent right of the students to receive foreign language instruction.[547] Since then, however, the Supreme Court definitive resolution on the merits in these cases has been frustrated by procedural impediments. Such was the case, for example, in Arizona, where the U.S. Supreme Court ultimately vacated a successful First Amendment challenge to Arizona's English-only statute in the Ninth Circuit. It did so on the basis that the case became moot when the plaintiff ceased to be a state employee.[548] As well, the U.S. Supreme Court vacated a successful discrimination Title VI of the Civil Rights Act of 1964 challenge against Alabama's English-only driving test policy in the Eleventh Circuit. It held there that there is no private right of action under the statute to enforce disparate impact regulations.[549] Since then, lawyers have largely replied on administrative complaints rather than using litigation to vindicate their client's title VI rights at least with regard to services provided by federal agencies.[550]

---

may remain unchallenged on constitutional grounds due to its apparent lack of impact, yet still cause pernicious injury to language minorities.").

[545] This was the case in Kansas, for example, where a school district barred students from speaking Spanish prior to that state's adoption of its English-only law. Rubio v. Turner Unified Sch. Dist. No. 202, 453 F. Supp. 2d 1295 (D. Kan. 2006). Kansas adopted its English-only statute in 2007. KAN. STAT. ANN. § 73–28 (2801–2807). Historically, schools have been used as the language battleground against non-native English speakers with the adoption of strict English-only policies. *See, e.g.*, Juan F. Perea, *Bucando America: Why Integration and Equal Protection Fail to Protect Latinos*, 117 HARV. L. REV. 1420, 1429 (2004) (discussing the no Spanish policies in Puerto Rican schools). *See also* Salinas, *supra* note 7, at 917 (discussing the history of No Spanish Rule in Texas public schools).

[546] Consider, for example, California's Proposition 227, adopted in 1998, which amended the California Education Code to replace bilingual education with immersion programs. California Teachers Ass'n v. Davis, 64 F. Supp. 2d 945, 948 (C.D. Cal. 1999).

[547] Meyer v. Nebraska, 262 U.S. 390 (1923).

[548] Arizonans for Official English v. Arizona, et al, 520 U.S. 43 (1997).

[549] Alexander v. Sandoval, 532 U.S. 275 (2001).

[550] Jessica Rubin-Wills, *Language Access Advocacy After Sandoval: A Case Study of Administrative Enforcement Outside the Shadow of Judicial Review*, 36 N.Y.U. REV. & SOC. CHANGE 465 (2012).

Despite this backdrop, free speech challenges have been successful when English-only laws broadly have required use of English by all government officials and employees in all levels of government.[551] Such laws have been found to infringe upon the rights of non-English speaking persons to petition their own government;[552] the speech rights of legislators and other elected official to communicate with their non-English speaking constituents;[553] and the right of employees to comment on matters of public concern.[554] Such was the case, for example, in Alabama, where the Department of Public Safety stopped its English-only administration of driving exams following the Eleventh Circuit ruling.[555] As well, an Arizona Superior Court[556], the Oklahoma[557] and the Alaska Supreme Courts[558] relied on the Ninth Circuit First Amendment holding to find similar free speech, as well as equal protection, violations in Arizona's English-only constitutional amendment.

In contrast, public employees' speech on matters of only personal interest is generally not thought to enjoy free speech protection. Specifically courts have held that bilingual public employees do not have a *per se* right to communicate to one another in Spanish, unless the employer intended to quash expression on a matter of public concern.[559] Further, these laws have been categorized as implicating more than merely form of speech regulations, since by their nature, they also regulate content. As such, these laws have been subjected to strict scrutiny.[560] Still, courts have found that the stated purpose of English-only laws — namely of promoting unity through a common language — is compelling.[561] The problem with the laws has really been their overly-broad scope.[562] More narrowly tailored laws, however, that impose an English-only requirement in highly specific situation could survive free speech scrutiny under the state-as-speaker doctrine, under which governments have been permitted to control the content, form, and manner of speech under certain circumstances.[563] As well, legislation that relieves states of the responsibility to provide services in languages other than English could also be upheld.[564]

---

[551] *Id.* at 197–99.

[552] *Id.* at 200; *Ruiz v. Hull*, 957 P.2d at 997.

[553] *Kritz*, 170 P.3d at 202–03; *Ruiz v. Hull*, 957 P.2d at 997–98.

[554] *Kritz*, 170 P.3d at 203–04; *Ruiz v. Hull*, 957 P.2d at 997–98.

[555] Cole et al., v. Riley, 989 So. 2d 1001 (Ala. 2008).

[556] Ruiz v. Hull, 957 P.2d 984, 988 (Ariz. 1998).

[557] In re Initiative Petition No. 366, 46 P.3d 123, 126 (Okla. 2002).

[558] Alaskans for a Common Language, Inc. v. Kritz, 170 P.3d 183, 200 (Alaska 2007).

[559] Maldonado v. City of Altus, 433 F.3d 1294, (10th Cir. 2006), *abrogated on other grounds by* Metzler v. Fed. Home Bank of Topeka, 464 F.3d 1164 (10th Cir. 2006) (rejecting a free speech challenge to English only policy applying to "all work related and business communications during the work day . . . with the exception of those circumstances where it is necessary and prudent to communicate with [the public]."). *See also Kritz*, 170 P.3d at 203.

[560] *Kritz*, 170 P.3d at 206; *Ruiz v. Hull*, 957 P.2d at 999.

[561] *Kritz*, 170 P.3d at 206–07.

[562] *Id.* at 207–08.

[563] *Id.* at 199.

[564] *Id.* at 208.

What these special circumstances may be is still largely undefined and likely to vary from jurisdiction to jurisdiction.[565] In 2009, however, an Iowa state court interpreted Iowa's English-only law as preventing the Iowa Secretary of State from providing non-English voter registration forms.[566] Scholars consider that such holdings run afoul of significant constitutional problems around the protection of voting rights.[567]

Equal protection challenges to Official English/English-Only laws have been fewer, in great part, given the difficult task of proving discriminatory intent in the adoption of language restrictions.[568] Moreover, most courts miss or reject the connection between language discrimination and race. Instead, they characterize language discrimination not as racist, but rather as discrimination based on national origin, culture, or worse, as "race-neutral."[569] Some courts, however, have applied strict scrutiny to equal protection challenges to English-Only laws when these laws have also been found to impinge on free speech[570] or because they have been found to be the product of intentional discrimination.[571]

Schools, whether public or private, have also become experimentation grounds of bilingualism or English-only instruction.[572] In general, deference to the education mission of schools has meant that courts are unwilling or hesitant to second-guess the choices made by schools either to insist on English-only or to promote bilingualism.[573] For example, the Ninth Circuit rejected that California's prohibition against bilingual education was racially motivated, even if it disproportionately affected Latinos. It found instead that it represented an effort to remedy a

---

[565] In dicta, for example, the Alaska Supreme court included the publication of official government documents and the administration of driving licensing examinations solely in English as permissible under the government-as-speaker doctrine. *Id.* at 199.

[566] King v. Mauro, King v. Mauro, No. CV6739, slip op. at 2 (Iowa Dist. Ct. Mar. 31, 2008), *available at* http://www.usefoundation.org/userdata/file/Ruling%20on%20Petition%20for%20Judicial%20Review.pdf.

[567] *See, e.g.*, Michael A. Zuckerman, *Constitutional Class: When English-Only Meets Voting Rights*, 28 Yale L & Pol'y Rev. 353 (2010).

[568] *See* Margaret Robertson, Comment, *Abridging the Freedom of Non-English Speech: English-Movement Legislation and the Free Speech Rights of Government Employees*, 2001 B.Y.U. L. Rev. 1641, 1645 (2001).

[569] Perea, *supra* note 545, at 1434–35.

[570] *See, e.g., Ruiz v. Hull*, 957 P.2d. at 1000–1001.

[571] Faith Action for Community Equity v. Hawaii, 2014 U.S. Dist. LEXIS 58817 (D. Haw. Apr. 28, 2014) (striking down policy that required that driver's examination test be given only in English).

[572] *See* Jennifer Bonilla Moreno, *¿Only English? How Bilingual Education Can Mitigate the Damage of English-Only*, 20 Duke J. Gender L & Pol'y 197, 197–99 (2012) and L. Darnell Weeden, *English Only Rules in Public Schools Should be Presumed Illegal*, 34 T. Marshall L. Rev. 379 (2009).

[573] *See, e.g.*, Coachella Valley Unified School District et al., v. State of California, 176 Cal. App. 4th 93 (2009) (upholding use of standardized tests only in English), Silva v. St. Anne Catholic School, 595 F. Supp. 2d 1171 (D. Kan. 2009) (upholding English-only rule among students to enforce discipline), and Broomer v. Huntington Union Free Sch. Dist. Carmen Casper, 2013 U.S. Dist. LEXIS 113971 (E.D.N.Y. Aug. 13, 2013), (dismissing suit by teachers who sued when they were fired for being monolingual when school instituted a fully bilingual curriculum).

"pedagogically flawed educational system."[574]

Another area of litigation has been the exclusion of jurors based on their bilingualism or multilingualism. For example, in 1991 in *Hernandez v. New York*, the U.S. Supreme Court upheld a prosecutor's use of peremptory strikes against bilingual jurors. It reasoned that the uncertainty of the juror's ability to accept the official translation of Spanish-language testimony provided a valid race-neutral reason for the practice.[575] Since then, the Fourth Circuit has rejected a defendant's argument that striking Spanish-speaking jurors violates the Sixth Amendment or due process.[576] These results have inspired critical scholarship primarily pointing out that the courts are ignoring the critical functions of language to cultural identity.[577] Other cases involving criminal defendants or prisoners involve the need to receive services or to communicate in other languages. The Tenth Circuit, for example, rejected the argument that failure to translate a plea agreement into Spanish violated due process.[578] In contrast, in prisoner lawsuits where inmates have claimed a right to receive mail from family based on first amendment grounds, the results have been mixed.[579]

In the private workplace, employers have responded to the increasing ethnic diversity in various ways, including by either embracing or rejecting the linguistic competence of their workers.[580] Any discussion of employee rights against discrimination must begin with Title VII of the Civil Rights Act of 1964.[581] The Act does not by its own terms provide legal protection for discrimination on the basis of language usage.[582] Instead, workers must prove that the language restriction is really aiming to discriminate workers on the basis of their ethnic or racial composition. With few

---

[574] Valeria v. Davis, 307 F.3d 1036, 1041 (9th Cir. 2002), *rehearing en banc denied by* Valeria v. Davis, 320 F.3d 1014 (9th Cir. 2003).

[575] 500 U.S. 352 (1991).

[576] U.S. v. Cabrera-Beltran, 660 F.3d 742 (4th Cir. 2011).

[577] *See, e.g.*, Jasmine B. Gonzalez-Rose, *Language Disenfranchisement in Juries: A Call for Constitutional Remediation*, 65 Hastings L.J. 811 (2014), Graham Douds, *International Human Rights Implications of Voire Dire Discrimination: Critical Examination of Contemporary Language Qualifications for Criminal Proceedings*, 47 Rev. Juridica U. Inter. P.R. 715 (2012–2013), and Jasmine B. Gonzales Rose, *The Exclusion of Non-English-Speaking Jurors: Remedying a Century of Denial of the Sixth Amendment in the Federal Courts of Puerto Rico*, 46 Harv. C.R.-C.L. L. Rev. 497 (2011).

[578] U.S. v. Sanchez-Leon, 764 F.3d 1248 (10th Cir. 2014).

[579] *Contrast* Novosel v. Wrenn, 2010 U.S. Dist. LEXIS 125973 (D.N.H. Nov. 18, 2010) (no discrimination when prisoner denied letters in Spanish) with Muthana v Hofbauer, 2013 U.S. Dist. LEXIS 44407 (W.D. Mich. Mar. 28, 2013) (and Novosel v. Wrenn, 2011 U.S. Dist. LEXIS 39332 (D.N.H. Apr. 11, 2011) (declining to dismiss lawsuits brought by inmate based on a first amendment challenge for the state refusal to provide him with mail in Arabic or Croatian respectively).

[580] *See* Bonilla Moreno, *supra* note 572, at 197–99.

[581] Title VII of the Civil Rights Act of 1964 (Pub. L. No. 88-352).

[582] Janet Ainsworth, *Language, Power, and Identity in the Workplace: Enforcement of 'English-Only' Rules by Employers*, 9 Seattle J. for Soc. Just. 233 (2010). For a critique of the U.S. legal regime for handlings language discrimination, see Tamar Brandes, *Rethinking Equality: National Identity and Language Rights in the United States*, 15 Tex. Hisp. J. L. & Pol'y 7 (2009). For a contrast with language protections under international human rights law, see Denise Gilman, *A "Bilingual" Approach to Language Rights: How Dialogue Between U.S. and International Human Rights Law May Improve the Language Rights Framework*, 24 Harv. Hum. Rts. J. 1 (2011).

exceptions,[583] many courts dismiss these claims on summary judgment so long as employer provides bona fide reason for the English-only policy. They have also dismissed them based on the employee's inability to show that the language restriction was a pretext for discrimination based on a protected class.[584] As well, the Equal Employment Opportunity Commission (EEOC) has issued guidelines that effectively require employees to speak English during operational times while protecting the right of immigrants to speak their native tongues at certain non-operational times in the workplace. Scholars debate the effectiveness of the regulation.[585] At least some courts have also held that the regulations violate Title VII.[586]

Beyond the rights-based legal challenges to language restrictive or discriminatory laws, scholars raise other policy-based concerns about the effect of such laws. These include the inability of government to provide culturally competent public services to persons with limited English proficiency.[587] English-only rules also interfere with individual's associative interests by obstructing the development of social relationships.[588] As well, such laws, particularly as enforced in schools, can result in language loss at a large disadvantage to the individual who must function in a globalized world.[589]

---

[583] *See, e.g.,*Wilkie v. Geisinger System Services, 2014 U.S. Dist. LEXIS 132162 (M.D. Pa. Sept. 18, 2014), Benhassine v. Star Taxi, Inc., 2013 U.S. Dist. LEXIS 84770 (M.D. Fla. June 17, 2013), and Reyes v. Pharma Chemie, Inc., 890 F. Supp. 2d 1147 (D. Neb. 2012).

[584] *See, e.g.*, Castillo v. Wells Fargo Bank, 2014 U.S. App. LEXIS 2809 (9th Cir. Feb. 14, 2014), Gonzales v. Eagle Leasing Co., 2014 U.S. Dist. LEXIS 134913 (D. Conn. Sept. 25, 2014), Rosa v. BMA Corp., 2013 U.S. Dist. LEXIS 180028 (D. Md. Dec. 24, 2013), Barucic v. Titan Tire Corp., 839 F. Supp. 2d 1038 (S.D. Iowa 2012), Lopez v. Flight Services & Systems, Inc., 881 F. Supp. 2d 431 (W.D.N.Y. 2012), El v. Max Daetwyler Corp., 2011 U.S. Dist. LEXIS 49645 (W.D.N.C. May, 9 2011), Aranda v. Renown South Meadows Medical Center, 2011 U.S. Dist. LEXIS 81709 (D. Nev. July 26, 2011), Joseph v. North Shore University Hospital, 2011 U.S. Dist. LEXIS 14926 (E.D.N.Y. Feb. 15, 2011), Penalver v. Resource Corporation of America, 2011 U.S. Dist. LEXIS 53330 (N.D. Tex. May 18, 2011), Polanco v. 34th Street Partnership, Inc., 724 F. Supp. 2d 420 (S.D.N.Y. July 2, 2010), Perez v. The New York Presbyterian Hospital, 2009 U.S. Dist. LEXIS 102139 (S.D.N.Y. Nov. 3, 2009), Pacheco v. New York Presbyterian Hospital, 593 F. Supp. 2d 599 (S.D.N.Y. 2009) and Colón v. Illinois Bell Telephone Co., 2009 U.S. Dist. LEXIS 89570 (N.D. Ill. Sept. 28, 2009).

[585] *Contrast* Ming Hsu Chen, *Governing by Guidance: Civil Rights Agencies and the Emergence of Language Rights*, 49 Harv. C.R.-C.L. L. Rev. 291 (2014) and James Leonard, *The Zero-Sum Game of Language Accommodation in the Workplace*, 33 Cardozo L. Rev. 1 (2011)

[586] *See e.g.*, Reyes v. PharmaChemie, Inc., 890 F. Supp. 2d 1147 (D. Neb. 2012).

[587] *See* Philip C. Aka and Lucinda M. Deason, *Culturally Competent Public Services and English-Only Laws*, 53 How. L.J. 53 (2000). *But see* Kevin Heinz, *Dismantling the Melting Pot: Evaluating the Effect of English-Only Ordinances Through the Lens of Resolution 10–68 of Lino Lakes, Minnesota*, 32 Hamline J. Pub. L. & Pol'y 179 (2010) (discussing the costs of states providing services in two or more languages).

[588] Cristina Rodriguez, *Language Diversity in the Workplace*, 100 Nw. U. L. Rev. 1689, 1692 (2006).

[589] Bonilla Moreno, *supra* note 572, at 206–208.

O.   LOCAL IMMIGRATION ENFORCEMENT

Since 1994, the then INS established the Law Enforcement Support Center (LESC), a clearinghouse based in Vermont that fields around the clock inquiries from law enforcement agencies concerning the immigration status of individuals under investigation or in custody.[590] From 1996 to 2012, the number of inquiries sent to LESC skyrocketed from 4,000 to over 1.3 million.[591] This trend coincides with the "force multiplier" that has resulted from the involvement of local law enforcement in enforcing federal immigration laws, particularly post-9/11.[592] Local police, state troopers, correctional facilities staff, and other law enforcement assist ICE to detect, arrest, detain, and turn-over foreign nationals who are present in the United States in violation of civil or criminal immigration laws. Local police are asking persons detained and/or arrested during their routine police work for their immigration status.[593] Police are also alone or in collaboration with ICE, executing immigration raids,[594] or conducting raids,[595] road blocks,[596] street sweeps, or other investigations that target noncitizens for violations of the federal immigration laws.[597]

To enforce federal immigration laws, local law enforcement agencies are either acting unilaterally or in collaboration with federal agencies.[598] Congress cannot compel local enforcement of immigration laws. It can, however, and has, conferred express authority to permit federal local law enforcement officers to voluntarily enforce certain provisions of the Immigration and National Act (INA). To date, Congress has chosen to confer this power only with respect to a limited number of criminal provisions in the INA. These sections are: (1) INA § 274 (Arrest authority

---

[590] Anil Kalhan, *Immigration Policing and Federalism Through the Lens of Technology, Surveillance, and Privacy*, 74 OHIO ST. L.J. 1105, 1117 (2013).

[591] *Id.*

[592] *See* Kris W. Kobach, *The Quintessential Force Multiplier: The Inherent Authority of Local Police to Make Immigration Arrests*, 69 ALB. L. REV. 179 (2005–2006). For a thorough and very helpful historical and modern account of local police involvement in the enforcement of immigrations laws, see also generally Kalhan, *supra* note 590.

[593] *See, e.g.*, Muelher v. Mena, 544 U.S. 93 (2005) (involving the questioning of detainee about her immigration status during the execution of a gang-related warrant in a home); Farm Labor Org. Comm. v. Ohio State Highway Patrol, 991 F. Supp. 895 (N.D. Ohio 1997) (involving asking occupants in a car during a traffic stop about their immigration status); U.S. v. Esparza-Mendoza, 386 F.3d 953 (10th Cir. 2004) (involving the discovery of an outstanding immigration warrant during a community care-function encounter).

[594] *See, e.g.*, Flores v. Walla Walla Police, 2006 U.S. Dist. LEXIS 71285 (E.D. Wash. Oct. 2, 2006) (involving local police arrest based on a federal immigration warrant).

[595] *See, e.g.*, U.S. v. Vite-Espinoza, 342 F.3d 462, 464 (6th Cir. 2003) (involving the execution of a home raid with a federal immigration search warrant during a joint federal, state, and local police task force investigating the counterfeiting of immigration and identification documents).

[596] *See, e.g.*, State v. Bolton, 905 F.2d 319 (10th Cir. 1990) (involving participation of ICE agents in state road block).

[597] U.S. v. Perez-Sosa, 164 F.3d 1082 (8th Cir. 1998) (involving state trooper's consensual encounter that lead to probable cause based on report that person was transporting undocumented persons).

[598] *See generally* Kalhan, *supra* note 590.

to enforce prohibitions against transporting and harboring certain aliens);[599] INA § 276 (Authority to arrest and detain re-entry offenders; that is, previously deported immigrants with a felony conviction who are found present in the United States);[600] and INA § 103(a)(8) (Emergency Powers authorizing "any State or local law enforcement officer" to enforce federal immigration laws in the event the Secretary certifies that "an actual or imminent mass influx of aliens arriving off the coast of the United States, or near a land border" exists.).[601]

In addition, the Illegal Immigration Reform and Immigrant Responsibility Act of 1996 ("IIRAIRA") added Section 287(g) to the INA. This provision authorizes the Secretary of the Department of Homeland Security ("DHS") to enter into agreements, known as Memorandum of Agreement ("MOA"), with state and local law enforcement agencies. It also permits trained officers to perform immigration enforcement functions under the supervision of ICE officers, at the expense of the state or political subdivision, and to the extent consistent with state and local law.[602] These MOAs have delegated to local law enforcement nearly all of ICE's enforcement powers, including the authority (1) to interrogate any person believed to be an alien as to his right to be or remain in the United States (INA § 287(a)(1) and 8 C.F.R. § 287.5(a)(1)); (2) to make warrantless arrest for unlawful entry at the border or within the U.S. for reasonable belief that a person has violated the immigration laws (INA § 287(a)(2) and 8 C.F.R. 287.5(c)(1)); (3) to make warrantless arrest for immigration felonies (INA § 287(a)(4) and 8 C.F.R. § 287.5(c)(2)); (4) to serve arrest warrants for immigration violations pursuant to 8 C.F.R. § 287.5(e)(3); (5) to administer oaths or take and consider evidence; book a noncitizen for immigration violations and interview and prepare affidavits and sworn statements from noncitizens (INA § 287(b) and 8 C.F.R. § 287(a)(2)); (6) to prepare charging documents (INA Section 239, 8 C.F.R. § 239.1; INA Section 238; 8 C.F.R. § 238.1; INA Section 241(a)(5), 8 C.F.R. § 241. INA Section 235 (b)(1), 8 C.F.R. § 235.3); (7) to issue immigration detainers (8 C.F.R. § 287.7) and I-213 Record of Deportable/ Inadmissible Alien, for processing aliens in categories established by ICE supervisors; and (8) to detain and transport arrested aliens to ICE-approved detention facilities (8 C.F.R. § 287.5(c)(6)).[603]

As of February 2014, ICE has 287(g) agreements with 35 law enforcement agencies in 18 states.[604] This number actually represents a drop in the number of 287(g) agreements. The last publication of this chapter in June 2008, ICE reported that 55 local law enforcement agencies, 765 officers in all, in 18 states had entered

---

[599] 8 U.S.C § 1324 (2000).

[600] 8 U.S.C. 1256(c) (2000), *amended by* Illegal Immigration Reform and Immigrant Responsibility Act of 1996 (IIRIRA), Pub. L. No. 104-208, § 372(3), 110 Stat. 3009.

[601] 8 U.S.C. § 1103(a)(8) (2000), *amended by* Illegal Immigration Reform and Immigrant Responsibility Act of 1996 (IIRIRA), Pub. L. No. 104-208, § 372(3), 110 Stat. 3009.

[602] 8 U.S.C § 1357(g) (2000).

[603] *See, e.g.,* Memorandum of Agreement between the ICE and the Arizona Department of Public Safety, at 2–3, *available at* http://www.ice.gov/doclib/foia/memorandumsofAgreementUnderstanding/arizonadepartmentofpublicsafety.pdf.

[604] ICE, Delegation of Immigration Authority Section 287(g) Immigration and Nationality Act, *available at* http://www.ice.gov/factsheets/287g (last visited Oct. 16, 2014).

into such agreements, with approximately 80 more with pending requests.[605] Since January 2006, the 287(g) program is credited with identifying more than 341,398 potentially removable aliens — mostly at local jails. ICE has trained and certified more than 1,500 state and local officers to enforce immigration law.[606]

The MOAs have differed greatly in terms of their nature and scope. The broadest of them take on all of the eight powers/functions to allow trained local law enforcement officers to enforce both civil and criminal immigration laws.[607] Others also pertain to all types of immigration violations, but may exclude certain of the delegated powers, usually the power to serve immigration warrants or the power to conduct warrantless arrests.[608] Most MOAs, however, restrict the cooperation agreement to assist ICE with criminal investigations in general or to certain types of criminal investigations, such as human trafficking, gangs, drugs, identity theft; to capture "criminal aliens;" or to address counter-terrorism and domestic security needs.[609] There are also quite a few agreements with detention facilities.[610] Thus, the MOA itself defines the scope and limitations of the authority to be designated to the local law enforcement agency, as well as the number of local officers trained and authorized to enforce federal immigration laws. Some MOAs are quite broad and grant all available powers to the local officers, while others are restricted to specific types of enforcement and adopt only some or a few of the enforcement powers. No one is monitoring how these agreements are actually being implemented, however, which raises concern over potential enforcement of immigration laws beyond those expressly spelled out in the agreement.[611]

In 2013 DHS announced it would reduce the 287(g) budget and suspend consideration of new requests for 287(g) agreements.[612] This is not at all surprising because by 2013, other federal enforcement initiatives — namely Secure Communities and the National Crime Information Center's Information Violation (NCIC) file — had essentially become a more effective and efficient means to detecting immigration violators across localities throughout the United States. Prof. Anil Kalhan calls this the rise of the automated immigration policing.[613] As he

---

[605] ICE, Partners, *Delegation of Immigration Authority Section 287(g) Immigration and Nationality Act*, April 18, 2008, http://www.ice.gov/factsheets/287g.

[606] ICE, Delegation of Immigration Authority Section 287(g) Immigration and Nationality Act, *available at* http://www.ice.gov/factsheets/287g (last visited Oct. 16, 2014).

[607] *See, e.g.*, Memorandum of Agreement between ICE and Washington County, Arkansas, Sheriff's Office, at 2–3, *available at* http://islandia.law.yale.edu/wirc/287g_foia.html.

[608] *See, e.g.*, Memorandum of Agreement between ICE and the State of Alabama at 2(no serving warrants, but power arrest without a warrant), *available at* http://islandia.law.yale.edu/wirc/287g_foia.html.

[609] *See, e.g.*, Memorandum of Agreement between ICE and State of Florida, at 2, (counter-terrorism and domestic security), *available at* http://www.ice.gov/doclib/foia/memorandumsofAgreementUnderstanding/r_287gfloridadeptoflawenforcement101609.pdf.

[610] *See, e.g.*, Memorandum of Agreement between ICE and the Jail Board of the Prince William — Manassas Regional Adult Detention Center, *available at* http://islandia.law.yale.edu/wirc/287g_foia.html.

[611] AMERICAN IMMIGRATION LAWYERS ASSOCIATION, FACT SHEET — "287(g)" Agreements, *available at* http://www.aila.org/search/default.aspx?searchterm=fact%20sheet%20287(g).

[612] U.S. Department of Homeland SEC., Budget-In-Brief: Fiscal Year 2013 at 16.

[613] Kalhan, *supra* note 590, at 1122.

documents, the NCIC, which had existed in computerized form sine 1967 — with its creation first authorized in 1930 — began to include hundreds of thousands of civil immigration records in the aftermath of the 2001 terrorist attacks. They did this to allow any law enforcement to identify immigration violators as part of traditional law enforcement.[614] To date, the database includes nearly half a million records of immigration violators. This includes those of individuals suspected of failing to register with the National Security Entry-Exist Registration System, a program that required certain nationals of predominantly Muslim countries and North Korea to register with immigration authorities.[615]

NCIC searches usually occur upon a traffic or pedestrian stop based on reasonable suspicion, but also before any stop takes place and without any suspicion — for example, using license plate or vehicle identification numbers.[616] Secure Communities was begun in 2008 when Congress directed ICE to develop a plan to identify incarcerated removable noncitizens.[617] As Prof. Kalhan describes, Secure Communities creates a "virtual presence in every jail" at the moment that every arrestee nationwide is booked.[618] Essentially, although practices vary widely among jurisdictions, particularly for minor offenses, during the booking process, the arrestee's fingerprints are taken and transmitted to the states' criminal records' repository but also to the FBI's IAFIS system. In turn, the FBI transmits these fingerprints to the DHS's Automated Biometric Identification System, a database generally referred to as IDENT, which is used for a range of immigration control functions and constitutes the main DHS-wide biometric and biographic information system of any noncitizen, including naturalized citizens, who have ever had an immigration process.[619] If the fingerprint check yield a match, LESC notifies the original law enforcement agency and relevant ICE field office. In turn, ICE decides, based on enforcement priorities and other factors, whether to interview the individual or issue a detainer requesting that the agency hold the individual.[620] Since its inception in 2008 with 14 jurisdictions, Secure Communities has expanded to all 3,181 jurisdictions within 50 states, the District of Columbia, and five (5) U.S. Territories. Full implementation was completed on January 22, 2013.[621] According to ICE, more than 283,000 noncitizens convicted of crimes have been removed through Secure Communities.[622]

Despite the success of the federal-state collaboration models for enforcing the immigration laws, most local law enforcement agencies still rely on claims of inherent authority to make arrests for violations to most federal immigration laws. Still a few others have passed their own laws to cement or expand their local

---

[614] *Id.*

[615] *Id.* at 1125.

[616] *Id.*

[617] *Id.* at 1126.

[618] *Id.* at 1127.

[619] *Id.*

[620] *Id.* at 1128.

[621] ICE, Secure Communities, *available at* http://www.ice.gov/secure-communities (last visited Oct. 26, 2014).

[622] *Id.*

authority to enforce the immigration laws. The most (in)famous of these laws is Arizona's SB1070 adopted in 2010. It, *inter alia*, criminalized the failure to carry proof of immigration registration when required. It also required that police investigate the immigration status of any person lawfully stopped, detained, or arrested, as well as permitted warrantless arrests of persons suspected of having committed a deportable offense.[623] Shortly after Arizona passed SB1070, at least 16 states moved to adopt copycat legislation.[624]

Back when Arizona adopted SB1070, there was already fierce disagreement on whether states could enforce immigration laws. Some defended states' inherent right to make both civil and criminal immigration arrests.[625] Others concluded that no such state inherent power exists because the enforcement of immigration law is an exclusive federal power that must be enforced uniformly by one sovereign in light of immigration laws' implications on foreign policy.[626] At a minimum, these scholars maintained that states can enforce federal immigration laws only to the degree that express congressional delegation authorizes.[627] At the time, only three federal circuit courts, the Ninth, the Tenth, and the Fifth, had weighed on the specific question of whether local law enforcement possessed inherent authority to make arrests for immigration offenses, which have not been preempted by federal law.[628] A circuit split existed between the Ninth Circuit, which recognized an inherent, non-preempted local law enforcement power to make such arrests but restricted it to violations of federal criminal immigration laws,[629] and the Fifth[630] and Tenth Circuits[631] which concluded similarly on the preemption issue, but without drawing the same distinction between civil and criminal offenses. In

---

[623] *See* Cianciarulo, *The "Arizonification" of Immigration Law, supra* note 243, at 85. For an article examining the road leading to the passage of SB 1070 in Arizona, see Kristina M. Campbell, *The Road to S.B. 1070: How Arizona Became Ground Zero for the Immigrant's Rights Movement and the Continuing Struggle for Latino Civil Rights in America*, 14 Harv. Latino L. Rev. 1 (2011).

[624] Seth Freed Wessler, *Bills Modeled after SB1070 Spread Through States, Colorlines*, March 2, 2010, *available at* http://colorlines.com/archives/2011/03/sb_1070_copycat_bills.html.

[625] *See, e.g.*, Kobach, *The Quintessential Force Multiplier, supra* note 592 and Seth M.M. Stodder and Nicolle Sciara Rippeon, *State and Local Governments and Immigration Law*, 41 Urb. Law 387 (2009).

[626] *See, e.g.*, Huyen Pham, *The Inherent Flaws in the Inherent Authority Position: Why Inviting Local Enforcement of Immigration Laws Violates the Constitution*, 31 Fla. St. U. L. Rev. 965, 978–1000 (2004). *See also* Gabriel J. Chin & Marc L. Miller, *The Unconstitutionality of Immigration through Criminal Law*, 61 Duke L.J. 251 (2011); Hiroshi Motomura, *The Discretion that Matters: Federal Immigration Enforcement, State and Local Arrests, and the Civil-Criminal Line*, 58 UCLA L. Rev. 1819 (2011) and Michael J. Wishnie, *State and Local Police Enforcement of Immigration law*, 6 U. Pa. J. Const. L. 1084, 1092–95 (2004).*See, e.g.*, U.S. Senator Jeff Sessions & Cynthia Hayden, *The Growing Role for State & Local Law Enforcement in the Real of Immigration Law*, 16 Stan. L. & Pol'y Rev. 323 (2005).

[627] Wishnie, *State and Local Police Enforcement of Immigration Law, supra* note 626, at 1092–95.

[628] Sessions & Hayden, *supra* note 626, at 332–336.

[629] Gonzalez v. City of Peoria, 722 F.2d 468, 475–77 (9th Cir. 1983). The Ninth Circuit held, for example, that the enforcement authority must distinguish illegal entry, which is a criminal immigration violation, from illegal presence, such as overstaying a visa, which is only a civil violation. *Id.* at 477.

[630] Lynch v. Cannatella, 810 F.2d 1363, 1366, 1371 (5th Cir. 1987).

[631] *See* U.S. v. Vasquez-Alvarez, 176 F.3d 1294, 1295–1300 (10th Cir. 1999); U.S. v. Santana-Garcia, 264 F.3d 1188, 1190–1194 (10th Cir. 2001).

addition, the Third Circuit had upheld the legality of a warrantless arrest executed by local law enforcement for an immigration criminal violation without expressly addressing local law enforcement's authority to engage in that type of law enforcement in the first place.[632]

The uncertainty of states' authority to make arrests for immigration violations has been made worse by conflicting opinions on the issue issued by the Office of Legal Counsel (OLC). In 1996, after the Ninth and Fifth, but before the Tenth Circuit opinions, the OLC accepted the Ninth Circuit limits. It concluded that state and local police may constitutionally detain or arrest persons who have violated criminal provisions of the INA, subject to state law, but may not do so solely for civil violations.[633] After the September 11 attacks on the World Trade Center and the Pentagon, however, the OLC issued a new 2002 opinion retracting its earlier position. It concluded instead that state and local police possessed inherent authority to make arrests for both criminal and civil violations which would render that person removable.[634] The 2002 OLC opinion remained unpublished until July 2005, when it was released after the Second Circuit granted a FOIA request,[635] although allowing some redactions to the opinion.[636]

In 2011, however, the United States federal government seemingly in retraction of its 2002 OLC opinion chose to challenge SB1070.[637] Interestingly, while the Mexican American Legal Defense Fund and other civil rights groups as well as the media has primarily decried the law as a recipe for racial and ethnic profiling,[638] the Solicitor General quickly distanced himself from the equality concerns and farmed his claim solely as a preemption challenge.[639] The Supreme Court granted certiorari after a California district court and the Ninth Circuit enjoined the enforcement of the law.[640] Professor Jennifer M. Chacón suggests that the United States perhaps ceded too much by focusing solely on the preemption claim. Moreover, this sole focus explains why the reaction of the Supreme Court to SB1070 was so mixed.[641] On the one hand, as Prof. Chacón suggests, the ruling was a pretty clear victory for the federal government, at least as far as preemption was concerned. The majority reaffirmed the constitutional doctrine known as obstacle preemption, endorsed the primacy of the federal government in immigration

---

[632] U.S. v. Laville, 480 F.3d 187 (2007).

[633] Theresa Wynn Roseborough, Deputy Assistant Att'y Gen., Office of Legal Counsel, U.S. Dep't of Justice, Assistance by State and Local Police in Apprehending Illegal Aliens (memorandum opinion for U.S. Attorney, S.D. Cal.) (Feb. 5, 1996), http://www.usdoj.gov/olc/immstopo1a.htm.

[634] Sessions & Hayden, *supra* note 626, at 337.

[635] Nat'l Council of La Raza v. Dep't of Justice, 411 F.3d 350 (2d Cir. 2005).

[636] Dep't of Justice, Office of Legal Counsel, *Non-preemption of the Authority of State and Local Law Enforcement Officials to Arrest for Immigration Violations* (Apr. 3, 2002), *available at* www.aclu. org/FilesPDFs/ACF27DA.pdf.

[637] For a discussion of the SB1070 litigation, see Cianciarulo, *supra* note 243, at 110–114.

[638] *See* Jennifer M. Chacón, *The Transformation of Immigration Federalism*, 21 WM. & MARY BILL RTS. J. 577 (2012).

[639] *Id.* at 578.

[640] Arizona v. United States, 132 S. Ct. 2492 (2012).

[641] Chacón, *supra* note 638, at 579–80.

control. It rejected the "mirror-image" theory proposed by the SB1070 (essentially that the law was simply a mirror-image of federal policies).[642] On the other hand, not all of SB1070 was struck down and the parts that survived were significant. The Court struck down Section 3, the provision of the law that created new state misdemeanor forbidding the "willful failure to completely or carry an alien registration document" in violation of federal law, on field preemption grounds, finding that the federal governments occupied the field of alien registration.[643] As well, the Court struck down Section 5(C) which made it a misdemeanor for "an authorized alien to knowingly apply for work, solicit work in a public place or perform work as an employee or independent contractor" also on field preemption grounds. It concluded the that federal government occupies the regulation of the employment of unauthorized workers.[644] Also the Court struck down Section 6 which provided that a state officer could arrest a person without a warrant if the officer had probable cause to believe that the person had committed a public offense that made him or her removable from the United States. The Court reasoned that in the absence of a federal warrant, arrests based on probable cause of removability are permitted only in a limited statutorily prescribed set of circumstances under federal law.[645] Essentially, the Court considered Arizona's arrest authority under SB1070 "far more capacious." It might have been possible for the Court to conclude simply that SB1070 was in consonant with federal law; instead, the Court applied a more robust obstacle preemption doctrine.[646] Yet, the Court rescued Section 2(B), perhaps the most controversial of the SB1070 law. This provision required that officers request proof of status during otherwise lawful seizures upon "reasonable suspicion" that a person is unlawfully present. The Court reasoned that Section 2(B) rests on a legitimate state enforcement justification since the initial stop or arrest has to be based on a violation of local law. Once this is done, the Court found no problem with the additional step of ascertaining immigration status since the federal government encourages this very type of enforcement through collaborative arrangements with local police.[647]

Some scholars optimistically read *Arizona v. United States* as a significant setback for supporters of SB 1070-type legislation. They read the decision as a rebuke to arguments of "inherent authority" to enforce the federal immigration violations at the sub-federal level.[648] Indeed, the *Arizona* case has already resulted in other similar laws in Alabama and Utah being struck down on preemption grounds. In 2012, the Eleventh Circuit enjoined several provisions of Alabama's

---

[642] *Id.* at 580. For a critique of the Court's ruling for its imposition of too many limits on the state law enforcement of immigration laws, see Roderick M. Hills Jr., *Arizona v. United States: The Unitary Enforcement Discretion as a Limit of Federalism*, 2012 Cato. Sup. Ct. Rev. 189 (2011–2012).

[643] *Arizona*, 132 S. Ct. at 2501.

[644] *Id.* at 2504–05.

[645] *Id.* at 2506.

[646] *Id.* at 2507.

[647] *Id.* at 2507–10.

[648] *See e.g.*, Lucas Guttentag, *Immigration Preemption and the Limits of State Power: Reflections of on Arizona v. United States*, 9 Stan. J. Civ. Rts. & Civ. Liberties 1 (2013) and Melissa Keaney and Alvaro M. Huerta, *Restrictionists States Rebuked: How Arizona v. United States Reins in States on Immigration*, 3 Wake Forest J.L. & Pol'y 249 (2013).

Omnibus law, mirrored after SB1070, H.B. 56.[649] However, not unlike the Arizona case, the Eleventh Circuit left intact the very same provision that allows police to inquire into a person's immigration status pursuant to a lawful stop or arrest.[650] In Utah, in 2014, a federal district court similarly enjoined certain provisions of HB497. It also left intact, however, provisions on verification of immigration status and those permitting that local police transport those believed to be in the country without authorization to secure facilities.[651] The open door to still some significant suitederal immigration enforcement has led some scholars to argue for an even stronger preemption doctrine or even for other doctrines, such as anti-commandering doctrine, to strike down what remains of these laws.[652]

Perhaps more importantly, the significant concerns over racial discrimination in the laws that remain in place have not gone away. It is important to clarify that concerns over equality and due process apply to laws like SB1070 where state unilaterally want to enforce the immigration laws. They also apply to the collaborative arrangements between the federal government and localities to enforce the immigrations laws together. Secure Communities, for example, has been criticized because it does not really target the most serious offenders as it purports to do. Instead it primarily targets Latinos who are caught up in the dragnet of over-arrests in the streets as they are profiled for such things are speaking Spanish, looking Mexican, or driving while Brown.[653] Similarly, several scholars have been documenting the racial disparity in the application of SB1070 type local immigration enforcement.[654] Meanwhile civil rights groups continue to raise racial profiling

---

[649] For a discussion of the history and implementation of H.B. 56 in Alabama see Kevin R. Johnson, *Immigration and Civil Rights: Is the "New" Birmingham the Same as the "Old" Birminham?*, 21 WM. & MARY BILL RTS. J. 367 (2012).

[650] United States v. Alabama, 691 F.3d 1269 (11th Cir. 2012) (striking down provisions that criminalized harboring, created employer sanctions or new causes of action against employers for affecting U.S. workers, prohibited contracts with undocumented immigrants, and created new driving-related felonies for undocumented persons). As a result of this ruling, the state of Alabama settled the lawsuit with the ACLU and other groups and agreed to pay $350,000 in attorney's fees and expenses. Daniel M. Kowalski, *Settlement Ends Alabama Immigration Lawsuit*, available at http://www.lexisnexis.com/legalnewsroom/immigration/b/insidenews/archive/2013/10/30/settlement-ends-alabama-immigration-lawsuit.aspx.

[651] Utah Coalition of La Raza v. Herbert, 2014 U.S. Dist. LEXIS 86614 (D. Utah June 18, 2014) (striking down state criminal harboring provision and the ability of police to make warrantless arrests for immigration violations).

[652] *See, e.g.*, Mary Fan, *Rebellious State Crimmigration Enforcement and the Foreign Affairs Power*, 89 WASH. U. L. REV. 1269 (2012) and Margaret Hu, *Reverse-Commandeering*, 46 U.C. DAVIS L. REV. 535 (2012).

[653] *See, e.g.*, Adam B. Cox and Thomas J. Miles, *Policing Immigration*, 80 U. CHI. L. REV. 87 (2013) (documenting the equal protection concerns raised in the way that the Secured Communities program was rolled out to target first communities with a substantial Latino presence) and Katarina Ramos, *Criminalizing Race in the Name of Secure Communities*, 48 CAL. W. L. REV. 317 (2012). *See also* TracImmigration, *Secure Communities and ICE Deportation: A Failed Program?*, available at http://trac.syr.edu/immigration/reports/349/ (concluding that only 12 percent of all deportees from Secure Communities have been found to have committed a serious "Level 1" offense based on the agency's own definition).

[654] *See, e.g.*, Maureen A. Sweeney, *Shadow Immigration Enforcement and its Constitutional Dangers*, 104 J. CRIM. L. & CRIMINOLOGY 227 (2014); Karla Mari. McKanders, *Federal Preemption and Immigrants' Rights*, 3 WAKE FOREST J. L. & POL'Y 333 (2013); Johnson, *Immigration and Civil Rights*,

claims on behalf of Latino clients.[655] Other critiques are based on the effect of suitederal local policing of immigrants on other important criminal justice goals. This includes building trust in the community and addressing the underreporting of crime by victims who fear deportation.[656]

Not all localities, however, have heeded the call to enforce immigration laws.[657] At the same time that localities and/or local law enforcement agencies are engaging in the enforcement of immigration laws, other local entities, including state and city governments, have adopted "sanctuary policies." Such policies restrict local law enforcement collaboration with ICE on the detection and detention of unauthorized immigrants. Most of the largest cities in the United States today have some variation of such sanctuary policies.[658] Sanctuary policies are generally of three types: (1) they limit inquiries into a person's immigration status (don't ask); (2) they limit arrests or detention for violation of immigration law (don't enforce); and (3) they limit provision to federal authorities of immigration status information (don't tell).[659] Localities promulgate these policies through various means, including by adopting city council resolutions, municipal ordinances, mayoral executive orders, and police chief memoranda.[660] The issues that arise with sanctuary policies are whether they are preempted by federal immigration law, or whether they are invalidated or made moot by conflicting local policies that seek greater local enforcement of immigration laws, including through adoption of INA § 287(g) agreements.

Several potential conflicts exist between sanctuary policies and federal law. Some suggest, for example, that sanctuary policies violate the federal anti-harboring

---

supra note 649; Kevin R. Johnson, *A Study of Color-Blindness: The Racially Disparate Impacts of Arizona's S.B.1070 and the Failure of Comprehensive Immigration Reform*, 2 UC IRVINE L. REV. 313 (2012) and L. Darnell Weeden, *It is Discriminatory for Arizona or Society to Engage in the Anti-Immigration Practice of Profiling Hispanics for Speaking Spanish*, 12 LOY. J. PUB. INT. L. 109 (2010).

[655] *See, e.g.* Ortega v. Arpaio, 836 F. Supp. 2d 959 (D. Ariz. 2011).

[656] *See, e.g.*, Ajmel Quereshi, *287(g) and Women: The Family Values of Local Enforcement and Federal Immigration Law*, 25 WIS. J. L. GENDER & SOC'Y 261 (2010).

[657] For a discussion of sanctuary policies, *see* Bill Ong Hing, *Immigration Sanctuary Policies: Constitutional and Representative of Good Policing and Goo Public Policy*, 2 UC IRVINE L. REV. 247 (2012); Kristina M. Campbell, *Humanitarian is Never a Crime: The Politics of Immigration Enforcement and the Provision of Sanctuary*, 63 SYRACUSE L. REV. 71 (2012); Rose CuisonVillazor, *"Sanctuary Cities" and Local Citizenship*, 37 FORDHAM URB. L.J. 573 (2010); and Pratheepan Gulasekaram and Rose Cuison-Villazor, *Sanctuary Policies & Immigration Federalism: A Dialectic Analysis*, 55 WAYNE L. REV. 1683 (2009).

[658] These include: Baltimore, Chicago, Denver, Detroit, Houston, Los Angeles, Minneapolis, New York City, Philadelphia, San Francisco, Seattle, and Washington, D.C. Orde F. Kittrie, *Federalism, Deportation, and Crime: Victims Afraid to Call the Police*, 91 IOWA L. REV. 1449, 1466–74 (2006). For a list of sanctuary cities, see http://www.ojjpac.org/sanctuary.asp (last visited Oct. 27, 2014).

[659] Kittrie, *supra* note 658, at 1455. *See also* Huyen Pham, *The Constitutional Right Not to Cooperate? Local Sovereignty and the Federal Immigration Power*, 74 U. CIN. L. REV. 1373, 1388–91 (2006) (describing the characteristics of sanctuary policies as follows: no discrimination; no enforcement civil immigration laws; no inquiry into citizenship status; and no notifying federal immigration authorities).

[660] *Id.* at 1474.

provision.[661] The resolution is likely to depend on the federal court that decides the issue given that circuit courts interpret the harboring provision quite differently.[662] The issue might turn on whether courts view "sanctuary policies" as active concealment, which has been required by the Sixth Circuit, as opposed to most other circuits (the Second, the Fifth, the Eighth, and the Ninth) that include in the definition of harboring the provision of services and the mere omission to report that person to immigration authorities.[663] From a political perspective, however, such challenge is unlikely.[664]

Congress, however, passed two laws in 1996 explicitly to counter local sanctuary policies.[665] The first, Section 1373, mandates that "a Federal, State, or local government entity or official may not prohibit, or in any way restrict, any government entity or official from sending to, or receiving from, [ICE] information regarding the citizenship or immigration status, lawful or unlawful, of any individual."[666] Section 1644 includes much of the same language as section 1373; it states that "no State or local government entity may be prohibited, or in any way restricted, from sending to or receiving from the Immigration and Naturalization Service information regarding the immigration status, lawful or unlawful, of an alien in the United States."[667] Essentially, the broader provision, Section 1373, prohibits a government entity or official from restricting disclosure of immigration status to ICE. Section 1644 only prohibits the proscription as applied to government entities. In 1999, the Second Circuit decided the only case to date, *City of New York v. United States*[668] that assesses the application of these provisions to sanctuary policies. In that case, the Giuliani administration sought to enjoin the 1996 laws arguing that these laws violated the Tenth Amendment by forcing New York City to collaborate with federal immigration enforcement and the Guarantee Clause of the Constitution by interfering with the City's chosen form of government.[669] The Second Circuit disagreed and found that the federal provisions preempted the City's sanctuary policy, which proscribed voluntary cooperation with ICE by local police in immigration enforcement. Essentially, "don't tell" sanctuary policies are vulnerable to preemption challenges in light of the Second Circuit opinion.[670] In contrast, "don't ask" and "don't enforce" sanctuary policies are not vulnerable to

---

[661] This provision imposes criminal penalties on "[a]ny person who . . . knowing or in reckless disregard of the fact that an alien has come to, entered, or remains in the United States in violation of law, conceals, harbors, or shields from detection, or attempts to conceal, harbor, or shield from detection, such alien in any place, including any building or any means of transportation." 8 U.S.C. § 1324(a)(1)(A)(iii) (2000).

[662] Kittrie, *supra* note 658, at 1493–95.

[663] *See id.*

[664] *Id.* at 1495.

[665] Pham, *The Constitutional Right Not to Cooperate?*, *supra* note 659, at 1384–85.

[666] 8 U.S.C. § 1373 (2000).

[667] 8 U.S.C. § 1644 (2000).

[668] 179 F.3d 29 (2d Cir. 1999).

[669] *Id.* at 33.

[670] Kittrie, *supra* note 658, at 1498. *See also* Pham, *The Constitutional Right Not to Cooperate*, *supra* note 659, at 1391–95.

preemption.[671] Federal prohibition of such sanctuary policies, moreover, would run afoul of the anti-commandeering doctrine, under which the federal government could not require that state and local officials engage in immigration law enforcement.[672] Local protection against immigration enforcement by local police responds to the strong policy objective of building trust and cooperation between immigrant communities and police.[673] The effectiveness of these so-called sanctuary policies, however, is weak for several reasons. For example, violations to these policies by local police are not enforced, and individual immigrants cannot prevent their removal once they have been turned over to ICE.[674]

Another more "narrow" type of resistance to collaborative immigration enforcement has come in the form of what Professor Christopher N. Lasch has called rendition resistance; that is, the refusal of certain localities to execute immigration detainers pursuant to the Secure Communities program.[675] Indeed, Professor Lasch has argued that immigration detainers are ultra vires (beyond constitutional authority) and raise constitutional questions, especially after the *Arizona v. United States* case.[676] The federal government, of course, contests these claims,[677] and in general, challenges in court to immigration detainers, are not successful.[678]

Nevertheless, detainers do raise significant concerns, including the detention of U.S. citizens, ineligibility for certain programs available to criminal defendants due to the immigration detainer, and prolonged detention.[679] In September 2014 a federal district court judge held that detainers are not mandatory.[680] Then, in October 2014, a federal district court certified a class action challenging immigration detainers based on similar due process concerns on behalf of thousands of men

---

[671] Kittrie, *supra* note 658, at 1499.

[672] *Id.* at 1487–93, 1499–1500.

[673] *Id.* at 1475–80.

[674] *Id.* at 1480–84.

[675] Christopher N. Lasch, *Rendition Resistance*, 92 N.C. L. Rev. 149 (2013).

[676] Christopher N. Lasch, *Federal Immigration Detainers after Arizona v. United States*, 46 Loy. L.A. L. Rev. 629 (2013) and Christopher N. Lasch, *Preempting Immigration Detainer Enforcement under Arizona v. United States*, 3 Wake Forest J.L. & Pol'y 281 (2013).

[677] Congressional Research Service, Kate M. Manuel, *Immigration Detainers: Legal Issues*, April 24, 2014.

[678] *See, e.g.*, Galarza v. Szalczyk, 745 F.3d 634 (3d Cir. 2014) (rejecting a challenge to a detainer beyond the 48 hours) and Nasious v. Two Unkown BICE Agents, 2010 U.S. App. LEXIS 3311 (10th Cir. Feb. 19, 2010) (rejecting equal protection and due process claim based on immigration detainer). *See also* Maphorisa v. Delaney, 2011 U.S. App. LEXIS 12308 (3d Cir. June 15, 2011) (challenging detention beyond 48 hours); Morales v. Chadbourne, 996 F. Supp. 2d 19 (D.R.I. 2014) (naturalized citizen challenging detainer); Quattara v. U.S. Citizenship & Immig. Svs., 2012 U.S. Dist. LEXIS 14464 (D.N.J. Feb. 2, 2012) (U.S. citizen challenging detainers); Quintero v. Immigration & Customs, 2012 U.S. Dist. LEXIS 140267 (D. Md. Sept. 27, 2012) (challenge to compel agency to execute detainer); Borrero v. Wells, 2010 U.S. Dist. LEXIS 85366 (S.D. Ga. Aug. 19, 2010) (challenging denial of home detention based on immigration detainer); and Hong Thi Le v. DHS, 2009 U.S. Dist. LEXIS 43196 (N.D.W. Va. May 13, 2009).

[679] *See id.*

[680] Moreno v. Napolitano, Case, 2014 U.S. Dist. LEXIS 138576 (N.D. Ill. Sept. 30, 2014).

and women.[681] Localities have either passed resolutions[682] or states have even passed laws expressing deep concerns over the civil rights of immigrants and opting to narrow the types of detainers it will enforce. An example of this is the Trust Act in California. In October 2013, California signed into law the Transparency and Responsibility Using State Tools Act. This law limits California law enforcement's discretion to prolong detention pursuant to an ICE detainer request only to cases that fall within a range of crimes.[683] An October 2014 ABC news story reported, in fact, that states have released thousands of immigrants after deciding to decline to enforce the immigration detainers.[684]

P. FAMILY LAW

Some states are denying couples marriage licenses or are considering legislation to do so on the basis of the immigration status of one or both persons.[685] Sometimes, the inability of at least one of the marriage license petitioners to produce certain types of identification only available to citizens, such as social security numbers or driver's licenses, becomes the basis for the denial.[686] In some states, however, existing practice or pending legislation does or would require proof of legal

---

[681] National Immigrant Justice Center, *Federal Court Certifies Class Action Challenging Immigration Detainers*, News Release (October 1, 2014).

[682] Examples of these are Broward County, the Colorado Sheriff, Santa Cruz County, San Diego County, Clark County Nevada, Nebraska, and nine counties in Oregon. *See, e.g.*, Amanda Peterson Beadle, *Avalanche of Local Detainer Limits Underscores Need for Federal Policy Reform*, July 24, 2014, Immigration Impact and Julia Preston, *Limit Detention of Immigrants*, April 18, 2014, THE NEW YORK TIMES.

[683] Recent Legislation, *Immigration Law-Criminal Justice and Immigration Enforcement — California Limits Local Entities' Compliance with Immigration and Customs Enforcement Detainer Requests — Tust Act, 2013 Cal. Sta. 4650 (codified, at Cal. Gov't Code 7282-7282.5 (WEST SUPP. 2014)*, 127 HARV. L. REV. 2593 (2014). The range of crimes is expansive and encompasses obstruction of justice, unlawful possession or use of a weapon, and any state felony, among other crimes. *Id.* at 2595.

[684] Associated Press, *Thousands Released After Immigration Holds Denied*, Oct. 17, 2014, ABC NEWS.

[685] Christopher D. Nelson, Comment, *Protecting the Immigrant Family: The Misguided Policies, Practices and Proposed Legislation Regarding Marriage License Issuance*, 4 U. ST. THOMAS L.J. 643, 644–656 (documenting marriage licenses denials and similar proposed legislation in Pennsylvania, Minnesota, Virginia, Tennessee, and Connecticut). Family law is not the only substantive area where immigration status has influenced local laws or local judicial decision-making. For instance, legislatures are increasingly considering immigration status to restrict discretionary leniency in criminal proceedings, such as probation or alternative punishment schemes or bail generally available to criminal defendants. *See, e.g.*, Ruvalcaba v. State, 143 P.3d 468, 470 (Nev. 2006) (considering undocumented status of defendant to deny him probation); Arizona 2006 Proposition 100 (amending the state Constitution to prohibit bail for illegal aliens who are charged with a serious felony (defined in statute as those of classes one, two, three and four, as well as aggravated DUI), *available at* http://www.azsos.gov/election/2006/ Info/pubpamphlet/english/Prop100.htm. As well, some localities have relied on immigration status to seek to deny or restrict certain tort remedies that are still available to citizens. Arizona 2006 Proposition 102 (amending the state Constitution to prohibit a person who is in Arizona in violation of federal immigration law from being awarded punitive damages in any civil lawsuit filed in the state. Eligibility of illegal immigrants to file for compensatory damages is not affected. Referred by Legislature (SCR 1001, 2006 Reg. Sess.), *available at* http://www.azsos.gov/election/2006/Info/pubpamphlet/english/ Prop102.htm.

[686] Nelson, *supra* note 685, at 645–651.

immigration status for the issuance of marriage licenses.[687] At least one federal district court in Pennsylvania enjoined the practice of requiring proof of legal immigration status to apply for a marriage license as unconstitutional based on a substantive due process and equal protection grounds.[688] In doing so, the court applied strict scrutiny analysis also to the equal protection challenge irrespective of whether the classification created a suspect class.[689]

Immigration status is also influencing the way that courts resolve traditional family matters, including determinations of divorce and child custody.[690] Professor David B. Thronson has documented that courts openly, or at times underhandedly, discriminate against undocumented immigrants to deny them family-based fundamental rights, including custody; or manipulate family proceeding outcomes purportedly to achieve certain immigration results, such as in divorce proceedings that could affect the legal status of the immigrant spouse; or simply tailor the decision to accommodate the immigration circumstances that follow from the family law decision, such as awarding alimony payments to a non-working spouse who is ineligible to work under immigration law.[691] Thronson cautions against this approach based on either its implications on equality or other family-based fundamental rights and on the erroneous assumption that judges make based on their poor understanding of complex immigration laws to make decisions.[692] Rather, Thronson advocates for a transformation of immigration law in ways that more fully recognize the "mixed status" immigration composition of U.S. families and the detrimental implications of immigration enforcement on the parent-child relationship.[693]

Finally, scholars have also begun to document how immigration detention and removal is affecting the fundamental rights of parents who end up losing their rights because they either lack access to the family justice system and legal representation.[694] Courts are actually also deciding whether allowing a U.S. citizen child to join the parent abroad is in the best interest of the child.[695] Unfortunately, this trend of relying on the best interest of the child in the context of removal runs

---

[687] *Id.* at 656.

[688] Buck v. Stankovic, 485 F. Supp. 2d 576, 582 (M.D. Pa. 2007) (citing Zablocki v. Redhail, 434 U.S. 374, 386 (1978) to affirm the fundamental character of the right to marry).

[689] *Id.* at 583.

[690] *See, e.g.,* David B. Thronson, *Custody and Contradictions: Exploring Immigration Law as Federal Family Law in the Context of Child Custody,* 59 HASTINGS L.J. 453 (2008); David B. Thronson, *Of Borders and Best Interests: Examining the Experiences of Undocumented Immigrants in U.S. Family Courts,* 11 TEX. HISP. J. L. & POL'Y 45 (2005). *See also* Soraya Fata et al., *Custody of Children in Mixed Status Families: Preventing the Misunderstanding and Misuse of Immigration Status in State-Court Custody Proceedings,* 47 FAM. L.Q. 191 (2013).

[691] Thronson, *Of Borders and Bests Interests, supra* note 690, at 54–71.

[692] *Id.*

[693] *See generally,* David B. Thronson, *Choice-less Choices: Deportation and the Parent-Child Relationship,* 6 NEV. L.J. 1165 (2006).

[694] Sarah Rogerson, *Lack of Detained Parents' Access to Family Justice System and the Unjust Severance of the Parent-Child Relationship,* 47 FAM. L.Q. 141 (2013).

[695] Marcía Yablon-Zug, *Separation, Deportation, Termination,* 32 B.C. J. L & SOC. JUST. 63 (2012).

afoul of the fundamental rights of the parents.[696]

Q. CONCLUSION

States have always engaged in the regulation of immigrants. The exponential increase in local laws pertaining to immigrants and immigration, a trend likely to continue in the face of failed immigration reform policies and continued migration, questions the premise, at least as a descriptive matter, that immigration control is the sole responsibility of the federal government. Indeed, in order to make sense of the recent explosion in immigration federalism, scholars have argued that there has always been a strong intersection of immigration and local government law. In addition, there is an interdependence of immigration and local government controls as both national and local sovereigns attempt to define borders and membership through the laws and power available to them.[697]

Normatively, however, immigration scholars cannot agree on whether this is a good or a bad trend. Further, immigration scholars (and judges) have been criticized for selectively choosing either federalism or national uniformity values based on their personal outcome preference, rather than a true commitment to a robust debate over the novel questions raised by immigration federalism.[698] Unfortunately, those immigration scholars, who have engaged in a more "functional account" (as opposed to outcome-determinative critique) of this new immigration federalism are still principally relying on selective anecdotal examples to support their functional value-claims. The the empirical evidence is either absent or mixed.[699] Thus, much more empirical research is needed to resolve the tensions created by localized immigration control.

One claimed benefit of decentralization of immigration powers is that it encourages experimentation and innovation.[700] Here, the claim is that such experimentation and innovation, by accommodating and reflecting a greater variety of view on citizens, could actually mitigate pressure on the federal government to enact legislation that reflects extreme positions at either end of the political spectrum.[701] Another cited benefit is that local experimentation can lead to quick lessons for states — i.e., a mass exit of workers from states — which could lead towns to repeal their anti-immigrant laws.[702] In short, there is no basis to favor uniformity over experimentation, at least not if the reason is that one level of

---

[696] *Id.*

[697] *See, e.g.,* Rick Su, *Local Fragmentation as Immigration Regulation*, 47 Hous. L. Rev. 367 (2010).

[698] Clare Huntington, *The Constitutional Dimension of Immigration Federalism*, 61 Vand. L. Rev. 787, 830 (2008).

[699] *See, e.g., id.* and Rodriguez, *The Significance of the Local, supra* note 16.

[700] Huntington, *supra* note 698, at 827.

[701] *Id.* at 831. The other side of the coin, that quenching decentralization through preemption, could lead to more restrictive immigration policies has been advanced by Peter Spiro with his "steam-valve" metaphor. *See* Spiro, *supra* note 311 and accompanying text.

[702] Huntington, *supra* note 698, at 832. *See also* Matthew Parlow, *A Localist's Case for Decentralizing Immigration Policy*, 84 Denv. U. L. Rev. 1061, 1069–73 (2007).

government will better protect the rights of citizens over another.[703] In contrast, those who favor preemption view a strong national government as serving an interest in uniformity, as well as fairness and equality, values that matter greatly in matters implicating foreign affairs.[704] The difficulty here is that the argument for uniformity has the most salience in areas of traditional immigration law — that is, the regulation of who comes in, must leave, or can become a full member of the U.S. society. This argument loses its value, however, the more immigration law touches on areas of traditional state concern, such as access to education or the distribution of state public resources.[705]

A second claimed federalism benefit is that competition among localities enhances efficiency and effectiveness; when local governments respond to local preferences the possibility of exit encourages efficiency.[706] As an example of economic efficiency, scholars cite the possibility that decentralized experimentation could fine-tune the connection between immigration and labor. It would do so in a way that localities could tailor their immigration supply to respond to the local demand for labor.[707] In contrast, those who favor preemption also claim that economic interests are better served by a strong national government, including by safeguarding against race-to-the-bottom phenomena.[708] Going back to the example of labor, the free movement of workers could be essential to a robust, globalized economy, and states could thwart immigration policy if immigrants allowed into the country are not welcomed by individual states.[709]

A third claimed benefit of decentralization of immigration laws is that it furthers political accountability and participation when the interests of smaller groups are satisfied and more individuals are able to participate.[710] In contrast, those who favor more centralized decision-making express worry over parochialism, as well as increasing negative externalities in the decision-making process.[711] More empirical data is necessary to examine whether the national or local governments are better placed to offer greater political accountability to immigrants. This argument is further complicated by the fact that noncitizens generally cannot vote in either federal or local elections. Thus, rather than electoral participation, data that must be examined includes non-electoral noncitizen participation, as well as the effec-

---

[703] Huntington, *supra* note 698, at 831. *But see* Keith Cunningham-Parmeter, *Forced Federalism: States as Laboratories of Immigration Reform*, 62 Hastings L.J. 1673 (2011) (challenging the assertion that states can serve as valuable laboratories of immigration reform because states that enact their own immigration laws do not internalize or yield replicable results — two conditions needed for viable experimentation).

[704] Huntington, *supra* note 698, at 828–29. *See also* Adam B. Cox and Eric A. Posner, *Delegation in Immigration Law*, 79 U. Chi. L. Rev. 1285 (2012) (citing as a cost of immigration delegation the fact that the federal government cannot always align the localities' preferences with those of the national government).

[705] Huntington, *supra* note 698, at 828–29

[706] *Id.* at 828.

[707] *Id.* at 833.

[708] *Id.* at 829.

[709] *Id.* at 834.

[710] *Id.* at 828.

[711] *Id.* at 835.

tiveness of immigrant civil rights groups vs. anti-immigrant groups to influence local vs. national politics.

Decentralization is also credited with better promoting states' rights or prerogatives. One such claimed state prerogative is the right of localities to define their cultural stability and preservation — i.e. deciding how to allocate scarce state resources — in the face of lax federal immigration enforcement. Some scholars point out, however, that resource-guarding rationales are really proxies for culture-based exclusion.[712] In fact, empirical findings into why states move to regulate immigrants also suggest that in fact most local immigration laws are not responding to pressing demographic challenges. Rather they are the by-product of more nuanced and politicized processes in which demographic or resource concerns are neither necessary nor sufficient factors.[713] These scholars, thus caution against functionalists accounts as an explanation for the rise in local immigration regulation and suggest the need to rethink traditional federalism frameworks for evaluating sub-federal attempts to regulate immigrants.[714]

The effect of decentralization on the individual rights of immigrants is also at times promoted as a benefit insofar as states act as a check against national power. Localities, some argue, promise to be an important site for progressive reforms on behalf of immigrants in response to restrictive federal immigration policies.[715] In direct conflict with this claim, some place greater faith that the national government is better placed to protect the fundamental rights of immigrants against vociferous, nativist local groups.[716] Here too, proponents on either side of the argument suffer from selectively pointing out to pro- or anti-immigrant local legislation to prove their claims.[717]

Many local immigration laws are quite harsh and seek to deny or severely restrict the rights of immigrants, especially the undocumented in the hope that immigrants will self-deport, but not all has been bad for immigrants. In fact, some studies suggest that the evidence as to whether immigration federalism has been bad or good for immigrants is quite mixed.[718] What is true, however, is that the

---

[712] Pratheepan Gulasekaram, *Sub-National Immigration Regulation and the Pursuit of Cultural Cohesion*, 77 U. Cin. L. Rev. 1441 (2009).

[713] Pratheepan Gulasekaram and S. Karthick Ramakrishnan, *Immigration Federalism: A Reappraisal*, 88 N.Y.U. L. Rev. 2014 (2013). *See also* S. Karthick Ramakrishnan and Pratheepan Gulasekaram, *The Importance of the Political in Immigration Federalism*, 44 Ariz. St. L.J. 1431 (2012).

[714] Gulasekaram and Pamakrishnan, *Immigration Federalism*, *supra* note 713, at 2075.

[715] *See, e.g.*, Rick Su, *The Promise and Peril of Cities and Immigration Policy*, 7 Harv. L. & Pol'y Rev. 299 (2003).

[716] *Id.* at 829. *See also* Lindsay Nasch, *Expansion by Ordinance: Preemption and Proxy Local Legislation*, 25 Geo. Immigr. L.J. 243 (2011) (documenting that suitederal laws often disfavor subgroups by treating them as nuisance).

[717] *See, e.g.*, Rodríguez, *The Significance of the Local*, *supra* note 16, at 569–70.

[718] The Migration Policy Institute (MPI) conducted an early study of this trend in 2007 that yielded surprising results. The MPI study found that state legislatures in all 50 U.S. states introduced more than 1,000 immigration-related measures in 2007. In all, 306 measures sought to expand the rights of immigrants, while 256 contracted the rights of immigrants. Christina Rodríguez, et al., *Testing the Limits: A Framework for Assessing the Legality of State and Local Immigration Measures* (Migration Policy Institute 2007). *See also* Raquel Aldana, *Immigration Federalism and Rights in Immigration*

different legal regimes governing the application of equal protection or due process doctrines as between the federal (i.e., rational review irrespective of classification and/or existence of a fundamental right) and state governments (strict scrutiny at least for suspect or quasi-suspect classifications and for fundamental rights) could mean greater judicial accountability at the local levels.[719] Unfortunately, as some scholars lament, traditional rights-based arguments rooted in equal protection or due process on behalf of immigrants have largely been replaced by structural arguments such as preemption.[720] Thus, whether judicial accountability could be sufficient to turn the anti-immigrant tide at the local level, or whether doctrines would eventually shift at the federal level to resemble those at the local level remains to be seen.[721]

Finally, a growing number of scholars reject an either or approach and find merit in both the national and subnational involvement in immigration regulation and favor a model generally known as cooperative federalism. For example, Professor Cristina Rodriguez has emphasized that states and local governments have a primary role in integrating immigrants into the body politic; thus, she suggests that for immigration there should develop legal doctrines and law making that simultaneously facilitate power sharing by the various levels of government and tolerate tensions between federal objectives and state and local interests.[722] Similarly, Professors Keith Aoki and John Shuford propose a model of immigration regionalism that would replace a binary approach to immigration regulation. This model seeks to involve representatives of the federal government, states, as well as private sector and civil society groups in order to promote more principled outcomes.[723] To some, however, the degree and scope of involvement of either the national or local sovereigns should vary according to the type of immigration regulation. For example, Professor Dale B. Thompson adopts what he calls an "optimal federalism" framework to compare economies and diseconomies of scale across, enactment, implementation, and enforcement institutions. This is done in order to determine the appropriate level of government for addressing these institutional aspects of immigration policy. Thompson concludes that in each of these areas the federal

---

Regulation in FEDERAL STATES: CHALLENGES AND RESPONSES IN COMPARATIVE PERSPECTIVES (Edited Collection of Essays) (Sasha Baglay & Delphine Nackache, eds., Springer 2013) (conducting a comparative analysis of the growing asymmetrical immigration federalism regimes that have surfaced in Australia, Canada, the European Union, Belgium, the United Kingdom, Switzerland, and the United States and concluding that the evidence as to whether such trends restrict or expand rights for immigrants is mixed).

[719] Aldana, *Federal Citizenship, supra* note 337, at 306.

[720] Geoffrey Heeren, *Persons Who Are Not the People: The Changing Rights of Immigrants in the United States,* 44 COLUM. HUM. RTS. L. REV. 367 (2013).

[721] *See, e.g.,* Lucas Guttentag, *The Forgotten Norm in Immigration Preemption: Discrimination, Harassment, and the Civil Rights Act of 1870,* 8 DUKE J. CONST. L. & PUBLIC POLICY 1 (2013) (based on the Civil Rights Act of 1870, arguing that preemption doctrine could be infused with an equality principle and assess the discriminatory consequences of sub-federal immigration measures).

[722] Rodriguez, *The Significance of the Local, supra* note 16, at 641.

[723] Keith Aoki & John Shuford, *Welcome to Amerizona — Immigrants Out!: Assessing "Dystopian Dream" and "Usable Futures" of Immigration Reform, and Considering Whether "Immigration Regionalisms" Is an Idea Whose Time Has Come,* 38 FORDHAM URB. L.J. 1 (2010). *See also* Christina M. Rodriguez, *Negotiating Conflict Through Federalism: Institutional and Popular Perspectives,* 123 YALE L.J. 2094 (2014) (arguing for the creation of a framework for ongoing negotiation of differences large and small between federal and local institutions to promote consensus on national integration).

government should have some dominant role across all phases; however, Thompson suggest that significant diseconomies of scale appear in both the implementation and enforcement phases, which implies that state and local governments should play important though limited roles in implementing and enforcing immigration policy.[724]

---

[724] Dale B. Thompson, *Immigration Policy through the Lens of Optimal Federalism*, 2 WM. & MARY POL'Y REV. 236 (2011).

Chapter 5

IMMIGRATION ACTORS: FEDERAL AGENCIES AND COURTS

A. THE POLITICAL BRANCHES OF THE FEDERAL GOVERNMENT IN REGULATING IMMIGRATION

1. Congress

It has long been recognized that Congress has plenary power over immigration matters. This power is derived from various provisions of the U.S. Constitution.[1] The plenary power of Congress also is based on the sovereign power of the federal

---

[1] U.S. Const., art. I, Sec. 8, Cl. 4 grants Congress the power to establish a uniform rule of naturalization; U.S. Const., art. I, Sec. 8, Cl. 3 grants Congress the power "to regulate Commerce with foreign Nations"; U.S. Const., art. I, Sec. 9, Cl. 1 the Migration and Importation clause; and U.S. Const., art. I, Sec. 8, Cl. 11 the War Power clause.

government; and it is shared by both the legislative and executive branches. The plenary power of Congress includes the authority to decide the requirements for entry into, the conditions for remaining in, and the grounds for removal from the United States. This power is quite broad and under this doctrine the actions of the federal government in immigration matters largely are immune from constitutional scrutiny. The plenary power doctrine is discussed in detail in Chapter 3.

2. The President and Executive Branch

The Executive Branch and the President, as the head of the branch, share immigration power with Congress. The President's power is derived from the U.S. Constitution, statutory authority, the delegated power of Congress, and the plenary power doctrine. The President of the United States directs several aspects of immigration law. Under the "take care" clause of the U.S. Constitution, the President has the authority to execute the laws of the U.S. and, therefore, direct the operations of all of the federal departments and agencies involved in the implementation of all aspects of immigration law.[2] This includes: the Department of State, the Department of Homeland Security, the Department of Justice, the Department of Labor, and the Department of Health and Human Services. The President directs the operation of the entire executive branch using the appointments power, with the advice and consent of the Senate, of Article II of the U.S. Constitution.[3]

The plenary power doctrine recognizes broad authority lies with both the Executive Branch and Congress.[4] The INA establishes a comprehensive immigration benefits and enforcement statutory scheme implemented by the various federal departments. The President's role in directing the executive branch immigration operations includes numerous discretionary decisions in the enforcement of immigration laws as well as in availability of immigration benefits. The DHS, under the direction of the President, in recent years has used prosecutorial discretion measures to grant temporary reprieves from deportation to address, in part, the failure of immigration reform legislative efforts.[5] Although Presidents have issued directives using prosecutorial discretion in the past, the measures established by the Obama Administration have been particularly criticized by anti-immigration groups.[6]

---

[2] U.S. Const., art. II, Sec. 3.

[3] Art. II, Sec. 2, Cl. 2.

[4] Ekiu v. United States, 142 U.S. 651 (1892). *See also*, Legomsky & Rodriguez, Immigration and Refugee Law and PolicyCh. 2 (2014).

[5] Hiroshi Motomura, *Perspectives: The President's Discretion, Immigration Enforcement and the Rule of Law* (American Immigration Council, August 2014). *See also* Hiroshi Motomura, Immigration Outside the Law 34–42 (Oxford University Press, 2014).

[6] This includes temporary relief granted to noncitizen students affected by Hurricane Katrina by President George W. Bush (2005), deferred enforcement for certain Liberian citizens by President George W. Bush (2007), deferred deportations under a family fairness policy by President George H. Bush (1990), and extended voluntary departure to Polish citizens by President Ronald Reagan (1981). *See*, Shoba Sivaprasad Wadhia, *Response, In Defense of DACA, Deferred Action and the DREAM Act*, 19 Tex. L. Rev. 59 (2013); Shoba Sivaprasad Wadhia, *My Great FOIA Adventure and Discoveries of Deferred Action Cases at ICE*, 27 Geo. Immigr. L.J. 345 (2013).

One prosecutorial discretion measure established in June 2012 by President Obama is a Deferred Action for Childhood Arrivals (DACA) relief from deportation directive.[7] This is covered in Chapter 14. The subsequent implementation of the DACA relief included instructions to ICE to facilitate granting deferred action to noncitizens already in removal proceedings or detention, as well as to USCIS to review applications and grant employment authorization. Another prosecutorial discretion measure is known as the Morton Memo. John Morton, Director of ICE, issued a memorandum in June 2011 outlining civil immigration enforcement priorities. The memo contained guidance for ICE to exercise of prosecutorial discretion.[8]

The measures garnered some vociferous internal DHS opponents, namely ICE officers, and a lawsuit challenging DHS authority, placing the issue of the President's executive power squarely in the midst of pro-immigration and anti-immigration debates. In August 2012, ICE officers filed an action seeking declaratory judgment on the constitutional and statutory validity of the DACA directive and the Morton Memo.[9] The ICE officers asserted that INA § 235(b)(2)(A) imposes a mandatory obligation on ICE immigration officers to initiate removal proceedings, and requested an injunction preventing implementation of the measures and prohibiting DHS from taking disciplinary action against officers for failure to comply.[10] The suit was dismissed as an internal employment issue barred from judicial review under the Civil Service Reform Act.[11]

The President establishes the number of refugees who may be admitted into the United States in each fiscal year under INA § 207(b). The President also may issue a proclamation to suspend the entry of all noncitizens or any group of noncitizens if their entry is deemed to be "detrimental to the interests of the United States" under INA § 212(f). This proclamation authority has been used by presidents to

---

[7] Under the directive, deferred action could be granted on a case-by-case basis to individuals who: came to the United States when they were younger than 16 and are under the age of 31; have continuously resided in the United States for at least five years; who are in school, have graduated from high school, have obtained a GED or are honorably discharged veterans of the armed forces; and who have not been convicted of a felony, significant misdemeanor offense or multiple misdemeanor offenses, or otherwise posed a threat to national security or public safety. A process to extend this benefit was established by DHS. http://www.uscis.gov/humanitarian/consideration-deferred-action-childhood-arrivals-daca.

[8] Memorandum of John Morton, ICE Director, *Exercising Prosecutorial Discretion Consistent with the Civil Immigration Enforcement Priorities of the Agency for Apprehension, Detention, and Removal of Aliens* (June 17, 2011) ("Morton Memo").

[9] Crane v. Napolitano, 920 F. Supp. 2d 724 (N.D. Tex. 2013). Crane v. Napolitano, 2013 U.S. Dist. LEXIS 187005 (N.D. Tex. July 31, 2013). The ICE officers asserted that the DACA directive and Morton Memo violates federal law that requires removal proceedings without discretion, prohibits a nonstatutory benefit to more than 1.7 million noncitizens, usurps Congress' authority, violates the Take Care Clause of the U.S. Constitution, Art. II, Sec. 3, and violates the Administrative Procedures Act.

[10] INA § 235(b)(2)(A) specifies that applicants for admission whom an examining immigration officer determines is "not clearly and beyond doubt entitled to be admitted . . . shall be detained for a proceeding under section 240."

[11] Crane v. Napolitano, 2013 U.S. Dist. LEXIS 187005 (N.D. Tex. July 31, 2013) (dismissed without prejudice).

further foreign policy goals of the U.S. In 1996 President Clinton banned the entry of noncitizens and their immediate family members from Burma who participated in political repression in that country.[12] Similar proclamations were issued by both President George W. Bush in 2001 and President Clinton in 1999 relating to Bosnia-Herzegovena and Kosovo.[13]

One of the most criticized uses of the presidential proclamation authority involves the interdiction of vessels containing migrants from Haiti and, later from Cuba.[14] Presidential proclamations to interdict vessels in international waters and return the noncitizen passengers were issued by President Reagan in 1981 and by President Bush in 1991 and 1992.[15] Those seeking asylum were forced to raise their claims in offshore refugee camps.[16] Chapter 10 covers refugees and asylum in the United States.

B. THE ADMINISTRATIVE STRUCTURE OF IMMIGRATION LAW

1. A Brief History of the Rise and Fall of the INS

Immigration functions are managed by a number of executive branch departments. Today, the Department of Homeland Security directs the majority of immigration functions. The Department of Labor, the Department of State, Department of Justice, and the Department of Health and Human Services also play an important role in the immigration system. Before 2003, most of the immigration functions were within the Department of Justice under the aegis of the Immigration and Naturalization Service (INS).

Federal regulation of immigration matters began during the late 1800s. The first 100 years of U.S. history, (1776–1875), generally was a period of open immigration. Immigrants were welcomed and admitted to the U.S. with minimal restrictions. States managed the admission processing during this time period. In 1891, the Superintendent of Immigration within the Department of Treasury began managing federal immigration matters, and took over this role from the states. The immigration function was transferred to the Department of Commerce and Labor in 1903. When a new Department of Labor was created in 1913, it housed two separate immigration operations: a Bureau of Immigration; and a Bureau of

---

[12] 61 Fed. Reg. 52,233 (1996) (The notice stated that "[t]he regime has failed to enter into serious dialogue with the democratic opposition and representatives of the country's ethnic minorities, has failed to move toward achieving national reconciliation, and has failed to meet internationally recognized standards of human rights.").

[13] 2001 Pres. Proc. No. 7452, 66 Fed. Reg. 34,775 (June 29, 2001); 1999 Pres. Proc. No. 7249, 64 Fed. Reg. 62561 (1999).

[14] *See* Harold Koh, *Americas Offshore Refugee Camps*, 29 U. Rich. L. Rev. 139 (1995).

[15] 1981 Pres. Proc. No. 4865, 46 Fed. Reg. 48,107 (1981); Executive Order No. 12801, 57 Fed. Reg. 2313. The Attorney General also has authority, in urgent circumstances, to direct state and local officials to respond to "an actual or imminent mass influx of aliens arriving off the coast" under INA § 103(a)(10).

[16] This policy was upheld in Jean v. Nelson, 472 U.S. 846 (1985).

Naturalization. In 1933, these two bureaus were consolidated into the Immigration and Naturalization Service (INS).

In 1940, the Attorney General of the Justice Department was assigned the role of supervising immigration matters including the INS which was transferred from the Department of Labor. The Attorney General directed both the INS and the Executive Office of Immigration Review. The INS managed both the enforcement of immigration law, and the processing of immigration benefits. The INS enforcement function included inspection of arriving passengers, prosecution at administrative hearings, border patrol, and detention of noncitizens. The INS immigration benefits function included the adjudication of petitions for naturalization, as well as other services relating to noncitizens in the U.S. on a temporary basis or those seeking lawful permanent resident status. Other immigration functions were housed in the Department of Labor as well as the Department of State.

The INS headquarters office in Washington D.C. directed a vast system of local district offices, regional adjudication centers and Border Patrol operations. This headquarters office managed operations, budget, policy-setting, the drafting of regulations, and liaising with Congress and other agencies. Local district offices operated throughout the United States, and regional offices primarily adjudicated immigration benefits applications. The district offices were divided into units relating to both enforcement functions, such as investigations, as well as adjudication functions such as the review of initial petitions for naturalization. Enforcement in the interior of the country also was managed through the district offices to apprehend unauthorized noncitizens in the United States, investigate employers who employed unauthorized workers, and detain noncitizens pending hearings before Immigration Judges. Asylum adjudicators were located in separate offices. Asylum adjudication was moved from the district offices in 1990 to ensure trained asylum officers adjudicated applications.

The Border Patrol also operated within the INS structure. The Border Patrol managed enforcement along the land borders of the United States with Mexico and Canada. The Border Patrol was separate from the district offices and its principal focus was to prevent unauthorized entry into the United States, including the apprehension of unauthorized noncitizens near the border. The district offices managed more than 350 ports of entry into the United States at airport terminals and land border crossings. Immigration officers admitted noncitizens into the United States after an inspection; generally, a brief series of questions about the noncitizen's plans in the U.S.

The INS also shared the management of immigration matters with other agencies within the Executive Branch, and the Department of Homeland Security continues to work with these agencies today. The Department of State was and continues to be involved in the issuance of visas in its embassies and consulate offices located worldwide. The Department of Labor was and continues to be involved in assessing labor needs for some lawful permanent residents and some temporary nonimmigrant workers.

Criticism of the large bureaucracy for immigration decision-making has been ongoing since the 1940s when the INS was consolidated within the Justice

Department. The 1997 Report of the Commission on Immigration Reform suggested a reorganization.[17] The primary issues included the dual mission of the INS (service and enforcement), the overlap of authority with other agencies within the federal government, and poor management.[18] In the 1990s, the INS had failing information management systems leading to significant backlogs in processing applications for immigration benefits. Regulatory and legislative attempts to reorganize the immigration benefits functions often created more inefficiencies. The enforcement function of the INS also was burdened as Congress increased funding in the late 1990s to enhance border protection. Many proposals were debated including whether to split apart the enforcement and immigration benefits functions entirely or whether a Cabinet level agency should be established.[19]

The impetus for change increased dramatically after September 11, 2001. Congress adopted a comprehensive reorganization of all national security functions, including immigration, as part of the Homeland Security Act of 2002 which was signed into law on November 25, 2002.[20] The Act abolished the INS and transferred nearly all of the functions to the newly created Department of Homeland Security.

2. Department of Homeland Security

The Homeland Security Act of 2002 (HSA) consolidated 22 federal agencies dealing with immigration and national security into one Executive Branch cabinet level department, including the Coast Guard, the Secret Service, the Federal Emergency Management Agency (FEMA), the Transportation Security Administration (TSA), and the Customs Service. HSA abolished the INS, and the immigration functions formerly within the Department of Justice were moved almost entirely to the new Department of Homeland Security (DHS). Congress restructured all of the immigration functions and mandated a complete separation of immigration benefits services from the enforcement operations. One immigration function has remained with the Department of Justice: the Executive Office of Immigration Review (EOIR).

As of March 1, 2003, the service and benefit functions of the INS transitioned into the Department of Homeland Security as the Bureau of Citizenship and Immigration Services which is now referred to as USCIS.[21] Two immigration enforcement units within DHS began operations on March 1, 2003: the Bureau of

---

[17] U.S. Commission on Immigration Reform, *Becoming An American: Immigration and Immigrant Policy* 148–169 (Report to Congress 1997).

[18] Papademetriou, Aleinikoff, & Meyers, *Reorganizing the U.S. Immigration Function: Toward a New Framework for Accountability*, Carnegie Endowment for International Peace (1998); *See also* Papademetriou, Aleinikoff, & Meyers, *Reorganizing the Immigration Function: Toward a New Framework For Accountability*, 75 INTER. REL. 501 (Apr. 13, 1998); Gene McNary, *No Authority, No Accountability: Don't Abolish the INS, Make It An Independent Agency*, 74 INTER. REL. 1281 (Aug. 25, 1997); David A. Martin, *Immigration Policy and The Homeland Security Act Reorganization: An Early Agenda for Practice Improvements*, 17 INTER. REL. 601 (Apr. 28, 2003).

[19] *Id.*

[20] Homeland Security Act of 2002 (HSA), Pub. L. No. 107-296, 116 Stat. 2135 (2002).

[21] HSA § 451; 69 Fed. Reg. 60, 937 (Oct. 13, 2004) (changing the name).

Immigration and Customs Enforcement (ICE); and the Bureau of Customs and Border Protection (CBP). ICE primarily deals with interior immigration enforcement operations, and CBP deals with border enforcement. This massive overhaul of all homeland security functions has required extensive, on-going oversight. For example, the Government Accounting Office and the DHS Office of Inspector General have issued numerous reports since 2003.[22]

The authority of the Secretary of Homeland Security relating to immigration matters is identified in INA § 103. HSA consolidated the authority to issue regulations, and administer and enforce the INA, under the Department of Homeland Security. HSA also transfers authority from the Department of State to DHS for final decisions regarding the issuance of visas, as discussed below. The immigration functions of the DHS remain governed by the Immigration and Nationality Act (INA) and the preexisting INS regulations. The HSA addresses these potential inconsistencies by deeming that all references in the INA and regulations to the agents or entities under the former system should be read as references to the new appropriate agents or entities.[23] For example, references to the "Immigration and Naturalization Service," the "Service," the "Commissioner," and other INS officials are deemed to refer to the appropriate DHS official or entity.

a.   Citizenship and Immigration Services — USCIS

USCIS began conducting the service and benefit functions of the INS on March 1, 2003.[24] It is responsible for the administration of immigration and naturalization adjudication functions, and establishing the policies and priorities for immigration services.[25] USCIS has oversight of approximately 223 offices and 19,000 government employees and contractors. USCIS is responsible for all of the adjudications formerly within the INS including decisions by immigration examiners, asylum officers, regional service centers and application support centers. These immigrant benefits decisions are made by district offices and regional offices throughout the United States.

USCIS approves or denies applications or petitions for nonimmigrant and immigrant status filed by or on behalf of noncitizens. Most immigration benefits applications or petitions are filed with one of four Regional Service Centers, with the National Benefits Center or with "lockbox" special intake facilities.[26] Field

---

[22] *See, e.g., Department of Homeland Security: Progress Report on Implementation of Mission and Management Functions* (GAO-07-454, August 2007); *Department of Homeland Security: Progress Report on Implementation of Mission and Management Functions* (GAO-07-454, August 2007) (noting over 400 GAO reports on DHS major departmental programs in 2003–2007). The DHS Office of the Inspector General (OIG) also conducts oversight through audits and investigations of DHS programs and operations, and regularly issues reports of its findings.

[23] HSA § 1517.

[24] The Director of USCIS reports directly to the Deputy Secretary of DHS.

[25] U.S. Citizenship and Immigration Services, http://www.uscis.gov/aboutus. USCIS adjudications include immigrant visa petitions, naturalization petitions, asylum and refugee applications, service center adjudications, and all other adjudications performed by the former INS.

[26] Some petitions are filed with a USCIS "lockbox" which is a post office box used to accelerate the

offices are located throughout the U.S. and internationally where interviews and other services are conducted. Application Support Centers take fingerprints for various applications and petitions. USCIS Asylum Offices are located throughout the U.S. and handle applicant interviews.[27] Immigration examiners make these decisions which are referred to as adjudications. These adjudications include citizenship petitions. USCIS covers its cost of operations using the fees imposed on applicants for immigration benefits.

There is an appellate review body located within USCIS for some benefits decisions: the Administrative Appeals Office (AAO). The AAO formerly existed within the INS to provide appellate review of decisions by regional offices regarding petitions for nonimmigrant status and permanent residence primarily under the employment-based immigrant categories.[28] Many other decisions are appealed to the AAO.[29] In recent years, the AAO has been criticized because of its lack of transparency, high denial rates, and lengthy processing times for appeals. As a result, AAO operations have been under scrutiny by the CIS Ombudsman (discussed below).[30] Other immigration benefits decisions are reviewed by Immigration Judges of the EOIR in the Department of Justice. Generally, appeals of removal orders are heard by the Board of Immigration Appeals (BIA) which operates within the EOIR. The regulations determine which decisions must be appealed to the BIA or to the AAO.[31] The EOIR is discussed in greater detail below.

The Office of the Secretary of DHS includes the Citizenship and Immigration Services (CIS) Ombudsman which is a position not within USCIS. The Ombudsman position was designed to resolve individual and employer problems with USCIS, as well as to recommend ways to fix systemic issues in administering citizenship and immigration services. The Ombudsman appoints local ombudsmen for each state. The CIS Ombudsman is required to issue an Annual Report to Congress that provides independent analyses, recommendations about systemic issues, and USCIS efforts to address past recommendations to improve programs and services.[32] The USCIS usually responds to the Annual Report recommendations annually as well.[33]

---

intake and initial processing. USCIS employees oversee Lockbox operations. *See* http://www.uscis.gov/about-us/find-uscis-office/field-offices/field-office-faqs/faq/what-lockbox.

[27] Asylum Offices handle scheduled interviews (INA § 208) and cancellation of removal under the Nicaraguan Adjustment and Central American Relief Act (NACARA). *See* USCIS Services Overview — Asylum Office *available at* https://egov.uscis.gov/crisgwi/go?action=offices.type&OfficeLocator.office_type=ZSY.

[28] Some family sponsored petitions can be appealed to the AAO including battered spouse and children self-petitions. *See* 8 C.F.R. § 103.1(f)(2014).

[29] 8 C.F.R. §§ 1003.1(b), 103.1, 103.3, 103.4 (2014) (certification of a case is possible to higher officials).

[30] 2013 and 2014 Ombudsman's Annual Reports to Congress *available at* http://www.dhs.gov/annual-report-congress.

[31] 8 C.F.R. §§ 1003.3(b), 103.3 (2014).

[32] *See, e.g.*, 2014 Ombudsman's Annual Report to Congress *available at* http://www.dhs.gov/annual-report-congress.

[33] USCIS Responses to Annual Reports to Congress *available at* http://www.uscis.gov/tools/ombudsman-liaison/uscis-responses-annual-reports-congress.

As of 2011, USCIS has been in the process of converting all of its operations to an electronic application and adjudication process under the supervision of its Office of Transformation Coordination. The office is charged with managing and directing the development of the Electronic Immigration System (ELIS) to improve operations, customer service, and national security systems.

b.   Immigration and Customs Enforcement — ICE

U.S. Immigration and Customs Enforcement (ICE) is engaged primarily in interior enforcement of federal law relating to border control, customs, trade and immigration. ICE operations include more than 20,000 employees in over 400 offices located throughout the U.S. and in internationally in 48 countries. As of 2014, ICE has an annual budget of approximately $6 billion, primarily devoted to two operational directorates: Homeland Security Investigations (HSI); and Enforcement and Removal Operations (ERO).[34]

ICE's immigration enforcement activities include: apprehending, detaining, and removing noncitizens who have committed crimes or are within the U.S. in unauthorized presence; disrupting and dismantling organized smuggling of humans and contraband as well as human trafficking; investigating and prosecuting those who engage in benefit and document fraud; conducting worksite investigations; and enforcing compliance with programs to monitor visitors.[35] ICE takes custody of noncitizens detained during and after removal proceedings, and serves as one of the largest jailors in the nation.[36] ICE is the largest investigative branch of DHS, and its detention system is the largest civil detention system in the nation. It is composed of special agents of the former INS and Customs Office, former INS detention and deportation officers, the former INS immigration litigation section, including trial attorneys representing the government in immigration court, and Federal Protective Service employees.

The Office of Enforcement and Removal Operations (ERO) transports noncitizens, detains noncitizens in removal proceedings or awaiting removal, and removes unauthorized noncitizens from the U.S. A noncitizen comes into ICE custody in a variety of ways: as an applicant for admission at a border port of entry who is denied admission and who is eligible for review by an Immigration Judge; as an individual who entered the U.S. without inspection and has been apprehended by a CBP officer and are transferred to ICE for detention pending review by an Immigration Judge; and as an individual who has been arrested by an ICE Officer, with or without a warrant, inside the U.S. Once a noncitizen is in ICE custody, ICE officers will either detain the individual or release her on bond, an order of supervision or an order on her own recognizance. If a noncitizen is detained, she may be detained

---

[34] A third directorate, Management and Administration (M&A), operates in a support function. *See* http://www.ice.gov/about.

[35] *See* 34 INTER. REL. 2137 (Sept. 17, 2007) (discussing GAO report entitled *Department of Homeland Security: Progress Report on Implementation of Mission and Management Functions* (GAO-07-454, August 2007)).

[36] *See* ALIENIKOFF, MARTIN, MOTOMURA & FULLERTON, IMMIGRATION AND CITIZENSHIP, PROCESS AND POLICY 245 (7th ed. 2012).

during the pendency of the removal hearing and while awaiting deportation after a removal order has been issued.

ICE manages the largest civil detention system in the U.S. under national guidelines. In 2000, the former INS adopted the National Detention Standards which are based on standards from the American Correctional Association. In 2008, ICE updated and revised these standards and now operates under Performance-Based National Detention Standards (PBNDS 2008). Most noncitizens detained by ICE are held in state and local jails with general population inmates.[37] ICE is authorized, as of 2011, to maintain an average daily population of approximately 33,400 detention beds. Noncitizens are detained in ICE-owned service processing centers, contract detention facilities operated by private contractors specifically for ICE detainees, contract detention facilities for juveniles, and contract family detention facilities. There is significant and ongoing criticism of the conditions in detention and the treatment of those detained.[38]

The detention of noncitizens has increased dramatically in recent years.[39] During FY 2013, ICE detained 440,557 noncitizens.[40] The number has been at this level for the past three years although the FY 2013 number is an eight percent decrease from FY 2012 total detentions.[41] The total number of noncitizens in removal proceedings who spend some time in detention per year increased from 95,214 in 2001 to 283,115 in 2006.[42]

In 2012, the agency instituted major reforms of the detention system prompted by years of criticism.[43] These reforms included: the creation of an Office of Detention Policy and Planning (ODPP) to manage the sprawling detention system; independent reviews by a medical expert of complaints of denials of medical services requests by detained noncitizens; an oversight structure with new detention managers at 23 facilities which house more than 40 percent of the noncitizens

---

[37] Nearly 67 percent of the ICE detained population are housed in 250 local or state facilities, 17 percent are housed in contract detention facilities, 13 percent are housed in ICE-owned facilities (service processing centers), and three percent are housed in Bureau of Prisons facilities, which are funded either through congressional appropriations to the bureau or through ICE reimbursement. See https://www.ice.gov/factsheets/detention-management. *See infra* note 39, GAO Report.

[38] *See, e.g., Additional Actions Could Strengthen DHS Efforts to Address Sexual Abuse,* GAO-14-38 (Nov. 20, 2013); *Alien Detention Standards: Observations on the Adherence to ICE's Medical Standards in Detention Facilities,* GAO-08-869T (June 4, 2008); National Immigrant Justice Center, Report, *Invisible in Isolation: The Use of Segregation and Solitary Confinement in Immigration Detention* (Sept. 2012); Amnesty International, Report, *USA: Jailed without Justice* (March 2009).

[39] The increase is due in part to the "detention bed mandate" requiring detention centers to fill the authorized number of beds annually. See Chapter 14 for further discussion.

[40] DHS Annual Report Immigration Enforcement Actions: 2013 (Sept. 2014) *available at* http://www.dhs.gov/publication/immigration-enforcement-actions-2013. 90 percent of the FY 2013 detentions were noncitizens from Mexico (56 percent), Guatemala (13 percent), Honduras (12 percent), and El Salvador (nine percent).

[41] FY 2012 total detentions were 477,523.

[42] *Alien Detention Standards: Telephone Access Problems Were Pervasive at Detention Facilities; Other Deficiencies Did Not Show a Pattern of Noncompliance,* GAO-07-875 (July 6, 2007) (In FY 2007, ICE received $953 million in funding for detention services).

[43] Detention Watch, *About the U.S. Detention and Deportation System, available at* http://www.detentionwatchnetwork.org/aboutdetention.

detained by ICE; an Office of Detention Oversight (ODO) to conduct inspections and investigate detainee complaints.[44]

The ODO is located in the Office of Professional Responsibility (OPR), which operates outside of the ERO structure. The 2012 reforms also included ongoing external oversight of healthcare and general policies by two advisory groups; and the closing of a family detention center at the T. Don Hutto Family Residential Facility in Texas. Family detention had been severely criticized leading to the closure of the Hutto family detention facility, however since Spring 2014 ICE has used family detention to address the large-scale migration of women and children from Honduras, Guatemala and El Salvador.[45] A 2014 GAO Report documents different detention standards used at government-operated and contract facilities and a lack of consistent oversight and cost management by ICE of these different types of facilities.[46]

The removal or deportation of noncitizens is also managed by ICE, if the individual is detained by ICE.[47] In FY 2013, ICE conducted a total of 368,644 removals, including 133,551 individuals arrested in the interior and 235,093 noncitizens apprehended at the border, generally by border patrol officials and then transferred to ICE custody.[48] The removal of a noncitizen occurs under a variety of statutory mechanisms. Removals orders are entered by Immigration Judges after a hearing, and are subject to appeal to the Board of Immigration Appeals. The removal of noncitizens who have prior orders of removal occurs through the reinstatement of these prior orders which accounted for 39 percent of all removals in FY 2013.[49] ICE removal statistics include noncitizens subject to expedited removal at the border[50] and those who choose to voluntarily return generally waiving their right to a hearing before an Immigration Judge.[51]

---

[44] As of September 2012, the ERO operates a Detention Reporting and Information Line to receive toll-free calls of complaints of sexual or physical abuse and serious or unresolved problems in detention; reports of victims of human trafficking and other crimes and of individuals with serious mental disorders or conditions; parental issues such as the separation of minor child or other dependent; inquiries from the general public, law enforcement officials and others; and requests for basic case information.

[45] *See* https://www.ice.gov/factsheets/2009detention-reform.

[46] *Additional Actions Needed to Strengthen Management and Oversight of Facility Costs and Standards* (GAO-15-153, Oct. 10, 2014) (recommending that ICE document reasons why all facilities cannot be transitioned to the most recent standards, review reasons for differences in inspection results, and assess the extent to which it has appropriate controls for tracking facility costs).

[47] Removals occur by bus or airplane. ERO operates a bus fleet for the removal of Mexican nationals, and others are removed via commercial flights, chartered flights or DHS planes. *See* ALIENIKOFF, MARTIN, MOTOMURA & FULLERTON, IMMIGRATION AND CITIZENSHIP, PROCESS AND POLICY 246 (7th ed. 2012).

[48] ERO Annual Report: FY 2013 ICE Immigration Removals *available at* http://www.ice.gov/removal-statistics.

[49] INA § 241(a)(5). DHS Annual Report Immigration Enforcement Actions: 2013 (Sept. 2014) *available at* http://www.dhs.gov/publication/immigration-enforcement-actions-2013.

[50] INA § 237. Expedite removals accounted for 44 percent of all removals. DHS Annual Report Immigration Enforcement Actions: 2013 (Sept. 2014) *available at* http://www.dhs.gov/publication/immigration-enforcement-actions-2013.

[51] Return can occur under INA § 240B (voluntary departure), INA § 217(b) (visa waiver program), and INA § 252(b) (crew members) and INA § 212(a)(5)(D) (stowaways). DHS Annual Report Immigra-

c. Customs and Border Protection — CBP

CBP is responsible for border enforcement including the inspection of goods, all cargo and agricultural products, and the screening of noncitizens requesting admission. CBP immigration inspectors review passports and visas at all ports of entry into the U.S. (both at airports and land borders), and at a select number of prescreening posts in Canada and the Caribbean. CBP immigration inspectors inspect and admit both noncitizens and U.S. citizens. In FY 2013, CBP officers processed more than 360 million travelers at 328 U.S. air, land and sea ports.[52] CPB is responsible for the 5,525 mile border with Canada and a 1,989 mile border with Mexico. CPB's border security activities also include: detecting and preventing terrorists and terrorist weapons from entering the U.S.; interdicting illegal drugs and other contraband; and apprehending individuals who attempt to enter the U.S. without inspection within a reasonable distance from the border.[53]

CPB oversees a large-scale effort to increase border security using enhanced technology, the construction of fencing along the Mexican border, and other measures. A 2007 GAO Report found that CPB had achieved modest progress on border security as a result of delays in the implementation of many new programs.[54] Currently, CPB operates under a 2012–2016 strategic plan that incorporates risk analysis identifying "high-risk areas and flows" for targeted responses.[55] The increased use of unarmed aerial surveillance on the border has led to concerns about privacy protections. A 2014 GAO report found that this surveillance technology is not used only in border and coastal areas.[56] This is covered in Chapter 13.

3. Department of State

The Department of State Bureau of Consular Affairs historically has managed the overseas process for noncitizens prior to entry into the United States. This process involves millions of visas issued annually. In FY 2013, the State Department issued a record total of 9,164,349 visas and an average of 7.5 million

---

tion Enforcement Actions: 2013 (Sept. 2014) *available at* http://www.dhs.gov/publication/immigration-enforcement-actions-2013.

[52] CBP Fiscal Year 2013 in Review *available at* http://www.cbp.gov/newsroom/national-media-release/2014-01-17-000000/cbp-fiscal-year-2013-review.

[53] *See* 34 INTER. REL. 2137 (Sept. 17, 2007) (discussing GAO report entitled *Department of Homeland Security: Progress Report on Implementation of Mission and Management Functions* (GAO-07-454, August 2007)).

[54] *Department of Homeland Security: Progress Report on Implementation of Mission and Management Functions* (GAO-07-454, August 17, 2007).

[55] *See,* LEGOMSKY & RODRIGUEZ, IMMIGRATION AND REFUGEE LAW AND POLICY, CHAPTER 10 (6th ed. 2014); Doris Meissner, Donald M. Kerwin, Muzaffar Chishti, & Claire Bergeron, *Immigration Enforcement in the United States*, at 2 (Jan. 2013), *available at* http://www.migrationpolicy.org/pubs/enforcementpillars.pdf.

[56] *Department of Homeland Security's Review of U.S. Customs and Border Protection's Use and Compliance with Privacy and Civil Liberty Laws and Standards* (GAO-14-849R, Sept 30, 2014) (analyzing CBP policies about unarmed aerial surveillance (UAS) on protection of civil rights and liberties and UAS flight data from FY 2011 through April 2014; finding that use is not confined to border and coastal areas with flight data indicating over 80 percent of hours in border and coastal areas).

visas in each of the last five fiscal years.[57] State Department consular officers in over 200 offices located worldwide perform this initial screening function.[58] DHS monitors the issuance of visas by consular officers and now has veto authority due to perceived weaknesses in the visa issuance system before September 11, 2001.[59] The authority of the Secretary of the State Department relating to immigration matters is in INA § 104.

Consular officers review applications for visas to enter the U.S. and issue visas allowing a noncitizen to present herself for entry into the U.S. under INA §§ 221 and 222. Consular officers have extraordinarily broad discretion in the issuance of visas.[60] Their visa decisions are subject to random review procedures by supervising officers at the consular post overseas. In any case where the denial of a visa raises a question of law, a consular officer's decision can be reviewed by a visa review board in Washington D.C.[61] There are noncitizens who are exempt from the visa requirement, however most noncitizens must apply for a visa prior to entry. This is covered in Chapter 11.

The visa does not guarantee admission into the United States. It is merely the first step in the process, and provides the required documentation for airline travel to the U.S.[62] Generally, a noncitizen must present her visa in order to request admission into the U.S. at a border port of entry. The various procedures for admission into the U.S. are covered in Chapter 10. The regulations for the State Department are set forth in 22 C.F.R. Parts 40–53 and interpretations relating to the code are published in the Foreign Affairs Manual (FAM).

The Visa Office of the State Department also tracks the annual number of immigrant visas issued under INA § 201 through the publication of a monthly visa bulletin.[63] The National Visa Center (NVC), created in 1994, manages the immigrant visa application process after USCIS approves the immigrant visa petition and until the final immigrant visa interview at a consular post overseas. As

---

[57] The total number of immigrant visas issued annually from FY 2009 to FY 2013 has remained constant as required by the INA, with an average annual issuance of 476,497 during this period. A record number of nonimmigrant visas was issued in FY 2013. Report of the Visa Office 2013 *available at* http://travel.state.gov/content/visas/english/law-and-policy/statistics/annual-reports/report-of-the-visa-office-2013.html.

[58] *See* INA §§ 221, 222. INA § 101(a)(9) defines consular officer to include any consular, diplomatic or other officer or employee designated under the regulations for the purpose of issuing immigrant or nonimmigrant visas, or adjudicating nationality of individuals outside of the U.S.

[59] DHS may not require a consular officer to issue a visa if the consular officer has refused.

[60] The doctrine of consular non-reviewability is covered in Chapter 10.

[61] INA § 104(a)(1). This lack of review by the Secretary of State, the chief officer of the department, is designed to insulate consular officers from political pressure in visa issuance decisions. The random review of decisions began in 2006 to ensure professionalism and uniformity of decisions. *See* 22 C.F.R. §§ 41.113(i), 41.121(c) (2014), 71 Fed. Reg. 37494 (2006).

[62] *See* INA § 273 (it is unlawful for any person, including any transportation company, to bring to the U.S. any alien who does not have a valid passport and unexpired visa, if a visa is required).

[63] The monthly visa bulletin charts immigrant visa availability by immigrant visa category under INA § 203, and, in some cases by country based on the per-country limit calculations under INA § 202. *See* U.S. Dept. of State, Visas, *available at* http://travel.state.gov/content/visas/english.html.

of September 1, 2013, all immigrant visa applicants apply online. This is covered in Chapter 11.

The State Department has other units dealing with immigration matters. The Bureau of Population, Refugee and Migration (PRM) manages key parts of the refugee admissions process including assistance to refugees in overseas camps, and the admission of refugees into the U.S. through refugee resettlement programs.[64] The Bureau of Educational and Cultural Affairs (ECA) offers exchange and other programs for noncitizens coming to the U.S. for cultural, educational, or professional exchange. It supervises exchange programs that send U.S. citizens overseas as well. Noncitizens who participate in these exchange programs are known as J-1 Exchange Visitors and they are admitted as nonimmigrants under INA § 101(a)(15)(J). Nonimmigrant visas and related matters are covered in Chapter 8.

4. Department of Justice

The Justice Department retained the Executive Office of Immigration Review (EOIR) after the HSA reorganization of immigration functions. The EOIR contains three units: the Office of the Chief Immigration Judge; the Board of Immigration Appeals (BIA); and the Office of the Chief Administrative Hearing Office (OCAHO). A Director of the EOIR is appointed by the Attorney General and manages all three units.[65] The Attorney General has direct authority over the EOIR.

All of the EOIR units hold hearings to make decisions on individual immigration matters. The Office of the Chief Immigration Judge supervises the immigration judges located throughout the United States. Appeals of the decisions by immigration judges are heard by the BIA. Trial attorneys, now within ICE, represent the government in these hearings. Both the BIA and Immigration Judges are discussed in more detail below.

The OCAHO consists of administrative law judges who hold hearings under the employer sanctions regime established by the Immigration Reform and Control Act of 1986 (IRCA).[66] IRCA prohibits the knowing hire of unauthorized noncitizens and imposes employer sanctions.[67] OCAHO judges also hold hearings to adjudicate civil penalties for document fraud.[68] A second office created by IRCA, the Office of Special Council for Immigration Related Unfair Employment Practices, ensures compliance with IRCA's antidiscrimination provisions.[69] A major concern when

---

[64] PRM's mission is "to provide protection, ease suffering, and resolve the plight of persecuted and uprooted people around the world on behalf of the American people by providing life-sustaining assistance, working through multilateral systems to build global partnerships, promoting best practices in humanitarian response, and ensuring that humanitarian principles are thoroughly integrated into U.S. foreign and national security policy." *See* http://www.state.gov/j/prm/about/index.htm.

[65] 8 C.F.R. § 1003.0 (2014).

[66] Immigration Reform and Control Act (IRCA), Pub. L. No. 99-603, 100 Stat. 3359 (1986).

[67] INA § 274A.

[68] INA § 274C.

[69] INA § 274B.

IRCA was enacted was the possibility of employer discrimination based on national origin or citizenship status when verifying employment eligibility of workers. This office is part of the Civil Rights Division of the Justice Department. ICE conducts the investigations for proceedings before OCAHO judges on IRCA and document fraud matters.

a. Immigration Courts

Many decisions about the removal of noncitizens from the United States are made by immigration judges who are defined in INA § 101(b)(4). Immigration Judges must be attorneys and they are appointed by the Attorney General.[70] The INA states that immigration judges shall conduct proceedings to make determinations about the inadmissibility or deportability of a noncitizen under INA § 240(a)(1).

Before 1956, decisions about immigration matters initially were made by inspections officials, not lawyers. Many were concerned about this dual authority of inspections officials, i.e. to make initial decisions at the point of entry into the U.S. and to conduct hearings after this initial decision. However, neither the Administrative Procedures Act nor the U.S. Constitution require the separation of enforcement and adjudication functions.[71] The Justice Department gradually imposed a separation of these functions. The HSA is the first statute to recognize the EOIR as a separate entity within the Justice Department. The HSA effectively has created a statutory separation of functions by housing the EOIR in the Justice Department and moving the rest of the INS functions to DHS.

Before HSA, the Justice Department used its regulatory authority to organize immigration court functions. As of 1956, some officers were assigned to present evidence on behalf of the government and other officers were assigned to render decisions. The INS required special inquiry officers to have law degrees in 1956. In 1962, the Justice Department established a staff of trial attorneys to represent the government. The special inquiry officers were designated as immigration judges in 1973 by regulation. In 1983, the Justice Department established the EOIR to separate immigration judges from the INS entirely. This change was designed to ensure neutral and independent decision-making by immigration judges.[72]

The Office of the Chief Immigration Judge provides overall program direction, articulates policies and procedures, and establishes priorities for immigration judges. As of 2014, there are over 260 immigration judges in 59 immigration courts. The corp of immigration judges has increased significantly in the last 20 years from 85 judges in 1992. The judges' have very large caseloads of removal proceedings,

---

[70] 8 C.F.R. § 1003.10 (2014) (immigration judges are attorneys appointed by the Attorney General as administrative judges who conduct specified classes of proceedings including removal proceedings under INA § 240).

[71] *See* Wong Yang Sung v. McGrath, 339 U.S. 33 (1950) (holding that the separation of enforcement and adjudication functions was required by the Administrative Procedures Act (APA)). In response to Wong Yang Sung v. McGrath, Congress amended the APA to specifically exempt immigration proceedings from this APA requirement.

[72] Uniform rules of practice were adopted by the EOIR in 1987.

bond and detention determinations, and motions decisions.[73] In FY 2013, judges received over 271,279 removal cases and completed 193,350 removal hearings.[74]

One on-going problem is the lack of secretarial and other administrative support; judges frequently issue long oral opinions from the bench because of this problem. Federal courts have highlighted the problems faced by immigration judges in terms of caseload and support, and some have criticized the of job performance of immigration judges.[75] Numerous media reports about abusive immigration judges were published in 2005 and 2006.[76] In response, Attorney General Gonzalez ordered a comprehensive review of immigration judge and BIA operations in January 2006. The Justice Department introduced a 22-point reform plan in August 2006 including better training of Immigration Judges and EOIR staff, a formal code of conduct, and regular performance evaluations of immigrations judges.[77] The reform plan also addressed BIA operations.

A 2008 report of the effectiveness of these 2006 reforms discovered that many reform measures were not implemented. The report stated that the EOIR failed to conduct performance evaluations of immigration judges, or review the summary appeals procedures of the BIA and had not implemented a code of judicial conduct.[78] Other issues exist within the EOIR as well. For example, in 2008, the Justice Department also was criticized for using political affiliation and other improper factors to appoint immigration judges.[79]

---

[73] EOIR statistics reports include all "immigration court matters" which includes cases (deportation, exclusion, removal, credible fear review, reasonable fear review, claimed status review, asylum only, rescission, continued detention review, Nicaraguan Adjustment and Central American Relief Act, and withholding only); bond redeterminations; and motions to reopen, reconsider, or recalendar. FY 2013 EOIR Statistical Yearbook *available at* http://www.justice.gov/eoir/statspub/syb2000main.htm.

[74] FY 2013 EOIR Statistical Yearbook *available at* http://www.justice.gov/eoir/statspub/syb2000main. htm.

[75] Judge Richard Posner has been a strong critic of the bureaucratic decision-making process within the EOIR. *See, e.g.*, Benslimane v. Gonzales, 430 F.3d 828, 829–30 (7th Cir. 2005); Iao v. Gonzales, 400 F.3d 530, 534–535 (7th Cir. 2005); Mekhael v. Mukasey, 509 F.3d 326, 328 (7th Cir. 2007); Kadia v. Gonzales, 501 F.3d 817, 821 (7th Cir. 2007).

[76] *See, e.g.*, Adam Liptak, *Courts Criticize Judges Handling of Asylum Cases*, N.Y. TIMES, Dec. 26, 2005, at A1; Pamela A. MacLean, *Immigration Judges Come Under Fire*, NAT'L L.J., Jan. 30, 2006, at 1; Errol Lewis, *It's Time for U.S. to Bridle Unfair Judges*, NEW YORK DAILY NEWS, Aug. 15, 2006, *available at* http://www.nydailynews.com/archives/opinions/time-u-s-bridle-unfair-judges-article-1.640236 (describing immigration judges as "incompetents, bigots and bullies").

[77] *See Attorney General Outlines Reforms for Immigration Courts*, 83 INTER. REL. 1725 (Aug. 14, 2006).

[78] The report was produced by the Transactional Records Access Clearinghouse (TRAC) supported by Syracuse University and the Carnegie Foundation and found that six of the twenty-two initiatives were not completed including performance evaluations for judges and BIA members, the completion of a code of judicial conduct, and a final rule limiting BIA affirmances without opinion. *See* Spencer S. Hsu and Carrie Johnson, *Effort on Immigration Courts Faulted*, WASHINGTON POST, Sept. 8, 2008, at A6; Pamela A. Maclean, *DOJ Falls Short on Promised Immigration Judge Reform, Report Says*, *available at* http://www.law.com (Sept. 17, 2008).

[79] A DOJ Inspector General Report found that internet searches to determine political campaign contributions, voting patterns and affiliations were part of the screening process for immigration judges. *See* Spencer S. Hsu and Carrie Johnson, *Effort on Immigration Courts Faulted*, WASHINGTON POST, Sept. 8, 2008, at A8.

Widespread criticism of EOIR operations continues,[80] despite almost a 12 percent increase in the FY 2010 EOIR budget by Congress. Significant backlogs in removal hearings continue.[81] The number of pending cases at the end of each of the last five fiscal years has increased from 262,799 at the end of FY 2010 to the predicted of pending cases at the end of FY 2014 of 408,037.[82] Inconsistent decisions by Immigration Judges in the interpretation and application of immigration law creates a lack of uniformity which is a key means to promote fairness and accountability in the system.[83] The call for major reform of the immigration adjudication system have continued unabated with a focus on the possibility of an Article I specialized federal court or an Article III court.[84] The Federal Bar Association supports the transfer of responsibilities for the adjudication of immigration claims from the Executive Office of Immigration Review within the Department of Justice to a specialized Article I court for immigration adjudications.[85]

The lack of legal representation in removal hearings before immigration judges has been a major concern especially in the case of unaccompanied minors and other vulnerable populations.[86] The 2013 Senate Bill (S. 744), its version of comprehensive immigration reform, contains a provision to provide free legal counsel to unaccompanied children.[87] National attention to the extraordinary difficulties faced by

---

[80] See TRAC, *Immigration Backlog, Wait Times, Keep Rising* (July 19, 2012) *available at* http://trac.syr.edu/immigration/reports/286/; TRAC, *Immigration Backlog Rises for Another Year* (Dec. 8, 2011) *available at* http://trac.syr.edu/immigration/reports/269/; American Bar Association, *Reforming the Immigration System: Proposals to Promote Independence, Fairness, Efficiency and Professionalism in the Adjudication of Removal Cases* (2010) *available at* http://www.americanbar.org/content/dam/aba/migrated/Immigration/PublicDocuments/aba&uscore.

[81] *See* TRAC, *Widespread criticism of EOIR operations continue, despite almost a 12% increase in the 2010 EOIR budget by Congress available at* http://trac.syr.edu/phptools/immigration/court_backlog/apprep_backlog.php.

[82] See TRAC, *Backlog of Pending Cases in Immigration Courts as of August 2014 available at* http://trac.syr.edu/phptools/immigration/court_backlog/apprep_backlog.php.

[83] *See,* Cristina M. Rodríguez, *Uniformity and Integrity in Immigration Law: Lessons from the Decisions of Justice (and Judge) Sotomayor,* 123 YALE L.J. FORUM 499 (2014); Philip G. Schrag, Andrew I. Schoenholtz, Jaya Ramji-Nogales, James P. Dombach, *Rejecting Refugees: Homeland Security's Administration of the One-Year Bar to Asylum,* 52 WM. & MARY L. REV. 651 (2010); Jaya Ramji-Nogales, Andrew I. Schoenholtz & Philip G. Schrag, *Refugee Roulette: Disparities in Asylum Adjudication,* 60 STAN. L. REV. 295, 305 (2007) (presenting data to document a system "refugee roulette" in adjudications where "the outcome of a refugee's quest for safety in America should be influenced more by law and less by a spin of the wheel of fate that assigns her case to a particular government official.").

[84] *See,* LEGOMSKY & RODRIGUEZ, IMMIGRATION AND REFUGEE LAW AND POLICY, CHAPTER 10 (6th ed. 2014); ALIENIKOFF, MARTIN, MOTOMURA & FULLERTON, IMMIGRATION AND CITIZENSHIP, PROCESS AND POLICY 258 (7th ed. 2012).

[85] *See,* Bruce Moyer, *Practicing Before Immigration Courts and Understanding Their Structure,* 61 Federal Lawyer 43 (August 2014).

[86] *See,* Legomsky, *Restructuring Immigration Adjudication,* 59 DUKE L.J. 1635, 1695 (2010) (proposing an Article III court for immigration adjudication with two term for judges serving on an immigration court of appeals to "minimize both the profit in lobbying and the opportunity for capture"); Lawrence Baum, *Judicial Specialization and the Adjudication of Immigration Cases,* 59 DUKE L.J. 1501 (2010); Leonard Birdsong, *Reforming the Immigration Courts of the United States: Why is There No Will to Make It an Article I Court?* 19 BARRY L. REV. 17 (2013)

[87] "Border Security, Economic Opportunity, and Immigration Modernization Act," S. 744, 113th

children was precipitated by a mass migration of unaccompanied children, as well as women and children, in spring 2014 from Honduras, Guatemala, and El Salvador. One response to this acute need for legal representation is an EOIR sponsored program known as "justice AmeriCorps."[88] This new grant program will enroll approximately 100 lawyers and paralegals as AmeriCorps members to provide legal services to unrepresented children in order "to better serve vulnerable populations such as children and improve court efficiency through pilot efforts aimed at improving legal representation." It is anticipated that the new program will help identify child victims of human trafficking or abuse to assist in law enforcement investigations and prosecutions.[89]

EOIR backlogs in removal hearings increased once again in 2014, when it redirected immigration judges from their current caseloads to rapid adjudications at detention centers housing the women and children migrants from Central America. The DHS also assigned additional ICE attorneys and asylum officers to the border with the goal to ensure "cases are processed fairly and as quickly as possible, ensuring the protection of asylum seekers and refugees while enabling the prompt removal of individuals who do not qualify for asylum or other forms of relief from removal."[90] This fast track effort was widely criticized as infringing on due process rights and has led to litigation.[91] The reallocation of immigration judges to the border has increased the backlog in the current removal docket with reports of hearings in other parts of the country rescheduled, due to lack of resources, as late as 2018.[92]

b. Board of Immigration Appeals

The BIA rules on appeals from decisions of immigration judges. A right of appeal to the BIA exists for noncitizens found removable by immigration judges under 8 C.F.R. 1003.1(b). The BIA has appellate jurisdiction to hear final decisions of immigration judges in most removal cases, cancellation of removal applications, decisions involving fines and penalties, waivers of inadmissibility for nonimmigrants, decisions relating to bonds and detention in removal, and asylum decisions.

Congress (2013–2014) (introduced Apr. 16, 2013) (provides the right to appointed counsel to unaccompanied minor children, immigrants with serious mental disabilities, and other particularly vulnerable individuals).

[88] "justice AmeriCorps" is a partnership between EOIR and the Corporation for National and Community Service (CNCS),which administers AmeriCorps. CNCS is a federal agency that manages over 5 million Americans in service through its AmeriCorps, Senior Corps, Social Innovation Fund, and other programs.

[89] EOIR Press Release, Justice Department and CNCS Announce New Partnership to Enhance Immigration Courts and Provide Critical Legal Assistance to Unaccompanied Minors (June 6, 2014) *available at* http://www.justice.gov/eoir/press/2014/JusticeAmeriCorpsRelease06062014.html.

[90] American Immigration Council, *Children in Danger: A Guide to the Humanitarian Challenge at the Border*, (July 10, 2014) *available at* http://www.immigrationpolicy.org/special-reports/children-danger-guide-humanitarian-challenge-border (last check Oct. 22, 2014).

[91] M.S.P.C. v. Johnson, No. 1:14-CV-01437, (Dist. D.C.) (filed Aug. 22, 2014) complaint *available at* http://www.nilc.org/nr082214.html.

[92] Nancy Lofholm, *Backlogged Denver immigration courts will take on glut of asylum cases*, The Denver Post, Sept. 22, 2014 *available at* http://www.denverpost.com/news/ci_26585035/backlogged-denver-immigration-courts-will-take-glut-asylum?source=pkg.

Some decisions by USCIS immigration examiners can be appealed to the BIA including family immigrant visa petitions other than adoptions.[93] The appeal of some DHS decisions are heard by the AAO of the DHS (discussed above) and are not reviewed in immigration court, other discretionary decisions by DHS.[94] Immigration Judges may consider matters when a removal hearing begins if an application is renewed. In that case, the application is considered de novo; for example, an asylum application or an adjustment of status application.[95]

An appeals process for immigration decisions regarding admission and removal has existed since 1921 when the Department of Labor managed immigration matters. The transfer of immigration functions to the Justice Department in 1940 included the transfer of the appeals board. It was named, at that time, the Board of Immigration Appeals and it operated independently from the INS. Decisions by the BIA were made by panels of three judges. As the caseload of appeals increased over the years so did the composition of the BIA from its original five members. In 1987, BIA membership increased to 15 members and later to 21 members. The backlog of cases continued to grow and the BIA was the subject of a great deal of criticism. In 1999, the Board adopted a streamlining mechanism to lessen the backlog of appeals.[96] A key feature of this streamlined procedure allowed one BIA member to review an appeal.

In 2002 further efforts to decrease the appeals backlog were adopted under Attorney General Ashcroft. Currently, the regulations permit review by a single member of the BIA in a majority of cases.[97] A single member of the BIA may summarily dismiss an appeal, affirm an immigration judge's decision without an opinion (AWO), or issue an abbreviated opinion. These summary procedures have been upheld.[98] The Attorney General exercises final review authority over BIA decisions, although this authority is rarely exercised. A case may be referred to the Attorney General for a final decision when the Chairman of the BIA or a majority of the BIA members decide a case should be referred, when the Attorney General decides to take a case on referral, or when the Secretary of DHS requests a referral.[99]

---

[93] 8 C.F.R. § 1003.1(b)(4)-(7) (2014) (DHS decisions regarding administrative fines on transportation, some waivers of inadmissibility, and the denial of some immigrant visa petitions).

[94] 8 C.F.R. §§ 1003.1(b), 103.3 (2014). For example, decisions on nonimmigrant extension of stay applications or nonimmigrant change of status applications under 8 C.F.R. §§ 214.1(c)(5), 248.3(g) (2014).

[95] 8 C.F.R. § 208.14(c)(1) (2014) (asylum applications); 8 C.F.R. § 245.2(a)(5)(ii) (2014) (adjustment of status applications to LPR).

[96] Single member review was permissible upon a finding "that the result reached in the decision under review was correct; that any errors in the decision under review were harmless or nonmaterial." 64 Fed. Reg. 56,135, 56,136 (Oct. 18, 1999).

[97] 67 Fed. Reg. 54,878 (Aug. 26, 2002).

[98] *See, e.g.,* Zhang v. U.S. Dept of Justice, 362 F.3d 155, 157 (2d Cir. 2004) (finding summary affirmance by one BIA member does not deprive an asylum applicant of due process and citing cases from the 10th, 8th, 9th, 7th, 11th, 5th and 1st circuits also upholding the streamlining provisions).

[99] 8 C.F.R. § 1003.1(h) (2014).

The substantial criticisms about immigration adjudications in 2005 and 2006 included the BIA streamlined procedures.[100] Proposed BIA reforms included increasing the size to 15 permanent judges and using temporary members assigned to the BIA for periods of up to one year. A 2006 Justice Department 22-point reform plan dealing with immigration judges and other EOIR reforms also included reform of AWO procedure to reduce the number of cases subject to this form of review.

During the same time, the streamlined adjudications resulted in a significant increase in appeals to federal court, which rose from 10 to 25 percent and were often appeals of BIA affirmances without opinions. Federal judges also were concerned about the rise in the federal judicial caseloads as reflected in greater number of remands back to the BIA. The increased number of permanent BIA judges seems to have addressed some issues. In May 2011, the EOIR Director reported that the number of AWOs had declined to two percent of decisions, and that federal court reversals dropped from 17.5 percent in 2006 to 11.5 percent in 2010.[101] Despite these improvements, there are numerous reform proposals for the entire immigration adjudication system as discussed above.

5. Department of Labor

The Department of Labor (DOL) is involved in immigration functions in three different areas. A substantial part of DOL's immigration function occurs in the labor certification process for many employment-based immigrants.[102] Labor certification from the DOL is required before the USCIS will process these immigrant visa petitions. Employers seeking to hire a noncitizen in these employment-based categories must first obtain DOL certification that there are no workers who are able, willing, qualified or available for a position and that the employment of the noncitizen will not adversely affect the wages and working conditions of U.S. workers similarly employed. Denials of certification are reviewed within DOL by the Board of Alien Labor Certification Appeals (BALCA). Three-judge panels of administrative law judges review these cases. The labor certification process is covered in Chapter 7.

A second area where DOL has a significant immigration function is the employment of certain temporary workers. DOL oversees the initial process for nonimmigrants who enter as H-1B specialty occupational temporary workers or as other lower-skilled H-2 temporary workers.[103] Employers of these temporary workers, who remain in the U.S. for an extended period of time, must first process

---

[100] *See e.g., Overwhelmed Circuit Courts Lashing Out at the BIA and Selected Immigration Judges: Is Streamlining to Blame*, 48 INTER. REL. 2005 (2005) (in the period ending March 2003 petitions for review for immigration cases filed in federal courts had increased 379 percent).

[101] *See* ALIENIKOFF, MARTIN, MOTOMURA & FULLERTON, IMMIGRATION AND CITIZENSHIP, PROCESS AND POLICY 258 (7th ed. 2012).

[102] INA §§ 212(a)(5)(A), 203(b)(2) (advanced degree professionals or persons of exceptional ability), 203(b)(3) (skilled workers, professionals and other workers).

[103] INA §§ 101(a)(15)(H)(i)(b) (requires a labor condition application to be filed with the DOL for H-1B specialty occupational workers); 101(a)(15)(H)(ii); 20 C.F.R. §§ 651.10, 655 (2014) (requiring temporary labor certification for H-2A agricultural workers and H-2B seasonal workers); 101(a)(15)(C) (crewmembers engaged in longshore work must be paid the prevailing wage).

an application with the DOL before filing a nonimmigrant visa petition with USCIS. The Office of Foreign Labor Certification (OFLC) manages the admission of noncitizens in employment related immigrant and nonimmigrant categories. It is located within the Employment & Training Administration (ETA). Nonimmigrants are covered in Chapter 8.

The third area of DOL immigration activity relates to the employment authorization of both citizens and noncitizens. The Wage and Hour Division monitors and investigates employer compliance with immigration control recordkeeping requirements, and minimum wage and maximum hour laws.

6. Department of Health and Human Services — Office of Refugee Resettlement

The Office of Refugee Resettlement (ORR) within the Department of Health and Human Services provides assistance to refugees who are resettled in the U.S. under INA § 412. ORR administers domestic refugee resettlement programs that provide assistance to new refugees including employment training, English language training, and financial assistance. The Homeland Security Act moved the jurisdiction over unaccompanied minors to ORR and it has the responsibility for the care and custody of unaccompanied minors in immigration proceedings.[104]

The ORR is tasked with ensuring compliance with the 2008 amendments to the Trafficking Victims Protection Act (TVPRA).[105] The Trafficking Victims Protection Reauthorization Act (TVPRA) of 2008 expanded and redefined HHS's statutory responsibilities to require that unaccompanied children "be promptly placed in the least restrictive setting that is in the best interest of the child."[106] The TVPRA was enacted in 2000 and the 2008 amendments were added to address the particular issues faced by young people. The 2008 TVPRA amendments require that all unaccompanied children: be screened as potential victims of human trafficking; are exempt from certain asylum limitations; and are precluded from the expedited removal procedure.

The availability of ORR protection for children is based on their country of origin. Children from non-contiguous countries are transferred to ORR for trafficking screening, and placed into ordinary removal proceedings under INA § 240.[107] Children in ORR care are generally housed through a network of state-

---

[104] An unaccompanied child is one who has no lawful immigration status in the United States; has not attained 18 years of age; and for whom; (1) there is no parent or legal guardian in the United States; or (2) no parent of legal guardian in the United States is available to provide care and physical custody.

[105] Trafficking Victims Protection Act of 2000 (TVPA) defines "Severe Forms of Trafficking in Persons" as: (1) Sex Trafficking: the recruitment, harboring, transportation, provision, or obtaining of a person for the purpose of a commercial sex act , in which a commercial sex act is induced by force, fraud, or coercion, or in which the person forced to perform such an act is under the age of 18 years; or (2) Labor Trafficking: the recruitment, harboring, transportation, provision, or obtaining of a person for labor or services, through the use of force, fraud or coercion for the purpose of subjection to involuntary servitude, peonage, debt bondage or slavery.

[106] INA § 232(b)(2).

[107] Fact Sheet: U.S. Department of Human Services, Administration for Children and Families, Office of Refugee Resettlement, Unaccompanied Alien Children Program (May 2014) *available at*

licensed, ORR-funded care providers. In contrast, Mexican and Canadian children remain in the custody of CBP immigration inspectors who make a determination of whether the child is unable to make independent decisions, is a victim of trafficking, or fears persecution in her home country. If not, the child from a contiguous country will be returned without a removal hearing or the opportunity to seek other forms of relief.[108]

In 2013 and 2014, the number of unaccompanied children who needed ORR care and supervision has risen exponentially. Generally, an average of between 7,000 and 8,000 children are served annually by ORR. In FY 2012 the number of unaccompanied noncitizen children seeking entry into the U.S. increased to 13,625 children. The number of unaccompanied children to 24,668 referrals from DHS for the 12-month reporting period in FY 2013, and the projection for 60,000 unaccompanied children needing services in FY 2014.

The children come primarily from Guatemala, El Salvador and Honduras. Most are over 14 and approximately three quarters of them are boys. In FY 2013, origin of youth in this program was as follows: Guatemala (37 percent); El Salvador (26 percent); Honduras (30 percent); Mexico (three percent); Ecuador (two percent); and Other (three percent). Over the years, the breakdown per country of origin has remained relatively constant. This is covered in Chapter 14 in greater detail.

C. THE JUDICIAL ROLE IN IMMIGRATION LAW

The judicial review of immigration decisions is not widely available due primarily to 1996 and 2005 amendments to the INA.[109] Despite this, federal courts have an important role in the review of removal orders and other immigration decisions. Federal courts do have jurisdiction using a writ of habeas corpus for persons "in custody in violation of the Constitution or laws . . . of the United States."[110] The availability of a writ of habeas corpus is guaranteed by the U.S. Constitution in the Suspension Clause of Article I.[111] Noncitizens seeking habeas review must be in physical custody and petitions for writs of habeas corpus traditionally were a primary source of jurisdiction for the review of agency decisions.[112] The 1952 initial codification of immigration laws did not have a judicial review provision for removal orders. After the passage of the INA, however, declaratory and injunctive relief to

---

http://www.acf.hhs.gov/programs/orr/spotlight#fact-sheets.

[108] An unaccompanied child could be eligible for asylum, a nonimmigrant "T" or "U" visa, or special immigrant juvenile status.

[109] REAL ID Act of 2005, Title B of the Emergency Supplemental Appropriations Act for Defense, The Global War on Terror, and Tsunami Relief, 2005, 109 Pub. L. No. 12, 110 Stat. 231 (2005); Illegal Immigration Reform and Immigrant Responsibility Act, Pub. L. No. 104-208, 110 Stat. 3009 (1996) (IIRIRA); Antiterrorism and Effective Death Penalty Act, Pub. L. No. 104-132, 100 Stat. 1214 (1996) (AEDPA).

[110] 28 U.S.C.A. § 2241(c)(3)(2008).

[111] U.S. Const., art. I, Sec. 9, Cl.2 states "The privilege of the writ of habeas corpus shall not be suspended, unless when in Cases of Rebellion or Invasion the public Safety may require it."

[112] See Heikkila v. Barber, 345 U.S. 229 (1953) (habeas corpus was the only way of challenging deportation under the INA at that time).

challenge an exclusion or deportation became available under the Administrative Procedures Act.[113]

For nearly 35 years, until 1996 amendments to the INA, the path for judicial review was defined by former INA § 106. In 1961, Congress enacted § 106 establishing a grant of judicial review in U.S. Courts of Appeal for final deportation orders and establishing an explicit habeas corpus review provision. Under the 1996 IIRIRA amendment to the INA, Congress adopted a new scheme for judicial review found in INA § 242, and eliminated § 106.

The 1996 IIRIRA legislation retains judicial review in U.S. Courts of Appeal by petition for review. Judicial review of many immigration decisions is barred through jurisdiction-stripping provisions.[114] Entire categories of cases are barred from judicial review under these amendments including those dealing with certain criminal offenses.[115] In addition, many of the numerous discretionary decisions by DHS and immigration judges are not subject to judicial review, including inadmissibility waivers, relief from removal, and the adjustment of status to permanent resident. Congress adopted extremely deferential standards in the new judicial review scheme as well.[116] This is discussed in greater detail in Chapter 6.

Federal courts of appeal have jurisdiction to review constitutional claims and questions of law such as applying the wrong standard.[117] As noted above, after 1996, district courts continued to have jurisdiction to decide habeas petitions, including those brought by criminal noncitizens.[118] The 2005 REAL ID Act revised the jurisdiction of federal courts and requires U.S. Courts of Appeal to function as the sole means for judicial review, thus eliminating district court habeas corpus jurisdiction in nearly all cases.[119] Now, petitions of review of removal orders must be filed with federal courts of appeal and jurisdiction extends only to questions of law or constitutional claims. Further, the federal courts of appeal must decide cases based on the administrative record alone without any factual development.[120] This is covered in Chapter 6.

---

[113] *See* Brownell v. Shung, 352 U.S. 180 (1956) (exclusion); Shaughnessy v. Pedreiro, 349 U.S. 48 (1955) (deportation). The Administrative Procedures Act, 5 U.S.C.A. § 701 *et. seq.* generally permitting judicial review of final administrative decisions unless specifically precluded from review or some other mechanism for review is provided by statute. Review under the APA eliminated the requirement of physical custody of the noncitizen required in habeas corpus review.

[114] INA § 242(a)(2).

[115] Antiterrorism and Effective Death Penalty Act, Pub. L. No. 104-132, 100 Stat. 1214 (1996) (AEDPA).

[116] *See, e.g.*, INA § 242(b)(4)(D) (asylum decisions by the Attorney General [through Immigration Judges and the BIA] are "conclusive unless manifestly contrary to the law and an abuse of discretion").

[117] *See* Liu v. INS, 508 F.3d 716, 720–22 (2d Cir. 2007); Jean-Pierre v. U.S. Att'y Gen., 500 F.3d 1315, 1320–22 (11th Cir. 2007).

[118] INS v. St. Cyr, 533 U.S. 289 (2001) (bar on judicial review in courts of appeal in INA § 242 does not preclude habeas corpus petitions in district courts).

[119] INA § 242(a)(2)(D) (added by the REAL ID Act) (eliminating habeas corpus jurisdiction, mandamus jurisdiction, and jurisdiction under the All Writs Act, 28 U.S.C. § 1651, but permitting district court jurisdiction over nationality claims).

[120] INA § 241(a)(1).

Currently, the appeals to federal courts of BIA decisions remain a significant part of the federal court docket. In 2011, there were more than 6000 immigration appeals filed of a total of approximately 55,000 total appeals filed with the federal courts of appeals.[121] In some recent years immigration cases constituted one out of every six cases on the federal appellate docket, and a third of the cases in the Second and Ninth Circuits[122] Moreover, there are concerns about errors and inconsistency in federal court immigration adjudications as well as concerns about EOIR adjudications as noted above. According to a recent empirical study, federal courts of appeal have denied stays of removal while an appeal from the BIA is pending in only about half of the appeals. The study found that appeals to federal court were ultimately granted in these cases, but the noncitizens had already been removed and, therefore, unnecessarily deported to countries where they might risk persecution or torture.[123]

---

[121] *See,* Admin. Office of the U.S. Courts, *2011 Annual Report of the Director: Judicial Business of the United States Courts* 9 (2012), *available at* http://www.uscourts.gov/uscourts/Statistics/JudicialBusiness/2011/JudicialBusiness2011.pdf.

[122] *See* Stephen H. Legomsky, *Restructuring Immigration Adjudication*, 59 DUKE L.J. 1635, 1646 (2010).

[123] *See* Fatma Marouf, Michael Kagan, Rebecca Gill, *Justice On the Fly: The Danger of Errant Deportations*, 75 OHIO ST. L.J. 337 (2014)

Chapter 6

JUDICIAL REVIEW

Judicial review of administrative agency decisions serves to safeguard individual liberty and property interests. Two doctrines require deference by the courts to the Executive and Legislative Branches of the federal government on immigration matters. These two doctrines weave themselves throughout the immigration caselaw.

1. **The "Plenary Power" Doctrine**: This doctrine requires the courts to defer to the substantive — and, at times, procedural — immigration judgments of Congress and the Executive Branch, which the Supreme Court has declared to possess "plenary power" over immigration. The doctrine in operation shields from judicial review determinations of Congress about which noncitizens to admit to, and deport from, the United States. In creating the plenary power doctrine, the Supreme Court refused to review the constitutionality of acts of Congress in the late 1800s known as the "Chinese Exclusion laws." *See* Chs. 2 and 3.[1] The cases upholding the laws remain binding precedent. Relying on plenary power principles, the courts refused to disturb various immigration measures directed at Arab and Muslim noncitizens put into place by the U.S. government following the events of September 11, 2001.[2] At the same time, however, consistent with the Supreme Court's intervention to ensure judicial review of U.S. government measures taken in the name of security after September 11,[3] the Court generally ensures some kind of judicial review of most of the U.S. government's immigration decisions.

2. **Deference to Administrative Action**: Under ordinary administrative law principles, the courts often defer to the decisions of administrative agencies. Such deference is not limited to agency fact findings but includes

---

[1] *See, e.g.*, Chae Chin Ping v. United States (*The Chinese Exclusion Case*), 130 U.S. 581, 609 (1889) (rejecting a constitutional challenge to the Chinese Exclusion Act and emphasizing that courts lack power to review exercise of congressional "plenary power" over immigration).

[2] *See, e.g.*, Kandamar v. Gonzales, 464 F.3d 65 (1st Cir. 2006) (rejecting the argument that evidence obtained through "special registration" program should be suppressed on constitutional grounds); Ali v. Gonzales, 440 F.3d 678, 681–82 (5th Cir. 2006) (finding that the special registration program did not violate Equal Protection guarantee); Roudnahal v. Ridge, 310 F. Supp. 2d 884, 892 (E.D. Ohio 2003) (rejecting constitutional challenge to special registration program).

[3] *See, e.g.*, Boumediene v. Bush, 553 U.S. 723 (2008) (holding that detainees possessed the right to seek a writ of habeas corpus to challenge their detention at Guantánamo Bay, Cuba); Hamdan v. Rumsfeld, 548 U.S. 557 (2006) (finding that military tribunals created by Bush administration violated the law); Hamdi v. Rumsfeld, 542 U.S. 507 (2004) (ruling that a U.S. citizen held as "enemy combatant" had the right to judicial determination of the propriety of that classification).

deference to agency interpretations of ambiguous statutes through what is known as *Chevron* deference.[4]

In addition to the doctrines requiring deference to agency immigration decisions, Congress has imposed various restrictions on the review of immigration decisions. Congress specifically limited judicial review of immigration decisions in reform legislation in 1996 and 2005. Congress intended the reforms to eliminate perceived excessive delays through limiting "frivolous" appeals to the courts. These "court stripping" provisions have provoked considerable commentary.[5]

A.   THE NEED FOR JUDICIAL REVIEW

1.   The Immigration Agencies

Until the spring of 2003, the Immigration & Naturalization Service (INS), an agency in the U.S. Department of Justice, was the primary federal agency in charge of administering the Immigration and Nationality Act (INA), the comprehensive federal immigration law. For decades, immigrant advocates contended that the INS over-emphasized enforcement to the detriment of providing fair and efficient service to immigrants (including, but not limited to, timely and careful processing of visa applications and naturalization petitions). One empirical study of the judicial review of immigration decisions concluded that successful class actions designed to remedy perceived patterns and practices of violation of the law by the government, "coupled with Congress' failure to overturn their results, provide a clear signal that some important aspects of the INS' administrative performance were deeply and systematically flawed."[6]

In the spring of 2003, the Department of Homeland Security (DHS) assumed responsibility for administration of the immigration laws.[7] Although separating enforcement and service functions in different agencies in the Department, *see* Chapter 5, the DHS is criticized just as frequently as the old INS was. Numerous commentators contend that the DHS mission of ensuring "homeland security" has resulted in enforcement dominating other immigration objectives.[8] DHS

---

[4] *See* Chevron USA, Inc. v. Natural Resources Defense Council, Inc., 467 U.S. 837 (1984).

[5] *See, e.g.*, Symposium, *Immigration Appeals and Judicial Review*, 55 Cath. U.L. Rev. 905 (2006). For analysis of the various limitations on judicial review of immigration decisions, see Jill E. Family, *A Broader View of Immigration Adjudication Problem*, 23 Geo. Immigr. L.J. 595, 611–43 (2009).

[6] Peter H. Schuck & Theodore H. Wang, *Continuity and Change: Patterns of Immigration Litigation in the Courts, 1979–1990*, 45 Stan. L. Rev. 115, 177 (1992).

[7] *See* Homeland Security Act, Pub. L. No. 107-296, 116 Stat. 2135 (2002).

[8] *See, e.g.*, Jennifer M. Chacón, *Unsecured Borders: Immigration Restrictions, Crime Control and National Security*, 39 Conn. L. Rev. 1827, 1884–87 (2007); Thomas W. Donovan, *The American Immigration System: A Structural Change With a Different Emphasis*, 17 Int'l. J. Refugee L. 574 (2005); Kevin R. Johnson & Bernard Trujillo, *Immigration Reform, National Security After September 11, and the Future of North American Integration*, 91 Minn. L. Rev. 1369, 1396–1403 (2007); M. Isabel Medina, *Immigrants and the Government's War on Terrorism*, 6 Centennial 225, 230–32 (2006); Victor Romero, *Race, Immigration, and the Department of Homeland Security*, 19 St. John's J. Leg. Comment. 51 (2004); Noel L. Griswold, Note, *Forgetting the Melting Pot: An Analysis of the Department of Homeland Security Takeover of the INS*, 39 Suffolk U.L. Rev. 207 (2005); *see also* Jeffrey Manns,

immigration enforcement programs are the subject of frequent criticism.[9]

2. The Immigration Courts and the Board of Immigration Appeals

Existing separately from the DHS, an administrative adjudicatory system decides cases brought by the U.S. government seeking removal of noncitizens from the United States and claims of those noncitizens seeking, among other things, to resist removal. The Executive Office for Immigration Review is housed in the U.S. Department of Justice. Immigration courts hear evidence and decide removal and related immigration matters; the Board of Immigration Appeals (BIA) decides administrative appeals of immigration court rulings.[10] *See* Ch. 5.

The decisions of the BIA and the immigration courts have been the subject of sustained criticism.[11] The Board has long been challenged for, among other things, a lack of independence and neutrality. Other criticisms run the gamut from poor quality rulings (most charitably attributed to a high volume of matters to review), to bias against noncitizens, to simple incompetence. Such criticism increased after, in an attempt to reduce a backlog of appeals, the BIA "streamlined" its procedures to expedite its rulings.[12]

Respected court of appeals judge Richard Posner, a law and economics conservative appointed to the federal bench by Republican President Ronald

---

Legislation Comment, *Reorganization as a Substitute for Reform: The Abolition of INS*, 112 YALE L.J. 145 (2002) (predicting that the reallocation of power from the INS to the DHS will refocus immigration priorities to national security concerns).

[9] *See, e.g.*, Katherine Evans, *The ICE Storm in U.S. Homes: An Urgent Call for Policy Change*, 33 NYU REV. L & SOC. CHANGE 561 (2009) (criticizing raids of homes of immigrants); Bill Ong Hing, *Institutionalized Racism, ICE Raids, and Immigration Reform*, 44 USF L. REV. 307, 310–23 (2009) (analyzing negative impacts of raids by Immigration & Customs Enforcement, an agency in the DHS); Laura Donohue, Note, *The Potential for a Rise in Wrongful Removals and Detention Under the United States Immigration and Customs Enforcement's Secure Communities Strategy*, 38 NEW ENG. J. CRIM. & CIV. CONFINEMENT 125 (2012) (criticizing the DHS Secure Communities program); Stephanie Francis Ward, *Illegal Aliens on I.C.E.: Tougher Immigration Enforcement Tactics Spur Challenges*, ABA J., June 2008, at 44 (questioning aggressive DHS immigration enforcement measures); *The Shame of Postville*, N.Y. TIMES, July 13, 2008, at WK11 (criticizing a DHS raid of meatpacking plant in Postville, Iowa); *see also* Philip G. Schrag et al., *Rejecting Refugees: Homeland Security's Administration of the One-Year Bar to Asylum*, 52 WM. & MARY L. REV. 651 (2010) (evaluating critically application of one year bar for filing asylum application).

[10] *See* 8 C.F.R. §§ 1002–1003.11 (2013).

[11] *See, e.g.*, Sukwanputra v. Gonzales, 434 F.3d 627, 637–38 (3d Cir. 2006); Wang v. Attorney General, 423 F.3d 260 (3d Cir. 2005); Nuru v. Gonzales, 404 F.3d 1207, 1229 (9th Cir. 2005); Pamela A. MacLean, *Immigration Judges Come Under Fire*, NAT'L L.J., Jan. 30, 2006, at 1; Christina B. LaBrie, *Third Circuit Describes "Disturbing Pattern of IJ Misconduct" in Asylum Cases*, IMMIGRATION DAILY, Oct. 22, 2005, *available at* http://www.ilw.com/articles/2005,1027-labrie.shtm (last visited July 21, 2014).

[12] *See* Stacy Caplow, *After the Flood: The Legacy of the "Surge" of Federal Immigration Appeals*, 7 NW. J.L. & SOC. POL'Y 1 (2012) (analyzing the impacts of the increase in the appeals to the federal courts following the BIA's streamlining measures); Jill E. Family, *Beyond Decisional Independence: Uncovering Contributors to the Immigration Adjudication Crisis*, 59 U. KAN. L. REV. 541 (2011) (studying the dilution of judicial review resulting from BIA streamlining measures); Scott Rempell, *The Board of Immigration Appeals' Standard of Review: an Argument for Regulatory Reform*, 63 ADMIN. L. REV. 283 (2011) (considering the impacts of the reforms of the BIA on the Board's standard of review).

Reagan, is one of the most vocal critics of the decisions of the BIA.[13] As Judge Posner succinctly stated in one immigration appeal, "[a]t the risk of sounding like a broken record, we reiterate our oft-expressed concern with adjudication of asylum claims by the Immigration Court and the Board of Immigration Appeals and with the defense of the BIA's asylum decisions in this court . . . ."[14] In another opinion, he stated "[w]e understand the Board's staggering workload. But the Department of Justice cannot be permitted to defeat judicial review by refusing to staff the Immigration Courts and the Board of Immigration Appeals with enough judicial officers to provide reasoned decisions."[15] Judge Posner in still another opinion emphasized that "[d]eference is earned; it is not a birthright. Repeated egregious failures of the Immigration Court and the Board to exercise care commensurate with the stakes in an asylum case can be understood, but not excused, as consequences of a crushing workload that the executive and legislative branches of the federal government have refused to alleviate."[16]

a. BIA "Streamlining"

The administration of President George W. Bush took a number of steps that made the agency adjudication of removal decisions even more controversial, adding concerns with political bias as well as incompetence. In 2002, then-Attorney General John Ashcroft reduced the number of members sitting on the Board of Immigration Appeals (BIA), the single appellate body in the immigration adjudicatory bureaucracy, from 23 to 11, expedited the review of cases, and increased the numbers of summary dispositions by the Board.[17] In downsizing the Board, "[t]he axe fell entirely on the most 'liberal' members of the BIA, as measured by percentages of their rulings in favor of noncitizens."[18]

The "streamlining" measures resulted in an increase in the number of appeals to the federal courts of appeals by noncitizens ordered removed from the country. Some circuits responded with special rules for expediting the review of immigration

---

[13] *See, e.g.*, Benslimane v. Gonzales, 430 F.3d 828, 829–30 (7th Cir. 2005); Iao v. Gonzales, 400 F.3d 530, 534–35 (7th Cir. 2005). For analysis of Judge Posner's immigration jurisprudence, see Adam B. Cox, *Deference, Delegation, and Immigration Law*, 74 U. Chi. L. Rev. 1671, 1679–87 (2007).

[14] Pasha v. Gonzales, 433 F.3d 530, 531 (7th Cir. 2005) (citation omitted).

[15] Mekhael v. Mukasey, 509 F.3d 326, 328 (7th Cir. 2007).

[16] Kadia v. Gonzales, 501 F.3d 817, 821 (7th Cir. 2007).

[17] *See* Attorney General Issues Final Rule Reforming Board of Immigration Appeals Procedure (Aug. 23, 2002), *available at* http://www.justice.gov/eoir/biainfo.htm (last visited July 21, 2014). For commentary on the streamlining of the Board of Immigration Appeals, see Susan Burkhardt, *The Contours of Conformity: Behavioral Decision Theory and the Pitfalls of the 2002 Reforms of Immigration Procedures*, 19 Geo. Immigr. L.J. 35, 80–83 (2004); Michael M. Hethmon, *Tsunami Watch on the Coast of Bohemia: The BIA Streamlining Reforms and Judicial Review of Expulsion Orders*, 35 Cath. U.L. Rev. 999 (2006); Shruti Rana, *"Streamlining" the Rule of Law: How the Department of Justice is Undermining Judicial Review of Agency Action*, 2009 U. Ill. L. Rev. 829.

[18] Stephen H. Legomsky, *Deportation and the War on Independence*, 91 Cornell L. Rev. 369, 376 (2006) (footnote omitted). The BIA currently is authorized to have up to 15 members. *See* Board of Immigration Appeals Practice Manual (2013), *available at* http://www.justice.gov/eoir/vll/qapracmanual/BIAPracticeManual.pdf (last visited July 21, 2014).

appeals.[19] Although the number of appeals has since stabilized,[20] the quality of BIA decision-making continues to be the subject of criticism.

An influential scholar has advocated the replacement of the Board of Immigration Appeals with an Article III Immigration Court of Appeals.[21] Such a court would specialize in immigration matters and have judges with the independence through life tenure like that other federal judges possess.

b. Bias in the Immigration Courts?

The immigration courts have been the subject of criticism. In late 2005, the *New York Times* ran a front page story about how immigration judges treated noncitizens callously.[22] In response, Attorney General Alberto Gonzales formally instructed the immigration judges to improve their conduct.[23] Besides questioning the immigration court's treatment of noncitizens, the Bush administration also were found to have employed political litmus tests for the selection of immigration court judges.[24]

Along these lines, an empirical study of asylum decision-making published in 2009 has shown widely disparate results in the asylum decisions of immigration judges.[25] *See* Ch. 10. The evidence suggests a problem in the quality and

---

[19] *See* Lenni Benson, *Introduction to Seeking Review: Immigration Law and Federal Court Jurisdiction Symposium*, 51 N.Y.L. Sch. L. Rev. 3, 5 (2006/07) (discussing increase in immigration appeals and special rules adopted in the Second Circuit designed to improve efficiency of deciding the appeals).

[20] *See* Caplow, *supra* note 12, at 2–3. Appeals from the BIA to the court of appeals fell from 17 percent of the overall caseload in 2006, *see BIA Appeals Still Significant Part of Appellate Caseload*, Third Branch, May 2007, *available at* http://www.uscourts.gov/news/TheThirdBranch/07-05-01/BIA_Appeals_Still_Significant_Part_of_Federal_Appellate_Caseload.aspx (last visited July 21, 2014) to less than 15 percent of *all* appeals from administrative agencies in 2012, *see* United States Courts, U.S. Courts of Appeals, *available at* http://www.uscourts.gov/Statistics/JudicialBusiness/2012/us-courts-of-appeals.aspx (last visited July 21, 2014).

[21] *See* Stephen H. Legomsky, *Restructuring Immigration Adjudication*, 59 Duke L.J. 1635 (2010). For commentary on this proposal, see Lawrence Baum, *Judicial Specialization and the Adjudication of Immigration Cases*, 59 Duke L.J. 1501 (2010); Russell R. Wheeler, *Practical Impediments to Structural Reform and the Promise of Third Branch Analytic Methods: a Reply to Professors Baum and Legomsky*, 59 Duke L.J. 1847 (2010).

[22] *See* Adam Liptak, *Courts Criticize Judges' Handling of Asylum Cases*, N.Y. Times, Dec. 26, 2005, at A1.

[23] For discussion of Attorney General Gonzales's memorandum to the corps of immigration court judges, see Cham v. Attorney General, 445 F.3d 683, 686–89 (3d Cir. 2006).

[24] The Office of the Inspector General concluded that, in the selection of immigration judges, the Bush administration took into account ties to the Republican Party and other political considerations. *See* Office of the Inspector General's, Special Report: An Investigation of Allegations of Politicized Hiring by Monica Goodling and Other Staff in the Office of the Attorney General, Chapter 6 (2008), *available at* http://www.justice.gov/oig/special/s0807/chapter6.htm (last visited July 21, 2014).

[25] *See* Jaya Ramji-Nogales, Andrew I. Schoenholtz, & Philip G. Schrag, Refugee Roulette: Disparities in Asylum Adjudication and Proposals for Reform (2009). For commentary on the study, see Stephen H. Legomsky, *Learning to Live with Unequal Justice: Asylum and the Limits of Consistency*, 60 Stan. L. Rev. 413 (2007); Margaret H. Taylor, *Refugee Roulette in an Administrative Law Context: The Deja Vu of Decisional Disparities in Agency Adjudication*, 60 Stan. L. Rev. 475 (2007); *see also* Kate Aschenbrenner, *Ripples Against the Other Shore: The Impact of Trauma Exposure on the Immigration*

consistency of asylum decisions, thereby placing their legitimacy in question.

Concerns with immigration adjudication persist. In 2014, the president of the National Association of Immigration Judges offered one possible solution:

> Immigration courts must be restructured as real courts under Article I of the Constitution, similar to Tax and Bankruptcy Courts, so we can maintain administrative independence and ensure total transparency in our proceedings. This would free them from any control or influence by the Attorney General or Department of Homeland Security. While seemingly technical, this change is essential to achieve the most fundamental expectation we American's hold about judges: that they are independent and protected from undue influence by any party to their proceedings. It is a reform which is much needed and long overdue.[26]

3. The Curious Response of Congress: Restrictions on Judicial Review

In immigration reform legislation in 1996 and 2005, Congress restricted the authority of the courts to review the removal decisions of the immigration bureaucracy — and, in some instances, purported to eliminate all judicial review of certain removal and other decisions.[27] The restrictions ostensibly were designed to limit delays caused by baseless appeals. After the 1996 reforms, litigation continued for years about what, if any, judicial review of various immigration decisions was permitted under the reforms. The U.S. government consistently argued for limited, or no, judicial review of the cases of noncitizens convicted of certain crimes.[28] As we shall see later in this Chapter, the immigration agencies today make numerous final immigration decisions on a variety of matters not subject to judicial review.

It might strike one as peculiar that, at the same time that the administrative immigration decision-making bodies have been the subject of regular and heated criticism, Congress has consistently moved toward *less* — not *more* — judicial review of agency decisions. Indeed, one could most forcefully argue that careful

---

Process Through Adjudicators, 19 Mich. J. Race & L. 153 (2013) (analyzing the impact of trauma suffered by immigrants on immigration adjudications); Elizabeth Keyes, *Beyond Saints and Sinners: Discretion and the Need for New Narratives in the U.S. Immigration System*, 26 Geo. Immigr. L.J. 207 (2012) (examining narratives of "good" and "bad" immigrants that affect exercise of discretion by immigration courts); Fatma E. Marouf, *Implicit Bias and Immigration Courts*, 45 New Eng. L. Rev. 417 (2011) (analyzing implicit bias that influences the decisions of immigration judges).

[26] Dana Leigh Marks, *Let Immigration Judges Be Judges*, The Hill, May 09, 2013, *available at* http://thehill.com/blogs/congress-blog/judicial/298875-let-immigration-judges-be-judges (last visited July 14, 2014).

[27] *See* REAL ID Act of 2005, Title B of the Emergency Supplemental Appropriations Act for Defense, the Global War on Terror, and Tsunami Relief, 2005, 109 Pub. L. No. 12, 110 Stat. 231 (2005); Illegal Immigration Reform and Immigrant Responsibility Act, Pub. L. No. 104-208, 110 Stat. 3009 (1996); Antiterrorism and Effective Death Penalty Act, Pub. L. No. 104-132, 100 Stat. 1214 (1996).

[28] *See* Lenni Benson, *Back to the Future: Congress Attacks the Right to Judicial Review of Immigration Proceedings*, 29 Conn. L. Rev. 1411, 1438 (1996); Nancy Morawetz, *Back to Back to the Future? Lessons Learned from Litigation over the 1996 Restrictions on Judicial Review*, 51 N.Y.L. Sch. L. Rev. 113 (2006).

judicial review is *most* necessary when the agency's competence, independence, and impartiality have been seriously questioned. Especially when critically important decisions affecting a discrete and insular minority — which noncitizens unquestionably are — are at stake, meaningful judicial review arguably is a necessary procedural safeguard.[29]

B. CONSTITUTIONAL SCOPE OF, AND LIMITS ON, JUDICIAL REVIEW OF IMMIGRATION DECISIONS

This section first reviews the constitutional requirements for judicial review of immigration decisions. It then proceeds to look at the Immigration and Nationality Act's provisions for judicial review.

1. The Constitutional Right to Judicial Review

Before the passage of reform legislation in 1996, there were two types of proceedings under the U.S. immigration laws.[30] In "exclusion" hearings, immigration courts decided the claims of noncitizens seeking admission into the United States; in "deportation" hearings, immigration courts adjudicated cases brought by the U.S. government to remove noncitizens from the United States.[31] Congress and the Supreme Court allocated different constitutional and other protections to noncitizens in each of these categories of hearings. In 1996, Congress combined these two hearings into a single "removal" hearing.[32]

Immigrants in removal proceedings, as well as certain categories of noncitizens facing denial of admission, have a right to a hearing that comports with the Due Process Clause of the Fifth Amendment.[33] Limited exceptions to this general rule are discussed at the end of this Chapter.

---

[29] *See* Kevin R. Johnson, *Hurricane Katrina: Lessons About Immigrants in the Administrative States*, 45 Hous. L. Rev. 11, 40–43 (2008). Commentators have advocated careful judicial review of laws affecting noncitizens, a "discrete and insular minority," who cannot vote and thus cannot participate directly in the political process. *See, e.g.*, John Hart Ely, Democracy and Distrust 135–79 (1980); David Cole, *Enemy Aliens*, 54 Stan. L. Rev. 953, 981 (2007); Neal K. Katyal, *Equality in the War on Terror*, 59 Stan. L. Rev. 1365, 1383–84 (2002).

[30] *See* Landon v. Plasencia, 459 U.S. 21, 25 (1982) (distinguishing between deportation hearings and exclusion hearings) (citing Leng May Ma v. Barber, 357 U.S. 185, 187 (1958)).

[31] *See* Leng May Ma v. Barber, 357 U.S. 185, 187 (1958).

[32] *See* INA § 240, 8 U.S.C. § 1229a.

[33] *See* Landon v. Plasencia, 459 U.S. 21 (1982) (holding that a lawful permanent resident was entitled to due process in an exclusion hearing). For a detailed analysis of the facts surrounding *Landon v. Plasencia* and the impacts of the decision, see Kevin R. Johnson, *Maria and Joseph Plasencia's Lost Weekend: The Case of* Landon v. Plasencia, *in* Immigration Stories (David A. Martin & Peter H. Schuck eds., 2005).

a. Admission

i.   The General Rule

Two Cold War decisions epitomize the traditional narrow conception of the constitutional rights of noncitizens seeking to enter the United States. In *United States* ex rel. *Knauff v. Shaughnessy,*[34] the Supreme Court refused to intervene in a case involving the denial of admission of a noncitizen spouse of a U.S. citizen based on secret evidence, emphasizing that "[w]hatever the procedure authorized by Congress, it is due process as far as an alien denied entry is concerned." In *Shaughnessy v. United States* ex rel. *Mezei,*[35] the Court reiterated this holding in an even more extreme case — a noncitizen who lived in the United States for about 25 years was denied re-entry into the United States faced the possibility of indefinite detention because his country of origin would not allow his return. Both of these cases are prime examples of the harsh consequences of the plenary power doctrine at work.

ii.   Returning Lawful Permanent Residents: *Landon v. Plasencia* (1982)

The Supreme Court's 1982 decision in *Landon v. Plasencia*[36] involved the denial of entry to the United States by a long term lawful permanent resident who had left the country for a weekend in Mexico. It is the most significant contemporary development in the due process rights of lawful permanent residents.

In *Landon v. Plasencia,* the Court restated the essence of the plenary power doctrine that "an alien seeking initial admission has *no* constitutional rights regarding his application, for the power to admit or exclude aliens is a sovereign prerogative."[37] The Court went on, however, to acknowledge that "once an alien gains admission to our country and begins to develop the ties that go with permanent residence, his constitutional status changes accordingly. Our cases have frequently suggested that a continuously present resident alien is entitled to a fair hearing when threatened with deportation . . . ."[38] The Court further emphasized

---

[34] 338 U.S. 537, 544 (1950).

[35] 345 U.S. 206 (1953); *see* Charles D. Weisselberg, *The Exclusion and Detention of Aliens: Lessons from the Lives of Ellen Knauff and Ignatz Mezei,* 143 U. Pa. L. Rev. 933 (1995). For criticism of *Knauff* and *Mezei,* see Henry Hart, *The Power of Congress to Limit the Jurisdiction of the Federal Courts: An Exercise in Dialectic,* 66 Harv. L. Rev. 1362, 1391–96 (1953); Stephen H. Legomsky, Immigration and the Judiciary: Law and Politics in Britain and America 199–201 (1987); T. Alexander Aleinikoff, *Aliens Due Process, and "Community Ties": A Response to Martin,* 44 U. Pitt. L. Rev. 237, 237–39, 258–60 (1983); David A. Martin, *Due Process and Membership in the National Community: Political Asylum and Beyond,* 44 U. Pitt. L. Rev. 165, 173–80 (1983).

[36] 459 U.S. 21 (1982).

[37] *Id.* at 32 (emphasis added).

[38] *Id.* (citations omitted). One of the authorities relied on by the Court for this proposition was *Johnson v. Eisentrager,* 339 U.S. 763, 770 (1950), a decision that was much-debated in connection with the indefinite detention of two U.S. citizens who the U.S. government classified as "enemy combatants." *See* Hamdi v. Rumsfeld, 542 U.S. 507 (2004) (ruling that a U.S. citizen held as "enemy combatant" had the right to a hearing to challenge that classification); Rumsfeld v. Padilla, 542 U.S. 426 (2004) (finding

that "[w]e need not now decide the scope of [the plenary power doctrine precedent]; it does not govern this case, for Plasencia was absent from the country only a few days, and *the United States has conceded that she has a right to due process.*"[39]

The Court stated that the *Mathews v. Eldridge* balancing test, which is the generally applicable test for evaluating whether governmental procedures comply with the Due Process Clause, applied to determining the specific procedures that due process required in Plasencia's immigration case:

> [T]he courts must consider the interest at stake for the individual, the risk of an erroneous deprivation of the interest through the procedures used as well as the probable value of additional or different procedural safeguards, and the interest of the government in using the current procedures rather than additional or different procedures.[40]

Although declining to strike the balance of the interests in the case before it, the Court noted that Plasencia, a lawful permanent resident, had a "weighty" interest at stake and "[stood] to lose the right 'to stay and live and work in this land of freedom,' with the possible loss of the right to rejoin her immediate family, a right that ranks high among the interests of the individual."[41] "The government's interest in efficient administration of the immigration laws at the border also is weighty."[42] The Court cautioned the lower court on remand to limit its decision to "whether the procedures meet the essential standard of fairness under the Due Process Clause and [could not impose] procedures that merely displace congressional choices of policy."[43]

The courts have understood *Landon v. Plasencia* to require that the *Mathews v. Eldridge* balancing test applies to evaluate whether immigration hearing procedures are consistent with Due Process.[44] In 1988, the Board of Immigration Appeals ruled that a lawful permanent resident returning to the United States must be given reasonable notice of the charges, as well as a procedurally fair hearing with the government bearing the burden of proof; the lawful permanent resident could be

---

that the court in which the action was filed lacked jurisdiction over Padilla and could not entertain a challenge to his detention as an "enemy combatant"). In *Eisentrager*, the Court acknowledged that the rights of a noncitizen who had resided in the United States ordinarily increased with the length of residence, and were different from the much more limited rights of "enemy aliens" in times of war.

[39] *Landon v. Plasencia*, 459 U.S. at 34 (citation omitted) (emphasis added).

[40] *Id.* (citing Mathews v. Eldridge, 424 U.S. 319, 334–35 (1976)); *see* Kevin R. Johnson, *an Immigration* Gideon *for Lawful Permanent Residents* 122 YALE L.J. 2394 (2013) (contending that *Mathews v. Eldridge* balancing test requires the guarantee of counsel to lawful permanent residents in removal proceedings); Nimrod Pitsker, Comment, *Due Process for All: Applying* Eldridge *to Require Appointed Counsel for Asylum Seekers*, 95 CAL. L. REV. 169 (2007) (making similar arguments for noncitizens seeking asylum in the United States).

[41] *Landon v. Plasencia*, 459 U.S. at 34 (citations omitted).

[42] *Id.*

[43] *Id.* at 34–35.

[44] *See, e.g.*, Zadvydas v. Davis, 533 U.S. 678, 694 (2002); Flores v. Meese, 934 F.2d 991, 1013 (9th Cir. 1990), *rev'd on other grounds*, 507 U.S. 291 (1993).

excluded rom the United States only upon a showing by clear, unequivocal, and convincing evidence of inadmissibility.[45]

Some courts have viewed *Landon v. Plasencia* as standing for the proposition that the rights of lawful permanent residents increase as the length of their time in the country grows and thus are greater than those of first-time entrants.[46] Other courts have taken language from the decision to support Congress's plenary power with respect to the procedures accorded certain noncitizens seeking initial entry into the country.[47]

Some immigration law scholars read *Landon v. Plasencia* as opening the door to expanded constitutional rights for noncitizens seeking entry into the United States.[48] Other commentators, however, are more circumspect, emphasizing that the Supreme Court reiterated the basics of the plenary power doctrine and failed to define with specificity the constitutional rights of lawful permanent residents.[49]

Congress in 1996 amended the Immigration and Nationality Act to ensure that returning lawful permanent residents seeking to enter the country are generally not subject to the same procedures and inadmissibility grounds as first-time entrants.[50] Most lawful permanent residents at the border now are entitled to a removal proceeding, with broader procedural protections than enjoyed before the Supreme Court's decision in *Landon v. Plasencia*.

b.   Removal

Noncitizens physically present in the United States — no matter the length of time or immigration status — are entitled to a hearing that complies with the Due Process Clause before they can be removed from the United States.[51] Such a

---

[45] *See* Matter of Huang, 19 I.&N. Dec. 749, 753–54 (BIA 1988); *see, e.g.*, Khodagholian v. Ashcroft, 335 F.3d 1003, 1006 (9th Cir. 2003); Rosendo-Ramirez v. INS, 32 F.3d 1085, 1090 (7th Cir. 1994).

[46] *See, e.g.*, Rhoden v. United States, 55 F.3d 428, 432 (9th Cir. 1995); Campos v. INS, 961 F.2d 309, 316 (1st Cir. 1992).

[47] *See, e.g.*, Cuban Am. Bar Ass'n v. Christopher, 43 F.3d 1412, 1428 (11th Cir.), *cert. denied*, 516 U.S. 913 (1995); Haitian Ctrs. Council v. McNary, 969 F.2d 1326, 1340 (2d Cir. 1992), *vacated sub nom. as moot*, 509 U.S. 918 (1993).

[48] *See, e.g.*, Martin, *supra* note 35, at 214–15; Hiroshi Motomura, *The Curious Evolution of Immigration Law: Procedural Surrogates for Substantive Constitutional Rights*, 92 COLUM. L. REV. 1625, 1652–56 (1992) [hereinafter Motomura, *The Curious Evolution of Immigration Law*]; Hiroshi Motomura, *Immigration Law After a Century of Plenary Power: Phantom Constitutional Norms and Statutory Interpretation*, 100 YALE L.J. 545, 578–580 (1990) [hereinafter Motomura, *Immigration Law After a Century of Plenary Power*]; Michael Scaperlanda, *Partial Membership: Aliens and the Constitutional Community*, 81 IOWA L. REV. 707, 744–45 (1996).

[49] *See* Aleinikoff, *supra* note 35, at 260 n.65; Stephen H. Legomsky, *Immigration Law and the Principle of Plenary Congressional Power*, 1984 S. CT. REV. 255, 260 nn.25–26; Peter H. Schuck, *The Transformation of Immigration Law*, 84 COLUM. L. REV. 1, 62–63 & n.342 (1984).

[50] *See* Immigration & Nationality Act § 101(a)(13)(C), 8 U.S.C. § 1101(a)(13)(C) (amended by the Illegal Immigration Reform and Immigrant Responsibility Act of 1996, Pub. L. No. 104-208 § 301(a), 110 Stat. 3009-546–3009-575 (1996)).

[51] *See* Yamataya v. Fisher (*The Japanese Immigrant Case*), 189 U.S. 86 (1903); *see also* Won Kidane, *Procedural Due Process in the Expulsion of Aliens Under International, United States, and European Union Law: A Comparative Analysis*, 27 EMORY INT'L L. REV. 285 (2013) (identifying minimal restrictions

hearing is justified by the weighty life and liberty interests of the noncitizen at stake in removal hearings.[52] As will be discussed, the Supreme Court has consistently emphasized that the general rule is that, even when Congress seeks to limit judicial review, the Constitution requires *some* judicial review of a removal order. Importantly, immigration removal proceedings and their review are not governed by the Administrative Procedure Act,[53] the law that generally governs procedures followed by administrative agencies.[54]

C. LIMITS ON JUDICIAL REVIEW

As outlined in the introduction to this Chapter, there are two important judicially created limits on the judicial review of immigration decisions — the "plenary power" doctrine, unique to immigration law, and the ordinary deference generally accorded the decisions of administration agencies. In addition, Congress has enacted specific restrictions on the review of immigration decisions by the courts.

1. Plenary Power Over Noncitizens Seeking Admission

The judicially created "plenary power" doctrine, emerging originally to shield from review the laws barring Chinese immigration in the late nineteenth century, has protected from judicial scrutiny the decisions of Congress on immigration admissions criteria as well as, in certain instances, the procedures afforded to noncitizens seeking entry into the United States.[55] In the seminal *Chinese Exclusion Case*,[56] the Supreme Court emphatically declared that

> [i]f . . . the government of the United States, through its legislative department, considers the presence of foreigners of a different race in this country, who will not assimilate with us, to be dangerous to its peace and security, ... *[i]ts determination is conclusive on the judiciary.*

Generations of scholars have roundly criticized the plenary power doctrine,[57] which allows noncitizens to be treated in ways that would be patently unconstitu-

---

under international law on the expulsion of aliens and comparing them to those in place in the United States and European Union).

[52] *See* Fong Haw Tan v. Phelan, 333 U.S. 6, 10 (1998) ("Deportation is a drastic measure and at times the equivalent of banishment or exile."); Bridges v. Wixon, 326 U.S. 135, 147 (1945) (emphasizing that "deportation may result in the loss 'of all that makes life worth living' ") (citation omitted).

[53] Pub. L. No. 79-404, 60 Stat. 237 (1946).

[54] *See* Marcello v. Bonds, 349 U.S. 302, 309–10 (1955).

[55] *See, e.g.*, Chae Chin Ping v. United States (*The Chinese Exclusion Case*), 130 U.S. 581, 609 (1889) (rejecting a constitutional challenge to the Chinese Exclusion Act and holding that courts lack power to review congressional exercise of its plenary power over immigration). *See generally* Gabriel J. Chin, Chae Chan Ping and Fong Yue Ying: *The Origins of Plenary Power in* IMMIGRATION STORIES, *supra* note 62, at 7; Ch. 3.

[56] *The Chinese Exclusion Case*, 130 U.S. at 606 (emphasis added).

[57] *See, e.g.*, T. ALEXANDER ALEINIKOFF, SEMBLANCES OF SOVEREIGNTY: THE CONSTITUTION, THE STATE, AND AMERICAN CITIZENSHIP (2002); GERALD L. NEUMAN, STRANGERS TO THE CONSTITUTION — IMMIGRANTS, BORDERS, AND FUNDAMENTAL LAW (1996); Michael Scaperlanda, *Polishing the Tarnished Golden Door*, 1993 WIS. L. REV. 965; Kif Augustine-Adams, *The Plenary Power Doctrine After September 11*, 38 UC DAVIS L. REV.

tional if they were citizens. Although the doctrine has been limited by the Supreme Court in certain respects, as seen in *Landon v. Plasencia*, its core remains the law of the land.

In *United States ex rel. Knauff v. Shaughnessy*,[58] a case involving the noncitizen spouse of a U.S. citizen, the Supreme Court emphasized that "[w]hatever the procedure authorized by Congress, it is due process as far as an alien denied entry is concerned." Reiterating this holding in *Shaughnessy v. United States ex rel. Mezei*,[59] the Court refused to intervene in a case in which the noncitizen denied entry into the United States faced the prospect of indefinite detention because his native country would not accept him.

One of the results of the hands-off approach of the courts in reviewing the Executive and Legislative Branches' immigration decisions is a body of immigration laws that permits discrimination against groups of noncitizens that could not survive constitutionally if they were citizens. As discussed in Ch. 2, the poor, unhealthy, political dissidents, disabled, gays and lesbians, and many other categories of noncitizens have been — and some continue to be — disadvantaged under the U.S. immigration laws.[60] Moreover, unlike other areas of constitutional law, there has been little dialogue between the courts and Congress on substantive immigration matters.[61]

Generally speaking, the courts historically have deferred to the major immigration decisions of Congress and the Executive Branch. In *Sale v. Haitian Centers Council, Inc.*,[62] for example, the Supreme Court in 1993 upheld the U.S. government's much-criticized interdiction on the high seas of Haitians fleeing widespread violence and crushing poverty, in the face of powerful arguments that it violated international and domestic law, and emphasized that "we are construing treaty and statutory provisions that may involve foreign and military affairs for which the President has unique responsibility." *See* Ch. 3.

a. Removal Grounds for Noncitizens

Besides invoking the doctrine in evaluating the *procedures* for admission in immigration cases, the Supreme Court, as it did in the *Chinese Exclusion Case*, also has applied the plenary power doctrine in upholding the substantive grounds for deportation of noncitizens from the United States established by Congress. For

---

701 (2005). For a capsule summary of "cracks" in the plenary power doctrine, see STEPHEN H. LEGOMSKY & CRISTINA M. RODRÍGUEZ, IMMIGRATION AND REFUGEE LAW AND POLICY 164–66 (5th ed. 2009).

[58] 338 U.S. 537, 544 (1950).

[59] 345 U.S. 206, 212 (1953). For criticism of *Knauff* and *Mezei*, see *supra* note 35 (citing authorities).

[60] *See generally* KEVIN R. JOHNSON, THE "HUDDLED MASSES" MYTH: IMMIGRATION AND CIVIL RIGHTS (2004) (analyzing the discriminatory history of U.S. immigration laws).

[61] For exploration of the results of the lack of a dialogue between the courts, Congress, and the Executive Branch, see Motomura, *Immigration Law After a Century of Plenary Power, supra* note 48, and Motomura, *The Curious Evolution of Immigration Law, supra* note 48.

[62] 509 U.S. 155, 188 (1993) (citing United States v. Curtiss-Wright Export Corp., 299 U.S. 304 (1936)). For critical commentary on the case, see Harold H. Koh, *The "Haiti Paradigm" in United States Human Rights Policy*, 103 YALE L.J. 2391, 2391 (1994); Harold H. Koh, *Reflections on Refoulment and Haitian Centers Council*, 35 HARV. INT'L L.J. 1 (1994).

example, in *Harisiades v. Shaughnessy*,[63] the Court upheld the deportation of lawful permanent residents who had been affiliated with the Communist Party (before the law provided that the affiliation could not result in removal) and emphasized that

> any policy toward aliens is vitally and intricately interwoven with contemporaneous policies in regard to the conduct of foreign relations, the war power, and the maintenance of a republican form of government. *Such matters are so exclusively entrusted to the political branches of government as to be largely immune from judicial inquiry or interference.*

In the 2003 decision of *Demore v. Kim*,[64] the Supreme Court upheld the mandatory detention of certain noncitizens pending their removal from the United States and restated the fundamental plenary power principle that "this Court has firmly and repeatedly endorsed the proposition that Congress may make rules as to aliens that would be unacceptable if applied to citizens."

The Bush administration expressly relied on the plenary power doctrine in targeting Arab and Muslim noncitizens for the special registration program put into place in response to the events of September 11, 2001.[65] The courts declined to disturb this program.[66]

b. Discrimination Against Noncitizens in the United States

As seen in the cases involving the deportation of alleged communists, the Supreme Court has held that, in certain instances, the plenary power doctrine serves to immunize from meaningful judicial review *federal* laws that discriminate against noncitizens who are physically present in the United States. In finding that Congress could limit the eligibility of lawful immigrants for a federal medical

---

[63] 342 U.S. 580, 586–89 (1952) (emphasis added) (footnote omitted); *see* Galvan v. Press, 347 U.S. 522, 531 (1954) (deporting lawful permanent resident who had been affiliated with an organization deemed to be communist). *See generally* Kevin R. Johnson, *The Anti-Terrorism Act, the Immigration Reform Act, and Ideological Regulation in the Immigration Laws: Important Lessons for Citizens and Noncitizens*, 28 St. Mary's L.J. 833 (1997) (analyzing the history of ideological exclusion and deportation under U.S. immigration laws).

[64] 538 U.S. 510, 522 (2003) (citations omitted).

[65] *See, e.g.*, Registration and Monitoring of Certain Nonimmigrants, 67 Fed. Reg. 52584, 52585 (Aug. 12, 2002) (announcing the special registration program directed at noncitizens from nations populated predominantly by Arabs and Muslims and emphasizing that "[t]he political branches of the government have plenary authority in the immigration area") (citing Fiallo v. Bell, 430 U.S. 787, 792 (1977); Mathews v. Diaz, 426 U.S. 67, 80–82 (1976)); *see also* David Cole, *Out of the Shadows: Preventive Detention, Suspected Terrorists, and War*, 97 Cal. L. Rev. 693, 703–07 (2009) (discussing the Bush administration's implementation of widespread preventive detention of Arabs and Muslims at home and abroad after the events of September 11, 2001); Cole, *supra* note 29 (criticizing the various security measures directed at noncitizens after September 11).

[66] *See, e.g.*, Kandamar v. Gonzales, 464 F.3d 65 (1st Cir. 2006) (rejecting the argument that evidence obtained through the "special registration" program should be suppressed on constitutional grounds); Ali v. Gonzales, 440 F.3d 678, 681–82 (5th Cir. 2006) (finding that the special registration program did not violate Equal Protection guarantee); Roudnahal v. Ridge, 310 F. Supp. 2d 884, 892 (E.D. Ohio 2003) (rejecting a constitutional challenge to the special registration program).

insurance program, the Court emphasized that

> [i]n the exercise of its broad power over naturalization and immigration, Congress regularly makes rules that would be unacceptable if applied to citizens. The exclusion of aliens and the reservation of the power to deport have no permissible counterpart in the Federal Government's power to regulate the conduct of its own citizenry. The fact that an Act of Congress treats aliens differently from citizens does not itself imply that such disparate treatment is "invidious."[67]

Other decisions demonstrate ambivalence in the Court's constitutional jurisprudence with respect to the rights of noncitizens, especially when it comes to *state* laws that discriminate against noncitizens.[68] In *Plyler v. Doe*,[69] for example, the Supreme Court found that a Texas law effectively barring undocumented children from the public elementary and secondary schools, violated the Fourteenth Amendment. Similarly, in *Graham v. Richardson*,[70] the Court applied strict scrutiny to strike down under the Equal Protection Clause a state law barring certain legal immigrants from receiving public benefits.

Ambivalence also can be seen in the review of federal law and policy concerning the rights of immigrants. For example, the Supreme Court in *Zadvydas v. Davis*[71] refused to invoke the plenary power doctrine to shield from review the indefinite detention of noncitizens awaiting deportation from the United States.

Despite the dictates of the plenary power doctrine, lower courts at times have employed limited rationality review in reviewing the constitutionality of the application of the immigration laws. In *Francis v. INS*,[72] for example, the U.S. Court of Appeals for the Second Circuit exercised rational basis review under the Equal Protection Clause to ensure that relief from removal was available to a category of noncitizens under the immigration laws that was available to other groups of noncitizens.

In sum, judicial intervention in the immigration laws has ordinarily been limited to ensuring that proper procedural protections are in place in removal hearings, but generally not guaranteeing meaningful review of substantive immigration decisions in the laws passed by Congress.[73] The Supreme Court has appeared to be less

---

[67] Mathews v. Diaz, 426 U.S. 67, 79–80 (1976) (footnotes omitted); *see* Reno v. Flores, 507 U.S. 292, 305–06 (1993) (invoking plenary power doctrine in upholding regulation limiting release from detention of juvenile noncitizens).

[68] *See generally* LINDA S. BOSNIAK, THE CITIZEN AND THE ALIEN: DILEMMAS OF CONTEMPORARY MEMBERSHIP (2006) (analyzing the ambivalence in American law about the legal status of aliens).

[69] 457 U.S. 202 (1982).

[70] 403 U.S. 365 (1971).

[71] 533 U.S. 678, 695–96 (2001). *But see* Demore v. Kim, 538 U.S. 510, 522 (2003) (invoking the plenary power doctrine to uphold mandatory detention of noncitizens pending removal).

[72] 532 F.2d 268 (2d Cir. 1976); *see, e.g.*, Cato v. INS 84 F.3d 597, 601–02 (2d Cir. 1996); Variamparambil v. INS, 831 F.2d 1362, 1364 (7th Cir. 1987); Augustin v. Sava, 735 F.2d 32 (2d Cir. 1984); Tapia-Acuna v. INS, 640 F.2d 223, 225 (9th Cir. 1981).

[73] *Compare* Landon v. Plasencia, 459 U.S. 21 (1982) (holding that a lawful permanent resident was entitled to due process in exclusion hearing), *with* Demore v. Kim, 538 U.S. 510, 517–33 (2003) (finding

deferential to state laws discriminating against immigrants.

c. Gender Distinctions in the Nationality Laws

Outside the immigration laws, the modern Supreme Court has not hesitated to invalidate outdated distinctions based on gender stereotypes.[74] However, in *Fiallo v. Bell*,[75] the Court in 1977 invoked the plenary power doctrine and upheld gender discrimination in the immigration and nationality laws, emphasizing that

> it is important to underscore the limited scope of judicial inquiry into immigration legislation. *This Court has repeatedly emphasized that "over no conceivable subject is the legislative power of Congress more complete than it is over" the admission of aliens* . . . . Our cases "have long recognized the power to expel or exclude aliens as a fundamental sovereign attribute exercised by the Government's political departments largely immune from judicial control." . . . .

In 2001, the Court upheld a distinction in the Immigration and Nationality Act concerning U.S. citizenship between illegitimate children of U.S. citizen fathers and mothers but did not invoke the plenary power doctrine; it applied the same scrutiny it generally applies to gender classifications under ordinary constitutional law.[76] A decade later, an equally divided 4-4 Court[77] affirmed a court of appeals' ruling rejecting a constitutional challenge to federal law establishing different standards for children born out of wedlock outside of the United States to obtain U.S. citizenship, depending on whether the child's mother or father was a citizen (with mothers favored over fathers with respect to bestowing citizenship on children).

---

that Congress could lawfully find that noncitizens subject to removal on certain criminal grounds could be detained pending deportation), *and* Kleindienst v. Mandel, 408 U.S. 753, 766 (1972) (refusing to intervene in a case in which U.S. government denied temporary entry to Belgian journalist allegedly because of his advocacy of communism and emphasizing that Congress has " 'plenary power to make rules for the admission of aliens and to exclude those who possess those characteristics which Congress has forbidden' ") (citation omitted).

[74] *See, e.g.*, United States v. Virginia, 518 U.S. 515 (1996) (striking down Virginia Military Institute's male-only admission policy); Mississippi Univ. for Women v. Hogan, 458 U.S. 718 (1982) (invalidating university's single sex admission policy).

[75] 430 U.S. 787, 792 (1977) (emphasis added).

[76] *See* Nguyen v. INS, 533 U.S. 53 (2001); *see also* Miller v. Albright, 523 U.S. 420 (1998) (declining to invalidate a similar gender-based distinction in nationality laws); Pierre v. Holder, 588 F.3d 767 (2d Cir. 2013) (rejecting the claim that gender discrimination in U.S. nationality law violated the Equal Protection Clause). For analysis of the caselaw, see Albertina Antognini, *From Citizenship to Custody: Unwed Fathers Abroad and at Home*, 36 Harv. J. L. & Gender 405 (2013); Nina Pillard, *Plenary Power Underground in* Nguyen v. INS: *A Response to Professor Spiro*, 16 Geo. Immigr. L.J. 835 (2002); Jessica Portness, Comment, *Until the Plenary Power Do Us Part: Judicial Scrutiny of the Defense of Marriage Act in Immigration After* Flores-Villar, 61 Am. U.L. Rev. 1825 (2012). Analysis of the genesis of the gender-based nationality distinctions as part of an effort to enforce racial exclusions in the immigration laws can be found in Kristin A. Collins, *Illegitimate Borders: Jus Sanguinis Citizenship and the Legal Construction of Family, Race, and Nation*, 123 Yale L.J. 2134 (2014).

[77] Flores-Villar v. United States, 131 S. Ct. 2312 (2011).

2. Agency Deference

Administrative agencies within the Executive Branch enforce U.S. immigration law. General administrative law principles call for significant deference to the factual and legal determinations of administrative agencies. In immigration cases, the Supreme Court typically follows these general principles.

a. Fact Finding

Judicial deference to the fact-finding of the immigration agencies is well-established. In *INS v. Elias Zacarias*,[78] for example, the Supreme Court articulated a potent form of deference to the fact-finding of the Board of Immigration Appeals. The Court held that, to reverse a Board fact determination, the asylum applicant must show that the evidence "was such that a reasonable fact-finder would have to conclude that the requisite fear of persecution existed." Congress in 1996 codified the Court's holding.[79]

b. *Chevron* Deference

In the landmark decision of *Chevron USA v. Natural Resources Defense Council, Inc.*,[80] the Supreme Court extended judicial deference to administrative agency interpretations of ambiguous statutes. The Court in that case pronounced that the courts must defer to the agency's reasonable interpretation of a statute that Congress has through ambiguous statutory language delegated it the power to interpret.[81] *Chevron* "dramatically expanded the circumstances in which courts

---

[78] 502 U.S. 478, 481 (1992) (citing NLRB v. Columbian Enameling & Stamping Co., 306 U.S. 292 (1939)) (footnote omitted). For analysis of *INS v. Elias Zacarias*, see Kevin R. Johnson, *Responding to the "Litigation Explosion": The Plain Meaning of Executive Branch Primacy Over Immigration*, 71 N.C. L. Rev. 413, 461–72 (1993); Stephen M. Knight, *Shielded from Review: The Questionable Birth and Development of the Asylum Standard of Review Under* Elias-Zacarias, 20 Geo. Immigr. L.J. 133, 133 (2005); Karen Musalo, *Irreconcilable Differences? Divorcing Refugee Protections from Human Rights Norms*, 15 Mich. J. Int'l L. 1179 (1994).

[79] *See* INA § 242(b)(4)(B), 8 U.S.C. § 1252(b)(4)(B) ("[T]he administrative findings of fact are conclusive unless any reasonable adjudicator would be compelled to conclude to the contrary.") (enacted as part of the Illegal Immigration Reform and Immigrant Responsibility Act of 1996 (IIRIRA), Pub. L. No. 104-208, 110 Stat. 3009-546); *see, e.g.*, Dia v. Ashcroft, 353 F.3d 228, 248 (3d Cir. 2003); Korytnyuk v. Ashcroft, 396 F.3d 272, 286 (3d Cir. 2005).

[80] 467 U.S. 837 (1984). For analysis of *Chevron* deference in immigration cases, see Shruti Rana, Chevron *Without the Courts?: The Supreme Court's Recent Chevron Jurisprudence Through an Immigration Lens*, 26 Geo. Immigr. L.J. 313 (2012); Brian G. Slocum, *The Immigration Rule of Lenity and* Chevron *Deference*, 17 Geo. Immigr. L.J. 515 (2003); Paul Chaffin, Note, *Expertise and Immigration Administration: When Does* Chevron *Apply to BIA Interpretations of the INA?*, 69 NYU Ann. Surv. Am. L. 503 (2013); *see also* Bassina Farbenblum, *Executive Deference in U.S. Refugee Law: Internationalist Paths Through and Beyond* Chevron, 60 Duke L.J. 1059 (2011) (contending that *Chevron* deference should not be applied to the interpretation of asylum laws by the Board of Immigration Appeals).

[81] In the Court's words,

Judges are not experts in the field, and are not part of either political branch of the government . . . . [A]n agency to which Congress has delegated policymaking responsibilities may, within the limits of that delegation, properly rely upon the incumbent administration's views of wise policy to inform its judgments. *While agencies are not directly accountable to the people, the Chief Executive is, and it is entirely appropriate for this political branch of*

must defer to agency interpretations of statutes."[82]

The courts frequently apply *Chevron*, as well as related forms of agency deference, to the Board of Immigration Appeals (BIA) immigration decisions. In *INS v. Aguirre-Aguirre*,[83] for example, the Supreme Court reversed a court of appeals ruling that the Board had improperly denied relief to an applicant for asylum and withholding of deportation because he had committed "serious nonpolitical crimes" that, under the applicable statutory language, rendered the applicant ineligible for relief:

> the Court of Appeals failed to accord the required level of deference to the interpretation of the serious nonpolitical crime exception adopted by the Attorney General and the BIA. Because the Court of Appeals confronted questions implicating "an agency's construction of the statute which it administers," the court should have applied the principles of deference described in *Chevron U.S.A. Inc. v. Natural Resources Defense Council, Inc . . . .*

The Court went on to explain that "we have recognized that judicial deference to the Executive Branch is especially appropriate in the immigration context where officials 'exercise especially sensitive political functions that implicate questions of foreign relations.' "[84]

In recent years, the Roberts Court has utilized *Chevron* and other forms of deference in a routine fashion in its review of BIA decisions.[85] In 2012, for example a unanimous Court[86] deferred to the Board's construction of the statutory provision that forbid the imputation of the years of a parent's residency in the United States to a minor child for the purpose of calculating the number of years necessary under the law to be eligible for relief from removal known as cancellation of removal. *See* Ch. 12. Concluding that the Board's position was a reasonable construction of the ambiguous statutory provision in question, the Court found that it was entitled to deference under *Chevron U.S.A. Inc. v. Natural Resources Defense Council, Inc.*[87]

---

the *Government to make such policy choices* — resolving the competing interests which Congress itself either inadvertently did not resolve, or intentionally left to be resolved by the agency charged with the administration of the statute in light of everyday realities.

Chevron USA v. Natural Resources Defense Council, Inc., 467 U.S. at 865–66 (emphasis added).

[82] Thomas W. Merrill & Kristin E. Hickman, Chevron's *Domain*, 89 Geo. L.J. 833, 833 (2001).

[83] 526 U.S. 415, 424 (1999) (citation omitted).

[84] *Id.* at 425 (quoting INS v. Abudu, 485 U.S. 94, 110 (1988)). Ch. 3 analyzes the foreign relations power as one possible constitutional rationale for the federal power to regulate immigration.

[85] *See* Kevin R. Johnson, *Immigration in the Supreme Court, 2009–13: A New Era of Immigration Law Unexceptionalism?*, 66 Okla. L. Rev (forthcoming 2015).

[86] *See* Holder v. Gutierrez, 132 S. Ct. 2011, 2014–15 (2012); *see also* Scialabba v. Cuellar de Osorio, 134 S. Ct. 2191, 2213 (2014) (plurality opinion) (deferring to the BIA's interpretation of family visa provisions of the Immigration and Nationality Act and finding that the case was ideally suited to *Chevron* deference).

[87] *See Holder v. Gutierrez*, 132 S. Ct. at 2021. For criticism of the Court's decision, see Johanna K.P. Dennis, *"Mommy, Where is Home?" Imputing Parental Immigration Status and Residency for Undocumented Immigrant Children*, 45 J. Marshall L. Rev. 991 (2012).

The Supreme Court, however, will not defer to an agency interpretation of the law that is contrary to Congressional intent. In *INS v. Cardoza-Fonseca*,[88] the Court rejected the Board of Immigration Appeal's interpretation of the Immigration and Nationality Act's provisions governing the burden of proof on a noncitizen seeking asylum in the United States. *See* Ch. 12. The Court found that Congress intended the "well-founded fear of persecution" standard for asylum to be "more generous" than the "clear probability of persecution" standard necessary to establish entitlement to another form of relief then known as withholding of deportation.[89] Because the Court found that the agency's interpretation was contrary to the intent of Congress as determined through reliance on "traditional tools of statutory construction," it refused to apply *Chevron* deference to the BIA's interpretation of the statute.[90]

Similarly, in *INS v. St. Cyr*,[91] the Supreme Court refused to extend *Chevron* deference to the BIA's interpretation of a provision of the 1996 immigration reforms restricting judicial review of removal decisions of the BIA because it found that "there was no ambiguity in the statute for an agency to resolve," a prerequisite for deference. The Court also found that "substantial constitutional questions" would arise if there was no avenue for judicial review of a removal decision.[92]

Judulang v. Holder[93] is another example of the Supreme Court's rejection of the BIA's interpretation of a statute. The U.S. government sought to remove a lawful permanent resident from the Philippines who had lived in this country since 1974, based on a criminal conviction. Former Section 212(c) of the Immigration and Nationality Act provided for a "waiver of excludability" allowing a noncitizen to relief preventing removal from the country despite a criminal conviction. The BIA ruled, and the court of appeals agreed, that Judulang was not eligible for relief from removal under Section 212(c).[94] Writing for a unanimous Court, Justice Elena Kagan emphatically disagreed:

> This case concerns the Board of Immigration Appeals' . . . policy for deciding when resident aliens may apply to the Attorney General for relief from deportation under a now-repealed provision of the immigration laws. We hold that the BIA's approach is arbitrary and capricious. The legal background of this case is complex, but the principle guiding our decision is anything but. *When an administrative agency sets policy, it must*

---

[88] 480 U.S. 421 (1987).

[89] *See id.* at 430.

[90] *See id.* at 446; *see, e.g.*, INS v. Aguirre-Aguirre, 526 U.S. 415, 427–28 (1999); Singh v. Gonzales, 451 F.3d 400, 403–04 (6th Cir. 2006); Ucelo-Gomez v. Gonzales, 448 F.3d 180, 185–88 (2d Cir. 2006); Zheng v. Gonzales, 422 F.3d 98, 112–20 (3d Cir. 2005); Soliman v. Gonzales, 419 F.3d 276, 281–86 (4th Cir. 2005); Gao v. Ashcroft, 299 F.3d 266, 271–72 (3d Cir. 2002); Chowdhury v. INS, 249 F.3d 970, 972–73 (9th Cir. 2001). In interpreting the statutory provision in question, the Court relied on the language of the statute, legislative history, and international law. *See INS v. Cardoza-Fonseca*, 480 U.S. at 427–43.

[91] 533 U.S. 289, 320 n.45 (2001).

[92] *See id.* at 300.

[93] 132 S. Ct. 476 (2011).

[94] Immigration and Nationality Act, § 212(c), 8 U.S.C. § 1182(c), repealed by Pub. L. No. 104-208, Div. C, Title III, § 304(b), (Sept. 30, 1996), 110 Stat. 3009-597.

provide a reasoned explanation for its action. That is not a high bar, but it is an unwavering one. Here, the BIA has failed to meet it.[95]

In reaching that conclusion, the Court applied mainstream administrative law principles borrowed from the Administrative Procedure Act[96] and found that the BIA's ruling "flunked" minimal judicial review.[97] The Court bluntly emphasized that "[w]e must reverse an agency policy when we cannot discern a reason for it. That is the trouble in this case."[98] The Court further noted that the BIA's arbitrary and capricious interpretation of the statute did not warrant deference under *Chevron*.[99]

D. JUDICIAL REVIEW UNDER THE IMMIGRATION AND NATIONALITY ACT

1. A Brief History of Judicial Review

The Immigration and Nationality Act provides for judicial review of removal orders as well as a variety of other immigration decisions. The general rule is that a noncitizen has a right to *some* form of judicial review of an order of removal by the Executive Branch.[100] The rule reflects the weighty interests of the noncitizens at stake.[101] The precise form of judicial review has changed over time.

---

[95] *Judulang v. Holder*, 132 S. Ct. at 479 (emphasis added).

[96] *See id.* at 483 (quoting Motor Vehicle Mfrs. Ass'n v. State Farm Mut. Auto Ins. Co., 463 U.S. 29, 43 (1983) and citing Citizens to Preserve Overton Park, Inc. v. Volpe, 401 U.S. 402, 416 (1971)). The Court did so even though the Administrative Procedure Act does not apply to removal proceedings. *See* Marcello v. Bonds, 349 U.S. 302, 309–10 (1955).

[97] *Judulang v. Holder*, 132 S. Ct. at 484.

[98] *Id.* at 490. For analysis of the Court's decision in *Judulang v. Holder*, see Adjoa Anim-Appiah, *Raising the Standard* Judulang v. Holder *Condemns the Use of Arbitrary and Capricious Policies When Determining Eligibility for the Section 212(c) Waiver*, 33 J. NAT'L ASS'N L. JUDICIARY 261 (2013); Patrick Glen, Judulang v. Holder *and the Future of 212(c) Relief*, 27 GEO. IMMIGR. L.J. 1 (2012); Jeffrey D. Stein, *Delineating Discretion: How* Judulang *Limits Executive Immigration Policy-Making Authority and Opens Channels for Future Challenges*, 27 GEO. IMMIGR. L.J. 35 (2012); *see also* Geoffrey Heeren, *Persons Who Are Not the People: The Changing Rights of Immigrants in the United States*, 44 COLUM. HUM. RTS. L. REV. 367, 403–07 (2013) (viewing the Supreme Court's reliance in *Judulang* on administrative law principles as a way of avoiding the recognition of the constitutional rights of noncitizens). The Board of Immigration Appeals implemented the Court's decision in *Judulang v. Holder*. *See* Matter of Abdelghany, 26 I.&N. Dec. 254 (BIA 2014).

[99] *See Judulang v. Holder*, 132 S. Ct. at 483 n.7.

[100] *See* Benson, *supra* 28 (discussing importance of judicial review in immigration proceedings and how recent legislation has purported to eliminate such review); David M. McConnell, *Judicial Review Under the Immigration and Nationality Act: Habeas Corpus and the Coming of REAL ID (1996–2005)*, 51 N.Y.L. SCH. L. REV. 75 (2007) (studying how courts have differed regarding the nature and extent of the judicial review available under reform legislation); M. Isabel Medina, *Judicial Review — A Nice Thing? Article III, Separation of Powers and the Illegal Immigration Reform and Immigrant Responsibility Act of 1996*, 29 CONN. L. REV. 1525 (1997) (noting constitutional problems created by statutes that limit judicial review of immigration decisions).

[101] *See* Fong Haw Tan v. Phelan, 333 U.S. 6, 10 (1998) ("Deportation is a drastic measure and at times the equivalent of banishment or exile."); Bridges v. Wixon, 326 U.S. 135, 147 (1945) (emphasizing that "deportation may result in the loss 'of all that makes life worth living' ") (citation omitted).

As originally enacted by Congress, the Immigration & Nationality Act of 1952 (INA) lacked any provision for judicial review of removal orders. The district courts reviewed deportation orders through, as guaranteed by the Constitution,[102] a writ of habeas corpus filed in the district court.[103]

In 1961, Congress created a specific statutory provision for judicial review.[104] Under that provision, the noncitizen directly filed a petition for review of a BIA ruling in the court of appeals, without any review in the district court.

2. Limits: "Court Stripping" Provisions of Immigration Reform Legislation

In 1996, Congress passed back-to-back pieces of immigration reform legislation that significantly narrowed judicial review of immigration decisions and resulted in years of litigation over the availability of judicial review of certain kinds of immigration decisions.[105] In Section 440(a) of the Antiterrorism and Effective Death Penalty Act (AEDPA), Congress provided that "[a]ny final order of deportation against an alien who is deportable by reason of having committed [certain crimes, including "aggravated felonies," *see* INA § 101(a)(43), 8 U.S.C. § 1101(a)(43)] *shall not be subject to review by any court.*" (emphasis added). Later that year, Congress passed the Illegal Immigration Reform and Immigrant Responsibility Act (IIRIRA), which incorporated and expanded the limitations on judicial review of immigration decisions.[106]

In *INS v. St. Cyr,*[107] the Supreme Court found that the bars on judicial review for noncitizens convicted of certain crimes in IIRIRA did not preclude challenges to removal through *habeas corpus* proceedings in the district courts and held that Congress had failed to make a "clear statement" eliminating habeas review. By so doing, the Court avoided what it characterized as "substantial constitutional questions."[108]

In response to the *St. Cyr* decision's guarantee of habeas corpus review of removal orders in the district court, Congress expressly eliminated such review in

---

[102] Article I, § 9, cl. 2 provides: "The Privilege of the Writ of Habeas Corpus shall not be suspended, unless when in Cases of Rebellion or Invasion the public Safety may require it." In 2001, the Supreme Court interpreted one of the statutory bars on judicial review in the 1996 immigration reforms as not foreclosing habeas corpus review. *See* INS v. St. Cyr, 533 U.S. 289 (2001).

[103] *See* Heikkila v. Barber, 345 U.S. 229, 235 (1953); *see, e.g.*, United States *ex rel.* Fells v. Garfinkel, 158 F. Supp. 524 (W.D. Pa. 1957), *aff'd*, 251 F.2d 846 (3d Cir. 1958); United States *ex rel.* Athanasopoulos v. Reid, 110 F. Supp. 200 (D.D.C. 1953).

[104] Congress added this provision in no small part in response to the perceived abuse of judicial review for purposes of delay by, among others, reputed mobster Carlos Marcello. *See* Daniel Kanstroom, *The Long, Complex, and Futile Deportation Saga of Carlos Marcello, in* IMMIGRATION STORIES, *supra* note 33, at 113.

[105] *See* Illegal Immigration Reform and Immigrant Responsibility Act, Pub. L. No. 104-208, 110 Stat. 3009 (1996); Antiterrorism and Effective Death Penalty Act, Pub. L. No. 104-132, 110 Stat. 1214 (1996).

[106] *See* INA § 242(a)(2)(B-C), 8 U.S.C. § 1252(a)(2)(B-C).

[107] 533 U.S. 289 (2001).

[108] *Id.* at 300.

the REAL ID Act of 2005.[109] The Act directed that the review of removal orders would proceed directly in the *court of appeals*, not the *district courts*.[110] Since passage of the REAL ID Act, courts have dismissed habeas corpus petitions filed in the district courts seeking review of removal orders.[111]

As amended, Section 242(a)(5) of the Immigration and Nationality Act, 8 U.S.C. § 1252(a)(5), which is entitled "exclusive means of review," now provides that "[n]otwithstanding any other provision of law (statutory or nonstatutory), . . . a petition for review filed with an appropriate court of appeals in accordance with this section *shall be the sole and exclusive means for judicial review . . . .*" (emphasis added).

INA § 242(a)(2)(D), 8 U.S.C. § 1254(a)(2)(D) further provides that:

> Nothing in [the provisions that limit or eliminate judicial review] shall be construed as precluding review of *constitutional claims or questions of law* raised upon a petition for review filed with an appropriate court of appeals in accordance with this section. (emphasis added).

Thus, the INA ensures review of "constitutional claims" and other "questions of law," but not agency fact-findings.

Judicial review of a removal order under Section 242, as amended by the REAL ID Act, thus rests in large part on whether a court classifies a claim as "factual" or "legal." As in many areas of law, the lines between questions of "law" and "fact" are often murky in immigration law.[112]

a.   Questions of "Law" (Review) or "Fact" (No Review)

As the REAL ID Act amended INA § 242, pure fact questions are not guaranteed judicial review.[113] In contrast, "constitutional claims" and "questions of law" generally can be reviewed by the courts. Courts have exercised jurisdiction

---

[109]   109 Pub. L. No. 12, 119 Stat. 231 (2005).

[110]   *See* Gerald L. Neuman, *On the Adequacy of Direct Review After the REAL ID Act of 2005*, 51 N.Y. SCH. L. REV. 133 (2006/07).

[111]   *See, e.g.*, Iasu v. Smith, 511 F.3d 881, 891 (9th Cir. 2007); Nunes v. Ashcroft, 375 F.3d 810, 811 (9th Cir. 2004); Zalawadia v. Ashcroft, 371 F.3d 292, 294 (5th Cir. 2004). For analysis, see Hiroshi Motomura, *Immigration Law and Federal Court Jurisdiction Through the Lens of Habeas Corpus*, 91 CORNELL L. REV. 459 (2006); Neuman, *supra* note 110.

[112]   *See* Rebecca Sharpless, *Fitting the Formula for Judicial Review: The Law-Fact Distinction in Immigration Law*, 5 INTERCULTURAL HUM. RTS. L. REV. 57 (2010); Aaron G. Leiderman, Note, *Preserving the Constitution's Most Important Human Right: Judicial Review of Mixed Questions Under the Real ID Act*, 106 COLUM. L. REV. 1367, 1369–77 (2006); Sarah A. Moore, Note, *Tearing Down the Fence Around Immigration Law: Examining the Lack of Judicial Review and the Impact of the Real ID Act While Calling for a Broader Reading of Questions of Law to Encompass "Extreme Cruelty"*, 82 NOTRE DAME L. REV. 2037, 2047–51 (2007).

[113]   *See, e.g.*, Rodrigues-Nascimento v. Gonzales, 485 F.3d 60, 62 (1st Cir. 2007) (holding that determination of "hardship" was finding of fact, and thus the court lacked appellate jurisdiction); Chen v. U.S. Dep't of Justice, 471 F.3d 315 (2d Cir. 2006) (holding that the REAL ID Act barred judicial review of agency fact-finding).

over constitutional challenges to the immigration laws.[114] Pure legal questions can be straight-forward. However, legal questions can be intertwined with factual determinations. For example, the U.S. Court of Appeals for the Seventh Circuit held that it had jurisdiction over a claim that the Board of Immigration Appeals applied the incorrect legal standard in the review of an immigration court fact-finding.[115]

The Ninth Circuit in *Ramadan v. Gonzales*[116] held that it had jurisdiction to challenge a determination that a noncitizen had failed to establish the changed circumstances necessary to excuse the untimely filing of an asylum application. The court found that it had jurisdiction to review "questions of law" including "questions involving the application of statutes or regulations to undisputed facts, sometimes referred to as *mixed questions of fact and law.*"[117] The court concluded that, under the REAL ID Act, it had jurisdiction to review these mixed questions.[118]

In contrast, the Second Circuit held that it lacked jurisdiction over an asylum claim that the immigration judge found was not filed in a timely manner.[119] It treated the issue as more factual than legal, and thus not subject to review under the immigration statute.

b. Standards of Review

Once judicial review has been established, the question then is the degree of scrutiny that the court of appeals will give the agency ruling or, in other words, how closely it will review the decision. The appropriate scrutiny is determined by the "standard of review" applied by the reviewing court.

INA § 242(b)(4), 8 U.S.C. § 1252(b)(4), sets forth deferential judicial review standards for factual determinations. "[A]dministrative findings of fact are conclusive unless any reasonable adjudicator would be compelled to conclude the contrary." INA § 242(b)(4)(B), 8 U.S.C. § 1252(b)(4)(B).[120] In addition, the INA provides that "[a] decision that an alien is not eligible for admission to the United

---

[114] *See* Patel v. Gonzales, 470 F.3d 216, 219–20 (6th Cir. 2006); Flores-Ledezma v. Gonzales, 415 F.3d 375, 380 (5th Cir. 2005).

[115] *See* Guevara v. Gonzales, 472 F.3d 972, 974–75 (7th Cir. 2007).

[116] 479 F.3d 646 (9th Cir. 2007); *see, e.g.*, Mirzoyan v. Gonzales, 457 F.3d 217, 220 (2d Cir. 2006) (per curiam) (reviewing de novo mixed questions of law and fact of whether mistreatment suffered by asylum applicant constituted persecution); Chen v. Ashcroft, 381 F.3d 221 (3d Cir. 2004) (holding that the court had jurisdiction to review BIA's determination that statutory asylum protection did not extend to women undergoing forced abortions to an unmarried partner).

[117] *Ramadan v. Gonzales*, 479 F.3d at 650 (emphasis added); *see, e.g.*, Vahora v. Holder, 641 F.3d 1038, 1042 (9th Cir. 2011); Khan v. Holder, 584 F.3d 773, 779–81 (9th Cir. 2009); Husyev v. Mukasey, 528 F.3d 1172, 1178–79 (9th Cir. 2008); Ghahremani v. Gonzales, 498 F.3d 993, 998–99 (9th Cir. 2007); *see also* Mirzoyan v. Gonzales, 457 F.3d 217, 220 (2d Cir. 2006) (per curiam) (reviewing "mixed" questions of law and fact de novo).

[118] *See Ramadan v. Gonzales*, 479 F.3d at 651–54.

[119] *See* Liu v. INS, 508 F.3d 716 (2d Cir. 2007).

[120] 502 U.S. 478, 481 (1992) The section is a codification of the Supreme Court's decision in *INS v. Elias-Zacarias.*

States is conclusive unless manifestly contrary to law."[121] For *asylum* decisions, the Attorney General's judgment whether to grant asylum "shall be conclusive unless manifestly contrary to the law and an abuse of discretion," a narrow standard of review. INA § 242(b)(4)(D), 8 U.S.C. § 1252(b)(4)(D).

Courts exercise "de novo," or independent, review of questions of law.[122] However, as discussed previously in this Chapter, courts must afford *Chevron* deference to an agency interpretation of the Immigration and Nationality Act in instances in which the statutory provisions are ambiguous.[123]

c. Commencing Proceedings and Stays of Removals

INA § 242(g), 8 U.S.C. § 1252(g), as added in 1996 by IIRIRA, bars judicial review of decisions as whether to commence removal proceedings and whether to stay a removal order.[124] In *Reno v. American-Arab Anti-Discrimination Committee*,[125] the Supreme Court ruled that Section 242(g) barred judicial review of a claim of selective prosecution of the immigration laws based on the political speech of the noncitizens.[126]

A stay of removal is available for noncitizens who have been ordered removed but seek time to conclude their affairs in the United States. Under current law, a stay is not automatically granted pending the appeal of a Board of Immigration Appeals'

---

[121] INA § 242(b)(4)(C), 8 U.S.C. § 1252(b)(4)(C).

[122] *See, e.g.*, Tista v. Holder, 722 F.3d 1122, 1125 (9th Cir. 2013); Mendoza-Pablo v. Holder, 667 F.3d 1308, 1312 (9th Cir. 2012); Federiso v. Holder, 605 F.3d 695, 697 (9th Cir. 2010); Lockhart v. Napolitano, 573 F.3d 251, 254 (6th Cir. 2009); Arca-Pineda v. Attorney General, 527 F.3d 101, 103–04 (3d Cir. 2008).

[123] *See, e.g.*, Estrada-Rodriguez v. Mukasey, 512 F.3d 517, 519–20 (9th Cir. 2007); Segran v. Mukasey, 511 F.3d 1, 5 (1st Cir. 2007); Ortega-Cervantes v. Gonzales, 501 F.3d 1111, 1113 (9th Cir. 2007); Abebe v. Gonzales, 493 F.3d 1092, 1100–01 (9th Cir. 2007); Vo v. Gonzales, 482 F.3d 363, 366 (5th Cir. 2007).

[124] *See* Reno v. American-Arab Anti-Discrimination Committee, 525 U.S. 471 (1999); *see, e.g.*, Barahona-Gomez v. Reno, 236 F.3d 1115, 1118 (9th Cir. 2001); Botezatu v. INS, 195 F.3d 311, 313 (7th Cir. 1999); Schaeuble v. Reno, 87 F. Supp. 2d 383, 392 (D.N.J. 2000); Maldonado v. Fasano, 67 F. Supp. 2d 1170, 1175 (S.D. Cal. 1999), *aff'd*, 225 F.3d 1100 (9th Cir. 2000). For analysis of § 242(g), see Hiroshi Motomura, *Judicial Review in Immigration Cases after AADC: Lessons from Civil Procedure*, 14 GEO. IMMIGR. L.J. 385 (2000); Leti Volpp, *Court-Stripping and Class-Wide Relief: A Response to Judicial Review in Immigration Cases after AADC*, 14 GEO. IMMIGR. L.J. 463 (2000).

[125] 525 U.S. 471 (1999). For analysis of the decision, see Berta E. Hernández-Truyol, *Nativism, Terrorism, and Human Rights-The Global Wrongs of Reno v. American-Arab Anti-Discrimination Committee*, 31 COLUM. HUM. RTS. L. REV. 521 (2000); John A. Scanlan, *American-Arab — Getting the Balance Wrong — Again*, 52 ADMIN. L. REV. 347 (2000) Adrien K. Wing, Reno v. American-Arab Anti-Discrimination Committee, 31 COLUM. HUM. RTS. L. REV. 561 (2000).

[126] Section 242(g), 8 U.S.C. § 1252(g), provides that

No courts shall have jurisdiction to hear any cause or claim on behalf of any alien arising from the decision or action by the Attorney General to commence proceedings, adjudicate cases, or execute removal orders against any alien under the Act.

For applications of § 242(g), see, for example, Chapinski v. Ziglar, 278 F.3d 718, 720–21 (7th Cir. 2002) (ruling that the court lacked jurisdiction to hear a class action to compel government to commence removal proceedings); Tefel v. Reno, 180 F.3d 1286, 1298 (11th Cir. 1999), *cert. denied*, 530 U.S. 1228 (2000) (finding that § 242(g) did not bar class action challenging rules for seeking relief from removal); Sadhvani v. Chertoff, 460 F. Supp. 2d 114, 121–25 (D.D.C. 2006) (holding that the court lacked jurisdiction to hear challenge to Immigration & Custom Enforcement decision to execute a removal order).

decision to the court of appeals. Rather a noncitizen who appeals a removal order affirmatively must request a stay. In *Nken v. Holder,*[127] the Supreme Court held that, despite limitations on judicial review in the 1996 immigration reforms, the court of appeals possess authority "to stay an order of removal under the traditional criteria governing stays . . . ."

Arguing that the case-by-case approach to a stay of removal pending appeal is too time consuming and ad hoc, one influential commentator contends that stays of removal should be automatically granted during the pendency of an appeal as was the rule before 1996.[128] Others might claim that automatic stays encourage frivolous appeals so that noncitizens can remain in the country pending the resolution of the appeals process.

d. Class Actions

Class actions long have been brought challenging the U.S. government's application of the immigration laws. In *McNary v. Haitian Refugee Center, Inc.,*[129] the Supreme Court addressed a class action in which the plaintiffs alleged a pattern or practice of procedural due process violations in the Immigration & Naturalization Service administration of a legalization program for agricultural workers created under the Immigration Reform and Control Act of 1986. The statutory provision at issue in that case, INA § 210(e), 8 U.S.C. § 1160(e), provides that

> [t]here shall be no administrative or judicial review of a determination respecting an application for [legalization] under this section except in accordance with this subsection . . . . *There shall be judicial review of such a denial only in the judicial review of an order of exclusion or deportation* . . . . (emphasis added).

The Court held that this language did not preclude the district court from exercising jurisdiction over the class action. As the Court observed, postponing adjudication until individual deportation orders were entered and reviewed " 'would foster the very delay and procedural redundancy that Congress sought to eliminate in passing' " the provision limiting judicial review.[130]

Since *McNary v. Haitian Refugee Center*, Congress has limited the courts' ability to order class-wide injunctive relief in immigration cases. The Immigration Reform and Immigrant Responsibility Act of 1996 added INA § 242(f)(1), 8 U.S.C. § 1252(f)(1), which provides that

---

[127] 556 U.S. 418, 422 (2009); *see, e.g.*, Leiva-Perez v. Holder, 640 F.3d 962 (9th Cir. 2011) (granting stay of a removal order pending the appeal of denial of asylum claim and related forms of relief from removal). The Court in *Nken v. Holder* reached this conclusion based on the statement by the Solicitor General that the U.S. government has a policy and practice of returning deportees who won their cases to pre-removal status, which it later in a rare admission confessed was not the case. *See* Nancy Morawetz, *Convenient Facts:* Nken v. Holder, *The Solicitor General, and the Presentation of Internal Government Facts*, 88 NYU L. Rev. 1600 (2013).

[128] *See* Legomsky, *supra* note 21, at 1719.

[129] 498 U.S. 479 (1991).

[130] *Id.* at 490 (quoting court of appeals decision) (citation omitted).

no court (other than the Supreme Court) shall have jurisdiction to enjoin or restrain the operation of [certain provisions of the immigration laws, as amended in 1996] other than with respect to the application of such provisions to an individual alien against whom proceedings . . . have been initiated.

Section 242(f)(1) has spawned considerable commentary.[131]

To this point, the Supreme Court after *McNary v. Haitian Refugee Centers, Inc.* has not addressed directly whether plaintiffs may bring class actions for injunctive or declaratory relief in challenges to the immigration laws. Immigration class actions continue to be brought and decided by the courts.[132]

e. Habeas Corpus

As discussed earlier, the Supreme Court has ensured, at a minimum, habeas corpus review of removal decisions in the district courts.[133] One benefit of habeas corpus in a removal case is that it allows for the development of a factual record. As amended by the REAL ID Act, however, Congress expressly precluded any fact-finding other than by the agency. Under INA § 242(a)(1), 8 U.S.C. § 1252(a)(1), a reviewing "court may not order the taking of additional evidence . . . ." INA § 242(b)(4)(A), 8 U.S.C. § 1252(b)(4)(A) further provides that "the court of appeals shall decide the petition only on the administrative record on which the order of removal is based."

There is one important exception, however, to the elimination of habeas corpus review. Courts have interpreted INA § 242(a)(2), 8 U.S.C. § 1252(a)(2) as authorizing habeas corpus review of the *detention* of noncitizens.[134]

---

[131] *See* Jill E. Family, *Another Limit on Federal Court Jurisdiction? Immigrant Access to Class-Wide Injunctive Relief*, 53 CLEV. ST. L. REV. 11 (2005–06); Gerald L. Neuman, *Immigration: Federal Courts Issues in Immigration Law*, 78 TEX. L. REV. 1661, 1679–87 (2000); Volpp, *supra* note 124, at 467–75; *see also* Benson, *supra* note 28, at 1454 ("Congress probably intended [8 U.S.C. § 1252(f)(1)] to prevent class-wide injunctions such as those which have prevented the [federal government] from removing large numbers of people or from implementing changes in the past."); Jill E. Family, *Threats to the Future of the Immigration Class Action*, 27 WASH. U. J.L. & POL'Y 71 (2008) (analyzing the threats to the future of immigration class actions).

[132] *See, e.g.*, Alli v. Decker, 650 F.3d 1007 (3d Cir. 2011) (seeking declaratory judgment that the continued detention of the class members without bond hearings violates the Immigration and Nationality Act and the Due Process Clause of the Fifth Amendment); Aparicio v. Blakeway, 302 F.3d 437 (5th Cir. 2002) (deciding class action involving applications for special agricultural worker status); Catholic Soc. Servs., Inc. v. Napolitano, 837 F. Supp. 2d 1059 (E.D. Cal. 2011) (addressing issues in class action challenging a provision of the Immigration Reform and Control Act of 1986).

[133] *See* INS v. St. Cyr, 533 U.S. 289 (2001). For study of habeas corpus review of detention and other measures taken in the name of national security, see Richard H. Fallon & Daniel J. Meltsner, *Habeas Corpus Jurisdiction, Substantive Rights, and the War on Terror,* 120 HARV. L. REV. 2029 (2007). Daniel A. Farber, *Justice Stevens, Habeas Jurisdiction, and the War on Terror*, 43 UC DAVIS L. REV. 945, 949 (2010), analyzes the opposing approaches to interpreting habeas jurisdiction adopted by Justices Stevens and Scalia.

[134] *See, e.g.*, Hernandez v. Gonzales, 424 F.3d 42, 42–43 (1st Cir. 2005); Del Toro-Chacon v. Chertoff, 2008 U.S. Dist. LEXIS 18807 (W.D. Wash. Mar. 10, 2008); Jeanty v. Bulger, 204 F. Supp. 2d 1366, 1373–74 (S.D. Fla. 2002), *aff'd sub nom.*, 321 F.2d 1336 (11th Cir.), *cert denied*, 540 U.S. 1016 (2003).

The REAL ID Act, as it amended Section 242(a), re-established petitions for review in the courts of appeals as the exclusive vehicle for court review of final removal orders,[135] and expressly eliminated habeas corpus jurisdiction over review of such orders.[136]

While removal proceedings are pending, administrative officials have the discretion to detain the noncitizen, release him or her on bond, or grant parole without bond. See INA § 236(a), 8 U.S.C. § 1226(a). Detention is mandatory for noncitizens who are subject to removal under most of the criminal provisions of the immigration laws. See INA § 236(c), 8 U.S.C. § 1226(c). The Supreme Court upheld this provision in the face of a constitutional challenge.[137]

Under INA § 236(e), 8 U.S.C. § 1226(e) "[n]o court may set aside any action or decision of the Attorney General under this section regarding the detention or release of any alien or the grant, revocation, or denial of bond or parole." The Supreme Court in *Demore v. Kim*[138] read the provision as permitting the use of habeas corpus to challenge the constitutionality of Section 236. The REAL ID Act did not amend the section, and the conference committee report to the legislation stated that the Act "would not preclude habeas review over challenges to detention that are independent of challenges to removal orders."[139]

3.   The Nuts-and-Bolts of Judicial Review

a.   The Petition for Review in the Court of Appeals

INA § 242(a)(1), 8 U.S.C. § 1252(a)(1) provides that "[j]udicial review of a final order of removal is governed only by chapter 158 of title 28 of the United States Code," a reference to the Hobbs Act, which permits a "petition for review" in the court of appeals. Such a petition, which is filed in the circuit that has jurisdiction over the geographical area in which the removal hearing was held, must be filed no later than 30 days after the final removal order.[140] This time limit has been treated as a jurisdictional bar, i.e., the court lacks jurisdiction to review the petition if it was not filed in a timely manner.[141]

INA § 242(a)(1), 8 U.S.C. § 1252(c)(1) makes the petition for review in the court of appeals the "sole and exclusive" procedure for reviewing removal orders. INA § 242(b)(9), 8 U.S.C. § 1252(b)(9), which the Supreme Court has referred to as an "unmistakable 'zipper' clause,"[142] consolidates for review all questions of law or fact

---

[135] For discussion of the various provisions of the REAL ID Act, see generally Motomura, *supra* note 111.

[136] *See* INA § 242(a)(5), 8 U.S.C. § 1252(a)(5).

[137] *See* Demore v. Kim, 538 U.S. 510, 516–17 (2003).

[138] *Id.* at 516–17.

[139] House Rep. No. 109-72, at 175, 109th Cong., 1st Sess. (2005).

[140] *See* INA § 242(b)(1),(2), 8 U.S.C. § 1252(b)(1), (2).

[141] *See, e.g.*, Stone v. INS, 514 U.S. 386, 394–95 (1995); Dakane v. United States Attorney General, 399 F.3d 1269, 1272 n.3 (11th Cir. 2005) (per curiam).

[142] Reno v. American-Arab Anti-Discrimination Committee, 525 U.S. 471, 483 (1999). "[T]he term

"arising from any action taken or proceeding brought to remove an alien from the United States . . . ." In *Madu v. Attorney General*,[143] however, the court of appeals found that Section 242(b)(9), 8 U.S.C. § 1252(b)(9) did not apply to a challenge to Madu's *detention* on the ground that there was no removal order in place. The court reasoned that Section 242(b)(9) applies only to the review of a *removal* order.[144]

As amended, the filing of a petition for review does not automatically stay the noncitizen's order of removal pending disposition of the appeal; the noncitizen must file a motion for a stay. *See* INA § 242(b)(3)(B), 8 U.S.C. § 1252 (b)(3)(B).[145] The Supreme Court in *Nken v. Holder*[146] held that a stay motion is subject to the traditional criteria for the granting of a stay.

b. Exhaustion of Administrative Remedies

Consistent with general administrative law principles, INA § 242(d)(1), 8 U.S.C. § 1252(d)(1) provides that "[a] court may review a final order of removal only if . . . *the alien has exhausted all administrative remedies* available to the alien as of right."[147] (emphasis added). This requirement is satisfied in most cases in which a removal order has been entered. Courts have recognized various exceptions to the exhaustion requirement.[148]

'zipper clause' comes from labor law, where it refers to a provision in a collective bargaining agreement that prohibits further collective bargaining during the term of the agreement or, more generally, that limits the agreement of the parties to the four corners of the contract." Gerald L. Neuman, *Jurisdiction and the Rule of Law After the 1996 Immigration Act*, 113 Harv. L. Rev. 1963, 1984–85 (2000).

[143] 470 F.3d 1362, 1367 (11th Cir. 2006).

[144] *See* Motomura, *supra* note 124, at 409–30 (urging a narrow reading of § 242(b)(9) that allows review of significant matters independent of removal).

[145] *See, e.g.*, Teshome-Gebreegziabher v. Mukasey, 528 F.3d 330, 331–32 (4th Cir. 2008); Rivera v. Mukasey, 508 F.3d 1271, 1277–78 (9th Cir. 2007); Tesfamichael v. Gonzales, 411 F.3d 169, 171–78 (5th Cir. 2005), *cert. denied sub nom.*, 128 S. Ct. 353 (2007); Mohammed v. Reno, 309 F.3d 95 (2d Cir. 2002); Bejjani v. INS, 271 F.3d 670 (6th Cir. 2001); Andreiu v. Ashcroft, 253 F.3d 477 (9th Cir. 2001) (en banc).

[146] 556 U.S. 418 (2009).

[147] The exhaustion requirement "is based on the need to allow agencies to develop the facts, to apply the law in which they are particularly expert, and to correct their own errors. The rule ensures that whatever judicial review is available will be informed and narrowed by the agencies' own decisions. It also avoids duplicative proceedings, and often the agency's ultimate decision will obviate the need for judicial intervention." Schlesinger v. Councilman, 420 U.S. 738, 756–57 (1975); *see, e.g.*, Soberanes v. Comfort, 388 F.3d 1305, 1309–10 (10th Cir. 2004); Jordan v. Ashcroft, 296 F. Supp. 2d 249, 251–53 (D. Conn. 2003); Beresford v. INS, 299 F. Supp. 2d 106, 109 (E.D.N.Y. 2004).

[148] *See, e.g.*, Zhong v. U.S. Dep't of Justice, 480 F.3d 104, 116–25 (2d Cir. 2007) (stating that cases can be considered in "extraordinary situations" even when remedies have not been exhausted); Beharry v. Ashcroft, 329 F.3d 51, 56 (2d Cir. 2003) (recognizing that "the judicial common law exhaustion doctrine is discretionary and includes a number of exceptions"); Iddir v. INS, 301 F.3d 492, 498–99 (7th Cir. 2002) (listing various exceptions to exhaustion requirement); Castro-Cortez v. INS, 239 F.3d 1037, 1044–45 (9th Cir. 2001) (finding that exhaustion requirement had been satisfied even though one avenue for contesting decision had not been pursued).

c. Exceptions to Judicial Review

i.   The Rule of Consular Absolutism

Although removal decisions ordinarily are subject to judicial review, a number of other immigration decisions are not. Importantly, visa denials by U.S. Department of State consular officers historically have generally been immune from judicial review.[149] The rule is that a consular officer's decision to deny a visa application cannot be subject to judicial review. See Ch. 11 for a description of admissions procedures. A visa denial thus is not subject to review by any court, a rule known as "consular absolutism" or the rule of consular nonreviewability[150]

"[C]ourts have identified a limited exception to the doctrine where the denial of a visa implicates the constitutional rights of American citizens."[151] The exception is founded in *Kleindienst v. Mandel*,[152] which stated that "when the Executive exercises [the] power [to exclude aliens] . . . on the basis of *a facially legitimate and bona fide reason*, the courts will neither look behind the exercise of that discretion nor test it by balancing its justification against First Amendment interest [of the U.S. citizen]." Courts have read that language as recognizing a limited exception to the consular nonreviewability doctrine in instances where the government does not have a "facially legitimate and bona fide reason" for denying a visa in cases in which a U.S. citizen's rights are implicated.[153]

---

[149] *See, e.g.*, Saavedra Bruno v. Albright, 197 F.3d 1153, 1156 (D.C. Cir. 1999); Li Hing of Hong Kong, Inc. v. Levin, 800 F.2d 970, 971 (9th Cir. 1986); United States *ex rel.* Ulrich v. Kellogg, 30 F.2d 984, 986 (D.C. Cir. 1929); United States *ex rel.* Ulrich v. Kellogg, 22 F.2d 984 (D.C. Cir. 1929); Ngassam v. Chertoff, 590 F. Supp. 2d 461, 466–67 (S.D.N.Y. 2008); *see also* Stephen H. Legomsky, *Fear and Loathing in Congress and the Courts: Immigration and Judicial Review*, 78 Tex. L. Rev. 1615, 1619–23 (2000) (mentioning well-settled precedent that courts lack jurisdiction to review visa denials by consular officers). For recommendations for reform of the rule of consular absolutism, see James A.R. Nafziger, *Review of Visa Denials by Consular Officers*, 66 Wash. L. Rev. 1 (1991).

[150] For criticism of the rule of consular absolutism based on perceived abuse of power in an individual case, see David Ngaruri Kenney & Philip G. Schrag, Asylum Denied: A Refugee's Struggle for Safety in America 319–22 (2008).

[151] Bustamante v. Mukasey, 531 F.3d 1059, 1061 (9th Cir. 2008) (citing Adams v. Baker, 909 F.2d 643, 647-48 (1st Cir. 1990); Burrafato v. United States Dept. of State, 523 F.2d 554, 556–57 (2d Cir. 1975); Saavedra Bruno v. Albright, 197 F.3d 1153, 1163 (D.C. Cir. 1999)). For analysis of the exceptions to the doctrine of consular absolutism, see Donald S. Dobkin, *Challenging the Doctrine of Consular Nonreviewability in Immigration Cases*, 24 Geo. Immigr. L.J. 113, 122–32 (2010). In its arguments to the Court, the U.S. government relied heavily on Cold War plenary power cases to justify the doctrine of consular nonreviewability; a number of questions from the Justices focused on how *Kleindienst v. Mandel* might apply to the case at hand. See Kevin R. Johnson, Argument Analysis: Review of Consular Visa Decisions for the Twenty-First Century, SCOTUSBlog, Feb. 24, 2014, *available at* http://www. scotusblog.com/2015/02/argument-analysis-review-of-consular-visa-decisions-for-the-twenty-first-century/.

[152] Kleindienst v. Mandel 408 U.S. 753, 770 (1972) (emphasis added).

[153] *See, e.g.*, Am. Acad. of Religion v. Napolitano, 573 F.3d 115, 123–25 (2d Cir. 2009) (relying on *Kleindienst v. Mandel* in holding that consular absolutism does not preclude a court from engaging in a "limited judicial review" when a visa denial by a consular officer implicates a U.S. citizen's First Amendment rights); *see also* Margaret Laufman, American Academy of Religion v. Napolitano, 55 N.Y.L. Sch. L. Rev. 1173 (2011) (claiming that the Second Circuit has opened the door for judicial review of visa denials that implicate *any* constitutional interest of U.S. citizens).

The Supreme Court has the opportunity in the 2014 Term to reconsider the consular nonreviewability doctrine. In *Din v. Kerry*,[154] the court of appeals addressed a case in which a U.S. citizen filed a visa petition on behalf of her husband, a citizen of Afghanistan. In denying the visa, consular officials stated with no explanation that the visa had been denied under Immigration and Nationality Act § 212(a)(3)(B), 8 U.S.C. § 1182(a)(3)(B), which broadly provides for the inadmissibility of noncitizens for "terrorist activities." The Ninth Circuit found that the U.S. government had failed to put forth a facially legitimate and bona fide reason to deny the visa. The Supreme Court granted *certiorari*.[155]

ii.   Expedited Removal

INA § 235(b)(1), 8 U.S.C. § 1225(b)(1) authorizes "expedited removal" of arriving noncitizens whom immigration inspectors believe to be inadmissible on documentary or fraud grounds. The Attorney General has the discretion to extend the expedited removal procedure to those who are present in the United States and are unable to prove two years continuous physical presence in the country, and has exercised that authority on several occasions.[156] INA § 242 (a)(2)(A), 8 U.S.C. § 1252(a)(2)(A) provides that courts lack jurisdiction to review expedited removal orders. However, INA § 242(e)(2), 8 U.S.C. § 1252(e)(2) provides that a court may exercise habeas corpus to review a claim that the person is a U.S. citizen (and thus not subject to expedited removal), that the person was not in fact the subject of an expedited removal order (such as a U.S. citizen), or that the expedited removal procedure should not have been used because the person was a returning lawful permanent resident.

Congress also imposed limits on class actions challenging the expedited removal provisions. INA § 235(e)(3), 8 U.S.C. § 1225(e)(3) prohibits actions to challenge the legality of INA § 235(b), or of any regulations or other written policies issued to implement Section 235(b), more than 60 days after the challenged section was implemented. A constitutional challenge to expedited removal filed within the time limit was dismissed on standing grounds.[157]

---

[154] 718 F.3d 856 (9th Cir. 2013).

[155] *See* Kerry v. Din, 2014 U.S. LEXIS 4911 (U.S. Oct. 2, 2014).

[156] *See* INA § 235(b)(1)(A)(iii), 8 U.S.C. § 1225(b)(1)(A)(iii). For a critical analysis of the discretion afforded to immigration inspection officers to make unreviewable admission and removal decisions, see Lisa J. Laplante, *Expedited Removal at U.S. Borders: A World Without a Constitution*, 25 NYU Rev. L. & Soc. Change 213, 213–16 (1999); Thomas J. White Center on Law & Government, *The Expedited Removal Study: Report on the First Three Years of Implementation of Expedited Removal*, 15 Notre Dame. J.L. Ethics & Pub. Pol'y 1, (2001); Ebba Gebisa, Comment, *Constitutional Concerns with the Enforcement and Expansion of Expedited Removal*, 2007 U. Chi. Legal F. 565, 566–67 (2007).

[157] *See* American Immigration Lawyers Ass'n v. Reno, 199 F.3d 1352 (D.C. Cir. 2000) (dismissing challenge to the expedited removal provision of 1996 reforms on standing grounds).

iii.   Criminal Grounds for Removal

Reflecting the fact that there are few defenders of "criminal aliens" in the political process, *see* Ch. 15, Congress has consistently imposed restrictions on the judicial review of removal orders of noncitizens on criminal grounds.[158] Under INA § 242(a)(2)(C), 8 U.S.C. § 1252(a)(2)(C), "no court shall have jurisdiction to review" a removal order if the person "is removable" on almost any of the crime-related grounds, such as the "aggravated felony" category. *See* INA § 101(a)(43), 8 U.S.C. § 1101(a)(43); Ch. 11. Importantly, INA § 242(a)(2)(D), 8 U.S.C. § 1252(a)(2)(D) specifies that the various limitations on judicial review do not preclude "review of constitutional claims or questions of law raised upon a petition for review . . . ."

Courts have consistently interpreted Section 242(a)(2)(C), 8 U.S.C. § 1252(a)(2)(C) as *not* barring review of whether the person is, in fact, subject to removal.[159] Thus, for example, if the removal ground is conviction of an "aggravated felony," the determination of whether the crime in question in fact constitutes an aggravated felony under the INA remains reviewable by a court.[160] The same holds true for crimes of moral turpitude, a ground for removal under INA § 237(a)(2), 8 U.S.C. § 1227(a)(2).[161]

In recent years, the Supreme Court on a number of occasions has addressed the

---

[158] *See, e.g.,* Gonzales v. Duenas-Alvarez, 549 U.S. 183 (2007); Lopez v. Gonzales, 549 U.S. 47 (2006); Leocal v. Ashcroft, 543 U.S. 1 (2004). *See generally* Andrew David Kennedy, Note, *Expedited Injustice: The Problems Regarding the Current Law of Expedited Removal of Aggravated Felons,* 60 VAND. L. REV. 1847 (2007). One commentator has observed that

> [t]he deportation of "criminal aliens" is now the driving force in American immigration enforcement. In recent years, the Congress, the Department of Justice, the Department of Homeland Security, and the White House have all placed criminals front and center in establishing immigration-enforcement priorities. By fostering immigration screening at local jails and courthouses, federal authorities have filled the deportation pipeline with migrants arrested by local police and prosecuted in county courtrooms. Criminals and others identified during criminal arrests, such as "repeat immigration violators" and "fugitives from warrants," now constitute a full ninety percent of all persons removed from the country. In effect, federal immigration enforcement has become a criminal removal system.

Ingrid V. Eagly, *Criminal Justice for Noncitizens: An Analysis of Variation in Local Enforcement,* 88 N.Y.U. L. REV. 1126, 1128 (2013) (footnotes omitted); see Jason A. Cade, *The Plea-Bargain Crisis for Noncitizens in Misdemeanor Court,* 34 CARDOZO L. REV. 1751, 1758–59 (2013) (summarizing expansion of "aggravated felony" under immigration law).

[159] *See, e.g.,* Mahadeo v. Reno, 226 F.3d 3, 9 (5th Cir. 2000) (recognizing that § 242(a)(2)(C) would not prevent courts from reviewing whether a defendant is "an alien, removable, and removable because of a conviction for a qualifying crime") (citations omitted); Fierro v. Reno, 217 F.3d 1, 3 (1st Cir. 2000) (to the same effect).

[160] *See, e.g.,* Ortiz-Magana v. Mukasey, 542 F.3d 653, 657 (9th Cir. 2008); Penuliar v. Ashcroft, 395 F.3d 1037, 1040 (9th Cir. 2005); Gomez-Diaz v. Ashcroft, 324 F.3d 913, 916 (7th Cir. 2003); Valansi v. Ashcroft, 278 F.3d 203, 207–08 (3d Cir. 2002); Dalton v. Ashcroft, 257 F.3d 200, 203 (2d Cir. 2001); Nehme v. INS, 252 F.3d 415, 419 (5th Cir. 2001); Guerrero-Perez v. INS, 242 F.3d 727, 729–30 (7th Cir. 2001); Drakes v. Zimski, 240 F.3d 246, 247–51 (3d Cir. 2001); Lewis v. INS, 194 F.3d 539, 541–46 (4th Cir. 1999).

[161] *See, e.g.,* Tall v. Mukasey, 517 F.3d 1115, 1118–19 (9th Cir. 2008); Marmolejo-Campos v. Holder, 558 F.3d 903 (9th Cir. 2009) (en banc), *cert. denied,* 558 U.S. 1092 (2009); Notash v. Gonzales, 427 F.3d 693, 695–96 (9th Cir. 2005); Sosa-Martinez, 420 F.3d 1338, 1340–41 (11th Cir. 2005); Patel v. Ashcroft, 401 F.3d 400, 405–07 (6th Cir. 2005); Carty v. Ashcroft, 395 F.3d 1081, 1082–83 (9th Cir. 2005).

question whether a crime constitutes an aggravated felony[162] subjecting a noncitizen to removal and rendering lawful permanent residents ineligible for cancellation of removal and other forms of relief from removal.[163] In *Carachuri-Rosendo v. Holder*,[164] the Court held that a minor drug possession offense, which was not enhanced to a felony because of a previous drug conviction, did not constitute an aggravated felony under the immigration laws. In *Kawashima v. Holder*,[165] the Court affirmed a court of appeals' holding that a tax crime was an aggravated felony under the U.S. immigration laws. In *Moncrieffe v. Holder*,[166] the Court held that the conviction under state law did not constitute an aggravated felony under the federal immigration laws because the Georgia statute encompassed crimes well beyond actual distribution of controlled substances, including mere possession of marijuana for personal use.[167] *See* Ch. 12.

iv.   Exercises of Discretion

One of the most important limits on judicial review concerns the exercise of discretion by the agency. INA § 242(a)(2)(B)(ii), 8 U.S.C. § 1252(a)(2)(B)(ii) denies judicial review of any form of relief "specified . . . to be in the discretion of the Attorney General or the Secretary of Homeland Security other than the granting of relief under section 208(a) [which governs asylum, *see* Ch. 10]." INA § 242(a)(2)(D), 8 U.S.C. § 1252(a)(2)(D) provides, however, that nothing "shall be construed as precluding review of constitutional claims or questions of law raised upon a petition for review filed with the appropriate court of appeals . . . ."

Section 242(a)(2)(B)(i), 8 U.S.C. § 1252(a)(2)(B)(i) bars judicial review of any judgment of relief under the waiver provisions in § 212(h), 8 U.S.C. § 1182 (h) and § 212(i), 8 U.S.C. § 1182(i), cancellation of removal, voluntary departure, and adjustment of status. *See* Ch. 12. INA § 242(a)(2)(B)(ii), 8 U.S.C. § 1252(a)(2)(B)(ii) bars judicial review of any other decisions or actions, not including nationality and naturalization decisions, to be in the discretion of the Attorney General or Secretary of Homeland Security.[168] Section 242(a)(2)(B), 8 U.S.C. § 1252(a)(2)(B)

---

[162] *See* Immigration & Nationality Act § 101(a)(43), 8 U.S.C. § 1101(a)(43). A difference of opinion exists about whether *Chevron* deference applies to the BIA's interpretation of an "aggravated felony" in light of the fact that the Board's expertise is in immigration, not criminal, law. *See* Michael Dorfman-Gonzalez, Note, Chevron's *Flexible Agency Expertise Model: Applying the* Chevron *Doctrine to the BIA's Interpretation of the INA's Criminal Law-Based Aggravated Felony Provision*, 82 FORDHAM L. REV. 973, 976–77 (2013).

[163] *See* Immigration & Nationality Act § 240A(a)(3), 8 U.S.C. § 1229b(a)(3).

[164] 560 U.S. 563 (2010). For analysis of the implications of the Court's decision in *Carachuri-Rosendo v. Holder*, see Asher Steinberg, Current Development, *Supreme Court Holds That a Finding of Recidivism Must be Made in Court of Conviction for Repeat Offenses to Qualify as Recidivist Offenses When Ruling on Applications for Cancellations of Removal*, 25 GEO. IMMIGR. L.J. 539 (2011); Inna Zazulevskaya, Comment, Carachuri-Rosendo v. Holder: *To Be Deemed Convicted of an Aggravated Felony, an Actual Conviction Is Required*, 44 LOY. L.A. L. REV. 1215 (2011).

[165] 132 S. Ct. 1166 (2012).

[166] 133 S. Ct. 1678, 1686–87 (2013); *see* Victor C. Romero, *A Meditation on* Moncrieffe: *On Marijuana, Misdemeanants, and Migrants*, 49 GONZ. L. REV. 23 (2013/14).

[167] *See Moncrieffe v. Holder*, 133 S. Ct. at 1686–87.

[168] *See, e.g.*, Singh v. Gonzales, 451 F.3d 400, 410 (6th Cir. 2006); Tang v. Chertoff, 493 F. Supp. 2d 148,

does not preclude judicial review of "constitutional claims or questions of law." In addition, an exception allows for judicial review of asylum decisions, but the statute specifies a highly deferential standard of review. *See* INA § 242(b)(4)(D), 8 U.S.C. § 1252(b)(4)(D) ("[T]he Attorney General's discretionary judgment whether to grant relief under section 208(a) [asylum] shall be conclusive unless manifestly contrary to the law and an abuse of discretion.").[169]

In *Montero-Martinez v. Ashcroft*,[170] the U.S. Court of Appeals for the Ninth Circuit held that Section 242(a)(2)(B)(i) permitted review of the question whether an immigrant was not eligible for cancellation of removal. *See* Ch. 12. However, the court held that whether the "exceptional and extremely unusual hardship" necessary for relief exists is a discretionary judgment not subject to judicial review.[171]

As for review of agency fact-finding, several courts construed the pre-REAL ID Act version of Section 242(a)(2)(B)(i), 8 U.S.C. § 1252(c)(2)(B)(1) as not barring judicial review of administrative findings of fact concerning eligibility for affirmative relief.[172] Nothing in the REAL ID Act purports to change those results.

In *Kucana v. Holder*,[173] the court of appeals dismissed a petition for review of the denial of the motion to reopen[174] for lack of jurisdiction based on the 1996 reforms. In the Supreme Court's estimation, the language of the statute, relevant legislative and regulatory history, and the presumption favoring judicial review of administrative action, militated in favor of judicial review of the denial of a motion to reopen the removal proceedings.[175] The Court ruled that Section 242 expressly

---

153 (D. Mass. 2007); Grinberg v. Swacina, 478 F. Supp. 2d 1350, 1353–54 (S.D. Fla. 2007); Zheng v. Pogash, 416 F. Supp. 2d 550, 554–56 (S.D. Tex. 2006).

[169] For a thorough analysis of judicial review of discretionary immigration decisions, see DANIEL KANSTROOM, DEPORTATION NATION: OUTSIDERS IN AMERICAN HISTORY 228–40 (2007); Daniel Kanstroom, *Surrounding the Hole in the Doughnut: Discretion and Deference in U.S. Immigration Law*, 71 TUL. L. REV. 703 (1997).

[170] 277 F.3d 1137, 1141–44 (9th Cir. 2002).

[171] *See, e.g.,* Fernandez v. Gonzales, 439 F.3d 592, 603 (9th Cir. 2006); Martinez-Rosas v. Gonzales, 424 F.3d 926, 929–30 (9th Cir. 2005); Sepulveda v. Gonzales, 407 F.3d 59, 62–63 (2d Cir. 2005); Morales-Morales v. Ashcroft, 384 F.3d 418, 423 (7th Cir. 2004); Romero-Torres v. Ashcroft, 327 F.3d 887, 889–92 (9th Cir. 2003).

[172] *See, e.g.,* Reyes-Vasquez v. Ashcroft, 395 F.3d 903, 907–09 (8th Cir. 2005) (holding that BIA finding of no "continuous physical presence" for cancellation of removal purposes was not discretionary and therefore subject to judicial review); Morales-Morales v. Ashcroft, 384 F.3d 418, 421–23 (7th Cir. 2004) (same); Sabido Valdivia v. Gonzales, 423 F.3d 1144, 1149 (10th Cir. 2005) (same); Mireles-Valdez v. Ashcroft, 349 F.3d 213 (5th Cir. 2003) (same); Sepulveda v. Gonzales, 407 F.3d 59, 63 (2d Cir. 2005) (holding that "INA did not bar judicial review of nondiscretionary, or purely legal, decisions regarding an alien's eligibility for adjustment of status").

[173] 558 U.S. 233 (2010).

[174] *See* 8 C.F.R. § 103.3 (2013).

[175] *See Kucana v. Holder*, 558 U.S. at 243–53. For analysis of the Supreme Court's decision in *Kucana v. Holder*, see Michelle R. Slack, *No One Agrees . . . But Me? An Alternative Approach to Interpreting the Limits on Judicial Review of Procedural Motions and Requests for Discretionary Immigration Relief After* Kucana v. Holder, 26 GEO. IMMIGR. L.J. 1 (2011); Michael A. Keough, Note, Kucana v. Holder *and Judicial Review of the Decision Not to Reopen Sua Sponte in Immigration Removal Proceedings*, 80 FORDHAM L. REV. 2075 (2012).

barred only the review of the discretionary judgments by the *Attorney General*, not discretionary decisions delegated by the Attorney General to the *Board of Immigration Appeals*.[176] Thus, the courts of appeals continue to have the jurisdiction under the 1996 reforms to review denials of motions to reopen by the BIA.

---

[176] *See Kucana v. Holder*, 558 U.S. at 252.

Chapter 7

IMMIGRANT VISAS

A. THE FUNDAMENTALS

The INA establishes an elaborate system to manage the total worldwide level of immigration for those seeking permanent residence in the United States. This chapter relates only to permanent residence — the system for immigrant visas. The term permanent resident[1] often is used interchangeably with the term immigrant or lawful permanent resident (LPR). The more common term used for immigrants is "green card" holder which is a reference to the government-issued registration

---

[1] INA § 101(a)(20).

card. Immigrants are distinguished under the INA from temporary visitors who are designated as nonimmigrants.[2]

There are worldwide annual numerical restrictions or quotas, per-country ceilings on the number of visas issued, and visa category restrictions. The worldwide allocation of visas is divided among the preference categories for family-sponsored and employment-based immigrants, and the diversity immigrant category. Immediate relatives of U.S. citizens are a distinct category of immigrants outside of the worldwide quota. Several categories of "special immigrants" also are treated differently in the allocation of immigrant visas. Refugees and asylees become lawful permanent residents under a separate numerical system. This Chapter covers immigrant visa categories and the visa allocation system.

1. Worldwide Quotas and Preference Categories

Worldwide numerical restrictions on immigrant admissions have existed since 1921 under the discriminatory national origins quota system. The national origins quota system from 1921 to 1965 favored certain countries by allocating more visas to Western European nations, and by excluding most Asian countries almost entirely. Chapter 2 covers the history and evolution of immigration law and policy.

Today, the immigrant visa system relies on an annual nondiscriminatory worldwide distribution as well as per-country quotas in each of the family-sponsored and employment-based immigrant visa preference categories. Diversity visas are within the worldwide quota but have different per-country limits. The current system was established by the 1990 amendments to the INA. The 1990 Act reorganized the family-sponsored preference categories, added new employment-based preference categories, and established the diversity visa category. It also increased the total number of annual immigrant visas.

The worldwide annual visa allocation system is set forth in INA § 201 and establishes a baseline for total annual immigrant visas of 675,000 for family-sponsored, employment-based, and diversity visas.[3] The per-country limits in INA § 202 ensure equal access to immigrant visas by all nations.

To understand the worldwide annual visa allocation system it is useful to think of immigrants as divided into two categories: (1) immigrants subject to numerical restrictions; and (2) immigrants who obtain immigrant visas without numerical limitation. Those admitted without numerical restriction include immediate relatives of United States citizens,[4] returning permanent residents[5] and special

---

[2] INA § 101(a)(15) defines the term immigrant to include any noncitizen who does not meet the requirements for classification as a nonimmigrant. This is confusing at first glance however the system presumes that all noncitizens are immigrants who are subject to more restrictive classification requirements than nonimmigrants. *See* Ch. 8.

[3] INA §§ 201(c)(1)(A)(i) (480,000 baseline for family-sponsored visas); 201(d)(1)(A) (140,000 baseline for employment-based visas); 201(e) (55,000 baseline for diversity visas).

[4] INA § 201(b)(2)(A).

[5] INA § 101(a)(27)(A).

immigrants as well as a limited group of other permanent residents.[6] Immediate relatives are a special class within the visa allocation system, and they represent the majority of immigrants entering without numerical restriction. The immediate relative category includes the children, spouses, and parents of U.S. citizens who are at least 21 years of age.[7]

The total worldwide number of immigrant visas issued in each fiscal year varies, and regularly is above the 675,000 baseline.[8] For example, in 2013, the total number of immigrant admissions was 990,553 and in 2012 the total number of immigrant admissions was 1,031,631.[9] The worldwide levels fluctuate due to a number of reasons. A major factor accounting for the range of total immigrant admissions is the number of immediate relatives and the statutory requirement of a minimum number of 226,000 visas for the family preference categories. This statutory minimum is discussed below. The system also is designed to capture unused visas in the employment-based and family-sponsored preferences, and reallocate those in the following fiscal year.[10] Another major reason is bureaucratic processing delays.

Immigrant visas are issued on a fiscal year basis beginning on October 1st each year.[11] An immigrant visa is assigned to an individual when a noncitizen is admitted at a port of entry after consular processing or when an adjustment of status application is approved.[12] Immigrant visas are assigned to the principal beneficiary of an immigrant visa petition and that person's spouse and children who generally are admitted at the same time as derivative beneficiaries.[13] Under INA § 203(d), a "spouse or child" who is "accompanying, or following to join" an immigrant receives an immigrant visa at the same time and in the same immigrant visa category when an immigrant visa is allocated under a family-sponsored

---

[6] INA § 201(b). Noncitizens not subject to the worldwide levels or numerical limits include: special immigrants who are returning from temporary visits abroad (INA § 101(a)(27)(A)) and former U.S. citizens who will apply to reacquire citizenship (INA § 101(a)(27)(B)); refugees under INA § 207 or asylees who have adjusted status under INA § 209; LPRs who were beneficiaries under IRCA under INA §§ 210 or 245A; LPRs who are beneficiaries of cancellation of removal under INA § 240A; and special registry LPRs who entered before 1972 under INA § 249.

[7] INA § 101(b)(1) (definition of a child); § 201(b)(2)(A) defines immediate relatives to include some widows and widowers; a lawful permanent resident's child born outside of the U.S. while on a temporary trip abroad; and a child who enters separately from a parent who was granted permanent residence, when the child is following to join that parent.

[8] INA § 201(c)(1)(A)(i) (480,000 baseline for family-sponsored visas); § 201(d)(1)(A) (140,000 baseline for employment-based visas); § 201(e) (55,000 baseline for diversity visas).

[9] Dept. of Homeland Sec., *Yearbook of Immigration Statistics, available at* http://www.dhs.gov/ yearbook-immigration-statistics. To compare: in 2006, total immigrant admissions were 1,266,264; in 2007, total immigrant admissions were 1,052,415; in 2000, total immigrant admissions were 849,807; in 2001 total immigrant admissions were 1,064,318. Dept. of Homeland Sec., *Archives, available at* http://www.dhs.gov/yearbook-immigration-statistics.

[10] INA § 201(c).

[11] The fiscal year is October 1 through September 31st.

[12] *See* Ch. 11.

[13] INA § 203(d). Noncitizen spouses and children may also "follow to join" the principal beneficiary of a petition who entered earlier as long as they are still eligible under the definition of "spouse" or "child" in INA § 101(b). *See infra* discussion of Child Status Protection Act.

preference category, an employment-based category, or the diversity category.[14] Visa numbers are used quickly in each preference category as visas are assigned to principal immigrants and their derivative beneficiaries.

a. Family-Sponsored Visas

The number of immediate relative admissions, although not subject to numerical restrictions, are tallied under the worldwide system. Immediate relatives represent the majority of immigrants entering without numerical restriction.[15] The immediate relative category includes the children (under the age of 21), spouses, and parents of U.S. citizens who are at least 21 years of age.[16]

The annual worldwide allocation of immigrant visas to the family categories is set at a baseline of 480,000.[17] These 480,000 visas are allocated to immediate relative admissions, which are not limited, and the family-sponsored preference category admissions which are numerically limited. There is a ceiling on the number of immediate relative admissions that can be allocated from the total 480,000 annual family-sponsored visas. The annual visas for the other family-sponsored preference categories may not be lower than 226,000.[18] This ensures that immediate relative admissions do not use up all of the family-sponsored preference visas in any fiscal year.[19]

This floor of 226,000 family-sponsored visas plus the unlimited immediate relative visas creates the annual variability in total immigrant visas. As a result, the total actual number of family visas issued in a fiscal year regularly is above the 480,000 family-sponsored baseline. Once immediate relative admissions rise above the floor of 226,000, then the total number of family visas issued will rise above 480,000, as needed, to accommodate all of the immediate relatives who seek admission in a given year. If immediate relative visas are below the floor, then more visas are available to the family-sponsored preferences categories.

The minimum number of 226,000 immigrant visas for the four family-sponsored preference categories are allocated under INA 203(a).[20] The four family-sponsored immigrant visa preference categories include:

---

[14] Under INA § 203(d), the spouse or child must have that status before the principal immigrant's admission as an LPR. 22 CFR § 42.53(c) (2014).

[15] Immediate Relative Admissions were 436,802 in 2005; were 581,106 in 2006; and were 494,920 in 2007. Dept. of Homeland Sec., *Yearbook of Immigration Statistics, available at* http://www.dhs.gov/yearbook-immigration-statistics.

[16] INA §§ 101(b)(1); 201(b)(2)(A)(i); 203(h).

[17] INA § 201(c). The annual allocation includes any unused employment-based visas from the prior fiscal year.

[18] INA § 201(c)(2) establishes a "floor" of 226,000 visas for the family-sponsored preference categories.

[19] INA § 201(c)(1)(B)(ii). Family-sponsored admissions also are reduced by the number of noncitizens who were paroled into the U.S. under INA § 212(d)(5) and who have not departed within 365 days and who did not acquire permanent residence in the preceding two fiscal years.

[20] Note more than 226,000 visas might be available in a fiscal year if immediate relative admissions are below the floor.

- **First Preference** for unmarried sons and daughters over the age of 21 of U.S citizens (23,400 visas per year);

- **Second Preference** for two categories: the spouses and children (2-A) and unmarried sons and daughters (2-B) of permanent residents (114,200 visas per year);[21]

- **Third Preference** for married sons and daughters of U.S. citizens and their spouses and children (23,400 visas per year); and

- **Fourth Preference** for brothers and sisters of U.S. citizens at least 21 years of age, and their spouses and children (65,000 visas per year).

Only one family-sponsored category is available to LPR petitioners to sponsor close family members. In the second preference category, the allocation of the family-sponsored visas favors LPR spouses and children under the age of 21. Seventy-five percent (75%) of the second preference visas must be allocated to the 2-A category for spouses and children.[22]

b. Employment-Based Visas

The worldwide level of employment-based immigrant visas allocated each fiscal year is 140,000.[23] The 1990 amendments to the INA increased the number of employment-based visas from 54,000 to the current level of 140,000. There are "spill-down" provisions to reallocate unused visas among the employment-based preference categories annually.[24]

The five employment based preference categories for immigrant visas are:

- **Priority Workers (EB-1)** including three types of workers: (1) persons of extraordinary ability in the sciences, arts, education, business or athletics; (2) outstanding researchers; (3) multinational executives and managers (28.6 percent of the total number or approximately 40,000);[25]

- **Members of the Professions with Advanced Degrees and Noncitizens with Exceptional Ability (EB-2)** including physicians working in shortage areas (28.6 percent of the total number plus any unused visas from the EB-1 category or approximately 40,000);[26]

---

[21] The INA provides more visas to the 2A group compared to the 2B group by setting aside at least 77 percent of the worldwide second preference visas for the 2A group. This establishes a floor for the 2A visa category annually. INA § 203(a)(2). In addition, 75 percent of the 2A floor is exempt from the per-country limits. INA § 202(a)(4).

[22] INA § 202(a)(2) establishes a floor for the second preference 2-A category for spouses and children of permanent residents to accommodate the demand for visas from the large number of petitions filed by permanent residents for their spouses and children, and the hardship caused by long delays in the availability of visas for close family members.

[23] INA § 201(d). The annual allocation includes any unused family-sponsored visas from the prior fiscal year. If not all of the employment-based numbers are used in a fiscal year, then the surplus visas are added to the total family-sponsored visas to be allocated in the following fiscal year.

[24] INA § 203(b).

[25] Each category of priority workers has equal access to the annual 40,000 visa allotment under INA § 203(b)(1). The terms "manager" and "executive" are defined in INA § 101(a)(44).

[26] *Id.*

- **Skilled Workers, Professionals and Other Workers (EB-3)** (28.6 percent of total number plus any unused visas in the EB-1 and EB-2 categories or approximately 40,000);[27]

- **Certain Special Immigrants** (7.1 percent of the total number or approximately 10,000; unused special immigrant visas are allocated to the EB-1 category); and

- **Employment Creation Visas** (7.1 percent of the total number or approximately 10,000).

2. Per-Country Ceilings and the Visa Bulletin

The annual per-country numerical ceiling on preference category immigrant visas for individual countries is set forth in INA § 202. The per-country limit system is extraordinarily complex. Generally, each country will receive seven percent of the total annual visas allocated to the immigrant visa preference categories. In 2015, this was 25,950 immigrant visas.[28] This does not mean that each of the 180+ countries of the world have 26,000 visas annually. The per-country limits exist to ensure that high demand in one country does not use up all of the available worldwide visas.[29] The per-country limits apply only to family-sponsored and employment-based categories with certain exceptions.[30] Immediate relatives are exempt from the per country limits, in addition to being exempt from the worldwide allocation limits. Diversity immigrant visas are allocated under an entirely different calculation of per country limits, as discussed below.

The Visa Office of the U.S. Department of State publishes a monthly visa bulletin that charts immigrant visa availability by preference category, and, in some cases by country based on a per-country ceiling calculation.[31] Some countries regularly reach the per-country limit for the allocation of visas in some preference categories. These backlogs are created because there are more approved immigrant visa petitions relative to the availability of visas under the per-country limits and worldwide allocation limits. The countries that typically have backlogs in the availability of visas include Mexico, India, China, and the Philippines. These backlogs and the disproportionate impact on countries of high immigration have been a consistent issue in immigration reform policy discussions.

An immigrant visa is available to each noncitizen according to the priority date noted in the Visa Bulletin. A priority date is assigned when the noncitizen's family

---

[27] The term "profession" is defined at INA § 101(a)(32).

[28] http://travel.state.gov/content/dam/visas/Statistics/Immigrant-Statistics/Web_Annual_Numerical_Limits.pdf.

[29] Under INA § 202(e) there is a separate complex formula to ensure that visas for countries with high demand are spread out among the family-sponsored and employment-based categories.

[30] Family-sponsored 2A immigrants (children of LPRs) also are exempt from the per country limits under INA § 202(a)(4). Employment-based immigrants are exempt from per-country limits during any calendar quarter in which the total worldwide ceiling for employment-based immigrants exceeds the worldwide number of qualified applicants under INA § 202(a)(5)(A).

[31] Dept. of State, *Visa Bulletin*, *available at* http://travel.state.gov/content/visas/english/law-and-policy/bulletin.html.

member files an immigrant visa petition or when the employer files a petition or labor certification application to begin the processing. Pending immigrant visa petitions will automatically convert to the appropriate preference category and retain the original priority date when that status of the petitioner or beneficiary changes.[32] For example, an LPR petitioner may become a U.S. citizen which would convert a family-sponsored second preference petition to an immediate relative petition for which there is no numerical ceiling.

The Visa Bulletin indicates the backlogs by immigrant visa preference category and by country. It is used to chart the movement of priority dates to identify the estimated waiting time for a visa and any other issues such as aging-out or automatic conversion benefits. For example, the May 2014 Visa Bulletin has a date of December 8, 2001 for the fourth preference family-sponsored visa category (brothers and sisters of U.S. citizens).[33] Immigrant visas are available to a noncitizen whose U.S. citizen brother or sister filed an immigrant visa petition on or before December 8, 2001. Noncitizens from the Philippines, for example, who are eligible under the fourth preference family-sponsored visa category have an even longer backlog in the availability of visas. The priority date on the May 2014 Visa Bulletin for Filipino fourth preference petition beneficiaries is November 1, 1990, representing a much greater backlog.

The backlogs in the family preference categories can particularly impact children, defined as those under the age of 21. Once the child reaches the age of 21, she is classified as an adult child, and the pending immigrant visa petition would automatically convert to the appropriate immigrant visa category. For example, the child of a U.S. citizen who reaches 21 would no longer be eligible for an immediate relative visa which is exempt from any numerical ceilings. Instead, the adult child is eligible for a first preference immigrant visa; a category for which there is a numerical ceiling and a backlog in availability. This is referred to as "aging-out" when a child's age makes her no longer eligible for the more favorable immigrant visa category. The Child Status Protection Act was passed by Congress in 2002 to amend the INA and address aging-out problems, as discussed below.[34]

B.   FAMILY IMMIGRATION

Family members of U.S. citizens and permanent residents are eligible for immigrant visas either as immediate relatives or within one of the family-sponsored preference categories set forth in INA § 203(a).

There are a few key issues that affect all of the family-sponsored preference categories. First, only U.S. citizens may petition for extended family members in the first, third and fourth preference categories. Permanent residents may only petition for their spouses, children under the age of 21, and adult, unmarried sons and daughters. Second, in most of the preference categories there are significant

---

[32] 8 C.F.R. § 204.2(i) (2014).

[33] Dept. of State, *Visa Bulletin*, *available at* http://travel.state.gov/content/visas/english/law-and-policy/bulletin.html.

[34] Child Status Protection Act, Pub. L. No. 107-208, 116 Stat. 927 (2002).

backlogs in the availability of immigrant visas. This situation has led to the suggestion that the third and fourth preference categories should be eliminated and those visas could be reallocated to close family members.[35] It is anticipated that this reallocation would eliminate the constant backlogs in the second preference category.

The four family-sponsored preference categories include:

- **First Preference** for unmarried sons and daughters over the age of 21 of U.S citizens (23,400 visas per year);

- **Second Preference** for the spouses, children and unmarried sons and daughters of permanent residents (114,200 visas per year);

- **Third Preference** for married sons and daughters of U.S. citizens and their spouses and children (23,400 visas per year); and

- **Fourth Preference** for brothers and sisters of U.S. citizens at least 21 years of age, and their spouses and children (65,000 visas per year).

1. Marriage-Based Immigration

Family unification is a principle goal of the immigration system, although many criticize the system for failing to fully support this goal.[36] Marriage is a key family relationship for immigration benefits under the INA, however the term "marriage" is not defined. Marriages are a major source of the annual immigrant admissions either as immediate relatives or within a preference category. Spouses and children also immigrate as derivative beneficiaries on employment-based petitions.[37]

There are two eligibility issues that arise in marriage-based immigrant cases. First, the marriage must be valid in the place where it took place. A common-law marriage is recognized as long as it is valid in the location where it existed.[38] Similarly, marriages that take place outside the United States are recognized if the marriage is valid under the laws of that country.[39]

Second, the marriage must qualify under the INA, even if the marriage is valid where it took place. For example, an otherwise valid marriage that was entered into to evade immigration laws or to obtain immigration benefits does not qualify

---

[35] U.S. Commission on Immigration Reform, *Becoming an American: Immigration and Immigrant Policy* (Report to Congress 1997).

[36] *See, e.g.*, Jennifer M. Chacón, *Citizenship and Family: Revisiting Dred Scott*, 27 WASHINGTON UNIV. J. L. & POLICY 45 (2008); Jennifer M. Chacón, *Loving Across Borders: Immigration Law and the Limits of Loving*, 2007 WISCONSIN L. REV. 345; Fernando Colon-Navarro, *Familia e Inmigración: What Happened to Family Unity?*, 19 FLORIDA J. INT'L L. 491 (2007); María Pabón López, *A Tale of Two Systems: Analyzing the Treatment of Noncitizen Families in State Family Law Systems and under the Immigration Law System*, 11 HARVARD LATINO L. REV. 229 (2008); Enid Trucios-Haynes, *"Family Values" 1990s Style: U.S. Immigration Reform Proposals and the Abandonment of the Family*, 36 BRANDEIS J. OF FAMILY L. 241 (1997–98); Hiroshi Motomura, *The Family and Immigration: A Roadmap for the Ruritanian Lawmaker*, 43 AMERICAN J. COMP. L. 511 (1995).

[37] INA § 203(b).

[38] Matter of Darwish, 14 I.&N. Dec. 307 (BIA. 1973).

[39] Matter of L___, 7 I.&N. Dec. 587 (BIA 1957); U.S. v. Gomez-Orozco, 28 F. Supp. 2d 1092 (C.D. Ill. 1998) *rev'd on other grounds*, 188 F.3d 422 (7th Cir. 1999).

under the INA.[40] Proxy marriages are not recognized unless there is proof of consummation.[41] Polygamous marriages do not qualify for immigration benefits.[42] For many years, same sex marriages were not recognized, although the marriage was valid in the locale where the ceremony occurred. This denial of immigration benefits was inconsistent with the immigration policies of many other nations.[43] For example, the United Kingdom has recognized same sex relationships of more than four years since 1997.

In *Adams v. Howerton*, 673 F.2d 1036 (9th Cir. 1982), *cert. denied*, 458 U.S. 1111 (1982), a gay couple was married after receiving a marriage license from the county clerk in Boulder, Colorado and a ceremony was performed by a minister. Adams filed an immediate relative petition for his same sex partner, Sullivan. The INS denied the petition and the BIA affirmed. The Ninth Circuit affirmed the BIA decision by interpreting the INA and Congressional intent in using the term marriage. The court concluded that the ordinary construction of the term marriage included only a man and a woman.[44]

There has been a vast change in the legal landscape regarding the right to marry for same sex couples since 1982, when these marriages were not recognized in any U.S. state or by any other nation. In the U.S. same sex marriages were recognized first in Hawaii by a Hawaiian Supreme Court decision based on state constitutional grounds.[45] A Hawaiian voter referendum amended the state constitution in 1998 to explicitly prohibit same sex marriages. As of October 2014, 29 states have similar state constitutional provisions.[46] In 2003, Massachusetts became the first state in the U.S. to recognize same sex marriages.[47] As of October 2014, 20 states recognize full marriage equality, and another 9 states provide some form of same sex relationship recognition.[48]

---

[40] INA §§ 204(c), 216(g).

[41] INA § 101(a)(35).

[42] Practicing polygamists are also inadmissible under INA § 212(a)(10)(A). For a discussion of these issues generally, see Kerry Abrams, *Polygamy, Prostitution, and the Federalization of Immigration Law*, 105 COLUMBIA L. REV. 641 (2005).

[43] *See* ALIENIKOFF, MARTIN, MOTOMURA & FULLERTON, IMMIGRATION AND CITIZENSHIP, PROCESS AND POLICY 310 (7th ed. 2012). As of 2011, same sex immigration benefits were available in at least 28 nations: Andorra, Australia, Belgium, Brazil, Canada, Colombia, Croatia, the Czech Republic, Denmark, Finland, France, Germany, Greenland, Iceland, Ireland, Israel, Luxembourg, the Netherlands, New Zealand, Norway, Portugal, Slovenia, South Africa, Spain, Sweden, Switzerland, the United Kingdom and Uruguay.

[44] The 1996 Defense of Marriage Act permits federal recognition only of marriages between a man and a woman. Pub. L. No. 104-199, 110 Stat. 2419 (Sept. 21, 1996).

[45] *See* Goodridge v. Dept. of Mental Health, 852 P.2d 44 (Haw 1993) (remanded to determine if a compelling government interest existed); Baehr v. Miike, 910 P.2d 112 (Haw. 1996) (finding state had no compelling government interest to ban same sex marriages); Baehr v. Miike, 950 P.2d 1234 (Dec. 19, 1997) (affirmed without a published opinion).

[46] Lambda Legal, *Status of Same-Sex Relationships Nationwide* available at http://www.lambdalegal.org/publications/nationwide-status-same-sex-relationships#2.

[47] Goodridge v. Dept. of Mental Health, 798 N.E.2d 941 (Mass. 2003).

[48] Lambda Legal, *Status of Same-Sex Relationships Nationwide* available at http://www.lambdalegal.org/publications/nationwide-status-same-sex-relationships#2.

Congress enacted the Defense of Marriage Act [DOMA] in 1996 to ensure that states would not be required to recognize valid same sex marriages under the "full faith and credit" clause of U.S. Constitution.[49] Section 3 of DOMA stated that the term marriage for purposes of federal law meant only "a legal union between one man and one woman" and that "spouse" referred only to a person of the opposite sex. DOMA, therefore, prohibited the recognition of same sex marriages for immigration benefits.

On June 26, 2013, the Supreme Court declared Section 3 of DOMA to be unconstitutional as a deprivation of liberty in *United States v. Windsor*.[50] On July 1, 2013, USCIS under the direction of President Obama, began to implement the decision and to review immigration visa petitions filed on behalf of a same sex spouse in the same manner as those filed on behalf of an opposite sex spouse.[51] The BIA confirmed a few weeks later that the *Windsor* decision removed any impediment to the recognition of lawful same sex marriages and spouses if the marriage is valid under the laws of the state where it was celebrated.[52]

The problem of sham marriages entered for immigration benefits has long been a concern of Congress. Before the 1986 amendments to the Act, the INS adopted two approaches to identify fraudulent marriages. A marriage was deemed fraudulent if the parties did not intend to establish a life together when they entered the marriage. Marriages also were deemed invalid if "factually dead" due to separation or other change in circumstances despite the intent of the husband and wife when they married. This resulted in lengthy, intrusive investigations of marriage relationships to determine whether a couple intended to establish a life together or to identify whether a marriage was factually dead.[53]

For example, in *Bark v. INS*, 511 F.2d 1200 (9th Cir. 1975), the Ninth Circuit reviewed an Immigration Judge's decision that a sham marriage existed. Bark and his wife were "sweethearts" in Korea before she immigrated. After Bark came to the U.S. in 1968 (as a business visitor and as a student), he and his wife renewed their relationship. The couple was married in 1969 (less than one year after his business visit). Both Bark and his wife testified at the hearing that they married for love and not to obtain immigration benefits. The couple had separated at one point and there was evidence before the Immigration Judge that "the wife could and did leave as she pleased when they were together."

In *Bark*, the Immigration Judge decided a sham marriage existed and the BIA affirmed. The Ninth Circuit reversed and remanded noting that a sham marriage exists if the couple did not intend to establish a life together, and the mere fact that

---

[49] Pub. L. No. 104-199, 110 Stat. 2419 (Sept. 21, 1996). U.S. Constitution, Art. IV, Sec. 1 provides that "the full faith and credit shall be given in each State to the public Acts, Records, and judicial Proceedings of every other State."

[50] 133 S. Ct. 2675 (2013).

[51] *See* http://www.uscis.gov/family/same-sex-marriages.

[52] Matter of Zeleniak, 26 I & N Dec. 158 (2013).

[53] *See* Dabaghian v. Civiletti, 607 F.2d 868 (9th Cir. 1979) (rejecting the INS denial of immigration benefits based on a finding that a marriage was "factually dead but legally alive" because, in part, of the likely invasion of privacy by INS investigators).

the couple separated is not an indication of whether they intended to establish a life together *when they are married*.[54] Further, a bona fide marriage does not require any particular kind of relationship between a couple.

Congress addressed the problem of fraudulent marriages and intrusive investigations in the 1986 Immigration Marriage Fraud Act [IMFA], and established an entirely new process.[55] Now, conditional permanent residence is granted to noncitizens who receive their LPR status based as an immediate relative or as a family-sponsored second preference if the marriage was entered into less than two years before the immigrant visa is issued under INA § 216.[56] Marriages over two years at the time an immigrant visa is issued are not subject to the conditional residency requirement. Conditional residence is accorded only to marriages in the family-sponsored second preference category and the immediate relative category, and the condition is not imposed the employment based preference categories.

IMFA establishes a procedure for removal of the condition. The conditional resident and petitioning spouse must file a joint petition to remove the condition during the ninety-day period prior to the second anniversary of obtaining permanent resident status.[57] The joint petition must establish that the couple has a qualifying marriage that: (1) is valid under the laws where it took place; (2) has not been judicially annulled or terminated other than through death of a spouse; and (3) was not entered for immigration benefits.[58] The couple may be required to appear for a personal interview before approval of the joint petition.[59]

Failure to file the petition before the two-year anniversary is permissible only if the noncitizen establishes good cause and extenuating circumstances.[60] Failure to file a joint petition or failure to appear for an interview, other than for good cause, results in termination of permanent residence as of the two-year anniversary.[61] If the joint petition is denied, permanent residence is terminated on the date of the second anniversary.[62] If the residence is terminated, then the noncitizen is removable under INA § 237(a)(1)(D).[63]

The noncitizen can request a waiver of the joint petition requirement.[64] A hardship waiver to remove the condition is available when one of the requirements of a qualifying marriage can not be established. The noncitizen's waiver application

---

[54] The case was remanded to the Immigration Judge to assess whether Bark and his wife intended to establish a life together at the time of their marriage. *Bark*, 511 F.2d at 1202.

[55] Pub. L. No. 99-639, 100 Stat. 3537 (Nov. 10, 1986).

[56] INA §§ 216(a), 216(g).

[57] INA § 216(c)(1)(a).

[58] INA § 216(d)(1)(A).

[59] INA § 216(d)(3). The personal interview requirement can be waived when deemed appropriate. 8 C.F.R. § 216.4(b)(1) (2014).

[60] INA § 216(d)(2)(B).

[61] INA § 216(c)(2).

[62] INA § 216(c)(3)(C).

[63] *See* Ch. 11.

[64] INA § 216(c).

must establish either: (1) extreme hardship would result if the noncitizen is removed; (2) the marriage was entered in good faith but has been terminated and the noncitizen was not at fault in failing to meet the requirements for removal of the condition; or (3) the marriage was entered in good faith by the noncitizen and during the marriage the noncitizen was subject to extreme cruelty or battery, and the noncitizen was not a fault in failing to meet the requirements for removal of the condition.[65]

The condition residency status can be terminated for several reasons during the noncitizen's first two years of permanent residence. If it is determined that the marriage was entered into for the purpose of procuring immigrant status, or that the marriage has been judicially annulled or terminated (other than by the spouse's death), or that a fee (other than an attorney fee) was given for the filing of the petition, then permanent resident status is terminated.[66]

Some spouses and children may self-petition to remove the condition or are otherwise exempt from the petition requirement although the marriage may be within two years of acquiring permanent residence. Victims of domestic violence are eligible to self-petition as discussed below. Widows and widowers married for less than two years may self-petition for immediate relative status based on a 2009 amendment to the INA.[67]

IMFA also limited the immigration benefits from marriages that occur while a noncitizen is in removal proceedings. Initially, as enacted in 1986, a petition for a noncitizen who was in removal proceedings would not be approved based on a marriage until the noncitizen had resided outside of the U.S. for a two-year period after the beginning of the marriage. This restriction was viewed as unnecessarily harsh and the constitutionality of the restriction was challenged in a number of cases.[68] In 1990, the Congress amended the provision to permit a noncitizen to receive immediate immigration benefits upon establishing by "clear and convincing" evidence that the marriage was bona fide and not entered for immigration benefits.

Another mechanism to prevent sham marriages, added in 1986, relates to subsequent marriages and immigration benefits.[69] An LPR who obtained residence based on a marriage is prohibited from filing a marriage petition for a new spouse until five years have elapsed, unless special circumstances exist.[70]

---

[65] INA § 216(c)(4).

[66] INA § 216(b)(1). The noncitizen may contest the finding at a removal hearing at which the government will have the burden of proof under INA § 216(b)(2).

[67] INA §§ 201(b)(2)(A)(i), 204(a)(1)(A)(ii). *See also*, Pub. L. No. 111-83, § 568, 123 Stat. 2142 (2009).

[68] *See, e.g.*, Manwani v. INS, 736 F. Supp. 1367 (W.D.N.C. 1990) (challenging the constitutionality under the 14th Amendment Equal Protection Clause).

[69] INA § 204(a)(2)(A).

[70] An LPR can avoid this bar if clear and convincing evidence exists that the prior marriage was not entered for purposes of obtaining immigration benefits or evading any provision of immigration laws. This spousal second preference petition limitation does not apply if the prior marriage was terminated by death of the U.S. citizen or LPR spouse. INA § 204(a)(2)(B).

The conditional residence status also applies to the children of the noncitizen who has married the U.S. citizen or LPR and received their LPR status in this manner. Thus, conditional residence is provided to anyone who acquires permanent resident status "by virtue of being the son or daughter of an individual through a qualifying marriage."[71]

2. Domestic Violence

One major concern about the conditional residence procedure was the possibility that victims of domestic violence might feel forced to stay with an abusive spouse in order to remove the condition on their permanent residence status. The 1990 Act added the third extreme hardship waiver ground to the joint petition requirement for battered spouses.[72] Subsequent amendments to the INA in 2000, 2005 and 2006 have expanded the protection of victims of domestic abuse.[73] Spouses, parents and children who are subject to extreme cruelty or are battered may file their own petitions for permanent residence.

Another domestic violence situation was addressed by 1994 amendments to the INA. The 1994 Violence Against Women Act (VAWA) permits a battered spouse, either documented or undocumented, who is eligible for a marriage-based immigrant visa petition to file a petition on her own behalf.[74] A battered spouse or child is eligible to self-petition if she is a person of "good moral character;" she entered the marriage in good faith, and resided in the United States with the U.S. citizen or permanent resident spouse; and the spouse or child was subject to a battering or extreme mental cruelty during the marriage.[75] Victims of violence are eligible based on physical and emotional abuse as well as the threat of abuse.[76] A self-petition also may be filed by: (1) battered children up to the age of 25 of a U.S. citizen or permanent resident, and (2) elderly abuse victims of a U.S. citizen or permanent resident.[77]

This self-petition process avoids the involvement of an abusive spouse, who may have refused to file a petition or threatened to withdraw a petition for an immigrant visa. The Battered Immigrant Women Protection Act of 2000 (VAWA 2000) amendments to the INA made it easier for battered spouses and children to self-petition in the event of a divorce before the self-petition is filed.[78] VAWA 2000

---

[71] INA §§ 216(a)(1), 216(h)(2).

[72] INA § 216(c)(4)(C).

[73] Victims of Trafficking and Violence Protection Act (VTVPA) (Battered Immigrant Women Protection Act, Pub. L. No. 106-386, 114 Stat. 1464 (Oct. 28, 2000); Violence Against Women and DOJ Reauthorization Act of 2005, Pub. L. No. 109-162, 119 Stat. 2960 (Jan. 5, 2006); Violence Against Women Reauthorization Act-Technical Corrections, Pub. L. No. 109-271, 120 Stat. 750 (Aug. 12, 2006).

[74] Violence Against Women Act (VAWA), Pub. L. No. 103-322, 108 Stat. 1902–1955 (Sept. 13, 1994).

[75] INA § 204(a)(1)(A)-(B).

[76] 8 C.F.R. § 216.5(e)(3)(i) (2014) defines extreme cruelty and a battered person to include, but not be limited to, forcible detention, psychological or sexual abuse, or exploitation which results in physical or mental injury or the threat of injury.

[77] INA §§ 204(a)(1)(D)(v); 204(a)(1)(A)(vii).

[78] INA § 204(a)(1)(B)(v). The marriage must be terminated within two years immediately preceding

also eliminated the requirement that the self-petitioning spouse or child establish deportation would result in extreme hardship.[79] Divorced victims of violence also are eligible to self-petition.

VAWA and other related amendments to the INA provide other forms of relief to battered spouses and children.[80] Certain grounds of inadmissibility and deportation may not apply if connected to the spousal battery or cruelty.[81] Special relief from removal provisions apply to battered spouses and children.[82] VAWA 2000 added two nonimmigrant visa categories for victims of trafficking and victims of other criminal activity.[83] These are discussed in Chapter 8.

3. Other Family Members

The INA recognizes only the closest family relations regardless of an individual's actual family situation.[84] Some family members of both lawful permanent residents and U.S. citizens are eligible for immigrant visas; namely spouses and children.[85] The extended family members of U.S. citizens may immigrate, including parents, married or unmarried sons and daughters, and siblings. The category of "immediate relative" includes spouses, children and parents of U.S. citizens.[86] The second preference category for LPR family members only includes children and unmarried sons and daughters. There are significant visa backlogs in some of these categories.[87]

Children are particularly affected by the backlog in visa availability. Children under the age of 21 are eligible for classification as immediate relatives and second preference 2A immigrants.[88] A frequent problem occurs when a child "ages-out"

---

the filing of the self-petition. The Battered Immigrant Protection Act of 2000 was enacted as §§ 1501–1513 of the Victims of Trafficking and Violence Protection Act of 0f 2000, Pub. L. 106-386, 114 Stat. 1464, 1518.

[79] Battered Immigrant Women Protection Act of 2000 (VAWA 2000), Pub. L. No. 106-386, 114 Stat. 1464 (Oct. 28, 2000). The Act also allows a self petition in the case of invalid marriages entered in good faith but found to be bigamous. *See* INA § 204(a)(1)(A)(iii).

[80] The International Marriage Brokers Regulation Act of 2005 requires certain international marriage brokers to conduct background checks on U.S. patrons and provide information to noncitizen spouses. 8 U.S.C. § 1375a (2006).

[81] *See* INA §§ 212(a)(6)(A)(ii); 212(a)(9)(B)(iii)(IV), 212(a)(9)(C)(ii), and 237(a)(7).

[82] INA § 240A(b)(2).

[83] INA §§ 101(a)(15)(T), (U).

[84] *See* Jessica Feinberg, *The Plus One Policy: An Autonomous Model of Family Reunification*, 11 NEVADA L. REV. 629 (2011) (suggesting individuals should have the freedom to decide with whom they have close relationships that would be some hardship from separation rather than relying on fixed categories, i.e., the choice of a "plus one.").

[85] *See* INA § 101(b)(1).

[86] INA § 201(b)(2)(A)(i).

[87] For example, in May 2014, visas were available for married sons and daughters of U.S. citizens who had filed petitions before September 1, 2003; visas were available for siblings of U.S. citizens who had filed petitions before Dec. 8, 2001. Dept. of State, *Visa Bulletin, available at* http://travel.state.gov/content/visas/english/law-and-policy/bulletin/2014/visa-bulletin-for-may-2014.html.

[88] INA §§ 201(b)(2)(A)(i), 203(a)(2)(A).

and turns 21 rendering her ineligible for an immigrant visa as a child.[89] The immigrant visa petition can be transferred to an adult son or daughter category, either as a first preference son or daughter of a U.S. citizen or as a second preference son or daughter of an LPR, but these categories often have even longer backlogs.[90] Longstanding bureaucratic processing delays had exacerbated the problem of children aging-out. The 2002 Child Status Protection Act, addressed this problem by changing the timeframe for determining whether a noncitizen is a child for derivative beneficiaries and the children of lawful permanent residents.[91]

Children under the age of 21 are subject to the aging-out problem discussed above. The aging-out issue became particularly problematic when administrative processing delays were causing many children to lose their eligibility for a more preferable immigrant visa category in the 1990s. Congress passed the Child Status Protection Act (CSPA) in 2002 to address the aging-out issue. The CSPA covers the aging-out problems for the sons and daughters of United States citizens and the sons and daughters of LPRs. Immediate relative children retains their child status as of the date the visa petition was filed and are treated as a "child" of a U.S. citizen regardless of actual age. The noncitizen child also retains her age on the date an immigrant visa petition is filed when a visa petition converts to an immediate relative petition. This occurs when an LPR files a visa petition for her child under the family-sponsored 2A category, and the LPR naturalizes which makes the child an immediate relative of the naturalized citizen. The pending 2A immigrant visa petition automatically converts to an immediate relative petition.

The CSPA covers LPR children which includes two different groups: children who may be beneficiaries in the family-sponsored 2A immigrant visa petition, and children who may be derivative beneficiaries who are "following to join." Children following to join as derivative beneficiaries are common in the employment-based preferences, but also exist in other family-based preferences (third and fourth). These noncitizens can retain their "child" status but this is not automatically set to the date the visa petition was filed as it is for immediate relative children. The LPR children retain their "child" status under a formula that accounts for the amount of administrative processing time for a visa petition but also looks at the noncitizen's age when the immigrant visa becomes available, which is usually determined when the priority date become current on the Department of State Visa Bulletin. LPR children retain their "child" status if they satisfy the formula and take steps to acquire the immigrant visa within one year of the visa becoming available.

---

[89] INA § 203(h).

[90] The child of a U.S. citizen who ages out will convert to the first preference unmarried son or daughter or the third preference married son or daughter family-sponsored category (INA § 203(a)(1)), and the child of an LPR who ages out will convert to the second preference adult unmarried son or daughter category (INA § 203(a)(2)(B)).

[91] Pub. L. No. 107-208, 116 Stat. 927 (Aug. 6, 2002). *See* INA § 203(h). The child's age for immediate relative petitions is deemed to be the age of the child when the parent filed the petition. The child's age for second preference petitions filed by permanent residents and derivative beneficiary admissions is the age of the child on the date on which an immigrant visa number become available, subject to some limitations. For a detailed explanation of these provisions, see 79 Interpreter Releases 1433, 1503, 1520 (2002) and 80 Interpreter Releases 243 (2003).

The CSPA also covers LPR children under 2A who age-out and are converted to the 2B category using the original petition. In this situation, when a child ages-out of the 2A category, the appropriate immigrant visa category would be the 2B category. The 2A petition submitted by the original, principal beneficiary is converted to a 2B petition. INA § 203(h) also makes following to join children eligible to retain their child status under the formula. However there is no automatic conversion of visa petitions when children age-out in an employment-based preference category or in the family based third or fourth preference category. In this situation, there is no other family or employment category for which the aged-out child is automatically eligible. Therefore the parent who becomes an LPR, as the principal beneficiary of an employment category or in the third/fourth family sponsored category, would need to file a new 2B petition for the aged-out child. It was unclear whether the aged-out derivative beneficiary who becomes the beneficiary of the new 2B visa petition could retain her child status and priority date.

In 2014, the U.S. Supreme Court addressed this question directly of whether following to join derivative beneficiaries could retain their "child" status and priority date after aging-out. In *Scialabba v. Cuellar de Osorio*, 573 U.S. ___, 134 S. Ct. 2191 (2014), the issue was whether section 203(h) permits the aged-out unmarried sons and daughters to retain their child status as derivative beneficiaries of family-sponsored 3rd preference (married sons and daughters of U.S. citizens) and the family-sponsored 4th preference (siblings of U.S. citizens). USCIS's position was that 203(h) did not allow these derivative beneficiaries to retain their "child" status because the petition originally filed did not automatically convert to another preference category. The BIA agreed with USCIS, and the Supreme Court agreed as well in a 5-4 decision resolving a circuit split. The Supreme Court found that the agency's interpretation was entitled to deference in this case. As a result, children who are following to join as derivative beneficiaries will not retain their child status nor the priority date when they age-out. Instead, the aged-out child must wait until the principal beneficiary becomes an LPR and files a new petition for the aged-out child. When the LPR files the new 2B immigrant visa petition for his or her aged-out son or daughter, the beneficiary will then have a new priority date.

Another major issue is the definitions of the key terms in the family-sponsored categories. The definitions of terms such as child, parent, spouse are extremely complex. A child must be unmarried and under age 21.[92] For example, the definition of a "child" includes children who are adopted, whose parents are unmarried, and stepchildren.[93] There is a large body of caselaw and administrative decisions interpreting these terms and other aspects of family relationships.[94]

---

[92] INA § 101(b)(1).

[93] INA §§ 101(b), 101(c).

[94] *See, e.g.,* Young v. Reno, 114 F.3d 879 (9th Cir. 1997) (adopted child may not apply for immigration benefits on behalf of a natural sibling); Matter of Martinez, 18 I.&N. Dec. 399, 400 (BIA 1983) (A noncitizen can be a "son or daughter" only if the noncitizen at one time had been that person's "child"). *See also,* INA § 101(b)(2) establishing that a noncitizen can qualify as a person's "parent" only if that person was at one time the noncitizen's "child." As a result, two people will be considered siblings only

Generally, Congress has broad, plenary power to draw distinctions among family members in creating preference categories. For example, in *Fiallo v. Bell*, 430 U.S. 787 (1977), unwed fathers challenged the constitutionality of the definition of those parents and children eligible for immigration benefits. In 1977, INA § 101(b)(1) defined the term child to only recognize nonmarital children and their natural mothers for immigration benefits.[95] The Supreme Court rejected the equal protection challenge and upheld the definition using only minimal scrutiny despite the apparent gender and illegitimacy classification.[96] The Court relied upon the plenary power doctrine and noted that only a facially legitimate and bona fide reason is required to support the gender discrimination against nonmarital natural fathers and their children.[97]

Foreign adoptions also are regulated by the INA. U.S adoptive parents must comply with the requirements designed, in part, to address the fear that "sham" adoptions could be arranged to evade the immigrant visa quotas.[98] The INA was amended in 1957 to include certain adopted children in the definition of a "child," and amended again in 1961 to add a special provision for the admission of "orphan" children.[99] An adoption will not be eligible for immigration benefits if it was entered into solely for immigration purposes, which reflects concerns similar to those in sham marriages.[100] U.S. citizens may seek LPR status for orphans defined to include children under age 16 who have experienced the death, disappearance, or abandonment of both parents or sometimes just one parent.[101] International law provides another method of adoption. The U.S. is a party to the Hague Convention on Protection of Children and Co-Operation in Respect of Intercountry Adoption[102] and the implementing U.S. legislation went into effect in 2000.[103] The treaty itself went into force for the U.S. on April 1, 2008.

---

if they were once "children" of a common parent. *See, e.g.*, Matter of May, 18 I.&N. Dec. 381 (BIA 1983).

[95] Before 1986, INA § 101(b)(1) defined "child" as "an unmarried person under the age of twenty-one who is a legitimate or legitimated child, a stepchild, an adopted child or an illegitimate child seeking preference by virtue of his relationship with his natural mother." A 1986 amendment to INA § 101(b)(1)(D) provided immigration benefits to natural fathers with bona fide relationships with their nonmarital children. *See* Matter of Vizcaino, 19 I.&N. Dec. 644 (BIA 1988).

[96] A dissenting opinion by Justice Marshall, joined by Justice Brennan, criticized the deference to Congress in the case of "invidious and irrational" discrimination among citizens. *Fiallo*, 430 U.S. at 800.

[97] *Cf.* Nguyen v. INS, 533 U.S. 53 (2001) upholding a gender classification regarding citizenship eligibility, but applying intermediate scrutiny, when nonmarital fathers and mothers were treated differently in regard to proof of parentage.

[98] Legomsky & Rodriguez, Immigration and Refugee Law and Policy, Chapter 3 (6th ed. 2014).

[99] Act of Sept. 11, 1957, Pub. L. No. 85-316, § 2, 71 Stat. 639; Act of Sept. 26, 1961, Pub. L. No. 87-301, 75 Stat. 650.

[100] *See*, Matter of Marquez, 20 I.&N. Dec. 160 (BIA 1990).

[101] INA § 101(b)(1)(F).

[102] 32 I.L.M. 1134 (1993) (requiring certain minimum procedures designed to protect children, biological parents, and adoptive parents within state parties to the treaty).

[103] Intercountry Adoption Act of 2000, Pub. L. 106-279, 114 Stat. 825 (Oct. 6, 2000) (providing the Department of State with authority over foreign adoptions and designated the categories of children who may be adopted from other states parties to the treaty). *See also*, INA § 101(b)(1)(G).

Other countries provide broader family reunification benefits. In Canada, grandparents, grandchildren, nieces, and nephews, and, in some cases, a more distant "relative" will be permitted to immigrate. In Great Britain, grandparents, uncles, and aunts in some circumstances are permitted to immigrate.[104]

4. Special Immigrant Juvenile Status

There is a special immigrant category, created in 1990, for children who are present in the United States and who have been declared dependents on a juvenile court or placed in the custody of a state. This Special Immigrant Juvenile (SIJ) category includes juveniles who have been placed in foster care for whom family reunification is no longer a viable option. This category principally applies to children who have been abandoned, neglected or abused.[105] There are several requirements: (1) presence in the U.S.; (2) a declaration of a juvenile court in the U.S. or placement by a juvenile court in the custody of a state agency or individual); (3) a determination that reunification with one or both of the noncitizen juvenile's parents is not viable due to abuse, neglect, abandonment, or a similar basis found under state law; (4) a prior administrative or judicial proceedings have determined that return to the home country would not be in the noncitizen juvenile's "best interest;" and (5) DHS consent to the grant of SIJ status. The INA only requires that reunification is not viable with one of the two parents even if the other parent is available for reunification. The juvenile noncitizen must be a "child" at the time of the application, unmarried and under age 21, and there is no aging-out of eligibility when the noncitizen reaches 21 years of age.[106]

Immigrant visas are available to a juvenile if there has been a determination, in an administrative or judicial proceeding, that it would not be in the juvenile's best interest to be returned to her or her parent's previous country of nationality or country of last habitual residence. State juvenile courts make this determination about whether family reunification is no longer viable. There are administrative difficulties in meeting these requirements. For example, juveniles in DHS or ORR custody, either actual or constructive, must receive DHS consent before a state juvenile court may assert jurisdiction. DHS will consent only if it determines that the jurisdiction of the state court is not for the purpose of obtaining permanent residence.

There are many advantages as well to applying for SIJ status.[107] Applicants for SIJ status are subject to much less restrictive requirements than other immigrant applicants. There are exemptions and waivers of many inadmissibility provisions.[108]

---

[104] LEGOMSKY & RODRIGUEZ, IMMIGRATION AND REFUGEE LAW AND POLICY, CHAPTER 2 (6th ed. 2014).

[105] INA § 101(a)(27)(J).

[106] TVPRA § 235(d)(6).

[107] One clear advantage is that the decision relies on the "best interest of the child" standard which is not used in other areas of immigration law where children are affected. *See generally* Bridgette A. Carr, *Incorporating a "Best Interests of the Child" Approach into Immigration Law and Procedure*, 12 YALE HUMAN RIGHTS & DEVELOPMENT L.J. 120 (2009); David B. Thronson, *Thinking Small: The Need for Big Changes in Immigration Law's Treatment of Children*, 14 U.C. DAVIS J. JUVENILE L. & POLICY 239 (2010).

[108] *See,* INA § 245(h)(2)(A) (exempt from INA § 212(a) grounds for public charge, lack of labor

As applicants who are present in the U.S., noncitizen juveniles are deemed to have been paroled into the U.S. and therefore a prior entry without inspection will not bar adjustment of status.[109] An applicant can apply affirmatively by submitting a petition to USCIS or defensively in removal proceedings.

The INA limits the possible immigration benefits that an SIJ immigrant can provide to her family members. Once SIJ status has been granted, "no natural parent or prior adoptive parent" will be eligible for any immigration benefit based on that parentage.[110] SIJ special immigrants, and all other special immigrants, become LPRs under the employment-based fourth preference.[111]

C. EMPLOYMENT-BASED PREFERENCE CATEGORIES

The 1990 amendments to the INA restructured the immigrant visa system and made major changes to the employment-based preference categories. The annual number of employment-based visas more than doubled to a total of 140,000. The 1990 Act also created new categories for immigrant investors who create employment in the U.S. and for advanced degree professionals. The employment-based preference categories include:

- **First Preference:** Priority Workers (EB-1) including three types of workers: (1) persons of extraordinary ability in the sciences, arts, education, business or athletics; (2) outstanding researchers; (3) multinational executives and managers;

- **Second Preference:** Members of the Professions with Advanced Degrees and Noncitizens with Exceptional Ability (EB-2) including physicians working in shortage areas;

- **Third Preference:** Skilled Workers, Professionals and Other Workers (EB-3);

- **Fourth Preference:** Certain Special Immigrants (discussed in Section D below); and

- **Fifth Preference:** Employment Creation Visas.

A key feature of the employment-based immigration system is the labor certification process which is the first step of the immigration process in many of the employment-based preference categories. It is managed by the U.S. Department of Labor and state workforce agencies. The employment-based preferences can be divided into those categories subject to labor certification and those categories exempt from labor certification. Typically those categories exempt from labor certification have a streamlined approval procedure and short visa backlogs, if any.

---

certification, presence without admission or parole, arrival at undesignated point, fraud, stowaway, lack of entry documents, and unlawful presence); INA § 245(h)(2)(B) (discretionary waiver available for all the other inadmissibility grounds, except certain of the criminal and national security grounds).

[109] INA § 245(h)(1).

[110] INA § 101(a)(27)(J)(iii)(II).

[111] INA § 203(b)(4).

Labor certification is designed to protect the wages and working conditions of U.S. workers by determining, on an individual basis, whether there are available, able, willing or qualified U.S. workers to fill positions offered to noncitizens.[112] Labor certification also is designed to determine whether the permanent employment of the individual noncitizen will adversely affect the wages and working conditions of U.S. workers.[113]

Another feature of the employment-based preference system is the similarity of the permanent resident categories to many nonimmigrant visa categories.[114] Often, a noncitizen will enter the U.S. as a nonimmigrant and later decide to pursue permanent residence. The nonimmigrant categories and immigrant categories interrelate and allow a seamless transition for some noncitizens from temporary status to permanent residence, including some EB-1 priority workers, some EB-2 exceptional and advanced degree professional workers, and some EB-3 professionals. For example, the O-1 outstanding person nonimmigrant visa category requires very similar evidence to the EB-1 employment-based person of extraordinary ability category.[115] There is a similar symmetry between the professionals in both the second and third employment-based preferences and the H-1B Specialty Occupational Worker nonimmigrant category.[116] This creates the possibility of a transition from nonimmigrant temporary worker to permanent resident worker for higher skilled workers which is unavailable to lower skilled workers for whom there is only one very limited nonimmigrant visa category.

Many employment-based immigrant categories do not have significant backlogs in visa availability. In 2000, Congress exempted most employment-based immigrants from the per-country limits.[117]

1. Priority Workers (EB-1)

Priority workers under the employment-based first preference (EB-1) immigrant visa category includes three types of workers, all of whom are exempt from the labor certification requirement. These are: (1) persons of extraordinary ability in the sciences, arts, education, business or athletics; (2) outstanding professors and researchers; and (3) multinational executives and managers. Regulations list the evidence required for each of these priority worker categories.[118]

---

[112] INA § 101(a)(31) defines "permanent" to mean "a relationship of continuing or lasting nature" even though the relationship may be dissolved eventually.

[113] INA § 212(a)(5)(i). A U.S. worker is defined as a U.S. citizen, U.S. national, or a noncitizen legally permitted to work permanently in the U.S., including refugees and asylees. 20 C.F.R. § 656.3 (2014).

[114] Compare priority worker multinational executives and managers under INA § 203(b)(1) with L intracompany transferees under INA § 101(a)(15)(L).

[115] INA §§ 101(a)(15)(0), 203(b)(1)(A).

[116] INA §§ 101(a)(15)(0), 203(b)(1)(A).

[117] INA § 202(a)(5)(A).

[118] 8 C.F.R. § 204.5(2014).

Persons of extraordinary ability are individuals "who have risen to the very top of the field of endeavor."[119] A noncitizen may establish eligibility with evidence of a one-time internationally recognized award (e.g., a Nobel Prize, Oscar Award or Pulitzer Prize) or combined evidence of lesser international or national recognition.[120] Noncitizens in the extraordinary ability category do not require a job offer from a U.S. entity and can self-petition to establish eligibility.[121] Outstanding professors and researchers who are internationally recognized, and who have at least three years of experience, are eligible if there is an offer of employment from a prospective U.S. employer.[122] Multinational executives and managers, who are intracompany transferees, are eligible if they function at a senior level in an organization as defined by the INA.[123] In many respects, the EB-3 category for multinational executives and managers mirrors the L-1 intracompany transferee nonimmigrant visa category.[124]

There is limited judicial precedent on what constitutes extraordinary ability aside from a relatively recent Ninth Circuit case, *Kazarian v. USCIS*.[125] The regulations define "extraordinary ability" as a "level of expertise indicating that the individual is one of those few who have risen to the top of the field of endeavor."[126] In this *Kazarian*, the USCIS and Administrative Appeals Office (AAO) denied the extraordinary ability petition because it rejected two types of evidence presented by a professor of theoretical physics from Armenia. The AAO determined that the 6 articles published were insufficient because "publication of scholarly articles is not automatically evidence of sustained acclaim." Similarly, the AAO rejected evidence of judging the work of others in the field because it found that serving as a Ph.D. thesis supervisor "is not persuasive evidence of acclaim beyond that university." The Ninth Circuit found the AAO rejection improper because the regulations specifically state that a noncitizen must have three of the listed types of evidence including publications and judging the work of others.[127] The AAO was found to add criteria not found in the regulations. The Ninth Circuit upheld the denial of the petition, however, because it did not contain three types of evidence as

---

[119]   8 CFR § 204.5(h)(2) (2014).

[120]   8 C.F.R. § 204.5(h)(3) (2014) allows evidence in at least three of the following categories: nationally or internationally recognized awards or prizes for excellence; membership in associations; published material about the noncitizen; participation by the noncitizen judging the work of other in his or her field; original contributions of major significance.

[121]   8 C.F.R. § 204(h)(5) (2014). A noncitizen demonstrating extraordinary ability must also demonstrate she will continue to work in her area of expertise.

[122]   8 C.F.R. § 204.5(i) (2014).

[123]   INA § 101(a)(44) defines managerial capacity and executive capacity for both employment-based priority workers and the L-1 intracompany transferee nonimmigrant visa category in INA § 101(a)(13)(L).

[124]   *See* INS § 101(a)(13)(L).

[125]   596 F.3d 1115 (9th Cir. Mar. 4, 2010); *see also* Rijal v. U.S. Citizenship and Immigration Services, 683 F.3d 1030 (9th Cir. 2012).

[126]   8 C.F.R. § 204.5(h)(2).

[127]   8 CFR §§ 204.3(h)(3)(vi), 204.5(h)(3)(iv) (2014) (listing specific criteria as evidence such as: "authorship of scholarly articles in the field, in professional or major trade publications or other major media" and "participation, either individually or on a panel, as a judge of the work of others in the same or an allied field").

required. The court also noted that while the evidence provided could not be rejected outright, the AAO's view of the persuasiveness of the evidence was relevant to the final merits determination about whether extraordinary ability has been established.

The *Kazarian* case may indicate a narrowing interpretation of the extraordinary ability criteria. The extraordinary ability visa has considerable advantages because it is not dependent on an offer for employment in the U.S., and is exempt from the labor certification process. USCIS has issued instructions to adjudicators to conduct a two-step analysis of whether the evidence meets the regulatory requirements of three types of evidence and whether the evidence in totality demonstrates extraordinary ability.[128]

2. Members of the Professions with Advanced Degrees and Noncitizens with Exceptional Ability (EB-2)

The second employment-based preference category (EB-2) includes noncitizens of exceptional ability in the sciences, arts or business, and advanced degree professionals.[129] The labor certification requirement applies to this preference category.[130] Advanced degree professionals must hold a degree beyond a baccalaureate degree or its equivalent.[131] Persons of exceptional ability must establish that their work in the U.S. will substantially benefit the national economy, cultural, educational interests, or welfare of the U.S.

National interest waivers are one way in which a noncitizen in the EB-2 category can avoid the lengthy labor certification process. These waivers are only available to second employment-based preference beneficiaries and the noncitizen may file a waiver application on his or her own behalf. The employment offer requirement is waived if the prospective work of the noncitizen is in the national interest.[132] If a waiver is granted, then the labor certification requirement also is waived.[133] These waivers are difficult to obtain because the noncitizen's prospective work must have a substantial and national impact.[134]

---

[128] *USCIS Issues Interim I-140 Guidance; Seeks Stakeholder Input*, 87 INTERPRETER RELEASES 1643 (2010); *USCIS Ombudsman Recommendations to Improve the Qualify in Extraordinary Ability and Other Employment-Based Petition Adjudications*, Dec. 29, 2011, *available at* http://www.dhs.gov/xlibrary/assets/cisomb-rec_extraordinaryability_petitions.pdf.

[129] INA § 203(b)(2) permits noncitizens with the equivalent of an advanced degree to petition under this category.

[130] INA § 212(a)(5)(A).

[131] 8 C.F.R. § 204.5(k)(2) (2014).

[132] National interest waivers are also available to physicians working in shortage areas or veterans facilities under INA § 203(b)(2)(B)(ii).

[133] INA § 203(b)(2)(B). The regulations specify that a national interest waiver of the job offer requirement also waives the labor certification requirement. 8 C.F.R. § 204.5(k)(4)(ii) (2014). Although the noncitizen who obtains a national interest waiver does not require a job offer, often, an employer is involved.

[134] In Matter of New York State Dept. of Transportation (NYSDOT), 22 I.&N. Dec. 215 (BIA 1998), the Administrative Appeals Office found that an employer seeking a national interest waiver of the job offer requirement and labor certification requirement, must establish that: the noncitizen will be

3. Skilled Workers, Professionals and Other [Unskilled] Workers (EB-3)

The third employment-based preference category (EB-3) includes skilled workers, professionals without advanced degrees and other workers (unskilled workers). The labor certification requirement applies to this category. A profession is defined in the INA to "include but not be limited to architects, engineers, lawyers, physicians, surgeons, and teachers in elementary or secondary schools, colleges, academies and seminaries."[135] The terms "profession" and "professional" are terms of art defined through a large body of caselaw and administrative decisions. Generally, a profession has been interpreted to include occupations for which at least a baccalaureate degree in the field is required for entry.

The skilled worker category is available to individuals who possess and are filling an employment position requiring at least two years of training or experience.[136] The "other workers" category is set aside for those performing unskilled labor which is not of a temporary or seasonal nature. There are only 10,000 visas allotted to the other worker category annually. In addition, the other worker annual limit is reduced to 5,000 beginning in FY 2002 under the Nicaraguan and Central American Relief Act (NACARA). NACARA states that the 10,000 other worker visas available are to be reduced by up to 5,000 annually as long as necessary to offset adjustments under the NACARA program. This has resulted in longstanding, severe backlogs in the availability of visas for these workers.[137]

4. Employment Creation [Investor] Visas (EB-5)

The fifth employment-based preference category (EB-5) includes immigrant investors who create employment in the United States. This category requires investment of one million dollars and the creation of at least ten full-time employment positions for U.S. citizens, permanent residents or other authorized noncitizen workers. The required investment is reduced in targeted rural or other high unemployment areas. More than the one million dollar investment can be required by the Attorney General in high employment areas. Investors are granted conditional permanent residence, similar to family-sponsored marriage cases, and there are INA criminal provisions prohibiting immigration-related entrepreneurship fraud.[138]

These entrepreneurship visas were not heavily used initially after the 1990 Act. More EB-5 visas were issued in the mid-1990s as investors created complex

---

employed in an area of substantial intrinsic merit; the proposed benefit of that employee will be national in scope; and the national interest would be adversely affected if labor certification were required for the noncitizen. The last prong of the test makes it virtually impossible for all but very few noncitizens to obtain national interest waivers.

[135] INA § 101(a)(32).

[136] INA § 203(b)(3)(A)(i); 8 C.F.R. § 204.5(l)(2) (2014).

[137] Nicaraguan Adjustment and Central American Relief Act (NACARA) Pub. L. No. 105-100, 111 Stat. 2160 (Nov. 19, 1997).

[138] INA § 275(d).

financing schemes to avoid putting their investments truly at risk. The AAO denied several cases on this basis in 1998, and fewer visas were issued until 2007. USCIS issued regulations permitting investors to pool their investments in regional centers located in a targeted employment area where indirect job creation would be sufficient and a lower investment is required. Local government and private partnerships have created "shovel ready" projects and the interest EB-5 visas has increased.[139] As of October 1, 2014, USCIS had approved approximately 588 regional centers in 53 states and U.S. territories with multiple regional centers in several states.[140]

5. Labor Certification

Labor certification is a prerequisite for many of the employment-based categories. The INA lists the lack of certification as an inadmissibility ground.[141] Labor certification applies to all of the employment-based third preference. Labor certification is required for the employment-based second preference category, except in the case of a national interest waiver or Schedule A precertification (discussed below). The labor certification process is a mechanism to evaluate the impact on the U.S. labor market of permanent employment offers to noncitizens.[142] The U.S. Department of Labor [DOL] determines whether the permanent employment of a particular noncitizen will produce an adverse impact on the wages and working conditions of U.S. workers. It is presumed that there is no adverse affect if there are no available, able, willing or qualified U.S. workers to fill the permanent position to be offered to the noncitizen.[143]

The labor certification requirement may be waived under Schedule A precertification. Schedule A is a list of occupations the DOL already has determined are shortage occupations, therefore the employment of a noncitizen would not adversely affect the wages and working conditions of U.S. workers.[144] Under Schedule A, Group I, licensed physical therapists and professional nurses are precertified occupations.[145] A noncitizen may be eligible as a person of exceptional ability in the sciences or arts under Schedule A, Group II. Only the labor certification requirement is waived; an offer of employment is still required. The Schedule A requirements for exceptional ability differ slightly from second preference employment-based exceptional ability.

The traditional labor certification process, from 1965 to March 2005, was a time-consuming procedure involving review by state workforce agencies and a regional

---

[139] *See* ALIENIKOFF, MARTIN, MOTOMURA & FULLERTON, IMMIGRATION AND CITIZENSHIP, PROCESS AND POLICY 342 (7th ed. 2012).

[140] http://www.uscis.gov/working-united-states/permanent-workers/employment-based-immigration-fifth-preference-eb-5/immigrant-investor-regional-centers

[141] INA § 212(a)(5)(i) (2014).

[142] INA § 101(a)(31) defines "permanent" to mean "a relationship of continuing or lasting nature" even though it may be dissolved eventually.

[143] INA § 212(a)(5)(i) (2014).

[144] 20 C.F.R. §§ 656.5(b)(1), 656.15 (2014).

[145] 20 C.F.R. § 656.15(c) (2014).

office of the DOL. The local state workforce agency (SWA) began the labor certification process by examining each individual job offer to determine whether it was a bona fide job opportunity. The SWA would supervise the employer's recruitment of workers to ensure a good faith process was used by the employer to assert that there were no available, able, willing or qualified U.S. workers for the offered permanent position. The DOL also would review the entire process, and determine whether additional information was needed, and ultimately whether to grant or deny certification. Significant processing backlogs developed during 1990s, creating problems for both employers and their noncitizen employees.[146]

As of March 28, 2005, the DOL has implemented a new system to address the enormous backlogs: PERM, the Program Electronic Review Management system.[147] The PERM system relies on the same substantive requirements as traditional labor certification, however, PERM significantly changes the procedure. SWAs only provide wage determinations to ensure an offered position reflects the prevailing wage in the local geographic area. The employer's recruitment process occurs before filing the labor certification application and, as a result, with no oversight by the SWA. Employers must attest to following the rules and they are required to maintain documentation of the recruitment effort.[148] The DOL will conduct audits on a random or selective basis to review this documentation.

The labor certification application includes information about the job offer and information about the noncitizen beneficiary on whose behalf certification is sought, including prior employment experience and education. The DOL will use the information about the noncitizen to review whether the employer has a valid job offer or one that is tailored to the noncitizen's background.

Employers are required to offer the prevailing wage for a position in the local geographic area.[149] The SWA determines the prevailing wage and an employer can challenge the SWA's determination.[150] Generally, a lower wage will not be accepted unless unusual circumstances exist. For example, in *Matter of Tuskegee University*, the DOL denied certification for an associate professor position

---

[146] Many noncitizens are employed in nonimmigrant status with a specific time limit, such as H-1B workers. The labor certification application is just the first step in the process of immigrant visa classification under the second and third employment-based categories. After certification, an immigrant visa petition (Form I-140) had to be filed, and in the 1990s backlogs in adjudicating these petitions also existed.

[147] Other attempts to streamline the labor certification process such as "Reduction-in-Recruitment," [RIR] were developed. RIR eliminated the state agency supervision of recruitment in straightforward cases. RIR was phased out when PERM was introduced, although some cases still remain in the adjudication pipeline.

[148] *See* 20 C.F.R. § 656.17 (2014). Regulations require advertising and posting requirements for the offered permanent employment position. The employer evaluates job applicants and prepares a detailed recruitment report specifying the recruitment steps taken, the job applicants, the number of hires, and the number of workers who were rejected based on lawful, job-related reasons.

[149] 20 C.F.R. § 656.40 (2014).

[150] The employer can challenge the SWA's prevailing wage determination. For example, the SWA conducts surveys and maintains databases of wages within its local area and this information is used to determine the appropriate prevailing wage. Employers may challenge the SWA's prevailing wage determination by providing their own surveys and other information.

because the university did not offer a wage comparable to other colleges in the local geographic area.[151] Tuskegee University argued that its offered wage was well-above the prevailing wage among the 43 schools in the United Negro College Fund and this group should be the comparison group for the prevailing wage determination. The Board of Alien Labor Certification Appeals [BALCA] agreed with Tuskegee University and granted certification.[152]

Employers may not tailor a job offer to the background of the noncitizen beneficiary of the labor certification application. The minimum requirements for offered positions may not be unduly restrictive in terms of the years and types of education or prior work experience required. The DOL makes its determinations about unduly restrictive requirements using the O*NET (Occupational Information Network), an online database of occupations with information about the normally required education and experience.[153] An employer can establish that its minimum requirements are justified by business necessity to counter a DOL finding of unduly restrictive requirements.[154]

O*NET contains job descriptions and the normal education and experience requirements for employment positions. The position descriptions include a number that corresponds to the years of education and experience required: the SVP (specific vocational preparation) number. If a job requires more experience and education than the SVP number in O*NET, or the job includes a combination of occupations or degree requirements, the employer may need to provide a business necessity justification.[155] Foreign language requirements are presumptively restrictive and, under PERM, a specific business necessity justification is required.[156]

Unduly restrictive requirements will cause a denial of certification.[157] After review of the application, the DOL Certifying Officer will approve the application, request additional information, select the application for audit, or deny the application. Denials are appealed to the Board of Alien Labor Certification Appeals [BALCA]. Employers are subject to sanctions for abuse of the process, such as

---

[151] 5 Imm. L. & Proc. Rep. B3-172 (BALCA, Feb. 23, 1988).

[152] BALCA did not follow *Matter of Tuskegee University* in later cases. In Matter of Hathaway Children's Services, 91-INA-388, 1994 WL 29778 (BALCA, Feb. 4, 1994), BALCA reviewed the wage for a "maintenance repairer" job in a nonprofit treatment center for disabled children. The Board stated it did not see any justification for paying a different wage for positions with the same job duties. The center argued that the comparison group for the prevailing wage determination should be other United Way non-profit organizations.

[153] *See* http://www.onetcener.org or www.flcdatacenter.com. O*NET incorporates information from the Dictionary of Occupational Titles which had been used for decades by DOL.

[154] Business necessity exists if the job requirements bear a reasonable relationship to the occupation in the context of the employer's business, and are essential to perform the job duties in a reasonable manner.

[155] 20 C.F.R. § 656.17 (2014).

[156] 20 C.F.R. § 656.17 (2014)states that business necessity for a foreign language may be based on the nature of the occupation, e.g., a translator, or the need to communicate with a large majority of the employer's customers, contractors, or employees who cannot communicate effectively in English.

[157] Denials also occur if the DOL determines that the noncitizen received on-the-job training for the offered position, and therefore was at an advantage compared to U.S. workers applying for the job.

misrepresentations or violation of the regulations pertaining to recordkeeping. Review in federal court is available after exhaustion of all administrative procedures under the Administrative Procedure Act. *In the Matter of Information Industries, Inc.* is the leading case on the issue of whether the job requirements in a labor certification application are unduly restrictive and tailored to the background of a noncitizen.[158] The employer sought certification for a systems engineer position requiring two specific educational degrees; both a B.S. in Engineering and an M.S. in Computer Science. The DOL Regional Office denied certification finding the dual degree requirement to be unduly restrictive and not justified by a business necessity.[159]

BALCA found that business necessity exists if an employer to demonstrate that the job requirements bear a reasonable relationship to the occupation in the context of the employer's business, and are essential to perform, in a reasonable manner, the job duties as described by the employer.[160] In *Information Industries*, BALCA found that the two degree requirement did not conflict with the Dictionary of Occupational Titles [now O*NET].[161] The Board remanded back to the DOL Regional Certifying Officer to determine whether the job requirements were justified by business necessity. On remand, certification was denied again because the two degree requirement was unduly restrictive.[162]

Upon approval of a labor certification application, an employer files an I-140 Immigrant Visa Petition on behalf of the noncitizen beneficiary. The employer files the immigrant visa petition with a USCIS Regional Service Center. The labor certification approval is valid for a period of 180 days.[163] The USCIS will examine whether the noncitizen meets the minimum job requirements for the offered position in the labor certification application. USCIS also will review whether the employer has the ability to pay the prevailing wage. The USCIS does not have authority to reevaluate the test of the labor market conducted by the DOL.

---

[158] In the Matter of Information Industries, Inc., 88-INA-82 (BALCA 1989).

[159] The DOL regulation at issue, 20 C.F.R. 656.21(b)(2) (2014), has a nearly identical provision under the PERM regulations, 20 C.F.R. 656.17(h) (2014). Under 20 C.F.R. 656.21(b)(2) (2014), the job opportunity cannot be unduly restrictive, unless justified by business necessity, and the requirements: "shall be those normally required for the job in the United States; shall be those defined for the job in the DOL Dictionary of Occupational Titles [incorporated today in O*NET] and shall not include requirements for foreign languages."

[160] BALCA adopted an interpretation of the business necessity standard after considering the use of the term in other statutory contexts. For example, under Title VII of the 1964 Civil Rights Act, business necessity is established only when the essence of a business operation is undermined.

[161] *See* http://www.onetcenter.org or www.flcdatacenter.com.

[162] The noncitizen subsequently moved to another DOL region and obtained certification. ALIENIKOFF, MARTIN, MOTOMURA & FULLERTON, IMMIGRATION AND CITIZENSHIP, PROCESS AND POLICY 375 (7th ed. 2012).

[163] An approved labor certification on or after July 16, 2007 expires if it is not filed in support of an I-140 Immigrant Visa Petition within 180 days. 20 C.F.R. 656.30(b)(1) (2014).

D. CERTAIN SPECIAL IMMIGRANTS (EB-4)

The fourth employment-based preference category (EB-4) includes certain special immigrants identified in INA § 101(a)(27)(C) through (M). This hodgepodge group includes: ministers and other religious workers; certain foreign medical graduates; certain overseas employees and retirees of the U.S. government, American Institute of Taiwan, Panama Canal Company or Canal Zone Authority, and specified international organizations including NATO; certain juvenile court dependents (SIJ); some members of the military; and certain broadcasters. Congress added translators with U.S. Armed Forces as a category of special immigrants in 2006.[164] Only Iraqi or Afghani translators are eligible and they must have worked for a period of at least 12 months. In 2008, Congress added another special immigrant category for Iraqis employed by or on behalf of the U.S. in Iraq after March 20, 2003.[165] The eligibility requirements for each of these categories of special immigrant are set forth in INA § 101(a)(27). Special immigrants file their own visa petitions (Form I-360) with USCIS.

Noncitizens eligible for special juvenile immigrant status are discussed in Section 4 of this Chapter.

E. DIVERSITY VISAS AS SET FORTH IN INA § 203(C)

Under the Diversity Visa Lottery Program, 55,000 visas are allocated using a random selection system.[166] This immigrant category was added to the system in 1990, in part, to address low immigration from Western European countries.[167] The diversity visas are allocated by dividing countries and regions of the world into high admission or low admission areas. Countries with fewer than 50,000 immigrants to the United States over the preceding five-year period may be designated low admission countries. High admission countries can not participate at all in the diversity immigrant visa system. Diversity visas are distributed differently to low admission countries in low admission regions and low admission countries in high admission regions. The high admission and low admission countries are identified annually.[168]

Noncitizens are eligible for diversity visas if they have at least a high school education or its equivalent, or at least two years of work experience in an occupation requiring two years of training or experience. There is a separate diversity visa

---

[164] Natural Defense Authorization Act for Fiscal Year 2006, Pub. L. No. 109-163, 119 Stat. 3136 (Jan. 6, 2006).

[165] Iraqis Providing Faithful and Valuable Service to U.S., Pub. L. No. 110-181, 122 Stat. 3 (Jan. 28, 2008).

[166] INA § 201(b)(2)(A). The number of diversity visas issued is reduced by up to 5,000 visas in order to allocate visas under NACARA. *See supra* note 137.

[167] Early lottery programs in 1988 and 1989 were ad-hoc measures available only to a narrow group of noncitizens. The history of the diversity immigrant category is discussed in Chapter 2.

[168] In FY 2008, the high admission countries included Brazil, Canada, China (mainland); Colombia; Dominican Republic; El Salvador; Haiti; India; Jamaica; Mexico; Pakistan; Philippines; Peru; Poland, Russia; South Korea; United Kingdom (except Northern Ireland); and Vietnam.

lottery each year. Only one application may be filed per year by a noncitizen.[169] The DOS website provides instructions and timetables for applications. If an applicant is selected, she is notified by the DOS. Spouses and children are eligible as derivative beneficiaries.[170] The immigrant visa must be issued within the fiscal year and more applicants are selected than the number of visas available. Delays in processing or an excessive number of applicants can use up all of the visas before the fiscal year ends. As a result, some selected applicants may not receive a diversity visa.

F.   ASYLEES AND REFUGEES

Noncitizens who have a "well founded fear of persecution based on race, religion, nationality, membership in a social group or political opinion" may become permanent residents.[171] Noncitizens who have been granted asylum in the United States or who have entered the U.S. as refugees are eligible to adjust status to permanent resident after one year under INA § 209. There is a separate system for the allocation of immigrant visas to refugees who have established a well-founded fear through an overseas refugee program. The President of the United States makes an annual recommendation of the number of refugee admissions.[172] Noncitizens who have applied for asylum in the United States based one of the five grounds above and have established a well-founded fear in the U.S. are asylees. Asylees are eligible to adjust status to LPR status without any numerical limit. Prior to the 2005 REAL ID Act, there were annual limits on the number of asylee adjustments.[173] This is covered in Chapter 10.

---

[169] The DOS usually specifies a one or two-month period for the online submission of applications. For example, the 2009 Lottery registration period was October 3 through December 2, 2007. Lottery winners were notified by mail between May and July 2008. DOS, *Diversity Visa (DV) Lottery Instructions, available at* http://travel.state.gov/visa/immigrants/types/types_1318.html.

[170] INA § 203(d).

[171] INA § 101(a)(42)(A).

[172] INA § 207.

[173] REAL ID Act of 2005, Pub. L. No. 109-13, 119 Stat. 231 (May 11, 2005).

Chapter 8

NONIMMIGRANT VISAS

Immigration law recognizes several categories of nonimmigrants who enter the United States, for specific purposes and for limited time periods, without an intent to remain in the country permanently. Nonimmigrant visas far outnumber immigrant visas. Criteria for admission to the United States with nonimmigrant visas are less restrictive than admission with immigrant visas because it is the nature of the activity and the permitted length of stay that restrict the nonimmigrant visa. Nonimmigrant visa applicants may seek waivers for most grounds of inadmissibility.[1]

INA § 101(a)(15) lists the categories of nonimmigrants allowed into the United States. These categories include family; business, employment and commercial; educational; and victims of violence. The name of the visa typically corresponds to the subsection of INA § 101(a)(15) in which each visa is described. For the most part, noncitizens seeking admission are presumed to be immigrants unless they can show they fit within one of the nonimmigrants categories listed in INA

---

[1] INA § 212(d)(3).

§ 101(a)(15).[2] Nonimmigrant visa applicants must show that their intended stay is temporary and that their activities in the United States are consistent with those allowed for the claimed nonimmigrant status. A nonimmigrant's long-term desire to remain in the United States permanently, however, has been recognized in the dual intent doctrine. The doctrine holds that a nonimmigrant may have both a long-term intent to immigrate to the United States permanently and a short-term intent to return to one's home country in compliance with the visa requirement.[3]

With certain exceptions, nonimmigrants can change status from one nonimmigrant category to another.[4] Nonimmigrants who overstay their visas or are otherwise unlawfully present in the United States for six months or more are ineligible to change status. The following categories of immigrants are not allowed to change status to another nonimmigrant classification: C (transit), D (crewmen), K (fiancée), J (exchange visitor/student, if subject to the two-year foreign residency requirement), S (informant), visa waiver program entrant or those who entered in transit without a visa. Moreover, M-1 (vocational student) visa holders cannot change status to F-1 (student) or to H-1, if H-1 is based on the training received as M-1. None of the restrictions on changing status apply to those who seek a change in status to T (trafficking) or U (crime victim) status.

A. FAMILY

1. The V Visa

Congress created the V visa in 2000 to allow for the reunification of families during the long wait time for an immigrant visa. The V visa allows spouses and children of permanent residents to live and work in the United States while awaiting either approval of an immigrant visa petition, processing of an immigrant visa, or adjustment of status. The V visa is a transitional visa that allows legal status in the United States until the visa holder can obtain immigrant status. Because the V visa was envisioned as a temporary measure, its provisions were made available only to those whose sponsors petitioned for them on or before December 21, 2000. The LIFE Act, which created the V visa, allowed beneficiaries of second preference petitions filed on or before December 21, 2000 to apply for nonimmigrant status as long as three years had passed since the petitions were filed. The visas were made available to those whose I-130 petitions were pending, those whose I-130 petitions were approved but whose visa numbers were not yet available, and those whose I-130 petitions were approved and whose adjustment of status was pending. It is not available to beneficiaries of petitioners who filed after December 21, 2000 so it is of limited practical use today.

There are three categories of V visas: the V-1 is reserved for spouses of permanent residents; the V-2 is reserved for children of the permanent resident

---

[2] INA § 214(b).

[3] Matter of H-R-, 7 I.&N. Dec. 651, 654 (R.C. 1958); Matter of Hosseinpour, 15 I.&N. Dec. 191, 192 (BIA 1975) (the "mere desire . . . to obtain permanent residence in the future does not, by itself, automatically disqualify an alien from admission as a nonimmigrant").

[4] INA § 248.

petitioner; the V-3 is reserved for derivative children of either a V-1 or V-2 visa holder. A person in V status can apply for work authorization as well.[5] A person can lose V status if the underlying I-130 petition or adjustment of status application is denied, withdrawn, or revoked.

2. The Fiancée Visa: K Visa

The K visa is sometimes known as a hybrid because the K visa holder is allowed to enter as a nonimmigrant and apply for permanent residence under certain conditions. K visas are available for fiancés of U.S. citizens and their children under 21 years of age, or for spouses of U.S. citizens and their children under 21.

There are four categories of K visa holders. The K-1 visa is reserved for fiancés of U.S. citizens. It allows a fiancé to enter the United States for a 90-day period to marry the petitioner and apply for permanent residence. A K visa can be issued only after a petition for sponsorship has been approved by DHS. The petitioner must show that the parties met previously, in person, within two years of the date of the filing of the petition (unless a waiver is granted).[6] This fraud prevention measure was implemented with the passage of the Immigration Marriage Fraud Amendments of 1986.[7] The requirement can be waived on a showing of extreme hardship to the petitioner, or a showing of long-held social, religious, or cultural custom.[8] The parties must also show that they have a bona fide intention to marry, and are legally able and willing to marry within 90 days after the fiancé's arrival in the U.S.

If the marriage does not occur within the 90-day period, the K nonimmigrant must leave the United States. The 90-day period is a strict time limit, although at least one court has held that the period can be tolled when circumstances beyond the control of the visa holder make it impossible to meet the deadline.[9] Once the marriage takes place, the K-1 nonimmigrant must apply for adjustment of status. If a divorce occurs, a K-1 may still apply to become an LPR under certain circumstances.[10] A child accompanying or following to join may be admitted as a K-2 nonimmigrant.

The K-3/K-4 visas were created by the LIFE Act of 2000 to speed the process of entry for spouses and children of U.S. citizens awaiting entry into the United States. The K-3/K-4 visas allow spouses and children of U.S. citizens who are the beneficiaries of approved I-130 petitions to be admitted to the U.S. initially as nonimmigrants while they wait to adjust status. Previously, these applicants had to wait outside the United States until their immigrant visas were processed. Applicants can enter the United States once an I-130 has been filed and await the

---

[5] INA § 214(o)(1)(A).

[6] INA § 214(d).

[7] Pub. L. No. 99-639, 100 Stat. 3537.

[8] 8 C.F.R. 214.2(k)(2).

[9] Moss v. INS, 651 F.2d 1091, 1093 (5th Cir. 1981) (court noted that purpose of K visa was to show intent to marry rather than to enforce an "absolute and mandatory period of time within which [to marry]").

[10] Matter of Sesay, 25 I.&N. Dec. 431, 441–444 (BIA 2011).

approval of the I-130 and the processing of the immigrant visa or adjustment of status in the United States. K-3/K-4 nonimmigrants are admitted for a period of two years, and can seek extensions.

B.   BUSINESS, EMPLOYMENT, AND COMMERCIAL

1.   Temporary Visitors for Business or Pleasure

Visas for temporary visitors, known as B-1/B-2 visitors, are reserved for those visiting the United States temporarily for business or pleasure.[11] The statute makes clear that this type of visa is not available for those planning to study in the United States, those performing skilled or unskilled labor, or those representing foreign media.[12] In other words, the B Visa is not meant to be catch-all available to all who wish to come to U.S. temporarily for whatever purpose.[13] A B-1/B-2 applicant must show that s/he has a residence in a foreign country which s/he has no intention of abandoning. The applicant must also show that s/he has an intention to depart at the expiration of his/her stay, permission to enter the foreign country s/he intends to depart to at the expiration of his/her stay, and that s/he has adequate financial resources to carry out the purpose of the visit. A B-1/B-2 visitor is admitted for up to one year with extensions of six months available.[14]

A B-1 visitor for business is admissible if entering the United States to engage in commercial transactions not involving gainful employment. Such activities as negotiating contracts, consulting with clients or business associates, attending conferences, and participating in board of directors meetings are considered activities of a commercial or business nature. If a business activity involves full-time management of a U.S. business, however, a B-1 visa is not appropriate.[15] The regulations governing nonimmigrant visas define business as a legitimate commercial or professional activity, not local employment or labor for hire.[16] The regulations require that the applicant show a clear intent to continue foreign residence, intent to enter the United States for a specified limited duration of time, and that the principal place of business and actual profit accrual occurs in a foreign country.[17] The B-1 applicant must show documentation that s/he meets each of these requirements.

B-2 visitors for pleasure can enter the United States temporarily and for specified periods of time. Pleasure is defined in the regulations as "legitimate activities of a recreational character, including tourism, amusement, visits with

---

[11] "Pleasure" is defined for B-2's as "Legitimate activities of a recreational character, including tourism, amusement, visits with friends or relatives, rest, medical treatment and activities of a fraternal, social or service nature." 22 C.F.R. § 41.31(b)(2).

[12] INA § 101(a)(15)(B).

[13] Matter of Healy and Goodchild, 17 I.&N. Dec. 22 (BIA 1979).

[14] 8 C.F.R. § 214.2(b)(1).

[15] Matter of Lawrence, 15 I.&N. Dec. 418, 420 (BIA 1975).

[16] 22 C.F.R. § 41.31(b).

[17] 22 C.F.R. § 41.31(b).

friends or relatives, rest, medical treatment and activities of a fraternal, social, or service nature."[18]

In addition to tourists, social visitors to see friends or relatives, or for health purposes, visitors for pleasure include convention participants, amateur sports or similar event participants, dependents of U.S. military personnel, and those entering the United States to marry U.S. citizens and depart.

A person entering as a B-1/B-2 visitor cannot attend school as an F-1 student without first obtaining a change in status within the United States, or an F-1/M-1 visa abroad.[19] Students who are attending a summer work and travel program whose principal component does not involve substantive academic instruction may receive a B-2.[20]

2. Visas for Business Personnel

There are several categories of visas available for those who enter the United States to work. This section discusses H, L, E, I, O, P, Q, and R visas. Each of these visas permits employment in the United States, and permits stays longer than the B visa allows. Some provide a path to permanent residency. The categories define the type of work, profession, or business that the applicant seeks to perform in the United States.

a. The Professional Visas: H-1, L, O, and P

H visa applicants are those coming temporarily to work in the United States in specialty occupations (H-1B); as professional nurses in health profession shortage areas (H-1C); as temporary agricultural workers (H-2A); as skilled/unskilled workers in occupations where U.S. citizens or residents are unavailable (H-2B); as trainees (H-3); or accompanying family members with H visas (H-4). Each visa category maintains a yearly cap. This section discusses the H-1 visa, which is reserved for specialty occupation employees.

The H-1B visa category includes persons in specialty occupations, fashion models of distinguished merit and ability, or persons participating in Department of Defense cooperative projects. A specialty occupation is defined as one that requires the application of highly specialized knowledge and a bachelor's degree or higher in that particular specialty.[21] The position must meet one of the following criteria: a bachelor's degree is the employer's minimum requirement for the entry into the position; a bachelor's degree is usually required of this position in the industry; the employer normally requires a degree or its equivalent, or the duties are so specialized and complex that the knowledge required for the position is associated with a degree.[22] Experience alone or "progressively responsible experience that is

---

[18] 22 C.F.R. § 41.31(b)(2).

[19] Memo, Williams, Ex. Assoc. Comm. Field Ops., HQISD 70/6.2.2 P (April 12, 2002), reprinted in 79 No. 17 Interpreter Releases 595, 605–07 (Apr. 22, 2002).

[20] Cable, State, 10-State-047061 (May 10, 2010) published on AILA InfoNet at Doc. No. 10051363.

[21] INA § 214(i)(1); 8 C.F.R. § 214.2(h)(4)(ii).

[22] 8 C.F.R. § 214.2(h)(4)(iii)(A).

equivalent to completion of a United States baccalaureate or higher degree in the specialty occupation"[23] may be sufficient to fulfill the education requirement. This experience must be with the "theoretical and practical application of specialized knowledge"[24] that the occupation requires.

This category of visas requires that the applicant submit a labor condition application (LCA), also known as an "attestation" to the U.S. Department of Labor (DOL).[25] Failure to comply with all LCA requirements may result in fine of $1,000–$35,000 and debarment of approvals for one year. The application must state that the employer will offer the greater of the actual wage paid to similar employees or the prevailing wage for the occupation in the area to the applicant seeking a visa; that the working conditions of similarly situated workers will not be affected; that there is not a strike or lockout at the place of employment; that the employer has provided notice of the filing of the visa application to the appropriate bargaining representative, or by public posting to affected employees. The employer must attest that it is not displacing and will not displace a U.S. worker within the period beginning 90 days before the filing and ending 90 days after the filing of the application.[26] The employer must show that it has taken good faith steps to recruit U.S. workers at the same or greater salary as is being offered to the noncitizen, and has offered the job to any U.S. worker who applies and is equally or better qualified.[27] An employer must show that it filed the attestation; DOL approval is not required.

Until 1990 there was no cap on nonimmigrant categories, including the H-1B category. When Congress passed the Immigration Act of 1990, it set caps for H-1B recipients at 65,000. This limitation caused much frustration for employers, especially those experiencing the industry boom and labor shortages in the information technology fields. Congress temporarily raised the H-1B caps for 1999, 2000, and 2001.[28] The caps were increased to up to 115,000 in 1999 and 2000, and 107,500 in 2001. Congress again raised the caps in 2000 to 195,000 for the fiscal years 2001 through 2003, and created a cap exemption for higher education institutions and government or nonprofit research institutions.[29] After an economic slowdown, Congress allowed the caps to revert to 65,000 in fiscal year 2004. For the past several years, the H-1B visa caps have been reached on the first day of the fiscal year or close to it. Every year, there are calls for a reform of the immigration system to address problems in labor flow caused by the caps. Congress has also responded to calls to address employer dependence on H-1B workers by imposing a markedly higher fee for H-1B petitions than for other petitions. The fees are used for workforce training programs for U.S. workers. Congress has also made H-1B

---

[23] 8 C.F.R. §214.2(h)(4)(iii)(C)(4).

[24] Matter of Sea, Inc. 19 I.&N. Dec. 817 (Comm. 1988).

[25] INA § 212(n).

[26] INA § 212(n)(1)(E).

[27] INA § 212(n)(1)(G).

[28] American Competitiveness and Workforce Improvement Act of 1998, Pub. L. No. 105-277, 112 Stat. 2681 (Oct. 21, 1998).

[29] American Competitiveness in the Twenty-First Century Act of 2000, Pub. L. No. 106-313, 114 Stat. 1251 (Oct. 17, 2000).

visas portable, allowing visa holders to change jobs after their arrival to avoid perceived employer exploitation of visa holders.

Although the visa requires intent to return to one's home country, it does not preclude seeking legal permanent residence for H-1B holders. Often, an H-1B visa holder also qualifies for an employment immigrant visa but, because the wait times for obtaining legal permanent resident status are so long, Congress made explicit in the Immigration Act of 1990 that a person whose skills are needed today can seek both permanent resident status and an H-1B visa. This dual intent is not considered, "evidence of an intention to abandon foreign residence for purposes of obtaining" an H-1B visa.[30]

The L visa serves functions similar to those of the H-1B visa but is reserved for intracompany transferees who are entering the United States to further the business needs of foreign or multinational corporations. An L Visa holder must be employed by a firm, corporation or other legal entity, or its parent, branch, affiliate, or subsidiary. This definition includes non-profits, religious, and charitable organizations. The purpose of the L visa is to facilitate transfers of executives or employees with specialized knowledge between foreign-based offices to U.S. branches or subsidiaries. Employees already working in the U.S. on an L Visa can be transferred from one U.S. affiliate to another, but a new I-129 must be filed for each transfer. The L visa requires that a person "render his services . . . in a capacity that is managerial, executive, or involves specialized knowledge."[31]

Specialized knowledge is defined by the statute as "special knowledge of the company product or its application in international markets or . . . an advanced level of knowledge of processes and procedures of the company."[32] L visa applicants must show that they have been employed continuously for one of the previous three years by the company that seeks their services.[33] L visa holders are granted up to three years' stay, and can extend their stay for up to seven years for managers or five years for those with specialized knowledge.[34] In addition, the L Visa requires full-time employment. Part-time or self-employment will not suffice to fulfill the L Visa requirements. However, full-time services divided among affiliate companies may be counted.

Concern over whether the L visa category was being used to circumvent the labor attestation requirements and caps of the H-1B category prompted Congress to limit eligibility for L visas based on specialized knowledge.[35] Congress limits the placement of employees with specialized knowledge to worksites principally controlled by the employer.[36]

---

[30] INA § 214(h).

[31] INA § 101(a)(15)(L).

[32] INA § 214(c)(2)(B).

[33] INA § 101(a)(15)(L).

[34] INA § 214(c)(2)(D); 8 C.F.R. § 214.2(l)(7); 8 C.F.R. § 214.2(l)(15)(ii).

[35] INA § 214(c)(2)(F).

[36] *Id.*

Closely related to the H-1B visa category are the O and P categories. The O category covers athletes, entertainers, and performers or others in the arts, sciences, business, or education, who have exhibited "extraordinary ability" demonstrated by "sustained national or international acclaim."[37] The O category also covers immediate relatives and support staff of the principal O visa recipient. An O visa is available initially for a three-year period with the possibility of one-year extensions.[38] There are three categories for the O Visa. The O-1 visa is for the athlete, entertainer, and performer. The O-2 visa is for the persons accompanying and assisting the O-1 artist, athlete or performer for a specific event or events. An O-2 holder must satisfy certain criteria, namely that he or she is 1) an integral part of such actual performance; 2) has critical skills and experience with the O-1 that are not of a general nature and which cannot be performed by other individuals; and 3) has foreign residence that he or she has no intention of abandoning. The O-3 visa is for spouses and children accompanying and following to join.

The P nonimmigrant category contains several subcategories of recognized athletes and entertainers. The P-1 category is reserved for internationally recognized athletes or entertainment groups performing in specific events. The P-2 category is reserved for artists and entertainers seeking to enter the United States under reciprocal exchange programs. The P-3 category is used by artists or entertainers providing "culturally unique" programs. For the P category, an entertainment group or athletic team may be as few as 2 persons and the manner in which the act is billed is not determinative of its eligibility for P status.

P-1 visa holders are admitted for up to five years, with the possibility of up to a five year extension.[39] The rest of the P categories are admitted initially for one year and can seek one year extensions.

b.   Lesser Skilled Workers: H-2 Visas

The H-2 visa category is reserved for low-skilled workers who enter the United States seasonally or for temporary work to fill a demonstrated temporary labor need. The H-2 category requires that an employer show that the nonimmigrant is needed on a seasonal or temporary basis "to perform agricultural labor or services"[40] or "to perform temporary service or labor if unemployed person capable of performing such service or labor cannot be found in this country."[41] Temporary employment is defined as employment that "last[s] no longer than 1 year" except in exceptional circumstances.[42]

The H-2A category is reserved for agricultural workers. This visa category carries the legacy of guest worker programs such as the "Bracero program,"

---

[37]   INA § 101(a)(15)(O).

[38]   8 C.F.R. § 214.2(o)(6)(iii); 8 C.F.R. § 214.2(0)(12)(ii).

[39]   8 C.F.R. § 214.2(p)(8)(iii)(A); 8 C.F.R. § 214.2(p)(14)(ii)(A).

[40]   INA § 101(a)(15)(H)(2)(A).

[41]   INA § 1019A)(15)(H)(2)(B).

[42]   20 C.F.R. § 655.103(d).

infamous for its lack of labor protections for its foreign workers.[43] Until 1986, employers could seek agricultural workers only through the general low-skill worker visa. Agricultural employers found the process for obtaining general visas too cumbersome, and, as a result, rarely sought visas for their workers. Much of the agricultural industry operated with undocumented workers. Congress attempted to remedy the problem by creating the H-2A program through the Immigration Reform and Control Act of 1986.[44] Congress made the process more accessible and streamlined. Each year DHS designates which countries are eligible for the H-2A program and the basis for the designation.[45]

An employer must file a labor certification application with the DOL showing that "(A) there are not sufficient workers who are able, willing and qualified, and who will be available at the time and place needed, to perform the labor or services involved in the petition and (B) the employment of the alien in such labor or services will not adversely affect the wages and working conditions of workers in the United States similarly employed."[46] Once a labor certification is granted, the USCIS must approve the petition before individual workers can obtain visas. The DOL establishes a yearly adverse effect wage rate that sets the minimum hourly wage for H-2A workers for each state. In 2013, the hourly wage ranged from $9.50 in Louisiana and Mississippi to $12.72 in Hawaii.[47] Also, H-2A workers must be provided with housing, meals or cooking facilities, return transportation, and workers' compensation insurance or its equivalent.[48] Employees who violate H-2A terms and conditions or overstay their approved stays are barred from the H-2A program for five years.

The H-2B program covers low-skilled workers outside of the agricultural industry. An H-2B visa is available for temporary employment for a job that is temporary in nature.[49] The need must be a "one-time occurrence, a seasonal need, or an intermittent need."[50] The period of employment must generally be one year or less unless it is a one-time event.[51] If employment is more than one year, a new Labor Certification is required.

---

[43] For history and analysis of the Bracero program and similar guest worker initiatives, *see* Mae Ngai, IMPOSSIBLE SUBJECTS 138–166 (2005); Michael A. Olivas, *The Chronicles, My Grandfather's Stories, and Immigration Law: The Slave Traders Chronicle as Racial History*, 34 ST. LOUIS U. L.J. 425, 435–39 (1989–1990); Gilbert Paul Carrasco, *Latinos in the United States — Invitation and Exile, in* IMMIGRANTS OUT! THE NEW NATIVISM AND THE ANTI-IMMIGRANT IMPULSE IN THE UNITED STATES 190–204 (Juan Perea, ed., 1997).

[44] *See* INA § 101(a)(15)(H)(ii)(a).

[45] 8 C.F.R. § 214.2(h)(5)(i)(F).

[46] INA § 218(a)(1).

[47] 73 Fed. Reg. 10289 (Feb. 26, 2008).

[48] INA § 218(c)(4); 20 C.F.R. §§ 655.102(b)(9), 655.107; 655.102(b)(4), 655.102(b)(5)(ii); INA § 218(b)(3).

[49] 8 C.F.R. § 214.2(h)(6)(ii); Matter of Artee Corp., 18 I.&N. Dec. 366 (BIA 1982); Sussex Engineering v. Montgomery, 825 F.2d 1084 (6th Cir. 1987). "Temporary" is defined as a year or less. 8 C.F.R. § 214.2(h)(6)(ii)(B).

[50] 8 C.F.R. § 214.2(h)(6)(ii)(B).

[51] *Id.*

H-2B visas are capped at 66,000, not including workers' families.[52] No more than 33,000 of the visas are available in each half of the fiscal year.[53] This six-month allocation reflects congressional desire to ensure that temporary visas are available throughout the year. An H-2B visa is available only if an "unemployed person capable of performing such service or labor cannot be found in this country."[54] Employers seeking H-2B workers must seek either a certification from the DOL that "qualified workers in the United States are not available and that the alien's employment will not adversely affect wages and working conditions of similarly employed United States workers," or a notice "detailing the reasons why such certification cannot be made. Such notice shall address the availability of U.S. workers in the occupation and the prevailing wages and working conditions of U.S. workers in the occupation."[55] As of 2013, landscaping was still the industry with the most H-2B certifications, with amusement park workers, forestry workers and maid and housekeeping cleaners in distant second, third and fourth place, respectively.[56]

c. Treaty Traders and Investors, and Free Trade Agreement Professionals: The E and TN Visas

The E and TN visas accommodate those who enter the United States pursuant to international trade and commerce and free trade agreements. E visas are available for those who seek to participate in international trade and investment opportunities in the United States. The E-1 category is for treaty traders; the E-2 category is reserved for treaty investors. The principal requirement for an E visa is that the visa holder be a citizen or national of a country that maintains a treaty of commerce or navigation which provides for the applicant's trade or investment. A treaty trader must carry out substantial international trade, principally between the United States and the treaty country. "Substantial" is defined as an amount of trade sufficient to ensure a continuous flow of international trade between the U.S. and treaty country for E-1 visa holders.[57] A treaty investor must invest, or be in the process of investing, significant capital in an enterprise s/he will direct and which will not be a marginal enterprise entered into solely to make a living.

Several treaties meet the definition of commerce and navigation, but the Immigration and Nationality Act itself also confers E visa benefits on citizens of Australia and Sweden. Trade is defined as transactions involving goods and services, as well as technology-related services.[58] A current list of countries which the U.S. allows E-1 and E-2 visas from can be found on the Bureau of Consular

---

[52] INA § 214(g)(2).

[53] INA § 214(g)(1)(B); INA § 214(g)(10).

[54] 8 C.F.R. § 214.2(h)(1)(ii)(D).

[55] 8 C.F.R. § 214.2(h)(6)(iv).

[56] OFFICE OF FOREIGN LABOR CERTIFICATION, H-2B TEMPORARY NON-AGRICULTURAL LABOR CERTIFICATION PROGRAM-SELECTED STATISTICS, FY 2013 YTD.

[57] 8 C.F.R. § 214.2(e)(10).

[58] INA § 101(a)(15)(E)(i).

Affairs website.[59]

An E visa holder is admitted for up to two years initially, and may remain indefinitely on two-year extensions as long as s/he continues to operate the activities for which entry was initially granted. This distinctive character of the E visa makes it preferable in some instances to an L or H-1B visa. As with H-1B and L visa holders, an E visa holder does not have to maintain a foreign residence that s/he does not intend to abandon.[60] An E visa holder's spouse may work.[61]

TN visas were created by Congress upon the passage of the North American Free Trade Agreement ("NAFTA"). There are four categories of businesspeople covered under NAFTA. They parallel the business visitor, the treaty trader or investor, the intra-company transferee, and the professional categories found in the general immigration statute. NAFTA incorporated free trade-related business-people into the general B-1, E-1, E-2, and L visa categories. NAFTA created a TN visa for professionals, which parallels the H-1B visa, except that employers seeking Canadian citizens need not file labor attestations or preliminary applications with DHS. Employers seeking Mexican citizens must go through a more involved process to obtain TN visas for their employees.[62]

Similar visa procedures have been set up pursuant to trade agreements with Chile and Singapore. Pursuant to these agreements Congress established a new H1-B1 "fast track" visa category that eliminates some of the procedural require-ments of the H-1B.[63]

d. Other Workers: I, Q, and R Visas

Workers who seek to come to the United States to exchange culture, history, or traditions of a country, as well as for employment and to provide practical training, are eligible for Q visas. These are popularly known as Disney visas, named after the company that lobbied for their creation in the Immigration Act of 1990. The visas allowed for sponsorship of an employee whose work inherently calls for the exchange of cultural information, regardless of skill level. The requirements for the visa include are twofold, with requirements for the employer and the employee. The employer must be actively engaged in the business of cultural exchange, and not merely an agent or broker and the employer must attest that it will provide Q visa holders with the wages and working conditions comparable to those afforded domestic workers. In short, there must be interaction with the American public, a cultural component and a work component.[64] The visa holder must be at least 18

---

[59] Bureau of Consular Affairs, *available at* http://travel.state.gov/content/visas/english/fees/treaty. html.

[60] 8 C.F.R. § 214.2(e)(5).

[61] 8 C.F.R. § 214.2(e)(6).

[62] Ranko Shiraki Oliver, *In the Twelve Years of NAFTA, the Treaty Gave to Me . . . What Exactly?: An Assessment of Economic, Social and Political Developments in Mexico Since 1994 and Their Impact on Mexican Immigration into the United States*, 10 HARV. LATINO L. REV. 53, 126–127 (2007) (describing the differences in procedures for obtaining TN visas between Canadians and Mexicans).

[63] INA § 101(a)(15)(H)(i)(b); § 214(g)(8).

[64] 8 C.F.R. § 214.2(q)(3)(iii).

years of age and have the skills and language ability to communicate the cultural attributes of the country and the visa holder must have resided and been physically present outside the U.S. for one year if previously admitted on a Q visa.[65] The program must be a structured program in a school, museum, or business; must contain a cultural component that is essential to the visa holder's employment or training; and cannot include training independent of a cultural component. The visa is available for up to 15 months initially, with extensions granted only up to a total of 15 months.

R visas are available to religious workers. Those who are eligible include ministers, persons in a professional religious capacity, persons working for religious organizations, and those who were, for two years before applying, a member of a bona fide religious organization. R visa holders may not work in the U.S. in any other capacity but as a minister or religious worker, but they may work for more than one qualifying employer as long as each files a petition.[66] An R visa holder is considered out of status if he/she works for a religious organization other than the petitioner. Entry is limited to five years and a visa is available for spouses and children accompanying or following to join the principal applicant as R-2. They may not work.

I visas are available to bona fide representatives of the foreign press, radio, television or information media entering solely to engage in their profession. The visa is available for those applicants whose countries have reciprocal agreements with the United States. A visa holder is admitted for up to one year, with indefinite one-year extensions. There are no restrictions on adjustment and no foreign residency requirements. Freelance workers may also apply as long as they have a valid and existing contract in place. Spouses and children can accompany or follow to join, but they must apply independently for employment authorization if they wish to work in the United States.

C. EDUCATIONAL: STUDENTS AND SCHOLARS

This section discusses academic and nonacademic student status in the United States. Academic student status is conferred through an F-1 visa. The F-1 visa is granted to an individual,

> having a residence in a foreign country which he has no intention of abandoning, who is a bona fide student qualified to pursue a full course of study and who seeks to enter the United States temporarily and solely for the purpose of pursuing such a course of study at an established college, university, seminary, conservatory, academic high school, elementary school, or other academic institution or in a language training program in the United States . . . .[67]

An applicant must show that s/he has no intention to immigrate into the United States. The applicant must be studying at a designated educational institution

---

[65] 8 C.F.R. § 214.2(q)(3)(iv).

[66] 8 C.F.R. § 214.2(r)(4)(i).

[67] INA § 101(a)(15)(F).

approved by U.S. Immigration and Customs Enforcement and in compliance with the Student and Exchange Visitor Information System ("SEVIS"). The SEVIS is a reporting and monitoring system that tracks student's status, reporting violations, school transfers, and course of study. The system reflects the government's views that student visa systems need more potent security dimensions, especially after 9/11. The system was implemented in order to more closely monitor the entry, exit, and movement of international students in the United States. Recently, ICE and DOS revised and modernized SEVIS and it is now commonly referred to as SEVIS II.

In order to apply for F-1 status, a student must submit a SEVIS Form I-20 issued by a school approved by USCIS.[68] The applicant must show that s/he has sufficient financial resources available to cover expenses while in the United States.[69] The applicant must show that s/he has the credentials to attend the chosen institution and that the applicant is proficient in English or will receive training to become proficient.[70] The applicant must show that s/he will carry a full course of study.[71]

F-2 status is available to spouses and children of F-1 visa holders. As this is a derivative status, F-2 visa holders lose their status if the principal F-1 visa holder violates his/her status. An F-2 visa holder cannot attend post-secondary educational institutions on an F-2 visa. A dependent child can attend elementary and high school, but cannot attend a post-secondary school without changing his/her status to F-1.

F-3 status is available to students from Canada and Mexico who are not residing in the United States.[72] These border commuting students are subject to SEVIS.[73] They cannot sponsor spouses or children for F-2 status.

Several activities may place an F-1 student out of status. A student who is employed without authorization, transfers schools without permission, or fails to complete a course of study in time and has run out of extensions is out of status and subject to removal.[74] Generally, F-1 visa holders cannot seek employment except for on-campus work during their first academic year. After the first year, F-1 visa holders can work if the student falls within one of several exceptions. A student who drops below a full course of study without prior permission of the designated school official is out of status.[75]

The M nonimmigrant visa is available for vocational students. The M visa is available for students who seek to study in a community college, a post-secondary

---

[68] 8 C.F.R. § 214.2(f)(1)(i)(A).

[69] 22 C.F.R. § 41.61(b)(1)(ii).

[70] 9 FAM 41.61 N. 7.

[71] A student can reduce his/her course load only once and with permission from the designated school official to no less than six semester/quarter hours, or a half-time load. 8 C.F.R. § 214.2(f)(6)(iii).

[72] INA § 101(a)(15(F)(iii).

[73] 68 Fed. Reg. 28129, 28130 (May 23, 2003).

[74] 8 C.F.R. § 214.2; Matter of Yazdani, 17 I.&N. Dec. 626 (BIA 1981).

[75] 8 C.F.R. § 214.2(f)(6)(iii).

vocational/business school which confers a degree, a vocational school such as a flight school, or a cooking school. An M applicant must present a SEVIS Form I-20 and is admitted for the time necessary to meet the course of study or one year, whichever is less.[76] The applicant may get extensions up to three years from the original start date to complete the program.[77]

Just as with the F visas, an M-1 visa holder may sponsor a spouse and children who are accompanying or following to join the applicant to the United States. These applicants hold M-2 visas. They cannot obtain employment or engage in full-time study without a change of status to M-1. A child with M-2 status can still attend elementary and high school. Similar to F-3, the M-3 visa is also available to commuters from Mexico and Canada.

M-1 status is more restrictive than F-1 status. An M-1 visa holder can only be authorized a reduced course load for medical reasons and only for a maximum aggregate period of five months. S/he can only attend school with extensions for a maximum of three years and can transfer schools only within the first 6 months unless circumstances beyond the student's control are involved.[78] Unlike F-1 visas holders, M-1 visa holders cannot accept employment, outside of practical training, after completing a course of study.[79] An M-1 visa holder cannot change status to H if the basis of the H was training received as an M-1 student.[80] Nor can an M-1 change status to F.[81]

The J visa is an education-related visa reserved for those who seek to enter the United States on a scholarly exchange. A J visa holder is one who has no intention of abandoning a foreign residence and is a bona fide student, scholar, trainee, teacher, professor, research assistant, specialist, or leader in a field of specialized knowledge. The J visa holder is coming temporarily to the United States on a program designated by the U.S. Information Agency for the purpose of teaching, training, studying or conducting research.[82] The J applicant must show that s/he has sufficient funds and English fluency to complete the intended program. The J program is administered by the U.S. Department of State's Bureau of Educational and Cultural Affairs ("ECA"), and its Office of Exchange Coordination and Designation ("ECD"). The ECD is responsible for designating qualifying governmental and private programs and maintaining an adequate participation process. The categories of potential participants range from secondary school students to scholars, and include trainees, au pairs, and camp counselors.

A J-1 visa holder may seek employment authorization with advance written approval if during her/his stay an urgent and unforeseen financial need has arisen

---

[76] 8 C.F.R. § 214.2)(m)(5).

[77] 8 C.F.R. § 214.2(m)(10).

[78] 8 C.F.R. § 214.2(m)(11).

[79] 8 C.F.R. § 214.2(m)(13).

[80] 8 C.F.R. § 248.1(d). This prohibition does not apply to M-2 visa holders.

[81] 8 C.F.R. § 248.1(c). This prohibition does not apply to M-2 visa holders.

[82] INA § 101(a)(15(J).

and the employment does not interfere with full-time progress toward the educational objective of the visit.[83]

J-2 visas are available for spouses and children following to join the principal visa holder. J-2 visa holders are eligible for employment authorization for the duration of the visa stay.[84]

Certain J visa holders are required to return to their home country for two years upon completion of their training in the United States before they can seek to adjust status, change status to H or L status, or apply for an immigrant visa.[85] These include visa holders whose participation was financed in whole or part by a U.S., or the participant's home country government, agency, or whose occupation was listed on the Department of State's skills list at the time of admission. Those who came to the U.S. or acquired J status after January 10, 1977 to receive graduate medical education are also required to meet the two-year foreign residency requirement.[86] A waiver of the 2-year residency requirement is possible. USCIS can grant a waiver upon a favorable recommendation from DOS. There are several possible bases for a waiver: 1) persecution on account of race, religion or political opinion; 2) exceptional hardship to the noncitizen's USC or LPR spouse or child; 3) a no-objection letter from the J holder's home country; or 4) a request by U.S. government agency or the State Department of Public Health.

The H-3 visa is available to workers who are invited to the United States by an individual or organization to receive instruction or training, other than graduate medical training. The training received in the United States must not be "designed primarily to provide productive employment."[87] An applicant seeking H-3 status must show that s/he has a foreign residence to which s/he will return. S/he must also show that the proposed training is not available in the home country, that the applicant will not be placed in a position that regularly employs U.S. citizens and residents, and that the training will benefit the applicant in pursuing a career outside the U.S.[88] An H-3 visa recipient will receive a visa for the length of time of the training, but no longer than two years.[89] An H-3 visa holder is limited in the type of extension or change of status s/he can seek. Importantly, the visa holder must remain and reside outside the country for at least six months before applying for an extension or change of status.[90]

---

[83] 22 C.F.R. § 62.23(g).

[84] 8 C.F.R. § 214.2(j)(1)(v)(B).

[85] The person may be able to obtain a waiver of the requirement. INA § 212(e).

[86] INA § 212(e).

[87] INA § 101(a)(15)(H)(iii).

[88] 8 C.F.R. § 214.2(h)(7)(ii)(A).

[89] 8 C.F.R. § 214.2(h)(9)(iii)(C)(1).

[90] 8 C.F.R. § 214.2(h)(13)(iv).

D. HUMAN TRAFFICKING AND OTHER VICTIMS OF VIOLENCE

In 2000, Congress passed the Victims of Trafficking and Violence Protection Act of 2000 ("VTVPA"),[91] which created two categories of nonimmigrant visas available to victims of human trafficking and serious crimes in the United States. The purpose behind the visas was largely humanitarian, but also law-enforcement related: to encourage undocumented noncitizens to step forward and cooperate in law enforcement investigations and/or prosecutions of criminal activity in the United States.[92] The T visa was meant to identify and capture perpetrators of forced sex and forced labor trafficking. The U visa was meant to identify and protect victims of an enumerated set of serious crimes.

1. T Visas

Congress made 5,000 nonimmigrant visas available pursuant to the VTVPA for victims of sex trafficking or of severe forms of trafficking. To be eligible, a T visa applicant must show that s/he is or has been a victim of a severe form of trafficking in persons, is physically present in the U.S. because of such trafficking, and is under the age of 18 or has complied with any reasonable request for assistance in the investigation or prosecution of trafficking. The applicant must also establish that s/he would suffer extreme hardship involving unusual or severe harm upon removal.[93]

A severe form of trafficking is defined under the Act as

(A) sex trafficking in which a commercial sex act is induced by force, fraud, or coercion, or in which the person induced to perform such act has not attained 18 years of age; or

(B) the recruitment, harboring, transportation, provision, or obtaining of a person for labor or services, through the use of force, fraud, or coercion for the purpose of subjection to involuntary servitude, peonage, debt bondage, or slavery.[94]

The Act defines sex trafficking as "the recruitment, harboring, transportation, provision, or obtaining of a person for the purpose of a commercial sex act."[95] If a T Visa applicant was not subject to forced labor in the U.S., she may still prove eligibility for the T-status by presenting evidence establishing that she was brought to the U.S. for the purpose of being subjected to involuntary servitude or peonage.

The T visa is available for four years, and allows for extensions as long as the person is still needed in the investigation or prosecution of a crime. Congress has

---

[91] Pub. L. No. 106-386, 114 Stat. 1464.

[92] *See* Victims of Trafficking and Violence Protection Act of 2000, section 102 (the purpose of this Act is to "combat trafficking in persons, . . . to ensure just and effective punishment of traffickers, and to protect their victims").

[93] INA § 101(a)(15(T)(i).

[94] 22 U.S.C. § 7102(9) (2013).

[95] 22 U.S.C. § 7108(10) (2013).

provided T visa holders the opportunity to seek adjustment to permanent resident status after three years.[96] If the principal T visa holder is under 21, T-2 through T-5 visas may be granted for spouses, siblings under 18, parent or child. If the principal is over 21, she can petition on behalf of a spouse and children.[97] T visa applicants are also exempt from public-charge in admissibility grounds and may seek to waive all other inadmissibility grounds, except for 212(a)(3) (related to security and terrorism), 212(a)(10)(C) (related to child abduction) and 212(a)(10)(E) (related to renunciation of citizenship). The T visa has been granted in few instances, even though up to 5,000 are available every year.[98] From 2002–2012, 6,206 T-Visas have been issued out of a possible 50,000, despite the fact that between 14,500 and 17,500 people are trafficked into the U.S. every year, according to State Department estimates.[99]

2. U Visas

The U visa is available to someone who "suffers substantial physical or mental abuse as a result of having been a victim of criminal activity." Enumerated in the immigration statute.[100] Physical or mental abuse means injury or harm to the victim's physical person, or harm to or impairment of the emotional or psychological soundness of the victim.[101] Documentation must be provided to show substantial abuse, with factors including: nature of the injury; severity of perpetrator's conduct; severity of harm; duration of infliction of harm; any permanent harm. To be eligible the victim must possess information concerning the criminal activity, and a law enforcement official must certify that the victim "has been helpful, is being helpful, or is likely to be helpful" in the investigation or prosecution of a crime. Any law enforcement agency may so certify, including police departments, prosecutors, judges, or other federal, state, and local authorities.[102] The regulations specifically name the EEOC, the DOL, and child protective services as agencies that can issue this certification. Furthermore, applicants for a U-Visa must be admissible. DHS can waive all grounds of inadmissibility except 212(a)(3)(E) (related to Nazi persecution, genocide and extrajudicial killings) if it is in the public or national interest.

The enumerated crimes range from sex-related crimes to labor-related crimes.[103] They include rape, torture, trafficking, incest, domestic violence, sexual assault, abusive sexual contact, prostitution, sexual exploitation, stalking, female genital mutilation, being held hostage, peonage, involuntary servitude, slave trade, kidnapping, abduction, unlawful criminal restraint, false imprisonment, blackmail,

---

[96] INA § 245(l).

[97] INA § 101(a)(15)(T)(ii).

[98] INA § 214(o)(2).

[99] 2014 Trafficking in Persons Report, Department of State Publication.

[100] INA § 101(a)(15)(U).

[101] 8 C.F.R. § 214.14(a)(8).

[102] INA § 101(a)(15)(U).

[103] *See* Leticia M. Saucedo, *A New U: Organizing Victims and Protecting Immigrant Workers*, 42 U. RICHMOND L. REV. 891 (2008).

extortion, manslaughter, murder, felonious assault, witness tampering, obstruction of justice, perjury, fraud in foreign labor contracting, or any similar activity considered criminal under local, state or federal law.[104] The provision also covers attempt, conspiracy or solicitation to commit any of the enumerated crimes.

A U visa recipient is eligible for the visa for four years. The visa holder is eligible to adjust to permanent resident status after three years.[105] Employment is authorized incident to status and USCIS will automatically issue an EAD when the U status is granted to the applicant. Extending or replacing the EAD requires filing an I-765. Family members of the principal U visa applicant are eligible for derivative status.

The U visa regulations were finally implemented in September 2007, seven years after the passage of the VTVPA. Before the regulations were in place, U visa-eligible persons were granted interim relief in the form of deferred action for one-year increments along with employment authorization documents. There are 10,000 U visas available per year. 2013 marked the fourth straight year that USCIS approved the maximum number of U visas allowed in a fiscal year.

Several critics of the U visa process point to the difficulty in balancing between the law enforcement purpose and the victim protection purpose of the Act in determining how U visas are disseminated.[106] Some of this balancing difficulty is evident in the regulations, which, for example, require each law enforcement agency to designate a person responsible for signing law enforcement certifications. Presumably this requirement limits the number of applicants who will receive law enforcement certification, which is the first step in seeking a U visa.

E. OTHER NONIMMIGRANT VISAS

There exist several visas that are very narrow in scope. The C visa covers those nonimmigrants in transit between two non-U.S. destinations. This category includes diplomats in transit and certain visitors to and from the United Nations headquarters in New York. D visas allow nonimmigrant crew members on airplanes and vessels to enter the United States temporarily in connection with their work or to take shore leave. The N visa is available to parents of special immigrants as defined in INA § 101(a)(27). The S visa is available to informants and witnesses in criminal and counter-terrorist investigations and prosecutions.

---

[104] INA § 101(a)(15)(U)(iii).

[105] INA § 214(p).

[106] See e.g., Grace Chang and Kathleen Kim, *Reconceptualizing Approaches to Human Trafficking: New Directions and Perspectives from the Field(s)*, 3 STAN. J.C.R.-C.L. 317 (2007); Dina Haynes, *(Not) Found Chained to a Bed in a Brothel: Conceptual, Legal and Procedural Failures to Fulfill the Promises of the Trafficking Victims Protection Act*, 21 GEO. IMMIG. L.J. 337 (2007); Jennifer Chacon, *Misery and Myopia; Understanding the Failures of U.S. Efforts to Stop Human Trafficking*, 74 FORDHAM L. REV. 2977, 3019 (2006).

Chapter 9

INADMISSIBILITY GROUNDS AND WAIVERS

Even though an applicant for admission may meet the requirements to qualify for a particular immigration category, for example, as the spouse of a U.S. citizen or professional of extraordinary ability, the person may still be precluded from the issuance of an immigrant visa if he or she falls within one of the grounds of inadmissibility. The grounds of inadmissibility are found in INA § 212.

A. IMMIGRATION CONTROL

A substantial number of inadmissibility grounds pertain to disqualifying factors related to immigration controls such as visa fraud, alien smuggling, and unlawful presence in the United States. In other words, violation of an immigration law itself can be a ground of inadmissibility.

1. Smugglers and Traffickers of Aliens

Under INA § 212(a)(6)(E), an alien who at any time "knowingly has encouraged, induced, assisted, abetted or aided" any other noncitizen to enter or try to enter the United States is inadmissible. Amendments in 1990 eliminated a requirement of smuggling "for gain" from the concept of alien smuggling. Thus, although the prior law was clearly aimed at punishing professional smugglers, the language of the current provision conceivably covers anyone who helps or encourages another alien to try to cross the border without inspection, even when payment is not contemplated. So individuals who have helped their own family members across the border surreptitiously are inadmissible under this provision. The provision is worded broad enough to include sending money to someone to pay a smuggler as well as merely encouraging someone to enter the United States illegally.

The Sixth and Ninth Circuits require an affirmative act of assistance or encouragement, such as paying alien smugglers, making the arrangements to get aliens across the border, or providing false information and documents to immigration officials.[1] Mere presence during the actual act of alien smuggling with knowledge that the act is being committed is insufficient. In contrast, the Second Circuit upheld smuggling inadmissibility where the noncitizen lied at the border about another person's residency and the whereabouts of his passport.[2] Agreeing to pay a smuggler after the person is already in the United States also is problematic.[3]

A waiver of this ground of admissibility is available only to a lawful permanent resident who assisted a spouse, parent, son, or daughter to enter illegally, or to an alien seeking admission or adjustment of status as an immediate relative or family preference immigrant (except for the sibling category).[4]

---

[1] *See, e.g.*, Altamirano v. Gonzales, 427 F.3d 586 (9th Cir. 2005); Aguilar-Gonzales v. Mukasey, 534 F.3d 1204 (9th Cir. 2008); Tapucu v. Gonzales, 399 F.3d 736 (6th Cir. 2005).

[2] Chambers v. Office of Chief Counsel, 494 F.3d 274 (2d Cir. 2007).

[3] *See, e.g.*, Covarrubias v. Gonzales, 487 F.3d 742 (9th Cir. 2007).

[4] INA § 212(d)(11).

There is a particular problem if the individual is actually criminally convicted of alien smuggling, harboring, or transporting under INA § 274(a)(1)(A) or (2). Such a conviction is considered an aggravated felony, even if the defendant was not paid and was simply helping a friend or relative, and even if no sentence was imposed. The only exception is for first offense smuggling of a spouse, child, or parent.[5]

Under INA § 212(a)(2)(H), an applicant is inadmissible if the government knows or has reason to believe that the person has been involved in "severe" forms of human trafficking. "Severe" trafficking refers to sex trafficking of persons under the age of 18, or trafficking of any persons who are forced by the traffickers to work as indentured laborers or slaves. Except for minor children, the trafficker's spouse, sons, or daughters who have benefited from the illicit activity also are inadmissible. No waiver is available for this ground of inadmissibility.

2. Visa Fraud

Under INA § 212(a)(6)(C), an alien who "by fraud or willfully misrepresenting a material fact, seeks to procure (or has sought to procure or has procured) a visa, other documentation, or admission into the United States" is inadmissible. Documentation includes not only the specified visa, but the supporting documents such as birth, marriage, and divorce certificates, work experience letters, and school records.

A charge based on procurement of a visa or other documentation is not sustainable unless the fraud was practiced on an authorized United States government official.[6] For example, a misrepresentation made to an airline official would not fall within this ground of inadmissibility.[7]

A willful misrepresentation must be made with knowledge of its falsity and with actual intent to deceive so that an advantage under the immigration laws might be gained to which the alien would not have otherwise been entitled.[8] The statement must have been "deliberate and voluntary."[9] A representation based on "innocent mistake, negligence or inadvertence" is insufficient.[10] The person must know that the statement was false at the time it was made.[11] Silence or the failure to volunteer information does not in itself constitute a misrepresentation.[12]

Even though the misrepresentation is willful, the alien is not inadmissible unless the misrepresentation is material. In determining whether a misrepresentation is material, the attorney general has suggested the following three-part inquiry:

---

[5] Matter of Ruiz-Romero, 22 I.&N. Dec. 486 (BIA 1999).

[6] *Cf.* Matter of Shirdel, 19 I.&N. Dec. 33 (BIA 1984).

[7] *See* Matter of D-L- & A-M-, 20 I.&N. Dec. 409 (BIA 1991).

[8] Matter of G-G-, 7 I.&N. Dec. 161 (BIA 1956).

[9] Matter of D-R-, 25 I.&N. Dec. 445 (BIA 2011).

[10] Emokah v. Mukasey, 523 F.3d 110, 117 (2d Cir. 2008).

[11] *See. e.g.*, Atunnise v. Mukasey, 523 F.3d 830, 834–38 (7th Cir. 2008); Forbes v. INS, 48 F.3d 439, 442 (9th Cir. 1995).

[12] 9 FAM 40.63 N4.2.

- Does the record establish that the alien is excludable on the true facts? If it does, then the misrepresentation was material; the inquiry ends. If it does not, then the second and third questions must be considered.

- Did the misrepresentation tend to shut off a line of inquiry which is relevant to the alien's eligibility? A misrepresentation as to identity or place of past residence, for example, would almost necessarily shut off an opportunity to investigate part or all of the alien's past history, and thus have shut off a relevant investigation. However, a remote, tenuous, or fanciful connection between a misrepresentation and a line of inquiry which is relevant to the alien's eligibility is insufficient to satisfy this aspect of the test of materiality.

- If a relevant line of inquiry has been cut off, might that inquiry have resulted in a proper determination that the alien be excluded? On this aspect of the question, the alien bears the burden of persuasion and proof. Having made a willful misrepresentation which tends to cut off a relevant line of investigation, he cannot now try out his eligibility as if nothing had happened. One who, by an intentional and wrongful act, has prevented or restricted an inquiry into relevant facts bears the burden of establishing the true facts and the risk that any uncertainties from the person's own obstruction of the inquiry may be resolved unfavorably.[13]

In order for the false statements to be material, they must have been predictably capable of affecting the decisions of the decision-making body.[14]

An applicant who timely and voluntarily retracts a misrepresentation may avoid inadmissibility. A retraction is only timely if made within a short period of time and not in response to the fact that the individual is about to be found out by a DHS or consular officer.[15]

A waiver of the visa fraud ground of inadmissibility is available to applicants if they are a spouse, son, or daughter of a U.S. citizen or lawful permanent resident and refusal of admission would result in extreme hardship to that relative.[16]

3. Document Fraud

Under INA §§ 212(a)(6)(F), a person who is subject to a final order and penalties related to document fraud proceedings is inadmissible. Under INA § 274C, it is unlawful for a person to knowingly forge or alter any document or to "use, attempt to use, possess, obtain, accept, or receive or provide" any false document for the purpose of obtaining any benefit under the immigration laws. This includes using a false document or borrowing someone else's document, such as a visa to gain entry or a social security card to complete an I-9 form to obtain a job. Document fraud also occurs when a noncitizen uses a false document to board an airplane or other transport and then destroys the document en route to the United States.

---

[13] Matter of S-&B-C-, 9 I.&N. Dec. 436, 448–49 (A.G. 1961).

[14] *See* Kungys v. United States, 485 U.S. 759 (1988).

[15] *See., e.g.*, Llanos-Senarrilos v. United States, 177 F.2d 164 (9th Cir. 1949).

[16] INA § 212(i).

Document fraud also covers those who assist others "to prepare, file, or assist another in preparing or filing, any application for benefits under this Act, or any document required under this Act, or any document submitted in connection with such application or document, with knowledge or in reckless disregard of the fact that such application or document was falsely made or, in whole or in part, does not relate to the person on whose behalf it was or is being submitted."[17]

INA § 274C defines document fraud and sets forth rules for a civil hearing before an administrative hearing officer. The officer will issue a final order against a person if the person either (a) waives the right to the civil hearing, or (b) is found to have committed document fraud. This is a civil penalty. For an applicant to be inadmissible for document fraud, the person must have been notified to attend the document fraud hearing and be subject to a final order from that hearing.[18]

A limited waiver exists for document fraud inadmissibility. The fraud must have been committed only to help support a spouse or child and is available to lawful permanent residents who temporarily left the country voluntarily and noncitizens seeking admission or adjustment of status based on a family visa petition.[19] The waiver will be granted as a matter of discretion for humanitarian purposes or to assure family unity.

4. False Claim to U.S. Citizenship

Any applicant who falsely claims to be a U.S. citizen is inadmissible under INA § 212(a)(6)(C)(ii). A noncitizen must not falsely claim to be a U.S. citizen for any purpose or benefit under the Immigration and Nationality Act, including the act's employment authorization attestation requirements or under any other federal or state law. This ground of inadmissibility requires a showing that the false representation was made for a specific purpose — to satisfy a legal requirement or obtain a benefit that otherwise would not be available to the noncitizen.

For purposes of this inadmissibility ground, a false claim to U.S. citizenship has been found when a person falsely claims to be a U.S. citizen to obtain a U.S. passport,[20] uses a false U.S. passport to enter the United States or obtain a state driver's license,[21] or claims U.S. citizenship on an I-9 form to obtain employment.[22] On the other hand, a false claim of U.S. citizenship to a police officer is not necessarily for any benefit or purpose under the INA,[23] and the BIA has held in an unpublished decision that the purchase of a firearm by making a false claim to U.S. citizenship also did not render the person inadmissible.

---

[17] INA § 274C(5).

[18] *See* Walter v. INS, 159 F.3d 1349 (2d Cir. 1998).

[19] INA 212(d)(12).

[20] Matter of Barcenas, 25 I.&N. Dec. 40 (BIA 2009).

[21] Almendarez v. Mukasey, 2008 U.S. App. LEXIS 12820 (5th Cir. June 17, 2008); Lara-Rivas v. Mukasey, 2008 U.S. App. LEXIS 6528 (9th Cir. Mar. 14, 2008).

[22] Kirong v. Mukasey, 529 F.3d 800 (8th Cir. 2008).

[23] Castro v. Attorney General, 671 F.3d 356 (3d Cir. 2012).

The inadmissibility ground related to false claims to U.S. citizenship does not apply in the following circumstances: (a) when each of the applicant's natural or adopted parents is or was a U.S. citizen; (b) if the applicant began to reside permanently in the United States prior to the age of 16; and (c) if the applicant reasonably believed at the time of such statement, violation, or claim that he or she was a U.S. citizen.[24] Also, a false claim to U.S. citizenship is excused if the person was (a) under the age of 18 at the time of the false claim, and (b) lacked the capacity to understand and appreciate the nature and consequences of a false claim to citizenship. Similarly, a false claim to citizenship does not apply if someone else made the false claim on behalf of the applicant, such as a parent making the claim for a child.

The statute does not provide a waiver for this ground of inadmissibility. However, a timely and voluntary retraction may cure a false claim to citizenship.[25] For example, an effective retraction was made when the person claimed citizenship before a border patrol officer, but promptly told the officer that he only had a work permit after being asked for documentation.[26]

5. Stowaways

Under INA § 212(a)(6)(D), a person who obtains transportation without consent and through concealment is inadmissible. A passenger with a valid ticket is not a stowaway. No waiver is available for this ground of inadmissibility. Stowaways do not have a right to a hearing, unless they apply for asylum and satisfy credible fear standards.[27]

6. Unlawful Presence in the United States

Under INA § 212(a)(9), an alien who has been unlawfully present in the United States may be barred from returning for three or 10 years once the person departs. If the person has been unlawfully present for a period of more than 180 days but less than a year, then the person is barred from admission for three years after departing. Any alien who has been unlawfully present in the United States for a year or more and who is seeking readmission will be barred for 10 years. The 180 days or year must be continuous. The penalty is worse, if the person goes through removal proceedings. Any person removed is subject to the 10 year bar if they were unlawfully present for more than 180 days.

In order to be subject to the three or 10-year bars, the person must have departed from the United States and is seeking readmission to the United States. Unlawful presence includes those who have overstayed their visas as well as those who entered without proper inspection. A person who has been unlawfully present does not fall within this inadmissibility category if he or she has not departed, is eligible for adjustment of status in the United States, and is applying for

---

[24] INA § 212(a)(6)(C)(ii)(II).

[25] Matter of M-, 9 I.&N. Dec. 118 (BIA 1960).

[26] Olea-Reyes v. Gonzales, 2006 U.S. App. LEXIS 10292 (9th Cir. Apr. 20, 2006).

[27] 8 C.F.R. §§ 208.2(c)(3); 208.30.

adjustment of status. Unfortunately, a person who entered the country without inspection is not eligible for adjustment of status under INA § 245(a).

Unlawful presence does not include any period of time that the person was under age 18, any time during which the alien had a bona fide asylum application pending, any time during which the alien had a nonfrivolous application pending for a change or extension of status and did not work without authorization, or any time during which the alien was a beneficiary of family unity protection. This ground of inadmissibility also does not apply to an alien who was a victim of spousal or parental abuse when the unlawful presence is related to the abuse. Individuals granted discretionary deferral of removal does not accrue unlawful presence during the period for which deferral is granted. Likewise, a person granted deferred action for childhood arrivals (DACA) will not accrue unlawful presence for the time that the deferral is in effect. However, if the person was older than age 18 when DACA was granted, the period of unlawful presence after turning 18 until the DACA grant will be counted.

Time spent in proceedings before an immigration judge or higher appellate authority is not necessarily a period of authorized stay. When a person enters without inspection, unlawful presence begins to accrue at entry and continues to accrue while such a person is in proceedings. On the other hand, when a nonimmigrant, like a student or tourist, bearing a date-certain Form I-94 (entry-departure form) remains in the United States beyond the date noted on that form, unlawful presence begins to accrue as of the date the Form I-94 expired. A nonimmigrant bearing a date-certain Form I-94 who is placed in removal proceedings will not begin to accrue time unlawfully present until the date noted on the Form I-94 has been reached or the immigration judge orders the alien removed, whichever is earlier. When an alien successfully contests the charges of inadmissibility or removability brought by ICE in a proceeding, the alien will be deemed not to have accrued any periods of unlawful presence in the United States during the pendency of the proceedings.

The unlawful presence ground of inadmissibility can be waived as a matter of discretion if the prospective immigrant is the spouse, son, or daughter of a U.S. citizen or lawful permanent resident and the refusal to admit would result in extreme hardship to the spouse or parent. The waiver is not available to a parent of a citizen or lawful permanent resident. The waiver decision is entirely within the discretion of immigration authorities and is not subject to judicial review.[28]

The family hardship waiver application can be filed prior to departing the United States.[29] In order to apply for this waiver — known as a "provisional" waiver, the prospective immigrant must be an immediate relative of a U.S. citizen, have an approved family petition, file an immigrant visa application at a U.S. consul, be physically present in the United States to file the application and complete biometric requirements (e.g., photos, fingerprints), not have been scheduled for an immigrant visa interview at the consul, not be in removal proceedings, and most importantly provide evidence that refusal of the waiver will

---

[28]　INA § 212(a)(9)(B)(v).

[29]　8 C.F.R. § 212.7(e).

cause extreme hardship to a citizen spouse or parent. The benefit of the provisional waiver process is that, if granted, the prospective immigrant can depart from the United States to attend a visa interview with confidence that he or she will be able to return right away. Without this advance knowledge, the applicant would have to proceed abroad to the consular interview without knowing if the three- or 10-year bar will be waived.

A more severe, permanent bar to admission applies to those who have been unlawfully present in the United States for an aggregate period of more than one year, depart, and then enter or attempt to reenter the United States without permission.[30] These individuals cannot even apply for a discretionary waiver of this provision until 10 years has elapsed since their last departure from the United States.

7. Prior Removal or Deportation

In general, any alien who has been ordered removed from the United States when attempting to seek admission is inadmissible for five years from the date of such removal. An alien who has been removed from the United States after having gained admission is inadmissible for 10 years from the date of such removal. However, if the person has already been removed at least once in the past, or if the alien was removed due to a conviction for an aggravated felony, the person is inadmissible for 20 years.[31] Aliens who were previously removed, deported, or excluded from the United States, and who reenter without permission are guilty of a felony under INA § 276. A waiver is available under INA § 212(a)(9)(A)(iii), however, the waiver must be sought from outside the United States.[32]

Under INA § 212(a)(6)(B), an alien who fails or refuses to attend a removal proceedings is inadmissible for five years.

A more severe, permanent bar to admission applies to those who have deported or removed and then enter or attempt to reenter the United States without permission.[33] These individuals cannot even apply for a discretionary waiver of this provision until 10 years has elapsed since their last departure from the United States.[34]

B POLITICAL AND NATIONAL SECURITY

Under INA § 212(a)(3), activities considered threatening to U.S. security trigger inadmissibility. Those activities include espionage, sabotage, terrorist activity, and genocide. The preclusion also applies to those who were Nazis or members in Communist or totalitarian parties. The law also excludes those whose entrance would have "serious adverse foreign policy consequences."

---

[30] INA § 212(a)(9)(C)(i)(II).

[31] INA § 212(a)(9).

[32] Matter of Torres-Garcia, 23 I.&N. Dec. 866 (BIA 2006).

[33] INA § 212(a)(9)(C).

[34] INA § 212(a)(9)(C).

Terrorist activity includes any activity that is unlawful under the laws of the place where committed involving highjacking or sabotage of any conveyance; seizing or detaining, and threatening to kill, injure, or continue to detain, another individual in order to compel a third person (including a governmental organization) to do or abstain from doing any act as an explicit or implicit condition for the release of the individual seized or detained; assassination; the use of any biological agent, chemical agent, or nuclear weapon or device, or explosive or firearm with the intent to endanger the safety of one or more individuals or to cause substantial damage to property.

The USA PATRIOT Act, enacted in response to 9/11, added new grounds of inadmissibility for representatives (and their spouses and children) of foreign terrorist organizations or any group that publicly endorses acts of terrorist activity. Noncitizens are denied admission if they "endorse or espouse terrorist activity," or "persuade others to support terrorist activity or a terrorist organization," in ways that the State Department determines impede U.S. efforts to combat terrorism. The Act defines "terrorist activity" expansively to include support of otherwise lawful and nonviolent activities of almost any group that used violence. Noncitizens are deportable for wholly innocent associational activity, excludable for pure speech, and subject to incarceration without a finding that they pose a danger or flight risk. Foreign nationals can be detained for up to seven days while the government decides whether or not to file criminal or immigration charges. The Attorney General has broad preventive detention authority to incarcerate noncitizens by certifying there are "reasonable grounds to believe" that a person is "described in" the antiterrorism provisions of the immigration law, and the individual is then subject to potentially indefinite detention. The Attorney General also can detain noncitizens indefinitely even after prevailing in a removal proceeding "until the Attorney General determines that the noncitizen is no longer a noncitizen who may be certified [as a suspected terrorist.]"

The Real ID Act of 2005 (effective May 11, 2008), expanded the terrorism grounds in the PATRIOT Act. Now INA § 212(a)(3)(B) renders an applicant inadmissible who "endorses or espouses" terrorist activity, anyone who has received "military-type training" from a terrorist organization, and anyone who is a member of a terrorist organization or has provided material support to a terrorist organization or a member of a terrorist organization.

INA § 219 allows the State Department to designate an organization as a terrorist organization if the group (1) is a foreign organization; (2) engages in terrorist activity; and (3) threatens the security of U.S. nationals or the national security of the United States. The State Department must notify Congress of the intent to designate a particular organization as terrorist and publish the designation in the Federal Register. The designation of an organization as a terrorist organization will last for two years, at which time the State Department may redesignate the organization for another two years. Congress, however, may block or revoke a designation at any time. An organization that is designated as a terrorist organization may, within 30 days of the date of designation, seek judicial review of the designation in the U.S. Court of Appeals for the District of Columbia Circuit.

The Secretary of State, after consultation with the Attorney General and the Secretary of Homeland Security, has sole, unreviewable discretion to waive inadmissibility related to material support of or membership in a terrorist organization. The spouse or child of a person who falls within the terrorism grounds of inadmissibility is not inadmissible if he or she did not know or should not reasonably have known of the person's actions. Inadmissibility also can be avoided if the spouse or child has renounced the person's actions.[35]

Supporters of certain groups can be exempted from the terrorism-related grounds of inadmissibility. For example, individuals who have helped the following groups are exempt: the Karen National Union/Karen Liberation Army, the Chin National Front/Chin National Army, or the Kayan New Land Party in Burma; Arakan Liberation Party or Karenni National Progressive Party in Myanmar; Tibetan Mustangs; Cuban Alzados; certain groups affiliated with the Hmong and some groups affiliated with the Montagnards.

Under INA § 212(a)(3)(E), any alien who has engaged in conduct defined as genocide for purposes of the International Convention on the Prevention and Punishment of Genocide is inadmissible. The convention defines the term "genocide" as any of the following acts committed with the intent to destroy, in whole or in part, a national, ethnic, racial, or religious group by killing members of the group: causing serious bodily or mental harm to members of the group, deliberately inflicting on the group conditions of life calculated to bring about its physical destruction in whole or in part, importing measures intended to prevent births within the group, and forcibly transferring children of the group to another group. Directing, inciting, or conspiring to commit genocide also fall within this section.

Applicants who are permanently ineligible for U.S. citizenship also are inadmissible under INA 212(a)(8). Draft dodgers and deserters fall within this provision.[36] However, the provision does not include those who merely failed to register with the Selective Service.

Unlawful voting contrary to federal, state, or local laws renders an applicant inadmissible under INA § 212(a)(10)(D)(i). Generally, these laws require that the person knew that he or she was not eligible to vote. This inadmissibility ground does not apply to a person (1) whose parents were U.S. citizens, (2) who began residing permanently in the United States prior to age 16, or (3) who reasonably believed that he or she was a U.S. citizen. Like false claims to U.S citizenship, the statute does not provide a waiver for illegal voting.

---

[35] INA § 212(a)(3)(B)(ii).

[36] Matter of Kanga, 22 I.&N. Dec. 1206 (BIA 2000).

C. CRIMINAL

1. Moral Turpitude Crime

Under INA § 212(a)(2)(A)(i)(I), an alien who has been convicted of, or who has admitted the commission of, a crime involving moral turpitude is inadmissible. The statute does not distinguish between misdemeanors and felonies. The term "moral turpitude" is difficult to define with precision. Various courts have suggested that the term includes crimes that evince depravity and baseness, that are malum in se, morally and inherently wrong, or that would be viewed as involving moral turpitude in the common conscience of the community.[37] Moral turpitude requires "a reprehensible act with some form of scienter, whether specific intent, willfulness, or recklessness."[38] Under this definition, a crime committed through negligence is not a crime involving moral turpitude.

Whether a crime involves moral turpitude depends on what must be proven to establish guilt. A crime involves moral turpitude if, from the statutory definition and the material allegations of the information or indictment, the crime necessarily or inherently involves moral turpitude. What happens when a case involves a criminal statute that is divisible as to moral turpitude? In those circumstances, if the record of conviction is inconclusive as to which offense the person was convicted of. The Third, Fourth, Fifth, Ninth, and Eleventh Circuits have ruled that convictions under such divisible statutes categorically do not involve moral turpitude.[39]

Crimes that have been determined to involve moral turpitude include murder, voluntary manslaughter, aggravated assault, rape, kidnapping, theft, lewd conduct, bigamy, fraud, and other crimes having as an element the intent to defraud. An aggravated assault against a peace officer that resulted in bodily harm to the victim and involved knowledge by the offender that his force was directed at an officer performing an official duty, has been held to involve moral turpitude.[40] Under certain circumstances, involuntary manslaughter could involve moral turpitude.[41] Being an accessory to murder can be a moral turpitude crime when the defendant admitted that he knew the principal had intentionally committed murder and that he intentionally assisted the principal in avoiding detention.[42] Making false statements on a driver's license application was a crime involving moral turpitude when the elements of materiality and knowledge were shown.[43] Furthermore, it makes no difference whether the moral turpitude offense was motivated by

---

[37] *See* Jordan v. DeGeorge, 341 U.S. 223 (1951).

[38] Matter of Silva-Trevino, 24 I.&N. Dec. 687, 706 (A.G. 2008).

[39] Jean-Louis v. Atty Gen., 582 F.3d 462 (3d Cir. 2009); Prudencio v. Holder, 669 F.3d 472 (4th Cir. 2012); Silva-Trevino v. Holder, 742 F.3d 197 (5th Cir. 2014); Olivas-Motta v. Holder, 716 F.3d 1199 (9th Cir. 2013); Fajardo v. US AG, 659 F. 3d 1303 (11th Cir. 2011).

[40] Matter of Danesh, Int. Dec. No. 3068 (BIA 1988).

[41] Franklin v. INS, 72 F.3d 571 (8th Cir. 1995).

[42] Cabral v. INS, 15 F. 3d 193 (1st Cir. 1994).

[43] Zaitona v. INS, 9 F. 3d 432 (6th Cir. 1993).

economic hardship or the need to feed a family during time of war.[44]

On the other hand, crimes such as voluntary manslaughter, joyriding, and simple assault have been held not to involve moral turpitude. Reckless assault that causes bodily injury, but not great bodily injury, is not necessarily a crime involving moral turpitude.[45] However, recklessly endangering another person with a "substantial risk of imminent death" can be a crime involving moral turpitude.[46] Thus, an involuntary manslaughter conviction for recklessly causing the death of one's child involved moral turpitude, because the statute required conscious disregard of substantial and unjustifiable risk to the life or safety of others.[47] However, structuring financial transactions to avoid currency reports was held to not involve moral turpitude because the statute did not make intent to defraud the government an essential element of the offense; the defendant could have been convicted even if he was not aware that his conduct was illegal.[48]

Under the statute, the alien's admission of all the essential elements of a crime involving moral turpitude to an immigration official is sufficient to trigger inadmissibility, notwithstanding the absence of a conviction.[49] The alien must understand the full nature and elements of the crime to which he or she is admitting.[50] If the alien was charged and acquitted, a subsequent admission by the alien should not render the person inadmissible.[51]

Two statutory exceptions to the moral turpitude ground of inadmissibility are contained in the statute.

    a. Youthful offense. Young offenders treated as adults are exempted from the moral turpitude exclusion if they have committed only one crime involving moral turpitude while under the age of 18.[52] However, at least five years must have elapsed since the date of commission of the offense since the date of release from confinement, whichever is later. Note that a young person whose case was handled in juvenile delinquency proceedings is admissible because juvenile proceedings do not result in convictions for immigration purposes. Similarly, conduct underlying a foreign conviction for an offense that constitutes an act of juvenile delinquency under U.S. standards, however treated by the foreign court, is not a crime for purposes of admission.

    b. Petty offense. An alien is exempted from the moral turpitude exclusion if convicted of only one crime and the maximum penalty for the crime did

---

[44] Chiaramonte v. INS, 626 F.2d 1093 (2d Cir. 1980); Matter of De La Nues, 18 I.&N. Dec. 140 (BIA 1981).

[45] Matter of Fualaau, 21 I.&N. Dec. 475 (BIA 1996).

[46] Matter of Leal, 26 I.&N. Dec. 20 (BIA 2012).

[47] Franklin v. INS, 72 F.3d 571 (8th Cir. 1995).

[48] Goldeshtein v. INS, 8 F.3d 645 (9th Cir. 1993).

[49] INA § 212(a)(2)(A)(i).

[50] Matter of K, 7 I.&N. Dec. 594 (BIA 1957).

[51] Matter of E.V., 5 I.&N. Dec. 194 (BIA 1953); Matter of C.Y.C., 3 I.&N. Dec. 623 (BIA 1950).

[52] INA § 212(a)(2)(A)(ii)(I).

not exceed imprisonment for one year and if the alien was not sentenced to a term of imprisonment in excess of six months.[53]

Under INA § 212(h), an alien inadmissible because of the commission of a crime involving moral turpitude may be admitted as a matter of discretion if one of two conditions is met: (1) the crime for which the person is inadmissible occurred more than 15 years ago, the admission would not be contrary to national safety and security, and the person has been rehabilitated; or (2) the person is the spouse, parent, son, or daughter of a U.S. citizen or a lawful permanent resident, and the admission would result in extreme hardship to the relative. The waiver is not available to someone who has been convicted of, or who admits committing, a murder or criminal acts involving torture.

2. Narcotics and Marijuana

Persons who have committed offenses relating to narcotics and marijuana are extremely disfavored under U.S. immigration laws. For example, under INA § 212(a)(2)(A)(i)(II), aliens convicted of violating any law or regulation relating to a controlled substance is inadmissible. This includes solicitation to commit a crime relating to a controlled substance.[54] Even minor offenses such as being under the influence of drugs or possessing a small amount of drugs will render the person inadmissible.

In the Ninth Circuit, a state's rehabilitative relief can eliminate the immigration consequences of a first conviction for certain minor drug offenses if the conviction occurred before July 15, 2011.[55] The qualifying offenses include: simple possession, possession of paraphernalia, and giving away a small amount of marijuana. The exception also applies to similar foreign relief for a first foreign conviction of these offenses.[56]

The statute also makes inadmissible aliens whom the consular or DHS official "knows or has reason to believe" are or have been traffickers.[57] For example, an arrest for a controlled substance offense that does not result in a conviction may form the basis for a reasonable belief that the alien was a trafficker.[58] The statute even renders inadmissible the illicit trafficker's spouse, son, or daughter who has received benefit from the illicit activity within the previous five years.[59]

As discussed below, aliens who are drug addicts or drug abusers also are inadmissible.

Waivers of inadmissibility for narcotics are quite limited. An INA § 212(h) waiver is available only to marijuana offenders who have committed a single offense

---

[53] INA § 212(a)(2)(A)(ii)(II).

[54] Matter of Beltran, Int. Dec. No. 3179 (BIA 1992).

[55] Nunez-Reyes v. Holder, 646 F.3d 684 (9th Cir. 2011).

[56] Dillingham v. INS, 267 F.3d 996 (9th Cir. 2001).

[57] INA § 212(a)(2)(C).

[58] Nunez-Payan v. INS, 815 F.2d 384 (5th Cir. 1987).

[59] INA § 212(a)(2)(C)(ii).

involving simple possession of not more than 30 grams. The waiver is a matter of discretion and one of two sets of conditions must be met: (1) the crime for which the person is inadmissible occurred more than 15 years ago, the admission would not be contrary to national safety and security, and the person has been rehabilitated; or (2) the person is the spouse, parent, son, or daughter of a U.S. citizen or a lawful permanent resident, and the denial of admission would result in extreme hardship to the relative.

3. Multiple Criminal Convictions

Aliens who have been convicted of two or more offenses, regardless of whether moral turpitude or drugs were involved, are inadmissible under INA § 212(a)(2)(B) if the aggregate sentence to confinement actually imposed was five years or more. This inadmissibility ground includes misdemeanors and felonies. It makes no difference if the convictions resulted from a single trial or involved offenses from a single scheme of misconduct.

The waivers available for the moral turpitude inadmissibility are also available for this ground of inadmissibility.

4. Prostitution and Commercialized Vice

Under INA § 212(a)(2)(D), aliens who come to the United States to engage in prostitution or who have engaged in prostitution within the last 10 years are inadmissible. There need not have been a conviction, and the alien is not exempt if prostitution was legal at the place engaged in or in the place to which the alien is coming to the United States.[60] The provision also covers aliens coming to the United States to engage in commercialized vice such as loan sharking or gambling.

A single act of prostitution does not amount to engaging in prostitution under this provision.[61] Prostitution is limited to providing sexual intercourse, not other lewd acts, for a fee. Solicitation of a prostitute by a customer does not fall within the prostitution inadmissibility ground.

Persons falling within the prostitution inadmissibility may apply for the discretionary family waiver of INA § 212(h). One of two conditions must be met: (1) the crime for which the person is inadmissible occurred more than 15 years ago, the admission would not be contrary to national safety and security, and the person has been rehabilitated; or (2) the person is the spouse, parent, son, or daughter of a U.S. citizen or a lawful permanent resident, and the denial of admission would result in extreme hardship to the relative.

D. ECONOMIC — PUBLIC CHARGE

One of the most commonly raised grounds of inadmissibility is under INA § 212(a)(4), which raises the issue of whether an applicant is likely to become a public charge. Consular and USCIS officials have tremendous discretion in deter-

---

[60] 22 C.F.R. § 40.24(c).

[61] Matter of Gonzalez-Zoquiapan, 24 I.&N. Dec. 549 (BIA 2008).

mining whether an applicant is likely to become a public charge. Yet that discretion is not absolute and there must be some support for the decision.[62] Some of the factors generally considered are age, health, family status, assets, resources, financial status, education and skills, promise of a job, and mental and physical health.[63] A healthy person in the prime of life ordinarily should not be considered likely to become a public charge.[64]

In making their likelihood of public charge determinations, consular and USCIS officials generally refer to income poverty guidelines published by the Department of Health and Human Services and updated annually. The applicant must establish a level of income or assets, essentially with income of at least 125 percent of the federal poverty guidelines.

Past receipt of public assistance can be relevant to whether the applicant is likely to become a public charge. DHS follows a set of interim rules that have been in place for a number of years:

- DHS may not consider use of non-cash benefits (such as Medicaid or Food Stamps) by an applicant as a basis for public charge. However, if a person has received, or is likely to receive long-term publicly funded institutionalization (such as placement in a nursing home or mental hospital), then DHS can consider that as one factor in a public charge decision.

- DHS may consider the receipt of cash benefits in the public charge determination if they are received for the purpose of income maintenance. This includes programs such as Temporary Assistance for Needy Families (TANF), General Assistance (GA), or Supplemental Security Income (SSI).

- If the cash benefits for maintenance were received by an applicant's family members, these cannot be considered in the applicant's public charge determination unless the applicant was relying on the cash benefits as his or her sole means of support.

- One-time cash grants and cash designated for other purposes such as child car or job training should not be considered in public charge decisions. Similarly, benefits that are earned, e.g., Social Security retirement or veterans benefits, are not to be considered.

Any applicant immigrating through a family visa petition must have an affidavit of support (Form I-864) submitted as part of the file from a U.S. family member. The affidavit of support is legally enforceable and is used to help the applicant establish sufficient assets and income. Under INA § 213A(f)(1), the sponsor who signs the affidavit of support must be a citizen or national of the United States or a lawful permanent resident, of at least 18 years of age. The sponsor must live in the United States or in a U.S. territory or possession. The U.S. citizen or lawful permanent resident who is filing the petition in a family immigration situation must file an affidavit of support, even if the petitioner's income is low.

---

[62] Matter of Perez, 15 I.&N. Dec. 136 (BIA 1974); Matter of Harutunian, 14 I.&N. Dec. 583 (Reg. Comm'r 1974).

[63] INA § 212(a)(4)(B).

[64] Matter of Martinez-Lopez, 10 I.&N. Dec. 409 (A.G. 1964).

The sponsor must establish that he or she has "the means to maintain an annual income equal to at least 125% of the federal poverty line" for his or her own household plus the intending immigrant and family members immigrating with the applicant.[65] Sponsors who are active in the U.S. Armed Forces only need to demonstrate support at 100 percent of the poverty line. To establish income, the sponsor must provide a social security number and copies of three years of tax returns.[66]

If the petitioner sponsor does not earn enough income alone to meet the 125 percent of the poverty income guidelines requirement, three other mechanisms are possible: (1) adding household members' income; (2) finding a joint sponsor; and/or (3) using significant assets.

The income of the petitioning sponsor's household members may be added to the sponsor's income in order to satisfy the applicant's public charge challenge. The income of these contributing household members can be added: any person (including the intending immigrant) who has lived in the sponsor's household for at least the previous six months and is related to the sponsor by birth, marriage or adoption, and dependents listed on the sponsor's tax return. These household members must also sign the I-864A affidavit of support, thereby become jointly and severally liable to help support the applicant.

Joint sponsors must meet the same requirements as the original petitioning sponsor. Under INA § 213A(f), the joint sponsor must be a lawful permanent resident or a U.S. citizen at least 18 years old who lives in the United States or a U.S. territory or possession. The joint sponsor must sign a separate affidavit of support and become legally obligated to support the applicant. The joint sponsor must make 125 percent of the income needed to support both his or her household and the intending immigrant.

When income is not sufficient, the availability of significant assets can still satisfy the public charge ground of inadmissibility. The intending immigrant's assets also can be counted. Savings accounts, stocks and bonds, certificates of deposit, life insurance policies, real estate, and personal property are examples of acceptable significant assets. There are two requirements: (1) the assets must be convertible to cash within one year, and (2) the net worth of the assets must be five times the difference between the sponsor's actual income and the income the sponsor is required to have. A sponsor, joint sponsor, or household member can use significant assets to meet or help meet the 125 percent requirement.

The Form I-864 affidavit of support is legally enforceable against the sponsor, as well as any joint sponsor or contributing household member.[67] Any federal, state, or local government can sue the sponsor to recover the costs of federal or state means-tested public benefits that were received by the immigrant during the period of enforcement of the affidavit of support. Reimbursement for benefits received by

---

[65] The 125 percent figure is published as Form I-864P, *available at* www.uscis.gov (under the Forms Menu).

[66] INA § 213A(6)(A)(i), (B).

[67] INA § 213A(a)(1)(B).

the immigrant more than 10 years earlier cannot be sought.[68] Federal mean-tested public benefits have been defined to include Medicaid, the State Children's Health Insurance Program (SCHIP), Temporary Assistance for Needy Families, SSI, and Food Stamps. The sponsored immigrant also can sue the sponsor to seek support at a level equivalent to 125 percent of the poverty guidelines.[69]

The sponsor's obligation under the affidavit of support ends when:

1. The sponsored immigrant becomes a U.S. citizen,

2. The sponsored immigrant is credited for 40 "qualifying quarters" of employment as reflected by social security payments (i.e., a minimum of 10 years),

3. The sponsored immigrant ceases to be a lawful permanent resident and has left the United States, or the sponsored immigrant dies, or

4. The sponsor files for bankruptcy.[70]

The sponsor's obligation does not end due to divorce, because the immigrant disappears and does not communicate with the sponsor, or for other personal reasons. Although the obligation ends if the sponsor dies, the sponsor's estate may have to pay obligations that arose before the sponsor died. Similarly, even after the sponsor's obligation ends, the sponsor remains liable for debts that arose before the support obligation ended.

The following groups are exempted from the I-864 Affidavit of Support requirement. Instead, they can submit Form I-864W, the Intending Immigrant's Affidavit of Support Exemption.

1. Self-petitioning battered spouses and children. A noncitizen who has been battered or abused by a U.S. citizen or permanent resident spouse or child can "self-petition" under the Violence Against Women Act (VAWA) provisions. Unlike other family immigrants, they need only meet the general public charge test.[71]

2. When the petitioner has died. If the prospective immigrant was married to a U.S. citizen at the time of the citizen's death but before the spouse immigrates, the prospective immigrant may file a petition on his or her own behalf, but must do so within two years of the petitioner's death.[72] The couple is not required to have been married for two years. The person will be immigrating as the widow(er) of a U.S. citizen and does not need a substitute sponsor. The exception applies regardless of whether the citizen spouse dies before or after approval of the petition.

   In non-spousal cases where the petitioner dies, an affidavit of support must be filed. However, a "substitute sponsor" is allowed. The substitute must be the souse, parent, mother-in-law, sibling, child (if over 18), son-in-law,

---

[68] INA § 213A(b)(2)(C).

[69] INA § 213A(a)(1)(B), (e)(1).

[70] INA § 213A(a)(3).

[71] INA § 212(a)(4)(C)(i)(III).

[72] INA § 201(b)(2)(A)(i).

daughter-in-law, grandparent, grandchild or legal guardian of the intended immigrant.[73]

3. Child automatically derives U.S. citizenship upon becoming lawful resident. Some noncitizen children automatically become U.S. citizens at the moment they become lawful permanent residents through the citizenship of the parent (derivative citizenship under INA § 340). Because they become citizens upon admission, an affidavit of support is not required.[74] An I-864W is required.

4. Immigrant has earned or inherits 40 quarters of qualifying income. Only an I-864W is required for applicants who already have or can be credited with 40 qualifying quarters of qualifying income.[75] Of course, many immigrants have worked in the United States with authorization. However, even those who worked without authorization can get credit for the quarters worked if they paid into the social security system; this requires working with the Social Security Administration to straighten out the records. And in some circumstances, some individuals can claim quarters of work done by relatives. For example, children can credit the quarters that their parents (including stepparents) earned from the date of the parent's birth until the date the child turns 18. A spouse can credit the quarters earned by the other spouse from the date of their marriage.

E. PUBLIC HEALTH AND MORALS

Inadmissibility grounds related to health can be divided into four categories: communicable diseases, failure to obtain vaccinations, mental or physical disorder, and drug addiction or abuse.

1. Communicable Diseases

Under INA § 212(a)(1)(A)(i), an applicant with a "communicable disease of public health significance" as determined by the Department of Health and Human Services (HHS) is inadmissible. For example, tuberculosis and sexually transmitted disease such as gonorrhea and syphilis are bases for inadmissibility. A person testing positive for these illnesses can have the disease treated and cured and then qualify to immigrate. In the alternative, if an illness such as tuberculosis cannot be quickly cured, under certain circumstances, the applicant may qualify for a waiver and gain admission.

Diseases that are designated as communicable diseases are listed in 42 CFR § 34.2(b). In addition to diseases like tuberculosis and sexually transmitted diseases, diseases that may trigger inadmissibility include: (1) quarantinable diseases designated by Presidential Executive Order, and (2) diseases that qualify as a "public health emergency of international concern which require notification to the World Health Organization (WHO) under the revised International Health

---

[73] 8 C.F.R. § 213a.1.

[74] 8 C.F.R. § 213a.2(a)(2)(ii)(E).

[75] 8 C.F.R. § 213a.2(a)(2)(ii)(C).

Regulations (IHR) of 2005." These categories only take effect when HHS directly notifies consular panel physicians in affected areas.

At one time, applicants with Acquired Immune Deficiency Syndrome (AIDS) were inadmissible. However, in 2010, HHS removed HIV from the definition of "communicable disease of public health significance." Prospective immigrants no longer are required to undergo IV testing as part of the required medical examination for immigration.

2. Failure to Prove Vaccinations

Under INA § 212(a)(1)(A)(ii), an applicant is inadmissible for failing to present evidence of vaccination against preventable diseases: mumps, measles, rubella, polio, tetanus and diphtheria toxoids, pertussis, influenza type B, and hepatitis B. This provision may be waived if the applicant obtains a vaccination, or if a civil surgeon or similar official certifies that the vaccination would not be medically appropriate, or if the vaccination would be contrary to the person's religious or moral beliefs.[76]

The required vaccinations are developed by the Advisory Committee for Immunization Practices (ACIP). The current vaccine tables based on the ACIP recommendations can be found at http://www.cdc.gov/vaccines/schedules/index. html. The vaccine must be age-appropriate and protect against a disease that has the potential to cause an outbreak or is against a disease that has been eliminated in the United States or is in the process of being eliminated.

3. Mental or Physical Disorder

Under INA § 212(a)(1)(A)(iii), applicants are inadmissible if they have a mental or physical disorder and related behavior that may threaten the property, welfare, and safety of themselves or others, or who have had such a disorder in the past that is likely to recur. For example, this ground of inadmissibility may apply to an applicant who has been committed to a mental institution for violent behavior, or to someone who has been diagnosed as a sexual predator, or even to someone who is suicidal. A waiver is available if the applicant can post a bond.[77]

Alcoholism can be a basis for inadmissibility under this provision, and a drunk driving conviction can serve as evidence of alcoholism. Some U.S. consulate offices have denied visa applications under this provision on the basis of one or two arrest for driving under the influence of alcohol. USCIS requires a medical evaluation for alcoholism if the applicant has a dingle drunk driving arrest or conviction within the last five years or two or more drunk driving arrests or convictions within the last 10 years.[78] However, the person is not inadmissible unless the examining physician finds (1) a diagnosis or mental disorder (alcohol abuse) and (2) current harmful behavior or a history of harmful behavior related to the disorder that is

---

[76] INA § 212(g)(2).

[77] INA § 212(g).

[78] *See* CIS Policy Update, *Physical or Mental Disorder with Associated Harmful Behavior* Ch. 7, *available at* http://www.uscis.gov/policymanual/HTML/PolicyManual-Volume8-PartB-Chapter7.html.

likely to recur in the future, such as drunk driving or domestic violence.[79]

Under INA § 212(a)(10)(B), an applicant who is accompanying a separate applicant who has been deemed inadmissible due to physical or mental disability also is inadmissible if the applicant is needed for the protection or guardianship of the helpless person.

4. Drug Addicts and Drug Abusers

Under § 212(a)(1)(A)(iv), drug addicts and drug abusers are inadmissible. This inadmissibility ground applies to current, not past, abuse or addiction. Drug abuse is defined as "the non-medical use of a controlled substance listed in §202 of the Controlled Substances Act, which has not necessarily resulted in physical or psychological dependence." Drug addiction is defined as "the non-medical use of a substance listed in §202 . . . which has resulted in physical or psychological dependence."[80] No waiver is available for this ground of inadmissibility.

The statute charges the Department of Health and Human Services with the responsibility of defining drug abuse or addiction. The Center for Disease Control, an HHS agency, has stated that a finding of substance dependence (drug addiction) or repetitively abusing substances (drug abuse) will only be made if the noncitizen meets current DSM (Diagnostic and Statistical Manual of Mental Disorders) diagnostic criteria for substance dependence or abuse with any of the specific substances listed in Schedules I through V of § 202 of the Controlled Substances Act.

In order to determine if an applicant for a visa is inadmissible under any of the health-related grounds, DHS requires the applicant to take a medical examination given by a doctor approved by DHS or, in consular processing, a doctor approved by the U.S. consulate. If the examining physician suspects the applicant of drug abuse, the applicant must be referred to a drug abuse expert for more evaluation. Only drug incidents that have occurred within the last three years are to be considered.

F. SPECIAL RULES

1. Asylum and Refugee Status

As we will see in Chapter 11, applicants with a well founded fear of persecution may qualify to remain in or enter the United States as asylees or refugees. However, even though a well founded fear of persecution is established, an applicant can still be barred from obtaining asylum or refugee status if the applicant has persecuted others, been convicted of a particularly serious crime, committed a serious non-political crime prior to entering the United States, or is a danger to U.S. security. Applicants may also be denied status if they have firmly resettled in a third country or have an offer of safe haven from a third country.

---

[79] 9 FAM 40.11 N8.3.

[80] 42 C.F.R. §§ (g), (h); *see also* 21 U.S.C. § 802.

a. Persecution of Others

Under INA § 208(b)(2)(A)(i), an applicant is ineligible for refugee status or asylum if the person has "ordered, incited, assisted, or otherwise participated in the persecution of any person on account of race, religion, nationality, membership in a particular social group, or political opinion." An applicant has not "persecuted others" if he or she simply participated as a regular soldier and fought against other combatants in a war. Also, in *Matter of Rodriguez-Majano*,[81] the BIA held that a truck driver who was forced to deliver supplies for the guerrillas, and who was later forced to join the guerrillas until he could desert after two months, was not ineligible for asylum. The Supreme Court also has suggested that there may be an exception when an individual was forced or coerced to persecute others.[82]

b. Conviction of a Particularly Serious Crime

Under INA § 208(b)(2)(A)(ii), no one who has been convicted of a particularly serious crime in the United States and therefore constitutes a danger to the community will be granted refugee or asylee status. In *Matter of Frentescu*,[83] involving an applicant who had been convicted of the crime of burglary in Illinois, the BIA ruled that the following factors should be considered in determining whether a particularly serious crime was involved: the nature of the conviction, the circumstances and underlying facts of the conviction, the type of sentence imposed, and whether the type and circumstances of the crime indicate that the alien will be a danger to the community. The BIA further stated that, although there may be instances when crimes against property will be considered "particularly serious," crimes against persons are more likely to be categorized as such. Also, the sentence imposed would be relevant to the issue of the seriousness of the alien's danger to the community.

Using these factors, the BIA concluded in *Frentescu* that the applicant had not been convicted of a particularly serious crime. The crime was an offense against property, the dwelling was not occupied, the applicant was not armed, and there were not aggravating circumstances. Furthermore, the applicant received a suspended sentence after serving only three months.

On the other hand, in *Matter of Garcia-Garrocho*,[84] the BIA held that a New York conviction for residential burglary in the first degree was per se a particularly serious crime because the statute involved one or more aggravating circumstances, including physical injury or potentially life-threatening acts. To the BIA, the determination of whether a crime is particularly serious essentially turns on whether the crime is one that, by its nature, represents a danger to the community.

Conviction of an aggravated felony is an absolute bar to asylum. As reviewed in Chapter 11, aggravated felonies include such things as drug trafficking, document fraud with a sentence of at least one year imposed, alien smuggling, crimes of

---

[81] Int. Dec. No. 3088 (BIA 1988).

[82] Negusie v. Holder, 555 U.S. 511 (2009).

[83] 18 I.&N. Dec. 244 (BIA 1982); *see also* Matter of N-A-M-, 24 I.&N. Dec. 336 (BIA 2007).

[84] Int. Dec. No. 3022 (BIA 1986).

violence or theft or burglary with a sentence of at least one year imposed, child molestation, money laundering (over $10,000), and murder.

Although unlawful trafficking in controlled substances presumptively constitutes a particularly serious crime, the Attorney General has stated that an exception can be made when there are extenuating circumstances that are both extraordinary and compelling.[85]

c.   Commission of a Serious Non-Political Crime

Under INA § 208(b)(2)(A)(iii), an applicant is ineligible for asylum if there are "serious reasons" to believe that the applicant has committed a serious non-political crime prior to entering the United States. The disqualification applies even without evidence of a conviction, and the crime can be less serious than a "particularly serious crime."

In *INS v. Aguirre-Aguirre*,[86] the Supreme Court reinstated a BIA decision holding that a serious non-political crime had occurred in an incident that involved throwing store merchandise on the floor and burning 10 buses, along with moving hesitant passengers off the buses before the vehicles were destroyed. The court rejected the use of a balancing test in such cases, maintaining that whether the applicant faced persecution in his home country had no bearing on whether a serious non-political crime had occurred.

The BIA considers the following factors when determining if an offense is a serious crime: (1) the immigrant's description of the crime; (2) the turpitudinous nature of the crime according to BIA precedent; (3) the value of any property involved; (4) the length of any sentence imposed and served; and (5) the usual punishments imposed for comparable offenses in the United States.[87]

d.   Danger to U.S. Security

Under INA § 208(b)(2)(A)(iv), an applicant is barred from asylum if "there are reasonable grounds for regarding the alien as a danger to the security of the United States." No person who has been involved in terrorist activity will be granted refugee or asylee status. After 9/11, the definition of who is a "terrorist" is quite broad. For example, the term could be interpreted to cover people who have provided food or other "material support" to guerillas or others trying to overthrow the government, or people who have given money to organizations whose aims the U.S. government believes are, at least in part, terrorist in nature.

The USA PATRIOT Act provisions are relevant here as well. Noncitizens are denied admission if they "endorse or espouse terrorist activity," or "persuade others to support terrorist activity or a terrorist organization," in ways that the State Department determines impede U.S. efforts to combat terrorism. The Act defines "terrorist activity" expansively to include support of otherwise lawful and nonviolent activities of almost any group that used violence. Noncitizens are deportable for

---

[85] Matter of Y-L-, A-G-,R-S-L-, 23 I.&N. Dec. 270 (A.G. 2002).

[86] 526 U.S. 415 (1999).

[87] Matter of Ballester-Garcia, 17 I.&N. Dec. 592 (BIA 1980).

wholly innocent associational activity, excludable for pure speech, and subject to incarceration without a finding that they pose a danger or flight risk. Foreign nationals can be detained for up to seven days while the government decides whether or not to file criminal or immigration charges. The Attorney General has broad preventive detention authority to incarcerate noncitizens by certifying there are "reasonable grounds to believe" that a person is "described in" the antiterrorism provisions of the immigration law, and the individual is then subject to potentially indefinite detention. The Attorney General also can detain noncitizens indefinitely even after prevailing in a removal proceeding "until the Attorney General determines that the noncitizen is no longer a noncitizen who may be certified [as a suspected terrorist.]."

After the Real ID Act of 2005, under INA § 212(a)(3)(B), an alien who "endorses or espouses" terrorist activity, anyone who has received "military-type training" from a terrorist organization, and anyone who is a member of a terrorist organization or has provided material support to a terrorist organization or a member of a terrorist organization is ineligible for asylum.

e.   Firm Resettlement or Offer of Safe Haven

Even though an asylum applicants may meet the definitional requirements for "refugee," under INA § 208(b)(2)(A)(vi), an applicant will be barred if he or she has "firmly resettled in another country prior to arriving in the United States."[88] The regulations provide the following guidance in determining whether the applicant has firmly resettled:

> An alien is considered to be firmly resettled if, prior to arrival in the United States, he entered into another nation with, or while in that nation received, an offer of permanent resident status, citizenship, or some other type of permanent resettlement unless he establishes: (a) that his entry into that nation was a necessary consequence of his flight from persecution, that he remained in that nation only as long as was necessary to arrange onward travel, and that he did not establish significant ties in that nation; or (b) that the conditions of his residence in that nation were so substantially and consciously restricted by the authority in the country of refugee that he was not in fact resettled. In making his determination, the Asylum Officer or Immigration Judge shall consider the conditions under which other residents of the country live, the type of housing made available to the refugee, whether permanent or temporary, the types and extent of employment available to the refugee, and the extent to which the refugee received permission to hold property and to enjoy other rights and privileges, such as travel documentation including a right of entry and/or reentry, education, public relief, or naturalization, ordinarily available to others resident in the country.[89]

---

[88] *See also* Matter of Lam, 18 I.&N. Dec. 15 (BIA 1981).

[89] 8 C.F.R. § 208.15.

In addition to these regulatory guidelines, a significant amount of existing case law interprets the firmly resettled concept,[90] which was upheld by the Supreme Court under prior law as a central theme of refugee legislation.[91] Arguably, the government bears the initial burden of establishing firm resettlement.[92]

In *Cheo v. INS*,[93] two brothers from Cambodia were denied their asylum claims because they had resided peacefully in Malaysia for three years prior to coming to the United States, suggesting that Malaysia had allowed them to stay indefinitely. Similarly, in *Matter of Portales*,[94] the applicants were Cubans requesting asylum. However, prior to their seeking asylum in the United States, they resided for 16 months in Peru, where they were granted refugee status. With that status, they were entitled to work, attend school, practice their religion, and were required to pay taxes. They were issued refugee documents by Peru that were valid for two years and could return to Peru. On those facts, the BIA concluded that the applicants were firmly resettled in Peru, especially because there was no indication that the Peruvian government intended to terminate their refugee status.

Related to, but quite distinct from, the firmly resettled preclusion is a discretionary basis for denial of asylum when there is an outstanding offer of resettlement by a third nation in which the applicant will not be subject to persecution. The policy has no basis in statute, and a regulatory reference to the policy was removed in 1990. The Ninth Circuit also disfavors such a policy, as evidenced by its decision in *Damaize-Job v. INS*.[95] In that case, a Nicaraguan Miskito Indian's claim was not undermined, even though he had stopped in other countries before entering the United States.

However, an applicant is barred from asylum if the Attorney General determines that the applicant may be removed, pursuant to a bilateral or multilateral agreement, to a country in which the person has access to a fair procedure for applying for asylum or equivalent protection. Of course, the person's life or freedom cannot be threatened in the third country.[96]

The safe haven bar does not apply to unaccompanied minors pursuant to the Trafficking Victims Protection and Reauthorization Act of 2008. That covers children who have no lawful immigration status in the United States, who are under 18 years of age, and who have no parent or legal guardian in the United States who is available to provide care and physical custody.[97] Those children can apply for asylum.

---

[90] *See, e.g.*, Matter of Guiragossian, 17 I.&N. Dec. 161 (BIA 1979).

[91] Rosenberg v. Chien Woo, 402 U.S. 49 (1971).

[92] Salazar v. Ashcroft, 359 F.3d 45, 50 n.3 (1st Cir. 2004).

[93] 162 F.3d 1227 (9th Cir. 1998).

[94] 18 I.&N. Dec. 239 (BIA 1982).

[95] 787 F.2d 1332 (9th Cir. 1986).

[96] INA § 208(a)(2)(A).

[97] 6 U.S.C. § 279.

2. Domestic Violence

Abused spouses and children of U.S. citizens and lawful permanent resident aliens who self-petition under VAWA are not inadmissible under the unlawful presence ground of inadmissibility (e.g., three and 10-year bars). They must, however, demonstrate a connection between the abuse and the unlawful status.[98]

Other grounds of inadmissibility under INA § 212(a) deserve special consideration. Under INA § 212(h), a special VAWA can be found those who are inadmissible because of a criminal past. The special waiver for VAWA self-petition set forth. In INA § 204(a)(1)(A), (B) relieves the applicant of a showing of extreme hardship to a qualifying relative. The waiver is discretionary, of course, and when the applicant's crime is violent or dangerous, favorable discretion is not likely unless there are extraordinary circumstances.[99]

When it comes to the public charge ground of inadmissibility, VAWA self-petitioners are exempted from the requirement of submitting an affidavit of support. Also, USCIS cannot consider for public charge purposes any benefits a self-petitioner received because of her status as an abused immigrant.[100]

A discretionary waiver is available to VAWA self-petitioners who have a disqualifying communicable disease. They must nonetheless comply with medical examination and vaccination requirements.

A VAWA-specific waiver for the fraud or misrepresentation ground of inadmissibility also is provided if the person can demonstrate extreme hardship to themselves or to a lawful parent or child.[101]

3. Special Juvenile Status

Children who are under the jurisdiction of a juvenile court and who are eligible for long term foster care may apply for adjustment of status as special immigrants. This means that they can become lawful permanent residents without having a U.S. citizen or permanent resident parent petition and without having to wait for a priority date. The court does have to rule that returning the child to the country of origin would not be in the child's best interest.[102]

Certain grounds of inadmissibility are waived (public charge, labor certification, documentation).[103] A waiver of most of the other noncriminal and nonsecurity grounds is available.

---

[98] INA § 212(a)(6)(ii).

[99] 8 C.F.R. 212.7(d).

[100] INA 212(p).

[101] INA § 212(i).

[102] INA §§ 101(a)(27)(J), 203(b)(4).

[103] INA § 245(h)(1); 8 C.F.R. § 245.1(e).

4. Nonimmigrant Visas

Nonimmigrants must also satisfy the grounds of inadmissibility in INS § 212(a). However, special mention must be made of INA § 214(b) which provides that "every alien . . . shall be presumed to be an immigrant until he establishes to the satisfaction of the consular officer . . . that he is entitled to a nonimmigrant status." Thus, the nonimmigrant bears the burden to establish that he or she qualifies. In other words, the nonimmigrant applicant must prove that he or she has a nonimmigrant intent to travel to the United States for temporary purposes. For example, a nonimmigrant visa could be denied if the applicant does not maintain a residence abroad.

Interestingly, some nonimmigrant categories allow the holder to have dual intent — to be in the United States on at temporary visa with intent of seeking immigrant status . . . do not require the maintaining nonimmigrant intent. Regulations appear to recognize dual intent for H-1b visas (specialty workers and their spouses), O visas (for workers who have extraordinary ability and their spouses and minor children), P visas (for athletes, artists or entertainers and their spouses and minor children), and E visas (for treaty traders or treaty investors and their spouses and minor children).[104]

Another ground of denial (INA § 221(g)) that provides that a consular officer should not issue a visa if (1) from the visa application or supporting documentation, it appears that the applicant is ineligible to receive it, (2) the application fails to comply with the statute or regulations, or (3) the consular officer knows or has reason to believe that the applicant is ineligible under INA § 212 or any other provision of law. Normally, consular officers rely on INA § 212(g) when an applicant fails to provide sufficient documentation to obtain a visa but there are insufficient grounds to deny it under INA § 214(b) and/or it appears that additional evidence could demonstrate the applicant's eligibility. Denials under INA § 221(g) also occur at border posts when the consular officer feels unable to adjudicate the application and wants the applicant to apply at his or her home post.[105]

---

[104] *See, e.g.*, 8 C.F.R. § 214.2(h)(16)(i).

[105] Susan K. Wehrer, M Mercedes Badia-Tavas, & Judy J. Lee, *Studies in Chaos Theory: Guiding Clients Through Appropriate Uses of the Temporary Visitor Visa Categories, in* IMMIGRATION & NATIONALITY LAW HANDBOOK, 2007–08 ED., at 314–15 (Richard Link, et. al, eds.).

Chapter 10

ASYLUM, WITHHOLDING OF REMOVAL, CONVENTION AGAINST TORTURE AND TEMPORARY PROTECTED STATUS

A. THE DEFINITION OF REFUGEE

U.S. asylum law arises largely out of international agreements that have been incorporated into immigration law. World War II left millions stateless and displaced. The need for international collaboration regarding this unique crisis eventually led to the creation of the Office of the United Nations High Commissioner for Refugees (UNHCR) in 1950. The following year, signatories adopted the United Nation Convention relating to the Status of Refugees (Convention), which attempted to provide an uniform protocol for refugee policy.[1]

According to the Convention, the definition of "refugee" emphasizes three main functions. First, a refugee is someone who is outside his or her country of nationality. Second, the refugee has fled and cannot return home because he or she faces the reality or the risk of persecution. Third, the persecution that an individual

---

[1] United Nations Convention relating to the Status of Refugees, July 28, 1951, http://www.refworld.org/docid/3be01b964.html (last visited Feb. 29, 2014).

faces is due to one's political opinion, race, religion, nationality, or membership in a particular social group. The definition of refugee was incorporated in the statute at INA § 101(a)(42).

The immigration statute requires the President of the United States to submit to Congress a report on proposed refugee admissions every year.[2] The report provides a description of the numbers of anticipated refugees, the country conditions from which refugees are expected, and the impact of the admission of refugees into the country. The President seeks authority to accept refugees from certain regions in the report. In its most recent report the President sought authority to accept 70,000 refugees.[3]

Although, in general, a refugee must be outside her country of nationality or stateless, the President has the authority to specify circumstances in which refugees still in their countries can seek refugee status.[4] This procedure is known as in-country processing. In its most recent report, the Obama administration sought to continue in-country processing for refugees in Iraq, Cuba, Eurasia and the Baltics, and to commence in-country processing for specified persons in Honduras, El Salvador and Guatemala.[5]

In order to qualify for asylum, the asylum seeker must meet the definition of a refugee as outlined in the statute. While the refugee does so from afar, the asylum seeker must present him or herself at the border, or be already present in the United States. The provisions for seeking asylum appear in INA § 208. Importantly, if the asylum seeker does not meet the requirements for asylum, she can seek other forms of relief based on humanitarian grounds. Article 33 of the Convention includes the principle of *non-refoulement*, which prohibits states from refusing entrance to an asylum seeker if doing so would force that person back to a country where he would likely face persecution on account of the five protected grounds, or torture whether or not based on the asylum grounds. Congress recognizes the doctrine of *non-refoulement* in INA § 241(b)(3), known as withholding of removal. Withholding of removal is also available for those who fear torture and who seek relief under the Convention Against Torture.

An asylum seeker can apply for asylum affirmatively or can seek asylum as a defense to removal. A grant of asylum entitles the applicant to remain in the country, authorizes employment, and allows travel abroad with prior consent.[6] It also requires an applicant acquire permanent residency[7] and to sponsor immediate relatives for immigrant petitions[8]

---

[2] INA § 207(d)(1).

[3] DEP'T OF STATE, PROPOSED REFUGEE ADMISSIONS FOR FISCAL YEAR 2015, REPORT TO CONGRESS (Sept. 18, 2014) (hereinafter Report on Proposed Refugees).

[4] INA § 101(a)(42)(B).

[5] Report on Proposed Refugees, *supra* note 3, at 5.

[6] INA § 208(c)(1).

[7] INA § 209.

[8] INA § 208(b)(3).

B. THE STANDARDS FOR ASYLUM

To be an asylee, a person must meet the definition of refugee under INA § 101(a)(42), which defined, in relevant part, as:

> any person who is outside any country of such person's nationality or, in the case of a person having no nationality, is outside any country in which such person last habitually resided, and who is unable or unwilling to return to, and is unable or unwilling to avail himself or herself of the protection of that country because of persecution or a well-founded fear of persecution on account of race, religion, nationality, membership in a particular social group, or political opinion.

In *Matter of Acosta*, the BIA set out the elements that applicants must demonstrate in order to meet the refugee definition when seeking asylum. The Board described these as follows: 1) the alien must have a "fear" of "persecution"; (2) the fear must be "well-founded"; (3) the persecution feared must be "on account of race, religion, nationality, membership in a particular social group, or political opinion; and (4) the alien must be unable or unwilling to return to his country of nationality or to the country in which he last habitually resided because of persecution or his well-founded fear of persecution."[9]

This section will discuss each of these element and its evolving standards.

1. "Fear" of "Persecution"

In *Matter of Acosta*, the BIA analyzed the meaning of fear by looking to its dictionary meaning, its use in the immigration statute and its definition in the United Nations High Commissioner for Refugees Handbook. It concluded that,

> [A]n alien seeking to qualify under section 101(a)(42)(A) of the Act must demonstrate that his primary motivation for requesting refuge in the United States is "fear," i.e., a genuine apprehension or awareness of danger in another country. No other motivation, such as dissent or disagreement with the conditions in another country or a desire to experience greater economic advantage or personal freedom in the United States, satisfies the definition of refugee created in the Act.[10]

The term "persecution" is not defined in the INA. Case law characterizes persecution "marked by the infliction of suffering or harm . . . in a way regarded as offensive." In *Matter of Acosta*, the BIA articulated guidelines when assessing persecution.[11] The BIA noted that persecution "contemplates that harm or suffering must be inflicted upon an individual in order to punish him for possessing a belief or characteristic a persecutor seeks to overcome."[12] It also noted that the harm "had to be inflicted by the government of a country or by persons or an

---

[9] Matter of Acosta, 19 I.&N. Dec. 211 (1985).

[10] *Id.* at 221.

[11] Matter of Acosta, 19 I.&N. Dec. 211 (BIA 1985).

[12] *Id.* at 223.

organization that the government was unable or unwilling to control."[13] Case law has identified multiple manifestations of persecution, including physical violence, torture, threats, detention, mental, emotional and psychological harm, and substantial economic deprivation.

2. "Well-Founded" Fear

An applicant must present evidence that establishes a well-founded fear of persecution as part of a claim for asylum under INA § 208. The Supreme Court decided in *INS v. Cardoza-Fonseca* the degree of risk of persecution that corresponds to the term "well-founded." In that case, the claimant sought asylum and withholding of removal based on her brother's political activities in Nicaragua. The immigration judge found that she could not show a clear probability of persecution in her home country and denied her asylum application, and the BIA agreed. The Ninth Circuit reversed the lower courts. The Supreme Court agreed with the Ninth Circuit, holding that for an asylum claim the risk of persecution need not rise to the level of the a "more likely than not" standard found in the statute's withholding of removal provision.[14] The Court noted that Congress provided for separate standards in its provisions, and that the asylum standard was meant to be more generous than the clear probability of persecution standard in withholding of removal cases.[15] The Court noted that, "One can certainly have a well-founded fear of an event happening when there is less than a 50% chance of the occurrence taking place."[16] The statute's regulations now state that a fear is well-founded if there is "a reasonable possibility of suffering such persecution" upon return to the applicant's country.[17] The BIA and lower courts have also interpreted a fear as well-founded if "a reasonable person in [the applicant's] circumstances would fear persecution," giving it both a subjective and objective character.[18] Courts have provided numerical expression to the "reasonable possibility" standard. In *Montecino v. INS*, the Ninth Circuit court noted that an applicant could meet the standard if "on the basis of objective circumstances personally known to him, believes that he has at least a one in 10 chance of being killed by the guerillas."[19]

Evidence of past persecution may satisfy the "well-founded fear" requirement. In order to establish past persecution, an applicant must show: (1) an incident, or incidents, that rise to the level of persecution; (2) that is on account of one of the statutorily-protected grounds; and (3) is committed by the government or forces the government is either "unable or unwilling" to control." Past persecution creates a presumption that the applicant has a well-founded fear of future persecution. The burden then shifts to the government to show that there has been a fundamental

---

[13] *Id.* at 222.

[14] INS v. Cardoza-Fonseca, 480 U.S. 421 (1987).

[15] *Id.* at 430.

[16] *Id.*

[17] 8 C.F.R. § 208.13(b)(2)(B).

[18] *See e.g.*, Matter of Mogharrabi, 19 I.&N. Dec. 439, 445 (BIA 1987).

[19] Montecino v. INS, 915 F.2d 518, 520 (9th Cir. 1990).

change in circumstances that mitigate against the applicant's fear.

An applicant may be eligible for asylum based on a well-founded fear of future persecution alone, even in the absence of past persecution. Acts of violence against the applicant, family members, and friends may establish a well-founded fear of persecution. An applicant need not show that she will be singled out individually for persecution if the applicant establishes that there is a "pattern or practice" of persecution of a group of persons similarly situated to the applicant and the applicant establishes his identification with this group such that his fear of persecution is reasonable.

The analogue to "well-founded" fear in the withholding of removal context requires that the applicant show that her life or freedom "would be threatened." The standard of proof for this requirement is a clear probability, or a "more likely than not" standard.[20]

3. 'On Account of'

An applicant's claim of persecution must be 'on account of,' or have a nexus to, race, religion, nationality, political opinion or membership in a particular social group.[21] The applicant's protected characteristic must be at least one central reason for persecution but does not have to be the central reason for the persecutor's motivation.[22] Previous case law precedent only required a showing that the persecution would be "at least in part" on account of a protected ground.

In determining whether the applicant has established a nexus between feared harm and a protected ground courts look to whether the applicant has established that the persecutor perceives the applicant to possess a protected characteristic. For example, it is not sufficient to show the persecutor's political opinion. The applicant must show that the persecutor is motivated to persecute because the applicant has (or is believed to have) a particular political opinion.[23] The applicant need not establish exact motive. The BIA has explained that "an applicant does not bear the unreasonable burden of establishing the exact motivation of a 'persecutor' where different reasons for actions are possible."[24] Instead, the applicant must establish "facts on which a *reasonable person* would fear that the danger arises on account of" one of the five protected grounds.[25]

---

[20] INS v. Stevic, 467 U.S. 407 (1984).

[21] INA § 208(b)(1)(A).

[22] REAL ID Act § 101(a)(30(B)(i), codified at INA § 208(b)(1)(B)(i); *see also,* Matter of J-B-N- & S-M-, 24 I.&N. Dec. 208, 213 (BIA 2007).

[23] INS v. Elias-Zacarias, 502 U.S. 478 (1992).

[24] Matter of J-B-N- & S-M-, 24 I.&N. Dec. 208, 211 (BIA 2007).

[25] Matter of Fuentes, 19 I.&N. Dec. 658, 662 (BIA 1988).

a. Race, Religion, or Nationality

The UNHCR Handbook defines race "in its widest sense to include all kinds of ethnic groups that are referred to as 'races' in common usage"[26] Recent cases use the term "ethnicity," which fits "between and within" race and nationality, interchangeably with race.[27] Racial discrimination may be the basis for persecution where "a person's human dignity is affected to such an extent as to be incompatible with the most elementary and inalienable human rights, or where the disregard of racial barriers is subject to serious consequences."[28]

Contemporary examples of religious persecution include prohibiting membership in a religious community, prohibiting worship in public or private, and prohibiting religious instruction.[29] The U.S. Commission on International Religious Freedom publishes annual reports about religious freedom conflicts, which serves as a resource for asylum claim adjudicators.[30]

Nationality includes membership in an ethnic or linguistic group in addition to citizenship.[31] Harm on account of nationality often overlaps with harm on account of race, religion, and/or political opinion.[32] Examples of claims based on nationality include Armenians in Azerbaijan,[33] Muslims, Croats, and Serbs in the former Yugoslavia,[34] and Tibetans in the People's Republic of China.[35]

b. Political Opinion

Persecution based on political opinion or imputed political opinion comprises one of the most-often claim forms of persecution. The applicant must show that he held, or that his persecutors believed that he held, a political opinion.[36]

In the classic political opinion case, the asylum seeker is a political dissident or participant in anti-government political activities. An applicant may manifest his political opinion by membership or participation in an organization with political purposes or goals, refusal to support an organization, participation in labor union membership and activities, or opposition to government corruption. With the rise of insurrections and civil wars, however, the political opinion claim has evolved from

---

[26] Handbook on Procedures and Criteria for Determining Refugee Status, U.N. Doc. HCR/IP/4/ Eng./REV.2 (ed. 1992) ("UNHCR Handbook"), para. 68.

[27] Duarte de Guinac v. INS, 179 F.3d 1156, 1159 n.5 (9th Cir. 1999); see also, Shoafera v. INS, 228 F.3d 1070, 1074 n.2 (9th Cir. 2000).

[28] UNHCR Handbook, para. 69.

[29] UNHCR Handbook, para. 72.

[30] Pub. L. 105-292 International Religious Freedom Act of 1998, Section 102(b).

[31] UNHCR Handbook, para. 74.

[32] UNHCR Handbook, para. 75.

[33] Avetova-Elisseva v. INS, 213 F.3d 1192, 1196 n.6 (9th Cir. 2000).

[34] Knezevic v. Ashcroft, 367 F.3d 1206 (9th Cir. 2004).

[35] Wangchuck v. Department of Homeland Security, Immigration, 448 F.3d 524 (2d Cir. 2006).

[36] In INS v. Cardoza-Fonseca for example, the court held that the applicant was persecuted based on a political opinion imputed to her by her persecutors because of her politically active brother in Nicaragua. INS v. Cardoza-Fonseca, 480 U.S. 421 (1987).

the traditional paradigm. Courts have been confronted with calls for a paradigm that better fits the realities of guerilla and non-traditional political upheaval. Two sorts of claims — political neutrality and imputed political opinion — have especially tested the paradigm. In *INS v. Elias-Zacarias*, the Supreme Court considered both of these sorts of claims as it addressed whether a guerrilla group's attempts to conscript an asylum seeker into military service constitutes persecution based on political opinion.[37] The Ninth Circuit court held that it was persecution based on imputed political opinion. The Supreme Court disagreed, holding that the asylum seeker in this case had failed to show that he was expressing a political opinion by refusing to be conscripted or that the guerilla group imputed a politically-based reason for his refusal too be conscripted.[38] The Court also noted that the political opinion prong of the statute required a showing of the asylum seeker's political opinion, not that of the persecutor.[39] The dissent noted that the majority in this case failed to consider that a political opinion could be expressed negatively as well as positively, and here refusal to join was its own political statement.[40] Since *Elias-Zacarias*, the BIA and several courts have concluded that the imputed doctrine remains a viable one.[41]

c.   Membership in a Particular Social Group

The Board of Immigration Appeals (BIA) set forth the definition of a particular social group in *Matter of Acosta*. For asylum purposes, a refugee must show that he or she is a member of a particular group that "share[s] a common, immutable characteristic . . . that the members either cannot change, or should not be required to change because it is fundamental to their individual identities and consciousness."[42] Examples of immutable characteristics include gender,[43] sexual orientation,[44] nuclear families,[45] and common past experiences, such as land ownership.[46] In addition to immutable qualities, courts also recognize that an applicant's body has immutable qualities, as in the context of an applicant's fear that she will be forced to undergo female genital mutilation.[47]

The BIA's approach to understanding membership in a particular social group is shifting.[48] In 2006, the BIA held in *Matter of C-A-* that a group could not be

---

[37] INS v. Elias-Zacarias, 502 U.S. 478 (1992).

[38] *INS v. Elias-Zacarias*, 502 U.S. at 483.

[39] *INS v. Elias-Zacarias*, 502 U.S. at 482.

[40] *INS v. Elias-Zacarias*, 502 U.S. at 486 (Stevens, J. dissenting).

[41] *See, e.g.*, In re T-M-B-, 21 I.&N. Dec. 775 (1997); Zhou v. Gonzales, 437 F.3d 860, 868–870 (9th Cir. 2006); Najjar v. Ashcroft, 257 F.3d 1262, 1289 (11th Cir. 2001); Morales v. INS, 208 F.3d 323, 331 (1st Cir. 2000); Sangha v. INS, 103 F.3d 1482 (9th Cir. 1997).

[42] Matter of Acosta, 19 I.&N. Dec. 211, 233 (BIA 1985).

[43] Matter of Kasinga, 21 I.&N. Dec. 357 (BIA 1996).

[44] Matter of Toboso-Alfonso, 20 I.&N. Dec. 819 (BIA 1990).

[45] Gebremichael v. INS, 10 F.3d 28 (1st Cir. 1993).

[46] Tapiero de Orjuela v. Gonzales, 423 F.3d 666 (7th Cir. 2005).

[47] Matter of Kasinga, 21 I.&N. Dec. 357 (BIA 1996).

[48] *See generally*, Jennifer Hess, *Social Visibility and Particularity in Asylum*: Gaitan v. Holder *and*

considered a "particular group" in the asylum context without being recognized in public view.[49] This definition focused on social visibility and particularity as conditions necessary to successfully show membership in a particular social group. The BIA reasoned that the inclusion of this element ensures that the particular social group ground is not a "catch-all" for asylum claims.[50] To date, the First,[51] Second,[52] Fourth,[53] Eighth,[54] and Ninth Circuits[55] all take into account visibility in varying degree. In contrast, the Third,[56] Sixth,[57] and Seventh Circuits[58] have found the BIA's new approach inconsistent with the previous approach stressing immutability.

The BIA's approach has an especially detrimental effect on the asylum claims of those fleeing gang warfare in Latin America. It is here that much of the litigation surrounding social visibility and particularity have occurred. In 2008, the BIA ruled on two cases that created a standard for immigration judge adjudications. In *Matter of S-E-G-*, the Board held that the essence of the "social visibility" requirement is whether the group would be recognized in a society as a discrete class of persons.[59] The Board found the characteristics of the social group as suggested by the male respondents — claiming that the group comprised male children who lack stable families and meaningful adult protection who are from middle and low income classes, who live in territories controlled by MS-13, and who refuse recruitment — too vague.[60] In *Matter of E-A-G-*, the BIA ruled that the male Honduran respondent failed to establish that members of Honduran society or even gang members themselves would perceive those opposed to gang membership as members of a social group.[61] Most recently, in *Matter of M-E-V-G*, the BIA reviewed and reaffirmed its requirement that a particular social group possess the element of particularity and social visibility.[62] It clarified at the same time that the social visibility test was never intended to require "ocular visibility" and renamed the element "social distinction."[63] The Board then held that an applicant seeking asylum based on particular social group must establish that the group is "(1)

---

the Ironic Requirement of Social Perception to Avoid Persecution, 33 B.C.J.L. & Soc. Just. 27 (2013); Adreanna Orlang, *Clearly Amorphous: Finding A Particular Social Group for Children Resisting Gang Recruitment*, 61 Cath. U. L. Rev. 621 (2012).

[49]   Matter of C-A-, 23 I.&N. Dec. 951, 959–960 (BIA 2006).

[50]   *Id.* at 960.

[51]   Scatambuli v. Holder, 558 F.3d 53 (1st Cir. 2009).

[52]   Fuentes-Hernandez v. Holder, 411 F. App'x 438, 438–39 (2d Cir. 2011).

[53]   Lizama v. Holder, 629 F.3d 440, 447 (4th Cir. 2011).

[54]   Gaitan v. Holder, 671 F. 3d 678 (8th Cir. 2012).

[55]   Ramos-Lopez v. Holder, 563 F.3d 855, 862 (9th Cir. 2009).

[56]   Valdiviezo-Galdamez v. Holder, 663 F.3d 582, 603–09 (3d Cir. 2011).

[57]   Urbina-Mejia v. Holder, 597 F.3d 360, 365–67 (6th Cir. 2010).

[58]   Gatimi v. Holder, 578 F.3d 611, 615–16 (7th Cir. 2009).

[59]   Matter of S-E-G-, et al., 24 I.&N. Dec. 579, 584 (BIA 2008).

[60]   *Id.* at 579.

[61]   Matter of E-A-G-, 24 I.&N. Dec. 591 (BIA 2008).

[62]   Matter of M-E-V-G, 26 I.&N. Dec. 227, 228 (BIA 2014).

[63]   *Matter of M-E-V-G*, 26 I.&N. Dec. at 228.

composed of members who share a common immutable characteristic, (2) defined with particularity, and (3) socially distinct with the society in question."[64] The board noted that the group must be perceived by society, and not just by the perpetrator, as socially distinct.

Domestic violence victims are at the forefront of particular social group litigation and regularly base their asylum claims on membership in a particular social group. Very recently, in 2014, the BIA decided in *Matter of A-R-C-G*, that "married women in Guatemala who are unable to leave their relationship" constitute a particular social group. The BIA applied its particularity test and the newly named social distinction test in this case. It found that both gender and marital status could be immutable characteristics where the individual is unable to leave the relationship for societal reasons. It found that evidence could be produced to show that Guatemalan society makes meaningful distinctions based on these immutable characteristics, such as by showing that its society recognizes a need to protect domestic violence victims. This case dealt with an ongoing issue in a series of cases in which the BIA, the Attorney General and the courts grappled with domestic violence as the basis for asylum claims.[65]

4. Unable or Unwilling to Return

In *Matter of Acosta*, the BIA described refugee status as one in which "an individual requires international protection because his country of origin or habitual residence is no longer safe for him."[66] The "unable or unwilling to return" prong of the refugee definition embodies this concept. The BIA has construed this requirement to mean that an asylum seeker must do more than establish a well-founded fear of persecution in a particular part of the country. To meet this requirement, the asylum seeker must show that "the threat of persecution exists for him countrywide."[67]

This standard is expressed in several asylum regulations that seek to determine whether an asylum seeker can reasonable relocate with the country of persecution.[68] Factors that courts or asylum officers consider include ongoing civil strife; strength or weakness of government infrastructures; geographical limitations; and social or cultural constraints.[69] Moreover, if the home government is the feared persecutor, or if past persecution has been shown, the burden to establish the reasonableness of internal relocation falls on the government.[70]

---

[64] *Matter of M-E-V-G*, 26 I.&N. Dec. at 237.

[65] *See, e.g.*, Matter of R-A, 24 I.&N. Dec. 629 (AG 2008); Dep't of Homeland Security's Supplemental Brief, Matter of L-R- (B.I.A. Apr. 13, 2009), *available at* http://graphics8.nytimes.com/packages/pdf/us/20090716-asylum-brief.pdf.

[66] Matter of Acosta, 19 I.&N. Dec. 211, 235 (1985).

[67] Matter of Acosta, 19 I.&N. Dec. 211 (1985).

[68] 8 C.F.R. § 208.13(b)(2)(ii).

[69] 8 C.F.R. § 208.13(b)(3).

[70] *See* 8 C.F.R. § 208.13(b)(3)(ii).

C. HUMANITARIAN ASYLUM

In cases of severe past persecution, an applicant may obtain asylum even without showing a well-founded fear of persecution in the future. The BIA held in *Matter of Chen* that based on the applicant's history of severe past persecution — which includes the Red Guard destroying the applicant's home, imprisoning and dragging his father through the streets, and badly burning him in a bonfire — an adjudicator may exercise discretion and grant asylum on this basis alone.[71] Additionally, victims of past persecution who no longer reasonably fear future persecution on account of a protected ground may be granted asylum if they can establish a reasonable possibility that they may suffer other serious harm upon removal to that country.[72] Serious harm could include civil strife,[73] severe mental or emotional harm,[74] and extreme circumstances of inadequate health care.[75]

D. WITHHOLDING OF REMOVAL

Withholding of removal, found at INA § 241(b)(3), is another remedy available to those whose life or freedom the immigration court determines would be threatened if removed to their home countries because of race, religion, nationality, membership in a particular social group, or political opinion.[76] It is a remedy that allows an applicant to stay in the United States to avoid removal to a country where the applicant will more likely than not face persecution. The same application for asylum covers a withholding of removal claim.[77]

Withholding of removal corresponds to the concept of *non-refoulement* in international law.[78] The concept of withholding first appeared in immigration law in 1950 in the context of deportation proceedings. At that time Congress prohibited deportation if a deportee would be subject to physical persecution.[79] The provision was made discretionary in 1952, and was changed to persecution on account of race, religion, or political opinion in 1965. In 1967 the United States agreed to abide by the 1967 U.N. Protocol Relating to the Status of Refugees, which itself incorporated the *non-refoulement* provisions of the 1951 Convention Relating to the Status of Refugees.[80] The Convention provides the basis for the current withholding provision, at INA § 241. The statute states, in accord with the Convention, "The Attorney

---

[71] Matter of Chen, 20 I.&N. Dec. 16, 21 (BIA 1989) (arguing that the particularity and social visibility prongs can be met by a nexus of gender, relationship status and society's perception of that status).

[72] Belishta v. Ashcroft, 378 F.3d 1078, 1081 (9th Cir. 2004).

[73] Mohammed v. Gonzales, 400 F.3d 785 (9th Cir. 2005).

[74] Kone v. Holder, 596 F.3d 141 (2d Cir. 2010).

[75] Pllumi v. Att'y Gen. of US., 642 F. 3d 155, 162 (3d Cir. 2011).

[76] INA § 241(b)(3).

[77] 8 C.F.R. § 208.1(a).

[78] *Non-refoulement* is an international law principle, codified in various international conventions, that protects refugees from being repatriated back to countries where their lives or their freedom would be in jeopardy.

[79] Internal Security Act of 1950, 64 Stat. 987, 1010 (Sept. 23, 1950).

[80] Article 33 of the Convention states that "No Contracting State shall expel or return ("refouler") a refugee in any manner whatsoever to the frontiers of territories where his life or freedom would be

General may not remove an alien to a country if the Attorney General decides that the alien's life or freedom would be threatened in that country because of the alien's race, religion, nationality, membership in a particular social group, or political opinion."[81]

Withholding requires a showing of "clear probability of persecution," a higher standard than the "past persecution" or "well-founded fear of persecution" required of asylum applicants. The Supreme Court held in *INS v. Cardoza-Fonseca* that the Congress made the asylum and withholding standards different and that the withholding standard, in accordance with the *non-refoulement* principle, was stricter than the asylum standard. Withholding's clear probability standard is defined as a greater than 50 percent chance of persecution. While a grant of asylum is discretionary, however, once an applicant meets the standard to the satisfaction of the judge, withholding is mandatory.

Withholding of removal is a more limited remedy than asylum. A recipient of a withholding of removal grant cannot become a lawful permanent resident. The remedy is only available to the individual applicant, moreover. By contrast, a grant of asylum under INA § 208 allows the permanent residence of the asylum seeker and his derivatives, and eventual citizenship. Additionally, if an applicant faces persecution in his homeland, § 241(b)(3) allows the Attorney General to deport him to a country that will accept him.

The following categories of noncitizens are ineligible for withholding of removal: persons who have persecuted others or participated in their persecution; persons convicted of a serious crime and who are a danger to the community; persons who have committed a serious non-political crime outside the United States; and persons who can reasonably be regarded as security risks.[82]

Whereas an applicant may apply for asylum both affirmatively and defensively, one can only receive withholding of removal in removal proceedings. A person applying for asylum does not need to file a separate application for withholding of removal since an application for asylum automatically constitutes an application for withholding of removal.

E. CONVENTION AGAINST TORTURE RELIEF

An applicant in fear of torture as defined in the United Nations Convention Against Torture (CAT). Under Article 3 of the Torture Convention, the United States has agreed not to return a person to a country where he or she could be tortured. In *Kamalthas v. INS*, the Ninth Circuit provided an excellent summary of the distinctions between CAT protection, asylum, and withholding of removal:

> [C]laims for relief under the Convention are analytically separate from claims for asylum under INA § 208 and for withholding of removal under INA § 241(b)(3). Put another way, a claim under the Convention is not

threatened on account of his race, religion, nationality, membership of a particular social group or political opinion."

[81] INA § 241(b)(3).

[82] INA § 241(b)(3).

merely a subset of claims for either asylum or whholding of removal. . . . [T]o be eligible for relief under the Convention, a petitioner must show that it is more likely than not that he or show would be tortured if removed to the proposed country of removal." . . . In an important sense, then, the Convention's reach is both broader and narrower than that of a claim for asylum or withholding of deportation: coverage is broader because a petitioner need not show that he or she would be tortured "on account of" a protected ground; it is narrower, however, because the petitioner must show that it is "more likely than not" that he or she will be tortured, and not simply persecuted upon removal to a given country.[83]

The guidelines for the implementation of CAT and for relief standards can be found in the regulations at 8 C.F.R. 208.16–18. The regulations define torture as:

[A]ny act by which severe pain or suffering, whether physical or mental, is intentionally inflicted on a person for such purposes as obtaining from him or her or a third person information or a confession, punishing him or her for an act he or she or a third person has committed or is suspected of having committed, or intimidating or coercing him or her or a third person, or for any reason based on discrimination of any kind, when such pain or suffering is inflicted by or at the instigation of or with the consent or acquiescence of a public official or other person acting in an official capacity.[84]

The regulations have further defined government acquiescence as a prior awareness of the torture and a subsequent breach of a legal duty to intervene to prevent the torture.

There are two types of CAT protection.[85] The first is withholding of removal and is referred to as Article 3 withholding. The second is called "deferral of removal" and is available to those who are barred from obtaining Article 3 withholding. The mandatory bars are the same as those for withholding under INA § 241(b)(3)(B). They include persecution of others based on a protected ground; conviction of a particularly serious crime; reason to believe the noncitizen committed a serious nonpolitical crime; reason to believe the noncitizen is a danger to the security of the United States. If even one of the bars exists, a judge must grant deferral of removal.

CAT benefits are narrow. CAT relief does not lead to permanent residency. Nor does it provide for family members to join the applicant. It also does not prevent removal to a third country. A grant of deferral of removal under CAT is subject to termination. Withholding or deferral under CAT may be terminated, moreover, if there is no longer a likelihood of torture in the person's country of origin.

---

[83] Kamalthas v. INS, 251 F.3d 1279, 1283 (9th Cir. 2001).

[84] 8 C.F.R. § 208.18(a)(1).

[85] 8 C.F.R. § 208.16(c)(2).

F. BARS TO ELIGIBILITY

There are several statutory bars to an applicant's ability to apply for asylum or withholding of removal. The statute requires that an asylum applicant file an application for asylum within one year of arriving in the United States. Procedurally, an applicant must show by "clear and convincing evidence" that an application for asylum was filed within one year of arrival,[86] that there are "changed circumstances which materially affect the applicant's eligibility for asylum,"[87] or that the delay in filing an application was because of "extraordinary circumstances."[88]

Other bars include: a safe third country,[89] submitting previous asylum application,[90] changed circumstances,[91] persecutor of others,[92] conviction of a particularly serious crime,[93] serious nonpolitical crime,[94] national security risk,[95] terrorist activity,[96] or firm settlement prior to arriving in the United States.[97] A person convicted of an "aggravated felony" is automatically considered to be convicted of a particularly serious crime.[98] If the crime is not an aggravated felony, it could still be a particularly serious crime.[99] To determine whether it is a particularly serious crime, the BIA considers several factors, including the nature of the conviction, the circumstances and underlying facts for the conviction, the type of sentence imposed, and whether the type and circumstances of the crime indicate that the individual will be a danger to the community.[100]

Some of the bars to withholding of removal are similar to those of asylum and include persecution of others,[101] conviction of a particularly serious crime,[102] reasons to believe the applicant has committed a serious nonpolitical crime outside the United States,[103] and reasonable grounds to believe the person is a danger to the security of the United States (including terrorist activity).[104] Neither the one

---

[86] INA § 208(a)(2)(B).

[87] INA § 208(a)(2)(D).

[88] INA § 208(a)(3).

[89] INA § 208 (a)(2)(A).

[90] INA § 208 (a)(2)(C).

[91] INA § 208 (a)(2)(D).

[92] INA § 208 (b)(2)(A)(i).

[93] INA § 208 (b)(2)(A)(ii).

[94] INA § 208 (b)(2)(A)(iii).

[95] INA § 208 (b)(2)(A)(iv).

[96] INA § 208 (b)(2)(A)(v).

[97] INA § 208 (b)(2)(A)(vi).

[98] INA § 208 (b)(2)(B)(i).

[99] INA § 208 (b)(2)(B)(ii).

[100] Matter of Frentescu, 18 I.&N. Dec. 244 (BIA 1982).

[101] INA § 241 (b)(3)(B)(i).

[102] INA § 241 (b)(3)(B)(ii).

[103] INA § 241 (b)(3)(B)(iii).

[104] INA § 241 (b)(3)(B)(iv).

year application deadline nor firm resettlement are bars to withholding of removal. A person convicted of an aggravated felony may still apply for withholding of removal unless sentenced to an aggregate term of at least five years imprisonment.[105]

Although there are no bars to eligibility for CAT relief, the regulations provide for deferral of removal — instead of withholding of removal — for those who would otherwise be ineligible for regular withholding because of crimes, persecution of others, or other threats to the community.[106]

G. TEMPORARY PROTECTED STATUS (TPS)

Under INA § 244, the Secretary of Homeland Security may designate a country, or parts of a country, for temporary protected status (TPS) if conditions temporarily prevent the country's nationals from returning safely or if a country cannot handle the return of its nationals adequately.[107] The Secretary may designate TPS for countries suffering from armed conflict, environmental disaster, or other extraordinary and temporary conditions. To date the Secretary has designated the following countries for TPS: El Salvador, Haiti, Honduras, Nicaragua, Somalia, Sudan, South Sudan, and Syria. The initial TPS designation lasts for a period of six to 18 months and can be extended if conditions continue to support the designation.[108] If the AG determines that the foreign state continues to meet the conditions for designation, the period of designation is extended for an additional period of six months (or 18 months in the AG's discretion).[109]

An alien who is a national of a state designated under Section 244(b)(1) is eligible for TPS only if the alien has been continuously physically present in the U.S. since the effective date of the most recent designation of that state.[110] An immigrant is not eligible for TPS if he or she is ineligible for admission because of certain criminal activity, has been convicted of any felony or two or more misdemeanors committed in the United States, or is ineligible for asylum.[111]

During the period for which a country has been designated for TPS, beneficiaries may remain in the United States and may obtain work authorization.[112] However, TPS does not lead to permanent resident status.[113] When the Secretary terminates a TPS designation, beneficiaries return to the same immigration status they had before TPS (unless expired).

---

[105] INA § 241(b)(3)(B).

[106] 8 C.F.R. § 208.17(a).

[107] INA § 244(b).

[108] INA § 244(b)(2)(B).

[109] INA § 244(b)(3)(C).

[110] INA § 244(c)(1)(A)(i).

[111] INA § 244(c)(2)(A-B).

[112] INA § 244(a)(1).

[113] INA § 244(f)(1).

Chapter 11

ADMISSION PROCEDURES

SYNOPSIS

A. OVERVIEW

Admissions procedures vary for the different categories of nonimmigrants and immigrants, and other noncitizens who request admission into the United States. Generally the noncitizen must establish eligibility for admission in one of the qualifying immigrant, nonimmigrant or other categories, and she must establish she is not inadmissible under INA § 212(a).

Most noncitizens are admitted into the United States using a two-stage procedure: applying for a visa at a U.S. Embassy or Consular Post overseas; and applying for admission into the United States at an approved port of entry. This two-stage procedure involves scrutiny by a Department of State (DOS) consular officer overseas and scrutiny by a CPB immigration inspector upon request for admission at the border. Some noncitizens are exempt from the visa requirement. In the case of admission into the U.S. by adjustment of status, available to some noncitizens changing from nonimmigrant to immigrant status, only the DHS USCIS adjudicator is involved in the process. Other noncitizens requesting admission into the U.S., including those fleeing persecution and unauthorized migrants, are addressed in Chapters 11 and 13. Lawful presence in the U.S. under a discretionary procedure such as parole or deferred action is discussed in this Chapter.

Noncitizens must possess appropriate travel documents to board an airplane bound for the U.S. and apply for admission at a port of entry. The required documentation varies. Generally, most noncitizens must possess a visa (either a nonimmigrant visa in their passport or the "green card" Form I-551 for LPRs). Most nonimmigrants must submit a visa application to a U.S. Embassy or Consular Office to obtain a visa before arriving at an approved port of entry into the United States. Nonimmigrants in certain categories may apply for admission directly at the border without a visa. Applicants for admission, as a result, bear the burden of establishing eligibility for admission in one of the immigrant or nonimmigrant categories.

Some nonimmigrant categories and nearly all immigrant visa categories require a visa petition approved by USCIS before submitting a visa application at a Consular Post overseas, and/or applying for admission into the United States. Visa petitions for nonimmigrants and immigrants are discussed separately below.

After the noncitizen receives the visa, or if a visa is not required, she may travel to a U.S. port of entry and apply for admission. A CPB immigration inspector conducts an inspection of each noncitizen requesting admission under INA § 235. The officer will determine if an inadmissibility ground under INA § 212(a) is applicable, and verify whether any computer system maintained by DHS has information about the individual.[1]

The term admission is defined in INA § 101(a)(13) to mean a lawful entry of a noncitizen into the U.S. after inspection and authorization by an immigration officer. All noncitizens who have not been admitted after inspection are deemed to be applicants for admission. This includes noncitizens who arrive a port of entry to apply for admission and those apprehended inside the United States.[2] The admission process at the border is discussed below.

---

[1] The DHS databases include the Arrival and Departure Information System (ADIS), the Interagency Border Inspection System (IBIS), and the National Automated Immigration Lookout System (NAILS), among others. The State Department maintains a database: the Consular Lookout and Support System (CLASS).

[2] INA §§ 101(a)(15), 235.

B. NONIMMIGRANTS

Most nonimmigrants who seek admission into the United States must follow the two-step procedure of applying for a visa at a U.S. Embassy or Consular Post overseas and applying for admission at an approved port of entry. Some nonimmigrants are exempt from the visa requirement, and, therefore, they may seek admission directly at a port of entry. This includes nationals of countries in the Visa Waiver Program, discussed below. Most nationals of Canada and Mexico also are exempt from the visa requirement.

1. Nonimmigrant Visa Applications and Admissions

Most nonimmigrants must obtain a visa by submitting a visa application to a U.S. Embassy or Consular Post abroad.[3] The visa application process identifies whether the noncitizen is eligible for the category under INA § 101(a)(15). Consular officers also must determine whether the nonimmigrant has the proper intent. Under INA § 214(b), all applicants for admission are presumed to be immigrants (lawful permanent residents).[4] The burden is on the noncitizen to establish the intent to visit the U.S. temporarily in a specific nonimmigrant visa category. For example, a B Tourist Visitor under INA § 101(a)(15)(B)(2) must intend to visit temporarily and to engage only in tourist activities.

The visa application process further requires the noncitizen to establish she is not inadmissible under any of the categories in INA § 212(a). The questions on a visa application mirror the INA § 212(a) inadmissibility provisions. Many nonimmigrant categories require the noncitizen to establish her intent to return to her home country. In some nonimmigrant categories, the DOS and DHS recognize a noncitizen may have a "dual intent" to remain in the U.S. temporarily and intend to remain permanently if, at some future time, the process for an immigrant visa is completed.[5]

Some nonimmigrant categories require an approved nonimmigrant visa petition prior to submitting a visa application to a U.S. Embassy or Consular Post abroad, and prior to applying for admission into the United States.[6] Other nonimmigrant categories may require additional documentation prior to applying for a visa.[7] For example, students in the F category, under INA § 101(a)(15)(F), must obtain a

---

[3] INA § 222 covers the requirements for a visa application. *See also*, INA §§ 212(a)(7)(A) (immigrant visa requirement), 212(a)(7)(B)(i)(II) (nonimmigrant visa requirement).

[4] INA § 214(b) presumes that a nonimmigrant applicant for a visa or admission into the U.S. is an immigrant (lawful permanent resident). Generally, this means the nonimmigrant must establish her intent to return to her home country. The INA § 214(b) presumption does not apply to nonimmigrant applicants under INA §§ 101(a)(15)(H), (L), and (V).

[5] The dual intent doctrine permits a nonimmigrant to begin the permanent residence process while maintaining valid nonimmigrant status. This doctrine only applies to nonimmigrants under INA §§ 101(a)(15)(E), (H)(i)(b), (L), (O), (P), and (V). *See also* Matter of Hosseinpour, 15 I.&N. Dec. 191 (B.I.A. 1975).

[6] Nonimmigrants under INA §§ 101(a)(15)(H), (L), (K), (O), (P), (Q) must file a nonimmigrant visa petition, Form I-129 with USCIS. Upon approval, a noncitizen may apply for the corresponding visa.

[7] Nonimmigrants under INA §§ 101(a)(15)(F), (M), (J).

document from the school they will attend in the United States.[8]

Visa applications are submitted in person at the U.S. Embassy or Consular Post overseas.[9] Congress requires everyone between the ages of 15 and 79 to appear for an in-person interview when requesting a nonimmigrant visa.[10] Visas are machine-readable, tamper-resident and use biometric identifiers.[11] As of October 2005, visa applicants must provide photos and fingerprints under the Biometric Visa Program [BIOVISA]. The State Department uses BIOVISA to create an electronic version of visa applications and this database is used by CPB immigration inspectors at ports of entry.[12]

Consular officers at U.S. Embassies and Consular Posts overseas have broad discretion in visa issuance and their scrutiny is the first screening of whether a noncitizen is inadmissible.[13] After September 11, 2001, there is greater oversight of visa issuance by the DHS.[14] DHS immigration officers are located in U.S. Embassies and Consular Posts abroad, and DHS officers can veto the issuance of a visa. There are few options if a visa application is denied including internal review at the consular post[15] and an applicant may request an advisory opinion on questions of law.[16] The denial of visas is covered in this chapter.

Upon approval of the visa application by the consular officer, a visa sticker is placed in the noncitizen's passport. Nonimmigrant visas have a specific validity period, generally determined by the statutory requirements for each nonimmigrant category. Often, visas allow multiple entries. For example, one might have an F-1 multiple-entry student visa valid for the duration of status as a student, or a three-year H-1B specialty worker visa based on the period of validity of the underlying H-1B nonimmigrant visa petition.[17] A multiple entry visa will allow an individual to travel to the U.S. on numerous visits.

The visa is a required travel document for most noncitizens. The visa allows a person to travel to the United States and apply for admission at a port of entry.

---

[8] An F-1 student must obtain a Form I-20 issued by the school in which she will enroll and this form must be presented to the DOS to obtain an F visa, and to the CPB immigration inspector at the port of entry to be admitted.

[9] INA §§ 221, 222.

[10] INA § 222(h) was added by the Intelligence Reform and Terrorism Prevention Act of 2004, Pub. L. No. 108-458, 118 Stat. 3638 (Dec. 17, 2004). Before this Act, the personal appearance requirement could be waived.

[11] The Enhanced Border Security and Visa Entry Reform Act of 2002 mandated the use of biometrics in U.S. visas. DHS established the U.S. standard for biometric screening as ten fingerprint scans which are collected at all U.S. Embassies and Consulates for visa applicants seeking to come to the United States. *See* http://travel.state.gov/content/visas/english/general/border-biometrics.html.

[12] INA § 221(a)(2), 8 U.S.C. § 1201(a)(2) (2014).

[13] INA § 101(a)(9) defines "consular officer" to mean any consular, diplomatic or other officer or employee of the U.S. designated for the purpose of issuing immigrant or nonimmigrant visas, and in some cases for the purpose of adjudicating nationality.

[14] DHS has authority over visa policy and regulations governing visas.

[15] 22 CFR §§ 41.121(c), 42.81(c) (2014).

[16] 22 CFR §§ 41.121(d), 42.81(d) (2014).

[17] INA §§ 101(a)(15)(F), (H)(1).

Airlines often perform the initial review of travel documents before an individual may board a flight to the U.S. The noncitizen will present the visa to a CPB immigration inspector to apply for admission at the port of entry. The visa does not guarantee admission into the United States.

2. Exceptions to the Visa Requirement

a. Visa Waiver Program Admissions

Under the Visa Waiver Program, business or tourist visitors from specified countries may apply for admission without a visa. The Visa Waiver Program [VWP] is set forth in INA § 217. Countries in the program are those Congress has determined have a low incidence of visa refusals, overstays or other immigration system abuses. Nationals of VWP countries may seek admission for up to 90 days. As of 2014, there are 38 countries in the VWP program.[18]

Only tourist or business visitors under INA § 101(a)(15(B) are admitted under the VWP. They waive their right to extend their stay, to change their nonimmigrant visa status under INA § 248, or to adjust status under INA § 245(a) (except immediate relatives). VWP visitors also waive their right to a removal hearing to contest an inadmissibility determination and (except in asylum cases) deportability under INA § 217(b).

The Visa Waiver Program was initially established as a pilot program in 1986. Congress made the program permanent in 2000. After September 11, 2001, amendments to the VWP enhanced the documentary requirements. Noncitizens entering under the VWP must satisfy either the e-Passport or machine-readable passport requirements in compliance with standards set by the International Civil Aviation Organization (ICAO). As of January 12, 2009, all VWP travelers must register in the Electronic System for Travel Authorization (ESTA) system prior to boarding a U.S. bound air or sea carrier. ESTA is a web-based system maintained by CPB.[19]

b. Western Hemisphere Admissions

Most Canadian noncitizens under the North American Free Trade Agreement [NAFTA] do not require a visa to apply for admission, however, most require a passport.[20] There are other longstanding systems for Western Hemisphere admissions designed to accelerate the admissions process for some noncitizens, for example, travel for citizens of the U.S., Canada, and Bermuda. Mexicans also may visit the U.S. for business or as tourists with a Border Crossing Card [BCC]

---

[18] As of 2014, the countries participating in the VWP include Andorra, Australia, Austria, Belgium, Brunei, Chile, Czech Republic, Denmark, Estonia, Finland, France, Germany, Greece, Hungary, Iceland, Ireland, Italy, Japan, Latvia, Liechtenstein, Lithuania, Luxembourg, Malta, Monaco, Netherlands, New Zealand, Norway, Portugal, San Marino, Singapore, Slovakia, Slovenia, South Korea, Spain, Sweden, Switzerland, Taiwan, and the United Kingdom.

[19] *See* http://www.cbp.gov/travel/international-visitors/esta.

[20] NAFTA categories for the admission of Mexicans and Canadians include tourist visitors, some intracompany transferees, and some professionals. 8 C.F.R. § 214.2(b)(4) (2014).

containing biometric data. Border Crossing Cards are issued citizens and residents in Mexico who meet the eligibility standards for a business or tourist visa. It functions as both a travel document and visa.[21]

The ease of travel within the Western Hemisphere has changed due to increased documentary requirements. As of January 2007, the Western Hemisphere Travel Initiative (WHTI) established by the DHS requires everyone (U.S. citizens and noncitizens) travelling by air from Canada, Mexico, the Caribbean and Bermuda to present a passport or other approved identification to enter the U.S.[22] The Global Entry Program began as a pilot program but now operates widely. Under the program, CPB provides expedited clearance for pre-approved, low-risk travelers who are U.S. citizens, LPRs or Mexican nationals. The NEXUS alternative inspection program is another CPB program available to registered U.S. and Canadian citizens. Participants receive an identification card used in lieu of a passport required under the WHTI program.

3. Nonimmigrant Visa Petitions

Generally, noncitizens who will work in the U.S. temporarily must have an approved visa petition. Those nonimmigrant categories requiring an approved visa petition prior to visa application and application for admission into the United States under INA § 101(a)(15) include:

- H Specialty Occupation Workers, Temporary Workers and Trainees;
- K Fiance, Fiancees, and Spouses of United States citizens;
- L Intracompany Transferees;
- O Outstanding Individuals in the sciences, arts, education, businesss, or athletics;
- P Artists and Entertainers; and
- Q International Cultural Exchange performers.

USCIS Regional Service Centers in the United States review nonimmigrant visa petitions to determine whether the petitioner (usually the employer) and the beneficiary of the petition (the noncitizen) meet the statutory requirements for that particular category. For example, H-1B specialty worker nonimmigrant visa petitions are filed by prospective employers who must establish the position to be filled is a "specialty occupation," and the noncitizen meets the statutory and regulatory requirements to fill the position.[23] Premium expedited processing of employment-related nonimmigrant petitions is available under INA § 286(u).[24]

---

[21] *See* http://travel.state.gov/content/visas/english/visit/border-crossing-card.html.

[22] 71 Fed. Reg. 68,412 (Nov. 24, 2006). WHTI is a joint Department of State (DOS) and Department of Homeland Security (DHS) plan to implement a 9/11 Commission recommendation for visa exempt noncitizens.

[23] INA § 101(a)(15)(H)(1)(B).

[24] Petitions submitted for premium processing pay that fee in addition to the regular processing fee. In 2014, the premium processing fee was $1225.00.

Upon approval of the visa petition by the USCIS Regional Service Center, a noncitizen may submit a visa application overseas to a Consular Post, or a change of status application in the United States.[25] For example, an F-1 student in the United States might change her status to H-1B specialty worker without leaving the country. The change of status application can be submitted at the same time as the H-1B visa petition, and the decision to approve the petition will occur simultaneously with the decision to change the noncitizen's status. The noncitizen in this example would apply for an H-1B visa on her next trip outside of the U.S. in order to return and be admitted in H-1B status.

C.   IMMIGRANTS

1.   Immigrant Visa Petitions

Generally, the first step in all immigrant visa cases is the submission of an immigrant visa petition to a USCIS Regional Service Center having jurisdiction over the petitioner under INA § 204(a).[26] The petitioner must establish the required relationship existing between the petitioner and beneficiary under the particular immigrant visa category. Some noncitizens may self-petition under the employment-based and family-sponsored categories.[27] Some employment-based categories require labor certification from the Department of Labor before the immigrant visa petition is filed.[28] In this case, an immigrant visa petition is filed with USCIS after a labor certification application is approved.

The burden of proof is on the petitioner to establish eligibility in the immigrant visa petition. The decision to approve or deny the petition is based only on the statutory criteria for the immigrant visa category (family-sponsored or employment-based) not the inadmissibility grounds of INA § 212(a). A petition is automatically revoked if the petitioner withdraws the petition or, generally, if the petitioner dies.[29]

Approval of the immigrant visa petition completes the first stage of the permanent resident process. Upon approval of the immigrant visa petition by a USCIS Regional Service Center, the beneficiary will opt for either consular visa

---

[25] INA § 248 allows change of status for nonimmigrants in lawful status who are admissible, except in certain categories (nonimmigrants under § 101(a)(15)(C), (D), (K), (S), (J) who are subject to a two-year foreign residence requirement; nonimmigrants in the VWP and tourist or business visitors to Guam are ineligible to change status).

[26] An I-130 Petition is submitted for the family-sponsored immigrant visa categories, and an I-140 Petition is submitted for the employment-based categories.

[27] INA §§ 204(a)(1)(A)(ii) (noncitizens who have been battered or subject to extreme cruelty), 204(e) (priority workers under INA § 203(b)(1)(A), 204(g) (certain special immigrants); 201(b)(2)(A) (the spouses, parent or child of a member of the armed forces killed in combat). An I-360 Petition is filed by many self-petitioners.

[28] The labor certification process in INA § 212(a)(5)(A)(i) is required for employment-based immigrant visas under INA §§ 203(b)(2) (advanced degree professionals), and 203(b)(3) (skilled workers, professionals, and other workers).

[29] There is a humanitarian exception to the revocation of a petition when the petitioner dies. 8 C.F.R. § 205.1(a) (2014).

processing at a U.S. Embassy or Consular Post abroad or adjustment of status in the United States. Lawful permanent residence status is granted upon admission into the U.S. at the conclusion of consular processing or upon approval of an adjustment of status application. Both consular processing and adjustment of status are discussed below.

a. Processing Delays

Lengthy delays in immigrant visa petition and adjustment of status application processing led Congress to adopt many ameliorative measures during the past 15 years. The long delays became a significant problem in the 1990s when resources were redirected to speed up the naturalization processing times. These delays created significant hardships for petitioners and noncitizen beneficiaries.

In 2000, a new K-3 nonimmigrant category was created for spouses of U.S. citizens in the Legal Immigration Family Equity Act [LIFE].[30] The K-1 visa category existed for fiancés and fiancées of U.S. citizens, but there was no category for the spouses of U.S. citizens.[31] Although immigrant visas are immediately available to immediate relatives, a backlog in processing petitions can cause a long separation for newly married couples. The K-3 nonimmigrant visa category is available to these spouses. The U.S. citizen must have filed an immigrant visa petition on behalf of his spouse and the spouse is admitted pending the approval of the petition. The LIFE Act also established the V nonimmigrant visa to address long processing delays for LPRs who file immigrant petitions. The V nonimmigrant category under § 101(a)(15)(V) is available to the spouses and children of LPRs when there is a delay of three years or more.[32]

The problem of processing delays and children aging-out of immigrant visa eligibility (turning 21 years of age) was also addressed by Congress.[33] The Child Status Protection Act of 2002 provides that a beneficiary of an immediate relative petition filed by a U.S. citizen will continue to be eligible for an immigrant visa even if she reaches the age of 21.[34] The children of lawful permanent residents who are beneficiaries of immigrant visa petitions also are aided by a relaxed determination of when a child ages out as a beneficiary. This is discussed in greater detail in Chapter 7.

Congress also adopted measures to assist H-1B nonimmigrant specialty occupation workers who have employment-based immigrant visa petitions filed by

---

[30] Pub. L. No. 106-553, 114 Stat. 2762 (Dec. 21, 2000).

[31] Before the LIFE amendment, spouses of U.S. citizens were forced to enter the U.S. using another nonimmigrant visa, usually a B-1 business or B-2 tourist visa. The spouses always faced the potential problem of violating their nonimmigrant visas because of their intent to become lawful permanent residents. The only other option was for the noncitizen spouse to endure a long separation from the U.S. citizen spouse pending the processing of the immigrant visa petition.

[32] Under § 101(a)(15)(V), a V nonimmigrant visa is available if an I-130 petition was filed prior to December 21, 2000 and the petition is pending for three years or more, or the petition was approved but three or more years have elapsed, and where an immigrant visa is not available or a jointly-filed visa petition and adjustment of status application is still pending.

[33] INA § 101(b)(1) defines a child to mean "an unmarried person under twenty-one years of age."

[34] Pub. L. No. 107-208, 116 Stat. 927 (Aug. 6, 2002).

employers. Employers can pay a substantial fee for premium expedited processing of the immigrant visa petition under INA § 286(u), although there is no mechanism to accelerate the visa issuance process (by adjustment of status or consular processing).[35]

2. Immigrant Visa Consular Processing

The final step of the permanent resident process for most noncitizens is the first admission into the U.S. as a permanent resident. There are two possible avenues for this first admission: consular visa processing or adjustment of status. Consular processing refers to a noncitizen's application for her immigrant visa abroad initially at the U.S. Embassy or Consular Post and then her application for admission at an approved port of entry into the United States. The alternative procedure, an application to adjust of status, usually from nonimmigrant to immigrant, occurs while remaining in the United States. Adjustment of status is a discretionary procedure and not all noncitizens are eligible as discussed below.

The consular processing begins after a visa petition is approved and the approved petition is forwarded to the National Visa Center [NVC] for management of the final stage of the process.[36] When an immigrant visa is available, based on the priority date established by the visa petition or labor certification application, the NVC will forward a notice to the noncitizen with detailed instructions about the submission of additional documents.[37] *See* Ch. 7. An affidavit of support is required for family-based immigrants to establish that the noncitizen is not likely to become a public charge, which would render her inadmissible.[38] All of the required documents are submitted to the NVC, and then the final immigrant visa interview is scheduled.[39] A medical exam must be performed overseas just prior to the final visa interview.

The second phase of consular processing is the visa interview at the consular post. Usually the interview is scheduled at the Consular Post in the last place of residence abroad.[40] At this interview, the consular officer will verify that the documents presented establish eligibility for the immigrant visa category.[41] The approval of the immigrant visa petition by USCIS establishes eligibility and the

---

[35] Other measures have eased the transition for H-1B workers to lawful permanent residents. *See* 21st Century Department of Justice Appropriations Act, Pub. L. No. 107-273, 116 Stat. 1758 (Nov. 2, 2002). In 2000, Congress had extended the six-year limit for beneficiaries of employment-based petitions filed under the first, second, or third preferences (INA § 203(b)(1)–(3)) if a backlog in immigrant visas existed due to per-country limits. American Competitiveness in the 21st Century Act, Pub. L. No. 106-313, 114 Stat. 1251 (Oct. 17, 2000); Pub. L. No. 106-311, 114 Stat. 1247 (Oct. 17, 2000).

[36] The visa petition is approved by a USCIS Regional Service Center and then forwarded to the USCIS National Visa Center.

[37] Certified copies of documents, police records from the jurisdictions in which the noncitizen has lived, evidence of the payment of U.S. taxes, if applicable, etc.

[38] INA § 212(a)(4).

[39] INA § 212(a)(4).

[40] 9 FAM 42.61.

[41] INA §§ 221, 222.

visa interview represents a verification of eligibility.[42] At this visa interview, the Consular Officer will evaluate whether the immigrant visa applicant is inadmissible under any of the categories in INA § 212(a).[43] The DHS is also involved in the immigrant visa interview. DHS, under the Homeland Security Act of 2002, also has authority to review any visa application, conduct investigations and require a denial of a visa.[44]

The final phase in consular processing of an immigrant visa is the initial application for admission into the United States as a permanent resident. Upon approval of the immigrant visa application at the Consular Post, the noncitizen is given a sealed packet to present to the CPB immigration inspector at an approved port of entry into the U.S.[45] At the border, the noncitizen again bears the burden of establishing she is admissible under INA § 212(a). Once the immigrant visa is issued at the Consular Post, it is only valid for six months, and, therefore the noncitizen must be admitted and inspected by a CBP immigration inspector at a U.S. port of entry within that time period.[46]

If the noncitizen is admissible, the CPB immigration inspector will place an I-551 stamp on the noncitizen's travel documents. The I-551 stamp on the card is the temporary "green card" verifying the individual is a lawful permanent resident. The actual card is mailed to the noncitizen usually within three to four months of the initial admission.

a. Review of Visa Denials

Consular officers will deny a visa application if it appears from statements in a visa interview, the application, or other documents, that the noncitizen is ineligible for either a nonimmigrant or immigrant visa.[47] A consular officer may also deny an immigrant or nonimmigrant visa if the officer has "reason to believe" the noncitizen is ineligible.[48] The noncitizen must be given a written explanation of the grounds for denial.[49]

Denials of immigrant and nonimmigrant visa applications at the U.S. Embassy or Consular Post historically have not been subject to judicial review.[50] State

---

[42] Approval of the petition by USCIS establishes prima facie eligibility for a particular immigrant visa, and consular officers are instructed to defer to this decision unless reasonable suspicion exists about its validity.

[43] The questions on the immigrant visa application mirror the inadmissibility provisions of INA § 212(a).

[44] INA § 221(a)(2).

[45] The noncitizen must apply for entry within six months of the issuance of this immigrant visa packet under INA § 221(c).

[46] INA §§ 221(c), 101(a)(13) (requirements for an admission into the U.S.).

[47] INA § 221(g).

[48] Id.

[49] See INA § 212(b), 22 C.F.R. § 42.81(b) (2014).

[50] See Pena v. Kissinger, 409 F. Supp. 1182 (S.D.N.Y. 1976); Saavedra Bruno v. Albright, 197 F.3d 1153, 1158–64 (D.C. Cir. 1999); Li Hing of Hong Kong, Inc. v. Levin, 800 F.2d 970 (9th Cir. 1986).

Department regulations require notice of the reasons for a visa denial.[51] Visa denials are reviewed by more senior consular officers.[52] If the denial is based on a question of law, an advisory opinion may be requested from the DOS Visa Office.[53] The Secretary of State does not have authority to review individual visa decisions under INA § 104.[54] Therefore, the only review of visa decisions by consular officers is the review by a supervisor, discretionary review by the Visa Office, or random reviews conducted by supervisors in a given Consular Post.[55]

The State Department regulations require reasonable facts and circumstances in order for a consular officer to determine a visa applicant is ineligible for a visa.[56] This broad discretionary authority of consular officers has led to abuses. In the 1990s, a consular officer was fired from his assignment to the U.S. Consulate in Sao Paulo, Brazil because he refused to follow an internal manual containing racial and economic stereotypes to characterize visa applicants and his refusal to follow the profiles to reach a 30 percent visa refusal rate.[57]

This "doctrine of consular nonreviewability," particularly in the case of immigrant visa denials, has been the subject of consistent scholarly criticism.[58] Under this system, an individual applying for an immigrant visa who has established eligibility through the immigrant visa petition approval process is in no better position than a tourist visitor applying for a nonimmigrant visa. The 1997 Report of U.S. Commission on Immigration Reform recommended formal administrative review of all immigrant visa denials and some nonimmigrant visa denials.[59]

---

[51] 22 C.F.R. § 42.81(b) (2014).

[52] 22 CFR §§ 41.121(c), 42.81(c) (2014).

[53] 22 CFR §§ 41.121(d) (nonimmigrants), 42.81(d) (immigrants).

[54] Under 6 USC § 236(a)(1), the DHS Secretary may not alter or reverse a consular officer's denial of a visa application, although the DHS but may refuse a visa that the consular officer had approved.

[55] 22 C.F.R. § 42.121(d)(2014).

[56] 22 CFR § 40.6 (2014): A visa can be refused only upon a ground specifically set out in the law or implementing regulations. The term "reason to believe," as used in INA § 221(g), shall be considered to require a determination based upon facts or circumstances which would lead a reasonable person to conclude that the applicant is ineligible to receive a visa as provided in the INA and as implemented by the regulations.

[57] *See* Olsen v. Albright, 990 F. Supp. 31 (D.D.C. 1997). The officer sued and won reinstatement relying, in part, on INA § 202(a)(1)(A) which provides that "no person shall receive any preference or priority or be discriminated against in the issuance of an immigrant visa because of the person's race, sex, nationality, place of birth, or place of residence (except as specifically provided by the INA)." The manual contained profiles that identified applicants as "rich kid," "looks poor," "talks poor," and "looks rough," and contained warnings about Korean and Chinese fraud and "known fraud" from applicants in certain Brazilian cities, most of which had predominantly black populations.

[58] *See* Stephen H. Legomsky, *Fear and Loathing in Congress and the Courts*, 78 Tex. L. Rev. 1615 (2001); James A.R. Nafziger, *Review of Visa Denials by Consular Officers*, 66 Washington L. Rev. 1 (1991); Leon Wildes, *Consular Nonreviewability — A Reexamination*, 64 IR 1012 (1987). *See also*, Legomsky & Rodriguez, Immigration and Refugee Law and Policy, Chapter 10 (6th ed. 2014) (using the term consular absolutism).

[59] U.S. Commission on Immigration Reform, *Becoming An American: Immigration and Immigrant Policy* 181–82 (Report to Congress 1997) (recommending review for nonimmigrant categories "where there is a petitioner in the United States who is seeking the admission of the visa applicant," such as employer petitioners for H-1B specialty occupations and L-1 intracompany transferees, or universities

In a few limited instances, judicial review of a visa denial has occurred. In *Kleindienst v. Mandel*, 408 U.S. 753 (1972), the Supreme Court found it had jurisdiction to hear a claim in which U.S. citizens asserted a First Amendment right to hear a noncitizen professor who was denied a nonimmigrant visa. The Supreme Court recognized the U.S. citizens' had standing to bring a claim into federal court, however, the Court upheld the Department of State's denial of the nonimmigrant visa by finding a facially legitimate, bona fide reason existed for the denial.[60]

The impact of immigrant visa denials on U.S. citizen rights is finally before the Supreme Court directly. It has granted a writ of certiorari in the 2014 Term to review whether a consular officer's visa refusal a U.S. citizen's noncitizen spouse infringes on a constitutionally protected interest of the U.S. citizen.[61] More specifically, the question is whether the U.S. citizen petitioner is entitled to judicial review of the visa denial and whether the government is required to identify a specific inadmissibility provision under INA § 212(a). In this case, the U.S. Consulate denied an immediate relative visa application based on national security under INA § 212(a)(3) but refused to indicate which of the 10 specific grounds for inadmissibility applied or the underlying facts for the decision. The Ninth Circuit found that a due process liberty interest existed, and the government was required to disclose the specific inadmissibility ground on which it based the visa denial.[62]

3. Adjustment of Status

Adjustment of status under INA § 245 is an alternative procedure to consular processing for the final stage of becoming a lawful permanent resident.[63] A noncitizen who applies to adjust status from nonimmigrant to immigrant is not required to attend a visa interview abroad. The noncitizen's application for initial admission as a lawful permanent occurs entirely inside of the United States. A nonimmigrant in the U.S. may apply for adjustment of status when his or her priority date is current and an immigrant visa, therefore, is immediately available.[64] The application, Form I-485, may only be filed after approval of the immigrant visa petition by USCIS. If the priority date is current, then an adjustment of status application can be filed concurrently with the immigrant visa petition.

---

for J-1 exchange visitors). Several bills have been introduced in Congress to create an administrative review board to hear appeals from designated categories of visa denials within DOS. *See* LEGOMSKY & RODRIGUEZ, IMMIGRATION AND REFUGEE LAW AND POLICY, CHAPTER 10 (6th ed. 2014)

[60] *See also* Academy of Religion v. Chertoff, 463 F. Supp. 2d 400, 416–19 (S.D.N.Y. 2006) (First Amendment challenge by academic organizations to denial of visa based on security concerns regarding an Islamic scholar); Abourezk v. Reagan, 785 F.2d 1043 (D.C. Cir. 1986), *aff'd per curiam by an equally divided court*, 484 U.S. 1 (1987) (District Court for the D.C. Circuit found it had jurisdiction to review a visa denial; INA provision at issue in this case has since been repealed); Martinez v. Bell, 468 F. Supp. 719 (S.D.N.Y. 1979).

[61] Kerry v. Din, 718 F.3d 856 (9th Cir. 2013), *cert. granted*, 135 S. Ct. 44 (2014).

[62] Kerry v. Din, 718 F.3d 856 (9th Cir. 2013). There are other recent federal court decisions addressing the issue of a U.S. citizen spouse's right to review. *See, e.g.*, Bustamante v. Mukasey, 531 F.3d 1059 (9th Cir. 2008); Jathoul v. Clinton, 880 F. Supp. 2d 168 (D.D.C. 2012).

[63] INA § 245.

[64] 8 C.F.R. § 245.1(g) (2014).

Adjustment of status is a discretionary procedure developed to accommodate nonimmigrants in the United States and avoid costly overseas visits to apply for an immigrant visa. These applications are a routine part of the permanent residence process, despite the DHS discretion whether to grant or deny adjustment. The vast majority of adjustments occur following the criteria set forth in INA § 245(a). Some noncitizens are eligible to adjust under the grandfathered provisions of INA § 245(i), discussed below. Adjustment also is available to noncitizens in special adjustment categories.[65] Adjustment of status is available to refugees and asylees.[66] Adjustment before an immigration judge through cancellation of removal is possible under INA § 240A.

An applicant for adjustment must establish she meets the separate requirements for adjustment, as well as all of the admissibility grounds of INA § 212(a) and requirements for the underlying immigrant visa category. The adjustment applicant, similar to the consular processing immigrant visa applicant, must provide certified copies of documents, police reports, an affidavit of support under INA § 212(d)(4), if required, and complete a medical exam. In addition, the adjustment applicant must pass security clearances. Noncitizens barred from adjustment of status must follow the consular processing procedure to become a permanent resident.

Eligibility for adjustment of status is determined by the noncitizen's current status in the U.S. when the application is filed, apart from immigrant visa eligibility and admissibility. Under INA § 245(a), the noncitizen must have maintained valid nonimmigrant status during all periods of stay in the United States with limited exceptions.[67] The adjustment applicant must have been inspected by a CPB immigration inspector, and admitted or paroled into the U.S. Those who enter without inspection or at a location other than an approved port of entry are not ineligible for adjustment of status under § 245(c).

Other noncitizens are barred from applying for adjustment of status under § 245(c).[68] Noncitizens, other than immediate relatives, who have engaged in unauthorized employment before filing or who are in "unlawful immigration status" are ineligible to adjust.[69] This means noncitizens are barred from adjusting status if they have violated the terms of their nonimmigrant visa, usually working without authorization for any period of time.[70] The INA provides a safe harbor for applicants who failed to maintain lawful status through no fault of their own or for

---

[65] Special adjustment categories include employment-based immigrants who have engaged in unauthorized employment or otherwise failed to maintain continuous lawful status (INA § 245(k)); victims of trafficking (INA § 245(l)), or victims of crimes with nonimmigrant "U" visas under INA § 101(a)(15)(U) (INA § 245(m)).

[66] INA § 209.

[67] INA §§ 245(c)(2), (7), and (8).

[68] INA § 245(c) lists all of the noncitizens who are barred from adjusting their status.

[69] Under INA § 245(c)(7) noncitizens who are beneficiary of an employment-based petition are barred from adjustment if they are "not in a lawful nonimmigrant status" thereby excluding those who entered without inspection or are otherwise present in the U.S.

[70] Under INA § 245(k) a noncitizen beneficiary of an employment-based petition may adjust if the failure to maintain lawful status, unauthorized employment or other violation is 180 days or less.

technical reasons.[71] Immediate relatives are exempt from this bar to adjustment of status under INA § 245(c)(2).[72] Other noncitizens are ineligible to adjust. For example, the INA bars business and tourist visitors who enter under the Visa Waiver Program from adjustment.[73]

There are some major benefits to the adjustment of status procedure. The applicant can be accompanied by an attorney to the adjustment of status interview in the United States. From a practical standpoint, the most important benefit is the opportunity to renew the adjustment of status application in a removal proceeding.[74] Therefore, greater procedural protection exists for the adjustment applicant vis-à-vis the consular processing applicant. A noncitizen may apply to adjust status in the first instance before an Immigration Judge as a form of relief from removal. This is discussed in Chapter 9.

There is no judicial review of the denial of an adjustment application. Adjustment of status is a discretionary decision by USCIS. Under INA § 242(a)(1)(B)(ii), there is no judicial review of discretionary decisions. Adjustment of status can be rescinded within five years if the noncitizen was not eligible to adjust. After five years, lawful permanent resident status may be terminated, effectively rescinding the adjustment application, if only an order of removal is entered.[75]

a. Adjustment Under § 245(i)

INA § 245(i) expanded the group of noncitizens eligible to adjust status in 1994. Under § 245(i), those individuals, who would have obtained lawful permanent residence through the consular processing procedure, could adjust status if they paid a substantially increased fee and were not otherwise ineligible.[76] This option was very popular among prospective immigrants because they could avoid the expense and inconvenience of traveling abroad. When Congress added this option in 1994, it included a three-year sunset provision. The 1994 expansion by Congress was part of a wide-ranging effort to increase funding for the INS. The INS was faced with major problems with its computer database and information systems. One solution was to increase its fee structure for many petitions and other benefits.

The INA § 245(i) adjustment option became a critical vehicle to obtain permanent residence after the 1996 IRRIRA amendments to the INA. The 1996 amendments added unlawful presence as a new ground of inadmissibility under § 212(a)(9)(B) with the possibility of being barred from admission for three or 10

---

[71] Technical violations of nonimmigrant status are permitted such as a USCIS delay in processing of a nonimmigrant extension of stay or change of status application. *See* 8 C.F.R. § 245.1(d)(2) (2014).

[72] Generally, immediate relatives, battered spouses and children, and special immigrants under INA § 101(a)(27)(H) are exempt from the requirement to maintain valid status in INA §§ 245(c)(2), (7), and (8).

[73] Immediate relatives who enter under the VWP are eligible to adjust under INA § 245(c)(4). INA § 245(c) also bars terrorists deportable under § 237(a)(4)(B), noncitizens transit without a visa under § 101(a)(15)(C), and criminal investigation informants under INA § 101(a)(15)(S).

[74] 8 C.F.R. §§ 103.5, 245.2(a)(5)(ii) (2014).

[75] INA § 246(a).

[76] Under INA § 245(i), a noncitizens must comply with the requirements of INA § 245(d)–(f).

years.[77] Prior to the 1996 IIRIRA amendments, noncitizens who violated their nonimmigrant status or entered the U.S. without inspection could become permanent residents using the consular processing method. These noncitizens, although ineligible to adjust, could satisfy the qualifying criteria for an immigrant visa as family-sponsored or employment-based immigrants and were admissible under INA § 212(a) before 1996. Consular processing was available because mere unlawful presence was not an inadmissibility ground before the 1996 IIRIRA amendments.

The 1996 IIRIRA amendment drastically altered the position of noncitizens who were beneficiaries of immigrant petitions but who had not maintained lawful status. If a noncitizen, who was never in lawful status or had fallen out of lawful status, was required to leave the United States to follow the consular processing procedure, then upon return she would be inadmissible under § 212(a)(9)(B) for three or 10 years, unless she obtained a waiver. For this group, the § 245(i) adjustment benefit became the only mechanism to become a lawful permanent resident unless they are eligible for a waiver under INA § 212(a)(9)(B)(v).[78]

In September 1997, just before the sunset provision of September 30, 1997, Congress adopted a grandfather clause to extend this benefit. The grandfather clause allowed any noncitizen to adjust under § 245(i) if a visa petition or labor certification application was filed on or before January 14, 1998. Congress chose not to extend 245(i) permanently although there was significant support for such action. Those opposed to a permanent extension argued that § 245(i) was similar to an "amnesty" provision.

Adjustment of status under § 245(i) was extended again by Congress in the 2000 Legal Immigrant Family Equity Act of 2000 (LIFE Act).[79] Under this extension, INA § 245(i) grandfathers noncitizens who were in the United States on December 21, 2000 and had a visa petition or labor certification application filed by April 30, 2001.[80] The extension of this benefit resulted in a tremendous surge in the filing of labor certification applications and family-sponsored petitions before the deadline. These cases are still winding their way through the system and decisions by Immigration Judges have limited § 245(i) adjustment in several decisions.[81]

---

[77] INA § 212(a)(9)(B)(i)(I)–(II) (unlawful presence of more than 180 days but less than one year means noncitizen may not seek readmission within three years of departure; unlawful presence of one year or more means noncitizen may not seek readmission within ten years of departure).

[78] INA § 212(a)(9)(B)(v) (waiver of unlawful presence inadmissibility ground requires extreme hardship to a citizen or LPR spouse or parent).

[79] Pub. L. No. 106-553, 114 Stat. 2762 (Dec. 21, 2000).

[80] The LIFE Act also created a new nonimmigrant V category to accommodate family members of § 245(i) adjustment applicants; it is available to spouses and children of lawful permanent residents who have filed a family-sponsored immigrant visa petitions prior to December 21, 2000. INA § 101(a)(15)(V).

[81] *See, e.g.*, Sattani v. Holder, 749 F.3d 368 (5th Cir. 2014) (noncitizen inadmissible under INA § 212(a)(6)(C)(i) ineligible for § 245(i)); Garfias-Rodriguez v. Holder, 702 F.3d 504 (9th Cir. 2012) (noncitizen inadmissible under § 212(a)(9)(C)(i)(I) ineligible for § 245(i)), In re Briones, 24 I & N Dec. 355 (BIA 2007); Mansour v. Holder, 739 F.3d 412 (8th Cir. 2014).

D. ACTUAL ADMISSION

1. Admissions at the Border

Generally, a noncitizen must either possess a visa or fit within one of the visa-exempt categories in order to board an airplane to travel to the U.S. The admission process at the border requires a noncitizen to present her passport with a biometric visa stamp at the port of entry to apply for admission. An individual is defined as an applicant for admission if: she is present in the U.S. but has not been admitted; if she is at the border seeking admission; she is interdicted and brought to the U.S. even if she is not seeking admission; or she is a returning lawful permanent resident deemed an applicant for admission under INA § 101(a)(13)(C).[82] All applicants for admission who are noncitizens must be inspected by an immigration officer.[83]

At the border, a CPB immigration inspector may admit a noncitizen, remove her under the expedited removal procedure of INA § 235 (discussed below),[84] parole her into the U.S. for humanitarian reasons under INA § 212(d)(5), require deferred inspection to obtain further information to make a decision about admission, or place her in ordinary removal proceedings under INA § 240.[85] The INA requires that the noncitizen "shall be detained" for the removal proceeding, however, all noncitizens are not detained.[86] Some are granted parole permitting the noncitizen into the United States temporarily.[87] A noncitizen may be permitted to withdraw her application for admission.[88] Noncitizens who seek entry from Canada and Mexico may be returned to Canada or Mexico pending the removal hearing.[89] Removal using expedited removal (INA § 235(b)(1)) or ordinary removal (INA § 240(b)) bars the noncitizen from seeking admission within five years of the date of the removal under INA § 212(a)(9)(A). The procedures for expedited removal are discussed below. Removal hearings are discussed in Chapter 12.

The inspections process for noncitizens is set forth in INA § 235. At the border, all noncitizens have the burden of proving they are eligible for admission. Possession of an immigrant or nonimmigrant visa does not guarantee admission into the U.S. The inadmissibility provisions of INA § 212(a) apply to all noncitizens

---

[82] INA § 235(a)(1).

[83] INA § 235(a)(3).

[84] If the noncitizen is found inadmissible because she lacks proper entry documentation or has committed fraud or misrepresentation then she will be subject to a separate expedited removal procedure under INA § 235(b)(1).

[85] Suspected terrorists and those admitted under the Visa Waiver Program are ineligible for removal hearings under INA § 240. Noncitizens who are suspected terrorists may be subject to removal without a hearing as a criminal or suspected terrorist, or subject to removal by a special Terrorist Removal Court.

[86] INA § 235(b)(2)(A).

[87] See INA §§ 212(d)(5), 236. Parole is granted for emergent reasons, subject to some exceptions barring parole for certain individuals who are removable on criminal or national security grounds.

[88] INA § 235(a)(4) (an applicant for admission may request to withdraw an application for admission and permission to withdraw is within the discretion of the DHS).

[89] INA § 235(b)(2)(C).

seeking admission, regardless of whether the noncitizen seeks admission as a lawful permanent resident, a nonimmigrant, a parolee, or a refugee. However, many returning LPRs, if not most, are not deemed applicants for admission as defined in INA § 101(a)(13).

All noncitizens requesting admission at the border also have the burden of establishing they are not intending immigrants. Under INA § 214(b) there is a presumption that all persons requesting admission or applying for a visa intend to become LPRs. As a result, the nonimmigrant bears the burden of establishing she has sufficient ties to her home country which she has no intention of abandoning in order to establish a true bona fide temporary intent. This presumption of intending immigrant status applies to all nonimmigrants.[90] Some nonimmigrants have a relaxed requirement to maintain ties to their home country.[91]

Lawful permanent residents are treated differently under the INA. LPRs who arrive at a port of entry are not deemed applicants for admission except in certain circumstances set forth in INA § 101(a)(13).[92] If a returning LPR is deemed an applicant for admission under INA § 101(a)(13), then she is subject to the inadmissibility provisions of INA § 212(a). This significantly alters the position of those LPRs who are defined as seeking admission upon return to the U.S. LPRs who must apply for admission under INA § 101(a)(13) include noncitizens: who have abandoned or relinquished their status; who are absent for a continuous period of more than 180 days; who have engaged in illegal activity after departing the U.S.; who depart from the U.S. during removal proceedings; who previously violated INA § 212(a) and have not received a waiver or received relief from removal; and those who attempted to enter at a place other than a port of entry.

Noncitizens arriving at a port of entry and seeking admission into the United States must establish "clearly and beyond doubt" they are entitled to be admitted under INA § 235(b)(2)(A), except returning LPRs. If a noncitizen cannot satisfy this burden of proof, then she will be placed in ordinary removal proceedings under INA § 240. The removal hearing process is covered in Chapter 12.

Nonimmigrants entering the U.S. fill out a I-94 Form (Arrival-Departure Record) containing basic biographical information. In 2013, CPB began an electronic process to gather this information automatically from the electronic travel records. Upon arrival, a CBP officer stamps the travel document (usually a passport) of each arriving nonimmigrant with the admission date, the class of admission, and term of authorized admission under that status. This I-94 Form is available online for noncitizens to verify immigration status or employment authorization.[93] As of 2014, the electronic process is used for travelers by air or

---

[90] INA § 214(b) presumes that a nonimmigrant applicant for a visa or admission into the U.S. is an immigrant (lawful permanent resident). Generally, this means the nonimmigrant must establish her intent to return to her home country.

[91] The INA § 214(b) presumption does not apply to nonimmigrant applicants under INA §§ 101(a)(15)(H), (L), and (V).

[92] INA § 101(a)(13) codifies, in part, the Supreme Court's decision in Rosenberg v. Fleuti, 374 U.S. 449 (1963) (brief, innocent, and casual trips abroad do not interrupt the lawful permanent residence presence in the U.S.).

[93] As of May 1, 2014, nonimmigrants have access to the CPB Nonimmigrant Information System

sea, and the paper Form I-94 continues to be used at land border ports of entry. The I-94 Form is a critical document because it's used as evidence of a lawful admission and the authorized term of stay in the U.S.[94] For example, a B Tourist Visitor under INA § 101(a)(15)(B) may request admission for a six month period, however, the notation on the I-94 Form will determine the end of the valid term of stay. Immigrants generally do not fill out I-94 Forms, except in connection with their first application for admission as a permanent resident. Thereafter, immigrants at the border present their immigrant visa card, Form I-551 (the "green card").[95]

A noncitizen applying for admission may request to withdraw her application for admission under INA § 235(a)(4). The option to withdraw an application for admission is available at the initial inspection, at a deferred inspection, and at a removal hearing to determine admission into the U.S.[96] The CPB immigration inspector has the authority to grant or deny the request to withdraw an application for admission. If a noncitizen withdraws the application for admission her visa can be cancelled and physically crossed out of her passport.[97] She must return to her home country on the next flight at her expense.[98]

Deferred or secondary inspection is another option available at the border. A secondary inspection occurs when further information is required from a noncitizen and the individual is taken aside at the port of entry for further questioning. A deferred inspection often will occur within a few days of the application for admission.[99] The CPB immigration inspector's decision to allow deferred inspection permits the noncitizen to present additional evidence of admissibility.

The inspections and admissions process at the border changed significantly after September 11, 2001. Many measures were introduced to address enhanced security concerns. Today, numerous databases are maintained by the DHS and are available to CPB immigration inspectors at border ports of entry. The USA PATRIOT Act contained a number of provisions designed to ensure data sharing among U.S. agencies and departments.[100] Information is available from the FBI,[101] the DOS,[102] and other interagency databases.[103] These and other systems used a

---

(NIIS) database containing their I-94 arrival/departure record and their arrival/departure history. Before, this information was only available through a Freedom of Information Act request. *See* http://www.cbp.gov/newsroom/spotlights/2014-04-30-000000/arrivaldeparture-history-now-available-i-94-webpage.

[94] *See* https://i94.cbp.dhs.gov/I94/request.html.

[95] INA §§ 211(g), 101(a)(13) (defining "admission" for LPRs).

[96] 8 C.F.R. § 235.4 (2014).

[97] 22 C.F.R. § 41.122(h) (2014).

[98] INA § 235(a)(4).

[99] 8 C.F.R. § 235.2 (2014).

[100] Pub. L. No. 107-56, 115 Stat. 343–45 (Oct. 26, 2001).

[101] The FBI National Crime Information Center database is used to check the criminal background of an applicant for admission or a visa applicant.

[102] The DOS provides an electronic version of each visa application to CPB immigration inspectors at ports of entry.

ports of entry are covered in Chapter 14.

The CPB also directs a number of trusted traveler programs to facilitate the entry of frequent travelers.[104] New systems to expedite entry are introduced regularly.[105] The Secure Electronic Network for Travelers Rapid Inspection (SENTRI) program provides expedited CBP processing for pre-approved, low-risk travelers. Applicants must voluntarily undergo a thorough biographical background check against criminal, law enforcement, customs, immigration, and terrorist indices; a 10-fingerprint law enforcement check; and a personal interview. The Global Entry Program provides expedited clearance for pre-approved, low-risk travelers who are U.S. citizens, LPRs or Mexican nationals enrolled in the program. The registered travelers use kiosks at airports to present their machine-readable documents and have fingerprint scan verifications. Noncitizens from countries with a bilateral trusted traveler arrangement with CBP may participate in the Global Entry program, however, there are significant exceptions.[106] The NEXUS alternative inspection program is available to registered U.S. and Canadian citizens. Participants receive an identification card used in lieu of a passport required under the WHTI program.

2.   Expedited Removal

Before the 1996 IRRIRA amendments, all noncitizens arriving at a port of entry and applying for admission could challenge their exclusion before an immigration judge. At the exclusion hearing, the noncitizen could be represented by counsel and some procedural protection was required by INS regulations.

The 1996 IRRIRA amendments redesigned the entire admissions process.[107] Separate exclusion hearings no longer take place. All hearings before an immigration judge are now called removal hearings, whether to decide the

---

[103] Other systems exist. An interagency database system, the Interagency Border Inspection System (IBIS), is available at the border. The DOS Consular Lookout and Support System (CLASS) is similar. The Arrival and Departure Information System (ADIS) is a centralized database containing information about each person's arrival and departure from the U.S. There are specialized databases for visa waiver admissions, refugees, and terrorists and others.

[104] In FY 2013, CBP has enrolled more than 1 million new travelers in its trusted traveler programs and expected with overall membership at more than 2.2 million people by the end of the FY 2014. *See* http://www.cbp.gov/newsroom/national-media-release/2014-01-17-000000/cbp-fiscal-year-2013-review.

[105] In August 2014, CPB launched a pilot project at the Hartsfield-Jackson Atlanta International Airport using an authorized smartphone/tablet "app," called Mobile Passport Control, allowing eligible travelers to submit their passport information and customs declaration prior to CBP inspection. *See* http://www.cbp.gov/newsroom/national-media-release/2014-08-11-000000/new-mobile-passport-control-app-available.

[106] As of 2014, CPB had bilateral arrangements with Australia, the Netherlands, South Korea and Mexico. *See* http://www.cbp.gov/global-entry/about.

[107] Congress was motivated by widespread media criticism following an explosive 1993 60 Minutes television report that many asylum seekers arrived without documents, after destroying the documents en route to the U.S., and they were admitted for subsequent exclusion hearings but rarely showed up. Congress sought to create some kind of summary exclusion procedure. *See* LEGOMSKY & RODRIGUEZ, IMMIGRATION AND REFUGEE LAW AND POLICY, CHAPTER 6 (6th ed. 2014).

admission of a noncitizen or to remove a noncitizen who is already admitted into the U.S.

More significantly, the 1996 IIRIRA amendments reclassified some applicants for admission and adopted a summary removal system. As a result, these noncitizens no longer have an opportunity to challenge the initial admission decision before an immigration judge. The separate procedure is called expedited removal and is set forth in INA § 235(b)(1). Noncitizen applicants for admission who lack proper documents, possess fraudulent or invalid documents, or committed fraud or misrepresentation at any time, are subject to expedited removal.[108] The CPB immigration inspector makes an inadmissibility determination at the border that INA § 212(a)(6)(C) or (7) applies to a noncitizen. For the noncitizen found inadmissible on these grounds, there are very limited exceptions to the expedited removal process.[109] Some Cubans and all unaccompanied minors are exempt from expedited removal.[110]

There are some alternatives to the expedited removal procedure for noncitizens inadmissible under INA § 212(a)(6)(C) or (7). The noncitizen may be permitted to withdraw her application for admission.[111] It is possible to obtain a waiver of the inadmissibility ground requiring proper documentation if unforeseen emergency circumstances exist. This waiver can be granted at the border by the CPB immigration inspector in lieu of entering an expedited removal order.[112] When a noncitizen expresses a fear of persecution if she were returned to her home country, or an intention to apply for asylum, there is an expanded inspection process involving a credible fear interview. The credible fear interview is discussed below.

Under the expedited removal procedure, the CPB immigration inspector immediately conducts the hearing at the port of entry by advising the noncitizen of the inadmissibility charges against her under either INA §§ 212(a)(6)(C) or (7), and gives the noncitizen an opportunity to respond. If a removal order is issued by the CPB immigration inspector, the order is reviewed by a supervisory officer before it is considered final. The INA precludes review of the inspector's decision and states "the officer shall order the alien removed from the United States without further hearing or review . . . " unless the noncitizen expresses intent to apply for asylum or a fear of persecution.[113]

---

[108] INA § 212(a)(6)(C) or (7).

[109] Nearly all noncitizens who are inadmissible under INA § 212(a)(6)(C) or (7) are subject to expedited removal. Under INA § 235(b)(1)(F), some Cubans and unaccompanied minors who may be inadmissible under § 212(a)(6)(C) or (7) are not subject to expedited removal. VWP applicants are also not subject to expedited removal. *See* 8 C.F.R. § 235.3 (2014).

[110] INA § 235(b)(1)(F).

[111] INA § 235(a)(4).

[112] INA § 212(d)(4)(A). Emergency documentary waivers may be granted when there is a medical emergency or the noncitizen's documents have been lost or stolen within 48 hours of departure to the U.S.

[113] INA § 235(b)(1)(A)(i).

Noncitizens present in the U.S., who have not been admitted or paroled as defined in INA 101(a)(13), are subject to expedited removal.[114] The Secretary of DHS has "sole and unreviewable discretion" to decide whether to apply expedited removal noncitizens in the interior of the U.S.[115] Under INA § 235(b)(1)(A)(iii)(II), expedited removal can apply to a noncitizen who has not been admitted or paroled and who cannot establish to the satisfaction of an immigration officer that she has been present in the U.S. continuously for the prior two years. Under this provision, DHS must decide whether to apply expedited removal to those with less than two years of continuous physical presence. The regulations require the Secretary of DHS to publish a notice in the Federal Register if he or she intends to apply expedited removal procedures to noncitizens apprehended within the United States who have not been admitted.[116]

DHS has applied expedited removal at locations other than an approved port of entry in two circumstances. In August 2004, the DHS published a notice explaining that the expedited removal procedure would be applied to noncitizens who are present in the U.S. within 100 miles of the U.S. border with Canada or Mexico, and who cannot establish that they have been physically present in the U.S. continuously for a 14 day period before the encounter.[117] DHS also has applied this expedited removal procedure in all coastal areas, specifically to exclude Haitian asylum seekers.[118]

Review of an expedited removal order is limited. Generally, there is no administrative appeal of the CPB immigration inspector's decision.[119] Judicial review is available only if a noncitizen claims she is a lawful permanent resident, refugee, asylee or a U.S. citizen.[120] In this case, a habeas corpus proceeding under INA § 242(e) is available but the scope of review is very limited.[121] The only other form of review of the expedited removal order is the limited review available to noncitizens who receive a negative credible fear determination as described below.

---

[114] INA § 235(b)(1)(A)(iii). Expedited removal also applies to other arriving noncitizens in addition to those applying for admission at a port of entry. These additional categories of arriving noncitizens include those seeking transit through the U.S., those interdicted in international or U.S. waters, and those brought to the U.S. by any means.

[115] INA § 235(b)(1)(A)(iii).

[116] 8 C.F.R. § 235.3(b)(1)(ii) (2014).

[117] 69 Fed. Reg. 488877 (Aug. 11, 2004). In January 2006 DHS announced that expedited removal was expanded to include the northern border of the U.S. Department of Homeland Security Streamlines Removal Process Along Entire U.S. Border, *available at* http://www.govtech.com/policy-management/Department-of-Homeland-Security-Streamlines-Removal.html.

[118] *See Secure Border Initiative, available at* http://www.cbp.gov/xp/cgov/border_security/sbi/sbi_information/.

[119] INA § 235(c). Administrative review is required for LPRs, asylees, and refugees.

[120] INA § 242(e) (judicial review by habeas corpus proceeding). 8 C.F.R. § 235.3(b)(5)(i) (2014).

[121] Under INA § 242(e)(2), the court may determine only: (1) whether the person is a noncitizen; (2) whether the noncitizen was ordered removed under the expedited review procedures; and (3) whether the noncitizen has shown by a preponderance of the evidence that she is a lawful permanent resident, is a refugee under INA § 207, or has been granted asylum under INA § 208 (and asylum status has not been terminated).

An expedited removal order issued by a CPB immigration inspector has the same weight as a removal order issued by an Immigration Judge. A noncitizen who was removed after an expedited removal order is inadmissible for five years under INA § 212(a)(9)(A)(i), unless a waiver is granted.

A distinct form of expedited removal under INA § 235(c) applies to suspected terrorists and noncitizens who threaten foreign policy or national security. Under this section, "[i]f an immigration officer or an immigration judge suspects that an arriving alien may be inadmissible under [INA §§ 212(a)(3)(A)(i or iii), (B), or (C)], the officer or judge shall order the alien removed (emphasis added)."[122] The Secretary of DHS is required to review these removal orders and is authorized to remove the noncitizen without further inquiry or hearing. The DHS may rely on confidential information and consultation with "appropriate security agencies of the United States Government" to determine whether a terrorist or national security ground of inadmissibility applies. Another special removal procedure for alleged terrorists applies to both inadmissible and deportable noncitizens before a special terrorist court. Both of these procedures are covered in Chapter 13.

a. Credible Fear Determinations

A modified expedited removal process exists for a noncitizen, inadmissible under INA § 212(a)(6)(C) or (7), who asserts a fear of persecution upon return to her home country or an intent to file an asylum application. Under INA § 235(b)(1)(B), the noncitizen must have an opportunity to demonstrate she possesses a credible fear of persecution. This occurs in an interview with a DHS asylum officer, usually in the airport or in a detention facility. An applicant demonstrates a credible fear if there is "a significant possibility, taking into account the credibility of the statements made by the alien in support of the alien's claim and such other facts as are known to the officer, that the alien could establish eligibility for asylum under section 208."[123]

If the DHS asylum officer finds no credible fear exists, then the applicant can request review by an immigration judge of the credible fear determination.[124] The review by an Immigration Judge must occur within seven days. No other administrative review is available of the initial credible fear determination. If the Immigration Judge agrees that no credible fear exists, there is no further administrative review on the merits of the fear of persecution. If the noncitizen establishes a credible fear of persecution, she will be referred for an ordinary removal hearing under INA § 240. The INA requires that a noncitizen "shall be detained pending a final determination of credible fear of persecution."[125] Once an applicant is referred for an ordinary removal hearing, she may be released from detention under discretionary parole. This is discussed below. Removal Hearings and Procedures are covered in Chapters 12 and 13.

---

[122] INA § 235(c)(1).

[123] INA § 235(b)(1)(B)(v).

[124] INA § 235(b)(1)(B)(iii)(III).

[125] *Id.*

There are on-going concerns about expedited removal, particularly the credible fear process.[126] A 2005 report of the U.S. Commission on International Religious Freedom [CIRF] expressed concern about potential asylum applicants feeling intimidated by the DHS initial questioning, or lacking comprehension about the significance of the interview as the only opportunity to convey a fear of persecution.[127] It recommended videotaping DHS initial interviews, and guidance for consistent assessments of whether a credible fear exists. A 2007 CIRF report confirmed that DHS had done little to implement the recommendations.

3. Before an Immigration Judge

Noncitizens who are found inadmissible generally may challenge the CPB immigration inspector's decision in an ordinary removal hearing under INA § 240. The 1996 IIRIRA amendments created one unified hearing, a removal hearing, for all inadmissibility or deportability determinations.[128]

As noted above, at the border, a CPB immigration inspector may admit a noncitizen, remove her under the expedited removal procedure of INA § 235, parole her into the U.S. for humanitarian reasons under INA § 212(d)(5), require deferred inspection to obtain further information to make a decision about admission, or place her in ordinary removal proceedings under INA § 240.[129] The INA requires that the noncitizen "shall be detained" for the removal proceeding, however, not all noncitizens are detained.[130] Some are granted parole permitting the noncitizen to enter the United States temporarily.[131] A noncitizen may be permitted to withdraw her application for admission.[132] Noncitizens who seek entry from Canada and Mexico may be returned to Canada or Mexico pending the removal hearing.[133] Removal, using expedited removal (INA § 235(b)(1)), or ordinary removal (INA § 240(b)) bars the noncitizen from seeking admission within

---

[126] *See* Tang v. Attorney General, 578 F.3d 1270 (11th Cir. 2009) (noting that inconsistencies between an asylum applicants statements during the airport credible fear interview and at the removal hearing may exist because at the airport, unlike a full due process removal hearing, the noncitizen "is not represented by counsel and may be markedly intimidated by official questioning, particularly if the alien has indeed been subject to government abuse in her country of origin."); Orantes-Hernandez v. Gonzales, 504 F. Supp. 2d 825 (C.D. Cal. 2007); *See also* Michele R. Pistone, *Justice Delayed Is Justice Denied: A Proposal for Ending the Unnecessary Detention of Asylum Seekers*, 12 HARV. HUM. RS. J. 197 (1999) (criticizing the detention of asylum seekers in the expedited removal process under INA § 235(a)).

[127] U.S. Commission on International Religious Freedom was created by the International Religious Freedom Act, Pub. L. No. 105-292, 112 Stat. 2787 (1998). It is a bipartisan independent agency.

[128] IIRIRA went into effect on April 1, 1997.

[129] Suspected terrorists and those admitted under the Visa Waiver Program are ineligible for removal hearings under INA § 240. Noncitizens who are suspected terrorists may be subject to removal without a hearing as a criminal or suspected terrorist, or subject to removal by a special Terrorist Removal Court.

[130] INA § 235(b)(2)(A).

[131] *See* INA §§ 212(d)(5), 236. Parole is granted for emergent reasons, subject to some exceptions barring parole for certain individuals who are removable on criminal or national security grounds.

[132] INA § 235(a)(4) (an applicant for admission may request to withdraw an application for admission and permission to withdraw is within the discretion of the DHS).

[133] INA § 235(b)(2)(C).

five years of the date of the removal under INA § 212(a)(9)(A). The procedures for expedited removal are discussed above. Removal hearings are discussed in Chapter 13.

Once ordinary removal proceedings have begun under INA § 240, the noncitizen may be able to prove that she is in fact admissible because the inadmissibility ground is inapplicable, or because she has been granted a waiver of inadmissibility. An arriving noncitizen bears the burden of proving admissibility, and she must prove he or she "is clearly and beyond doubt entitled to be admitted and is not inadmissible."[134] The Immigration Judge will decide whether an inadmissibility ground applies. Some waiver applications can be decided by an IJ in a removal hearing and others must be decided by USCIS. An applicant for admission who is placed in removal proceedings before an Immigration Judge may seek to adjust status. As noted above, she may renew her adjustment application if it was denied by DHS, or she may file an application initially before the Immigration Judge.[135] Appeals of an Immigration Judge's decision are submitted to the Board of Immigration Appeals (BIA).[136]

If a noncitizen is ordered removed by an IJ, because she is found inadmissible, then she is barred from readmission to the U.S. for five years under INA § 212(a)(9)(A)(i).[137] The noncitizen may be admitted sooner if the Secretary of DHS consents to her readmission.

4. Detention and Parole

Detention is required for many noncitizens seeking admission into the United States if they are denied admission.[138] An individual is an applicant for admission if she is present in the U.S. but has not been admitted or if she is at the border seeking admission under INA § 101(a)(13)(C).[139] All applicants for admission must be inspected by immigration officers.[140]

There are a variety of removal procedures for applicants seeking admission.[141] Detention pending removal is determined by the reason for removal in a particular case. Most often, a noncitizen who is found inadmissible by an immigration officer will be placed either in ordinary removal proceedings under INA § 240 or expedited removal proceedings under INA § 235(b)(1). Other removal proceedings exist for criminals and suspected terrorists. All removal procedures are discussed in Chapter 13. Detention is covered in more detail in Chapter 14.

---

[134] INA §§ 291, 240(c)(2)(A).

[135] 8 C.F.R. § 245.2(a)(1) (2014).

[136] 8 CFR § 1003.1(b)(1, 3) (2014).

[137] The bar to readmission is longer for noncitizens with a second removal order and the bar is permanent for those removed as aggravated felons.

[138] INA § 235(b)(2).

[139] INA § 235(a)(1). Applicants for admission also includes noncitizens interdicted and brought to the U.S., and returning lawful permanent residents deemed applicants for admission under INA § 101(a)(13).

[140] INA § 235(a)(3).

[141] See supra Section D(iii) discussing Denial of Admission.

The DHS decision whether to detain or release a noncitizen on parole may depend on the availability of detention facilities, and the concern about the likelihood of a noncitizen appearing at future hearing dates. This can result in different parole policies of various DHS districts across the country. Priority is given to noncitizens subject to mandatory detention under the INA including noncitizens who are criminals or suspected terrorists.[142] Those in expedited removal proceedings, including lawful permanent residents, are subject to mandatory detention.[143] Mandatory detention is discussed in Chapter 12.

Noncitizens placed in ordinary removal proceedings under INA § 240, may request parole for release from detention under INA 212(d)(5).[144] Historically, parole was granted regularly to arriving noncitizens pending a hearing before an Immigration Judge. A noncitizen applying for admission at the border may be paroled into the U.S. for "urgent humanitarian reasons" or if a significant public health benefit exists under INA § 212(d)(5)(A).[145] Parole permits a noncitizen to enter the territory of the United States, however, it is not an admission into the U.S. as defined in INA § 101(a)(13). It is often granted during the pendency of a removal hearing or other DHS determination, or for emergency medical reasons. A noncitizen may reside for many years in the U.S. as a parolee under the "legal fiction" of an applicant for admission. Immigration Judges do not have jurisdiction to review parole decisions regarding noncitizens arriving at a port of entry and seeking admissions, including those who claim to be lawful permanent residents.[146]

Noncitizens subject to expedited removal must be detained pending any challenge to expedited removal and pending the execution of the removal order. This mandatory detention requirement is applied to all noncitizens including lawful permanent residents.[147] Detention also is required for noncitizens asserting a credible fear until a final decision is made whether a credible fear exists, and if a negative decision is made, until the order is executed.[148] Release from mandatory detention through parole is available but only for a medical emergency or for a legitimate law enforcement objective, or if the noncitizen is referred for an ordinary removal hearing under INA § 240.[149]

---

[142] INA § 236(c).

[143] 8 C.F.R. 235.3(b)(5)(i) (release from mandatory detention through parole is available but only to meet a medical emergency or for a legitimate law enforcement objectives).

[144] INA § 212(d)(5). Parole is available to those inspected by an immigration officer under INA § 235(b) and those apprehended inside the U.S. who are deemed to by "arriving" under INA § 235(a).

[145] Prior to the 1996 IIRIRA amendments, the criteria for parole were either the existence of "emergent reasons" or "reasons deemed strictly in the public interest."

[146] INA § 236(c); 8 C.F.R. § 236.1(c)(11) (2014).

[147] See Matter of Collado-Munoz, 21 I&N Dec. 1061 (BIA 1997) (an LRP arriving at a border post of entry and seeking admission is not entitled to a bond hearing before an Immigration Judge).

[148] INA § 235(b)(1)(B)(iii)(IV).

[149] 8 C.F.R. 253.3(b)(5)(i) (2014) (2014).

Chapter 12

REMOVAL

    c. Asylum, Withholding of Removal and Convention Against Torture

    d. Registry (INA § 249; 8 U.S.C. 1259)

    e. Private Bills

2. Limited Relief

    a. Deferred Action and Prosecutorial Discretion

    b. Voluntary Departure

    c. Stays of Removal

A. GENERAL CONSIDERATIONS

Before 1996, removal proceedings were categorized as either deportation or exclusion proceedings, depending on the presence of the noncitizen within the United States. Noncitizens who were seeking admission into the United States and were not physically present within the borders of the country were subject to exclusion proceedings. Those who had entered and were present, with or without authorization, were subject to deportation proceedings. In 1996, Congress passed the Illegal Immigration Reform and Immigrant Responsibility Act ("IIRAIRA"), which, among other things, replaced deportation and exclusion proceedings with removal proceedings. The grounds of inadmissibility and deportability remain in the statute, however. The biggest practical consequence of the shift has been that those who have entered without inspection and are found inside U.S. borders are now subject to the grounds of inadmissibility rather than the grounds of deportability.[1]

1. History and Theory of Deportation

Originally, deportation was the method used to correct errors in admission or to expel alien enemies.[2] Until the mid-nineteenth century, immigration control was considered a police power of the individual States rather than of the federal government.[3] States continued to control immigration exclusively or in conjunction with the federal government until the passage of the first comprehensive federal immigration law, the Immigration Act of 1882.[4] The law mandated the exclusion of several undesirable categories of noncitizens, including convicts, "lunatics," and people unable to care for themselves.[5]

The Supreme Court solidified the power of the federal government to control immigration and exclusion policies in *Chae Chan Ping v. United States*.[6] There, the Supreme Court held that the power to exclude foreigners is an "incident of

---

[1] INA § 212(a)(6) (a).

[2] Alien and Sedition Acts of 1798.

[3] DAN KANSTROOM, DEPORTATION NATION: OUTSIDERS IN AMERICAN HISTORY 92 (2007).

[4] KANSTROOM, *supra* note 3, at 94.

[5] Immigraton Act of Aug. 3, 1882, 22 Stat. 214; KANSTROOM, *supra* note 3, at 94.

[6] 130 U.S. 581 (1889).

sovereignty belonging to the government of the United States."[7] The 1891 Immigration Act further consolidated immigration power in the federal government, and extended deportation policy to cover those who were later discovered to have been subject to exclusion at entry. That law was followed in 1892 by a law requiring all Chinese to register and to prove their legality. To prove their legality, Chinese had to produce the testimony of at least one credible white witness. The Supreme Court found the law constitutional in *Fong Yue Ting v. United States*.[8] The *Fong Yue Ting* Court reaffirmed and expanded the holding of *Chae Chan Ping*, finding "[t]he right to exclude or to expel all aliens, or any class of aliens . . . [is] an inherent and inalienable right of every sovereign and independent nation."[9] The Court established that the federal government has as much of a right to expel and deport foreigners as it has to prevent them from entering in the first place.

Ever since the passage of the Alien and Sedition Acts of 1798, Congress has continued to enhance the government's power to expel aliens for violating entry laws and to expel temporary aliens.[10] This power has incrementally increased over the years to include the deportation of those who had entered with proper documentation, but who behaved improperly once within the United States. Thus, despite the Supreme Court's proclamation in *Fong Yue Ting* that an "order of deportation is not a punishment for crime,"[11] deportation's punitive character has assumed greater and greater significance over time as Congress adds to the list of grounds for which a noncitizen may be expelled once in the United States with proper documentation.

Before Congress changed the landscape with its passage of IIRAIRA in 1996, the law classified a noncitizen according to whether s/he had "entered" the United States. If the noncitizen had not entered, s/he was considered someone seeking admission and was subject to the inadmissibility grounds under INA § 212. If the noncitizen had physically entered, whether lawfully or not, s/he was not seeking admission, but rather was subject to the deportation grounds of INA § 237.

IIRAIRA and its companion, the Antiterrorism and Effective Death Penalty Act ("AEDPA"), have substantially altered immigration policy, moving it radically toward a policy that punishes criminal behavior through deportation. Nonetheless, deportation policy and deportation procedures have never carried the constitutional protections reserved for criminal proceedings because the Supreme Court has held that both exclusion and deportation proceedings are civil in character.[12] Several commentators, both before and after passage of the 1996 law, have reasoned that to the extent that deportation procedures are increasingly used

---

[7] *Id.* at 609.

[8] Fong Yue Ting v. United States, 149 U.S. 698 (1893).

[9] *Id.* at 711.

[10] CHARLES GORDON, STANLEY MAILMAN, AND STEPHEN YALE-LOEHR, IMMIGRATION LAW AND PROCEDURE, § 71.01[2].

[11] *Fong Yue Ting*, 149 U.S. at 730.

[12] Chae Chan Ping v. United States, 130 U.S. 581 (1889) (exclusion proceedings are civil in nature); Fong Yue Ting v. United States, 149 U.S. 698 (1893) (expulsion proceedings are civil in nature).

to punish, they should be accompanied by the constitutional protections of criminal proceedings.[13] Recently, courts have begun to agree. The U.S. Supreme Court held in *Padilla v. Kentucky* that a defendant made a successful ineffective assistance of counsel claim when he was not advised of the immigration consequences of his guilty plea.[14]

2. The 1996 Law

When Congress passed IIRAIRA in 1996, it created several obstacles to admission and to lawful presence in the United States, all relevant to the deportation and exclusion categories. The following are some of the highlights of IIRAIRA relevant to removal:

a. Bars to Admissibility

Congress added a provision to the inadmissibility grounds of the INA prohibiting the re-entry of certain noncitizens who had entered the country unlawfully and who subsequently left the country. The provision is known as the "three- and ten- year bar" because of the sanctions it imposes. The law states that any alien who was unlawfully present for a period of more than 180 days but less than one year, and who voluntarily departed the United States before commencement of removal proceedings, is barred from seeking admission into the United States for three years from the date of his or her departure.[15] Persons who depart after commencement of proceedings are not subject to the three-year bar for unlawful presence.[16] Any alien who was unlawfully present for one year or more is barred from seeking admission for 10 years.[17] Unlike the three-year bar, a person is subject to the 10-year bar whether they leave during or after proceedings.[18] For purposes of this provision, unlawful presence means presence after the expiration of an authorized stay, or presence without admission or parole.[19] The statute defines certain periods that do not count as unlawful presence.[20] These include the time period before a noncitizen turns 18, the time period that an asylum applicant's application is pending, and the time period that a beneficiary of family unity protection holds such status.[21] The unlawful presence definition does not apply to victims of domestic

---

[13] *See, e.g.*, Gabriel J. Chin and Richard W. Holmes Jr., *Effective Assistance of Counsel and the Consequences of Guilty Pleas*, 87 Cornell L. Rev. 697(2002); Daniel Kanstroom, *Deportation, Social Control, and Punishment: Some Thoughts About Why Hard Laws Make Bad Cases*, 113 Harv. L. Rev. 1889, 1898 (2000); Peter L. Markowitz, *Straddling the Civil-Criminal Divide: A Bifurcated Approach to Understanding the Nature of Immigration Removal Proceedings*, 43 Harv. C.R.C.L. L. Rev. 289, 290–295 (2008); Stephen H. Legomsky, *The Alien Criminal Defendant*, 14 San Diego L. Rev. 105, 121–127 (1977).

[14] Padilla v. Kentucky, 559 U.S. 356 (2010).

[15] INA § 212(a)(9)(B)(i)(I).

[16] INA § 212(a)(9)(B)(i)(I).

[17] INA § 212(a)(9)(B)(i)(II).

[18] Matter of Lemus-Losa, 24 I.&N. Dec. 373, 376–77 (BIA 2007).

[19] INA § 212(a)(9)(B)(ii).

[20] INA § 212(a)(9)(B)(iii).

[21] INA § 212(a)(9)(B)(iii)(I), (II), (III).

violence who violated the terms of their nonimmigrant visas because of the domestic violence.[22] It also does not apply to a noncitizen who demonstrates a central reason for unlawful presence is that he was a victim of a severe form of trafficking.[23] This inadmissibility ground can be waived by the Attorney General if the noncitizen can show that refusal of admission will result in extreme hardship to the citizen or lawful permanent resident spouse or parent of the noncitizen.[24]

b. Expedited Removal

IIRAIRA created a new expedited removal process that allows government authorities to summarily remove anyone attempting to enter the country with no or invalid documents,[25] or with false documents.[26] The statute requires that a noncitizen who has not been admitted or who arrives in the United States be deemed an applicant for admission.[27] The Attorney General has the discretion to allow an applicant to withdraw her application for admission and depart immediately.[28] An immigration officer can also order the noncitizen removed without further hearing or review unless the noncitizen seeks asylum or makes a credible claim of fear of persecution.[29] This is known as expedited removal.

An immigration officer can also apply expedited removal to persons who have not been admitted or paroled, and who cannot show to the officer's satisfaction that they have been physically present in the United States continuously for two or more years.[30] In 2004, DHS broadened expedited removal to include persons present in the U.S. without having been admitted or paroled, who are encountered within 100 miles of the southern border, and who cannot show that they have been physically present in the U.S. continuously for the preceding 14 days. There are several exceptions to the expedited removal process in addition to asylum seekers, including Cuban citizens, lawful permanent residents or persons lawfully admitted, and minors who are not aggravated felons or who have not been formerly removed.

c. Removal Proceedings

IIRAIRA replaced the pre-1996 procedures of "deportation" and "exclusion" with the "removal" proceeding, which now covers both those cases in which a noncitizen has not been admitted and those in which an admitted noncitizen is being expelled.[31] Where someone is not covered by expedited removal procedures, s/he is entitled to removal proceedings pursuant to INA § 240. While the statute no longer

---

[22] INA § 212(a)(9)(B)(iii)(IV).

[23] INA § 212(a)(9)(B)(iii)(V).

[24] INA § 212(a)(9)(B)(v).

[25] INA § 212(a)(7).

[26] INA § 212(a)(6)(C).

[27] INA § 235(a)(1).

[28] INA § 235(a)(4).

[29] INA § 235(b)(1)(A).

[30] INA § 235(b)(1)(A)(iii)(II).

[31] INA § 240.

makes distinctions between those seeking admission and those subject to deportation, it does continue to differentiate between the burden of proof for someone who is seeking admission and someone subject to deportation. In addition, the grounds of removal still depend on one's status with respect to admission.

d. Cancellation of Removal

The 1996 law replaced the pre-1996 relief from expulsion known as "suspension of deportation" with the procedure now known as "cancellation of removal."[32] Cancellation of removal applies when the government seeks to remove lawful permanent residents[33] or when the government seeks to remove various categories of noncitizens.[34] Significantly, the cancellation of removal procedure is more stringent than its predecessor. The suspension of deportation rules allowed a noncitizen who had been present in the United States for at least seven years to show that the noncitizen or his/her citizen or LPR spouse, parent, or child would suffer extreme hardship upon deportation. An immigration judge would then have the discretion to suspend the deportation. Under the cancellation of removal procedure, a nonpermanent resident must show that s/he has been in the United States for at least 10 years, and that removal will cause an "exceptional and extremely unusual" hardship to a citizen or LPR spouse, parent, or child. Unusual hardship to the noncitizen is not sufficient for cancellation of removal under the new standard. Cancellation of removal will be discussed in more detail later in this chapter.

e. Meaning of "Entry" and "Admission"

IIRAIRA replaced "entry" with "admission" as a determinative factor in removal proceedings.[35] Before IIRAIRA was enacted, a noncitizen seeking "entry" into the United States was subject to exclusion proceedings, while a noncitizen who had already entered was subject to deportation proceedings. Many important deportation grounds used the term entry, e.g., "entry without inspection" and "inadmissible at entry."

Nonetheless, admission is now a key concept in immigration law. Admission is defined in INA § 101(a)(13) as, "the lawful entry of the alien into the United States after inspection and authorization by an immigration officer." Both admitted and non-admitted noncitizens are now subject to removal proceedings. However, admission is important in determining whether the noncitizen will be subject to the grounds of inadmissibility found at INA § 212(a) or the grounds of deportability found at INA § 237(a). Thus, physical presence within the United States has become less important than legal presence, i.e., one's status as admitted or not admitted. The admission definition also applies to returning lawful permanent residents in certain circumstances. The statute lists the following instances in which a returning LPR will be deemed to seek admission:

---

[32] INA § 240A.

[33] INA § 240A(a).

[34] INA § 240A(b).

[35] INA § 101(a)(13).

1. The LPR has abandoned or relinquished LPR status;

2. The LPR has been absent from the United States for a continuous period of 180 days or more;

3. The LPR has engaged in illegal activity after having departed the United States;

4. The LPR has departed while removal proceedings were under way;

5. The LPR has committed a crime involving moral turpitude;

6. The LPR has not entered the United States without authorization.[36]

Some of these scenarios codify prior case law surrounding the entry doctrine. For example, in *Rosenberg v. Fleuti*,[37] the Supreme Court held that a brief, casual, and innocent absence from the country would not subject a lawful permanent resident to exclusion grounds because he was not seeking entry. The statute now defines the time periods for such absences as 180 days or less.

The concept of entry remains important because the Supreme Court recently held in *Vartelas v. Holder* that the admission definition for returning lawful permanent residents at INA § 101(a)(13) is not retroactive and that the concepts surrounding re-entry were still valid. In *Vartelas*, the petitioner, a lawful permanent resident, took a one-week trip to Greece in 2003. On his return he was denied admission and placed in removal proceedings because he had been convicted of a crime involving moral turpitude in 1994, before the law changed in 1996. The statute stated that a returning lawful permanent resident would be considered seeking admission if he had committed a crime involving moral turpitude. The Supreme Court held that the statute was impermissibly retroactive if it imposed a consequence — inadmissibility — that was not foreseen at the time of conviction. Before the law changed, Vartelas would not have been deemed to seek entry after such a short trip. For noncitizens like Vartelas who pled to offenses before the law changed, the entry doctrine still applies.

B.   REMOVAL GROUNDS AND WAIVERS

This section explores the three broad categories of deportability grounds that could subject noncitizens to removal proceedings, all of which are found at INA § 237. Grounds of removal, whether for inadmissibility or for deportability, fall into three conceptual categories: immigration control, criminal grounds, and other grounds. This section covers the removal grounds that are based on deportability. The separate section on inadmissibility in this book covers parallel removal grounds based on inadmissibility.

---

[36] INA § 101(a)(13)(C)(i)–(vi).

[37] Rosenberg v. Fleuti, 374 U.S. 449 (1963).

1. Immigration Control Grounds

Immigration control rationales for exclusion and expulsion can be found in the inadmissibility[38] as well as in the deportability grounds for removal.[39] These sets of rules are meant to maintain the integrity of the immigration control system established in the statute. Some of the provisions deal with errors upon entry, while others deal with post-entry immigration control issues.

a. Correcting Errors in Admission upon Entry

INA § 237(a)(1) contains several grounds of deportability related to immigration control upon entry. The most comprehensive of these, INA § 237(a)(1)(A), states that a noncitizen who was inadmissible at the time of entry or adjustment of status is deportable. The provision itself reflects the immigration control function of deportation. If someone gains admission because of fraud, for example, the government invokes the error-correcting function of INA § 237(a)(1)(A) to deport.

The statute specifically addresses marriage fraud as an example of fraud for which an admitted noncitizen can be deported. The statute makes a noncitizen admitted on the basis of a marriage entered into less than two years prior deportable if she terminates or annuls the marriage within two years after obtaining admission, unless the noncitizen establishes that the marriage was not entered into for the purpose of evading immigration laws.[40] The statute also provides that a noncitizen is deportable if he fails to fulfill a marriage agreement and the Attorney General finds that the marriage was made for the purpose of procuring his admission into the United States.[41]

Congress implemented other forms of error-correction into INA § 237(a)(1). A noncitizen who is present in the United States in violation of the Act or after a nonimmigrant visa has been revoked can be deported under INA § 237(a)(1)(B). Similarly, a noncitizen holding a nonimmigrant visa can be deported if he violates the conditions of his status of the terms and conditions of entry.[42] A conditional residence whose status is terminated is also deportable.[43]

Waivers are available for the immigration control grounds that involve certain forms of misrepresentation.[44] The statute waives deportability for those who were inadmissible at the time of admission because of fraud or misrepresentation in the procurement of a visa or other documentation or admission into the United States.[45] There are two types of waivers available under the statute. The first is for a spouse,

---

[38] *See, e.g.*, INA § 212(a)(6); INA § 212(a)(7).

[39] *See, e.g.*, INA § 237(a)(1); INA § 237(a)(3).

[40] INA § 237(a)(1)(G)(i).

[41] INA § 237(a)(1)(G)(ii).

[42] INA § 237(a)(1)(C).

[43] INA § 237(a)(1)(D). The provision does not apply to conditional residents who obtain waivers of conditional residence requirements. INA § 216(c)(4).

[44] INA § 237(a)(1)(H).

[45] INA § 237(a)(1)(H). The waiver is available unless the noncitizen is also deportable for having participated in Nazi persecution, genocide, or the commission of any act of torture or extrajudicial killing.

parent, son, or daughter of a citizen or lawful permanent resident who possessed and immigrant visa at the time of admission and was otherwise admissible but for the inadequate documentation resulting from the fraud. The second is available to VAWA self-petitioners. Notably, a waiver of the deportability ground also waives the underlying inadmissibility grounds resulting from the fraud or misrepresentation occurring at admission.

b. Post-Entry Immigration Control

The grounds of deportability apply to actions taken after entry, such as noncompliance with the conditions of entry. In keeping with the immigration control function, the INA deems any non-citizen who smuggles, or encourages, induces, or aids and abets smuggling, deportable.[46] This deportability ground has a humanitarian waiver provision for LPRs who smuggled immediate family members — spouse, parent, son, or daughter.[47] It also makes exceptions for immigrants who were present in the United States and who smuggled immediate family members who were eligible for family reunification immigration benefits under the Immigration Act of 1990.[48]

There are several provisions in the statute that require those who have lawfully entered to maintain their status by registering with the government, reporting address changes, and similar activities aimed at facilitating the monitoring of immigrants.[49] Violations of these provisions render a noncitizen deportable.[50]Willful violations of these provisions are also criminal offenses subject to fines or imprisonment.[51]

2. Criminal Grounds

The criminal grounds of removal have continued to grow through the years, as Congress increasingly relies on deportation to punish those who acquire criminal records after admission. Most of these require a conviction. The criminal deportability grounds apply to crimes involving moral turpitude, multiple criminal convictions, aggravated felonies, high-speed flight, sex offender convictions, controlled substance and firearms convictions, and domestic violence convictions.

a. Crimes Involving Moral Turpitude

A noncitizen convicted of a crime involving moral turpitude (CIMT) that was committed within five years after the date of admission is deportable if the crime is one for which a sentence of one year or longer may be imposed.[52] A similar

---

[46] INA § 237(a)(1)(E).

[47] INA § 237(a)((1)(E)(iii).

[48] INA § 237(a)(1)(E)(ii).

[49] INA § § 261–266.

[50] INA § 237(a)(3)(A); INA § 237(a)(3)(B).

[51] INA § 266.

[52] INA § 237(a)(2)(A)(i). The statute states that for those who obtained permanent residence through S visas, a CIMT conviction will trigger deportation if committed ten years after admission.

provision makes a noncitizen inadmissible, although the deportability ground is more stringent; it focuses on the *possible* sentence rather than the *actual* sentence in determining a noncitizen's deportability. Even if a noncitizen is actually sentenced to less than one year, s/he is still deportable under this provision for a crime involving moral turpitude if the offense carried a possible term of one year or more.

The CIMT provision states that the crime must have been committed within five years after the date of admission. The Ninth Circuit has defined admission under INA § 101(a)(13)(A) for the purposes of a crime of moral turpitude as the prior "lawful entry [of the alien into the United States after] inspection and authorization by an immigration officer."[53] Admission, therefore, is a key factor in determining the relevant time period for deportability.

The term "moral turpitude" has never been legislatively defined. The Supreme Court held that the term was not unconstitutionally vague in a case involving the deportation of a noncitizen for criminal convictions involving fraud. In *Jordan v. DeGeorge*, the Court was asked to decide whether the term "moral turpitude" was unconstitutionally vague in a case involving the crime of conspiracy to defraud the United States of taxes on distilled spirits, the elements of which involve fraud.[54] That particular crime, the Court held, was squarely within the definition of a crime involving moral turpitude, "[w]hatever else the phrase 'crime involving moral turpitude' may mean in peripheral cases."[55] Since then, courts have consistently defined moral turpitude as involving "an act of baseness, vileness or depravity in the private or social duties which a man owes to his fellow men, or to society in general, contrary to the accepted and customary rule of right and duty between man and man."[56] Extensive case law has been developed around what constitutes a crime of moral turpitude. Volumes have been written cataloguing the crimes that courts have held involve moral turpitude.[57] In general, however, crimes that involve murder, fraud, or aggravated forms of assault have been found to be crimes of moral turpitude.

Under INA § 237(a)(2)(A)(ii), a noncitizen who, any time after admission, commits two or more crimes involving moral turpitude is deportable. There is an exception for purely political offenses and for multiple offenses arising out of a single scheme of criminal misconduct. The BIA has interpreted the single scheme provision to cover separate and distinct crimes performed in furtherance of a single criminal episode, lesser included offenses, and instances where two crimes flow from and are the natural consequence of a single act of criminal misconduct.[58] The Ninth Circuit has rejected this approach, noting that the statute refers to a single "scheme" rather than a single act. In the Ninth Circuit, a single scheme includes

---

[53] Shivaraman v. Ashcroft, 360 F.3d 1142 (9th Cir. 2004).

[54] Jordan v. De George, 341 U.S. 223 (1951).

[55] *Id.* at 232.

[56] Marciano v. INS, 450 F.2d 1022, 1025 (5th Cir. 1971); *see also*, Sosa-Martinez v. U.S. Attorney General, 420 F.3d 1338, 1341 (11th Cir. 2005); Navarro-Lopez v. Gonzales, 503 F.3d 1063, 1068 (9th Cir. 2007).

[57] *See e.g.*, GORDON, MAILMAN & YALE-LOEHR, 6 IMMIGRATION LAW AND PROCEDURE § 71.05; NORTON TOOBY, CRIMES OF MORAL TURPITUDE (2008).

[58] Matter of Adetiba, 20 I.&N. Dec. 506, 509 (BIA 1992).

two or more crime that "were planned at the same time and executed in accordance with that plan."[59]

b. Aggravated Felonies

Another category of general crimes for which admitted noncitizens can be deported is the aggravated felony category. While this category was initially a narrow one, it has expanded to include behaviors and actions that are not considered particularly egregious or aggravated or even felonies in the criminal law context. The statute defines "aggravated felony" for immigration purposes at INA § 101(a)(43). The definition includes what are traditionally considered egregious crimes, such as murder, rape, sexual abuse of a minor, illicit trafficking in a controlled substance, crimes of violence, and theft offenses. It also includes activities such as forging a passport, counterfeiting, obstruction of justice or perjury, and failure to appear in court to answer for a felony charge. Importantly, an aggravated felony does not have to be committed within five years of admission, as with a crime involving moral turpitude. Whether a crime is an aggravated felony sometimes depends on the length of imprisonment imposed. Certain crimes like forgery, burglary, theft, or obstruction of justice will not be considered aggravated felonies if they carry a sentence of less than a year, or 364 days or less. Other offenses in the aggravated felony category do not depend on the sentence imposed.

Aggravated felony convictions also make a noncitizen ineligible for most discretionary relief from removal and trigger mandatory detention throughout the removal process. A person with an aggravated felony conviction who is removed cannot ever return to the United States without special permission from DHS.[60] Such persons who return unlawfully are subject to a 20-year prison term.[61]

As with crimes of moral turpitude, whether a crime is an aggravated felony depends on a categorical analysis of the convicted offense.[62]

i. The Categorical Approach

In determining whether an offense (state or federal) falls within a category of aggravated felony offenses listed in the aggravated felony definition, the courts have historically used a "categorical approach." Under this approach, courts ignore

---

[59] Gonzalez-Sandoval v. INS, 910 F.2d 614, 616 (9th Cir. 1990).

[60] INA § 212(a)(9)(A)(ii).

[61] INA § 276(b)(2).

[62] The Attorney General issued an opinion in 2008 that altered the categorical analysis for crimes of moral turpitude. In Matter of Silva-Trevino, 24 I.&N. Dec. 687 (AG 2008), the Attorney General found that determining whether a given crime was a crime involving moral turpitude was within the scope of the executive agency, and such a determination deserved *Chevron* deference. The AG then held that if a record of conviction is inconclusive as to whether a crime involved moral turpitude, the immigration judge could consult evidence outside the record of conviction. Several circuits have overruled Matter of Silva-Trevino, including the Ninth, Third, Fourth, Fifth and Eleventh Circuits. *See*, Olivas-Motta v. Holder, 716 F.3d 1199 (9th Cir. 2013); Prudencio v. Holder, 669 F.3d 472 (4th Cir. 2012); Fajardo v. U.S. Attorney General, 659 F.3d 1303(11th Cir. 2011); Jean-Louis v. Attorney General of U.S., 582 F.3d 462 (3d Cir. 2009). The Seventh and Eighth Circuits have upheld the decision. *See* Ali v. Mukasey, 521 F.3d 737, 739 (7th Cir. 2008); Bobadilla v. Holder, 679 F.3d 1052, 1057 (8th Cir. 2012).

the facts of a particular case, and instead look to whether the statute defining the crime fits categorically within the generic definition of the enumerated crime in the statute. In *Moncrieffe v. Holder*, the Supreme Court noted that "generic" means that, "the offenses must be viewed in the abstract, to see whether the state statute shares the nature of the federal offense that serves as a point of comparison."[63] There is a categorical match only if a conviction necessarily involved facts equating to the generic federal crime. Because the actual facts of the case are irrelevant, the court must presume when conducting a categorical analysis that the conviction rested on the minimum conduct punishable under the statute. The court then compares that minimum conduct with the generic offense. In *Moncrieffe*, the Court noted that in defining the minimum conduct criminalized by the statute in question, "there must be a realistic probability, not a theoretical possibility, that the State would apply its statute to conduct that falls outside the generic definition of a crime."[64]

The Court in *Moncrieffe* applied the categorical approach to the generic crime of "illicit trafficking in a controlled substance" which is an aggravated felony under the INA. It analyzed a Georgia statute making it a crime to "possess, have under [one's] control, manufacture, deliver, distribute, dispense, administer, purchase, sell, or possess with intent to distribute marijuana."[65] Moncrieffe pleaded guilty to possession with intent to distribute marijuana. The Court noted that while possession with intent to distribute a controlled substance is a federal crime, the generic crime did not include distribution of a small amount of marijuana with no remuneration, which is treated as simple possession.[66] The Court then analyzed the Georgia courts' treatment of possession with intent to distribute marijuana and found that courts punished the distribution of a small amount of marijuana as well as distribution with no remuneration under the statute. The Court then found that because the minimum conduct criminalized by the statute fell outside the federal generic definition of illicit trafficking in a controlled substance, the Georgia statute did not categorically fit and therefore, conviction under the Georgia statute could not be an aggravated felony.

ii.   The Modified Categorical Approach

When a criminal statute contains more than one offense, it is known as a divisible statute. That is, the statute may include some crimes that carry and some that do not carry an immigration consequence. The court must then determine the offense for which the noncitizen was convicted. The Supreme Court has endorsed a modified categorical approach to determining the basis for the conviction. The modified categorical approach allows the court to look to the record of conviction to determine whether it bears light on the convicted offense. The Supreme Court recently reiterated in *Descamps v. United States* that the modified categorical approach can only be used when a statute is divisible, and should be used as a tool to "identify, from among several alternatives, the crime of conviction so that the

---

[63] Moncrieffe v. Holder, 133 S. Ct. 1678, 1684 (2013).

[64] *Moncrieffe*, 133 S. Ct. at 1685.

[65] *Id.*

[66] *Moncrieffe*, 133 S. Ct. at 1693.

court can compare it to the generic offense."[67] This approach is used to determine whether the conviction was for a particular statutory offense, and not to determine the factual basis for a plea.

The record of conviction for purposes of applying the modified categorical approach includes the statutory definition of the crime, the charging document, the written plea agreement, a transcript of the plea colloquy, and any finding by the judge to which the defendant assented.[68] For a jury conviction the court can review the complaint, the jury instructions and the verdict.[69]

c. Controlled Substances, Firearms, Domestic Violence, and Other Crimes

In addition to the general CIMT and aggravated felony provisions, the statute names specific crimes that make a noncitizen deportable. These provisions are far-reaching in their scope and effect, and they reflect a congressional purpose to regulate the activities of noncitizens even after admission.

A noncitizen who at any time after admission has been convicted of any state, federal, or foreign country law related to controlled substances, other than possession for personal use of 30 grams or less of marijuana, is deportable.[70] The statute covers convictions for conspiracy or attempt as well as direct convictions. The statute also makes a noncitizen who at any time after admission becomes a drug abuser or addict deportable.[71] This provision is triggered simply by behavior rather than a conviction.

Just as broad in its application is the provision which makes conviction of a firearms offense after admission a deportable offense. The statute states that "[a]ny alien who at any time after admission is convicted under any law of purchasing, selling, offering for sale, exchanging, using, owning, possessing, or carrying . . . any weapon, part, or accessory which is a firearm . . . in violation of any law is deportable."[72] This provision also covers conspiracy and attempt offenses.

Probably the most far-reaching criminal deportability ground is the domestic violence ground. A noncitizen convicted of any domestic violence offense at any time after admission is deportable.[73] Domestic violence offenses include domestic violence, stalking, and child abuse, and neglect or abandonment. Moreover, the statute makes anyone who violates a protection order involving threats of violence, whether civil or criminal, deportable.[74]

---

[67] Descamps v. United States, 133 S. Ct. 2276, 2285 (2013).

[68] Shepard v. United States, 544 U.S. 13, 16 (2005).

[69] Taylor v. United States, 495 U.S. 575, 602 (1990).

[70] INA § 237(a)(2)(B)(i).

[71] INA § 237(a)(2)(B)(ii).

[72] INA § 237(a)(2)(C).

[73] INA § 237(a)(2)(E)(i).

[74] INA § 237(a)(2)(E)(ii).

The statute enumerates several other offenses for which conviction makes a noncitizen deportable, including failure to register as a sex offender; high speed flight from an immigration checkpoint; crimes related to espionage, treason and sedition; and certain violations of the Trading with the Enemy Act or the Military Selective Service Act.

d. Defining a Conviction

The statute defines the term conviction for the crimes in which a conviction triggers deportability. A conviction is now defined under INA § 101(a)(48) as a formal judgment of guilt by a court, or if adjudication has been withheld, where (1) a judge or jury has found the alien guilty or the alien has entered a plea of guilty or *nolo contendere* or has admitted sufficient facts to warrant a finding of guilt, and (2) the judge has ordered some form of punishment, penalty, or restraint on the alien's liberty. This definition applies retroactively.

Under this definition, dismissals, juvenile court dispositions, and convictions that are on direct appeal are not considered "convictions." Completion of a pre-trial diversion program, upon which charges are dismissed, is not a conviction, as long as no plea of guilty or *nolo contendere* has been entered at any time.

A conviction that is vacated on the basis of procedural or substantive legal infirmities is not a conviction for immigration purposes.[75] A conviction vacated for rehabilitative or immigration reasons, however, will still be considered a conviction for immigration purposes.[76]

Expungements do not generally eliminate the negative immigration consequences of a criminal conviction.[77] Convictions dismissed under the Federal First Offender Act were not considered convictions for immigration purposes before the conviction provision was altered in 1996. Since then, several circuit courts have declined to decide whether IIRAIRA changes the rule that FFOA expungements do not count as convictions.[78] The BIA considers expungements under state first offender statutes, however, convictions for immigration purposes in most jurisdic-

---

[75] In re Adamiak, 23 I.&N. Dec. 878, 880–81 (BIA 2006) (The BIA held that a conviction vacated by the trial court because of a defect in the underlying criminal proceedings, i.e., the failure of the court to advise the defendant of possible immigration consequences of a guilty plea, was no longer a conviction for immigration purposes. In so holding, the BIA recognized that it did not "share the view" of the Fifth Circuit Court of Appeals on the effectiveness of vacating a conviction for immigration purposes.). *But see* Renteria Gonzalez v. I.N.S., 322 F.3d 804, 813–14 (5th Cir. 2002) ("a vacated conviction, federal or state, remains valid for the purposes of the immigration laws").

[76] Pickering v. Gonzales, 465 F.3d 263, 266 (6th Cir. 2006) (holding that the BIA "correctly interpreted the law by holding that, when a court vacates an alien's conviction for reasons solely related to rehabilitation or to avoid adverse immigration hardships . . . the conviction is not eliminated for immigration purposes").

[77] Matter of Marroquin, 23 I.&N. Dec. 705 (AG 2005).

[78] *See* Acosta v. Ashcroft, 341 F.3d 218, 224 (3d Cir. 2003); Gill v. Ashcroft, 335 F.3d 574, 578–79 (7th Cir. 2003). The Attorney General has also declined to decide whether either the FFOA or its state equivalents are recognized as eliminating a conviction for immigration purposes. Matter of Marroquin-Garcia, 23 I.&N. Dec. 705, 717 (AG 2005).

tions.[79] There is one narrow exception for expungements under state statutes that correspond to analogous federal juvenile delinquency provisions.

3. Other Removal Grounds

The statute includes several miscellaneous removal grounds that do not fit into the immigration control or criminal categories. These grounds include health-related, economic, and moral grounds for removing admitted noncitizens. For example, the deportability grounds target nonimmigrant status violators or those who entered lawfully but have since failed to comply with the requirements imposed by a health-related waiver upon entry.[80] A noncitizen can be removed under certain circumstances if he or she becomes a public charge within five years after entry.[81]

C. RELIEF FROM REMOVAL

Noncitizens in removal proceedings may be eligible for several forms of relief from removal that allow them to stay in the United States. The concept of relief from removal is analogous to an affirmative defense in a civil judicial setting. The noncitizen can demonstrate that other factors, such as length of stay in the United States, should outweigh the grounds of removability s/he faces. This section discusses the eligibility requirements as well as the possible obstacles to relief from removal. Some obstacles are common to several forms of relief. For example, aggravated felons cannot seek forms of relief such as cancellation of removal, voluntary departure, or registry.[82] Likewise, anyone who (1) receives a Notice to Appear (NTA) at a removal hearing and fails to appear, (2) accepts voluntary departure but fails to depart, or (3) re-enters the United States without authorization after being removed, is rendered ineligible for these remedies for 10 years.[83]

1. Lasting Relief

a. Cancellation of Removal

IIRAIRA added section 240A to the INA in 1996, creating a type of relief known as cancellation of removal. At the same time, Congress eliminated suspension of deportation and section 212(c) relief, both of which existed under previous versions

---

[79] Matter of Roldan, 22 I.&N. Dec. 512 (BIA 1999); the Ninth Circuit initially reversed Matter of Roldan and the BIA maintained its policy in all but the Ninth Circuit. *See* Lujan-Armendariz v. INS, 222 F.3d 728 (9th Cir. 2000). In 2011, however, the Ninth Circuit held that an expunged conviction under a state first offender statute would still be a conviction for immigration purposes, albeit prospectively. Nunez-Reyes v. Holder, 646 F.3d 684, 688 (9th Cir. 2011).

[80] INA § 237(a)(1)(C).

[81] INA § 237(a)(2)(B)(ii).

[82] *See* INA § 240A(a)(3); § 240A(b)(1)(c) (cancellation of removal); § 240B(a)(1) (voluntary departure); § 249 (registry). Section 212(c) relief continues to be available for persons in proceedings prior to April 1, 1997, the date of IIRAIRA's enactment. It is also available to those who pled guilty to a crime prior to April 1, 1997. INS v. St. Cyr, 533 U.S. 289 (2001).

[83] INA § 240(b)(7), § 240B(d), § 241(a)(5).

of the statute.[84] These forms of relief were folded into the now-existing cancellation provisions of the statute. Congress capped the number of cancellations available each year at 4,000.[85]

Section 240A of the INA describes several forms cancellation of removal available to noncitizens. Cancellation Part A, found in section 240A(a), allows certain lawful permanent residents to remain in the United States after an order of removal. Cancellation Part B, found in section 240A(b)(1), is available to "certain nonpermanent residents," and is available either to out-of-status noncitizens, or to lawful permanent residents who do not fit into the requirements of section 240A(a). A third type of cancellation, with its own rules, applies to victims of domestic violence. The rules for this VAWA cancellation are found at INA § 240A(b)(2). The statute also contains a form of cancellation available to Central Americans and others fleeing unrest in their home countries.

Cancellation of removal is more restrictive than either suspension of deportation or relief under section 212(c). In particular, unlike previous similar relief provisions, the new provision requires that any nonpermanent resident seeking relief must show exceptional and extremely unusual hardship to a citizen or LPR spouse, parent, or child.[86] On the other hand, the provision resolves many questions that had historically arisen under the interpretation of section 212(c) regarding its differential applicability in deportation and exclusion cases.[87] Years of legal debate surrounding when and how section 212(c) could be used to protect deportable or inadmissible noncitizens was resolved when Congress implemented the cancellation of removal provision, which applies both to noncitizens subject to deportation and those subject to exclusion.

i.   Lawful Permanent Residents (Cancellation of Removal Part A)

Cancellation of removal is available for certain lawful permanent residents who can show that they (1) have been admitted for permanent residency at least five years; (2) have resided continuously in the United States for seven years after having been admitted in any status; and (3) have not been convicted of an aggravated felony. A person who was admitted temporarily or as a nonimmigrant

---

[84] For a description of the remedies available before cancellation of removal, see Elwin Griffith, *The Road Between the Section 212(c) Waiver and Cancellation of Removal under Section 240A of the Immigration and Nationality Act — The Impact of the 1996 Reform Legislation*, 12 GEO. IMMIGR. L.J. 65 (1997); Lory D. Rosenberg and Denise Sabagh, *A Practitioners' Guide to INA § 212(c)*, IMMIGRATION BRIEFINGS (April 1993).

[85] INA § 240A(e). The cap does not include grants of cancellation for certain nationals of Guatemala, El Salvador, the Soviet Union and its successor republics, and most Eastern European countries. INA § 240(e)(3)(A).

[86] INA § 240A(b)(1)(D).

[87] The Supreme Court resolved some of these issues in *Judulang v. Holder*, 132 S. Ct. 476 (2011). The Court held that the BIA's practice of allowing 212(c) relief for LPRs only when the charged deportation ground was comparable to an inadmissibility ground was arbitrary and capricious in violation of the Administrative Procedure Act.

will be considered to have been "admitted in any status" for purposes of the seven year requirement.

In defining periods of continuous residence, and continuous presence under cancellation part B, the statute stops the clock when the noncitizen is issued a notice to appear in immigration court. The clock also stops when a noncitizen commits an offense that renders her inadmissible under INA § 212(a)(2) (i.e., a crime of moral turpitude or controlled substance offense) or removable under INA § 237(a)(2) (i.e., a one or more crimes of moral turpitude, aggravated felony, high speed flight offense, sex offender registration offense, controlled substance offense, firearms offense, domestic violence offense, trafficking offense, or espionage offense, as defined in the statute), or § 237(a)(4) (i.e., a security-related ground).[88]

In determining whether a noncitizen should be granted cancellation of removal, the discretionary criteria previously used in section 212(c) relief cases continues to be used in cancellation of removal cases to determine eligibility. The positive criteria include family ties in the United States, residency of long duration in the country, evidence of hardship to the respondent's family if deportation occurs, military service, history of employment, existence of value and service to the community, proof of genuine rehabilitation if a criminal record exists, and evidence of good character. Negative factors include the nature and underlying circumstances of exclusion grounds, additional significant violations of the INA, existence of a criminal record, and other evidence of bad character. Once cancellation of removal is granted, the noncitizen returns to his/her previous LPR status.

ii.   Nonpermanent Residents (Cancellation of Removal Part B)

Cancellation of removal is available for nonpermanent residents, although the eligibility requirements render it a more limited remedy for this class of noncitizens. Cancellation of removal is available for nonpermanent residents who can show they (1) have been physically present in the United States continuously for 10 years immediately prior to the cancellation application; (2) have exhibited good moral character for the 10 year period; (3) have not been convicted of a crime listed in the criminal provisions of the inadmissibility and deportability grounds in the INA; and (4) can show that removal would result in exceptional and extremely unusual hardship to a citizen or LPR spouse, parent, or child.[89]

Cancellation of removal for nonpermanent residents is available for those who are deportable or inadmissible. Those whose removal is cancelled under this provision can also seek adjustment of status as part of their relief.[90] The statute requires that the 10-year continuous presence period end when an NTA is served on the noncitizen.[91] The statute also defines continuous physical presence for

---

[88] INA § 240A(d)(1)(B).

[89] INA § 240A(b)(1).

[90] INA § 240A(b)(1).

[91] INA § 240A(d)(1).

purposes of this provision. It states that a single departure of more than 90 days destroys continuous physical presence, as do cumulative absences totaling more than 180 days.[92] Courts have held that voluntary departure in lieu of removal will also destroy continuous physical presence.[93]

The hardship requirement in this provision of cancellation is more restrictive than the requirement for suspension of deportation, its predecessor relief mechanism. Under previous versions of suspension of deportation, eligibility for relief required a showing of *economic detriment* to the citizen/LPR spouse, parent, or child of the respondent. It was later transformed to a showing of *extreme hardship* to the applicant. With the passage of IIRAIRA, Congress now requires the applicant to show *exceptional and extremely unusual hardship* to the applicant's USC or LPR spouse, parent, or child. Not only is this standard more restrictive than the previous standards, but a judge's decision on whether the standard has been met is not reviewable.[94]

In *Matter of Recinas*, the BIA considered several factors in deciding whether this hardship standard had been met, including: 1) the citizen children do not know any other way of life than in U.S. and do not read or write in the language or country of deportation, and don't speak the language either; 2) citizen children are entirely dependent upon respondent for financial and emotional support; 3) lack of family in country of deportation and care of child in the U.S. will be substantially hampered if respondent is deported; 4) strong family system in U.S. that provides financial and emotional support to U.S. citizen child, without which respondent's hardship would increase and would affect hardship of the child; 5) prospects of the respondent immigrating are unrealistic due to backlog of visa availability.[95] While courts can and do consider other factors these are the typical factors courts consider today.

This form of relief is not available to certain categories of noncitizens, including crew members, J visa exchange visitors, and those who are inadmissible or deportable on political or national security grounds.[96]

iii.   Victims of Domestic Violence

Certain victims of domestic violence are eligible for cancellation of removal under special rules that apply because of their victim status. This form of relief is available for a noncitizen who can show s/he has been battered or subjected to extreme cruelty by a citizen or LPR spouse or parent.[97] The noncitizen must also show continuous physical presence for the three years immediately preceding the

---

[92] INA § 240A(d)(2).

[93] Matter of Romale-Alcaide, 23 I.&N. Dec. 423 (BIA 2002); Reyes-Vasquez v. Ashcroft, 395 F.3d 903, 907 (8th Cir. 2005).

[94] INA § 242(a)(2)(B)(i); Romero-Torres v. Ashcroft, 327 F.3d 887 (9th Cir. 2003); Gonzalez-Oropeza v. U.S. Attorney General, 321 F.3d 1331, 1332–33 (11th Cir. 2003).

[95] Matter of Recinas, 23 I.&N. Dec. 467 (BIA 2002).

[96] INA § 240A(c).

[97] INA § 240A(b)(2)(A). This relief is also available to battered spouses whose marriage is not legitimate because of bigamy. INA § 240A(b)(2)((A)(i)(III).

application. The issuance of an NTA does not toll the three-year continuous residence period as it does for those seeking cancellation of removal under INA § 240A(b).[98] The noncitizen must show good moral character during the three-year period as well. S/he is ineligible for relief if s/he has committed an aggravated felony, a crime defined in INA § 212(a)(2) or 212(a)(3), marriage fraud, or a crime defined under INA § 237(a)(2)-(4). The noncitizen must also show "extreme hardship" (as opposed to "exceptional and extremely unusual hardship") to him/herself, or to the noncitizen's child or parent.[99] The parent of an abused child, even if he or she is not married to the abuser, may make a claim under cancellation of removal based on the abuse of the child by the child's other U.S. citizen or LPR parent.[100]

The continuous physical presence requirement in the domestic violence provision allows an exception for those who cannot meet the requirement for reasons related to the violence or abuse. Any absence shown to be linked to the violence or abuse will not be counted in determining whether the noncitizen meets the continuous physical presence requirement. With respect to good moral character, the Attorney General can waive any conviction for a crime that was connected to the noncitizen having been abused or battered if it may otherwise be a bar to a finding of good moral character. In addition, the children of battered spouses who obtain cancellation of removal will be paroled and considered beneficiaries of an application for adjustment of status once the cancellation applicant has been granted adjustment.[101]

iv.   NACARA

In 1997, Congress passed the Nicaraguan Adjustment and Central American Relief Act (NACARA), providing relief to thousands of Central Americans and others fleeing civil unrest in their home countries.[102] NACARA provides for a form of cancellation of removal, known as special rule cancellation. It is available to nationals of Guatemala, El Salvador, the Soviet Union and its successor republics, and most Eastern European nations, who entered before a specified date in 1990. The requirements for special rule cancellation are less restrictive than the general cancellation of removal requirements. They are the same as the requirements for the pre-IIRAIRA suspension of deportation. Special rule cancellation requires seven years of continuous physical presence, compared to 10 under regular cancellation for nonpermanent residents. It also requires "extreme hardship" to oneself or immediate relatives, rather than the strict "exceptional and extremely unusual" standard in regular cancellation. The rule that continuous physical presence ends with the filing of an NTA or with the commission of a crime does not apply to special rule cancellation. The applicant must also show good moral

---

[98] INA § 240A(b)(2)(A)(ii). The 90 day continuous absence and 180 days in the aggregate rules still apply to victims of domestic violence.

[99] INA § 240A(b)(2)(a)(v).

[100] Lopez-Birrueta v. Holder, 633 F.3d 1211 (9th Cir. 2011).

[101] INA § 240A(b)(4).

[102] Pub. L. No. 105-100; 111 Stat. 2160, 2193.

character for the seven years immediately preceding the filing of the application.[103]

A separate provision of NACARA created an amnesty program for Nicaraguan and Cuban nationals who were continuously present in the United States since December 1995. Applications had to be filed by April 1, 2000. The person had to be admissible, although certain inadmissibility grounds, such as public charge, lack of labor certification, and present without admission, were waived.

b. Adjustment of Status

As seen in the cancellation of removal context, adjustment of status for nonpermanent residents is available as affirmative relief from removal. A noncitizen in removal proceedings is eligible for adjustment of status if s/he is otherwise admissible. Waivers are available for certain grounds of inadmissibility. As with affirmative applications for adjustment of status, those who are out of status are not eligible for adjustment, unless they are immediate relatives of citizen sponsors, or are employment-based preference immigrants who have not been out of status more than 180 days.

An eligible noncitizen already in removal proceedings can apply for adjustment of status with the immigration judge directly.[104] The judge has the discretion to deny removal and grant adjustment of status; that decision is reviewable by the Board of Immigration Appeals.[105]

c. Asylum, Withholding of Removal and Convention Against Torture

Asylum and withholding of removal, and withholding of removal under the Convention Against Torture may be sought in removal proceedings by persons fleeing persecution in their home countries. Typically, those in removal proceedings apply for three forms of protection, with each form of protection in the alternative: Asylum, Withholding of Removal under INA § 241(b)(3), and Withholding of Removal pursuant to the Convention Against Torture. The United States is a signatory to the 1967 United Nations Protocol Relating to the Status of Refugees, which governs the treatment of asylees and refugees. Although the Protocol and similar international agreements are not self-executing,[106] they do provide persuasive authority for issues that arise in asylum-related cases.

An applicant who seeks asylum or withholding will typically also seek protection under the Convention Against Torture (CAT). The United States became a party to the United Nations Convention Against Torture and other Forms of Inhuman or Degrading Treatment or Punishment in 1994. Pursuant to the international agreement, Congress enacted legislation stating that "it will be the policy of the United States not to expel, extradite, or otherwise effect the involuntary return of

---

[103] Cuadra v. Gonzales, 417 F.3d 947, 950–52 (8th Cir. 2005).

[104] 8 C.F.R. § 245.2(a)(1).

[105] 8 C.F.R. § 1003.1(b)(3).

[106] They do not go into full effect without action by Congress to enact them through accompanying legislation. *See* Haitian Refugee Center v. Baker, 949 F.2d 1109 (11th Cir. 1991).

any person to a country in which there are substantial grounds for believing the person would be in danger of being subjected to torture, regardless of whether the person is physically present in the United States."[107] INS promulgated rules to implement the legislation in 1999. CAT is not limited to protection for those who fit within the five protected grounds of asylum and withholding of removal.

A more robust discussion of these forms of relief is found in a separate asylum chapter in this book.

d. Registry (INA § 249; 8 U.S.C. 1259)

If a respondent in removal proceedings entered the United States before January 1, 1972 and has maintained continuous presence since then, that respondent may be eligible for a form of relief known as registry.[108] The purpose of registry is to "create a legal record of entry for those who have none."[109] The registry provision allows those who have been in the United States in unauthorized status for a period of time to register and become lawful permanent residents. Originally, registry was a form of relief available to those who remained in the United States for at least five years. Consistent with this purpose, the dates of entry for registry eligibility were advanced periodically until 1972. Since then, Congress has failed to update the cut-off date for registry eligibility.

In addition to continuous residence, a registry applicant must show that s/he is a person of good moral character (including not falling into the more serious inadmissibility categories), is not ineligible for citizenship, and is not inadmissible under INA 212(a)(3)(E) (relating to Nazi persecution or terrorist activity) or under INA 212(a)(2) (relating to criminals, immoral persons, subversive and controlled substance violators, and smugglers).

e. Private Bills

Congressional legislators have the power to grant equitable relief from removal in the form of private legislation. Any member of Congress can introduce a bill to provide lawful permanent resident status for a private individual who cannot otherwise get relief. This is a very limited form of relief because very few private bills are introduced and passed each year. A stay of removal is not automatic with the introduction of private legislation, so an applicant must make a separate application for such a stay. Once a congressional committee seeks a report from DHS, a stay is usually granted.

The first step in obtaining this relief is to seek a Congressional sponsor to introduce a bill. The bill then goes to the immigration subcommittees of the Judiciary committees in each house of Congress. There are rules and protocols for

---

[107] PL 105-277, Title XXI Foreign Affairs and Restructuring Act of 1998, § 2242(a), 112 Stat. 2681–822, 105th Cong. 2d Sess. (1998); *see also* regulations relating to definition of torture at 8 C.F.R. § 208.16–18.

[108] INA § 249.

[109] Angulo-Dominguez v. Ashcroft, 290 F.3d 1147, 1149 (9th Cir. 2003).

granting such relief, which is usually predicated on extreme hardship.[110]

2.   Limited Relief

a.   Deferred Action and Prosecutorial Discretion

Deferred action is the result of prosecutorial discretion, or, an administrative decision by the USCIS District Director, the Regional Commissioner, or their designees, not to prosecute or deport an individual who is otherwise removable. It does not confer any right to remain in the United States. Instead, it is considered an administrative decision to give a particular case or set of cases lower priority when setting priorities for removal. Among the factors that the agency considers in determining whether to grant deferred action are whether the person is an LPR, the duration of her residence, any criminal history, humanitarian concerns, past immigration violation, the likelihood of ultimate removal, the availability of alternative courses of action, how long a bar to future return removal would create, past cooperation with authorities, military service, the person's role in the community, and the availability of detention space.[111] The decision to grant deferred action is discretionary and cannot be judicially reviewed.[112]

The government can effect its prosecutorial discretion not to bring removal proceedings or it can affirmatively grant deferred action. DHS regulations define deferred action as "an act of administrative convenience to the government which gives some cases lower priority."[113]

Deferred Action for Childhood Arrivals (DACA)

DACA is a form of deferred action available to certain undocumented youth who have lived in the United States for an extended period of time. DACA is the Obama administration's response to calls from immigration advocates to legalize the status of undocumented youth who came to the United States at an early age. On June 12, 2012, President Obama announced that the Department of Homeland Security would grant deferred action to those youth who met the criteria laid out by the agency. The DHS subsequently laid out the criteria for eligibility and quickly put in place a program for adjudicating individual cases. Under the program, a DACA applicant must show that s/he: 1) was under the age of 31 as of June 15, 2012; 2) came to the United States before age 16, and must be at least 15 years old at the time of application; 3) has continuously resided in the United States since June 15, 2007; 4) was physically present in the United States on June 15, 2012, and at the time of applying for DACA; 5) had no lawful status on June 15, 2012; 6) is currently

---

[110] *See* Ryan Quinn and Stephen Yale-Loehr, *Private Immigration Bills: An Overview*, 9 BIB 1147 (Oct. 1, 2004) for an overview of the private bill process. *See* Robert Hopp and Juan P. Osuna, *Remedies of Last Resort: Private Bills and Deferred Action*, IMMIGRATION BRIEFINGS (June 1997) for an overview of criteria and procedures for private bills.

[111] *See* INS Commissioner Doris Meissner, Exercising Prosecutorial Discretion, HQOPP (Nov. 17, 2000), reprinted in 77 Interpreter Releases 673, 1680 (Dec. 4, 2000).

[112] Reno v. American-Arab Anti-Discrimination Comm., 525 U.S. 471 (1999).

[113] 8 C.F.R. § 274a.12(c)(14).

in school, has graduated from high school or obtained a GED, or has been honorably discharged from military service; and 7) has not been convicted of a felony, significant misdemeanors, or three or more other misdemeanors, and do not otherwise pose a threat to national security or public safety.[114]

DACA deferred action status lasts for two years. DACA recipients are eligible for employment authorization, and their unlawful presence is tolled during the period that they have deferred action. Over 500,000 DACA requests have been granted thus far. Many of the initial DACA applicants are in the process of renewing their DACA requests, as the initial two year periods have begun to expire.

Expanded DACA and Deferred Action for Parents of Americans and Lawful Permanent Residents (DAPA)

On November 20, 2014, President Obama announced an expansion of the existing DACA program and the initiation of a deferred action program for parents of U.S. citizens and lawful permanent residents. Under guidelines announced by the Department of Homeland Security at the President's direction, DACA was to be extended to those who, in addition to meeting the current criteria, entered the United States and maintained continuous residence since January 1, 2010.[115] The Deferred Action for Parents of Americans and Lawful Permanent Residents program was to be available to parents who have lived continuously in the United States since January 1, 2010; who were present in the United States without lawful status on November 20, 2014; and who have not been convicted of certain crimes, including felonies and misdemeanors.[116]

On February 16, 2015, a federal district court in Texas temporarily blocked the implementation of both programs.[117] As of this writing, an injunction blocking the programs remains in place and is on appeal to the Fifth Circuit Court of Appeals.

b. Voluntary Departure

Voluntary departure is a form of relief that allows those who have received a notice to appear in removal proceedings to leave the United States on their own, rather than through a removal order.[118]An immigration judge may grant voluntary departure at the beginning or at the end of removal proceedings as an alternative to issuing a removal order. Leaving the United States through voluntary departure avoids the 10-year inadmissibility ground, which is triggered with a removal

---

[114] *See* Janet Napolitano, Secretary of Homeland Security, Excercising Prosecutorial Discretion with Respect to Individuals Who Came to the United States as Children (June 15, 2012), *available at* http://www.dhs.gov/xlibrary/assets/s1-exercising-prosecutorial-discretion-individuals-who-came-to-us-as-children.pdf; *see also*, USCIS, Consideration of Deferred Action for Childhood Arrivals (DACA), *available at* http://www.uscis.gov/humanitarian/consideration-deferred-action-childhood-arrivals-daca.

[115] Department of Homeland Security, *Jeh Johnson Memo: Exercising Prosecutorial Discretion with Respect to Individuals Who Came to the United States as Children and with Respect to Certain Individuals Who Are the Parents of U.S. Citizens or Permanent Residents* (November 20, 2014), *available at* http://www.dhs.gov/sites/default/files/publications/14_1120_memo_deferred_action.pdf.

[116] *Id.*

[117] State of Texas v. U.S., 1:14-cv-00254 (S.D. Texas) (Feb. 16, 2015).

[118] INA § 240B

order.[119] It also avoids reinstatement of removal actions in the event the person returns to the United States illegally.

If a noncitizen seeks voluntary departure at the beginning of removal proceedings, s/he must be able to pay his/her own way out the country and must not be deportable as an aggravated felon or on terrorist grounds.[120] The respondent who seeks voluntary departure at the beginning of proceedings must concede removability, must make no other requests for relief from removal, and must waive all appeals. Because voluntary departure is discretionary relief, the respondent must show evidence of favorable factors and must explain away negative factors.[121] A judge may grant up to 120 days for voluntary departure if it is sought before the completion of proceedings.

Voluntary departure may also be sought at the conclusion of removal proceedings. The requirements at this stage of litigation are more stringent. The applicant must show that s/he has been physically present in the United States for at least one year prior to the initiation of removal proceedings, demonstrate good moral character for at least five years prior to the application, and s/he must not be deportable as an aggravated felon or terrorist.[122] The applicant must establish by clear and convincing evidence that s/he intends to, and has the means to, depart the United States.[123]

Voluntary departure at the conclusion of proceedings may be granted for no more than 60 days.[124] The applicant must post a departure bond within five days of the voluntary departure grant.

c. Stays of Removal

A stay of removal is available for those who have been ordered removed and need more time in the United States. It is discretionary and is granted by U.S. Immigration and Customs Enforcement.[125] A stay is not automatically granted on appeal of an immigration judge's decision. Therefore, an applicant who appeals must also seek a stay of removal to avoid removal while an appeal is pending.

---

[119] INA § 212(a)(9)(A). Note that it does not avoid the separate 3- and 10-year bars that are a result of a noncitizen's unlawful presence within the United States for more than 180 days and one year, respectively.

[120] INA § 237(a)(2)(A)(ii) & § 237(a)(4)(B).

[121] Matter of Arguelles, 22 I.&N. Dec. 811 (BIA 1999).

[122] INA § 240B(b).

[123] INA § 240B(b)(1)(D).

[124] INA § 240B(b)(2).

[125] 8 C.F.R. § 1003.6(b).

Chapter 13

THE REMOVAL PROCESS

A. OVERVIEW OF THE REMOVAL PROCESS

The 1996 amendments to the INA established one administrative hearing system for noncitizens under INA § 240.[1] In a removal hearing an Immigration Judge decides issues relating to admissibility, deportability (removal after admission) and the grounds of relief from removal, including asylum. There are some key exceptions to the use of "ordinary" removal proceedings under INA § 240. These include: removal proceedings at federal, state and local prisons;[2] summary removal proceedings for aggravated felons;[3] summary procedures applied to crew members; and special terrorist removal court procedures.[4] Expedited removal, another exception to the ordinary removal procedure under INA § 240, applies to some applicants for admission into the U.S. This is covered in Chapter 10.[5]

This Chapter includes a review of these removal procedures as well as detention under the INA. The constitutional issues, including due process requirements, are covered in Chapter 3.

B. THE REMOVAL HEARING

1. Notice to Appear

Removal proceedings begin when DHS files a charging document with the Office of the Immigration Judge called a Notice to Appear [NTA].[6] The NTA is served on the noncitizen in person or by mail.[7] Under INA § 239, the NTA must provide notice about the nature of the proceeding, the specific alleged violations of law and information about the right to be represented by counsel at no expense to the government. The noncitizen also must be provided a list of free legal services.[8] The NTA requires the noncitizen immediately to provide an address and telephone number (if any) where she may be contacted by the Immigration Judge.[9] Issues relating to notice often arise in *in absentia* hearings and are discussed below.

---

[1] Illegal Immigration Reform and Immigrant Responsibility Act of 1996, Pub. L. No. 104-208, 110 Stat. 3009 (IIRIRA), effective as of April 1, 1997. The term removable means, as defined in INA § 240(e)(2), that a noncitizen is either inadmissible under INA § 212(a) if she has not been admitted or that a noncitizen is deportable under INA § 237 if she has been admitted to the U.S.

[2] INA § 238(a)(1).

[3] INA § 238(a)(2).

[4] INA § 236A (mandatory detention of suspected terrorists). Under INA § 236A(5) detention up to seven days is permitted before an NTA or criminal arrest warrant must be issued.

[5] INA § 235.

[6] Form I-862, formerly referred to as an Order to Show Cause.

[7] Before IIRIRA, the charging document had to be served by certified mail. Under INA § 239(a)(1), (a)(2), personal service of any hearing notice is required if practicable, including changes of hearing dates and times. *See* In re M-D-, 23 I.&N. Dec. 540, 542 (BIA 2002).

[8] A hearing may not be scheduled until at least 10 days after service of the NTA in order to provide the noncitizen the opportunity to obtain counsel.

[9] INA § 239(a)(1)(F)(i) & (ii) (Immediate notice also is required upon a change of address or telephone number.). Under INA § 239(c), service by mail on the noncitizen or his or her attorney is sufficient if sent to the address provided by the noncitizen when the NTA was initially issued.

An NTA may be issued in a variety of circumstances. An NTA may be issued to a noncitizen after an arrest, to an arriving noncitizen, or to an individual who is already present in the United States, in order to begin removal proceedings. The INA distinguishes between those who have not been admitted deemed "arriving" noncitizens and other noncitizens who have not been admitted.[10] Noncitizens apprehended within the U.S. are not in the category of arriving noncitizens.

The INA covers both an arrest with a warrant (INA § 236) and an arrest without a warrant upon reasonable suspicion, (INA § 287(a)). Arrest without a warrant, under INA § 287(a), may be made by an employee or officer authorized by the Secretary of Homeland Security, typically an Immigration and Customs Enforcement (ICE) officer but other DHS officials also can issue an NTA.[11] If a noncitizen is arrested without a warrant, an NTA must be issued to begin removal proceedings within 48 hours of the arrest.[12] The decision whether to grant bond and release, or continue detention also must be made within 48 hours. The subject of interior enforcement and the enforcement powers of DHS are covered in Chapter 14.

There is broad prosecutorial discretion to decide when and whether to issue an NTA.[13] An immigration officer may permit the noncitizen to depart the U.S. voluntarily rather than begin removal proceedings.[14]

Once the NTA is issued and removal proceedings begin, there are typically two stages to the proceedings. First, there is a master calendar hearing. At the master calendar hearing the noncitizen usually is asked to concede deportability or challenge the allegations and deportability charges in the NTA, and designate the country of removal if a removal order is entered at the conclusion of the proceeding. There might be several master calendar hearing dates set by the Immigration Judge while the noncitizen tries to seek legal representation. Second, when a noncitizen contests removal, an individual merits hearing is scheduled. In

---

[10] INA §§ 235(a)(1), 101(a)(13). A noncitizen is an arriving alien whether or not she arrives at a designated port of arrival and this includes aliens brought to the U.S. after having been interdicted in the international or U.S. waters.

[11] INA § 287 (a)(2) (The authority to arrest an individual without a warrant exists if the officer or employee has reason to believe a noncitizen is entering, attempting to enter or is present in the U.S. in violation of any law or regulation and the noncitizen is likely to escape before an arrest warrant can be obtained.).

[12] 8 C.F.R. § 287.3(d) (2014). The DHS regulations provide this procedural protection and in the case of emergency or extraordinary circumstances the removal hearing may begin with the issuance of the NTA after 48 hours. If a criminal arrest warrant is issued, in lieu of an NTA, it too must be issued within the 48 hours of the arrest of a noncitizen.

[13] Generally, an NTA will not be issued when a noncitizen is in some kind of deferred action program, if an immigrant visa is pending and, upon approval, the noncitizen will be eligible to adjust status, if a conviction is vacated or about to be vacated, if the noncitizen is a member of the armed forces, or if the noncitizen is an asylee. Recent challenges to the President's authority to exercise prosecutorial discretion and instruct or provide guidance to DHS officers in their exercise of discretion are covered in Chapter 5.

[14] INA § 240B(a) a noncitizen may voluntarily depart "in lieu of being subject to removal proceedings" as long as the noncitizen is not removable for an aggravated felony or terrorist activities. This has been described as similar to a plea bargain. ALIENIKOFF, MARTIN, MOTOMURA & FULLERTON, IMMIGRATION AND CITIZENSHIP, PROCESS AND POLICY 789 (7th ed. 2012).

an uncontested case, where the noncitizen admits the allegations and waives any relief, the case can be resolved at the master calendar hearing. After the master calendar and before the individual hearing, applications for relief from deportation or motions may be entered in the case, e.g., for a continuance,[15] to change venue,[16] or other matters.[17]

2. Bond and Detention

The detention of noncitizens arriving at a border port of entry and seeking admission traditionally has been within the exclusive power of Congress and the Executive Branch implementing the INA.[18] Many provisions of the INA require or permit detention by ICE during the removal process of both arriving noncitizens seeking admission into the U.S. and noncitizens apprehended inside the U.S.[19] Release from detention may occur by posting a bond under INA § 236(a) or by parole under INA § 212(d)(5). Each of these options is discussed below.

A noncitizen comes into ICE custody in a variety of ways: as an applicant for admission at a border port of entry who is denied admission and who is eligible for review by an Immigration Judge; individuals who entered the U.S. without inspection and have been apprehended by a border patrol officer and are transferred to ICE for detention pending review by an Immigration Judge; and individuals who have been arrested by an ICE Officer, with or without a warrant, inside the U.S. Once a noncitizen is in ICE custody, ICE officers will either detain the individual or release her on bond, an order of supervision or an order on her own recognizance. If a noncitizen is detained, she may be detained during the pendency of the removal hearing and while awaiting deportation after a removal order has been issued.

Detention was expanded dramatically in 1996 by the addition of harsh mandatory detention provisions to the INA.[20] Initially, this was an effort to ensure that noncitizens appear at their removal hearings and leave the U.S. if a removal order is issued. Detention while the removal proceedings are pending may last for months, and the noncitizen often is held in facilities far away from family and friends. The INA detention requirements, policies and administration have been the subject of significant and on-going criticism based on the conditions in facilities and broad use of these policies.[21] One concern has been detention in remote

---

[15] 8 C.F.R. § 1003.29 (2014) (granted for "good cause shown")

[16] 8 C.F.R. § 1003.20(b) (2014).

[17] Motions to remand to DHS for consideration of an application for relief or to suppress evidence can be submitted, as well as requests for limited discovery (including depositions). 8 C.F.R. § 1003.35 (2014).

[18] Wong Wing v. U.S., 163 U.S. 228 (1896); Schaughnessy v. United States ex rel. Mezei, 345 U.S. 206 (1953).

[19] INA §§ 235(a)(1), 101(a)(13). A noncitizen is an arriving alien whether or not she arrives at a designated port of arrival and this includes aliens brought to the U.S. after having been interdicted in the international or U.S. waters.

[20] INA § 236(c) requires mandatory detention of noncitizens who are inadmissible for any criminal offense under INA § 212(a)(2), deportable under be detained after they are released from criminal custody and remain detained pending removal.

[21] See Additional Actions Needed to Strengthen Management and Oversight of Facility Costs and

locations which can compromise an attorney's capacity to adequately represent clients because of the distance and lack of regular contact.[22]

Mandatory detention during removal proceedings under INA § 236(c) applies to noncitizens who are inadmissible or deportable for a wide range of criminal offenses and terrorist activities and these noncitizens are ineligible for bond.[23] Mandatory detention applies to noncitizens if they are deportable under INA § 237(a)(2)(A) because: (1) they have committed two crimes of moral turpitude after admission; (2) are aggravated felons; (3) have committed drug crimes, firearms offenses, or miscellaneous crimes; (4) have committed a crime involving moral turpitude for which the sentence is at least one year; or (5) are deportable on terrorist grounds. Mandatory detention also is required for any individual who is inadmissible under INA § 212(a)(2). Mandatory detention, therefore, is imposed on a large number of individuals who are in removal proceedings for being inadmissible because INA § 212(a)(2) includes any person who has been convicted of a crime involving moral turpitude (CIMT) as well as a many other crimes. Finally, the 1996 amendments also imposed mandatory detention on persons in expedited removal who are applying for asylum but who have not established that they have a credible fear of persecution.[24] There are very limited grounds for release from custody under INA § 236(c)(2).[25] This statutory mandate has been upheld in by the Supreme Court.[26]

Generally, all other noncitizens placed in removal proceedings are eligible for release in a bond hearing before an Immigration Judge under INA § 236(a). Generally, noncitizens applying for admission are not eligible for release on bond. If a noncitizen has been arrested, a decision whether to continue detention pending removal or release on bond pending removal must be made within 48 hours of an

---

Standards (GAO-15-153 , Oct. 10, 2014) (recommending that ICE document reasons why all facilities cannot be transitioned to the most recent standards, review reasons for differences in inspection results, and assess the extent to which it has appropriate controls for tracking facility costs); *Additional Actions Could Strengthen DHS Efforts to Address Sexual Abuse*, GAO-14-38 (Nov. 20, 2013); *Alien Detention Standards: Observations on the Adherence to ICE's Medical Standards in Detention Facilities*, GAO-08-869T (June 4, 2008); National Immigrant Justice Center, Report, *Invisible in Isolation: The Use of Segregation and Solitary Confinement in Immigration Detention* (Sept. 2012); Amnesty International, Report, *USA: Jailed Without Justice* (Mar. 2009); M. Dow, American Gulag: Inside U.S. Immigration Prisons (2004); Pistone, *Justice Delayed Is Justice Denied: A Proposal for Ending the Unnecessary Detention of Asylum Seekers*, 12 HARV. HUMAN RIGHTS L.J. 197 (1999) (criticizing the detention of asylum seekers in the expedited removal process under INA § 235(a)).

[22] *See, e.g.*, Detention Watch, *About the U.S. Detention and Deportation System, available at* http://www.detentionwatchnetwork.org/aboutdetention; Taylor, *Promoting Legal Representation for Detained Aliens: Litigation and Administrative Reform*, 29 CONN. L. REV. 1647 (1997).

[23] INA §§ 236(c); 235(b)(1)(A); 235(b)(2); 235(b)(1)(B)(ii) (after a credible fear determination in expedited removal).

[24] INA § 236(c). Noncitizens subject to expedited removal under INA § 235(b) are also subject to mandatory detention.

[25] INA § 236(c)(2) permits release to assist in a major crime investigation, if release does not pose any risk to the safety of other persons or property, and if the noncitizen is likely to appear at any scheduled proceeding.

[26] Demore v. Kim, 538 U.S. 510 (2003) (upholding mandatory detention pending removal proceedings under INA § 236(c) of a lawful permanent resident who had conceded deportability based on a criminal conviction).

arrest.[27] This time limit does not apply to noncitizens detained as certified suspected terrorists under INA § 236A.

Bond is available to other noncitizens for release from detention under INA 236(a).[28] The initial determination is made by the DHS District Director and the District Director may impose any other conditions of release in addition to the payment of security for the bond. The noncitizen has the burden to establish that she does not present a danger to persons or property, is not a threat to national security and does not pose a risk of flight under INA § 236(a).[29] The decision about whether to grant a bond usually is based on local family ties, prior arrests, convictions, appearances at hearings, employment or lack of employment, membership in community organizations, manner of entry and length of time in the U.S., and financial ability to post bond.[30]

Detention pursuant to an arrest with or without a warrant is possible.[31] Under § 236(a), a noncitizen may be arrested and detained on a warrant issued by ICE. An arrest without warrant is authorized under INA § 287(a).[32] Detention after an arrest is only permissible for 48 hours, at which point a decision must be made whether: (1) to begin removal proceedings by issuing an NTA; (2) to file criminal charges; or (3) to release the noncitizen from custody.[33] Detention up to seven days is permissible for certified suspected terrorists under INA § 236A. The procedures applied to certified terrorists under INA § 236A are discussed below.

Arriving noncitizens seeking admission into the U.S. must be detained under INA § 235(b)(2) and are not eligible for release on bond under INA § 236(a).[34] This includes lawful permanent residents who seek admission as defined in INA § 101(a)(13). Release on parole for very limited reasons is possible for arriving

---

[27] 8 C.F.R. § 287.3(d) ("except in the event of an emergency or other extraordinary circumstance in which case a determination will be made within an additional reasonable period of time, whether the alien will be continued in custody or released on bond or recognizance").

[28] INA § 236(a)(2). The noncitizen's release on either bond or conditional parole is subject to revocation, resulting in re-arrest under the original warrant and detention. The bond amount must be at least $1,500.00.

[29] 8 CFR § 1003.19(a)–(c). See Matter of D.J., 23 I.&N. Dec. 572 (A.G. 2003) (denial of bond premised on a general immigration policy issue represented a national security concern, i.e., the possibility of mass migration from Haiti and the Dominican Republic).

[30] Matter of Patel, 15 I.&N. Dec. 666 (BIA 1976).

[31] INA § 287(a) permits interrogation and arrest by any officer or authorized employee of DHS if the noncitizen enters or attempts to enter unlawfully in view of the officer or if reasonable suspicion exists that the noncitizen is in the U.S. in violation of any law or regulation and is likely to escape before a warrant can be obtained.

[32] Under INA § 236(a), after a warrant has been issued, a noncitizen may be released from detention on a bond (minimum bond of $1,500 and any other conditions imposed by the Attorney General) or released on conditional parole.

[33] 8 C.F.R § 287.3(d) (2014).

[34] Under INA § 235(b)(2)(A) arriving noncitizens seeking admission, other than LPRs, must establish they are "clearly and beyond a doubt entitled to be admitted." An arriving noncitizen who is not clearly and beyond doubt entitled to admission "shall be detained" for a removal hearing under INA § 240. 8 C.F.R. § 236.1(c)(2).

noncitizens.[35] Decisions about parole of an arriving noncitizen are made by ICE District Directors and there is no review by an Immigration Judge of this determination even in the case of a lawful permanent resident.[36]

Noncitizens who are apprehended and detained under INA § 236 may seek review of the DHS detention decision before an Immigration Judge in a bond hearing. The noncitizen can request a de novo bond redetermination hearing before an Immigration Judge.[37] The decision of the Immigration Judge at the bond redetermination hearing can be appealed to the BIA.[38] There is no review by an Immigration Judge of a DHS decision to deny bond and release if the noncitizen is detained under INA § 236(c) on criminal or terrorism grounds. All Immigration Judge decisions about bond or parole are discretionary judgments and are precluded from judicial review under INA § 236(e), which includes discretionary judgments regarding detention, release, and the grant or denial of parole or bond.[39] Arriving noncitizens who are detained by ICE under INA § 235 may not appeal a DHS custody decision to an Immigration Judge.[40]

3. Legal Representation

At the removal hearing, the Immigration Judge must inform the noncitizen of the right to representation by counsel.[41] INA § 240(b)(4)(a) specifies that noncitizens "have the privilege of being represented, at no expense to the Government, by counsel of the alien's choosing who is authorized to practice in such proceedings."[42] The Immigration Judge must verify on the record whether or not the noncitizen wishes to be represented by counsel.[43] The noncitizen also must be informed by the Immigration Judge about the availability of free legal services, and the right to present evidence, cross examine witnesses, and appeal.[44]

---

[35] INA § 212(d)(5). (Noncitizens applying for admission are eligible discretionary parole for on a case-by-case basis for "urgent humanitarian reasons or significant public benefit." Refugees are eligible only if there are "compelling reasons in the public interest."); 8 C.F.R. § 212.5 provides for the release on parole of an arriving noncitizen in the case of a serious medical condition; a pregnant woman; certain juveniles; and witnesses in government proceedings; and if detention is not in the public interest.

[36] See 8 C.F.R. § 236.1(c)(11) (2014). See also Matter of Collado-Munoz, 21 I.&N. Dec. 1061 (BIA 1997) (an LPR arriving at a border post of entry and seeking admission is not entitled to a bond hearing before an Immigration Judge).

[37] 8 C.F.R. § 1003.19 (2014).

[38] 8 C.F.R. §§ 1003.1(b)(7), 1003.19(f) (2014) (both the noncitizen and DHS may appeal the Immigration Judge's custody decision to the BIA).

[39] Judicial review is still available to raise constitutional or statutory challenges by habeas corpus.

[40] Arriving noncitizens are eligible for parole only and there is no renew by IJs of this discretionary decision. 8 C.F.R. §§ 236.1(c)(2), 212.5(b), 235.1(d) (2014).

[41] 8 C.F.R. § 1240.10(a)(1) (2014).

[42] See also INA § 292.

[43] 8 C.F.R. § 1240.10(a)(1) (2014).

[44] 8 C.F.R. § 1240.11(a)(2) refers to an Immigration Judge's obligation to inform of benefits for which the respondent has apparent eligibility if the record raises the reasonable possibility of eligibility. See, e.g., U.S. v. Arrieta, 224 F.3d 1076 (9th Cir. 2000) (apparent eligibility for INA § 212(h) relief).

There is no constitutional right to appointed counsel under the Sixth Amendment because deportation from the U.S. is not viewed as punishment akin to a criminal conviction.[45] Fifth Amendment procedural due process requirements must be met in deportation hearings. A right to the effective assistance of counsel exists under the Fifth Amendment, but a lack of representation does not violate due process.[46] In *Aguilera-Enriquez v. INS*, 516 F. 2d 565 (6th Cir. 1975), *cert. denied*, 423 U.S. 1050 (1976), the Sixth Circuit held that the "fundamental fairness" required under the Fifth Amendment is satisfied even when an indigent noncitizen, who requested appointed counsel, lacks any representation in a deportation hearing.[47]

Noncitizens who are not represented by counsel are at a substantial disadvantage in removal proceedings, although lack of representation is not a denial *per se* of procedural due process.[48] A lack of representation, in some instances, can violate due process because of a lack of fundamental fairness. For example, in *Jacinto v. INS*, 208 F.3d 735 (9th Cir. 2000), the court of appeals found that a noncitizen who was unrepresented was denied procedural due process because the Immigration Judge did not fully explain the right to representation by counsel or give her a full opportunity to present testimony.[49] In this case, the noncitizen requested asylum, withholding of deportation and voluntary departure. There was confusion because the noncitizen did not appear to understand she could be represented by counsel and also speak for herself and present testimony in support of her applications.

Ineffective assistance of counsel can violate principles of fundamental fairness and procedural due process guarantees. The due process right to representation includes a right to competent representation. The BIA has identified criteria for ineffective assistance of counsel claims to determine whether competent counsel would have acted otherwise and whether counsel's performance was so inadequate that it *may* have affected the outcome.[50] From 1988 to January 2009, under the BIA decision *Matter of Lozado*, an ineffective assistance of counsel claim must have been supported by: (1) an affidavit setting forth the agreement that was entered into with former counsel with respect to the actions to be taken, as well as any representations made by counsel to the alien; (2) proof that the movant has informed former counsel of the allegations in writing as well as any response received; and (3) a statement detailing whether a complaint has been filed with

---

[45] *See* Fong Yue Ting v. United States, 149 U.S. 698 (1893), discussed in Chapter 2.

[46] U.S. v. Gouveia, 467 U.S. 180 (1984).

[47] There are no cases applying the *Aguilera-Enriquez* criteria to find that government paid counsel was required in a deportation/removal case. ALIENIKOFF, MARTIN, MOTOMURA & FULLERTON, IMMIGRATION AND CITIZENSHIP, PROCESS AND POLICY 1155 (7th ed. 2012).

[48] Fundamental fairness does not require that children are represented by counsel. *See, e.g.*, Machado v. Ashcroft, No CS-02-066-FVS (E.D. Wash. 2002), 79 Interp. Rel. 1044–45 (2003).

[49] *See also* Biwot v. Gonzales, 403 F.3d 1094, 1099 (9th Cir. 2005) (finding a violation of procedural due process when a noncitizen in detention was given only five days to find counsel).

[50] The Ninth Circuit has held that the BIA criteria should not be applied rigidly when other information sufficiently indicates the ineffective assistance of counsel may have affected the outcome of the case. Morales Apolinar v. Mukasey, 514 F.3d 893, 898 (9th Cir. 2008).

appropriate disciplinary authorities and if not, why not.[51]

In January 2009, shortly before the inauguration of President Obama, the Attorney General overruled *Matter of Lozado* by finding there was no constitutional or statutory right under procedural due process guarantees of the Fifth Amendment to effective counsel, only discretionary authority of the BIA to reopen proceedings if egregious conduct occurred. In *Matter of Compean*, a new set of criteria for deficient performance of counsel were identified. A person must show: (1) the lawyer's failing were egregious; and (2) prejudice resulted from the lawyer's errors.[52] One of the first actions of Attorney General Holder was to vacate the *Compean* decision. The *Lozada* decision was reinstated and the EOIR required to propose a new rule in order to revise the ineffective assistance of counsel criteria.[53] The EOIR has not proposed a new rule, and, therefore, the *Lozada* case continues to be followed.[54]

The lack of legal representation in removal hearings before Immigration Judges has been a major concern especially in the case of unaccompanied minors and other vulnerable populations.[55] Cases where mental incompetency is an issue warrant special concern under the INA, although there is no requirement of appointed counsel.[56] Recent cases challenging mandatory detention of mentally incompetent without legal representation have been successful in enjoining the government's continued detention unless the noncitizen had "qualified" representation (although not necessarily legal representation) was available.[57]

---

[51] Matter of Lozada, 19 I.&N. Dec. 637, 639 (BIA 1988).

[52] Matter of Compean, 24 I.&N. Dec. 710 (A.G. 2009), *vacated*, 25 I.&N. Dec. 1 (2009).

[53] *See*, LEGOMSKY & RODRIGUEZ, IMMIGRATION AND REFUGEE LAW AND POLICY, CHAPTER 9 (6th ed. 2014). The courts of appeals are split on the question of whether a constitutional right to the effective assistance of counsel exists in removal proceedings. Most courts have recognized such a right. *See, e.g.*, Nehad v. Mukasey, 535 F.3d 962, 967 (9th Cir. 2008); Aris v. Mukasey, 517 F.3d 595, 600–01 (2d Cir. 2008); Zeru v. Gonzales, 503 F.3d 59, 72 (1st Cir. 2007); Fadiga v. AG of the United States, 488 F.3d 142, 155 (3d Cir. 2007); Sene v. Gonzales, 453 F.3d 383, 386 (6th Cir. 2006); Dakane v. United States Attorney General, 399 F.3d 1269, 1274 (11th Cir. 2005). Others have not recognized this right. *See, e.g.*, Rafiyev v. Mukasey, 536 F.3d 853, 861 (8th Cir. 2008); Afanwi v. Mukasey, 526 F.3d 788, 798–99 (4th Cir. 2008); Magala v. Gonzales, 434 F.3d 523, 525 (7th Cir. 2005).

[54] *See generally* Aliza Kaplan, *A New Approach to Ineffective Assistance of Counsel in Removal Proceedings*, 62 RUTGERS L. REV. 345 (2010); Jean Pierre Espinoza, Note, *Ineffective Assistance of Counsel in Removal Proceedings — Matter of Compean and the Fundamental Fairness Doctrine*, 22 FLORIDA J. INTERNAT'L L. 101 (2010).

[55] *See*, Legomsky, *Restructuring Immigration Adjudication*, 59 DUKE L.J. 1635, 1695 (2010) (proposing an Article III court for immigration adjudication with two term for judges serving on an immigration court of appeals to "minimize both the profit in lobbying and the opportunity for capture"); Lawrence Baum, *Judicial Specialization and the Adjudication of Immigration Cases*, 59 DUKE L.J. 1501(2010); Leonard Birdsong, *Reforming the Immigration Courts of the United States: Why Is There No Will to Make It an Article I Court?* 19 BARRY L. REV. 17 (2013).

[56] INA § 240(b)(3). *See also* Matter of M-A-M-, 25 I.&N. Dec. 474 (BIA 2011) (discussing various safeguards available including appearance of a friend, custodian or attorney on behalf of the noncitizen).

[57] *See also*, Franco-Gonzales v. Holder, 767 F. Supp. 2d 1034 (C.D. Cal. 2010) (class action lawsuit challenging the detention of mentally incompetent noncitizens; a preliminary injunction granted to two named plaintiffs barring continued detention unless the noncitizens were represented by a "qualified representative" (although not necessarily legal counsel) as required by § 504 of the Rehabilitation Act which requires reasonable accommodation to the disabled); Franco-Gonzales v. Holder, 2011 U.S. Dist.

The situation of unaccompanied minors in removal proceedings also demands attention. Appointed counsel is not required for unaccompanied minors despite the understanding that children possess more "limited understanding and decision-making ability" and may be more susceptible to the "inherently coercive nature" of the immigration process.[58] The 2013 Senate Bill (S 744), it's version of comprehensive immigration reform, contains a provision to provide free legal counsel to unaccompanied children.[59] In Spring 2014, national attention to the extraordinary difficulties faced by children in ICE custody and removal proceedings was precipitated by a mass migration of unaccompanied children, as well as women and children, from Honduras, Guatemala, and El Salvador. One response to this acute need for legal representation is an EOIR sponsored new grant program known as "justice AmeriCorps,"[60] designed to provide legal services to unrepresented children in order "to better serve vulnerable populations such as children and improve court efficiency through pilot efforts aimed at improving legal representation."[61]

The lack of legal representation is a critical issue for all noncitizens in removal proceedings who are often detained in remote locations and must rely on *pro bono* representation. A 2005 study by the Migration Policy Institute found that 24 percent of detainees represented by counsel in removal proceedings were successful in their claims for relief from removal compared to only 15 percent of unrepresented detainees.[62]

Legal assistance to noncitizens by federally funded Legal Services Corporation [LSC] agencies is very limited. LSC-funded organizations may only provide services to noncitizens who are permanent residents, immediate relatives of U.S. citizens who have applied for adjustment of status, noncitizens granted refugee status or asylum, or noncitizens granted withholding of removal under INA § 241(b)(3). There is an exception to the ban allows an entity to use non-LSC funds to serve victims of domestic abuse and for persons who have established a credible fear of persecution.[63]

LEXIS 139148 (C.D. Cal. Aug. 2, 2011) (granting permanent injunction against continued mandatory detention for one petitioner in class action lawsuit on behalf of mentally incompetent detainees).

[58] Perez-Funez v. District Director, 619 F. Supp. 656, 664–65 (C.D. Cal. 1985).

[59] "Border Security, Economic Opportunity, and Immigration Modernization Act," S. 744, 113th Congress (2013–2014) (introduced Apr. 16, 2013) (provides the right to appointed counsel to unaccompanied minor children, immigrants with serious mental disabilities, and other particularly vulnerable individuals).

[60] "justice AmeriCorps" is a partnership between EOIR and the Corporation for National and Community Service (CNCS),which administers AmeriCorps. CNCS is a federal agency that manages over five million Americans in service through its AmeriCorps, Senior Corps, Social Innovation Fund, and other programs.

[61] EOIR Press Release, Justice Department and CNCS Announce New Partnership to Enhance Immigration Courts and Provide Critical Legal Assistance to Unaccompanied Minors (June 6, 2014) *available at* http://www.justice.gov/eoir/press/2014/JusticeAmeriCorpsRelease06062014.html.

[62] *See* Kerwin, *Revisiting the Need for Appointed Counsel*, Migration Policy Institute Insight 6 (April 2005). The disparity has been particularly pronounced for asylum seekers. Non-detained applicants for asylum represented by counsel were granted relief in 39 percent of cases while unrepresented non-detained applicants were granted relief in only 14 percent of cases.

[63] 45 CFR §§ 1626.4, 1625.5 (2014).

Non-lawyers may represent noncitizens. Qualified organizations may practice before the Immigration Court and DHS if recognized by the Board of Immigration Appeals [BIA].[64] Law students and law graduates not yet admitted to practice also may represent noncitizens under the rules.[65] Group rights presentations by lawyers and other volunteers now occur in many detainee facilities where noncitizens are detained pending removal. Detention pending removal is covered later in this Chapter. The need for adequate legal assistance is critical as the detainee population increases. These presentations inform noncitizens about the general process and issues in a removal hearing. These are conducted by lawyers and others who provide written materials, some counseling about individual cases, and, in some cases, pro bono legal representation.[66]

4. Evidence, Burden of Proof and Hearing Procedures

This section covers how the removal hearing is conducted by the Immigration Judge. The hearing procedures used by an Immigration Judge can be challenged under procedural due process protections of the Fifth Amendment to U.S. Constitution if these violate fundamental fairness.[67] This section also covers evidence, the burden of proof and standard of proof in removal hearings.

a. Hearing Procedures

The removal hearing is conducted by the Immigration Judge who administers oaths, receives evidence, and may interrogate, examine and cross-examine the noncitizen and any witnesses.[68] The noncitizen has a right to present evidence and cross-examine witnesses, including the right to present expert testimony.[69] The noncitizen must receive a full and fair hearing, and if a noncitizen is prejudiced by the Immigration Judge's conduct of the hearing then there may be a violation of due process.[70] This requires the Immigration Judge to fully develop the record, and an Immigration Judge's refusal to allow the presentation of evidence may be a denial

---

[64] 8 C.F.R. § 292.2(a) (2014). Qualified organizations include any non-profit religious, charitable, social service or similar organization demonstrating it has at its disposal adequate knowledge, information and experience, and charges only nominal fees.

[65] The law student must be directly supervised by a faculty member, attorney or other accredited representative.

[66] *See EOIR Adds 12 new Legal Orientation Program Sites*, 85 INTER. REL. 2781 (Oct. 20, 2008); Andrew I. Schoenholtz, *The State of Asylum Representation: Ideas for Change*, 16 GEO. IMM. L.J. 739 (2002); Christopher Nugent, *Strengthening Access to Justice: Prehearing Rights Presentations for Detained Respondents*, 76 INT. REL. 1077, 1078 (1999).

[67] *See* Goldberg v. Kelly, 397 U.S. 254 (1970); Matthews v. Eldridge, 424 U.S. 319 (1976).

[68] INA § 240(b)(1). The Immigration Judge has authority to issue subpoenas for witnesses and the presentation of evidence. The EOIR has adopted formal procedures for the timing, presentation and acceptance of evidence by IJs. *See* Immigration Court Practice Manual, *available at* www.usdoj.gov/eoir. There are separate guidelines for proceedings involving unaccompanied minors.

[69] INA § 240(b)(4)(B).

[70] *See* Jacinto v. INS, 208 F.3d 725 (9th Cir. 2000); United States v. Mendoza-Lopez, 481 U.S. 828, 837 (1987) (recognizing the possible defense against a criminal charge of illegal reentry after removal under INA § 276 of fundamentally unfair hearing procedures in the first removal hearing).

of procedural due process.[71] The Immigration Judge also must notify the noncitizen of her apparent eligibility for any forms of relief from removal. Relief from removal is covered in Chapter 12.

In *Jacinto v. INS*, a case involving an unrepresented person, the Immigration Judge did not clearly explain that the noncitizen had the right to testify and present evidence in support of her case, rather than give testimony only by examination of the DHS Trial Attorney. The Ninth Circuit found that the noncitizen was denied the opportunity to testify fully in her own behalf and suffered prejudice in her ability to present her asylum application. In *Sosnovskaia v. Gonzalez*, 421 F.3d 589, 592 (7th Cir. 2005), a decision denying asylum was reversed where the Immigration Judge refused to allow any evidence of one claim and ignored other evidence presented.[72]

A removal hearing may be held by video or telephone conference in some instances under INA § 240(b)(2). Telephone and video conference hearings also present issues relating to the effectiveness of hearing procedures.[73] The Immigration Judge must evaluate the demeanor of a noncitizen to make a credibility determination, and this is difficult in a video or telephone conference hearing.

Noncitizens with limited English language ability will give testimony through a translator and the noncitizen may only have portions of the removal proceeding translated.[74] A full or simultaneous translation is not required by procedural due process.

b. Evidence

The formal rules of evidence do not apply in removal hearings. Hearsay is admissible but only if it is probative and no fundamental unfairness will result from its admission.[75] Unauthenticated documents also are admissible.[76] The leading case

---

[71] The Ninth Circuit in *Jacinto* compared the removal hearing to social security hearings where there is an unfamiliar setting for the applicant, especially pro se applicants, who may not possess the legal knowledge to fully appreciate which facts are relevant, lack of English language proficiency and the possibility of being removed to a situation where a noncitizen could face a threat to life, safety and well-being.

[72] 421 F.3d at 592 the procedure used by the Immigration Judge was an "affront to [the applicant's] right to be heard.").

[73] Rusu v. United States INS, 296 F.3d 316, 322–23 (4th Cir. 2002) (rejecting the due process challenge; although "asylum hearing was conducted in a haphazard manner, we conclude that Rusu suffered no prejudice as a result"). *See also* Kalin, *Troubled Communications: Cross-Cultural Misunderstandings in the Asylum Hearings*, 20 INT'L MIGRATION REV. 230 (1986).

[74] *See* Amadou v. INS, 226 F.3d 724, 726–28 (6th Cir. 2000) (an incomplete or incorrect translation of a noncitizen's testimony can deny a full and fair hearing and due process if prejudice results). *See also* El Rescate Legal Services, Inc. v. EOIR, 959 F.2d 742, 752 (9th Cir. 1991) (no denial of due process if translation is limited to the questions directed to non-English speaking persons); United States v. Leon-Leon, 35 F.3d 1428, 1431 (9th Cir. 1994) (no denial of due process from failure to translate crucial parts of a hearing).

[75] 8 C.F.R. § 240.7(a) (2014). *Compare* Bustos-Torres v. INS, 898 F.2d 1053 (5th Cir. 1990) (admission of hearsay because unimpeachable).

[76] Rosendo-Ramirez v. INS, 32 F.3d 1085, 1087–89 (7th Cir. 1994) (no denial of due process where a form was admitted into evidence even after the Immigration Judge stated it was "obviously, carelessly drafted").

on the admission of hearsay is *Ezeagwuna v. Ashcroft*, 325 F.3d 396, 405–408 (3d Cir. 2003).[77]

In *Ezeagwuna*, the admission of "multiple" hearsay violated due process. The Immigration Judge relied almost entirely on a letter from the Vice Consul of a U.S. Embassy summarizing the results of an investigation of five documents and concluding that each document was fraudulent. The Immigration Judge did not have the investigative report, any information about the investigator, or the details about the investigation. The letter contained multiple hearsay, e.g., a summary of statements by three declarants who had stated to the investigator that certain aspects of the documents appeared to be fraudulent. The Third Circuit was concerned about the government's attempt to "use the prestige of the State Department letterhead to make its case and give credibility to the letter's contents."[78]

A noncitizen is entitled to "a reasonable opportunity" to present evidence, and examine and cross-exam witnesses under INA § 240(b)(4)(B). An Immigration Judge's reliance on undisclosed national security information can be a denial of due process. In *Kiareldeen v. Reno*, 71 F. Supp. 2d 402 (D.N.J. 1999), an Immigration Judge violated procedural due process by relying on classified evidence presented by the government, *ex parte* and *in camera*, to establish that the noncitizen was a suspected member of a terrorist organization and to oppose his request for adjustment of status.[79] The government had introduced unclassified summaries of the information and the federal court found these to be insufficient. Confidential information can be used in some cases. This is discussed below in Section D.5. of this Chapter.

c. Burden of Proof and Standard of Proof

The burden of proof varies based on the nature of the charges and the status of the noncitizen in the removal proceeding. Since the 1996 IIRIRA amendments, removal hearings may address either inadmissibility under § 212(a) or deportability under INA § 237. The first issue in any removal proceeding, either for inadmissibility or deportability, is whether the respondent is a noncitizen. The DHS bears the burden of proof to establish that the respondent is a noncitizen and that the Immigration Judge has jurisdiction.[80] In most cases, alienage is easily established and the issue before the Immigration Judge is eligibility for relief from removal.

---

[77] *See also* Alexandrov v. Gonzales, 442 F. 3d 395, 404–07 (6th Cir. 2006) (denial of due process by relying on two highly unreliable hearsay memoranda from the U.S. Embassy in Sofia, Bulgaria to prove that the respondent's documents were fraudulent); Cunanan v. INS, 856 F.2d 1373, 1374–75 (9th Cir. 1988) reversing denial of voluntary departure because of the reliance on a hearsay declaration from the noncitizen's wife without providing the opportunity to cross-examine the wife.

[78] *Id.* at 407.

[79] 71 F. Supp. 2d at 413. The BIA procedures violated procedural due process, failing the constitutional requirement of Matthews v. Eldridge, 424 U.S. 319 (1976), because the private interest in physical liberty, the weighty national security interest of the government, and the risk of an erroneous decision due to the one-sided presentation of evidence was likely to result in erroneous deprivations.

[80] INA § 291. 8 C.F.R. § 1240.8(c) (2014) (the Service bears the burden to first establish alienage if a noncitizen charged with being in the U.S. without being admitted or paroled).

Relief from removal is covered in Chapter 11.

After alienage is established, the burden shifts to the noncitizen to prove by *"clear and convincing evidence"* that she is present in the U.S. based on a prior lawful admission.[81] The burden of proof is on the noncitizen to show the time, place, and manner of entry into the U.S.[82] If the noncitizen cannot establish a prior lawful admission, then she is deemed an applicant for admission. An applicant for admission in removal proceedings bears the burden of establishing she is *"clearly and beyond doubt"* entitled to be admitted and is not inadmissible under INA § 212.[83]

Noncitizens have a Fifth Amendment due process right to refuse to answer questions if the answers would incriminate them in a criminal proceeding.[84] Unlawful entry is a crime under INA § 275. Silence alone is insufficient evidence for the government to meet its evidentiary burden of establishing by clear and convincing evidence that the noncitizen is deportable.[85] However, adverse inferences can be drawn from silence when a noncitizen has failed to respond to evidence offered by the government. For example, if the government introduces evidence about alienage or the circumstances of entry into the U.S., then it is permissible to draw an inference from a noncitizen's silence.[86] Further, when a noncitizen chooses to remain silent or fails to establish the time, place and manner of entry into the U.S. for lawful presence, she will be found to be either present without admission, which is now an inadmissibility ground, INA § 212(a)(6)(A)(i), or otherwise inadmissible.[87]

If the noncitizen can establish a prior lawful admission, she is no longer in the position of an applicant for admission. Under INA § 240(c)(3)(A), the government then has the burden of establishing by clear and convincing evidence that the noncitizen is deportable under one of the grounds in INA § 237. This standard was incorporated in the 1996 amendments and codifies the Supreme Court's decision in

---

[81] INA § 240(c)(3)(A).

[82] *See also* INA § 291 (burden of proof is on the noncitizen in any application for any document required for entry or an application for admission and if she does not meet this burden, it is presumed the noncitizen is in the United States in violation of law).

[83] INA § 240(c)(2)(B).

[84] A noncitizen could refuse to testify about an unlawful entry into the U.S. since this is a criminal ground under INA § 275.

[85] *See* Matter of Guevara, 20 I.&N. Dec. 238 (BIA 1990, reconsideration denied 1991); Matter of Perez-Gonzales, A73 128 867 (BIA, Apr. 28, 2000) (unpublished decision) (silence alone does not establish "clear and convincing evidence" of deportability, however an Immigration Judge may draw negative inferences from the silence and, when combined with other evidence, could meet the government's burden of proof).

[86] *See, e.g.*, United States ex rel. Bilokumsky v. Tod, 263 U.S. 149, 153–54 (1923) (no rule prohibits immigration officers from drawing an inference from silence); INS v. Lopez-Mendoza, 468 U.S. 1032, 1044 (1984) (quoting/following *Bilokumsky*). *See* Daniel Kanstroom, *Hello Darkness: Involuntary Testimony and Silence in Deportation Proceedings*, 4 GEO. IMMIG. L.J. 599 (1990) (analyzing constitutional right against self-incrimination and the lack of Fifth Amendment protection in civil deportation proceedings).

[87] *See* LEGOMSKY & RODRIGUEZ, IMMIGRATION AND REFUGEE LAW AND POLICY, ch. 9 (6th ed. 2014).

Woodby v. INS with a minor modification.[88] The BIA has held that this standard is viewed as somewhere between "preponderance of the evidence" and "beyond a reasonable doubt."[89]

In *Woodby v. INS*, 385 U.S. 276 (1966), the Supreme Court required a high standard of proof for deportation once the noncitizen has established she has been lawfully admitted and is subject to INA removal provisions rather than the inadmissibility provisions. The Court held that the government must establish by *clear, unequivocal and convincing evidence* that the facts alleged by the government as the grounds for deportation are true. The rationale for this heightened standard of proof was the severe burden and "drastic deprivations that may follow" upon deportation. Several courts of appeal have relied upon the *Woodby* clear, unequivocal and convincing evidence standard in the review of deportation decisions.[90] Other federal courts have relied on the clear and convincing evidence standard in INA § 240(c)(3)(A).[91]

The Immigration Judge's decision must be based on "reasonable, substantial, and probative evidence" under INA § 240(b)(3)(A).[92] The Immigration Judge is required to interpret the removal grounds in favor of the noncitizen, and thus construe these narrowly. This is referred to as the rule of lenity. In *Leocal v. Ashcroft*, 543 U.S. 1 (2004), the Supreme Court applied this rule of lenity and the presumption in favor of the noncitizen because of the longstanding principle of interpreting statutes in favor of noncitizens.[93]

If the DHS establishes by clear and convincing evidence that a deportation ground applies to a noncitizen, then the burden of proof shifts to the noncitizen for relief from removal. The REAL ID Act of 2005 altered the burden of proof for applications for relief from removal filed as of May 11, 2005 by amending INA § 240(c). Under INA § 240(c)(4), the applicant for relief from removal has the burden to establish that she satisfies the applicable eligibility requirements; and that she merits a favorable exercise of discretion with respect to the relief requested. Therefore the noncitizen also must present an argument that discretion

---

[88] *See* LEGOMSKY & RODRIGUEZ, IMMIGRATION AND REFUGEE LAW AND POLICY, Ch. 9 (6th ed. 2014).

[89] Matter of Patel, 19 I.&N. Dec. 774, 783 (BIA 1988) (applying the "clear and convincing evidence" standard set out in INA § 204(a)(2) in the case of the remarriage of a noncitizen who had attained her LPR status by marriage, and noting: "[t]he clear and convincing standard imposes a lower burden than the clear, unequivocal, and convincing standard applied in deportation and denaturalization proceedings because it does not require that the evidence be unequivocal or of such a quality as to dispel all doubt.").

[90] Jaggernauth v. U.S. Atty. General, 432 F.3d 1346, 1352–56 (11th Cir. 2005); Hernandez-Guadarrama v. Ashcroft, 394 F.3d 674, 678–83 (9th Cir. 2005); Murphy v. INS, 54 F.3d 605 (9th Cir. 1995); Gameros-Hernandez v. INS, 883 F.2d 839 (9th Cir. 1995).

[91] Singh v. DHS, 517 F.3d 638, 643–46 (2d Cir. 2008); Bigler v. U.S. Att'y Gen., 451 F.3d 728, 732–33 (11th Cir. 2006).

[92] INA § 240(c)(3)(A). Woodby v. INS, 385 U.S. 276 (1966) (the government must establish by "clear, unequivocal and convincing evidence" that the facts alleged as grounds for deportation are true).

[93] Leocal v. Ashcroft, 543 U.S. 1 (2004) (in a deportation premised on an aggravated felony, the underlying crime of violence must include the element of intent rather than a simple showing of negligence). *See also* INS v. St. Cyr, 533 U.S. 289 (2001) (1996 repeal of discretionary relief from deportation did not apply retroactively); Fong Haw Tan v. Phelan, 333 U.S. 6 (1948) (doubts resolved in favor of the noncitizen).

should be exercised in her case. The REAL ID Act also permits an Immigration Judge to require corroborating evidence in some instances when making a credibility determination of an applicant for relief from removal.[94]

5. Administrative Review

The Board of Immigration Appeals (BIA or the Board) receives appeals of the final decisions of Immigration Judges in most removal cases; both the government and noncitizen respondent can appeal the Immigration Judge's removal decision.[95] An appeal must be received by the Board within 30 calendar days of the Immigration Judge's decision with the specific reasons for appeal, including the findings of fact and conclusions of law being challenged.[96]

The ongoing problem of a backlog in BIA decisions led the BIA, in 1999, to adopt a streamlining mechanism to reduce it.[97] In 2002, the Attorney General further revised the streamlined procedure. As discussed in Chapter 5, a key feature of these reforms is the authority of one BIA member to review an appeal, and review by a single member occurs in a majority of cases.[98] One Board member may decide cases involving procedural or ministerial matters. Appeals decided by one member are handled in one of three ways: a case may be summarily dismissed, summarily affirmed without opinion (AWO), or decided using an abbreviated decision affirming, modifying or remanding back to the Immigration Judge.

A case will be referred to a three-member panel for a decision when: (1) there are inconsistencies among decisions; (2) a need to establish a precedent ruling exists; (3) a decision by an Immigration Judge or the DHS was made in violation of law; (4) a matter involves a national impact; or (5) a clearly erroneous factual determination was made by an Immigration Judge.[99]

A summary dismissal of an appeal by a single board member can occur if: (1) the notice does not state the specific reasons for appeal; (2) the appellee states it will

---

[94] INA § 240(c)(4)(B).

[95] *See* 8 C.F.R. § 1003.3. 8 C.F.R. 1003.1(b)(3) bars BIA appellate jurisdiction from some removal decisions including: (1) where the sole ground is the length of time of voluntary departure; (2) where there is an *in absentia* order of removal entered under either INA § 240(b)(5)(C) or former INA § 242B(c).

[96] 8 C.F.R. § 1003.3(b). *See also* Board of Immigration Practice Appeals Manual at http://www.usdoj. gov/eoir/vll/qapracmanual/apptmtn4.htm. Presently it is unclear whether the 30 day time limit is jurisdictional (may not be waived) or mandatory (waiver possible). *See* Eberhart v. U.S., 546 U.S. 12 (2005) (some mandatory time limits are not jurisdictional and can be waived) and Bowles v. Russell, 551 U.S. 205 (2007) (filing deadlines for cases in lower federal courts are jurisdictional and, therefore, can not be waived). As of 2008, most courts of appeal have found that the 30 day time limit in 8 C.F.R. § 1003.38(b) is not jurisdictional and can be waived. *See* Liadov v. Mukasey, 518 F.3d 1003 (8th Cir. 2008); Khan v. DOJ, 494 F.3d 255 (2d Cir. 2007); Huerta v. Gonzales, 443 F.3d 753 (10th Cir. 2006). *But see* Magtanong v. Gonzales, 494 F.3d 1190 (9th Cir. 2007).

[97] Single member review was permissible upon a finding "that the result reached in the decision under review was correct; that any errors in the decision under review were harmless or nonmaterial." 64 Fed. Reg. 56,135 (Oct. 18, 1999).

[98] 67 Fed. Reg. 54,878 (Aug. 26, 2002).

[99] 8 C.F.R. § 1003.1(e)(6).

file a brief and fails to do so without notice to the BIA; (3) the relief requests on appeal has been granted already; (4) if a finding of fact or conclusion of law has already been conceded by the appellee; (5) the Board lacks jurisdiction; (6) the appeal was filed late; or (7) the right to appeal was waived at the conclusion of the removal hearing.[100]

Affirmance without an opinion by a single Board member is permissible if three criteria are met: (1) the Immigration Judge's decision is correct; (2) any errors in the decision below are harmless or immaterial; and (3) the issue is either controlled by existing precedent or the factual or legal questions do not merit review by a three member panel.[101] AWO is authorized when a full and complete record, including specific findings of fact by the Immigration Judge, is available.[102]

These summary AWO decisions have quickened the pace of BIA adjudication. Federal court challenges to these summary proceedings as a denial of procedural due process have been unsuccessful.[103] As discussed in Chapter 5, criticism about immigration adjudications in 2005 and 2006 referred to the affirmance without opinion procedures as an example of the inconsistency in adjudication.[104] The 2006 Department of Justice 22-point reform plan dealing with Immigration Judges and other EOIR reforms included reform of the affirmance without opinion procedure. The plan noted the need to reduce the number of cases subject to this form of review.

During the same time, the streamlined adjudications resulted in a significant increase in appeals to federal court, which rose from 10 to 25 percent and were often appeals of BIA affirmances without opinions. Federal judges also were concerned about the rise in the federal judicial caseloads as reflected in greater number of remands back to the BIA. The increased number of permanent BIA judges seems to have addressed some issues. In May 2011, the EOIR Director reported that the number of AWOs had declined to two percent of decisions, and that federal court reversals dropped from 17.5 percent in 2006 to 11.5 percent in 2010.[105] Despite these improvements, there are numerous reform proposals for the entire immigration adjudication system as discussed Chapter 5.

Decisions of an Immigration Judge prior to the removal determination also may be appealed including determinations on bonds and detention pending removal,

---

[100] 8 C.F.R. § 1003.1(d)(2).

[101] 8 C.F.R. § 1003.1(e)(4).

[102] *In re S-H-*, 23 I.&N. Dec. 462, 465 (BIA 2002). *See also* Gallegher, *Practice and Procedure Before the Board of Immigration Appeals*, 03-02 IMM. BRIEFINGS (Feb. 2003).

[103] Soadjede v. Ashcroft, 324 F. 3d 830, 831–32 (5th Cir. 2003); Gonzalez-Oropeza v. United States Attorney General, 321 F.3d 1331, 1333–34 (11th Cir. 2003); Albathani v. INS, 318 F.3d 365, 375–79 (1st Cir. 2003); Capital Area Immigrant's Rights Coalition v. U.S. Dept. of Justice, 264 F. Supp. 2d 14, 25–36 (D.D.C. 2003).

[104] *See, e.g., Overwhelmed Circuit Courts Lashing Out at the BIA and Selected Immigration Judges: Is Streamlining to Blame*, 48 INTER. REL. 2005 (2005) (in the period ending March 2003 petitions for review for immigration cases filed in federal courts had increased 379 percent); Spencer S. Hsu and Carrie Johnson, *Effort on Immigration Courts Faulted*, WASHINGTON POST, Sept. 8, 2008, at A6.

[105] *See* ALIENIKOFF, MARTIN, MOTOMURA & FULLERTON, IMMIGRATION AND CITIZENSHIP, PROCESS AND POLICY 1258 (7th ed. 2012).

except for those detained as inadmissible or subject to mandatory detention. Immigration Judge decisions about requests for relief from removal such as cancellation of removal, adjustment of status, and asylum may be appealed to the BIA.

6. Judicial Review

Judicial review of administrative agency action is the cornerstone of the modern administrative state. As a society we have come to trust and depend on the expertise that agencies gather to address complex problems, but we rely on the judicial system to ensure that due process is accorded to all whose lives are impacted by agency decisions and to ensure accountability to the public of these agencies. Federal agency action therefore is presumptively subject to judicial review, however Congress can limit judicial review in a specific category of cases.[106]

Before 1996 amendments by IIRIRA and AEDPA, the federal courts generally had the power to review BIA decisions. Federal circuit courts of appeal had jurisdiction to hear appeals of deportation decisions by the BIA. Appeals of exclusion (inadmissibility) decisions were heard by federal district courts.

The 1996 IIRIRA and AEDPA amendments and the more recent 2005 REAL ID Act changes to the INA have severely restricted judicial review. The 1996 amendments stripped federal courts of jurisdiction over many critical, life-changing decisions by both Immigration Judges and what is now USCIS. The impetus to deny judicial review reflects a distrustful view of federal courts particularly their immigration decisions. The competing views of the role of the judiciary has been described as "an ideological minefield" pitting those "who perceive the judiciary as an obstructive, anti-democratic institution that delays the removal of deportable noncitizens and displays undue sympathy toward undeserving violators of our laws" against others "who perceive the judiciary as a principled and dispassionate dispenser of justice and a bulwark against unlawful government action, particularly important when the litigants (noncitizens) are distinctively exposed to volatile and often hostile political sentiments."[107]

Under INA § 242 there is one avenue for judicial review of removal orders relating to deportability or inadmissibility which is by petition for review in the court of appeals where the immigration proceedings occurred.[108] A petition for review must be filed within 30 days of the date of the final order of removal.[109] A separate motion for a discretionary stay of removal must be filed with the circuit court.[110] Before 1996, an appeal resulted in an automatic stay of removal. If the noncitizen is removed from the United States prior to a judicial decision, the court

---

[106] ALIENIKOFF, MARTIN, MOTOMURA & FULLERTON, IMMIGRATION AND CITIZENSHIP, PROCESS AND POLICY 1271–2 (7th ed. 2012), citing Abbott Laboratories v. Gardner, 387 U.S. 136, 140–41 (1967), Lincoln v. Vigil, 508 U.S. 182 (1993).

[107] LEGOMSKY & RODRIGUEZ, IMMIGRATION AND REFUGEE LAW AND POLICY, CHAPTER 9 (6th ed. 2014).

[108] INA §§ 242(a)(1), 242(b).

[109] INA § 242(b).

[110] INA § 242(b)(3)(B).

retains jurisdiction. Before 1996, when a noncitizen left or was removed from the U.S. the jurisdiction of the court ceased.

INA § 242 governs judicial review of removal orders by Immigration Judges and the BIA. Other immigration agency action may occur entirely within DHS and the avenue for review of these decisions is under the Administrative Procedures Act.[111] For example, USCIS denial of a visa petition or an adjustment of status application after, appeal to the Administrative Appeals Office, would be challenged under the APA. Generally the review of agency action is in the form of a request for injunctive or declaratory relief in federal district court.[112] In some cases, both an Immigration Judge and USCIS may consider the same application e.g., adjustment of status applications under INA § 245. Some applications for immigration benefits that may be renewed de novo if a noncitizen is placed in removal proceedings, e.g., adjustment of status applications under INA § 245 and the avenue for judicial review would be through INA § 242 review of the final removal order.

See Chapter 6 for in-depth coverage of judicial review.

C. MOTIONS TO REOPEN OR RECONSIDER

Motions to reconsider and motions to reopen are permitted under INA §§ 240(c)(6) and (c)(7) and may be submitted to either the Immigration Judge or the BIA.[113] Most motions are filed directly with the BIA which usually has jurisdiction over a case after an appeal has been filed.[114] Motions to reopen to an *in absentia* order of removal are covered in INA § 240(b)(5)(c). *In absentia* orders of removal are discussed below in this Chapter.

Motions to reconsider a determination are based on errors in the underlying decisions, the availability of additional legal arguments, a change of law, or further development of an aspect of the case that was overlooked. Motions to reopen are based on new factual information and must be supported by this new evidence. The new evidence must be material and must have been unavailable and undiscoverable at the time of the original hearing.[115]

Generally, only one motion to reconsider and one motion to reopen may be filed by a noncitizen with several exceptions. Motions are governed by statutory deadlines and jurisdictional requirements, regulations prescribing the form and

---

[111] 5 U.S.C. § 702 provides that "[a] person suffering a legal wrong because of agency action, or adversely affected or aggrieved by agency action within the meaning of the relevant statute, is entitled to judicial review."

[112] *See* ALIENIKOFF, MARTIN, MOTOMURA & FULLERTON, IMMIGRATION AND CITIZENSHIP, PROCESS AND POLICY 1274 (7th ed. 2012).

[113] 8 C.F.R. § 1003.23 (2014). The Immigration Judge may retain jurisdiction over a matter or the BIA may receive jurisdiction as a result of the appeal. The BIA will consider motions to reopen, motions to reconsider, motions to remand, motions to stay removal, as well as other motions permitted by the rules or Board of Immigration Practice Appeals Manual, *available at* http://www.usdoj.gov/eoir/vll/qapracmanual/apptmtn4.htm.

[114] 8 C.F.R. §§ 1003.2, 1003.23(b)(1) (2014).

[115] 8 C.F.R. § 1003.2 (2014).

timing of motions, as well as the Board of Appeals Practice Manual.[116] The deadline for filing a motion to reconsider is 90 days from the date of entry of a final administrative order of removal.[117] This filing deadline does not apply to a motion to reopen to apply for asylum based on a material change of circumstances.[118] Filing deadlines also do not apply to battered spouses, children or parents.[119] An Immigration Judge's decision to grant or deny a motion to reopen or reconsider is discretionary.[120] Motions filed with the Immigration Judge will not stay the execution of the decision to remove unless a stay of execution of the removal order is granted.[121] The BIA, as well as Immigration Judges and District Directors of the DHS, have discretionary authority to stay removal pending a decision.

Motions to reopen claiming an ineffective assistance of counsel and a denial of Fifth Amendment due process must meet certain requirements. The 90 day filing deadline does not apply in some cases involving ineffective assistance of counsel claims. It is possible to file a motion to reopen for ineffective assistance of counsel after the filing deadline under an equitable tolling doctrine until a noncitizen learns of counsel's incompetence.[122]

If the noncitizen leaves the U.S. while a motion to reopen or a motion to reconsider is pending before the BIA or Immigration Judge, she is deemed to have withdrawn the motion.[123] The regulations also prohibit a noncitizen from filing a motion to reopen after leaving the United States while in removal proceedings.[124]

D. SPECIAL REMOVAL PROCEDURES

1. Criminal Cases

a. Prison Hearings

The removal of noncitizens convicted of crimes has been a major focus of Congress over the last two decades. In 1988, Congress amended the INA and established a removal procedure for noncitizen criminals who commit aggravated

---

[116] INA §§ 240(c)(6), (c)(7); 8 C.F.R. 1003.

[117] INA § 240(c)(7)(C)(i). A different filing deadline applies to motions to reopen *in absentia* orders of removal under INA § 240(b)(5)(c).

[118] INA § 240(c)(7)(C)(ii) imposes no time limit on a motion to reopen to apply for asylum if: (1) it is based on changed country conditions arising in the country of nationality or the country to which removal has been order; and (2) such evidence is material and was not available or "would not have been discovered or presented at the previous proceeding."

[119] INA § 240(c)(7)(C)(iv).

[120] 8 C.F.R. § 1003.23(b)(1)(ii) (2014).

[121] 8 C.F.R. § 1003.23(b)(1)(v) (2014). A stay can be granted by the Immigration Judge, BIA, or ICE.

[122] Iavorski v. INS, 232 F.3d 124 (2d Cir. 2000).

[123] 8 C.F.R. § 1003.2(d) (2014). *But see* William v. Gonzales, 499 F.3d 329 (4th Cir. 2007) (invalidating this regulation as conflicting with the statutory language that governs motions to reopen).

[124] 8 C.F.R. § 1003.23(b)(1) (2014). At least one court has held that the rule preventing a noncitizen from filing a new motion to reopen after leaving the U.S. only applies when a person leaves while still in removal proceedings. Lin v. Gonzales, 473 F.3d 979 (9th Cir. 2007).

felonies, which required deportation hearings for aggravated felons before they completed their criminal sentences.[125] The 1990 Immigration Act amendments expanded the definition of an aggravated felony and decreased the avenues of relief from deportation for noncitizen criminals.[126] The 1996 AEDPA and IIRIRA amendments expanded the prison hearing procedure to a longer, wide-ranging list of criminal removal grounds in INA § 237(a) including drug and firearm offenses, two crimes of moral turpitude (under certain circumstances), and other miscellaneous crimes.[127]

Removal hearings under INA § 238(a)(1) in prison occur when states send certified court records for noncitizens with state law convictions to DHS. The enhanced communication among local, state and federal agencies is coordinated by the Criminal Alien Tracking Center and the Law Enforcement Support Center. The DHS issues detainers using information from these agencies. Detainers are a request by DHS to local, state and federal prison officials to hold a noncitizen rather than release her from custody.[128]

Currently the special removal process for criminal noncitizens is designed to avoid any DHS detention after the completion of a prison sentence. Criminal convictions falling within INA § 238(a)(1), subject to the prison hearing process, include aggravated felonies, drug and firearm offenses, two crimes of moral turpitude committed within five years of entry, and the miscellaneous crimes under INA § 237(a)(2)(D).[129] These special prison removal hearings occur in federal, state and local correctional facilities. The hearings are initiated and completed, if possible, while the noncitizen is incarcerated. The right to counsel and access to counsel often is limited in prison removal hearings. The DHS is required to ensure that the right to counsel and access to counsel is not impaired during the process.[130]

Aggravated felony prison removal hearings are expedited proceedings conducted under INA § 238(a)(3). These aggravated felony prison hearings must be initiated and completed, to the extent possible, including any administrative appeals, before the aggravated felon's release from incarceration.[131] Aggravated felons in these special hearing procedures are subject to the conclusive presumption of deportability under INA § 238(c).

A noncitizen who is incarcerated may be eligible for early removal before the end of a criminal sentence in limited circumstances. This option is available under INA

---

[125] INA § 101(a)(43). The Omnibus Anti-Drug Abuse Act of 1988, Pub. L. No. 100-690, 102 Stat. 4181 (Nov. 18, 1988), identified certain crimes as aggravated felonies, added new removal grounds for persons convicted of aggravated felonies, and established a special deportation procedure using prison hearings.

[126] Pub. L. No. 101-649, 104 Stat. 4978 (Nov. 29, 1990).

[127] INA § 238(a)(1).

[128] 8 C.F.R. §§ 236.1, 287.7 (2014).

[129] INA § 238(a)(1) makes available special removal proceedings in federal, state and local correctional facilities for noncitizens convicted of any criminal offense covered in INA §§ 237(a)(2)(A)(iii), (B), (C) or (D), or any offense covered in INA § 237(a)(2)(A)(ii).

[130] INA § 238(a)(2).

[131] INA § 238(a)(3).

§ 241(a)(4)(B), and permits early removal if the noncitizen was convicted of a nonviolent offense.[132]

b. Administrative Removal

Administrative removal is available to remove aggravated felons who are not lawful permanent residents or who are not conditional permanent residents under INA § 216. Under INA § 238(b), these aggravated felons may be removed without a hearing before an Immigration Judge. The procedure must include reasonable notice to the noncitizen of the charges and an opportunity to inspect the evidence and rebut the charges.[133] The noncitizen may be represented by counsel. The INA further requires that the immigration official issuing the charges may not be the official who determines whether to issue a final order of removal.

In administrative removal proceedings there is a conclusive presumption of deportability under INA § 238(c). Noncitizens in administrative removal are not eligible for any discretionary relief.[134] A noncitizen subject to administrative removal may seek judicial review under INA § 242.[135] Review by the court of appeals is only available to consider constitutional questions and questions of law under INA § 242(a)(2)(D).

Federal courts have upheld the constitutionality of this administrative removal process finding that there is no violation of procedural due process. For example, *United States v. Benitez-Villafuerte*, 186 F.3d 651, 657 (5th Cir. 1999), *cert. denied* 528 U.S. 1097 (2000), involved a criminal prosecution for illegal reentry based on a prior administrative removal. The defendant claimed that the prior administrative removal violated procedural due process guarantees. The Fifth Circuit rejected the due process challenge and found that the administrative removal procedure provides a full and fair opportunity to be heard.

c. Stipulated Removal

Another form of administrative removal is authorized under INA § 240(d) and is referred to as stipulated removal. INA § 240(d) permits Immigration Judge to enter a removal order based on a noncitizen's stipulation that she has requested "voluntary removal" and waived her right to a removal hearing. The regulations state that the "stipulated determination shall constitute a conclusive determination of the alien's removability from the United States."[136] The rationale for this procedure is that it allows noncitizens to have their cases decided expeditiously and avoid prolonged detention pending removal. The EOIR has provided guidance and

---

[132] INA § 241(a)(4)(B). Early removal is available, and the Attorney General has discretion whether or not to grant a request. The INA specifically states there is no private right of action to compel early removal. *See* Peter H. Schuck, *Immigrant Criminals in Overcrowded Prisons: Rethinking an Anachronistic Policy*, 27 Geo. Immigration L.J. 597 (2013) (proposing bilateral prisoner transfer treaties and expanded early release so noncitizens can complete their prison sentences in their home countries).

[133] INA § 238(b)(4).

[134] INA § 238(b)(5); relief under the Convention Against Torture is available. *See* Ch. 11.

[135] The DHS must wait at least 14 days following the removal order to allow judicial review.

[136] 8 C.F.R. § 1003.25(b).

created a template for the form that is signed by the noncitizen to be used by ICE officers for noncitizens in detention.[137]

In practice, there are many criticisms of the procedure and whether noncitizens understand the impact of accepting a voluntary removal order. A 2011 Report, *Deportation Without Due Process*, found that more than 160,000 noncitizens have signed stipulated removal orders in the last decade, often unknowingly waiving their rights to a removal hearing and usually without legal representation.[138] Noncitizens in detention agree to these stipulated orders, often called "voluntary deportation," because ICE officers tell them that they will be released more quickly if they sign a stipulated order and they will remain in detention much longer during a removal hearing, although many of these individuals would be eligible for a bond.[139] The report found that some Immigration Judges have expressed concerns about whether the stipulated waivers of a removal hearing are voluntary, knowing and intelligent, and, as a result have been resistant to approving these removal orders.[140]

d. Judicial Removal

Federal courts have the power to enter an order of removal.[141] Judicial removal occurs when a U.S. District Court enters an order of removal at the time of sentencing in a federal criminal case. Under INA § 238(c)(1), a U.S. district court has jurisdiction to enter a judicial order of removal at the time of sentencing if the "order has been requested by the U.S. attorney with the concurrence of the [DHS] Commissioner." If the District Court denies the U.S. Attorney request for a judicial order of removal, the Attorney General may begin removal proceedings under INA § 240 based on the same ground of deportability or another ground of deportability.[142]

Under this judicial removal procedure, the U.S. Attorney must provide notice of the intent to seek judicial deportation and this must be served on DHS and the noncitizen criminal defendant. The U.S. District Court can decide whether to grant relief from removal after considering the DHS's recommendation and report about the noncitizen's eligibility for relief.[143] A person who is convicted of an aggravated felony is conclusively presumed to be deportable under INA § 238(c). The U.S.

---

[137] ALIENIKOFF, MARTIN, MOTOMURA & FULLERTON, IMMIGRATION AND CITIZENSHIP, PROCESS AND POLICY 1210 (7th ed. 2012).

[138] J. Koh, J. Srikantiah, & T. Tumlin, *Deportation Without Due Process* (National Immigrant Law Center 2011).

[139] National Immigrant Justice Center, *Human Rights Report Exposes ICE's Deceptive Deportation Practices* (Sept. 2011) *available at* http://www.immigrantjustice.org/press_releases/human-rights-report-exposes-ices-deceptive-deportation-practices.

[140] *See also* ALIENIKOFF, MARTIN, MOTOMURA & FULLERTON, IMMIGRATION AND CITIZENSHIP, PROCESS AND POLICY 1210 (7th ed. 2012).

[141] INA §§ 238(c)(2), (c)(5). A stipulated judicial order of removal under INA § 238(c)(5) permits the U.S. Attorney's may enter a plea agreement, if DHS agrees, and the noncitizen waives the right to notice and hearing on the issue of deportability and relief from removal.

[142] INA § 238(c)(4).

[143] INA § 238(c)(2)(C).

District Court has final authority whether to grant or deny relief. Both the noncitizen defendant and the government may appeal the decision of the District Court to the Court of Appeals.

2. In Absentia Removal

The 1990 amendments to the INA included the possibility of *in absentia* orders of removal to address the problem of noncitizens failing to appear at their hearings.[144] If a noncitizen does not attend any hearing date during a removal proceeding, the INA permits an order of removal to be entered *in absentia* under INA § 240(b)(5). *In absentia* orders of removal are permissible only if the noncitizen has received proper written notice of the hearing date and any subsequent change in the date and/or time of a hearing.[145]

An *in absentia* order of removal can be rescinded only through a motion to reopen before an Immigration Judge.[146] The motion to rescind the removal order must establish either a lack of proper notice of the hearing, exceptional circumstances caused the failure to appear, or the noncitizen was in state or federal custody.[147] A motion based on failure to appear due to exceptional circumstances must be filed within 180 days after the date of the order. In the case where a noncitizen claims a lack of proper notice, a motion to reopen can be filed at any time.[148]

A lack of proper notice is established if there is a failure to provide notice and there is a failure to receive notice by the noncitizen. Recall that an NTA contains a notice of the obligation to immediately provide an address to the Immigration Court. Prior to April 1, 1997, the effective date of the IIRIRA amendments, the *in absentia* removal hearing process required notice by certified mail.[149] In this circumstance, a noncitizen could claim she had not received notice using the evidence provided by the certified mail process. Today, the noncitizen may not have evidence of the failure to receive notice because certified mail is not required.[150] In an *absentia* hearings, the government must prove by clear, unequivocal, and

---

[144] In FY 2002 approximately 25 percent of Immigration Judge decisions involved noncitizens who failed to appear and for whom an *in absentia* order of removal was entered. In FY 2005 and FY 2006 *in absentia* orders of removal were 39 percent of the total Immigration Judge decisions. In FY 2007, the nonappearance rate fell to 17 percent and in FY 2010 it was 12 percent. The lower number of these orders can be attributed to the expanded use of detention. *See* ALIENIKOFF, MARTIN, MOTOMURA & FULLERTON, IMMIGRATION AND CITIZENSHIP, PROCESS AND POLICY 1197 (7th ed. 2012). (citing EOIR, Department of Justice, FY 2006 Statistical Yearbook at H1-H2).

[145] INA §§ 239(a)(1), (a)(2). Personal service of any hearing notice is required if practicable, including changes of hearing dates and times. Service by mail on the noncitizen or his or her attorney is also sufficient if sent to the address provided by the noncitizen when the NTA was initially issued.

[146] INA § 240(c)(7)(C)(iii).

[147] INA § 240 (b)(5)(c).

[148] Under INA § 240(b)(5)(C), a motion to reopen also can be filed at any time if the noncitizen was in state or federal custody and the failure to appear was not the noncitizen's fault.

[149] Former INA § 242B added to the INA by the Immigration Act of 1990, Pub. L. No. 101-649, 104 Stat. 4978 (Nov. 29, 1990).

[150] See Lopes v. Mukasey, 517 F.3d 156 (2d Cir. 2008) (holding that the change in mailing procedures lessens the strength of the presumption of receipt).

convincing evidence that the required hearing notice was provided, or couldn't be provided because the noncitizen had not notified DHS of an address or telephone change, and that the person is deportable.[151]

A motion to reopen claiming exceptional circumstances must satisfy the statutory definition in INA § 240(e). Exceptional circumstances are beyond the control of the noncitizen such as battery or extreme cruelty to the noncitizen or the serious illness or death of a spouse, parent or child of the noncitizen. The INA further states that less compelling circumstances are not considered exceptional.[152] Exceptional circumstances can include ineffective assistance of counsel.[153] The Immigration Judge will evaluate the totality of the circumstances to decide whether exceptional circumstances exist.[154]

Equitable tolling of the 180 day statute of limitations for filing motion to reopen is possible under INA § 240(c)(7)(C)(iii) based on a claim of ineffective assistance of counsel. The rationale for equitable tolling is the view that the 180 day deadline is a statute of limitations rather than a jurisdictional requirement. In *Anin v. Reno*, 188 F.3d 1273 (11th Cir. 1999), the Court of Appeals rejected an ineffective assistance of counsel claim as an exceptional circumstance because the motion to reopen was filed after the 180 day deadline. The *Anin* court held that the deadline is mandatory and jurisdictional. Other circuits courts of appeal have found the 180 day deadline is subject to equitable tolling when there is an ineffective assistance of counsel challenge to an *in absentia* order of removal.[155] The Supreme Court's decision in *Bowles v. Russell*, 127 S. Ct. 2360 (2007) also adds to the confusion. In *Bowles*, the Supreme Court held that time limits for appealing judgments in civil cases to federal courts of appeal are jurisdictional and no equitable exceptions are permitted.

There is no appeal to the BIA of an *in absentia* order of removal.[156] The only vehicle for review is a motion to reopen. The denial of a motion to reopen an *in*

---

[151] INA § 240(b)(5)(A, B).

[152] Morales v. INS, 116 F.3d 145 (5th Cir. 1997) (exceptional circumstances did not exist when a noncitizen failed to appear because his car engine broke on the 60 mile drive to the hearing although the noncitizen began the drive one and one-half hours before the hearing, got a ride back home after leaving the car because he could not afford to repair it, and attempted to call the immigration court but could not find a telephone number in the phone book nor on the hearing notice).

[153] Matter of Grijalva, 21 I.&N. Dec. 472 (BIA 1996) (ineffective assistance of counsel established when noncitizen told by counsel not to attend proceeding, noncitizen filed complaint with state Bar, and noncitizen's claims corroborated by former counsel's affidavit).

[154] Herbert v. Ashcroft, 325 F.3d 68 (1st Cir. 2003) (totality of circumstances indicate exceptional circumstances when counsel filed emergency continuance request, noncitizen's relative arrived in court on time, and noncitizen's 30 minute delay resulted from a combination of ill child, bad weather, heavy traffic, and long line at courthouse security checkpoint).

[155] *See* Aris v. Mukasey, 517 F.3d 595 (2d Cir. 2008) (paralegal misinformed noncitizen about whether a hearing was scheduled, and, after he was deported *in absentia*, law firm failed to inform him of deportation); Pervaiz v. Gonzales, 405 F.3d 488 (7th Cir. 2005); Borges v. Gonzales, 402 F.3d 398 (3d Cir. 2005). In Saakian v. INS, 252 F.3d 21 (1st Cir. 2001), the First Circuit held that a noncitizen was denied procedural due process when his appeal from denial of motion to reopen *in absentia* deportation order based on ineffective assistance of counsel was not heard on the merits.

[156] INA § 240(b)(7).

absentia removal order can be appealed to the BIA. A BIA decision to grant or deny a motion to reopen or reconsider is discretionary. It is not an abuse of discretion to deny a motion even if the movant established a prima facie case for relief.[157] Judicial review of an *in absentia* removal order is limited to specific claims.[158] A motion to reopen to rescind an *in absentia* removal order based on exceptional circumstances or failure to obtain notice will result in an automatic stay of deportation.[159]

There are severe consequences stemming from an *in absentia* order of removal. A noncitizen against whom an *in absentia* removal order has been entered is ineligible for discretionary relief for 10 years.[160] This includes voluntary departure, cancellation of removal, adjustment of status, change of nonimmigrant classification, and registry. The noncitizen also is inadmissible for 10 years as a person previously removed.[161]

3. Reinstatement of Removal

A summary removal procedure is used for noncitizens who reenter the U.S. unlawfully after a removal order.[162] The summary procedure, under INA § 241(a)(5), applies to those who have been physically removed or have voluntarily departed under an order of removal.[163]

The summary removal procedure based on reinstatement of a prior removal order was established by the 1996 IIRIRA amendments. The summary removal process reinstates the prior removal order from its original date and expedites the removal of the noncitizen who has reentered the U.S. This reinstatement of the prior removal order is performed solely by a DHS officer. The regulations for reinstatement of a prior removal order require that the DHS officer determines: (1) the noncitizen is the person ordered removed using a fingerprint check if needed; (2) there was a final removal order; and (3) the noncitizen reentered the U.S. unlawfully.[164] DHS must give the noncitizen a written statement of the determination and give the noncitizen an opportunity to challenge the determination.

---

[157] Anin v. Reno, 188 F.3d 1273 (11th Cir. 1999) (relying on 8 C.F.R. § 3.2(a)(1999)).

[158] INA §§ 240(b)(5)(D), 242(b)(5). Judicial review of the order can address nationality claims, and the underlying elements of the *in absentia* order including validity of the notice, the reasons for not attending the hearing, and whether or not the noncitizen is removable.

[159] INA § 240(b)(5)(C).

[160] INA § 240(b)(7).

[161] INA § 212(a)(9)(A)(ii)(I). This applies to all removals.

[162] INA § 241(a)(5) requires that the noncitizen has "reentered illegally" after removal, however reinstatement has been applied in a case where a noncitizen was removed and reentered at a port of entry where her inadmissibility was not identified by the CPB immigration inspector. Cordova-Soto v. Holder, 659 F.3d 1029 (10th Cir. 2011) (although the noncitizen entered with an inspection, the entry was deemed an illegal reentry for purposes of reinstatement of removal).

[163] INA § 241(a)(5) applies to those who were removed and reentered unlawfully before 1997 when the 1996 amendment became effective. Fernandez-Vargas v. Gonzales, 548 U.S. 30 (2006).

[164] 8 C.F.R. § 241.8 (2014).

There is no right to a hearing before an Immigration Judge and no right to counsel. The noncitizen is not eligible for any relief from deportation, including adjustment of status. Further, the noncitizen may not file any motion to reopen or review the prior removal order. Only very limited relief from removal is available to the noncitizen subject to reinstatement.[165]

Judicial review of the summary removal based on reinstatement of a prior removal order is available in the Circuit Court of Appeal under the REAL ID Act amendments to the INA.[166] The REAL ID amendments added INA § 242(a)(2)(D) to permit judicial review of legal and constitutional challenges.[167]

Federal courts have upheld this summary removal procedure despite due process concerns about the underlying removal order.[168] In *Morales-Izquierdo v. Gonzales*, 486 F.3d 484 (9th Cir. 2007) (*en banc*), the Court of Appeals upheld the reinstatement of an *in absentia* order of removal.[169] The case involved a Mexican who was deported and reentered without inspection, who married a U.S. citizen, and had a reinstatement of the prior removal order when he and his wife attended the final interview for his LPR status. The immigrant visa petition was denied and he was issued a notice of intent to reinstate the prior removal order. The Ninth Circuit confirmed that the regulation permitting reinstatement by an immigration officer, rather than an Immigration Judge, followed the intent of Congress to establish a summary procedure. Further, the Ninth Circuit determined that this decision by an immigration officer satisfies Fifth Amendment procedural due process.[170] The court was satisfied with the procedural safeguards against an incorrect decision in reinstatement cases including the use of fingerprints and obtaining the prior order. Reinstatement does not violate due process, even in the case where the process afforded in the underlying removal order is challenged, because reinstatement does not change a noncitizen's rights or remedies. As a result, the only effect of the reinstatement order is to cause removal rather than any civil or criminal penalties or any additional obstacles to attacking the removal order.

The Supreme Court also has upheld the retroactive application of INA § 241(a)(5) to noncitizens who reentered the U.S. before the effective date of this

---

[165] 8 C.F.R. §§ 208.31, 241.8(d) (2014) (withholding of removal, claims under the Convention Against Torture and HRIFA or NACARA benefits).

[166] INA § 242(a)(2)(D).

[167] INA § 241(a)(5) states reinstatement of the prior removal order is not subject to being reopened or reviewed.

[168] *See also* U.S. v. Arias-Ordonez, 597 F.3d 972 (9th Cir. 2010); U.S. v. Rodriguez-Ocampo, 664 F.3d 1275 (9th Cir. 2011).

[169] The noncitizen challenged the DHS regulation permitting an immigration officer, rather than an Immigration Judge, to reinstate the order of removal as contrary to the statutory requirements for removal hearings under INA § 240. He argued that the INS explicitly exempts certain proceedings from this hearing requirement, such as expedited removal under INA § 235(b).

[170] The Ninth Circuit found that the regulation was a valid interpretation of the INA by applying both prongs of the test articulated in Chevron USA Inc. v. Natural Res. Def. Council, Inc., 467 U.S. 837 (1984): (1) the regulation follows the intent of Congress to establish a summary proceeding; and (2) the DHS interpretation is a permissible construction.

IIRIRA amendment (April 1, 2007).[171] Applications for relief filed after April 1, 1997, the effective date of INA § 241(a)(5) also are barred. A noncitizen who reenters before IIRIRA but applies for relief after IIRIRA is subject to the ban on relief included in the reinstatement provision. This can occur if a noncitizen reentered and is apprehended after April 1, 1997 and applies for relief.

According to ICE removal statistics, reinstatements of prior removal orders account for large percentages of total removals.[172] In FY 2013, 39 percent of all ICE removals were reinstatements of prior removal orders.[173] Among those removed with one or two misdemeanor convictions (Level III), 60 percent of these noncitizens were removed based on reinstatement or *in absentia* removal orders.[174] ICE categorizes its interior enforcement efforts according to different levels of criminal removal grounds under INA § 237.[175]

4. Crew Members

Crewmembers are subject to a summary removal procedure under INA § 252(b). Crewmembers are noncitizens serving in good faith on board a vessel in a capacity required for normal operation and service of the vessel.[176] Crewmembers are permitted to "land temporarily" in the U.S. using a 29 day conditional landing permit under INA § 252(a), if the crewmember is admissible.[177]

Noncitizens who are not bona fide crewmembers or who do not intend to depart may have their conditional permit to land in the U.S. revoked by an immigration officer. If a conditional landing permit is revoked, then the crewman will be detained on board the vessel or aircraft and will be removed from the U.S. at the expense of the transportation line. This summary removal procedure applied to crewmembers is separate from the removal procedures under INA § 240.[178]

---

[171] *See* Fernandez-Vargas v. Gonzales, 548 U.S. 30 (2006). This case applied reinstatement to a noncitizen who initially came to the U.S. in the 1970s, had been deported for immigration violations and made his last unlawful reentry in 1982. He had been in the U.S., on and off, for over 30 years and his last unlawful reentry occurred nearly 20 years before his adjustment of status application was filed based on an immediate relative petition after a marriage to a U.S. citizen in 2001. This case resolved a split in the circuits on this issue of retroactive application prior to the effective date of the IIRIRA amendments.

[172] *See also* Jennifer Stepp Breen & Stephen Yale-Loehr, *Reinstatement of Removal: New Developments in a Growing Form of Removal*, 19 BIB 396, 396–97 (Apr. 15, 2014).

[173] DHS, *Office of Immigration Statistics, Annual Report of 2013 Immigration Enforcement Actions* (Sept. 2014) *available at* http://www.dhs.gov/publication/immigration-enforcement-actions-2013.

[174] ICE ERO Annual Report, *FY 2013 ICE immigration Removals available at* http://www.ice.gov/removal-statistics.

[175] Level 1 offenders are noncitizens convicted of aggravated felonies, or two or more crimes punishable by more than one year. Level II offenders are noncitizens convicted of other felonies or three or more misdemeanor crimes punishable by less than one year. Level III offenders are those convicted of one or two misdemeanor crimes. ICE ERO Annual Report, *FY 2013 ICE immigration Removals available at* http://www.ice.gov/removal-statistics.

[176] INA § 101(a)(15)(D).

[177] Parole of the crew member into the U.S. under INA § 212(d)(5) is also possible.

[178] INA § 252(b) ("nothing in this section [252] shall be construed to require the procedures prescribed in section 240 [8 U.S.C.A. § 1229a] to cases falling within the provisions of this subsection").

5. National Security

Suspected terrorists are subject to a summary removal procedure under INA § 501 or under INA § 235(c). These terrorist removal procedures operate independently from the removal procedure under INA § 240.

Suspected terrorists and noncitizens who threaten foreign policy or national security are subject to a distinct form of expedited removal under INA § 235(c).[179] If an immigration officer or an Immigration Judge suspects that an arriving noncitizen is inadmissible under terrorist or national security grounds, then a removal order will be issued and the immigration officer or Immigration Judge may "not conduct any further inquiry or hearing until ordered by the Attorney General."[180] The Attorney General is required to review these removal orders and is authorized to remove the noncitizen without further inquiry or hearing.[181] The Attorney General may rely on confidential information and consultation with "appropriate security agencies of the United States Government" to determine whether a terrorist or national security ground of inadmissibility applies. If the Attorney General does not order removal, then the A.G. must specify the type of further inquiry or hearing to be conducted.

The second type of summary removal was established by the 1996 Anti-Terrorism and Effective Death Penalty Act (AEDPA). It established the Special Terrorist Removal Court under INA § 501.[182] This only applies to noncitizens "certified" as terrorists and provides another option to the DHS in its use of classified information about a noncitizen.[183] Suspected terrorists are those who are removable under INA § 237(a)(4)(B).[184] The Chief Justice of the Supreme Court must publicly designate five district court judges to serve on the terrorist court to conduct these removal proceedings.[185] Proceedings are initiated by the Attorney General who files an application with the terrorist court.[186]

---

[179] INA § 235(c) applies to those inadmissible under security grounds (espionage, sabotage, unlawful overthrow of the government), terrorist grounds, and foreign policy grounds under INA §§ 212(a)(3)(A) (other than clause (ii)), (B) or (C).

[180] INA § 235(c)(1)(C).

[181] A noncitizen may request consideration of a claim based on the Convention Against Torture under 8 C.F.R. § 208.18(d).

[182] Pub. L. No. 104-132, 110 Stat. 1214 (Apr. 24, 1996); Suspected terrorists are defined in INA § 237(a)(4)(B).

[183] DHS officers can rely on classified information in expedited removal based on natural security grounds of INA § 212(a)(3) or to oppose discretionary relief in ordinary INA § 240 removal proceedings. *See* above discussion of Kiareldeen v. Reno, 71 F. Supp. 2d 402 (D.N.J. 1999).

[184] INA 237(a)(4)(B) is the deportation ground and refers only to noncitizens described in INA §§ 212(a)(3)(B) (terrorist activities) or (3)(F) (association with terrorist organizations).

[185] INA § 502(a). The same five judges may also be designated by the Chief Justice to serve under the Foreign Intelligence Surveillance Act (50 U.S.C. § 1803(a)).

[186] INA § 503(a)(1)(D). The application must include a statement of facts and circumstances with probable cause that the noncitizen is a terrorist, that the noncitizen is physically present in the U.S. and that the standard removal procedures would pose a risk to national security. The judge's decision to grant the application can include *ex parte*, *in camera* review of classified information system.

The Special Terrorist Removal Court statute provides some enhanced noncitizen procedural protections designed to counterbalance the summary process. Removal hearings by the terrorist removal court must be conducted in open court as expeditiously as practicable.[187] A noncitizen has a right to be present and to be represented by counsel at the hearing. A noncitizen who is financially unable to obtain counsel is entitled to have counsel assigned. Nevertheless, the process limits the noncitizen's procedural protections. The Federal Rules of Evidence do not apply. There is no right to review any classified evidence presented or a right to suppress information, even if it is unlawfully obtained.[188] The government's burden of proof for deportation is reduced to a preponderance of the evidence rather than the burden of clear and convincing evidence standard in ordinary removal proceedings under INA § 240.[189]

Special procedures apply when an lawful permanent resident has a case in the terrorist removal court under INA § 504(e)(3)(F). A special attorney will be assigned to assist the permanent resident and this special attorney may review classified information on behalf of the noncitizen and challenge the veracity of the evidence contained in the classified information. It is a criminal offense for the special attorney receiving classified information to disclose any information to the noncitizen or any other attorney representing the noncitizen.[190] Appeal of the decision of the terrorist removal court is available under an expedited procedure. The noncitizen must file a notice of appeal within 20 days and the D.C. Court of Appeals must render a decision within 60 days.[191]

To date, the Special Terrorist Removal Court has never been convened.

E. DETENTION

Detention related to removal proceedings can occur during the removal hearing process, after a final removal order has been entered, and, when physical removal is unlikely although a final order of removal has been issued. Each of these types of detention is addressed below.

Detention is authorized for arriving noncitizens who have never entered as well as long-term LPRs in certain circumstances. Generally, indefinite detention is not authorized. Long-term detention has come under much greater judicial scrutiny in recent years as discussed below.

DHS relies on detention to ensure noncitizens appear at hearings, because nonappearance has been an ongoing concern, and to ensure physical removal upon the conclusion of proceedings. There are tremendous costs of detention to noncitizen including impaired access to counsel, and the potential economic and other

---

[187] INA § 504(a).

[188] INA §§ 504(e)(3)(A), (e)(1)(B). The government can introduce as evidence "the fruits of electronic surveillance and unconsented physical searches authorized under the Foreign Intelligence Surveillance Act."

[189] INA § 504(g).

[190] INA § 504(e)(1)(F).

[191] INA §§ 505(a)(1), (c)(4)(B).

hardships for the detainee's family members.[192] In addition there is the expense of detention which is increasing as more noncitizens are placed in detention.[193] There are numerous criticisms about the nature of immigration detention.[194] Detention facility operations are similar to a prison setting and frequently are located in remote areas. There are national detention standards for ICE-operated facilities and contractor detention facilities. Numerous reports both from the government and non-governmental organizations have documented the failures of the current detention system.[195] This is covered in detail in Chapters 5 and 14.

1. Pending Removal

Many provisions of the INA require or permit the detention of noncitizens. The INA treats noncitizens differently if they are arriving to request admission into the U.S., or if they are apprehended while already present in the U.S. Some are subject to detention but remain eligible for bond and release. Others are subject to mandatory detention and are ineligible for an individualized bond determination. Both types of detention are discussed below.

Detention can occur when a noncitizen applies admission into the U.S. at the border under INA § 235. Under INA § 235(b)(2), the inspection process for arriving noncitizens in the U.S. requires a determination by the DHS officer whether a noncitizen is "clearly and beyond a doubt entitled to be admitted." An arriving noncitizen who is not clearly and beyond doubt entitled to admission "shall be detained" for a removal hearing under INA § 240.[196] Despite the restrictive language of this INA provision, immigration officers do regularly grant release on parole under INA §212(d)(5). Release on parole of arriving noncitizens is permitted in the case of: (1) serious medical conditions; (2) pregnant women; (3) certain juveniles; (4) witnesses in government proceedings in the U.S.; and (5) if continued detention in not in the public interest.[197] These decisions are made by ICE officers and Immigration Judges do not have jurisdiction to review bond decisions of arriving noncitizens, including arriving LPRs.[198] Arriving noncitizens in expedited removal under INA § 235(b)(1), such as a credible fear determination, are subject to mandatory detention pending removal.

---

[192] Stephen H. Legomsky, *The Detention of Aliens: Theories, Rules, and Discretion*, 30 Univ. Miami Inter-American L. Rev. 531 (1999).

[193] The costs, statistics and current concerns about detention covered in Chapter 5.

[194] *House Judiciary Subcommittee Take Testimony of Medical Provided to ICE Detainees*, 85 Inter. Rel. 1737 (June 16, 2008); 85 Inter. Rel. 1477 (May 19, 2008).

[195] Detention Operations Manual, *available at* https://www.ice.gov/detention-standards/2000.

[196] INA § 235(b)(2)(A). Under INA § 235(b)(2)(C), Mexicans and Canadians requesting admission may be returned to Mexico or Canada pending removal proceedings under INA § 240.

[197] INA § 236. 8 C.F.R. § 212.5 permits release on parole of arriving noncitizens in the case of: (1) serious medical conditions; (2) pregnant women; (3) certain juveniles; (4) witnesses in government proceedings in the U.S.; and (5) if continued detention in not in the public interest.

[198] 8 C.F.R. §§ 236.1(c)(11), 1003.19(h)(2)(i)(B).

Detention can also occur upon apprehension inside the United States.[199] The detention requirements for these noncitizens are covered in INA § 236. If a noncitizen is arrested, the decision whether to issue an NTA to begin removal proceedings must be made within 48 hours of the arrest.[200] ICE officers' initial decisions whether to detain, release on recognizance, or release after payment of a bond must be made within 48 hours.

Noncitizens who are *not arriving*, under INA § 236, may be released on bond. Release decisions are based on whether the noncitizen poses a flight risk or a danger to the community. The noncitizen has the burden to show release on bond is warranted. Release on bond is a discretionary decision and there is no constitutional right to release on bond. Appeal of the DHS District Director's bond decision to an Immigration Judge and the BIA is available.[201] A noncitizen must establish that she does not present a danger to persons or property, is not a threat to national security and does not pose a risk of flight under INA § 236(a).[202] In addition, a bond determination will include evidence of the noncitizen's employment history, length of residence in the community, family ties, record of appearance or nonappearance at immigration court proceedings, and previous criminal or immigration law violations.[203]

Some noncitizens are ineligible for bond and release and are subject to mandatory detention pending removal under INA § 236(c). Mandatory detention during removal proceedings under INA § 236(c) applies to noncitizens who are inadmissible or deportable for a wide range of criminal offenses and terrorist activities and these noncitizens are ineligible for bond.[204] Mandatory detention applies to noncitizens if they are deportable under INA § 237(a)(2)(A) because: (1) they have committed two crimes of moral turpitude after admission; (2) are aggravated felons; (3) have committed drug crimes, firearms offenses, or miscellaneous crimes; (4) have committed a crime involving moral turpitude for which the sentence is at least one year; or (5) are deportable on terrorist grounds.

Mandatory detention also is required for any individual who is inadmissible under INA § 212(a)(2). Mandatory detention, therefore, is imposed on a large number of individuals who are in removal proceedings for being inadmissible because INA § 212(a)(2) includes any person who has been convicted of a CIMT as well as a many other crimes. Finally, the 1996 amendments also imposed mandatory detention on persons in expedited removal who are applying for asylum

---

[199] INA § 287(a) (providing authority to interrogate and arrest any person believed to be an alien).

[200] 8 C.F.R. § 287(3)(d). If a criminal arrest warrant is issued, it too must be issued within the 48 hours of the arrest of a noncitizen.

[201] 8 C.F.R. §§ 236.1(d)(3), 1003.19(i).

[202] *See* Matter of Patel, 15 I.&N. Dec. 666 (BIA 1976) (factors in bond determinations include local family ties, prior arrests, convictions, appearances at hearings, employment or lack of employment, membership in community organizations, manner of entry and length of time in the U.S., and financial ability to post bond).

[203] *See* Matter of Aguilar-Aquino, 24 I.&N. Dec. 747 (BIA 2009).

[204] INA §§ 236(c); 235(b)(1)(A); 235(b)(2); 235(b)(1)(B)(ii) (after a credible fear determination in expedited removal).

but who have not established that they have a credible fear of persecution.[205] There are very limited grounds for release from custody under INA § 236(c)(2).[206] Release from detention is only permitted for witness protection or cooperation, and only if there is no national security risk or risk of flight. This statutory mandate has been upheld by the Supreme Court.[207]

In *Demore v. Kim*, 538 U.S. 510 (2003) the Supreme Court rejected a due process challenge and upheld the constitutionality of INA § 236(c). In *Demore*, an LPR had conceded deportability as an aggravated felon and did not request a hearing to challenge whether he was properly subject to INA § 236(c) mandatory detention. The constitutional issue was the lack of an individualized determination of whether Kim posed a flight risk and thus should be detained. The plurality relied on the nature of detention pending removal which usually is a relatively short period of time. Justice Kennedy's concurring opinion, creating the fifth vote, stated an LPR in mandatory detention could be entitled to an individualized hearing as to his risk of flight and dangerousness if the continued detention became unreasonable or unjustified.

Recent judicial decisions have limited the government's authority to continue mandatory detention in cases where mentally incompetent individuals are detained. In *Franco-Gonzales v. Holder*, 2011 U.S. Dist. LEXIS 139148 (C.D. Cal. 2011), an injunction against continued mandatory detention was issued for one petitioner in a class action lawsuit on behalf of several immigration detainees with mental-health issues. The petitioner, an LPR in removal proceedings on an aggravated felony charge, was diagnosed with a schizoaffective disorder and was receiving mental-health care and medication, and had been detained for almost one year. The court enjoined his further detention under either INA § 236(a) or (c) unless he was provided a bond hearing at which he could request conditional, supervised release.[208]

There is extensive recent litigation to determine when ICE may begin mandatory detention. INA § 236(c)(1) provides that ICE "shall take into custody" any noncitizen who has committed a qualifying offense "when the alien is released." Those in ICE custody under this section may not seek judicial review of detention decisions.

---

[205] INA § 236(c). Noncitizens subject to expedited removal under INA § 235(b) are also subject to mandatory detention.

[206] INA § 236(c)(2) permits release to assist in a major crime investigation, if release does not pose any risk to the safety of other persons or property, and if the noncitizen is likely to appear at any scheduled proceeding.

[207] Demore v. Kim, 538 U.S. 510 (2003) (upholding mandatory detention pending removal proceedings under INA § 236(c) of a lawful permanent resident who had conceded deportability based on a criminal conviction).

[208] *See also*, Franco-Gonzales v. Holder, 767 F. Supp. 2d 1034 (C.D. Cal. 2010) (class action lawsuit challenging the detention of mentally incompetent noncitizens and a preliminary injunction granted to two named plaintiffs barring continued detention unless the noncitizens were represented by a "qualified representative" (although not necessarily legal counsel) as required by § 504 of the Rehabilitation Act which requires reasonable accommodation to the disabled). *See* Bill Ong Hing, *Systemic Failure: Mental Illness, Detention, and Deportation*, 16 U.C. Davis J. Internat'l L. & Policy 341 (2010).

For example, in *Diomedes Martinez-Done v. Diane McConnell*, Asst Field Director, ICE, 14 Civ. 3071 (S.D.N.Y. Oct. 8, 2014), an LPR's request for a bond hearing was granted although he was subject to mandatory detention under INA § 236(c). Martinez-Done had been an LPR since 1993. He had two drug conviction and was sentenced to five years of probation in each conviction.[209] In March 2014, when ICE officers arrested him, it was six years after his most recent arrest and nearly 10 years since he was released from post-conviction custody. ICE determined Martinez-Done was subject to mandatory detention under INA § 236(c) because of his criminal history.

Martinez-Done challenged the mandatory detention asserting he was subject to detention under INA § 236(a) in which case detention is not mandatory and he would be entitled to an individualized bond hearing. He provided three reasons: (1) he never served a custodial sentence and therefore was never "released" from custody as required by § 236(c); (2) he was not taken into custody *"when* [he was] released" violating the implicit timeliness requirement of § 236(c); and (3) mandatory detention as applied to his case violates the Due Process Clause of the U.S. Constitution.[210] The district court agreed and found that, although Martinez-Done was "released," he was not taken into custody "when [he was] released." The court also determined that Martinez-Done has a right under the Due Process Clause of the Fifth Amendment to have an impartial adjudicator decide if he may be released during his removal proceedings.

The District Court made a number of observations about the pre-removal mandatory detention system. First, among the nearly 400,000 noncitizens detained annually as of FY 2009, nearly two-thirds were subject to mandatory detention and many were taken into custody under INA § 236(c) long after they had reintegrated into their communities and our society. Second, mandatory detention devastates the families of the detained by imposing emotional and economic hardship. Third, ICE frequently waits many years to take noncitizens into custody under INA § 236(c) "despite the fact that, with so much time elapsed, they often pose little to no risk of flight, and even less danger to 'public safety.'" And, fourth, when courts grant habeas petitions and bond hearing are provided, many noncitizens originally detained under § 236(c) are released.

As of October 2014, there is a split in the circuits on this issue. The First Circuit has found that the phrase *"when* the alien is released" under INA § 236(c) creates a time limit for ICE to detain a noncitizen. *Castaneda v. Souza* involved a class action filed on behalf of noncitizens subject to mandatory detention under INA § 236(c) in which each of the noncitizens had not been taken into custody by the ICE until years after being released from state custody.[211] The First Circuit held

---

[209] He was serving a five year term of probation for a 2012 drug possession conviction (second) when he was arrested by ICE in March 2014. This was his second drug possession conviction and he was sentenced to five years of probation for each convictions. At one point, Martinez-Done was remanded into custody for violating his first probation after a 2006 conviction (first).

[210] The government argued that "when the alien is released" is not a time limit but rather triggers the duty of ICE to arrest for mandatory detention, and that Martinez-Done was released from custody after his initial criminal arrest.

[211] 769 F.3d 32 (1st Cir. 2014).

that INA § 236(c) mandatory detention only applies to noncitizens who are detained "when . . . released" from criminal custody. Here, the court found that the noncitizens were not timely detained under any reasonable interpretation of this provision; therefore they could not be subject to mandatory detention and were entitled to an individualized bail hearing.

Other circuits have determined that "*when* the alien is released" triggers a duty for the government to exercise mandatory detention authority. The Third and Fourth Circuits have adopted the "duty-triggering" construction,[212] as well as the BIA. [213]

There is another form of mandatory detention for suspected terrorists under INA § 236A. This special terrorist removal process permits detention up to seven days under USA PATRIOT Act amendments. INA § 236A(a) permits the Secretary of Homeland Security to certify a noncitizen is a terrorist if there is reasonable grounds to believe the individual is excludable under INA §§ 212(a)(3)(A)(i) (espionage/sabotage/export), (3)(A)(iii) (violent overthrow, opposition, control of government), (3)(B) (terrorist activities), 237(a)(4)(A)(i) (espionage or sabotage), 237(a)(4)(A)(iii) (violent overthrow, opposition, control of government), (4)(B) (terrorist activities), or is engaged in any other activity that endangers the national security.

Unaccompanied minors are no longer held in ICE detention facilities, however they were subject to detention until 2008.[214] The 2002 Homeland Security Act transferred the care and custody of unaccompanied minors to the Department of Health and Human Services from the former INS to move towards a child welfare-based-model of care for children and away from the adult detention model. The Trafficking Victims Protection Reauthorization Act (TVPRA) of 2008, expanded and redefined HHS's statutory responsibilities, to require that unaccompanied minors must "be promptly placed in the least restrictive setting that is in the best interest of the child."[215]

The TVPRA was enacted in 2000 and the 2008 amendments were added to address the particular issues faced by young people. The 2008 TVPRA amendments require that all unaccompanied children: be screened as potential victims of human trafficking; are exempt the children from certain asylum limitations; and are precluded from the expedited removal procedure.

Juveniles also may be detained when a noncitizen parent is taken into custody by DHS. Prior to 2001, families were rarely detained because of the lack of bed space, and the INS had a policy of releasing families to avoid the detention of

---

[212] *See* Hosh v. Lucero, 680 F.3d 375 (4th Cir. 2012); Sylvain v. Attorney Gen., 714 F.3d 150 (3d Cir. 2012).

[213] Matter of Rojas, 23 I.&N. Dec. 117 (BIA 2001).

[214] Unaccompanied minors are covered in Chapter 5. *See* Reno v. Flores, 507 U.S. 292 (1993). Juveniles are defined as noncitizens under the age of 18. 8 C.F.R. § 236.3. In Reno v. Flores, 507 U.S. 292 (1993), a constitutional challenge to the restraint on the liberty of noncitizen children upon a request for release to non-relatives was rejected by the Supreme Court. The juvenile detention regulations were upheld on procedural due process grounds as well.

[215] INA §232(b)(2).

children.[216] After September 11, 2001, the INS began this detention policy, although alternatives exist to detention such as the Intensive Supervised Appearance Program (electronic monitoring). Concerns continue about the detention of children.[217] In 2007 a federal district court, in a lawsuit filed against DHS regarding the detention conditions for families with children at the Hutto detention facility in Taylor, Texas, found that the conditions were substandard and the case was settled.[218] Family detention was expanded in Spring 2014 when a large-scale humanitarian migration from Central America occurred which included women and children, as well as unaccompanied minors.

In 2013 and 2014, the number of unaccompanied children who needed HHS care and supervision has risen exponentially with children fleeing violence in Honduras, Guatemala and El Salvador. Generally, an average of between 7,000 and 8,000 children are served annually by ORR. FY 2012 the number of unaccompanied noncitizen children seeking entry into the U.S. increased to 13,625 children. The number of unaccompanied children rose to 24,668 referrals from DHS for the 12-month reporting period in FY2013, and the projection for 60,000 unaccompanied children needing services in FY2014. This is discussed further in Chapter 5 and 14.

2.   After an Order of Removal

The statutory provision applying to the detention and removal of noncitizens after a removal order are set forth in INA § 241. Removal is required within 90 days of the order of removal.[219] This 90 day time period is referred to as the removal period. The removal period begins either: (1) when the order becomes administratively final; (2) when a court's final order is entered if a judicial appeal is sought and the administrative order was stayed; or (3) when a noncitizen is released from detention or confinement unrelated to the immigration process.[220]

Continued detention and suspension of the 90 day removal requirement is possible in three circumstances. First, continued detention is authorized if the noncitizen refuses or fails to obtain required documents for departure from the U.S.[221] The INA states that the noncitizen may "remain in detention during such extended period" while making travel arrangements. Second, noncitizens deemed inadmissible or deportable under any criminal or terrorist ground must be detained during the removal period.[222] "Under no circumstances" may the DHS

---

[216] *A District Court Finds Conditions at Hutto Family Residential Center Substandard*, 84 INTER. REL. 936 (Apr. 23, 2007).

[217] *See House Judiciary Subcommittee Takes Testimony of Medical Care Provided to ICE Detainees*, 85 INTER. REL. 1737 (June 16, 2008); Office of the Inspector General, Dept. of Homeland Security, A Review of DHS' Responsibilities for Juvenile Aliens (2005); Amnesty International USA Unaccompanied Children in Immigration Detention (2003), *available at* http://www.amnestyusa.org/refugee/pdfs/children_detention.pdf.

[218] Bunikyte v. Chertoff, 2007 U.S. Dist. LEXIS 26166 (W.D. Tex. Apr. 9, 2007).

[219] INA § 241(a)(1) (". . . the Attorney General shall remove the alien from the United States within a period of 90 days. . . . ").

[220] INA § 241(a)(1)(B).

[221] INA § 241(a)(1)(C).

[222] INA § 241(a)(2).

release these noncitizens from custody during the removal period.[223] Third, continued detention is authorized for any noncitizen who is ordered removed and is inadmissible on any ground, and for any noncitizens who are found by DHS to be a risk to the community or unlikely to comply with the removal order.[224]

The INA specifies that after the 90-day removal period has ended, the noncitizen is "shall be subject" to DHS supervision.[225] The conditions that may be imposed for supervision are set forth in the INA and include: regularly appearing at an immigration office; submitting, if necessary, to medical and psychiatric exams; and providing information under oath about activities and any other information deemed appropriate. A bond may be required as part of an order of supervision.

The indefinite detention of a noncitizen after an order of removal because the noncitizen's home country will not accept her return has been challenged. The indefinite detention of inadmissible noncitizens has long been accepted in the U.S. immigration system.[226] Moreover, as discussed above, the continued detention after the 90 day removal period is also contemplated under INA § 241(a)(6). In *Zadvydas v. Davis*, 533 U.S. 678 (2001), the Supreme Court addressed the authority of the Attorney General when the removal period was extended indefinitely. The Court held there is a limit on continued detention under INA § 241(a)(6) when a noncitizen had been admitted to the U.S. in contrast to an applicant for admission. The 90 day removal period can be suspended and continued detention is authorized only in limited circumstances. The government had argued that indefinite detention was justified to prevent flight and protect the community from dangerous individuals.

In *Zadvydas*, the Court held there is an implicit limit on continued detention and the DHS is only authorized to detain a noncitizen after the removal period for a reasonable time period. A period of six months is the presumptive time limit for post-removal detention. A noncitizen for whom there is no significant likelihood of reasonably foreseeable removal must be released. The Court's decision was premised on the idea that "[f]reedom from imprisonment . . . lies at the heart of the liberty that [the due process] protects and indefinite detention for persons with final order who can not be removed to any country is impermissible."

After *Zadvydas* the Attorney General issued a memorandum to guide detention decisions. The Department of Justice published an interim regulation in November 2001 establishing procedures for the review of detention on a six months basis if removal was unlikely in the reasonably forseeable future.[227] Noncitizens have been released under these procedures, primarily noncitizens from Cuba, Laos, Vietnam and Cambodia.

---

[223] INA § 241(a)(2). Under no circumstances may a noncitizen be released if inadmissible or deportable under §§ 212(a)(2), (3)(B) or §§ 237(a)(2), (a)(4)(B), including all criminal grounds and terrorism grounds.

[224] INA § 241(a)(6) permits detention of those inadmissible under INA § 212(a) or removable under INA §§ 237(a)(1)(C), (a)(2), and (a)(4).

[225] INA § 241(a)(3).

[226] *See* Shaughnessy v. United States ex rel. Mezei, 345 U.S. 206 (1953).

[227] 66 Fed. Reg. 56,967, Nov. 14, 2001.

A 2004 GAO report about detention after the *Zadvydas* decision concluded that ICE does not have readily available information to determine whether custody reviews are held in a timely manner.[228] The GAO report also concluded this lack of information made it difficult for ICE to ensure that custody determinations were consistent with the *Zadvydas* requirement of determining whether the likelihood of removal was reasonably forseeable.

In *Clark v. Martinez*, 543 U.S. 371 (2005), the Supreme Court addressed the issue of continued detention of noncitizens who are inadmissible under INA § 212 after the removal period. The Court held that the *Zadvydas* rule interpreting INA § 241(a)(6) to limit detention beyond the removal period applies to noncitizens who are inadmissible. As a matter of statutory interpretation, the detention authorized under INA § 241(a)(6) was applicable to noncitizens who were inadmissible and deportable. There was no distinction between the two groups included. The case involved two Cubans who arrived in the U.S. in 1990 and had been paroled into the U.S. Their parole had been revoked in 2000 and 1993 and they were both inadmissible due to criminal convictions.

3. Indefinite Detention

Continued detention of certified terrorists under INA § 236A after the removal period is permissible. Certified terrorists are not protected under the *Zadvydas* and *Clark* interpretations of INA § 241(a)(6) discussed above. Congress has expressly authorized mandatory, indefinite detention in INA § 236A.

A noncitizen detained as suspected terrorist under INA § 236A, who has not been removed and who is unlikely to be removed in the reasonably foreseeable future, may be detained for an additional six months if release will threaten national security of the U.S. or the safety of the community or any person.[229]

---

[228] Immigration Enforcement: Better Data and Controls are Needed to Ensure Consistency with the Supreme Court Decision on Long-Term Detention, GAO 2004.

[229] INA § 236A(a)(6).

Chapter 14

ENFORCEMENT AGAINST UNDOCUMENTED IMMIGRANTS

A. UNDOCUMENTED IMMIGRATION

The undocumented population in the United States has begun to grow again since the end of the Great Recession in June 2009. Researchers at the Pew Hispanic Center estimated that 11.7 million undocumented immigrants resided in the United States in 2012, compared to 11.3 million in 2009.[1] 1 Of that figure, 52 percent were from Mexico, 24 percent from other parts of Latin America, 9 percent from Asia, 6 percent from Europe and Canada, and 4 percent from Africa and other areas. Almost two-thirds (60 percent) of the unauthorized population lives in six states: California (2.45 million), Florida (950,000), Illinois (450,000), New Jersey (525,000), New York (875,000), and Texas (1.75 million). Almost a third of the undocumented population (32 percent) is spread throughout other parts of the country. States such as Georgia, Colorado, Maryland, Massachusetts, Virginia, and Washington have

---

[1] Jeffrey S. Passel, et. al., *Population Decline of Unauthorized Immigrants Stalls, May Have Reversed*, Sept. 23, 2013.

more than 200,000 undocumented immigrants. Nevada, Oregon, Pennsylvania, Michigan, Ohio, Wisconsin, and Tennessee each have more than 100,000. Connecticut, Utah, Minnesota, Kansas, New Mexico, Indiana, Iowa, Oklahoma, and Missouri have more than 55,000 undocumented immigrants.

Most undocumented immigrants are adults (8.8 million); 56 percent of these adults are men, and 44 percent are women. About 1.5 million families have at least one parent who is undocumented along with children who are all U.S. citizens. Another 460,000 are mixed-status families in which some children are U.S. citizens and some are undocumented.

Undocumented immigrants account for about 5.2 percent of the civilian labor force — about 8.4 million workers out of a labor force of 161 million. Although they can be found throughout the workforce, undocumented workers tend to be overrepresented in certain occupations and industries. They are much more likely to be in broad occupation groups that require little education or do not have licensing requirements. The share of undocumented immigrants who work in agricultural occupations (Department of Labor estimates 53 percent; growers estimate 70 percent) and construction and extractive occupations is about three times the share of native workers in these types of jobs. In contrast, undocumented immigrants are conspicuously sparse in white collar occupations. Whereas management, business, professions, sales, and administrative support account for half of native workers (52 percent), fewer than one-fourth of the undocumented workers are in these areas (23 percent).

Unfortunately, in spite of the social and economic contributions that undocumented immigrants make to the United States, anti-immigrant fervor — largely aimed at the undocumented population — is at an all-time high. The sentiment is manifested in at least three ways: President Obama's administration set deportation records, easily surpassing any administration in history, House Republicans — many in response to the Tea Party — blocked any efforts at reform that would include legalization or at least a legalization with a path to citizenship, and many state and local municipalities have enacted anti-immigrant laws and ordinances.

This Chapter is an overview of U.S. immigration enforcement. Throughout the country's history, the U.S. has become increasingly determined to keep people from entering the country without inspection and apprehend those who have entered and are undocumented. That history set the stage for gun-wielding raids during the George W. Bush administration and the record-setting removal actions of the Obama era.

B. AT THE U.S./MEXICO BORDER

1. Creation and Expansion of the Border Patrol

By the 1960s, the flow of undocumented Mexicans was rapidly increasing and straining the resources of the Border Patrol. In 1962, after a severe drought in northern and central Mexico leading to high unemployment, U.S. officials estimated that the number of aliens who crossed the border without inspection increased by 41 percent and reported a 2.9 percent increase in the number of deportable Mexicans apprehended by the Border Patrol. In addition, U.S. wage rates attracted Mexican laborers. In lower Texas, for instance, cotton pickers were paid $2.50 per hundred pounds, while cotton pickers in Mexico were paid 75 cents.[2] Within two years, 59 percent of the deportable aliens arrested were Mexican, a 13 percent increase over 1963, attributable to the termination of the Bracero program.[3]

During this era, the Border Patrol used airplanes to monitor the border and seek out concentrations of aliens in places such as ranch areas. These strategies helped to locate over 4,000 deportable aliens in 1963.[4] By 1964, over 56,000 aliens were transported back to Mexico using an airlift in order to return people closer to their homes in southern Mexico. Another 54,000 were transported back to Mexico via train to Chihuahua.[5]

Attempts to smuggle aliens also increased at the time. In 1966, for example, three small boats of smuggled aliens were found in Mission Bay near San Diego; a rental truck was parked nearby waiting to take people to interior points of California. The aliens had paid $125 to $150 each.[6] In 1967, more aliens were found, concealed in trucks, as well as in new cars being freighted across the Canadian border.[7] In 1977, the INS established an Office of Anti-Smuggling to reduce alien smuggling in hopes of "immobilizing criminal conspiracies responsible for bringing in and transporting undocumented aliens."[8] No one knows, of course, how many similar attempts succeeded.

During the last four months of fiscal year 1977, 100 extra Border Patrol agents were sent to Chula Vista to augment the permanent force. During that period, about 145,000 aliens were apprehended, compared to 96,000 the previous year.[9]

Procedural restrictions on lawful residency disadvantaged Mexicans, thereby increasing the attraction of illicit entry. The ability to apply for lawful permanent resident status through adjustment of status without having to exit the United States was added by the 1965 amendments. Aliens, other than crewmen and natives of contiguous countries (i.e., Mexico and Canada) and islands, who had been admitted or paroled (i.e., entered with inspection), could apply for adjustment of status to permanent resident status without leaving the country to get an immigrant visa. The act specifically excluded any aliens born in any country of the Western Hemisphere.[10] In 1977, adjustment of status became available to Western Hemisphere immigrants if they qualified under an immigration category, but the provision does not apply to most undocumented Mexicans because the law requires

---

[2] Immigration and Naturalization Service, 1963 Annual Report.

[3] Immigration and Naturalization Service, 1964 Annual Report.

[4] Immigration and Naturalization Service, 1963 Annual Report.

[5] Immigration and Naturalization Service, 1964 Annual Report.

[6] Immigration and Naturalization Service, 1966 Annual Report.

[7] Immigration and Naturalization Service, 1967 Annual Report.

[8] Immigration and Naturalization Service, 1977 Annual Report.

[9] Immigration and Naturalization Service, 1966 Annual Report.

[10] Immigration and Naturalization Service, 1977 Annual Report.

that the person must have initially entered with inspection.[11] The procedural challenges to obtaining lawful permanent residence status contributed to the decision on the part of many undocumented Mexicans to simply enter without inspection even though they may have been able to qualify under a lawful immigrant category.

A different procedural option became available for some Mexican citizens crossing the U.S. border in 1966. Despite the increased fears of smuggling, the United States started to issue border-crossing cards to alleviate travel difficulties. Border, passport, and visa requirements were waived for Mexican nationals with border-crossing cards. These allowed individuals to remain in the United States for up to six months. The Mexican government reciprocated with a card valid from 30 days to six months.[12]

Today, the Border Patrol (formerly part of INS) is the mobile and uniformed enforcement arm of the U.S. Customs and Border Protection of the Department of Homeland Security, responsible for protecting more than 8,000 miles of international land and water boundary. The Border Patrol contains twenty-one sectors, including nine southwest border sectors, sectors on the northern border, and those in Livermore, California; Miami, Florida; New Orleans, Louisiana; and Mayaguez, Puerto Rico.

In spite of general problems with the federal budget since the 1990s, money for immigration enforcement steadily increased. For example, while a general federal hiring freeze was experienced in 1992 and 1993, in 1994 the Border Patrol was able to hire 350 new officers (300 were added to San Diego and 50 to El Paso, where the need was regarded as greatest), and 700 new positions were added in 1995. Close to 1,000 more were added in 1996. The agency doubled its ranks between 2006 and 2013, when its ranks swelled to 60,000 agents, making it the largest federal law enforcement program. The Senate-passed immigration reform bill in 2013 (S. 744) would have added another 19,000 Border Patrol agents.

Since 9/11, the government has funneled $100 billion into border weapon and surveillance systems for the Border Patrol. Customs and Border Protection has its own air and marine forces, a special operations branch, and a separate tactical unit. Its rapid-response teams have 500 agents ready to deploy anywhere within 48 hours. Its Predator B drones and Blackhawk helicopters are patrolling the desert southwest as if they were in an Afghanistan war zone. It has armored personnel carriers and uses forward operating bases like those in U.S. wars to secure positions in remote areas. Roughly 700 miles of walls have scarred the landscape of the Mexican borderlands, backed by increasingly sophisticated surveillance towers, cameras, and more than 12,000 motion sensors.

The Border Patrol is engaged in a variety of activities, including boat patrol operations, anti-smuggling operations, and employer sanctions. Even before the creation of the Homeland Security Department, the Border Patrol was involved in intelligence work. It also has desert-area rescue teams, emergency response

---

[11] Immigration and Naturalization Service, 1977 Annual Report.

[12] Immigration and Naturalization Service, 1966 Annual Report.

teams, canine units, drug awareness programs for schools, and scouting activities for youth, and is involved in the detection of aliens with criminal backgrounds. Of course, the Border Patrol is best known for border surveillance (or "linewatching"), transportation and traffic checks, and interior enforcement.

Though the Border Patrol is involved in myriad functions, patrolling the southern border is its primary task and that is where resources have been constantly added since the 1970s. In the late 1980s, an estimated 11.3 to 3.9 million undocumented crossings along the southern border occurred annually; 1.2 to 3.2 million were Mexicans crossing the southwest border. By the mid-1990s, some 88 percent of the Border Patrol's agents were stationed along the Mexican border, and southern border apprehensions accounted for 98 percent of all border apprehensions. And while the Border Patrol has always believed that the simple, large presence of an organized force would serve as a deterrent to some Mexicans contemplating an illicit crossing, a substantial portion of linewatch time has been spent in the apprehension and deportation of undocumented Mexican immigrants.

The apprehension aspect of linewatch operations continues to be a part of the Border Patrol routine. When deterrence does not work and persons suspected of surreptitious entry are observed, agents pursue and arrest. Although such agents usually work with partners, often pursuing individuals, sometimes four or five agents can effectuate the arrest of groups of up to 70 immigrants who have been detected in safe houses used by smuggling operations.

Once numerical limitations began being applied to Mexico in 1965 and in 1976, waiting lists developed and there was more pressure for Mexicans to enter surreptitiously in response to available seasonal work and recruitment efforts by U.S. growers. Much of the public and policy makers reacted negatively to 'the illicit entries by Mexicans, and the rise of anti-immigrant sentiment in the 1970s was conspicuous. Although INS officials acknowledged that Mexicans did not make up the majority of undocumented aliens in the country, Mexicans were targeted by INS sweeps. In the mid-1970s, as exclusionists advanced a labor displacement theory, Congress considered an employer sanction law that was referred to as the Rodino Bill, named after Congressman Peter Rodino, a powerful immigration policy figure in Congress. Exclusionists persistently complained about undocumented workers coming across the United States-Mexico border, and the commissioner of the INS routinely alleged that 12 million undocumented aliens were in the United States. In 1977, for example, of the deportable aliens arrested by the INS, more than 80 percent were Mexican. Mexicans also continued to be the targets of highly publicized INS raids in the interior of the country.

2. Operation Gatekeeper

Beginning in 1994, the Clinton administration implemented Operation Gatekeeper, a strategy of "control through deterrence" that involved constructing fences and militarizing parts of the southern border that were most easily traversed. Instead of deterring migrants, their entry choices were shifted to treacherous terrain — the desert and the mountains. The number of entries and apprehensions were not at all decreased, and the number of deaths because of dehydration and sunstroke in the summer or freezing in the winter dramatically surged. In 1994, fewer than 30 migrants died along the border; by 1998, the number was 147; in 2001, 387 deaths were counted; and in 2007, 409 died.[13]

a. Development of Operation Gatekeeper

The San Diego Sector of the DHS Border Patrol covers the section of the United States-Mexico border that historically has been the preferred site of entry for those entering the United States without inspection.[14] This sector contains 66 miles of international border.[15] Tijuana, Mexico's third largest city, lies directly south of San Diego, California, the sixth largest city in the United States.[16] A smaller Mexican city, Tecate, is situated in the eastern end of the sector.[17]

In 1994, over 450,000 apprehensions of illicit border crossings were made in the San Diego sector. This number far surpassed the sectors with the next highest apprehension: Tucson (139,473) and McAllen, Texas (124,251). In the period prior to the end of 1994, undocumented border crossers in the San Diego sector commonly entered in the western part of the sector near the city of San Diego. Often, many of these individuals traveled through private property, and some were even seen darting across busy freeways near the international border inspection station. Clearly, most of the illicit crossers entered along the 14-mile area from Imperial Beach (at the Pacific Ocean) to the base of the Otay Mountains.[18] Most of the stretch involves "easy terrain and gentle climbs," where the crossing lasts only 10 or 15 minutes to a pickup point.[19] Even individuals who were apprehended and turned back across the border were just as likely to attempt reentry in the westernmost part of the sector at that time.[20]

These highly visible border crossings resulted in tremendous public pressure on the INS to act. Residents of San Diego complained. Anti-immigrant groups demanded action. Politicians decried lack of border control. President Clinton came up with an answer and an approach to the question of "illegal immigration." In his State of the Union address on January 24, 1995, Clinton signaled a renewed get-tough policy against undocumenteds, including "mov[ing] aggressively to secure our borders by hiring a record number of border guards" and "cracking down on illegal hiring."[21] Knowing that Clinton faced reelection in 1996, administration officials hoped that renewed enforcement effort against undocumented aliens would

---

[13] California Rural Legal Assistance Foundation, Charts on page 191 of Defining America Through Immigration Policy; Frontera NorteSur, *2008 Migrant Death Count*, July 8, 2008, *available at* http://newspapertree.com/news/2630-2008-migrant-death-count.

[14] GUSTAVO DE LA VINA, U.S. BORDER PATROL SAN DIEGO SECTOR STRATEGIC PLANNING DOCUMENT, April 29, 1994, at I.

[15] *Id.* at 3.

[16] *Id.*

[17] *Id.*

[18] Border Patrol, *Operation Gatekeeper: 3 Years of Results in a Glance* (1997).

[19] *Id.*

[20] INS Fact Sheet, *Frustrating Illegal Crossers at Imperial Beach and Moving the Traffic Eastward*, October 17, 1997.

[21] *72 Interpreter Releases 169*, January 30, 1995.

shore up the president's support among voters in California, who overwhelmingly passed the anti-immigrant Proposition 187 in 1994.[22]

Operation Gatekeeper was one of several operations that resulted from the Clinton administration's commitment to a new aggressive enforcement strategy for the Border Patrol. In August 1994, the INS Commissioner Doris Meissner approved a new national strategy for the Border Patrol.[23] The heart of the plan relied on a vision of "prevention through deterrence," in which a "decisive number of enforcement resources [would be brought] to bear in each major entry corridor" and the Border Patrol would increase the number of agents on the line and make effective use of technology, raising the risk of apprehension high enough to be an effective deterrent."[24] The specific regional enforcement operations that resulted included (1) Operation Blockade (later renamed Hold the Line), which commenced in September 1993 in the Greater El Paso, Texas areas; (2) Operation Gatekeeper, which commenced in October 1994, south of San Diego, California; (3) Operation Safeguard, which also commenced in October 1994 in Arizona; and (4) Operation Rio Grande, which commenced in August 1997 in Brownsville, Texas.[25] The idea was to block traditional entry and smuggling routes with border enforcement personnel and physical barriers.[26] By cutting off traditional crossing routes, the strategy sought to deter migrants or at least channel them into terrain less suited for crossing and more conducive to apprehensions.[27] To carry out the strategy, the Border Patrol was to concentrate personnel and resources in areas of highest undocumented alien crossings, increase the time agents spent on border-control activities, increase use of physical barriers, and carefully consider the mix of technology and personnel needed to control the border.[28]

In the San Diego sector, efforts would be concentrated on the popular fourteen-mile section of the border beginning from the Pacific Ocean (Imperial Beach) stretching eastward.[29] That stretch had been the focus of some resources before Gatekeeper. Steel fencing and bright lighting were already in place in sections of this corridor, erected in part with the assistance of the U.S. military.[30] Yet because of the persistent traffic of undocumented entrants along this corridor, phase I of Gatekeeper continued to concentrate on increased staffing and resources along the fourteen mile area.[31]

---

[22] *Clinton Will Seek Spending to Curb Aliens, Aides Say: Political Balancing Act*, N.Y. TIMES, January 22, 1995, at AI; Matthew Jardine, *Operation Gatekeeper*, 10 PEACE REV. 329, 333 (1998).

[23] U.S. Border Patrol, *Border Patrol Strategic Plan: 1994 and Beyond-National Strategy*, July 1994.

[24] *Id.* at 6.

[25] Petition on the Inter-American Commission on Human Rights of the Organization of American States (Feb. 9 1999), at 16, n.4.

[26] *National Strategy*, at 6–9.

[27] *Id.* at 7; U.S. General Accounting Office, *Illegal Immigration: Status of Southwest Border Strategy Implementation 3* (May 1999).

[28] *Id.*

[29] *Id.* at 1, 4, 8.

[30] *Id.*

[31] *Id.* at 8.

As the INS implemented its national border strategy, Congress supported these efforts; between 1993 and 1997, the INS budget for enforcement efforts along the southwest border doubled from $400 million to $800 million.[32] The number of Border Patrol agents along the southwest border increased from 3,389 in October 1993 to 7,357 by September 1998 — an increase of 117 percent.[33] State-of-the-art technology, including new surveillance systems using electronic sensors linked with low-light video cameras, infrared night-vision devices, and forward-looking infrared systems for Border Patrol aircraft, were installed.[34]

Given these additional resources, Operation Gatekeeper buildup was impressive. Before Gatekeeper, the San Diego sector had 19 miles of fencing. By the end of 1999, 52 miles were fenced. Half of this fencing runs from the Pacific Ocean to the base of the Otay Mountains. Fourteen miles contain primary fencing (a 10-foot wall of corrugated steel landing mats left over from the Vietnam War.) Two backup fences, each 115 feet tall, have been constructed. The first backup fence is made of concrete pillars. The second backup fence is made of wire mesh, with support beams. Both are topped with wire. Almost 12 miles of this stretch are illuminated by stadium lights. Some fencing has been erected on sections of the Otay Mountains, as well as around various East San Diego communities along the border.[35] The Department of Defense's Center for Low Intensity Conflicts as well as the Army Corps of Engineers provided guidance to INS on the development of Gatekeeper features.[36]

In contrast, in areas other than San Diego, the construction was not as significant. The El Centro sector covers 72 miles of the border and is sparsely populated on the U.S. side and has only seven miles of fence — all of it between the contiguous border cities of Calexico and Mexicali. Arizona has 17 miles of fencing — six in the Yuma sector and nine in the Tucson sector. That fencing was erected exclusively in the towns and cities. Texas has the Rio Grande River and seven miles of fencing from El Paso/Ciudad Juarez area — two miles of primary and five of secondary. Thus, 73 miles of fencing was erected on the 2,000 mile and the 66-mile San Diego sector had 72 percent of it, as well as 54 percent of the illumination.[37] The 144-mile long San Diego and El Centro sectors have almost a third of the Border Patrol agents stationed on the 2,000 mile of southwest border.[38]

b. Results of Operation Gatekeeper

In implementing its national strategy beginning in 1994, the INS made a key assumption about its "prevention through deterrence" approach: "alien apprehensions will decrease as [the] Border Patrol increases control of the border."[39] In

---

[32] *Operation Gatekeeper: New Resources, Enhanced Results*, INS Fact Sheet, July 14th, 1998.

[33] 1999 GAO report, at 7.

[34] INS Fact Sheet, February 2, 1998.

[35] November 19, 1999 letter to Mary Robinson.

[36] *Id.*, 1999 GAO Report, at 12.

[37] November 19, 1999 letter to Mary Robinson.

[38] October 6, 2000 letter to Gabriela Rodriguez Pizarro.

[39] *National Strategy*, at 4.

other words, the INS anticipated that as the show of force escalated by increasing agents, lighting, and fencing, people would be discouraged from entering without inspection so that the number of apprehensions naturally would decline. In fact, the Border Patrol predicted that within five years, a substantial drop in apprehension rates border-wide would result.[40] The deterrence would be so great that "many will consider it futile to continue to attempt illegal entry."[41] These assumptions and predictions have not borne out.

Apprehension levels did not decline. The enforcement strategies began with Operation Gatekeeper in San Diego and Operation Blockade in El Paso in 1994. True, apprehension levels for those two sectors were considerably lower in 1998 than in 1993 (e.g., 531,689 apprehended in San Diego in 1993 compared to 248,092 in 1998). However, the apprehension levels surged in El Centro, Yuma, and Tucson during the same period (e.g., from 92,639 to 387,406 in Tucson; from 30,508 to 226,695 in El Centro; and from 23,548 to 76,195 in Yuma).[42]From 1994 to 1999, total apprehensions statistics along the southwest border actually increased by 57 percent![43] The increase continues. The number of apprehensions for all of the fiscal year 2000 was 1.64 million, which was an all-time high.[44] In sum, after Gatekeeper sealed the western most section of the border, apprehensions in San Diego declined, but crossers moved east and overall apprehensions actually increased substantially.

The INS thought that with the combination of fencing and increased spending on border patrols at the most frequently traveled routes, undocumented immigration would slow if not come to a complete halt altogether. But migrants were not deterred, and began looking for other areas to penetrate the border. However, the new areas of travel were risky; they were more dangerous and life threatening. Given the challenges, more migrants turned to costly smugglers to help them cross the border.

As Operation Gatekeeper closed the Imperial Beach corridor, the border-crossing traffic moved east. Frustrated crossers moved first to Brown Field and Chula Vista, and subsequently to the eastern sections of the San Diego sector.[45] Before Gatekeeper began in 1994, crossers were just as likely to make their second try at the westernmost part of the sector; but that changed very quickly. By January 1995, only 14 percent were making their second try near Imperial Beach. The illicit border traffic had moved into "unfamiliar and unattractive territory."[46] The tragedy of Operation Gatekeeper is the direct link of its prevention through deterrence strategy to an absolutely horrendous rise in the number of deaths among border-crossers who were forced to attempt entry over terrain that even the

---

[40] September 30, 2000 letter to Mary Robinson.

[41] *National Strategy*, at 23.

[42] *Id.* at 18–20.

[43] *Apprehension Statistics for the Southwest Border*, Oct. 7, 1999 (Chart prepared by California Rural Legal Assistance Foundation).

[44] 1999 GAO report, at 17–18, 20.

[45] *Id.* at 18–20.

[46] November 19, 1999 letter to Mary Robinson.

INS knew to present "mortal danger" due to extreme weather conditions and rugged terrain.

The death statistics are revealing. In 1994, 23 migrants died along the California-Mexico border. Of the 23, two died of hypothermia or heat stroke and nine from drowning. By 1998, the annual total was 147 deaths — 71 from hypothermia or heat stroke and 52 from drowning. Figures for 1999 follow this unfortunate trend, and in 2000, 84 were heat stroke or hypothermia casualties. In spite of the aid of smugglers, the new routes were simply too dangerous for many border-crossers and death of migrants surged. The number of migrant deaths increased 600 times from 1994 to 2000; a number that could be attributed to Operation Gatekeeper's pushing surreptitious entries toward treacherous eastward routes.

From 2007 to 2013, over two thousand known migrant deaths occurred along the Mexico-Arizona border. The remains of 100 and 77 people were found in 2012 alone. Many more bodies likely go unfound, and of the ones that are found, many go unidentified.

3. The Secure Fence Act of 2006

The Secure Fence Act was signed by President Bush on October 26, 2006. The statute's main goals in regards to the U.S.-Mexico border were to "achieve operational control on the border" and "the construction of fencing and security improvements in the border area from the Pacific Ocean to the Gulf of Mexico."[47]

The Secure Fence Act defines "operational control" as the prevention of all unlawful U.S. entries, including entries by terrorists, other unlawful aliens, instruments of terrorism, narcotics, and other contraband.

The Secure Fence Act amended the Illegal Immigration Reform and Immigrant Responsibility Act of 1996 to direct the Secretary of Homeland Security to provide for at least two layers of reinforced fencing, the installation of additional physical barriers, roads, lighting, cameras, and sensors on over 700 miles of the U.S.-Mexico Border.[48] The surveillance measures were to be installed by May 30, 2007, and the fence construction was to be completed by May 30, 2008.[49] But in 2007, senators slipped language into a spending bill to water down those requirements, giving Homeland Security officials the leeway to determine how much and what type of fencing. As of 2013, DHS had built just 36 miles of two-tier fencing, 316 miles of single-tier fence, and another 299 miles of vehicle barriers that still allow pedestrians and wildlife to cross, but is meant to keep out smuggling vehicles.

The extremely high cost of complying with the Secure Fence Act's mandate — estimated at US$4.1 billion, or more than the Border Patrol's entire annual budget of US$3.55 billion — is one reason that it has not been fulfilled. Congress has failed to fund the project sufficiently in order to finish building the fence.

---

[47] The Secure Fence Act of 2006, Pub. L. No. 109-367, Oct. 26 2006, *available at* http://frwebgate. access.gpo.gov/cgi-bin/getdoc.cgi?dbname=109_cong_public_laws&docid=f:publ367.109.pdf.

[48] *Id.* at Sec. 3.

[49] *Id.*

4. Operation Streamline

Operation Streamline is an umbrella term for a number of related criminal proceedings in which unauthorized entrants to the United States are criminally prosecuted and deported or sentenced to prison. A joint initiative of the Department of Homeland Security and the Department of Justice, Operation Streamline was first implemented in the Border Patrol's Del Rio, Texas sector in 2005 before being expanded to Border Patrol sectors in Arizona, New Mexico and across Texas. Operation Streamline is a zero-tolerance enforcement policy designed to criminally prosecute every undocumented migrant apprehended in certain zones under two federal statutes which prohibit entry into the United State without inspection and entry after deportation. Although many sentences are reduced through plea agreements, those prosecuted for the first time face a misdemeanor charge and may receive sentences up to six months in federal prison while those charged with a felony following a prior deportation may face up to two years, or up to twenty years with certain prior convictions.

The criminal prosecution of undocumented migrants represents a dramatic departure from previous practices. Until 2005, noncitizens apprehended by Border Patrol were removed from the country under a "voluntary departure" or were detained and formally deported through the civil immigration system without facing criminal prosecution. However, under Operation Streamline and other fast-track programs, thousands of people are criminally prosecuted each month for entering the U.S., with as many as 70–80 defendants processed simultaneously in some district courts. Due to the *en masse* nature of the proceedings, meeting with counsel, arraignment, plea and sentencing are condensed into the space of a few hours, depriving defendants of due process and effective assistance of counsel. Furthermore, defendants are virtually compelled to accept a guilty plea to avoid prolonged detention periods and the criminal conviction and removal order that result from a guilty plea may make it impossible for a defendant to later regularize their status in the United States.

Operation Streamline and related programs have led to an unprecedented rate of federal criminal prosecutions against immigrants. By 2009, 54 percent of all federal criminal prosecutions were for immigration-related offenses and "illegal re-entry" had become the most commonly filed federal charge. The resulting mass incarceration of noncitizens has been a boon for the private prison industry which has reaped millions of dollars through imprisoning Operation Streamline defendants. In addition, the preponderance of federal prosecutions for immigration violations has driven a major demographic shift within the federal penal system: by 2011 Latinas/os represented over 50 percent of new federal inmates sentenced for felony offenses. The sentences handed down by the courts under Operation Streamline compound the distress of those apprehended by Border Patrol and unnecessarily separate defendants from their homes and families for prolonged periods while denying them any recourse to legal methods of entering the United States. By the end of fiscal 2012, more than 200,000 people were processed through the program.

The backstory of Operation Streamline begins on a chilly December day in 2005 in west Texas. Until then, most undocumented immigrants were sent voluntarily back to their countries or processed through civil immigration courts. Occasionally, large groups of immigrants would wade across the river together in broad daylight and walk up to Border Patrol agents to surrender. The Border Patrol lacked the detention center bed space and money to house the immigrants while they waited to appear before an immigration judge. So thousands of non-Mexicans were issued paperwork instructing them to return for their court hearings in 30 days. Many never came back.

A fed-up Randy Hill, then the sector chief for the Border Patrol in Del Rio, and several fellow agents started pushing for a new "zero tolerance" strategy. The agents wanted to use sections of the INA since 1952 criminalizing illegal entry to prosecute every undocumented immigrant, unless there was a compelling humanitarian reason to spare them. First-time offenders could be sentenced to up to six months in prison. Another arrest could lead to a felony charge and up to two years in prison. The strategy would solve the Border Patrol's detention space problem by sending undocumented immigrants into the federal criminal justice system, which would pick up the tab for their incarceration. Most importantly, Hill reasoned, it would finally deliver a concrete consequence for illegal entry. Nearly all those caught would be funneled into the federal criminal justice system, prosecuted, imprisoned and sent home as convicted criminals.

Operation Streamline mainly targets migrant workers with no criminal history, causing skyrocketing caseloads in many federal district courts along the border. Prior to the program the U.S. Attorney's Office reserved criminal prosecution for migrants with criminal records and for those who made repeated attempts to cross the border. Operation Streamline removed that prosecutorial discretion, requiring the criminal prosecution of all undocumented border crossers, regardless of their history.

The program's voluminous prosecutions have forced many courts to cut procedural corners. Magistrate judges conduct *en masse* hearings, during which as many as 80 defendants plead guilty at a time, depriving migrants of due process. Indeed, in December 2009, the U.S. Court of Appeals for the Ninth Circuit raised concerns that Operation Streamline's *en masse* plea hearings in Tucson, Arizona violate federal law.[50]

First-time offenders are prosecuted for misdemeanor illegal entry under 8 U.S.C. § 1325, which carries a six-month maximum sentence. Any migrant who has been deported in the past and attempts to reenter can be charged with felony reentry under 8 U.S.C. § 1326, which generally carries a two-year maximum penalty but can involve up to a 20-year maximum if the migrant has a criminal record. Defense attorneys estimate that 99 percent of Operation Streamline defendants plead guilty.

The sheer number of defendants requires nearly all judges to combine the initial appearance, arraignment, plea, and sentencing into one *en masse* hearing. Many Operation Streamline defendants complete the entire criminal proceeding — meeting with counsel, making an initial appearance, pleading guilty, and being sentenced after waiving a presentence report — in a single day.

---

[50] United States v. Roblero-Solis, 588 F.3d 692 (9th Cir. 2009).

Federal defenders report that many of their clients are caught off guard by the criminal prosecution and cannot begin to grasp how it will affect them in the longer term because they do not, at a basic level, understand the concept of bars to reentry or what it means to be charged with a misdemeanor or a felony in the United States. Defense attorneys also emphasize that many of their clients have traveled a great distance and spent a good deal of money to reach the border. Some have family members already residing in the United States with whom they wish to reunite. Others are caring for children, sick family members, or aging parents and are unable to find work to support those relatives in their own country.

To the extent that migrants are aware of Operation Streamline's zero-tolerance zones, as DHS claims, several additional concerns arise. First, Operation Streamline may drive more migrants to use professional human smugglers out of a belief that *coyotes* can identify border areas where migrants are least likely to be apprehended. About 90 percent of the migrants interviewed for a San Diego study had hired a *coyote* for their most recent border crossing. This increased reliance on professional smugglers heightens border violence and may make it more difficult for Border Patrol agents to apprehend unlawful entrants. Second, as in the case of Operation Gatekeeper, zero-tolerance zones may force migrants to attempt to cross along stretches of the border that are remote and physically hazardous and therefore less likely to be heavily monitored by Border Patrol agents. This can lead to more migrant deaths from harsh conditions, including heat exhaustion and drowning.

According to a report by UC Berkeley Law School, despite their best efforts, it is extremely difficult for border jurisdictions to implement Operation Streamline without depriving migrants of procedural due process and effective assistance of counsel.[51] The high volume of daily prosecutions requires proceedings in which dozens of defendants appear at once, and not all migrants receive timely appearances. As a result, in this assembly-line justice system, most defendants receive just one court appearance, which serves as an arraignment, plea, and sentencing. Defendants are processed in groups, with up to 80 defendants arraigned each day in Del Rio, 70 in Tucson, and an average of 20 in El Paso. A defense attorney may have as little as a few minutes (in Del Rio) or as much as half an hour (in El Paso and Tucson) to meet her Operation Streamline client, assess the client's competency, explore potential defenses or claims to immigration relief (including whether the client may face persecution if returned to his home country), obtain mitigating information, and advise her client whether to accept a plea. The client's ability to ever legally reside in the United States may hang in the balance during these few minutes, as a removal order and a conviction under 8 U.S.C. §§ 1325 or 1326 can make it impossible for a client to later obtain permanent residency or U.S. citizenship.

---

[51] Joanna Lydgate, Assembly-Line Justice: A Review of Operation Streamline, Jan. 2010, *available at* https://www.law.berkeley.edu/files/Operation_Streamline_Policy_Brief.pdf.

C. HUMAN TRAFFICKING

Human trafficking is the world's fastest growing criminal activity.[52] It is a modern-day form of slavery. Measured by profitability, human trafficking ranks third only behind the arms and drug industries.[53] Human trafficking generates an estimated $9.5 billion in annual revenue and affects over 12.3 million people worldwide.[54]

Victims of human trafficking are subject to force, fraud or coercion for the purposes of sexual exploitation or forced labor. There are two major forms of human trafficking. As defined by the Trafficking Victims Protection Act of 2000 (TVPA), "Severe Forms of Trafficking in Persons" involves either:

- Sex Trafficking: the recruitment, harboring, transportation, provision, or obtaining of a person for the purpose of a commercial sex act, in which a commercial sex act is induced by force, fraud, or coercion, or in which the person forced to perform such an act is under the age of 18 years; or

- Labor Trafficking: the recruitment, harboring, transportation, provision, or obtaining of a person for labor or services, through the use of force, fraud or coercion for the purpose of subjection to involuntary servitude, peonage, debt bondage or slavery.[55]

According to the Department of State, between 14,500 and 17,500 are trafficked into the United States annually.[56] Prior to 2000, no comprehensive federal law existed to protect victims of human trafficking or prosecute traffickers.[57] Punishment of human trafficking occurred through legislation aimed at specific components of the offense, such as immigration offenses or violations of involuntary servitude.[58] Prosecution of human trafficking using these means were minimal, and victims of human trafficking were frequently re-victimized because they were most often deported back to a country where they would be stigmatized and ostracized.[59]

Congress passed the Trafficking Victims Protection Act in October 2000 (TVPA), in the hopes of combating human trafficking more effectively and better protecting victims. TVPA allowed for easier prosecutions of human traffickers. The TVPA was reauthorized in 2003, 2005, and 2008 by the Trafficking Victims Protection Reauthorization Act (TVPRA) of 2003 (P.L. 108-193), the TVPRA of 2005 (P.L. 109-164),

---

[52] Office to Monitor and Combat Trafficking in Persons, U.S. Department of State, Trafficking in Persons Report 6 (June 3, 2005), *available at* http://www.state.gov/documents/organization/47255.pdf [hereinafter TIP Report 2005].

[53] Office to Monitor and Combat Trafficking in Persons, U.S. Department of State, Trafficking in Persons Report 13 (June 5, 2006), *available at* http://www.state.gov/documents/organization/66086.pdf [hereinafter TIP Report 2006].

[54] *Id.* at 6.

[55] Victims of Trafficking and Violence Prevention Act of 2000, Pub. L. 108-396, Oct. 28, 2000.

[56] U.S. Dep't of Health and Human Servs., Fact Sheet: Human Trafficking, *available at* http://www.acf.hhs.gov/trafficking/about/fact_human.html.

[57] http://www.acf.hhs.gov/trafficking/about/fact_human.html.

[58] Angela D. Giampolo, *The Trafficking Victim's Reauthorization Act of 2005: The Latest Weapon in the Fight Against Human Trafficking*, 16 TEMP. POL. & CIV. RTS. L. REV. 195. at 197 (Fall 2006).

[59] *Id.*

and the William Wilberforce Trafficking Victims Protection Reauthorization Act of 2008 (P.L. 110-457).Court decisions have interpreted the TVPA as expanding the Thirteenth Amendment anti-slavery provisions to apply to human traffickers.[60] In addition, the TVPA also revised the United States Code adding new crimes involving peonage and slavery, thereby expanding the definition of "involuntary servitude" to apply to human trafficking.[61]

The TVPA also increased maximum penalties for crimes relating to human trafficking. A life sentence is now allowed for death, kidnapping, an attempt to kidnap, aggravate sexual abuse, an attempt to commit aggravated sexual abuse, or an attempt to kill occurring in conjunction with a trafficking violation.[62] Sex trafficking also is made a crime punishable by life imprisonment when force, fraud or coercion is used to cause a person to engage in commercial sex acts.[63] The TVPA also augmented the penalties for kidnapping, inducing an individual into slavery, placing a person into peonage or selling someone into voluntary servitude from a 10 to 20-year maximum sentence, a fine, or both.[64] Moreover, the Act enhanced provisions safeguarding restitution to the victims for the full amount of the victim's losses and permitting victims to bring an action against their traffickers in federal district court.[65]

The FBI's efforts to investigate human trafficking are coordinated by the Civil Rights Unit (CRU) and the Violent Crimes Against Children Section (VCACS) of the Department of Justice. The CRU investigates forced labor; sex trafficking by force, fraud, or coercion; and the sexual exploitation of foreign minors, while the VCACS focuses on the commercial sexual exploitation of domestic children under the age of 18. Sex trafficking prosecutions involving children do not require proof of the use of force, fraud, or coercion.

By 2013, the FBI task forces have rescued more than 2,800 children. Investigations have led to the conviction of more than 1,400 pimps, madams, and their associates who commercially exploit children through prostitution. These convictions have resulted in lengthy sentences, including multiple life sentences and the seizure of real property, vehicles, and monetary assets.

TVPA also allowed for better prosecution of human traffickers by adding provisions protecting their victims. The most important of these provisions was the creation of the "T" and "U" visas. Congress wanted to strengthen the ability of law enforcement agencies to detect, investigate and prosecute trafficking and crimes against immigrants. Congress recognized that in order to achieve this goal the victim's cooperation and assistance was necessary. Moreover, where the victims are undocumented immigrants, their status in the United States can directly affect their ability to cooperate and assist in investigation and prosecution efforts. The TVPA therefore provided specific avenues for victims of human trafficking and

---

[60] TIP Report 2005, *supra* note 52; and *see* Giampolo, *supra* note 58 at 200.

[61] TVPA § 7102(5).

[62] Giampolo, *supra* note 58, at 200.

[63] *Id.*

[64] *Id.* at 201 and *see* TVPA § 7109(b)(2)(B).

[65] 18 U.S.C.A. § 1593, and *see* Giampolo, *supra* note 58, at 201.

certain crimes to obtain lawful immigration status through the T and U Visas.

T visas grant legal status to victims of severe form of trafficking in persons.[66] The applicant must be on U.S. territory and must be willing to comply with reasonable requests for assistance in the investigation and prosecution of their traffickers.[67] The applicant must have a law enforcement official attest to their cooperation.[68] T visa holders are eligible to apply for permanent residency after three years if they can show that they would suffer "extreme hardship involving unusual and severe harm" if they were deported.[69]

The U Visa grants temporary legal status for a period of three years, after which an applicant can apply for adjustment of status to lawful permanent resident.[70] In order to qualify for a U Visa, applicants must demonstrate that they meet the requirements set forth in INA § 101(a)(15)(U), 8 U.S.C. § 1101(a)(15)(U). In order for an application to be successful, U Visa applicants must demonstrate that they 1) were a victim of a qualifying crime, such as assault, domestic violence, false imprisonment;[71] 2) and demonstrate that "the victim has been helpful, is being helpful, or is likely to be helpful" in the investigation or prosecution of the criminal activity.[72] In order to prove their cooperation, applicants must have a qualifying law enforcement official certify in writing that they were helpful in the investigation of the crime(s). U Visas are also available for qualifying relatives. A victim's spouse, child, or if the victim is a child, their parents and minor siblings may be granted U status.

D.   LEGALIZATION

1.   Amnesty Under IRCA (1986)

On November 6, 1986, President Reagan signed into law The Immigration Reform and Control Act of 1986 (IRCA).[73] IRCA was adopted after almost a decade of intensive, highly visible public debate punctuated by several bills that passed one or both houses by slim margins only to die without final approval. When the IRCA did pass, it did so only in the waning hours of the 99th Congress, after an exceedingly fragile compromise was stitched together, and then only by thin margins.[74]

---

[66]   INA § 101(a)(15)(T)(i)(I), 8 U.S.C.A. § 1101 (a)(15)(T)(i)(I).

[67]   *Id.*

[68]   INA § 101(a)(15)(T)(i) (III), 8 U.S.C.A. § 1101(a)(15)(T).

[69]   Giampolo, *supra* note 58, at 200.

[70]   INA § 101(a)(15)(U), 8 U.S.C.A. § 1101(a)(15)(U).

[71]   INA § 101(a)(15)(U)(iii), 8 U.S.C.A. § 1101(a)(15)(U)(iii).

[72]   INA § 101(a)(15)(U)(i)(III), 8 U.S.C.A. § 1101(a)(15)(U)(i)(III).

[73]   Immigration Reform and Control Act of 1986, Pub. L. No. 99-603, codified as 8 U.S.C. § 1101.

[74]   Juan P. Osuna, *Amnesty in the Immigration Reform and Control Act of 1986: Policy Rationale and Lessons from Canada*, 3 AM. U. J. INT'L. & POL'Y 145, at 148.

This legislation contained two key provisions: employer sanctions and legalization, or amnesty, of undocumented aliens. This section focuses on the amnesty provisions of IRCA.

IRCA contained legalization programs for several groups. First, the general legalization provision granted amnesty to persons who had resided in the United States since before January 1, 1982. Second, the Special Agricultural Worker (SAW) program gave amnesty to agricultural workers, and lastly a program that gave Cubans and Haitians who had resided in the United States since before 1982 immediate permanent residence.

Before the 1970s, the United States government had never employed amnesty to address immigration problems.[75] The controversial nature of legalizing the status of millions of people illegally present in the country accounted for much of this reluctance.[76] Despite this controversy, Congress viewed an amnesty program as the least costly alternative, politically as well as financially and administratively.[77]

The debates over IRCA focused on three main questions.[78] The first question was whether to enact an immediate amnesty or a 'triggered' amnesty. A triggered amnesty would delay the legalization of aliens until a presidential commission had determined that adequate enforcement mechanism were in place.[79] The rational behind a 'triggered' amnesty was that without adequate enforcement, an amnesty would offer an invitation to thousands of aliens to cross the borders of the United States seeking legal status.[80] Some groups expressed support for a triggered amnesty, however widespread criticism quickly followed.[81] Many argued that the complexity of the provision would preclude its enactment and instead they advocated for a simplified administrative program.[82] Congress rejected a triggered amnesty in the final version of the bill in favor of a program beginning almost immediately.[83]

The cutoff date was the second major concern in the amnesty debates. Supporters of a restrictive amnesty wanted a date further in the past, whereas supporters of a liberal amnesty argued for a date closer to the date of enactment.[84] Ultimately, congress established a compromise between these two positions.[85] IRCA would grant amnesty to all undocumented immigrants present in the United States prior to January 1, 1982.[86]

---

[75] *Id.*

[76] *Id.*

[77] *Id.*

[78] *Id.* at 162.

[79] *Id.*

[80] *Id.*

[81] *Id.*

[82] *Id.*

[83] *Id.*

[84] *Id.*

[85] *Id.*

[86] *Id.*

The third issue discussed in the debates was whether to provide benefits and services to undocumented immigrants who were to receive amnesty.[87] The final version of the IRCA excluded aliens from receiving benefits for five years, except for a few selected programs such as disability benefits.[88]

a. Amnesty for Persons Residing in the United States Since Before January 1, 1982

Title II of IRCA established an amnesty provision for undocumented aliens residing in the United States and directed the Attorney General to promulgate implementing regulations. Although Title II is divided into four sections, it is the first one, the legalization status sections, that is the most important for amnesty purposes.

IRCA established that the Attorney General shall adjust the undocumented status of "an alien to that of an alien lawfully admitted for temporary residence" if the alien meets certain requirements.[89] First, in order to be granted amnesty, undocumented immigrants had to have resided in the United States continuously since before January 1, 1982 in an unlawful status. According to INA § 245A(b)(1)(B)(ii), aliens are deemed to have 'resided continuously' if they were not absent from the United States for more than "brief, casual and innocent absences" since January 1, 1982.[90] In addition, the undocumented immigrant must have been maintaining a residence in the United States and their departure must not have been based on a deportation order.[91] This section was problematic because applicants had to provide tangible documentation that they had resided in the United States for more than five years.[92] According to the regulations, this documentation included such items as past employment records, such as paycheck stubs or tax forms; utility bills; school records; hospital or medical records; attestation by churches, unions or other organizations; or any other supporting documents, like money order receipts, bank books, social security cards, automobile registrations, deeds or contracts, or insurance policies. Many undocumented immigrants in the United States, however, avoided accumulating such documentation for fear of being discovered and deported.[93] Consequently, many applicants had a difficulty proving that they arrived before 1982.[94]

Another obstacle to proving continuous residence was that undocumented individuals who entered as nonimmigrants before January 1, 1982 had to establish that their periods of authorized stay expired before that date through the passage

---

[87] *Id.*

[88] *Id.*

[89] Immigration and Nationality Act, § 245A, 8 U.S.C.A. § 12255a.

[90] INA § 245A(3)(B).

[91] INA § 245A(g)(2)(B).

[92] INA § 245A(g)(2)(D).

[93] Wilentz, *Harvest of Confusion*, TIME, Nov. 3, 1986, at 28.

[94] *Id.*

of time or that their unlawful status was known to the government as of that date.[95] The phrase 'known to the government' was a source of controversy.[96] The implementing regulations defined the phrase as meaning 'known to the INS,' despite considerable public opposition.[97] The regulations provided that an alien's unlawful status was known to the government in only four situations: 1) if the INS received information on the alien from another federal agency; 2) if the INS made an affirmative determination prior to January 1, 1982 that the alien was subject to deportation proceedings; 3) if the INS responded to an inquiry by another agency regarding the individual's status; 4) if the applicant produces documentation from a school stating that he or she had violated his or her nonimmigrant status.[98]

A lawsuit was filed to challenge the INS definition of the phrase "known to the Government." In Farzad v. Chandler, 670 F. Supp. 690 (N.D. Tex. 1987), the court held that the INS definition was inconsistent with IRCA and outside the scope of authority of the INS. In a different case, Kalaw v. Ferro, 651 F. Supp. 1163, 1170 (W.D.N.Y. 1987), the court endorsed the INS definition of the phrase. The decision in *Kalaw*, however, did express some concern that the INS interpretation of the phrase would make IRCA legalization difficult to administer.[99]

Second, applicants for amnesty under IRCA also had to show that they had not committed any felonies or more than two misdemeanors, and that they were otherwise admissible under INA § 212(a).[100]

Finally, in order to be granted amnesty, undocumented immigrants had to file an application for temporary residence between May 5, 1987 and May 4, 1988. Individuals granted amnesty under these provisions became temporary residents. They could only apply for permanent residence 18 months after they first applied for temporary residence. Moreover, in order not to lose their legal status, temporary residents were required to adjust their status to permanent residents within 12 months of becoming eligible to file.[101] That deadline was extended 12 months for each applicant by the Immigration Act of 1990.

b. Amnesty Program for Special Agricultural Workers (SAW)

The IRCA Amnesty Program for Special Agricultural Workers permitted aliens who had worked on perishable commodities for a specified period of time prior to May 1, 1986 to apply for temporary resident status. The SAW program's eligibility, benefit and application requirement provisions are somewhat more liberal than those in the general legalization program.

---

[95] INA § 245A(a)(2)(B).

[96] Juan P. Osuna, *Amnesty in the Immigration Reform and Control Act of 1986: Policy Rationale and Lessons from Canada*, 3 Am. U. J. Int'l. & Pol'y 145, at 8.

[97] *Id.*

[98] *Id.* at 140, and *see* 52 Fed. Reg. 43,845 (1987).

[99] *Id.*

[100] INA § 245A(a)(4).

[101] INA § 245A(b)(1)(A).

The SAW program was designed to maintain the availability of agricultural labor, while "protect[ing] workers to the fullest extent of all applicable federal, state, and local laws . . . to provide them with a status that insures their employment is fully governed by all relevant law without exception."[102] SAWs were not required to continue working in agriculture to gain permanent residency and could freely travel outside the United States in a manner similar to permanent resident aliens.[103]

In order to be eligible for amnesty under the SAW program, an applicant had to establish that: 1) they resided in the United States, and 2) had performed seasonal agricultural work for at least 90 man-days between May 1, 1985 and May 1, 1986.[104]

Under INA § 210(a)(1)(A), an applicant had to file for temporary residency during the 18-month period which began on June 1, 1987, and ended on November 30, 1988. Moreover, the agricultural worker had to be admissible under INA § 212(a). The provision that barred any individual convicted of a felony or more than two misdemeanors did not originally apply to SAWs, but it was added later.[105]

SAW contained a two-phase temporary residency provision. Applicants who had performed agricultural labor for 90 days during the prior three consecutive years fell into Group 1.[106] 112 Group 1 had a cap at 350,000.[107] These SAWs became legalized for permanent residency on December 1, 1989.[108] Group 2 covered all other qualified applicants all those SAWs who would be eligible for Group 1 but for the cap, and all other agricultural workers with temporary residency status under INA § 210.[109] Group 2 SAWs obtained permanent residency status on December 1, 1990.[110] SAW temporary residents were adjusted automatically on that date and had to complete only a simple form to get their permanent resident cards.[111]

At the time that the application period had closed on November 30, 1988, more than 1.1 million undocumented immigrants had applied for amnesty under SAW, and more than half of them were in California.[112]

2. Cubans and Haitians (1986)

For decades, Cubans and Haitians have been migrating to the United States seeking to flee the political turmoil and extreme poverty of their native countries. In the early months of 1980, declining economic conditions in Cuba cumulated in "a rising tide of dissatisfaction, particularly among those with relatives in the United

---

[102] H.R. REP. NO. 682, 99th Cong., 2d Sess., pt. 1, at 46, *reprinted in* 1986 U.S.C.C.A.N. 5649, 5650.

[103] INA § 210(a)(4).

[104] INA § 210(a)(1)(B).

[105] *Id.*

[106] *Id.*

[107] *Id.*

[108] *Id.*

[109] *Id.*

[110] *Id.*

[111] *Id.*

[112] Schuck, *supra* note 6, at 6.

States."[113] In response, Fidel Castro announced on April 4, 1980 that anyone who wished to leave Cuba could do so.[114] Thousands chose to do so through chartered flights to Costa Rica.[115] Yet due to the number of émigrés and their increasing publicity, Castro soon suspended air travel.[116] On April 20, 1980, he announced that anyone who wished to emigrate to the United States could, but only by boat and only through the port of Mariel.[117]

Within hours of this broadcast, fleets of boats left southern Florida to pick up relatives and others seeking to leave Cuba.[118] The Mariel boatlift began as a small boat exodus of several thousands of Cubans that were welcomed into the United States as refugees from the Castro government. After President Carter offered an "open arms" welcome to the initial group, however, these numbers swelled to over 125,000. All of the refugees were called "Marielitos" because of the port of Cuba from which they launched to sea.

The Carter administration had a hard time classifying this large group of Cubans, and declined to assign them refugee status.[119] The Cubans of the Mariel boatlift were already in the United States but the administration wanted to avoid setting a precedent that might encourage people from other countries to enter the United States without documents and claim to be refugees.[120] The Refugee Act of 1980 allowed for asylee status to be granted to those already in the United States, but the status was meant for individual applicants and not large groups of people.[121]

Cubans were arriving from Mariel joined a number of boats crowded with Haitians émigrés. These Haitian boats had been arriving in southern Florida since the early 1970s, but the attention given to the Cuban refugees sparked public debate and controversy. Since Haiti and Cuba are neighboring islands that were both ruled by dictators (one leftist and anti-American, the other right-wing and pro-American),[122] the situation of their citizens fleeing to the United States had to be compared. Successive U.S. administrations had consistently contended that most Haitians were illegal immigrants while virtually all Cubans were refugees and asylees.[123] This disparate treatment of Haitians and Cubans had caused political and legal difficulties and evoked charges of racism because the Cubans tended to be white whereas Haitian immigrants were exclusively black.[124] Over the

---

[113] Vernon M. Briggs, Jr., Mass Immigration and the National Interest 143 (M.E. Sharpe Publishers 2003).

[114] *Id.*

[115] *Id.*

[116] *Id.*

[117] *Id.*

[118] *Id.*

[119] *Id.* at 144.

[120] *Id.*

[121] *Id.*

[122] *Id.* at 145.

[123] *Id.*

[124] *Id.*

years, the INS had returned several hundred prospective immigrants to Haiti because they did not believe they were seeking protection from political persecution.[125]

As the number of Haitian immigrants increased during the Mariel Era, the Carter administration refused to exercise its authority to parole for Haitians as a group.[126] Instead, they were given the same status as Cubans who entered during this time. On June 20, 1980, the U.S. attorney general administratively established a new temporary status for the immigrants from both countries. They were designated as "Cuban-Haitian Entrants (Status Pending)" and were given a six-month parole into the United States.[127] This status was later extended to all those who entered as of October 10, 1980. In total, over 6,000 Haitians and 123,000 Cubans entered the United States during this six-month period and their immigration status remained uncertain.[128]

When Reagan replaced Carter in 1981, the Reagan administration began to take a strong stand against Haitians trying to enter the United States by sea.[129] The U.S. Coast Guard was ordered to interdict Haitians on the high seas and turn them back before they could enter U.S. territorial waters and claim asylum.[130] The U.S. government also simultaneously started placing all mass arrivals of people into detention centers rather than releasing them to sponsors, as had been the practice up to that time.[131] Lawsuits were filed to challenge this detention policy as racially discriminatory against Haitians, but the U.S. Supreme Court ultimately decided that detention policy was legal and not discriminatory.[132]

The Reagan administration continued to give Cubans preferential treatment and announced that all Cubans whose status was pending could adjust their status to become legal permanent residents under the Cuban Adjustment Act of 1966.[133] Efforts were also made by advocates to grant status to Haitians who had entered during the Mariel era, but these failed.[134]

IRCA was ultimately the legislation that concluded the controversy over the status of "Cuban-Haitian Entrants." Section 202 of the IRCA granted amnesty to Cubans and Haitians who had resided in the United States since before 1982.[135] The applicant had to : 1) have received an immigration designation as "Cuban/Haitian Entrant" or, 2) be a Cuban or Haitian national with respect to

---

[125] *Id.*

[126] *Id.*

[127] *Id.* at 146.

[128] *Id.*

[129] *Id.*

[130] *Id.*

[131] *Id.*

[132] *Id.*

[133] *Id.*

[134] *Id.* at 147.

[135] IRCA, *supra* note 79, at section 202.

whom any record was established with the INS before January 1, 1982.[136]

In order to qualify, the Cuban or Haitian had to apply within a two year window, which ended on November 6, 1988.[137] Haitians and Cubans who applied and qualified became immediately eligible for permanent residence as of January 1, 1982, and were therefore immediately eligible for naturalization as well.[138]

3. Nicaraguans and Cubans (1997)

Several political groups sympathetic to the plight of undocumented immigrants after the passage of IIRIRA in 1996 petitioned Congress to enact reforms.[139] The establishment of IIRIRA posed a threat of mass deportation of immigrants throughout the United States.[140] In 1997, Central American advocates launched a new campaign to win legal permanent residency for Salvadorans and Guatemalans.[141] Salvadoran and Guatemalan authorities concerned with the destabilizing effects that would result from deportations also lobbied for a remedy.[142] Several months into the campaign, Salvadorans and Guatemalans joined forces with Nicaraguans who had fled the Sandinista government and were also victims of IIRIRA.[143] These lobbying efforts resulted in the passage of Nicaraguan Adjustment and Central American Relief Act of 1997 (NACARA).[144]

Congress passed NACARA to provide relief to select groups of immigrants and protect long-time residents from deportation. NACARA used separate provisions to address two statutorily distinct groups of immigrants. The first provision applies to Cubans and Nicaraguans, and the second applies to Guatemalans, Salvadorans and Eastern Europeans.

a. NACARA Provisions for Nicaraguans and Cubans

NACARA enables certain eligible noncitizens who are physically present in the United States to adjust to legal permanent residency status, regardless of whether they had been inspected and admitted or paroled.[145] In order to be eligible for adjustment of status under NACARA 202(a), an applicant must: 1) be a national of Nicaragua or Cuba; 2) have been physically present in the U.S. continuously from at least December 1, 2005 until the date the application is filed; 3) be otherwise

---

[136] Id.

[137] Id.

[138] Id.

[139] 14 Cardozo J. Int'l & Comp. L. 177, at 191.

[140] Id.

[141] Susan Coutin, *The Odyssey of Salvadoran Asylum Seekers, North American Congress on Latin America Report on the Americas*, May 1, 2004, at 38 (noting that more than one million Salvadorans fled to the United States from 1980 to 1992 during El Salvador's civil war).

[142] Id.

[143] Id.

[144] Id.

[145] Nicaraguan Adjustment and Central American Relief Act, Pub. L. No. 105-100, 111 Stat. 2160, Tit. II, Div. A (1997) [hereinafter NACARA].

admissible to the United States; and 4) have filed an application for adjustment of status before April 1, 2000.[146]

Pursuant to § 202, Cubans and Nicaraguans seeking permanent residency status under NACARA only had to complete an adjustment of status form. Applicants did have to show proof of continuous physical presence through reliable documentation. For the purposes of the statute, "continuous physical presence" meant physical presence in the United States with total absences not exceeding 180 days. Absences between November 19, 1997 and June 22, 1998, however, were not counted for continuous presence purposes.[147] Moreover, on March 17, 2000, the Department of Justice issued various final regulations that establish a more flexible standard for proving initial presence and continuous residence in the United States.[148]

Applicants for permanent residency under NACARA faced few bars to their adjustment. A Cuban or Nicaraguan applicant under NACARA was not subject to several inadmissibility requirements, such as public charge and labor certification provisions. Moreover, these applicants could be granted permanent residence even if they were in exclusion, deportation, or removal proceedings. If there had been a final administrative determination to deny their application, however, the applicant could not adjust their status under NACARA.

NACARA also allowed Nicaraguans and Cubans to file derivative claims for adjustment of status and obtain work authorization for their spouses and children.[149] In order to apply, the spouse or child had to be present in the United States.[150] If the individual was not in the United States, the primary applicant could file a parole application to request that their spouse or child be admitted into the country in order to apply for NACARA adjustment.[151]

4. Haitians (1998)

NACARA allowed for the adjustment of status for certain Nicaraguan and Cuban national, and more limited immigration relief for immigrants from other countries. NACARA, however, failed to address the status of Haitian nationals who were in a similar position.[152] Advocates for Haitian immigrants made immediate calls for action.[153] President Bill Clinton responded by granting certain Haitian nationals Deferred Enforced Departure (DED) status pending congressional action to address their plight.[154] The Clinton Administration and a bipartisan coalition of members of Congress worked together to establish relief for at least

---

[146] *Id.*

[147] *Id.*

[148] *See* 65 Fed. Reg. 15,846–15,925, reprinted in Interpreter Releases, March 24, 2000, Appendix II

[149] *Id.* at § 202(d)(1)(B).

[150] *Id.*

[151] *Id.*

[152] Austin T. Fragomen, IMMIGRATION FUNDAMENTALS: A GUIDE TO LAW AND PRACTICE 4–49 (Practicing Law Institute).

[153] *Id.*

[154] *Id.*

some Haitian nationals who had entered the United States.[155] The Haitian Refugee Immigration Fairness Act of 1998 (HRIFA) was the result of these efforts. HRIFA was enacted as part of an omnibus bill for the fiscal year 1999.

HIFRA provides that certain Haitian nationals can adjust their status to permanent residence. HIFRA established that to be eligible for adjustment of status, a Haitian national must have been present in the United States on December 31, 1995, and 1) have filed for asylum before December 31, 1995, and 2) have been paroled in the United States prior to December 31, 1995, after having been identified as having a credible fear of persecution, or paroled "for emergent reasons deemed strictly in the public interest."[156] A Haitian could also be eligible for adjustment of status if they were a child, as defined by the INA, at the time of arrival and on December 31, 1995, who 1) arrived without parents and remained without parents in the United States since arrival; 2) became orphaned subsequent to arrival in the United States; or 3) was abandoned by parents or guardians prior to April 1, 1998, and had remained abandoned since that date.[157]

The statute also required that an eligible Haitian be physically present continuously from at least December 31, 1995 to the date the application was filed.[158] Again, aggregate absences of not more than 180 days did not affect the continuous physical presence required by the provision. Also, applicants were exempt from similar inadmissibility provisions as NACARA applicants. Haitians were still able to qualify for HRIFA if they were 1) considered a public charge; or 2) had labor certification or other special qualifications; 3) were present in the United States without admission or parole; 4) were immigrants without proper documents; 4) had been unlawfully present in the United States.[159]

Derivate applications were also allowed. HRIFA allowed an applicant's spouse, child, or unmarried son or daughter to also be eligible for status under the act provided that the qualifying relative was: 1) a national of Haiti, 2) was otherwise admissible, and 3) applied for such adjustment and was physically present in the U.S. on the date the application was filed.[160] There was an exception to this last requirement for unmarried sons and daughters: they had to establish continuous physical presence from December 31, 1995 to the date of application. Spouses and children of the applicant only had to be physically present in the United States on the date the application was filed.[161]

Haitian HRIFA applicants faced certain obstacles to filing their applications. First, applications had to be filed between June 11, 1999 and April 1, 2000.[162]

---

[155] *Id.*

[156] Haitian Refugee Immigration Fairness Act of 1998, Pub. L. 105-277 (Oct. 21, 1998).

[157] *Id.*

[158] *Id.*

[159] *Id.*

[160] *Id.*

[161] *Id.*

[162] *Id.*

However, this limited application window only applied to principal applicants.[163] The period for eligible family members to apply remains open indefinitely.[164] A second obstacle applicants faced was dealing with the burdensome document requirements.[165] HRIFA applicants had to present a birth certificate.[166] They also needed documentary evidence that they had been present in the United States on December 31, 1995, and documents proving their residence for each 90 period since then.[167]

5. Proposed Legalization Programs

While President Bush's guestworker proposal was not introduced as independent legislation, his plan was incorporated into a bipartisan compromise in early April 2006 written largely by Senators Mel Martinez (R-Florida) and Chuck Hagel (R-Nebraska) (Hagel-Martinez bill). The compromise is best understood in the context of a number of other guestworker proposals that have been proposed in Congress. Some, like the Hagel-Martinez bill, have included a separate path toward legalization (permanent residence and eventual citizenship) for undocumented workers. Others are limited to agricultural workers. Their approaches to wages vary. The most noteworthy are summarized in the following sections.

a. AgJOBS

In 2003, the Agricultural Jobs Opportunity, Benefits and Security (AgJOBS) Act was introduced in the House (H.R. 3142) and the Senate (S. 1645) after several years of bipartisan efforts and earlier iterations. The sponsors of the House Bill were Representatives Chris Cannon (R-Utah) and Howard Brennan (D-California). Senators Edward Kennedy (D-Massachusetts) and Larry Craig (R-Idaho) sponsored the Senate version. The bill would have granted lawful permanent residency to as many as 500,000 undocumented farmworkers and revised the current H-2A agricultural worker program. The bill represented a compromise between the farmworker advocates and their employers and contained several concessions on both sides.

After six years, a worker would be eligible for legalization. Under the legislation, temporary resident status would be granted to undocumented farmworkers who could establish proof of 575 hours of agricultural work or 100 workdays during the 18-month period preceding the introduction of the legislation. After the grant of temporary resident status, the farmworker would be required to complete an additional 2,060 hours of agricultural work or 360 workdays during the next six years to be eligible for lawful permanent residency.

---

[163] *Id.*

[164] *Id.*

[165] *Id.*

[166] *Id.*

[167] *Id.*

The proposed changes to the current H-2A guestworker program by AgJOBS was significant. The legislation would replace the labor certification process of the present H-2A program (requiring that recruitment efforts of available U.S. workers have been attempted and failed) with the labor attestation found in the H-1B program (where the employer simply attests in a statement that U.S. workers are unavailable). This was a major concession by farmworker advocates who believe that the present labor certification process is more protective of farmworker wages than the proposed labor attestation process.

Changes to the wage structures were also contemplated by AgJOBS. The legislation would effectively freeze the Adverse Effect Wage Rate (AEWR) for three years. AEWR is used to determine the wages that farmworkers receive. Employers wanted to eliminate AEWR altogether. Currently, employers must pay workers the highest of three rates: the state or federal minimum wage, the AEWR, or the local prevailing wage. The AEWR was created under the Bracero program as a necessary protection against the depression in prevailing wages that results from guestworker programs.

The proposal also would expand the H-2A program by allowing temporary workers to enter the United States for a period of up to three years. After three years, these guestworkers would be obligated to return to their countries of origin. This provision sounded very familiar to the guestworker reform proposed by President Bush. However, AgJOBS' opportunity for legalization after six years was not part of the president's plan.

b. Hagel-Daschle

Soon after President Bush announced his temporary worker proposal in January 2004, Senators Chuck Hagel (R-Nebraska) and Tom Daschle (D-South Dakota) unveiled their bipartisan immigration reform package that contained a temporary worker provision. [Note: Senator Daschle was not reelected to the Senate November 2004.]

A new H-2C category would be open to 250,000 nonimmigrant workers per year for five years and would not be limited to agricultural workers. Workers would be admitted for an initial period of two years, and employers would be allowed to petition for extensions for workers for an additional two years. Spouses and children of willing workers would be eligible for derivative status. Employers would be required to pay the prevailing wage, and H-2C employees would be allowed to maintain status and change employers after three months.

The legislation also contained a path to legalization ("earned adjustment of status") for undocumented immigrants who had resided in the United States for at least five years prior to the introduction of the legislation. They must also demonstrate aggregate employment in the United States for at least three of the five years immediately preceding the introduction of the legislation and for at least one year following the enactment. An alien who filed an application for earned adjustment of status would be required to pay a fine plus a $1,000 application fee.

An alien who was physically present in the United States on the date the legislation was introduced, but who did not satisfy the five-year physical presence requirements, would be able to apply for "transitional worker status." Transitional workers would be eligible for adjustment of status to permanent residence if they were lawfully employed in the United States for an aggregate of more than two but fewer than three of the five years immediately preceding the introduction of the legislation and are employed for at least two years following the enactment.

c. Goodlatte-Chambliss

In November 2003, Congressman Bob Goodlatte (R-Virginia) introduced legislation that would substantially alter the H-2A agricultural worker program. The program's application process would be streamlined to become a labor attestation program, rather than the current labor certification program. Employers would simply promise to comply with requirements (e.g., temporary nature of the work, benefits, wages, recruitment of domestic workers). The Department of Labor would have seven days to review and approve the employer's petition for workers. The employer would still need to engage in "positive recruitment" (i.e., private market efforts) in areas of labor supply but would no longer be required to recruit U.S. workers through government job services efforts. The legislation would eliminate the AEWR. A special "prevailing wage" would apply that could be determined by the employers' own prevailing wage survey. Currently, H-2A employers must provide free housing to nonlocal U.S. and foreign workers, but under this legislation, employers could choose to provide a monetary housing allowance if the state's governor has certified that there is sufficient farmworker housing available in the area. With philosophical undertones similar to that of President Bush, Congressman Goodlatte felt that his legislation was a good way to address the problem of undocumented workers in the United States, by providing a streamlined temporary visa program through which farmworkers could be hired. Workers currently in the United States in undocumented status would be given a one-time chance to return home and apply for the program legally.

Senator Saxby Chambliss (R-Georgia) introduced a Senate bill in March 2004 that was almost identical to the Goodlatte bill. The Chambliss bill added a couple of noteworthy provisions. Currently, employers must reimburse workers for their transportation costs to and from their place of recruitment. This bill would allow employers to pay for travel costs to and from the place where the worker was approved to enter the United States, which could be the U.S. consulate hundreds of miles from the worker's home. The bill sought to overrule the decision in *Arriaga v. Florida Pacific Farms*,[168] regarding the Fair Labor Standards Act. It would essentially allow H-2A employers to reduce worker's wages below the federal minimum wage by imposing on the workers the obligation to absorb visa, transportation, and other costs related to entering the United States. Although the current H-2A program is intended to fill agricultural jobs that last fewer than 11 months, the Chambliss bill would distort the definition of "seasonal" employment by allowing an employer to file an unlimited number of applications for guestworkers during a 12-month period.[169]

---

[168] 305 F.3d 1228 (11th Cir. 2002).

[169] Farmworker Justice Fund, Inc. Policy Brief, September 2004.

d. SOLVE Act

In May 2004, congressional Democrats introduced the Safe, Orderly, Legal Visas and Enforcement Act of 2004 (SOLVE Act), sponsored by such legislators as Senator Edward Kennedy (D-Massachusetts) and Representatives Bob Menedez (D-New Jersey) and Luis Gutierres (D-Illinois). The comprehensive package proposed changes to facilitate family reunification in the immigrant visa categories and reductions in the waiting lists (backlog reduction) as well as adjustment to the income tests for sponsors and would have established a "future worker program." New programs would be established for workers in low skilled positions. H-1D visas would be available to 250,000 workers for a period of two years, and the visas would be renewable for two additional terms (six years total). H-2B visas would be available to 100,000 workers for a period of nine months and renewable for up to 40 months. After three months with one employer, the workers in each category could change employers (job portability). The Department of Labor would have to agree through the "strengthened" attestation process that U.S. workers are not available and that the employment of foreign workers will not adversely affect the wages and working conditions of U.S. workers. H-2B and H-1D workers would be paid the prevailing wage, as determined by the shop's collective bargaining agreement or, in its absence, under federal labor laws.

The programs would include a path to permanent residency for undocumented immigrants. Immigrants who have been in the United States for five or more years as of the date the legislation was introduced are eligible, if they can demonstrate 24 months in aggregate employment in the United States and payment taxes. Applicants here fewer than five years are eligible for transitional status of five years, during which time they can work and travel abroad if necessary. After 24 months, they too would be eligible for permanent residence.

e. Arizona Bill

Republican members of the Arizona congressional delegation came up with their own plan. H.R. 2899 was introduced by Congressmen Kolbe and Flake in the House and Senator McCain (S. 1461) in the Senate in July 2003. The legislation would have created a new nonimmigrant worker visa category, H-4A. Employers would have to provide the same benefits, wages, and working conditions provided to other employees similarly employed; the visa would be portable — employers could not prevent nonimmigrants from accepting work for a different employer. The employer would have to verify that the worker did not or would not displace a U.S. worker. The visa would be valid for an initial period of three years and could be extended once for another three years. The spouse and children of the worker would not be given a special visa to join the worker. A filing fee plus a $1,500 penalty would be required. Adjustment to legal permanent resident (LPR) status would be available to the H-4A nonimmigrant either by petition of employer or through self-petition, if the alien has maintained status for three years.

Critics of the McCain/Kolbe/Flake proposal included another Arizona Republican congressman, J.D. Hayworth. He claimed that the legislation was a "transparent path to amnesty" that would "only encourage a new wave of illegal aliens and make America's uncontrolled and unacceptable immigration debacle even worse than it is now." A local resident complained that the legislation was "not a solution because it does not address the true problem of uncontrolled borders with Mexico and Canada. It is a surrender because politicians from both parties are pandering to the Latino vote."[170]

f. McCain-Kennedy

With some fanfare and timed when the Migration Policy Institute announced the formation of an Immigration Task Force to analyze immigration policy, Senators McCain and Kennedy and Representatives Kolbe, Flake, and Gutierrez introduced sweeping immigration reform in May 2005 that included major guestworker components: H-5A and H-5B.

A new temporary worker visa (H-5A) would be created for nonagriculture or high skilled jobs. To qualify, the person must have a job offer. H-5A workers would have the same rights as U.S. workers under applicable federal, state, and local government and employment laws; they would not be treated as independent contractors. For the first year, at least 400,000 visas will be made available, with up to 80,000 more depending on demand. Available visas in subsequent years will follow similar formulas. After four years of work, H-5A visa holder may apply for lawful permanent resident status through an employer or through self-petition.

The H-5B program is for aliens (including undocumented) who are in the United States before the date of introduction of the legislation (May 2005). The person's spouse and children may also apply. The applicant must pay an initial $1,000 fine. The initial period of authorized stay is for six (three plus three) years. After a period of time, the person eligible for adjustment to LPR status if still working, must pay an additional $1,000 fine, must submit to security checks, and must demonstrate knowledge of English and U.S. civics.

While Senator McCain went through great pains to make sure that the legislation is not viewed as an amnesty by emphasizing the penalties that undocumented workers would have to pay to participate in the program, Representative Tancredo immediately expressed opposition: "There might be a little more lipstick on this pig than there was before," he said, "but it is most certainly the same old pig. Time and time again, history has shown us that amnesty actually increases illegal immigration."[171] Similarly, Rosemary Jenks, director of government affairs for Numbers USA, which advocates reducing the undocumented immigrant population, said her group also opposed the McCain-Kennedy proposal and only "would support an exit amnesty, like a tax amnesty, that would allow illegal immigrants to leave and not apply a ban on future reentry."[172]

---

[170] John P. Hoeppner, *Border Proposal Is a Surrender*, Arizona Republic, Aug. 5, 2003, at 8B.

[171] Darryl Fears, *Immigration Measure Introduced*, Washington Post, May 13, 2005, at A8.

[172] *Id.*

g. Hagel-Martinez

For much of March 2006, the U.S. Senate wrangled over the issue of immigration. Although the McCain-Kennedy proposal sparked much of the debate that occurred first in the Judiciary Committee, Committee Chair Senator Arlen Specter (R-Pennsylvania) came up with his own legislation that attempted to balance McCain-Kennedy provisions with pressure from others to include strong enforcement provisions. For example, Republican Senate Majority Leader Bill Frist threatened to come up with his own Sensenbrenner-type bill if the Judiciary Committee failed to produce something. In fact, even though the committee did put forward a bill, Frist introduced his own bill (S. 2454) anyway, threatening to make his the central bill if an accord was not reached by Easter break. The Senate debate raged on.

Two days prior to the congressional break, a major breakthrough was made when a bipartisan compromise was cobbled together by Senators Hagel and Martinez. The Hagel-Martinez bill (S. 2611) was embraced by two-thirds of the senators, including Senators Frist, McCain, Kennedy, and Reid. The deal came after days of negotiations designed to persuade Republicans who had supported the more lenient measure that emerged from the Senate Judiciary Committee to shift their backing to a bill with more Republican ownership. The Democrats thought they still had enough votes to pass the Judiciary Committee version until two of the Judiciary Committee bill's primary sponsors, Senators McCain and Lindsey Graham (R-South Carolina), informed Kennedy that they were no longer with him and, instead, would back the Hagel-Martinez compromise. Able to secure a few changes in the compromise, Kennedy went to the Senate floor to urge Democrats to endorse the deal.

The Hagel-Martinez compromise in early April addressed the issue of undocumented immigrants in a number of manners. For those who could prove that they had been in the country for five years or more (perhaps eight million), a renewable work visa would be granted after paying a $2,000 penalty, back taxes, and undergoing a criminal background check. After five years, those individuals could apply for legalization provided they remained employed, learned English, and did not commit crimes. For those undocumented who were in the country for more than two years but less than five (perhaps three million), a temporary work visa was available if they left the country and applied for the visa outside. The bill also provided for a Bush-type guestworker program for 325,000 visas annually.

The compromise immediately received criticism from the right and the left. Senator John Kyle (R-Arizona) dismissed the deal as "artificial and meaningless," and former House speaker Newt Gingrich (R-Georgia) called it "a cave-in" to the Democrats. Congressman Tancredo chimed in, "The Senate amnesty deal is miserable public policy."[173] On the other hand, the AFL-CIO President John Sweeney, desiring a broader legalization program, said the agreement "tears at the heart of true immigration reform."[174] Immigrant rights advocates were opposed

---

[173] Jonathan Weisman, *Senate Offers Permits to Most Illegal Immigrants*, WASHINGTON POST, Apr. 7, 2006, at A1.

[174] *Id.*

because of provisions such as those that would preclude the participation of anyone who had used a false Social Security number to obtain employment in the past, permit indefinite and possibly permanent detention of deportable immigrants, expand the use of expedited removal proceedings, give local and state police the authority to assist the federal government in enforcing federal immigration laws, and permit the deportation of someone who has never committed a crime if the attorney general had reason to believe that the person is a member of a gang.

On April 7, 2006, the day before Congress took its break, the agreement on Hagel-Martinez appeared to fall apart. Republicans blamed the Democrats and vice versa. The disagreement was over whether amendments could be introduced to the bill floor of the Senate and what rules would be used in a Senate-House conference that would ultimately reconcile the Senate bill with the enforcement-only Sensenbrenner House bill. The Democratic leadership also was concerned about the rules that would govern the conference between the two bodies of Congress. They feared that without a bipartisan agreement on rules limiting concessions to the House, Congressman Sensenbrenner, who certainly would be one of the House conferees, would have his way and the legislation would come out of the negotiations intensely anti-immigrant. With no agreement over process, the Senate took its Easter break.

However, discussions continued. President Bush met with a bipartisan group in late April that included Senators Martinez, McCain, Kennedy, Reid, Specter, and Frist, signaling to many that the president was willing to endorse the legalization provisions of Hagel-Martinez. When the Senate reconvened on April 24, 2006, these senators were committed to bringing the legislation provisions of Hagel-Martinez. When the Senate reconvened on April 24, 2006, these senators were committed to bringing the legislation to the Senate floor by Memorial Day. They worked tirelessly and considered countless amendments. On May 15, President Bush delivered a major primetime address to the nation on the immigration issue, reiterating his earlier message but acknowledging that undocumented immigrants with "roots in the country" deserve a path to citizenship. By May 25, Hagel-Martinez passed the Senate by a 62–63 margin.

The May 25 legislation differed somewhat from the early April bill. Undocumented immigrants who have been in the country five years or more can continue working and eventually become lawful permanent residents and citizens after paying at least $3,250 in fines, fees, and back taxes and learning English. Those here from two to five years would have to depart the country and apply to reenter under a guestworker program. Anyone convicted of a felony or three misdemeanors is barred from these programs. Those undocumented here less than two years would have to leave the United States. AgJOBS was incorporated, which would put a million undocumented farmworkers on the path to legalization. A guestworker program would be created for up to 200,000 workers per-year; visas would be good for three years with a possible three-year extension. An additional 370-mile, triple layer fence along the U.S.-Mexico border would be constructed. The president is authorized to send six thousand National Guardsmen to help at the border. Employers are subject to increased fines and criminal penalties for hiring unauthorized workers. The names of overstayed nonimmigrants would be added to a national crime database.

A Senate-House conference committee was formed to try to reconcile the enforcement-only Sensenbrenner House bill with the more comprehensive Hagel-Martinez Senate bill that contains a path to legalization for millions of undocumented, a compromise that would include legalization appeared doubtful. Certainly, Senator Frist's support remained important. Although he once supported the House version that would make illegal immigration a felony, he changed his position, remarking on how "a mature understanding" of the handling of undocumented immigration emerged in the Senate after weeks of debate. But Congressman Sensenbrenner, the chief negotiator for the House, stated that he would not accept any legislation that would put the undocumented immigrants on a path to citizenship, and his intransigence could prevail.

h. DREAM Act

The Development, Relief, and Education for Alien Minors Act, or "DREAM Act" first introduced in 2001, would provide a pathway to legal status for the thousands of undocumented students who graduate from high school each year. Under the DREAM Act, most undocumented students who came to the United States at age 15 or younger at least five years before the date of the bill's enactment and who have maintained good moral character since entering the country would qualify for conditional permanent resident status upon acceptance to college, graduation from a U.S. high school, or being awarded a GED in the U.S. Students would not qualify for this relief if they had committed crimes, were a security risk, or were inadmissible or removable on certain other grounds. Under various versions, qualifying students must be under age 30 or 35.

Each year, approximately 65,000 undocumented students graduate from high school, but cannot go to college, join the military, work, or otherwise pursue their dreams. They belong to the 1.5 generation — any (first generation) immigrants brought to the United States at a young age who were largely raised in this country and therefore share much in common with second-generation Americans. These students are culturally American, growing up here and often having little attachment to their country of birth. They tend to be bicultural and fluent in English. Many did not even know that they are undocumented immigrants until they apply for a driver's license or college, and then learn they lack Social Security numbers and other necessary legal documents.

The DREAM Act addresses the plight of young undocumented immigrants growing up in the United States who wish to go to college and obtain lawful employment. The bill allows current, former, and future undocumented high-school graduates and GED recipients a pathway to U.S. citizenship through college or the armed services.

An undocumented high-school graduate or GED recipient would be eligible to adjust to conditional lawful permanent resident (LPR) status if they have been physically present in the United States for at least five years and were younger than 16 when they first entered the country.

This LPR status would be granted on a conditional basis and valid for six years, during which time the student would be allowed to work, go to school, or join the military. The conditional status would be removed and the person granted LPR status after six years once the student has either completed two years in a program for a bachelor's degree or higher degree or has served in the uniformed services for at least two years and, if discharged, has received an honorable discharge.

DREAM Act students would not be eligible for federal education grants. Students would, however, be eligible for federal work study and student loans, and individual states would not be restricted from providing financial aid to the students.

An estimated 2.1 million undocumented children and young adults in the United States would be eligible for legal status under the DREAM Act. For many of these young people, the United States is the only home they know and English is their first language. The DREAM Act would provide an opportunity for them to live up to their full potential and make greater contributions to the U.S. economy and society. Research has shown that the DREAM Act would be a boon to the economy and the U.S. workforce.

If enacted, under the DREAM Act:

- 114,000 potential beneficiaries with at least an associate's degree would be immediately eligible for conditional LPR status.

- 612,000 potential beneficiaries would be immediately eligible for conditional LPR status because they already have a high-school diploma or GED (and would have the incentive to complete two years of college or two years of military service to be eligible for permanent status).

- 934,000 children under 18 could be eligible for conditional LPR status in the future, which would provide them with incentives to finish high school and pursue a post-secondary education or join the military.

- 489,000 potential beneficiaries could be eligible for conditional LPR status in the future if they obtain a GED.

DREAM Act-eligible immigrants live in all 50 states, but some states have far more potential beneficiaries than others. The top 10 states with the largest number of potential DREAM Act beneficiaries are California (26 percent of the national total), Texas (12 percent), Florida (9 percent), New York (7 percent), Arizona (5 percent), Illinois (4 percent), New Jersey (4 percent), Georgia (3 percent), North Carolina (2 percent), and Colorado (2 percent). All other states combined are home to one-quarter of potential DREAM Act beneficiaries.

The DREAM Act came close to passage in 2010. On December 8, 2010, the House passed the legislation by a vote of 216 to 198. However, on December 18, 2010, a minority of Senators blocked the DREAM Act from being considered in the Senate, by rejecting a cloture motion (to end a filibuster) by a vote of 55 to 41; 60 votes were needed to prevent a filibuster.

Of course, DREAMers and their supporters were disappointed and called on President Obama to act administratively.[175] So on June 15, 2012, President Obama announced that DREAMers would be granted deferred action and employment

---

[175] *President Obama to Halt Deportation of DREAMers*, June 15, 2012, *available at* http://immigrationimpact.com/2012/06/15/president-obama-to-halt-removal-of-dreamers/.

authorization for at least two years.[176] Not coincidentally, his decision came after DREAM activist Gaby Pacheco met with Republican Senator Marco Rubio and a weeklong protest and sit-in at the Obama campaign office in Denver, Colorado.[177]

Under the directive, deferred action could be granted on a case-by-case basis to individuals who meet the following criteria: they came to the United States when they were younger than 16, they have continuously resided in the United States for at least five years, and they are in school, have graduated from high school, have obtained a GED or are honorably discharged veterans of the armed forces. The individuals could qualify if they had not been convicted of a felony, significant misdemeanor offense or multiple misdemeanor offenses, or otherwise posed a threat to national security or public safety.[178] And they had to be under age 31.

Deferred Action for Childhood Arrivals (DACA) status was granted to 553,197 applicants by March 2014. Only 20,311 applicants were denied. After the initial two-year period, individuals could request DACA renewal if they continued to meet the initial criteria and these additional guidelines: (a) did not depart the United States on or after Aug. 15, 2012, without advance parole; (b) continuously resided in the United States since they submitted their most recent DACA request that was approved; and (c) had not been convicted of a felony, a significant misdemeanor or three or more misdemeanors, and do not otherwise pose a threat to national security or public safety.

i.   Border Security, Economic Opportunity and Immigration Modernization Act of 2013

In President Obama's second term, a bipartisan group of Senators forged a broad agreement on immigration, and the Senate passed the Border Security, Economic Opportunity and Immigration Modernization Act of 2013 (S.744), which, if enacted, would comprise the largest-scale overhaul of our immigration system in more than 25 years. Significantly, the bill would provide a road to U.S. citizenship for perhaps as many as 11 million unauthorized immigrants, allocate billions for militarization of

---

[176] *Id.* When the Morton memo was issued, supporters of same-sex couples sought explicit assurances from DHS and the White House that the foreign-born partner of a U.S. citizen would be granted prosecutorial discretion. Administration officials had stated that being in a same-sex relationship would be considered in the context of the "community contributions" and "family relationships" factors in the Morton memo. But activists and Democratic lawmakers sought additional assurances that bi-national same-sex couples would not be left out. Chris Johnson, *Lawmakers seek added protections for bi-national gay couple*, WASHINGTONBLADE.COM, Sept. 27, 2011, http://www.washingtonblade.com/2011/09/27/lawmakers-seek-added-protections-for-bi-national-gay-couples/. Finally, more than a year later, DHS Secretary Napolitano announced: "In an effort to make clear the definition of the phrase 'family relationships,' I have directed ICE to disseminate written guidance to the field that the interpretation of the phrase 'family relationships' includes long-term, same-sex partners." Miranda Leitsinger, *US Immigration Chief: Same-sex ties are family ties*, NBC NEWS.COM, Sept. 28, 2012, http://usnews.nbcnews.com/_news/2012/09/28/14140024-us-immigration-chief-same-sex-ties-are-family-ties?lite.

[177] Julia Preston, *Young Immigrants Say It's Obama's Time to Act*, N.Y. TIMES, Nov. 30, 2012; Julianne Hing, *DREAMers Stage Sit-Ins at Obama Office to Force Deportation Standoff*, COLORLINES, June 13, 2012, http://colorlines.com/archives/2012/06/dreamers_planned_obama_campaign_office_sit-ins_force_deportation_standoff.html.

[178] *A Breakdown of DHS's Deferred Action for DREAMers*, June 18, 2012, *available at* http://immigrationimpact.com/2012/06/18/a-breakdown-of-dhss-deferred-action-for-dreamers/.

the southern border, and restructure the family immigration system. The bill also would create stringent enforcement and deportation measures, and ramp up workplace enforcement by mandating that employers use an electronic employment eligibility verification system (E-Verify). The main portions of S. 744 relating to undocumented immigrants were as follows:

TITLE I: BORDER SECURITY

Initial implementation. Within six months of the bill's passage, the secretary of the U.S. Department of Homeland Security (DHS) would be required to craft a strategy to increase surveillance at all southern border sectors and to extend the existing barriers along the U.S.-Mexico border so that they total 700 miles of barriers/fencing. The goal of the strategy would be to apprehend nine out of every 10 immigrants who attempt to enter the country at these border sectors without permission (also known as a 90 percent effectiveness rate).

Funding. The bill allocates an astronomical $46.3 billion for border enforcement.

Commission. An advisory Southern Border Security Commission would be established no later than one year after the bill's enactment. The DHS secretary may use $2 billion in funding to carry out the activities recommended by the commission.

Use of force. Use-of-force policies and trainings would be implemented, along with a complaint procedure. U.S. Customs and Border Patrol officers, along with other federal law enforcement officials, would be subject to a prohibition on racial or ethnic profiling.

Trigger to begin legalization. Before registered provisional immigrant (RPI) status is granted to unauthorized immigrants, the DHS secretary must certify that implementation of the U.S.-Mexico border strategy has begun.

LPR trigger. Before RPIs can adjust to lawful permanent resident (LPR) status (i.e., obtain a "green card"), the DHS secretary must:

- Certify that the U.S.-Mexico border surveillance and fencing strategy has been "substantially deployed" and is "substantially operational";

- Deploy 38,405 full-time active-duty Border Patrol agents along the southern border;

- Implement a mandatory electronic employment eligibility verification system (E-Verify), to be used by all employers in the U.S.; and

- State that DHS is using an electronic system to identify those who are exiting the country at air and sea ports of entry.

TITLE II: IMMIGRANT VISAS

Registered Provisional Immigrant (RPI) Status

In order to be eligible for RPI status, a person must:

- Have been physically present in the U.S. on or before Dec. 31, 2011,

- Have maintained continuous presence up until the date of application,

- Have settled any assessed federal tax liability,

- Not have been convicted of certain criminal offenses, and

- Not have been a lawful permanent resident, asylee, refugee, or present in the U.S. in a lawful nonimmigrant status.

- After six years of having RPI status, the person to whom it was granted must apply to renew it. After 10 years in RPI status, the person would be eligible to apply for LPR (or "green card") status. An additional three years in LPR status is required before individuals may apply for U.S. citizenship.

Fees and fines. Fees paid by the applicant must cover the cost of the application process, and fines would be assessed as follows: $1000 at RPI application ($500 may be paid when filing the initial application and $500 at renewal), and $1000 at adjustment to a green card.

Back taxes. A person with RPI status must also pay any back taxes owed since he or she was granted the status.

Time limit to file. Immigrants may file for RPI status up to one year after the time that the final regulations are published by DHS. The DHS secretary may extend this limit for an additional 18 months.

Ability to apply for family members. A person with RPI status would also be able to apply for RPI status for dependent children or his/her spouse, provided they were in the U.S. on the date the RPI status was granted to the principal applicant and also that they were present in the U.S. on or before Dec. 30, 2012.

Individuals in custody or removal proceedings. Individuals who are apprehended by immigration authorities before the application period, are in removal proceedings, or have been ordered removed would be able to apply after establishing eligibility for RPI status.

Individuals outside the U.S. Individuals who departed from the U.S. subject to an order of exclusion, deportation, removal, or voluntary departure, and who are outside the U.S. or who reentered unlawfully after Dec. 31, 2011, without receiving DHS consent to reapply for admission would not be eligible to apply for RPI status. However the DHS secretary may waive this bar for spouses or children of a U.S. citizen or LPR, parents of a child who is a U.S. citizen or LPR, or individuals who meet certain requirements under the DREAM-related provisions that are included in the bill. In addition, prior to granting this waiver, DHS must determine whether the person has a criminal conviction, notify and consult with any victim to determine whether to grant the waiver, and notify the victim that the waiver was granted.

Who is not eligible. Those who have been convicted of the following are not eligible for RPI status: a felony, an aggravated felony, three or more misdemeanors (other than immigration status-related convictions), certain foreign offenses, and unlawful voting. Aggravated felonies can include minor offenses such as shoplifting.

Nationality-based additional security screening. DHS is required to conduct an additional security screening of RPI applicants, spouses, and children who resided in a country or region "known to pose a threat, or that contains groups or organizations that pose a threat to the U.S."

Requirements for renewal. At renewal, RPIs must demonstrate that they have been employed regularly and are not likely to fall below the federal poverty level.

Requirements for lawful permanent residence (LPR status or "green card"). At the stage of applying for adjustment to LPR status, RPIs must demonstrate that they are employed regularly and show that they are likely to have income or resources at 125 percent of federal poverty level wages or satisfy certain education requirements. They must also demonstrate that they are pursuing a course of study in English and U.S. history/civics.

Waiver. The DHS secretary would have the authority to waive certain restrictions for humanitarian purposes, to ensure family unity, or if it is in the national interest.

DREAM

An expedited road to citizenship would be available to those who entered the U.S. before the age of 16, graduated from high school (or received a GED) in the United States, and attended at least two years of college or served four years in the uniformed services. DREAMers would apply for RPI status, and, after five years, would be eligible to apply for adjustment to LPR status. They then would be able to apply immediately for U.S. citizenship.

No age cap. There would be no upper-age limit for those who apply under this provision. This makes sense, since the relevant issue is the person's age at the time of entry into the U.S., not his or her current age.

DACA streamlining. The DHS secretary would have the discretion to establish streamlined procedures for people already granted Deferred Action for Childhood Arrivals (DACA).

No penalty for offering in-state tuition. The bill would repeal a provision of the Illegal Immigration Reform and Immigrant Responsibility Act of 1996 that prohibited public universities from offering in-state tuition rates to undocumented students on the basis of residence in the state, unless they offered the same rates to nonresidents of the state.

Educational loans. RPIs who entered the U.S. prior to age 16 (and agricultural workers with blue card status) may qualify for federal work-study and federal student loans. They remain ineligible for federal Pell grants until they adjust to LPR status.

TITLE III: INTERIOR ENFORCEMENT

This title contains many subparts, including: a section that requires employers to use an electronic employment eligibility verification system; worker protections, including the POWER Act; asylum and refugee provisions; immigration court reform; and new provisions related to violations of immigration law that constitute crimes.

Electronic Employment Eligibility Verification System (EEVS)

The bill would require all employers to use the federal government's EEVS to verify the employment eligibility of newly hired employees; the requirement would be phased in by employer size. The EEVS provision contains significant due process and worker protections for U.S. citizens and employment-authorized individuals who are affected by a system error. An example of an electronic employment eligibility verification system is E-Verify.

Implementation. Employers with more than 5,000 employees must begin using the EEVS, for newly hired employees and employees with expiring work-authorization documents, within two years after the regulations are published. Similarly, employers with more than 500 employees must begin using the EEVS within three years, and agricultural employers and all other employers must begin using the EEVS within four years.

S. 744 was attacked from the right and from the left. The Tea Party, the Center for Immigration Studies, and the Federation for American Immigration Reform (FAIR) remain staunchly opposed to any legislation that provides legalization — especially one that provides a path to citizenship — to undocumented immigrants. Many immigrant rights organizations opposed S.744 because of billions in increased funding for border militarization as well as a nebulous path to citizenship that could take up to 15 years for undocumented immigrants.

In contrast to the Senate's successful bipartisan efforts on a broad immigration bill, efforts in the House of Representatives languished. More than a year after S.744 passed the Senate, the prospects for immigration reform legislation in the House were declared dead. In response, immigrant rights advocates focused on pressuring President Obama to expand his executive actions to benefit more undocumented immigrants. These efforts continued in the midst of the unaccompanied immigrant children challenge at the border that provided another basis for anti-immigrant politicians and organizations to oppose legislation, blaming the president for the crisis.

E. ENFORCEMENT AT PORTS OF ENTRY

1. The Automated Entry-Exit System

Illegal Immigration Reform and Immigration Responsibility Act, § 110, 8 U.S.C.A. § 1221 was passed on September 30, 1996. Section 110 of IIRIRA required that within two years the Attorney General develop an "automated entry and exit control system" capable of (1) recording the departure of every alien from the United States and matching the record of departure with the record of the alien's arrival in the United States; and (2) enabling the Attorney General to identify, through on-line searching procedures, lawfully admitted nonimmigrants who remain in the United States beyond the period authorized by the Attorney General.[179]

There were many critics of Section 110 of IIRIRA who thought that Congress had not sufficiently considered a cost-benefit analysis when passing this provision. Opponents of the automated entry-exit system worried that these controls would have detrimental effects on cross-border commerce and would be ineffective in controlling the drug trade or other criminal activities at the border. One opponent of Section 110, Bronwyn Lance, summarized the major concerns with regard to the automated entry-exit system, when he wrote:

> This new requirement, made with little forethought, will not prevent illegal immigration, but will be expensive to implement and cause inordinate delays at border crossings for both persons and transport. Additionally, the new law will not affect drug enforcement or terrorism prevention, and shows a willful disregard for America's diplomatic agreements with our neighbors.[180]

Another important issue raised by opponents of section 110 was that the automated entry-exit system failed in its other goal of helping to detect the whereabouts of visa overstays. Critics explained that even if the automated entry-exit system recorded information at the time of entry about a visitor's identity and expected place of stay in the United States, six or more months later the alien may not be at the same location.[181]

Following the passage of the IIRIRA, Congress extended the deadline for the automated entry-exit system to October 15, 1998.[182] In the Fiscal Year 1999 Omnibus Consolidated and Emergency Supplemental Appropriations Act, Congress further extended the deadline for implementation of the automated entry-exit system. The deadline for land border ports of entry and seaports was extended to

---

[179] IIRIRA, Pub. L. No. 104-208, § 110, 110 Stat. 3009.

[180] Bronwyn Lance, *The Traffic Jam and Job Destruction Act: Why Congress Must Do Away With Border-Clogging Provision Slipped Into 1996 Law,* Issue Brief #171, June 1999, *available at* http://www.adti.net/imm/Section110.html.

[181] A June 1998 Senate Judiciary Committee Report (Senate Judiciary Report 105-197 on S. 1360, Border Improvement and Immigration Act of 1997, June 1, 1998).

[182] The "Extension of Date of Development of Automated Entry-Exit Control System" Act, Pub. L. No. 105-259, 112 Stat. 1918.

March 30, 2001; however, the October 15, 1998, deadline for air ports of entry remained unchanged.[183] Congress also added language prohibiting significant disruption of trade, tourism, or other legitimate cross-border traffic once the entry-exit system was in place.[184]

In June 2000, Congress amended IIRIRA § 110 in by passing the Naturalization Service Data Management Improvement Act of 2000 (DMIA), which renamed the entry-exit system the "Integrated Entry and Exit Data System."[185] 246 The new entry-exit system included provisions that: (1) rewrote § 110 to require the development of a system using data collected with no new documentary require-ments; (2) set staggered deadlines for the implementation of the system at air, sea, and land border ports of entry; (3) established a task force to evaluate the implementation of the system and other measures to improve legitimate cross-border traffic; and (4) expressed the sense of Congress that federal departments charged with border management should consult with foreign governments to improve cooperation.[186]

Immediately following the terrorist attacks of September 11, Congress voted to allocate more funds for border and interior enforcement of the immigration laws by passage of the USA PATRIOT Act of 2001.[187] Entry-exit tracking became viewed as a national security asset. Soon thereafter, biometric identifiers (such as finger-prints, photographs, or iris scans) became part of the entry-exit mandate. Previ-ously, only biographic data (text data including names and birthdates) were required. The entry-exit system was further developed through the implementation of the United States Visitor and Immigrant Status Indicator Technology program (U.S.-VISIT) discussed in the next section.

An entry-exit system's essential function is to match foreign visitors' arrival records to subsequent departure records. If the system included all arrivals and all departures, DHS could determine whether and when individuals depart the country and identify those who overstay their period of admission. In order to establish a high level of confidence in the entry-exit data, the system would have to cover all land, air, and sea ports of entry. The more ports of entry or travelers are omitted from entry or exit tracking, the less confident DHS can be that an individual actually overstayed.

Today, biometric entry capability is fully deployed, and biographic exit capability is deployed everywhere but the land border with Mexico, where vehicle travelers depart the country at speed and no systematic or mandatory collection occurs. This is a large gap, since about 45 percent of all entry inspections — land, air, or sea — occur at the southwest land border. The southwest land border presents the greatest challenge to completing the entry-exit system. Land ports of entry have

---

[183] Pub. L. No. 105-277, 112 Stat. 2681.

[184] Pub. L. No. 105-277, 112 Stat. 2681.

[185] Pub. L. No. 106-215, 114 Stat. 337.

[186] *Id.*

[187] The "Uniting and Strengthening America by Providing Appropriate Tools Required to Intercept and Obstruct Terrorism (USA PATRIOT) Act," Pub. L. No. 107-56, 115 Stat. 272, was signed into law on October 26, 2001.

about five entry lanes for each exit lane, and a variety of challenges, most notably insufficient space and economic impacts, prevent the construction of an exit infrastructure that mirrors the entry system. Other potential southern border solutions may be years away.

At airports and seaports, a biometric solution appears technologically feasible. A large gap exists, however, between technological feasibility and real-world implementation. In the air and sea environments, DHS is still working to develop and test a concept of operations that fulfills biometric identifiers' considerable potential to produce accurate matches, while minimizing impacts to the already crowded travel environment.[188]

2. U.S.-Visit

The United States Visitor and Immigrant Status Indicator Technology program (U.S.-VISIT) was launched on January 5, 2004 and is intended to complement and reinforce the automated entry-exit system first established under IIRIRA.[189] U.S. VISIT is meant to electronically record the entry of non-U.S. citizen visitors into the country and their exit from the United States, as well as verify each visitor's identity through the use of biometric identifiers encoded in their travel documents.[190] In theory, the system also is supposed to warn immigration officials when foreign visitors have failed to leave the country on the date they were expected to. U.S.-VISIT is currently in effect at 116 airports and 15 seaports, and the 154 land ports of entry.[191]

U.S.-VISIT requires the collection of personal data, photos and fingerprints at consular posts abroad and at ports-of-entry, as well as extensive database and information sharing.[192] Upon arrival in the United States, a foreign national who is subject to U.S.-VISIT is inspected by Customs and Border Protection (CBP) inspectors at a port-of-entry.[193] The individual's travel documents are scanned, and a digital photograph and inkless fingerprints of all ten fingers are taken.[194] Depending on the results the CBP officer receives in the system, the officer either admits the visitor or requires the visitor to undergo more thorough examination.[195] DHS expected that U.S.-VISIT would assist in combating fraud and protecting the integrity of the U.S. visa.[196] However, questions were raised about whether U.S.-VISIT could enhance the nation's security. Specific concerns were raised regarding whether U.S.-VISIT really has anything to do with countering drug trafficking,

---

[188] Bipartisan Policy Center, Entry-Exit System: Progress, Challenges, and Outlook, May 2014, *available at* http://bipartisanpolicy.org/library/immigration-entry-exit-system/.

[189] Bernard P. Wolfsdorf, Secure Borders, Open Doors: Consular Processing Issues in 2007.

[190] http://www.dhs.gov/xtrvlsec/programs/editorial_0527.shtm.

[191] http://www.dhs.gov/xtrvlsec/programs/editorial_0685.shtm.

[192] http://www.dhs.gov/xtrvlsec/programs/content_multi_image_0006.shtm.

[193] http://www.dhs.gov/xtrvlsec/programs/editorial_0525.shtm.

[194] *Id.*

[195] *Id.*

[196] http://www.dhs.gov/xtrvlsec/programs/content_multi_image_0006.shtm

halting the entry of terrorists into the United States, or with any other illegal activity near the borders.

In 2013, U.S.-Visit was reorganized into a new Office of Biometric Identity Management within DHS in response to its failure to fulfill the longstanding mandate to produce the biometric exit-tracking component to help track visa overstays.[197] Some functions were also moved to the Border Patrol and ICE in hopes of making the biometric tracking system more efficient. The Border Patrol is responsible for implementing the biometric collection program at exits if it ever comes to fruition. ICE's role is to match arrival and departure data, part of the overstay analysis that the U.S.-VISIT program previously performed. ICE also investigates the overstays indicated by the data.

The Office of Biometric Identity Management began operating March 27, 2013 within the National Protection and Programs Directorate, where U.S.-VISIT was located. OBIM manages one system that tracks arrival and departure records and another that maintains the biometric information collected at the country's entry points. The aim is to provide an interoperable system for DHS and the departments of Defense, Justice and State to share biographic and biometric data. The goal is to achieve a whole of government approach to identity services.

3.   NSEERS and Special Registration

The main goal of the National Security Entry-Exit Registration System (NSEERS), launched on September 11, 2002, was to subject a targeted minority of noncitizen visitors to a detailed registration process. NSEERS was designed to enable mass tracking of individual entries, departures, and domestic whereabouts. According to the Department of Justice memo authorizing the program, 'nonimmigrant aliens' were to be selected for registration according to four criteria: (1) all citizens or nationals of certain designated countries, (2) individual notification through a tracking database known as the "Interagency Border Inspection System" (IBIS), (3) pre-existing criteria defined by the Attorney General, and (4) officer discretion. Individuals registered under this program were to be questioned, fingerprinted, and provided with a special form complete with a "fingerprint identification number."

Questions asked during such registration go far beyond the routine and universal questions travelers answer while crossing international borders. Immigration officials have been instructed to ask individuals for e-mail addresses, personal details about parents and other family members, contact points in the United States, employers' addresses, school addresses, bank accounts, and credit card numbers. Before such visitors are allowed to enter the United States, officers are encouraged to provide extra comments and observations on the questioning form, while such travelers are instructed to sign a sworn statement verifying the accuracy of information provided.

---

[197] Zach Rausnitz, *US-VISIT reorganized but not diminished, DHS official says*, FIERCE HOMELAND SECURITY, Aug. 26, 2013.

Such monitoring does not end upon entry into the United States. Once individuals have been enrolled in this program, they are expected to report in person to an immigration office between day 30 and day 40 of their visit, report to an immigration office again within 10 days of the one-year anniversary of their arrival should they stay that long, notify the immigration authorities of every change of address while present in the United States within 10 days of that change of address, and appear before an immigration inspecting officer at certain designated ports of departure prior to leaving. At each of these follow-up interviews, individuals are required to prove that they have done what they came to the United States to do, by showing hotel and gas station receipts, employment contracts, class schedules, and other documents. Any individual failing to comply fully with such instructions is to be classified as "out of status," and thus subject to potential, and sometimes immediate, deportation.

At all ports of entry, this "special registration" initiative has evolved in progressive stages since its public launching on the one-year anniversary of September 11, 2001. The most controversial piece of NSEERS required all males on temporary nonimmigrant visas who were 16 years old or older from 25 countries to register at local immigration offices, be fingerprinted, photographed, and subjected to lengthy interrogations. Most of the countries listed have predominantly Muslim populations. Initially, the only nationals subjected to such registration procedures were those of Iran, Iraq, Libya, Syria, and Sudan. In October 2002, Saudi Arabia, Yemen, and Pakistan were added to the list of designated countries.[198] At the same time, the IBIS system was implemented in consular offices throughout the world and the Attorney General's pre-existing criteria for "special registration" were specified. These criteria concentrate on what the United States government would consider security risks: unexplained trips to 15 countries, including frequently visited United States allies such as Egypt, Saudi Arabia, and Pakistan; previous overstaying of non-immigrant visas; fitting current intelligence profiles; and demonstrating either suspicious behavior or personal information upon arrival. Significantly, those considered dual nationals by the Immigration authorities — such as Syrian-born French citizens or Iraqi-born UK citizens — are also subject to such registration procedures despite the fact that the Attorney General's office has indicated that the nationality or citizenship used to enter the United States will be the one considered for special registration procedures.[199]

In November 2002, the NSEERS program was greatly expanded through implementation of what the immigration authority innocuously designated 'call-in registration' — ostensibly designed to track those admitted to the United States prior to implementation of the NSEERS 'special registration' program at all ports of entry. In this program, all 'nonimmigrant alien' adult male nationals — 16 years and older — of the original five countries covered by the 'special registration'

---

[198] *See* U.S. Department of State International Informational Program, Fact Sheet: National Security Entry-Exit Registration System (June 5, 2002), *available at* http://www.ice.gov/pi/specialregistration/archive.htm#what.

[199] *See, e.g.*, Statement of Barbara Comstock, Director of Public Affairs, Regarding the National Security Entry-Exit Registration System, Department of Justice Press Release (Nov. 1, 2002), *available at* http://www.ice.gov/pi/specialregistration/archive.htm#what.

program (Iran, Iraq, Libya, Syria, and Sudan) were instructed to make a physical appearance at designated INS offices and register prior to December 16.

This initiative was internally justified as applying to "certain aliens, whose presence in the United States requires closer monitoring in the national security and/or law enforcement interests of the United States"[200] — initially defined only as all nationals of the five countries listed above. Individuals who failed to register, or registered late, were subject to deportation, and potentially vulnerable to criminal prosecution as well. Any information encountered during the registration process which might subject an interviewee to removal proceedings would cause the individual to be referred to the "investigations section" for "appropriate action" — meaning interrogation and potential detention or deportation.

In the very poorly distributed INS public announcement concerning these registration procedures, no mention was made of interrogation or deportation following compliance with "call-in" procedures. As a result, when thousands of male nationals from the five designated countries turned up at various INS offices, several hundred were detained nationwide — which resulted in an impromptu demonstration by nearly 1,000 relatives in Los Angeles, protest letters by several civil liberties, human rights, and ethnically-based advocacy organizations, and the assignment of volunteer escorts to record who was detained and for how long. Detentions, deportations, and personal abuses reportedly took place following referrals to "investigation sections."

In spite of widespread protest by affected communities, the Attorney General's office expanded the "call-in registration" program in the weeks following the December fiasco. Following the original five affected countries (Iran, Iraq, Libya, Syria, and Sudan), three more groups of countries were singled out for enforced "call-ins." The second group, whose nationals were obliged to visit INS offices prior to February 7, 2003 consisted of Afghanistan, Algeria, Bahrain, Eritrea, Lebanon, Morocco, North Korea, Oman, Qatar, Somalia, Tunisia, United Arab Emirates, and Yemen. The third group, instructed to visit INS offices by February 21, 2003 consisted of Pakistan and Saudi Arabia. Nationals of the fourth and final group — Bangladesh, Egypt, Indonesia, Jordan, and Kuwait — were instructed to visit the newly formed Department of Homeland Security offices by April 25, 2003.[201]

In its first term, the Obama administration made efforts to end the NSEERS program, but NSEERS still exists and the impact of these policies is still being felt in immigrant communities. In April 2011, the Obama administration "de-listed" the 25 countries and announced that males from those countries would no longer have to comply with the program. In April 2012, DHS released a memo on individuals impacted by NSEERS, granting limited relief to those who failed to comply if they can prove the noncompliance was not willful. However, NSEERS is still on the books, and the regulations that created the program are still intact. While no one is

---

[200] *See* U.S. Department of State, Attorney General Ashcroft Announces Implementation of First Phase of the National Security Entry-Exit Registration System (Aug. 12, 2002), *available at* http://www. usdoj.gov/opa/pr/2002/August/02_ag_466.htm.

[201] Mae M. Cheng, *Final Day for INS Registry; Immigrant Advocates Continue to Criticize Program*, NEWSDAY, Apr. 25, 2003.

currently required to comply, the program could be resurrected at any point.

F. INTERIOR ENFORCEMENT OF THE IMMIGRATION LAWS

1. Employer Sanctions

Under IRCA, for the first time Congress prohibited employers from hiring workers who are not authorized to work in the United States, imposing civil and criminal penalties on violators. IRCA was the product of years of debate regarding the impact of undocumented immigrant workers on the United States. As part of the compromise that IRCA represented, amnesty (legalization) was granted to about three million undocumented aliens, and employers also became subject to penalties for new employment discrimination laws.

In response to intensive lobbying by civil rights advocates and concerned members of Congress who feared that employer sanctions would cause employment discrimination, protections were included in the law intended to safeguard against discrimination. In other words, IRCA contained provisions that attempted to ensure that employers would not use the new employer sanctions law as a pretext for discriminating against lawful immigrant workers. Prior to IRCA, private employers could require employees to be U.S. citizens, but after IRCA, employers had to hire a qualified immigrant job applicant, unless a citizen who was equally qualified applied for the job. Employers could be fined for such discriminatory hiring practices, as well as for requiring new immigrant employees to come up with more proof than necessary to establish eligibility to work.

IRCA's employer sanctions provisions placed great responsibilities upon the business community. Employers must verify that a new employee is authorized to work in the United States. The employer and the employee must complete an I-9 form. Employers who "knowingly hire" undocumented workers are subject to penalties, which can include fines ranging from $250 to $10,000 per unauthorized worker, as well as criminal penalties against the employer for pattern and practice violations.

IRCA mandated the General Accounting Office (GAO), the investigative arm of Congress, to conduct three annual studies from 1987 to 1989 to determine whether employer sanctions had resulted in "widespread discrimination." A "sunset" provision further stipulated that employer sanctions could be repealed if the GAO concluded that compliance caused employers to discriminate.

The first two status reports on employer sanctions by the GAO found that "one in every six employers in GAO's survey who were aware of the law may have begun or increased the practice of (1) asking only foreign looking persons for work authorization documents or (2) hiring only U.S. citizens." In spite of the fact that almost 17 percent of employers admitted to practices that violated the discrimination provisions of IRCA, GAO concluded that the findings did not establish a pattern of "widespread discrimination," citing lack of conclusive evidence that the employer sanctions requirements were the cause of discrimination.

Upon the release of its second report, the GAO came under fire from both governmental and nongovernmental entities for using shoddy methodology in its evaluation of the possible discriminatory impacts of sanctions. The U.S. Commission on Civil Rights identified several problems inherent in both the methodology and the findings. For one thing, the commission argued that Congress needed to clarify the meaning of "widespread pattern of discrimination." Legal service providers and immigrant and refugee advocacy groups had been collecting evidence of IRCA-related discrimination since the law's inception. Organizations in New York, Chicago, San Francisco, Los Angeles, and Fresno established multilingual information and referral telephone hotlines upon the passage of IRCA to provide information to immigrants about the amnesty program and employer sanctions. Their experience revealed that employment discrimination as a result of employer sanctions was pervasive.

In 1989, a number of groups across the country began to compile information that they had received from individuals of mostly Asian, Latino, and Middle Eastern descent regarding discriminatory treatment they had experienced while seeking new employment or working in their current positions. Several civil rights organizations issued reports of the anecdotal evidence collected. While the reports documented disturbing accounts of discrimination, proponents of employer sanctions dismissed the data collected by advocacy groups as unreliable. Eventually, some of the independent research could not be ignored by the GAO. A methodological survey of 416 San Francisco employers was conducted in San Francisco, revealing that an overwhelming 97 percent of the firms regularly engaged in at least one employment practice that could be discriminatory under IRCA or other antidiscrimination laws. Another 53 percent reported that they engaged in three or more such practices. The research was submitted to the GAO in September 1989, and influenced the GAO's third report.[202] The GAO significantly improved the research methodology for its third and final report. Its staff used both direct contact with employers and teams of job search testers. Its new findings showed that as a direct result of IRCA, 461,000 employers nationwide (10 percent) discriminated on the basis of national origin, and 430,000 employers (9 percent) discriminated on the basis of citizenship status. These findings meant that an estimated 2.9 million employees were discriminated against based on national origin, and 3.9 million based on citizenship status. The research found that rates of discrimination were somewhat higher in cities with high Latino or Asian populations: "Our survey suggests that persons of Hispanic and Asian origins may have been harmed by employers' citizenship discrimination practices." As part of the same report, the GAO contracted with Washington, D.C-based Urban Institute to conduct a "hiring audit," by using a job applicant tester survey utilizing Latino and Anglo U.S. citizen college students to apply for a sample of 360 low skilled, entry-level jobs in Chicago and San Diego. The study found that the Anglo testers received 52 percent more job offers and 33 percent more interviews than the Latino testers, and that overall, the Latino testers were three times as likely as Anglo testers to encounter unfavorable treatment.

---

[202] Lina M. Avidan, *Employment and Hiring Practices Under the Immigration Reform and Control Act of 1986; A Survey of San Francisco Businesses* (Coalition for Immigrant and Refugee Rights and Services, 1989).

Despite the GAO's findings of "widespread" IRCA-related employment discrimination and similar evidence by independent researchers, Congress did not repeal employer sanctions. The findings were routinely dismissed by anti-immigrant groups, Senator Alan Simpson (a co-sponsor of IRCA), and the AFL-CIO as insignificant or unreliable. Several bills to repeal employer sanctions were introduced in Congress in 1990 and 1991, but none reached the floor of Congress (in spite of bipartisan support from Senators Kennedy and Hatch).

Although employer sanctions were not repealed, the Immigration Act of 1990 did strengthen IRCA's antidiscrimination provisions. The law increased employer and employee education, added special agricultural workers to the category of protected workers, changed the penalties for discrimination to conform with those for employer sanctions penalties, made document abuse an unfair immigration-related employment practice, prohibited retaliation against those who file charges, made it easier to prosecute for document abuse by adding civil as well as criminal penalties, and eliminated the requirement that a noncitizen who makes a discrimination charge must have filed an official "declaration of intent" to become a citizen.

By the early 1990s, many members of Congress, most notably Senator Simpson, contended that no further employer education was necessary to decrease employment discrimination. In fact, Simpson argued at a 1992 Senate judiciary Committee hearing that the employer sanctions provisions, both the documentation requirements and the antidiscrimination protections, were as familiar to employers as was the requirements to pay taxes.

While many politicians and business leaders claimed that compliance with employer sanctions had become a "regular part" of doing business in the United States, the experiences of immigrants and ethnic minorities suggested otherwise. Employer sanctions were often implemented and enforced selectively, discriminatorily, and as a means of intimidating undocumented workers who sought union representation or who complained about unfair labor practices, such as sexual harassment, wage and hour violations, and unsafe working conditions. Only a fraction of U.S. employers and workers have received education from the Office of Special Counsel (OSC). OSC's education program did not begin in earnest until 1990, when it initiated a grants program, contracting with local groups to conduct educational campaigns. The OSC is located in Washington, D.C., with no branch offices. Between 1987 and 1996, the OSC received 4,868 charges of discrimination from workers, but only 145 formal complaints were filed by the OSC against employers, 83 of who were fined for IRCA-related unfair employment practices. Distribution of INS's Handbook for Employers that explains the regulations and has pictures of acceptable documents also has been inadequate. Only two nationwide distributions of the handbook took place by 1996: one in 1987 and one in 1991.

Since 1990, no government-sponsored research examining the possibly discriminatory effects of employer sanctions has occurred. Lina Avidan's private survey of 422 employers in New York, Los Angeles, Chicago, and San Francisco conducted in 1992 revealed that 91 percent regularly engage in at least one employment practice prohibited under IRCA's antidiscrimination provisions, and

48 percent regularly engage in three or more. Half of the employers feel that the INS documentation requirements make it riskier to hire people who speak limited English, and more than a third (38 percent) feel it is riskier to hire Latinos, Asians, and people from the Caribbean.[203]

Although employer sanctions remain part of the immigration laws, by 2001, the concept had lost one of its ardent supporters. As organized labor, including the AFL-CIO, realized that its future viability rested solidly on the shoulders of immigrant workers, unions called for the repeal of employer sanctions and for the legalization of undocumented workers.

By the 1980s, contentious congressional debate over how to handle the problem of undocumented aliens, particularly Mexicans, took center stage. Clear support for employer sanctions was evident, but when IRCA was finally passed, support for legalization of undocumented immigrants was not as clear. The ambivalence over amnesty reflected the policy makers' desire to keep out undocumented Mexicans and not demonstrate any sign of approval for those already here.

Legalization applicants faced several challenges. Procedural hurdles discouraged many from even applying. The most difficult hurdle was obtaining documentation to approve the duration of time an applicant lived in the United States or worked in agriculture. Furthermore, each applicant was required to pay a filing fee as high as $420 per family — not an insignificant amount for many.

The implementation of legalization through INS and community agencies was inconsistent. Outreach efforts did not reach many eligible immigrants, the INS suffered from long-standing distrust in immigrant communities, and community service agencies miscalculated the needs of many applicants and suffered from bureaucratic problems themselves. Yet, important partnerships were formed, and the efforts INS officials finally implemented were impressive in many parts of the country. Most observers agree that the three million immigrants who benefited from legalization represent less than half of those who were actually eligible, and the ongoing employer sanctions provisions result in discrimination against lawful immigrants of color.

Congress and Employer Sanctions

Blame for continued migration might also be placed at the feet of Congress. Responding to public complaints about undocumented migration, Congress simply threw more border enforcement funds at the issue, while encouraging migration with weak employer sanction laws. Certainly many who support, as well as many who oppose, Gatekeeper claim that the failure to prosecute employers for hiring undocumented workers is a problem. Between 1992 and 1997, the number of INS fines levied against employers decreased from 2,000 to 888, and the amount of fines levied decreased from $17 million to $8 million.[204] Further, the Department of

---

[203] Lina M. Avidan, *Employment and Hiring Practices Under the Immigration Reform and Control Act of 1986; A Survey of Businesses in Los Angeles, New York, Chicago and San Francisco* (Master's Thesis, Public Administration Department, 1992).

[204] Claudia E. Smith, *Operation Gatekeeper Report*, May 10, 2000, at 41 (unpublished paper on file with author).

Labor had only 900 investigators to enforce workplace requirements such as minimum wage laws in seven million U.S. workplaces in 1995.[205] Broadly speaking, however, criticism of weak employer sanction laws is misplaced. Enforcement of employer sanctions will not deter undocumented migration. U.S. employers' need for low-wage workers is too strong, and migrant motivations for entering are too great.

The conventional wisdom goes like this: if the country seriously enforces the laws that make it illegal for employers to knowingly hire undocumented workers, employers will stop hiring undocumented workers, undocumented migrants will get the message and stop migrating, and environmental deaths at the border will disappear. The Clinton administration argued that to control illegal immigration effectively, the federal government must "remove the magnet of illegal employment that draws illegal aliens" to the United States.[206] INS Commissioner Meissner said that border enforcement should be coupled with workplace disincentives."[207] The U.S. Commission on Immigration Reform (USCIR) similarly argued that since "employment opportunity is . . . the principal magnet which draws illegal aliens to the United States," the best thing to do is improve the system of employer sanctions enforcement, and labor standards enforcement should be enhanced as well.[208] USCIR's executive director observed that as a "nation we have a basic ambivalence about workplace enforcement."[209] Thus, Clinton's border czar Alan Bersin complained: "We have not been given the tools ñ a matter of deliberate policy ñ to have effective worksite enforcement. . . . Because people can show an employer phony documents, there's no reliable way to correctly identify [the immigration status of] people seeking work."[210] Similarly, although the *San Diego Union Tribune* applauded efforts that resulted in fewer crossings in urban areas, its editors were troubled by the environmental deaths, concluding that as "long as we continue to hire illegal aliens, we will continue to have rampant illegal immigration."[211] Wayne Cornelius, a longtime' observer of the border, also notes that "work site enforcement is without doubt the weakest element of the current U.S. strategy for controlling illegal immigration."[212] In his view, "large numbers are still getting in, and because of low employer sanctions enforcement, they are just as employable today as they were before the current buildup of border enforcement capabilities began."[213] A binational body of experts chimed in,

---

[205] *Id.* at 43.

[206] *Id.* at 40.

[207] *Id.* at 42.

[208] U.S. Commission on Immigration Reforms, U.S. Immigration Policy: Restoring Credibility 50–53 (1994). The commission criticized the current verification process as "time-consuming and confusing," and urged a more efficient use of resources. *Id.* at 53.

[209] Smith, *Operation Gatekeeper Report*, at 14 (citing Susan Martin).

[210] Brae Canlen, *The Border Honcho*, 17 California Lawyer 34, 37 (1997).

[211] *A Losing Battle: Border Patrol Scores Tactical Gains, Strategic Losses*, San Diego Union Tribune, November 5, 1999, B8. The editors noted: "Gatekeeper's physical measures have slowed the flow in San Diego County, replacing the chaos that once defined the border here [illegals] dashing across freeways or stampeding checkpoints." *Id.*

[212] Smith, *Operation Gatekeeper Report*, at 41.

[213] *Id.* at 22.

suggesting that the United States should assess the extent to which the demand of U.S. employers can be reduced through enhanced enforcement of labor standards, including wage and hour requirements, child labor prohibitions, and employer sanctions.[214] Even representatives of the California Rural Legal Assistance Foundation, ardent critics of Operation Gatekeeper, while not supporting employer sanctions, note the inconsistencies of U.S. policies: "During the last five years the INS has done virtually nothing to counteract the employer magnet that pulls migrants here — the undeniable hypocrisy of its immigration policy. For example, since the start of Gatekeeper, only a half-dozen employers of undocumented laborers have been prosecuted in either of California's border counties,"[215] and "the agency devotes only two percent of its enforcement man-hours to enforcing immigration laws at the work site."[216]

Could the employment of undocumented workers really be stopped? What would it take? Would the enforcement of employer sanctions really deter the employment of undocumented workers and their continued migration? It's doubtful. The fortitude, drive, and unbelievable desire to migrate north among border-crossers given the economic disparities, family ties, and tradition are factors that cannot be discounted lightly. And the labor market that relies on such workers is ingrained in our economy. In sum, assuming that employer sanctions will discourage further migration and the hiring of undocumented workers is unrealistic and simplistic. Employer sanctions enforcement, even with greater resources, faces insurmountable challenges.

Employer sanctions create additional problems as well. Many employers use employer sanctions as an excuse to discriminate. The General Accounting Office has reported that nearly one-fifth of employers discriminate against foreign-appearing or foreign-sounding job applicants because of employer sanctions. This is too much of a price to pay for a regime that has little incentive to discourage the hiring of undocumented workers anyway.

2. Detection Strategies

Immigration enforcement officials use various tactics to detect and apprehend people who are out-of-status. This section will discuss five main detection strategies: 1) how DHS uses immigration petitions to uncover undocumented individuals living in the country, 2) how ICE picks up people after criminal arrests, 3) how workplace sweeps are carried out to apprehend large groups of undocumented workers, 4) how the use of social security numbers are used for "silent raids" to threaten employers with sanctions if certain employees are not fired, and 5) the Criminal Alien Removal Initiative. The Secure Communities Program and INA § 287(g) agreements are discussed in Chapter 2 .

---

[214] Binational Study on Migration (1997), at 66.

[215] December 14, 1999. Letter to Gabriela Rodriguez Pizarro.

[216] CRLAF Fact Sheet.

a. Petitions

Whenever an application for an immigration benefit is filed on behalf of an individual, an "alien registration file" is created for that person. Immigration petitions often involve disclosing a substantial amount of information about a person's identity, family and whereabouts. This information is then kept on file with DHS. It is an easy task for an ICE-Investigation officer to use this information to apprehend the applicant or their family members.

b. Criminal Custody

Immigrants who are in criminal custody are particularly likely to be picked up by Immigration and Customs Enforcement. ICE often contacts local police to see if there are any immigrants being held on criminal charges.

ICE uses a system of "immigration holds" to facilitate their cooperation with local police. Immigration holds, or immigration detainers as they are sometimes called, are issued for people who are in criminal custody and who are suspected of being deportable or inadmissible. Once an immigration hold is issued to a person, the local police have the power to temporarily detain the immigrant beyond the time of their completed jail sentence in order for ICE to pick the person up.

According to 8 CFR § 287.7(d), immigration holds allow police to detain an immigrant who has completed their criminal sentence for 48 hours, excluding Saturdays, Sundays and holidays. After this period, the immigration hold expires and the immigrant can no longer be legally detained. The immigrant must be released whether or not ICE has had time to pick them up.

c. Workplace Sweeps

Agriculture and other workplace sweeps for undocumented Mexican workers have been common immigration enforcement strategies since the mid twentieth century. Consider Operation Jobs, that occurred in April 1982. Five thousand people, primarily of Latin appearance, were arrested in nine metropolitan areas across the country. Critics of the raids charged that the operation was directed at Mexicans, whipped up anti-alien hysteria, and caused much fear in the Latino community, while providing no jobs for native-born citizens. Curiously, Operation Jobs was launched during the same week that restrictive legislation (the Simpson-Mazzoli Bill that contained employer sanctions provisions) was being marked up in the Senate subcommittee on immigration. The raids also coincided with Congress' consideration of additional funds for the old Immigration and Naturalization Service. Operation Jobs highlighted what had been going on for many years — focused sweeps by the INS at locations with large numbers of persons of Latin descent.

The constitutionality of the operation was challenged in northern California in *International Molders' and Allied Workers' Local Union No. 164 v. Nelson*,[217] the facts of which are representative of what happened nationwide. During the operation, the INS and Border Patrol conducted approximately 50 workplace raids

---

[217] 643 F. Supp. 884 (N.D. Cal. 1986).

in northern California as part of a nationwide campaign. During these raids, agents arrived at various workplaces, such as the Petaluma Poultry Processors, Mammoth Lakes Lodge, and Pacific Mushroom Farm. The agents carried with them "warrants of inspection" authorizing entry into the nonpublic areas of particular premises. Typically, the warrants named one or more individuals thought to be undocumented aliens who were working at a specified location, but then went on to allow the INS to seek and seize unspecified and unlimited "others" on the premises who might also be undocumented aliens. During Operation jobs, warrants were obtained for eight of the approximately 50 raids. Although a warrant might list from four to 13 suspected undocumented aliens, as many as 70 people would be arrested, and few if any of these were the people named in the warrant. In the eight warrants used for the raids described in the case, 192 individuals were arrested. Of these, 179 were "others" not identified in the warrants. Of the 51 persons named in the various warrants, only 13 were found on the premises.

The warrants said nothing about how the searches would be carried out, other than permissible hours of entry, or how INS agents would determine which persons were to be interrogated or seized as suspected "others." The warrants neither directed nor limited agents to the portions of the premises where the named suspects were likely to be found.

Officials admitted that they used the warrants to gain entry into workplaces for generalized searches for undocumented aliens. In many raids the INS agents made no particular effort to apprehend the suspects named in the warrants, but rather based their decisions as to which workers to question, detain, or seize solely on information or observation gained *after* they had entered.

Given these facts, the federal judge issued the following order against INS officials in northern California:

Good cause appearing therefor, the Court preliminarily enjoins defendants and their officers, agents, and employees in the San Francisco District of the United States Immigration and Naturalization Service and the Livermore Border Patrol Sector as follows:

1. Each INS workplace entry, other than in public areas and open fields, must be based on at least one of the following: a valid warrant, a valid consent, or exigent circumstances not deliberately provoked by defendants' own conduct.

2. Every INS warrant must particularly describe each suspect to be questioned or seized pursuant to the particularity requirement of the Fourth Amendment. There must be probable cause to believe each such person is an alien illegally present in the United States. A warrant need not in every case identify the suspect(s) by name, but the warrant and its supporting affidavits must contain enough specific identifying information to assure that the search for that person is reasonably likely to result in finding that person.

3. A warrant may not provide that "others" may be searched and seized, if such "others" are unnamed or only conclusorily described by any supporting affidavits.

4. When possible, each warrant must describe the particular area(s) of the workplace where the suspect(s) are likely to be found, in light of the information available to the defendants.

5. Each warrant must provide that the agents executing the warrant, before searching any work area, must show the warrant to an authorized company representative, and ask that representative to produce the suspect(s) named or described in the warrant. Before the suspects are produced, agents may position themselves at exits and question or detain any workers attempting to flee. If the representative is unwilling or unable to produce those suspects within a reasonable time, agents may then enter the work area to search for the suspects. Such searches must be directed at finding the named or described suspects as quickly as possible, rather than for general questioning of the entire workforce. This does not preclude agents from questioning or detaining workers who attempt to hide or flee.

6. Each warrant must provide that the agents executing the warrant, before searching any work area, must show the warrant to an authorized company representative, and ask that representative to produce the suspect(s) named or described in the warrant. Before the suspects are produced, agents may position themselves at exits and question or detain any workers attempting to flee. If the representative is unwilling or unable to produce those suspects within a reasonable time, agents may then enter the work area to search for the suspects. Such searches must be directed at finding the named or described suspects as quickly as possible, rather than for general questioning of the entire workforce. This does not preclude agents from questioning or detaining workers who attempt to hide or flee.

7. Agents may not deliberately provoke flight by workers in order to justify entries onto workplace premises.

8. Absent a valid warrant or genuine exigent circumstances not deliberately precipitated by the agents themselves, agents may not detain workers without reasonable, articulable suspicion of illegal alienage. During non-detentive questioning, and before agents detain a worker, agents must give the worker a reasonable opportunity to produce his or her relevant documents, even if those documents are not on the worker's person but are in his constructive possession somewhere on the premises. Agents may accompany a worker who must retrieve his documentation.

9. Absent a valid warrant or genuine exigent circumstances not deliberately precipitated by the agents' own conduct, agents may not arrest a worker except upon probable cause, based on articulable facts and reasonable inferences drawn therefrom, that the worker is an alien unlawfully present in the United States and is likely to escape before a warrant can be obtained for his arrest.

Nevertheless, government workplace raids were emboldened by the Supreme Court in 1984. In *INS v. Delgado*,[218] INS officials, acting pursuant to warrants issued on a showing of probable cause that numerous unidentified undocumented

---

[218] 466 U.S. 210 (1984).

aliens were employed at a garment factory, conducted two "factory surveys" of the workforce in search of undocumented aliens. A third factory survey was conducted with the employer's consent at another garment factory. During each survey, which lasted from one to two hours, INS agents positioned themselves near the factory exits, while other agents moved systematically through the factory, approaching most, but not all, employees at their work stations and, after identifying themselves, asking the employees one to three questions relating to their citizenship. The agents displayed badges, carried walkie-talkies, and were armed, although at no point during any of the surveys was a weapon ever drawn. If an employee gave a credible reply that he or she was a U.S. citizen or produced immigration papers, the agent moved on to another employee. During the survey, employees continued with their work and were free to walk around within the factory. Employees who were U.S. citizens or permanent resident aliens, and who had been questioned during the surveys and their union complained that the factory surveys violated their Fourth Amendment rights. They argued that the surveys constituted a seizure of the entire workforce, and that the INS could not question an individual employee unless its agents had a reasonable suspicion that the employee was an undocumented alien.

The Supreme Court disagreed with the plaintiffs, holding that the factory surveys did not result in the seizure of the entire workforce, and the individual questioning of the employees by INS agents concerning their citizenship did not amount to a detention or seizure under the Fourth Amendment. The Court ruled that interrogation relating to one's identity or a request for identification by the police does not, by itself, constitute a Fourth Amendment seizure. Unless the circumstances of the encounter are so intimidating as to demonstrate that a reasonable person would have believed he or she was not free to leave if he or she had not responded, such questioning does not result in a detention under the Fourth Amendment. In the Court's view, the entire workforce was not seized for the duration of the surveys, even though INS agents were stationed near the exits of the factory sites. The record indicated that the agents' conduct consisted simply of questioning employees and arresting those they had probable cause to believe were unlawfully present in the factory. This conduct should not have given employees any reason to believe that they would be detained if they gave truthful answers to the questions put to them or if they simply refused to answer. If mere questioning did not constitute a seizure when it occurred inside the factory, it was no more a seizure when it occurred at the exits.

The plaintiffs argued that the positioning of agents near the factory doors showed the INS's intent to prevent people from leaving. But the Court saw nothing in the record indicating that this is what the agents at the doors actually did. To the Court,

> The obvious purpose of the agents' presence at the factory doors was to insure that all persons in the factories were questioned. The record indicates that the INS agents' conduct in this case consisted simply of questioning employees and arresting those they had probable cause to believe were unlawfully present in the factory. This conduct should have given respondents no reason to believe that they would be detained if they gave truthful answers to the questions put to them or if they simply refused to answer.

One worker described an incident that occurred during the October factory survey at Mr. Pleat, in which an INS agent stationed by an exit attempted to prevent a worker, presumably an undocumented alien, from leaving the premises after the survey started. The worker walked out the door and when an agent tried to stop him, the worker pushed the agent aside and ran away. But the Court felt that this was "an ambiguous, isolated incident" failing to provide any basis on which to support the plaintiffs.

Likewise, as to workers inside the buildings, the Court felt that the mere possibility that they would be questioned if they sought to leave the buildings should not have resulted in any reasonable apprehension by any of them that they would be seized or detained in any meaningful way. The INS conduct simply did not create a psychological environment that made employees reasonably afraid they were not free to leave.

As the backlash against undocumented immigrants heightened after 9/11, raids and other internal enforcement efforts were stepped up by ICE. The methods included worksite operations, home invasions, and even monitoring of public schools. In the process, U.S. citizens and lawful permanent residents were detained along with undocumented immigrants, resulting in a multitude of lawsuits against DHS. And while several thousand deportable aliens were arrested as a result of these efforts, the totals were a far cry from the estimated millions of undocumented immigrants living in the country. Were such tactics really worth the effort? Consider these operations.

Stillmore, Georgia

One ICE raid in Stillmore, Georgia, the Friday before Labor Day weekend in 2006, evoked outcry from local residents who labeled the ICE action as nothing short of "Gestapo tactics."[219] Nestled amid pine trees and cotton fields, undocumented Mexican immigrants supplied a stable workforce for a thriving poultry industry and for the onion fields in Vidalia a few miles away. Descending shortly before midnight, then over a three-day period, ICE agents swarmed throughout the area, arresting and deporting 125 undocumented workers.[220] Most of those rounded up were men, while their wives fled to woods to hide with their children in tow.[221] In the weeks after the raid, at least 200 more immigrants left town. Many of the women whose husbands were deported used their spouse's final paycheck purchase bus tickets to Mexico.[222] The impact was evident, underscoring just how vital the undocumented immigrants were to the local economy. Trailer parks lie abandoned. The poultry plant scrambled to replace more than half its workforce. Business dried up at stores where Mexican laborers once lined up to buy food, beer and cigarettes. The community of about a thousand people became little more than a ghost town. The raid included a trailer park operated by David Robinson, where immigrants

---

[219] Dahleen Glanton, *Raid Exposes Ethnic Fault Lines; Town Grapples with Illegal Immigrant Crackdown*, Chicago Trib., Dec. 11, 2006.

[220] *Id.*

[221] *Id.*

[222] Dahleen Glanton *For Immigrants, Raid Dims Hope for a Better Life*, Chicago Trib., Dec. 11, 2006.

were handcuffed and taken away. Robinson bought an American flag and posted it by the pond out front — upside down, in protest: "These people might not have American rights, but they've damn sure got human rights. There ain't no reason to treat them like animals."[223]

In May 2006, ICE launched Operation Return to Sender, an aggressive effort to rapidly increase deportation of undocumented immigrants violating removal orders. At this time ICE officials also began discussing enforcement issues with the Stillmore-based Crider poultry plant. Stillmore is a quiet community with few small businesses, a gas station and two convenience stores, intended to service local employees of the Crider plant, the largest employer of a community with roughly a thousand inhabitants. The plant employed slightly over 900 people, about 700 who had work documentation discrepancies when ICE began discussions with Crider's senior management in mid-2006.

On a state level the immigration debate in Georgia was intensifying. The state attracted attention after a federal report noted that Georgia had the fastest growing undocumented immigration population in the country.[224] In early 2006, the state legislature passed what many considered to be some of the most far-reaching immigration legislation in the nation, the Georgia Security and Immigration Compliance Act. The legislation has been likened to California's Proposition 187 and includes several strict requirements to curb immigration into the state and the hiring of undocumented workers. These provisions include requiring employers to use a federal database system (E-Verify) to verify employee documentation, requiring corrections officials to notify the state of any undocumented incarcerated persons, and requiring proof of citizenship for recipients of many medical and welfare benefits.[225]

In the summer months preceding the raid, the Crider plant began firing employees and pressuring others to resign upon suspecting improper work documentation. ICE officials swiftly cracked down at summer's end. The agency took the unusual approach of researching employee home address information and raided several homes shortly before midnight on Friday, September 1, the first day of Labor Day weekend. ICE's Labor Day weekend raid launched what became a series of raids lasting three weeks in the Stillmore area and the surrounding counties. The Stillmore raid focused mainly on male employees from the Crider plant, leaving many female and child family members stranded. Many remaining family members fled into the nearby woods in the hopes of avoiding detection. There was one report of a family hiding in a tree for two nights to avoid capture.[226]

---

[223] Story cited in immigrationprof blog.

[224] Russ Bynum, *Immigration raids leave Georgia town bereft, stunned*, SEATTLE TIMES, Sept. 16, 2006, *available at* http://seattletimes.nwsource.com/html/nationworld/2003261371_immigaftermath16.html.

[225] Rick Lyman, *In Georgia Law, a Wide-Angle View of Immigration*, N.Y. TIMES, May 12, 2006, *available at* http://www.nytimes.com/2006/05/12/us/12georgia.html?_r=1&oref=login.

[226] Patrick Jonsson, *Crackdown on Immigrants Empties a Town and Hardens Views*, CHRISTIAN SCIENCE MONITOR, Oct. 3, 2006, *available at* http://www.csmonitor.com/2006/1003/p01s01-ussc.html?s=hns.

Local residents witnessed the events, as ICE officials raided local homes and trailer parks, forcing many members of the community out of Stillmore. Officials were seen stopping motorists, breaking into homes and there were even reports of officials threatening people with tear gas.[227] Witnesses reported seeing ICE officials breaking windows and entering homes through floorboards.[228] Mayor Marilyn Slater commented, "This reminds me of what I read about Nazi Germany, the Gestapo coming in and yanking people up."[229]

The Crider Poultry plant was the primary employer in the town of a thousand. Other local businesses complained that they faced a severe drop in business in the weeks after the raids. One local caregiver in the community, a legal resident, took in a two-year old boy, a U.S. citizen born to undocumented Mexican parents, because his mother feared she could no longer sufficiently provide for him. The caregiver noted all her other customers disappeared after the raid, having been forced to leave Stillmore.[230]

San Rafael, California

On March 6, 2007, ICE officials raided the small communities of San Rafael and Novato in Marin County, arresting roughly 30 undocumented immigrants. This raid was also part of ICE's "Operation Return to Sender," the federal effort to crack down on immigrants who have stayed past their deportation orders. ICE officials parked several vans outside apartment complexes before dawn the Tuesday morning of the raids. Armed with warrants, many bearing dated and/or incorrect information, the police stormed homes and began arresting violators regardless of whether they were named in the original warrant. Many children were handcuffed along with their parents. The San Rafael raid drew criticism at the local and national level because of the nature and timing of the operation.

The San Rafael raid became a national symbol of the negative effects raids have on children. Juan Rodriguez, principal of Bahia Vista Elementary School, noted that on a typical day the school might have eight to 10 children absent, but 77 children were absent the day of the raid.[231] Another local principal, Kathryn Gibney of San Pedro Elementary, testified before a congressional committee on the effect of ICE raids upon her school's children and their families. Stressing the level of fear the ICE raids placed on the community, Gibney noted that families kept kids at home and in hiding, describing an increased level of paranoia in the community. Gibney recounted instructions from the wife of man who had just been arrested to her daughter to pack a backpack and leave it by the door. If the child came home and found no one present she was to take the backpack to her aunt's house and stay with

---

[227] *SPLC Files Federal Lawsuit Challenging Constitutionality of Immigration Raids that terrorized Latino residents of Southeast Georgia Towns PR NEWSWIRE*, PUBLIC INTEREST SERVICES, Nov. 1, 2006, *available at* http://w3.lexis.com/lawschoolreg/researchlogin08.asp?t=y&fac=no

[228] *Id.*; Jonsson, *supra* note 226.

[229] *Id.* Russ Bynum, *Immigration Raids Leave Georgia Town Bereft, Stunned*, SEATTLE TIMES, Sept. 16, 2006.

[230] *Id.*

[231] Mark Prado, *30 Illegal immigrants targeted in Canal neighborhood raid*, MARIN INDEPENDENT JOURNAL, Mar. 7, 2007, *available at* http://www.marinij.com/marin/ci_5372749.

her in case her mother was also arrested and deported.[232] Gibney further lamented the long term effects of the raids, describing a frightened community with children asking teachers whether police would be coming to school, as well as "higher absenteeism, lower test scores and increased counseling for her students . . . '[ICE] left behind them a trail of fear.' "[233]

A young boy, Kebin Reyes, a U.S. citizen, symbolizes one of ICE's more egregious actions. Kebin, six-years-old the day of the raid, was seized along with his father, who did not have citizenship, and held at an ICE processing center in San Francisco. Kebin and his father, Noe Reyes, were held for over 10 hours with only bread and water. Noe Reyes' requests to contact a family member to take Kebin home were repeatedly denied. Eventually, Kebin's uncle was able to pick up Kebin and remove him from the processing center. The American Civil Liberties Union has filed a lawsuit on Kebin's behalf.[234]

San Rafael's Mayor Alberto Boro criticized the raid's effect on the entire community. Boro was particularly disturbed by the broken relationship between local law enforcement and San Rafael's immigrant community. He criticized federal officials for identifying themselves simply as police, noting this caused confusion within the community that thought local law enforcement was responsible for the raids. He noticed that the raid resulted in a drop in calls to local law enforcement agencies and signaled a heightened level of mistrust of police within the community.[235]

New Bedford, Massachusetts

In March 2007, nearly 500 ICE officials descended upon the small southern New England community of New Bedford, Massachusetts. ICE officials targeted the local Michael Bianco, Inc. plant, a leather goods manufacturer that had manufactured goods for brands such as Coach, Rockport and Timberland.[236] Recently, however, the factory had contracted with the government to produce goods for military operations in Iraq. Officials arrested 361 factory employees during the raid.

As with other larger raids, the event split families and underscored the negative effects the raids have on communities. Many of Bianco's employees were women, creating a crisis with caring for their children. Roughly 100 children were stranded with babysitters and other caregivers as their mothers were seized during the

---

[232] *Id.*

[233] *Workforce Protections Subcom. Hearing: "ICE Workplace Raids: Their Impact on U.S. Children, Families and Communities,* 110th Cong., 2d Session, v. 154 Cong Rec D., No 83, May 20, 2008 (Statement of Kathryn Gibney, Principal, San Pedro Elementary School).

[234] Press Release, American Civil Liberties Union, Civil Rights Groups Sue Immigration Officials for Unlawfully Detaining Six-Year-Old U.S. Citizen (Apr. 26, 2007) (on file with Author) *available at* http://www.aclu.org/immigrants/detention/29526prs20070426.html.

[235] Jesse McKinley, *San Francisco Bay Area Reacts Angrily to Series of Immigration Raids.* N.Y. TIMES, Apr. 27, 2008, *available at* http://www.nytimes.com/2007/04/28/washington/28immig.html?n=Top/Reference/Times%20Topics/People/M/McKinley,%20Jesse&pagewanted=all.

[236] Ken Maguire, *Factory Struggles After Immigration Raid,* WASHINGTON POST Mar. 28 2007, *available at* http://www.washingtonpost.com/wp-dyn/content/article/2007/03/28/AR2007032801392_pf.html.

raid.[237] The majority of those arrested were moved to detention centers half-way across the country in Texas. Eventually, about 60 employees were released on humanitarian grounds, such as Rosa Herrara who was 8 1/2 months pregnant at the time of her arrest.[238] Representatives from the Massachusetts State Department of Social Services went to Texas to lobby for the additional release of 21 detainees who were parents of children who had been left behind in New Bedford. Additional pleas from Governor Deval Patrick and two U.S. Senators had to be made before ICE released a handful of detainees back to Massachusetts so they could care for their children.[239] A seven-month-old infant who had been nursing became dehydrated after her mother's arrest; the baby lacked milk and needed urgent medical care.[240]

In communities across the country where raids occurred, local churches often provided safe haven and advocacy for the affected families. The National Council of La Raza released a report in late 2007, *Paying the Price: The Impact of Immigration Raids on America's Children*, documenting the effects of ICE raids, including community response, and used the events in New Bedford as part of their case study. The report noted a common theme throughout towns where raids had occurred — the use of local churches as a resource to affected communities. In New Bedford, St. James and Our Lady of Guadalupe became gathering places and refuge for those affected. The report pointed out that in the short term the Church provided a recognizable meeting point, central to the lives of members within the Latino community and was able to provide quick short term relieve without being slowed by bureaucratic gathering of information for statistical purposes or fear of offending partner organizations. In the long term however they were ill equipped and limited by small staff to meet the long term needs of immigrant communities.[241]

The La Raza study also analyzed the emotional and mental side effects upon children. While the long-term effects of the raids are still unraveling, psychologists have already observed and are concerned about long-term depression and other mental illness in family members. Psychologists have observed a level of fear among children resulting from separation from one or both parents. Children feared leaving the parent who was not seized and also questioned their parents' feelings for them. The report found that because younger children do not think in conceptual terms of citizen versus noncitizen, they translated the temporary parental absence as abandonment. Parents also noticed changes in behavior, such as children becoming more fearful and sometimes even more aggressive. One parent repeated

---

[237] Ray Henry, *Children Stranded After Immigration Raid*, Boston Globe, Mar. 7, 2007, *available at* http://www.boston.com/news/local/massachusetts/articles/2007/03/07/children_stranded_after_immigration_raid/.

[238] Alexandra Marks, *After New Bedford Immigration Raid, Voices Call for Mercy and Justice*, Christian Science Monitor, Mar. 16, 2007, *available at* http://www.csmonitor.com/2007/0316/p01s02-ussc.html?page=1.

[239] National Council of La Raza, Paying the Price: The Impact of Immigration Raids on America's Children 28–29 (2007).

[240] Anahad O'Connor, *Immigration Agency Learns from '07 Raid*, N.Y. Times.com, March 6, 2006, *available at* http://thelede.blogs.nytimes.com/2008/03/06/a-year-later-debate-continues-about-raid/?scp=1-b&sq=%22New+Bedford%22+AND+Ice&st=nyt.

[241] National Council of La Raza, Paying the Price: The Impact of Immigration Raids on America's Children 36–37 (2007).

that her child said "the parent 'love[es] money more than he loves me."[242]

Postville, Iowa

One of the largest immigration raids in U.S. history occurred in April 2008 in the small Midwestern town of Postville, Iowa. Postville represents the quintessential American melting pot in a community with a population of roughly 2,600 people. The community houses a mix of Hasidic Jews, who originally moved to Postville to open up a kosher meatpacking plant. They work alongside immigrant workers from Mexico and parts of Central American who staff the plant, along with other residents including descendants of German Lutheran migrants. The raid occurred at the kosher meat plant, Agriprocessors, Inc., the largest employer in town, and one of the largest in northeastern Iowa. ICE seized over 400 undocumented workers, including 18 juveniles.[243]

Agriprocessors employed approximately 970 workers, 80 percent of whom were believed to have fraudulent identification.[244] After the raid both Agriprocessor and the entire Postville community were in recovery mode. The company brought in a skeleton crew from New York to meet their staffing needs. Community residents observed the sudden drop in business and worried about the town's future. Postville is home to many Latino businesses, and in the days after the raids many storefronts posted signs in Spanish reading "closed".[245] Postville Mayor, Robert Penrod speculated on the effect of a possible Agriprocessor plant closure upon the town, estimating that "two-thirds of the homes here will sit empty [and] 95 percent of downtown business . . . will dry up."[246]

As in other communities the school system also felt the immediate impact of the raids. The local school district estimated that 150 of the 220 students from immigrant families were absent the day after the raid.[247] As in other communities, the Catholic Church became a refuge for the local immigrant population. One local nun, Sister Kathy Thrill, of nearby Waterloo where the detainees were being held at a local fairground, spoke out against the raids. She participated in an effort to collect donations for the affected families but noted the fear in the community. Many residents heard a story of someone who was stopped while shopping at a local Wal-Mart, and tales like these were scaring many families into hiding. Sister Thrill also spoke of her own apprehension as she got word of possible check points set up

---

[242] *Id.* at 50–51.

[243] Antonio Olivio, *Immigration raid roils Iowa Melting Pot*, CHICAGO TRIBUNE, May 18, 2008, *available at* http://www.chicagotribune.com/news/nationworld/chi-iowa-plant-raidmay19,0,3571577.story.

[244] *Id.*

[245] *Raids Could Make Postville a Ghost Town*, KAALTV.com, May 14, 2008 *available at* http://kaaltv.com/article/stories/S443938.shtml?cat=0.

[246] *Id.*

[247] Mary Ann Zehr, *Iowa School District Left Coping with Immigration Raid's Impact*, EDWEEK May 20, 2008, *available at* http://www.edweek.org/ login.html?source=http%3A%2F%2Fwww.google.com%2Fsearch%3Fhl%3Den%26client%3Dfirefox-a%26channel%3Ds%26rls%3Dorg.mozilla%253Aen-US%253Aofficial%26hs%3Di5G%26q%3DImmigration%2Braids%26btnG%3DSearch&destination=http%3A%2F%2Fwww.edweek.org%2Few%2Farticles%2F2008%2F05%2F21%2F38immig.h27.html&levelId=2100&baddebt=false.

by ICE officials while she was en route to deliver donated items to families.[248]

One witness to the effects of the ICE raid in Postville labeled the government strategy "criminal," as the women were made to wear restrictive "humiliating GPS bracelets" while caring for their children, and hundreds of women and children were faced with the threat of being left "homeless and starving."[249]

This raid also sparked criticism for the potential aftershocks on the American Jewish population who observes kosher dietary practice. Approximately one million American Jews follow kosher law. The slowdown of Agriprocessors — the nation's largest Kosher food provider — took time to recover; there were reports of increased meat prices and hoarding of food in the days following the raid.[250]

The May raid was not the first sign of trouble for Agriproessors, Inc. The company had been under scrutiny for numerous violations of environmental laws, labor laws, and was on notice that there was an alleged methamphetamine lab being run from inside the plant. The owners were eventually convicted of bank fraud charges and went bankrupt, and a new owner took over the operations.[251]

d. Silent Raids

Workplace ICE raids by gun-wielding agents resulting in the mass arrests of dozens and sometimes hundreds of employees that were common under the George W. Bush administration were purportedly eliminated under the Obama administration. Legally questionable mass arrests continued to occur in neighborhoods under the pretext of serving warrants on criminal aliens. However, disruptive, high-profile worksite raids began to subside. When a Bush administration-style ICE raid took place in Washington State in February 2009 soon after Janet Napolitano took the helm as Secretary of the Department of Homeland Security, she expressed surprise and ordered an investigation. These types of raids were not in her strategy plan she noted; instead enforcement in her regime would focus on employers who hire undocumented workers, not on the workers themselves.[252] As we will see in the next section, however, the Criminal Alien Removal Initiative of the Obama Administration has been implemented in a manner that is strikingly similar to Bush era ICE raids.

Make no mistake, although deportations related to worksite operations decreased under the Obama approach in contrast with that under George W. Bush, actual deportation numbers are not down. The Obama administration removed more than two million individuals by the middle of its second term, far surpassing

---

[248] Jayne Norman, *Immigrants feel distress, shock, nun says*, DES MOINES REGISTER, May 21, 2008, *available at* http://www.desmoinesregister.com/apps/pbcs.dll/article?AID=/20080521/NEWS/805210358.

[249] Jonah Newman, Minneapolis, Letter to the Editor, NY TIMES, June 3, 2008.

[250] Michelle Boorstein, *Raid on Slaughterhouse May Mean Shortage of Kosher Meat*, WASHINGTON POST, May 22, 2008, at A02, *available at* http://www.washingtonpost.com/wp-dyn/content/article/2008/05/21/AR2008052102471.html?hpid=sec-religion.

[251] *Ripple effect continues five years after immigration raid on Iowa plant*, CATHOLIC NEWS SERVICE, May 17, 2013; Orlan Love, *Two years after Agriprocessors raid, Postville is flush with new optimism*, THE GAZETTE, May 14, 2010.

[252] *Secretary Seeks Review of Immigration Raid*, N.Y. TIMES, Feb. 26, 2009.

deportation totals of any other president. According to ICE, the increase was partly a result of deporting those persons picked up for other crimes and expanding the search through prisons and jails for deportable immigrants already in custody.[253] Unlike the worksite raids that lead to arrests and deportation, the "silent raids," or audits of company records by federal agents, usually result in firings. Thus, for example, 765 undocumented workers were arrested by ICE at their jobs in 2010 through early summer, compared with 5,100 in 2008.[254]

However, the Obama administration's focus-on-employers-rather-than-workers strategy in fact falls squarely on the shoulders of the workers. Immigration raids at factories and farms were replaced with a quieter enforcement strategy: sending federal agents to scour companies' records for undocumented immigrant workers. While the sweeps of the past commonly led to the deportation of such workers, the "silent raids," as employers call the audits, usually result in the workers being fired, although in many cases they are not deported.[255] The idea is that if the workers cannot work, they will self-deport, leaving on their own. However, they actually do not leave because they need to work. They become more desperate and take jobs at lower wages. Given the increasing scale of enforcement, this can lead to an overall reduction in the average wage level for millions of workers, which is, in effect, a subsidy to employer. Over a 12-month period, ICE conducted audits of employee files at more than 2900 companies.[256] The agency levied a record $3 million in civil fines in the first six months of 2010 on businesses that hired unauthorized immigrants. Thousands of workers were fired.[257]

The audits reach more companies than the work-site roundups of the Bush administration. The audits force businesses to fire every suspected undocumented worker on the payroll — not just those who happened to be on duty at the time of a raid — and make it much harder to hire other unauthorized workers as replacements. Auditing is effective in getting unauthorized workers fired for sure.

Consider some examples. An audit of Gebbers Farms in the orchard town of Brewster, Washington is typical. Immigration inspectors scoured the records of Gebbers Farms and found evidence that approximately 550 of its workers, mostly immigrants from Mexico, did not have proper documentation.[258] So, those workers were fired. ICE officials also pressured one of San Francisco's major building service companies, ABM, into firing hundreds of its own workers.[259] ICE agents told ABM that they had flagged the personnel records of those workers. Weeks

---

[253] Peter Slevin, *Deportation of Illegal Immigrants Increases Under Obama Administration*, WASH. POST, July 26, 2010.

[254] Roy Maurer, *Undocumented Workers Fired, Firms Audited in 'Silent Raids,'* Soc'y for Human Resource Mgmt. (July 22, 2010), http://www.shrm.org/hrdisciplines/global/Articles/Pages/SilentRaids. aspx.

[255] Julia Preston, *Illegal Workers Swept from Jobs in "Silent Raids,"* N.Y. TIMES, July, 9, 2010.

[256] *Id.*

[257] *Id.*

[258] Melissa Sanchez, *Massive Firings in Brewster, and a Big Debate about Illegal Immigration*, SEATTLE TIMES, Feb. 13, 2010.

[259] Lauren Smiley, *Janitors Descend From Skyscrapers to Protest Immigration Raids*, SFWEEKLY BLOG, Apr. 27, 2010, http://blogs.sfweekly.com/thesnitch/2010/04/janitors_descend_from_skyscrap.php.

earlier, the agents sifted through Social Security records and the I-9 immigration forms all workers have to fill out when they apply for jobs. They then told ABM that the company had to fire 475 workers who were accused of lacking legal immigration status.[260] Similar ICE actions resulted in the firing of 1200 ABM janitors in Minneapolis, and 100 janitors in Seattle in the Fall of 2009.[261]

Advancing a theme of focusing on employers who use undocumented workers to "drive down wages" and "mistreat" workers, President Obama and ICE chief John Morton claimed to be looking primarily for "egregious employers who commit both labor abuses and immigration violations."[262] But American Apparel, also a target for a silent raid, ABM, and Gebbers Farms did not appear to fit that profile. While American Apparel is a huge corporation that makes hundreds of millions of dollars a year, the workers dismissed were "long-term employees being paid decent wages."[263] The company was proud of their "Made in America" labels and had a reputation for paying more than most garment shops. Before the audit, its CEO, Dov Charney, took to the streets and stood shoulder to shoulder with workers in protesting and demanding legalization for workers who have been "victimized by our broken immigration system."[264]

Similarly, Gebbers Farms had a general reputation for "doing right by their employees."[265] The company built housing and soccer fields for its workers and, unlike many other growers, provided stable year-round work."[266] After the firings, Gebbers Farms advertised hundreds of jobs for orchard workers. But there were few takers in the state. Finally, the company applied to the federal guest worker program to import about 1200 legal temporary workers — most from Mexico.[267] The guest workers, who can stay for up to six months, also included about 300 from Jamaica.[268] Thus, one thing that silent raids do accomplish is to support those who advocate for expanded guest worker programs.

As for ABM, the building service has been a union company for decades, and many of the workers had been there for years. According to Olga Miranda, President of Service Employees Local 87: "They've been working in the buildings downtown for 15, 20, some as many as 27 years. They've built homes. They've provided for their families. They've sent their kids to college. They're not new workers. They didn't just get here a year ago."[269]

---

[260] *Id.*

[261] Lornet Turnbull, *Illegal Workers Quietly Let Go*, Seattle Times, Nov. 23, 2009.

[262] Preston, *supra* note 255.

[263] Ben Johnson, *Crackdown on American Apparel Workers Another Wasted Effort*, Alternet.org, Oct. 6, 2009, http:// www.alternet.org/immigration/143116/crackdown_on_american_apparel_workers_another_wasted_effort/.

[264] *Id.*

[265] Preston, *supra* note 255.

[266] Sanchez, *supra* note 258.

[267] Preston, *supra* note 255.

[268] *Id.*

[269] David Bacon, *Fighting the Firings*, In These Times, Aug. 23, 2011, *available at* http://inthesetimes.com/article/11857/fighting_the_firings.

e. Criminal Alien Removal Initiative

In spite of the Obama Administration's use of "Silent Raids" to target undocumented immigrants, in 2012, ICE launched a program called the Criminal Alien Removal Initiative (CARI) that evolved in a manner that took on the characteristics of Bush era ICE raids. ICE had announced a focus on deporting violent or convicted criminals, and immigrants who posed a threat to national security. Its targets included returned deportees, as well as "immigrant fugitives," meaning immigrants who failed to appear for a court date. These were the purported targets of CARI.

CARI was established in May 2012 as part of a broad agency push to boost deportations of immigrants with criminal records. But when details about the initiative's operations in New Orleans came to light in September 2013 — after the New Orleans Workers' Center for Racial Justice (NOWCRJ) requested an ICE case review of Erlin San Martin Gomez, a father with no criminal record who was swept up as part of a raid and placed into deportation proceedings, CARI was exposed as a program that also sweeps up immigrants without criminal records.[270]

Gomez was leaving his house to pick up his two-year-old son at day care when two plainclothes immigration agents approached him. The agents had one question for the 27-year-old Honduran immigrant: whether he had an ID. The agents handcuffed him, led him to an ICE vehicle and scanned his fingerprints with a mobile biometrics unit that searches immigration and criminal databases. Gomez had not criminal record, but ICE discovered that he had been previously deported. His feet were shackled and he was put in the back of the ICE vehicle, where he would stay for several hours. During that time, the agents stopped for a meal, met with other ICE officers and then drove around New Orleans arresting people until the vehicle was full. One agent boasted, "This is like going hunting." The devices used by ICE were first developed for U.S. military use in Iraq and Afghanistan, allowing ICE agents to perform immediate biometric record checks during community raids.

ICE has found willing partners for the CARI strategy in local law enforcement agencies, many of which had their own handheld biometric devices with instant access to databases. In Jefferson Parish, the ad hoc collaboration between the locals and the feds has made it difficult to determine why some Latinos have been stopped and questioned by police; advocates suspect pure racial profiling. The ICE agents who scanned Gomez's fingerprints were members of a CARI PROGRAM "fugitive team." Federal indictments from stops in the county describe the CARI team members "assisting" sheriff's officers on "routine patrols."

CARI, has sparked immigration raids at grocery stores, Bible study groups and parks both noncitizens and citizens have complained to her office about stops and arrests. Like Gomez, they are asked for ID, then handcuffed and fingerprinted, while walking on the street, standing in their front yard, or driving through checkpoints. Latino U.S. citizens have also reported being fingerprinted by ICE agents, then let go, after the scans of their prints show their legal status.

---

[270] *See* New Orleans Workers' Center for Racial Justice, The Criminal Alien Removal Initiative in New Orleans: The Obama Administration's Brutal New Frontier in Immigration Enforcement, Dec. 2013, *available at* http://nowcrj.org/wp-content/uploads/2008/11/CARI-report-final.pdf.

As a result, Louisiana has the highest per capita deportation rate in the country and the highest per capita rate of immigration arrests of any non-border state. CARI deportees have included Hurricane Katrina reconstruction workers engaged in labor disputes, parents of U.S. citizen children, and a crime victim with a U-visa certification. CARI has become a regime of indiscriminate and terrifying community raids based on racial profiling: "driving while Latino" stops on major roads and highway exists, raids at stores and social settings, and open discussions by ICE agents about racial profiling and quota-based arrests.

The CARI program in New Orleans are not the only ICE raids undertaken by ICE under the Obama administration. Soon after news of the CARI program in New Orleans broke out, immigrants and community advocates around the country reported significant increases of individuals detained as "collateral" arrestees during similar raids. This increase was especially acute in places like, New York, Philadelphia, Wisconsin, Washington, Alabama, Massachusetts, Florida, and Illinois. Reports from Georgia and Connecticut also documented sharp increases of collateral arrests of people with old criminal convictions or prior deportation orders. In places like Arizona, local organizers were aware of home raids and collateral arrests for a long time.[271]

ICE officials do not label these policies "raids." Instead, in its terminology, ICE conducts "targeted enforcement" operations to arrest "priority" individuals who present a danger to the public. On the ground, however, there is little difference. As implemented by ICE, "targeted enforcement" looks very much like a raid. In a targeted enforcement operation, ICE stakes out a single home, apartment building, business, or — in some cases — an entire neighborhood in search of its target. Along the way, ICE agents request identification from anyone they encounter, often arresting and placing in deportation proceedings individuals who were not the stated target of the operation. A variety of branches of ICE, including Fugitive Operations teams conduct the operations under the direction of the local Field Office Director.[272] These operations are not limited to businesses. In the words of one day laborer organizer in New Orleans, "Before ICE used to round people up in the community. Now, they go to people's houses. They show them a picture of a person they usually don't know. Even if the person isn't there, everyone in the house still gets fingerprinted using the biometric machines. The only difference is ICE makes sure to show people a photograph so that they can say it is targeted enforcement and not a raid."[273]

To make matters worse, community organizers and immigrants have experienced retaliation from ICE in response to their advocating for improved conditions, a moratorium on removals, or protection of rights of those in custody. An Arizona advocate reports that "In retaliation for organizing, ICE has denied people's visitation rights, gone out of their way to keep people in detention even when granted bond, and even put people's family members in solitary confinement," or

---

[271] Tania Unzueta Carrasco & B. Loewe, Destructive Delay: A Qualitative Report on the State of Interior Immigration Enforcement and the Human Costs of Postponing Reforms 6 (2014), *available at* http://www.notonemoredeportation.com/wp-content/uploads/2014/10/Destructive-Delay-final1.pdf.

[272] *Id.* at 7.

[273] *Id.* at 9.

deny visitation rights.[274] Organizers in Tacoma, Washington working with immigrants who participated in a detention center hunger strike reported similar retaliation against families of those who led these actions. Family visits are often reduced to 10 or 20 minutes.[275]

f. National Security

i. SEVIS and Other Student-Related Programs

The government has a history of monitoring and tracking foreign students in the United States under the pretext of protecting national security. Even though student visitors make up a small percentage of nonimmigrant admissions annually, the involvement of Eyad Ismoil in the World Trade Center bombing on February 26, 1993, sparked widespread concern about the INS's ability to track student whereabouts.[276] Ismoil, a Jordanian national, entered the U.S. on a student visa in 1989 but had dropped out of school and overstayed his visa.[277]

This incident and the public's response led to the passage of section 641 of IIRIRA in 1996.[278] This section of the statute provided that the Attorney General, in consultation with the Secretaries of State and Education, develop and conduct a program to collect certain information about F, J and M visa holders or applicants for such status who were nationals of five designated countries.[279] This information was collected from the approved schools and exchange programs, and was to be collected electronically when practicable.[280] The program was to be funded by fees of no more than $100 per student or exchange visitor.[281]

The Coordinated Interagency Partnership Regulating International Students (CIPRIS) was developed to implement section 641. CIPRIS is an internet based reporting system that was used cooperatively by the INS, the Department of State, the Department of Education, and members of the educational and exchange programs.[282] CIPRIS was a pilot project that began in June 1997 to test the concepts of electronic data collection and reporting methods.[283] This pilot project ended in October 1999.[284]

The Student and Exchange Visitor Program (SEVP) started developing in 2000 and was designed to incorporate the permanent version of CIPRIS. The terrorist attacks of September 11, 2001, however, led to renewed anxiety in regards to

---

[274] *Id.* at 12.

[275] *Id.* at 12.

[276] Susan N. Burguess, *Sevis: Is It Academic?*, 04-02 IMMIGR. BRIEFINGS 1, 1 (Feb. 2004).

[277] *Id.*

[278] *Id.*

[279] Pub. L. No.104-208, 110 Stat. 3009, Sec. 641 (Sept. 30, 1996) codified at 8 U.S.C.A. § 1372.

[280] *Id.*

[281] *Id.*

[282] Burguess, *supra* note 271, at 4.

[283] *Id.*

[284] *Id.*

foreign students and let to a perceived need to accelerate a more thorough tracking and monitoring system.[285]

The USA PATRIOT Act of 2001 amended Section 641 of IIRIRA and it accelerated the earlier program by (1) requiring that it be fully implemented prior to January 1, 2003, (2) authorizing funding to accommodate the accelerated implementation, and (3) imposing additional data collection requirements. In addition, the Enhanced Border Security and Visa Entry Reform Act of 2002 added to the requirements pertaining to data collection and reporting. Schools and exchange visitor programs were now required to report to ICE any student or exchange visitor who were supposed to enroll but failed to do so.

The Student and Exchange Visitor Information System (SEVIS) became an integral part of this new monitoring system. SEVIS is an internet-based program that is intended to enhance the government's ability to "manage and monitor" foreign students and exchange program visitors and their dependents. DHS monitors and tracks these individuals by requiring that, in order to accept foreign students or exchange visitors, the schools and exchange programs must be certified and enrolled in SEVIS and must adhere to its data collection requirements. SEVIS functions were given to the Immigration and Customs Enforcement (ICE) branch of DHS, as it is supposed to be a tool to protect national security.

SEVIS affects several nonimmigrant groups. In order to admit F-1, F-3, M-1 or M-3 students, schools are required to be enrolled in SEVIS. Similarly, in order to admit a J-1 exchange visitor, a program must register with SEVIS. Spouses and children of any of these nonimmigrants who enter the United States as dependents of the principal applicant are also subject to SEVIS reporting.

SEVIS imposed stringent reporting and record keeping requirements, which are codified in various laws and regulations. IIRIRA, The Patriot Act, the Enhanced Border Security and Visa Entry Reform Act, as well as DHS Regulations and Department of State Regulations all require the reporting of different types of information. For example, IIRIRA established that the identity and current U.S. address of the nonimmigrant had to be provided, as well as their nonimmigrant 1) classification and the date on which a visa was issued, extended, or approved; 2) the nonimmigrant's current academic status; and 3) any disciplinary action taken against the nonimmigrant as a result of his or her being convicted of a crime.[286] DHS regulations require an even longer list of information such as whether a student failed to maintain status or complete his or her program, or whether they graduated early.[287]

The Accreditation of English Language Training Act of 2010 ensures that all colleges, universities, and other educational institutions that provide English language training ("ESL") programs also are subject to SEVIS. The schools must obtain accreditation from a regional or national accreditation agency recognized by

---

[285] *Id.* at 1.

[286] 8 U.S.C.A. § 1372(c)(1)(A)–(D).

[287] 8 C.F.R. § 214.3(g)(3)(ii).

the United States Department of Education. The Accreditation Act applies to two types of ESL programs: Stand-Alone ESL Schools and Combined Schools.

SEVIS was established with the goals of improving national security, and as a way to modernizing the old paper system of tracking student visa recipients. It is unclear whether SEVIS has been able to achieve either of its main goals.

ii.   The Penttbom Investigation

Immediately after the September 11 attacks, the FBI, in cooperation with several other law enforcement agencies, launched the Pentagon/Twin Towers Bombing Investigation (PENTTBOM).[288] Officials questioned and frequently detained individuals possibly involved in the September 11 attacks or other terrorist activities, as well as anyone who might have information of use to the investigation.[289] Undocumented immigrants were sometimes encountered fortuitously during the course of the investigation.[290] Even if they had no link to, or knowledge of, terrorist activities, they too were arrested, turned over to the former INS and detained.[291] Of the detainees held on immigration-related grounds (whether or not suspected of terrorism), the overwhelming majority were males, between ages 26 and 40, from Arab or Muslim countries.[292] About one-third were from Pakistan.[293]

To compound the controversy, the government steadfastly refused to disclose to the public the names or whereabouts of the detainees, a policy that the D.C. Circuit Court of Appeals upheld.[294] 332 In addition, a federal Bureau of Prisons regulation rooted in the PENTTBOM investigation authorized the monitoring of inmate-attorney conversations, sometimes with the inmate's knowledge and sometimes without it, in certain cases of suspected terrorism.[295]

The racial profiling used in this investigation, the government tactics, and secrecy were gravely concerning. Many individuals' constitutional and human rights seemed to be compromised. Widespread criticism of the PENTTBOM investigation developed. One of the most critical reports of post 9/11 anti-terrorism performance and its impact on immigrants, especially Muslim males, came from the Office of the Inspector General (OIG) of the Department of Justice (DOJ). The OIG testified before the Congress as to the plight of 9/11 detainees:

---

[288] Dan Eggen, *FBI's 9/11 Team Still Hard at Work; Dwindling Group Wants to See Probe Through to the End*, WASH. POST, June 14, 2004.

[289] *See* OFFICE OF THE INSPECTOR GENERAL, U.S. DEPARTMENT OF JUSTICE, THE SEPTEMBER 11 DETAINEES: A REVIEW OF THE TREATMENT OF ALIENS HELD ON IMMIGRATION CHARGES IN CONNECTION WITH THE INVESTIGATION OF THE SEPTEMBER 11 ATTACKS 69–70 (2003), *available at* http://www.usdoj.gov/oig/special/0306/full.pdf [hereinafter OIG REPORT].

[290] Stephen H. Legomsky, *The Ethnic and Religious Profiling of Noncitizens: National Security and International Human Rights*, 25 B.C. THIRD WORLD L.J. 161, 165 (2005).

[291] *Id.*

[292] *Id.*

[293] *Id.*

[294] *Id.*

[295] *Id.*

> Our review determined that 762 aliens were detained on immigration charges in connection with the PENTTBOM investigation in the first 11 months after the terrorist attacks. . . . Our review found that many September 11 detainees did not receive notice of the charges against them in a timely manner. . . . More than a quarter of the 762 detainees' clearance investigations took longer than 3 months. . . . Our review found serious problems in the treatment of the September 11 detainees housed at the MDC . . . the BOP imposed a total communications blackout for several weeks on the September 11 detainees held at the MDC. . . . Most of the September 11 detainees did not have legal representation prior to their detention at the MDC . . . detainees were placed in full restraints whenever they were moved, including handcuffs, leg irons, and heavy chains. . . . The detainees also were subjected to having two lights illuminated in their cells 24 hours a day. . . . We concluded that on occasion staff members used strip searches to intimidate and punish detainees.[296]

The government's high handed counter-terrorism measures and tactics were egregious enough to also attract the intervention of the courts.[297] In United States v. Awadallah, 202 F. Supp. 2d 55, (S.D.N.Y. 2002), the Court opined:

> Having committed no crime — indeed, without any claim that there was probable cause to believe he had violated any law — [the witness] bore the full weight of the prison system designed to punish convicted criminals as well as incapacitate individuals arrested or indicted for criminal conduct . . . .[He was] repeatedly strip-searched, shackled whenever he [was] moved, denied food that complies with his religious needs . . . prohibited from seeing or even calling his family over the course of 20 days and then [pressured into] testifying while handcuffed to a chair.

The PENTTBOM investigation again exemplified that the U.S. government is willing to compromise immigrants' human rights and constitutional protections under the pretext of protecting national security. There was little connection between the government's detention and deportation of these immigrants and the investigation of terrorist activities. As the PENTTBOM investigation ensued, human rights violations occurred by the U.S. government against many immigrants.

3.   The Scope of Enforcement Powers

There are certain provisions in our constitution that protect all individuals living in the United States, regardless of their immigration status. The following rights apply in the immigration enforcement context and are important to understand the scope of enforcement powers. First, under the Fourth Amendment of the Constitution, every person has the right not to be "unreasonably" searched or seized by the government. An arrest warrant can only be issued if there is a

---

[296] Detainees: Hearing Before the Sen. Comm. on the Judiciary, 109th Cong. (2005) (statement of Glenn A. Fine, Inspector Gen. U.S. Dep't of Justice).

[297] Kam C. Wong, *The USA Patriot Act: A Policy of Alienation*, 12 Mich. J. Race & L. 161, 168 (2006).

"probable cause" that a person has violated the law. Second, the Fifth Amendment established that no person can be deprived of life, liberty, or property without due process of law. Third, the Fourteenth Amendment guarantees "equal protection" under the law for any person affected by actions of local or state government. The Fourteenth Amendment ensures that people in similar situation are treated equally under the law. These constitutional provisions, along with certain sections of the INA and other statutes, grant immigrants certain rights and should limit the scope of the government's immigration enforcement power.

The rights and protections outlined in the Constitution, however, are dependent on court interpretation. Courts across the United States have differed in their interpretation of what these rights mean. Moreover, in general, courts have interpreted the Constitution and these laws to only narrowly protect immigrant rights and to give the government broad immigration enforcement power. The following sections of this Chapter will explore the scope of the government's immigration enforcement powers as defined by the courts in the context of stops and arrests, search and seizure, interrogations, and detention.

a. Interrogations

The Immigration and Nationality Act (INA) provides that INS officers "shall have power without warrant . . . to interrogate any alien or person believed to be an alien as to his right to be or to remain in the United States."[298] The Fourth Amendment, which the Supreme Court has applied to Border Patrol searches and seizures of all persons in the United States, circumscribes this power. An official can therefore only legally stop someone, for interrogation purposes, if they have good reason to believe that the individual is undocumented.

Courts use a balancing test to determine if a stop and interrogation is reasonable under the Fourth Amendment. Courts weigh how much an enforcement officer's conduct impedes a person's freedom against how strong a reason the officer has to suspect that the individual is undocumented. The more an enforcement officer's conduct interferes with a person's freedom, the greater the justification the officer needs to question that person.

This balancing test falls into three categories based on the intensity of the interrogation. An immigration enforcement officer can briefly question an individual if the officer has "articulable facts to justify a suspicion" that the individual is an "alien."[299] This type of interrogation is referred to as "casual questioning." For this test to apply, the officer must question the individual without a show of force, and the person being questioned must be free to walk away.

When an immigration enforcement official stops an individual for longer than "brief questioning," it is a detentive stop. In most parts of the United States, the officer in this situation must have a "reasonable suspicion" that the person is an undocumented immigrant. Only a very short period of questioning is allowed during a detentive stop, however the person is not free to walk away. If during this

---

[298] INA § 287(a); 8 U.S.C. § 1357(a).

[299] United States v. Brignoni-Ponce, 422 U.S. 873, 884 (1975).

questioning, the officer finds "probable cause" to believe the person is undocumented, the officer can arrest the person.

An agent can only legally arrest a person if they have "probable cause" to believe that the individual is undocumented. Because an individual's freedom is being curtailed, the officer needs strong evidence to meet this requirement. A person can be "under arrest" if they reasonably believe that they are not free to leave. A person does not have to be told they are under arrest or be hand-cuffed.

The difference between a "detentive stop" and an arrest is sometimes hard to recognize. Usually, if an immigration enforcement officer uses force against a person, displays weapons, questions the individual in a threatening manner, or uses coercive language, the courts will determine that a person has been arrested.

The Supreme Court, however, has found that use of coercive language or behavior by the police does not always constitute an arrest. In *California v. Hodari D*,[300] the Supreme Court held that an arrest was not made until the coercion was complete — that is, until the person has completely submitted to the show of force or authority.

The scope of immigration enforcement power is subject to courts interpreting the Fourth Amendment and other statutes. As we will see in the following sections, courts have usually used their powers to broaden the scope of enforcement power and limit the protections of individuals within the immigration context.

b.   Stops and Arrests

i.   Immigration Checkpoints

As the INS enforcement budget grew larger and larger, the Supreme Court, swayed by arguments that the undocumented alien problem was worsening, allowed more flexibility to INS enforcement strategies.

In 1973, the Supreme Court appeared to have put an end to the Border Patrol practice of "roving" near the United States-Mexico border to search vehicles, without a warrant or probable cause. In *Almeida-Sanchez v. United States*,[301] INS officials unsuccessfully argued that as long as they were in the proximity of the border, their efforts in following and stopping cars located near the border was the "functional equivalent" of the border; on that theory, the Border Patrol felt that inhabitants of such vehicles were subject to the same intrusions as those at the border. But within two years, the Supreme Court was overwhelmed by government claims of a crisis at the border opened the door to stops by roving patrols near the border under certain circumstances.

In *United States v. Brignoni-Ponce*,[302] two Border Patrol officers were observing northbound traffic from a patrol car parked at the side of Interstate Highway 5 north of San Diego. The road was dark, and they were using the patrol

---

[300] 499 U.S. 621 (1991).

[301] 413 U.S. 266 (1973).

[302] 422 U.S. 873 (1975).

car's headlights to illuminate passing cars. They pursued Brignoni-Ponce's car and stopped it, saying later that their only reason for doing so was that its three occupants appeared to be of Mexican descent. The officers questioned the three occupants about their citizenship and learned that the passengers were aliens who had entered the country illegally. All three were then arrested, and Brignoni-Ponce was charged with two counts of knowingly transporting undocumented immigrants. At trial he moved to suppress the testimony of and about the two passengers, claiming that this evidence was the fruit of an illegal seizure because the officers did not have the authority to stop his car. The Court of Appeals agreed, holding that the Fourth Amendment, as interpreted in *Almeida-Sanchez*, forbids stopping a vehicle, even for the limited purpose of questioning its occupants, unless the officers have a founded suspicion that the occupants are aliens illegally in the country. The appellate court refused to find that Mexican ancestry alone supported such a founded suspicion and held that Brignoni-Ponce motion to suppress should have been granted.

The Supreme Court agreed that a roving patrol generally should not be allowed to stop a vehicle near the Mexican border and question its occupants about their citizenship and immigration status, when the only ground for suspicion is that the occupants appear to be of Mexican ancestry. But the Court carved an important exception: patrolling officers may stop vehicles if they are aware of specific articulable facts, together with rational inferences, reasonably warranting suspicion that the vehicles contain aliens who may be illegally in the country and the occupants can be questioned. Any number of factors may be taken into account in deciding whether there is reasonable suspicion to stop a car in the border area. Officers may consider the characteristics of the area in which they encounter a vehicle. Its proximity to the border, the usual patterns of traffic on the particular road, and previous experience with alien traffic are all relevant. They also may consider information about recent illegal border crossings in the area. The driver's behavior may be relevant; erratic driving or obvious attempts to evade officers can support a reasonable suspicion. Aspects of the vehicle itself may justify suspicion. For instance, officers say that certain station wagons, with large compartments for fold-down seats or spare tires, are frequently used for transporting concealed aliens. The vehicle may appear to be heavily loaded, it may have an extraordinary number of passengers, or the officers may observe persons trying to hide. The Court also acknowledged that trained officers can recognize the characteristic appearance of persons who live in Mexico, relying on such factors as the mode of dress and haircut.

The Court was willing to give more latitude to Border Patrol officers in response to government claims that undocumented Mexican migration was getting out of hand:

> The Government makes a convincing demonstration that the public interest demands effective measures to prevent the illegal entry of aliens at the Mexican border. Estimates of the number of illegal immigrants in the United States vary widely. A conservative estimate in 1972 produced a figure of about one million, but the INS now [in 1975] suggests there may be as many as 10 or 12 million aliens illegally in the country. Whatever the number, these aliens create significant economic and social problems,

competing with citizens and legal resident aliens for jobs, and generating extra demand for social services. The aliens themselves are vulnerable to exploitation because they cannot complain of substandard working conditions without risking deportation. . . .

The Government has estimated that 85% of the aliens illegally in the country are from Mexico. . . . The Mexican border is almost 2,000 miles long, and even a vastly reinforced Border Patrol would find it impossible to prevent illegal border crossings. Many aliens cross the Mexican border on foot, miles away from patrolled areas, and then purchase transportation from the border area to inland cities, where they find jobs and elude the immigration authorities. Others gain entry on valid temporary border-crossing permits, but then violate the conditions of their entry. Most of these aliens leave the border area in private vehicles, often assisted by professional "alien smugglers." The Border Patrol's traffic-checking operations are designed to prevent this inland movement. They succeed in apprehending some illegal entrants and smugglers, and they deter the movement of others by threatening apprehension and increasing the cost of illegal transportation.[303]

ii.   Racial Profiling

A case in Illinois illustrates enforcement strategy by INS investigators that focuses on individuals with "Latin" appearance in both employment and nonemployment settings. In *Illinois Migrant Council v. Pilliod*,[304] the federal court of appeals upheld an order of a lower court critical of such INS tactics. The case involved six individuals and the Illinois Migrant Council (IMC), a nonprofit corporation, who brought a class action against officials of the INS. IMC was a community service agency that served as an advocate for illiterate migrant agricultural workers of Mexican heritage; the individual plaintiffs were U.S. citizens or permanent residents of Mexican descent. The plaintiffs alleged that INS officials were unconstitutionally stopping and questioning individuals simply on the basis of physical appearance, and without any basis for concluding that they were aliens.

One part of the case involved three street encounters between INS agents and four individuals. On September 18, 1974, plaintiffs Sandoval and Montanez were driving in Sandoval's car to the IMC office in Rochelle, Illinois. As they parked outside the office and were leaving the car, an INS car pulled alongside and the agents got out of their car. When Montanez was asked where he was born, he replied, "Mexico." He was asked for his identification and produced a satisfactory permanent resident alien card after being threatened otherwise with jail in Chicago. When Sandoval, a U.S. citizen of Mexican descent, was asked to produce identification, and refused to do so, the agents said they would have to take him to Chicago and forced him into the back seat of their car. He again refused to produce

---

[303] United States v. Brignoni-Ponce, 422 U.S. 873, 879 (1975).

[304] 540 F.2d 1062 (7th Cir. 1976).

identification, but was ordered out of the car when he implied that he was a U.S. citizen.

During the first week of October 1974, plaintiff Lopez was walking to his office at 19 West Jackson Boulevard in Chicago when he was asked by two strangers if he lived in the area. He responded "No" but said that he worked around there. Then he was asked where he was born. When he inquired why he was being interrogated, the agent said he was from the INS and flashed his identification. Lopez then said that he was born in New Mexico. He is an American-born citizen of Mexican descent. At the time, he was attired in boots made in New Mexico, Levis jeans, an Illinois shirt, and a Mexican jacket.

Jose Ortiz, a member of the plaintiff class, stated that when he was walking with a friend on September 18, 1974, in Rochelle, Illinois, two INS agents stopped them and asked for Ortiz's papers. He was allowed to leave upon complying.

Other incidents involved "area control operations" conducted by agents without search or arrest warrants. At 4:30 A.M. on September 18, 1974, defendant Theodore Glorgetti, an INS employee, and 32 armed INS agents began simultaneous operations on preselected targets in Rochelle, Illinois. First, they knocked on the unlocked doors and entered two La Hacienda buildings where 55 female employees of the Del Monte Food Company were sleeping. The agents proceeded from bedroom to bedroom, demanding that the women occupants produce their papers. Afterward they left the buildings without making any arrests.

The agents also searched the Del Monte cottages where male immigrant employees resided. The INS agents used essentially the same method of operation in those cottages. When one of the residents, the same Jose Ortiz mentioned before, was unable to produce his green card evidencing legal residency, he was forced to accompany the INS agents on their search and was released only when another Del Monte employee assured them that Ortiz's papers were in order.

At the same time, an INS agent repeatedly kicked on the door of a small farmhouse near Rochelle occupied by Alonzo Solis, a U.S. citizen migrant worker. The agent tried to force his way into the house but desisted only when the Solis's child cried and Solis ordered him out. Solis dressed and showed the agent his "certificate" outside the house, whereupon the agent left.

At 5:00 A.M., INS agents also conducted similar operations at Del Monte plants 109 and 110. They questioned everyone who appeared to be of Latino heritage. Two Del Monte supervisors offered no resistance because they believed they had to allow the agents to search the plants.

In Mendota, Illinois, at 8:00 A.M. on September 26, 1974, defendant Giorgetti and 30 agents first went to the Motor Wheel plant. Nineteen employees were interviewed by Giorgetti, 10 were arrested, and five of the 10 were subsequently permitted to return to work. The agents then proceeded to several other industrial targets in Mendota and to hotels, boardinghouses, and private dwellings, resulting in the apprehension of 108 undocumented aliens, 104 of whom were still in detention at the time of the hearing below.

The court ruled that these INS enforcement strategies were improper, because a person should not be stopped by an INS agent unless the agent reasonably suspects that he or she is an alien illegally in the country, or at least that the person is an alien. Latin appearance alone is not sufficient basis for INS agents to stop and question.

Another brazen government example involved the sweep of an entire downtown area of a California town in conjunction with local law enforcement officials. On September 8, 1984, a raid of bars in the central valley town of Sanger, California, resulted in the deportation of 255 undocumented aliens. Five law enforcement agencies blockaded the main street downtown, swept through bars, and arrested 40 people on criminal charges. Officers from the Fresno County Sheriff's Department, Sanger Police Department, Fresno Police, Department, state Department of Alcoholic Beverage Control (ABC), and Border Patrol closed off downtown Sanger streets and entered 16 bars. For the next two hours, they served 35 warrants and made 40 arrests, mostly for misdemeanor offenses, while. Border Patrol agents asked bar patrons for identification and arrested 255 undocumented aliens. Officers entered bars and ordered that no one leave. An agent from ABC searched for liquor law violations and police officers attempted to serve individual arrest warrants on charges of B-girl activities, receiving stolen property, prostitution, gambling, and narcotics.

Meanwhile, a Border Patrol agent asked in English who had citizenship or legal residency documents. Those with documents were detained in another room for about 40 minutes, while other patrons were searched and questioned. Of the hundred patrons in the bar, 47 were undocumented. One was arrested for having a concealed weapon. The other 52 patrons were detained although they were U.S. citizens or legal residents and were accused of no crime.

One bar owner (who was not cited for any wrongdoing) was appalled by what he saw: "Officers came in like Hitler's police or the police in South Africa. [Those suspected by the INS] were herded like cattle. I can't believe this can happen in the United States." What happened was clear to William Kennedy, an attorney with California — Rural Legal Assistance, who investigated: "These are *racist raids*. There's no way to characterize them any other way. They're looking for *brown-skinned people*, not any others."[305]

Antonio Martinez fell prey to one of the more unusual INS enforcement, strategies also directed primarily at Mexicans in southern California in 1993. Martinez received a letter from the INS and read it several times, getting, an uneasy feeling each time. After two years of battling the INS to legalize his status so he could remain here with his American wife and daughter, the offer seemed too good to be true. Come to the Federal Building, bring some identification, and we'll give you a work permit good for a year, the letter said. How could the letter not be authentic? asked Martinez's wife, Ariel, a California native. It was written on INS stationery and said Martinez qualified under the "Immigration and Nationality Act of 1993."

---

[305] Julie Charlip, *Sanger Sweep Stirs Questions on Civil Rights Violations*, THE FRESNO BEE, October 14, 1984, at A1 (emphasis added).

In the end, Ariel's optimism and belief in the INS's credibility won out. On July 20, Martinez, his wife, and the couple's 18-month-old daughter drove to the INS office in downtown San Diego to pick up his permit. But instead of being welcomed by their adopted country, Martinez and dozens of others were promptly arrested and deported. The sting letter was sent to Martinez and more than 600 others, resulting in 60 apprehensions, though 18 immigrants were released for a variety of technical reasons. Attorneys who saw the letter quickly determined that it was an INS sting because the law referred to in the letter does not exist. INS officials in San Diego said the operation targeted people who were under judges' orders of deportation, though several who received letters disputed this. After promising a work permit, the letter said: "Since this is a one-time event, failure to report to this office at this time will render you ineligible to receive your employment authorization."

Immigration officials avoided sending copies of the letters to immigrants' attorneys because they feared that the lawyers would alert their clients to the sting. They also said that two of the immigrants apprehended but later released were freed because they had pending appeals to their deportation orders. In addition, two others were released because they had become permanent residents. Four immigrants who received the letter were also released because they were "the right names but wrong persons."[306]

In border cities and areas, the former INS also engaged in some rather devious enforcement "sting" strategies. In the late 1980s in El Paso, Texas, the INS used a phony letterhead from "Argim" Ford. Argim is *migra* spelled backward, a Spanish word used by Mexicans to describe the INS. The bogus letters were sent to Spanish — surnamed individuals indicating that they might win a Ford Bronco if they showed up for a drawing. When letter recipients showed up, their immigration documentation was checked. Fifty-five of those who showed up turned out to be undocumented immigrants, and were deported.[307] There have even been reports of Border Patrol agents disguised as saguaro cacti waiting at the border to catch illicit border crossers.

Of course, in the past decade, as noted earlier in this chapter, racially profiling of immigrants has continued since 9/11 with the targeting of Arabs, Muslims, and South Asians, as well as in the conventional work place raids that occurred.

c. Search and Seizure

In 1976, the Court articulated a major exception to the Fourth Amendment's protection against search and seizure to accommodate the Border Patrol even further. The case, *United States v. Martinez-Fuerte*,[308] involved the legality of a fixed checkpoint located on Interstate 5 near San Clemente, California, the principal highway between San Diego and Los Angeles. The checkpoint is 66 road miles north of the Mexican border. Approximately one mile south of the checkpoint

---

[306] H.G. Reza, *Immigrants Deported in INS Sting Operation*, L.A. Times, July 31, 1993, at A1.

[307] *Id.* J. Michael Kennedy, *Aliens Fear Massive Deportations; at El Paso Border, Rumor Mill is the Biggest Worry*, L.A. Times, March 14, 1987, at I-1.

[308] 428 U.S. 543 (1976).

is a large black-on-yellow sign with flashing yellow lights over the highway stating "ALL VEHICLES, STOP AHEAD, 1 MILE." Three-quarters of a mile farther north are two black-on-yellow signs suspended over the highway with flashing lights stating "WATCH FOR BRAKE LIGHTS." At the checkpoint, which also is the location of a State of California weighing station, are two large signs with flashing red lights suspended over the highway. These signs each state "STOP HERE-U.S. OFFICERS." Placed on the highway are a number of orange traffic cones funneling traffic into two lanes where a Border Patrol agent in full uniform, standing behind a white on red "STOP" sign, checks traffic. Blocking traffic in the unused lanes are official U.S. Border Patrol vehicles with flashing red lights. A building that houses the Border Patrol office and temporary detention facilities are at the site. Floodlights are turned on for nighttime operations.

The "point" agent standing between the two lanes of traffic visually screens all northbound vehicles, which the checkpoint brings to a virtual, if not a complete, halt. Most motorists are allowed to resume their progress without any oral inquiry or close visual examination. In a relatively small number of cases the "point" agent will conclude that further inquiry is in order. He directs these cars to a secondary inspection area, where their occupants are asked about their citizenship and immigration status. The average length of an investigation in the secondary inspection area is three to five minutes. A direction to stop in the secondary inspection area could be based on something suspicious about a particular car passing through the checkpoint, but in the three situations that were challenged in *Martinez-Fuerte*, the government conceded that none of the three stops was based on any articulable suspicion.

In the first situation, Amado Martinez-Fuerte approached the checkpoint driving a vehicle containing two female passengers. The women were undocumented Mexican aliens who had entered the United States at the San Ysidro port of entry by using false papers. They rendezvoused with Martinez-Fuerte in San Diego to be transported northward. At the checkpoint their car was directed to the secondary inspection area. Martinez-Fuerte produced documents showing him to be a lawful resident alien, but his passengers admitted being present in the country unlawfully. He was criminally charged with two counts of illegally transporting aliens.

The second situation involved Jose Jimenez-Garcia, who attempted to pass through the checkpoint while driving a car with one passenger. He had picked up the passenger by prearrangement in San Ysidro after the latter had been smuggled across the border. Questioning at the secondary inspection area revealed the illegal status of the passenger, and Jiminez-Garcia was charged with two counts of illegally transporting an alien.

The third case involved Raymond Guillen and Fernando Medrano-Barragan. They approached the checkpoint with Guillen driving and Medrano-Barragan and his wife as passengers. Questioning at the secondary inspection area revealed that Medrano-Barragan and his wife were undocumented aliens. A subsequent search of the car uncovered three other undocumented aliens in the trunk. Medrano-Barragan had led the other aliens across the border at the beach near Tijuana, Mexico, where they rendezvoused with Guillen, a U.S. citizen. Guillen and Medrano-Barragan were jointly indicted on four counts of illegally transporting aliens and four counts of inducing the illegal entry of aliens.

The defendants argued that the routine stopping of vehicles at a checkpoint was invalid because *Brignoni-Ponce* must be read as prohibiting any stops in the absence of reasonable suspicion. However, the Court recognized that maintenance of a traffic-checking program in the interior is necessary because "the flow of illegal aliens cannot be controlled effectively at the border." The Court noted the "substantiality of the public interest in the practice of routine stops for inquiry at permanent checkpoints, a practice which the Government identifies as the most important of the traffic-checking operations." The checkpoints (similar ones are in Texas and Arizona) were located on important highways; in their absence such highways would offer undocumented aliens a quick and safe route into the interior. Routine checkpoint inquiries apprehend many smugglers and undocumented aliens who succumb to the lure of such highways. And the prospect of such inquiries forces others onto less efficient roads that are less heavily traveled, slowing their movement and making them more vulnerable to detection by roving patrols. Therefore, the Court held:

> A requirement that stops on major routes inland always be based on reasonable suspicion would be impractical because the flow of traffic tends to be too heavy to allow the particularized study of a given car that would enable it to be identified as a possible carrier of illegal aliens. In particular, such a requirement would largely eliminate any deterrent to the conduct of well-disguised smuggling operations, even though smugglers are known to use these highways regularly.

Thus, fixed checkpoints, even though more than 50 miles away from the border, were constitutional. Again, the Court cited the importance of supporting the Border Patrol's efforts in enforcing immigration laws that were being violated by Mexicans.

> It has been national policy for many years to limit immigration into the United States. Since July 1, 1968, the annual quota for immigrants from all independent countries of the Western Hemisphere, including Mexico, has been 120,000 persons. Act Of Oct. 3, 1965, § 21(e), 79 Stat. 921. Many more aliens than can be accommodated under the quota want to live and work in the United States. Consequently, large numbers of aliens seek illegally to enter or to remain in the United States. We noted last Term that "[e]stimates of the number of illegal immigrants [already] in the United States vary widely. A conservative estimate in 1972 produced a figure of about one million, but the Immigration and Naturalization Service now suggests there may be as many as 10 or 12 million aliens illegally in the country." *United States v. Brignoni-Ponce*, 422 U.S. 873, 878 (1975) (footnote omitted). It is estimated that 85% of the illegal immigrants are from Mexico, drawn by the fact that economic opportunities are significantly greater in the United States than they are in Mexico.

> Interdicting the flow of illegal entrants from Mexico poses formidable law enforcement problems. The principal problem arises from surreptitious entries. . . . The United States shares a border with Mexico that is almost 2,000 miles long, and much of the border area is uninhabited desert or thinly populated and land. Although the Border Patrol maintains person-

nel, electronic equipment, and fences along portions of the border, it remains relatively easy for individuals to enter the United States without detection. It also is possible for an alien to enter unlawfully at a port of entry by the use of falsified papers or to enter lawfully but violate restrictions of entry in an effort to remain in the country unlawfully. Once within the country, the aliens seek to travel inland to areas where employment is believed to be available, frequently meeting by prearrangement with friends or professional smugglers who transport them in private vehicles.

The Supreme Court majority was not concerned with the racial overtones of its decision even though the Border Patrol essentially was picking out those who looked Mexican for secondary inspection. A dissenting opinion by Justice William Brennan warned: "Every American citizen of Mexican ancestry and every Mexican alien lawfully in this country must know after today's decision that he travels the fixed checkpoint highways at [his] risk." In response, the majority encouraged lower courts to act against the Border Patrol if evidence of "the misuse of checkpoints to harass those of Mexican ancestry" surfaced.

Less than a decade later, in 1984, the Supreme Court made it quite clear that the Fourth Amendment's protection against illegal search and seizure was not available to aliens fighting deportation, even if INS officials acted illegally. In *INS v. Lopez-Mendoza*,[309] Adam Lopez-Mendoza was arrested by INS agents at his place of employment, a transmission repair shop. Responding to a tip, INS investigators arrived at the shop shortly before 8:00 A.M. The agents had not sought a warrant to search the premises or to arrest any of its occupants. The proprietor of the shop firmly refused to allow the agents to interview his employees during working hours. Nevertheless, while one agent engaged the proprietor in conversation, another entered the shop and approached Lopez-Mendoza. In response to the agent's questioning, Lopez-Mendoza gave his name and indicated that he was from Mexico with no close family ties in the United States. The agent then placed him under arrest. Lopez-Mendoza underwent further questioning at INS offices, where he admitted he was born in Mexico, was still a citizen of Mexico, and had entered the United States without inspection. While the arrest was illegal, the Supreme Court refused to exclude Lopez-Mendoza's admission that he was not a legal resident. It was important to the Court that deportation proceedings were civil rather than criminal proceedings, and the Court also felt that applying the Fourth Amendment exclusionary rule in the deportation context would have little deterrent effect on illegal police activity. Also, the Court felt that excluding evidence after an illegal arrest by INS officials would have great societal costs.

> The first cost is one that is unique to continuing violations of the law. Applying the exclusionary rule in proceedings that are intended not to punish past transgressions but to prevent their continuance or renewal would require the courts to close their eyes to ongoing violations of the law. This Court has never before accepted costs of this character in applying the exclusionary rule.

---

[309] 468 U.S. 1032 (1984).

> Presumably no one would argue that the exclusionary rule should be invoked to prevent an agency from ordering corrective action at a leaking hazardous waste dump if the evidence underlying the order had been improperly obtained, or to compel police to return contraband explosives or drugs to their owner if the contraband had been unlawfully seized.

Once again, the Court was influenced by the perceived need to support INS activities to combat the problem of undocumented aliens.

> Immigration officers apprehend over one million deportable aliens in this country every year . . . A single agent may arrest many illegal aliens every day. Although the investigatory burden does not justify the commission of constitutional violations, the officers cannot be expected to compile elaborate, contemporaneous, written reports detailing the circumstances of every arrest. At present an officer simply completes a "Record of Deportable Alien" that is introduced to prove the INS's case at the deportation hearing; the officer rarely must attend the hearing. Fourth Amendment suppression hearings would undoubtedly require considerably more, and the likely burden on the administration of the immigration laws would be correspondingly severe.
>
> . . .
>
> There comes a point at which courts, consistent with their duty to administer the law, cannot continue to create barriers to law enforcement in the pursuit of a supervisory role that is properly the duty of the Executive and Legislative Branches.

Apparently, that point is reached when the issue of controlling the problem of undocumented Mexicans is before the Court.

Thus, when it comes to the southwest border, the Border Patrol conducts three kinds of inland traffic-checking operations in an effort to minimize undocumented immigration. Permanent checkpoints, such as the one at San Clemente, are maintained at or near intersections of important roads leading away from the border. They operate on a coordinated basis designed to avoid circumvention by smugglers and others who transport the undocumented aliens. Temporary checkpoints, which operate like permanent ones, occasionally are established in other strategic locations. Finally, roving patrols are maintained to supplement the checkpoint system.

d. Detention

Even before the 2014 surge of unaccompanied children arriving at the border, ICE detained 400,000 adults and children every year: immigrants, refugees, and newcomers.[310] This costs taxpayers $1.7 billion at an average of $122 a day per bed. They are detained because they are in removal proceedings, because a final order of removal has been entered against them, or because they are suspected of being involved in terrorist related activities. Without the right to government-appointed

---

[310] Detention Watch, About the U.S. Detention and Deportation System, *available at* http://www. detentionwatchnetwork.org/aboutdetention.

counsel, an estimated 90 percent of these immigration detainees go unrepresented in their cases before the Immigration Court-often due to poverty and the limited pro bono resources available to this population. Detainees, often with limited English skills and limited education, have to face a trained immigration prosecutor in adversarial administrative proceedings before an Immigration Judge without any help.

Over the course of the Obama Administration, DHS officials detained record numbers of immigrants, driven by a little-known congressional directive known on Capitol Hill as the "bed mandate." Congressional appropriations language covering ICE's detention budget, for example in the Continuing Appropriations Act of 2014, states "[t]hat funding made available under this heading shall maintain a level of not less than 34,000 detention beds." The policy has been interpreted as requiring ICE to keep an average of 34,000 detainees per day in its custody, a quota that has steadily risen since it was established in 2006 by conservative lawmakers who insisted that the agency was not doing enough to deport unlawful immigrants.

ICE detention is considered civil — as opposed to criminal — in nature. So while they await their administrative immigration proceedings, detainees are held at hundreds of facilities nationwide- the majority of which are local and county jails under DHS contract. Immigration detainees, including innocent asylum seekers, may be commingled with criminal convicts.

Over the course of the Obama Administration, DHS officials detained record numbers of immigrants, driven by a little-known congressional directive known on Capitol Hill as the "bed mandate." Congressional appropriations language covering ICE's detention budget, for example in the Continuing Appropriations Act of 2014, states "[t]hat funding made available under this heading shall maintain a level of not less than 34,000 detention beds." The policy has been interpreted as requiring ICE to keep an average of 34,000 detainees per day in its custody, a quota that has steadily risen since it was established in 2006 by conservative lawmakers who insisted that the agency was not doing enough to deport unlawful immigrants.

But before the unaccompanied immigrant children crisis occurred in 2014, illicit crossings from Mexico had fallen to near their lowest levels since the early 1970s, and ICE began meeting Congress' immigration detention goals by reaching deeper into the criminal justice system to arrest foreign-born, legal U.S. residents convicted of any crimes that could render them eligible for deportation. The agency also greatly expanded the number of undocumented immigrants taken into custody after traffic stops by local police, often via the Secure Communities Program. Four countries — Mexico, Guatemala, Honduras and El Salvador — accounted for 88 percent of all immigration detainees in 2011.

The majority of ICE detainees are not violent offenders. A 2009 internal ICE review found that only 11 percent of detainees had been convicted of violent crimes. Almost half of all potential deportees who appear in immigration court are allowed to remain in the United States. But many end up spending months, even years, in costly federal custody while they await a ruling, even when far cheaper alternatives are available, such as ankle bracelets and other forms of electronic monitoring. Those alternatives can cost less than $10 a day, while the cost of keeping someone in ICE custody exceeds $150.

With federal spending on immigration detention and deportation reaching $2.8 billion a year, more than doubling since 2006, the mandate has met growing skepticism from budget hawks in both parties, particularly after DHS officials told Congress during the "sequestration" debate in April 2014 that the agency could save money by lowering the bed mandate to 31,800 and relying on cheaper alternatives to jails. But House Republicans successfully pushed back, set the mandate at 34,000 detainees and ordered ICE officials to spend nearly $400 million more than they requested. Congress' expanding detention goals and consistently high funding for DHS detention have been a boon to private prison contractors, especially Florida-based GEO Group and Tennessee-based Corrections Corp. of America. The two companies have won hundreds of millions of dollars' worth of ICE contracts in recent years while lobbying Congress on immigration enforcement issues.

ICE officials argue that they have limited discretion over which detainees are eligible for alternative forms of supervision. The Illegal Immigration Reform and Immigrant Responsibility Act of 1996 greatly expanded the scope of crimes that could trigger deportation. According to ICE, more than two-thirds of the immigrants in custody are "mandatory detention" cases, including drug offenders, violent offenders and anyone involved in prostitution-related crimes, among other violations that trigger automatic detention. INA § 236(c) requires that noncitizens be detained after they are released from criminal custody, and that they remain detained while removal proceedings are pending against them.

The conditions in the detention facilities are often abhorrent.[311] Since detention is contracted out and the system is decentralized, ICE is unable to ensure access to counsel and uniform and fair treatment of detainees.[312] In November 2000, after numerous lawsuits attempting to force the government to change and years of advocacy by concerned organization, a more comprehensive set of "Detention Standards" was issued that became effective in 2001.[313] These "Detention Standards" apply to DHS detention facilities and contract centers, such as local or county jails.[314] Despite these new standards, however, detention facilities continue to provide inadequate food and medical treatment to their detainees, and many detainees suffer severe human rights abuses in these facilities.[315]

According to a national investigation published by Detention Watch Network at the end of 2013, none of the 250 detention centers can guarantee the detainees basic medical care, adequate protection against physical and sexual abuse and enough contact with the outside to preserve their families and adequately prepare their legal defense. Two of the main problems in the system are the lack of independent oversight and the fact that detention centers do not apply the same standards because of contractual reasons. Although standards for immigrant detention have

---

[311] *Id.*

[312] *See* Steven Neeley, *Immigration Detention: The Inaction of the Bureau for Immigration and Customs Enforcement*, 60 ADMIN. L. REV. 729, 730 (2008).

[313] *Id.*

[314] *Id.*

[315] *Id.* at 731–32.

been updated to provide better conditions and services, the 250 centers operate under three different versions of ICE guidelines. The reason for that discrepancy is the contractual agreements signed over the years with different counties and states, some of which are binding to old standards and even renew automatically with those provisions. While the 2000 and 2008 guidelines only guarantee medical attention in case of emergencies, the 2011 version ensures medical services for "serious conditions."[316]

e. Mandatory Detention During Removal Proceedings

Courts have long held that detention incidental to removal proceedings is allowed. Courts have justified broad detention provisions as necessary to protect the public safety and ensure that immigrants ordered removed actually leave the country.

In 1996, during a period of rampant anti-immigrant sentiment, Congress enacted several draconian immigration laws, and along with other harsh enforcement provisions, Congress imposed mandatory detention on several groups of noncitizens. Mandatory detention means that an individual is not entitled to bond and must remain in detention while their removal proceedings are under way. These detention provisions, which went into effect in 1998, imposed mandatory detention on many individuals because of their criminal history. INA § 236A(c) requires mandatory detention of individuals if they are deportable under INA § 237(a)(2)(A) because: 1) they have committed two crimes of moral turpitude after admission; 2) are aggravated felons; 3) have committed drug crimes, firearms offenses, or miscellaneous crimes; 4) have committed a crime involving moral turpitude for which the sentence is at least one year; 5) or are deportable on terrorist grounds. INA § 236A(c) also imposes mandatory detention on any individual who is inadmissible under INA § 212(a)(2). Mandatory detention is therefore imposed on a large number of individuals who are in removal proceedings for being inadmissible as INA § 212(a) includes any person who has been convicted of a CIMT as well as a slew of other crimes.

The 1996 laws also imposed mandatory detention on persons in expedited removal who are applying for asylum but who have not established that they have a credible fear of persecution.

Immigration advocates voiced their concerns regarding these broad mandatory detention provisions. Once an individual is in immigration detention, it becomes incredibly difficult to find representation, or communicate with their attorney if they do manage to find someone to take their case. Moreover, once in detention, hearings are expedited. These barriers made it difficult for individuals to raise any valid immigration claim they might have in court.

Unfortunately, in 2003, the Supreme Court reviewed these mandatory detention provisions under INA§ 236(c) and upheld them as constitutional, even when applied

---

[316] Alonso Yáñez, *Living in the Shadows: Detention Centers Deaths Raise Immigrant Rights Questions*, New American Media, Feb. 19, 2014.

to lawful permanent residents. In *Demore v. Kim,*[317] the majority asserted that "Congress was justifiably concerned that deportable criminal aliens, who are not detained continue to engage in crime and fail to appear for their removal hearings in large numbers, may require that they be detained for the brief period necessary for their removal proceedings."

Because of the prolonged nature of immigration court cases, this lengthy detention raises serious questions. However, based on the statute and *Demore v. Kim,* Immigration Courts across the nation have routinely refused to consider bond in these cases, even where the noncitizen has been detained for six months or longer. But a class action lawsuit certified in the District Court of Massachusetts, as well as a preliminary injunction upheld by the Ninth Circuit in a class action filed in California, gives hope for those detained for excessive periods. In the California (Ninth Circuit) case, that Court upheld a preliminary injunction, ordering ICE to give a bond hearing to anyone who was detained for more than six months (after completing their sentence for their criminal conviction).[318] The order requires the Immigration Judge to release the person (under reasonable bond and/or supervision conditions) unless the government can prove by clear and convincing evidence that the person was a flight risk, a danger to society, or the person fell within a ground of removability concerning national security concerns. The Massachusetts case certified a class action lawsuit based on similar concerns.[319]

f.   Mandatory Detention After a Final Order of Removal

Once a final order of removal has been entered, removal of that individual must be carried out within a 90 day period.[320] INA § 241(a)(2) established that persons subject to final removal orders may be detained during this removal period. Moreover, the statute requires that persons who have been found inadmissible or removable for criminal or security grounds be mandatorily detained during this time.[321]

Many noncitizens who have final orders of removal against them are placed in detention. However, for various reasons, some of these individuals cannot be removed within the 90 day window. For example, countries such as Laos and Cuba do not take people after they have been ordered removed, and so natives of those countries have a hard time finding a country that will accept them. Many immigrants therefore found themselves in indefinite detention, with no hope of leaving the United States or of being released from immigration detention.

In 2001, the Supreme Court addressed the issue of indefinite detention of noncitizens ordered removed. In *Zadvydas v. Davis,* the Supreme Court reaffirmed that at least in regards to aliens living inside the United States, substantive due

---

[317] 538 U.S. 510, 513 (2003).

[318] Rodriguez v. Robbins, 715 F.3d 1127 (9th Cir. 2013).

[319] Reid v. Donelan, 13-cv-30125-MAP, *available at* 2014 U.S. Dist. LEXIS 16223 (Feb. 10, 2014).

[320] INA § 241(a)(2).

[321] INA § 241(a)(2).

process applies to immigration detention.[322] Moreover, INA 241(a)(6) did not authorize indefinite detention.[323] The Court determined that detention is only permissible for a period reasonably necessary to secure the noncitizen's removal.[324] The Court read the statute as having a presumptive six-month limit on detention, and also held that when there is no reasonable likelihood of removal, there cannot be a basis for continued detention.[325]

This was one of the few decisions by the Court in recent years that has limited the scope of enforcement powers with regards to immigration detention.

g.   Mandatory Detention for Suspected Terrorists

In the wake of the terrorist attacks of September 11, 2001, Congress passed the USA-PATRIOT Act. The PATRIOT Act allowed the Attorney General (AG) and the Deputy Attorney General (DAG) to detain any suspected terrorists, regardless of the provision discussed above.

Under INA § 236A(a)(3), the AG and the DAG can certify an individual if there are reasonable grounds to believe that the person falls within one of the terrorism grounds of inadmissibility or deportability. The AG and the DAG can also certify an individual when there are reasonable grounds to believe that the person is engaged in any other activity that will endanger the national security of the United States.[326]

Once the AG or DAG certifies someone, that person is subject to special detention provisions. Under these special provisions, the AG must place the person in removal proceedings, or charge the person with a criminal offense within seven days of commencement of detention, or the person must be released.

While proceedings are pending, the person must remain in custody, even if they are eligible for, or granted, relief from removal. The only way a person can be released from detention under these provisions is if the AG determines that the individual no longer falls within one of the specified grounds of terrorist related activity.

Moreover, even if an individual is ordered removed, they can still be detained if the person's release will threaten the national security of the United States, or the safety of the community, or any person. Their detention needs to be reevaluated every six months.[327]

---

[322] 533 U.S. 678 (2001).

[323] *Id.*

[324] *Id.*

[325] *Id.*

[326] INA § 236A(a)(3).

[327] INA § 236A(a)(7).

Chapter 15

CRIMMIGRATION

D. Conclusion

In a 2011 article titled *Deportation Is Different,* Professor Peter L. Markowitz, traced the origins of how U.S. immigration law received the label of civil as opposed to criminal law.[1] Markowitz explained that at the time of the framing of the Constitution, there was no concept known as "deportation" in U.S. law. The earliest precursor to modern deportation was banishment, which dated back to ancient times and was widely used as a form of criminal punishment for citizens and noncitizens alike. Similarly, U.S. colonies never utilized any civil method to expel citizens. The only method by which citizens or noncitizens were removed from the colonies was through the criminal punishment of banishment. Accordingly, the dominant historical models of common law England and the U.S. colonies were exclusively and explicitly criminal in nature. However, starting in 1889, with the decision of *Chae Chan Ping v. United States,*[2] commonly known as the *Chinese Exclusion Case,* the U.S. Supreme Court articulated immigration power differently. This new articulation would now rest largely in sovereignty as a means to regulate the border against foreign intrusion and thus not subject to constitutional limits, including those relevant to criminal proceedings.[3] Thus, Chae Chan Ping, the petitioner and a returning lawful resident from China who had lived in the U.S. for 1 years, was unable to challenge his "exclusion."[4] Even though he had been granted permission to travel to China and the infamous Chinese Exclusion Act[5] that would proscribe his re-entry was not adopted until after his departure, Chae Chan Ping remained "excluded."[6]

Four years later in 1893, the U.S. Supreme Court affirmed the doctrine that became known as the "plenary power doctrine."[7] The Court held in *Fong Yue Ting v. United States,*[8] commonly known as the *Chinese Deportation Case,* that deportation was not punishment. It thereby refused to apply proscriptions against *ex post facto* and other due process guarantees that would have applied to criminal defendants, despite strong dissents to the contrary.[9] In *Fong Yue Ting,* three long-term lawful residents in the U.S. would be unable to challenge their expulsion to China based on a law that retroactively applied to them.[10] This law required that each petitioner produce a "white witness" who could attest to their lawful presence in the U.S. prior to the passage of the Chinese Exclusion Act.[11] Only three years

---

[1] The origins of the treatment of the immigration power as civil has been explored in several writings. *See, e.g.,* Javier Bleichmar, *Deportation as Punishment: A Historical Analysis of the British Practice of Banishment and Its Impact on Modern Constitutional Law,* 14 Geo. Immigr. L.J. 115 (1999).

[2] 130 U.S. 581 (1889).

[3] Peter L. Markowitz, *Deportation is Different,* 13 U. Pa. J. Const. L. 1299, 1308–11 (2011).

[4] 130 U.S. 581 (1889).

[5] Sess. I, Chap. 126; 22 Stat. 58. 47th Congress (1886).

[6] 130 U.S. 581 (1889).

[7] 149 U.S. 698 (1893).

[8] *Id.*

[9] *Id.* at 740–741.

[10] *Id.* at 703.

[11] *Id.*

after *Fong Yue Ting*, in *Wong Wing v. U.S.*,[12] a case involving the application of different provisions of the same Chinese Exclusion Act that excluded Chae Chan Ping, the Court had to acknowledge that immigration's enforcement could be criminal when and if it involved "true" punishment. Wong Wing, like the three plaintiffs in *Fong Yue Ting*, was found unlawfully residing in the U.S.[13] He was sentenced by a Commission of the Circuit Court, not a judge, to 60 days of hard labor followed by his deportation to China.[14] The Court distinguished between deportation and the 60 days of hard labor, largely viewing the latter as retributive against Wong Wing for having broken the immigration laws. Thus, this punishment required a judicial trial to establish guilt.[15] In contrast, it viewed Wong Wing's deportation solely as a measure incident to the sovereign's power to control its border.[16]

The harshness of deportation has led several scholars to critique its treatment as non-punishment.[17] This is particularly true as scholars have documented the way in which immigration and criminal law have become increasingly intertwined, while still leaving significant asymmetry in the rights that attach to noncitizens facing expulsion from the United States in contrast to criminal defendants.[18] "Crimmigration," a term coined in 2006 by Professor Juliet Stumpf, refers to the ways in which immigration laws increasingly overlap in substance and enforcement,[19] a shift that had been noted even earlier by other scholars.[20] More specifically, the substantive overlap refers to the treatment of immigration violations as crime and the treatment of crime as deportable offenses not only federally but also increasingly by states.[21] The enforcement parallels refer not only the way in which immigrant violators are treated like criminals (including prolonged and mandatory detention), but also by the involvement of criminal law enforcement agencies (including local police in the enforcement of immigration violations).

---

[12] 163 U.S. 228 (1896).

[13] 149 U.S. at 981.

[14] *Id.*

[15] *Id.*

[16] *Id.*

[17] *See, e.g.*, Beth Caldwell, *Banishment for Life: Deportation of Juvenile Offenders as Cruel and Unusual Punishment*, 34 Cardozo L. Rev. 2261 (2013); Michael J. Wishnie, *Proportionality: The Struggle for Balance in U.S. Immigration Policy*, 72 U. Pitt. L. Rev. 431 (2011); Peter L. Markowitz, *Straddling the Civil-Criminal Divide: A Bifurcated Approach to Understanding the Nature of Immigration Removal Proceedings*, 43 Harv. C.R.-C.L. L. Rev. 289 (2008); Daniel Kanstroom, *Deportation, Social Control, and Punishment: Some Thoughts About Why Hard Laws Make Bad Cases*, 113 Harv. L. Rev. 1890 (2000); and Robert Pauw, *A New Look at Deportation as Punishment: Why At Least Some of the Constitution's Criminal Procedure Protections Must Apply*, 52 Admin. L. Rev. 305 (2000).

[18] *See, e.g.*, Stephen Legomsky, *The New Path of Immigration Law: Asymmetric Incorporation of Criminal Justice Norms*, 64 Wash. & Lee. L. Rev. 469 (2007).

[19] Juliet Stumpf, *The Crimmigration Crisis: Immigrants, Crime, and Sovereign Power*, 56 Am. U. L. Rev. 367 (2006).

[20] *See, e.g.*, Teresa A. Miller, *Citizenship & Severity: Recent Immigration Reforms and the New Penology*, 17 Geo. Immigr. L.J. 611, 616 (2003) (discussing a number of scholars documenting the trend to criminalize immigrants).

[21] *Id.* at 614–15 and 618–19.

It is historically inaccurate to suggest that crimmigration is solely a modern phenomena. As even the discussion of *Wong Wing* indicates, the overlap between immigration and crime came early in the history of U.S. immigration laws. However, most scholars date the exponential growth of immigration's criminal regime to the mid-1980s, when Congress moved to expand the criminal grounds for removal.[22] Furthermore, immigration violations would be treated as crimes, at the same time that the use of detention grew to enforce the immigration laws while the grounds and procedures for seeking immigration relief from removal narrowed.[23] According to Professor Teresa A. Miller, "a confluence of factors, including post-industrial economic decline, skyrocketing unemployment, the ascendancy of right-wing political conservatism, negative public attitudes toward the dramatic increase of legal immigration made possible by legislative changes in 1965 and 1980, and trepidation about rising illegal immigration, contributed to a fundamental shift in policy toward legal and illegal immigration."[24]

The punitive shift in immigration law continued and was solidified in the series of transformative pieces of legislation adopted in 1996. This legislation included the Illegal Immigration Reform and Immigration Responsibility Act (IIRIRA)[25] and the Anti-Terrorism and Effective Death Penalty Act (AEDPA)[26] which came at the heels of certain terrorist attacks on U.S. soil. During the next decade that followed, the harshness and fiscal impact of these laws, including the mass incarceration and removal of long-term permanent residents, started a movement that might have possibly turned the tide.[27] However, the September 11 attacks on the United States solidified the trend to retain and expand crimmigration if not as the sole face of immigration enforcement, certainly as its priority.[28]

Other chapters in this book already discuss important aspects of crimmigration.[29] This chapter discusses three additional important areas of

---

[22] *See, e.g., id.* at 622–23. *See also* Jennifer M. Chacón, *Unsecured Borders: Immigration Restrictions, Crimes Control and National Security*, 39 Con. L. Rev. 1827 (2007); Stumpf, *The Crimmigration Crisis, supra* note 19, at 369.

[23] Miller *supra* note 20, at 622–23.

[24] *See, e.g., id* at 625. Professor César Cuauhtémoc García Hernández has offered a different explanation for the rise of crimmigration, namely that in the aftermath of the civil rights movement, when overt racism became impermissible, the country turned to other more subtle ways to perpetuate nativists and racists policies, this time against growing immigrant communities perceived as a threat to the fabric of U.S. society. *See generally* César Cuauhtémoc García Hernández, *Creating Crimmigration*, B.Y.U. L. Rev. 1457 (2013).

[25] Jennifer M. Chacón, *Over Criminalizing Immigration*, 102 J. Crim. L. & Criminology 613, 642 (2012); Dawn Marie Johnson, *The AEDPA nd The IIRIRA Treating Misdemeanors as Felonies for Immigration Purposes*, 27 J. Legis. 477 (2001); Allegra M. McLeod, *The U.S. Criminal-Immigration Convergence And Its Possible Undoing*, 49 Am. Crim. L. Rev. 105, 120 (2012).

[26] Miller *supra* note 20, at 622–23.

[27] *Id.* at 624.

[28] *Id.* at 643–45.

[29] Chapter 4 on Immigration Federalism documents the rise in local police enforcement of the immigration laws through their own laws, like Arizona's SB 1070, or in collaboration with federal agencies, such as through Secure Communities. Chapter 9, 12 and 17 discuss respectively the growing use of criminal conduct as a ground for exclusion, removal from the United States or denial of citizenship. Chapter 11 and 12 discuss how exclusion and removal proceeding offer fewer procedural due process

crimmigration. Part A discusses the history and evolution of the federal criminalization of immigrants and those who associate with immigrants through the federal immigration power. Part B discusses what some scholars have termed the nascent procedural due process revolution triggered by the seminal U.S. Supreme Court case of *Padilla v. Kentucky*,[30] which recognized a limited right to counsel at the point where immigration and crime intersect as part of the criminal justice process. Part C turns to a discussion of the history, evolution, and constitutionality of state criminalization of immigrants and those who associate with them through the state policing function.

A.   FEDERAL IMMIGRATION CRIMES

The very first federal law to emerge in the new age of federal regulation of immigrants began not as a deportation law but rather a law — The Naturalization Act of 1870.[31] The 1870 Naturalization Act imposed criminal sanctions of incarceration, fines and hard labor for persons who committed perjury in order to obtain a fraudulent certificate of citizenship.[32] Soon after, Congress moved for the first time to control immigration beyond regulating naturalization and also employed incarceration, fines, and hard labor as tools to enforce the newly passed immigration laws, rather than deportation.[33] Deportation as a means to enforce the immigration laws did not appear until 1888, when Congress mandated that noncitizens who landed in violation to contract labor laws were to be deported at their own expense and at the expense of the owner of the importing vessel.[34]

By the early 1890s, Congress had constructed a patchwork of penalties for immigration violations that included deportation, incarceration, and fines.[35] By 1929, deportation became the central immigration sanction for violation of immigration laws. However, deportation continued to be significantly intertwined with crime not only in that persons who committed crimes were subject to deportation, but also in a number of federal immigration violations that became sanctioned with both criminal punishment and deportation.[36]

Especially since the 1980s, Congress substantially expanded the categories of federal crimes criminalizing noncitizens and at times those who associate with them. Moreover, the prosecution of immigration-related offenses exploded in the wake of

---

protections and relief from removal and often impose mandatory detention to persons in removal based on alleged criminal conduct.

[30] Hiroshi Motomura, *The Curious Evolution Of Immigration Law: Procedural Surrogates For Substantive Constitutional Rights*, 92 Colum. L. Rev. 1625, 1638–1649 (1992).

[31] 16 Stat. 214.

[32] Juliet Stumpf, *Fitting Punishment*, 66 Wash. & Lee L. Rev. 1683, 1711 (2009).

[33] *Id.* at 1711–12 (discussing the Chinese Exclusion Act of 1882 which created the following sanctions: up to a year of hard labor for the master of any vessel who knowingly transported a Chinese laborer; up to five years of similar incarceration and hard labor for fraudulently obtaining an immigration certificate; and a year's confinement for aiding a Chinese person entered the U.S. unlawfully).

[34] *Id.* at 1712.

[35] *Id.* at 1713.

[36] *Id.* at 1716–17.

September 11, 2001.[37] By 2005, immigration-related crimes represented the single largest group of federal prosecutions, outpacing even drug and weapons prosecutions.[38] As Professor Ingrid V. Eagly described in a 2010 article, prosecuting immigration crimes, "which now constitutes over half of the federal criminal workload, has eclipsed all other areas of criminal federal prosecution. Noncitizens have become the face of federal prisons."[39] Indeed, at nearly 100,000 immigration prosecutions in fiscal year 2013, immigrations prosecutions reached an all-time high, with illegal re-entry crimes dominating the numbers.[40]

The growth of federal immigration crimes fall into three broad categories: (1) the expansion or imposition of enhanced criminal penalties for existing immigration-related crimes; (2) the criminalization of immigration violations that either previously were treated only as civil violations or were not considered immigration violations at all; and (3) the use of federal non-immigration crimes, such as identity theft statutes, to criminalize immigrants. The Transactional Records Access Clearinghouse (TRAC), a data gathering, research and distribution organization at Syracuse University, has identified over 60 federal crimes most frequently used in immigration prosecutions that include a combination of immigration and non-immigration federal crimes.[41] This chapter only addresses a few of the most important of these crimes.

1. The Expansion or Enhancement of Old Immigration Crimes

a. Entry/Re-Entry

In 1929, unlawful entry became a misdemeanor, and unlawful re-entry (the crime of entering or attempting to enter, or remaining in the U.S. after a deportation) a felony.[42] Illegal reentry became a separate and more serious offense in 1952.[43] With the Anti-Drug Abuse Act, penalties for the crime of re-entry were also increased in

---

[37] Jennifer M. Chacón, *Managing Migration Through Crime*, 109 COLUM. L. REV. SIDEBAR 135, 139 (2009).

[38] Stumpf, *The Crimmigration Crisis, supra* note 19, at 369.

[39] Ingrid V. Eagly, *Prosecuting Immigration*, 104 Nw. U. L. REV. 1281, 1281–82 (2010). *See also* Sklansky, *Crime, Immigration, and Ad Hoc Instrumentalism*, 15 NEW CRIM. L. REV. 157, 166–75 (2012) (documenting the rise of federal immigration prosecutions).

[40] TracImmigration, *At Nearly 100,000, Immigration Prosecutions Reach All-Time High in FY2013: Illegal Re-entry Prosecutions Jump 76% During Obama Administration, available at* http://trac.syr.edu/immigration/reports/336/, (last visited June 11, 2014).

[41] TracImmigration, *Criminal Statutes Most Frequently Used in Immigration Prosecution, available at* https://trac.syr.edu/immigration/aboutLaw/ (last visited June 11, 2014).

[42] For a historical backdrop of the crime of entry and re-entry, *see generally* Doug Keller, *Re-Thinking Illegal Entry and Re-Entry*, 44 LOY. U. CHI. L.J. 65 (2012). *See also* Mae N. Ngai, *The Strange Career of the Illegal Alien: Immigration Restriction and Deportation Policy in the United States, 1921–1965*, 21 LAW & HIST. REV. 69 (2003) and Stumpf, *Fitting Punishment, supra* note 32, at 1717 (explaining that unlawful entry was punishable by up to one year in jail, or $1000 fine, or both and a second unlawful entry doubled the sanctions).

[43] Keller, *Re-Thinking Illegal Entry and Re-Entry, supra*, note 42, at 83–92.

1988[44] from up to two years to a maximum of five or 15 years, depending on whether the noncitizen had been previously deported as an aggravated felon.[45] With the adoption of the Violent Crime Control and Law Enforcement Act[46] in 1994, Congress increased the penalties for these crimes once more to a maximum of 10 or 20 years where it remains today (the higher penalty again applying to aggravated felons).[47] Today the crimes of illegal entry (a misdemeanor) and illegal reentry (a felony) are codified at 8 U.S.C. §§ 1325 and 1326 respectively. Of these two, the charge leading the way today in all federal immigration convictions is for the misdemeanor illegal entry crime.[48] Scholars criticize this trend because that these crimes essentially criminalize immigration status and racializes crime.[49] The prosecutions occur almost exclusively in districts along the U.S.-Mexico border where prosecutors, defense counsel, and court personnel are overwhelmed by the tidal wave of cases.[50]

A significant issue in the prosecution of illegal entry crimes has been its disproportionate and uneven punishment. This is because the degree of punishment largely depends on the underlying crime which had been the basis of the original deportation.[51] In the mid-1980s, Congress adopted Sentencing Guidelines, and the Sentencing Commission specifically attempted to address sentencing disparities of re-entry crimes through Section 2L1.2.[52] However, in 1998 Congress dramatically increased the potential sentence a defendant could receive for illegal re-entry (up to 15 years for those previously removed as "aggravated felons") in 1988.[53] The Sentencing Commission responded to the crime of illegal entry and created an unprecedented four-level enhancement for defendants previously deported after being convicted of a felony offense (other than a purely immigration crime).[54] Then,

---

[44] Doug Keller, *Why The Prior Conviction Sentencing Enhancements In Illegal Re-Entry Cases Are Unjust And Unjustified (And Unreasonable Too)*, 51 B.C. L. Rev. 719, 731–733 (2010).

[45] The same Anti-Drug Abuse Act of 1988 actually introduced the term aggravated felon into the Immigration and Nationality Act. At this time, the category only included murder, drug trafficking and firearms trafficking crimes. Miller, *supra* note 20, at 633.

[46] Pub. L. No. 103-322, § 13001, 108 Stat. 1796, 2013 (codified at 8 U.S.C. § 1324 (1994)).

[47] 8 U.S.C. § 1326(b)(2). By 1994, the category of aggravated felony had again been expanded in 1990 to include, in addition to those listed in *supra* note 26, the crime of violence and money laundering. Chacón, *Unsecured Borders*, *supra*, note 22, at 1684.

[48] TracImmigration, *Despite Rise in Felony Charges, Most Immigration Convictions Remain Misdemeanors*, available at http://trac.syr.edu/immigration/reports/356/, last checked June 11, 2014.

[49] *See generally* Gabriel J. Chin, *Illegal Entry as a Crime, Deportation as Punishment: Immigration Status and the Criminal Process*, 58 UCLA L. Rev. 1417 (2011) and Victor C. Romero, *Decriminalizing Border Crossings*, 38 Fordham Urb. L.J. 273 (2010).

[50] Doug Keller, *Re-Thinking Illegal Entry and Re-Entry*, *supra*, note 42.

[51] Linda Drazga Maxfield, *Aggravated Felonies and § 2L1.2 Immigration Unlawful Reentry Offenders: Simulating the Impacts of Proposed Guideline Amendments*, 11 Geo. Mason L. Rev. 527, 527 (2003). Prior to some sentencing reforms, there were also significant critiques over the confusion and unfairness of punishing the crime when not all underlying felonies that triggered it were considered equal. *See id.* See also James P. Fleissner and James A. Shapiro, *Federal Sentences for Aliens Convicted of Illegal Reentry Following Deportation: Who Needs the Aggravation?*, 9 Geo. Immigr. L.J. 421 (1995).

[52] Keller, *Re-Thinking Entry and Re-Entry*, *supra* note 42, at 94–96.

[53] *Id.* at 100.

[54] *Id.*

just two years later in 1991, the Sentencing Commission dramatically increased the harshness of its prior-conviction scheme by creating a sixteen-level enhancement for illegal re-entry defendants deported after a conviction for an "aggravated felony."[55] The harshness of the new sentencing scheme would not significantly play out until the 1990s, when the Department of Justice decided to adopt a "fast track" system to prosecute illegal entry and re-entry cases along the border.[56] Under this system, an illegal re-entry defendant received a "charge bargain" plea offer within 24 hours of arraignment.[57] It was nearly impossible to turn down the plea given that how easy it would be for the prosecutor to prove the crime and how harshly the crime could be punished under the Sentencing Guidelines.[58] In essence, the incentives to plea out and waive a number of constitutional rights became "too good" to pass up given the alternatives. This process significantly increased the number of prosecutions for this crime, and still each year that number gets even higher.[59]

Then, in the aftermath of the Supreme Court's holding in *Booker v. United States* in 2005,[60] which held that the mandatory nature of the Guidelines could violate a defendant's Sixth Amendment right to trial, the Sentencing Guidelines became advisory. This opened the way for illegal re-entry defendants to challenge the defects in the illegal re-entry sentencing scheme.[61] Today, some circuits have permitted such challenges, while most have not; in essence missing the opportunity to attempt to redress the harshness of the Sentencing Guidelines applying to illegal re-entry crimes.[62]

Also in 2005, the Department of Homeland Security adopted a plan known as "Operation Streamline," designed to resurrect the idea of prosecuting mass illegal entry and re-entry cases as a way to deter unauthorized migration.[63] Operation Streamline, like its predecessor fast-track, attempted to obtain convictions by reducing the amount of process afforded to defendants.[64] Essentially under this new system, with most of these crimes charged now as misdemeanors (illegal entry only), magistrates are able to hold mass guilty plea hearings in which a single defense counsel represents dozens of defendants who get a defense counsel at most for a few minutes.[65] With the help of these procedural shortcuts, the number of prosecutions have unsurprisingly imploded.[66]

---

[55] *Id.* at 101. *See also* Keller, *Why the Prior Conviction Sentencing Enhancements in Illegal Re-Entry Cases Are Unjust and Unjustified, supra* note 44 and Note, Zoey T. Jones, *Prescribing Disproportionate Punishment: The Federal Sentencing Guidelines for Illegal Entry*, 33 Cardozo L. Rev. 1217 (2012).

[56] Keller, *Rethinking Illegal Entry and Re-Entry, supra* note 42, at 105–107.

[57] *Id.* at 107–108.

[58] *Id.*

[59] *Id.* at 109–110.

[60] 543 U.S. 220 (2005).

[61] Keller, *Re-Thinking Illegal Entry and Re-Entry, supra* note 42, at 122–125.

[62] *Id.* at 123–25.

[63] *Id.* at 125.

[64] *Id.* at 126–28.

[65] *Id.* at 127.

[66] *Id.* at 129.

The mechanisms in place to expedite illegal entry and re-entry crimes have lead critics to describe the process as turning criminal proceedings into an assembly-line.[67] To date, only the Ninth Circuit has begun to question the legality of some of these procedures.[68] Moreover, despite the government's significant reliance on these broader crimes, scholars question their effectiveness in either deterring unauthorized migration or targeting dangerous immigrants.[69]

b. Harboring, Smuggling, "Aiding and Abetting," and Transporting Undocumented Immigrants

Prior to 1917, immigration statutes prohibited only the bringing in or landing of undocumented aliens into the United States. The Immigration Act of 1917,[70] however, extended immigration enforcement inland by additionally proscribing the harboring and concealing of undocumented aliens.[71] However, in 1948, the Supreme Court held in *United States v. Evans*[72] that while this statute was intended to regulate harboring and concealing undocumented immigrants, the penalty provisions of the statute applied only to the offense of landing or bringing foreigners into the country. The court declined to interpret the statute as creating a penalty for harboring and concealing immigrants. In response to this decision, and also in response to heightened concern for economic displacements caused by the growing influx of undocumented alien workers from Mexico, Congress expanded the crime, including by penalizing the transporting of undocumented immigrants. Congress intended to ensure that application of the law would extend not solely to border crossings but to actions within the border that might encourage undocumented immigration.[73] These same crimes were again rewritten as part of the 1986 Immigration Reform and Control Act (IRCA) legislation,[74] with the significant change that employers could now be charged with these crimes.[75] Then, the Immigration Act of 1990,[76] the Violent Crime Control and Law Enforcement Act of 1994,[77] the Violent Crime Control and Law Enforcement Act of 1994, and the IIRIRA of 1996 raised the sentences for harboring undocumented immigrants and for aiding the entry of noncitizens inadmissible under the immigration laws.[78]

---

[67] *See id.* at 114 and 126–27.

[68] *See, e.g.*, U.S. v. Arqueta-Ramos, 730 F.3d 1133 (9th Cir. 2013); U.S. v. Aguilar-Vera, 698 F.3d 1196 (9th Cir. 2012); and United States v. Roblero-Solis, 588 F.3d 692, 700 (9th Cir. 2009). Keller, *Re-Thinking Illegal Entry and Re-Entry, supra* note 42, at 68.

[69] Keller, *Re-Thinking Illegal Entry and Re-Entry, supra* note 42, at 68.

[70] Act of Feb. 5, 1917, Ch. 29, 39 Stat 874.

[71] William G. Phelps, J.D., *Validity, construction, and application of § 274(a)(1)(A)(iii) of Immigration and Nationality Act (8 U.S.C.A. § 1324(a)(1)(A)(iii)), making it unlawful to harbor or conceal illegal alien*, 137 A.L.R. Fed. 255 § 2 (originally published in 1997).

[72] 333 U.S. 483 (1948).

[73] Phelps, *supra* note 71, at § 2.

[74] Pub. L. No. 99-603, 100 Stat. 3445 (1986).

[75] Phelps, *supra* note 71, at § 2.

[76] Pub. L. No. 101-649, 104 Stat. 4978 (1990).

[77] H.R. 3355, Pub. L. No. 103-322 (1994).

[78] Sklansky, *Crime, Immigration, and Ad Hoc Instrumentalism, supra* note 39, at 165.

Currently, the Immigration and Nationality Act (INA) contains several criminal prohibitions against the smuggling, harboring and transport of undocumented immigrations, found in INA § 274. INA section 274(a)(1)(A)(i) criminalizes "bring-[ing] or attempt[ing] to bring [an alien] to the United States." INA Section 274(a)(1)(A)(ii) criminalizes the transportation of unlawfully present alien. The federal harboring provision is found in INA Section 274(a)(A)(iii) and prohibits anyone from "conceal[ing], harbor[ing], or shield[ing and alien] from detection." Subsection (B) of INA 274 prescribes the punishment for these offenses and in general, the range in punishment is from a minimum of five years for the enumerated crimes (except smuggling) that are not committed with pecuniary gain; 10 years if the enumerated crimes are committed for financial gain; 20 years if the enumerated crimes result in serious injury; and death or life imprisonment if the enumerated crimes result in death. Moreover, the penalty is imposed for each unauthorized person who is either smuggled, harbored or transported.

The crime of smuggling, in general, applies only to intentional and active conduct to aid an unauthorized person enter the United States in violation of the immigration laws.[79] The crime of harboring is broader than smuggling as it extends to acts within the border directed at assisting unauthorized persons in the breaking of the immigration laws. In general, persons have been convicted of harboring when they have willfully prevented the detection of unauthorized persons from law enforcement or immigration agencies.[80] Although, the courts are more divided on whether (intentionally or knowingly) substantially facilitating a persons' unauthorized stay in the U.S. would meet the definition.[81] Interestingly, and despite IRCA, the employment of unauthorized workers, even if knowingly, has not constituted harboring under federal law,[82] although states have attempted to punish this conduct.[83]

Furthermore, several scholars have documented reliance on all of these federal immigration crimes to target humanitarian and religious workers considered to be assisting or encouraging unauthorized migration in to the U.S.[84] For example, the prosecution of persons of faith who provided humanitarian aid to asylum seekers as part of the Sanctuary Movement of the 1980s has been well-documented.[85] Humanitarian and religious workers unsuccessfully attempted to argue that their actions should have been shielded from prosecution because they were motivated by

---

[79] Dan Kesselbrenner and Lory D. Rosenberg, *Chapter 7. Crime-Related Deportation Grounds and Criminal Offenses Under the INA*, III. Smuggling, Transporting, or Harboring; Illegal Entry, Immigra. Law & Crimes §7:16 (2014).

[80] Phelps, *supra* note 71, at § 20.

[81] *Id.* at § 3.

[82] *Id.* at § 6.

[83] *See infra* Part C.

[84] Kristina M. Campbell, *Humanitarian Aid is Never a Crime? The Politics of Immigration Enforcement and the Provision of Sanctuary*, 63 SYRACUSE L. REV. 71 (2012); Emily Breslin, Note, *The Road to Liability Is Paved with Humanitarian Intentions: Criminal Liability for Housing Undocumented People Under 8 U.S.C. §1324(A)(1)(A)(III)*, 11 RUTGERS J. L. & RELIGION 214 (2009) and Gregory. A. Loken and Lisa R. Babino, *Harboring, Sanctuary and the Crime of Charity Under Federal Immigration Law*, 28 HARV. C.R.-C.L. L. REV. 119 (1993).

[85] *See generally* Loken and Babino, *supra*.

humanitarian concerns, which were founded largely in religious beliefs and thus protected by the First Amendment.[86] Today there are growing fears that the new sanctuary movement, which grew post-911 in large parts as a response to attempts to pass H.R. 4437 — a draconian interior federal immigration enforcement law — will start to face similar prosecutions.[87]

c. Human Trafficking

As early as 1875, Congress made it a felony, punishable by imprisonment not exceeding five years and by a fine not exceeding $5,000, for anyone who knowingly and willfully imported women into the United States for purposes of prostitution.[88] Then in 1903, the crime was expanded to include the importation of girls for prostitution.[89] It was again expanded in 1907 to prohibit importation of women and girls for any other immoral purpose, not just prostitution.[90] Then, in 1910, Congress amended the law to include not only the importation but also the harboring of women and girls for prostitution.[91]

The broadening of the crime of trafficking beyond sex crimes, however, did not arise until much later. In 2000, Congress adopted the Trafficking Victims Protection Act (TVPA) as its centerpiece legislation to combat "severe forms of trafficking in persons."[92] By expanding the definition of involuntary servitude so as to encompass the crime of human trafficking, the TVPA created new crimes involving peonage and slavery.[93] For example, the TVPA makes it a crime to obtain the labor and services of a person by way of "any scheme, plan, or pattern intended to cause the person to believe that, if the person did not perform such labor or services, that person would suffer serious harm or physical restraint."[94] In addition, the TVPA increased penalties for several crimes associated with human trafficking, including up to life sentences, as well as strict restitution and forfeiture provisions.[95] Additionally, in 2005, Congress attempted to improve the protections offered by the TVPA and passed the Trafficking Victims Protection Reauthorization Act (TVPRA).[96] The most significant amendment to the TVPRA was to include extraterritorial jurisdiction to try the crime of human trafficking. In 2008, the William Wilberforce

---

[86] Campbell, *supra* note 84, at 102.

[87] *Id.* at 104–06.

[88] U.S. v. Bitty, 208 U.S. 393, 397 (1908).

[89] *Id.*

[90] *Id.* at 398.

[91] U.S. v. Elie Portale, 235 U.S. 27 (1914).

[92] H.R. Rep. No. 106-386, at 24–33, § 7101 (2000).

[93] Angela D. Giampolo, *The Trafficking Victims Protection Reauthorization Act of 2005: The Latest Weapon in the Fight Against Human Trafficking*, 16 Temp. Pol. & Civ. Rts. L. Rev. 195, 200 (2006).

[94] 18 U.S.C.A. § 1589, amended by the TVPA, § 112. For a fuller discussion of the types of conduct penalized by the TVPA, *see* Comment, Kendal Nicole Smith, *Human Trafficking and RICO: A New Prosecutorial Hammer in the War on Modern Day Slavery*, 18 Geo. Mason L. Rev. 759, 773–75 (2011).

[95] *Id.* at 200–01. *See also* Bo Cooper, *A new Approach to Protection and Law Enforcement Under the Victim of Trafficking and Violent Protection Act*, 51 Emory L.J. 1041, 1050 (2002).

[96] H.R. 972 (109th 2005).

Trafficking Victims Protection Reauthorization Act[97] instituted several more prosecutorial reforms, including adding a conspiracy provision and punishing obstructions of trafficking investigations.[98]

Perhaps due to the relative recency of the anti-trafficking criminal laws, relatively few writings explore the effectiveness of addressing the growing problem of human trafficking through prosecutions. In 2007, however, Journalist Anthony M. DeStefano wrote a book titled the *War on Human Trafficking: A U.S. Policy Assessed.* He offered at least two insightful critiques for why the effort has not been as effective: first, that a shift in priorities post-9/11 has meant that few resources have actually been devoted to the prosecution of these cases and second that, even in the few prosecutions that have been carried out, there is too much focus on sex trafficking, which distorts the nature of the most common types of labor trafficking.[99] As well, in 2010, Professor Jennifer M .Chacón focused on a different problem that undermines the effectiveness of the anti-trafficking effort: the criminalization of the unauthorized immigrants themselves (such as through illegal entry and re-entry crimes), which makes potential victims of trafficking even more reluctant to come forward to report crimes.[100]

2. The Creation of New Federal Immigration Crimes

Many immigration-related conduct has been criminalized only since the 1980s. This includes employer sanctions, immigration fraud, citizenship-related crimes, and other miscellaneous crimes.

a. Border Crimes in the U.S. Workplace

The Immigration Reform and Control Act of 1986 (IRCA), the same law that granted amnesty to thousands of undocumented immigrants, would become the first legislation to impose sanctions on workplace immigration violations. The first time the proposal to criminalize employers for hiring undocumented workers was introduced in Congress was more than a decade earlier in 1972.[101] However, it was largely unpopular, not only among employers but also among civil rights advocates who worried the laws would lead to discrimination against those perceived to be foreigners.[102] Although opposition to IRCA remained strong in 1986, Congress appeased dissent by enhancing protections against discrimination on the basis of national origin.[103]

---

[97] H.R. 7311 (110th 2008).

[98] Smith, *supra* note 94, at 774.

[99] ANTHONY M. DESTEFANO, THE WAR ON HUMAN TRAFFICKING: U.S. POLICY ASSESSED at xx–xxiv (Rutgers U. Press 2007).

[100] Jennifer M. Chacón, *Tensions and Trade-Offs: Protecting Trafficking of Victims in the Era of Immigration Enforcement,* 158 U. PA. L. REV. 1609 (2010).

[101] María Isabel Medina, *The Criminalization of Immigration Law: Employer Sanctions and Marriage Fraud,* 5 GEO. MASON L. REV. 669, 680–81 (1997).

[102] *Id.*

[103] *Id.* at 681. IRCA also legalized over 3 million undocumented workers and did so with the promise that tougher immigration enforcement would deter future unauthorized migration. Hearing before the

IRCA singled out employers, not the undocumented immigrants, for punishment (as well as civil sanctions). The rationale of this approach was the idea that employer sanctions would do more to discourage undocumented immigration with employers refusing to risk both civil and potentially criminal liability by hiring undocumented workers.[104] Under IRCA, U.S. employers are prohibited from hiring, recruiting or referring for a fee noncitizens known to be unauthorized to work in the United States. In addition, employers are required to complete the Employment Verification Form (I-9) for all employees, which includes, verifying their identity and employment status, and making a good faith effort to determine whether the documents appear to be genuine.[105] Employers who violate the law are subject to a series of civil fines (not more than $3000) and to criminal penalties, including incarceration (not more than six months), when there is a pattern or practice of violations.[106] The Violent Crime Control and Law Enforcement Act of 1994 raised sentences for immigration-related employment fraud.[107] In addition, in 1996, the IIRIRA created a new employment criminal offense by amending the immigration harboring criminal provision to include a new offense: knowingly hiring at least 10 individuals during a 12-month period with actual knowledge that the individuals are unauthorized workers.[108] This new crime would now carry stiffer sentences contemplating substantial fines and a term of imprisonment of not more than five years.[109]

Writing in 1997, Professor María Isabel Medina noted that IRCA's employer sanctions, including its criminalization provisions, had done little to deter the practice a decade later.[110] Most attributed to the failure was under-enforcement of the law, although Professor Medina cast doubt that criminalizing a practice that is highly valued by U.S. employers would have any meaningful effect in curtailing the practice.[111] Today, nearly three decades since IRCA's adoption, some of the same critiques remain. In a 2013 study, the Migration Policy Institute concluded that IRCA has largely failed to regulate the workplace because its employer sanction provisions are inherently difficult to enforce. First, employers can largely be in compliance with the law while still employing unauthorized workers and thus feel little incentive to comply with the law.[112] Moreover, the availability of counterfeit work documents makes enforcement difficult.[113] If IRCA's success is measured by

---

Senate Judiciary Committee on "Comprehensive Immigration Reform II," Oct. 18, 2005, *available at* http://www.aila.org/content/default.aspx?docid=17760.

[104]   Miller, *supra* note 20, at 630.

[105]   Medina, *supra* note 101, at 683–90.

[106]   *Id.* at 683.

[107]   Sklansky, *Crime, Immigration, and Ad Hoc Instrumentalism*, *supra* note 39, at 165.

[108]   Medina, *The Criminalization of Immigration Law*, *supra* note 101, at 691 (discussion 8 U.S.C. § 1324).

[109]   *Id.*

[110]   *Id.*

[111]   *Id.* at 672.

[112]   Doris Meissner, *et al.*, *Immigration Enforcement in the United States: The Rise of a Formidable Machinery*, 76 (Migration Policy Institute 2013).

[113]   *Id.* at 77.

a decrease in undocumented workers in the U.S. labor force, it has not happened. Since 2000, in fact, the population has steadily increased reaching a peak in 2007 at 12 million, although with a steady decline since.[114] In 2010, an estimated 8 million unauthorized workers worked in the United States constituting approximately 5.2 percent of the U.S. labor force.[115]

Especially since 2007, however, there has been greater and different enforcement of workplace immigration violations with the establishment and expansion of E-verify, a federal government's online work authorization verification system.[116] While it is still largely a voluntary program, it is now mandatory at the federal level at least for federal employers,[117] while some states require its use by all employers.[118] As well, in 2009, workplace enforcement shifted away from workplace raids targeting workers to scrutiny of employer hiring practices, accompanied by several high profile prosecutions of businesses that persistently violate the immigration laws in their hiring practices.[119] Some view these changes to IRCA enforcement patterns as having a greater potential to deter immigration violations in the workplace.[120]

b. Immigration Marriage Fraud

Prior to the Immigration Marriage Fraud Act (IMFA) of 1986,[121] knowingly entering into a marriage to seek immigration benefits or to evade immigration law's enforcement subjected only the noncitizen to removal. Since 1986, however, the same conduct is now treated as a felony and could mean substantial fines (up to $250,000) and/or incarceration (up to five years) not only for the noncitizen but also for his or her U.S. citizen or lawful permanent resident allegedly fraudulent spouse.[122] There are at least two significant critiques to IMFA: that it was an exaggerated response to poorly documented claims of marriage fraud[123] and that it significant meddles into the private sphere of family life by forcing that marriages satisfy traditional notions of marriage before they satisfy the definition of bona fide marriage under the immigration laws.[124]

Two decades after IMFA's adoption, scholars found it difficult to measure its impact based on the absence of reliable data on the frequency of immigration marriage fraud.[125] However, IMFA's enforcement and the few reported cases of

---

[114] *Id.* at 76 (citing to Pew Hispanic Center Data).

[115] *Id.*

[116] *Id.* 77.

[117] *Id.* at 77–78.

[118] For a discussion of state workplace immigration regulation, *see* Ch. 4 on Immigration Federalism.

[119] Meissner, *et al.*, *supra* note 112, at 82–83.

[120] *Id.* at 83.

[121] Public Law 99-639 (1986).

[122] Miller, *supra* note 20, at 640. *See also* Kerry Abrams, *Immigration Law and the Regulation of Marriage*, 91 Minn. L. Rev. 1628 (2007) for a comprehensive explanation of IMFA.

[123] Medina, *The Criminalization of Immigration Law*, *supra* note 101, at 709–10.

[124] *Id.* at 698–700.

[125] Abrams, *supra* note 122, at 1686–87.

IMFA prosecutions reveal inherent challenges of prosecution marriage fraud. This includes the difficulties of drawing lines between valid and fraudulent marriages and the limited resources by immigration agencies to investigate the multitude of marriage-based petitions for fraud.[126] The critiques remain the same today with little faith in the ability of immigration agencies to weed out the good faith marriages from the fraudulent ones[127] as well as concerns over uneven enforcement.[128]

c. Citizenship-Related Crimes

In 1996, Congress passed the IIRIRA which created a series of new immigration crimes, including those pertaining to alleged false claims of citizenship. The IIRIRA penalized noncitizens for voting in a federal election[129] as well as for making false claims to citizenship to obtain a benefit of employment in the U.S.[130] Scholars have criticized in particular the harshness of the false claim to citizenship provisions, which in addition to constituting a crime results in a life-time banishment from the U.S. and a permanent bar to citizenship.[131] As well, scholars question the legitimacy of these provisions, which were motivated in great part on unfounded claims of voter fraud.[132] The true effect of the provisions, instead, has been to target unnecessarily and unduly punish lawful permanent residents who are viable candidates for citizenship.[133]

3. The Use of Non-Immigrant Crimes to Target Immigrants

a. Identity Theft

A recent trend is for prosecutors to rely on general criminal statutes to prosecute undocumented immigrants. Specifically, the federal identity theft statute, which carries a minimum two-year sentence, has been a particularly potent prosecutorial tool to go after workers using other person's social security numbers to work.[134] At first, federal prosecutors charged the crime irrespective of whether the worker knew that the social security number belonged to someone else. This was

---

[126] *Id.*

[127] Nina Bernstein, *Do You Take This Immigrant*, N.Y. Times, June 10, 2010, *available at* http://www.nytimes.com/2010/06/13/nyregion/13fraud.html?pagewanted=all.

[128] Callum Borchers and Stephen Kurkjian, *Few Resources, Uneven Enforcement: Illegal Marriage Scams Fall Through the Cracks*, Watchdog New England: The Initiative for Investigative Reporting at Northeastern University, Sept. 17, 2011, *available at* http://nuweb9.neu.edu/watchdognewengland/featured_articles/few-resources-uneven-enforcement-illegal-marriage-scams-fall-through-the-cracks/.

[129] Pub. L. No. 104-208, 110 Stat. 3009-546, at § 215.

[130] *Id.* For a description of IIRIRA's citizenship crimes provisions, *see* Anne Parsons, *A Fraudulent Sense of Belonging: The Case for Removing the "False Claim to Citizenship,"* 6 Mod. Am. 4 at Part III (2010).

[131] *See e.g.*, Parsons, *supra* note 130.

[132] *Id.*

[133] *Id.*

[134] 18 U.S.C. § 1028A (2006).

particularly the case following the Postville raids that led to hundreds of arrests.[135] However, in 2008, the U.S. Supreme Court held in *Flores-Figueroa v. United States* that the government must show that defendants charged under the identity theft statute had knowledge that the identity at issue belonged to another person.[136] Prior to *Flores-Figueroa*, federal prosecutors used the aggravated identity theft statute often and effectively against undocumented workers who used others' identity to obtain employment without proof of intent.[137] Now, federal prosecutors are forced to rely instead on immigration crimes that penalize intentional fraud, which some argue better preserves the objectives of the crime of identity theft of penalize those who knowingly usurp someone else's identity with a purpose to do harm.[138]

b. Targeting the "Terrorist" Immigrant for "Material Support"

Post 9/11, material-support prosecutions have played a major role in the prosecution of alleged terrorists, many of them noncitizens from Arab and predominantly Muslim nations.[139] Congress first enacted a material-support prohibition in 1994 to criminalize knowingly aiding or abetting enumerated terrorist acts, which were defined in relation to offenses that were already enumerated in the U.S. Code.[140] Congress added a second material-support crime in the Antiterrorism and Effective Death Penalty Act of 1996.[141] This second material-support offense applies to knowingly aiding foreign organizations designated as "terrorist" by the secretary of state.[142] The provision that prohibits providing material support to designated groups survived a constitutional challenge in the Supreme Court in 2010.[143] After the September 11 attacks, Congress further amended the material-support statute to extend its reach to terrorism financing and attendance at foreign terrorist training camps.[144] While the material support provision applies equally to citizens, what make its employment against noncitizens more effective is the use of

---

[135] *See* Donna Ackermann, *A Matter of Interpretation: How the Language Barrier and the Trend of Criminalizing Illegal Immigration Caused a Deprivation of Due Process Following the Agriprocessors, Inc. Raids*, 43 COLUM. J.L. & SOC. PROBS. 363 (2010).

[136] 129 S. Ct. 1886 (2009).

[137] Note, Kristina Glithero, *Picking Members Out of Thin Air: Federal Aggravated Identity Theft Prosecutions in Light of Flores-Figueroa*, 37 AM. J. CRIM. LAW 69, 72 (2009).

[138] *Id.* at 71.

[139] *See* Aziz Z. Huq, *Forum Choice for Terrorism Suspects*, 61 DUKE L.J. 1415, 1433–34 (2012). Federal criminal prosecutions for "material support" is just one of a multitude of strategies involving both immigration and criminal law used to target noncitizen Arabs and Muslims. *See generally* Susan M. Akram and Maritza Karmely, *Immigration and Constitutional Consequences of Post 9/11 Policies Involving Arabs and Muslims in the United States: Is Alienage a Distinction Without a Difference?*, 38 U.C. DAVIS L. REV. 609 (2005).

[140] Huq, *supra* note 139.

[141] Pub. L. No. 104-132, 110 Stat. 1214 (1996).

[142] *Id.*

[143] Holder v. Humanitarian Law Project, 130 S. Ct. 2705, 2710 (2010) (rejecting the plaintiff's challenge to the applications of 29 U.S.C. § 2339B (2006), one of several material-support provisions).

[144] Huq, *supra* note 139, at 1434.

the federal immigration enforcement machinery in a multitude of ways that facilitate prosecutions targeting alleged noncitizen terrorists.[145]

c. Targeting "Humanitarian Workers" for Prosecution

In addition to the use of "harboring" immigration crimes to target humanitarian workers who assist undocumented immigrants in the United States, federal prosecutors have also relied on non-immigration crimes to attempt to curtail practices commonly known as "sanctuary movements." In September 2010, for example, the United States Court of Appeals for the Ninth Circuit reversed the federal criminal conviction of Daniel Mills for placing water for migrants crossing the United States-Mexico border in the Buenos Aires National Wildlife Refuge.[146] Mills conviction was based on a federal statute that made it a crime to dispose of waste on federal land, and the appellate court reversed solely on the narrow issue that the statute was ambiguous on whether jugs full of life-sustaining water constituted waste.[147] While Ninth Circuit ruling represented a personal victory for Mills, the narrow statutory construction holding in the case means that the case will not have a broader impact to shield the criminalization of aid to immigrants whether at the state or federal level.[148]

B.   THE *PADILLA* DUE PROCESS "REVOLUTION"?

Scholars criticize the treatment of immigration law as civil for two principal reasons. First, substantively, the fact that deportation — or its accompanying harsh enforcement practices[149] — is not viewed as punishment — has meant that many of the fundamental principles of criminal law that attempt to limit its application, such as the principal of proportionality, are missing from immigration law's enforcement.[150] In immigration proceedings, neither the Eight Amendment proscription against cruel and unusual punishment nor the *ex post facto* clause limit the deportation power.[151] As Professor Julie Stumpf has observed, "[n]either the gravity of the violation nor the harm that results governs whether deportation is a consequence for an immigration violation."[152] A second critique relates to what Professor Stephen Legomsky described as the asymmetric incorporation of criminal law approaches into the realm of civil immigration enforcement and adjudication in the absence of a parallel incorporation of greater procedural due process rights

---

[145] *Id.* at 1434–35. *See also* Akram and Karmely, *supra* note 139.

[146] U.S. v. Mills, 621 F.3d 914 (9th Cir. 2010).

[147] *Id.* at 918.

[148] State efforts to criminalize aid to immigrants is discussed in Part C *infra*.

[149] *See, e.g.*, Peter H. Shuck, *Immigrant Criminals in Overcrowded Prisons: Rethinking an Anachronistic Policy*, 27 Geo. Immigr. L.J. 597 (2013) and Mary Bosworth and Emma Kaufman, *Foreigners in a Carceral Age: Immigration and Imprisonment in the United States*, 22 Stan. L. & Pol'y Rev. 429 (2011).

[150] *See, e.g.*, Juliet Stumpf, *Fitting Punishment*, *supra* note 32.

[151] Jennifer M. Chacón, *A Diversion of Attention? Immigration Courts and the Adjudication of Fourth and Fifth Amendment Rights*, 59 Duke L.J. 1563, 1604–07 (2010).

[152] Stumpf, *Fitting Punishment*, *supra* note 32, at 1684.

for immigrants.[153] In U.S. immigration enforcement, for example, the Fourth Amendment protections against unreasonable searches and seizures apply but those protections are much narrower than in the criminal context and when these occur, the exclusionary remedy is largely unavailable.[154] The Fifth Amendment protections against self-incrimination also do not apply in civil proceedings, nor is the *Miranda* warning required when executing civil arrests.[155] In addition, there is no constitutional right to counsel at government expense in immigration proceedings, although noncitizens have a statutory right to counsel at their own expense.[156] Finally, judicial review is significantly curtailed in most areas of the immigration law in order to give deference to the other branches of government.[157]

Even if immigration law today resembles criminal punishment a great deal both in substance and procedure, there may be strong reasons why immigration law should still be considered civil. Some still insist on the theoretical distinctions that distinguish punishment from deportation as a matter of law.[158] Another reason relates to the concern that the rhetoric of criminalization and punishment as applied to immigrants has a greater potential to contribute to the erosion not the improvement of rights.[159] Among these scholars, thus, some argue that while courts should insist on heightened procedural protections in immigration proceedings, they should do so under the Fifth Amendment's Due Process Clause rather than by importing Sixth Amendment protections from the criminal context, in part to avoid the potential pitfalls of converging the two systems.[160] Indeed, this path has already started to happen. In April 2013, a U.S. Federal District Court judge in California

---

[153] *See generally* Legomsky, *supra* note 18.

[154] *See, e.g.*, Devon W. Carbado and Cheryl I. Harris, *Undocumented Criminal Procedure*, 58 UCLA L. REV. 1543 (2011); Irene Scharf, *The Exclusionary Rule in Immigration Proceedings: Where it Was, Where It Is, and Where It May Be Going*, 12 SAN DIEGO INT'L L.J. 53 (2010); Stella Burch Elias, *"Good Reason to Believe": Widespread Constitutional Violations in the Course of Immigration Enforcement and the Case for Revisiting Lopez-Mendoza*, 2008 WIS. L. REV. 1109 (2008); Raquel Aldana, *Of Katz and "Aliens": Privacy Expectations and the Immigration Raids*, 41 U.C. DAVIS L. REV. 1081 (2008).

[155] Chacón, *A Diverson of Attention?*, *supra* note 151, at 1604–07. *See also* The Honorable Karen Nelson Moore, *Aliens and the Constitution*, 88 N.Y.U.L. REV. 801, 845–876 (2013) (discussing aliens due process rights in contrast to the rights of criminal defendants) and Anjana Malhotra, *The Immigrant and Miranda*, 66 SMU L. REV. 277 (2013).

[156] Michael Kaufman, *Detention, Due Process, and the Right to Counsel in Removal Proceedings*, 4 STAN. J. CIV. RTS. & CIV. LIBERTIES 113 (2008). As well, for immigrants with language barriers, there is no constitutional right to an interpreter, though there is a statutory right to a court interpreter in cases where the detainee does not speak English. *See* Department of Justice Immigration Practice Manual § 4.11.

[157] *See, e.g.*, Sarah A. Moore, *Tearing Down the Fence Around Immigration Law: Examining the Lack of Judicial Review and the Impact of the Real ID Act While Calling for Broader Readings of Questions of Law to Encompass "Extreme Cruelty"*, 82 NOTRE DAME L. REV. 2037 (2007). *See also* Chapter 6 of this book discussing judicial review in immigration proceedings.

[158] *See, e.g.*, Ethan Verner Torrey, *"The Dignity of Crimes": Judicial Deference of Aliens and the Civil-Criminal Distinction*, 32 COLUM. J. L. & SOC. PROBS. 187 (1999) (discussing especially judicial insistence that deportation is not punishment).

[159] Thomas Hammarberg, *Criminalization of Migration in Europe: Human Rights Implication*, CommDH/Issue Paper (2010), https://wcd.coe.int/ViewDoc.jsp?id=1579605.

[160] *See, e.g.*, Anne R. Traum, *Constitutionalizing Immigration On Its Own Path*, 33 CARDOZO L. REV. 491 (2011).

ordered in a landmark case, *Franco-González v. Holder*, that the federal government provide legal representation for immigrant detainees in California, Arizona and Washington who have serious mental disabilities and are unable to represent themselves in immigration court.[161] As well, the exclusionary rule as a remedy for policing civil rights violations in immigration enforcement is not available, at least in particularly egregious cases.[162]

Inevitably, however, the increasing convergence of immigration and criminal law will create spaces where it is impossible to acknowledge that immigration law and criminal law co-exist in detrimental ways to due process. One area where this is obviously true is where the noncitizen or someone who associates with him is being criminally prosecuted for an immigration crime. In general, in this space, noncitizen criminal defendants as a matter of law enjoy the same constitutional protections as other criminal defendants facing non-immigration crimes. However, as Professor Jennifer Chacón has documented, inevitably the lower standards of procedural protections that apply in removal proceedings have made "ultra-vires incursions into the criminal realm."[163] A few examples of this is Operation Streamline and Fast Track which have permitted the prosecution of dozens of persons charged with entry/re-entry crimes in a single trial or in mass plea agreements with a single defense lawyer appointed to all defendants.[164] As well, as Professor Ingrid Eagly has argued, criminal prosecutors are able to take advantage of the resources of the immigration system, which are largely unconstrained by the Constitution, to supplement their criminal prosecutions.[165] This includes detention without bond, interrogation without *Miranda*, arrest without probable cause of a crime, and sentencing without probation.[166] Further, at least half of the criminal immigration cases are adjudicated through the prosecution of illegal entry as a "petty crime" in magistrate courts, a practice that places immigrants squarely outside the realm of Article III courts and other due process rights, such as the right to a jury trial and grand jury indictments.[167] The exposure of noncitizens to second-class criminal justice treatment raises the question of whether in practice the criminal-civil divide is any longer justifiable.[168]

Another area of clear convergence is when a noncitizen charged with a non-immigration crime, whether in federal or state court, faces adverse immigra-

---

[161] Case No. CV 10-02221 DMG (DTBX), Partial Judgment and Permanent Injunction, April 23, 2013.

[162] *See, e.g.*, Irene Scharf, *The Exclusionary Rule in Immigration Proceedings: Where It Was, Where It Is, Where It May Be Going*, 12 SAN DIEGO INT'L L.J. 59 (2010).

[163] Chacón, *Managing Migration Through Crime, supra* note 37, at 141.

[164] *Id.* at 142. *See also* García Hernández, *Creating Crimmigration, supra* note 24, at 1475–79.

[165] Eagly, *Prosecuting Immigration, supra* note 39, at 1288. *See also* David Alan Sklansky, *Crime, Immigration and Ad Hoc Instrumentalism, supra* note 39, at 161 (using the term ad hoc instrumentalism to refer of the growing trend in law and legal institutions to use "tools" interchangeably across different fields of law so long as these provide instrumental advantages to satisfy their objectives) and Malhotra, *supra* note 155 (discussing the use of immigration law enforcement procedures to circumvent criminal rights for noncitizen defendants).

[166] Eagly, *Prosecuting Immigration, supra* note 39, at 1288.

[167] *Id.*

[168] *Id.* at 1286.

tion consequences based on the outcome of the criminal case, whether in the context of plea agreements or trials. Until 2010, and despite the harsh consequences affecting noncitizen criminal defendants who were sometime ill-advised for their defense lawyers about the immigration consequences of their pleas, courts refused to recognize an ineffective assistance of counsel remedy under the Sixth Amendment, treating the issue as a collateral issue that did not involve protections available in the criminal realm. Then, the U.S. Supreme Court decided *Padilla v. Kentucky*,[169] a case that has been both categorized as revolutionary and disappointing.

1. Padilla's Story and Holding

José Padilla, who came to the United States from Honduras in the 1960s, served in the Vietnam War, became a lawful permanent resident, and settled in California with his family. Padilla pled guilty to marijuana trafficking and to a sentence of five years plus an additional five years probation, his first offense, after his defense lawyer told him that his plea would not have adverse immigration consequences.[170] His defense lawyer was flatly wrong. Indeed, the plea made Padilla deportable as an aggravated felon, which triggered mandatory detention, rendered him ineligible for any relief from deportation based on family unity, and forever barred him from reentering the United States, with the prospect of facing up to 20 years in jail if he reentered illegal after his removal.

The Supreme Court agreed with Padilla that his attorney engaged in ineffective assistance of counsel and for the first time recognized that criminal defense counsel have a duty to inform a noncitizen of the immigration consequences of a guilty plea if it is clear that the crime may constitute a basis for deportation.[171] As is explained later, more than the narrow holding of *Padilla*, which has not resulted in the transformation of the status quo, the revolutionary aspects of *Padilla* rested in the Court rejecting the treatment of immigration consequences simply as a collateral consequences as many lower courts had done and recognizing a Sixth Amendment ineffective assistance claim. To do this, the Court reasoned as follows:

> We have long recognized that deportation is a particularly severe "penalty," but it is not, in a strict sense, a criminal sanction. Although removal proceedings are civil in nature, deportation is nevertheless intimately related to the criminal process. Our law has enmeshed criminal convictions and the penalty of deportation for nearly a century. And, importantly, recent changes in our immigration law have made removal nearly an automatic result for a broad class of noncitizen offenders. Thus, we find it "most difficult" to divorce the penalty from the conviction in the deportation context. Moreover, we are quite confident that noncitizen defendants facing a risk of deportation for a particular offense find it even more difficult.

---

[169] 559 U.S. 356 (2010).

[170] Padilla v. Kentucky, 559 U.S. 356, 359 (2010).

[171] *Id.* at 369.

Deportation as a consequence of a criminal conviction is, because of its close connection to the criminal process, uniquely difficult to classify as either a direct or a collateral consequence. The collateral versus direct distinction is thus ill suited to evaluating a Strickland[172] claim concerning the specific risk of deportation. We conclude that advice regarding deportation is not categorically removed from the ambit of the Sixth Amendment right to counsel. Strickland applies to Padilla's claim (citations omitted).[173]

2. The Meaning of *Padilla*

Immediately after *Padilla* was decided, a number of scholars wrote to try to explain its scope and potential for transformation not only in bridging the due process gap between the treatment of deportation and punishment — e.g., recognizing a right to counsel for immigrants in removal proceedings or applying the proportionality principle to deportation — but also potentially in expanding its holding to other types of collateral consequences for criminal defendants.[174] There were also significant questions about its implementation, including whether its holding would be applied retroactively and whether resources limitations plaguing defense counsel would function to significantly limit its impact.[175]

One issue related to *Padilla*'s scope was its creation of a two-tiered Sixth Amendment advising function that hinged on the simplicity or complexity of immigration law.[176] *Padilla* essentially created only a right to advise on the immigration consequences when immigration law is "succinct, clear, and explicit": otherwise, all that is required is for counsel to give general advice that the plea may have adverse effects on his/her immigration status.[177] Of course, immigration law is hardly ever straightforward, which raised concern that its more concrete mandate would apply in too few cases. Consequently, the response from overburdened criminal defense institutions ill-equipped to implement a more robust *Padilla* holding would likely be simply to provide a general warning to noncitizen clients of potential adverse immigration consequences.[178] Thus, scholars predicted that the long-term fate of *Padilla* would rely primarily with the defense bar,[179] but also on important partnerships between immigration lawyers, the

---

[172] Strickland v. Washington, 466 U.S. 668 (1984).

[173] *Padilla*, 559 U.S. at 365–66.

[174] *See, e.g.*, Maureen A. Sweeney, *Where Do We Go from Padilla v. Kentucky? Thoughts on Implementation and Future Directions*, 45 NEW ENG. L. REV. 353 (2011).

[175] *Id.*

[176] Yolanda Vazquez, *Realizing Padilla's Promise: Ensuring Noncitizen Defendants are Advised of the Immigration Consequences of a Criminal Conviction*, 39 FORDHAM URB. L.J. 169, 171 (2011).

[177] *Id. See also* Maurice Hew, Jr., *Under the Circumstances: Padilla v. Kentucky Still Excuses Fundamental Fairness and Leaves Professional Responsibility Lost*, 32 B.C. J. L. & SOC. JUST. 31 (2012) and César Cuauhtémoc García Hernández, *Criminal Defense After Padilla v. Kentucky*, 26 GEO. IMMIGR. L.J. 475 (2012).

[178] Sweeney, *supra* note 174, at 357–64.

[179] *See* Malia Brink, *A Gauntlet Thrown: The Transformative Potential of Padilla v. Kentucky*, 39 FORDHAM URB. L.J. 39 (2011). Another insightful observation is that Padilla alone would make little difference in the lives of noncitizens because its effect could never address the inherent unfairness of the

defense bar, and non-profits.[180] Other scholars rightly note, however, that prosecutors cannot be ignored in the *Padilla* equation, especially in light of prosecutorial discretion.[181] As well, scholars have focused on the need to improve in particular state criminal courts ill-equipped to handle *Padilla* as a preventative measure and as a remedy.[182] Some initial assessments of how *Padilla* has worked as implemented are mixed. In North Dakota, for example, a public defender concluded that *Padilla* had changed some practices in the state but hardly enough because in few cases are the immigration consequences clear.[183] A study of Brooklyn New York District Attorney's, however, suggested that interest convergence, including limited prosecutorial resources or ensuring case outcomes that are proportionate to the charged offense have great potential to involve prosecutors in crafting immigration-neutral pleas when appropriate.[184]

Other legal issues left unresolved in *Padilla* included whether its mandate applied retroactively; what the standard was to demonstrate prejudice resulting from counsel's ineffective assistance of counsel; and whether a *Padilla* violation could be cured by a warning intervention provided by a judge.[185] On the retroactivity issue, immediately after its decision, lower courts disagreed on whether the decision applied to cases pled out prior to the date *Padilla* was decided.[186] Then in 2013, the U.S. Supreme Court decided *Chaidez v. U.S.* and held that *Padilla* did not apply retroactively to cases already final on direct review when *Padilla* was decided.[187] To do so, the Court reasoned that when the Court announces a "new rule," a person whose conviction is already final may not benefit from its protection.[188] Writing for the dissent, Justice Sotomayor disagreed that *Padilla* articulated a new rule because it should be read as an extension of *Strickland v. Washington*,[189] a case decided in 1984 in which the Court first

---

immigration consequences flowing from crime. Darryl K. Brown, *Why Padilla Doesn't Matter (Much)*, 58 UCLA L. REV. 1393 (2011).

[180] *See* Joel M. Schumm, *Padilla and the Future of the Defense Function: Conference Report*, 39 FORDHAM URB. L.J. 3 (2011).

[181] Heidi Altman, *Prosecuting Post-Padilla: State Interests and the Pursuit of Justice for Noncitizen Defendants*, 101 GEO. L.J. 1 (2012).

[182] *See, e.g.*, César Cuauhtémoc García Hernández, *When State Courts Meet Padilla: A Concerted Effort is Needed to Bring State Courts up to Speed on Crime-Based Immigration Law Provisions*, 12 LOY. J. PUB. INT. L. 299 (2011). *See also* Note, Alison L. Carruthers, *Guilty Plea Colloquies in Michigan After Padilla*, 90 U. DET. MERCY L. REV. 303 (2013) (discussing Michigan's failure to adopt a procedure requiring judges to provide a warning to noncitizens about immigration consequences as part of plea agreements).

[183] Nicholas D. Thornton, *The Failing Promise of Padilla: How Padilla v. Kentucky Should Have Changed the Game in North Dakota, But Did Not*, 87 N. DAK. L. REV. 85 (2011).

[184] Altman, *supra* note 181, at 32–54.

[185] RAQUEL ALDANA, ET AL., IMMIGRATION POLICING AND RIGHTS IN GLOBAL ISSUES IN IMMIGRATION LAW 366–67 (2011).

[186] *Id.*

[187] 133 S. Ct. 1103 (2013).

[188] *Id.* at 1105.

[189] 446 U.S. 668 (1984).

recognized a remedy based on ineffective assistance of counsel.[190] Some states, however, including New Mexico and Massachusetts, have disagreed with *Chaidez* and have decided to apply *Padilla* retroactively based on state law grounds.[191]

Other scholars have expressed doubt that *Padilla*, even when available, could result in adequate reparation to the criminal defendants already deported based on both restrictions on the availability of post-conviction relief for persons no longer inside U.S. territory and the inability of remaining former immigration status once excluded.[192]

3. Beyond *Padilla*?

At the same time that *Padilla*'s limitations were scrutinized, scholars also explored its potential for its expansion in other contexts. Many scholars, for example, suggested that *Padilla* could be the beginning of a right to counsel for certain noncitizens facing deportation.[193] Others read *Padilla* as reversing the treatment of deportation as non-punishment and infusing its application with greater constitutional limits.[194] Others hoped that *Padilla* would mean a similar transformation of Sixth Amendment rights applied to other types of collateral consequences facing criminal defendants, such as loss of parental rights or voting.[195] These hopes for *Padilla* less than five years after its holding perhaps are too early to assess.[196]

C. CRIMINALIZATION OF IMMIGRATION VIOLATIONS AND IMMIGRANTS

In the early days of U.S. history when the federal government had yet to occupy the field of immigration law and declared it a federal power, states governed migration across state borders states did so in part through the imposition of punishment to the immigrant and those who aided immigrants in the violation of

---

[190] 133 S. Ct. at 1115–18. *See also* Christopher N. Lasch, *Redress in State Postconviction Proceedings for Ineffective Assistance of Counsel*, 63 DEPAUL L. REV. 959, 984–94 (2014) (critiquing the *Chaidez* majority).

[191] Lasch, *Redress in State Postconviction Proceedings*, *supra* note 190, at 994–1000. *See also* Note, Kate Lebeaux, *Padilla Retroactivity on State Law Grounds*, 94 B.U.L. REV. 1651 (2014).

[192] Rachel E. Rosenbloom, *Will Padilla Reach Across the Border?*, 45 NEW ENG. L. REV. 327 (2011).

[193] *See, e.g.*, Christopher N. Lasch, *"Crimmigration" and the Right to Counsel at the Border Between Civil and Criminal Proceedings*, 99 IOWA L. REV. 2131 (2014); Ingrid V. Eagly, *Gideon's Migration*, 122 YALE L.J. 2282 (2013); Daniel Kanstroom, *The Right to Deportation Counsel in Padilla v. Kentucky: The Challenging Construction of the Fifth-And-A-Half Amendment*, 58 UCLA L. REV. 1461 (2011); and Alice Clapman, *Petty Offenses, Drastic Consequences: Toward a Sixth Amendment Right to Counsel for Noncitizen Defendants Facing Deportation*, 33 CARDOZO L. REV. 585 (2011).

[194] Anita Ortiz Maddali, *Padilla v. Kentucky: A New Chapter in Supreme Court Jurisprudence on Whether Deportation Constitutes Punishment for Lawful Permanent Residents?*, 61 AM. U. L. REV. 1 (2011).

[195] *See, e.g.*, McGregor Smyth, *From "Collateral" to "Integral": The Seismic Evolution of Padilla v. Kentucky and Its Impact on Penalties Beyond Deportation*, 54 HOW. L.J. 795 (2011).

[196] Some disappointment has already been expressed in terms of Padilla not extending to non-immigration collateral consequences. *See, e.g.*, Thornton, *supra* note 183, at 125–35.

immigration restrictions on entry or based on the post-entry conduct of individuals who were not "citizens" of that state.[197] Then, when the federal government moved to federalize the immigration laws, with some exceptions, states ceased their own attempts to regulate immigration through the criminal laws. More recently, however, as immigration federalism has imploded,[198] states and localities have added crimes that "mirror" or expand on the crimes that already exist under federal law or have relied on traditional state criminal laws such as anti-loitering or housing and zoning ordinances for criminal immigrants and those who associate with them.[199]

In the wake of *Arizona v. U.S.* decided in 2012,[200] however, it is likely that state efforts to criminalize noncitizens will be under significant constitutional scrutiny on preemption grounds. In *Arizona v. U.S.*, the U.S. Supreme Court struck down as preempted the two provisions that created the immigration crimes of punishing undocumented immigrants for working in the state or for being present in the state but having failed to register under federal immigration law.[201] As described in this section, preemption challenges have already started to narrow the ability of states to regulate immigration through immigration crimes, but it has not ended the enactment or enforcement of state immigration criminal laws. States are also starting to legislate in this area in ways to avoid conflicts with federal immigration laws. As well, some laws remain simply due to the structural impediments of raising constitutional challenges against such laws since most defendants plea out.[202] This section is not an exhaustive treatment of state immigration crimes. Rather, it provides examples of both successful and unsuccessful emblematic state criminal immigration laws that some states have enacted particularly in recent years.

1. State Immigration Crimes that "Mirror" Federal Immigration Crimes

Some state immigration crimes purport to be simply enacting similar legislation that already exists under federal immigration law. Professors Gabriel J. Chin and Marc L. Miller label this approach the mirror-image theory. They question the alleged premise of cooperative enforcement that underlies the mirror-image theory, suggesting instead that substantive variations and more importantly enforcement variations make these more like the evil twin.[203]

---

[197] Stumpft, *Fitting Punishment*, *supra* note 32, at 1707–1710.

[198] *See* Ch. 4 in this book.

[199] *See, e.g.*, Jennifer M. Chacón, *Overcriminalizing Immigration*, 102 J. Crim. L. & Criminology 613, 628–30 (2012) and Jennifer M. Chacón, *Managing Migration Through Crime*, *supra* note 37, at 138–39.

[200] Arizona v. U.S., 132 S. Ct. 2492 (2012).

[201] *Id.* at 2503–05.

[202] Ingrid V. Eagly, *Local Immigration Prosecution: A Study of Arizona Before SB 1070*, 58 UCLA L. Rev. 1749, 1754 (2011).

[203] Gabriel J. Chin and Marc L. Miller, *The Unconstitutionality of State Regulation of Immigration Through Criminal Law*, 61 Duke L.J. 251, 255 (2011).

a.   Employer Sanctions

Prior to the passage of IRCA, eleven states and one city has already adopted employer sanctions; however, these were largely unenforced and contemplated solely civil sanctions.[204]More recently, however, states like Arizona and Alabama adopted laws that criminalized undocumented workers for working in the state. Section 5(C) of Arizona's SB 1070 made it a state misdemeanor for an "authorized alien to knowingly apply for work, solicit work in a public place or perform work as an employee or independent contractor."[205] Violations to this law could be punished by a $2500 fine and incarceration for up to six months.[206] In Alabama Section 11 criminalized an unauthorized "alien's application for, solicitation of, or performance of work, whether as an employee or independent contractor, inside the state of Alabama."[207]

In 2012, however, the U.S. Supreme Court struck down Arizona's provision as preempted by federal law, even as it recognized that Arizona did not replicate any comparable federal immigration law.[208] In fact, the Court reasoned that Congress was very deliberate not to impose criminal penalties on immigrants who seek or engage in unauthorized employment when it adopted IRCA.[209] IRCA, in fact, provided that information employees submit as their immigration status "may not be used" for purposes other than prosecution under specified federal criminal statutes for fraud, perjury, and related conduct.[210] The Court acknowledged that this express preemption provision applied to employers who hired unauthorized workers and was silent on employees themselves.[211] However, the Court applied conflict preemption analysis to hold that Arizona's law could interfere with the careful balance struck by Congress with respect to attempting to regulate violations of immigration law in the workplace.[212] Unsurprisingly, a few months after the Supreme Court's holding, the Eleventh Circuit would declare Alabama's comparable provision preempted for the same reasons.[213]

---

[204] Miller, *supra* note 20, at 630. Just a day earlier, in fact, the Department of Justice announced the issuance of new regulations on "Safeguards for Unrepresented Immigration Detainees with Serious Mental Disorders or Conditions." The policy concluded that EOIR "will make available a qualified representative to unrepresented detainees who are deemed mentally incompetence to represent themselves in immigration proceedings." EOIR News, April 22, 2013, *available at* http://www.justice.gov/eoir/press/2013/SafeguardsUnrepresentedImmigrationDetainees.html.

[205] Ariz. Rev. Stat. Ann. § 13-2928(C) (West Supp. 2011).

[206] *Id.* at 2928(f).

[207] Ala. Code § 31-13-10(f).

[208] *Arizona v. U.S.*, 132 S. Ct. at 2503.

[209] *Id.* at 2504.

[210] 8 U.S.C. §§ 1324a(b)(5), (d)(2)(F)–(G).

[211] 132 S. Ct. at 2504–05.

[212] *Id.* at 2505.

[213] U.S. v. Alabama, 691 F.3d 1269, 1283 (11th Cir. 2012).

b. Human Trafficking

Especially since 2005 when Congress enacted anti-trafficking laws,[214] dozens of states including Arizona,[215] California, Florida,[216] Kansas,[217] Illinois,[218] Indiana,[219] Massachusetts,[220] Missouri,[221] Nevada,[222] New York,[223] Texas,[224] Utah,[225] Virginia,[226] and Wisconsin,[227] have enacted laws to bolsters prosecutions against alleged human traffickers. California probably enacted the most comprehensive state human trafficking legislation when it passed the California Trafficking Victims Protection Act in 2005.[228] The Act makes human trafficking a crime punishable with up to eight years in prison and provides for civil remedies to victims and their families.[229] It also created the California Alliance to Combat Trafficking and Slavery Taskforce (California ACTS) whose members include the state attorney general,

---

[214] *See supra* Part A.1.c.

[215] For a discussion of Arizona's human trafficking legislation, *see* Note, Anaru Hall, *The Uniform Act on Prevention of and Remedies for Human Trafficking*, 56 ARIZ. L. REV. 853 (2014).

[216] For a discussion of Florida's human trafficking legislation, *see* Note, Adam S. Butkus, *Ending Modern-Day Slavery in Florida: Strengthening Florida's Legislation in Combating Human Trafficking*, 37 STETSON L. REV. 297, 326–37 (2007).

[217] For a discussion of Kansas' human trafficking legislation, *see* Note, Leslie Klaassen, *Breaking the Victimization Cycle: Domestic Minor Trafficking in Kansas*, 52 WASH. L.J. 581 (2013).

[218] For a discussion of Illinois' human trafficking legislation, *see* Sabena Auyeung, *"How Much Are You Worth?" The Effects of Human Trafficking on the Sex Trade in Illinois and the Remedies Designed to Eliminate it*, 18 PUB INT. L. REP. 191 (2013).

[219] For a discussion of Indiana's human trafficking laws, *see* Notes, May Li, *Did Indiana Deliver in Its Fight Against Human Trafficking?: A Comparative Analysis Between Indiana's Human Trafficking Laws and the International Legal Framework*, 23 IND. INT'L & COMP. L. REV. 277 (2013).

[220] For a discussion of Massachusetts human trafficking laws, *see* Note Melissa Dess, *Walking the Freedom Trail: An Analysis of the Massachusetts Human Trafficking Statute and Its Potential to Combat Child Sex Trafficking*, 33 B.C. J.L. & SOC. JUST. 147 (2013).

[221] For a discussion of Missouri's human trafficking laws, *see* Comment, Abby Duncan, *A Tale of Two Districts: Lessons Learned from Missouri's Human Trafficking Task Forces*, 33 ST. LOUIS U. PUB. L. REV. 191 (2013).

[222] For a discussion of Nevada's human trafficking laws, *see* Note, Chariane K. Forrey, *America's "Disneyland of Sex": Exploring the Problem of Sex Trafficking in Las Vegas and Nevada's Response*, 14 NEV. L.J. 970 (2014).

[223] For a discussion of New York's human trafficking laws, *see* Notes and Comments, Marisa Nack, *The Next Step: The Future of New York State's Human Trafficking Law*, 18 J. L. & POL'Y 817 (2010).

[224] For a discussion of Texas human trafficking laws, *see* Cheryl Nelson Butler, *Sex Slavery in the Lone Star State: Does the Texas Human Trafficking Legislation of 2011 Protect Minors?* 45 AKRON L. REV. 843 (2011–2012).

[225] For a discussion of Utah's human trafficking legislation, *see* Note, Lenora C. Babb, *Utah's Misguided Approach to the Problem of Sex Trafficking: A Call for Reform*, 14 J. L. & FAM. STUD. 277 (2012).

[226] For a discussion of Virginia's human trafficking legislation, *see* Nicole Tutrani, *Open for the Wrong Kind of Business: An Analysis of Virginia's Legislative Approach to Combating Commercial Sexual Exploitation*, 26 REGENT U. L. REV. 487 (2013–2014).

[227] For a discussion of Wisconsin's human trafficking laws, *see* Comment, Lisa Holl Chang, *Reaching Safe Harbor: A Path for Sex-Trafficking Victims in Wisconsin*, 2013 WIS. L. REV. 1489 (2013).

[228] A.B. 22 (2005).

[229] Cal. Penal Code Ann. § 236.1 and Cal. Civ. Code Ann. § 52.5(a) (2006)

prosecutors, public defenders, and social providers. The task force issued an important report in 2007 to provide insights and recommendations to address the problems of human trafficking in the state.[230] Then in 2012, the Attorney General Pamela Harris convened a new group to issue a new report in lights of significant changes to the face of human trafficking in the state in just five years. [231]

Unlike other areas of immigration crimes, anti-trafficking state laws have been encouraged by the federal government.[232] To date, there are no reported cases seeking to invalidate the laws on preemption grounds.

c. Harboring, Transporting, and Smuggling

Several states, including Alabama, Arizona, Georgia, Oklahoma,[233] and South Carolina, have adopted laws that criminalize conduct such as harboring, transporting, and/or smuggling of unauthorized persons, which are supposed to mirror but often go way what federal law intended.

The state leading the way in these types of laws is Arizona. Since 2005, Arizona has authorized state prosecutors to impose criminal sanctions on those who transport undocumented immigrants into the state.[234] Since its passage, local prosecutors have used it to pursue hundreds of criminal cases.[235] In fact, in order to enhance these prosecutions, Arizona has developed a sophisticated alienage-based criminal procedural system with special rules on issues of bail, sentencing, material witnesses, jails and policing functions.[236] As Professor Ingrid V. Eagly has documented, through these smuggling prosecutions gives local prosecutors, *inter alia*, the authority to control their own prosecutions in ways that federal law and policy would not allow, altering as such the federal power over immigration.[237]

Both the Arizona and federal smuggling crimes prohibit the transportation and movement of undocumented migrants within the United States, but they also differ

---

[230] Human Trafficking in California, Final Report of the California Alliance to Combat Trafficking and Slavery Task Force (2007) *available at* http://oag.ca.gov/sites/all/files/agweb/pdfs/publications/Human_Trafficking_Final_Report.pdf.

[231] The State of Human Trafficking in California (2012), *available at* http://oag.ca.gov/sites/all/files/agweb/pdfs/ht/human-trafficking-2012.pdf.

[232] Butkus, *supra* note 216, at 321–322 (discussing a U.S. DOJ memorandum proposing model anti-trafficking state laws).

[233] In 2007, the Oklahoma Taxpayer and Citizen Protection Act, an omnibus legislation that, *inter alia*, made it a felony for an individual to provide even casual transportation — such as a ride to school — if that individual knows or suspects the person is an undocumented immigrant. It also made it a felon to harbor undocumented immigrants. To date, attempts to challenges the constitutionality of these provisions have been dismissed by two federal district courts for lack of standing. National Coalition of Clergy, Inc. v. Henry, 2007 U.S. Dist. LEXIS 78658 (N.D. Okla. Oct. 22, 2007) and National Coalition of Clergy, Inc. v. Henry, 2007 U.S. Dist. LEXIS 91487 (N.D. Okla. Dec. 12, 2007) .

[234] S. 1372, 47th Leg., 1st Reg. Sess. (Ariz. 2005) codified as amended at Ariz. Rev. Stat. Ann. §13-2319 (2010).

[235] Ingrid V. Eagly, *Local Immigration Prosecution: A Study of Arizona Before SB 1070*, 58 UCLA L. Rev. 1749, 1752 (2011).

[236] *Id.* at 1753.

[237] *Id.* at 1754.

in important respects which make the Arizona law more flexible.[238] One difference pertains to the *mens rea* requirements, which under federal law require at a minimum reckless disregard of the person's immigration status and only "reason to know" in Arizona.[239] As well, the Arizona law does not include the requirement under the federal law that the transportation be "in furtherance" of the smuggling offense.[240] Moreover, as implemented, and in contrast to the federal smuggling provision, the Arizona law has been employed to charge the persons being smuggled, which has earned it the label of a self-smuggling law.[241]

The Arizona smuggling law had survived preemption challenges in state court prior to *U.S. v. Arizona*, with Arizona courts viewing the law as core to state police powers, compatible with federal enforcement and duplicative of federal objectives.[242] The law, however, has not fared well in federal court. In 2013, a federal district court struck down as impliedly preempted the employment of the Arizona smuggling law against non-smugglers working with undocumented immigrants who had been convicted for conspiracy under the statute.[243] As well, in 2013, the Ninth Circuit certified a class and allowed the litigation challenging the Arizona smuggling law as applied to community pro-immigrant groups to move forward, finding that the litigation is likely to succeed based on field and conflict preemption with federal immigration laws.[244] Arizona received another blow when the U.S. Supreme Court refused *certiorari* to review the Ninth Circuit ruling in 2014.[245]

In 2011, Alabama signed into law H.B. 56, also known as the "Beason-Hammon Alabama Taxpayer and Citizen Protection Act," whose stated purpose was to discourage undocumented immigration within the state.[246] An omnibus legislation, one of its ten provisions created three new state crimes: first, it criminalized the actual or attempted concealment, harboring, or shielding from detection of any undocumented person; second it criminalized the act of encouraging or inducing an undocumented immigrant from residing in Alabama and third, it criminalized transporting, attempting to transport, or conspiring to transport an undocumented immigrant within the state.[247] In 2012, however, after the Department of Justice brought suit, the Fourth Circuit struck down the provisions as being field preempted because a comprehensive federal framework for dealing with the same crimes already exist.[248]

Also in 2011, Georgia lawmakers enacted H.B. 87, known as the Illegal Immigration Reform and Enforcement Act, also an omnibus legislation, which,

---

[238] *Id.* at 1768.

[239] *Id.*

[240] *Id.*

[241] *Id.* at 1770.

[242] *Id.* at 1753.

[243] We Are America v. Maricopa County Board of Supervisors, 297 F.R.D. 373 (D. Ariz. 2013).

[244] Valle Del Sol Inc., v. Whiting, 732 F.3d 1006 (9th Cir. 2013), *cert. denied*, 134 S. Ct. 1876 (2014).

[245] Arizona v. Valle del Sol, Inc., 134 S. Ct. 1876 (2014).

[246] U.S. v. Alabama, 691 F.3d 1269, 1276 (11th Cir. 2012) (discussing the content of H.B. 56).

[247] *Id.* at 1277.

[248] *Id.* at 1285–86.

inter alia, codified in Section 7 three separate crimes for interactions with undocumented immigrants, including "transporting or moving an illegal alien," "concealing or harboring an illegal alien," and "inducing an illegal alien to enter into [Georgia]."[249] In 2012, however, the Eleventh Circuit recognized standing of the undocumented immigrants and nonprofit organizations providing services to Latino communities and also affirmed the district court's injunction of the law based on the likelihood of a preemption challenge.[250]

Finally, also in 2011, South Carolina passed into law an omnibus law, S.B.20, that, *inter alia*, made it a state felony for an unlawfully present person to allow himself or herself to be "transported or moved" within the state or to be harbored or sheltered to avoid detection, punishable by a fine up to $5,000 or up to five years in prison or both.[251] A different subsection criminalized the same acts and imposed the same punishment for persons who assisted the immigrants in those acts.[252] Immediately thereafter, however, the Department of Justice filed suit against these and certain other criminal provisions of the law and in 2013, the Fourth Circuit declared the provisions preempted.[253]

d. Identity Theft Laws

Unlike federal attempts to criminalize noncitizens for the use of someone else's identity documents, some states have gone further to expressly criminalize noncitizens for unknowingly using someone else's identity. One example of this type of crime is Arizona's "Taking identity of another person or entity," which creates criminal culpability for the use of an alternative identify whether or not the defendant knows that he is using the identity of an actual person or whether or not another person with such identity.[254] This offense can be used to prosecute noncitizens who have used false identities to obtain false employment in cases where there is no loss to anyone as a result of the use of that identity.[255] The law has been used successfully to prosecute undocumented workers who have used false documents to obtain employment in the state.[256] Other states have relied on forgery laws to prosecute undocumented workers for the use of false documents.[257] Since the law does not create *per se* an immigration crime, preemption challenges against the law have not been successful.[258]

---

[249] *See* Georgia Latino Alliance for Human Rights v. Governor of Georgia, 691 F.3d 1250, 1256 (11th Cir. 2012) (discussing the harboring provisions of the Georgia's H.B. 87).

[250] *Id.*

[251] U.S. v. South Carolina, 720 F.3d 518, 523 (4th Cir. 2013) (discussing Subsection 4(B) of the S.B. 20).

[252] *Id.* (discussing Subsection D. of S.B. 20).

[253] *Id.*

[254] *See* Ariz. Rev. Stat. Ann. § 13-2008 (Supp. 2008) and § 13-2009.

[255] Chacón, *Managing Migration Through Crime*, *supra* note 37, at 138.

[256] *See, e.g.*, State v. Parker, 2009 WL 1065988 (Ariz. Ct. of App. 2009).

[257] *See, e.g.*, Missouri v. Diaz-Rey, 397 S.W.3d 5 (Mo. Ct. App. 2013) and Minnesota v. Reynua, 807 N.W.2d 473 (Minn. Ct. App. 2011) (relying on state forgery law to successfully convict workers who used false documents to obtain employment).

[258] *See, e.g.*, *id.*

2. State Immigration Crimes that Innovate Beyond Federal Immigration Crimes

a. Housing

Some states and localities have created new housing crimes to target landlords and tenants who reside in the state. The City of Farmers Branch Texas, for example, adopted Ordinance 2952, which *inter alia*, imposed criminal sanctions on persons who occupied a rented apartment or a single-family residence without first obtaining a valid license from the City, which they could only do by proving lawful immigration status.[259] In turn, landlords were prohibited from knowingly renting an apartment to persons who lacked the valid licenses.[260] Finally, the Ordinance also criminalized creating, possessing, selling or distributing a counterfeit license.[261] These offenses constituted Class C criminal misdemeanors and were punishable by a fine of $500 upon conviction.[262] In Alabama, the state criminalized as part of H.B. 658 certain instances of entering into a rental agreement with an undocumented immigrant.[263] These provisions, however, have not survived constitutional scrutiny under preemption grounds. Both the Eleventh Circuit and the Fifth Circuits have considered Alabama's and Farmer Branchs's laws respectively conflict preempted because similar crimes are not contemplated under federal immigration laws[264] and/or because such laws disrupt the federal anti-harboring immigration framework already in place by applying a whole new enforcement mechanisms for crimes that could be tried federally.[265]

b. Trespass/Unlawful Presence

Since around 2005, states and localities, including New Hampshire, California, and Florida, have relied on criminal trespass charges to target undocumented immigrants for unlawful presence.[266] For example, the New Hampshire law applied to undocumented immigrants penalizes a person who "knowing he is not licensed or privileged to do so, [. . .] enters or remains in any place."[267] As well, some states and localities are creating new crimes that penalize being unlawfully present in the United States. For example, Arizona's SB 1070[268] and Alabama's H.B. 56[269] omnibus legislations, specifically penalized undocumented immigrants for being present in

---

[259] Ordinance 2952, §§ 1(C)(2); 3(C)(2).

[260] *Id.* at §§ 1(C)(7); 3(7).

[261] *Id.* at §§ 1(C)(3); 3(C)(3).

[262] Tex. Penal Code Ann. §12.41(3) (West 2009).

[263] U.S. v. Alabama, 691 F.3d at 1277.

[264] *Id.* at 1288.

[265] Villas at Parkside Partner v. The City of Farmers Brach, Texas, 726 F.3d 524, 528–30 (5th Cir. 2013).

[266] Karla Mari McKanders, *Unforgiving of Those who Trespass Against U.S.: State Law Criminalizing Immigration Status*, 12 Loy. J. Pub. Int. L. 331 (2011).

[267] N.H. Rev. Stat. Ann. § 635:2 (1971).

[268] S.B. 1070, 49th Leg., 2d Reg. Sess. (Ariz. 2010); Ariz. Rev. Stat. Ann. § 13-1509 (2010).

[269] H.B. 56 § 10; Ala. Code § 31-13-10(a).

their respective states without lawful immigration status. In each case, to avoid the crime being struck down as unconstitutional as a status crime,[270] Arizona[271] and Alabama made the prohibited conduct, the failure to register with the federal immigration agencies or failure to carry the required registration documents.[272] In Arizona, the first offense of this law is a class one misdemeanor, punishable by up to six months of jail time and an additional $500 fine, as well as jail costs. The second offense is a class four felony, which is also punishable by up to six months of jail time with an additional $1000 fine and jail costs.[273] In Alabama, a violation carries a fine of up to $100 and not more than 30 days in prison.[274]

These laws have also not overcome preemption challenges. As to Arizona's law, the U.S. Supreme Court rejected Arizona's argument that the law simply followed existing federal law and noted that the Arizona law was both field and conflict preempted since it imposed its own penalties for federal offenses that conflicted with Congress's existing framework.[275] The Court went on to observe that under federal law, failure to register is only a misdemeanor that may be punished by only a fine or probation; in contrast, the Arizona law ruled out probation.[276] Following the holding of the Supreme Court, the Eleventh Circuit cited the Arizona case Court's language that "even complimentary state regulation is impermissible" to hold that the City of Farmer's Branch law would dilute federal control over immigration enforcement and detract from Congress's comprehensive scheme.[277]

c.   "Driving While Undocumented"

Following the attacks of September 11, 2001, the Louisiana legislature enacted the Prevention of Terrorism on the Highways Act, which includes the felony of operating a vehicle without lawful presence.[278] The law had as its purpose "to complement federal efforts to uncover those who seek to use the highways of [Louisiana] to commit acts of terror."[279] Specifically, the law provided that "[n]o alien student or nonresident alien shall operate a motor vehicle in the state without documentation demonstrating lawful presence."[280] Violating the law resulted in

---

[270] *See, e.g.*, Robert J. Cottrol, *Outlawing Outcasts: Comparative Perspectives on the Differing Functions of the Criminal Law of Slavery in the Americas*, 18 CARDOZO L. REV. 717 (1996).

[271] *Arizona addressed trespass also through enforcement. Section 2 of SB 1070 provided that "trespassing by illegal aliens, if present on any public or private land in the state," required police officers to determine an individual's immigration status.*

[272] Section 3 of SB 1070 provides that "a person is guilty of willful failure to complete or carry an alien registration document if the person is in violation of [8 U.S.C. §§] 1304(e) or 1306(a)." In Alabama, an unlawfully present immigrant violates section 10 when he or she is found to be in violation of the same provisions.

[273] Ariz. Rev. Stat. Ann. § 13-1509.

[274] Ala. Code § 31-13-10(f).

[275] *Arizona v. U.S.*, 132 S. Ct. 2492 at 2504–05.

[276] *Id.* at 2505.

[277] *U.S. v. Alabama*, 691 F.3d at 1282.

[278] La. Rev. Stat. § 14:100.13 (2013).

[279] State v. Sarrabea, 126 So. 3d 453, 457 (La. 2013) (discussing the law's legislative history)

[280] La. Rev. Stat. § 14:100.13 (2013).

license suspension and punishment of not more than a year incarceration and/or a fine of not more than $1000.[281] The law had been used consistently to target Latino immigrants initially stopped for minor offenses such as speeding, malfunctioning brake lights, or driving with an expired license plate.[282] However, in 2013, the state's Supreme Court put the issue to rest when it abrogated several state of appeals holdings that had declined to hold that the Louisiana law was preempted.[283] In doing so, the court rejected the state's argument that regulating the highways is a state police function by noting that the law targeted only noncitizens and had little to do with road safety; moreover, the law imposed punishment for failure to carry documents solely regulated under the federal immigration laws, which made the law field preempted.[284]

d. Bail Restrictions

Some states, including Arizona and Oklahoma[285], have attempted to restrict bail for criminal defendants believed to lack authorization to be present in the United States.[286] Arizona voters passed Proposition 100, which amended the state constitution to forbid courts from setting bail in certain cases involving undocumented immigrants.[287] Under the law, persons charged with "serious felony offenses as prescribed by the legislature" were to be categorically denied bond if they had "entered or remained in the United States, illegally."[288] Shortly after its passage, the Arizona legislature defined a "serious felony" offense to include any class one, two, three, or four felony.[289]

Constitutional challenges to Proposition 100 based on substantive and procedural due process received mixed treatment by the Arizona Court of Appeals.[290] However, in October of 2014, the Ninth Circuit upon rehearing en banc struck down Proposition 100 by recognizing that the law infringed on a fundamental constitutional right to liberty and should be subject to strict scrutiny, which it did not satisfy.[291]

---

[281] *Id.*

[282] Comment, Annalisa Cravens, *"This Is Not the System Congress Created": Rethinking Louisiana's Immigration Law After Arizona v. United States*, 88 TUL. L. REV. 161, 162 (2013).

[283] *State v. Sarrabea*, 126 So. 3d at 453.

[284] *Id.* at 464.

[285] The Oklahoma Taxpayer and Citizens Protection Act also included a provision that permitting a rebuttal presumption of flight risk for undocumented criminal defendants. The Oklahoma Supreme Court in 2013, however, invalidated the provision as unconstitutional. Thomas v. Henry, 260 P.3d 1251 (Okla. 2013).

[286] García Hernández, *Creating Crimmigration, supra* note 24, at 1474.

[287] H.R. Con. Res. 2028, 47th Leg., 1st Reg. Sess. (Ariz. 2005) (amending Ariz. Const. art. II, § 22.

[288] *Id.*

[289] H.R. 2580, 47th Leg., 2d Reg. Sess. (codified as amended at Ariz. Rev. Stat. Ann. § 13-3961(A)(5)(b)).

[290] Contrast Hernández v. Lynch, 167 P.3d 1264 (Ariz. Ct. App. 2007) (upholding Propostion 100 as serving a substantial state interest) with Segura v. Cunanan, 196 P.3d 831 (Ariz. Ct. App. 2008) (holding that noncitizen criminal defendants must get a hearing to determine the legality of their detention).

[291] Lopez-Valenzuela v. Arpaio, 770 F.3d 772 (9th Cir. 2014).

D. CONCLUSION

The justifications of the criminal-immigration convergence have usually touted its usefulness, legitimacy and rationality.[292] The Obama administration, for example, offers two reasons for focusing on the "criminal alien": (1) the need to allocate limited enforcement resources in a politically palatable manner and (2) and the assumption that a focus on criminals will capture the worst and less deserving noncitizens.[293] Each of these justification have been theorized and applauded by scholars, including Professors Adam Cox and Eric Posner who view criminality as a useful proxy for non-belonging and undesirability.[294] As well, Professors Peter Schuck and Williams focus on the efficiency in enforcement that results when criminal and immigration enforcement agencies combine forces both federally and locally to maximize their effectiveness to rid the country to immigration law breakers.[295]

Other scholars caution, however, that the increased penology of immigration law is perpetuating the treatment of noncitizens not only as non-members but, further, as criminals, despite the fact that there is little empirical support for the conclusion that immigrants are more prone to crime than the native born.[296] Like citizen "criminals," the result is a separation and isolation of the "criminal element" from society, either through incarceration or other collateral consequences that do little to reintegrate them as members of society.[297] Unlike citizens, however, noncitizens criminalization ultimately results in their physical expulsion and/or banishment from United States and from their family and communal ties. Not surprisingly, many attempt to come back given that their criminal histories cannot erase the significant ties they have built in the United States.[298] When they do come back, they encounter new and tougher re-entry crimes, resulting in increased costs to the criminal justice system. As well, for nearly all immigrants and especially those with a criminal record, reintegration as a goal once in their country of birth, now a strange land after years in the United States, is even more elusive.[299] Furthermore,

---

[292] Allegra M. McCleod, *The U.S. Criminal-Immigration Convergence and its Possible Undoing*, 49 AM. CRIM. L. REV. 105, 126 (2012).

[293] *See id.* at 125.

[294] *See generally* Adam B. Cox & Eric A. Posner, *The Second-Order Structure of Immigration Law*, 59 STAN. L. REV. 809 (2007).

[295] *See generally* Peter H. Shuck & John Williams, *Removing Criminal Aliens: The Pitfalls and Promises of Federalism*, 22 HARV. J. L. & PUB. POL'Y 367 (1999).

[296] *See* Chacón, *Unsecured Borders*, *supra* note 22, at 1840–41 and 1850–56 and 1879–80. *See also* Kirk Semple, *Deportations Have "No Observable Effect" on Crime Rate, Study Concludes*, N.Y. TIMES, Sept. 3, 2014.

[297] Stumpft, *The Crimmigration Crisis*, *supra* note 19, at 403–05. *See also* Miller, *supra* note 20, at 654–55.

[298] McLeod, *The U.S. Criminal-Immigration Convergence*, *supra* note 292, at 133–35 (questioning the legitimacy of using criminality as proxy for non-belonging).

[299] M. Kathleen Dingeman and Rubén G. Rumbaut, *The Immigration-Crime Nexus And Post-Deportation Experiences: Encountering Stereotypes In Southern California And El Salvador*, 31 U. LA VERNE L. REV. 363, 388–401 (2010) (case study of El Salvador deportees); Bryan Lonegan, *American Diaspora: The Deportation of Lawful Residents from the United States and The Destruction of their Families*, 32 N.Y.U. REV. L. & SOC. CHANGE 55, 72–77 (2007) (making the case deportees and their children

removal is seldom an effective security tool.[300] First, many who are labeled a security threat in the immigration context simply are not, even when they have committed crimes given how vast the removal net is casted even against low level offenders.[301] Second, removal can even aggravate the commission of crime whose effects, which, even if committed abroad, are transnational.[302] At least those expelled for having committed non-immigration property crimes, their expulsion aggravates the factors that would make them likely to reoffend. Rehabilitation literature strongly points to substance abuse, mental illness, and a lack of social support as the primary causes of crime and recidivism.[303] Addressing these problems call for substantial resources. Indeed, the convergence of immigration and criminal law enforcement often means that limited law enforcement resources are diverted away from the pursuit of more serious crimes.[304] As well, criminal removals have also aggravated transnational crime and violence, particularly in nations ill-equipped or unwilling to address the challenges of rehabilitation.[305] Not unlike the recidivism as a symptom of the failed criminal justice system,[306] physical expulsion, even when it means life banishment, does not disappear, but rather aggravates, the underlying problems of violence in the sending nations. For the United States, the problem returns as thousands of victims attempt to flee unfettered violence, in part caused or aggravated by the mass removal of criminals from the United States.[307]

---

have suffered high levels of Post-Traumatic Stress Disorder).

[300] *See* Chacón, *Unsecured Borders, supra* note 22, at 1857–61.

[301] *Id.* at 1861–65 and 1880–83.

[302] *Id.* at 1875–79 and 1884–1888.

[303] E. Lea Johnston, *Theorizing Mental Health Courts*, 89 Wash. U. L. Rev. 519, 564 (2012); Wendy Heller, *Poverty, Poverty the Most Challenging Condition of Prisoner Release*, 13 Geo. J. On Poverty L. & Pol'y 219 (2006).

[304] McLeod, *The U.S. Criminal-Immigration Convergence, supra* note 292, at 130–31.

[305] Daniel Kanstroom, *Post-Deportation Human Rights Law: Aspiration, Oxymoron, or Necessity?*, 3 Stan. J. Civ. Rts. & Civ. Liberties 195, 218–220 (2007); Randall Richard, *AP Investigation: 500,000 Criminal Deportees from America Wreak Havoc in Many Nations*, A.P., Oct. 25, 2003.

[306] *See, e.g.*, Robert Weisberg, *Reality-Challenge Philosophies of Punishment*, 95 Marq. L. Rev. 1203 (2012).

[307] *See* N.C. Aizenman, *More Immigrants Seeking Asylum Cite Gang Violence*, Wash. Post, Nov. 15, 2006, at A8.

Chapter 16

THE RIGHTS AND RESPONSIBILITIES OF IMMIGRANTS

A. PUBLIC BENEFITS

With the implementation of recent sweeping welfare reform legislation, the Personal Responsibility and Work Opportunity Reconciliation Act of 1996, federal public assistance programs became unavailable to permanent resident and undocumented aliens alike. The law authorized state and local governments to deny locally-funded benefits to legal immigrants, transgressing the long-standing tradition of treating citizens and legal immigrants alike in terms of public benefits eligibility.[1]Although a budget compromise in 1997 allowed refugees and lawful immigrants who were in the United States prior to the 1996 reform to continue receiving benefits, new immigrants and refugees would be severely affected.

The law bars new immigrants from "federal means-tested public benefits" during the five years after they secure qualified immigrant status. Those benefits include Medicaid (except for emergency medical care), State Children's Health Insurance Program (SCHIP), Temporary Assistance to Needy Families (TANF), Food Stamps, and Supplemental Security Income (SSI). SSI provides monthly cash grants to low-income persons who are aged, blind, or disabled. Food Stamps are vouchers, redeemable for food at participating vendors. The only classes of

---

[1] *See* Graham v. Richardson, 403 U.S. 365 (1971).

immigrants exempted from these restrictions are (1) refugees, asylees, and individuals granted withholding of deportation, but only for the first five years after being granted that status; (2) active duty service members, veterans, and their direct family members; and (3) lawful permanent residents who can prove that they have worked at least 40 qualifying quarters (10 years) for social security purposes.

Since welfare reform legislation authorizes states to exercise the option to pass legislation denying legal immigrants access to state-administered federal programs, a range of benefits can be affected: nonemergency Medicaid, Title XX social services block grants, and Temporary Assistance to Needy Families (TANF), the state block grant program that replaced Aid to Families with Dependent Children (AFDC). States use Title XX social services block grants for a variety of purposes, including child care, programs to combat family violence, and in-home care for disabled persons. As the costs of social welfare programs shift to the states, states will face increasing temptations to exercise their option to deny legal immigrants assistance under these programs. The same classes of legal immigrants exempt from federal SSI and Food Stamps restrictions are shielded from state-adopted restrictions.

"Not qualified" immigrants remain eligible for emergency Medicaid, if they are otherwise eligible for their state's Medicaid program. The 1996 law does not restrict access to public health programs providing immunization and/or treatment of communicable disease symptoms (whether or not those symptoms are caused by such disease). School breakfast and lunch programs remain open to all children regardless of immigration status, and every state has opted to provide access to the Special Supplemental Nutrition Program for Women, Infants, and Children (WIC). Also exempted from the restrictions are in-kind services necessary to protect life or safety, as long as the program is not conditioned on a person's income or resources.

Undocumented immigrants are barred from receiving any of the chief federal public benefit programs: TANF, Food Stamps, Medicaid, SSI, unemployment compensation, school loans and grants, and subsidized housing. Many of these programs have been historically closed to undocumented immigrants. However, under former law, immigrants were eligible to receive Medicaid, SSI, and AFDC if they were considered to be "permanently residing in the United States under color of law,"[2]a category eliminated by welfare reform's blanket bar against unqualified immigrants. Prior law also enabled immigrants to qualify for social security benefits and unemployment compensation if they had employment authorization and a valid social security number. These programs are not completely foreclosed to all unqualified immigrants.

Many states have worked to fill in some of the gaps in non-citizen coverage mandated by the 1996 laws. In fact, over half of the states spend their own money to cover at least some of the immigrants who are ineligible for federally funded services. A growing number of states or counties provide health coverage to children and/or pregnant women, regardless of their immigration status. State-funded programs are often temporary or at risk of being cut or eliminated, in state

---

[2] *See* Holley v. Lavine, 553 F.2d 845 (2d Cir. 1977). *See generally* Bill Ong Hing, *Don't Give Me Your Tired, Your Poor: Conflicted Immigrant Stories and Welfare Reform*, 33 Harv. C.R.-C.L. L. Rev. 159 (1998).

budget battles. In determining an immigrant's eligibility for benefits, it is important to understand the federal rules as well as the rules of the state in which an immigrant resides.[3]

The 1996 welfare law created two categories of immigrants for benefits eligibility purposes: "qualified" and "not qualified." Contrary to what these names suggest, the law excluded most people in *both* groups from *eligibility* for many benefits, with a few exceptions. The qualified immigrant category includes:

- Lawful permanent residents, or LPRs (persons with green cards).

- Refugees, persons granted asylum or withholding of deportation/removal, and conditional entrants.

- Persons granted parole by the Department of Homeland Security (DHS) for a period of at least one year.

- Cuban and Haitian entrants.

- Certain abused immigrants, their children, and/or their parents.[4]

All other immigrants, ranging from undocumented immigrants to many persons lawfully present in the United States, are considered "not qualified."[5]

In 2000, Congress established a new category of non-U.S. citizens, *victims of trafficking*, who, while not listed among the qualified immigrants, are eligible for federal public benefits to the same extent as refugees.[6] In 2003, Congress clarified that "derivative beneficiaries" listed on trafficking victims' visa applications (spouses and children of adult trafficking victims; spouses, children, parents, and

---

[3] Updates on federal and state rules are available at the website of the National Immigration Legal Center, www.nilc.org.

[4] In order for an immigrant to be considered to be a "qualified alien" under the battered spouse or child category, the immigrant must have an approved visa petition filed by a spouse or parent, a self-petition under the Violence Against Women Act (VAWA) that sets forth a prima facie case for relief, or an application for cancellation of removal under the VAWA. The spouse or child must have been battered or subjected to extreme cruelty in the United States by a family member with whom the immigrant resided, or the immigrant's parent or child must have been subjected to such treatment. The immigrant must demonstrate a "substantial connection" between the domestic violence and the need for the benefit being sought. And the battered immigrant, parent, or child must have moved out of the household of the abuser.

[5] Before 1996, some of these immigrants were served by benefit programs under an eligibility category called "permanently residing in the U.S. under color of law" (PRUCOL). PRUCOL is not an immigration status, but a benefit eligibility category that has been interpreted differently depending on the benefit program and the region. Generally, it means that DHS is aware of a person's presence in the United States but has no plans to deport or remove him or her from the country. Some states continue to provide services to these immigrants using state or local funds.

[6] The Victims of Trafficking and Violence Protection Act of 2000, Pub. L. No. 106-386 § 107 (October 28, 2000). Federal agencies are required to provide benefits and services to individuals who have been subjected to a "severe form of trafficking in persons," without regard to their immigration status. To receive these benefits, the victim must be either under 18 years of age or certified by the U.S. Department of Health and Human Services (HHS) as willing to assist in the investigation and prosecution of severe forms of trafficking in persons. In the certification, HHS confirms that the person either (a) has made a bona fide application for a T visa that has not been denied, or (b) is a person whose continued presence in the United States is being ensured by the attorney general in order to prosecute traffickers in persons.

minor siblings of child victims) also may secure federal benefits.[7]

With some important exceptions detailed below, the law prohibits not-qualified immigrants from enrolling in most federal public benefit programs.[8] Federal public benefits include a variety of safety-net services paid for by federal funds.[9] But the welfare law's definition does not specify which particular programs are covered by the term, leaving that clarification to each federal benefit-granting agency. In 1998, the U.S. Department of Health and Human Services (HHS) published a notice clarifying which of its programs fall under the definition.[10] The list of 31 HHS programs includes Medicaid, the State Children's Health Insurance Program (SCHIP), Medicare, Temporary Assistance for Needy Families (TANF), Foster Care, Adoption Assistance, the Child Care and Development Fund, and the Low-Income Home Energy Assistance Program.

The welfare law also attempted to force states to enact new laws, after August 22, 1996, if they choose to provide state or local public benefits to not-qualified immigrants.[11] Such micromanagement of state affairs by the federal government is potentially unconstitutional under the Tenth Amendment.

The law includes important exceptions for certain types of services. Regardless of their status, "not qualified" immigrants remained eligible for emergency Medicaid,[12] if they are otherwise eligible for their state's Medicaid program.[13] The law did not restrict access to public health programs providing immunizations and/or treatment of communicable disease symptoms (whether or not those symptoms are caused by such a disease). School breakfast and lunch programs remain open to all children regardless of immigration status, and every state has opted to provide access to the Special Supplemental Nutrition Program for Women, Infants and Children (WIC).[14] Also exempted from the restrictions are in-kind services necessary to protect life or safety, as long as no individual or household

---

[7] Trafficking Victims Protection Reauthorization Act of 2003, Pub. L. No. 108-193, § 4(a)(2) (December 19, 2003).

[8] Welfare law § 401 (8 U.S.C. § 1611).

[9] "Federal public benefit" is described in the 1996 federal welfare law as (a) any grant, contract, loan, professional license, or commercial license provided by an agency of the United States or by appropriated funds of the United States, and (b) any retirement, welfare, health, disability, public or assisted housing, postsecondary education, food assistance, unemployment, benefit, or any other similar benefit for which payments or assistance are provided to an individual, household, or family eligibility unit by an agency of the United States or appropriated funds of the United States.

[10] HHS, Personal Responsibility and Work Opportunity Reconciliation Act of 1996 (PRWORA), "*Interpretation of 'Federal Public Benefit,'*" 63 FR 41658–61 (August 4, 1998). The HHS notice clarifies that not every benefit or service provided within these programs is a federal public benefit.

[11] Welfare law § 411 (8 U.S.C. § 1621).

[12] Emergency Medicaid cover the treatment of an emergency medical condition, which is defined as: "a medical condition (including emergency labor and delivery) manifesting itself by acute symptoms of sufficient severity (including severe pain) such that the absence of immediate medical attention could reasonably be expected to result in: (A) placing the patient's health in serious jeopardy, (B) serious impairment to bodily functions: or (C) serious dysfunction of any bodily organ or part." 42 U.S.C. § 1396b(v).

[13] Welfare law § 401(b)(1)(A) (8 U.S.C. § 1611(b)(1)(A)).

[14] Welfare law § 742 (8 U.S.C. § 1615).

income qualification is required. In January 2001, the attorney general published a final order specifying the types of benefits that meet these criteria. The attorney general's list includes child and adult protective services; programs addressing weather emergencies and homelessness; shelters, soup kitchens, and meals-on-wheels; medical, public health, and mental health services necessary to protect life or safety; disability or substance abuse services necessary to protect life or safety; and programs to protect the life or safety of workers, children and youths, or community residents.[15]

States can receive federal funding for TANF, Medicaid, and SCHIP to serve qualified immigrants who have completed the federal five-year bar.[16] "Humanitarian immigrants," refugees, persons granted asylum or withholding of deportation/removal, Cuban/Haitian entrants, certain Amerasian immigrants (described below), and victims of trafficking — are exempt from the five-year bar, as are "qualified" immigrant veterans, active duty military, and their spouses and children.

Approximately half of the states use state funds to provide TANF, Medicaid, and/or SCHIP to some or all of the immigrants who are subject to the five-year bar on federally funded services, or to a broader group of immigrants.[17]

Congress restricted eligibility even for many qualified immigrants by arbitrarily distinguishing between those who entered the United States before or "on or after" the date the law was enacted, August 22, 1996. The law barred most immigrants who entered the United States on or after that date from "federal means-tested public benefits" during the five years after they secure qualified immigrant status.[18] Federal agencies clarified that "federal means-tested public benefits" are Medicaid (except for emergency care), SCHIP, TANF, Food Stamps, and Supplemental Security Income (SSI).[19] No other programs are subject to a five-year bar.

---

[15] U.S. Dept. of Justice (DOJ), "Final Specification of Community Programs Necessary for Protection of Life or Safety under Welfare Reform Legislation," A.G. Order No. 2353-2001, published in 66 FR 3613–16 (Jan. 16, 2001).

[16] States were also given an option to provide or deny federal TANF and Medicaid to most qualified immigrants who were in the United States before August 22, 1996, and to those who enter the United States on or after that date, once they have completed the federal five-year bar. Welfare law § 402 (8 U.S.C. § 1612). Only one state, Wyoming, denies Medicaid to immigrants who were in the country when the welfare law passed. Colorado's proposed termination of Medicaid to these immigrants was reversed by the state legislature in 2005 and never took effect. In addition to Wyoming, six states (Alabama, Mississippi, North Dakota, Ohio, Texas, and Virginia) do not provide Medicaid to all qualified immigrants who complete the federal five-year ban. Five states (Indiana, Mississippi, South Carolina, Texas, and Wyoming) fail to provide TANF to all qualified immigrants who complete the federal five-year ban.

[17] See GUIDE TO IMMIGRANT ELIGIBILITY FOR FEDERAL PROGRAMS, 4th ed. (Los Angeles: National Immigrant Law Center, 2002), and updated tables at http://www.nilc.org/guideupdate.html. See also Shawn Fremstad and Laura Cox, Covering New Americans: A Review of Federal and State Policies Related to Immigrants' Eligibility and Access to Publicly Funded Health Insurance (Washington, DC: Kaiser Commission on Medicaid and the Uninsured, November 2004), retrieved from http://kff.org/medicaid/report/covering-new-americans-a-review-of-federal/.

[18] Welfare law § 403 (8 U.S.C. § 1613).

[19] HHS, Personal Responsibility and Work Opportunity Reconciliation Act of 1996 (PRWORA), Interpretation of "Federal Means-Tested Public Benefit," 62 Fed. Reg. 45256 (Aug. 26, 1997); U.S. Dept. of Agriculture (USDA), Federal Means-Tested Public Benefits, 63 Fed. Reg. 36653 (July 7, 1998). The SCHIP program, created after the passage of the 1996 welfare law, was later designated as a federal

Although the 1996 law severely restricted immigrant eligibility for food stamps, subsequent legislation restored access for many of these immigrants. Qualified immigrant children, the humanitarian immigrant and veterans groups described above, lawful permanent residents with 40 quarters of work history, certain Native Americans, lawfully residing Hmong and Laotian tribe members, and immigrants receiving disability-related assistance[20] are now eligible regardless of their date of entry into the United States. Qualified immigrant seniors who were born before August 22, 1931, may be eligible if they were lawfully residing in the United States on August 22, 1996. Other qualified immigrant adults, however, must wait until they have been in qualified status for five years before their eligibility for food stamps can be considered.

Several states provide state-funded food stamps to some or all of the immigrants who were rendered ineligible for the federal program.[21]

Congress imposed its most harsh restrictions on immigrant seniors and immigrants with disabilities who seek assistance under the SSI program.[22] Although advocacy efforts in the two years following the welfare law's passage achieved a partial restoration of these benefits, significant gaps in eligibility remained. SSI, for example, continues to exclude not-qualified immigrants who were not already receiving the benefits, as well as most qualified immigrants who entered the country after the welfare law passed[23] and seniors without disabilities who were in the United States before that date.

"Humanitarian" immigrants (refugees, persons granted asylum or withholding of deportation/removal, certain Amerasian immigrants, or Cuban and Haitian entrants) can receive SSI, but only during the first seven years after having obtained the relevant status. The main rationale for the seven-year time limit is that it was supposed to provide a sufficient opportunity for humanitarian immigrant seniors and those with disabilities to naturalize and retain their eligibility for SSI as U.S. citizens. However, a combination of factors, including immigration backlogs, processing delays, former statutory caps on the number of asylees who can adjust their status, language barriers, and other obstacles have made it impossible for most of these individuals to naturalize within seven years. During the 2007–2008 Congressional term, the House and Senate passed different bills providing a two-year extension of SSI eligibility to humanitarian immigrants who are approaching or were terminated from assistance due to the seven-year time limit, but as of

---

means-tested public benefit program. *See* Health Care Financing Administration, *The Administration's Response to Questions About the State Child Health Insurance Program*, Question 19(a) (September 11, 1997).

[20] For this purpose, disability-related programs include: SSI, Social Security disability, state disability or retirement pension, railroad retirement disability, veteran's disability, disability-based Medicaid, and disability-related General Assistance, if the disability determination uses criteria as stringent as those used for SSI.

[21] *See* NILC's updated tables on state-funded services, at http://www.nilc.org/guideupdate.html.

[22] Welfare law § 402(a) (8 U.S.C. § 1612(a)).

[23] Most new entrants cannot receive SSI until they become citizens or secure credit for 40 quarters of work history (including work performed by a spouse during marriage, persons "holding out to the community" as spouses, and by parents before the immigrant was 18 years old).

this writing no new law had been enacted.[24]

A few states provide cash assistance to immigrant seniors and persons with disabilities who were rendered ineligible for SSI; some others provide much smaller general assistance grants to these immigrants.[25]

Many immigrants fear that use of public benefits could jeopardize their immigration status. As we saw in Chapter 9, current immigration laws allow officials to deny applications for permanent residence if the authorities determine that the prospective immigrant is "likely to become a public charge." In deciding whether an immigrant is likely to become a public charge, USCIS or consular officials look at the "totality of the circumstances," including an immigrant's health, age, income, education and skills, and affidavits of support. Receipt of health care and other noncash benefits will not jeopardize the immigration status of recipients or their family members by putting them at risk of being considered a public charge.

Some immigrants and their families are deterred from using public benefits because they fear that their use of benefits will have negative repercussions for their "sponsors." Under the 1996 welfare and immigration laws, family members who file a petition to help a person immigrate must become financial sponsors of the immigrant by signing a contract with the government (an affidavit of support). Under this affidavit, the sponsor promises to support the immigrant and to repay certain benefits that the immigrant may use. The particular federal benefits for which sponsors may be liable have been defined to be TANF, SSI, food stamps, nonemergency Medicaid, and SCHIP. States are not obligated to pursue sponsors and states cannot collect reimbursement for services used prior to publication that they are considered means-tested public benefits for which sponsors will be liable.

B.   HEALTHCARE

Background

On March 23, 2010, President Obama signed the Patient Protection and Affordable Care Act ("ACA") into law,[26] with the purpose of expanding health insurance coverage through: (1) an individual mandate; (2) state-run health exchanges; (3) federally run high risk pools; (4) premium credits and cost-sharing subsidies; (5) expanded Medicaid coverage for families earning up to 133 percent of the federal poverty line.[27]

---

[24] The SSI Extension for Elderly and Disabled Refugees Act (H.R. 2608 and S. 821).

[25] *See* GUIDE TO IMMIGRANT ELIGIBILITY FOR FEDERAL PROGRAMS, 4th ed. (Los Angeles: NILC, 2002), and updated tables, *available at* http://www.nilc.org/guideupdate.html.

[26] Patient Protection and Affordable Care Act, Pub. L. No. 111-148, 124 Stat. 119 (2010) (codified in scattered sections of 21, 25, 26, 29, and 42 U.S.C.).

[27] Allison K. Hoffman, *Three Models of Health Insurance: The Conceptual Pluralism of the Patient Protection and Affordable Care Act*, 159 U. PA. L. REV. 1873, 1915–16 (2011).

In June 2012, the Supreme Court[28] upheld the constitutionality of the ACA's individual mandate,[29] which requires that all individuals maintain "minimum essential coverage" or pay a penalty for noncompliance. However, the Court held that requiring states to either expand Medicaid or lose existing funding was not a valid exercise of its spending power.[30]

Eligibility

Under the ACA, individuals who are citizens, nationals, or "lawfully present" in the United States are eligible for new affordable health insurance coverage options after January 1, 2014.[31] The U.S. Department of Health and Human Services defined "lawfully present" to include individuals who are: lawful permanent residents; humanitarian immigrants; survivors of domestic violence, trafficking, and other serious crimes; nonimmigrant visa holders; and longtime residents.[32] Humanitarian immigrants include refugees, asylees, applicants for relief under the Convention Against Torture Treaty, Cuban and Haitian Entrants, U.S. parolees, and individuals with temporary protected, deferred action, or special immigrant juvenile status.[33] Undocumented immigrants are ineligible for ACA and other federally funded health care benefits.[34] Although the "lawfully present" definition includes deferred action grantees, the Centers for Medicare and Medicaid Services (CMS) changed the rule in 2012 to explicitly exclude Deferred Action for Childhood Arrivals ("DACA") grantees from eligibility for the Pre-Existing Condition Insurance Plan ("PCIP") Program.[35] In response to this rule, U.S. Representative Michelle Lujan Grisham introduced the Health Equity and Access under the Law ("HEAL") for Immigrant Women and Families Act of 2014.[36]

Federally Funded Health Care Services

An individual's eligibility for federally funded health care services may vary depending on their immigration status. Generally, legally present immigrants are subject to the ACA's individual mandate and are eligible for premium tax credits, lower copayments, PCIP, and enrollment in qualified health plans from state insurance exchanges.[37] Medicaid and CHIP also are available to legally present immigrants who have resided in the United States for five or more years. Some states may opt to waive the five-year waiting period for children and pregnant

---

[28] Nat'l Fed'n of Indep. Bus. v. Sebelius, 132 S. Ct. 2566, 2584 (2012).

[29] 42 U.S.C.A. § 5000A (2012).

[30] *Sebelius*, 132 S. Ct. at 2607.

[31] 42 U.S.C § 18001 (2012).

[32] National Immigrant Law Center, *"Lawfully Present" Individuals Eligible under the Affordable Care Act, available at* http://www.nilc.org/document.html?id=809 (last visited July 10, 2014).

[33] *Id.*

[34] National Immigrant Law Center, *Immigrants and the Affordable Care Act (ACA), available at* http://www.nilc.org/immigrantshcr.html (last visited July 10, 2014).

[35] 45 C.F.R. § 152.2(8); 77 FR 52614 (Aug. 30, 2012).

[36] H.R. 4240 113th Cong. (2014) (would provide DACA grantees access to Medicaid, CHIP, and tax credits provided through the ACA).

[37] *Id.*

women who are legally present and offer those individuals Medicaid and CHIP benefits.[38] DACA grantees and undocumented immigrants are ineligible for non-emergency Medicaid and CHIP.[39] Although the Emergency Medical Treatment and Active Labor Act ("EMTALA")[40] offers emergency treatments to individuals who are ineligible for ACA, CHIP, or preventative Medicaid benefits, the ACA makes significant aggregate reductions in the funding hospitals use to offset EMTALA costs.[41] Additionally, undocumented individuals are ineligible for Medicare.[42]

Access to State and Local Health Care Services

In 2012, lawfully present and undocumented immigrants made up 19.7 percent of the over 47 million uninsured individuals in the United States.[43] Although federal funds may not be used to provide nonemergency health care to DACA grantees, recent immigrants, and undocumented immigrants, some states and local governments offer health care services to these populations. States may choose to offer Medicaid and CHIP coverage to children and pregnant women who are lawfully residing in the United States.[44] As of March 2014, 21 out of 50 states offer CHIP coverage to children and 31 out of 50 states offer Medicaid to children and/or pregnant women.[45] Additionally, 18 states offer at least one or more health care services to individuals "regardless of status."[46]

In the District of Columbia, for example, adults may be eligible for health care coverage through the DC Health Care Alliance, regardless of immigration status.[47] Additionally, children in the District of Columbia may be eligible for the Immigrant Children's Program regardless of their immigration status, if they are ineligible for

---

[38] Personal Responsibility and Work Opportunity Reconciliation Act of 1996, 8 U.S.C. § 1613 (2008).

[39] National Immigrant Law Center, *Immigrants and the Affordable Care Act (ACA)*, *available at* http://www.nilc.org/immigrantshcr.html (last visited July 10, 2014).

[40] *Id.*

[41] Emergency Medical Treatment and Active Labor Act , 42 U.S.C. § 1395dd (2006) (requires hospitals to offer treatment to anyone in need of emergency medical care, regardless of their citizenship status or their ability to pay for services).

[42] Michelle Nicole Diamond, *Legal Triage for Healthcare Reform: The Conflict Between the ACA and EMTALA*, 43 COLUM. HUM. RTS. L. REV. 255, 257 (2011); *see* 42 U.S.C. § 1396r-4 (2014) (stating that DSH funds will be reduced by "$1.8 billion for fiscal year 2017, $4.7 billion for fiscal year 2018, $4.7 billion for fiscal year 2019, and $4.7 billion for fiscal year 2020").

[43] National Immigrant Law Center, *Immigrants and the Affordable Care Act (ACA)*, *available at* http://www.nilc.org/immigrantshcr.html (last visited July 12, 2014).

[44] The Henry J. Kaiser Family Foundation, *Key Facts About the Uninsured Population*, *available at* http://kff.org/uninsured/fact-sheet/key-facts-about-the-uninsured-population/ (last visited July 12, 2014).

[45] Children's Health Insurance Program Reauthorization Act of 2009, H.R. 2, 111th Cong. (2009) (allowing states to offer CHIP and Medicaid services to children and pregnant mothers, including those who are within the federally required five-year waiting period).

[46] InsureKidsNow.gov, *Medicaid and CHIP Coverage of Lawfully Residing Children and Pregnant Women*, *available at* http://www.insurekidsnow.gov/professionals/eligibility/lawfully_residing.html (last visited July 12, 2014).

[47] National Immigrant Law Center, *Medical Assistance Programs for Immigrants in Various States*, *available at* http://www.nilc.org/immigrantshcr.html (last visited July 12, 2014).

Medicaid.[48] In San Francisco, California, "Healthy San Francisco" was launched in 2007 to provide universal health care for the city's residents — regardless of employment status, pre-existing medical conditions, or immigration status.[49] The program is not as good as health insurance because it does not provide medical care outside the city's borders.

Furthermore, uninsured or underinsured immigrants rely on the health care safety net, which includes federally funded community health centers, public hospitals, academic hospitals, local health departments, free clinics, family centers, and school-based programs.[50]

C. GENERAL EMPLOYMENT-RELATED RIGHTS AND BENEFITS

Except for certain areas when making U.S. citizenship a prerequisite to employment is considered proper (e.g., federal civil service jobs or state public functions jobs), for the most part, aliens have the same employment-related rights as those enjoyed by U.S. citizens. For example, federal minimum wage laws apply to employers who hire documented as well as undocumented workers.[51] Similarly, the federal Occupational Safety and health Act does not differentiate between documented and undocumented workers in its requirement that employers provide a safe place of employment.[52]

Undocumented as well as documented workers also are covered by the National Labor Relations Act. In *Sure-Tan, Inc. v. NLRB*,[53] the Supreme Court held that it was an unfair labor practice to constructively discharge undocumented alien workers by reporting them to INS in retaliation for participating in union activities. In accordance with *Sure-Tan*, the NLRB placed the burden of proof on employers to show that unlawfully fired alien workers were not entitled to be in the United States or eligible to work, and the only acceptable evidence was a final INS ruling to that effect.[54] The Supreme Court has added a serious wrinkle here, however. In *Hoffman Plastics Compounds, Inc. v. National Labor Relations Board*,[55] the Court held that undocumented workers discharged during a union organizing drive cannot sue for back pay for wrongful terminations under the National Labor Relations Act, at least under the fact circumstances of the case, in which the worker had given the employer false documents to get work and the employer did not discover that they were false until the time of the National Labor Relations Board proceedings. The court held that a back pay award was not an appropriate remedy. The Court found

---

[48] *Id.*

[49] *Id.*

[50] Sen. Bill No. 1005, Reg. Sess. (Ca. 2013–14) (held in Senate Appropriations).

[51] Nathan Cortez, *Embracing the New Geography of Health Care: A Novel Way to Cover Those Left Out of Health Reform*, 84 S. Cal. L. Rev. 859, 872–73 (2011).

[52] 29 U.S.C. § 201–219.

[53] 29 U.S.C. § 651–678.

[54] 467 U.S. 216 (1984).

[55] 535 U.S. 137 (2002).

that awarding back pay to "illegal aliens runs counter to policies underlying IRCA."[56].

Usually all workers, whether citizens or aliens, are entitled to worker's compensation benefits for work-related injuries. In determining eligibility, most state statutes are concerned with residence rather than immigration status. For example, in Florida, the definition of "employee" for worker's compensation purposes includes aliens, whether lawfully or unlawfully employed.[57] Alaska is one state that limits worker's compensation benefits to citizens, permanent residents, or aliens in the United States under "color of law."[58]

Unemployment insurance benefits are made available to workers who have quit work with good cause or who have been discharged without good cause. Benefits are drawn from a fund financed by state and federal taxes. The federal statute restricts these benefits to aliens who are lawful permanent residents, authorized to work, or who are in the United States under "color of law."[59] Furthermore, the unemployment insurance programs usually require that the person be "able and available for work," a requirement that undocumented workers who do not have DHS permission to work cannot meet. In contrast, unemployment disability benefits may be available even to undocumented workers because for disability purposes, the claimant does not have to be able and available for work.[60]

Social Security benefits are usually available to all former workers as long as they have contributed their share to the Social Security program and are aged, blind, or disabled.[61] Therefore, Social Security disability and old age retirement benefits are generally available to eligible citizens, permanent residents, and aliens permanent residing in the United States under color of law. Visitors and students, for example, would not qualify. Benefits also are payable to surviving widows and widowers who are undocumented or who did not even reside in the United States with the wage-earner spouse. However, the removal of an otherwise qualified alien can operate to terminate benefits under these Social Security programs.[62] Furthermore, Medicare benefits for retired wage earners are conditioned on five years of permanent residency in the United States.[63]

One of the difficulties in becoming eligible for Social Security insurance benefits today, however, is that the issuance of a Social Security number is forbidden to an alien who is not a permanent resident or refugee, or who has not been granted employment authorization from DHS. Note, however, that employers cannot avoid paying their FICA and FUTA contributions for employees on the grounds that the

---

[56] 535 U.S. at 149.

[57] 237 F.3d 639 (D.C. Cir. 2001).

[58] Fla. Stat. 440.02.

[59] Alaska Stat. 23.20.381(b).

[60] 26 U.S.C. § 3304(a)(14)(A).

[61] 42 U.S.C. § 401–431.

[62] *Id.* 402(n).

[63] *Id.* 1395o; *see* Mathews v. Diaz, 426 U.S. 67 (1976).

employees are undocumented and do not have Social Security numbers.[64]

D. EMPLOYMENT AND LICENSES

Most employment and licensing restrictions imposed by the federal government, state governments, and private employers have come in the form of limiting certain occupations to U.S. citizens. Some state licenses are limited to U.S. citizens or lawful permanent resident aliens. Whether such restrictions are proper usually depends on which entity has imposed the restriction and/or what the occupation or license entails.

1. State Restrictions

As a general rule, state restrictions limiting state jobs and the issuance of licenses to U.S. citizens have been subjected to strict equal protection scrutiny by the U.S. Supreme Court. For example, in *In re Griffiths*,[65] the exclusion of lawful permanent residents from the practice of law in Connecticut was invalidated, and in *Sugarman v. Dougall*,[66] a New York law providing that only U.S. citizens could hold permanent state civil service positions was struck down.

However, in the state employment area, beginning with *Foley v. Connelie*,[67] the Supreme Court has deferred to the state requirement of U.S. citizenship when the position entails a public function, or involves the "formulation, execution, or review of broad public policy." Thus, in *Foley*, the Court held that New York could bar aliens from holding state law enforcement positions. In *Ambach v. Norwick*,[68] the court ruled that public school teaching fell within the public functions exception as well. Similarly, in *Cabell v. Chavez-Salido*,[69] the Supreme Court indicated that probation officer positions in California could be limited to U.S. citizens. Note that some citizen-only statutes, such as the one in *Ambach*, provide that lawful permanent residents who file declarations of intent to become citizens under INA § 334(f) can also qualify for the employment.

Without the showing of the involvement with a public function or broad public policy, however, the state cannot require U.S. citizenship as a condition of state employment.

State laws that attempt to limit the issuance of certain licenses to U.S. citizens have followed the fate of the Griffiths case and have been struck down. In *Bernal v. Fainter*,[70] for example, the Supreme Court ruled that it was unconstitutional for Texas to require citizenship of notary publics in the state. In *Examining Board of*

---

[64] Rev. Rul. 82-116, 1982-1 C.B. 152.

[65] 413 U.S. 717 (1973).

[66] 413 U.S. 634 (1973).

[67] 435 U.S. 291 (1978).

[68] 441 U.S. 68 (1979).

[69] 454 U.S. 432 (1982).

[70] 467 U.S. 216 (1984).

Engineers v. Flores de Otero,[71] Puerto Rico's citizenship requirement for engineer and architect licenses was also ruled invalid. Similarly, it has been held that state liquor and dental licenses cannot be conditioned on U.S. citizenship.[72] Similarly, in *Raffaelli v. Committee of Bar Examiners*,[73] the California Supreme Court ruled that a lawful permanent resident alien who passed the bar examination should be issued a license to practice law.

The federal government takes the position that in order for undocumented immigrants to be issued professional licenses, the state legislature must enact legislation authorizing the issuance of such licenses. Under 8 U.S.C. § 1621(a), an undocumented immigrant "is not eligible for any State or local public benefit," defined in 8 U.S.C. § 1621(c) as "any grant, contract, loan, professional license, or commercial license provided by an agency of a State or local government." A public benefit can be provided under 8 U.S.C. § 1621(d), however, through the enactment of a state law. For example, the Department of Justice has argued under 8 U.S.C. § 1621 that an undocumented immigrant who has passed the barred examination is not eligible for a license to practice law unless the state legislature passes legislation allowing admission. Thus, in *In re: Sergio C. Garcia in California*,[74] the California Supreme Court admitted the applicant for admission to practice only after the state legislature passed legislation allowing undocumented immigrants to practice law in the state.

The issuance of driver's licenses to undocumented immigrants has been a topic of fierce debate. While the Tenth Amendment affords States the constitutional authority to issue driver's licenses,[75] in 2005, Congress enacted the REAL ID Act, which established standards for state-issued driver's licenses to prevent certain immigrants from obtaining these documents.[76] Many states have resisted this federal intrusion. Currently, 11 states — California, Colorado, Connecticut, Illinois, Maryland, New Mexico, Nevada, Oregon, Utah, Vermont, and Washington — and the District of Columbia allow undocumented immigrants to acquire driver's licenses.[77] State eligibility requirements typically include certain documents and proof of residence in the state.[78] Colorado, for example, allows individuals, regardless of lawful presence in the United States, to obtain driver's licenses, permits, or identification cards if they sign an affidavit declaring current residency and proof of Colorado income tax return filing for the previous year.[79] The applicant must also provide an Individual Taxpayer Identification Number and sign

---

[71] 426 U.S. 572 (1976).

[72] Kalra v. Minnesota, 580 F. Supp. 971 (D. Minn. 1983); Szeto v. Louisiana State Bd. of Dentistry, 508 F. Supp. 268 (E.D. La. 1981).

[73] 496 P.2d 1264 (Cal. 1972).

[74] Bar. Misc. 4186 (Calif. Supreme Court, Jan. 2, 2014).

[75] U.S. Const. amend. X.

[76] REAL ID Act of 2005, Pub. L. No. 109-13, 119 Stat. 302 (2005).

[77] National Conference of State Legislatures, *States Offering Driver's Licenses to Immigrants*, *available at* http://www.ncsl.org/research/immigration/states-offering-driver-s-licenses-to-immigrants. aspx (last visited July 15, 2014).

[78] *Id.*

[79] *Id.*

an affidavit stating that the applicant has applied or will apply for lawful status.[80] Georgia and Maine offer limited driving privileges to certain immigrants.[81]

2. Federal Restrictions

Unlike the strict scrutiny the courts give to state employment and licensing restrictions, similar federal restrictions are usually given great deference when it comes to noncitizen rights to federal employment or licenses. For example, an executive order limiting federal civil service jobs to U.S. citizens has been upheld.[82] A federal statute limiting all federal employment to citizens and aliens who have applied for naturalization has similarly been held constitutional,[83] although nationals of the People's Republic of China who were protected by an April 1990 executive order were granted special permission to apply for federal civil service jobs.[84] In addition, the limitation of FCC broadcasting licenses to U.S. citizens has also been upheld.[85]

E. EMPLOYMENT DISCRIMINATION

Prior to 1986, private employers could require job applicants to be United States citizens. However, as part of the political compromise that led to the passage of the Immigration Reform and Control Act of 1986 (IRCA), private employers can no longer limit job openings to U.S. citizens.

It is an unfair immigration-related employment practice for an employer to discriminate against a person authorized to work with respect to hiring the individual for employment or discharging the individual from employment on the basis of:

- The individual's national origin; or

- The individual's citizenship status, as long as the person is a *protected* citizen or alien.[86]

An employment discrimination provision was made part of IRCA for two basic reasons:

- Concern that some unsavory employers will use the law against hiring unauthorized workers (employer sanctions) as an excuse to not hire individuals "who look like aliens"; and

---

[80] *Id.*

[81] *Id.* (Georgia offers noncitizen applicants, who have filed a request for an extension to remain lawfully in the United States, a temporary driving permit. Maine allows individuals, who are older or long-time driver's license holders, to be exempt from proving legal presence in the United States for renewing a license or identification card.).

[82] Mow Sun Wong v. Campbell, 626 F.2d 739 (9th Cir. 1980), *cert denied*, 450 U.S. 959 (1981).

[83] Yuen v. Internal Revenue Serv., 649 F.2d 163 (2d Cir. 1981), *cert denied*, 454 U.S. 1053 (1981).

[84] *See OPM Clarifies Government Work Restrictions of PRC Nationals*, 69 INTERPRETER RELEASES 508 (Apr. 27, 1992).

[85] Campos v. FCC, 650 F.2d 890 (7th Cir. 1981).

[86] 8 U.S.C. § 1324b(a)(1).

- Concern that some employers will not bother to learn the employer sanctions rules carefully and simply "take the easy way out" by not hiring someone who "looks" foreign or who does not present a particular document.

The term *protected* individual includes the following:

1. Citizens or nationals of the United States;

2. Lawful permanent resident aliens;

3. Aliens lawfully admitted for temporary residence;

4. Refugees; and

5. Asylees.

An alien ceases being a *protected* individual if

- He or she fails to apply for naturalization within six months of the date of becoming eligible to apply for naturalization (usually after being a lawful permanent resident for five years); or

- He or she has filed for naturalization in a timely fashion but has not become naturalized as a citizen within two years of the application. This essentially covers applicants who fail to pursue their application after being called in for the naturalization exam or interview. Processing time utilized by INS in handling the application does not count toward the two-year period.[87]

Although *national origin* is not defined in the immigration laws, in the Title VII employment discrimination context, the term refers both to "the country where a person was born" and to "the country from which her ancestors came."[88] Thus, employers cannot favor one nationality group over another in their work force.

The IRCA immigration-related employment discrimination law does not apply to every employer. Exceptions include:

1. Employers with less than four employees;

2. Where the discrimination based on national origin is covered by Title VII of the Civil Rights Act of 1964, 42 U.S.C. § 2000e-2; or

3. Where the discrimination based on citizenship status is required or essential for an employer to do business with an agency of the federal, state, or local government.[89]

It is not an unfair immigration-related employment practice for an employer to hire a citizen or national of the United States over another individual who is an alien if the two individuals are equally qualified.[90]

Thus, an employer cannot limit job openings to U.S. citizens, but if two applicants — one a citizen, one a lawful permanent resident — are equally qualified, the law

---

[87] 8 U.S.C. § 1324b(a)(3).

[88] Espinoza v. Farah Mfg., 414 U.S. 86, 88–89 (1973).

[89] 8 U.S.C. § 1324b(a)(2).

[90] 8 U.S.C. § 1324b(a)(4).

permits (but does not require) the employer to hire the citizen over the alien. The employer must be prepared to show that he or she has specifically evaluated the qualifications of the two job applicants.

An unfair immigration-related employment practice does occur, however, if the lawful permanent resident is better qualified than the citizen, and the employer hires the citizen.

Employers who try to interfere with the rights of an employee or job applicant under the IRCA employment discrimination rules face penalties for that interference. An employer who fears that an employee is going to file a complaint against the employer risks making things worse if he or she tries to dissuade the employee from complaining. The law provides that an unfair immigration-related employment practice occurs when an employer intimidates, threatens, coerces, or retaliates against any individual for the purpose of interfering with any right or privilege under the general rule.

This interference is prohibited whether it occurs in response to an individual's intent to file or actual filing of charges under the law, or simply if the individual is helping someone else who is complaining by testifying or assisting in the investigation. An individual who has been intimidated, threatened, or retaliated against also can claim discrimination under the law.[91] Retaliation by employers against employees for availing themselves of state and federal labor rights is always a bad idea — even when the employee is undocumented.[92]

An employer can also be accused of an unfair immigration-related employment practice if he or she:

- Requests more or different documents than are required for purposes of the I-9 process (*see* Ch. 2); or

- Refuses to honor documents offered by the employee that on their face appear reasonably genuine.[93]

In order for an employer to actually be found liable for an unfair immigration-related practice in one of these situations, the government must show that the employer intended to discriminate.

Citizenship discrimination occurs when an employer disfavors a person because of the individual's citizenship or immigration status. One blatant form of citizenship discrimination that is a clear violation occurs when a private employer requires that all job applicants be U.S. citizens while none of the statutory exceptions apply to the employer's situation.

To consider whether citizenship discrimination has occurred, these questions should be considered:

1. Is the employer treating an applicant or worker differently than other workers because of the person's citizenship or immigration status?

---

[91] 8 U.S.C. § 1324b(a)(5).

[92] *See* Contreras v. Corinthian Vigor Ins. Brokerage, Inc., 103 F. Supp. 2d 1180 (N.D. Cal. 2000).

[93] 8 U.S.C. § 1324b(a)(6).

2. Is the person eligible to work?

3. Is the person a protected individual — U.S. citizen, national, lawful permanent resident, lawful temporary resident, refugee, or asylee?

Citizenship discrimination has occurred if the answer to all three inquiries is affirmative.

Thus, in addition to a "citizens-only-need-apply" rule, the employer can be liable for citizenship discrimination if

1. The employer says that only citizens and "green-card holders" can work for the employer.

2. The employer has a policy of not hiring refugees.

3. The person does not hire an applicant because the EAD has an expiration date, and the person is a protected individual.

Illegal citizenship discrimination by the employer is a prohibited activity that occurs in the context of hiring, firing, recruiting, or referring the person to work for someone else for a fee. The citizenship discrimination provision does not apply to other work issues that relate to the "terms and conditions" of employment, such as:

1. Promotions,

2. Salary increases,

3. Vacations, or

4. Work assignments.

If a worker is treated badly because of her citizenship or immigration status and that person resigns due to the mistreatment, the employer also may be liable for citizenship discrimination. Thus, an employer who hires a worker but then proceeds to not provide equal pay, or demotes the worker in terms of seniority, may be liable. If the employer's actions are so extreme that the worker has no choice but to quit, this may be the equivalent of firing someone based on citizenship status. This is called constructive discharge. Workers also are protected from retaliation by employers if the workers have filed a charge against the employer, or if they support the charges of another worker.

IRCA employment discrimination provisions cover only hiring, firing, recruitment or referral for a fee, and retaliation. However, changes in a person's working conditions also can be so bad that they would be considered a constructive discharge.

F. NATIONAL ORIGIN DISCRIMINATION

A person's national origin refers to the person's place of origin (or that of the person's ancestors) as well as those things (physical features, dress, language) that are identified specifically with the people of that place of origin. Thus, the Equal Employment Opportunity Commission (EEOC), which handles discrimination claims under Title VII of the Civil Rights Act of 1964, finds national origin discrimination when an individual is treated differently from others because of the "individual's, or his or her ancestor's, place of origin; or because an individual has the physical, cultural or linguistic characteristics of a national origin group." If a person is discriminated against because he or she is associated by marriage or in other ways with a particular national origin group, that discrimination also is considered to be national-origin based.

An employer who is guilty of discrimination based on national origin may be subject to a claim under the IRCA employment discrimination laws or Title VII of the Civil Rights Act of 1964. The injured party must elect only one of these routes. The main difference in the protections afforded by these two laws is that the immigration-related provision covers smaller employers while Title VII covers mainly larger employers.

Specifically, Title VII covers employers with 15 or more full or part-time workers, who work for at least 20 out of 52 weeks during the year. In contrast, the IRCA employment discrimination provision covers employers employing four to 14 part or full-time workers, and larger employers not covered by Title VII. For example, seasonal employers who have more than 14 workers, but do not employ them for at least 20 weeks a year are covered by the IRCA provision. Note that most states also have laws that protect against discrimination based on national origin.

The most common example of national origin discrimination is when an employer refuses to hire someone who is from a particular country. Thus if an employer does not want to hire people from Japan, or Mexico, or France, or Iran, that would constitute national origin discrimination. Similarly, if an employer does not want to hire a person who was born in the United States because that person's parents are from Iran, that too would be national origin discrimination.

An employer would also be in violation of the law if the job applicant in a sense represents a particular national origin. For example, if an applicant's spouse is from Mexico, many of the applicant's friends are of Mexican origin, and the employer refuses to hire the applicant due to those reasons, that would be problematic. Similarly, if one spouse has adopted the Japanese surname of the other spouse and the employer refuses employment because of the surname, discrimination has occurred.

Some jobs require a higher level of English proficiency than others. If an employer requires a certain level of English proficiency for a particular position, the employer must be able to provide justification for the particular level of proficiency required. A secretary is generally required to know more English than a janitor. If an employer requires more English than is reasonably required for a particular job, national origin discrimination may have occurred. Such a practice is discrimination if the effect of the requirement is that some qualified workers are treated differently than other qualified workers solely on the basis of their ability to speak English. The goal of the law is to ferret out those employers who are simply using English proficiency as a pretext for not hiring applicants of particular national origins. For example, in *Rivera v. Nibco, Inc.*,[94] 23 immigrant women who spoke Spanish, Hmong, Lao, or Khmer as their primary language were arbitrarily terminated because of their limited English proficiency. The women were laid off from manufacturing plant jobs they had successfully performed for years because

---

[94] CV-F-99-6443 (E.D. Cal. 2011).

they had failed to score 100 percent on an improvised written test of their English language skills. The plaintiffs reached a large monetary settlement after filing their lawsuit alleging discrimination under both Title VII of the Civil Rights Act of 1964 and the California Fair Employment Housing Act.

Discriminating against an applicant because of what is perceived as an "accent," can also be problematic. Generally, an accent should only be taken into account only if it interferes with the worker's ability to do the job. The employer cannot use an applicant's purported accent simply as a pretext for not hiring applicants from a particular country or region of the world.

An employer may be guilty of committing unlawful discrimination if he or she imposes a rule that requires workers to speak only English at certain times. Some courts allow English-only rules if the employer can show that the rule is required by a legitimate business necessity. For example, there may not be a legitimate business necessity for imposing a rule that workers cannot speak Spanish to each other during their breaks or at any time during work hours. But requiring that everyone helping on a surgical team in a hospital speak only English during surgery might be legitimate.

Some courts do not require employers to justify English-only rules by showing a business necessity unless

- The persons to whom the rule is applied have difficulty speaking English, or

- The rule is applied in such a way as to create a work environment that is hostile to workers from minority national origin or language groups.

G.　INCOME TAX CONSIDERATIONS

For federal income tax purposes, if aliens are considered a resident, their entire worldwide income is taxable, but nonresidents are subject to tax on income earned in the United States.[95] The determination of whether an alien is considered a resident or nonresident for federal income tax purposes is not, however, controlled by immigrant or nonimmigrant status.

The Tax Reform Act of 1984[96] provides a definition of resident alien for U.S. income tax purpose. Under § 7701(b) of the Internal Revenue Code, aliens will be considered residents if they have either (1) been a lawful permanent resident of the United States during the calendar year, or (2) meet the requirements of a substantial preference test.

In general, the substantial preference test is met if the alien has been present in the United States for 31 days or more during the current calendar year and for 183 days within the last three years, as computed under a formula that counts each day present in the country in the current calendar year as a full day, each day in the first preceding year as one-third of a day, and each day in the second preceding year as one-sixth of a day.

---

[95] IRC § 871; 26 C.F.R. § 1.1; Di Portanova v. United States, 690 F.2d 169 (Ct. Cl. 1982).

[96] Pub. L. No. 98-369, 98 Stat. 494 (1984).

If an individual is present in the United State for fewer than 183 days during the calendar year and establishes that he or she has a closer connection with a foreign country than with the United States and a tax home in that country for the year, the individual will usually not be subject to tax as a resident on account of the substantial preference test. Maintenance of a U.S. abode will not automatically prevent an individual from establishing a tax home in a foreign country.[97] But if an individual is present for as many as 183 days during a year, this closer connections/ tax-home exception will not be available.

The closer-connections/tax-home exception is also not available if the alien has an application for lawful permanent residence pending, or has taken steps to apply for lawful permanent residence. Filing preliminary forms is considered an affirmative step toward seeking permanent residence status.

The closer-connections/tax-home exception does apply to an alien who could not physically leave the United States because of a medical condition that arouse during the person's presence, even if the person was present for more than 182 days during the year.

Time spent in the United States on a valid F-1, J-1, or diplomatic visa is not counted for purposes of the substantial preference test. However, this exemption does not apply if the alien was exempted on this basis for any part of two of the six preceding calendar years.

Resident and nonresident aliens are also subject to state income tax, depending on the state residence.

Provisions in 26 C.F.R. §§ 301 *et seq.* provide an additional gloss on the definition of resident alien for tax purposes. For example, generally, aliens are deemed to be resident aliens with respect to a calendar year if they are lawful permanent residents of the United States at any time during that year.

Aliens who do not qualify for a Social Security number cannot claim the earned income tax credit (EIC). The EIC is a federal tax credit for working families who have moderately low incomes. To qualify for the tax credit, the family unit must contain at least one child, who must have resided in the taxpayer's home for at least half the year.

Until 1993, aliens who did not have a Social Security number were able to file a tax return and claim the EIC by writing in the words "applied for" or "section 503(c)" in lieu of providing a Social Security number. Beginning with the 1994 tax year, the IRS required each taxpayer, spouse, dependent, and EIC-qualifying child to provide a valid number, or be subject to delays and penalties. The practice varied, however, depending upon the particular IRS office processing the claim.

Only aliens who have DHS-issued employment authorization may obtain a Social Security number that allows them to post earnings and qualifying quarters to their Social Security account. Aliens who are residing lawfully in the United States, such as nonimmigrants, but who do not have employment authorization, may obtain a non-work Social Security number for certain limited purposes. But this non-work

---

[97] IRC §§ 162(a)(2), 911(d)(3).

card will not be acceptable proof of employment eligibility for purposes of satisfying the I-9 employment verification requirements, posting earnings to a Social Security account, or claiming the EIC. Only persons who include their taxpayer identification number (defined as the Social Security number) and that of their spouse may claim the EIC.[98]

H. EDUCATION BENEFITS

Children in the United States, citizens, permanent residents, refugees, and undocumented alien children have a right to attend elementary public schools. *Plyler v. Doe.*[99] The importance of such education is too great to deny to children as a class on the basis of immigration status. Similarly, in institutions of higher education, it is unconstitutional for a state to require lawful permanent residents or refugees who have met all other residency requirements to pay additional nonresident tuition.[100]

Higher Education

Nonimmigrants who enter the United States to attend school, such as with F-1 visas, are usually charged a higher nonresident tuition fee in state colleges and universities because by virtue of their status they do not hold the requisite intent to establish domicile.[101] However, there is support for the proposition that loan, scholarship, and financial aid programs for colleges and universities cannot be limited solely to U.S. citizens.[102]

The Supreme Court established that access to free primary and secondary public education to all students, regardless of their immigration status, was a right protected under the Equal Protection Clause of the Fourteenth Amendment.[103] The Court, however, did not specify whether these rights extended to the postsecondary education context. In 1996, Congress enacted section 505 of the Illegal Immigration Reform and Immigrant Responsibility Act ("IIRIRA"),[104] which states

> [A]n alien who is not lawfully present in the United States shall not be eligible on the basis of residence within a State (or a political subdivision) for any postsecondary education benefit unless a citizen or national of the United States is eligible for such a benefit (in no less an amount, duration, and scope) without regard to whether the citizen or national is such a resident.

---

[98] IRC § 32(c)(1)(F).

[99] 457 U.S. 202 (1982).

[100] Jagnandan v. Giles, 379 F. Supp. 1178 (N.D. Miss. 1974).

[101] *Cf.* Toll v. Moreno, 458 U.S. 1 (1982).

[102] Nyquist v. Mauclet, 432 US. 1 (1977); Chapman v. Gerard, 456 F.2d 577 (3d Cir. 1972).

[103] Plyler v. Doe, 457 U.S. 202, 220–22 (1982) (holding that the "denial of education to some isolated group of children poses an affront to one of the goals of the Equal Protection Clause: the abolition of governmental barriers presenting unreasonable obstacles to advancement on the basis of individual merit.").

[104] Illegal Immigration Reform and Immigrant Responsibility Act, 8 U.S.C. § 1623(a) (applies to any benefit provided after July 1, 1998) (1996).

This statute applies to state or local postsecondary education benefits, including qualifying for in-state tuition rates.[105] However, the Personal Responsibility and Work Opportunity Reconciliation Act of 1996 ("PRWORA") allows states to provide any State or local public benefit to individuals who are not lawfully present in the United States through the enactment of a State law, which provides for such eligibility.[106]

State Laws

In response to federal legislation, Texas[107] and California[108] passed state laws that allow undocumented students who meet specific requirements to qualify for in-state tuition. Since 2001, 18 states have enacted similar state laws extending in-state tuition to qualified undocumented students.[109] In Rhode Island and Hawaii, the respective governing boards have voted to offer in-state tuition to the states' public colleges and universities to eligible students, regardless of immigration status.[110] Furthermore, although undocumented students are ineligible for federal financial aid, states like California, Minnesota, New Mexico, Texas, and Washington, allow undocumented students to receive state financial aid.[111] For example, California's AB 130 allows students who meet the in-state tuition requirements to apply for and receive scholarships derived from non-state funds; AB 131 allows such students to receive Cal Grants and other state aid.

Generally, state laws use similar eligibility requirements including: (1) attendance at a state school for a certain number of years; (2) graduation from high school in the state; and (3) signed affidavit stating they have either applied or will apply to legalize their status.[112] However, state laws granting in-state tuition to undocumented students may be categorized into one of two models: the California Model or the Texas Model.[113] The California Model offers an exemption to students from paying non-resident tuition and does not classify undocumented students as residents, whereas the Texas Model classifies qualified undocumented students as

---

[105] 8 U.S.C. § 1621(c)(1)(B) (1998).

[106] 8 U.S.C § 1621(d) (1998).

[107] TEX. EDUC. CODE § 54.052.

[108] CAL. EDUC. CODE § 68130.5 (2002).

[109] National Conference of State Legislatures, *Undocumented Student Tuition: Overview,* available at http://www.ncsl.org/research/education/undocumented-student-tuition-overview.aspx (last visited July 12, 2014) (states offering in-state tuition to undocumented students include: California, Colorado, Connecticut, Florida, Illinois, Kansas, Maryland, Minnesota, Nebraska, New Jersey, New Mexico, New York, Oklahoma, Oregon, Texas, Utah, Washington, and Wisconsin, with Wisconsin revoking its law in 2011).

[110] National Immigrant Law Center, *Basic Facts About In-State Tuition for Undocumented Immigrant Students,* available at http://www.nilc.org/basic-facts-instate.html (last visited July 12, 2014).

[111] National Conference of State Legislatures, *Undocumented Student Tuition: Overview,* available at http://www.ncsl.org/research/education/undocumented-student-tuition-overview.aspx (last visited July 12, 2014).

[112] National Immigrant Law Center, *Basic Facts About In-State Tuition for Undocumented Immigrant Students,* available at http://www.nilc.org/basic-facts-instate.html (last visited July 12, 2014).

[113] Jessica Salsbury, Comment, *Evading "Residence": Undocumented Students, Higher Education and the States,* 53 AM. U. L. REV. 459, 474 (2003).

residents.[114] States using the California Model include Maryland,[115] New York,[116] and Utah.[117] States using the Texas Model include Connecticut,[118] Kansas,[119] and Washington.[120]

While a growing number of states offer in-state tuition to undocumented students, states like Arizona, Georgia, and Indiana have enacted states laws explicitly prohibiting undocumented students from receiving in-state tuition.[121] Additionally, Alabama[122] and South Carolina[123] ban undocumented students from enrolling in public postsecondary institutions.

Legal Challenges to In-State Tuition Benefits for Undocumented Students

As states approve tuition and financial aid benefits for undocumented students, they also face legal challenges to those laws. For example, in 2010, both the California and Texas laws were challenged.[124] In *Martinez v. Regents of the University of California*,[125] students paying nonresident tuition brought suit, claiming that California law granting undocumented students in-state tuition violated IIRIRA, PRWORA, and the Privileges and Immunities Clause.[126] The *Martinez* court rejected the federal preemption claim that IIRIRA prohibited the California statute by noting that the statute offered a nonresident tuition exemption based on criteria other than residence.[127] The *Martinez* court also rejected the claim state law must specify that "illegal aliens" are eligible for in-state tuition and expressly reference PRWORA.[128] Finally, the court rejected the claim that the California statute violated the Privileges and Immunities Clause, stating that "[t]he fact that the clause does not protect aliens does not logically lead to the conclusion

---

[114] *Id.*

[115] MD. CODE ANN. EDUC. § 15-106.8 (2012).

[116] N.Y. EDUC. LAW § 355(2)(h)(8) (2012).

[117] UTAH CODE ANN. § 53B-8-106 (2012).

[118] CONN. GEN. STAT. § 10a-29(9) (2012).

[119] KAN. STAT. ANN. § 76-731a(2) (2012).

[120] WASH. REV. CODE § 28B.15.012(2)(e) (2012).

[121] ARIZ. REV. STAT. § 15-1803(B) (2012) ("[A] person who was not a citizen or legal resident of the United States or who is without lawful immigration status it not entitled to classification as an in-state student."); GA. CODE § 20-3-66(d) (2012) ("Noncitizen students shall not be classified as in-state for tuition purposes unless the student is legally in this state and there is evidence to warrant consideration of in-state classification as determined by the board of regents."); IND. CODE § 21-14-11-1(1) (2012) ("[a]n individual who is not lawfully present in the United States is not eligible to pay the resident tuition rate").

[122] ALA. CODE § 31-13-8 (2012) ("An alien who is not lawfully present in the United States shall not be permitted to enroll in or attend any public postsecondary education institution in this state.").

[123] S.C. CODE § 59-101-430 (2012) ("An alien unlawfully present in the United States is not eligible to attend a public institution of higher learning in this State.").

[124] Martinez v. Regents of the University of California, 241 P.3d 855, 861 (Cal. 2010); Immigration Reform Coalition of Texas v. Texas, 706 F. Supp. 2d 760, 765 (S.D. Tex. 2010).

[125] *Martinez*, 241 P.3d 855, 861 (Cal. 2010).

[126] *Id.*

[127] *Id.* at 863.

[128] *Id.* at 866.

that it also prohibits states from treating unlawful aliens more favorably than nonresident citizens."[129]

I. BENEFITS FOR DACA RECIPIENTS

Background

On June 15, 2012, the Obama administration implemented the Deferred Action for Childhood Arrivals ("DACA") policy.[130] Under DACA, the U.S. Department of Homeland Security ("DHS") can exercise prosecutorial discretion in granting administrative relief from deportation for young people who receive deferred action status.[131] Although DACA grantees are considered to be "lawfully present," this status does not confer any "substantive right, immigration status, or pathway to citizenship."[132] An individual's DACA status is valid for two years and may be renewed for an additional two years.[133]

DACA Eligibility

To be considered for deferred action under the DACA program, an individual must: (1) have been under the age of 16 when they came to the United States; (2) have continuously resided in the United States for at least five years since June 15, 2007; (3) be currently present in the United States; (4) be currently in school, graduated from high school, obtained a general education development certificate, or is an honorably discharged veteran of the Coast Guard or Armed Forces of the United States; (5) not have been convicted of a felony offense, significant misdemeanor offense, multiple misdemeanor offense, or pose a threat to national security or public safety; (6) not be older than 30 years old.[134]

Public Benefit

All DACA grantees may be eligible to apply for a work permit and a social security number,[135] however, access to other federal public benefits are severely limited. DACA grantees are lawfully present in the United States, however, under the Personal Responsibility and Work Opportunity Reconciliation Act of 1996, they are not considered "qualified" immigrants[136] and are ineligible to receive federal

---

[129] *Id.* at 869.

[130] Memorandum from Janet Napolitano, Sec'y of Homeland Sec., *Exercising Prosecutorial Discretion with Respect to Individuals Who Came to the United States as Children* (June 15, 2012), *available at* http://www.dhs.gov/xlibrary/assets/s1-exercising-prosecutorial-discretion-individuals-who-came-to-us-as-children.pdf (last visited July 17, 2014).

[131] *Id.*

[132] *Id.* (DACA grantees are not eligible for CHIP or Medicaid).

[133] *Id.*

[134] *Id.*

[135] National Immigration Law Center, *Frequently Asked Questions: The Obama Administration's Deferred Action for Childhood Arrivals* (June 13, 2014), *available at* http://nilc.org/FAQdeferredactionyouth.html (last visited July 17, 2014).

[136] 8 U.S.C. § 1641(b) (2008).

benefits including "any retirement, welfare, health, disability, public or assisted housing, postsecondary education, food assistance, unemployment, benefit, or any other similar benefit for which payments or assistance are provided" by federal funds.[137] As a result, the public benefits available to DACA grantees depend largely on state laws, programs, and eligibility requirements.[138]

Health Care

Currently, DACA grantees are not eligible for health care benefits under Medicaid, CHIP, or the ACA.[139] However, Congress is currently considering legislation that would provide DACA grantees access to Medicaid, CHIP, and ACA benefits.[140] DACA grantees may also access emergency Medicaid services and may be eligible to receive services through state-funded programs.[141]

Driver's Licenses

As noted above, eligibility requirements vary from state to state and DACA status alone is insufficient to obtain a driver's license. Still, DACA grantees are better positioned than undocumented immigrants because most states require a Social Security number, evidence of lawful presence in the United States, identity and date of birth, and state residency.[142] With the exception of states like Arizona and Nebraska, DACA grantees are eligible for driver's licenses.[143] Both Arizona and Nebraska state policies have been challenged.[144] In July 2014, the Ninth Circuit granted a preliminary injunction against Arizona Motor Vehicle Division's policy to deny DACA grantees driver's licenses.[145] The Ninth Circuit held that Arizona's driver's license policy violated DACA grantee's constitutional right to equal protection of the laws and that the Plaintiffs were "likely to suffer irreparable harm" due to the state policy.[146]

---

[137] 8 U.S.C. § 1611 (1998) (stating that "an alien who is not a qualified alien is not eligible for any Federal public benefit").

[138] 8 U.S.C § 1621(d) (1998).

[139] National Immigration Law Center, *Health Care and DACA Deferred Action* (Sept. 25, 2013), *available at* http://nilc.org/acadacafaq.html (last visited July 18, 2014).

[140] H.R. 4240 113th Cong. (2014) (would provide DACA grantees access to Medicaid, CHIP, and tax credits provided through the ACA).

[141] Children's Health Insurance Program Reauthorization Act of 2009, H.R. 2, 111th Cong. (2009) (allowing states to offer CHIP and Medicaid services to children and pregnant mothers, including those who are within the federally required five-year waiting period).

[142] National Immigrant Law Center, *Are Individuals Granted Deferred Action Under the Deferred Action for Childhood Arrivals (DACA) Policy Eligible for State Driver's Licenses?* (June 19, 2013), *available at* http://www.nilc.org/document.html?id=831 (last visited July 20, 2014).

[143] *Id.* (state officials in Arizona and Nebraska announced that DACA grantees will be ineligible for state driver's licenses.)

[144] *Id.*

[145] Arizona Dream Act Coalition v. Brewer, 757 F.3d 1053 (9th Cir. 2014).

[146] *Id.*

Educational Benefits

As "unqualified" immigrants, DACA grantees face similar challenges as undocumented students with regard to federally subsidized funding or financial aid for postsecondary education. However, like undocumented students, DACA grantees may be eligible for in-state tuition if they meet state requirements.

Chapter 17

CITIZENSHIP

E. Denaturalization

A. THE MEANING OF CITIZENSHIP

Citizenship is more than simply a formal legal status. Citizenship characterizes modes of participation and governance, embodies identities and commitments, and confers rights and duties.[1] Defined this broadly, citizenship also is not confined to any single nation; and within nations, to any single governmental unit, as it includes states, provinces, and other localities.[2] Nevertheless, the possession of formal legal citizenship in the United States, while it does not guarantee equality under the law or belonging[3] and despite pleas to narrow its significance,[4] remains fundamentally important and may even function as a precondition to rights and membership, particularly in a post 9/11 context.[5] This Chapter focuses on the types of formal

---

[1] Linda Bosniak, *Citizenship Denationalized*, 7 IND. J. GLOBAL LEGAL STUD. 447, 450 (2000). *See also generally* Kitty Calavita, *Law, Citizenship, and the Construction of (Some) Immigrant "Others,"* 30 LAW & SOC. INQUIRY 401 (surveying the literature on the various dimensions of citizenship); ROGERS M. SMITH, CIVIC IDEALS: CONFLICTING VISIONS OF CITIZENSHIP IN U.S. HISTORY 30 (1997) (describing citizenship laws as designating the criteria for membership in a political community and the key prerogatives that constitute membership); GERALD L. NEUMAN, STRANGERS TO THE CONSTITUTION: IMMIGRANTS, BORDERS AND FUNDAMENTAL LAW 3 (1996) (concluding that membership questions in the U.S. define the "domain of constitutionalism."); Stephen H. Legomsky, *Why Citizenship?*, 35 VA. J. INT'L. L. 279, 287–300 (1994) (analyzing the functions of citizenship in terms of political participation, rights and disabilities, symbolism and community, allegiance, sovereignty, and the world order).

[2] Linda Bosniak, *Multiple Nationality and Postnational Transformation of Citizenship*, 42 VA. J. INT'L L. 979, 1000 (2002). *See also* Yishai Blank, *Spheres of Citizenship*, 8 THEORETICAL INQUIRIES L. 411 (2007) (arguing that, contrary to its state-centered conception, citizenship is determined, managed, and controlled in three distinct yet intertwined territorial spheres: the local, the national, and the global).

[3] *See, e.g.*, S. David Mitchell, *Undermining Individual and Collective Citizenship: The Impact of Exclusion Laws on the African-American Community*, 34 FORDHAM URB. L.J. 833 (2007) (documenting especially the exclusionary effect of felon exclusion laws on African-Americans) and Rebecca Tsosie, *The Challenge of "Differentiated Citizenship": Can State Constitutions Protect Tribal Rights?*, 64 MONT. L. REV. 199, 200 (2003) (discussing the challenge of differentiated citizenship for Native Americans). *See also generally* William E. Forbath, *Caste, Class, and Unequal Citizenship*, 98 MICH. L. REV. 1 (1999) (critiquing the limited view of equal citizenship among modern liberal constitutional scholars which leave out social and economic rights and documenting the rise and loss of a conception of a broader conception of social citizenship in U.S. history) and Goodwin Liu, *Education, Equality, and National Citizenship*, 116 YALE L.J. 330 (2006) (proposing to address educational inequality among states by advancing a constitutional right to equal national citizenship).

[4] *See e.g. generally*, Rachel E. Rosenbloom, *The Citizenship Line: Rethinking Immigration Exceptionalism*, 54 BOSTON COLLEGE L. REV. 1965 (2013) (arguing for the erasure of the citizenship divide in the context of procedural protections); HIROSHI MOTOMURA, AMERICANS IN WAITING: THE LOST STORY OF IMMIGRATION AND CITIZENSHIP IN THE UNITED STATES, OXFORD U. PRESS (2008) (arguing that legal immigration should serve as a meaningful transition to citizenship and, as such, the gap between lawful permanent residents' access to public goods and political participation and that of citizens should narrow) and LINDA BOSNIAK, THE CITIZEN AND THE ALIEN: DILEMMAS OF CONTEMPORARY MEMBERSHIP, PRINCETON U. PRESS (2008) (arguing for treating noncitizens residing within the U.S. territory as closely to citizens as possible).

[5] *See e.g.*, The Honorable Karen Nelson Moore, *Aliens and the Constitution*, 88 N.Y.U. L. REV. 801 (2013) (discussing the constitutional distinctions created between citizens and noncitizens and also as between different classes of noncitizens); Nan D. Hunter, *Health Insurance Reform and Intimations of Citizenship*, 159 U. PENN. L. REV. 1955 (2011) (arguing that the exclusion of undocumented residents from the Patient Protection and Affordable Care Act reignites the fervor around what the relationship should be between membership in the U.S. community and meaningful access to health care); Catherine

citizenship available in the United States and examines how its acquisition, legal standing, and loss has been intimately tied to U.S. national identity struggles, including the ebbs and flows of racialized, exclusionary politics in times of heightened national security.[6]

B. ACQUIRING CITIZENSHIP

The United States recognizes three types of citizenship: (1) by birth in the country, or *jus solis*; (2) by descent or being the child of at least one U.S. citizen parent, also known as *jus sanguinis*; or (3) through naturalization. Every year, about 680,000 persons are naturalized as citizens, while about four million or so are born as citizens either here in the U.S. or by having U.S. citizen parents.[7]

1. Jus Solis

a. Its Origins

The United States is among a few nations, mostly in the Western Hemisphere, that assign citizenship on the circumstance of birth within the territorial boundaries of the nation, regardless of the parents' citizenship.[8] The United States adopted the doctrine of birthright citizenship directly from the British common law, which itself was derived from England's medieval past.[9] The Calvin Case, decided in 1608,[10] became the earliest, most influential theoretical expression of what became the

---

Dauvergne, *Citizenship with a Vengeance*, 8 THEORETICAL INQUIRIES L. 489 (2007) (asserting that citizenship as a formal status is enjoying resurgence of authority at present that is directly linked to a worldwide crackdown on undocumented migration); Audrey Macklin, *Who Is the Citizen's Other? Considering the Heft of Citizenship*, 8 THEORETICAL INQUIRIES L. 333 (2007) (noting the strong link between legal and social citizenship); and Linda Bosniak, *Constitutional Citizenship Through the Prism of Alienage*, 63 OHIO ST. L.J. 1285 (2002) (arguing that while " 'alien citizen' is not an entirely incoherent notion within the terms of conventional constitutional thought . . . the citizenship that noncitizens can aspire to remains limited in scope . . . because the constitutional ideal of equal citizenship is committed not only to universal rights . . . but also to an ethnic and national solidarity and to a practice of bounded national membership"). *But see generally* Peter J. Spiro, *The (Dwindling) Rights and Obligations of Citizenship*, 21 WM. & MARY BILL RTS. J. 899 (2013) and PETER J. SPIRO, BEYOND CITIZENSHIP: AMERICAN IDENTITY AFTER GLOBALIZATION, OXFORD U. PRESS (2008) (arguing that as the nation state and concepts of citizenship are diluted by the rise of international law and political institutions, citizenship has come to matter much less in ways that make citizenship a status with distinctive privileges, obligation, values, and attachments); and CHRISTIAN JOPPKE, CITIZENSHIP AND IMMIGRATION, POLITY PRESS (2010) (concluding that as human rights become more important than citizen rights, the future of citizenship is bound to be light).

[6] *See, e.g.*, Mae M. Ngai, *Birthright Citizenship and the Alien Citizen*, 75 FORDHAM L. REV. 2521 (2007) (documenting the nullification of birth citizenship for the " 'unassimilable' Chinese, 'enemy-race' Japanese, Mexican 'illegal aliens,' and Muslim 'terrorists.' ")

[7] U.S. Citizenship & Immigration Services, Naturalization Fact Sheet, Oct. 24, 2012, *available at* www.uscis.gov/news/naturalization-fact-sheet.

[8] Polly J. Price, *Natural Law and Birthright Citizenship in Calvin's Case* (1608), 9 YALE J. L. & HUMAN. 73, 74, 77 (1997).

[9] *Id. See also* Note, Lisa Maria Perez, *Citizenship Denied: The Insular Cases and the Fourteenth Amendment*, 94 VA. L. REV. 1029 (2008).

[10] Calvin v. Smith, 77 Eng. Rep. 377 (K.B. 1608).

common law birthright citizenship.[11] Sir Edward Coke, along with 14 other leading members of the English bench, conferred birthright citizenship on Robert Calvin, a child born in Scotland after James I of England acceded to the Scottish throne as James VI.[12] In doing so, Sir Coke held that all persons born within any territory ruled by the King of England were subjects of the King and owed their allegiance to him and were therefore entitled to all the benefits of English law.[13] Sir Coke further rooted his decision in the divine law of nature, [14] giving his theory of birthright citizenship the strongest possible foundation.[15]

Remarkably, birthright citizenship in the United States remained a status conferred by the common law for centuries, as opposed to through statutory or constitutional law.[16] The 1787 Constitution references birth citizenship but does not define it or confer it as a right. Even the Act of 1790,[17] the first law to address citizenship by descent and through naturalization, did not codify it as a right.[18] In 1830, thus, the U.S. Supreme Court affirmed that "[n]othing is better settled at the common law than the doctrine that the children even of aliens born in a country, while the parents are resident there under the protection of the government, and owing temporary allegiance thereto, are subjects by birth."[19] It was not until the aftermath of the U.S. Civil War, a struggle in part over slavery, that three constitutional amendments were adopted to foster racial equality: the Thirteenth Amendment, which abolished slavery; the Fifteenth, which prohibited race-based voting restrictions; and the Fourteenth, which, in addition to conferring citizenship rights, included a due process and equal protection clause. The Fourteenth Amendment, ratified in 1868, overturned *Scott v. Sandford*, which had declared that Black slaves and free Blacks were not "citizens," even if born in U.S. territory.[20] The pertinent parts of the Fourteenth Amendment read: "All persons born or naturalized in the United States, and subject to the jurisdiction thereof, are citizens of the United States and of the State wherein they reside."[21]

---

[11] Price, *supra* note 8, at 74.

[12] Calvin, 77 Eng. Rep. at 379.

[13] *Id.* at 409.

[14] *Id.* at 392.

[15] James H. Kettner, The Development of American Citizenship 1608–1870, at 17 (1978).

[16] Price, *supra* note 8, at 74.

[17] An Act to Establish a Uniform Rule of Naturalization, 1 Stat. 103 (Mar. 26, 1790), repealed by Act. of Jan. 29, 1795, 1 Stat. 414.

[18] *See infra* notes 124–130 and 172–177 and accompanying text (discussing the jus sanguinis and naturalization provisions of the 1790 Act respectively).

[19] Inglis v. Trustees of the Sailor's Snug Harbor, 28 U.S. (3 Pet.) 99, 164 (1830).

[20] 60 U.S. 393 (1857).

[21] U.S. Constitution, Fourteenth Amendment, § 1.

b. Birthright Citizenship for Undocumented Children

In recent years, citizenship by birth of children born in the U.S. to undocumented parents has come under attack by scholars and members of Congress alike.[22] Some who favor the restrictionist measures argue that a liberal policy of *jus solis* has encouraged unauthorized migration into the United States and rewards those who break U.S. immigration laws.[23] Others question the legitimacy of citizenship that attaches by birth for it involves no assent by the new citizen or by the parents when the parents themselves are foreign citizens. The concept of birthright citizenship is seen as medieval in origin and contravening the trend of contemporary political theory of citizenship by consent.[24] In contrast, some nations, like Germany, have moved in recent years toward introducing some aspects of *jus solis* citizenship in order to promote the greater integration to their increasing immigrant communities.[25]

Among those favoring a more restrictive doctrine of *jus solis*, some uphold the constitutional standing of birthright citizenship. They are, therefore, proposing a constitutional amendment to abolish birthright citizenship to children born to the undocumented in order to eliminate incentives for unauthorized immigration.[26] Others, however, argue that the phrase "subject to the jurisdiction thereof" understood historically and in light of the Fourteenth Amendment's legislative history, rejects a classical *jus solis* understanding of birthright citizenship under English common law.[27] Rather, they argue, the phrase "subject to the jurisdiction" imposed an additional connection to the nation requirement, measured in terms not

---

[22] The contemporary debates favoring the exclusion of children of undocumented parents from U.S. citizenship can be traced back 30 years ago to a book by PETER H. SCHUCK AND ROGERS M. SMITH, CITIZENSHIP WITHOUT CONSENT: ILLEGAL ALIENS IN THE AMERICAN POLITY (1985). However, attempts to restrict birthright citizenship in the U.S. is not new. For a historical account of this movement, *see* Rachel E. Rosenbloom, *Policing the Borders of Birthright Citizenship: Some Thoughts on the New (and Old) Restrictionism*, 51 WASHBURN L.J. 311 (2012).

[23] *See, e.g.*, Ron Paul, *Rethinking Birthright Citizenship*, LEWROCKWELL.COM, Oct. 2, 2006, http://www. lewrockwell.com/paul/paul346.html. *But see* Rosenbloom, *supra* note 22, at 314 (concluding that the persistent phenomenon of mixed-status families (those with documented and undocumented members) questions the premise of the "anchor baby" (babies birthed in the U.S. by their undocumented parents in order to gain legal status)).

[24] Schuck & Smith, *supra* note 22 at 4. *But see* Garrett Epps, *The Citizenship Clause: A "Legislative History"*, 60 AM. U. L. REV. 331, 372 (2010) (distinguishing the jus solis concept criticized by John Locke and others which locked in the allegiance of anyone born into the territory of the King to the evolved concept of jus solis citizenships recognized by the drafters of the Fourteenth Amendment). *See also* D. Carolina Núñez, *Beyond Blood and Borders: Finding Meaning in Birthright Citizenship*, 78 BROOK. L. REV. 835 (2013) (arguing that birthright citizenship is a more accurate indicator of membership than as when citizenship is derived from the status of parents).

[25] Citro Avitabile, et al., *The Effect of Birthright Citizenship on Parental Integration Outcomes*, 56 J. L. & ECON. 777 (2013). A problem that attaches to the more restrictive jus sanguinis citizenship model in the context of global migration is the growth in the population of stateless persons. *See, e.g.*, Polly J. Price, *Stateless in the United States: Current Reality and Future Prediction*, 46 VAND. J. TRANSNAT'L L. 443 (2013) (arguing that if birthright citizenship in the United States is amended to exclude the children of undocumented parents, it would exacerbate statelessness in the next generation).

[26] Price, *supra* note 8, at 78–79.

[27] William Ty Mayton, *Birthright Citizenship and the Civic Minimum*, 22 GEO. IMMIGR. L.J. 221, 224–225 (2008).

of the child at birth but through his or her parent.[28] To some, this requires that the child's parent/s be citizens or lawful permanent residents to claim a meaningful affiliation with the nation on the basis of consent and reciprocity, in contrast to the undocumented parents who usurped their way into the nation.[29]

Critiques to the revisionist interpretation of the Fourteenth Amendment include the textual meaning of jurisdiction, since the word does not usually mean allegiance or consent of the subject but refers instead to the power of a sovereign or of law over the subject.[30] A rebuttal to this textual meaning is that since the Fourteenth Amendment already requires birth in the U.S. territory, and, thus, territorial presence, interpreting "subject to the jurisdiction thereof" as merely subject to the sovereign or laws prescribes constitutional redundancy.[31] Other scholars contest the value of an ahistorical textual interpretation of the Fourteenth Amendment, although different historical facts are cited to reach different meanings. For example, the historical fact that undocumented persons were here, namely illegally smuggled slaves, who were nonetheless conferred citizenship under the Fourteenth Amendment, is cited as casting doubt on the reciprocal allegiance theory.[32] The proposed re-interpretation of the Fourteenth Amendment must also contend with evidence of a strong precedential value of the Calvin case in the U.S. colonies.[33] Prior to 1868, for example, the U.S. Supreme Court referenced the Calvin *jus solis* doctrine on five occasions,[34] as did also federal courts.[35] State courts especially transformed the doctrine from a medieval concept of kings and subjects to a

---

[28] *Id.* at 242–47. Rather than a constitutional amendment, thus, some legislators would seek only to clarify the meaning of the Fourteenth Amendment through statute. One example of such law is the Birthright Citizenship Act, which was last introduced in the Senate February 2013. The law would redefine the phrase "subject to the jurisdiction thereof" to include only (1) a citizen or national of the United States; (2) a lawful permanent resident whose residence is in the United States; or (3) a foreign national performing active service in the armed forces. To find the text of the bill, visit: https://www.govtrack.us/congress/bills/113/s301. A few states, including Texas, have also proposed to refuse to issue birth certificates to children whose parents could not establish U.S. citizenship or lawful residency status.

[29] *Id.* at 223 and 257–58. *See also generally* Schuck & Smith, *supra* note 22.

[30] Gerard N. Magliocca, *Indians and Invaders: The Citizenship Clause and Illegal Aliens*, 10 U. Pa. J. Const. L. 499, 512–13 (2008). Critiques to the revisionist argument also suggest normative reasons against it, including protecting egalitarian and equality principles, the nation's commitment to political justice, the desirability of governmental responsiveness to the interests of all over whom it exerts general jurisdiction. *See, e.g.*, Chistopher L. Eisgruber, *Birthright Citizenship and the Constitution*, 72 N.Y.U. L. Rev. 54, 72–96 (1997) and Jonathan C. Drimmer, *The Nephews of Uncle Sam: The History, Evolution, and Application of Birthright Citizenship in the United States*, 9 Geo. Immigr. L.J. 667, 671 (1995).

[31] Lino A. Graglia, *Birthright Citizenship for Children of Illegal Aliens: An Irrational Policy*, 14 Tex. Rev. L. & Pol. 1 (2009).

[32] Magliocca, *supra* note 30, at 513–14.

[33] *See* Price, *supra* note 8, at 141.

[34] *Id.* at 139 (citing to Inglis, 28 U.S. 99 (1830)); The Venus, 12 U.S. (14 Cranch) 253 (1814); Dawson's Lessee v. Godfrey, 8 U.S. (8 Cranch) 321 (1807); Lambert's Lessee v. Paine, 7 U.S. 97 (1805); M'Ilvaine v. Coxe's Lessee, 6 U.S. (5 Cranch) 280 (1804). *But see* Mayton, *supra* note 27, at 235–238 (arguing that two Supreme Court cases decided in the 1830s, Shanks v. Dupont, 28 U.S. 242, and Inglis v. Sailors' Snug Harbour, 28 U.S. at 99, departed from the jus soli doctrine to approve instead an "election" doctrine by which, in the wake of the Revolutionary War, persons might of their own will choose either British or U.S. citizenship) and Patrick J. Charles, *Decoding the Fourteenth Amendment's Citizenship Clause: Unlawful Immigrants, Allegiance, Personal Subjection, and the Law*, 51 Washburn L.J. 211, 218 (2012) (arguing that the first U.S. case to address directly the subject of citizenship by birth, Lynch v. Clarke,

doctrine of citizenship by birth in the U.S.[36]

A different counter-argument to the reinterpretation of the constitutional birthright provision rests on the historical and textual context surrounding the Fourteenth Amendment's adoption, including the co-terminus debates of the adoption of the Civil Rights Act of 1866 and the Amendment itself.[37] The birthright citizenship provision was adopted first in the 1866 Act, whose principal purpose was to recognize the citizenship of freed blacks.[38] Senator Lyman Trumbull proposed the language of the bill and then made substantial changes to the language without adequate (and at times confusing) explanations, which has caused a great deal disagreement among scholars as to the bill's original intent.[39] Originally, the language simply declared that "all persons of African descent born in the United States are hereby declared to be 'citizens of the United States'" but subsequently changed to "all persons born in the United States, and not subject to any foreign power, are hereby declared to be citizens of the United States."[40] In a letter to President Lyndon Johnson, Senator Trumbull declared that the 1866 Act made all persons born of parents domiciled in the U.S., except untaxed Indians, citizens of the United States,[41] leading some scholars to conclude that "not subject to any foreign power" in the bill simply meant domiciled in the U.S.[42] Other scholars, however, reject this interpretation because it would have meant defiance of the then prevailing international law that recognized the right of every nation to define its own citizenship rules with language in the bill that actually suggests deference to foreign powers.[43] Thus, to these scholars, the language supports an interpretation of citizenship that excludes those persons born in the United States but who are also subjects or citizens of other nations.[44] Senator Trumbull's later comments, however, cast even more doubt on this more restrictive interpretation since he simply replied "undoubtedly" when asked by Senator Cowen if the "gypsies of Pennsylvania" and the "Chinese of California" would be citizens under the bill.[45] The debates then

---

1 Sand. Ch. 583 (1844), did not hold that citizenship by birth vests automatically upon territorial presence).

[35] Price, *supra* note 8, at 139 (citing to U.S. v. Rhodes, 27 F. Cas. 785 (C.C. Ky. 1866) (No. 16, 151)); Case of Williams, 29 F. Cas. 1330 (C.C. Conn. 1799) (No. 17, 708). *See also* Bernadette Meyler, *The Gestation of Birthright Citizenship, 1868–1898, State's Rights, the Law of Nations, and Mutual Consent*, 15 Geo. Immigr. L.J. 519, 528–32 (2001) (discussing numerous federal and state cases that adopted the Calvin case jus solis doctrine, despite claims by certain revisions scholars of a single decision in 1844 of Lynch v. Clarke).

[36] Price, *supra* note 8, at 139–44.

[37] Mayton, *supra* note 27, at 241–47.

[38] Robert E. Melsel, *Jurisdiction in Nineteenth Century International Law and Its Meaning in the Citizenship Clause of the Fourteenth Amendment*, 32 St. Louis U. Pub. L. Rev. 329, 354 (2013).

[39] *Id.* at 356.

[40] Cong. Globe, 39th Cong., 1st Sess. 474 (Jan. 29, 1866) at 475–98.

[41] Melsel, *supra* note 38, at 355.

[42] Mark Shawhan, *The Significance of Domicile in Trumbull's Conception of Citizenship*, 119 Yale L.J. 1351, 1352–53 (2010).

[43] *See, e.g.*, Melsel, *supra* note 38, at 356.

[44] Melsel, *supra* note 38, at 357.

[45] *Id.* at 360.

turned on whether Native American should gain birthright citizenship.[46] Then the consensus became that only those Native Americans who lived outside tribal jurisdiction, and not those who lived within tribes and under tribal government, should gain birthright citizenship through the Act.[47] To achieve that, the text of the Act became: "[A]ll persons born in the United States and not subject to any foreign power, excluding Indians not taxed, are hereby declared to be citizens of the United States."[48] The argument here becomes that "Indians not taxed" meant to exclude Native Americans born under tribal jurisdiction, while "subject to any foreign power," included, according to the debates, "children born on our soil to temporary sojourners."[49] Some would interpret this latter phrase to mean "any child born on U.S. soil to parents who were temporary visitors to this country and who, as a result of the foreign citizenship of the child's parents, remained a citizen or subject of the parents' home country."[50] To other scholars, this interpretation ignores that during the debate common law precedent was cited to reject the claim that birthright citizenship would impose additional political or allegiance requirements on parents.[51] Read in this light, the phrase "subject to any foreign power" referred to the traditional exception under common law, which referred to children of ambassadors and enemy aliens in hostile occupation.[52]

As to the Fourteenth Amendment, Senator Jacob Howard proposed what would become the text of the amendment, including the wording "subject to the jurisdiction thereof."[53] There does not exist an explanation for the change in wording from the 1866 Act, but some argue that the single phrase was intended to capture both the "Indians not taxed" and the "not subject to any foreign power" of the Civil Rights law,[54] while others insist that the different wording of the Fourteenth Amendment emerged from a different political situation and its meaning should stand on its own.[55] A great deal of debate remains as to the meaning of the term and the Amendment's legislative history is far from conclusive, despite statements to the contrary.[56] When introducing the phrase, Senator

---

[46] Mayton, *supra* note 27, at 243.

[47] *Id.*

[48] Civil Rights Act of 1866, Ch. 31, § 1, 14 Stat. 27 (1866) (Senator Trumbull).

[49] Mayton, *supra* note 27, at 244 (citing to Cong. Globe, 39th Cong., 1st Sess. 2896 at 1117 (1866)).

[50] John C. Eastman, *Politics and the Court: Did the Supreme Court Really Move Left Because of Embarrassment over Bush v. Gore?*, 94 Geo. L.J. 1475, 1486 (2006). *See also* Melsel, *supra* note 38, at 358 (arguing that at the time, under British law, a British man born in the United States would still be subject to the Crown to the second generation).

[51] Cong. Globe, 39th Cong., 1st Sess. 2896 at 1832 (1866) (Rep. Lawrence) ("In the great case of Lynch v. Clarke, 1 Sand [Ch. 583 (N.Y. Ch. 1844)], it was conclusively shown . . . that all 'children born here are citizens without any regard to the political condition or allegiance of their parents.'"). *But see* Charles, *supra* note 34, at 223–224 (arguing that the common understanding of birthright citizenship at the time of the 1866 Act's adoption included compliance with the doctrine of allegiance as a precondition).

[52] Magliocca, *supra* note 30, at 507.

[53] Mayton, *supra* note 27, at 244–45.

[54] *Id.*

[55] Garrett Epps, *supra* note 24, at 350 (arguing that the drafters of the Fourteenth Amendment was a considerable more radical Joint Committee seeking to expand rights).

[56] *See id.* at 245–47.

Howard explained that it meant to exclude "persons born in the United States who are foreigners, aliens, who belong to the families of ambassadors or foreign ministers accredited to the Government of the United States."[57] Professor William Ty Mayton reads this explanation to deny birthright citizenship to aliens generally,[58] but that is far from clear as a different explanation is that the final qualifier means that only children of ambassadors or foreign ministers born in the U.S. would be excluded. On the floor debate of the Fourteenth Amendment, when the question turned again to Native Americans, Senator Howard provided the same distinction that was made during the 1866 Civil Rights Act debate, and it was in this context that Senator Howard explained that "subject to the jurisdiction" "ought to be construed so as to imply a full and complete jurisdiction . . . that is to say, the same jurisdiction in extent and quality as applies to every citizen of the United States now."[59] Those who would read a "connection" or "consent" requirement to the Fourteenth Amendment birthright citizenship suggest that this explanation of the "subject to the jurisdiction" phrase denotes a reciprocal relationship between the sovereign and subject at the time of birth or contributive responsibilities between them, such as to limit birthright citizenship to children of lawful permanent residents and perhaps citizens.[60] Professor Gerard N. Magliocca, however, challenges this reliance on the Native American citizenship debate to limit citizenship to undocumented children in that the framers of the Fourteenth Amendment intended the "subject to the jurisdiction" clause "as a way of enhancing trial autonomy, not as a tool for limiting citizenship."[61] Native American tribes, Magliocca explains, were differently situated than slaves because, while they lived within the U.S., most Native Americans retained their tribal identity and considered themselves as co-equal sovereigns; that is, they were on the same legal plane as foreign ambassadors with respect to citizenship.[62]

Perhaps more importantly, the U.S. Supreme Court has affirmed the conventional view that the Civil Rights Act of 1866 and the Fourteenth Amendment sought to affirm the common law approach to birthright citizenship and extend the rule to newly freed slaves.[63] In 1898, the Court upheld the birthright citizenship of children born to Chinese immigrants with permanent lawful status but no eligibility for naturalization.[64] Then, the Court observed that birthright citizenship for aliens had not been "contested or doubted until more than 50 years after the adoption of the Constitution." The Court resolved that "subject to the jurisdiction thereof" meant

---

[57] Cong. Globe, *supra* note 40, at 2890.

[58] Mayton, *supra* note 27, at 245.

[59] Cong. Globe, *supra* note 40, at 2895.

[60] Mayton, *supra* note 27, at 246 and Schuck & Smith, *supra* note 22, at 5. *See also* ohn *C. Eastman, Born in the U.S.A.? Rethinking Birthright Citizenship in the Wake of 9/11*, 42 U. RICH. L. REV. 955, 960–61 (2008) and Charles, *supra* note 34, at 227–231 (citing the statements of other Senators, including Senator Trumbull to argue that "complete jurisdiction" embraced the doctrine of allegiance).

[61] Magliocca, *supra* note 30, at 501–02.

[62] *Id.* at 505–06.

[63] For a historical discussion of the crucial 30-year period that elapsed between the ratification of the Fourteenth Amendment and the Supreme Court's justification of jus solis in *Wong Kim Ark, see generally* Meyler, *supra* note 35 and Charles, *supra* note 34.

[64] United States v. Wong Kim Ark, 169 U.S. 649 (1898).

to exclude only Native Americans, children of diplomatic representatives in a foreign state, and children born of "alien enemies in hostile occupation" in the U.S.[65] *Wong Kim Ark* remains the Court's final pronouncement on the issue of birthright citizenship for children of "aliens" born in the U.S., and lower courts citing to it continue to affirm it,[66] even when the U.S. born child has grown up outside the U.S.,[67] and, implicitly, in cases defining the scope of rights of U.S. citizenship children born to undocumented parents.[68] As some scholars have pointed out, however, *Wong Kim Ark* does not resolve definitely the question of the citizenship of children born from persons who do not satisfy the requisite temporary or local allegiance to the United States, or lawful residence or domicile.[69] Indeed, in 2004, in the case of *Hamdi v. Rumsfeld*, which turned on whether Hamdi, a U.S. citizen by birth, could be detained as an "enemy combatant" without the full due process guaranteed by the U.S. Constitution, friends of the court argued that Hamdi, the son of two Saudi citizens temporarily residing in the United States, was not a U.S. citizen under the proper interpretation of the Fourteenth Amendment.[70] While the Court neither adopted nor addressed the argument, Professor John C. Eastman, the counsel of record in the amicus curiae brief, celebrated the fact that Justice Anthonin Scalia referred to Hamdi in his dissent as a "presumed" citizen of the United States.[71]

---

[65] *Id.* at 682. Some suggest that it might be possible to equate undocumented immigrants to the "enemy alien" in hostile occupation exception to jus solis that already existed under common law. *See* Magliocca, *supra* note 30, at 522–26.

[66] The early cases between 1898 through the early 1900's citing to *Wong Kim Ark* concern Chinese individuals born in the U.S. *See, e.g.*, Lee Sing Far v. U.S., 94 F. 834 (9th Cir. 1899) (affirming citizenship of child born in the U.S. of Chinese parents who had permanent domicile and residence in the U.S.); and In re Giovanna, 93 F. 659 (S.D. N.Y. 1899) (children of Chinese nationals born in the U.S. are citizens and not subject to exclusion under the immigration laws on their return when their parents return from a temporary visit abroad).

[67] *See, e.g.*, Dos Reis ex rel. Camara v. Nicolls, 161 F.2d 860 (1st Cir. 1947) (child born in the U.S. of a Portuguese father and a Brazilian mother, who was taken by them as a child to a Portuguese island remained a U.S. citizen and did not lose citizenship through involuntary service in the Portuguese military); Perkins v. Elg., 99 F.2d 408 (C.A.D.C. 1938) (minor child born in U.S. of a naturalized U.S. citizen who took on his father's foreign citizenship as a child when his father abandoned U.S. residence and returned to his country of birth could elect to restore his birthright citizenship).

[68] These cases concern, for example, the entitlement of U.S.-born citizen children to stay deportation proceedings of their parents or to confer immigration benefits to "immediate relatives." *See, e.g.*, Coleman v. U.S., 454 F. Supp. 2d 757 (N.D. Ill. 2006) (holding that a removal order for the mother would not impinge on the child's Fourteenth Amendment right because he would remain free to live in the U.S.); Acosta v. Gaffney, 558 F.2d 1153 (3d Cir. 1977) (holding that parent's deportation order did not deny U.S. citizen child the right to live in the U.S. because her return to Colombia would merely postpone, but not bar, her residence in the U.S. were she to choose to return); Perdido v. INS, 420 F.2d 1179, 1181 (5th Cir. 1969) (deportation order against parents of a citizen child did not deprive child of a constitutional right); and Lopez v. Franklin, 427 F. Supp. 345 (E.D. Mich. 1977) (holding that not giving native-born citizens under the age of 21 the privilege to confer the "immediate relative" immigration benefit on their parents did not violate their rights as citizens). Other cases involve the citizen child's eligibility for social service benefits, despite their parent's undocumented status. *See, e.g.*, Intermountain Health Care, Inc. v. Board of Comm'rs of Blaine County, 707 P.2d 1051 (Idaho 1985).

[69] Charles, *supra* note 34, at 252.

[70] Epps, *supra* note 24, at 335–36.

[71] *Id.* at 336.

c.   Native Americans and Their Birthright Citizenship

As to Native Americans, their birthright citizenship today is recognized only through statute.[72] Even prior to *Wong Kim Ark*, in *Elk v. Wilkins*, a case involving a Native American born in a reservation, the Supreme Court held that an "Indian" born in the U.S. but within tribal authority was not born "subject to the jurisdiction" of the U.S. and thus did not acquire U.S. citizenship at birth.[73] Congressional conferral of birthright citizenship to Native Americans, moreover, was a gradual process that occurred over a considerable period of time.[74] Congress first granted citizenship to certain tribal nations through treaties as an incentive to remove them from the West,[75] or even as part of U.S. territorial acquisition of Mexico.[76] Congress also granted citizenship through legislation to certain tribes, and through the passage of the General Allotment Act in 1887, which codified for most American Indians the idea of dividing Indian lands into individual holdings to promote assimilation and destroy tribal relations.[77] The 1924 Indian American Citizenship Act[78] granted concurrent U.S. citizenship with their respective tribes on all Native Americans.

d.   Birthright Citizenship and the Territories

Birthright citizenship is also only statutorily recognized with regard to persons born in the U.S. "unincorporated territories," as such places do not form part of the U.S. within the meaning of "born in the United States" under the Fourteenth Amendment.[79] Today, these places include Puerto Rico,[80] American Samoa, Guam, the Northern Mariana Islands, and the United States Virgin Islands.[81] In a series

---

[72] INA § 301(b). For a thoughtful treatment on the exclusion of Native American from the Fourteenth Amendment, *see* Earl M. Maltz, *The Fourteenth Amendment and Native American Citizenship*, 17 CONST. COMMENT. 17, 555 (2000).

[73] 112 U.S. 94 (1884).

[74] Ediberto Roman, *The Citizenship Dialectic*, 20 GEO. IMMIGR. L.J. 557, 583 (2006).

[75] *Id.*

[76] The Pueblo Indians became citizens through the Treaty of Guadalupe Hidalgo. *Id.*

[77] *See id.*

[78] 43 U.S. Stats at Large, Ch. 233, at 253 (1924).

[79] Perez, *supra* note 9, at 1029. *See also e.g.*, Tuaua v. U.S., 951 F. Supp. 2d 88 (D.D.C. 2013) (Citizenship Clause does not guarantee birthright citizenship to American Samoans) and Nolos v. Holder, 611 F.3d 279 (5th Cir. 2010) (holding that persons born in the Philippines during its status as a United States territory were not "born in the United States" under the Fourteenth Amendment).

[80] At the time of U.S. acquisition of Puerto Rico from Spain, the U.S. insisted upon ratification of the Treaty of Paris in 1898 that the citizenship status of Puerto Rican people was subject to the will of Congress. Treaty of Peace Between the United States of America and the Kingdom of Spain, U.S.-Spain, Dec. 10, 1898, 30 Stat. 1754. In 1900, Congress passed the Foraker Act, Ch. 191, 31 Stat. 77, and declared that Puerto Ricans were "citizens of Porto Rico," a meaningless citizenship given that Puerto Rico did not retain any sovereignty. Perez, *supra* note 9, at 1036–37. It was not until 1917 with the Jones Act, Ch. 145, 39 Stat. 951, 953 (1917) that Puerto Ricans were declared citizens of the United States, although the grant was only derivative as the acquisition of future U.S. citizenship depends on the Puerto Rican parentage and not mere birth in the island. Perez, *supra* note 9, at 1037.

[81] Roman, *supra* note 74, at 586–88. Congress granted citizenship to the residents of the Virgin Islands in 1927, to the residents of Guam in 1950, and to the residents to the Northern Mariana Islands

of cases that became known as the Insular Cases, the U.S. Supreme Court adopted the doctrine of territorial incorporation, and thus sanctioned the exclusion of residents of unincorporated territories from Fourteenth Amendment birthright citizenship.[82] Combined, the Insular Cases hold that the term "United States" as used in the Constitution, excludes all territories which Congress has opted under its powers not to incorporate as part of the United States.[83] Some scholars question the constitutional validity of the Insular Cases, arguing that the common law codification of *jus solis* rule by the Fourteenth Amendment would confer citizenship on any person born in a place where the United States has actual exercise of power.[84]

The exclusion of persons born in unincorporated territories from Fourteenth Amendment citizenship has relegated the territorial citizens to what scholars label second-class citizenship.[85] In the most important of the Insular Cases, *Downes v. Bidwell*,[86] the Court abandoned the old rule that the U.S. Constitution follows the flag to the territories *in toto*, and, instead, granted Congress near plenary power to decide which constitutional provisions would apply.[87] Professor Gerald Neuman has critiqued the Insular Cases for creating a "geographically restrictive social compact approach" which limits the applicability of constitutional provisions to a territorially defined class of beneficiaries while excluding any peoples whom Congress is not prepared to regard as equals.[88] The critique is especially poignant when the Court's assumption about the temporary nature of the unincorporated territories is significantly tested by the lasting legacy of places like Puerto Rico and Guam which remain territories despite the passage of time.[89] Indeed, as Professor Pedro A. Malavet has documented with regard to the residents of the existing territories "over four million citizens of the United States [have had to live] with the rule of the Insular Cases for the 109 years since it was first articulated in *Downes v. Bidwell*."[90] The residents of the U.S. territories, for example, lack full representation in the U.S. House of Representatives and Senate and are not allowed to vote in presidential elections, even when some constitutional rights have been recognized to

---

in 1976. The residents of American Samoa are treated as nationals, rather than citizens. *Id.* *See also* Guam Organic Act of 1950, 48 U.S.C. § 1421 et seq.

[82] Downes v. Bidwell, 182 U.S. 244, 287 (1901); Dorr v. U.S., 195 U.S. 138 (1904); Balzac v. Porto Rico, 258 U.S. 298 (1922).

[83] For a discussion of the Insular Cases, *see* Perez, *supra* note 9, at 1036–46.

[84] *Id.* at 1055–57.

[85] *See, e.g.*, Pedro A. Malavet, *The Inconvenience of a "Constitution [that] Follows the Flag . . . but Doesn't Quite Catch Up with It": From Downes v. Bidwell to Boumediene v. Bush*, 80 Miss. L.J. 181, 182 (2010).

[86] 182 U.S. at 287.

[87] Malavet, *supra* note 85, at 185–86.

[88] Neuman, Strangers to the Constitution, *supra* note 1, at 83–85. *See also* Roman, *supra* note 74, at 586–89.

[89] Malavet, *supra* note 85, at 192–195.

[90] *Id.* at 182. *Downes v. Bidwell* dealt with the Philippines and Cuba as well as Puerto Rico but only Puerto Rico remains a territory. The Philippines gained its independence 45 years after the Court's ruling, and Cuba was granted independence by the treaty that ended the Spanish-American War, although its sovereignty would remain limited for decades to come. In addition to Puerto Rico, Guam is the other territory which has been and remains a territory since the Insular Cases were decided more than a century ago. *Id.* at 188–89.

apply in the territories on a case-by-case basis.[91]

Recently, the ongoing relevance of the Insular Cases was reaffirmed in *Boumediene v. Bush*, a case that involved the application of constitutional habeas to the detainees at Guantanamo Bay.[92] According to the Court, Guantanamo Bay, not unlike the unincorporated territories, is a place that the U.S. does not intend to govern indefinitely. Some scholars question this conclusion given the indefiniteness and scope of jurisdiction that the U.S. exercises over the territory.[93] In *Boumediene*, the Court did hold that Art. I, § 9, cl. 2, of the Constitution has full effect at Guantanamo Bay and as such, Congress cannot deny the detainees the privilege of habeas corpus without complying with the requirements of the Suspension Clause.[94] Because *Boumediene* applies to non-U.S. citizen detainees, some scholars read the case as departing from the Insular Cases precedent and embracing global constitutionalism — the view that the Constitution protects even non-U.S. citizens outside the territory of the United States — and universal human rights.[95] Other scholars, however, suggest that this view largely exaggerates the implications of *Boumediene*.[96] First, *Boumediene* treats the Suspension Clause as a structural separation-of-powers issue, and not as an individual right such as due process, and, thus, is not extending the Constitution *en toto* to the territories.[97] Second, *Boumediene* does little to grant formal equal citizenship to the millions of residents in the territories; rather, it affirms that the scope of rights they enjoy remains subject to a case-by-case treatment with deference to Congress.[98]

e.   The Meaning of "Natural Born"

A separate question has been whether the term "natural born Citizen" as used in Article II of the U.S. Constitution to describe who is eligible for the office of President[99] requires birth in U.S. territory.[100] The meaning of "natural-born

---

[91] In 1979, for example, the U.S. Supreme Court decided that the Fourth Amendment — and any other provision of the Bill of Rights — applied to the Commonwealth of Puerto Rico. Torres v. Puerto Rico, 442 U.S. 465, 475–76 (1979).

[92] Boumediene v. Bush, 553 U.S. 723 (2008).

[93] *See, e.g.*, Malavet, *supra* note 85, at 185.

[94] Boumediene, 553 U.S. at 771.

[95] *See, e.g., Andrew Kent, Boumediene, Munaf, and the Supreme Court's Misreading of the Insular Cases*, 97 Iowa L. Rev. 101 (2011).

[96] Stephen I. Vladeck, *Insular Thinking About Habeas*, 97 Iowa L. Rev. Bull. 16, 18 (2012).

[97] *Id.* at 19.

[98] Malavet, *supra* note 85, at 243–250. *See also* Juan R. Torruella, *Ruling America's Colonies: The Insular Cases*, 32 Yale L. & Pol'y Rev. 57, 74–93 (discussing the historical and modern political, economic, and cultural implications of the colonial relationship between the U.S. and Puerto Rico) and Sean Morrison, *Foreign in a Domestic Sense: American Samoa and the Last U.S. Nationals*, 41 Hastings Const. L. Q 71 (2013) (discussing the rights implications of being merely a national and a resident of American Samoan).

[99] U.S. Const. art. II, § 1, cl. 5.

[100] *See* Lawrence Friedman, *An Idea Whose Time Has Come — The Curious History, Uncertain Effect, and Need for Amendment of the "Natural Born Citizen" Requirement for the Presidency*, 52 St. Louis U. L.J. 137, 143 (2007) (qualification of foreign-born U.S. citizen as "natural born Citizen" "is an open question").

Citizen" has never been definitively interpreted by the courts and is unlikely to be taken up given its political character,[101] despite that many candidates to the U.S. presidency have been born abroad to U.S. citizen parents.[102] Most scholars agree, however, that it includes any person who was a citizen at the time of his or her birth, under then-current law, whether by birth in the United States within the meaning of the Fourteenth Amendment or through statutory conferral.[103] This interpretation is based on the history of the adoption of Article II's "natural born Citizen" at the Constitutional Convention of 1787, as well as an examination of British common law in effect at the time of its adoption.[104] Evidence on the meaning of the "natural born Citizen" clause is scant in the 1787 Convention's debates,[105] but it appears to have been introduced to prevent the erection of a monarchy headed by a foreign ruler.[106] As well, the conferral of *jus sanguinis* citizenship through statute by the British well before the U.S. Revolution also suggests that the Framers understood the term "natural born" to include both a *jus solis* and *jus sanguinis* conception of

---

[101] *See, e.g.*, Adam Clanton, *Born to Run: Can an American Samoan Become President?*, 29 UCLA PAC. BASIN L.J. 135, 159–173 (2002) (concluding that while technically an American Samoan would be ineligible to become U.S. President since they are nationals, not citizens when they are born, jurisdiction doctrines of political question and standing would prevent litigation to resolve the issue in court).

[102] J. Rebekka S. Bonner, *Who May Be President? Constitutional Reinterpretation of Article II's "Natural Born" Presidential Eligibility Clause, available at* http://ssrn.com/abstract=1133663. Such presidential candidates have included Lowell Weiker, born in Paris to a U.S. father and English mother; Barry Goldwater, born in the territory of Arizona before it became a state; George Romney, born in a Mormon colony to U.S. parents in Chihuahua, Mexico; Christian Herter, born to U.S. parents in France; Franklin D. Roosevelt, Jr., born in Canada to U.S. parents; and John McCain, who was born to U.S. parents in the Panama Canal. *Id.* Most recently, Senator Ted Cruz, who was born in Canada to a U.S. citizen mother has announced his bid for the Presidency. *Is Ted Cruz Allowed to Run since he was Born in Canada?*, npr.org, Mar. 23, 2015.

[103] *See* Stephen E. Sachs, *John McCain's Citizenship: A Tentative Defense* (unnumbered manuscript), *available at* http://ssrn.com/abstract=1236882; Sarah Helene Duggin & Mary Beth Collins, *"Natural Born" in the USA: The Striking Unfairness and Dangerous Ambiguity of the Constitution's Presidential Qualifications Clause and Why We Need to Fix It*, 85 B. U. L. REV. 53, 83 (2005); Jill A. Pryor, *The Natural-Born Citizen Clause and Presidential Eligibility: An Approach for Resolving Two Hundred Years of Uncertainty*, 97 YALE L.J. 881, 896 (1988); Peter J. Spiro, *McCain's Citizenship and Constitutional Method*, 107 MICH. L. REV. FIRST IMPRESSIONS 42 (2008); and Charles A. Gordon, *Who can be President of the United States: The Unresolved Enigma*, 28 MD. L. REV. 1, 31 (1968).

[104] Bonner, *supra* note 102 (unnumbered manuscript).

[105] The records that exist include the proposed text introduced by Alexander Hamilton on June 18, 1787, which read "[n]o person shall be eligible to the office of President of the United States unless he is now a Citizen of one of the States, or hereafter be born a Citizen of the United States. Second, notes prepared by Pierce Butler on August 31, 1787 provide a similar construction: "No person shall be eligible to the Office of President . . . who shall not be a natural born Citizen of the United States, excepting those who now or at the time of the Adoption of This Constitution shall be a citizen of the said States of whom may be President." Third, the phrase also appears in a letter from John Jay to George Washington (and possibly others attending the Convention) urging Washington that "it would be wise and seasonable to provide a strong check to the admission of Foreigners into the administration of our National Government; and to declare expressly that the Command in Chief of the American Army shall not be given to nor devolve on, any but a natural born Citizen." Finally, there were at least two proposed revisions, including the imposition of residency requirements on top of the "natural born" provision that were not adopted. *See* Bonner, *supra* note 102 (unnumbered manuscript).

[106] *See* Gordon, *supra* note 103, at 5.

citizenry.[107] Included in the "natural born Citizen," then, are children born in the United States within the meaning of the Fourteenth Amendment, as well as children who are born citizens under the then-existing statute conferring citizenship at birth,[108] which today includes Puerto Ricans born in Puerto Rico,[109] Native American born in a U.S. reservation,[110] and certain children of U.S. citizen parent/s born abroad.[111] It does not, however, include naturalized citizens because they are not citizens at birth.[112] A less clear issue is whether "natural born citizen" would include American Samoans who, though born on U.S. soil, are statutorily treated as nationals and not as citizens at birth.[113] At least one scholar has argued that "natural born" should be understood to refer to "natural born subjects" as the term was used under the common law.[114] Under the English common law, "natural born subject" is someone who owes permanent allegiance to a nation; moreover, Congress has defined national in the Immigration and Nationality Act as a person who "owes permanent allegiance to the United States."[115] This interpretation, however, has to contend with the use of "citizen" rather than "subject" in the actual text of Article II.[116] Unfortunately, what that intended different meaning might have been is also not clear since the U.S. Constitution did not define the word citizen until its adoption of the Fourteenth Amendment. Moreover, as explained above, the meaning of birthright citizenship under the Fourteenth Amendment has excluded persons born in the U.S. territories, including American Samoans.[117]

---

[107] Bonner, *supra* note 102 (unnumbered manuscript).

[108] In fact, the debate over whether Senator John McCain is a "natural-born" citizen has principally been about the meaning of the statute in effect at the time of his birth. For different views on the topic contrast Gabriel J. Chin, *Why Senator John McCain Cannot Be President: Eleven Months and a Hundred Yards Short of Citizenship*, ARIZONA LEGAL STUDIES, DISCUSSION PAPER No. 08-14 (July 2008) with Stephen E. Sachs, *John McCain's Citizenship: A Tentative Defense*, Manuscript, *available at* http://ssrn.com/abstract=1236882 and Spiro, *supra* note 103.

[109] INA § 302.

[110] INA § 301(b).

[111] INA § 301(c)-(h) (jus sanguinis citizenship generally) and INA § 303 (jus sanguinis citizenship for persons born in the Panama Canal).

[112] Merlinda L. Seymore, *The Presidency and the Meaning of Citizenship*, 2005 B.Y.U. L. REV. 927, 930 (2005).

[113] Clanton, *supra* note 101, at 142.

[114] *Id.* at 143.

[115] *Id.* at 144 (citing to 8 U.S.C. § 1101(a)(22)).

[116] Adam Clanton argues that the change from citizen to subject did not intend to change the meaning of "natural born subject" but rather was simply to embody a different political concept of government, namely to distinguish the U.S. as a republican form of government from Britain, which was still a monarchy. *Id.* at 145.

[117] Clanton acknowledges this predicament and ultimately concludes that it is likely that the Insular Cases and the case law excluding persons born in the U.S. territories from Fourteenth Amendment birthright citizenship are likely to prove insurmountable to a broader interpretation of Article II. *Id.* at 149–59.

2. Citizenship by Descent for Children Born Abroad

a. Its Origins

Jus sanguinis citizenship has been available under U.S. law from the beginning, and today approximately two and a half million U.S. citizens are derivative citizens born abroad to at least one U.S. citizen parent.[118] Even so, there is disagreement on whether its conferral has been solely through statute, rather than through constitutional or common law.[119] There is agreement that at common law the British recognized that children born abroad to subjects serving in the military were citizens at birth.[120] In addition, beginning in 1350, England enacted a series of statutes that provided that persons born abroad to British parents would have the same rights of inheritance available only to natural born children.[121] Scholars have since disagreed on whether these statutes codified the common law or augmented it.[122]

Despite British history, the U.S. Constitution was silent on citizenship by descent. Congress first conferred a right to derivative citizenship in 1790 when it declared that "the children of citizens . . . that may be born beyond the seas . . . shall be considered as natural born citizens," except for those "persons whose fathers have never been resident in the United States."[123] This act by Congress could suggest that *jus sanguinis* was not part of the fundamental law in the U.S. on citizenship, although, here too, others argue that Congress merely codified what had already existed as law.[124] This is at least consistent with an 1863 ruling by the New York Court of Appeals, which declared *jus sanguinis* to be an organic rule of U.S. citizenship[125] and conferred such right on children who, perhaps inadvertently, had been left out of the definition in the 1802 reenactment of the 1790 Act.[126] However, at various times, as early as 1898, the U.S. Supreme Court has chosen to interpret the Naturalization Clause to include the conferral of citizenship by descent, although not without strong dissents.[127] Scholars have also questioned this

---

[118] American Community Survey Briefs, Nativity Status and Citizenship in the United States: 2009, *available at* http://www.census.gov/prod/2010pubs/acsbr09-16.pdf.

[119] *Id.* at 77–78.

[120] Sachs, *supra* note 103, at 6–10.

[121] *Id.* at 7. *See also* Bonner, *supra* note 102 (unnumbered manuscript).

[122] *Id.*

[123] 1 Stat. 103 (1790).

[124] Mayton, *supra* note 27, at 233.

[125] Ludlam v. Ludlam, 26 N.Y. 356 (N.Y. 1863).

[126] The 1802 Act declared that "children of persons who are not, or have been citizens of the United States, shall, though born out of the limits and jurisdiction of the United States, be considered as citizens of the United States," which meant that children born abroad to persons who became citizens after 1802 could not gain citizenship. Mayton, *supra* note 27, at 235.

[127] In dictum, the Court held in *Wong Kim Ark* that "[the Fourteenth Amendment] has not touched the acquisition of citizenship by being born abroad of American parents; and has left that subject to be regulated, as it had always been, by Congress, in the exercise of the power conferred by the Constitution to establish an uniform rule of naturalization." 169 U.S. at 701–02. The Court has adopted this same interpretation, not without objection, in the more recent cases of Miller v. Albright, 523 U.S. 420, 426

interpretation because it would require that derivative citizenship be considered a form of naturalized or elective citizenship after birth,[128] as opposed to an automatic birth citizenship that would be covered under the "natural born Citizen" clause of Art. II of the U.S. Constitution.[129]

Despite the Court's prevailing view that Congress' power to confer derivative citizenship rests with the Naturalization Clause, the Court, has not equally granted derivative citizens Fourteenth-Amendment status as naturalized citizens. Instead, it has read the Fourteenth Amendment as requiring that naturalization occur inside U.S. territory[130] In 1971, in *Rogers v. Bellei*, the Court declined to recognize Bellei's Fourteenth Amendment citizenship right as a foreign-born man who had one citizen-parent but who failed to meet the post-birth statutory residency requirement for derivative citizenship, thus relinquishing the right.[131] If Bellei could establish a Fourteenth Amendment right to derivative citizenship at birth, then his failure to meet the residency requirement would have been immaterial. The Court, however, considered Bellei neither born in nor naturalized in the U.S., nor subject to its jurisdiction and concluded that "[h]e is simply not a Fourteenth-Amendment-first-sentence-citizen." By focusing on Bellei's location outside the U.S., the Court avoided the question of whether derivative citizenship was a form of naturalization. In his dissent, Justice Black argued for a broader interpretation of the word "in" to include being "naturalized into it," based on his understanding of the legislative history of the Citizenship Clause:[132]

Thus, Congress has the power to grant derivative citizenship, although the source of this power is not entirely settled. The prevailing view continues to be that such power rests with the Naturalization Clause, which would grant Congress plenary power to define the terms of derivative citizenship.[133] And while derivative citizenship does not fall within the meaning of the Fourteenth Amendment's naturalization citizenship clause, its plausible treatment as part of the fundamental meaning of citizenship at the time of the Constitution's adoption would argue for greater judicial intervention.[134] Determining whether and how much this power is subject to judicial review is important, especially when such statutes have traditionally included provisions that discriminate on the basis of gender.[135] The 1790 statute, for example, created the first distinction between citizen-fathers and

---

(1998), and Nguyen v. INS, 533 U.S. 53, 61 (2001). *See infra* notes 147–155 and accompanying text.

[128] The INA defines the term naturalization as the "conferring of nationality of a state upon a person after birth, by any means whatsoever." INA § 101(a)(23).

[129] *See supra* notes 99–112 and accompanying text (discussing the meaning of "natural born").

[130] The Clause provides: "All persons born or naturalized in the United States."

[131] 401 U.S. 815 (1971).

[132] *Id.* at 843. "That clause was added in the Senate rather late in the debates of the Fourteenth Amendment and as originally introduced its reference was to all those 'born in the United States or naturalized by the laws thereof.' The final version of the Citizenship Clause was undoubtedly intended to have this same scope" (citations omitted).

[133] *See infra* notes 180–189 and accompanying text.

[134] *Id.*

[135] *See* Notes, Michael G. McFarland, *Derivative Citizenship: Its History, Constitutional Foundation, and Constitutional Limitations*, 63 N.Y.U. ANN. SURV. AM. L. 467, 478 (2008).

citizen-mothers, and citizen-mothers were not able to pass citizenship to their foreign-born children when they married a foreign national, for instance.[136] Then in 1855, the amended statute precluded mothers altogether from passing citizenship to their foreign-born children, a provision that was not rescinded until 1934.[137] Gender-based distinctions exist also under current law; this time, however, to burden certain U.S. citizen fathers, not mothers, in their conferral of derivative citizenship to their children.[138]

b. The Statute

The statute in effect at the time of the child's birth determines the requirement for derivative citizenship.[139] The statutory conferral of *jus sanguinis* citizenship depends on several factors, including the marital status of the child's citizen parent, and the length of time the citizen parents have resided in the U.S. Both the requirements for *jus sangunis* citizenship and the procedures for acquiring it are quite onerous.[140] As documented by some scholars, many who have derived U.S. citizenship from their parents are unable to prove it even if the law recognizes them as citizens.[141]

Under current U.S. law, adopted since 1952 and supplemented by later amendments, citizenship by descent is provided for primarily in sections 301(c), 301(g), 309(a), and 309(c) of INA.[142] Sections 301(c) and 301(g) of the INA list universally applicable conditions for acquisition of citizenship by descent, and sections 309(a) and 309(c) provide overriding rules for persons born out of wedlock.

Citizenship by descent for children born to a married couple requires that at least one parent be a U.S. citizen at the time of the child's birth abroad. Citizenship by descent may also be conferred on a child who is adopted internationally and subsequently admitted as a child of a U.S. citizen.[143] The Child Citizenship Act of 2000 grants automatic citizenship to a child born abroad who (1) was fully and finally adopted; (2) is under 18 years of age; (3) was admitted to the U.S. as an LPR; and (4) is in the legal and physical custody of at least one parent who is a U.S. citizen.[144]

---

[136] It read: "[T]he right of citizenship shall not descend to persons whose fathers have never been resident in the United States." Act of March 26, 1790, ch. 3, § 1, 1 stat. 103, 104.

[137] McFarland, *supra* note 135, at 480–81.

[138] *See infra* notes 147 and accompanying text.

[139] For a good historical discussion of U.S. derivative citizenship statutes, *see* McFarland, *supra* note 135, at 477–82.

[140] For a detailed discussion of the procedures for establishing derivative citizenship, *see* Lee J. Terán, *Mexican Children of U.S. Citizens: "Viges Prin" and Other Tales of Challenging of Asserting Acquired U.S. Citizenship*, 14 SCHOLARS 583, 617–75 (2012).

[141] *See, e.g., Id.* at 594.

[142] *Id.* at 482.

[143] INA § 320.

[144] Pub. L. No. 1-06-395, 8 U.S.C. §§ 1431–33. For an insightful discussion and critique of the Child Citizenship Act, *see* Victor C. Romero, *The Child Citizenship Act and the Family Reunification Act: Valuing the Citizen Child as Well as the Citizen Parent*, 55 FLA. L. REV. 489 (2003).

In addition, laws require residency or physical presence in the U.S. by the citizen parent(s). The laws differ depending on whether the child was born to two U.S. citizen parents or to one U.S. citizen parent and a foreign national. If the child is born abroad to two U.S. citizen parents, then at least one of them must have resided in the U.S. or its outlying possessions prior to the birth of the child at any time and for however long.[145] If the child is born to only one U.S. citizen parent, the U.S. citizen parent must have been physically present in the U.S. or its outlying possessions for cumulative periods totaling not less than five years, at least two of which were before the U.S. citizen parent was 14 years old.[146] The logic behind the physical presence requirement is that a citizen parent who spends enough time in the U.S. will absorb U.S. customs and values, which will then be transmitted to the child.

The INA definition imposes additional requirements for U.S. citizen fathers when the child is born outside the context of a traditional marriage. If the child is born out of wedlock, the father (though not the mother) must demonstrate a bona-fide parent-child relationship with the mother.[147] Before a child born abroad can gain U.S. citizenship, INA § 309(a) requires the unwed U.S. citizen father to establish that: (1) clear and convincing evidence proves a blood relationship between father and child; (2) the father had U.S. nationality at the time of child's birth; (3) the father (unless deceased) agrees in writing to provide financial support until the child reaches the age of 18; and (4) the father legitimated, recognized, or had a court declare parentage with the child. For children born out of wedlock to a U.S.-citizen mother, INA section 309(c) does not provide conditions for the application of sections 301(c) and 301(g), but rather, supersedes them. According to section 309(c), "[n]otwithstanding the provision of subsection [309](a)," an out-of-wedlock child will be a citizen if its mother was a U.S. citizen at the time of its birth and "the mother had previously been physically present in the United States or one of its outlying possessions for a continuous period of one year."

c. Gender Discrimination[148]

U.S. citizen plaintiffs have brought to the U.S. Supreme Court three equal protection challenges to the derivate citizenship laws based on the additional requirements that attach to unwed fathers but not mothers who wish to transfer

---

[145] INA § 301(c). The term "the United States" as used here also includes the U.S. territories of Puerto Rico, Guam, and the U.S. Virgin Islands, as well as the Commonwealth of the Northern Mariana Islands. INA § 101(a)(38). The term outlying possessions means Samoa and Swains Islands. INA § 101(a)(29).

[146] INA § 301(g). Physical presence includes time in the military or employment in the U.S. foreign service. INA § 301(g).

[147] INA § 101(b)(D).

[148] In a fascinating recent article, Professor Kristin A. Collins argues and documents the relationships between gender-asymmetrical jus sanguinis citizenship and racially nativist policies that were central to U.S. nationality law until 1965. Professor Collins traces the origins of the gender discrimination applied to unwed parents of a child born abroad imposed on fathers to a case decided by the Maryland Court of Appeals in 1864, Guyer v. Smith, 22 Md. 239 (1864). Guyer denied jus sanguinis citizenship to two brothers born in St. Barthélemy to a U.S. white citizen with a mother of reportedly African descent. This influential case would ultimately result in the 1940 codification the gender

their citizenship to their children born abroad; all three have been unsuccessful. First in 1998, in *Miller v. Albright*, a U.S. citizen father challenged the additional requirements relating to children born out of wedlock to citizen-fathers, but the Court's plurality opinion held that the statute could easily satisfy even heightened scrutiny.[149] Interestingly, Justice Scalia's concurrence, joined by Justice Thomas, concluded, without citing authority, that Congress' exclusive authority to confer derivative citizenship rests in the Naturalization Clause.[150] In his dissent, Justice Breyer vehemently disagreed with the inclusion of derivative citizenship in the Naturalization Clause; instead, Justice Breyer viewed derivative citizenship as part of the original understanding of citizenship at the time of adoption of the U.S. Constitution, and, as such, subject to greater constitutional scrutiny.[151]

Two years later, in *Nguyen v. INS*, a case that involved the same legal challenge, this time raised by the child claiming derivative citizenship, a divided Supreme Court (5-4) upheld the law as constitutional, and to do so applied intermediate scrutiny standard to the law without actually deciding what standard of review would apply in such cases.[152] Rather, the Court concluded that since INA's differing treatment of them under equal protection "serves important governmental objectives and . . . the discriminatory means employed are substantially related to the achievement of those objectives," it was unnecessary to decide whether only a rational-basis of review should apply. The holding was particularly jarring as applied to the facts in the case because Nguyen had been abandoned by his mother at birth and raised by his U.S. citizen father in the U.S. from the age of six.[153] Here, it was Justice O'Connor, joined by Justices Souter, Ginsberg, and Breyer, who dissented, no doubt concerned over the watering down of equal protection review as applied to gender-based discrimination.[154] Justice O'Connor also, moreover, disagreed that derivative citizenship means the same thing as "naturalization," where Congress has enjoyed plenary power.[155] Rather, Justice O'Connor urged the Court to consider and resolve the question of whether Congress should have the same deference in cases involving derivative citizen cases as they have in cases involving aliens where the underlying question is whether the person is a citizen in the first place.[156]

---

discrimination jus sanguinis rule applied to children born out of wedlock. Professor Collins explains that this coincided and was meant to work in tandem with the race-based immigration laws and race-based military marriage policies to exclude Amerisian children from citizenship. Kristin A. Collins, *Illegitimate Borders: Jus Sanguinis Citizenship and the Legal Construction of Family, Race, and Nations*, 123 YALE L.J. 2134, 2136–43 (2014).

[149] 523 U.S. 420, 426 (1998).

[150] *Id.* at 453.

[151] *Miller*, 523 U.S. at 481.

[152] 533 U.S. 53, 61 (2001).

[153] *Id.* at 70.

[154] *Id.* at 73 ("In a long line of cases spanning nearly three decades, this Court has applied heightened scrutiny to legislative classifications based on sex. The Court today confronts another statute that classifies individuals on the basis of their sex. While the Court invokes heightened scrutiny, the manner in which it explains and applies this standard is a stranger to our precedents.")

[155] *Id.* at 95.

[156] *Id.* at 96–97.

In 2011, in *Flores-Villar v. United States*, in a 4-4 split decision,[157] the Court affirmed without opinion the Ninth Circuit's decision to uphold the INA's disparate physical presence requirements in the *jus sanguinis* statute that applied to unwed fathers but not mothers.[158] Not unlike the facts in *Nguyen*, Ruben Flores-Villar, who was born in Mexico out of wedlock to a U.S. citizen father and a Mexican mother, was raised by his father and paternal grandmother (also a U.S. citizen) in the United States and had little if any contact with his mother.[159] Yet, while Ruben's father had legitimated his son before he turned 21, he could not satisfy the additional requirements that applied to him under statute in 1970, the year of Ruben's birth. Under 1970 law, Ruben's father must have lived in the United States for a total of 10 years, five of which must be after he turned 14 but before Ruben was born.[160] In fact, Ruben's father could not have met the requirements because he was only 16 at the time of Ruben's birth.[161] The rule, in effect, prevented Ruben's father from conveying citizenship until at least age 19. The issue in the case, thus, was whether Congress exceeded its authority by imposing an age-based requirement in the statute. Because of the 4-4 split, however, the Court did not decide the issue. Interestingly, the Ninth Circuit's decision assumed, without deciding, that intermediate scrutiny applies INA provisions governing citizenship conferred at birth.[162] The Ninth Circuit attributed two purposes to the residency-requirement gender-asymmetrical distinction.[163] The first was to protect children against statelessness, reasoning that because many nations do not recognize *jus solis* citizenship, a child born out of wedlock can acquire no citizenship other than through his mother's derivative citizenship at birth.[164] Petitioners acknowledged the legitimate purpose of preventing statelessness but challenged why such protection necessarily dictated penalizing the father.[165] The Ninth Circuit, however, turned to the second purpose of the lengthier residency requirement for the father, namely developing a tie between the child, his or her father, and this country.[166]

---

[157] 131 S. Ct. 2312 (2011), Justice Kagan recused herself due to her earlier involvement in the case as Solicitor General.

[158] U.S. v. Flores-Villar, 536 F.3d 990, 993 (9th Cir. 2008), *affirmed*, 131 S. Ct. 2312 (2011).

[159] Brief for Petitioner at 2, Flores-Villar, 131 S. Ct. 2312 (2011).

[160] *See* 8 U.S.C. §§ 1401(g), 1409(a) (1970).

[161] Brief for Petitioner, *supra* note 159, at 1–2.

[162] 536 F.3d at 995. While some scholars have argued that the intermediate scrutiny applied in the context of gender-discrimination in the jus sanguinis cases is more exceptional than that applied in other context, Professor Albertina Antognini disagrees. Albertina Antognini, *From Citizenship to Custody: Unwed Fathers Abroad and at Home*, 36 Harv. J. L & Gender 405 (2013) (arguing that the citizenship transmission cases are not examples of immigration law exceptionalism but rather are remarkably consistent with the Court's treatment of unwed fathers and mothers in its equal protection jurisprudence generally).

[163] Under the statute, Ruben's mother would only have had to establish a one-year residency requirement in the U.S. before she turned 14 and prior to Ruben's birth. *See* 8 U.S.C. §§ 1401(g), 1409(a) (1970).

[164] *Id.* at 996.

[165] *Id.* at 997.

[166] *Id.* at 997–98.

3. Citizenship Through Naturalization

Today, every year, between half a million and one million foreign nationals become U.S. citizens through naturalization,[167] motivated in part by such factors as the gain in civil and legal rights that flow from full membership, family unification goals, and a desire for greater social integration.[168] Hundreds of thousands more, however, are eligible to naturalize but either choose not to or increasingly are unable to do so based on the requirements for naturalization.[169]

a. Its Origins

Congress is authorized by the U.S. Constitution to establish a "uniform Rule of Naturalization."[170] In the exercise of this power, in 1790, Congress established that "any alien, being a free white person . . . may be admitted to become a citizen,"[171] The "white person" requirement remained in effect through 1952,[172] Although Congress amended the Act in 1873 to allow naturalization to "aliens of African nativity and to persons of African descent."[173] During this period, and at least until the 1920s when immigration national quotas severely restricted immigration from southern and eastern Europe and barred immigration from Asia,[174] courts entertained requests for a finding of whiteness from a number of naturalization claimants. In the absence of a Congressional meaning of the term "free white persons" in the 1790 Act, courts struggled to come up with standards to assess

---

[167] U.S. Department of Homeland Security, Yearbook of Immigration Statistics 2012, Naturalizations, *available at* http://www.dhs.gov/yearbook-immigration-statistics-2012-naturalizations.

[168] Ana Gonzalez-Barrera et al., *The Path Not Taken: Two-thirds of Legal Mexican Immigrants are not U.S. Citizens*, Feb. 2013, at 7 *available at* http://www.pewhispanic.org/files/2013/02/Naturalizations_Jan_2013_FINAL.pdf.

[169] In 2011, Mexican immigrants had a comparatively lower rate of naturalization, 36 percent of those eligible, compared with 61 percent for all immigrants and 68 percent for all non-Mexican immigrants. When asked in an open-ended question in a survey conducted by the Pew Hispanic Center why they had not naturalized, 26 percent of Latino immigrants identified personal barriers such as a lack of English proficiency, and an additional 18 percent identified administrative barriers, such as the financial cost of naturalization. *Id.* at 6.

[170] U.S. Const. art. 1, § 8, cl. 4.

[171] The 1790 Act, *supra* note 17, at Ch. 3, § 1, 1 Stat. 103 (repealed 1952).

[172] Congress selectively lifted naturalization's racial restrictions in the twentieth century. First, for foreign policy reasons, Congress allowed the Chinese to naturalize in 1943. Next were Filipinos and Indians who were allowed to naturalize in 1946, followed by persons from Guam in 1950. In 1952, Congress removed all racial barriers to naturalization. Leti Volpp, *"Obnoxious to Their Very Nature": Asian American and Constitutional Citizenship*, 8 ASIAN L.J. 71, 74 (2001).

[173] J. Allen Douglas, *The "Priceless Possession" of Citizenship: Race, Nation, and Naturalization in American Law, 1880–1930*, 43 DUQ. L. REV. 386, 394–426 (2005) (discussing the range of legal reasons employed by courts to define "whiteness," from physical identification based on appearance to the ethnography of family lineage, and from geographic origin to community sentiment).

[174] The Immigration Act of 1924, restructured the criteria for admission and limited immigration from any particular country to 2 percent of their nationality in 1890. The law struck most deeply at Jews, Italians, Slavs, and Greeks who immigrated particularly after 1890. The 1924 Act also provided for the permanent exclusion of any "alien ineligible for citizenship," which again meant non-whites, and primarily Asians. BILL ONG HING, DEFINING AMERICA THROUGH IMMIGRATION POLICY 46–47 (2004).

"whiteness."[175] These cases reveal a desire to achieve white hegemony, including through the assimilation of certain groups (i.e., Mexicans), as well as racial exclusion altogether for other groups (i.e., the Japanese).[176] Racial ineligibility for naturalization, moreover, affected women beyond those who were racially barred from naturalization. In 1907, Congress stripped of citizenship any woman who married a foreign national, since that wife would take the nationality of her husband.[177] Congress partially repealed this law in 1922, but the law continued to apply to women who married men ineligible to naturalize, usually those who married Asian men, until 1931.[178]

Congress enjoys broad discretion to legislate the requirements for naturalization, as Courts have treated its conferral as a privilege, not a right.[179] The constitutionality of the racial and gender bars to naturalization were never directly challenged in court. In 1923, however, the U.S. Supreme Court, at least *in dicta*, upheld the validity of the "white person" requirement in a case involving a challenge by a Japanese national ineligible to Naturalize under Washington's Constitution, which prohibited the ownership of land by "aliens other than those who in good faith have declared intention to become citizens."[180] The Court declared that "Congress is not trammeled" by the Naturalization Clause and "may grant or withhold the privilege of naturalization upon any grounds or without any reason, as it sees fit."[181] Subsequent direct challenges to the unqualified oath requirement promising to bear arms in defense of the United States failed because "[n]aturalization is a privilege, to be given, qualified or withheld as Congress may determine."[182] This precedent

---

[175] Douglas, *supra* note 173, at 394–426.

[176] *Id. See also generally* George A. Martinez, *Immigration and the Meaning of United States Citizenship: Whiteness and Assimilation*, 46 WASHBURN L.J. 335, 336–43 (2007) and Note, John Tehranian, *Performing Whiteness: Naturalization Litigation and the Construction of Racial Identity in America*, 109 YALE L.J. 817 (2000) and IAN F. HANEY LOPEZ, WHITE BY LAW: THE LEGAL CONSTRUCTION OF RACE (1996).

[177] Expatriation Act, ch. 2534, § 3, 34 Stat. 1228, 1228–29 (1907).

[178] Leti Volpp, *Divesting Citizenship: On Asian American History and the Loss of Citizenship Through Marriage*, 53 UCLA L. REV. 405, 407–410 (2005). *See also* Deenesh Sohoni, *Unsuitable Suitors: Anti-Miscegenation Laws, Naturalization Laws, and the Construction of Asian Identities*, 41 LAW & SOC'Y REV. 587 (2007); Kevin R. Johnson, *Racial Restrictions on Naturalization: The Recurring Intersection of Race and Gender Immigration and Citizenship Law*, 11 BERKELEY WOMEN'S L.J. 142 (1996).

[179] Professor James E. Pfander and Theresa R. Wardon have documented, however, two limitations on Congress' naturalization power since the early Republic: the first is that the law had to be public, and thus precluding private naturalization bills, and two, that it had to be prospective such that a person who relied on the Naturalization law at the time of legal immigration should not be disqualified from subsequently adopted requirements. James E. Pfander and Theresa R. Wardon, *Reclaiming the Immigration Constitution of the Early Republic: Prospectivity, Uniformity, and Transparency*, 96 VA. L. REV. 359 (2010). Neither of these restrictions, however, are applied in the modern context.

[180] Terrace v. Thompson, 263 U.S. 197 (1923).

[181] *Id.* at 220. Similarly, when eligible Asians attempted to naturalize through the more generous 1862 law that permitted the naturalization of any "alien honorably discharged" from U.S., lower courts upheld the earlier race-based naturalization restriction to deny them citizenship. *See* Deenesh Sohoni and Amin Vafa, *The Fight to Be American: Military Naturalization and Asian Citizenship*, 17 ASIAN AM. L.J. 119 (2010).

[182] U.S. v. Macintosh, 283 U.S. 605, 615 (1931), *reversed on statutory grounds*, Girouard v. U.S., 328

have significant relevance in today's debates around comprehensive immigration reform given the 2014 Republic Party leadership proposal to confer a path to legalization to unauthorized immigration without a path to naturalization.[183] One study examining the implications of the GOP proposal estimates that between 4.4 and 5.6 million unauthorized foreign nationals would be left with some path to legalization but without a clear path to citizenship.[184] While historically, Congress has imposed race-based restrictions on citizenship through naturalization, were this proposal to become law, this would be the first time that Congress would preclude naturalization of foreign nationals who gained their lawful residency through special legislation commonly known as amnesty. Case precedent suggests, moreover, that courts could well uphold such a law in light of Congress' broad discretion to define the parameters of who is eligible for naturalization.

Citizenship through naturalization, once conferred, becomes a constitutional right in the same standing as birthright citizenship.[185] The U.S. Supreme Court defines naturalization as the "act of adopting a foreigner, and clothing him with the privileges of a native citizen."[186] Naturalized citizens, however, cannot become President,[187] and, moreover, face different challenges from the Native born on such issues as loss of citizenship[188] or dual nationality.[189]

b. The Statute

Over the course of the nineteenth Century, Congress amended the naturalization laws several times to attach certain requirements, including lawful entry, enumerated years of continuous residence, intention to reside in the U.S. permanently, ability to write his or her name, ability to speak English, good moral character, and attachment to the principles of the U.S. Constitution.[190] These naturalization requirements are intended to promote and maintain cohesion within

---

U. S. 61 (1946) (petitioners found not to be attached to the principles of the Constitution when he would not promise in advance to bear arms in defense of the United States unless he believed the war to be morally justified). *See also* U.S. v. Schwimmer, 279 U.S. 644, 649 (1929) (same), *reversed on statutory grounds*, Girouard v. U.S., 328 U.S. 61 (1946).

[183] On January 28, 2014, House Speaker Boehner released a set of Standards for Immigration Reform which read in part: "Our national and economic security depend on requiring people who are living and working here illegally to come forward and get right with the law. There will be no special path to citizenship for individuals who broke our nation's laws." Standards for Immigration Reform, *available at* http://www.nytimes.com/2014/01/31/us/politics/text-of-republicans-principles-on-immigration.html?_ r=0.

[184] Stuart Anderson, *National Foundation for American Policy Brief, a Path to an Agreement?: Analyzing House and Senate Plans for Legalizing the Unauthorized Immigrant Population*, (Jan. 2014), *available at* http://www.nfap.com/pdf/NFAP%20Policy%20Brief.Analyzing%20House%20and% 20Senate%20Plans%20for%20Legalization.January%202014.pdf.

[185] Schneider v. Rusk, 377 U.S. 163, 165 (1964). *See also* Knauer v. U.S., 328 U.S. 654, 657 (1946) (declaring that "naturalization is not second-class citizenship").

[186] Boyd v. State of Nebraska, 143 U.S. 135, 162 (1892).

[187] Seymore, *supra* note 112, at 932 (arguing that the Natural-Born Citizen Clause perpetuates second-class citizenship status for naturalized citizens).

[188] *See infra* notes 300–397 and accompanying text.

[189] *See infra* notes 277–299 and accompanying text.

[190] Douglas, *supra* note 175, at 385.

the national community, as well as to promote the political assimilation of foreign nationals into U.S. democracy.[191] The English Language and Civics requirement, as well as the requirement of attachment to constitutional principles especially have been questioned, even if national cohesion and assimilation are deemed legitimate objectives, for failing to meet their objectives, for conflicting with U.S. liberal traditions, or for serving, instead, an exclusionary agenda.[192]

Currently, there are eight basic statutory requirements to naturalization.[193] Some of these rules apply differently to special groups, such as to foreign members of the U.S. military, which are explained below.

1. Lawful Permanent Residence

Only persons lawfully admitted as lawful permanent residents (LPRs) are eligible for naturalization.[194] INA § 318 also specifies that naturalization may not be conferred while removal proceedings are pending or while a final finding of removability is outstanding. If a person has honorably served in time of war or declared hostility, LPR status as a precondition is unnecessary.[195]

2. Residence and Physical Presence

The durational residency requirement has been around since the passing of the first Citizenship Act in 1790.[196] Under current law, the applicant must have "resided continuously" after being admitted as an LPR in the United States for either (1) a five-year period immediately preceding the filing of the application;[197] or (2) a three-year period immediately preceding the filing of the application when the applicant became an LPR through marriage to a U.S. citizen and has been living in that marital union during that three-year period.[198] The INA defines residence as a "person's principal, actual dwelling place in fact, without regard to intent."[199] However, because residence must also be continuous, long absences, even if the person meets the principal residence requirements, can disqualify the

---

[191] *See* Peter J. Spiro, *Questioning Barriers to Naturalization*, 13 Geo. Immigr. L.J. 479, 480 (1999).

[192] *Id. See also generally* Gerald L. Neuman, *Justifying U.S. Naturalization Policies*, 35 Va. J. Int'l L. 237 (1994).

[193] In addition to these basic requirements, at times, immigration agencies have imposed additional requirements not included in the statute based on factors such as heightened national security measures. In response to the attacks of September 11, 2001, for example, as part of the naturalization process, immigration agencies must now also conduct a name check through the FBI. For many applicants, it has resulted in significant delays, leading some to file class action lawsuits against the CIS. *See* Amber Pershon, Outstanding Student Article, *Processing Citizenship: Jurisdictional Issues in the Unreasonable Delay of Adjudication of Naturalization Applications*, 5 Phoenix L. Rev. 259, 261 (2011).

[194] INA § 318.

[195] INA § 329.

[196] Spiro, *Questioning Barriers to Naturalization*, *supra* note 191, at 509. The period was first five years, then extended to five, and for a brief period was increased to 14 under the Alien and Sedition Acts of 1798. *Id.*

[197] INA § 316(a).

[198] INA § 319(a).

[199] INA § 101(a)(33).

person from citizenship. Generally, "continuous residence" means the applicant cannot have traveled outside the U.S. for more than six months, unless the applicant can establish that he did not intend to abandon his residence in the U.S. for such period.[200] Absences for longer than a year break the continuity automatically, and the clock must begin anew.[201] In addition, the applicant must be physically present in the U.S. for at least half of the five- or three-year residency requirement.[202] There are more flexible requirements for children of U.S. citizens or for applicants who have served in the U.S. military.[203] The durational residency requirement, along with lawful entry, are among the least controversial, and is usually justified in that societal integration requires time and presence in a country, even when globalization is making the world smaller and U.S. culture transnational.[204]

3.   Good Moral Character

The applicant must demonstrate that he is of good moral character, at minimum for the periods for which residence and physical presence are required.[205] Congress imposed the "good moral character requirement" as early as 1790,[206] but did not define it.[207] Instead, the term was judicially defined and assessed character; i.e., conduct, as well as reputation; i.e., perceptions of conduct by the community for about 150 years.[208] In 1952, Congress provided the first definition of good moral character in the citizenship context.[209] Especially since 1990, moreover, Congress has added numerous bars to a good moral character finding, generally triggered by criminal conduct. Under current law, INA § 101(f) defines what acts would preclude a finding of good moral character, although the list is not exhaustive. These categories include alcoholism, the commission of specified crimes, being a professional gambler, the commission of fraud to obtain immigration benefits, and having been incarcerated for an aggregate period of 180 days or more. Some categorized activities, such as the commission of an aggravated felony as the term

---

[200] INA § 316(b). The regulations at 8 C.F.R. 316.5(c)(1)(i) provide examples which would support a claim that residence had not been interrupted even with an absence of between six and 12 months: (a) the applicant did not terminate her employment in the U.S.; (b) the applicant's immediate family remained in the U.S.; (c) the applicant retained full access to her U.S. abode; or (d) the applicant did not obtain employment while abroad.

[201] INA § 316(c).

[202] INA § 316(c).

[203] INA §§ 322 and 328.

[204] Spiro, *Questioning Barriers to Naturalization*, *supra* note 191, at 511–12. *See also* Elizabeth F. Cohen, *Citizenship and the Law of Time in the United States*, 8 DUKE J. CONST. L. & PUB. POL'Y 53, 54 (2013) (arguing that the temporal requirements of naturalization can represent a wide array and at times divergent norms associated with citizenship including assimilation, civic knowledge, social connection, loyalty, and also has the virtue of equality since time is equally available to all people).

[205] INA § 316(a)(3).

[206] Spiro, *Questioning Barriers to Naturalization*, *supra* note 191, at 509.

[207] Douglas, *supra* note 175, at 391.

[208] *Id.* at 392–94.

[209] Kevin Lapp, *Reforming the Good Moral Character Requirement for U.S. Citizenship*, 87 IND. L.J. 1571, 1589–90 (2012).

is defined in INA § 101(a)(43), preclude a permanent finding of good moral character. Where no statutory bar applies, immigration officers may still deny an applicant on character grounds in their discretion.[210] Some scholars critique the recent changes finding that the requirement has become a powerful exclusionary device that has subverted the statutory and regulatory process by grating broad discretion on individual immigration officers to deny applicants based on character grounds.[211]

From a policy standpoint, the character qualification seems grounded in the protection of the political process, although felony disenfranchising laws are able to fulfill that objective quite well.[212] A different rationale appears to be ensuring the country's ability to remove the foreign national from U.S. soil, as citizens cannot be deported. The character deportation rationale, however, especially for U.S. long-term residents, is questionable, since it is difficult to allocate responsibility to the criminal's original national community, as opposed to other factors, including perhaps the place where the person grew up.[213] Further, the nature of transnational crime today does not at all guarantee that removal is safer to U.S. communities.[214] Furthermore, a growing number of long-term permanent residents ineligible to naturalization based on character grounds remain in the United States unable to naturalize. Professor Kevin Lapp identifies the failures of this current scheme since long-term residents are relegated to a subordinate, outsider status, with fewer rights, and without the prospect of greater integration or of redemption.[215]

4.   Age

The applicant must be at least 18 years old to apply for naturalization.[216] However, under the Child Citizenship Act of 2000, any child who: (a) has a U.S. citizen parent; (b) is under age 18; and (c) resides in the U.S. as an LPR, in the legal and physical custody of the citizen parent, automatically becomes a citizen when the naturalization petition is approved for the parent.[217] This provision applies to both biological and adopted children. To qualify as a child under immigration laws, the child must have been adopted prior to reaching the age of 16.[218] For children who do not qualify for automatic citizenship, INA § 322 allows parents to file on their behalf for naturalization, as long as (1) the children have a U.S. citizen parent who files the application; (2) either the citizen parent or the children's citizen grandparent (parent of the citizen parent) has been physically present in the U.S. for five years, at least two of which were before either the

---

[210] *Id.* at 1573.

[211] *Id.* at 1606–1614.

[212] *See* Spiro, *Questioning Barriers to Naturalization, supra* note 191, at 516.

[213] *Id.* at 512.

[214] *Id.*

[215] Lapp, *supra* note 209, at 1614.

[216] INA § 334(b).

[217] INA § 320.

[218] INA § 101(b)(E)(i).

parent or grandparent reached the age of 14; (3) the children are under the age of 18; and (4) the children reside outside the U.S. in the legal and physical custody of the citizen parent but are temporarily present in the U.S. after a lawful admission.

5. English Language

Congress first adopted the ability to speak the English language requirement in 1906, and subsequently added in 1950, a literacy component, which remains to today.[219] Under current law, the petitioner must demonstrate during an interview with an immigration officer "an understanding of the English language, including an ability to read, write, and speak words in ordinary usage."[220] Generally, this involves conversing and responding in English to questions on the civics test, described below. There are a few exceptions to the English language requirement based on physical or mental disability, which must be substantiated through a medical examination.[221] The exception also applies to a person who is over 50 years of age and has been living in the U.S. for at least 20 years as an LPR, or a person who is over 55 years of age and has been living in the U.S. for at least 15 years as an LPR.[222] Even with these exceptions, the English language requirement represents the most formidable obstacle to naturalization. Some defend the requirement as consistent with encouraging immigrant's broad and political assimilation. The argument is that a common language is constitutive of the community and provides an important bond among its members, and the latter insofar as language is important for responsible political participation.[223] Those who oppose it question not only the premise that the English language has defined or unified the U.S. community but also because it fails to achieve its unifying purpose for the substantial numbers of those who learn it for purposes of naturalization but still do not make English their primary language.[224]

6. Knowledge of Civics

This requirement grew out of the early naturalization requirement that an applicant show an attachment to constitutional principles, and it was ultimately codified in 1950, as part of the anti-Communist Internal Security Act.[225] The current statute requires the applicant to demonstrate "knowledge and understanding of the fundamentals of the history, and of the principles and the form of government, of the United States."[226] Persons with a medically demonstrated physical or developmental condition can be exempted from this

---

[219] Spiro, *Questioning Barriers to Naturalization, supra* note 191, at 489–91.

[220] INA § 312(a)(1).

[221] INA § 312(b)(1).

[222] INA § 312(b)(2).

[223] *See* Neuman, *Justifying U.S. Naturalization Policies, supra* note 192, at 263–68. *See also* Spiro, *Questioning Barriers to Naturalization, supra* note 191, at 492–95.

[224] Spiro, *Questioning Barriers to Naturalization, supra* note 191, at 494–95.

[225] Internal Security Act of 1950, ch. 1024, § 30, 64 Stat. 984, 1013. *See also* Spiro, *Questioning Barriers to Naturalization, supra* note 191, at 497–98.

[226] INA § 312.

requirement,[227] as can, at the discretion of the interviewing immigration officer, persons over 65 years old who have lived in the U.S. for more than 20 years.[228] Even those applicants who have been exempted from the language requirement must pass the civics portion of the test in their own language, however.

An official naturalization test was first implemented in 1986, and remained unchanged until 2006.[229] In September 2007, United States Citizenship and Immigration Services (CIS) unveiled the final 100 questions to the new citizenship test, created to be "more standardized, fair, and meaningful."[230] The new test, implemented nationwide as of October 2008, includes 100 revised questions, from which 10 are randomly selected.[231] The English reading and writing portions of the examination remained the same but it contains more civic-based questions.[232] CIS described this new test as emphasizing "the fundamental concepts of American democracy and the rights and responsibilities of citizenship."[233] CIS stated goal is to "inspire immigrants to learn about the civil values of this nation so that after they take the oath of citizenship they will participate fully in our great democracy."[234] The test has pleased some groups who perceive the new test as a better tool to encourage civic participation among immigrants.[235] Others, however, view the new test either as a meaningless barrier to naturalization,[236] while other critique it for its perpetuation of a bounded construction of citizenship that, by its nature, promotes a universalist citizenship ideology that particularly disfavors minority groups.[237]

---

[227] INA § 312(b)(1).

[228] INA § 312(b)(3).

[229] Keun Dong Kim, *Citizenship Exam Redesigned to Focus on Concepts Rather than Trivia*, 21 GEO. IMMIGR. L.J. 155, 155 (2006).

[230] USCIS, Redesigned Naturalization Test, http://www.uscis.gov/us-citizenship/naturalization-test.

[231] The test is *available at* http://www.uscis.gov/sites/default/files/USCIS/Office%20of%20Citizenship/Citizenship%20Resource%20Center%20Site/Publications/100q.pdf

[232] The vocabulary lists for the reading and writing components are *available at* http://www.uscis.gov/sites/default/files/USCIS/Office%20of%20Citizenship/Citizenship%20Resource%20Center%20Site/Publications/PDFs/reading_vocab.pdf and http://www.uscis.gov/sites/default/files/USCIS/Office%20of%20Citizenship/Citizenship%20Resource%20Center%20Site/Publications/PDFs/writing_vocab.pdf.

[233] Press Briefing, *USCIS, Pen and Pad: New Naturalization Test* 30–33 (Sept. 27, 2007), *available at* http://www.uscis.gov/files/pressrelease/natzndtbl_72sep07.pdf.

[234] Press Release, *USCIS Issues Questions and Answers for New Pilot Naturalization Exam* (Nov. 30, 2006), *available at* http://www.uscis.gov/files/pressrelease/NatzTestQs113006.pdf.

[235] Kim, *supra* note 229, at 157.

[236] *Id.* at 156. *See also* Liav Orgad, *Creating New Americans: The Essence of Americanism under the Citizenship Test*, 47 HOUS. L. REV. 1227 (2011) (arguing that the new U.S. citizenship test failed to create a more meaningful test by requiring new citizens to memorize esoteric issues, such as the location of the Statute of Liberty, while ignoring the understanding of important ideas, such a liberty and equal protection).

[237] Julian Wonjung Park, *A More Meaningful Citizenship Test? Unmasking the Construction of a Universalist, Principled-Based Citizenship Ideology*, 96 CAL. L. REV. 999, 1002 (2008).

7.   Political or Ideological Requirements

The history of ideological exclusion from naturalization began in 1906, when Congress adopted what became known as an anti-anarchist provision [i.e., those opposed to organized government] following the assassination of President Mckinley.[238] That provision was applied broadly to deny naturalization to members of the Industrial Workers of the World, a global workers' union.[239] Then it was expanded in 1940 to include those who believed in the overthrow of the U.S government, or belonged to an organization advocating such action, which was applied broadly to members of the Communist Party.[240] Under current law, applicants who, either during the 10-year period immediately preceding the filing of the application or during the interval between the filing and the taking of the final oath of citizenship, have been affiliated with "communist, totalitarian, or terrorist groups or have advocated their ideals, including through speeches and publications" are disqualified from naturalization.[241] The requirement is controversial especially because it relies on proxies, most notably membership in the Communist Party, as conclusive evidence that a person, if granted citizenship, would undermine U.S. polity.[242] As well, ideological qualifications conflict with bedrock principles of U.S. liberal tradition, including freedom of thought, speech, and association.[243] They may be justified, however, insofar as the applicant's acceptance of the republican framework is a pre-requisite to the person's political incorporation, if the ideological criteria are compatible with U.S. national identity.[244]

8.   Attachment to the Principles of the U.S. Constitution

An applicant must demonstrate an attachment to the principles of the U.S. Constitution and allegiance to the U.S. government by taking an oath both in writing on the application and during the induction ceremony. The oath is a promise that the applicant supports the Constitution, renounces all foreign allegiances, is willing to defend all federal laws against all enemies, will bear true allegiance to those laws, and will bear arms for the U.S. if required by law.[245] The oath was first introduced as part of the naturalization act of 1795[246] and evidences a strong norm against dual citizenship[247] as discussed below.

---

[238] Spiro, *Questioning Barriers to Naturalization*, *supra* note 191, at 501–02.

[239] *Id.* at 502.

[240] *Id.*

[241] INA § 313.

[242] Spiro, *Questioning Barriers to Naturalization*, *supra* note 191, at 503–04.

[243] *See* Neuman, Justifying U.S. Naturalization Policies, *supra* note 192, at 256–60.

[244] *Id.* at 260–63.

[245] INA § 337(a).

[246] Act of Jan. 29, 1795, ch. 20, § 1, 1 Stat. 414. For a discussion of the original oath requirement, *see* Neuman, *Justifying U.S. Naturalization Policies*, *supra* note 192, at 253–54.

[247] Spiro, *Questioning Barriers to Naturalization*, *supra* note 191, at 504.

Beyond these eight statutory requirements for naturalization, DHS has imposed a few additional requirements. Non-statutory criteria that may be considered include: non-support of dependents; adultery; and failure to register with the Selective Service between 18 and 26 years of age, but only if the applicant knowingly and willfully failed to register during the period for which the applicant must establish a history of good moral character. A person who fails to file taxes or to pay back-taxes prior to filing an application for naturalization could also be denied, especially since the failure to do so could be considered a crime.

c. Adjudication and Judicial Review

Finally is the question of adjudication. Congress also has broad discretion to allocate by statute the functions of administrative agencies and courts in the adjudication of Naturalization petitions. For more than a century, courts had an exclusive role in granting or denying citizenship. In 1906, however, Congress for the first time established an administrative agency, the Bureau of Immigration and Naturalization, responding to concerns over the absence of a uniform naturalization process, including the intermittent acceptance by courts of non-white immigrants as citizens. The Bureau "provided for a uniform rule for the naturalization of aliens throughout the United States."[248] Overtime and especially under the current statute, the adjudicatory function by administrative agencies over Naturalization petitions has increased. The current statutory scheme was put in place in 1990, when Congress transferred the authority to grant naturalization to the Attorney General (now the Secretary of Homeland Security through the Department of Homeland Security). This was the first time that Congress provided an executive agency the formal power to award citizenship without court intervention.[249]

Courts, however, continue to possess robust powers to ensure the speedy resolution of citizenship cases, as well as to review denials. First, the statute provides that courts have jurisdiction over matters in which the agency has failed to adjudicate within 120 days, in which case the court "may either determine the matter or remand the matter, with appropriate instructions."[250] Second, when a person has been denied naturalization following an administrative appeal,[251] courts retain jurisdiction to conduct de novo review, and the court "shall make its own findings of fact and conclusions of law and shall, at the request of the petitioner, conduct a hearing de novo on the application."[252] Both the express authority in a statute for courts to take jurisdiction before the administrative process is completed and the de novo review standard are unusual in administrative law, and especially in immigration law.[253] Congress views citizenship, including its acquisition through naturalization, an important right such that enhanced procedures should protect

---

[248] Law of June 29, 1906. *See* Douglas, *supra* note 175, at 389–90. *See also* Nancy Morawetz, *Citizenship and the Courts*, 2007 U. CHI. LEGAL F. 447, 451–54 (2007).

[249] *Id.* at 454.

[250] INA § 336(b).

[251] The 1990 Acts introduced an administrative appellate review process for the first time. Morawetz, *supra* note 248, at 455.

[252] INA §§ 310 (b), (c).

[253] Morawetz, *supra* note 248, at 451.

those seeking citizenship.[254] The current judicial review process, however, has not consistently achieved its intended results. One problem has been that the current statute permits judicial intervention only when delays occur between an initial examination and a decision, but it says nothing about delays during other stages of the proceedings.[255] Thus, courts have not always remedied administrative delays in the adjudication of naturalization.[256] Second, courts have taken different approaches to their fact-finding role, with some courts reviewing cases solely on the agency record while others conduct their own fact-finding.[257]

To file for Naturalization, applicants must submit Form N-400 to the U.S. Citizenship & Immigration Services (CIS). Beginning on May 5, 2014 all naturalization applicants must use a new N-400 form that is 21 pages long, or twice as long as the old form. The increased length is due to a number of additional questions,[258] formatting changes, and the new bar code that appears at the bottom of each page. Some have expressed concern that the new form will create an undue burden for applicants and lead to longer adjudication times and processing delays.[259] Of particular concern is the inclusion of a number of new or amended questions to reflect the inadmissibility grounds added by the Intelligence Reform and Terrorism Prevention Act of 2004.[260] These questions, in general, ask very broadly about a person's association with any type of potentially armed group, about past work or activities in a prison, detention facility or similar camp, or about involvement with the use or transfer of weapons. The concern here has been that while some of the questions are relevant to inadmissibility, many are overly broad and encompass lawful activity.[261]

d. Military Naturalization

Since 2002, nearly 90,000 foreign nationals have become naturalized through their military service in the U.S. armed forces.[262] Noncitizens filing for naturalization based on their service with the U.S. military must meet some but not all of the

---

[254] *Id.*

[255] *Id.* at 457.

[256] *See, e.g.*, Pershon, *supra* note 193 (attributing blame to the inability of the courts to resolve the undue delays caused by the FBI name check requirement for naturalization on Congress stripping the courts of their power to adjudicate naturalization applications until the administrative process is complete).

[257] *Id.* at 459–60.

[258] Additional questions, for example, pertain to the applicant's parents but it is unclear as to whether the intent of these questions is for the agency to adjudicate derivative citizenship when a different N-600 form already exists for this purpose. The questions also seek more detailed information regarding prior spouses or current spouses that some consider irrelevant to the, naturalization application. American Immigration Lawyers Association and Catholic Legal Immigration Network Inc., *Comments to the proposed changes to the N-400 Application*, dated Feb. 15, 2013, *available at* http://www.aila.org/content/default.aspx?docid=43342.

[259] *Id.*

[260] *Id.*

[261] *Id.*

[262] CIS, *Naturalization Through Military Service: Fact Sheet*, *available at* http://www.uscis.gov/news/fact-sheets/naturalization-through-military-service-fact-sheet.

requirements applicable to all other applicants for naturalization. There are two separate military naturalization statutory provisions that operate either in peacetime [INA §328] or wartime [INA §329] that create significant differences that make them quite attractive options for many noncitizens.[263] The two provisions contain common features but also differ in significant ways. Both provisions still require that all qualified U.S. military personnel[264] satisfy the requirements of attachment to the U.S. Constitution, knowledge of civics and the English language as described above. Both provisions also generally waive or modify the normal age, good moral character, and residence and physical presence requirements that apply to other applicants for naturalization. As to the residence, lawful permanent residents who serve in the U.S. military have traditionally been permitted to obtain U.S. citizenship in an expedited fashion. First, qualified members of the U.S. Armed Forces are permitted to apply for U.S. citizenship after one year of service or immediately when a Presidential executive order regarding wartime hostilities is in effect.[265] As to physical presence, since 2004, current service members overseas are still eligible to naturalize.[266] The good moral character requirement is in effect but the period is reduced to one year for most applicants, except as to those bars that are permanent.[267] Another unique aspect of the special military naturalization rules is that it allows for naturalization notwithstanding the pendency of removal proceedings.[268] In addition, since October 1, 2004, current qualified military service members and veterans can apply for naturalization without paying any application or biometric fee.[269] As well, since 2009, military personnel may file their naturalization applications, with support from the CIS, when they report to Basic Combat Training (BCT) and complete the entire naturalization process while they are at BCT.[270]

The significant divergence between the peacetime [INA §328] and wartime [INA §329] military naturalization provisions pertains to the requirement of lawful permanent residence. Under INA § 328, qualified military applicants must have had LPR status during their military service or within six months of leaving the service.[271] Under INA § 239, however, qualified military applicants may also naturalize without obtaining lawful residency status first. INA § 329, however, only applies during specified statutory periods or when a presidential executive order exists that invokes the statute.[272] Currently, an Executive Order issued by President George W. Bush on July 3, 2002, retroactive to September 11, 2001,

---

[263] Margaret D. Stock, *Recent Developments in Military Enlistment and Naturalization Law*, 11-03 Immigration Briefings 1, 6 (2011).

[264] The key to military naturalization is that the military service must have been "honorable" as determined by the branch of the U.S. Armed forces in which the person served or is serving. *Id.* at 10.

[265] *Id.* at 6.

[266] *Id.*

[267] *Id.* at 7. *See also supra* Part B.3.b.3.b, discussing the good moral character requirement.

[268] *Id.* at 10.

[269] *Id.* at 6 (discussing the National Defense Authorization Act).

[270] *Id.* at 11.

[271] *Id.* at 7.

[272] *Id.* at Appendix II.

remains in effect as of this writing.[273] Another interesting aspect of INA § 329 is that someone who is ineligible to adjust status based on grounds of inadmissibility may still potentially naturalize so long as they can show the requisite good moral character and meet the law's other requirements.[274] It is important to note, however, that, with few exceptions, lawful residency status is a requirement for enlistment into the U.S. military.[275] Despite this bar, however, there are reports of noncitizens serving in the U.S. military who have died in combat while undocumented and who have been granted citizenship posthumously.[276]

C. DUAL NATIONALITY

Dual nationality, defined simply as the formal possession of citizenship in at least one more nation, has long been disfavored in the United States.[277] Over the past decades, many foreign countries have liberalized their laws regarding retention of citizenship after naturalization in another country.[278] As well, U.S. laws have evolved to accommodate dual nationals in most instances, even as distaste for its possession or retention remains.[279]

Initially, dual nationality resulted when the birth countries of immigrants who naturalized in the United States refused to release them from the perpetual allegiance doctrine that then attached to common law *jus solis* citizenship.[280] In the early nineteenth century, the United States recognized the prerogative of other states to restrict expatriation, and, in effect refused request for diplomatic intervention from dual nationals against their birth country, even from those who might find themselves drafted into the military after a temporary visit abroad.[281] By the mid-nineteenth century, however, as U.S. immigration grew, U.S. authorities found themselves having to more firmly protect naturalized U.S. citizens from military service obligations.[282] The issue intensified in 1868 when Britain arrested several naturalized U.S. citizens and tried them for treason in connection with an

---

[273] CIS, *Naturalization Through Military Service: Fact Sheet*, *available at* http://www.uscis.gov/news/fact-sheets/naturalization-through-military-service-fact-sheet.

[274] *Id.* at 9.

[275] The exceptions apply for citizens of the Republic of the Marshall Islands, Palau, and Micronesia, who may enlist owing to a treaty between the United States and their countries. As well, some foreigners who are present legally in the United States and have a valid Social Security Number may enlist if their enlistment is "vital to the national interest." Margaret D. Stock, *Hidden Immigration Benefits for Military Personnel*, 30 GPSolo, no. 5 (2013), *available at* http://www.americanbar.org/publications/gp_solo/2013/september_october/hidden_immigration_benefits_military_personnel.html.

[276] *See* America's Voice Education Fund, Fact Sheet: Immigrants and the Military (2010), *available at* http://amvoice.3cdn.net/385e1d33bde48f4d3e_znm6b9k3x.pdf.

[277] Peter J. Spiro, *Dual Nationality and the Meaning of Citizenship*, 46 EMORY L.J. 1411, 1415 (1997).

[278] U.S. Citizenship and Naturalization Handbook, § 15–18 (2013).

[279] *Id.*

[280] *Id.* at 1418–25.

[281] *Id.* at 1425–26.

[282] *Id.* at 1427.

Irish uprising.[283] Congress moved quickly to enact legislation affirming expatriation as "a natural and inherent right of all people, indispensable to the enjoyment of the rights of life, liberty, and the pursuit of happiness,"[284] and directed the President to employ all means short of war to secure the release of U.S. citizens.[285] This act marked the beginning of the decline of the perpetual allegiance doctrine for birth citizens also in much of Europe.[286]

Compelled dual nationality, thus, was largely resolved by the late nineteenth century, but dual nationality by choice remained, even as they faced little toleration and were perceived as threats to the community.[287] These dual nationals included not only naturalized citizens but also an increasing number of children born to immigrant parents yet to naturalize as well as children born abroad to U.S. citizen parents.[288] U.S. laws responded to each of these in turn. By 1907, for example, Congress codified the existing administrative practice of requiring a renunciation oath upon naturalization, with the intended effect of triggering denationalization by the birth country.[289] In practice, however, the oath requirement has not resulted in denationalization and many naturalized citizens retain their dual nationality despite taking the oath.[290] For dual nationals born abroad or living abroad, the U.S. imposed a type of informal election requirement by requiring residence in the U.S.[291] As well, Congress passed a series of lax expatriation laws, such that the payment of taxes or the holding of agricultural land or the participation of politics abroad, and even the return of naturalized citizens to their homeland past a certain period, could result in the loss of nationality.[292] The enforcement of some of these laws intensified, of course, during the Cold War, during which time any active political identification with a foreign state provided grounds for expatriation.[293] Courts, including the U.S. Supreme Court upheld much of these practices against constitutional attack.[294] Eventually, the U.S. Supreme Court reined in these laws by imposing substantive restrictions on what acts could result in a loss of nationality, but also by imposing a requirement that the act be done with the specific intent of relinquishing citizenship.[295] Thus, the United States has softened significantly in its

---

[283] *Id.*

[284] Act of July 27, 1868, sh. 249, 15 Stat. 223 (codified at 22 U.S.C. § 1732 (1976)).

[285] Spiro, *Dual Nationality, supra* note 277, at 1428.

[286] *Id.* at 1429–30.

[287] *Id.* at 1431–32.

[288] *Id.* at 1435–36.

[289] *Id.* at 1435.

[290] *Id.* at 1457–60.

[291] *Id.* at 1437–38.

[292] *Id.* at 1440–41.

[293] *Id.* at 1443–44.

[294] *Id.* at 1445–46 (discussing MacKenzie v. Hare, 239 U.S. 299 (1915) (upholding the expatriation of a U.S. born woman citizen by virtue of her marriage to a foreign national) and Perez v. Brownell, 356 U.S. 44 (1958) (upholding the expatriation of a naturalized citizen who voted in a foreign political election)).

[295] *See infra* notes 300–397 and accompanying text on Loss of Citizenship.

legal attitudes against dual nationality, even as it remains unpopular.[296] Mexico's adoption in 1998 of a constitutional grant of dual nationality at the heels of similar changes by other countries (such as El Salvador) that have traditionally sent large numbers of immigrants to the United States, has provoked renewed fervor against . dual nationality.[297] Some political scientists, for example, have argued that the dual nationality of naturalized citizens, especially Latinos, disconnects immigrants from the U.S. political system.[298] Moreover, some post 9/11 practices suggest increased intolerance for the perceived divided loyalties that attach to dual nationality.[299]

D. EXPATRIATION OR LOSS OF CITIZENSHIP

Citizenship acquired through birth or naturalization may be lost through a process formerly known as expatriation and now simply called loss of citizenship.[300] The U.S. Supreme Court considers relinquishment of U.S. citizenship a right.[301] Loss of citizenship can also occur through statutory revocation, although the Fourteenth Amendment protects individuals from governmental abridgment of a right to citizenship.[302]

1. The History of Expatriation Laws

Congress has legislated to denationalize only sparingly.[303] Expatriation laws have existed since 1865, when Congress declared deserters as having abandoned their U.S. citizenship.[304] In 1868, Congress passed the Expatriation Act and to declare expatriation a natural and inherent right, though its purpose was primarily to protect naturalized U.S. citizens with dual nationality who returned to their countries of origin.[305] In 1907, Congress set out the actions that would effect this

---

[296] Spiro, *Dual Nationality*, *supra* note 277, at 1456 (discussing State Department policies disfavoring dual nationality).

[297] *See e.g.*, David A. Martin, *New Rules on Dual Nationality for a Democratizing Glove: Between Rejection and Embrace*, 14 Geo. Immigr. L.J. 1 (1999) and Notes and Comments, Chris Dangaran, *The Duel Over Dual Nationality Amendments*, 7 Sw. J. L. & Trade Am. 47 (2000).

[298] Jeffrey K. Staton, et al., *Costly Citizenship? Dual Nationality Institutions, Naturalization, and Political Connectedness* (June 19, 2007), *available at* SSRN: http://ssrn.com/abstracts=995569. *See also* Jeffrey K. Staton, et al., *Dual Nationality Among Latinos: What are the Implications for Political Connectedness?*, 69 J. of Politics 470 (2007).

[299] The issue comes up frequently with regard to the availability to U.S. jobs that require a security clearance, for example U.S. Department of State Policies on Security Clearance states that "[d]ual nationality is a relevant element in some cases." And while DOS does not adopt a blanket rule against dual citizens in making security clearances, the issue is considered on a case by case basis. U.S. Department of State, Dual Citizenship: Security Implications, *available at* https://careers.state.gov/ uploads/8f/f7/8ff7b0bab879946e78f30e62c859c0f1/DualCitizenship.pdf.

[300] In 1994, Congress amended the Immigration and Nationality Act to replace the reference to expatriation with the phrase loss of citizenship. INTCA § 105.

[301] *See* Afroyim v. Rusk, 387 U.S. 253, 263–66 (1967).

[302] *Id.*

[303] T. Alexander Aleinikoff, *Theories of Loss of Citizenship*, 84 Mich. L. Rev. 1471, 1476–78 (1986).

[304] Sec. 21, Act of March 3, 1865, 13 Stat. 487.

[305] *See supra* notes 198–204 and accompanying text.

expatriation.[306] The 1907 Expatriation Act was also aimed at solving problems occasioned by dual nationality, although this time the aim was to restrict the right of persons to retain their original nationality upon naturalizing as U.S. citizens.[307] Between 1907 and 1922, women who married U.S. citizens who naturalized in another country lost their citizenship because women acquired the nationality of their husbands.[308] In 1940, Congress added several new grounds for loss of nationality, such that citizenship could be lost by voting in a political election of a foreign state, or accepting the duties of an office or employment under the government of a foreign state for which only nationals of the state were eligible, desertion in a time of war, and for conviction of treason or attempting to overthrow the U.S. government.[309] In 1944, Congress also moved to denationalize a person for departing the United States in time of war in order to avoid military service. Congress also made minor changes in 1952, including amending the provision relating to employment in a foreign government to read as the provision reads under current law.[310] Also in 1954, Congress authorized denationalization for certain convictions under the Smith Act.[311] Generally, all statutes repealing a prior expatriation law have provided that citizenship lost under the former statute is not restored by its repeal, unless that prior statute would be unconstitutional under current constitutional doctrine; as such, the law in effect at the time of the person committed the expatriating act could apply, unless it is declared unconstitutional.[312]

Post 9/11, some members of Congress attempted but failed to pass legislation that would have stripped of citizenship to anyone becoming members or providing material support to a terrorist organization.[313] Professor Peter J. Spiro suggests that an explanation for this failure turns on the fact that the judicially-defined constitutional restrictions on the scope of permissible expatriation limited the utility of such laws.[314] Despite the failure, *Hamdi*, at least renounced his citizenship as part of his settlement agreement upon his release as an "enemy

---

[306] Act of March 2, 1907, Pub. L. No. 59-193, 34 Stat. 1228.

[307] *See supra* notes 207–209 and accompanying text.

[308] Daniel Levy, *U.S. Citizenship and Naturalization Handbook*, § 15:6 (2008).

[309] Ch. 876, 54 Stat. 1137 (1940).

[310] Aleinikoff, *supra* note 303, at note 28. The Smith Act or the Alien Registration Act of 1940, 8 U.S.C. § 2385, makes it a crime to "knowingly or willfully advocate, abet, advise, or teach the duty, necessity, desirability or propriety of overthrowing the Government of the United States or of any State by force or violence, or for anyone to organize any association which teaches, advises, or encourages such an overthrow, or for anyone to become a member of or to affiliate with any such association."

[311] Ch. 1256, § 2, 68 Stat. 1146 (1954).

[312] Levy, *supra* note 308, at §§ 15:1 and 15:3.

[313] In May 2010, for example, Joe Liberman proposed the Terrorist Expatriation Act which would have amended the Immigration and Nationality Act to add a new ground for loss of citizenship for engaging in hostilities against the United States or providing material support to a foreign terrorist organization. Peter J. Spiro, *Expatriating Terrorists*, 82 FORDHAM L. REV. 2169, 2169–71 (2014). Similar legislation was introduced but never passed to denationalize U.S. citizens of Japanese ancestry indicating loyalty to the Emperor of Japan. *See, e.g.*, Expatriation of Certain Nationals of the United States: Hearings before the House Committee on Immigration and Naturalization, 78th Cong., 2d Sess. (1944).

[314] Spiro, *Expatriating Terrorists*, *supra* note 313, at 2170.

combatant."[315] Saad Gul has argued that Hamdi's renunciation clause would be unconstitutional under current Supreme Court doctrine, which requires that expatriation be voluntary, as explained below.[316]

2. Constitutional Scrutiny of Expatriation Statutes

The courts have not always scrutinized Congress for enacting expatriation laws. In 1915, for example, the U.S. Supreme Court upheld the constitutionality of the then expatriation regime that considered a woman's loss of citizenship upon marriage to a noncitizen.[317] In a series of cases following WWII, the courts entertained some challenges by expatriated U.S. citizens who claimed that their service in the armed forces of Axis states, the basis for losing their citizenship, had not been voluntary.[318] Those cases, however, were to the application of the law but not to the substance of the law itself. In the 1950's, however, Congress' expatriation laws met fierce judicial hostility. In 1958, the Court issued three rulings in a single day that started to change the way courts would consider expatriation laws. In *Trop v. Dulles*, the Court rejected the use of the 1940 law in cases of desertion, considering the law punitive.[319] In *Nishikawa v. Dulles*, a case in which Japanese U.S. citizens claimed duress when they served in the Japanese armed forces, the Court required the government to bear the burden of proof to establish the voluntariness of an expatriation act.[320] In contrast, in *Perez v. Brownell*, the Court upheld expatriation for voting in a political election.[321] Still, this trilogy of cases did not significantly alter Congress' discretion to exercise the expatriation power. This changed, however, after the Cold War. In 1967, the Court held that the Constitution did not confer on Congress an affirmative power to expatriate any citizen and affirmed that persons cannot lose their citizenship unless they relinquished it voluntarily.[322] To the contrary, the Fourteenth Amendment protected persons from any governmental abridgment of his or her citizenship rights.[323] Then in 1980, the Court clarified its earlier holdings to affirm that expatriation also requires an independent showing of intentionality to relinquish U.S. citizenship by the person who commits the expatriating act.[324] In addition, since the 1950's, the Court has disallowed certain acts, even when committed voluntarily, to become the sole basis for expatriation.[325] These include deserting armed forces during wartime,[326]

---

[315] Saad Gul, *Return of the Native? An Assessment of the Citizenship Renunciation Clause in Hamdi's Settlement Agreement in the Light of Citizenship Jurisprudence*, 27 N. ILL. U. L. REV. 131, 155–57 (2007).

[316] *Id.* at 134–163.

[317] Mackenzie v. Hare, 239 U.S. 299 (1915).

[318] Spiro, *Expatriating Terrorists, supra* note 313, at 2172–73.

[319] 356 U.S. 86 (1958).

[320] 356 U.S. 129 (1958).

[321] 356 U.S. 44 (1958).

[322] *Afroyim*, 387 U.S. at 253. Earlier cases had also required voluntariness. *See, e.g.*, Nishikawa v. Dulles, 356 U.S. 129, 133(1958).

[323] *Afroyim*, 387 U.S. at 261–62.

[324] Vance v. Terrazas, 444 U.S. 252, 261 (1980).

[325] In contrast, in 1915, the Court upheld a statute that stripped a woman of her birthright citizenship

departing or remaining outside the United States to avoid military service,[327] voting in a foreign political election,[328] and possessing dual nationality.[329] In 1986, Congress revised the expatriation sections of the Immigration and Nationality Act to comport with Constitutional requirements. Congress made the 1986 amendments retroactive so that current determinations of whether a person expatriated himself by acts committed before 1986 must be based on the current statute.[330]

3. The Current Law

Currently, the INA has seven grounds that, if performed voluntarily and "with the intention of relinquishing United States nationality,"[331] results in a loss of nationality. In general terms, these are (1) obtaining naturalization in another country; (2) taking an oath of allegiance for a foreign sovereign; (3) serving in the armed forces of a foreign state as an officer or in any capacity when those forces are engaged in hostilities against the U.S.; (4) accepting a government post with another state after acquiring the nationality of that state or when the post requires an oath of allegiance to that foreign country; (5) making a formal renunciation of nationality; (6) making a written renunciation of nationality; or (7) committing of treason or attempting to overthrow the U.S. government.[332] When citizenship is lost under the statute, it also divests in the same sense that U.S. citizenship vests upon a child when both parents naturalize.[333] Thus, a child who acquired or would have acquired citizenship through the parent also loses his or her citizenship with the parent who is expatriated. In addition, because voluntary expatriation could have tax advantages, Congress passed a law in 1996 to penalize persons who voluntarily relinquished citizenship to obtain tax advances by barring them from seeking admission to the U.S. in the future.[334] Since, there have been a series of tax laws that attach tax consequences to expatriates.[335]

---

solely by virtue of her marriage to a foreign national. Mackenzie v. Hare, 239 U.S. 299 (1915). Marriage-based expatriation has not existed since 1931 because Congress repealed it outright. Sec. 3(a) Act of March 3, 1931, Pub. L. No. 71-829, 46 Stat. 1511.

[326] Trop v. Dulles, 356 U.S. 86, 86 (1958).

[327] Kennedy v. Mendoza-Martinez, 372 U.S. 144 (1963).

[328] *Afroyim*, 387 U.S. at 253.

[329] Kawakita v. U.S., 343 U.S. 717, 724 (1952).

[330] Immigration and Nationality Act, Amendment of 1986, Pub. L. 99-653, 100 Stat. 3655, at § 23(g).

[331] INA § 349(a).

[332] *Id.* Except for six and seven, the person must have taken up residence outside the United States and its outlying possessions before expatriation can take effect. INA § 351(a).

[333] Levy, *supra* note 308, at § 15:1.

[334] Illegal Reform and Immigrant Responsibility Act, Pub. L. 104-208, 110 Stat. 3009-546, § 352(b). In addition, under current tax laws, persons who renounced their citizenship to avoid tax liability face serious adverse consequences. IRS Notice 97-19, Guidance for Expatriates Under §§ 877, 2501, 2107, and 6039F (Mar. 10, 1997) reproduced in 74 Intepreter Releases (May 23, 1997).

[335] *See* Michael F. Pfeifer, *The State of Expatriation 2012(3)*, SU013 ALI-CLE 547 for an explanation of the tax regime that governs U.S. expatriates.

Congress also created more flexible evidentiary requirements for establishing the voluntariness and intentionality that appeared to modify the burden of proof standard required in earlier Court cases. In 1961, the INA established an evidentiary presumption that a person who has performed any expatriating act has done so voluntarily, which can be rebutted upon showing by the preponderance of the evidence that the acts were not undertaken voluntarily.[336] In 1980, the Court upheld this evidentiary presumption and expressly rejected that the Government must prove voluntariness with clear and convincing evidence,[337] a standard the Court had required in earlier rulings.[338] In other words, under current law, proving with a preponderance of the evidence that the person has committed one of the expatriating acts in the INA is sufficient, and it is the citizen who must prove with a preponderance of the evidence that he or she committed the act under duress.[339]

With regard to intentionality, the Court also affirmed the statutory requirement that intent is proved with the preponderance of the evidence rather than higher burden of proof.[340] The Court explained, moreover, that any of the specified acts for expatriation could be highly persuasive evidence of a purpose to abandon citizenship.[341] The Court did not, however, define what conduct would support a finding that a citizen who performed a statutory imperative act intended to terminate citizenship. As a result, lower court decisions on loss of citizenship cases have tended to be fact-specific, and there is no simple certainty when it comes to assessing the issue of intent to relinquish citizenship.[342] Then in 1990, the Department of State made a policy decision to presume that the U.S. citizen does not intend to relinquish citizenship when obtaining naturalization in a foreign state, subscribing to routine declaration of allegiance to a foreign state, or accepting non-level employment with a foreign government.[343] This standard in effect has allowed certain U.S. citizens not only to vote in foreign elections but even to assume a high political post without risking denationalization.[344]

E.　DENATURALIZATION

In addition to loss of citizenship through expatriation, naturalized citizens may have their naturalization revoked. Denaturalization statutes have also encountered judicial resistance because a liberty interest that accrues as soon as naturalization is conferred[345] and consequently the Court has held that "it should not be lightly

---

[336] Vance v. Terrazas, 444 U.S. 252, 254–55 (1980) (citing to then Section 349(a)(2) of the INA, 66 Stat. 267, as amended, 75 Stat. 656).

[337] *Terrazas*, 444 U.S. at 254.

[338] *See, e.g.*, *Nishikawa*, 356 U.S. at 133 and *Kawakita*, 343 U.S. at 724.

[339] *Terrazas*, 444 U.S. at 268–70.

[340] *Id.* at 267.

[341] *Id.* at 261.

[342] Alan G. James, *Expatriation in the United States: Precept and Practice Today and Yesterday*, 27 SAN DIEGO L. REV. 853, 893–94 (1990).

[343] *Id.* at 895–96.

[344] Spiro, *Dual Nationality*, *supra* note 277, at 1454–55.

[345] *Schneiderman*, 320 U.S. at 125. *See also* Chaunt v. U.S., 364 U.S. 350, 354 (1960).

revoked."[346] As well, First Amendment values have influenced the Court's rulings to interpret or apply statutes to favor the person facing a loss of citizenship.[347] This has been the result of the Court's concern over denaturalization proceedings being employed as part of a broader campaign to stamp out perceived disloyalty during times of heightened national security periods in the United States. Such was the case, for instance, when the government targeted alleged communists or pro-Nazi sympathizers for denaturalization.[348]

Denaturalization rulings, however, also reveal deep disagreement among the Justices about how much individual rights considerations should trump Congressional intent to denaturalize,[349] at least insofar as denaturalization retains a relationship to Congress' powers to grant naturalization in the first place.[350] Denaturalization generally can occur at any time post-naturalization[351] whenever the recipient of the privilege procured it invalidly. The Court has long affirmed Congress' power to strip a person of his citizenship by naturalization when it has been unlawfully or fraudulently procured.[352] In contrast, statutes that would impose substantive restrictions on the acts of naturalized citizens post-naturalization are generally invalid.[353]

Currently the INA permits "setting aside the order admitting [a] person to citizenship and canceling the certificate of naturalization on the ground that such order and such certificate were illegally procured or were procured by concealment of a material fact or by willful misrepresentation."[354] Person who claimed U.S.

---

[346] *Schneiderman*, 320 U.S. at 125.

[347] *See, e.g., Schneiderman*, 320 U.S. at 134 and 137.

[348] *See, e.g.,* Charles H. Hooker, *The Past as Prologue: Schneiderman v. United States and Contemporary Questions of Citizenship and Denationalization*, 19 EMORY INT'L L. REV. 305, 319–46 (Discussing the historical context of the *Schneiderman*, 320 U.S. at 134, case, which involved the denaturalization of Schneiderman because of his affiliation with the Workers Party of the America and the Young Workers League of America), and the Baumgartner v. U.S., 322 U.S. 665 (1944), and Knauer v. U.S., 328 U.S. 654 (1946) cases, which involved the denaturalization of a German nationals essentially for their support of the Nazi regime.

[349] *See, e.g., Schneiderman*, 320 U.S. at 194 (three dissenting justices stating that the Court cannot change or modify the will of Congress by reading a freedom of thought prescription to statutory interpretation) and Klapprott v. U.S., 335 U.S. 601 at 625 (1949) (three justices disagreeing that Court can disallow default judgments in denaturalization proceedings where Congress has not expressly invalidated them in the statute).

[350] *See, e.g.,* Johannessen v. U.S., 225 U.S. 227, 238 (1912).

[351] Costello v. U.S., 365 U.S. 265, 282 (1961) (disallowing a challenge to denaturalization proceedings 27 years after the conferral of naturalization).

[352] *See, e.g., Johannessen*, 225 U.S. at 238; U.S. v. Ginsberg, 243 U.S. 472 (1917); and *Knauer v. U.S.*, 328 U.S. at 1336.

[353] *Schneider*, 377 U.S. at 163 (striking down a 1952 statute that denaturalized citizens shown to have had continuous residence for three years in the territory of the foreign state in which they were formerly a national after becoming citizens). *But see* discussion of a few remaining post-naturalization denaturalization statutory grounds discussed *infra* in notes 359–61.

[354] INA § 340(a). The INA also allows revocation of admission to citizenship when there has been a criminal conviction for procuring naturalization by fraud. INA § 340(e). Commentators of immigration law also identify a third avenue for denaturalization known as "administrative denaturalization." This power to "correct, reopen, alter, modify, or vacate an order naturalizing the person" is found in INA

citizenship as the spouse or child of the denaturalized person will also automatically lose their citizenship as of the time of the order setting aside the principal's citizenship.[355] "Illegally procured" and "concealment of a material fact or by willful misrepresentation" constitute two separate grounds for denaturalization.[356] Thus, the government has generally relied on applicants' omissions or misrepresentations to start denaturalization, which were also the circumstances of denaturalization proceedings that targeted alleged communists or Nazi supporters. These are also the circumstances, in fact, in denaturalization cases today against alleged terrorists who may have failed to disclose all of their associations with any group that could be perceived as supporting terrorism or misrepresented any fact, including biographical ones, that could have led the government to discover damning facts.[357]

Congress responded to the Courts' limitations on denaturalization based on omitting or misrepresenting past membership in communist organizations by enacting the Internal Security Act of 1950.[358] This Act, which remains law,[359] creates a presumption of lack of attachment to the U.S. Constitution if within five years after a person naturalizes, he or she becomes "members of or affiliated with organization, membership in or affiliation with which at the time of naturalization would have been precluded . . . ." This provision, which has not been invoked, is likely unconstitutional, insofar as it creates post-Naturalization conditions found unconstitutional in *Scheiderman*.[360] A separate denaturalization ground that creates post-Naturalization conditions applies to person who received their naturalization based on their service in the U.S. armed forces. Such persons are subject to denaturalization proceedings if at any time subsequent to naturalization the person is separated from the military under other than honorable conditions.[361] The constitutionality of this provision is also uncertain.

In order to balance individual rights concerns against Congress' naturalization powers, the Court has at times imposed strict procedural safeguards in favor of persons facing denaturalization on the bases of alleged fraud. The Court has required the Government to prove by "clear, unequivocal, and convincing" evidence

---

§340(h) and rests with the Secretary of the Department of Homeland Security (DHS). DHS regulations on administrative denaturalization — *see* 8 C.F.R. §340.1 — contain limited procedural safeguards and allow denaturalization based on minimal proof. Based on this, the Ninth Circuit — Gorbach v. Reno — 219 F.3d 1087 (9th Cir. 2000) has upheld a challenge to the agency's authority to reopen and revoke naturalization orders. *See* Sarah B. Ignatius and Elisabeth S. Stickney, *Revocation or Loss of Citizenship, Immigration Law & Family*, § 15:54 (2014 ed.).

[355] INA § 340(d).

[356] Under all prior statutes from 1906 to 1952, the basis of denaturalization was fraud or illegality. Levy, *supra* note 308, at § 14:3. The Court, however, has not drawn a distinction between fraud and the new terms under the statute. Costello, 365 U.S. at 287.

[357] *See, e.g.*, Lety Volpp, *Citizenship Undone*, 75 FORDHAM L. REV. 2579, 2583 (2007) (noting several cases involving denaturalization proceedings against Muslim-Americans for their alleged association with terrorists organizations).

[358] Ch. 1024, 64 Stat. 987, amended by Immigration and Nationality Act, ch. 477, 66 Stat. 163 (1952).

[359] Current version INA § 340(c).

[360] *See supra* note 353 and accompanying text. *See also* Comment, *Charles H. Hooker, The Past as Prologue: Schneiderman v. United States and Contemporary Questions of Citizenship and Denationalization*, 19 EMORY INT'L L. REV. 305, 340–44 (2005).

[361] INA § 329(c).

that the applicant sought to obtain naturalization illegally or fraudulently.[362] This standard of proof is very strict and has required that facts be construed in favor of the citizen, insofar as it is reasonably possible.[363] Moreover, more often than not, on appeal the Court will not accept the concurrent findings of fact of two lower courts, but will examine the facts de novo.[364] When the Government proves either ground for denaturalization, the Court, however, has rejected the application of equitable discretion to consider mitigating factors in favor of the denaturalizing the defendant.[365] Such factors could include the circumstances surrounding the omitted or misrepresented facts, such as whether the association with a particular group was with knowledge or compelled or mitigating factors in cases involving the commission of crimes.[366]

The U.S. Supreme Court has not distinguished doctrinally between willful misrepresentation and concealment, even though the statute speaks of both "concealment of material fact" and "willful misrepresentation." Instead, the Court holds that misrepresentation must also be of a material fact and that concealment must also be willful.[367] Following this approach, the Government must prove four separate factors: (1) that the naturalized citizen concealed or misrepresented a fact; (2) that the misrepresentation or concealment was willful; (3) that the fact was material; and (4) that the naturalized citizen procured citizenship as a result of the misrepresentation or concealment.[368] Concealment means that the petitioner for naturalization has sworn under oath that the person lacks a record of misconduct or has never done certain actions, usually by failure to list these in the naturalization application.[369] Misrepresentation refers to lies or false answers to questions in the naturalization application that generally require the disclosure of certain facts or conduct.[370] When questions in the naturalization application are ambiguous, however, the alleged concealment or misrepresentation cannot be the basis for denaturalization. For example, in several cases where petitioners belonged to communist organizations but answered no in a question pertaining to belief in or affiliation to anarchism, the Court rejected the finding of denaturalization.[371] Willful means simply that the applicant must have purposefully concealed or misrepresented a material fact. It is sufficient that the applicant knowingly concealed or

---

[362] The Court first declared the rule in Schneiderman, 320 U.S. at 125. *See also* Fedorenko v. U.S., 449 U.S. 490, 505 (1981) and Knauer v. U.S., 328 U.S. at 657–58.

[363] *Schneiderman*, 320 U.S. at 121.

[364] *See, e.g., Knauer*, 328 U.S. at 657. *But cf.* Berenyi v. INS, 385 U.S. 630, 635 (1967).

[365] Fedorenko v. U.S., 449 U.S. 490, 517 (1981). For a critique of the preclusion of equitable discretion in denaturalization cases *see* Amy D. Ronner, *Denaturalizatin and Death: What it Means to Preclude the Exercise of Judicial Discretion*, 20 Geo. Immigr. L.J. 101 (2005).

[366] Ronner, *supra* note 365, at 111–115.

[367] *Fedorenko*, 449 U.S. at 507.

[368] Kungys v. U.S., 485 U.S. 759, 767 (1988).

[369] *See* U.S. v. Oddo, 314 F.2d 115, 116 (2d Cir. 1963), *cert. denied*, 375 U.S. 833 (1963).

[370] *Costello*, 365 U.S. at 272 (representing that person was a real estate agent when in fact he was a bootlegger). In Costello, the Court treated the misrepresentation as concealment, despite finding that the real estate business was no more than a cover up for his real occupation. *Id.* at 276.

[371] *See* Maisenberg v. U.S., 356 U.S. 670, 672 (1958) and Nowak v. U.S., 356 U.S. 660 (1958).

misrepresented material facts in the naturalization process, without actual proof of intent to deceive.[372]

The Supreme Court's holdings regarding the requirement that the omission or misrepresentation must also be material have created confusion. In *Chaunt v. U.S.*, the Court concluded that the Government proved the elements of concealment and willful misrepresentation when the applicant did not disclose his criminal record.[373] Nevertheless, the Court reversed the lower courts to deny denaturalization on the basis that the criminal record was immaterial to the determination of denaturalization given that the offenses charged were of extremely light consequence.[374] The Court's early holdings on the meaning of material concealment or misrepresentation, however, created confusion among the lower courts, and in 1988, the Court decided *Kungys v. US* in order to clarify its definition.[375] Many scholars have noted *Kungy's* failure to do so.[376] In part, the problem resides in that the *Kungy's* Court produced five different written opinions, in addition to Justice Scalia's plurality holding.[377] Justice Scalia interpreted material fact to parallel the same requirement in criminal fraud statutes,[378] and treated it as a question of law to be determined by judges.[379] To be material, the statement needs only to "be predictably capable of affecting" or have a "natural tendency to influence" the agency's determinations.[380] A finding of material concealment or misrepresentation, converts the procurement prong into a rebuttable presumption against the petitioner of disqualification for naturalization.[381] To overcome the presumption, the petitioner must establish with a preponderance of the evidence that he or she in fact met the requirement affected by the misrepresentation or concealment.[382] Justice Brennan's concurrence held that the burden-shifting presumption should only arise when the Government produces "evidence sufficient to raise a fair inference [and not merely a possibility] that a statutory disqualifying fact actually existed," coupled with the fact that the concealment or misrepresentation necessarily frustrated the Government's investigative efforts.[383] Justice Brennan, therefore, would impose a stricter evidentiary burden on the government, which is more consistent with the Court's stricter application of the materiality test.[384] As applied to the facts, the Court still reversed

---

[372] *Chaunt*, 364 U.S. at 355. *See also* Levy, *supra* note 308, at § 14.3 (citing to lower court holdings).

[373] *Chaunt*, 364 U.S. at 352.

[374] *Id.*

[375] 485 U.S. at 768–69 (Justice Scalia discussing the confusion created by the Court's earlier decision in Chaunt and Costello).

[376] *See* Levy, *supra* note 308, at § 14:7.

[377] Only Justice Brennan and Chief Justice Rhenquist fully joined Justice Scalia's opinion. In addition, Justice Brennan, Justice O'Connor, and together Justices Marshall, Stevens, and Blackmun wrote separate concurring opinions, while Justice White dissented.

[378] *Kungys*, 485 U.S. at 769–70.

[379] *Id.* at 771.

[380] *Id.*

[381] *Id.* at 777.

[382] *Id.*

[383] *Id.* at 783.

[384] Levy, *supra* note 308, at §§ 14.10 and 14.11.

the Court of Appeals and affirmed the district court to disallow denaturalization.[385] Kungys made false statements about his date and place of birth in his visa and naturalization applications. The Court did not consider that the government proved with clear, unequivocal, and convincing evidence "that had petitioner disclosed the information, it would have likely produced either outright denial or an investigation regarding the discrepancy in the original visa application."[386] "Even a high probability," the Court held, is not enough.[387]

Beyond concealment or misrepresentation, "*illegally procured*" can also include unwitting ineligibility for naturalization.[388] The Supreme Court has allowed denaturalization proceedings when the applicant did not strictly comply with all the conditions precedent to naturalization, on the basis that the certificate was "*illegally procured.*"[389] Probably the single most important basis for "illegally procured" naturalization is when the applicant committed fraud in the original petition for permanent residence.[390] In *Fedorenko*, the Court held that fraudulently procured visas are not valid and would render illegal any subsequent naturalization derived from those visas.[391] In *Kungys*, however, the Court rejected this rationale,[392] considering instead, whether providing "false testimony" during the visa procurement stage would bar the person from establishing good moral character, which would have made naturalization "illegally procured."[393] Good moral character is a statutory prerequisite to naturalization and disqualifies, *inter alia*, any person who within the required permanent residence period (usually five years) "has given false testimony for the purpose of obtaining any benefits under the [INA § 101(f)(6)]." As applied, Kungys was not disqualified because his misrepresentation at the time of applying for his visa had occurred beyond the statutory period required under the good moral character provision.[394] In addition, only oral testimony triggers the good moral character bar.[395] *Kungys* did not require the misrepresentation, however, to have to be material for purposes of establishing good moral character.[396] Some lower courts, however, are not reading *Kungys* as replacing the holding in *Fedorenko*, but as supplementary. Therefore, post-*Kungys*, some lower courts have continued to denaturalize relying on *Fedorenko* based upon material misrepresentations in the original visa process.[397]

---

[385] *Kungys*, 485 U.S. at 759.

[386] *Id.* at 774.

[387] *Id.*

[388] Levy, *supra* note 308, at § 14.16.

[389] *Fedorenko*, 449 U.S. at 506.

[390] Levy, *supra* note 308, at § 14.17.

[391] *Fedorenko*, 449 at 515.

[392] *Kungys*, 485 U.S. at 779.

[393] *Id.* at 773–74.

[394] *Id.*

[395] *Id.*

[396] *Id.* at 759 (J. Stevens concurring in judgment).

[397] *See, e.g.*, U.S. v. Demjanjuk, 367 F.3d 623 (6th Cir. 2004).

It is possible, moreover, that "illegally procured" could lead to denaturalization based on misrepresentation that was not necessarily material.[398] In the *Fedorenko* decision, the Court stated that "strict compliance with all the congressionally imposed prerequisites to the acquisition of citizenship" was required for "naturalization." [399] At least two Circuits have relied on this language to allow the denaturalization of persons who unwittingly failed to report conduct in their naturalization applications that rendered them ineligible to naturalize as a matter of law.[400] These holdings open the possibility that unwitting ineligibility for permanent residency or citizenship could be used as a basis for denaturalization years after the fact.[401]

---

[398] *See* Daniel Levy, *Revocation of Naturalization, Bases of Denaturalization, Illegal Procurement, U.S. Citizenship and Naturalization Handbook* § 14:19 (2013).

[399] *Fedorenko*, 449 U.S. at 506.

[400] *See* Levy, *supra* note 398 (discussing U.S. v. Jean-Baptiste, 395 F.3d 1190 (11th Cir. 2005) and U.S. v. Dang, 488 F.3d 1135 (9th Cir. 2007)).

[401] *Id.*

Chapter 18

THE FUTURE OF AMERICAN IMMIGRATION LAW

This chapter speculates about the future of American immigration law. It first looks at the Supreme Court and proceeds to consider possible congressional and regulatory reforms.

A. IMMIGRATION IN THE SUPREME COURT[1]

1. The Future of the Plenary Power Doctrine

For better or worse, immigration law is perhaps most well-known for its marked departures from mainstream American constitutional law. *See* Chs. 1, 2, 6. That reputation traces its genesis to the late 1800s with the Supreme Court's creation of the "plenary power" doctrine, which was originally invoked to protect from judicial review the laws designed to exclude Chinese immigrants from the United States.[2] The doctrine generally immunizes the substantive immigration judgments of Congress, such as which immigrants to admit into, and deport from, the country. The doctrine allows the courts to permit the U.S. immigration laws to discriminate against noncitizens in ways that would be patently unconstitutional if the rights of U.S. citizens were at stake.[3] The plenary power doctrine's deviation from fundamental conceptions of judicial review epitomizes what immigration law scholars have termed "immigration exceptionalism."[4]

Commentators criticize the plenary power doctrine for being out of synch with modern constitutional norms.[5] Despite having had the opportunity, the Supreme Court has failed to eliminate, or substantially limit, the doctrine. *See* Ch. 6. At the same time, the Court at times has struggled to creatively avoid application of the plenary power doctrine.[6] Lower courts sporadically employ the doctrine as a

---

[1] This section of this chapter summarizes a more detailed analysis of the Supreme Court's contemporary immigration decisions in Kevin R. Johnson, *Immigration in the Supreme Court, 2009–13: The New Era of Immigration Law Unexceptionalism*, 66 OKLA. L. REV. (forthcoming 2015).

[2] *See, e.g.*, Chae Chan Ping v. United States (*The Chinese Exclusion* Case), 130 U.S. 581 (1889). For cogent criticism of *The Chinese Exclusion Case*, see Louis Henkin, *The Constitution and United States Sovereignty: A Century of Chinese Exclusion and Its Progeny*, 100 HARV. L. REV. 853 (1987).

[3] *See generally* KEVIN R. JOHNSON, THE "HUDDLED MASSES" MYTH: IMMIGRATION AND CIVIL RIGHTS (2004) (analyzing the history of discrimination against people of color, women, political minorities, and other disfavored groups in U.S. immigration laws).

[4] *See, e.g.*, Hiroshi Motomura, *Federalism, International Human Rights, and Immigration Excep-tionalism*, 70 U. COLO. L. REV. 1361, 1392–94 (1999); Rachel E. Rosenbloom, *The Citizenship Line: Rethinking Immigration Exceptionalism*, 54 B.C. L. REV. 1965, 1981–89 (2013).

Besides immunizing from judicial review the substantive immigration judgments of Congress, immigration exceptionalism also afflicts the Supreme Court's Fourth Amendment decisions and allows race to be relied upon in border enforcement. *See* Devon W. Carbado & Cheryl I. Harris, *Undocumented Criminal Procedure*, 58 UCLA L. REV. 1543 (2011); Alfredo Mirandé, *Is There a "Mexican Exception" to the Fourth Amendment?*, 55 FLA. L. REV 365 (2003). The emergence of that form of immigration exceptionalism, as well as its racially disparate impacts on particular communities, is analyzed in Kevin R. Johnson, *How Racial Profiling in America Became the Law of the Land: United States v. Brignoni-Ponce and Whren v. United States and the Need for Truly Rebellious Lawyering*, 98 GEO. L.J. 1005 (2010). *See* Ch. 14.

[5] *See, e.g.*, T. ALEXANDER ALEINIKOFF, SEMBLANCES OF SOVEREIGNTY: THE CONSTITUTION, THE STATE, & AMERICAN CITIZENSHIP (2002); GERALD L. NEUMAN, STRANGERS TO THE CONSTITUTION: IMMIGRANTS, BORDERS, & FUNDAMENTAL LAW (1996).

[6] *See, e.g.*, Landon v. Plasencia, 459 U.S. 21 (1982) (finding that lawful permanent resident returning to United States after a brief trip outside the country was entitled to Due Process in seeking to return.); Rosenberg v. Fleuti, 374 U.S. 449 (1963) (interpreting immigration law in a manner to avoid deciding the constitutionality of the exclusion of homosexuals under the U.S. immigration laws from admission into

justification for not subjecting an immigration matter to judicial review.[7]

Over the course of the twentieth century, immigration law inched toward greater congruency with the expansion of constitutional rights.[8] Not long before 2001 — and even after, influential scholars predicted that the plenary power doctrine was destined for its demise.[9]

However, in response to national security fears after September 11, 2001, the political power of the Executive Branch and Congress came back. In promulgating a regulation allowing for exceptional immigration procedures that required certain Arab and Muslim noncitizens to register in person with the Immigration and Naturalization Service, Attorney General John Ashcroft expressly invoked the plenary power doctrine in an attempt to immunize the facially discriminatory measure from judicial review.[10] Deferring to the Executive Branch's policy choice, the courts rejected constitutional challenges to the special registration program.[11]

National security worries ultimately translated into calls for enhanced enforcement of the U.S./Mexico border.[12] The renewed focus on public safety appears to have influenced the Supreme Court's approach to immigration enforcement measures, rendering it, for example, more tolerant than it had been not long before September 11, 2001 of the long-term detention of immigrants convicted of criminal offenses.[13]

---

the United States). *See generally* Hiroshi Motomura, *The Curious Evolution of Immigration Law: Procedural Surrogates for Substantive Constitutional Rights*, 92 COLUM. L. REV. 1625 (1992) (analyzing reliance by the Supreme Court on procedural due process norms in immigration cases as "surrogates" for substantive constitutional rights to achieve fair results); Hiroshi Motomura, *Immigration Law After a Century of Plenary Power: Phantom Constitutional Norms and Statutory Interpretation*, 100 YALE L.J. 545 (1990) (offering examples of the Supreme Court invoking "phantom norms" in interpreting the immigration laws in order to avoid the harsh results of application of the plenary power doctrine).

[7] *See, e.g.*, Angov v. Holder, 736 F.3d 1263, 1273 (9th Cir. 2013) (Kozinski, C.J.); Diop v. ICE, 656 F.3d 221, 232 (3d Cir. 2011); Johnson v. Whitehead, 647 F.3d 120, 126 (4th Cir. 2011), *cert. denied*, 132 S. Ct. 1005 (2012); United States v. Loaiza-Sanchez, 622 F.3d 939, 941 (8th Cir. 2010).

[8] *See generally* Peter H. Schuck, *The Transformation of Immigration Law*, 84 COLUM. L. REV. 1 (1984) (analyzing the evolution of immigration law in the modern era).

[9] *See, e.g.*, Gabriel J. Chin, *Is There a Plenary Power Doctrine? A Tentative Apology and Prediction for Our Strange but Unexceptional Constitutional Immigration Law*, 14 GEO. IMMIGR. L.J. 257 (2000); Cornelia T. L. Pillard & T. Alexander Aleinikoff, *Skeptical Scrutiny of Plenary Power: Judicial and Executive Branch Decision Making in Miller v. Albright*, 1998 SUP. CT. REV. 1 (1998); Peter J. Spiro, *Explaining the End of Plenary Power*, 16 GEO. IMMIGR. L.J. 339 (2002). For questioning of the assertion that the end of the plenary power doctrine was imminent, see Kevin R. Johnson, *Race and Immigration Law and Enforcement: A Response to Is There a Plenary Power Doctrine?*, 14 GEO. IMMIGR. L.J. 289 (2000).

[10] Registration and Monitoring of Certain Nonimmigrants, 67 Fed. Reg. 52584, 52585 (Aug. 12, 2002) (emphasizing that "the political branches of the government have *plenary authority* in the immigration area.) *See* Fiallo v. Bell, 430 U.S. 787, 792 (1977); Mathews v. Diaz, 426 U.S. 67, 80–82 (1976). *In the context of immigration and nationality laws, the Supreme Court has particularly "underscored the limited scope of judicial inquiry." Fiallo*, 430 U.S. at 792.) (emphasis added).

[11] *See, e.g.*, Kandamar v. Gonzales, 464 F.3d 65 (1st Cir. 2006); Ahmed v. Gonzales, 447 F.3d 433 (5th Cir. 2006).

[12] *See* Kevin R. Johnson & Bernard Trujillo, *Immigration Reform, National Security After September 11, and the Future of North American Integration*, 91 MINN. L. REV. 1369, 1387 (2007).

[13] *See* Margaret H. Taylor, *Demore v. Kim: Judicial Deference to Congressional Folly*, in IMMIGRATION

As the events of September 11 fade slowly in the nation's collective memory, the push for extraordinary immigration enforcement measures in the name of national security has diminished. Invocation of the plenary power doctrine by the Executive Branch and the Supreme Court has returned to being a relatively rare phenomenon.

2. The Roberts Court's Approach to Immigration Cases: Careful Textual Analysis and Agency Deference

An analysis of the Roberts Court's immigration decisions from 2009 to the present supports the idea that the plenary power doctrine may again be on its way out.[14] What is perhaps most noteworthy from the review of the Court's decisions is that a conservative Court[15] unquestionably has *not* taken an extreme approach to immigration law and its enforcement. The Court regularly applies routine legal doctrines in ordinary ways in its immigration decisions. Nor has the Court stretched the usual rules to review immigration cases with decidedly ideological overtones.[16] Rather, the Roberts Court generally has adhered to its standard practice of resolving circuit splits and considering legal questions of national importance.[17]

Consider a few examples. Rather than blindly defer to the judgments of the Executive Branch, the Roberts Court has decided several cases rejecting the U.S. government's efforts to remove lawful permanent residents convicted of crimes from the United States.[18] In a time in which increasing numbers of states have attempted to participate in immigration enforcement, the Court decided a pair of cases in consecutive Terms arising out of immigration enforcement laws passed by the Arizona legislature.[19] The state of Arizona saw mixed results in two decisions on the constitutionality of its immigration enforcement laws. In *Chamber of Commerce v. Whiting*,[20] the Court upheld a narrow Arizona immigration

---

Stories 343, 344–45 (David A. Martin & Peter H. Schuck eds., 2005) (contending that the Supreme Court's decision upholding mandatory detention of noncitizens convicted of certain categories of crimes in Demore v. Kim, 538 U.S. 510 (2003) was influenced by national security fears following September 11, 2001 and explained the decision's apparent departure from Zadvydas v. Davis, 533 U.S. 678 (2001), which was decided only months before September 11).

[14] *See* Johnson, *supra* note 1.

[15] *See, e.g.*, H. Jefferson Powell, *Reasoning About the Irrational: The Roberts Court and the Future of Constitutional Law*, 86 Wash L. Rev. 217, 218 (2011).

[16] *See, e.g.*, Arizona v. Valle del Sol, Inc., 732 F.3d 1006 (9th Cir. 2013), *cert. denied*, 134 S. Ct. 1876 (2014); Villas at Parkside Partners v. City of Farmers Branch, 726 F.3d 524 (5th Cir. 2013) (en banc), *cert. denied*, 134 S. Ct. 1491 (2014); City of Hazleton v. Lozano, 724 F.3d 297 (3d Cir. 2013), *cert. denied*, 134 S. Ct. 1491 (2014). Keller v. City of Fremont 719 F.3d 931 (8th Cir. 2013) , *cert. denied*, 134 S. Ct. 2140 (2014); United States v. Alabama, 691 F.3d 1269 (11th Cir. 2012), *cert. denied*, 133 S. Ct. 2022 (2013).

[17] *See* Johnson, *supra* note 1.

[18] *See, e.g.*, Moncrieffe v. Holder, 133 S. Ct. 1678 (2013); Judulang v. Holder, 132 S. Ct. 476 (2011); Carachuri-Rosendo v. Holder, 560 U.S. 563 (2010).

[19] For analysis of the decisions as well as the law of federal preemption of state and local immigration laws generally, *see* Ch. 4.

[20] 131 S. Ct. 1968 (2011).

enforcement law. In *Arizona v. United States*,[21] the Court struck down much of a more expansive — and controversial — Arizona immigration enforcement law known as SB 1070. Adding clarity to the relative spheres of state and federal power with respect to modern immigration enforcement, the two decisions represent generally unremarkable applications of federal preemption doctrine to state immigration enforcement laws.

While not yet eliminating the plenary power doctrine, the Court has slowly but surely moved away from anything that might reasonably be characterized as immigration exceptionalism. The trend in the Roberts Court's immigration jurisprudence is entirely consistent with its practice over more than a decade to, whenever possible, interpret the immigration laws to avoid serious constitutional questions, and ensure judicial review of removal orders in the face of stringent congressional restrictions.[22]

Today, in applying the U.S. immigration laws, both conservative and liberal Justices on the Court ordinarily look first to the text of the statute and debate the proper interpretation of the provision in question.[23] They occasionally differ about the proper application of conventional legal doctrines to immigration cases, but rarely debate whether those generally applicable doctrines apply to immigration cases.[24] Similarly, the arguments on an all-important question central to administrative law mirror the general ones surrounding the propriety of deference to the rulings of the immigration agencies.[25] Arguments by even a single Justice, much less a majority of the Court, for extreme deference, or anything that looks like immigration exceptionalism, to the agency or the Executive Branch are exceedingly rare.[26]

---

[21] 132 S. Ct. 2492 (2012).

[22] *See, e.g.*, Kucana v. Holder, 558 U.S. 233 (2010) (holding that 1996 immigration reforms failed to eliminate judicial review of motions to reopen removal proceedings); INS v. St. Cyr, 533 U.S. 289, 298 (2001) (acknowledging the "strong presumption in favor of judicial review of administrative action" that requires "a clear statement of congressional intent to repeal habeas jurisdiction" and holding that habeas corpus review of removal orders remained). Other modern Supreme Court decisions have ensured judicial review of Board of Immigration Appeals' removal orders in the face of congressional attempts to restrict, if not eliminate, judicial review. *See, e.g.*, Demore v. Kim, 538 U.S. 510, 516–17 (2003); Zadvydas v. Davis, 533 U.S. 678, 687 (2001). This pattern of avoiding constitutional questions by ensuring judicial review of immigration matters can be understood as an effort by the Court to avoid invoking the plenary power doctrine, with the process justifications for maintaining judicial review arguably creating more substantive rights for noncitizens. *See* Jenny S. Martinez, *Process and Substance in the "War on Terror*," 108 Colum. L. Rev. 1013 (2008) (making similar observation about litigation over the rights of enemy combatants in the "war on terror").

[23] *See* Johnson, *supra* note 1.

[24] *See id.*

[25] *See, e.g.*, Scialabba v. Cuellar de Osorio, 134 S. Ct. 2191 (2014) (plurality) (deferring to agency interpretation of immigration laws in the issuance of immigrant visas); Holder v. Gutierrez, 132 S. Ct. 2011, 2014–15 (2012) (holding that BIA's interpretation of the immigration statute was entitled to *Chevron* deference).

[26] An exception is Justice Scalia's dissent in Arizona v. United States, 132 S. Ct. 2492, 2521 (2012) (Scalia, J., dissenting), which calls for great deference to the state's sovereign power over immigration enforcement, is what commentators have characterized as a high-pitched, ideologically-driven opinion. *See* Ch. 4.

In applying conventional methods to its review of immigration cases, the Roberts Court has on a regular basis — although not always — rejected the U.S. government's positions and thus has not generally shown what might fairly be characterized as undue deference to the Executive's immigration decision-making.[27] Some might even contend that the Court is less deferential in some instances than conventional administrative law principles require it to be.[28]

Extreme approaches to immigration for the most part appear to be something of the past, not current, Supreme Court. Consequently, one might predict that such approaches will not likely return in the foreseeable future — except perhaps in truly exceptional instances, such as cases implicating an imminent mass migration,[29] or responses taken by the government to another major act of terrorism.

In sum, a Supreme Court clearly on the conservative side of the ideological spectrum consistently takes a lawyer-like, case-by-case approach to the judicial review of immigration decisions and brings to bear generally applicable legal doctrines to the review of those decisions. The trend in the Roberts Court's immigration decisions reflects what can be viewed positively as bringing immigration law more into line with traditional notions of judicial review. If the trend continues, immigration exceptionalism — and ultimately the plenary power doctrine itself — in the near future may be relegated to the history books.

B. IMMIGRATION REFORM IN CONGRESS

In 1952, Congress passed the comprehensive federal immigration statute, the Immigration Nationality Act (INA),[30] the intricacies of which have been discussed extensively in this book. The law has been amended almost annually since its original enactment, sometimes in minor ways and other times with major overhauls. *See* Ch. 2.

The last decade has seen repeated calls for major immigration reform. Congress has debated many different reform bills. To this point, efforts to pass significant — referred to by many observers as "comprehensive" — immigration reform have failed.[31]

---

[27] *See, e.g., supra* note 18 (citing cases refusing to affirm Board of Immigration Appeal removal orders).

[28] *See, e.g.,* Judulang v. Holder, 132 S. Ct. 476 (2011) (rejecting the Board of Immigration Appeals' interpretation of the immigration statute as arbitrary and capricious).

[29] *See, e.g.,* Sale v. Haitian Ctrs. Council, Inc., 509 U.S. 155 (1993) (upholding U.S. government program in which the Coast Guard interdicted Haitian migrants on the high seas before they could reach the shores of the United States and apply for asylum and other forms of relief that would permit them to remain in the country). In 2014, an increase in the migration of unaccompanied minors from Central America drew national attention. *See* Frances Robles, *Fleeing Gangs, Children Head to U.S. Border,* N.Y. TIMES, July 9, 2014. Public concern decreased as the number of migrants decreased so that it does not appear that this much-publicized migration flow will affect the enactment of immigration reform or the Supreme Court's approach to immigration cases.

[30] Pub. L. No. 82-414, 66 Stat. 163 (1952) (codified as amended in scattered sections of Titles 8, 18, and 22 U.S.C.).

[31] For different perspectives on "comprehensive" immigration reform, see Steven W. Bender,

The politics of immigration are complex with public debate of the issue often heated. Importantly, immigration often lacks a clear divide between the Republican and Democratic parties. For example, labor unions, generally considered to be politically liberal, at times have supported immigration restrictions in hopes of protecting domestic workers while the *Wall Street Journal*, known for its conservatism, has championed liberal admission of immigrants (and cheap labor). *See* Ch. 1.

The events of September 11, 2001, at least for a time, significantly influenced the immigration debate. Any proposal that does not focus on border enforcement and greater removal efforts, almost assuredly will be challenged by some partisans as posing undue risks to the national security and public safety.[32]

1. The Status Quo

To appropriately evaluate potential immigration reforms, one must consider the operation of the modern U.S. immigration laws and policy and their impacts.

a. Undocumented Immigration

As President George W. Bush observed in calling for immigration reform, *"illegal immigrants live in the shadows of our society . . . . [T]he vast majority . . . are decent people who work hard, support their families, practice their faith, and lead responsible lives.* They are part of American life, but they are beyond the reach and protection of American law."[33]

Compassionate Immigration Reform, 38 Fordham Urb. L.J. 107 (2010); Sheila Jackson Lee, *Why Immigration Reform Requires a Comprehensive Approach that Includes Both Legalization Programs and Provisions to Secure the Border*, 43 Harv. J. Legis 267 (2006); Christopher J. Walker, *Border Vigilantism and Comprehensive Immigration Reform*, 10 Harv. Latino L. Rev. 135 (2007). John D. Skrentny & Micah Gell-Redman, *Comprehensive Immigration Reform and the Dynamics of Statutory Entrenchment*, 120 Yale L.J. Online 325 (2011), *available at* http://www.concurringopinions.com/archives/2011/03/ylj-online-symposium-a-republic-of-statutes.html (last visited July 7, 2014) (attempts to explain the failure of Congress to enact comprehensive immigration reform).

Of course, there are possibilities for more incremental reform, such as, for example, guaranteeing counsel to noncitizens (or some category thereof), in removal proceedings. *See, e.g.*, Kevin R. Johnson, *An Immigration Gideon for Lawful Permanent Residents*, 122 Yale L.J. 2394 (2013). The City of New York has endeavored to create a pilot public defender program guaranteeing representation to indigent noncitizens in removal proceedings. *See* New York Immigrant Family Unity Project, *available at* http://www.bronxdefenders.org/programs/new-york-immigrant-family-unity-project/ (last visited July 21, 2014).

[32] *See* Bill Ong Hing, Deporting Our Souls: Values, Morality, and Immigration Policy 140–63 (2006); Jennifer M. Chacón, *Unsecured Borders: Immigration Restrictions, Crime Control and National Security*, 39 Conn. L. Rev. 1827 (2007); *see also* Jonathan Hafetz, *Immigration and National Security Law: Converging Approaches to State Power, Individual Rights, and Judicial Review*, 46 Rev. Jur. U.I.P.R. 787 (2011) (discussing the relationship between immigration policy and national security after September 11, 2001); Donald Kerwin & Margaret D. Stock, *The Role of Immigration in a Coordinated National Security Policy*, 21 Geo. Immigr. L.J. 383 (2007) (analyzing how immigration law can serve national security ends); Karen C. Tumlin, Comment, *Suspect First: How Terrorism Policy is Reshaping Immigration Policy*, 92 Cal. L. Rev. 1173 (2004) (evaluating how post-September 11 terrorism concerns reshaped U.S. immigration law and policy).

[33] Address to the Nation on Immigration Reform, Presidential Papers of the Presidents (May 22, 2006) (emphasis added).

Somewhere in the neighborhood of 12 million undocumented immigrants currently live in the United States.[34] Generations of migrants from Mexico have migrated to this country.[35] In modern times, migrants literally risk life and limb to come to this land of freedom and opportunity. Absent dramatic economic, political, and social changes, immigrants will continue to come lawfully and unlawfully to the United States in pursuit of employment and to reunite with family members. The United States would benefit if its immigration laws better addressed the modern political, economic, and social realities currently fueling undocumented immigration and contributing to the millions of people who live and work in communities across the country in contravention of the U.S. immigration laws. *See* Ch. 1.

As outlined in Chapters 1 and 7, many unskilled and medium-skilled workers have no line to wait in to lawfully immigrate to the United States. The limited legal avenues under U.S. law for labor migration encourage migration in violation of the law by noncitizens who seek to work in the country.

The fact that so many undocumented immigrants live in the United States confirms what most Americans know — that the immigration laws are routinely violated and, as currently configured, are effectively unenforceable. The magnet of jobs unquestionably attracts many undocumented immigrants to the United States. Undocumented workers understand that if they are able to make the often-arduous journey to the United States, they will be able to obtain work and that the job will pay more than most of them would have been able to earn in their native countries. Employers willingly hire undocumented workers. Day laborer pick up points found in many American, if not most, cities demonstrate both undocumented immigrants' ability to obtain work and employers' willingness to hire them.[36]

Recent years have seen increasingly aggressive efforts by the U.S. government to close the southern border with Mexico. *See* Ch. 14. Over the last decade or so, *increased* border enforcement efforts, to the surprise of many, have been accom-

---

[34] Jeffrey S. Passel, D'Vera Cohn and Ana Gonzalez-Barrera, Population Decline of Unauthorized Immigrants Stalls, May Have Reversed (Pew Research Center 2013), *available at* http://www.pewhispanic.org/2013/09/23/population-decline-of-unauthorized-immigrants-stalls-may-have-reversed/ (last visited July 14, 2014) (estimating that, as of March 2012, 11.7 million unauthorized immigrants lived in the United States). The U.S. government estimated that, in 2011, 11.5 million undocumented immigrants lived in the United States compared to 11.6 million in 2010. *See* U.S. Dep't of Homeland Security, Estimates of the Unauthorized Population Residing in the United States: January 2011, at 3 (2012).

[35] *See* Gerald P. López, *Undocumented Mexican Migration: In Search of a Just Immigration Law and Policy*, 28 UCLA L. Rev. 615, 641–72 (1981); JoAnne D. Spotts, *U.S. Immigration Policy on the Southwest Border from Reagan Through Clinton, 1981–2001*, 16 Geo. Immigr L.J. 601 (2002); *see also* Gerald P. Lopez, *Don't We Like Them Illegal?*, 45 UC Davis L. Rev. 1711 (2012) (analyzing critically how the operation of the U.S. immigration laws has facilitated the creation of the undocumented immigrant population in the United States).

[36] For studies of day laborers, see Abel Valenzuela, Jr., et al., On the Corner: Day Labor in the United States (2006); Abel Valenzuela, Jr. & Edwin Melendez, Day Labor in New York: Findings From the NYDL Survey (2003); *see also* Justin McDevitt, *Compromise Is Complicity: Why There Is No Middle Road in the Struggle to Protect Day Laborers in the United States*, 26 ABA J. Lab. & Emp. L. 101 (2010) (advocating for increased protection of the rights of day laborers in the United States); Kim McLane Wardlaw, *The Latino Immigration Experience*, 31 Chicana/o-Latina/o L. Rev. 13, 30–35 (2012) (discussing the impacts of state and local regulation of day laborers on Mexican immigrants).

panied by an *increase* in the overall size of the undocumented population. One study concluded that "[t]here is *no* evidence that the border enforcement build-up . . . has substantially reduced unauthorized border crossings"; "[d]espite large increases in spending and Border Patrol resources . . . , the number of unauthorized immigrants increased to levels higher than those" before 1986.[37] The bottom line is that the undocumented population in the United States has more than doubled since the mid-1990s.[38]

Employer sanctions, which bar the employment of undocumented immigrants, added to the immigration laws in 1986 have failed to end the employment of undocumented immigrants.[39] Computer systems designed to allow employers to easily verify work authorization, such as E-Verify, continue to have high error rates.[40]

Incremental enforcement measures have had a limited impact on undocumented immigration from Mexico.[41] The U.S. government simply has been unable to keep migrants — who are so determined that they are willing to risk their lives, from unlawfully entering, and remaining in, the country.[42]

The U.S. government generally has made few efforts to remove noncitizens that lawfully entered the country on temporary visas, such as students and tourists, but overstayed their terms. Visa overstays likely constitute somewhere between 25 and 40 percent of the undocumented population.[43] Increased monitoring of nonimmigrant visa holders implemented after September 11, 2001 does not appear to have had much of an impact. Increased interior enforcement, including workplace raids,

---

[37] BELINDA I. REYES ET AL., HOLDING THE LINE? THE EFFECT OF THE RECENT BORDER BUILD-UP ON UNAUTHORIZED IMMIGRATION, at viii, xii (2002) (emphasis added).

[38] *See* ESTIMATES OF THE U.S. UNAUTHORIZED IMMIGRANT POPULATION, 1990–2012 (Pew Research Center 2013), *available at* http://www.pewhispanic.org/2013/09/23/population-decline-of-unauthorized-immigrants-stalls-may-have-reversed/ph-unauthorized-immigrants-1-01/ (last visited July 7, 2014).

[39] For analysis of the failure of employer sanctions to deter the employment of undocumented immigrants, see Cecelia M. Espenoza, *The Illusory Provisions of Sanctions: The Immigration Reform and Control Act of 1986*, 8 GEO. IMMIGR. L.J. 343 (1994); Michael J. Wishnie, *Prohibiting the Employment of Unauthorized Immigrants: The Experiment Fails*, 2007 U. CHI. LEGAL F. 193 (2007).

[40] *See* Westat, *Findings of the E-Verify Program Evaluation* 114 (2009), *available at* http://www.uscis.gov/sites/default/files/USCIS/E-Verify/E-Verify/Final%20E-Verify%2012-16-09_2.pdf (last visited July 7, 2014); Emily Patten, Note, *E-Verify During a Period of Economic Recovery and High Unemployment*, 2012 UTAH L. REV. 475, 482–83; *see also* T. Alexander Aleinikoff, *Administrative Law: Immigration, Amnesty, and the Rule of Law*, 36 HOFSTRA L. REV. 1313, 1314 (2008) (acknowledging that the United States is years away from creating some kind of computerized system that can reliably identify undocumented workers: "There is not a clear way to fix employer sanctions anytime soon. The widely discussed 'smart cards' or 'swipe cards' will be years in the making. Meanwhile massive work will need to be done on government databases to clean up misspelled, duplicate, and false names.") (footnote omitted).

[41] *See* Belinda I. Reyes, *U.S. Immigration Policy and Unauthorized Mexican Immigration*, 2007 U. CHI. LEGAL F. 131 (2007).

[42] *See* PETER ANDREAS, BORDER GAMES: POLICING THE U.S.-MEXICO DIVIDE (2001) (analyzing the difficulties of border enforcement reducing undocumented immigration).

[43] *See* Pew Hispanic Center, *The Size and Characteristics of the Unauthorized Migrant Population in the U.S.* (Mar. 2006), *available at* http://pewhispanic.org/files/reports/61.pdf (last visited July 24, 2014).

pursued by the Bush administration also failed to reduce the undocumented population in the United States.[44]

Resistance to interior enforcement from employers, as well as immigrant rights advocates, makes such enforcement politically challenging.[45] In any event, increased border enforcement without any effort to tighten the availability of jobs to undocumented immigrants, will ultimately do little to change the status quo, with availability of jobs continuing to fuel migration to this country. *See* Ch. 1.

Laws and policies promoting more liberal admissions to decrease the incentives for undocumented immigration are often characterized as sacrificing national security, a concern that grew paramount after September 11, 2001. In response, commentators claim that flexible immigration admission systems would in fact better ensure national security.[46] A scheme that better matches the demand for immigration — while minimizing the incentive for undocumented immigration and thus limiting the creation and maintenance of a population of millions of undocumented immigrants living "in the shadows" — arguably would better ensure public safety.[47] An immigration system that ensures that the U.S. government has the basic identifying information, such as name and address, of as many residents in the United States as possible, would improve criminal and immigration law enforcement and allow the nation to better protect national security.

b. Labor Exploitation

The contemporary operation of the immigration laws has negative labor market consequences. Unscrupulous employers can exploit undocumented immigrants in the workplace. Reports of involuntary servitude of immigrants in the modern United States — for example, immigrants forced to work off debts to smugglers who brought them here — have increased over time.[48]

---

[44] *See* Raquel Aldana, *Of Katz and "Aliens": Privacy Expectations and the Immigration Raids*, 41 UC Davis L. Rev. 1081, 1092–96 (2008) (discussing raids of meatpacking plants); Sandra Guerra Thompson, *Immigration Law and Long-Term Residents: A Missing Chapter in American Criminal Law*, 5 Ohio St. J. Crim. L. 645, 655 (2008) (mentioning raids); Anil Kalhan, *The Fourth Amendment and Privacy Implications of Interior Immigration Enforcement*, 41 UC Davis L. Rev. 1137 (2008) (analyzing legal impacts of raids and other forms of interior immigration enforcement); Shoba Sivaprasad Wadhia, *Under Arrest: Immigrants' Rights and the Rule of Law*, 38 U. Memp. L. Rev. 853, 862–88 (2008) (same); *see also* David B. Thronson, *Immigration Raids and the Destabilization of Immigrant Families*, 43 Wake Forest L. Rev. 391 (2008) (identifying negative impacts of immigration raids on families).

[45] *See* Lori Nessel, *Undocumented Immigrants in the Workplace: The Fallacy of Labor Protection and the Need for Reform*, 36 Harv C.R.-C.L. L. Rev. 345, 359–61 (2001); Michael J. Wishnie, *Emerging Issues for Undocumented Workers*, 6 U. Pa. J. Lab. & Emp. L. 497, 516–21 (2004).

[46] *See, e.g.*, Bill Ong Hing, *Misusing Immigration Policies in the Name of Homeland Security*, 6 New Centennial Rev. 195, 207–16 (2006); Jan Ting, *Immigration Law Reform After 9/11: What Has Been and What Still Needs to Be Done*, 17 Temple Int'l & Comp. L.J. 503, 512–15 (2003).

[47] *See* Jeffrey Manns, *Private Monitoring of Gatekeepers: The Case of Immigration Enforcement*, 2006 U. Ill. L. Rev. 887, 930–72 (2006).

[48] *See* Human Rights Center (University of California, Berkeley), Freedom Denied: Forced Labor in California 1 (2005); Free the Slaves & Human Rights Center of the University of California, *Hidden Slaves: Forced Labor in the United States*, 23 Berkeley J. Int'l L. 47 (2005); Ellen L. Buckwalter, Maria Perinetti, Susan L. Pollet & Meredith S. Salvaggio, *Modern Day Slavery in Our Own Backyard*, 12 Wm. & Mary Women & L. 403 (2006).

More commonly, exploited in the workplace,[49] undocumented workers have legal rights that go unenforced.[50] Because many are people of color, the nation's labor market has a racial caste quality to it. The secondary labor market for undocumented workers operates outside of the confines of law, with undocumented workers receiving few legal protections and often working for low wages in poor (often unlawful) conditions. More realistic immigration law and policy, combined with better workplace enforcement, that allow labor migration could help eliminate this secondary labor market.

As Professor Leticia Saucedo has written, the nation has seen the emergence of a "brown collar" workplace, with many Mexican migrants working in low wage jobs.[51] The new "Jim Crow" in the employment market sees undocumented immigrants working for low wages in poor conditions — and virtually unprotected by law — in one labor market and all others in a superior, more law-abiding, labor market.[52]

c. Human Trafficking and Death on the Border

Demand for evasion of the law by millions of undocumented immigrants has contributed to the emergence of highly organized trafficking and smuggling networks.[53] The trafficking of human beings today is a booming industry, with the

---

[49] See Maria L. Ontiveros, *To Help Those Most in Need: Undocumented Workers' Rights and Remedies Under Title VII*, 20 N.Y.U. REV. L. & SOC. CHANGE 607 (1993–94); Donna E. Young, *Working Across Borders: Global Restructuring and Women's Work*, 2001 UTAH L. REV. 1 (2001).

[50] See, e.g., Hoffman Plastic Compounds, Inc. v. NLRB, 535 U.S. 137 (2002) (holding that undocumented immigrant lacked full legal rights under federal labor law and was not entitled to reinstatement and back pay despite being unlawfully terminated for union organizing activities). For critiques of the *Hoffman Plastic* decision, see, for example, Christopher David Ruiz Cameron, *Borderline Decisions: Hoffman Plastic Compounds, the New Bracero Program, and the Supreme Court's Role in Making Federal Labor Policy*, 51 UCLA L. REV. 1 (2003); Robert I. Correales, *Did Hoffman Plastic Compounds, Inc. Produce Disposable Workers?*, 14 BERKELEY LA RAZA L.J. 10 (2003); Ruben J. Garcia, *Ghost Workers in an Interconnected World: Going Beyond the Dichotomies of Domestic Immigration and Labor Laws*, 36 U. MICH. J.L. REF. 737 (2003); María Pabón López, *The Place of the Undocumented Worker in the United States Legal System After Hoffman Plastics: A Comparative Analysis*, 15 IND. INT'L & COMP. L. REV. 301 (2005); *Developments in the Law — Jobs and Borders*, 118 HARV. L. REV. 2171 (2005); James Lin, Note, *A Greedy Institution: Domestic Workers and a Legacy of Legislative Exclusion*, 36 FORDHAM INT'L L.J. 706 (2013).

[51] See Leticia M. Saucedo, *Addressing Segregation in the Brown Collar Workplace: Toward a Solution for the Inexorable 100%*, 41 U. MICH. J.L. REF. 447 (2008); Leticia M. Saucedo, *The Browning of the American Workplace: Protecting Workers in Increasingly Latino-ized Occupations*, 80 NOTRE DAME L. REV. 303 (2004); Leticia M. Saucedo, *The Employer Preference for the Subservient Worker and the Making of the Brown Collar Workplace*, 67 OHIO ST. L.J. 961 (2006); *see also* Leticia M. Saucedo, *Anglo Views of Mexican Labor: Shaping the Law of Temporary Work Through Masculinities Narratives*, 13 NEV. L.J. 547 (2013) (analyzing narratives of race and masculinity used to justify the exploitation of Mexican immigrant workers).

[52] See Karla M. McKanders, *Sustaining Tiered Personhood: Jim Crow and Anti-Immigrant Laws*, 26 HARV. J. RACIAL & ETHNIC JUST. 164 (2010).

[53] See Morgan Brown, *Targeting Demand: A New Approach to Curbing Human Trafficking in the United States*, 11 RICH. J. GLOBAL L. & BUS. 357 (2012); Jennifer M. Chacón, *Misery and Myopia: Understanding the Failures of U.S. Efforts to Stop Human Trafficking*, 74 FORDHAM L. REV. 2977 (2006); Jayashri Srikantiah, *Perfect Victims and Real Survivors: The Iconic Victim in Domestic Human Trafficking Law*, 87 B.U. L. REV. 157 (2007).

problem not limited to the U.S./Mexico border region but extending across the entire United States. Deaths regularly occur as migrants try to cross the border with and without the assistance of smugglers.[54] *See* Ch. 14.

Besides risking life and limb, some immigrants are forced to work to pay off smuggling fees, with thousands of immigrant women forced into the sex industry and other exploitative work arrangements that amount to involuntary servitude.[55] The trafficking of human beings — with its devastating impacts — flows immediately from heightened immigration enforcement. Congress has passed laws in response to human trafficking but continue to employ border enforcement strategies that in effect encourage the unlawful trafficking of labor. *See* Ch. 8.[56]

d. A Disrespected Immigration Bureaucracy

The American immigration bureaucracy frequently is accused of being unfair and biased. *See* Chs. 5, 6. As discussed in Chapter 6, many commentators currently lack respect and confidence in the agencies that enforce the U.S. immigration laws..

The Immigration and Naturalization Service (INS), which until the spring of 2003 had primary responsibility for enforcing the immigration laws, had long been criticized as inefficient, arbitrary, and incompetent, emphasizing enforcement over all other immigration goals.[57] The new Department of Homeland Security appears as enforcement-oriented as the old INS. This is not altogether surprising because the agency, as its very name connotes, was created with the primary purpose of

---

[54] For a sampling of literature analyzing the deadly impacts of increased border enforcement, see TIMOTHY J. DUNN, THE MILITARIZATION OF THE U.S.-MEXICAN BORDER, 1978–1992: LOW INTENSITY CONFLICT DOCTRINE COMES HOME (1996); KARL ESCHBACH, JACQUELINE HAGAN, & NESTOR RODRIGUEZ, CAUSES AND TRENDS IN MIGRANT DEATHS ALONG THE U.S./MEXICO BORDER, 1985–1998 (2001); JOSEPH NEVINS, OPERATION GATEKEEPER (2002); Wayne A. Cornelius, *Death at the Border: Efficacy and Unintended Consequences of US Immigration Control Policy*, 27 POPULATION & DEV. REV. 661 (2001); Karl Eschbach et al., *Death at the Border*, 33 INT'L MIGRATION REV. 430 (1999); Bill Ong Hing, *The Dark Side of Operation Gatekeeper*, 7 UC DAVIS J. INT'L L. & POL'Y 121, 123 (2001); Guillermo Alonso Meneses, *Human Rights and Undocumented Migration Along the Mexican-U.S. Border*, 51 UCLA L. Rev. 267 (2003); Jorge A. Vargas, *U.S. Border Patrol Abuses, Undocumented Mexican Workers, and International Human Rights*, 2 SAN DIEGO INT'L L.J. 1 (2001). Much popular literature focuses on the travails of immigrants seeking to unlawfully enter the United States from Mexico. *See, e.g.*, SONIA NAZARIO, ENRIQUE'S JOURNEY (reprint ed. 2013); LUIS ALBERTO URREA, THE DEVIL'S HIGHWAY: A TRUE STORY (2004).

[55] *See* AMERICAN CIVIL LIBERTIES UNION, HUMAN TRAFFICKING: MODERN ENSLAVEMENT OF IMMIGRANT WOMEN IN THE UNITED STATES (2007), *available at* https://www.aclu.org/womens-rights/human-trafficking-modern-enslavement-immigrant-women-united-states (last visited July 7, 2014); Rosy Kandathil, *Global Sex Trafficking Victims Protection Act of 2000: Legislative Responses to the Problem of Modern Slavery*, 12 MICH. J. GENDER & L. 87 (2005); Susan W. Tiefenbrun, *Sex Slavery in the United States and the Law Enacted to Stop it Here and Abroad*, 11 WM. & MARY J. WOMEN & L. 317 (2005); Susan W. Tiefenbrun, *The Domestic and International Impact of the U.S. Victims of Trafficking Protection Act of 2000: Does Law Deter Crime?*, 2 LOY. U. CHI. INT'L L. REV. 193 (2005).

[56] *See* Trafficking Victims Protection Act of 2000, Pub. L. No. 106-386, 114 Stat. 1464, 1466 (codified as amended at 22 U.S.C. §§ 7101–7110 (2000)); Trafficking Victims Protection Reauthorization Act of 2003, Pub. L. No. 108-93, 117 Stat. 2875 (2003).

[57] *See* Nancy Morawetz, *Understanding the Impact of the 1996 Deportation Laws and the Limited Scope of Proposed Reforms*, 113 HARV. L. REV. 1936, 1948–50 (2000); Margaret H. Taylor, *Promoting Legal Representation for Detained Aliens: Litigation and Administrative Reform*, 29 CONN. L. REV. 1647, 1698–1700 (1997).

better protecting "homeland security," and enforcing the borders, not serving the needs of immigrants

Nor has the dismantling of the INS seen any dramatic improvement in the efficiency of administrative operations.[58] Unless the DHS is reformed to better balance its enforcement and service functions, pouring increasing resources into the agency is unlikely to improve matters. Specifically, regular infusion of additional funding to increase the number of Border Patrol officers without significantly improving their training, is likely to make matters worse, not better.[59]

Moreover, as discussed in Chapter 6, the immigration courts and Board of Immigration Appeals have been the subject of sustained criticism. Consideration of reform to the agency adjudicatory process seems in order if the results are to even have the perception of the legitimacy and fairness.

e.   The Need for Reform

Consider the available evidence. Despite record levels of deportations in the years since September 11, 2001,[60] officials at the highest levels of the U.S. government recognize that removal of all undocumented immigrants from the country is simply not possible. In 2006, President George W. Bush himself acknowledged that *"[m]assive deportation of the people here is unrealistic. It's just not going to work."*[61] President Obama continues to make similar statements.[62] One study estimated that it would cost $41 billion a year for five years to fund a serious effort to remove all undocumented immigrants from the country.[63]

---

[58] For a sampling of criticism of the Department of Homeland Security's handling of immigration matters, see M. Isabel Medina, *Immigrants and the Government's War on Terrorism*, CENTENNIAL, 225, 230–32 (2006); Thomas W. Donovan, *The American Immigration System: A Structural Change with a Different Emphasis*, 17 INT'L. J. REFUGEE L. 574 (2005); Victor Romero, *Race, Immigration, and the Department of Homeland Security*, 19 ST. JOHN'S J. LEG. COMM. 51, 52 (2004); Noel L. Griswold, Note, *Forgetting the Melting Pot: An Analysis of the Department of Homeland Security Takeover of the INS*, 39 SUFFOLK U.L. REV. 207, 227–28 (2005); Jeffrey Manns, Legislation Comment, *Reorganization as a Substitute for Reform: The Abolition of INS*, 112 YALE L.J. 145 (2002).

[59] *See* Ruchir Patel, *Immigration Legislation Pursuant to Threats to US National Security*, 32 DEN. J. INT'L L. & POL'Y 83, 97 (2003) (criticizing USA PATRIOT Act for increasing the number of Border Patrol agents but failing to ensure better training); Gabriela A. Gallegos, Comment, *Border Matters: Redefining the National Interest in U.S. Matters*, 92 CAL. L. REV. 1729, 1757–58 (2004) (stating that 1996 immigration reforms failed to ensure adequate training in light of "the Border Patrol's checkered history of abuse in the Southwest") (footnote omitted).

[60] For statistics on the number of unauthorized immigrants removed from the United States since 2001, *see*, DEPARTMENT OF HOMELAND SECURITY, IMMIGRATION ENFORCEMENT ACTION (2013), *available at* http://www.dhs.gov/sites/default/files/publications/ois_enforcement_ar_2012_1.pdf (last visited July 7, 2014).

[61] Elisabeth Bumiller, *In Immigration Remarks, Bush Hints He Favors Senate Plan*, N.Y. TIMES, Apr. 25, 2006, at A22 (quoting President Bush) (emphasis added).

[62] *See Obama Addresses the National Council of La Raza*, WASH. POST (CQ Transcript), July 15, 2008, (advocating a path to legalization for undocumented immigrants: "[w]e cannot and should not deport 12 million people"), *available at* http://www.washingtonpost.com/wp-dyn/content/article/2008/07/15/AR2008071501138_pf.html (last visited July 24, 2014).

[63] RAJEEV GOYLE & DAVID A. JAEGER, DEPORTING THE UNDOCUMENTED: A COST ASSESSMENT 2 (2005). It further concluded that

A system that allows for easier migration of labor to the United States would likely decrease the incentive for circumventing the immigration laws. A good first step would be to liberalize the admissions criteria to allow more workers to legally enter and to move permanently decreasing the incentives for undocumented migration.

At the same time, more liberal admissions of immigrants to the United States arguably would benefit the national economy. The Economic Reports of the President in both the Bush (Republican) and Obama (Democratic) administration's extolled the economic benefits of immigrants.[64] The Obama administration has argued that immigration reform would bring substantial economic benefits to the American economy.[65]

Narrower exclusion grounds in the U.S. immigration laws would be more realistic than the current blanket exclusions that, for example, bar the immigration of poor and working people from the developing world.[66] With relaxation of the grounds of inadmissibility, the nation could devote scarce enforcement resources to efforts to bar the entry into the United States of criminals, terrorists, and other serious dangers to society. More focused enforcement has a greater likelihood of rooting out public safety risks than scattershot efforts that infringe on the civil rights of large numbers of people.[67]

A system in which undocumented migration is reduced would allow for improved tracking of all noncitizens entering and living in the United States. It is difficult to see how the existence of millions of undocumented immigrants could in any way be in the national interest. Nor is there sufficient evidence that the U.S. government as a practical matter could end undocumented immigration under the current laws

---

While the net benefits of adopting such a policy are largely speculative, we do know that spending $41 billion annually over five years ($206 billion in total) would:

- Exceed the *entire* budget of the Department of Homeland Security for FY 2006 ($34.2 billion);
- Approach the *total* amount of money required by the 33 federal agencies responsible for homeland security activities for FY 2006 ($49.9 billion);
- *More than double* annual spending on border and transportation security ($19.3 billion); Comprise half the annual cost of the Iraq War ($74 billion); and more than double the annual cost of military operations in Afghanistan ($16.8 billion).

Id. (some emphasis in original) (some emphasis added).

[64] *See* ECONOMIC REPORT OF THE PRESIDENT 154, 156 (2013); ECONOMIC REPORT OF THE PRESIDENT 93 (2005).

[65] *See* EXECUTIVE OFFICE OF THE PRESIDENT, THE ECONOMIC BENEFITS OF FIXING OUR BROKEN IMMIGRATION SYSTEM (2013), *available at* http://www.whitehouse.gov/sites/default/files/docs/report.pdf (last visited July 7, 2014).

[66] See Immigration & Nationality Act § 212(a)(4), 8 U.S.C. § 1182(a)(4) (providing that "[a]ny alien . . . likely at any time to become a public charge is inadmissible"). *See generally* KEVIN R. JOHNSON, OPENING THE FLOODGATES: WHY AMERICA NEEDS TO RETHINK ITS BORDERS AND IMMIGRATION LAWS 91–108 (2007) (analyzing the history of excluding poor and working noncitizens from the United States). Statistics for fiscal year 2013 show that the public charge exclusion was a substantive ground frequently relied upon in the denial of immigrant visas by State Department officials, see DEPARTMENT OF STATE, REPORT OF THE VISA OFFICE 2013 (2013) (Table XX), *available at* http://travel.state.gov/content/dam/visas/Statistics/AnnualReports/FY2013AnnualReport/FY13AnnualReport-TableXX.pdf (last visited July 7, 2014).

[67] *See* Kevin R. Johnson, *U.S. Border Enforcement: Drugs, Migrants, and the Rule of Law*, 47 VILL. L. REV. 897, 912–15 (2002) (reviewing the experience of the U.S. Customs Service and its adoption of a policy limiting searches resulting in fewer searches and increased rate of searches finding contraband).

and remove all undocumented immigrants from the country. At a most fundamental level, the nation needs modern immigration laws that avoid the creation and re-creation of an undocumented immigrant population numbering in the millions.

2. Constraints on Reform

a. National Security Concerns

The events of September 11 and fears of terrorism led to tighter immigration restrictions, ranging from stricter monitoring of foreign scholars and students seeking to enter the United States on nonimmigrant visas[68] to new immigration requirements and procedures. Many measures targeted Arab and Muslim immigrants, including the "special registration" program, mass detentions, and focused removal operations.[69] Ultimately, all immigrants, including those from Mexico, felt the impacts of the various security measures and greatly bolstered immigration enforcement.[70]

In 2006, Professor Enid Trucios-Haynes observed that

[i]mmigration dominates policy discussions in the post-September 11, 2001 world in a manner that has distorted traditional issues and concerns relating to noncitizens. To some, the perception or reality of porous U.S. borders requires the most strenuous methods of border enforcement. *In the eyes of many, immigration reform proposals since 2001 have focused exclusively on enforcement without sufficient acknowledgment of the human consequences on the noncitizens, both authorized and unauthorized, throughout our community.*[71]

---

[68] *See* Michael A. Olivas, *The War on Terrorism Touches the Ivory Tower — Colleges and Universities After September 11: An Introduction*, 30 J. C. & U. L. 233 (2004); Victor C. Romero, *Noncitizen Students and Immigration Policy Post-9/11*, 17 Geo. Immigr. L.J. 357 (2003).

[69] For a sampling of criticism of the various measures, see Raquel Aldana-Pindell, *The 9/11 "National Security" Cases: Three Principles Guiding Judges' Decision-Making*, 81 Or. L. Rev. 985 (2002); Sameer M. Ashar, *Immigration Enforcement and Subordination: The Consequences of Racial Profiling After September 11*, 34 Conn. L. Rev. 1185 (2002); Bill Ong Hing, *Vigilante Racism: The De-Americanization of Immigrant America*, 7 Mich. J. Race & L. 441 (2002); Thomas W. Joo, *Presumed Disloyal: Executive Power, Judicial Deference, and the Construction of Race Before and After September 11*, 34 Colum. Hum. Rts. L. Rev. 1 (2002); Victor C. Romero, *Decoupling "Terrorist" From "Immigrant": An Enhanced Role for the Federal Courts Post 9/11*, 7 J. Gender, Race, & Just. 201 (2003); Leti Volpp, *The Citizen and the Terrorist*, 49 Ucla L. Rev. 1575 (2002). *See generally* Symposium, *Citizenship, Immigration, and National Security After 9/11*: Editor's Foreword, 82 Fordham L. Rev. 2037 (2014).

The response to the bombing that killed and injured hundreds of people in 2013 by two Chechen immigrants generated responses, most of which generally bore little resemblance to the more generalized fears immediately after September 11, 2001. *See* Leti Volpp, *The Boston Bombers*, 82 Fordham L. Rev. 2209 (2014).

[70] *See* Kevin R. Johnson, *September 11 and Mexican Immigrants: Collateral Damage Comes Home*, 52 Depaul L. Rev. 849, 866–67 (2003).

[71] Enid Trucios-Haynes, *Civil Rights, Latinos, and Immigration: Cybercascades and Other Distortions in the Immigration Reform Debate*, 44 Brandeis L.J. 637, 638 (2006) (emphasis added).

Passionate arguments have been made about the need to close the borders to immigrants in the fight against terrorism.[72] However, not one of the September 11 terrorists entered without inspection (much less from Mexico), and there is little evidence suggesting that there is a realistic threat of terror from Mexico.[73] Nonetheless, it has been alleged that the entry of undocumented immigrants from Mexico into the United States poses a substantial security risk.[74]

Serious discussions of a bilateral agreement regularizing migration between the United States and Mexico, such as will be discussed later in this Chapter, ended abruptly on September 11, 2001.[75] Efforts to remove the harshest provisions of 1996 immigration reform laws, *see* Ch. 2 — characterized by one influential scholar as "the most radical reform of immigration law in decades — or perhaps ever"[76] — also ended in the wake of September 11. The political climate has made congressional liberalization of the immigration laws exceedingly difficult.[77]

b. Popular Fed of the Proverbial "Floodgates"

The intuitive reaction to any suggestion that the United States liberalize immigration admissions is that we cannot open the "floodgates" to people from all over the world.[78] These fears have been exacerbated by modern national security concerns following the events of September 11, 2001.

As discussed in Chapter 1, even if immigration laws might encourage somewhat greater rates of lawful migration, realistic immigration laws that are efficiently enforced might improve, not undermine, the security of the nation. Immigration laws that better fulfill the nation's labor needs would eliminate a powerful magnet to circumvent the law. Serious reform of the immigration laws to liberalize immigration would thus improve adherence to the law. Increased compliance in turn

---

[72] *See, e.g.*, Patrick J. Buchanan, State of Emergency: the Third World Invasion and Conquest of America (2006); Michelle Malkin, Invasion: How America Still Welcomes Terrorists, Criminals, and Other Foreign Menaces to our Shores (2002); Jan C. Ting, *Unobjectionable but Insufficient — Federal Initiatives in Response to the September 11 Terrorist Attacks*, 34 Conn. L. Rev. 1145 (2002).

[73] One study found that "[n]ot one terrorist has entered the United States from Mexico." Peter Beinart, *The Wrong Place to Stop Terrorists*, Wash. Post, May 4, 2006, at A25 (discussing the study making this finding); *see* Robert S. Leiken, the Quantitative Analysis of Terrorism and Immigration: an Initial Exploration 2 (2006) ("Despite media alarms about terrorists concealed in the illegal traffic crossing the Mexican border, *not a single [person charged or convicted of terrorist acts, or killed in such acts] entered from Mexico.*") (emphasis added) (footnote omitted). There has not been nearly as much of a focus on the U.S. border with Canada despite the fact that a bona fide terrorist was apprehended seeking to cross the border from the North. *See* Sam Howe Verhovek, *2nd Man Sought for Questioning in Bomb Plot*, N.Y. Times, Dec. 19, 1999, at § 1, p. 42.

[74] *See, e.g.*, Kris W. Kobach, *The Quintessential Force Multiplier: The Inherent Authority of Local Police to Make Immigration Arrests*, 69 Alb. L. Rev. 179, 179 (2005). In a comment consistent with the tenor of the debate, Senator John Cornyn emphasized that the debate over immigration reform "is . . . and I would say first and foremost about our Nation's security. *In a post-9/11 world, border security is national security.*" 152 Cong. Rec. S2551 (Mar. 30, 2006) (Cornyn, Sen.) (emphasis added).

[75] *See* Johnson, *supra* note 70, at 866–67.

[76] Peter H. Schuck, Citizens, Strangers, and in-Betweens 143 (1998).

[77] *See* Johnson, *supra* note 70, at 866–67.

[78] *See* Johnson, *supra* note 66, at 26–31.

would add to the law's perceived legitimacy.

Border controls that are more focused on national security and public safety than those found in the current U.S. immigration laws, might well improve our security. Efforts could be focused on barring serious criminals and those reasonably suspected of terrorist activities from entering the United States while admitting other immigrants more liberally.

As this reasoning suggests, liberal admissions of immigrant workers that better fulfill the demand for labor in the United States[79] are consistent with efforts to protect the nation from terrorism. More liberal migration with fewer time-consuming bureaucratic requirements would allow the U.S. government to focus its enforcement efforts on, true dangers to public safety and national security. Rather than routine checks on mundane matters such as income and assets, *see* Chapter 10, U.S. immigration authorities could focus on terrorists, dangerous criminals, drugs and other contraband, and public health risks.[80]

3. Recent Proposals for Immigration Reform

For roughly a decade, the nation has engaged in a fractious national debate over reform of the immigration laws, with a special focus on undocumented immigration from Mexico. The proposals frequently call for legalization of undocumented immigrants, guest worker programs,[81] and a myriad of enforcement measures. The granting of "amnesty" to undocumented immigrants in some of the proposals became nothing less than a charged political accusation and contributed to political opposition to any reform proposal with a path to legalization for undocumented immigrants.[82]

In December 2005, the House of Representatives passed what was known as the Sensenbrenner bill,[83] named after sponsor Representative James Sensenbrenner. The tough nature of the bill sparked protests of thousands of immigrants and their

---

[79] *See* Special Feature, *Working Features: Linking Debates About Insourcing and Outsourcing of Capital and Labor*, 40 Tex. Int'l L.J. 691 (2005); Jennifer Gordon, *We Make the Road by Walking: Immigrant Workers, the Workplace Project, and the Struggle for Social Change*, 30 Harv. C.R.-C.L. L. Rev. 407 (1995); Jennifer Gordon, *Transnational Labor Citizenship*, 80 S. Cal. L. Rev. 503 (2007).

[80] *See* Johnson, *supra* note 66, at 200–11.

[81] For critical analysis of guest worker programs, see Cristina M. Rodriguez, *Guest Workers and Integration: Toward a Theory of What Immigrants and Americans Owe One Another*, 2007 U. Chi. Leg. F. 219 (2007); Karla M. Campbell, *Guest Worker Programs and the Convergence of U.S. Immigration and Development Policies: A Two-Factor Economic Model*, 21 Geo. Immigr. L.J. 663 (2007); *see also* Enid Trucios-Haynes, *Temporary Workers and Future Immigration Policy Conflicts: Protecting U.S. Workers and Satisfying the Demand for Global Human Capital*, 40 Brandeis L.J. 967 (2002) (reviewing policies designed to protect U.S. workers from noncitizen labor). For a partial defense of such programs, see Howard F. Chang, *Liberal Ideals and Political Feasibility: Guest-Worker Programs as Second-Best Policies*, 27 N.C. J. Int'l L. & Com. Reg. 465 (2002).

[82] *See* Bryn Siegel, Note, *The Political Discourse of Amnesty in Immigration Policy*, 41 Akron L. Rev. 291 (2008). For a defense of the concept of amnesty for certain categories of undocumented immigrants, see Bill Ong Hing, *The Case for Amnesty*, 3 Stan. J. C.R. & C.L. 233 (2007).

[83] *See* Border Protection, Antiterrorism, and Illegal Immigration Control Act of 2005, H. Rep. 4437, 109th Cong. 1st Sess. (2005). The Sensenbrenner bill, among other things, would have made the status of being an undocumented immigrant a felony subject to imprisonment and would have imposed criminal

supporters across the United States.[84] Shortly thereafter, the Senate passed a more moderate reform proposal, which included legalization and guest worker programs in addition to less extreme enforcement measures.[85] Ultimately, Congress failed to enact immigration reform. It instead agreed only to extend the fence along the United States's southern border with Mexico.[86] Congress did so even though there is no evidence that this, or any other border enforcement measure alone, will decrease the flow of undocumented immigrants to the United States.[87]

In the 2008 election campaign, President Obama expressed support for immigration reform, with a majority of Latina/o voters supporting his candidacy.[88] His administration renewed calls for comprehensive immigration reform.[89] In 2013, the Senate passed the Border Security, Economic Opportunity, and Immigration Modernization Act (S. 744),[90] which was co-sponsored by a bipartisan group of Senators. The bill generally focuses on four basic objectives:

> (1) creating a path to citizenship for the approximately 11 million undocumented aliens currently living in the United States; (2) reforming America's immigration system to better recognize characteristics that will help build the economy; (3) implementing an effective employment verification system; and (4) establishing an improved process for admitting future workers.[91]

---

sanctions on persons who provided humanitarian assistance to undocumented immigrants. See *id.* §§ 203, 205.

[84] For analysis of the spring 2006 immigrant rights marches, see Bill Ong Hing & Kevin R. Johnson, *The Immigrant Rights Marches of 2006 and the Prospects for a New Civil Rights Movement*, 42 HARV. C.R.-C.L. L. REV. 99 (2007); Sylvia R. Lazos Vargas, *Emerging Latina/o Nation and Anti-Immigrant Backlash*, 7 NEV. L.J. 685 (2007).

[85] *See* Comprehensive Immigration Reform Act of 2006, S. 2611, 109th Cong, 2d Sess (2006).

[86] *See* Secure Fence Act of 2006, Pub. L. No. 109-367, 120 Stat. 2638 (2006). For analysis of the political symbolism of the U.S./Mexico border fence, see Pratheepan Gulasekaram, *Why a Wall?*, 2 UC IRVINE L. REV. 147 (2012)

[87] *See* JOHNSON, *supra* note 66, at 114–15.

[88] *See* Pew Research, The Hispanic Vote in the 2008 Election (stating that Latina/os voted by Democratic presidential ticket by a 2:1 margin over Republican), *available at* http://www.pewhispanic. org/2008/11/05/the-hispanic-vote-in-the-2008-election/ (last visited July 28, 2014).

[89] *See Building a 21st Century Immigration System* (2011), *available at* http://www.whitehouse.gov/ issues/immigration (last visited July 7, 2014).

[90] *See* S. 744, 113th Cong. (2013), *available at* http://www.gpo.gov/fdsys/pkg/BILLS-113s744pap/pdf/ BILLS-113s744pap.pdf (last visited July 7, 2014). The Senate passed the bill by a margin of 68-32. *See* U.S. Senate, U.S. Senate Roll Call Votes 113th Congress — 1st Session, *available at* http://www.senate. gov/legislative/LIS/roll_call_lists/roll_call_vote_cfm.cfm?congress=113&session=1&vote=00168 (last visited July 24, 2014). For analysis of recent immigration reform efforts in Congress, see Maria Pabón López & Natasha Ann Lacoste, *Immigration Reform in 2013–14: An Essay on the Senate's Bipartisan Plan, the House's Standards for Immigration Reform, Interest Convergence and Political Realities*, 17 HARV. LATINO L. REV. 121 (2014).

[91] Brandon E. Davis, *The Border Security, Economic Opportunity, and Immigration Modernization Act an Overview of the Changes Employers May Expect Following Comprehensive Immigration Reform*, FED. LAW., Jan./Feb. 2014, at 26. For analysis of the bill's provisions, see CONGRESSIONAL BUDGET OFFICE, THE ECONOMIC IMPACT OF S.744, THE BORDER SECURITY, ECONOMIC OPPORTUNITY AND IMMIGRATION MODERNIZATION ACT (2013), *available at* http://www.cbo.gov/sites/default/files/cbofiles/attachments/44346-

Despite bipartisan support, as this book goes to press, the House of Representatives has not voted on the Senate bill or any alternative comprehensive immigration reform proposal.[92]

a.　The DREAM Act

Congress has considered many versions of a bill narrower in scope than comprehensive immigration reform that would expressly permit states to allow undocumented students to pay in-state fees to attend public colleges and universities and would allow them to regularize their immigration status.[93] Members of Congress almost annually sponsor legislation known as the Development, Relief and Education for Alien Minors (DREAM) Act, which undocumented college students known as DREAMers have championed.[94]

Immigration restrictionists harshly criticize the many iterations of the DREAM Act, contending, among other things, that it rewards unlawful conduct and amounts to an "amnesty" for undocumented immigrants.[95]

In 2007, the DREAM Act was part of a comprehensive Senate immigration bill that ultimately failed.[96] The U.S. Senate failed to pass a subsequent version of the Act, which would have permitted a path to legalization for undocumented high school graduates who attend college or serve in the military.[97] To date, although activists aggressively push for enactment of the law, Congress has not passed any version of the DREAM Act.

Immigration.pdf (last visited July 14, 2014); Claire Bergeron, Current Development, *Development in the Legislative Branch: Bipartisan "Gang of Eight" Bill Would Dramatically Alter US Immigration Law*, 27 Geo. Immigr. L.J. 431 (2013).

[92] *See* Wesley Lowery, *House Democrats Need 27 Signatures to Force Vote on Comprehensive Immigration Reform Bill*, Wash. Post, Apr. 15, 2014; David Nakamura, *U.S. Chamber of Commerce Pushes House GOP on Immigration Reform*, Wash. Post, Feb. 25, 2014.

[93] *See* Michael A. Olivas, *IIRIRA, The DREAM Act, and Undocumented College Student Residency*, 30 J.C. & U.L. 435, 452–56 (2004); Thomas R. Ruge & Angela D. Iza, *Higher Education for Undocumented Students: The Case for Open Admissions and In-State Tuition Rates for Students Without Lawful Immigration Status*, 15 Ind. Int'l & Comp. L. Rev. 257, 266–274 (2005).

[94] *See* Kevin R. Johnson, *A Handicapped, Not "Sleeping," Giant: The Devastating Impact of the Initiative Process on Latina/o and Immigrant Communities*, 96 Cal. L. Rev. 1259, 1280–82 (2008). For analysis of the DREAM Act and arguments favoring its enactment, see Berta Hernandez-Truyol & Justin Luna, *Children and Immigration: International, Local, and Social Responsibilities*, 15 B.U. Pub. Int. L.J. 297, 314–16 (2006); Victor Romero, *Postsecondary School Education Benefits for Undocumented Immigrants: Promises and Pitfalls*, 27 N.C. J. Int'l & Com. Reg 393 (2002); *see also* Maria Pabón López, *Reflections on Educating Latino and Latina Undocumented Children: Beyond Phyler v. Doe*, 35 Seton Hall L. Rev. 1373, 1400–04 (2005) (summarizing the status of undocumented student access to higher education).

[95] *See* Julia Preston, *In Increments, Senate Revisits Immigration Bill*, N.Y. Times, Aug. 3, 2007, at A1. *Compare* Kris W. Kobach, *Immigration Nullification: In-State Tuition and Lawmakers Who Disregard the Law*, 10 NYU J. Legis. & Pub. Pol'y 473 (2007) (criticizing state and federal DREAM Acts), with Michael A. Olivas, *Lawmakers Gone Wild? College Residency and the Response to Professor Kobach*, 61 SMU L. Rev. 99 (2008) (advocating passage of these laws).

[96] *See* Preston, *supra* note 95.

[97] *See* Karin Brulliard, *Bill Aimed at Immigrant Children Fails*, Wash. Post, Oct. 25, 2007, at A12.

Although lacking authority to provide a path to legalization for undocumented immigrant students, some states, including California, have expanded access to public colleges and universities.[98] In contrast, Arizona voters passed an initiative that barred public universities from providing undocumented students with in-state fee eligibility, state financial aid, or enrollment in adult education classes.[99]

b. Prosecutorial Discretion, Deferred Action for Childhood Arrivals, and the 2014 Expansion of Deferred Action

With Congress failing to pass immigration reform, the Obama administration took a number of steps to fine-tune its immigration enforcement efforts. While focusing its efforts on immigrants with brushes with the criminal law, it administratively employed its discretion to designate certain removal cases a low priority. *See* Ch. 12.

In June 2012, U.S. Department of Homeland Security announced the Deferred Action for Childhood Arrivals program (DACA), an exercise of prosecutorial discretion that provides temporary relief in the form of deferred action from removal on a case-by-basis to noncitizens who entered the United States as children.[100] *See* Ch. 12. Those eligible for DACA must have entered the United States before the age of 16; continuously resided in the Unites States since June 15, 2007; been physically present in the United States and not over the age of 30 when DACA was announced; have not been convicted of a felony, a significant misdemeanor, or multiple misdemeanors; must not pose a threat to national security or

---

[98] *See, e.g.*, Martinez v. Regents of the University of California, 241 P.3d 855 (Cal. 2010), *cert. denied*, 131 S. Ct. 2961 (2011) (rejecting a challenge to a California law that allows certain graduates of California high schools, including undocumented immigrants, to pay the same fees as state residents to attend the University of California, state universities, and community colleges). For analysis of the *Martinez* decision, see Kyle William Colvin, Note, *In-State Tuition and Illegal Immigrants: An Analysis of Martinez v. Regents of the University of California*, 2010 B.Y.U. Educ. & L.J. 391 (2010); Beverly N. Rich, Note, *Tracking AB 540's Potential Residence: An Analysis of the In-State Tuition for Undocumented Students in Light of Martinez v. Regents of the University of California*, 19 S. Cal. Rev. L. & Soc. Just. 297 (2010).

[99] *See* Friendly House v. Napolitano, 419 F.3d 930 (9th Cir. 2005); Yes on Prop 200 v. Napolitano, 160 P.3d 1216 (Ariz. Ct. App. 2007). Arizona Governor Jan Brewer later issued an order that prohibited public colleges and universities from allowing undocumented students granted relief by the U.S. government under the Deferred Action for Childhood Arrivals program to be eligible for in-state university fees. *See* Ariz. Exec. Order No. 2012-06, 18 Ariz. Admin. Reg. 2237 (Sept. 7, 2012), *available at* http://www.azsos.gov/aar/2012/36/governor.pdf (last visited July 24, 2014); Daniel Gonzalez, *Young Migrants May Get Arizona College Tuition Break*, Ariz. Rep. Sept. 12, 2012.

[100] U.S. Dep't of Homeland Security Memorandum, Exercising Prosecutorial Discretion with Respect to Individuals Who Came to the United States as Children (June 15, 2012), *available at* http://www.dhs.gov/xlibrary/assets/s1-exercising-prosecutorial-discretion-individuals-who-came-to-us-children.pdf [hereinafter DHS Memorandum] (last visited July 7, 2014); *see* Ch. 12. For debate over the legality of the DACA program, compare Robert J. Delahunty & John C. Yoo, *Dream On: The Obama Administration's Nonenforcement of Immigration Laws, the DREAM Act, and the Take Care Clause*, 91 Tex. L. Rev. 781, 784–85, 856 (2013) (arguing that by authorizing the DACA program, President Obama breached his responsibility to faithfully enforce the immigration laws), *with* Shoba Sivaprasad Wadhia, *In Defense of DACA, Deferred Action, and the DREAM Act*, 91 Tex. L. Rev. 59, 62–68 (2013) (defending the program as consistent with the executive exercise of prosecutorial discretion by the Executive Branch in the immigration matters), *available at* http://www.texaslrev.com/wp-content/uploads/Wadhia.pdf (last visited July 7, 2014).

public safety; and be currently in school, graduated from high school, obtained a General Educational Development (GED) certification, or be an honorably discharged veteran of the U.S. Coast Guard or Armed Forces. DACA recognizes its beneficiaries to be "low priority cases" for removal from the United States.[101]

By the end of the first quarter of fiscal year 2014, the U.S. Citizenship and Immigration Services reported that the U.S. government received a total of 638,054 DACA applications, approved 521,815, and denied 15,968.[102] In 2014, DHS announced a renewal program for DACA recipients.[103]

DACA recipients are able to obtain employment authorization, a Social Security number, and, in many states, a driver's license.[104] However, the relatively high $465 filing fee and the difficulty of providing evidentiary support establishing continuous presence in the United States serve as impediments to successful applications.[105] Those factors may explain why many eligible noncitizens have not applied for DACA relief.

Thus far, DACA has helped more than a half million immigrants "who were brought to this country as children and know only this country as home."[106] As one commentator has noted, however, it "is not a permanent solution and does not grant [recipients] any long-term immigration status stability."[107]

In response to Congress's repeated failure to pass immigration reform, the Obama administration after the 2014 midterm elections took a number of steps to revise its immigration enforcement efforts. The President expanded the existing DACA program and created a new deferred action program for undocumented parents of U.S. citizens and lawful permanent residents.[108] Notably, the new initiatives did not, as some had hoped, provide deferred action status to the

---

[101] *See id.*

[102] *See* U.S. Citizenship and Immigration Services Number of I-821D, Consideration of Deferred Action by Fiscal Year, Quarter, Intake Biometrics and Case Status: 2012–2014 First Quarter, *available at* http://www.uscis.gov/sites/default/files/USCIS/Resources/Reports%20and%20Studies/Immigration%20Forms%20Data/All%20Form%20Types/DACA/DACA-06-02-14.pdf (last visited July 7, 2014).

[103] *See* U.S. Citizenship and Immigration Services, Secretary Johnson Announces Process for DACA Renewal, June 5, 2014, *available at* http://www.uscis.gov/news/secretary-johnson-announces-process-daca-renewal (last visited July 24, 2014).

[104] *See* National Immigration Law Center, Frequently Asked Questions: The Obama Administration's Deferred Action for Childhood Arrivals (DACA), *available at* http://www.nilc.org/FAQdeferredactionyouth.html (last visited July 7, 2014).

[105] *See* Audrey Singer & Nicole Prchal Svajlenka, *Metropolitan Policy Program at Brookings at 2, Immigration Facts: Deferred Action for Childhood Arrivals (DACA)*, Aug. 14, 2013, *available at* http://www.brookings.edu/research/reports/2013/08/14-daca-immigration-singer (last visited July 7, 2014).

[106] DHS Memorandum, *supra* note 100.

[107] Mariela Olivares, *Renewing the Dream: DREAM Act Redux and Immigration Reform*, 16 Harv. Latino L. Rev. 79, 91 (2013).

[108] *See* U.S. Dep't of Homeland Security, *Fixing Our Broken Immigration System Through Executive Action — Key Facts* (last published Dec. 5, 2014), *available at* http://www.dhs.gov/immigration-action?utm.

undocumented parents of DACA recipients.[109]

The President's actions sparked a contentious national debate. Although previous Presidents had engaged in similar (although not identical) measures,[110] critics complained that the new deferred action program was unprecedented in scope.[111] Texas and 25 other states filed a lawsuit challenging the new program, claiming among other things that it violated the constitutional requirement that the President "shall take care that the laws be faithfully executed."[112] A federal district court in February 2015 entered a preliminary injunction barring the expanded deferred action program from going into effect.[113]

4. Future Possibilities for Reform

Future possibilities for immigration reform run the gamut. Reform could represent incremental changes to the current immigration laws, with "comprehensive" immigration reform similar to S. 744 a possibility.[114] One commentator observed that

> [a] thoughtful and responsible reform package must accomplish a few things. First, it must address the dilemma of the existing undocumented immigrant population in our country. Second, it must regulate future flows of immigrants consistent with our labor market needs and economic interests in an increasingly inter-dependent world. Third, it must advance the protection of both U.S. and foreign workers. Finally, it must reflect the deeply engrained American value of fairness.[115]

One of the co-authors of this book has argued that economic, moral, and policy arguments militate in favor of more liberal admissions of immigrants to the United

---

[109] The Justice Department's Office of Legal Counsel had concluded that such relief might violate the law. See Memorandum on the Department of Homeland Security's Authority to Prioritize Removal of Certain Aliens Unlawfully Present in the United States and to Defer Removal of Others, Karl R. Thompson, Principal Deputy Assistant Attorney General, Office of Legal Counsel dated Nov. 19, 2014, *available at* http://www.justice.gov/sites/default/files/olc/opinions/attachments/2014/11/20/2014-11-19-auth-prioritize-removal.pdf.

[110] *See American Immigration Council, Immigration Policy Center, Executive Action on Immigration: A Resource Page, available at* http://www.immigrationpolicy.org/executive-action-immigration-resource-page (last visited Dec. 8, 2014).

[111] *See* Editorial, *President Obama's Unilateral Action on Immigration Has No Precedent,* Wash. Post, Dec 3. 2014.

[112] *See* Texas v. United States, Civil No. B 14-254 (S.D. Tex., filed Dec. 3. 2014), *available at* http://www.texasattorneygeneral.gov/files/epress/files/20141203ImmigrationExecutiveOrderLawsuit.pdf.

[113] *See* Texas v. United States, 2015 U.S. Dist. LEXIS 18551 (S.D. Tex. Feb. 16, 2015). As this book goes to press, the injunction is being appealed to the U.S. Court of Appeals for the Fifth Circuit.

[114] *See, e.g., Comprehensive Immigration Reform Symposium,* 55 Wayne L. Rev. 1599 (2009); Symposium, *Immigration Reform and Policy in the Current Politically Polarized Climate,* 16 Temp. Pol. & Civ. Rts. L. Rev. 309 (2007); Asa Hutchinson, *Keynote Address: Holes in the Fence: Immigration Reform and Border Security in the United States Symposium,* 59 Admin. L. Rev. 533, 537–38 (2007).

[115] Muzaffar Chishti, *A Redesigned Immigration Selection System,* 41 Cornell Intl L.J. 115, 116 (2008); *see* Kevin R. Johnson, *Ten Guiding Principles for Truly Comprehensive Immigration Reform: A Blueprint,* 55 Wayne L. Rev. 1599 (2009).

States than current law provides.[116] A related possibility is the greater economic integration, including the integration of labor markets, of the United States, Canada, and Mexico modeled after the successful European Union, an alternative discussed at the end of this chapter.

Discussion of immigration reform often neglects strategies that might improve the integration of legal, as well as undocumented, immigrants into U.S. society.[117] Facilitating naturalization of immigrants is one way to provide for the legal integration of immigrants into American social life. The U.S. government, however, has been inconsistent with respect to promoting naturalization as well as other programs, such as ensuring access to federal public benefits programs, which might facilitate immigrant integration.[118] *See* Chs. 16, 17.

Although often focusing primarily on strategies to facilitate immigration enforcement, *see* Chapter 4, state and local governments can play an important role in the integration of immigrants into civil society.[119] Issuing driver's licenses to undocumented immigrants or recipients of deferred action, which has proven to be hotly contested in the states,[120] is one strategy that facilitates noncitizen integration. A number of states have passed laws allowing undocumented high school graduates to pay in-state fees at public universities.[121] *See* Ch. 16. Providing additional English as a second language classes, which are chronically over-enrolled,[122] and bilingual education,[123] also would facilitate English language acquisition by immigrants and thus promote immigrant integration.

---

[116] *See* JOHNSON, *supra* notes 66.

[117] *See, e.g.*, SECURING THE FUTURE: U.S. IMMIGRANT INTEGRATION POLICY: A READER (Migration Policy Institute, Michael Fix ed., 2007).

[118] *See* Judith Bernstein-Baker, *Citizenship in a Restrictionist Era: The Mixed Messages of Federal Policies*, 16 TEMP. POL. & CIV. RTS. L. REV. 367, 381–84 (2007).

[119] *See* Cristina M. Rodríguez, *The Significance of the Local in Immigration Regulation*, 106 MICH. L. REV. 567, 581–609 (2008).

[120] *See* Kevin R. Johnson, *Driver's Licenses and Undocumented Immigrants: The Future of Civil Rights Law?*, 5 NEV. L.J. 213 (2004); Sylvia R. Lazos Vargas, *Missouri, the "War on Terrorism," and Immigrants: Legal Challenges Post 9/11*, 67 MO. L. REV. 775, 798–807 (2002); María Pabón Lopez, *More than a License to Drive: State Restrictions on the Use of Driver's Licenses by Noncitizens*, 29 S. ILL. U. L.J. 91 (2004/05); Kari E. D'Ottavio, Comment, *Deferred Action for Childhood Arrivals: Why Granting Driver's Licenses to DACA Beneficiaries Makes Constitutional and Political Sense*, 72 MD. L. REV. 931 (2013); Steven J. Escobar, Note, *Allowing Undocumented Immigrants to Obtain Driver's Licenses in New Mexico: Revising, Not Abandoning, the System*, 43 WASH. U. J.L. & POL'Y 285 (2013); Joelle P. Hong, Current Development, *Development in the Legislative Branch: Illinois Joins Three States in Granting Driving Privileges to Undocumented Immigrants*, 26 GEO. IMMIGR. L.J. 713 (2012).

[121] *See, e.g.*, Martinez v. Regents of the University of California, 241 P.3d 855 (Cal. 2010), *cert. denied*, 131 S. Ct. 2961 (2011) (upholding California law permitting California high school graduates including undocumented immigrants to pay in-state fees at public universities); *see* Rodriguez, *supra* note 119, at 605–09; Michael A. Olivas, *IIRIRA, the DREAM Act, and Undocumented College Student Residency*, 30 J.C. & U.L. 435 (2005).

[122] *See* James Thomas Tucker, *The ESL Logjam: Waiting Times for ESL Classes and the Impact on English Learners; English as a Second Language*, NAT'L CIVIC REV., Mar. 22, 2007, vol. 96, No. 1. Increasingly, the private sector has promoted immigrant assimilation with employers, among other policies, promoting English language acquisition. *See* Pamela Constable & N.C. Aizenman, *Companies Take Lead in Assimilation Efforts*, WASH. POST, Aug. 9, 2008, at B1.

[123] *See* Kevin R. Johnson & George Martínez, *Discrimination by Proxy: The Case of Proposition 227*

5. Increased Economic Integration of Canada, Mexico, and the United States

Some contend that incremental reform will not work and that bolder initiatives are necessary to cure the ills of U.S. immigration law. In that vein, the possibility of more open borders has been analyzed.[124] In an era of an increasingly integrated world economy, the United States arguably requires a system of immigration admissions that better comports with social, political, and economic factors contributing to the demand for immigration than the current system.[125]

At the tail end of the twentieth century, regional common markets gained popularity. Many nations perceived the economic benefits of more integrated economies. At the same time, there was reluctance to move from a restricted to a more open scheme immediately. In several important instances, with the European Union the most well-known labor migration between the member nations evolved out of increased trade of goods and services.

The U.S. government at some point may consider regularizing the flow of labor from Mexico into the United States.[126] The North American Free Trade Agreement (NAFTA) might be expanded to permit labor migration to mirror the free trade of goods and services among the member nations. A North American Union modeled on the European Union could permit labor migration among Canada, Mexico, and the United States.[127]

---

and the Ban on Bilingual Education, 33 UC Davis L. Rev. 1227 (2000) (analyzing the elimination of bilingual education in California).

[124] *See* Johnson, *supra* note 66; Jason Riley, Let Them In: the Case for Open Borders (2008); Satvinder Juss, International Migration and Global Justice (2006); Teresa Hayter, Open Borders: the Case Against Immigration Controls (2d ed. 2004).

[125] *See* Walter A. Ewing, *From Denial to Acceptance: Effectively Regulating Immigration to the United States*, 16 Stan. L. & Pol'y Rev. 445, 445 (2005) ("U.S. immigration policy is based on denial. Most lawmakers in the United States have largely embraced the process of economic 'globalization,' yet stubbornly refuse to acknowledge that migration, especially from developing nations to developed nations, is an integral and inevitable part of this process.")

[126] Considerable attention has been paid to the growing economic integration of North America. *See, e.g.*, The Future of North American Integration: Beyond NAFTA (Peter Hakim & Robert E. Litan eds., 2002); Eric Helleiner, Towards North American Monetary Union? (2006). Opposition in some quarters to any such union is strong. *See, e.g.*, Jerome R. Corsi, The Late Great USA: The Coming Merger with Mexico and Canada, (2007); Colin D. Standish & Russell R. Standish, The European Union, the North American Union, the Papacy, & Globalism (2007).

[127] *See* T. Alexander Aleinikoff, *Legal Immigration Reform: Toward Rationality and Equity*, *in* Blueprints for an Ideal Legal Immigration Policy 5, 5–6 (Richard D. Lamm & Alan Simpson eds., 2001); Naomi Gal-Or, *Labor Mobility Under NAFTA: Regulatory Policy Spearheading the Social Supplement to the International Trade Regime*, 15 Ariz. J. Int'l & Comp. L. 365 (1998); Emily Gibbs, Comment, *Free Movement of Labor in North America: Using the European Union As a Model for the Creation of North American Citizenship*, 45 USF L. Rev. 265, 286–88 (2010); *see also* Ernesto Hernandez-Lopez, *Sovereignty Migrates in U.S. and Mexican Law: Transnational Influences in Plenary Power and Non-Intervention*, 40 Vand. J. Transnat'l L. 1345 (2007) (noting that the United States and Mexico have been acting in increasingly transnational ways with respect to migration); Katie E. Chachere, Comment, *Keeping America Competitive: A Multilateral Approach to Illegal Immigration Reform*, 49 S. Tex. L. Rev. 659 (2008) (contending that the United States must work with other nations on immigration). *See generally* Bill Ong Hing, Ethical Border: Nafta, Globalization, and Mexican Migration (2010) (analyzing immigration in North America after NAFTA); L. Ronald Scheman, Greater America: a New Partnership

Some preliminary steps might need to be taken before the implementation of a North American regional migration arrangement. Noting that the European Union invested billions of dollars in the infrastructure of new member nations before permitting labor migration, one observer contends that the United States must consider an economic adjustment strategy for Mexico to decrease migration pressures and allow for the possibility of more manageable free movement into the United States.[128]

a. The European Union

The most well-known example of a regional migration system exists in Europe. After gaining experience with the free trade of goods and services, the member nations of the European Union (EU) agreed that the economic benefits of relatively easy labor migration would, as a whole, also benefit the member states.[129] Today, labor migration is generally permitted within the EU. The elimination of border controls between the member nations did not result in mass migration.

Several regions of Northern Europe, South America, and Africa have allowed, or are considering allowing, relatively freer migration between member states.

b. The Political Feasibility of a Regional Arrangement

Regional migration arrangements, such as the one that exists in much of Europe, represent a more politically viable alternative — at least in the first instance — to completely open borders. As a purely practical matter, it is far easier to obtain popular consent to regional arrangements because the people in the region are more likely to share cultural, racial, and other commonalities and have experience interacting with each other.[130]

Because a regional arrangement only provides entry to more "local" immigrants, it offers the appearance of more control over the numbers of migrants coming into a nation. In addition, greater racial and cultural homogeneity among populations in a region would tend to moderate opposition to a regional arrangement and blunt the concern that the nation would be overrun by migrants.

In negotiating the North American Free Trade Agreement in the early 1990s, the U.S. government adamantly opposed discussing immigration between the United States, Canada, and Mexico. Although concern with Mexican migration continues to exist in the United States, the tripartite trading relationship holds the promise of

---

FOR THE AMERICAS IN THE TWENTY-FIRST CENTURY (2003) (advocating generally greater cooperation between nations in the Americas); THE FUTURE OF NORTH AMERICAN INTEGRATION: BEYOND NAFTA (Peter Hakim & Robert E. Litan eds., 2002) (analyzing integration of North America).

[128] *See* Timothy A. Canova, *Closing the Border and Opening the Door: Mobility, Adjustment, and the Sequencing of Reform*, 5 GEO. J. L. PUB. POL'Y 341 (2007).

[129] *See* Randall Hansen, *Migration to Europe Since 1945: Its History and Its Lessons*, POL. Q., 2005, at 25.

[130] For similar reasons, regional arrangements have been advocated as a politically viable alternative to the current system for admitting *refugees* to the United States, with nations allowing for the resettlement of refugees facing persecution in nearby nations. *See* James C. Hathaway, *A Reconsideration of the Underlying Premise of Refugee Law*, 31 HARV. INT'L L.J. 129 (1990).

evolving into an EU-like labor migration relationship.[131]

The nations of North America have worked together on migration-related issues on a small scale. Canada and the United States, for example, have increasingly cooperated with respect to migration controls.[132]

Over the course of the twentieth century, the United States and Mexico as a result of NAFTA developed a closer economic and political relationship.[133] The U.S. government has worked with the Mexican government to assist in border enforcement efforts.[134] To this end, the Mexican government, at the behest of the U.S. government, has taken steps to limit Central American migrants from traveling through Mexico to this country.[135] The burgeoning relationship between the two neighbors creates the potential for future cooperation on migration issues.[136]

The highest levels of the U.S. and Mexican governments have at times discussed possible bilateral measures addressing migration, a sharp turnaround from the early 1990s, when NAFTA's approval hinged on *not* addressing immigration. Only days before September 11, 2001, an agreement to regularize migration between the United States and Mexico appeared to be on the immediate horizon. Serious

---

[131] *See* JASON ACKLESON, ACHIEVING "SECURITY AND PROSPERITY"; MIGRATION AND NORTH AMERICAN ECONOMIC INTEGRATION (Immigration Policy Center, 2006); Kevin R. Johnson, *Free Trade and Closed Borders: NAFTA and Mexican Immigration to the United States*, 27 UC DAVIS L. REV. 937 (1994); John A. Scanlan, *A View From the United States — Social, Economic, and Legal Change, the Persistence of the State, and Immigration Policy in the Coming Century*, 2 IND. J. GLOBAL LEG. STUDS. 79, 123–25 (1994).

[132] *See* Johnson & Trujillo, *supra* note 12, at 1391–92. The United States and Canada, for example, entered into an agreement involving refugees and cooperation on a variety of immigration measures designed to tighten security after September 11, 2001. *See* Agreement for Cooperation in the Examination of Refugee Status Claims from Nationals of Third Countries, Aug. 30, 2002, U.S.-Canada *available at* http://www.cic.gc.ca/english/department/laws-policy/safe-third.asp (last visited July 7, 2014); Audrey Macklin, *Disappointing Refugees: Reflections on the Canada-U.S. Safe Third Country Agreement*, 36 COLUM. HUM. RTS. L. REV. 365 (2005); *see also Special ABA Committee Report on the Canada-U.S. Border: Balancing Trade, Security, and Migrant Rights in the Post-9/11 Era: ABA Immigration and Nationality Committee, International Law Section*, 19 GEO. IMMIGR. L.J. 199 (2004) (discussing increased cooperation between the United States and Canada on migration issues); Adam Centner, *Strengthening North American Perimeter Security: An Analysis of United States and Canadian Immigration and Refugee Laws and the Collaboration Required to Harmonize Those Laws*, 37 CAN.-U.S. L.J. 493 (2012) (discussing the North American perimeter security concept that seeks to facilitate trade across the border while maintaining national security measures).

[133] *See* Johnson & Trujillo, *supra* note 12, at 1391–92. *See generally* CONGRESSIONAL RESEARCH SERVICE, MEXICO BACKGROUND AND U.S. RELATIONS (Jan. 30, 2014) (analyzing issues of mutual interest to United States and Mexican governments).

[134] *See* CONGRESSIONAL RESEARCH SERVICE, MEXICO'S IMPORTANCE AND MULTIPLE RELATIONSHIPS WITH THE UNITED STATES (2006); CONGRESSIONAL RESEARCH SERVICE, MEXICO-UNITED STATES DIALOGUE ON MIGRATION AND BORDER ISSUES, 2001–2005 (updated June 2, 2005); Elizabeth A. Whitaker, *U.S. Governments Efforts with Mexico to Address Immigration Issues*, Testimony before the House International Relations Committee, *available at* http://2001-2009.state.gov/p/wha/rls/rm/2006/69604.htm (last visited July 7, 2014).

[135] *See* Steven W. Bender, *Sight, Sound, and Stereotype: The War on Terrorism and Its Consequences for Latinas/os*, 81 OR. L. REV. 1153, 1161–64 (2002); Bruce Zagaris, *International Criminal and Enforcement Cooperation in the Americas in the Wake of Integration: A Post-NAFTA Transition Period Analysis With Special Attention to Investing in Mexico*, 3 SW. J.L. & TRADE AM. 1, 51–54 (1996).

[136] *See* CONGRESSIONAL RESEARCH SERVICE, U.S.-MEXICAN SECURITY COOPERATION: THE MÉRIDA INITIATIVE AND BEYOND (Apr. 8, 2014); Alan D. Bersin, *El Tercer Pais: Reinventing the U.S./Mexico Border*, 48 STAN. L. REV. 1413 (1996).

consideration of this option ceased on September 11.[137]

In 2005, the United States, Canada, and Mexico embarked on the Security and Prosperity Partnership of North America to work on common economic and security issues.[138] This increased cooperation may help facilitate long term collaboration on labor and migration issues common to the three nations.

After a hiatus of several years following the events of September 11, the United States and Mexico in 2005 again began to discuss migration between the two nations.[139] However, the antipathy for immigrants — especially those from Mexico, see Ch. 2 — in the United States, and concerns with mass migration, continue to be major stumbling blocks.

c.　The Costs of a Regional Migration Arrangement

Despite their political advantages, regional regimes are not cost-free. Regional blocs almost necessarily lead to border fortifications at the outer perimeter of the union of nations. For example, with internal controls between the EU member nations eased, border controls were erected around the EU's outer perimeter to keep noncitizens from outside Europe from entering.[140] Border controls sought to thwart a mass migration from North Africa into France and Germany. As a condition of EU membership, Spain created its first comprehensive immigration law in an effort to restrict migration from North Africa.[141] The result of the EU's labor migration arrangment was the creation of the so-called "Fortress Europe."[142]

Migrants seeking entry into Europe face perils like those encountered by undocumented Mexican immigrants attempting to enter the United States. Like Mexican migrants, undocumented migrants to Europe evade border fortifications by making a hazardous journey across the Mediterranean Sea.[143] Migrants from

---

[137] See Johnson, supra note 70, at 866–67.

[138] See Johnson & Trujillo, supra note 12, at 1391–92. See generally JASON ACKLESON & JUSTIN KASTNER, ROUTINIZING COOPERATION AND CHANGING NARRATIVES: THE SECURITY AND PROSPERITY PARTNERSHIP OF NORTH AMERICA (2006); GREG ANDERSON & CHRISTOPHER SANDS, NEGOTIATING NORTH AMERICAN: THE SECURITY AND PROSPERITY PARTNERSHIP (HUDSON INSTITUTE WHITE PAPER 2007); ALEXANDER MOENS WITH MICHAEL CUST, SAVING THE NORTH AMERICAN SECURITY AND PROSPERITY PARTNERSHIP: THE CASE FOR A NORTH AMERICAN STANDARDS AND REGULATORY AREA (2008).

[139] See David Stout, Bush and Neighbors Promise to Cooperate, INT'L HERALD TRIB., Mar. 24, 2005, at 5

[140] See Kevin R. Johnson, Regional Integration in North America and Europe: Lessons About Civil Rights and Equal Citizenship, 9 U. MIAMI INT'L & COMP. L. REV. 33, 40–43 (2000–01).

[141] See Kitty Calavita, Immigration, Law, and Marginalization in a Global Economy: Notes From Spain, 32 LAW & SOC'Y REV. 529, 542–48 (1998). See generally KITTY CALAVITA, IMMIGRANTS AT THE MARGINS: LAW, RACE, AND EXCLUSION IN SOUTHERN EUROPE (2005).

[142] See Lydia Esteve Gonzalez & Richard Mac Bride, Fortress Europe: Fear of Immigration? Present and Future of Immigration Law and Policy in Spain, 6 UC DAVIS J. INT'L L. & POL'Y 153 (2000); Bob Hepple, Race and Law in Fortress Europe, 67 MOD. L. REV. 1 (2004).

[143] See Michael A. Becker, Note, Managing Diversity in the European Union: Inclusive European Citizenship and Third-Country Nationals, 7 YALE HUM. RTS. & DEV. L.J. 132 (2004); Aristides Diaz-Pedrosa, Note, A Tale of Competing Policies: The Creation of Havens for Illegal Immigrants and the Black Market Economy, 37 CORNELL INT'L L.J. 431 (2004).

North Africa who make it into the EU encounter increased discrimination and at times, even violence.[144]

d. A Possible North American Union

In the end, the signals are decidedly mixed as to whether there will be any kind of U.S./Mexico migration agreement in the near future. Indeed, as the discussion of a possible agreement with Mexico fell by the wayside after September 11, Congress has moved in the opposite direction of facilitating labor migration from Mexico and progressively fortified the U.S./Mexico border and increased border enforcement.

There are signs that, in the long run, some kind of migration accord will be reached between the United States and Mexico. Both Mexico and the United States have much at stake in continued labor migration between the two nations. The Mexican economy annually receives billions of dollars in remittances from Mexican nationals living and working in the United States.[145] It needs these resources to subsidize economic growth, and dampen political unrest, in Mexico. The Mexican government thus has much to gain by ensuring that its citizens have access to jobs in the United States.[146]

At the same time, many sectors of the U.S. economy rely on undocumented labor. The U.S. economy benefits handsomely from such labor, particularly in the service, agriculture, and other low skill, labor-intensive industries.[147] Reliance on immigrant labor has been built over generations. Consequently, it is unlikely that labor migration will end with mere changes to the immigration laws.

Ultimately, the key ingredient to significantly reducing migration from Mexico is economic growth in Mexico.[148] Policies that foster this growth are likely to diminish

---

[144] *See* Manuel Caro, *Tying Racism In El Ejido To Spanish And European Politics*, 54 RUTGERS L. REV. 893, 897–902 (2002); Jane E. Larson, *Class, Economics, and Social Rights*, 54 RUTGERS L. REV. 831, 833–37 (2002); Maria Pabón López, *Immigration Law Spanish-Style: A Study Of Spain'S Normalización Of Undocumented Workers*, 21 GEO. IMMIGR. L.J. 571, 591–93 (2007).

[145] *See* Pia M. Orrenius, Madeline Zavodny, Jesus Canas, & Roberto Coronado, *Do Remittances Boost Economic Development? Evidence from Mexican States*, 16 L. & BUS. REV. AM. 803 (2010); Matthew C. Wilson, *The Economic Causes and Consequences of Mexican Immigration to the United States*, 84 DEN. U.L. REV. 1099, 1118–20 (2007); Martin Chavez, Note, *Remittances and the Charitable Deduction: A New Approach to Encouraging Development in Mexico*, 14 NYU J. LEGIS. & PUB. POL'Y 565, 582–602 (2011); Victoria Lehrfeld, Comment, *Patterns of Migration: The Revolving Door From Western Mexico to California and Back Again*, 8 LA RAZA L.J. 209, 245–50 (1995); Alexander C. O'Neill, Note, *Emigrant Remittances: Policies to Increase Inflows and Maximize Benefits*, 9 IND. J. GLOBAL LEGAL STUD. 345 (2001).

[146] The Mexican government's interest in protecting migrant labor in the United States thus is not solely humanitarian; increasing wages and benefits for Mexican migrants also increases remittances to Mexico. *See* Richard Griswold del Castillo, *Mexican Intellectuals' Perception of Mexican Americans and Chicanos, 1920–Present*, 27 AZTLÁN 33, 49 (2002); Deanna Ford, *Tapping the Development Potential of Migration Through MFIs*, 12 GEO. PUB. POL'Y REV. 11, 11–14 (2006); Xinying Chi, Note, *Challenging Managed Temporary Labor Migration as a Model for Rights and Development for Labor-Sending Countries*, 40 N.Y.U. J. INT'L L. & POL. 497, 505–06 (2008).

[147] *See* JOHNSON, *supra* note 66, at 131–67.

[148] *See* U.S. COMM'N FOR THE STUDY OF INT'L MIGRATION AND COOPERATIVE ECON. DEV., UNAUTHORIZED MIGRATION: AN ECONOMIC DEVELOPMENT RESPONSE (1990); Philip L. Martin, *Economic Integration and*

migration pressures. However, economic growth is a slow process and requires substantial investment of capital.

Labor integration between the United States and Mexico in fact is occurring. Market forces have driven U.S. employers and Mexican workers in this direction for years. Immigration law has been a minor hindrance to immigrants and employers but has not been an effective deterrent to conduct inconsistent with the U.S. immigration laws. Efforts to bar the employment of undocumented workers have been largely ineffective.[149] Certain industries in the United States, such as the agriculture, construction, and many service industries rely on low wage labor provided by immigrants. Unlike other industries, which have increasingly moved operations overseas to exploit low wage labor, jobs in these industries cannot be exported.

C. CONCLUSION: THE FUTURE OF U.S. IMMIGRATION LAW

The future of U.S. immigration law is difficult to predict. The Supreme Court seems to be firmly committed to applying generally applicable legal doctrines to immigration cases. One possible ultimate outcome is the elimination of the plenary power doctrine. Major changes to immigration law, however, are likely to come through Congress and the political process. It is at best uncertain whether Congress will be able to pass a major overhaul of the immigration laws in the near future.

Migration: The Case of NAFTA, 3 UCLA J. Int'l L. & Foreign Aff. 419 (1998).

[149] *See supra* note 39 (citing authorities).

TABLE OF CASES

[References are to pages]

[References are to pages]

[References are to pages]

[References are to pages]

[References are to pages]

[References are to pages]

[References are to pages]

[References are to pages]

[References are to pages]

INDEX

[References are to sections and to the Federal Rules of Evidence.]

[References are to sections and to the Federal Rules of Evidence.]

[References are to sections and to the Federal Rules of Evidence.]

[References are to sections and to the Federal Rules of Evidence.]

[References are to sections and to the Federal Rules of Evidence.]

HEARING (See REMOVAL PROCESS, subhead: Hearing)

HOMELAND SECURITY, DEPARTMENT OF (See DEPARTMENT OF HOMELAND SECURITY)

HUMANITARIAN AND HUMAN RIGHTS PRINCIPLES
International human rights limitations on sovereign power over borders
    Refugees . . . 1[C][2]
    Rights of immigrants (See RIGHTS OF IMMIGRANTS)
Refugees . . . 1[C][2]
Rights of immigrants (See RIGHTS OF IMMIGRANTS)

HUMAN TRAFFICKING
Border control, human trafficking and death on border . . . 18[B][1][c]
Enforcement against undocumented immigrants . . . 14[C]
Old immigration crimes, expansion or enhancement of . . . 15[A][1][c]

I

ICE (See IMMIGRATION AND CUSTOMS ENFORCEMENT (ICE))

IIRIRA (See ILLEGAL IMMIGRATION REFORM AND IMMIGRANT RESPONSIBILITY ACT OF 1996 (IIRIRA))

ILLEGAL IMMIGRATION REFORM AND IMMIGRANT RESPONSIBILITY ACT OF 1996 (IIRIRA)
Generally . . . 2[I][3]

IMMIGRATION AND CUSTOMS ENFORCEMENT (ICE)
Generally . . . 5[B][2][b]

IMMIGRATION AND NATIONALITY ACT OF 1952
Generally . . . 2[F]
Immigration Reform and Control Act of 1986 (IRCA) (See IMMIGRATION REFORM AND CONTROL ACT OF 1986 (IRCA))

IMMIGRATION LAW (GENERALLY)
African workers as forced immigration policy, enslavement of . . . 2[C]
Blacks . . . 2[B][3]
Criminals . . . 2[B][1]
Early state and federal law and policy regarding criminals
    Generally . . . 2[B]
    Blacks . . . 2[B][3]
    Criminals . . . 2[B][1]
    Paupers . . . 2[B][2]
    Religious views . . . 2[B][4]
    Unorthodox views . . . 2[B][5]

IMMIGRATION LAW (GENERALLY)—Cont.
Economic impacts
    Demand for labor . . . 1[D][1][b]
    Poverty and limited economic opportunity . . . 1[D][1][a]
Immigration and Nationality Act of 1952 . . . 2[F]
Immigration Reform Act of 1990 (See IMMIGRATION REFORM ACT OF 1990)
Immigration Reform in 1996
    Antiterrorism and Effective Death Penalty Act of 1996 (AEDPA) . . . 2[I][1]
    Illegal Immigration Reform and Immigrant Responsibility Act of 1996 (IIRIRA) . . . 2[I][3]
    Welfare reform . . . 2[I][2]
Impacts on United States
    Generally . . . 1[E]; 1[E][5]
    Costs of immigration, economic
        Generally . . . 1[E][6]
        Downward wage pressures . . . 1[E][6][a]
        Inequality, economic . . . 1[E][6][c]
        Minorities, wage costs to . . . 1[E][6][b]
        Wage costs to minorities . . . 1[E][6][b]
    Crime . . . 1[E][9]
    Employers and business, economic benefits for . . . 1[E][2]
    Immigrant workers, benefits to . . . 1[E][3]
    Labor market . . . 1[E][1]
    National economy, aggregate benefits to . . . 1[E][4]
    Public benefits . . . 1[E][7]
    Social and cultural impacts (See SOCIAL AND CULTURAL IMPACTS)
International human rights limitations on sovereign power over borders
    Refugees . . . 1[C][2]
    Rights of immigrants (See RIGHTS OF IMMIGRANTS)
Jekyll and Hyde Obama era
    Generally . . . 2[K]
    Deferred action for childhood arrivals (DACA) . . . 2[K][5]
    Detention . . . 2[K][3]
    Immigration and Customs Enforcement (ICE) detainers . . . 2[K][2]
    Prosecutorial discretion . . . 2[K][4]
    Same-sex, binational couples . . . 2[K][6]
    Secure communities . . . 2[K][1]
Morality of immigration restrictions . . . 1[A]
National identity . . . 1[E][8][b]
National origins quota system . . . 2[E]
National security and post-9/11 measures . . . 2[J]
National sovereignty and national borders
    Generally . . . 1[B]
    Borders and border controls . . . 1[B][2]
    Expansive notions of sovereignty . . . 1[B][1]
    Social contract and community membership . . . 1[B][3]
Paupers . . . 2[B][2]
Policy, and
    African workers as forced immigration policy, enslavement of . . . 2[C]
    Blacks . . . 2[B][3]
    Criminals . . . 2[B][1]

[References are to sections and to the Federal Rules of Evidence.]

[References are to sections and to the Federal Rules of Evidence.]

[References are to sections and to the Federal Rules of Evidence.]

[References are to sections and to the Federal Rules of Evidence.]

[References are to sections and to the Federal Rules of Evidence.]

[References are to sections and to the Federal Rules of Evidence.]

[References are to sections and to the Federal Rules of Evidence.]

[References are to sections and to the Federal Rules of Evidence.]